P9-DFI-017

The
BEGGAR
and the
PROFESSOR

The
BEGGAR
and the
PROFESSOR

A Sixteenth-Century Family Saga

EMMANUEL LE ROY LADURIE

TRANSLATED BY
Arthur Goldhammer

THE

UNIVERSITY

OF CHICAGO PRESS

·

CHICAGO & LONDON

The University of Chicago Press, Chicago 60637
The University of Chicago Press, Ltd., London
© 1997 by The University of Chicago
All rights reserved. Published 1997
Paperback edition 1998
Printed in the United States of America
06 05 04 03 02 01 00 99 98   5 4 3 2
ISBN: 0-226-47323-6 (cloth)
ISBN: 0-226-47324-4 (paperback)

Originally published as *Le siècle des Platter, 1499–1628. Tome premier: Le mendiant et le professeur,* © Librairie Arthème Fayard, 1995.

Library of Congress Cataloging-in-Publication Data

Le Roy Ladurie, Emmanuel.
   [Mendiant et le professeur. English]
   The beggar and the professor : a sixteenth-century family saga /
Emmanuel Le Roy Ladurie ; translated by Arthur Goldhammer.
     p.   cm.
   Includes bibliographical references and index.
   ISBN 0-226-47323-6 (alk. paper)
   1. Platter family. 2. Platter, Thomas, 1499–1582. 3. Platter,
Felix, 1536–1614. 4. Platter, Thomas, 1574–1628. 5. Protestants—
Switzerland—Basel-Stadt—Biography. 6. Physicians—Switzerland—
Basel-Stadt—Biography. 7. Authors, Swiss—16th century—
Biography. 8. Basel-Stadt (Switzerland)—Genealogy.
I. Goldhammer, Arthur. II. Title.
DQ398.54.P53L413 1997
949.4'3203'0922—dc20
[B]   96-23340

♾ The paper used in this publication meets the minimum requirements of the American National Standard for Information Sciences—Permanence of Paper for Printed Library Materials, ANSI Z39.48-1992.

CONTENTS

AUTHOR'S NOTE

Many of the notes, including both endnotes and (in the majority of cases) notes incorporated into the body of the text, use references of the following type: (T 54) or (F 21) or (T2 383). These refer, respectively, to pages 54, 121, and 383 of the 1944 German-Swiss edition of the *Lebenbeschreibung* by Thomas Platter Sr. (T); the 1976 edition of the *Tagebuch* by Felix Platter (F), edited by Valentin Lötscher; and the 1968 edition of the *Beschreibung der Reisen* by Thomas Platter Jr. (T2), edited by Rut Reiser. (Full references to these works can be found in the bibliography.)

In quotations from the works of the Platters, which were written in a "Basel dialect" of German, I have followed the authors' practice of not capitalizing nouns (in contrast to contemporary High German usage).

In the text, moreover, the reader will find a few rare quotations of actual dialogue among the personages. Although invented dialogue is an accepted practice in certain literary histories that aim to achieve verisimilitude, as well as in historical fiction, this book, as a purely historical work, belongs to a very different genre, and I have refrained from inventing any dialogue here. Dialogue fragments were included verbatim in the texts of the Platters themselves, particularly those of Thomas Sr. and Felix, and I have simply quoted them as I found them.

Finally, all dates prior to 1582 are cited according to the "old style" of the Julian Calendar. In that year the Gregorian Calendar was instituted, and subsequent dates refer to it.

Platter Family Tree

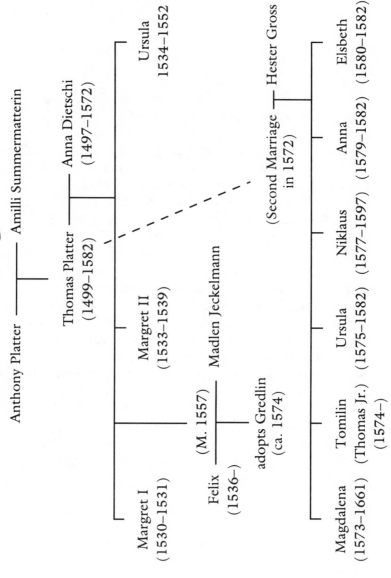

PART ONE

Father and Son: Thomas and Felix Platter

CHAPTER ONE

Pilgrimage to the Valais

In 1563, in the final weeks of spring (F 401), Thomas Platter, an erstwhile highland shepherd and vagabond who had gone on to become first a printer and later a boarding-school teacher and headmaster in Basel, decided, at the age of sixty-four, to leave Basel on a pilgrimage of reminiscence to the land of his birth: the German-speaking Upper Valais, situated downstream from the Rhone glacier and upstream from Lausanne and Geneva, the heartland of francophone Switzerland. Linked to the Helvetic Confederation since the fifteenth century, the Valais region had long been divided between the Francophile party of Georg Supersaxo and the "minions" of the Milanese state, to which a powerful personage, Cardinal Matthaeus Schiner (1465–1522) had thrown his support, only to end up as one of the biggest losers at Marignano in 1515.* Since the 1550s, the Valais, whose bishopric and central town had long been Sion (or Sitten), had been (relatively) hospitable to "heresy." The silent majority remained Catholic, but the nobles, including several of Thomas Platter's former boarders, inclined toward Protestantism. The area remained basically rural and pastoral, if only because of its mountainous terrain.

On June 1, 1563, in Basel, Thomas sat down to a meal, probably the evening repast. To this feast he had issued a neighborly invitation to his son Felix Platter, a fashionable young doctor and graduate of the University of Montpellier, who had already begun to attract a considerable clientele among the aristocracy or at the very least the bourgeoisie of Basel and its environs, drawing patients from even as far away as southern Alsace, Wurtemberg, and the Black Forest. Felix lived a short distance from Thomas in a house on Freie Strasse, or "free street," near the city walls and the so-called Gate of Ashes (Innere Aeschentor). He came to dinner with his shy, pretty young wife, Madlen. Although married for more than five years, the couple still had no children. They were joined by Madlen's father, Franz Jeckelmann, a surgeon. Anna Dietschi, the elder Platter's

---

*The battle in which King Francis I of France defeated the Swiss allied with the Duke of Milan.—TRANS.

wife, probably served the diners, but her presence (on this occasion at least) is not mentioned in our sources. No surprise about that.

During dinner Thomas brought up an idea he had been mulling over for some time: "Madlen," he told his daughter-in-law, "you should make the journey with me and take the baths in the Valais. You have no child, and as you know, the Valaisian waters are effective against sterility."[1] Madlen had only to nod her assent. In this house the old man's words were generally taken as orders, and in any case the young woman was not averse to the journey he proposed. Surgeon Jeckelmann, who on this occasion was in uncharacteristically good spirits (*lustig*), immediately chimed in: "I'm coming too." He owned his own horse, which solved one transportation problem. Felix, who also owned a horse, quickly made up his mind to join the group as well. Thomas, who was fond of asinine creatures, had brought back a mule from a previous trip to the Valais: just the animal for Madlen to ride. The headmaster himself was an indefatigable walker: he had not forgotten his youth as a mountain climber and hiker. Hence he would travel on foot. Anna, his wife, would stay home and keep an eye on the house on Freie Strasse. Preparations for the trip were quickly completed.

In fact, the group set out the very next day, on the afternoon of Wednesday, June 2, 1563. The four travelers were joined by Pierre Bonet of Porrentruy, Felix's French-speaking servant. From his long sojourns among the "Welches,"[2] the young doctor had retained a fondness for the French language, even if he used it only in conversation with his servants. A pharmacist from Sion, the principal town of the Valais, accompanied the spa-bound tourists; his first name was Hans (we cannot be sure of his last name). Hans and Thomas, the two Valaisians, both traveled on foot yet always reached the inn ahead of their companions on horseback. Because Madlen was a delicate, nervous city girl, whenever the group came to a difficult ford, one of the men took hold of her mule's bridle to make sure that nothing would go awry.

On June 3, in an arduous stretch of the Jura not far from the craggy rim of the "Wasserfall," Pierre Bonet stepped on a nail. His foot became so infected that he could not go on. Felix, a surgeon as well as a physician, took charge of the case. Knife in hand, he dug out the wound and cleaned away the mud and pus. In pain and frightened, the injured man fainted and then, overwhelmed by his ordeal, defecated on Madlen's apron as she tried to nurse him. By the time the others had finished their picnic dinner, however, Pierre had regained consciousness and seemed to have recovered his strength. The caravan was able to proceed.

From June 4 to June 6, the travelers worked their way southward, staying with friends or friends of friends from Basel, people with connections to various city officials and Protestant clergymen. In Erlenbach (F 404), they ate for the first time a sort of cracker made from dried bread and stacked up by the dozen on long needles.

On June 8, near Saanen, Jeckelmann, accompanied by a pastor who was the son of a monk, drank his first Valais wine and gave signs of being quite pleased with it, indeed slightly inebriated. His joy was not to last: after losing one of his gloves, he vented his wrath on the rocky trail and declared the Valais a place fit for devils. This was the first of what would prove to be a series of angry outbursts. The day's journey ended in Gsteig (altitude 1,200 meters), at an inn where there was no one to greet the travelers but the wife of the innkeeper, who was away. The woman had just given birth. She had, she said, neither money nor food. Madlen was obliged to improvise a meal from eggs and milk. Apparently there was no shortage of protein.

On June 9, Thomas and his family (F 404) climbed to the peak of Sanetsch (2,243 meters). The peasants were cutting hay. It was hot and dry. Pink willow-herb flowered amid the grass and boulders. The horses stumbled. The travelers passed wine merchants headed north, their packhorses laden with tall kegs of wine for the people of the highlands. Jeckelmann shamelessly quaffed several glassfuls straight from the keg and ate cheese provided by Hans, the apothecary. As if by miracle, the surgeon's foul mood vanished: he even forgot about the glove he had lost. Meanwhile, the travelers admired an astonishing irrigation system built by the local peasants, not unlike the irrigation systems that exist today on the lower slopes of the Himalayas. The water came from a glacier and flowed directly by gravity into a series of larchwood conduits, which directed the irrigating flow into gardens and pastures. As they drew near a bridge, Felix was astonished to see a woman astride a packhorse. She carried a keg of wine on her back while spinning yarn with a distaff under her arm as easily as another woman might knit. Meanwhile, the horse, with scarcely any prodding from its rider, fearlessly crossed a bridge so narrow and dangerous that Felix himself scarcely dared set foot on it. The plainsman was terrified to go where the mountain woman moved easily. (This equestrian spinner calls to mind the Giantesses of Provence, mythical creatures about whom Thomas Platter Jr. would learn, much later, while traveling in the south of France. These Giantesses could supposedly spin or weave while at the same time carrying heavy stones on their heads—stones to be used for the construction of a great Roman monument.)

Felix tossed a stone over the side of the bridge, counting to eighteen before observing its splash in the rapids below. Characters in Shakespeare's *Hamlet* also counted to measure time; in Catholic countries, people used to use the time it took to say an *Ave Maria* or a *Pater Noster* for the same purpose. Given the height of the bridge that we can deduce from this scientific observation, it is easy to understand why the young doctor from Basel was so impressed by the courage of the woman on the horse.

A short while later, Felix, overcome by dizziness and heat, fainted. His wife thought he was dead. She shouted at her father and father-in-law to turn back. But the young doctor came to and—always the professional—asked for a blanket or cloak. This was to make him sweat, which would then lower his body temperature. He was soon back on his feet. At four in the afternoon, the group reached Savièse (F 405), in a region of irrigated fields and isolated farms with fine views of the Alps. The recovered patient drank a healthy draft, a *trunck,* which fully restored his strength. After climbing a steep, arduous path strewn with loose pebbles, the three urban riders (Felix, Jeckelmann, and Madlen) and the two highland hikers (Thomas and Hans) at last arrived at Sitten, alias Sion, toward the end of the afternoon.

Sion was different. Relaxed men in shirtsleeves strode about with bare swords at their sides; scabbards were not used. Such liberties were permissible in the highlands. Captain Marc Wolff, formerly one of Thomas's boarders and a local "castellan,"[3] was the secret (?) lover of the wife of a local scholar, a pharmacist by trade. He proposed to put the travelers up. Thomas, always somewhat puritanical, refused. The group stayed instead at the inn of Franz Gröli, another graduate of the Platter boarding school. Thomas had former students everywhere. Gröli was the castellan's son and married to a noblewoman; he was the father of a medical student soon to become a doctor. In other words, this was the high society of Sion. On their very first night in town, the visitors from Basel drank canteens of wine by the dozen. They were in high spirits. Felix and his wife slept on the first floor, near the "noble room," which could be heated in winter. The stove, unlike stoves in Basel, was covered with stone rather than ceramic tile. The two fathers, Jeckelmann and Thomas, shared a room on the second floor.

The whole week was amusing and pleasant. The saffron and pomegranate were in bloom in the countryside. The four visitors from Basel received countless invitations, especially from Captain Wolff, who harbored no ill will toward Thomas for his haughty attitude. Always the lady's man, the captain offered Madlen some lovely items of clothing as a gift. Captain Heinrich in Albon, who belonged to a family, soon to become Protestant, that had distinguished itself in war, notarial practice, and humanism, also spared no effort. His wife, a woman with a yen for wine and men, did everything she could to get Felix into bed, but the great physician politely declined (she would repeat the offense a few weeks later at the baths in Leuk, where the promiscuity of bathing gave her new opportunities but with no greater success than before). All this reveling was highly ecumenical: religious differences were forgotten around the massive silver mugs made by the great silversmith Exuperantius. The Catholic bishop invited the visitors to dine with him and offered to stable their horses. What sweet revenge for Thomas, the former shepherd of the Valais, who had been so poor in his childhood! The canons invited the surgeon Jeckelmann to dinner. Of course one of them, a future bishop, had also been a boarder at Thomas's school. An easygoing Catholicism, a papistry of good cheer, reigned in this small highland town, which in this respect differed from the surrounding flatland, from the rather stiff climate of Basel and Zurich.

Eventually, however, the visitors had to move on. From Sion they headed northeast along the Rhone. An escort accompanied them, as was customary for travelers of some importance. They stopped in Saint-Leonhard at the home of Alexander Jossen, an episcopal treasurer and an old friend of the Platters, as well as the bishop's grandson by the left hand: they were delighted by the gorgeous woodwork in his home, paid for perhaps by the money of the faithful. Across slopes and vineyards they made their way toward the baths at Leuk. They stopped at the home of a veteran of the battle of Marignano, a man wounded in the thigh in 1515 and still paralyzed. This gentleman, Petermann Hengart of Platea (F 410), had accumulated any number of blessings, civil as well as military. He was both sheriff and ensign as well as the bishop's nephew and the son-in-law of the great Supersaxo. The visitors were received sumptuously. After another, similar stop at the home of yet another gentleman, Peter Allet, the Platter-Jeckelmann quartet, father, son, daughter-in-law, and father-in-law, finally reached Leuk (known as Loèche in Romansch). At the inn the four travelers shared a room with three beds. It would be pretentious to call Leuk a "spa," but there were numerous hotels in the town. The baths at Leuk had regained some of their importance as a tourist spot and a locale for real-estate investment as the Renaissance economy flourished in the second half of the fifteenth century. Said to be good for gout and skin diseases, Leuk's waters also attracted infertile women, as was mentioned earlier. An unpleasant joke had it that the promiscuity of the bathers at Leuk had something to do with the observed increase in *post festum* natality. In any case, Jeckelmann and his daughter arranged to stay at the Hotel Ours for three crowns each for four weeks, including room and baths. Felix and Thomas continued on to the highlands of Upper Valais. Old Thomas planned to visit the house in which he had been born, or at any rate the old family homestead. The two men proceeded on foot; Pierre Bonet, Felix's servant, having recovered from his foot infection, took his master's horse from Leuk back to Sion, to the providential stables of the bishop, where the animal would be kept until its owner returned. For this pilgrimage to his mountain roots, Felix had literally disguised himself: he wore a red silk doublet, red pantaloons, and a fuzzy velvet hat. One can only assume that he wished to dazzle his highland kinsmen with the sumptuousness of his attire (this was not the most attractive side of his personality). Thomas, who knew and liked the highland natives from childhood and experience, dressed more soberly.

On the first stretch of this final stage of their journey, Felix and Thomas planned to stop at Visp (also known as Viège), on a tributary south of the upper Rhone. Felix wrote that Viège was "a pretty place," but in saying this his intention was primarily to disparage what came afterward. A first delegation of the Platter family, or that portion of the family that had not emigrated from its native region, came to greet the two visitors at the inn. One imagines the country folk doffing their hats before these "successful" cousins from another world. Early in the morning of June 19, the two visitors proceeded upstream along the Visp river valley. They crossed bridges of wood and stone, some of them quite recent and high enough so that Felix had to count to sixty before the stone splashed in the water below. The most noteworthy of these was the stone bridge of the Matter Visp, built in 1544 by the architect Ulrich Ruffiner, whose upper arch stood 65 meters above the rapids (F 416). Here is evidence of the architectural vitality of the sixteenth century, a time when even the remotest of valleys showed signs of the increased pace of commerce and trade. Although the trail narrowed as it climbed, it was still wide enough for caravans of pack animals to pass. To Felix, who lacked experience, it seemed at times little more than a footpath cut into the rock. His right hand hugged the cliff, his left hand hovered over the abyss. At times his courage amazed him. Meanwhile, riding a horse down this same narrow path, a cousin came down from Grächen to meet the two visitors. His name was Hans in der Bünde, and he belonged to one of the better-off peasant families of Grächen, the birthplace of the original Platters.[4] To be sure, at this altitude (Grächen stood at 1,610 meters), the wealthier families were hardly any better off than other people. Cousin Hans was dressed in the old style. He wore trousers and a jacket and seemed disconcerted by Felix's provocative scarlet outfit. He greeted the elder Platter (F 411), whom he knew by hearsay, with a question: "Welcome by God, Cousin Thomas. Is that your son?"

Hans used the familiar form of the second-person pronoun as a matter of course. He then jumped off his horse, which he rode practically bareback and guided with just a plain rope, eschewing bit and reins. Always helpful, the skilled horseman offered to ride double with Felix, who strenuously declined for fear that he might fall off and plummet to his death. The two Platters proceeded on foot to Grächen, accompanied by Hans, who continued to ride. Along the way, Thomas showed Felix the spot where his grandfather Summermatter, also named Hans (and, if we are to believe him, 126 years old at the time), had answered little Thomas's question in 1504 or 1505: "Grandfather, do you want to die?" "Yes, little one, if only I knew what kind of food they would cook for me up there" (F 412).

As they drew near their destination, the route, wending its way among the larches, grew arduous. Felix had to agree to mount his cousin's horse. To have maintained his refusal would have seemed impolite. Once the doctor was in place, Hans jumped on behind him, holding him by the waist while Felix, frozen with terror, shut his eyes. His cousin, riding behind, guided the horse with his strange rig. The travelers next crossed a relatively flat field and a dark pine forest that served as a lair for the bears still numerous in the region. Snowy peaks loomed in the distance. And then came the first human contact with Grächen: a blind centenarian (?) and his grown, white-haired children, all living in the same house as an extended family, watched as the three men passed. The elderly man served up the old story of the Platters' ancestor, Thomas's grandfather, more than a hundred years old, who was supposed to have lived this way in Grächen with ten other old men in 1505. Thomas had known this story by heart since childhood and even believed it. Then a female cousin of the Platters, a "Platterin," wearing a gray skirt and with her hair down, served a milk soup in a house occupied by very elderly peasants, a hut with larch beams. Milk and cheese dishes were the staple of the highlands. Tired, Felix collapsed in this old-folks' hut and briefly lay down on a straw mattress. Hans in der Bünde's house was located a short distance away from the home of the woman in the gray skirt. He invited his cousins over for another meal. Thomas Platter asked after a beautiful girl who had tended geese and with whom he had spent part of his childhood, and someone showed him the way to her house. Now very ugly, she was busy smashing pine cones. The reunion, after more than fifty years of separation, came as something of a disappointment. Nevertheless, the former goose-tender was a good-hearted woman: she clasped Felix to her bosom and called him "dear cousin" (*laube vetter* rather than *liebe vetter*). This dialectal dissonance caused the not very charitable physician to burst out laughing. After this sentimental interlude, Thomas and Felix returned to the home of Hans in der Bünde, the fearless horseman. Was Hans's wife perhaps put out that Felix had fallen asleep in the midst of the earlier family reunion? In any case she was unfriendly to the two men from the city and even to her own husband: "You've brought me guests, eh? Well, then, you take care of them, in the devil's name!"

Once again she served them milk, but this time generously sprinkled with pepper. Felix's throat burned. He cooled it down with excellent Val d'Aosta wines, which Hans had in his cellar. So the village was not as autarchic as it might have seemed, nor was Hans's house as wretched as it appeared. Pepper and wine were semiluxury or luxury items imported from Liguria and the Piedmont, carried up from Aosta and Genoa on the backs of pack animals in direct or indirect exchange for local products such as wood, livestock, and cheese. The bedding was rustic, however. After the evening meal, straw was spread on the floor close to the fire (nights were cool at this altitude), and the guests were invited to lie down.

Although old Thomas's highland simplicity had survived four decades of urban life, he could not stop himself from discreetly letting his son know how disappointed he felt at this treatment: "As you see, Felix, they make quite a fuss over me."

A further surprise awaited Felix the following morning. A crowd of little girls from the various hamlets of Grächen milled about the house where the two men from Basel had spent the night. Each of the girls was carrying a chamber pot full of urine. They wanted the great doctor from Basel to inspect the liquid—in other words, to provide them with a free consultation. Felix, who ordinarily preferred to treat nobles or wealthy clients, obligingly complied. More moving was the visit to the home of the brother of the late Simon Steiner, an old friend and probably a cousin of Thomas's. When Felix looked back on the occasion in his memoirs, however, he mainly recalled the wretchedness of the surroundings: the tourist clad in red silk liked to see himself as a civilized emissary among the barbarians of the forests and mountains. With antiquarian pedantry he referred, for instance, to Simon Steiner as Lithonius.[5] Steiner had been born in Grächen into a poor peasant family. Like Thomas, he had scored a "success" in town: in Strasbourg he had been the *famulus* (assistant) of the great local reformer Martin Bucer and later a teacher in Johannes Sturm's Latin school. To honor his memory, Thomas and Felix called on his brother, who had remained in the country on a plot of land that belonged to the family. Unlike Simon, the brother had never known success in the city. Thomas offered him his affection. Felix offered him alms of ten shillings.

The high point of this "homecoming" was the pilgrimage to the Platter family home, which Thomas had left in the first decade of the sixteenth century. Like many other dwellings in the area, it was a stout, simple cabin of larch logs, comfortable enough in its distinctive style. Wood was plentiful in these high Alpine valleys. The construction was old, probably dating back to the thirteenth century. The cabin stood close to a high crag or plateau (*platte*), a circumstance that may have been the origin of the name Platter: in these parts, the family was named after the house rather than the house after the family (F 415). In his memoirs Felix described this august dwelling as the birthplace of his father Thomas— but he was mistaken: Antony Platter, Thomas's father, mired in debt, was forced to flee his creditors shortly before 1499. He moved into a house some distance away but still within the limits of Grächen, a witch's house known as *Auf den Gräben* (By the Grave). It was there that Thomas Platter was born. But Thomas and Felix ignored this episode, important as it was, and focused their attention exclusively on the fifteenth-century family homestead at the place known as *An der Platte*. The visit took place on the beautiful day of June 18, 1563. Taking advantage of the sun, the two men, accompanied by acquintances and kin from the village, cousin Hans among them, took the noon meal at the house and washed down their food with a good deal of drink. Then they moved on from the cabin to the nearby *Platte,* whose dominating view made Felix dizzy. There they drank some more: afternoon and evening flagons, *trunck* and *abendtrunck*. Felix dug into his purse for another crown, this one for a local artisan whose name was not recorded, to carve his (newly acquired) coat of arms into the rock. Felix's blazon consisted of a white rock in relief with a white dove taking off from the rock against a background of blue sky. Rock on rock: of course there was no thought of coloring the bas-relief carved on stone in the open air. But the symbols spoke for themselves: the flat rock was Thomas, faithful to his roots; the dove was Felix, who, being fond of doves anyway, used one to symbolize how high he had already climbed in the world and how much higher he still dreamed of going. The physician never knew for sure whether the work of art he had commissioned was completed. To tell the truth, the ground he walked on scorched his feet. He was eager to leave this mountain eyrie, to which he never returned. Once the last goblet of wine was downed, the young doctor hastened that very evening down the mountain to Saint-Niclaus below. From there he returned as quickly as possible to the company of his wife, who was waiting at Leuk with her father. Thomas, who accompanied his son on this return journey, was preoccupied with very different thoughts. This brief excursion home had given him a new lease on life; it was his last contact, for he was now an old man, with a childhood for which he remained nostalgic despite its frequent misery, a childhood that had begun some sixty years before in this remote, not to say God-forsaken, parish of Grächen, where "little Thomas" had indeed been born into extreme poverty in 1499.

PART TWO

Childhoods and Undertakings
(1499–1551)

CHAPTER TWO

The Platter Childhoods: Thomas

Tomilin (little Thomas) was born in the ninety-ninth year of the fifteenth century. The boy's father, Antony Platter, still lived in his native Grächen. His mother, Amilli Summermatterin, was the daughter of Hans Summermatter, an elderly man said to have celebrated his one hundred and twenty-sixth birthday in the year of Thomas's birth. At one hundred he had married a woman of thirty, who had borne him a son, or so the story went. That is more or less all Thomas has to say about his maternal grandfather.

Amilli could not breast-feed her child. Did Thomas truly survive the first years of his life on nothing but cow's milk sucked from a pierced horn?[1] The boy must have had an iron constitution not to have succumbed, in the absence of breast milk from his mother or a wet nurse, to the raging infant mortality of the time. Death was commonplace: Antony, Thomas's father, died of plague in Thun, near Bern, where he had gone, as the men of the Valais customarily did, to obtain wool for his wife to spin and weave. After Antony's death, Amilli Summermatterin remarried and had several more children. Two of Thomas's elder sisters also died, one of them of the plague. Amilli personally buried two other children cut down by the same disease. And two brothers died in battle, as Swiss mercenaries. "From pestilence, war, and famine, preserve us, O Lord!" Hunger was never very far from the Platter household, which was on occasion victimized by usurers. Yet the extreme mortality in the Platter family was not a consequence of poverty alone: even after Thomas became a well-to-do burgher, he lost nearly all his children to the pestilential conditions common at the time in the cities of Germanic Switzerland.

Not knowing what to do with the surviving children of at least two marriages, Amilli sent little Thomas to board with his father's two sisters. Essentially his mother abandoned him (abandonment being fairly common at the time). While living with his aunts, Thomas had a frightening experience. One night, after the grownups had gone out for an evening with neighbors, the boy, who had been left sleeping on a tabletop bed of straw, ventured out alone. He lost his way in the snow, and for a time no one could find hide nor hair of him. When they did find him, it took some doing to warm his nearly frozen body. (Other rural memoir-writers looking back on their earliest memories mention similar experiences.)

Shortly after his third birthday, Thomas was presented to Bishop (soon to be Cardinal) Schiner, himself the son of a goatherd and a man of some considerable importance in the politics of the Valais.[2] An inveterate enemy of the French, Schiner was a prelate who wore the boots and helmet of a soldier, a bishop who rode into battle as readily as other bishops bestowed benedictions. (Schiner, by the way, was of great help to the future "heretic" Ulrich Zwingli in the early stages of Zwingli's brilliant career. But let us not get ahead of ourselves.) Did the bishop, seated on an armchair in the parish church of Grächen in 1502, really predict that Thomas had a future as a priest? The belief that such a prediction had been made was one reason why people in the village encouraged the boy to consider acquiring an ecclesiastical education, this being a traditional (though by no means easy) avenue of advancement for peasant lads who showed precocious intellectual ability. Thomas's family, though impoverished, had a number of prominent kin in the region, and his relatives were pious. Hence the boy's ecclesiastical vocation was encouraged if not foreordained: if joining the clergy (or becoming a printer, teacher, or doctor) was what it took to climb back up the social ladder, then so be it.

At age seven or eight, Thomas tended goats for one of his aunts. Like many a malnourished country boy, he was a small child, and his goats, no more than a few dozen in number, could easily knock him down when they came bounding out of his aunt's barn before dawn. One time he lost his shoes in the muddy snow. Often he went barefoot. In embarking on the hard life of the goatherd or shepherd, which in those days was the common fate of the pauper's child, he came to know older shepherds, some of whom treated him kindly. Once, when some of his companions mistakenly surmised that he had fallen from a mountain trail and vanished, their tender concern for his safety touched him. Between playing quoits on the slopes and enjoying snacks of rye bread and cheese, Thomas discovered the perversity of goats: they climbed so high up the steep terrain in their search for greenery that the goatherd could barely keep up. One day, Tomilin had a terrifying experience: after a fall, he found himself lying flat on a rock, clinging to a few tufts of grass as his feet flailed above a yawning abyss. Too young for pants, he wore only a short tunic, which he kept with him throughout his extensive later travels in Germany. He owed his life to an "older" friend, also named Thomas and already an experienced rock climber, who somehow managed to make his way down to the treacherous rock and grab the younger boy by the fingers. In later life the rescuer came to claim his reward, but Thomas, by then grown up, insisted that if he had survived, the Almighty deserved all the credit: it was sometimes easier to repay debts with prayers of thanksgiving than with cash. "God preserved me," Thomas wrote (other peasant scribblers used virtually the same words).[3] Divine protection was useful: vultures and crows scoured the slopes, to say nothing of bears, which were everywhere in Thomas's nightmares.

Tomilin at some point moved to the home of another peasant, a safe enough place as far as he could tell. There he played with the farmer's daughter, who was socially a cut above him because her father owned a herd of goats. The games they played were typical of rural children's games: they rode wooden horses and built mock irrigation systems like those found throughout Europe (and not just in the south). *Claudite jam ripas pueri, sat prata biberunt.* While working for his new master, Thomas again came to know the perils of the mountains, which were as deadly for the shepherds and goatherds of the past as they are for mountain climbers today.[4] Once, he spent a whole day searching for a lost herd of goats. Another time he spent an entire night clad only in a tunic, without hat or shoes, clinging to the roots of a larch tree: he had fallen again, and it was not until morning that he realized how deep was the chasm into which he had nearly plunged. While holding on for dear life, he had also had to fend off bears, real or imagined, and a goat antelope that he mistook for a stray buck. The life of the goatherd, he decided, was not for him. So he made another change: he found work tending cows, which was safer since these animals, unlike goats, preferred the lower, gentler slopes. Yet pleasant memories from his goat-tending years stayed with him: one day he lay on his back and dreamt of soaring above the mountain peaks until the sight of a huge hawk overhead brought him back to earth. He also hunted for "crystals," a sometimes lucrative pastime for young highlanders in the sixteenth century and later. And of course he participated in games: throwing stones, blowing shepherds' horns, and pole vaulting. Close calls were commonplace: falling rocks passed just inches above the climber's head. Thirst was harder to bear than hunger: shepherds were known to drink their own urine, and the baskets of food they carried on their backs were often almost empty. The straw pads they carried for sleeping (in wintertime) were infested with lice and bugs. One got used to these pests, but the louse, which carried typhus, had its role in history too.

Thomas's work tending cows on the lower slopes soon came to an end. The boy was not stupid, as his family was quick to realize. No one had forgotten Bishop Schiner's prediction. Aunt Fansy, the benefactress who had already employed the boy in several capacities, now took him to her elderly cousin Antony Platter, a priest who happened to have the same name as Thomas's late father. Thomas thus gave up tending cows after a brief stint, only to find himself treated like an animal: Antony, a pitiless teacher of the old school, boxed him on the ears and made him cry out, as Thomas described it, "like a stuck goat." Tomilin became even more depressed than he had been while risking his miserable neck on steep mountainsides. By now he was ten or eleven years old. In the home of this uncle, who may have run a small school, Thomas learned very little. All he could remember was learning to sing the *Salve Regina:*

Salve Regina, mater misericordiae,
Vita, dulcedo et spes nostra, salve.

(Hail, Queen [Mary], mother of mercy
Our life, sweetness, and hope, hail.)

Whatever schooling Tomilin may have received from his uncle, it did not last long. The elderly priest gave the boy a gold piece and sent him on his way, essentially casting him out into the world on his own. As we know from the work of distinguished scholars, West European attitudes toward childhood have changed considerably since the sixteenth century. In other parts of the world, such as Brazil (where more than six million children live on their own) and the Andes, things may not be so different today from what they were in Europe in the sixteenth century. In any event, Thomas set off to beg for his bread, but also to study. With his older cousin Paulus, also a grandson of the allegedly centenarian grandfather—the stalwart trunk of the Platter family tree (and still a source of strength, pride, and virility some fifty years later)—Thomas headed for Germany. His mother's brother, Simon zu den Summermatten, advised him that this was the best thing for him, even if it meant permanent exile.

The child therefore left his native Valais and discovered, on the other side of the Grimsel pass, still in mountainous country but at a lower altitude, civilization, or at any rate what passed for civilization in this part of Switzerland: tile roofs, ceramic stoves (which Montaigne, two generations later, so admired during his travels in this region), and geese, which the child had never encountered in the highlands. The little highlander, now on his way to Germany, at first found these geese almost as diabolical as a boy named Carl, who beat him cruelly after giving him a small coin, then demanding it back almost before Thomas had had time to put it in his pocket. After several days on the road, Thomas also discovered the rules of chess, a game he had never before seen played. In order to eat, Thomas had to beg: his Upper Valaisian dialect, extremely rare in these parts, made the boy popular with potential benefactors. Begging proved marginally profitable. Paulus, who was living off the fruits of his little cousin's labors and did not hesitate to beat him if he found the proceeds insufficient, was delighted.

But to get back to the geese: the journey from Grimsel (via Lucerne and Zurich) to Breslau survived in Thomas's (selective) memory as one long confrontation with these birds. Having left his "savage" fellow citizens of Upper Valais behind, the boy perceived the goose as the symbol of a culture, or, rather, of a sophisticated agriculture: a discovery. Soon, however, they became living targets, to be killed or stolen. This prey supplemented the meager rations of a group of young travelers led at times by a young, vigorous, and incontestable leader, Antony Schallbetter, a stout fellow capable of dissuading any would-be marauders that might turn up on German highways. Schallbetter somehow managed to obtain candles and a tinder-box. Did he steal them from a church? In any case, he was the only member of the group with the means to provide light at night. At his beck and call he had five or six older boys, close to twenty years old, known as "graduates," along with three younger lads, referred to as "schoolboys" (although they attended no school), who ranged in age from eleven to thirteen, Platter among them. Intermediate in age between the schoolboys and the scamps was Cousin Paulus: he disciplined the younger boys by pinching their calves and behinds and continued thrashing Thomas as before. The younger Platter, with his highlander's skill at tossing quoits and rings, specialized in chasing ducks and geese whenever the gang came upon a village. To believe Thomas, such bird-hunting was tolerated provided one took care not to get caught: that, at any rate, was the case in free Silesia, where age-old communal customs were still in force. Before reaching that province, however, the gang of boys first had to make their away across most of Germany. Along the way they feasted on geese, which they either stoned (a sport at which Thomas's son Felix would also excel) or liberated from the sheds in which farmers fattened the birds to serve as dowry for their daughters. No sooner was a goose pinched than it was plucked and made ready, its head, feet, and innards destined for the stew pot and the remainder for the spit, to be broiled along with turnips. The meal might be rounded out with fish snatched from the bottom of a freshly drained pond and boiled in beer obtained from an obliging farmer in exchange for a share of the looted fish. Thomas also hunted geese with a sort of boomerang and shared his take with his friends and with a "schoolmaster" who joined the group for a while and apparently had no scruples about partaking of filched fowl. Indeed, it was the *magister* himself who encouraged the boys to go after the indispensable birds, though he knew that what they were doing was illegal.

Generally speaking, the diet of our little wanderers seems to have been variable rather than uniformly miserable, though on many days it was deplorably unhealthy.[5] During certain stretches of the journey, between Dresden and Breslau, for example, Paulus and Thomas subsisted mainly on what they could gather: true, they ate onions, both raw and salted, but they also survived on grilled nuts, crab apples, and the like. At other times, within the walls of Breslau, for instance, they dined royally: it was probably a year of abundant harvest and low grain prices. In any case, Breslau (today Wroclaw in Poland) was well supplied because it was the center of a farming region, a market town for the lands bordering on the southern Baltic. Better yet, the ready availability of grain in the city meant that beer was plentiful, and the Polish peasants amused themselves by getting Tomilin and his companions drunk. In his memoirs, written much later, Thomas never alludes to the fact that Silesia was partially Polish except when he describes these drinking bouts: the German traveler, availing himself of a common expression, says that on feast days he got "drunk as a Pole." By the time Thomas wrote, of course, the Slavic nation had already come under military pressure from the Russians. Meanwhile, in Frauenburg (Frombork), Copernicus was beginning to work out his heliocentric cosmology. Modernity—the "Age of Copernicus"—was about to dawn.[6] But Platter had other things on his mind.

*   *   *

Food and drink varied, but the vermin were ever-present. In Dresden, bedrooms were full of lice: one could hear swarms of them moving in the straw. In Breslau, the lice in the bedding were so thick that Tomilin preferred to sleep on the floor. Every now and then he deloused his cloak, washed his tunic in the Oder, and threw the crushed lice into a hole dug for the purpose. Whether out of piety or for a joke, he covered the insects with earth and planted a small cross on the mound. The slaughter of the bugs was Christianized: these lice died a sanctified death.

Crime was another scourge. Although Silesia was by no means a hotbed of vice, at this level of society and among this mobile population, criminality was commonplace. Thomas himself engaged in petty thievery in rural areas, where minor stealing was tolerated but thieves were punished if caught. Once he was spotted with the feet of a goose sticking out from underneath his tunic; a group of hatchet-wielding peasants bent on recovering their property chased him in vain. Itinerant children were vulnerable to all the perils of the road, which sometimes claimed the lives of travelers.

Thomas mentions two brushes with danger. One time, at an inn near Nuremberg, he and his friends crossed paths with a self-professed murderer. The other incident took place near Naumburg,[7] when the young itinerants ran into eight shady characters armed with crossbows (petty criminals like these could not afford firearms). In both instances the youngsters escaped with nothing more than a fright. There were other frightening moments as well: in the forests of Thuringia and Silesia, for example. Europe in the early sixteenth century was still thinly populated, although the population was rapidly returning to the level it had attained before the Black Plague; much of Germany still resembled a vast, often dangerous forest interspersed with ample clearings. In trading the mountains for the forest, Thomas did not always come out ahead. Between Nuremberg and Breslau, however, he no longer had to worry about his old mountain enemy, the bear: here, *batzen* (bear) was simply the name of a coin, equivalent to one-fifteenth of a florin, just about the price of a duck or goose.

At first Thomas's ideas about geography were vague and imprecise. As if in a dream, the boy traveled from Zurich to Nuremberg and from Nuremberg to Naumburg, Dresden, and Breslau, not without side trips that we have no way of tallying up. All this hiking may have taken several months or several seasons or several years—it is hard to know just how long he was on the road. In the course of his travels he visited, or at any rate passed through, eastern Switzerland, Bavaria, Franconia, Prussia, Saxony, Silesia, and perhaps Hungary: at the time he had other things on his mind than mastering geography. We cannot even be sure of the chronological order in which the narrator visited the "eastern" provinces. How different are the travelogues of Thomas's two sons, Felix and Thomas Jr., whose "higher" social and cultural status ensured that from early youth they would share the geographical concerns of other Renaissance humanists: their accounts detail their routes village by village. Of course they kept running logs of their journeys, which was not the case with Thomas Sr., who at this time was still almost illiterate. In any case he did not carry a notebook suitable for keeping records of his travels.

What about school in all these travels? In the case of our Valaisian vagabond, it was intermittent at best. In Naumburg, Thomas begged while his companions sang. The local schoolteacher, accompanied by a group of poor children, tried to force the young Helvetians to sign up for his courses (for which they would have had to pay). The young nomads proved recalcitrant: they ambushed the teacher and assailed him with stones. Then they beat a hasty retreat, but not before making off with some geese. In Halle (Saxony) another attempt was made to get the boys into school. But the older boys treated Thomas and his cousin Paulus miserably, and the two fled to another school in Dresden, which proved so lousy in both the literal and figurative senses that they ran off a second time, to Breslau, pursued by dogs and accompanied by hunger. In the capital of Silesia, where food was plentiful, the visitors from the west took courses at a school connected with St. Elizabeth's Church, where the Swiss influence was strong. Each of the city's seven parishes had its own school. The classroom was heated, and pupils sang and took dictation. The schoolmasters no more had printed books than the "primitive" bandits encountered on the road months earlier had had firearms. Only one of the dozen teachers in the school possessed a text of Terence, one of the classics of the day. The older boys had notebooks and could thus take better advantage of the teaching than younger children like the Platters. Did the ex-goatherd from Grächen have any means of taking notes? Apparently not. Did he know how to write? In any case, he seems to have spent much of his time in Breslau begging. He also met various distinguished individuals, including, if we believe his account, one of the Fuggers (the famous banking family). Thomas proved rather successful as a beggar, benefitting from the popularity of the unfortunate Swiss, thousands of whom had been massacred at Marignano by the troops of Francis I: Germans felt an instinctive sympathy for them. By the time of that crucial battle (1515), Thomas had lived a full fifteen years. He must have spent several years roaming Germany from west to east. Soon he would travel the same routes in the opposite direction. To be sure, sixteenth-century hikers were a hearty lot, and for them covering a vast territory was not an unthinkable feat.

The culmination of Thomas's fitful schooling came in Munich (somehow the boy had continued on, or returned, to Bavaria). To gain access to this heavily fortified and guarded city, one had to show proof (genuine or counterfeit) of having a relative, friend, or place to stay inside the walls. Thomas, who arrived from Dresden, became an assistant to a soapmaker, who was married to a pleasant enough woman and happened to be an anticlerical (which was a problem in this ultra-Catholic region). The young Helvetian helped his master boil the mixture from which soap was made. In the course of his work he purchased ashes in the countryside, which prevented him from completing elementary school, or so he claimed. School also served as a pretext: as a "student," Thomas was able to persuade the local authorities, who were strict in such matters, to grant him the right to sing in the streets, which helped in his begging (the boy's voice had already changed, and he made progress in his singing). Apparently soapmaking didn't provide enough to feed him, and in any case Paulus's insatiable appetites had to be looked after, for this disagreeable cousin was still living off Thomas's earnings. The reformer Luther had also been a singing beggar in his youth. Did he meet with similar misadventures?[8]

From Munich, Thomas moved on to a place that was even worse: Ulm. He traveled there with Hildebrand Kalbermatter, the illegitimate young son of a Valaisian priest. The two boys remained—voluntarily or involuntarily—under the thumb of Paulus and an older boy, Achacius of Mainz. Evidently non-Swiss youths were allowed to join the gang. But Thomas and Hildebrand did not stay in Ulm for long. They returned briefly to the Valais and then went back to Munich. During this phase of Thomas's travels, schooling was out of the question. The former "schoolboys" had grown up. By now Thomas must have been sixteen, and despite repeated efforts he still did not know how to read. Still working for the indefatigable Paulus, he spent his time displaying a piece of cloth to passersby and offering to make them a vest in exchange for a cash payment. This dodge worked well enough until the swindlers were fingered. Thomas seems to have been particularly miserable during his stays in Munich subsequent to his initial stint with the soapmaker (who had treated him well). The two older boys went on (or back to) forcing the younger ones to beg. Paulus and Achacius even made Hildebrand spit into a bowl to prove that he had not consumed any of the food he had begged on behalf of his tormentors. Thomas was forced to snatch bones from dogs in the street just to survive. Like a servant, he picked crumbs out of cracks in the floor—but to eat. As luck would have it, his picaresque adventures led him to a room in the home of a kindly widow, a saddle-maker by trade. Widowhood and the trades were the only avenues to emancipation available to the women of the time. The sympathetic hostess gave the young man a bowl of soup and wrapped his feet in furs that had been hung beside the stove to warm (another advantage of these German stoves compared to decrepit French fireplaces).

*   *   *

By now Thomas was sixteen and eager to be rid of Paulus. He was nearly grown, and his bitterness toward his older companion had built up over the years. Paulus, meanwhile, was bent on exploring new territory of his own: he had begun to chase girls, in particular the soapmaker's servant, and the soapmaker showed him the door when he found out. In Munich Thomas slept on grain sacks in the market. He met a butcher's wife, a former barmaid and convinced Helvetophile, who judged him to be a bright lad and gave him a room. She often sent him out to buy beer and to deliver hides and meat. After a beating from Paulus, who was still trying to hang on to his erstwhile "slave," Thomas made up his mind to leave Munich. With a heavy heart, he left the kindly butcher's wife: once again his desire for schooling was his excuse for moving on. After bidding (a discreet) farewell to the great Bavarian city, Thomas decided to head for Salzburg, despite the absence of any festival at the time (as a professional nomad, his geographic knowledge was by this time considerable, though not at all systematic). So after Switzerland, Bavaria, Saxony, Prussia, and Poland, it was on to Austria—or so Thomas thought. To hasten his journey, he attempted to hitch a ride, as we would say nowadays, in the wagon of a drunken peasant. The ground was covered with heavy frost, and Thomas had no shoes, only torn stockings. In Passau, the sentinels on duty at the city gates turned him back. He then decided to head for Switzerland by way of Freising. There he was warned that Paulus was looking for him, halberd in hand. Thomas was ready to do anything to avoid falling once again under the sway of the older boys. For years his begging had kept them alive. So he set out at once for Ulm, dozens of miles away, and covered the whole distance without stopping. There he tended turnips for a widow who had taken him in before. He worked in a garden not far from the city walls, where the widow grew turnips, cabbages, and other vegetables. Of course Paulus soon turned up, and Thomas fled again, this time toward Konstanz, in the direction of home. Along the way he had a scare: he thought he was going to be attacked by a stonecutter, who turned out to be a practical joker. The man liked to scare people but was not a real threat. Finally, Thomas reached Konstanz and was delighted to see Swiss country children in their white blouses. With his conventional (though not indelible) Catholic upbringing, Thomas thought he had died and gone to heaven. From there he went to Zurich, a city in the grip of the plague, and once again it was the same old cycle: beg first and then, in the hope of picking up a bit more learning, feed the "graduates," who were perpetually ready to "haze" would-be scholars starved for wisdom. Once again he had to endure threats from Paulus, who tried to lure Thomas back by sending Hildebrand, the priest's bastard, as his emissary. But enough of this.

*   *   *

Thomas returned to the Valais two or three times in these difficult years: he stayed either with an aunt or cousin ("extended family" was not just a word) and visited his mother. She was a sturdy woman, on her third marriage after being twice widowed, who survived by taking farm jobs such as haymaking and threshing—jobs normally reserved for men. She had a blunt manner: when her son ate unripe grapes that made his hair stand on end and gave him colic, she said, "Eat them if you like, and die for all I care." Another time she asked if the devil had brought him. But everyone agreed that she was honest, upright, and pious. What mother hasn't lost her temper when her son ate too much green fruit? Thomas tasted the milk of human kindness while staying with aunts or among good German burghers but not at home with his own mother.

* * *

One thing is missing in all these accounts of Thomas's travels: death. It is unthinkable that there were no deaths among the adolescents and children, the "graduates" and "schoolboys," who roamed Switzerland and the still more dangerous Germany in the company of young Platter. Thomas, who during hard Silesian winters had been obliged to discover the discomforts of the hospital, does not mention losing any of his comrades. Was this a taboo subject? A blind spot in Thomas's memory? Or a matter of indifference? In any case, Thomas was a sensitive boy, and at times even tender.

If death is absent from Thomas's memoirs, childhood is perforce amply represented. Peter Laslett, the author of the widely read *World We Have Lost,* lamented that few documents from before 1800 deal with childhood as such. Platter's memoirs would have served him well. They are among our three or four most important sources concerning the lives of peasant children in early modern Europe. The others are the hard-hitting texts of Jamerai Duval and the future Captain Coignet, both of whom begged as boys, and Rétif de La Bretonne's *Monsieur Nicolas,* which deals with peasants in somewhat easier circumstances.

* * *

In Zurich, though, Thomas was unable to make much intellectual progress. His new friend Antonius Venetz invited him to head back north, to Strasbourg. Alsace in this period was experiencing an intellectual and religious transformation along with substantial economic and demographic growth.[9] Thomas has nothing to say about any of this: his interests did not extend that far. About Strasbourg, the Alsatian metropolis, he is laconic: "Many poor schoolchildren, wretched school." From Strasbourg, the two boys moved on to Sélestat. There, they received valuable instruction in the local school, but there was too much competition for food among the large number of impoverished pupils. Platter reached Sélestat in September 1520. Shortly before, he had suffered another attack of colic after eating unripe walnuts that had fallen to the ground: always short of money and good food, Thomas was perpetually ready to swallow anything. He was then twenty-one (and not, as he claimed, eighteen, for he had somehow miscounted the years). He left Sélestat around Pentecost of 1521—the year, as he expressly notes, of the Diet of Worms. This was when Luther, summoned to appear before the imperial diet, declared to Charles V: "Here I stand, I can do no other." Clearly Thomas was beginning to take an interest in the Reformation. That he was aware of such an event was not unusual: Sélestat was in a German-speaking region, and Thomas was a poor youth who, though not yet an intellectual, hoped to become one. Openness to reform was fairly widely shared. A few years later, in a different social setting, it found a rather different issue in the Peasants' War, whose causes were at once evangelical and "communalist."

In any case, the school at Sélestat was good for Thomas Platter. It was there that he really learned to read—in Latin, of course, and none too soon. The school was run by Johannes Sapidus (whose real name was Witz). A competent Hellenist, Sapidus was hostile to obscenities and barbarisms, which offended his sense of propriety. He favored methods that some people nowadays consider old-fashioned: his students were required to learn texts by heart and study grammar diligently. He was a fervent teacher of "the Donatus," a grammar dating from Late Antiquity that was still quite popular in medieval and Renaissance schools. It was the work of the fourth-century writer Aelius Donatus, who also taught Saint Jerome and wrote a commentary on Terence. Sapidus was an adept of the Rhenish strand of humanism, which was greatly influenced by the *devotio moderna,* a form of piety that flourished in Flanders and the Rhineland between 1300 and 1500. Christocentric, the *devotio moderna* emphasized the inward, subjective, emotional aspects of religion: enthusiasm, meditation, virtue, asceticism. It frowned upon interminable prayer, hierarchy, formalistic charity and ritual, the apostolic succession, and proselytism.[10] *The Imitation of Christ* made its tenets familiar to a broad audience. Adepts of the *devotio moderna* were deathly afraid of any rift with Catholicism, however, in contrast to Thomas, who did ultimately break with the Church. Sapidus was more cautious. To be sure, he detested the corruption of the clergy, but he rejected any radical reform of religion along Lutheran or other Protestant lines that might have challenged the dogma or temporal structure of the Church.

The Alsatian teacher's methods were simple, if stringent: "In my school, if you work, everything is free. If you are lazy, you will pay through the nose." In a school full of children, Platter and Venetz were already grown men. Both were mangy, especially Venetz, whose clothes Thomas peeled off in the morning as if skinning a goat. A former goat-herd who had been beaten like a kid and who now skinned men as if they were goats—was Thomas's destiny set out in advance? In front of the other schoolchildren Sapidus described in gruesome detail the physical disgrace that had befallen Antonius and Thomas on account of a tiny mite (the cause of mange). Yet Thomas retained fond memories of the Sélestat schoolmaster, whom he would later describe as his "dear *Praeceptor.*" In this small Alsatian town, whose sixteenth-century cultural splendor is often evoked by humanist scholars even now,[11] Thomas learned, if not to write, at least to read tolerably well—and even to stumble his way through the inevitable Donatus, which, over a period of a thousand years, initiated some thirty generations of schoolchildren into the arcana of Latin. Eventually Thomas learned the Donatian *Ars major* by heart, even though he could not yet write: it was not for nothing that the six-teenth century cultivated the arts of memory. By the time he felt ready to leave Sélestat, Platter possessed a good basic knowledge of spoken Latin: according to the methods then in use, writing and reading were distinct objects of study. This distinction would persist among the literate well into the eighteenth or even nineteenth century.[12] In Thomas's day, to be a decent reader at age twenty-one was no mean feat. What extraordinary lengths he had gone to—over more than a decade—to attain a level of education that even the indifferent student achieves today without much difficulty.

Eventually Thomas had to leave Sélestat because begging, that source of most "scholarships" in the waning Middle Ages, had ceased to pay. Some 900 schoolchildren, many of them beggars, had strained the gener-osity of the town's fairly small population. By attracting several hundred students to his school, Sapidus had precipitated a crash in the "alms mar-ket." Some of his "graduates" would later carry on his work, going on to become excellent teachers in what is today the French *département* of the Haut-Rhin.

By Pentecost of 1521 Thomas had returned to Switzerland. He went first to Soleure, where there was a good school and the food was decent but he wasted many hours in interminable religious services. Lutheraniz-ation was just beginning to make inroads. Growing restless, Thomas de-cided to revisit his Valaisian roots. While staying with two aunts, he had clear proof that now, in his early twenties, and having overcome many obstacles, he was at last well on the way to literacy: in twenty-four hours (by his own account), he taught a young cousin his *abc*'s. The lad, Simon

Steiner by name, clearly had the right stuff. Following in the footsteps of his modest master, he grew up to become a teacher in Strasbourg and a friend of Bucer. Obviously, a child did not have to attend school to acquire the rudiments of an education. A friend or relative could teach anyone eager enough to learn.

Thomas soon learned how to write as well. His progress was unstoppable: a Valaisian priest taught him "a little" about writing, and he quickly made rapid strides in the art of inscribing marks on vellum and paper, if not in the actual composition of texts. The following spring (1522?), our young man once again quit the high valleys of southern Switzerland, but not before bidding his mother a tearful farewell: perhaps she was not quite so hard-hearted as he makes her out to be elsewhere in his book. "May God have mercy on me," she cried. "I have had to watch three sons leave home for lives of poverty!" At that moment the other children she had lost to plague and war were surely on her mind as well. For all its gruff exterior, the Platter family preserved a discreet fund of affection for its "needy" members. But standards of family feeling in those days were very different from what they are now and even more different from what they were in our parents' and grandparents' day. Certain stereotypes should be banished from our minds. In an interesting recent book, the sociologist Michel Fize writes: "From ancient Rome to 1945, the model of family authority governing relations between parents and adolescents changed little. The father reigned as head of the family."[13] This may be an overstatement. In fact, Thomas, like many of his contemporaries, scarcely knew his father. And while his mother did not abandon him entirely, she did leave him with aunts and cousins. Authority, though, generally came from the male side. While still very young, Thomas worked for a living or at any rate helped to support his various patrons. He earned an income, unlike children in the late twentieth century, who cost their parents money. The Platter clan, with its flexible, interlocking networks, treated him harshly but also accorded him a measure of affection and care without which he could not have survived. And when he left the Valais yet again in 1522 or 1523, he did so in the company of two of his brothers (he had a whole slew of them, of whom several had survived childhood). The journey nearly proved disastrous, for Thomas came close to dying one sparklingly clear, bitter-cold night on a snowy slope that he tried to descend too quickly. Perhaps in his horizontal peregrinations around the Holy Roman Empire he had lost some of his mountaineering skills, unlike his brothers, who retained the surefootedness that went with the highland lifestyle. But Thomas quickly regained his footing.

Leaving his two brothers in Entlebuch, where they found modest employment, Thomas once again settled in Zurich. There, in a plague year, he stayed with a woman named Gwalther and tended her baby, Rudolf. Little Rudolf would grow up to become the learned pastor of Saint Peter's Church in Zurich. Apart from his part-time chores as baby-sitter, Thomas sampled the teaching of several masters, among them a certain Knöwell, who had studied in Paris, where he acquired a taste for pretty girls. Platter's favorite teacher was Myconius, whose real name was Oswald Geisshüssler, from Lucerne. Myconius was an original: a very learned man whose motto was not "study or pay" [T 60] but "work (intellectually) or die." He did not beat his students (some of whom were twenty years old or more, after all), but he did require them, and Thomas in particular, to go beyond what they had memorized from Donatus. They were obliged to learn Latin declensions and conjugations and to check their knowledge against the texts of Terence, a playwright for whom Thomas's appetite had been whetted at Saint Elizabeth's school in Breslau. Myconius proved to be a vigilant but not abusive teacher: a cuff on the ears and a backhand slap on the cheek were the only blows that Thomas received. He did sweat, though: by dint of hard work, he eventually learned to distinguish the nominative from the genitive and the third declension from the first.

Above all, Myconius became a kind of friend for Thomas, though his affection could be gruff and condescending. The young man, often malnourished, found a way to pay his master for meals by recounting tales of his wanderings in Germany, at that time still fresh in his mind. In addition, the two men together became acquainted with the early stages of the Protestant Reformation (Myconius being only slightly ahead of his pupil in this regard). The light of the Gospel had begun to shine; the struggle against "false idols" was under way. Myconius, a cantor (though not a priest), was obliged to take part regularly in masses, matins, and vespers at the Church of Our Lady. He, too, sang for his dinner! Such jobs were a mainstay of young clerics of the period.

Myconius much preferred teaching to officiating in the Roman style, which he disliked. He accordingly delegated some of his responsibilities to Thomas, who took his place as cantor or sacristan and "bellowed" (*sic*) requiems in his master's stead. Bellowing was no longer what was wanted, however: the urgent task of the hour was to explain the Gospel text in the new manner of the Lutherans and, before long, the Zwinglians. Myconius thus played an important role in Thomas's career, because he was also a friend of Zwingli's and aided him in the early stages of his work. Zwingli (who shared Myconius's dislike of certain hymns) was at times more extreme than the German reformers. He had nevertheless forged ties with Luther on the basis of their passionate mutual interest in such subjects as grace and free will, the psalms, and Saint Augustine.[14]

To believe Platter, moreover, Myconius was quite different from the hordes of would-be priests who went to ordination with little in their heads beyond a few notions about how to sing hymns. Such men knew nothing of Latin grammar and had never meditated on sacred texts. To Myconius these men of counterfeit learning were worse than ignorant.

*　*　*

In 1522, some five or six years after Luther's emergence into the public arena, Thomas Platter experienced a religious crisis. Thomas explicitly describes himself as a follower of Luther, although he knew little at the time about Luther's ideas, with which Zwingli, the spiritual and political leader of Zurich reformers, was far from being in total agreement. Until this sudden turn in Thomas's religious beliefs, brought on in part by the general spiritual ferment in Switzerland's large cities, he had been a good boy, respectful of traditional religious notions that are sometimes described as naive. He had aspired to become a priest, and that ambition had led him to roam Europe, from Switzerland to Germany to Poland and back again, in order to learn how to read and write—abilities that long eluded him for want of competent, devoted teachers. Then, suddenly, during his stay in Sélestat, basic literacy came to him like a bolt out of the blue, suffusing his whole being and transforming him through and through. His original religious vocation had not lacked sincerity, yet all it took was a thunderous sermon by Zwingli, who flayed Christendom's corrupt shepherds for losing so many of Christ's lambs, for Thomas to become a wholehearted partisan of the Reformation.

As a child, however, Thomas had dreamed of serving zealously at a handsomely decorated altar. He had invoked the Virgin along with Saints Catherine, Barbara, and Peter, the patrons, respectively, of childhood, education, a pious death, and the entry into the hereafter. Here was a full program, an itinerary, for life and death. The ecclesiastical calling, which had been drilled into the Valaisian goatherd's soul from a tender age, was also linked very early to a desire for social advancement and even social revenge. Thomas and his mother were very poor, and all the boy wanted was a chance to bounce back. He came of good stock: there were people of substance among his forebears and collateral kin. The Platters on his father's side and the Summermatters on his mother's owned homes and farms on the rocky plateaus. One of Thomas's cousins, old Antony Platter, was a priest. More than that, the boy's uncle (his mother's brother) was a castellan in the Visp district (being a castellan meant, as we saw earlier, not that he was a nobleman but rather an official responsible for law and order in a handful of villages, something between a steward of the castle and a local chieftain). Modest clerical ambitions such as Thomas's were traditional and perfectly legitimate in this milieu of substantial peasants and minor officials. But now, all at once, the New Testament and even the Old Testament had struck the young man like a thunderbolt, descending out of the blue like the eagles and bears that snatched young goats from the highland herds.

Now that Thomas could read, he kept a copy of the New Testament, which for some seasons now the printers had made widely available, in his knapsack. He took it out and brandished it frequently. And he learned it by heart, as he had once swallowed the Donatus: from Latin grammar to the grammar of the heavens. Platter also took counsel from Myconius and the sermons of Zwingli. He felt sufficiently well educated to refute the cult of the saints, starting with Saint Peter (Saint John came later). Thomas joined a large group of recent "heretics," who attacked doctrines that had been professed in Latin Christendom for a millennium. Catholics had joined heaven to the fallen world below through the mediation of the host on the altar; through the real presence of God in the sanctuary; through the sovereign pontiff; and through saints whose relics were piously preserved. Together, these things gave celestial sanctity a *point of contact* with the terrestrial life of mankind, an incarnation here below.[15] Unfortunately, perhaps, the Lutherans, Zwinglians, and men like Thomas Platter confused this Roman suture, this Catholic structure, with the cult of Baal and other idols condemned by the Bible, which their cumbrous Germanic intelligences assimilated all too rapidly. And so the clear Latin unities, the harmonious fusions of Heaven and Earth, were replaced by a dramatic German dichotomy between the old Teutonic folklore of forests and elves and the pure light of the Gospel. During one stay in the Valais, for example, Platter decided to consign a statue of Saint John to the oven; the paint on the heavy wooden figurine sputtered horribly before the object was totally consumed.[16] The statue must have been one of those handsome Rhenish Swiss icons of the late Middle Ages that are nowadays so highly prized by art lovers and dealers.[17] At the age of twenty-two Thomas thus underwent a cultural transformation: to learn to read and write, to enter the world of letters, manuscripts, and printed editions, meant nothing less.

Having passed through the looking-glass, the Helvetian was ready to turn on "wicked priests" he had known, like the one in Silesia who, be-

cause Thomas had eaten cheese one morning, refused to grant him abso-
lution, which barred him from taking communion and thus in good logic
kept him from partaking of the substantial postcommunion meal.
Thomas thus joined the flock of the Good Shepherd who "giveth his life
for the sheep" (John 10:11). He traded his rural "ignorance" (which in fact
hid a considerable fund of knowledge of pastoral agriculture) for new
ideas from the city. After his sacrilegious sojourn in the Valais, Thomas
returned to Zurich (around 1525).[18] The journey was a pious pilgrimage
to Zwingli's new Jerusalem and a farewell (though not a permanent one)
to the Valaisians. Good-bye to all those country bumpkins, intellectually
vacuous people good for nothing but milking cows, as Zwingli, himself
of rural background, derogatorily observed. It was so tempting for
Thomas to "spit in the soup" that had tasted so good back in the days
when he was a young boy romping with his goats in green mountain pastures. Zurich with its bracing spiritual climate drew Thomas as a light
draws a moth. In the city he met new people, but soon he was off again on
a month-long excursion to Lake Uri. He traveled by boat as well as on
foot. Along the way he found time for a monumental "bender," made
possible by the generosity of a wine merchant. The journey was also
marked by a storm on Lake Uri that nearly sank the frail bark carrying
Platter and all his worldly possessions. We are reminded that the existence of memoirs from the past is a matter of chance: the writer has to be
lucky in both life and death. Following this excursion, Thomas returned
to Zurich. There he lived chastely in a friend's room in the house of an old
woman, the hospitable and shrewd Adelaide, who seems to have had the
manners of a madam in a brothel. The two youths were famished. At
times they were compelled to stave off starvation by eating what they
could scrape off the bottoms of pots. So Thomas was not out of the
woods yet: he still had no real home. One could hardly treat one's body
worse than Thomas treated his, but then the body is but a wretched carcass, a miserable tabernacle that the immortal soul makes its temporary
abode. And who was to blame for Thomas's plight? Street-singing was
scorned as a priestly custom hence no longer serviceable as a way of begging alms. Soon the people of Zurich would take up a general collection
to provide for the poor now that individual begging was looked upon as
an outdated practice, a relic of the past.

Thomas eked out a living by working the land outside the city walls,
hauling logs for food and wages, and performing the duties of a sacristan.
These activities brought in just enough to pay old Adelaide the rent on
his half of the tiny room he shared with his friend. Platter meanwhile
risked his neck carrying letters from Zwingli, Myconius, and other Protestant leaders to their heretical disciples in the Five Cantons. This mes-

senger work became even riskier at the time of the Baden conference (1526). The Catholics, still very powerful in the Empire and even in the Confederation, sought to silence the rapidly growing Helvetian and Zwinglian heterodoxy. French agents were numerous in Zurich, as were francophiles generally. It was in Zurich, in fact, that Thomas first encountered the powerful influence of the great kingdom that loomed so large on the western horizon of his new homeland. The "Welch" factions would not have been unhappy to see Zwingli consigned to the flames without trial. Of course the great man was well aware of the danger. He never left Zurich, where he was protected by supporters and bodyguards from would-be assassins who, riding horses with padded shoes, prowled the city by night in search of the heretic leader. Zwingli was present at the Baden conference, however, if not in body then at least in spirit, for he was represented by his friend Œcolampadius, who received his instructions and acted as his spokesman.

Communication between Zurich and Baden was maintained by messengers, who were at times literally runners. Volunteers, including Platter and other young men and even boys, ran the roads between the two cities and arrived, as was only fitting, covered with dust and sweat. Thus reports from the Baden conference reached Zurich, and Zwingli's reactions were then carried back to Œcolampadius. Sometimes Thomas or one of the other messengers drove a hay wagon or accompanied a shipment of chickens as cover on the dangerous journey. There were nevertheless many close calls; Thomas himself had quite a few. As always in underground resistance operations, children were less likely to be suspected than adults. It was a little boy, for example, who carried one batch of urgent letters from Zwingli to Baden. Arriving at his destination in the evening, he found the gates of the city closed and promptly climbed into a hay wagon and fell asleep. At dawn, the carter, unaware of his sleeping passenger, drove his wagon into the city. Meanwhile, the messenger boy, slumbering soundly on his soft bed of hay, did not awaken until the wagon had come to rest right in the middle of town. Rubbing the sleep from his eyes, he slid down the hay stack into the street, quickly scouted out the scene, and set off to deliver his message—all under the noses of the soldiers charged with arresting and locking up Protestant emissaries. No one was any the wiser.

*   *   *

Thomas's sudden change of religion was followed by a period of intense intellectual and, more precisely, linguistic fermentation. Platter was typical of a certain kind of self-made man: instead of amassing a quick fortune, he discovered culture, rose in society, and fathered a family of distinguished children. There were many such men in early modern France: think of the ancestors of Louvois, Colbert, Villeroy, and others like them. In Thomas's case, however, we have the unique good fortune of being able to examine the beginnings of such a saga of social ascent in the story of an ex-goatherd. So many families have, out of misplaced pride, obliterated all traces of the humble but ingenious ancestor who started them on their way up the social ladder. Disdainful of such snobbery, Felix Platter instead asked his aging father to dictate his memoirs, for which we owe him a debt of gratitude.

*　*　*

But the year is still 1526. Thomas, his appetite whetted by his perilous exploits as a secret agent, set out to master three languages simultaneously: Latin, Greek, and Hebrew. (Learning classical German, or *Hochdeutsch,* with which young Thomas was certainly familiar—he quotes the Lutheran Bible—was the least of his concerns. Virtually all of his writing is in the Basel dialect. It was not given to everyone to become a Luther, the man who made the German tongue anew.) When it came to the three ancient languages, Thomas, always short of time to study, spared no effort. At night he chewed on raw turnips and even sand and drank cold water to keep himself awake in order to spend more time with his eyes open and his nose in a book. (Graduate students might find these tips worth noticing.) Platter even bought a Hebrew Bible from Venice with the modest inheritance he received from his mother. This experience with the Bible was among his first completely private and personal relationships with a book—with The Book. Thomas was fed, housed, and kept warm at first by Myconius and later by others in Zurich and nearby towns in return for teaching them the language of the Old Testament.[19] He taught them what he had learned the day before. During the Renaissance, culture was transmitted at a prodigious rate. It spread from person to person by contagion, like the plague.

Hebrew, however, did not suffice to keep this teacher alive—though merely to call him a teacher shows the extraordinary strides made by this former illiterate, now a humanist and scholar of sorts. Other things interested him as well: Thomas was susceptible to the "workerist" propaganda put out by Zwingli and other reformers who believed in the eminent dignity of manual labor (Adam hoed, Eve sewed, and Jesus was a carpenter). They also worried, as Richelieu, Colbert, and Voltaire would do after them, about the possible overproduction of priests and Latinists—in a word, intellectuals. Earn thy bread in the sweat of thy brow! Had such ideas been taken seriously, sixteenth-century universities might well have found themselves without students. And in a sense they were taken seriously. Anticlericalism, which was rampant between 1525 and 1529, did not bother to distinguish between students, or readers generally, and those who were studying specifically to become priests: all were derided as "priestlings." After spending some time as a teacher of Hebrew, an experience, as we shall see, that would have its importance later on, Thomas embarked on a new phase of his life in which he sought to apprentice himself to a master craftsman while also continuing his studies, "pounding the books" and working with his hands at the same time.

*   *   *

As it happens, Platter chose to take up the art of ropemaking, a choice dictated by a chance encounter with a young master ropemaker. The ex-Valaisian used part of his inheritance to purchase a quintal of hemp (and it is because of this that we learn of his mother's death, which must have occurred some time in 1525 or 1526 and apparently had little emotional impact on her son). Thomas began training with his new "master." Hemp in hand, he braided rope. His young master, though elegantly dressed, must have been close to broke, because he was unable to provide his new employee with raw material. Or perhaps it was just one of those old guild rules according to which a newly hired apprentice has to add some capital to the business, in this case a quantity of hemp. This investment was supposed to cover the cost of training the neophyte.[20] Platter worked at a frightening pace: when the master slept (Thomas had rooms in his employer's house), the apprentice read and took notes on Homer and Pindar at breakneck speed. The former goatherd thus emulated, on a more modest scale, Rabelais's Gargantua, improving himself both intellectually and manually.

When he finally learned, more or less, how to make rope (and he was never to become very good at it), Thomas decided it was time to leave the shop owner's employ, just as he had earlier left the "protection" of his older cousin Paul. He hastened to the disreputable house of his former landlady, the affable Adelaide. But Platter had no intention of wooing the bevies of young women who presumably worked for the elderly madam. He simply took lodging in the bordello: in that oasis of carnal indulgence, he merely rented a room where he could read Euripides. His copy of the playwright's works is filled with notes made during six weeks of non-stop reading, during which no one knew where he was. One wonders if the puritanical Zwingli knew similar pleasures. If our neophyte ropemaker also indulged in fornication while reading in the brothel, he kept no record of it. At the end of his stay with Adelaide, he made up his mind to take to the road once again, this time heading for Basel. Did he fear the wrath of the employer he had left in the lurch? In any case, he decided to make himself ready for such an important departure by bathing his entire body, something he surely had not done in quite some time. His contacts in the world of prostitution may have been useful, because the bawdy houses now controlled the baths. In a bathhouse run by a woman, Thomas took a hot dip, which made him sick, and injured himself in a fall, topping it all off with a nocturnal mudbath. Was it unwise to scour away all at once the filth of months if not years? Having thus warmed, cooled, and deodorized himself (if the final mud bath did not restore some of the odor that the scouring had removed), Thomas picked up his bundle of clothes and set out for Basel, which he reached in two days. There he decided to pitch his tent and ply his new trades, teaching and ropemaking.

At first things were difficult in Basel. Thomas found work with Master Hans Stähelin, the Swabian ropemaker whose shop was located near the cattle market. Stähelin, a violent man always ready with an insult, was not popular among workers. Here we find one of the rare allusions in Thomas's prose if not to class struggle then at least to the bitterness of relations between different social groups. Later, his son Felix would not be much more loquacious on this subject. In any case, Master Stähelin was unpopular. Thomas had no difficulty finding a job in his shop: there was little competition for the spot. The "red ropemaker," as Stähelin was known, now employed an apprentice and two workmen, one of whom was Thomas, who with some exaggeration claimed to have completed an apprenticeship in ropemaking in Zurich. Stähelin treated his workers very badly, giving them rotten cheese which his wife hastened to throw out the window the moment her husband's back was turned. Because there was virtually no heat, the winters were hard. The boss's young apprentice called Thomas, whose ropemaking skills were minimal, a "cow's mouth" (T 80). The master was, as one might imagine, hardly more ingratiating: he disliked the fact that the new man from Zurich spent his Sundays and holidays, nights, and even working hours reading Plautus in the original. Plautus, Platter: Thomas unstitched his edition of the Latin comic writer and cleverly stashed its pages in bundles of hemp until Stähelin discovered his secret, which provoked a stream of frightful invective.[21] "Priestling" was the supreme insult in those days, and Thomas heard it on this occasion. Obviously Zwinglian propaganda had had an impact here too: clerical work, and indeed intellectual work generally, enjoyed no better reputation in Basel than it did in Zurich. Eventually, however, the ropemaker grew used to Thomas. He was the only man in the shop who could read and write and therefore keep the books, recording inflows and outflows of raw materials, finished goods, wages, and the like.

*   *   *

Stähelin even allowed Thomas time off to teach Hebrew, though he may have reduced his wages accordingly. In any case, Thomas taught for an hour every Monday at the school connected with Saint Leonhard's Church. He had eighteen pupils, who in the beginning giggled at the filthy workman's attire in which their new teacher was obliged to appear before them. Most likely the students paid for their lessons. Valaisians counted their pennies, and the young "teacher" gave nothing away for free. His dress may have been odd, but he was more than competent. Thomas for the first time enjoyed the status, and stature, of an intellectual: he was part of the small but luminous circle of Basel humanists. Among them was one Cratander, alias Andreas Hartmann of Strasbourg, a printer, bookseller, and publisher of Plautus. There were close ties at the time between Basel Protestants and religious dissidents in Strasbourg, all of whom had the German language in common. By contrast, French-speaking Geneva was less closely connected with Basel than were German-speaking cities on the banks of the Rhine. But things would soon change: Calvin was coming—Calvin, that slender but sturdy Picardian bridge between "heretical" Germans and Gauls. Thomas also saw a great deal of that prodigious scholar Beatus Rhenanus, who worked with Amerbach, another important local printer. Beatus would soon become one of the scientific luminaries of Sélestat and Upper Alsace.[22]

Thomas Platter also had close ties to another resident of Basel, Oporinus (Johann Herbster), who would later produce an admirable edition of Vesalius's treatise on anatomy. Johann was first a teacher and later a printer. In his teaching Thomas used a Hebrew grammar published in 1524 by Sebastian Münster, a linguist and cosmographer. Münster did not actually set up in Basel as a professor of Hebrew until the summer of 1529. Hence we may assume that Thomas's career as a teacher in Basel must have ended by 1528 at the latest, at which time the erstwhile ropemaker was at most twenty-nine. The chronology I am proposing here can easily be checked against the established facts: Thomas states that he never knew Münster except through his celebrated grammar, from which he had taught students without having met the author. On one occasion Thomas even crossed paths with Erasmus, who lived in Basel for a time. The great humanist offered the former goatherd a few words of encouragement. Erasmus left Basel (where he had been since November 1521) in April 1529, a date compatible with my proposed chronology. Platter also met a young man who came to him to study Hebrew and who had something of a propensity to tell tall tales. Subsequently this man traveled for almost a decade, making the rounds of Jewish rabbis in Crete, Asia, and Arabia, or so he claimed after returning to the bosom of his Swiss family.

During his lectures on Hebrew, which brought him into contact with so many people, Platter liked to comment on the Book of Jonah, the prophet who spent three days in the belly of a whale or sea monster before being cast upon a shore. In Zwinglian propaganda this monster was often equated with the Anti-Christ or the Church of Rome, as the occasion required. Topical or not, the allusion was colorful and pleased Thomas, who passed it on to his audience.

Following his mystical phases in the Valais and in Zurich, Thomas became a confirmed teacher in Basel and would remain so until the end of his life. He no longer gave private lessons in Hebrew to a few pupils from the city's outlying districts. Now he delivered full-blown lectures to twenty-odd fledgling Hebrew scholars who met in Saint Leonhard's Church. The timing could not have been better for a convinced anti-papist like Thomas, for Basel, under the leadership of Œcolampadius, was just experiencing its Protestant revolution, which would culminate, to the detriment of local "papism," in February 1529.[23]

* * *

Thomas's first experience as a teacher was cut short by the brief little war that Basel Protestants and their allies from Zurich and elsewhere waged against five Catholic cantons (Lucerne, Uri, Schwyz, Unterwalden, and Zug) in the late spring of 1529. Platter, not quite thirty, was active in the tiny Protestant army. He wore his employer's breastplate, hauled wine for combatants and merchants, and carried messages to captains in the field. At Kappel in midsummer a cease-fire was declared. Catholics and Protestants shared a huge pot of milk soup, symbolizing the end of hostilities. The conflict, though relatively insignificant, nevertheless left a legacy of rancor and hatred. The Basel forces insisted on a ceremonial burning of the treacherous anti-heretic treaty that the papist cantons had signed with the "king of the Romans," Ferdinand of Hapsburg. The treasonous document was reduced to ash as Thomas looked on. A few moderates in the Protestant camp wanted to examine the accursed treaty before it was incinerated, but anti-Catholic extremists threatened violence if the offending parchments were not burned immediately. Zwingli, a maximalist, denounced the Treaty of Kappel as a hasty mistake, an "appeasement" that would only sow the seeds of another war (in which, when it came in 1531, he was to meet his death). Although the spirit of moderation did not prevail in 1529, it did eventually take hold in Switzerland, where Protestants and Catholics found it possible to coexist in peace. Thus despite a brief resurgence of religious combat in 1531, the Confederation managed to avoid the fanaticism and horror of the religious warfare that would devastate its neighbor France some thirty or forty years later.

* * *

The clatter of arms and the impassioned rhetoric of Zwingli gave way to a period of greater calm in Thomas's life. These were relatively idyllic years, although Thomas still lived quite modestly. He returned to Zurich and Hut Macherin's inn of ill repute, where he shared a room with Simon Steiner, the cousin to whom he had taught his *abc*'s. The two men remained close even after Steiner went off to teach in Strasbourg. When they were rooming together in Zurich in the late summer of 1529, Simon was living on free food that was handed out to the poor in a deconsecrated Dominican monastery. Had Thomas tired of the old life? In any case, he took a significant step: he married Anna Dietschi, the servant of his master Myconius. Born in 1497, Anna was two or three years older than her husband. She came from a family that included, in Zurich alone, burghers, goldsmiths, and nobles, whose coat of arms bore a gold crown. But the pedigree is misleading: Anna married without dowry and brought few resources into the marriage. She belonged to a penniless rustic branch of the prestigious Dietschi clan. Her parents had lived in the country, and her brother earned a living making baskets, seats, and brooms in Lucerne.

Left an orphan, young Anna soon found work as a maid. She worked hard as a servant and spinner and helped her employer, Myconius, by processing hemp; meanwhile, she filled her trousseau with tunics she made herself out of coarse fabric. She was no pauper: until her marriage she had never slept on straw (but later would share a bed of straw on occasion with Thomas, a man quite familiar with rude accommodations in three countries). A shy woman, Anna was as pious as her husband. The newlyweds, though well past adolescence, observed a postnuptial custom that was widespread in Christian Europe: they went two months without sleeping together. Housing problems may have been the reason for their abstinence: the couple continued to live separately, Anna with Myconius, Thomas at Macherin's "inn." Whether out of choice or necessity, therefore, they continued to abstain longer than was strictly required (if indeed abstinence was required at all). They finally decided to take the plunge only after being egged on by Myconius in his characteristic friendly, good-natured way: "Wen wil tu by dim Anni ligen?" (When will you lie with Anna? [T 86]). After some weeks they made up their minds, not least because they were afraid of seeming ridiculous in the eyes of a priest to whom Thomas had once taught Hebrew and who now offered them a place where they could spend nights together. Much later, when Thomas was an old man thinking back on Anna's past, he remarked how wages had risen over the course of the sixteenth century: at the time of the couple's marriage in 1529, servants earned roughly two-thirds of what they were paid in 1572, when Thomas came to write his memoirs. But Platter's reckoning failed to take account of inflation: rising prices would probably have more than offset these increased wages, leaving domestic servants worse off than before.

More prosaically, Thomas and Anna's life together was punctuated by quarrels over money and debts. In the long run, however, these fights only made their marriage stronger. I would not go as far, however, as those who say that marital squabbling is "an excellent form of therapy, an antidote against divorce and a kind of nuptial life insurance policy"[24]— though it is true that Thomas and his wife would remain together without serious rift until Anna's death. After several weeks in Zurich, the couple decided to head south, to Platter's native Valais, where they hoped to find work in the teaching and ropemaking trades. As ropemakers they were a team: Anna worked with the distaff and spinning wheel, while Thomas braided rope. One of their first stops was in Sarnen, a canton of Unterwalden, which, to believe the possibly exaggerated Swiss folktales of the period, was a region full of inveterate drunkards. The local innkeeper, a lutist, and his wife, both completely drunk, could barely manage to make up a bed for the young couple; the two hosts then spent the night sprawled on benches in the tavern. At the break of dawn, the innkeeper, recovered from his monumental binge, managed to present our student of ancient languages with a bill (possibly a little stained with wine). With some annoyance Thomas paid what he owed.

The journey from Unterwalden to Visp (in the Valais), across the Alps and through the Grimsel pass, was made in two stages. The traveling was unpleasant at first. Thomas and his wife were not accustomed to stale bread, and at high altitudes they ran into snow. Snowflakes adhered to their clothes and skin. They also met with hostility from the still-Catholic natives of the Upper Valais, who were not overly fond of Zurich or Zwinglians. Nevertheless, on the descent into Visp (also known as Viège), they met good people (T 88). At the baths in Brigg, reputed to be good for injured limbs, nasal fluxes, the shakes, deafness, and cramps, they met a friendly barber, who also kept an inn and was in charge of the baths, and his mistress, who helped him in his various capacities. After giving birth to a child in Zurich, this woman had fled her father's wrath. (The father, incidentally, became a national hero in the next outbreak of religious war: he died for Switzerland, presumably but which Switzerland?) A little farther on, and at a somewhat higher altitude, Thomas was reunited with one of his sisters, Christine, who was accompanied by her husband, nine children, and two of her husband's elderly aunts, each said to be over one hundred years old. Christine gave Thomas what she could spare from their mother's modest legacy: some linen and an ass. The animal allowed Thomas and Anna to continue their journey in comfort, carrying their baggage the rest of the way to Visp.

*   *   *

In Visp Thomas knew true prosperity for perhaps the first time in his young life (the date was approximately 1530). He worked as a ropemaker and schoolteacher and earned additional money selling wine and apples to his students (the money to buy apples came from a loan from his uncle, Antony Summermatter). In rural and mountainous areas in those days, schoolteaching was a prestigious profession: a teacher commanded respect and often received gifts in kind from his pupils' parents. Thomas and Anna lived in a fine house that had been set aside for the local schoolteacher, a house with glass windows and a borrowed bed supplied free of charge. The parents of Thomas's students (of whom there were some thirty during the summer but only six during the winter) paid him a cash fee supplmented by gifts of milk, vegetables, and quarters of mutton. Platter's many unmarried female cousins (of whom there were at least seventy-two in the region) kept him supplied with butter, cheese, and eggs. The schoolmaster even found it possible to put some money aside. When Thomas left Visp after a relatively brief stay, he took with him thirteen pieces of gold. For the time being his debts were no more than a bad memory. At the time, learning was hard to come by in such plebeian surroundings, but it could help to pull the person who did manage to acquire it out of poverty.

Thus Thomas enjoyed a newfound prosperity, but he was hardly a hedonistic materialist. People in town also had certain expectations of him. Ever since he was a child, they had believed that he would become a priest: this reputation had spread far and wide, to villages well beyond his birthplace and among his seventy-two still virginal female cousins (T 90). It was expected that he would celebrate a memorable first mass in a parish in the Valais, at which time dozens of young ladies taking part in the traditional procession would heap him with gifts. While Thomas was still off acquiring an education, this wonderfully exciting event had often been discussed in anticipation by the women of the highland hamlets when they gathered in the evening around the fire. So one can easily imagine the disappointment these Catholics still in awe of their clerics must have felt when Thomas returned home with a wife who helped him sell apples to schoolchildren, a woman who had to be something of a *huren* (whore, T 50). The word shocked poor Thomas, whose wife was in fact absolutely virtuous, like her husband. What is more, in this bigoted, backwater community, Thomas would have been expected to attend mass and even chant prayers: in those days attendance at mass was a duty incumbent upon any schoolmaster worthy of the name. But he found the Catholic mass a burdensome and vexing chore. He did not like to violate what he called his "conscience" by faking conventional piety, insisting instead on freedom of expression, though he himself had left precious little liberty to poor Saint John, whose effigy he had consigned to the oven's flames.

At some point Thomas could no longer bear the pressure. He returned to Zurich to consult his spiritual master, Myconius, who was also a kind of father-in-law, for he had given Platter his own servant as a wife (and as a matter of fact still owed Anna a considerable sum in unpaid back wages, which he never did pay: it was possible to be learned and pious and still be dishonest—or broke). Myconius recommended that Thomas pitch his tent somewhere else, outside a Valais that still worshiped idols. Perhaps he ought to return to Basel, where there were opportunities to be found. So much for the good life in the Valais: no more quarters of mutton, no more butter or cheese. Thomas had tasted plenty, but not for long.

In looking back on this period before heading north to stay, Thomas reflected on life in the highlands, and indeed in Switzerland and Europe generally, in light of his experiences. His account is not simply another version of the usual sixteenth century triptych: famine, pestilence, war. For him the things that stood out were cold (or, more precisely, snow), pestilence (to be sure), and, more surprisingly, childbirth (which all too often spelled death). Snow was an affliction of high altitudes: on his return to the Valais from Zurich after seeking Myconius's advice concerning his troubled conscience, Thomas, accompanied by one of his students, had a bitter journey through the Grimsel pass. The two travelers almost froze to death in deep snow (T 91). Like modern mountain climbers, they fended off disaster by moving all the time, continuing to walk in order to avoid freezing. This episode probably took place in early August 1530.

Platter recounts another bout with cold at high altitude in which he came close to "giving up the ghost." Buried in snow, he experienced an almost pleasant sensation as the heat drained from his heart to warm his extremities (such, at any rate, was the "physiological" explanation he gave after the fact). A man appeared to him as if in a dream and earnestly admonished him as in the Gospel, "Rise and walk." He did so, and thus managed to avoid the fate of one *Hibernatus,* who lost his life in the Tyrolean Alps some four thousand years ago.[25]

And then there was pestilence. Earlier in his memoirs Thomas remarked on the broad swathe that the epidemics of the early sixteenth century had cut through his family, claiming his father and several sisters among others. In 1530, the curé of the parish in the Valais where Thomas and Anna were living died of plague: when the disease struck, everyone shunned the man except for one young boy. Anna, already a good Protestant and afraid for her own life, rejoiced at this death, because the priest was unfriendly and widely disliked. In recalling this story, Thomas mentions two other serious outbreaks of plague that he witnessed in Zurich.[26] (Incidentally, he always introduces passages of remembrance with the same turn of phrase: "Speaking of boots," "speaking of plagues.") The two plague epidemics filled a pair of common graves with some 1,600 bodies. On the first occasion, Thomas himself seems to have been infected: a boil or bubo appeared on his thigh. One of his aunts healed him with God's help and a dressing of cabbage leaves. To reach the home of this merciful and skillful relative, he had been obliged to hike for miles. Walking was difficult because of his abscess, and he was so weak that he fell asleep eighteen times in half a day, although he was ordinarily a man who could hike all day without tiring. During the second episode of plague, Thomas had no bed of his own; he slept between two young women, both of whom soon showed symptoms of the disease. They died, he says, yet he emerged unscathed. A tall if tragic tale? There is perhaps a grain of truth to the story: Platter might have developed an immunity to plague after his earlier bubo responded to the cabbage-leaf cure.

The birth of Anna's first child, probably in the fall of 1530,[27] also proved dramatic for both the mother and her husband. As was customary in the

Valais in the Middle Ages and Renaissance, the mother was assisted by an aristocratic midwife who engaged in this kind of work "for joy" (*freid*) and who offered her services for free, for it would have been a sin to receive payment for bringing a new soul into the world (T 93). This was an old-fashioned attitude: in the more modern Basel, midwives were paid for their services. But not even old-fashioned good will could insure against infant mortality. The noble midwife was assisted by several other "distinguished" women, proof that Thomas had risen several notches in the social hierarchy of the Valais. While Anna was in labor, Thomas sweated profusely, to the point where his shirt became soaked: Henri IV was in a similar state when little Louis XIII was born. Thomas actually witnessed the birth, although the women, bent over Anna, kept him from seeing what was going on. Religious conflict continued around the birthing bed: the midwives, all of whom carried wooden rosaries, prayed to Saint Margaret and urged Anna to sponsor a mass in the hope that she might be favored with a relatively painless birth. To these entreaties she simply responded: "I am faithful to my devoted God!" Neither Thomas nor Anna approved of the worship of "idols." Her time with the very Zwinglian Myconius had clearly had its impact on her. The baptism was inevitably Catholic, of course, and the baby, a little girl, was named Margretlin ("little Margaret" [T 94]), reflecting the hagiographic tastes of the respectable midwives. Yet while the baptism was Catholic, the godfather (flanked by the same "distinguished" godmothers who had assisted at the birth) was Protestant, a "friend of the truth." Thomas once again scandalized the "conformists" of Visp by publicly announcing to anyone who wished to listen that, should he be widowed, he would sooner become an executioner or "carcass butcher" than a "priestling" (*sic*). The anticlericalism that would become such a prominent feature of French politics in the late nineteenth and early twentieth century clearly had deep roots.

Ultimately, Thomas was unable to appreciate the priest-ridden Upper Valais for its scenic beauty. His wife, though a "heretic," was physically comfortable there but unwilling to remain for long. Toward the end of 1530 or the beginning of 1531, Thomas packed his bags and moved on. The locals did all they could to encourage him to stay. The bishop, a man named von Riedmatten, even sent a cousin with flattering offers of advancement that would have launched Platter on his way to some of the better-paid posts in the diocese. Thomas's reply was full of modesty: "I am too young and ignorant." Of course it is difficult to take this reply seriously, since Thomas, a teacher of thirty-two and a man risen from the common lot and determined not to fall back into it, already knew Hebrew, Greek, and Latin. The bishop guessed that Thomas was hiding something and saw his refusal as a sign that he harbored dark (heretical) intentions. Yet Thomas remained on good terms with the bishop's family, and some of the prelate's nephews, including a future bishop, became boarders in the school that Thomas founded fifteen or twenty years later—in Basel, however, not in the Valais. The local bishop was not the only one to regret Thomas's departure: the ex-Valaisian's sister was also unhappy and blamed Anna Dietschi-Platter for orchestrating the move. To be sure, relations between the two sisters-in-law, one a city girl from Zurich, the other a country girl from the Valais, were not always good. But in this case Thomas's sister was wrong: it was Thomas who wore the pants in the family and made all the plans. Thomas was no homebody, and he was restless. The only people happy to see the Platters go were the local curés: there was a whiff of heresy about this family, and the priests were glad to see them leave.

* * *

So Thomas set out once more, carrying his clothing and his baby on his back in an improvised wooden carrier. He led his wife, also on foot, by a rope, as a peasant might lead a cow. This expedient was necessary because Anna had only recently given birth and, being a city girl, was not sure-footed on mountain paths. In effect, husband and wife were tied together as two mountain climbers might tie themselves together today. As a fare-well gift, one of the respectable godmothers had given the Platters' child, Margretlin, two ducats. Catholic, German-speaking Upper Valais had not done badly by Thomas: he left with thirteen pieces of gold, which he had managed to save out of his earnings as a teacher and merchant. This time the destination was Basel, but the family stopped for a brief visit with Myconius in Zurich. They stayed just long enough to take advan-tage of the good master's hospitality, for Myconius was as generous a host as he was tightfisted as an employer. Of course he owed Anna back wages from her time as a servant, and putting up the itinerant couple was also a way for the "elderly" scholar to discharge his debt.

* * *

From Zurich the Platters moved on to Basel. Thomas again carried the baby, who at six months was bigger now than when they left the Valais. Anna, assisted by a schoolboy, caried the family's belongings, except for the things that Thomas arranged to have carted from Visp to Basel by way of Bern. The man who agreed to carry those things was a friend by the name of Thomas Roten, who also came from a prominent family in the Valais—apparently these family contacts among people from the same area were quite important. In Basel, Platter was no longer the lonely, shivering schoolboy he had been when he first visited the city. By this time he had many contacts and substantial support. "Pious people," local supporters of Œcolampadius, strongly recommended him for a position as tutor (*provisor*) with his old friend and protector Oporinus, who had settled in Basel without difficulty. Thomas thus became a sort of assistant schoolmaster in the school run by Oporinus. Now, Oporinus, who had adopted a Greek pseudonym in place of his real name, Johannes Herbster, was involved in a campaign to rebaptize as many individuals as possible in this fashion: in Basel, the "renaissance of Latin and Greek" meant just that.

In 1526, Thomas had made the acquaintance of Oporinus, who was then teaching at Saint Leonhard's school in Basel. Besides being associated with the first-rate Hebrew scholar and cosmographer Sebastian Münster (T 163), Oporinus was also a secretary to Paracelsus, the "Doctor Faustus" of sixteenth-century Swiss medicine. His career began brilliantly. By 1538 Oporinus had become a professor at the University of Basel. Then, in 1542, he embarked on a new career as a printer. In 1543 he produced a typographic masterpiece: the admirable treatise on anatomy by the eminent Renaissance anatomist, Vesalius—"seven books on the construction of the human body"—in a superb folio edition of 700 pages with a woodcut title page.[28] After a long history of indebtedness and poverty, the printer-professor at last achieved a comfortable position by marrying a third and then a fourth wife—both women with substantial dowries. His career as teacher, printer, and paramedic served as a model for Thomas Platter, who, when his wander-years were over, became first a teacher, then a printer, and then again a teacher. Platter also exhibited a constant interest in medicine, as we shall see, and his two sons would later follow medical careers: medicine was a means of social advancement.

In 1530–31 Platter was still on the best of terms with the Basel elite. His mentor Oporinus lived in an imposing house near the bishop's residence, a location that afforded him a kind of preeminence. The new arrival in Basel also enjoyed the friendship of Heinrich Billing, the son of an innkeeper whose fine voice had earned him a position as a member of Saint Leonhard's chorus. By his mother's second marriage, he was also the stepson of the Bürgermeister of Basel, Jacob Meyer zum Hirzen, one of the lay leaders of the Œformation in the city. Billing had helped Thomas Platter land his first "stable" teaching job in the city. Of course the word "stable" has to be taken with a grain of salt, for Thomas's roaming days were not yet over, and who knew what tomorrow might bring? One day

Billing offered a gift to his "excellent friend" Thomas and his wife Anna: a glass shaped like a boot and as big as a bottle. With this misshapen goblet the Platters could conveniently tap the keg of wine that was the principal ornament of their cellar (*keller*). Husband and wife both drank, and the ritual at the keg was at times comical: "Drink," Thomas commanded his wife, "because you are breastfeeding" (Margretlin was well past six months at the time). "No, you drink," Anna replied, "because you're studying and no one can say that you're frittering your time away."

Indeed, the couple, though not wealthy by any means, had at last risen from poverty: never again did the Platter table want for wine or bread. In the early modern period, the consumption of wine marked a person's ascent into the lower middle class, as the case of Vauban (who rose to become Marshal of France in the seventeenth century) would corroborate. The Platters liked to drink after bathing in the public baths. In their present situation they washed more frequently than Thomas had done ten years earlier. The teacher earned a good salary: forty livres a year. The city was not stingy with teachers of Thomas's caliber. But he had to pay a quarter of that as rent on his small home at the sign of the Lion's Head (near Oporinus's house and the bishop's residence).

If the Platters ate reasonably well and were lodged decently, their furniture, picked up second-hand, was rudimentary at best, apart from a chair and a good bed (purchased for five livres not far from Heinrich Billing's house). As for the kettle and cistern, Thomas had retrieved these items, both with holes in them, from the scrapheap at the city hospital.

This rather happy existence was not to last, however: Thomas had problems with his health, and he had not yet rid himself of the wanderlust of the eternal student. As a scholar he burned the candle at both ends. A glutton for work, he survived on just a few hours' sleep. To have gone from complete illiteracy to a post as teacher of Hebrew, Latin, and Greek had obviously required an effort that might have ruined the health of many a man. Thomas suffered from dizzy spells. Occasionally he stumbled about the classroom, supporting himself on a bench or wall. Neither bloodletting nor powders of ginger, nutmeg, and sugar, Galenists nor Hippocratics, brought him much relief.

Seeking advice about these troublesome but not life-threatening spells, Thomas went to see the "celebrated" Doctor Johannes Epiphanius (who, despite his supposed celebrity, has vanished from the historical record except for the incident I am about to recount). Epiphanius was a Venetian who had lived for a long time in Munich, where he had married a pretty woman. Later he was obliged to flee the Bavarian capital with his wife in order to escape persecution and possible decapitation at the hands of Duke Wilhelm IV von Wittelsbach, who suspected the physicians of his duchy of harboring Lutheran ideas and of eating meat during Lent. Although not initially hostile to the "heretics," the duke soon changed his mind when it dawned on him that the reformers might well be political as well as religious dissidents. In 1522 he banned anything having the remotest connection with Lutheranism. In 1524 he sought and received from Pope Clement VII special powers to maintain surveillance over abbeys and bishoprics. In 1541 he invited the Jesuits into his territory. Under such a ruler, anyone who wished to deviate from sound doctrine was well advised to tread carefully or take to the road. Epiphanius chose the latter course.

In Basel, where everyone knew everyone else, the members of the small but illustrious intellectual elite were of course aware of one another. Thomas Platter, who was fascinated by medicine (it was one of his "hobbies"), soon struck up a friendship with the Italian-Bavarian émigré Epiphanius (whose Latinate name had more to do with the influence of the Renaissance and the Reformation than with his Venetian roots, which had long since been forgotten or severed). Thomas described his dizzy spells to the illustrious physician, who was certain he could cure them. The two men immediately struck a bargain. Anna and Thomas Platter agreed to serve as maid and valet in the doctor's new home in the still-Catholic town of Porrentruy, where Epiphanius had become the personal physician of the bishop (T 98). The prelate in question was none other than the dashing and corpulent Philip von Gundelsheim, an ecclesiastic in his forties who had begun his career in the cathedral at Basel. Epiphanius was also a hearty, vigorous fellow: with the bishop's permission, he had taken to selecting bottles from the cellar of the episcopal residence and then having them transported to his home, where he liked to remain in his garden until midnight, clad only in a nightshirt while drinking his wine uncut and consuming quantities of food. Hence this episode must have taken place in the warm season of 1531, for winters in the Jura were cold and hardly conducive to semi-clad nocturnal revels. By day, Epiphanius found time to take an interest in the dizzy spells of his valet-patient, who also became his student, for he undertook to teach Thomas the rudiments of medicine, which the student was all the more eager to learn because he knew that medical knowledge was even more apt to lead to social advancement than knowledge of Hebrew or Greek. (Later, his son Felix would share this utilitarian attitude toward learning. Neither the father nor the son was any less solicitous or charitable toward the sick because of this, but their concern for the health of others was only an incidental consequence of their interest in the art of medicine, which they saw primarily as a way of getting rich.)

In any case, Thomas's health problems were the immediate reason for his decision to leave Basel for Porrentruy. Once again he took his wife by the hand and hoisted his daughter onto his back: it was the child's third "journey by backpack," after her earlier trips from Visp to Zurich and Zurich to Basel. The people who had gone to so much trouble to find Thomas a teaching post in Basel were most unhappy about his departure. Their protégé was more erratic than they had realized. But after the move Thomas saw them only rarely, on his visits to Basel to purchase drugs for his new master. Epiphanius's treatments did wonders for the health of his new servant, but his methods proved less effective in his own case: Physician, heal thyself! The cure for Thomas's dizziness was simple: Epiphanius eschewed both bloodletting and potions in favor of natural medicine. "Go to bed early with your wife, who will be your doctor." Broadly speaking, this was the Venetian doctor's prescription. "Remain in bed in the morning as long as you please, until someone knocks, and when you wake up have your Anna serve you a nice big bowl of soup." *Natura sanat, medicus curat:* medicine treats, nature heals. The care of women was preferable to bloodletting, enemas, and apothecaries' preparations. The Epiphanian "pharmacopoeia" appears to have been effective: Thomas's dizzy spells disappeared, never to return, except when he stayed up too late at night. Thomas later taught the same proven methods of treating dizziness to his friends in Basel, who apparently had gotten over their anger about his departure. Among them were the *bürgermeister* zum Hirzen, the father of Thomas's friend Heinrich Billing; dear old Myconius; and, some years later, one Cellarius, also known as Martin Borrhaus, a client and colleague of Thomas's (F 92).[29] Born in Stuttgart, Borrhaus was a curious fellow who had started out as the protégé of an important family. He spent time in Tübingen and Cracow as an itinerant student, befriended Melanchthon, quarreled with Luther, and married three times. After arriving in Basel in 1536, he worked as a glassmaker, alchemist, and professor. His efforts to decompose complex compounds into simpler constituents made him one of the (many) precursors of modern chemistry.

Comedy (the Molièresque doctors confounded by the gentle remedies of natural medicine) turned into tragedy: the plague returned in the summer of 1531. The hot months were the season of epidemics. The Platters had been in Porrentruy for almost three months. The first victim to be claimed by the lurking germs was Margretlin Platter. The little girl had just celebrated her first birthday (and was just beginning to walk).[30] She died after much suffering. Her parents were in tears: they proved to be more affectionate and understanding than Thomas's mother had been in similar circumstances: Amilli Summermatter had suffered too much in her own wretched life to be deeply affected by the tribulations of her children; when all is said and done, she was a woman not much moved by the woes of her offspring, or even by their deaths. Margretlin was buried by a colleague of Thomas's, a schoolmaster in Porrentruy. Anna, though overwhelmed by her daughter's death, found the strength to make a wreath of flowers for her, but the joy had gone out of her life and for a time she lost all interest in the singing that her husband loved so much. Her sadness (which was typical, according to Thomas, of families stricken or threatened by plague) bothered the normally jovial Epiphanius: "Your wife is sad," he told Thomas in substance. "This probably means that she will soon come down with the plague, or else that my wife will. So do what you must to get her out of my house." Thomas had no choice but to follow the orders of Herr Doktor (as Epiphanius was called). He took Anna to Zurich, probably to Myconius, her former employer. Epiphanius's fears proved to be well-founded. Margretlin had contaminated the doctor's entire household, except for Thomas, who may have acquired immunity to the plague when the (supposed) bubo on his thigh was successfully treated some years earlier. The doctor's wife, who also developed a bubo on her thigh, was the first adult to take to her bed (on the second floor). The great doctor himself, terrified by his wife's affliction and well aware of what that lay in store, began a drinking bout that lasted for days.

On his return from Zurich one Sunday night, Platter found his master sitting in front of a bottle with his face down on the table; he was "choking on wine." Between hiccups, Epiphanius lashed out at Thomas for having obeyed his orders, as if, through some mysterious alchemy, Anna's departure had caused the dubious doctor's wife to become ill. Epiphanius's own fatal odyssey began the next morning: the doctor awoke with the plague. He fled the afflicted town and his sick wife without a word, hastening after his bishop, who had taken refuge some time earlier at his summer residence in Delémont, close to forests and plains in which the prelate liked to hunt. Outbreaks of plague were opportunities for heroism, and more than one bishop rose to the occasion: witness the case of Archbishop de Belzunce in Marseilles in 1720. Philip von Gundelsheim, however, was a coward who turned tail and ran at the first sign of danger, despite his exalted position among the Jurassians of Helvetia.

Did Epiphanius, accompanied as was only fitting by his servant Thomas Platter, really hasten after the bishop? It was certainly his intention to do so, but in the event he was unable. The sick physician could barely walk. In a day he managed to cover only a mile after leaving Porrentruy, a community that now found itself without a doctor for body or soul. That night Epiphanius could not keep food down. The second day of his calvary, Tuesday, was even worse. After renting a horse—not a charger but a litter-bearer—the two men continued on to Delémont only to be turned back at the town's gates. In time of plague, communities barricaded themselves behind walls—the only protection to be had.

Epiphanius, so delirious from the sickness and the summer heat that he fell from his horse several times, was not in great shape. The bishop, safe in his residence inside the walls, was informed that his doctor was at the gates, however, and ordered the townspeople, or at any rate the guards who enforced the townspeople's wishes, to admit the ailing physician, whom he invited to dine with him that evening. His guest's pallor, so different from his usual ruddy complexion, worried him. Epiphanius explained that he was suffering from sunstroke and from the aftereffects of his drinking bout. Evidently Gundelsheim, who knew the Venetian's capacity for wine, found this explanation convincing. The bishop and the doctor, who had occasionally hunted together, ceremoniously addressed each other as Herr and Herr Doktor. As men of distinction, members, respectively, of the clerical and medical orders, they used the formal second-person pronoun with each other but addressed Thomas with the informal pronoun. Epiphanius grew worse during the night: he soiled his bed. Platter, always the devoted servant, slept in the same room as his master, on an adjoining mattress. At dawn he obligingly washed the sick man's sheets so that "people would not see right away" (*das man nit glich sähe*). The two men were afraid that someone would realize that Epiphanius was sick with the plague. The next morning, the bishop, who had gone out early to hunt, jumped from his horse the moment he returned and immediately began to "grill" Thomas: "Does your master have the plague?" Someone had told His Eminence (*gnädiger Herr*) that Thomas's daughter had died of the plague and that Epiphanius's wife still lay agonizing in Porrentruy with a bubonic infection. The news did not travel from Porrentruy to Delémont, it flew.

Confronted directly by the bishop, Thomas hemmed and hawed. He spoke vaguely of a malady brought on by a sudden chill when the doctor drank a large quantity of cold water durring the torrid journey, but no one was fooled. The bishop summarily threw Master Epiphanius and his valet Thomas out of his house. In search of a room, the two men made the rounds of the village, but nobody would take them in. In the end, however, they found shelter at the White Cross Inn and a bed befitting the station of a "lord" of Epiphanius's rank. The innkeeper, a woman, was sympathetic to their plight: throughout this episode, certain women proved more merciful than any man, but not everyone of the female gender proved kind. The desperate physician's thoughts turned, a bit late, to the wife he had left behind in Porrentruy. Thomas, to whom he spoke from time to time in Latin, was sent to fetch the ailing "Epiphania" and bring her to Delémont, dead or alive. Understandably, the lady (who apparently had recovered from her illness, her bubo having disappeared) sent the messenger packing and denounced her husband as a scoundrel, indeed a *welche,* that is, a Latin (whether she meant French or Venetian hardly matters)—a supreme insult in the mouth of a Bavarian woman. The age-old antagonism between Germans and Latins often came out in dramatic moments. Epiphanius could die, for all she cared. She washed her hands of him. Let God deal with him.

Platter, however, would not be deterred. In his usual reasonable style, he reminded the lady from Munich of the realities: "Woman, I think he is going to die" (*Frow, ich gloub, er werde sterben*). He then reminded her that she—or at any rate she and her husband—had debts in Basel. Their creditors, such as the apothecary, a certain elderly gentleman, and the fornicating host of the Swan Inn might well insist on immediate payment. Epiphanius was a political—or, if you prefer, religious—refugee in Basel, where he had arrived from Munich with nothing to his name but his medical skills. He had not had time to attract a clientele, let alone amass a fortune. After being recalled to her senses by Platter, "Frau Epiphanius" had no choice but to see the situation as it was, namely, unpleasant. When she calmed down, she gave Thomas, whom she trusted (not altogether justifiably, as we shall see), a small consignment of things to sell in Basel in order to prevent her creditors from seizing her property: the consignment included fine linen and a small quantity of silver. Thomas, whose feet were firmly planted on the ground, also "borrowed" his master's medical formulae (*experiment buch*), which he planned to copy in his spare time for his own use. He had not given up the hope of one day becoming a physician, if not actually a doctor of medicine. In that way he hoped to avoid ending his days as a schoolmaster, as with good reason he suspected he might.

With "cargo" in tow, Thomas returned to his stricken master's side on Friday evening. The bishop, still afraid of the contagion, had meanwhile ordered that the doctor be placed on a horse and led by a servant to Münster, also known as Moutier, a short distance from Delémont (T 167). This village, succumbing to reformist currents emanating from Basel and to an impetuous French evangelist named Guillaume Farel, had gone over to the Protestants. Thomas, though a Zwinglian, knew when to softpedal his religious preferences: in Porrentruy he had managed to coexist with a "papist" bishop and the prelate's personal physician, a Lutheran. In Moutier, however, the only religious decision that was likely to arise was that of choosing last rites: Epiphanius hovered near death. Despite being accompanied by a servant, he had fallen from his horse on the short ride from Delémont.

A night passed, and then a day. Saturday night was terrible. The innkeeper in Moutier, totally in the dark about what was going on, agreed to take in the corpulent, sickly gentleman who arrived on horseback from Delémont. When he finally understood that plague was involved, he flew into a rage, attacking among other people his wife, who had registered the sick guest. The bedrooms being on the second floor, the innkeeper threatened to throw Platter and his master down the stairs (*die Stägen ab werffen* [T 102]). Answering in similarly heated terms, Thomas refused to budge. So there he was, with Epiphanius and a reform pastor who had come to Moutier to celebrate the Sunday service. More Christian than the bishop, this minister of God tried to console the dying Venetian and exhort him to die a good death. He had less success with the parishioners of Moutier: none would offer the dying man so much as a stable or pigsty (*süwstellin*) in which to die in peace. The only person Thomas could find to do his master this one last favor was, once again, a woman. Originally from Basel, this lady was pregnant and close to giving birth. She lived a stone's throw from the inn where Epiphanius lay dying. The fact that all three—the charitable lady, the dying physician, and the Valaisian servant—had all lived recently in Basel obviously had something to do with her generous gesture. She was friendly to Platter, to whom she referred as "my good neighbor" (*gsell*); with the more eminent physician she was more formal. In any case, her patent good will contrasts sharply with the disagreeable attitude of the natives.

Another woman (this one paid by Platter) helped transport the doctor to the pregnant woman's nearby home. In tears, this Good Samaritan kissed the dying Epiphanius twice on the lips—a moving gesture that involved real risk. She seated her stricken guest on a comfortable chair and later had him placed on a carefully prepared bed, worthy of a man of Epiphanius's social station and medical reputation. She even coaxed him to eat two bowls of soup. While transporting the dying man from the inn to the home of the good woman from Basel, Platter had heaped abundant insults on the local peasants, who lined both sides of the main street. He castigated them for having cast God out of their hearts, a charge to which it seems they listened without reacting.

Thomas was now torn between contradictory imperatives. His devoted friendship for Epiphanius, of which he had given ample proof (though, to be sure, he was also performing his duties as a valet), demanded that he remain at the dying man's side to the end, but his own interests had become pressing. Eventually the latter won out. In a choking voice, speaking in a pidgin that was half Latin and half dialect, Epiphanius himself urged Thomas to return to Basel. He gave his valet a gold toothpick that he removed from a neck chain as well as several rings, which he hoped would provide enough money to keep "Epiphania" alive for a while. About to succumb to the plague, the alcoholic old doctor's brain was clouded: had love for his wife really been rekindled? The question did not occur to Platter. With a few kind words he bade his benefactress farewell. Although the woman's baby arrived on the very day of Epiphanius's death, she nevertheless saw to it that the old man received the first-class burial appropriate to his status "as a doctor" (*wie ein doctor*). Meanwhile, Platter made sure to pack Epiphanius's medical notes, which he still planned to copy, and went straight to Oporinus's house in Basel.

After Epiphanius died, the good woman reimbursed herself for her expenses and kindnesses by selling the sumptuous garments he left behind. She had no trouble at all converting the doctor's wardrobe into hard cash. Epiphanius, who died like a pauper, without surgeon or pharmacopoeia (*weder schärer noch artnzy*), was laid out on a bier like a rich man but as naked as the day he was born. His cast-off finery could be seen on the backs of the village worthies, who took what blessings fortune brought their way (much as coastal dwellers appropriated the cargo of ships driven onto the reefs by a storm). Platter came away from the experience with something like a medical apprenticeship under his belt. This was worth more than the few florins in wages of which the plague had deprived him. But Thomas's medical education was to proceed no farther; later, his two sons would easily surpass him.

Now came two weeks of legal wrangling in the courts of Basel, an ordeal that Platter claims to have survived with honor intact. But we have only his version of the facts, which is all to his advantage. The dead man's creditors (the apothecary, the innkeeper, and perhaps others) hoped to settle Epiphanius's debts by seizing his worldly belongings, including the gold toothpick and the thick book of medical secrets. Oporinus and Platter did what they could to delay the proceedings and meanwhile duplicated the disputed book, each copying half its pages. Later, each made a second copy of the half originally copied by the other. In the end, the original of this much-coveted formulary wound up in the collection of one of the creditors, probably the apothecary, while the modest "libraries" of Thomas and Oporinus were both enriched by the addition of handsome handwritten reproductions: the golden age of the manuscript was not yet over. The dispute over the disposition of Epiphanius's property apparently left no rancor. Twenty years later, Thomas's son Felix became the godfather of the illegitimate son of Klingenberg, the innkeeper who was among the doctor's creditors. The child was the product of the hosteler's fling with the servant of the man who had been Thomas's attorney in the case and who had since then become a friend of Klingenberg's.

Throughout this legal wrangling Epiphanius's young widow was all but forgotten. She had survived the horrible plague of 1531 but was ruined nonetheless.[31] All her property had been seized (*alle ding iren genummen werin* [T 105]). Much later she paid a call on Thomas: she wanted her husband's formula for a purgative made from dried grapes (*purgatz mit den rosinlinen* [T 105]), which he had recorded in his book. Did she plan to sell it? She hadn't a penny to her name. Thomas sent her on her way with a twinge of regret: she was pretty (*sy was hüpsch*). He never heard of her again. All she got out of this short and brutish tale was the scar on her thigh left by the bubo.

These few plague-ridden weeks, and particularly the week of Epiphanius's death, occupy a disproportionate place in Thomas's narrative, roughly 7 percent of the total number of pages. As he explicitly states, he always regretted not having followed the medical calling. The best he could do now was to pass his interest in medicine on to his sons.

* * *

For Thomas Platter, the summer of 1531 was a time of plague. The following fall was a time of war, a conflict that Thomas managed to squeak through more or less unscathed. In early October, the five "papist" or "forest" cantons—Lucerne, Uri, Schwyz, Unterwalden, and Zug— spurred on from Vienna by the Hapsburgs, decided that they had had enough of Zwingli's aggressively imperialistic theocracy. Over the years Zwingli had established a dictatorship of virtue in Zurich. He had withdrawn from the city's Catholics the toleration that he rightly claimed for his fellow Protestants living under the authority of the Roman Church. The five cantons had mustered a small but well-trained army. Attacking from the south, these troops marched on the territory over which Zurich claimed authority. Things went badly for the Protestants (*es übell erging*). The Zurich troops, badly organized, politically divided, and militarily ineffective despite the presence of courageous Zwinglians in the ranks, were defeated at Kappel on October 11, 1531. Zwingli himself, wearing a helmet and armed with sword, axe, and mace, fought like a wild man but lost his life in the battle. In the nineteenth century the prophet's smashed helmet and weaponry found their way into the Swiss national museum.

Kappel awakened Swiss Protestants to the limits of their power. They reined in their expansionist impulses and resigned themselves to coexistence with the "papists." (The peace would endure, largely without friction, until the so-called War of the Sonderbund in 1847. This shifted the balance of power in favor of the Protestants without giving them a political and religious monopoly that might have undermined the subtle equilibrium on which the stability of the Swiss Confederation depended.) On the night of October 11, 1531, just as lamps were being lit in the early evening, news of the disaster of Kappel reached Zurich. The alarm was sounded. On that day Platter happened to be in the city visiting Myconius. Was this just a friendly call, or did Thomas want to be on the scene at a moment when the fate of religious reform in German-speaking Switzerland hung in the balance? As news of the defeat spread, many men of fighting age took up positions on the bridge. Obviously some number of men capable of bearing arms had remained in the city. Was their failure to join the army one of the reasons for the defeat? In any case, Thomas was among those who now took up defensive positions. His conscience was easy, for he was not a citizen of Zurich. The defenders occupied the bridge and its approaches and before long fanned out along the river bank as well. They were on the lookout for enemy marauders: emboldened by victory, the enemy might try to attack and occupy the city. But no marauders appeared. The Catholic cantons had no interest in exploiting their victory. Their aim had been to restrain the imperialism of the reformers, not to annihilate them—a goal that would have been beyond their means in any case.

The night was cold. The defenders lit huge fires, and those with shoes, including Thomas Platter, removed them to warm their feet: no longer was Thomas one of those poor wretches obliged to go barefoot in summer or to wear clogs in winter. In the early morning hours the wounded could be seen in the torchlight, limping home. It was a horrifying sight: one man had lost a hand, another supported his wounded head unsteadily with his hands, and a third held his own guts, which were spilling out of his body. Even small wars are tragic, be they between Greek city-states or Swiss burgs. Meanwhile, the halberd Thomas had borrowed from Myconius was nearly stolen. Platter remained confident, however. The few captains (*houptlüt*) who had survived the rout of the Zurich "army" straggled home, some having lost their way in the fields, others accused of treason or at any rate of cowardice in the face of the papist enemy. Although Thomas's stomach was growling, no one offered him food, since he was not a member of any of the city's regular militias. With the courage of a philosopher, he decided to return to the city, which meant crossing a bridge guarded by sentinels armed to the teeth. They kept a close eye on everyone entering the city: not only were the authorities afraid of a "Trojan horse" tactic on the part of the enemy, they also feared the arrival of useless mouths to feed and of wounded outsiders in need of care. Thomas had a hard time making his way back to Myconius's residence.

Such stunning reverses were common in the 1530s. A few years later, French Protestants had their turn: in 1534, after the Affaire des Placards, Francis I abandoned his relatively benevolent policy toward the Protestants and moved toward a more discriminatory position. In German-speaking Switzerland, the situation was less grave, yet the expansion of Protestantism had clearly been stopped. The treaty that was signed shortly after the Battle of Kappel had the effect of freezing the boundaries between the rival religions for a long time to come. Hopes of a new surge of reformist sentiment on one side and of a total Catholic victory on the other proved unfounded. The peace, quickly established *de facto* and soon ratified *de jure,* did not immediately put an end to every alarm. In late November 1531 the Catholic peasants of Schwyz who had been among the victors at Kappel began their homeward march. Choosing the shortest path between two points, their army passed close to the walls of Zurich.

For the defeated but still inviolate city (no enemy had ever breached its walls), this was a humiliating affront and a terrifying provocation. Zurich was afraid. Rumors of treachery and impending slaughter swept the city. A month earlier Zurich had lost a battle. This time it might lose its "virginity" (it was in such terms that people spoke of the honor of a city not yet polluted by the invasion of an assailant).[32] The fear proved salutary, because it gave rise to a defensive reaction: citizens poured into the streets. Myconius issued an order to his faithful disciple: "Thomas, you will lie by my side tonight" (*Thoma, lig du hinacht by mier*). Thomas did as he was told. In their shared bed, both men lay with one eye open. Each kept a halberd by his side. In the morning the "Schwyzians" abandoned their bivouacs outside the city and moved out in the direction of home. The alert, though very real, was now over.

Even though Zwingli was now gone, many people in Zurich still smelled the flames of inquisition. The ground burned their feet. Take, for instance, Georg Göldli, one of the leaders of the Protestant "army." He had led his troops badly enough to hasten defeat and was in fact accused of treason by his men, since, as it happened, his brother was serving in the Catholic ranks. Charges were brought against Captain Göldli in 1532, a year after the battle, but he managed to fend off his accusers. No sooner was he released from prison than he moved to Constance, where he died in 1536. He had found it wise to put as much distance as possible between himself and Zurich (T 168).

Myconius would soon leave Zurich as well, but for different reasons: there was nothing left for him to do in that threatened and dangerous city. Unemployment, a scourge less dire than plague but serious nonetheless, loomed. In addition, the death of Master Ulrich (Zwingli) had deeply upset Myconius the teacher: he and Zwingli had long been close, and Myconius had always respected the slain Protestant leader as a man of superior intellect and spirituality. Platter claimed to have strenuously encouraged Myconius to leave for Basel and to have used his contacts with the Billing family to try to get his former teacher a position as (reformed) preacher at Saint Alban's that had been left vacant by the death of Hieronymus Bothanus, also known as Bothan, at Kappel.

Platter may well have embellished his role in this case and made himself out to be more important than he actually was, but it is indeed true that the "bald preacher," as Myconius was known, left Zurich at the time Thomas mentions. We find him in Basel in December 1531, where he had become acting pastor. His career as teacher and minister had thus taken him from Basel (where he had been earlier) to Zurich to Lucerne, back to Zurich and then once more to Basel. There, from 1531 until his death of plague in 1552, Oswald Geisshüssler, known as Myconius, would achieve all that a Protestant could hope to achieve in both his ecclesiastic and teaching careers. The two friends, Oswald and Thomas, were still young by our standards (one was in his forties, the other in his thirties), and their journey from Zurich to Basel in the fall of 1531 did not lack for suspense or excitement. In the village of Mumpf they encountered a party of four rather disreputable-looking noblemen on horseback. One of these stout fellows, the Junker Hans Egloff Offenburg, was "one of the most ornery rascals and drunkards recorded in the fighting annals of that time" (T 110, 169). And Myconius was not wrong to have been somewhat suspicious of these men. A few weeks earlier the quartet had attended the solemn funeral for Zwingli and others who had fallen at Kappel and elsewhere in the holy war against papism—not to mourn but secretly to celebrate the deaths of these "heretics." Apparently, Offenburg and his three friends had entered into a pact with the pro-papist opposition in Zurich, an opposition that was only too glad to be rid of the pious dictator.

The four noblemen were even more suspect in the eyes of a loyal Protestant like Thomas because at least one of them had family ties to the Catholic bishops of the region. Platter was therefore glad he had seen through the thin disguises of these papists, who were in any case rarely sober. In the inn at Mumpf the Junker "squadron" drained flagon upon flagon and raised a dreadful ruckus. One of the younger nobles tried to force Myconius to have a drink with him, drawing an indignant protest from the "elderly" professor (the geriatric epithet was applied to the forty-year-old professor by the the jolly topers) (T 110).

"That will do, my friend," Myconius retorted. "I already knew how to drink before you knew how to do your business on the wood shavings." (Were wood shavings used in outhouses for the same purpose as sawdust or leaves?) Late that night, as a final round was being drunk, one of the revelers had the audacity to put his elbows on the table, a gesture that incurred the wrath of his father, Wolfgang Daniel von Landenberg, who was even drunker than his son. Drunkenness was one thing, but putting one's elbows on the table—why, the very idea! Platter and his companion, mute witnesses to these proceedings, quaked with stifled laughter. A commoner, Myconius had little respect for the nobility, or at any rate for certain crude, pretentious, uncouth gentlemen who wore swords at their sides, for whom he had almost as much disdain as for Catholic priests.

In Basel, Myconius found lodging with Oporinus (*by dem Oporino,* as Thomas put it in his mixture of German and Latin). Oporinus had been a benefactor of many a "right-thinking" visitor from Zurich. Soon thereafter, toward the end of 1531, Myconius was named minister and schoolmaster of Saint Alban's. Platter rather indiscreetly lets drop that he occasionally assisted the new preacher by "ghostwriting" sermons on particularly delicate topics such as "why God got us all into this mess" (the mess in question being the defeat and death of Zwingli). Whether Thomas had anything to do with it or not, Myconius's sermons drew crowds and pleased men of learning, including those whose predilection was the Greeks as well as those whose specialty was theology.

So successful was Myconius that in the summer of 1532 he succeeded Œcolampadius as the spiritual if not political leader of Basel. Œcolampadius had died at almost the same time as Zwingli, in the fall of 1531, but of nonviolent causes. A replacement was needed, and Platter's friends took advantage of the situation. In general, the movement of religious reform drew much of its leadership and support from the middle to lower strata of society: there were sons of the middle class (such as Luther and Calvin), of the relatively well-to-do peasantry (Zwingli), and even the poorer peasantry (Platter). The rise of Protestantism among Saxons and Anglo-Saxons, Alemannis and Welches, was more than just a change in spiritual behavior. It was also quite simply a social upheaval affecting class status and marriage (the successive marriages of King Henry VIII of England are a case in point, to say nothing of the marriages of nuns and clerics) and provoking violent rebellion (such as the Peasants' War in Germany).

At a more modest level, Thomas clearly wanted to persuade his readers that he was responsible for Myconius's brilliant career. It was through his "contacts," he says, that Myconius obtained his ministry. He had accompanied his teacher from Zurich to Basel and even financed the journey (which had not cost very much). And he claims to have provided Myconius with the subjects (and even texts) of some of his sermons. We are not obliged to take Thomas at his word: he sometimes wrote to impress any members of his family who might read his memoirs. In all this story about Myconius's departure from Zurich, we almost fail to notice another "permanent" move to Basel: that of Thomas himself. (To be sure, he did not altogether forgo the pleasures of the road, but Basel henceforth became his home.) By the end of 1531, Zurich held no further prospects for Thomas, civilian or military. He judged that he would be better off returning to Basel to study and earn his living. Anna would rejoin her husband later. It was far easier for her to move now after the unfortunate death of little Margretlin, for the baby, though much loved, had greatly complicated the couple's travels.

Thomas thus continued his education in Basel. Truth to tell, he found his studies more amusing than the company of his rather ill-tempered wife, who for the time being was providentially separated from her husband. Thomas enrolled in the Untern Collegium am Rheinsprung, which for centuries remained the central institution of the University of Basel. His "good master" at the time, in whose course he enrolled officially in the summer of 1534 (later than he implies, but he may have attended lectures as early as 1531–32), was Phrygio, whose real name was Konstantin Sydenstricker. Born in Sélestat in the 1480s, Phrygio grew up in the humanist ambiance created in this Athens or Florence of the north by the scholar Beatus Rhenanus, a friend of Erasmus, enlightened lover of the ancient classics and writings of the Church Fathers, connoisseur of ancient and Germanic geography, and editor, coeditor, or annotator of the works of Pliny, Seneca, Tacitus, Velleius Paterculus, Livy, Augustine, Jerome, Chrysostom, Tertullian, Thomas Aquinas, and Erasmus. With this background Phrygio became first a curate in Basel and later, in 1532, a professor at the university, from which he moved to Tübingen in 1535, but before that it fell to him to transmit to Thomas the lessons of the Renaissance.

The Valaisian not only attended lectures at the university but also seems to have been provided by his *alma mater* with a small room or at any rate a bed. He slept at the university as other men sleep in barracks. Without a wife to cook for him (Anna having stayed behind in Zurich), Thomas ate for three denarii at the Pilger Stab (Pilgrim's Staff), an execrable student restaurant that left diners feeling almost as hungry when they came out as when they went in. But his teacher Phrygio often invited Platter to his table along with another teacher, Christian Herbort, who was considerably older. To Thomas, Herbort was a parasite (a specialist in *schmorotzen* [T 115]) as well as a turncoat, with his "butt firmly between two stools," as Platter put it, half-Catholic and half-Protestant and always ready to turn with the prevailing winds: a Protestant in Basel and a Catholic in Freiburg or the Valais. When Montaigne visited Basel in 1580, he was still struck by the number of such "flexible" spirits in Switzerland.

In the early years of this latest residence in Basel, Thomas met with circumstances that contributed to his success. The university had been profoundly disrupted by the triumph of the Reformation in the city in 1529. Normal academic activities did not resume until 1532 or so, and then only slowly and of course under new masters professing new beliefs. Times had changed, and Platter had come a long way since his revolutionary phase, when he had supported iconoclasm (burning the statue of Saint John) and embraced working-class populism (choosing ropemaking as his trade). He had matured: at age thirty-five, in the summer of 1534, he ceased to be an eternal student, an advanced though impecunious disciple, and accepted a teaching position, which he would thereafter hold, with brief interruptions, to the end of his life. He of course had the requisite professional experience: he had taught at many levels, from familiarizing his cousin with the *abc*'s to giving lessons in the Hebrew language. But Thomas's promotion was not solely the result of his personal merits. He also benefited from the fact that many Catholic professors had abandoned their posts in disgust at the triumph of "heresy" in the city. In addition, many people, including members of the intellectual elite, had been cut down by the plague, and this also improved Thomas's chances.

In 1534, then, Thomas became almost a full-fledged teacher, a sort of lecturer or senior lecturer holding a post superior in status to that of a secondary (or elementary) schoolteacher but below that of a full university professor. He taught what we would now describe as first-year undergraduate courses in Greek (a language that he knew well, along with Latin and Hebrew). In his teaching he used the *Dialogues* of Lucian, a writer impatient of human ambitions and celestial deities. Did continual study of such texts make Thomas a skeptic, or at any rate less of a mystic than he had been ten or fifteen years earlier? For Greek grammar he relied on the work of Ceporinus (Jacob Wiesendanger). A native of the Winterthur region and former teacher at the monastery school in Basel, Ceporinus had published his grammar in that city in 1522. The work went through numerous editions and proved to be a lasting success, at least in Switzerland. Its style was modern, Cartesian *avant la lettre*, with "its long chains of simple, easy arguments." Grammar was explored in all its dimensions: nouns, accents, declensions, adjectives, adverbs, prepositions, and so on. Thomas, having left the mountains and their traditional culture behind, now discovered, and filled his students' heads with, subtle classifications. When necessary he concentrated the minds of his students with a smart box on the ears. Such methods were common at the time (everywhere but in Montaigne's château, apparently).

At this point, however, Thomas embarked on yet another temporary but important excursion: he learned the art of printing. The plague, still lurking about, claimed the life of one Jacob Ruber (or Ruberus in pedantic Latin), a close friend of Thomas and Oporinus. Ruber had been a proofreader in the print shop of Johannes Herwagen (or Hervagius), a native of Austria who in 1527 had married Gertrud, the widow of the illustrious printer Johannes Frobenius. For some years Herwagen had been in partnership with other members of the Frobenius family, renowned among typographers, but since 1531 he had been on his own, employing helpers but doing business without partners. After losing Ruber, Herwagen managed to replace him for a short time with a local student (or intellectual) of remarkable intelligence, Simon Sulter or Sulzer. It was but a short step in those days from scholar to proofreader, because scholarship alone was not enough to keep the pot boiling. But Sulzer may have had other sources of income, or perhaps he was simply enamored of pure research and culture, regardless of the cost (F 170). Typesetting was not compatible with his real interests. He therefore passed his job as printer's assistant on to Thomas Platter.

Though reluctant at first to accept the job, Thomas allowed himself to be talked into it, "giving in to the warm urgings of my friend." It may be worth mentioning that even so illustrious a scholar as Oporinus was not loath to earn extra money from time to time as a proofreader. For four long years, from 1536 to 1539, Thomas thus worked as both a teacher and a proofreader. Out of toil and woe came a new calling for Thomas: that of fully qualified printer and indeed publisher. This was Basel, after all, a center of German printing, much as Lyons became the center of French printing in the sixteenth century. Before long Platter was filling in for his employer: when Herwagen traveled to Frankfurt for the book fair, it was

Thomas, back in Basel, who supervised the shop in the master's absence. Thomas had certainly acquired an impressive variety of skills in his first thirty-six years: he had been a shepherd, goatherd, cowherd, mountaineer, schoolboy, beggar, nomad, student, singer, professor of three ancient languages, ropemaker, typographer, and proofreader, and he was not yet done: he would end his life as a school headmaster and real-estate entrepreneur. He was a Renaissance man in the full sense of the term. Yet like many of his contemporaries he had little use for the calendar: rarely does he give precise dates for any of the important events in his life, except his birth (for which the date 1499 may have been approximate)—and of course we know the exact date of his death thanks to his son Felix, who took the trouble to record it in the manuscript.

For the time being, however, Thomas was still very much alive: indeed, he was making children. After a more or less obligatory period of separation, he resumed married life with Anna. His first daughter, Margretlin, born in the Valais in 1530, had died of plague in 1531, as we have seen. His second daughter, Margretlin II, was born in 1533 (F 50 and T 144). Thomas, having taken the cure at the baths in Brig, was working for Herwagen as a proofreader and living with his wife in the schoolmaster's house attached to Saint Peter's Church. At the time the schoolmaster was a man named Antony Wild, a defrocked Franciscan, who would soon move to the Collegium, where his distinguished career was cut short by the plague in 1541. Little Margetlin II preceded him to the grave, also succumbing to a rather nasty if brief resurgence of the disease in 1539 after the major outbreak of 1538.[33] A third daughter, Ursula, was born in 1534, after the Platters, having come up in the world, had moved once more. In fact, Ursula's story reveals just how far they had come: the new house, which adjoined Wild's, had a window, and the little girl (*kindlin*) was about to fall out of it one day when a certain Marc Wolff, who boarded with Thomas, saved her by grabbing her tiny feet (*fiesslinen* [T 119]).

Thus it may have been as early as 1535 or 1536 that Platter began his lucrative business of taking in boarders: students who paid to sleep under his roof, eat his food, and take his lessons. Thomas became a surrogate father (and when necessary a stern father) to the growing number of boys and youths who lived with him in a series of houses. Anna played a major role: who else (apart from any servants they could afford to hire) was to make the beds, do the laundry, and prepare meals for this host of noisy young men who had other things on their minds besides rhetoric? Platter of course taught. Glutton for work that he was, he also began printing under his own name in 1536. These years thus marked a clear advance for the family both socially and professionally. Long gone were the days when little Thomas, the mangy schoolboy, had begged for his supper on country roads and city streets, though his memories of those days remained vivid. In 1536 he became the father of a fourth child: it was on October of that year that his son Felix—aptly named, for this was the "happy" child—was born (F 52). Felix would outlive his three sisters: Ursula, too, died of plague in 1551, exactly like her two elder siblings. And he would carry the memoir-writing tradition inaugurated by his father into the second half of the century.

Paternity, of course, has religious significance. God—the "devoted God" of the Protestants—bestowed his blessings on it. Yet Thomas did not blame God for the deaths of his three daughters. "Margretlin also died of plague," he wrote (*Margretli starb mir ouch an der pesetelentz* [T 144]). Thomas extolled the supernatural force that overwhlemed him. He felt no need to offer even a pious explanation for the judgment of heaven that had decreed the deaths of so many of his relatives and children. He was in this respect closer to the "enlightened" and often optimistic theology of Zwingli than to the neurasthenic ideas of Luther, imbued as those ideas were with fatalistic notions of predestination to disease or death on express orders of the Creator.

CHAPTER THREE

The Platter Childhoods: Felix

Felix Platter, the only son of Thomas and Anna, was thus born in Basel in October 1536, shortly before the city's annual fair. Indeed, the traditional "gifts from the fair" were placed on the new mother's bed. As for the father, Felix himself was his mother's gift to her husband. And what a present he turned out to be! Over the next half century, the boy would bring his father all the honor and happiness a man could wish for. The year of Felix's birth, 1536, was also the year in which Thomas printed with his own hands the first Latin edition of Calvin's *Institutes of the Christian Religion*. But, as everyone knows, once a child is born, its parents love it more and more, whereas a person who makes a book (whether author or printer) is concerned with it only as long as it takes to produce it: once the book is out in the world, it consumes less of one's thought. If Felix was aware that his birth coincided, as if by Calvinist predestination, with his father's edition of Calvin's work, it surely would have encouraged him in his decision to describe his coming into the world as a sign of God's grace.

Felix provides certain interesting details concerning his mother and father. Thomas, he says, was the owner of a print shop, the scion of a "large and respectable family" from the Valais. Anna, we are told, came from an "old and honorable family, several of whose members were ennobled" (*dorunter ettlicher geadlet worden* [F 50]). Technically, these assertions are not false. Thomas, as we have seen, did indeed come from a line of substantial Valaisian peasants with some distinguished relatives. And Anna's family, the Dietschis, did include nobles, goldsmiths, and other burghers from Zurich and the surrounding region. Yet a few lines later Felix concedes that before her marriage his mother was illiterate and employed as a servant by Myconius, who had suggested that he be named "Felix," a forecast of the happiness he would later enjoy in considerable measure. He also tells us that Thomas, in the prime of life, often thrashed his apprentice, Balthasar Lazius (also known as Ruch).

Little Felix was baptized by Benedikt Wydmann, the pastor's vicar. Felix's godfathers were Simon Grynaeus, a native of Sigmaringen in Germany and distinguished professor of theology and Greek, and Johann

Walder, a printer. Here we see both the division and the unity of labor: Grynaeus edited the Greek classics, Walder printed them. The boy's godmother was Ottilia Nachpur, the wife of a wealthy cloth merchant (F 52–53). Thus the university, the printing trade, and commerce were all represented: these were the spheres of society that Thomas moved in or aspired to enter. By contrast, when his second wife brought him additional children some forty years later, nearly all the godparents were drawn from outside the economic sphere, from the world of judges, ecclesiastics, intellectuals, and municipal government. Slowly but surely, Thomas had made his way up the social ladder.

Felix's birth was a great joy for Thomas's cousin Simon Steiner, known as Lithonius, who, like Thomas, sprang from a peasant background in the Valais. He had assisted the reformer Bucer in Strasbourg and gone on to become a professor of Greek at the Gymnasium in the Alsatian capital. Married but without children, Lithonius, with Thomas's blessing, intended to treat Felix *de facto* as his own adoptive son, but his premature death in 1545 put an end to this dream. Felix did, however, inherit his cousin's fine library, the books from which were marked with a cloverleaf. It is remarkable to observe how illiterate peasant children like Simon and Thomas grew up to be astonishing bibliophiles.

Unusually for the time, Felix, in recounting his childhood, set out to be a conscientious historian. He drew a distinction between his own authentic memories (from his later years, obviously) and things that he had learned from others about himself (mostly having to do with his early years, of which he had no personal recollection: as he put it, "'36, '37, '38, up to 1539"). Many of these memories concern either pranks or injuries or both. In 1539, for example, in a time of plague (the first of many epidemics mentioned by Felix), some practical jokers interrupted his mother as she sat spinning thread with a distaff and showed her a skull stolen from a nearby cemetery with a candle inserted in one of its eye sockets. Frightened, Anna leapt up and knocked over Felix's cradle, resulting in an injury that left a scar on his nose. Another time, while slicing bread, Anna slipped and cut the tip of the middle finger of little Felix's right hand, leaving him with another scar for life. As a result, the little boy was frightened by the sight of wounds and bruises. A little later he had a nanny with a mutilated finger, and his refusal to eat porridge served by a hand thus truncated led to the woman's dismissal. For years Felix continued to exhibit an obsessive dislike of people with mutilated limbs or broken bones.

Looking back, decades later, on his first three years, Felix recalled one authentic personal memory as if it had happened the day before: his elder sister Margret was carried into the house unconscious after being accidentally struck with a pickax by a servant digging in the yard. The grownups gathered in a panic around the senseless child. She sooned regained consciousness, however, and before long was running around the table in her nightshirt. A few months later, however, she died of the plague. Perhaps the superimposition of these two "snapshots" (the first, of Margret unconscious, masking the second, of her actual death) accounts for the vividness of this image in Felix's mind. In 1539, an amazed Felix looked on as the artist Matthäus Han, age twenty-six, from a family of master glaziers, decorated the facades of the house that Thomas Platter had purchased the year before, which bore the resonant name *Zum Gejägd* (To the Hunt) (F 55–56). Han drew an outline of a stag with its horns, then of a hunter with his dog (*hundt und jeger*). On the facade of the house across the street, the same artist drew a scene depicting a number of Moors. The Moors figured frequently in the folklore of the time, owing to their important role in the wars of the early sixteenth century: they almost captured Vienna in 1529. The king of France became their ally in 1532.[1] In one of the heated rooms of the Platter home, moreover, there was a small birdcage made of iron wire painted all the colors of the rainbow. Much later, Felix would have his own home painted in the gaudy French style.

The summer of 1540 was very hot, hot enough to advance the date of the grape harvest by two weeks and to melt glaciers and snow fields in the mountains. This sweltering summer left Felix with other memories as well: a woman invited to Sunday dinner at the Platters' gave him a handful of pretzels, and a friendly carpenter took him by the hand and bought him white bread for a few pennies (the daily bread in Switzerland and adjacent regions of Germany was usually black). Another memory also involved eating—and indigestion: little Felix ate too many cherries in celebration of his first pair of pants, which were as red as the cherries themselves; his new trousers paid the price for his overindulgence. Until then Felix's regular costume had been a tunic, which he wore much longer than his father had worn his. Felix's childhood had little in common with Thomas's rude beginnings some thirty to thirty-five years earlier. One thing remained the same, however: little Felix became fascinated very early with horses and horsemen.[2] One of Thomas's brothers, a soldier, had given him a toy horse in the early years of the sixteenth century. A soldier named Meltinger, about whom we know nothing except that he lived in a house in the middle of the block the Platters lived in (at what would later be 92, Obere Freie Strasse), had a horse that he kept in a stable rented from Thomas, and Felix always looked on with great pleasure whenever the steed was led in or out.

Distractions also stuck in Felix's mind. He remembered his father's workmen playing skittles; a wooden doll, purchased at the fair, which was flexible enough to use in fencing games; and riding perched on the shoulders of his father's boarders, students from the leading families of the Valais, who lifted him high enough to touch the ceiling. Grownups sometimes bantered with the boy: every snowflake, they said, was an old woman, falling, falling, falling. On Christmas Eve, Saint Nicholas came riding on an ass and handed out gifts to all the laughing children, Felix among them. Here, then, is evidence of a long-standing opposition between Christmas customs in the north and south, dating back to at least the sixteenth century: in German-speaking countries, good Saint Nick was the focus of attention, whereas in Provence and Romansch-speaking areas, the "yule-log" was the centerpiece of the winter celebration. Thomas Platter Jr., Felix's younger brother, would discover this for himself while traveling in the south of France during the winter season a half-century later.

Another miracle was Felix's discovery of eggs on the straw bed occupied by Canis, the dog belonging to Herr Grauwenstein, a vintner and Latinist who lived across the street. Grauwenstein and his wife liked to invite Felix for dinner and serve him eggs, which they of course claimed had been laid by Canis. The story shows that the Platters continued to frequent common folk—craftsmen and vine growers—even though Thomas, with his grand ideas, would have preferred to give the impression that he hobnobbed exclusively with distinguished clergymen and professors. Unfortunately we have no access to the vast wealth of folktales that little Felix must have heard from the grandmothers of other children (his own grandparents were long since dead). The Platters' only son delighted in the ghost stories that these old women told, which terrified him. He was afraid to sleep alone (night terrors are of course common among children), and was obsessed with thoughts of screech owls, which were said to peck at people's heads (to steal their souls, perhaps?). He also worried about the black cow that provided milk to a nearby hospital, because he was afraid it might swallow him whole. In the end Felix was allowed to sleep in Thomas's bed to put an end to his nocturnal frights.

Felix's earliest memory of a political or religious kind is precisely dated (and partially reconstructed from the testimony of others): it concerned his one and only meeting with Calvin in 1541. The Picardian theologian was on his way from Strasbourg to Geneva. In 1541 his path crossed that of Thomas Platter, who, with his boy in tow, was escorting his old friend Hans Rust to the new house Rust had just bought at Kalchmatt in Simmental. The three travelers from Basel met the future dictator of Geneva in Liestal (F 93). Thomas Platter and Calvin spoke at length (their conversation had to have been in Latin). They discussed the *Institutes of the*

Christian Religion, which Thomas had of course printed in 1536. Felix's account of the meeting is partially reconstructed from the later testimony of Rust and his father, but the young narrator also remembers having drunk several glasses of sugared or sweet wine served to him by Jacob Murer, the son of Liestal's innkeeper, in whose establishment the meeting took place. Jacob, who was a student in Basel, returned to the city with Felix and Thomas, while Rust continued on to his new home.

This episode from Felix's childhood is actually the culmination of a long digression involving Hans Rust. Using fragmentary personal memories fleshed out with family stories, Felix brings Rust's saga to life. Hans Rust was the son of a former abbot, Thüring Rust, who quit the monastery, became a Protestant pastor, and took a wife. His boy Hans later became a court clerk, alchemist, and poet. In the 1520s, when people around Bern were destroying "papist idols," he developed a technique that thrust him into the front ranks of iconoclasts. The religious idols that the reformers wished to destroy had of course been gilded and regilded many times over. Rust invented a special powder which, when burned, gave off fumes that could be used to remove the gold from statues slated for destruction. He was thus able to recover the precious metal without having to scrape each object by hand, as Protestant goldsmiths had been doing previously. Once scraped bare of all its gold, the pious object could be consigned to the flames.

Moreover, Rust, a master alchemist, kept his furnaces running full blast, transforming mercury into silver—or so the sometimes credulous Felix Platter believed.[3] The profits from this activity had supposedly made him a wealthy man, and, being wealthy, Rust lent to the poor in order to avoid the sin of avarice, which would have damned him otherwise. He even laid out a handsome sum to buy the buildings (*gebäulichkeiten*) of the old Trub monastery where his father had been abbot before taking off his habit (F 92). Certain forms of privilege carried over, apparently, from Catholicism to Protestantism; in any case, the abbatial infrastructure remained in the family. Hans Rust's marriage to Sara Rimlenen, a seamstress employed by the Platters, was quite a raucous occasion. Thomas's boarders, dressed as clowns, were such a riot that Myconius, the grave pastor who succeeded Œcolampadius as the Protestant spiritual leader of Basel, nearly peed in his pants. Rust had a number of children with biblical names like Sarah and Rebecca who threw snowballs with Felix, as well as a son Hermes, whose name recalled the divine magic of Antiquity. Rust also had two other sons, one of whom, a student in Paris, died young and penniless; the other, despite being a student in Catholic Bologna, was destined to become a Protestant pastor. Hans Rust was friendly with Martin Borrhaus, an associate of Thomas Platter's (F 92). An alchemist who also liked to travel,

Borrhaus claimed to be able to decompose compounds into simpler elements. Felix, the future physician, would remember what he had learned from Borrhaus when he later became interested in medicinal formulas while studying at the University of Montpellier.

* * *

Plague and death, meanwhile, continued their macabre dance. Plague struck in the middle of the annual Basel crossbow contest in 1541. Archers from the city and throughout the Confederation competed on Petersplatz.[4] They tried to hit moving targets shaped like men and painted black and white. Little Felix actually believed they were men (F 57). Masked revelers mingled with the fife-and-drum corps and flailed at young spectators with slapsticks, hurting some, including Felix, badly enough to send them to the hospital. In the middle of the competition, one well-known archer, Hans Knüttel, a member of the Saffron Guild, collapsed: he had been stricken with the plague and died a short while later. The crowd fled in panic, and the festival ended abruptly. Another victim of plague that year was Simon Grynaeus, the Hellenist and theologian in whose home Felix remembered having cavorted in his tunic when he was four or five years old. Platter's cousin Simon Steiner returned to Basel from Strasbourg, where he was teaching, for a brief visit. Felix recalled this visit as in a dream: it was among his earliest memories, he says. He paints a picture of Simon in lederhosen emerging from the washroom on the second floor of Zum Gejägd. Steiner, too, would die of plague a few years later, in 1545.

* * *

Felix felt a particular loathing for a washtub in the middle bedroom of Zum Gejägd. The bottom of the tub still showed traces of blood where a baby, the son of the previous owner or tenant, had fallen into it. The child had been left unattended in its cradle and had somehow toppled into the tub, whose cover had then fallen on the tiny victim. For several days it was feared that the child had been kidnapped, until his body was found lying on its stomach in the washtub. The child's nurse had been negligent (many Basel burghers, including the Platters, employed nannies). Felix never entered this "accursed" room without feeling a shiver down his spine.

* * *

As the elderly gentleman looked back in 1612 on the child he had been between 1540 and 1545, fear sometimes gave way to nostalgia. He remembered, for instance, the little green writing case that had been kept on a dresser seventy years before. As a child he had stood on tiptoe trying to reach it, but he was always told that he could not have it, despite his tears.

*   *   *

Memories often ran together and were sometimes misdated. A "Welch" (that is, French- or Romansch-speaking) vintner by the name of Mumelin, who lived close to the Platter's house, a married man and a father, used a pickax to murder another neighbor who had mocked his mediocre German, his incomplete mastery of the local dialect—an incident of Renaissance racism. In punishment for this killing, Mumelin was beheaded. On another occasion, in 1549, a person named Vetterlin, who lived across the street from Zum Gejägd, committed a robbery. He, too, lost his head. Two capital crimes committed by two residents of Felix Platter's street make one wonder if the crime rate at the time was particularly high, or if beheadings were particularly common. The latter seems more likely, because houses in Basel were not always locked.

*   *   *

Felix also remembered having been dandled on the knees of some of Switzerland's, and indeed Europe's, leading intellectuals and physicians. We have already encountered Professor Steiner of Strasbourg. In 1543 the boy met Vesalius, the great anatomist, whose assistant, Franz Jeckelmann, a surgeon, would fifteen years later become Felix's father-in-law. And then there was Hieronymus Gschmus, also known as Gemuseus, the son of an Alsatian merchant, who had roamed Switzerland, France, and the Piedmont in pursuit of an education before becoming a physician, professor, philosopher, naturalist, editor, and son-in-law of the renowned bookseller Cratander; his brother became the Protestant reformer of Mulhouse. In short, Gemuseus was a typical Renaissance man, whose obscurity today is undeserved (F 61).

*   *   *

Felix often played with toys that Thomas's boarders bought for him at the town fair. He was particularly fond of a puppet swordsman that Heinrich Billing the bürgermeister's son and a close friend of Thomas's, had brought from Strasbourg. When Felix remembered pulling this puppet's strings, he was truly revisiting his early childhood, because Heinrich Billing died in 1541, before the boy's sixth birthday (F 62).

*   *   *

This remembrance of the toy soldier leads here, as so often when military memories are evoked, to an image of paternal glory: Felix remembers Thomas as a robust man of forty, armed with a lance or halberd and buckled into his uniform. The printer-professor marched in step with other burghers of the municipal guard on holidays and in drills just outside the city walls. His friend Heinrich Petri, a master typographer, was also fond of sticking his chest out. Petri, the son of a Basel printer, had been a student in Luther's Germany. It will come as no surprise, then, that he was married to a widowed former nun. He later remarried, taking the widow of the bookbinder Hieronymus Frobenius as his second wife. He was thus a part of the group of printers and typographers that included Frobenius, Hervagius, and Episcopius—the very milieu in which Thomas Platter launched his brief career as a printer. By the 1540s, Thomas, having shed his crude highland ways, enjoyed the full confidence of his fellow citizens, as evidenced by his admission to the Bear Guild, of which he and Petri were both members. Recognized by all as an honest man, Platter was entrusted with the guild's silver, two basketfuls of which were kept in his home (T 62). (In English universities, whose colleges of fellows are the direct descendants of medieval communities, one can find similar corporate hoards of silver today.)

*   *   *

Felix also has many detailed things to say about the plague, though his chronology is rarely precise. Many of his memories date from the fourth to ninth years of his life; some are later. At least two women in the neighborhood died of plague. One, whose last name was Wettenspiessen, died sometime between 1539 and 1542 (T 62). The other, Christelin von Ougstall, had married into a family of vintners on Freie Strasse and was the mother of a girl named Pascasia (from the Latin *pascha*, Passover, hence Easter) because she was born on Easter Sunday in 1542, shortly before her mother's tragic death.

In 1539, the first year of the great epidemic that cost little Margret Platter her life,[5] Thomas and Anna for obvious reasons sent Felix to live in a house some distance away with a printer named Görg, about whom little is known (F 62). Felix mingles personal memories with stories he heard from others. He was not frightened by the infection, he tells us, but was afraid of the sun. The sun's rays entered through a slit in the windowshade, revealing motes of dust in the air that made the little boy anxious. His elder sister Ursula, who shared his exile from home, apparently put ideas into his head: the two children imagined that the dust could turn into a monster that liked to snap off people's heads and eat them. Was it now that Felix first became interested in saws and planes for making wooden toys and even musical instruments such as lutes? Most likely memories of different periods ran together in Felix's mind; it seems doubtful that he learned woodworking in 1539, when he was only three or four years old.

In any case, the child who so disliked mythical monsters returned from Görg's as a budding carpenter with his miniature adze and plane. Though forbidden to do so by his father, Felix, three or four years old at the time, surreptitiously entered the front room of the house which contained the body of his sister Margret, who had died a few hours earlier. (Despite what some historians have argued, apparently not all children in this period were expected to acquire firsthand knowledge of the dead.) Pears were piled on a bench in the death chamber. Felix filched a few, then hid behind the oven and ate them: love of fruit was a constant of his childhood. Like many children, Felix believed that people could easily return from the dead: lift a piece of slate from the roof and his sister would fall from heaven into his arms. The same image would occur to him in a dream thirty-five years later, when he was thinking of "adopting" a baby.[6]

* * *

At a very tender age Felix showed signs of an artistic sensibility; his father, as a poor mountain lad, had not had an opportunity to develop any of his artistic talents except for singing. Felix took an interest in the lute and the violin. He secretly liked to leaf through illuminated parchment prayerbooks, whose colorful pages were pleasing to the eye. Among them perhaps, was a Fouquet or a Bourdichon, destined for destruction by Thomas Platter, who used the vellum for bindings. Today, any antiquarian bookseller would be horrified at the thought that such masterpieces, any one of which would easily fetch millions at Christie's or Sotheby's, were so casually destroyed. Little Felix apparently had good taste, as did the princes and patrons who had commissioned the beautiful works that the boy's father recycled without a second thought.

Many plague deaths (including perhaps that of the Wettenspiessen woman and certainly that of Christelin von Ougstall) occurred in 1542, most likely in the summer. The following February, the young nobleman (*junker*) Gedeon von Ostheim rented a room in Thomas's house (F 64). The name Gedeon (or Gideon) comes from the Book of Judges: Gideon is the hero who smashes the altars of Baal and other idols despised by the ancient Hebrews (see Judges 6). Such a name identified him as a second-generation Protestant, born in the 1520s, when his parents were smashing idols and defying the papists. The scion of an Alsatian noble family that had distinguished itself in the wave of Helvetic iconoclasm in 1529, Gedeon later participated in the Reformation "reconstruction" of Basel: in 1566 he began building a town house for himself, a fine dwelling in which Prince Henri de Condé, a leader of the French Huguenots, stayed in 1575 while traveling between Strasbourg, Basel, and Bern in search of allies (F 64).[7]

Felix's contacts with Gedeon von Ostheim in 1543–44, when the young nobleman took his meals at Thomas Platter's table, were on a rather less lavish scale than Ostheim's relations with the Prince de Condé. Essentially all that Felix remembered was that his father's noble boarder had given him a velvet hood or cape (*sammat schlepplin*) that proved quite durable.

Felix received another gift in 1544 from Captain Georg Summermatter. As the name suggests, the captain was a relative of Thomas's mother, but their destinies could not have been more different. Amilli Summermatterin had slipped, through her own or her family's misfortune, into the ranks of the impoverished peasantry. Captain Georg, however, came from a more prosperous branch of this increasingly prominent family. He became first a notary and later a castellan-officer before rising to the rank of regional captain in the Valais (F 63). In April 1544 (after the plague epidemic had ended in Basel), the effects of war elsewhere in Europe began to make themselves felt: the conflict between Charles V and Francis I had resumed some years earlier. Captain Georg Summermatter was a Swiss officer, and Swiss troops were fighting in Italy with a French army under the command of a Bourbon, the Prince d'Enghien. At Ceresole Alba in the Piedmont, some 15,000 French troops, including 4,000 Swiss foot soldiers, clashed in a bloody battle with nearly 20,000 soldiers of the Empire, including 7,000 German lansquenets commanded by the Marquis del Vasto. The French victory cost Charles V 10,000 men killed or taken prisoner, against losses of only 2,000 dead on the "royal" side. The battle demonstrated the superiority of a force of infantry (especially Swiss infantry) equipped with harquebuses and pikes over cavalry. The victory at Ceresole enabled France to hold on to the Piedmont for another fifteen years (until 1559). The French held some of their Piedmont fortresses, such as Pinerolo, even longer, until the seventeenth century, when the Bourbons, successors of the Valois, finally gave them up—but then France's future did not really lie in Italy, not even northern Italy (if we exclude Savoy).

Of course Felix, at age nine, had no notion of such geopolitical consid-erations. He mostly remembered seeing the Swiss Confederates—limping, ragtag veterans—marching up Bäumleingasse to the Cathedral of Our Lady. The conquering troops' uniforms and banners were in tat-ters (*zerlumpet*). Among the soldiers was Captain Georg Summermatter, Thomas Platter's kinsman and friend. Hence it was only natural that he should give Felix a present of a doublet and a multicolored pair of trou-sers in the outdated fifteenth-century Roman or Florentine Renaissance style—the fruit of his Italian campaign. Felix was quite proud of these gifts. He wore them as long as he could, but he was a growing boy. Thus the date 1544 stood out in Felix's mind as the year of the glorious home-coming of the veterans of Ceresole. It was also the year in which one of the city's inner gates, the Aeschentor, was demolished. The bricks and timbers from this structure, which formed part of Basel's wall, were re-used in the construction of a new residence for a noble family.

*   *   *

From the colors of the clothing he wore as a boy Felix moved by analogy, if not logic, to the changing color of his skin: epidemic, not to say epider-mic, matters were once again on his mind. Felix came down first with smallpox (certainly before 1544, when his father went out of the printing business) and then with measles, two diseases that killed millions of people at about this time: the natives of the Antilles and the Americas, who were not immune to European "affections." In Felix's case, the dis-eases turned his skin many shades of red but did not kill him. When sick he lay on a "couch" (*gutschen*) in the print shop (*stube*), a room that could be heated in winter; apparently it was located toward the back of the Plat-ter house. The typographers teased the sick little boy about his scarlet complexion.

The child had a "sweet tooth," and people spoiled him by bringing him sweets (*sieuss, siess, süss*), which apparently played an important part in the dietary preferences of the middle and upper classes as early as the fifteenth century. Sugar was imported from southern Spain, the Canary Islands, and other islands off the coast of West Africa, but not yet from the Carib-bean. Its production inevitably involved the use of black, or at any rate dark-skinned, slaves to plant and cut cane. True to form, Felix also ate fruit. While sick with either smallpox or measles, Felix was allowed as a special favor to eat a superb pear brought to him by a noble lady, Mag-dalena Münch, the wife of Ludwig von Reischach. Reischach, a Protes-tant exiled for religious reasons, had been living in Basel for more than fifteen years. He had been granted the rights of a burgher of the city in 1529, a turning point in the fortunes of "heresy" in Basel. He lived in a fine house on the cathedral square. As usual, Felix tries to impress us with his father's relations with eminent nobles while concealing his humble origins.[8] He mentions several times that Magdalena was a Valaisian: this was not true, but it allowed him to narrow the gap between the blue blood of this generous lady and the more rustic blood of his own forebears. But the child in him soon returns to the fore: like so many other children, Felix, at age eight, liked to be sick because it meant he would be pampered. "Would that you could stay sick for a long time," he told himself. "Then you could eat sweets." (When he talked to himself, he used the familiar form of the second-person pronoun: many people in southern France do the same thing today.)

Did smallpox and measles leave any traces? For a long time, when Felix worked outdoors, people noticed that his eyes were red and that he had red stripes on his nose (*rote strick über die nassen*). More serious were his urinary troubles, of which Felix, like Montaigne, does not spare us a single detail. When he urinated, he experienced a burning sensation. This was most often a problem in the afternoon. His acidic urine left a white trace, like the salt from seawater. Although there were privies on the second floor of Zum Gejägd, Felix urinated outside more often than not. His bladder frequently felt bloated, and as a result the child hopped from one foot to the other so often that he became embarrassed when people noticed. But with his travels in France, marriage, and quite simply the passage of time, his symptoms gradually disappeared. What had caused them? Much later, while in Speyer, he consulted Dr. Johannes Crato, a moderate Protestant who, after being educated in Lutheran Saxony and papist Italy, served as physician to two emperors: Ferdinand and Maximilian (F 65). Crato suspected kidney spasms, a diagnosis that thrust Felix into a depression that lasted all the way back to Basel. Although Felix no longer suffered from the problem, he continued to think about it, and it figured in the learned treatise on micturition that he published in 1614. Most likely young Felix had suffered from a urinary tract infection spread by dirty hands and linen.

* * *

Thomas Platter's house was home to any number of boarders, who literally broke bread with Felix and other members of the family. Some of these boarders were the sons of nobles or other prominent individuals who went on to distinguished careers. One of them was Christoph

Efinger, the scion of a noble family and a man who would later father twelve children of his own (F 65). In 1552 his castle burned on the eve of his eldest son's birth. Thanks to primogeniture, his descendants remained major landowners in the canton of Aargau for three centuries. Another boarder was Ludwig von Diesbach, a scion of the Helvetic nobility who later sold his services as a soldier in Germany and France. He would enjoy the friendly patronage of the Duc d'Alençon and the Prince de Condé.

Then there were four brothers from the illustrious Truchsess von Rheinfelden family, which could trace its history in Basel back twelve generations. During the Renaissance, members of this family served Basel and other communities along the Rhine in various official and military capacities. One of the brothers, Jacob, a friendly practical joker, was especially close to Felix. To round out this survey, we should also mention Gedeon von Ostheim, whom we encountered earlier, and Ludwig von Schoenau, whose kinsmen held important episcopal and administrative posts. These students constituted the Platters' links to the aristocracy, of which they liked to boast (F 66). Felix above all prided himself on his frequentation of the "upper crust." These young nobles were more "suitable" than his previous companions, the crude and uncouth apprentice printers who were such a lively presence at Zum Gejägd until 1543 or 1544 and perhaps even longer.

* * *

Besides their democratic relations with typographers and their snobbish hobnobbing with bluebloods, Thomas and Felix also had dear friends of intermediate social status, among the (non-noble) patrician bourgeoisie. At Zum Gejägd, among Thomas's students, there were above all the brothers Paul and Johann-Ludwig Höchstetter, who belonged to a family of wealthy Augsburg merchants, dealers in "grains, fabrics, spices, and metals of all kinds" (F 66). The Höchstetters were ruined, however, by an economic crash that affected much of Europe in 1529, at which point the two boys bade farewell to the business world and made the familiar move into the more secure world of the professions (public or private): see Thomas Mann's *Buddenbrooks*. Paul took up law, while Johann-Ludwig went into medicine. With Thomas, who, though well into his forties, still liked to amuse himself, the two boys liked to play *Spickspeck,* a game that involved throwing a knife at a board. The same trio—the "old" man and the two young boys—also shot at artificial birds on a pole with a small harquebus (or was it a miniature crossbow?): a game of "popinjay." The brothers also bet on who could knock the other off a table.

The room in which the two brothers played this rough game, as Felix looked on admiringly, also served as an aviary. One day, while fighting, the Höchstetters left the window open and allowed all the turtledoves to escape. Felix was wrongly accused of having opened the window and severely scolded (*übel gescholten*) by his father, but the truth came out later. Thomas, though a harsh and at times brutal father, was capable of acknowledging his mistakes. In any case, he was not the only person to try his hand at raising birds along with his other occupations: the printer Görg, with whom Felix had stayed during one plague outbreak, also kept birds in his house. But to get back to the Höchstetters, the episode in which they shot artificial birds with Felix's father must have taken place in 1548, given the date that they registered at the university and the periods during which they were students of Thomas's (F 66–67). Felix was then twelve or thirteen. Paul Höchstetter later embarked on a career in the judiciary, only to die of plague in 1563, before his fortieth birthday, in Thomas's house (F 66). Johann-Ludwig studied medicine at Montpellier with Felix, at which time the two became close friends. Having settled in Württemberg as a physician, Johann-Ludwig Höchstetter would drown himself in the Neckar three years after the death of his eldest son.

It is at this point in the memoirs, when Felix is twelve or thirteen, that he first mentions prayer—and shortly thereafter recounts a dream. Felix was a friend of another boarder in his father's house, a boy named Stelli (also spelled Stelle, Stölli, or Stellin—the spelling of proper names was not yet fixed). The boy was the nephew of the *junker* Captain Wolfgang Stelli of Solothurn, where he was a city official (*Obervogt*) in a family of officials (*Schultheiss*). He also owned a house in Basel known as Zum Samson. The two boys, Felix and Stelli, went almost every Sunday for breakfast prepared by Wolfgang Stelli's wife, née Salomé Baer (a "Berin," as people said—one of the Baer girls, in other words). She was the daughter of a hero of Marignano and of course young Stelli's aunt. A stubborn, authoritarian woman of breeding, she was not well liked by her neighbors. She became the butt of malicious laughter when she fell from a horse while crossing the Rhine bridge en route to her country estate and landed sprawling on the pavement with her skirts above her waist. Her foul temper frightened Stelli, who incurred her wrath frequently because he was often dirty—hygiene, as we have seen, was not the Platter household's strong suit. In the hope of warding off the usual scolding, Felix and Stelli prayed fervently on Sunday mornings before breakfast on wooden blocks set up in Saint Peter's square.

As for the dream, Felix dreamt that he had fallen asleep on a stone bench near Zum Samson where he often slept, and that he remained asleep there for years. Riders used this same bench as a convenient place to tie up their horses. (People in the past dreamt frequently of horses; in this motorized age we have lost touch with the connection between dreaming and horses, to which we owe the English word *nightmare*.) In later life Felix was able to decipher this dream easily. In 1574 he bought Captain Wolfgang Stelli's house, Zum Samson, and made it his home. Meanwhile, in 1565, having become one of Basel's leading physicians, he had treated the captain, whose wife had lost none of her irascible temper, for plague, from which he subsequently died, clearing the way for Felix to acquire his house ten years later. In his glory days, the captain had also been the owner of a noble estate not far from Basel in a place called Kliben or Klybeck. Salomé, who managed this estate along with her husband, invited Felix and Stelli to come work there during the harvest season. The boys expected to have a gay old time, but once the harvest was in, the mistress of the house sent them packing without so much as a crust of bread. Felix never again set foot in the inhospitable countryside. Had the aristocratic Salomé Stelli looked down on the young commoner whose father had been a beggar? Disagreeable as some of his encounters with the Stellis were, they were yet another link to the aristocracy and there-fore invaluable as long as relations could be kept up. At their home Felix met another noblewoman, Catharina von Reinach, who was so tall that she had to bend down to pass through some of the house's door-ways (F 68).

*   *   *

The digging of a well at Zum Gejägd on Thomas's orders and before little Felix's amazed eyes provides an occasion with which to measure the dif-ferences in style and vision between father and son: Thomas is concrete, precise, and brief, whereas Felix often digresses to recall various details of his childhood. "At the time I had twenty boarders," writes Thomas in his characteristically concise style, "so that I was making a good deal of money." (The remark is worth noting: the boarders so improbably crowded together in the ramshackle house were crucial in allowing Thomas to amass enough of a fortune to suspend at least part of his activ-ity in the risky printing business in 1544 and settle into the pedagogical branch of the more secure world of the gown). "I gradually paid off my debts. Immediately after buying the house [1541?], I dug a well.[9] Not counting the food for the workers, it cost me one hundred florins" (T 124). Thomas is just as succinct when he describes the construction of the second well (T 139), on his suburban property in Gundeldingen in the

second half of 1549. "Shortly after buying the Hugwald estate in Gundeldingen, I began digging a well and then building, or rather rebuilding, the house, barn, and stable. I planted vines, I paid the workers, I
bought three acres of pasture," and so on. Clearly the experience of the
first well-drilling at Zum Gejägd served Thomas well in the second at
Gundeldingen.

Felix, who revels in his memories and is more of a writer than Thomas,
gives us a more detailed description of the scene. He was no more than
eight and a half when the first well was dug at Zum Gejägd. Seven decades later, he recalled the extraction of sand from the hole, along with a
few grains of silver and gold: he called the substance thus recovered *acry-
moso,* embellishing it with a word taken perhaps from Pliny the Elder or
Isidore of Seville (F 69). Felix fully depicts Thomas's understandable joy
when his workers finally strike water: the elder Platter fills a fur cap with
the fresh liquid and generously anoints his friend Lux Iselin, who came
from a family of grocers and politicians.

Another scene connected with the well strikes a sadder note. It involved Gertrud (or perhaps Anna) Lachner, who had been the wife of
two prominent members of the print trade, first the binder Hieronymus
Frobenius and later Johannes Herwagen. Gertrud suffered from gout
and was in the habit of treating the disease, as others treated gallstones,
by drinking abundant quantities of water. She therefore had herself carried on a chair to the Platters' new well and eagerly drank the slightly
carbonated water. The treatment proved ineffective, however: she died a
few months later (F 69).

*   *   *

Felix also remembered the mason Michael, whose job was to smoothe the
inner wall of the well. While he was busy at this task, someone accidentally dropped a sizable stone down the well, grazing his head and shoulders. The workman was hauled up, and his wounds were dressed by the
surgeon Franz Jeckelmann, Felix's future father-in-law. But the incident
led to disaster: unable to work in the building trades after his accident,
the handicapped former mason found work as a mounted courier. But his
horse lost its footing on a narrow mountain trail and plunged, together
with its rider, into a raging torrent. The man's body was never found.
Divers later recovered his mail sack, still attached to the carcass of the
horse, which had snagged on a rock.

According to Felix, the well also earned his father a certain amount of
abuse from other burghers. One substantial citizen mocked the

professor-printer for sinking a hundred gulden into an investment like a well rather than lending the money out at interest. With the interest rate at 5 percent, Thomas was forgoing an income of five gulden annually for the pleasure of drinking his own water. Thomas heatedly objected that he was no banker, that moneylending and usury were not for him. Felix's subsequent report of this virtuous indignation is all the more interesting in that a quarter of the substantial income he earned in his forty-four years as a physician in Basel came from interest on loans.[10]

Every year, Thomas organized a lavish dinner for his colleagues in the book trade, including Frobenius and many others. For some reason this was referred to as the "executioner's meal": perhaps the name had to do with some hazing ritual for apprentice typographers. Taken in by the name, the son of one of Platter's friends, a young man also named Thomas, went so far as to hide in an oven for fear that he would be hanged (F 70).

* * *

After the narrative reaches 1543 or 1544, Felix's chronological notations become considerably more precise. In the summer of 1543, he notes, an inn known as Zum Goldenen Kopf collapsed, killing several people. A little girl was retrieved from the wreckage safe and sound: a beam had protected her. The owners, a man and a woman, had the inn rebuilt, and it was back in business the following year as if nothing had happened (F 70).

* * *

Meanwhile, Felix's future—and even his future marriage—began to take shape. A sore toe and a toothache were the first signs. Jeckelmann treated him again, this time for an infected ingrown toenail. This probably took place before the fall of 1545, when Jeckelmann was still living in the Aeschenvorstadt district (F 70). He did not move to the more spacious house known as Zum Schöneck until October 1545. Slightly younger than Thomas, Jeckelmann, the son of a surgeon, was a member of the professional and municipal elite. He had at least five children, of whom three survived. One of them, a daughter named Madlen, would marry Felix in 1557, while the two sons, Franz and Daniel, became surgeons like their father. Daniel, while still young, tried his hand by pulling a tooth from Felix's upper jaw, an experience so traumatic that he refused to have a tooth pulled ever again. Was he immune to tooth decay despite his fondness for sugar? Daniel, who married fifteen years later, lost two children in the plagues of 1563 (F 70).

* * *

In 1543 or 1544 Felix took his first music lessons.[11] These suited his tastes and talents. His father sang, as we know. Felix, being the son of a prosperous man, learned to play an instrument. He was eight years old (*ich nur acht ieri wass* [F 71]) when Thomas paid for him to take lute lessons from Peter Dorn, a professional lutenist. Was this Peter perhaps a relative of the carpenter Ambrosius Dorn, whose shop, humming with saws and planes, adjoined the Platter house on the side of the Aeschentor? Or was he a son of the Flemish doctor Gerhard Dorn, a disciple of Paracelsus, who practiced medicine for a time in Frankfurt before coming to Basel (F 71)? There is no way to know for sure. In any case, Thomas hired Peter Dorn to teach Felix and other boarders at Zum Gejägd to play the lute. Together they formed a sort of musical circle, a hotbed of culture in which our budding music lover learned to play his first notes.

Felix's memoirs cast doubt on the standard view among musicologists that the lute was primarily a court instrument in the sixteenth century and did not gain popularity among the bourgeoisie until the seventeenth century, at which time it became common in salons as well as in theater and opera.[12] Clearly the instrument was already in widespread use among the middle and even lower-middle classes of Switzerland. The musicologists are right, however, when they say that in Basel and elsewhere the Protestant liturgy had a decisive influence on musical practice. But it was not the only influence. From early childhood, Felix was fond of hymns, but he also liked folksongs and mountain tunes. Unlike his father, Felix did not sing much, although he played a number of instruments. He was afraid that if he sang loudly he would show his teeth "to the back of his mouth." He would sing only when he was in a good mood or on horseback or accompanied by others in a choir. But he took great pleasure in listening to lute music during carnival or by moonlight after dinner, and he studied the instrument in depth under several teachers. He concluded his study in Montpellier, where other medical students called him *den Teutschen lutenisten,* the German lutenist (which proves that Occitan was not the only language in use in Montpellier, where many students chose to speak French). As an adolescent, Felix also played the lute for girls and at the inn for peasants; such evenings must have been reminiscent of a Brueghel painting. He also played at "concerts and banquets" (F 71). His lute cost him nearly two hundred crowns. In addition, he played other instruments such as the clavichord and possibly the spinet.

In Montpellier, Felix took harp lessons from a Dutch physician and anatomist and then from an Englishman whom he had cured of a bladder infection. When he died in 1614, Felix owned forty-two musical instruments (including seven violas da gamba), enough to equip an orchestra (F 73). As a child, he made and strummed all sorts of stringed instruments of his own design. Before 1541 (or was it 1544?) he liked to listen to his father's workmen playing the Jew's harp and dulcimer. A few years later, after the same typographers had benefited from the lute lessons of Peter Dorn, Felix delighted in their musical abilities. The traditional Swiss love of music runs in an unbroken line from Felix Platter to Frédéric Amiel.[13] Felix's musical memories from this period are more vivid than his memories of learning to read or write (the first book he mentions is not an ordinary printed book but a set of bound, illuminated parchments). What a difference from Thomas, for whom primers were precious objects, all the more so because in his life they were for so long forbidden fruit.

Felix's received instruction in the rudiments of Latin from a private teacher, Johannes von Schallen, a young man only a dozen or so years older than his pupil. The teacher was the bastard son of a notary-captain (in those days it was not uncommon for professionals to marry the pen and the sword). A former student of Thomas's, von Schallen went on to become a teacher in Platter's school, and it was then that he took it upon himself to teach the language of Cicero as well as the lute to Felix and Ursula.

* * *

It was also in 1543 or 1544 that Felix became aware of political and military matters extending beyond his local community. The battle of Ceresola Alba (1544), which he experienced intensely if at a distance, was a key factor in the child's politicization and acculturation. Meanwhile, in 1543, Vesalius, whom Felix had met, published his *Seven Books on the Structure of the Human Body*. To be sure, the great anatomist resorted to some unusual methods to obtain his cadavers, some of which were snatched from the gallows, others from their graves. As a medical student in Montpellier, Felix hastened to imitate the master's techniques: he frequently dug up newly buried bodies for use in his study of anatomy. Thomas Platter was a reader of Vesalius, and so was his son. Thomas was also Calvin's printer. In Geneva, some distance from Basel, the French reformer had inaugurated a theocratic government—or should we call it theodemocratic? In 1549 he reached an agreement with the Zwinglians of northern Switzerland about the theology of the Last Supper and the meaning of the Eucharist. In nearby France, which the two Platter sons would visit forty years apart (although their father would never set foot in the country), Francis I had resumed his war against Charles V in 1542, in alliance with the Turks and against the Anglicans of Henry VIII. The situation was perhaps less confused than it might appear, however. Along with this geopolitical maneuvering, the second "wave" of antiheretical repression is also notable for the massacre of the nonconformists of the Vaud and the execution of Etienne Dolet, the Huguenot and perhaps freethinker (1546).

Meanwhile, the workingman's standard of living fell as both prices and population increased. The French language made inroads among officialdom and the elite but failed to win the allegiance of the masses. The Protestant Clément Marot translated the psalms into French. The age of cathedrals was not yet over, as the continuing construction work on the steeple of Beauvais indicates. But the age of palaces had already begun: these new edifices symbolized the monarchy's assertion of sovereignty, although at this stage the monarchy was still relatively modest compared with what it became later in the age of absolutism. Construction and renovation were under way at the Louvre of Francis I; Henri II would continue what his predecessor began.

Felix, though an antipapist like his father, was more moderate on religious matters than Thomas. Had his travels taken him as far as Rome, however, he would have found numerous justifications for his congenital anticlericalism. Pope Paul III was in the process of reviving the Inquisition, the future Holy Office. His Holiness also approved—and who can blame him?—the creation of the Company of Jesus, that training ground for the Catholic teachers of the future. And last but not least, the pontiff convoked the Council of Trent. It was a time of feverish activity despite nascent or renascent manifestations of heresy and still fresh memories of papal revels from the time when the Borgias were in the Vatican. In a single year, 1541, Ignatius Loyola became leader of the Jesuits, Calvin settled in Geneva, and John Knox launched the Scottish Reformation. In Britain the antipapist offensive continued: the theological aims of the monarchy were modest, but in the economic sphere the government was resolute (it confiscated monastic property), and it was no less determined to have its way in the realm of liturgy and language (prayers were Anglicized). Out of these reforms came the "Anglican" Church, a narrowly nationalistic institution that also proved to be a useful tool in the hands of a monarch with hegemonic designs. Later, however, it would also demonstrate its capacity to shelter or tolerate new dissident tendencies. The anti-Roman offensive was also, to varying degrees, a confrontation between the central power of London and the Celtic or semi-Celtic periphcries (Ireland, Wales, Scotland). A certain papism often persisted in these regions—a papism that was also a reaction against English conquest. Henry VIII enjoyed moderate success in extending his authority to Ireland in 1541–42. English control of Scotland was far from assured despite frequent military forays. The Scots wavered between an old-line Catholic militancy and a new Protestant radicalism inspired by the preaching of John Knox and his notion of justification by faith. Would the Anglican Church be routed on its right (by pro-Roman, pro-French forces) or on its left (that is, before long, by Puritans and even Calvinists)? To ask the question is to answer it: Scotland, allying itself with England, chose the second path.

Henry VIII's goal was to build an insular monarchy. His forays on the Continent were risible: in 1544, the king of England, in alliance with Charles V, seized Boulogne—a precarious triumph that led nowhere. A more intelligent move was the decision to develop the navy, which Henry VIII took in 1545–46. Britain's future lay on the high seas, and it was a future that augured well in view of the country's already considerable demographic, cultural, and economic growth. Henry's bizarre behavior as an elderly, paranoid tyrant, when he imprisoned and executed former wives and allies, changes the picture only slightly. After his death, a brief resurgence of Catholicism under Edward and Bloody Mary soon subsided, leaving the Anglican Church dominant. Great Britain was thus able to develop peacefully on its own, on the fringes of a Europe often torn apart by warring dogmas and armies.

Thomas and his family, indifferent to these insular British concerns, saw themselves as "Alemannic," hence Teutonic and Continental. Charles V, the head of the Germanic Holy Roman Empire, is barely mentioned in the early memories of either Thomas or Felix. Still, it is convenient to use the emperor as a touchstone for discussing the fate of the German territories, among which confederated Switzerland, though not strictly speaking a part of the Empire, is always included.

The period 1542–44 was a turning point in the history of the imperial lands. After the failure of knights and peasants to enforce their claims, the period from 1525 to 1542 was the "age of princes," dominated by the landgrave Philip of Hesse and Prince Johann Friedrich of Saxony.[14] In 1542, the religious map of a Germany made powerful by its population, its precious and nonprecious metals, and its great merchants was already clear: the Prussian east was all Luther's, as were the center (Hesse, Thuringia, and Saxony) and the Hanseatic and lower-Saxon north, to which must be added the duchy of Brunswick-Wolfenbüttel, "evangelical" after 1542.[15] By contrast, the regions south of the Main and close to the Rhine had traditional ties to the emperor.[16] They have remained, broadly speaking, Catholic to this day. The religious choices made by the princes followed the old Roman *limes*.[17]

But the religious choices of the people were different, for the Reformation had flourished on both sides of the old frontier inherited from the Roman legions. The year 1543 marked the beginning of what Michael Stürmer and his collaborators call the "decade of the Emperor" (*das Jahrzehnt des Kaisers*). That decade began with two victories by Charles V. The first, over Wilhelm von Jülich, extended Hapsburg influence into the Netherlands, thus keeping "heresy" out of the lower Rhine region. Then, after the Treaty of Crépy (of 1544, in which Charles gave up his claims to the duchy of Burgundy, in return for which France ceded, along with other territories, Flanders and Artois to the Empire), Charles scored a major personal victory at Mühlberg, defeating the Protestant armies under Johann Friedrich of Saxony (1547). The landgrave of Hesse and the prince of Saxony were both prisoners of the emperor, who was further blessed by the death of his old enemy Francis I in 1547.

It would be a mistake, however, to exaggerate the consequences of the imperial decade. The Protestant princes had been humilated but were not permanently defeated. Furthermore, the Treaty of Augsburg (1555) consecrated the principle of *cujus regio, ejus religio:* "Tell me which prince or sovereign you are the subject of, and I will tell you which religion, Catholic or Protestant, you are firmly admonished to profess." The Treaty of Augsburg established a geographical equilibrium and more or less peaceful coexistence between the German Catholics of the west and south and the Protestants of the north and east. It fixed the balance of power between the territorial princes, who were much more powerful on German soil than in France or England, and the emperor, whose influence was limited but in principle unchallenged. All this took place through the mediation of the Reichstag: although its recruitment was narrow, this assembly was nevertheless one of the matrices from which today's parliamentarism emerged (though to a lesser extent, to be sure, than in Britain's House of Commons). This is not the place for subtle distinctions: however one sees the matter, the imperial star shone more brightly in 1543 than it had for a generation, and it would continue to shine for the next ten years, spanning roughly the middle of the sixteenth century.

To this point in his narrative, Felix (like Thomas) has said little about the great emperor in the first twenty-five years of his reign. Will he be more expansive about the remainder of Charles's imperial tenure, from 1543 until his abdication in 1556? For obvious reasons, the Platters have even less to tell us about the emperor's great enemy, the Turks, who were now close to the height of their power and whose sailors, allied with the French, were harassing the Mediterranean coast from Catalonia to Nice. The only sign of them thus far in Felix's text is the mention of his neighbor's having painted the head of a Moor on the wall of his house. Felix was also completely in the dark concerning another part of the Hapsburg domain (later to be known as Austria-Hungary), which in 1543 was also under attack by the ubiquitous Turks. Neither Thomas nor Felix knew anything about what was happening in Russia, which for the time being, until Ivan the Terrible regained sovereignty after his coronation in 1547, was subject to the anarchic rule of the boyars. The two Platters knew even less about China, about whose internal politics few Westerners had any inkling. Yet dramatic events were taking place there: in November 1542, several palace women attempted (unsuccessfully) to strangle Emperor Chia Ching, a startling crime that left its victim traumatized. In the following year, 1543, Mongolian cavalrymen launched raids into Shansi, with detrimental effects on trade and on an economy already suffering in the northern provinces from the effects of drought and famine.

Despite such setbacks, conditions in the Celestial Empire, as in Europe, were conducive to increases in agricultural output, textile production, and other craft and manufacturing activities.[18] Whether the Platters were aware of it or not, they were in indirect communication with the southern and eastern coasts of Asia via Portuguese vessels that had been transporting cargoes of oriental spices to Europe for decades. Thomas and Felix knew little about these expeditions, but thanks to their many friends among Basel grocers they were familiar with the taste of pepper. Over the past half-century ships from Lisbon had established a chain of ports and military and commercial bases along the coasts of India (Diu, Goa), Ceylon, Burma, and Indonesia, with Japan at the end of the line. In 1542, even as Felix was beginning to open his eyes to the wider world, a certain Francis Xavier was beginning missionary work in Goa, which had been in Portuguese hands since 1510. Meanwhile, a shipwreck led to the first Portuguese contact with southern Japan, and Portuguese businessmen then pursued this opening systematically from 1542 on. They introduced the Japanese to European goods and firearms and later to Catholic doctrine, which the same Francis Xavier preached in Japan after 1549. Across the Pacific, the Spanish had by now conquered Mexico and Peru and were pressing inland along the great rivers of North and South America, the Amazon and the Mississippi. Moving northward along the coast of California, they reached the places known today as San Diego and San Francisco and pushed as far north as Oregon.

The Spanish colonizers also explored Florida, the Mayan lands, Bogota, and Chile. On the microbial level the world was unified: smallpox, accompanied by other pandemics, wreaked havoc on Mexican plateaus. The Amerindians, who received no quarter from either microbes or conquerors, found a defender in Bartolomé de Las Casas, who, after denouncing the "destruction of the Indies" in 1540, was named bishop of Chiapas in 1544. In the meantime, and closer to home, in Poland (which Thomas had already visited), Copernicus published *De revolutionibus orbium coelestium,* which dethroned the Earth, and man along with it, from their position at the center of the universe.

* * *

Felix's reminiscences naturally fail to mention any of the major ideological and political "discontinuities" that emerged in 1543–44. If he was aware of the non-European world at all, it was chiefly through the "colonial" or tropical taste of sugar, which figures in an episode involving the boy's teacher, Scalerus (Johannes von Schallen [F 71]). Scalerus was essentially Felix's tutor. In addition, from 1538 to 1551 he was associated with the school of Thomas Platter, first as a boarding student and later as an assistant teacher. The episode I am about to recount probably occurred well after 1543: at the time in question, Felix owned books and had his own pocket money. Like most children, he also liked fruit. He was particularly fond of exotic fruits, such as Corinthian grapes and figs, which his father's prosperity placed within his reach, to say nothing of juniper and other preserves that his mother made. Preserves were in any case one of the great passions of the sixteenth century.[19] It only stands to reason that little Felix was also fond of sugar and sweets. Since the sugar plantations of the New World (the Caribbean and Brazil) were barely established, most cane was still grown on the Canary Islands, Madeira, or Cape Verde.

Such geographic details were of little interest to Felix, who nevertheless spent every penny he had on sweets. He became so dependent on the sugary drug,[20] in fact, that he fell victim to the blackmail scheme of a classmate, Amandus Langbaum, the son of a Basel bureaucrat (an official in the grain office), who went on to study medicine (F 74). Langbaum threatened to reveal the extravagance of Felix's craving for sugar to his father unless Felix turned over certain printed books from his personal collection. Scalerus settled the matter by persuading Felix to confess his peccadilloes to his father. The assistant teacher thus kept peace in the household.

Once, after consuming an overdose of sugar, Felix fell deathly ill in the bed he shared at night with his father. Thomas, who had no idea what was happening, became alarmed. Sometimes Felix ate candied fruits and bonbons colored with lead oxide, copper sulfate, and other chemicals, which probably killed other children with less robust constitutions.

* * *

Writing later of his time in Montpellier, Felix frequently speaks of drunken German students who passed out, snored, pissed in their pants, and sprawled over kegs whose contents they imbibed straight from the tap. Felix, for his part, preferred sugar to alcohol. As a young man, he got drunk once or twice. His head spinning, he collapsed onto his bed and "puked his guts out." But such incidents were rare. In Languedoc Felix did not even count a wine flagon among his personal possessions (F 75). When he drank water tinged with wine (*drüncklin*), he sipped directly from a pitcher that his mother had given him.

* * *

Sugar, wine, girls. One winter, Felix decided to build a snowman or snow fort in his father's yard. The two daughters of Thomas's friend Hans Rust, girls who bore the fine biblical names Sarah and Rebecca, made fun of his work from a turreted tower behind the house. Annoyed, Felix tried to run up the stairs to where they were but slipped on an icy step. Two of his teeth tore through his lip, resulting in a permanent scar. Incidentally, the father of the girls, and of many other children besides, was a poet, speculator in church property, and alchemist who made silver out of mercury (F 92). Another time, when he was fifteen, Felix injured himself in the thigh with a sharp instrument while visiting Rötteln in the Black Forest, where he had taken refuge from a plague epidemic in 1551 (F 75–76).

* * *

Three years earlier, Felix may have had a crush on his cousin Margret Madlen Erbsin, a pretty girl from Strasbourg who was one of Thomas's boarders. This Madlenlin was the niece of Margret Erbsin, a widow, who, through another niece, introduced Basel to the beautiful yellow Strasbourg dresses that were a Lutheran symbol of sorts. Thomas and the widow Erbsin had secretly arranged a marriage between the two children, who soon suspected that something was up.

Felix's friends, who somehow found out about this premature romance, gave him a hard time about it. He was fond of the girl and liked to wheel her about in a cart. After returning home to Strasbourg, however, she died of the plague. Another wife would have to be found, and as it happens her name also turned out to be Madlen.

"Engaged" or not, Felix soon discovered a fondness for the caresses of beautiful women. While still very young, he allowed himself to be fondled by an attractive maid from Solothurn who worked for a time as a servant in his father's household. But he rejected the advances of his mother's lame elder sister, for whom Anna Dietschi-Platter had no use. The woman later disappeared without a trace, to no one's great regret. Family ties in these old Swiss clans were not always as important as some historians claim. In any case, the old hag, whom Anna always greeted with the words "Come in, by the devil,"[21] had predicted a brilliant future for the boy: "Felix, you will be an important person." Both father and son thus enjoyed rosy forecasts for their futures.

*   *   *

Optimism was vital for instilling confidence, but children were still treated harshly: punishment, maternal as well as paternal, was an integral part of childrearing. Felix mentions an extreme case: the printer Henri Aliot, who came from a family of Welch Anabaptists from Moûtiers, France, beat his young son, who then ran to the attic and hanged himself (F 79). Originally Felix concealed the name Aliot (suicide was dishonorable), but he later wrote it in the margin of his *Tagebuch*.

Felix's scolding by his mother had less dire consequences. One fall day, Thomas gave his son a quarter of a gulden to buy a dagger he had been eyeing for some time. Impatient, the boy hastened to the market and wound up buying all sorts of things in addition to the knife: dolls, toys, what have you. When he ran into his mother on his way home, she took him to task right then and there, after which she returned to the market and let the merchants who had taken advantage of her son have a piece of her mind before demanding her money back. Back home, the boarders, as usual playing the role of a Greek chorus, made fun of the boy. Thomas and his cousin (Aunt Margret) found the story quite amusing and managed to cool everyone's tempers (F 78). On another occasion, which must have been before Felix's eighth birthday because he was wearing a red tunic at the time, his mother slapped him for losing a small coin she had given him. He had tucked the money into his tunic and it had somehow disappeared. "You should have been paying more attention" was the philosphical advice he received from Chrischona Jeckelmann (the surgeon's wife), who did not yet know that she would become his mother-in-law *in partibus.*[22] In any case it is worth noting that Anna's outbursts against both her husband and her son chiefly concerned issues of money. The Platter household was heavily in debt.

* * *

His father's anger was a more serious matter, and Felix took it more deeply to heart even when the occasion was trivial. We are reminded of Henri IV whipping the future Louis XIII, or ordering him to be whipped, "for his own good."[23] Felix was punished by his father on at least three occasions. The first time was because he had thrown rocks onto the roof of the carpenter Philip, whose shop was located next to the Gymnasium, resulting in several broken tiles. Another time he was beaten for using chalk to deface the partition between two classrooms in his father's school. In both cases the malefactor was turned in by a classmate, the snitch Langbaum, whom we encountered earlier in the role of blackmailer (F 80). In punishing these schoolboy pranks, Thomas was acting as both father and schoolmaster. Mama administered slaps at home; papa administered whippings at school. But the worst was yet to come. The date of the third episode is difficult to pin down: Felix, advanced for his age, was already in his last year at his father's school. He may have been twelve at the time, in which case the incident would have occurred in 1548. In the middle of a Greek class, Thomas, standing at the podium, became incensed that his son knew nothing about the *alpha purum,* that is, the fact that in the Attic dialect one said *chora* instead of *chore* as in Ionian Greek. Such subtleties were beyond the boy, and Thomas felt called upon to beat the lesson into him. Although he aimed to hit Felix's back, his switch caught the boy's face, almost taking out an eye. Felix was left with a puffy, swollen face, which caused his mother to become incensed in turn at her husband's brutal conduct.

Thomas, overcome with remorse, never beat his son again. Until then he had not hesitated to whip or kick the child. Chastened by the event, however, Felix's father now gave in to his kindly natural bent. Was it common for fathers to put away the whip when a son reached the age of twelve or thirteen? In any case, the headmaster of the Burgschule always treated Felix well when he was sick: the boy was his only son, after all. And after Felix went off to medical school in Montpellier, his father's letters revealed numerous signs of paternal affection (F 81).

Before that, his father had expressed his affection by buying the boy nice clothes. If children of relatively modest background often dress better today than do children of more prosperous parents, the same was true in the sixteenth century. Thomas never forgot the rags he had worn as a child and how they had stuck to his mangy skin. He therefore commissioned the tailor Wolf Eblinger, or Master Wolf, to make a tunic for Felix in the medieval style, half in one color, half in another (F 81). When the boy was a little older, Thomas had the same tailor make him two pairs of breeches, one white, the other yellow. The boy paced back and forth in the new marketplace, impatient for the tailor to arrive for his scheduled fitting. This scene had to have taken place before March 1550, by which time Eblinger was already dead. The new clothes evidently left an impression on young Felix, who in later life, whether studying in Montpellier or traveling in the Valais, always liked to dress well. Indeed, he was so much the elegant dresser that he was unpleasant if not downright hostile to his distant highland cousins, who were hardly in a position to vie with him in matters of luxurious attire.

A good father loved well and punished well; he dressed his children appropriately; and he did what he could to provide them with a sound religious education. Among the various paragraphs in Felix's memoirs that begin with the words *mein vater,* symbolizing Felix's strong family ties, those that deal with his father's role as a preacher could not be more eloquent. In a time before Sunday services were customary in Protestant churches, Thomas, the erstwhile itinerant beggar, read the Bible at home and preached a sermon to his wife and children (F 79). This practice was common to Lutherans and Zwinglians and soon to Calvinists as well. Huguenot farmers were also great Bible readers.[24] Thomas's sermons hinged on three main themes. First, the hardening of Pharaoh's heart: the Egyptian ruler refused to allow the Jews to leave Egypt, and Jehovah was obliged to visit the valley of the Nile with no fewer than ten plagues before the sovereign of the pyramids could be persuaded, temporarily, to relent. The second theme was that of grace, or the absence of grace: for it was God himself who had hardened the heart of a Pharaoh who was thus excluded from the company of the elect. One is reminded of Racine's hymn:

> Divin Sauveur, jette sur nous les yeux!
> Répands sur nous le feu de Ta grâce puissante.

> (Divine Savior, cast your eyes on us! Visit us with the fire of
>   Thy powerful grace.)

The third and final theme of the Platter sermons was really a set of themes, a method of biblical interpretation based on types and antitypes: the oppression of the Israelites, for instance, was the ancient type, or prefiguration, of the persecution of the Protestants in the Netherlands in the early sixteenth century.[25] Felix indignantly notes that a number of girls were sent to the stake there on orders of Charles V (F 79). Such thoughts tell us a great deal about the spiritual evolution of the Platter family. Thomas, as we saw earlier, had been an iconoclast in his youth: he once burned a statue of Saint John, one act in the devastating wave of iconoclasm that engulfed parts of Switzerland and Germany and put an end to the great religious sculpture of the late fifteenth century.[26] Later, Thomas moderated these radical views, but he remained as pious as he had been, first in his clerical and Catholic childhood and subsequently in his Zwinglian Protestant youth. Felix, looking back on his long life, has vivid memories of his father's preaching. In retrospect, however, he sees himself as having been much more devout when he dressed in yellow trousers in the 1540s than he was later as a student in Montpellier or as a successful doctor caught up in a busy career. As a medical student in Languedoc, Felix seems to have been largely unmoved by the persecution of the "Lutherans" of Montpellier, or at any rate much less moved than he had been as a child by the story of the little girls consigned to the flames in the Netherlands—a story spread far and wide by Protestant propaganda at the time. Yet Felix would remain a Protestant.

* * *

A lively, imaginative boy fond of amusements in which his family allowed him to indulge in the evening, Felix took advantage of the whole range of activities that urban culture made available to children of the middle class. When his father had been a poor country lad, he had played with hobby horses and pretended to irrigate miniature fields; a little later he had moved on to simple games involving red tiles and flocks of geese. Felix, a city boy from a prosperous family, had heard of the sea; he actually saw it for the first time at Palavas during the time he was studying medicine at Montpellier. He was already dreaming of ocean voyages long before that, however, and sailing wooden boats in the family well. His chief passion was the theater, and there was ample opportunity to indulge it in Basel. In this respect, Montpellier, though a large city, lagged behind. Felix was not impressed by the theater when he was there in 1555: executions of criminals were more entertaining. It was not until later in the century that his younger brother Thomas was able to attend decent productions of plays in the capital of Languedoc. Felix was already enjoying plays at home as early as 1546, however, and in Basel admission was free: was the Swiss city particularly advanced, or was the Languedoc metropolis particularly retarded?

The first precise date that Felix gives for a theatrical production in

Basel was May 23, 1546: he was nine and a half at the time. From his tailor's house he watched a performance of "Chaste Susanna" at the fish market (F 83). This biblical play features the misadventures of a pretty woman surprised in her bath by two randy old men ("elders" of the community). When they falsely accuse her of adultery with a young man, she is saved by the skillful arguments of a child, who grows up to be the prophet Daniel. The themes of the play, with its allusion to the Old Testament prophet, reflect some of the favorite themes of the Swiss Reformation: chastity, prophecy, reverence for the Bible, and so on. The play, now forgotten, was the work of one Sixtus Birk, or Sixtus Betulejus in Latin. A Basel schoolmaster and native of Swabia, Birk published the play (well before it was performed) in two successive editions, one of them in Latin, in the 1530s. The performance that Felix witnessed in 1546 was the work of a group of young actors. The director was a student in his twenties, Ulrich Koch, also known as Coccius and Essig, a native of Freiburg, who went on to a successful career as a teacher (F 83). He became a professor first of Greek, then of dialectics, and finally of theology (his talents as an impresario took him from the theater to the lectern). By his fortieth birthday he had also become a minister. For the role of Susanna, Koch chose his fiancée, Margret Merian, who was the same age as he and the thirteenth child of a sailor from Basel. According to the customs of the Renaissance, Margret should have played the role in the nude, but the Reformation did not tolerate such licentiousness. Ulrich therefore had his actress appear in a red costume in a zinc tub filled with water from the fish market fountain: since the performance took place in May, the weather was not so cold as to make this staging unbearable. The role of Daniel was played by a young boy (*bieblin*) not much older than Felix: Ludwig Ringler, aged eleven. He later became a glass-painter and sheriff of Lugano. The players were thus drawn from Basel's elite, or at any rate its middle class.

*   *   *

Two weeks later, on June 6, 1546, another play captivated Felix: "The Conversion of Saint Paul" was performed at the grain market on a bright, sunny day. The city spared no effort, erecting wooden barriers around the space set aside for the players. The play is the story of Paul on the "road to Damascus," where Christ appears in a radiant vision to the young man of twenty-five, who is instantly converted from persecutor to apostle. The Alsatian Valentin Boltz, who had been a pastor in Württemberg and Basel, wrote and directed the work. Paul was played by Bonaventura von Brunn, aged twenty-six, a merchant who later became mayor of Basel. The glass-painter Balthasar Han, a militant corporatist not quite forty years old, played Hergoth, a character embodying, as Felix recounts it, both the Father and the Son of the Trinity. Finally, Captain Hans Rudolf Fry (or Frey), a robust man in his forties and a prominent member of the local elite, commanded a hundred burghers in colorful uniforms who, along with their standard-bearers, formed the saint's escort. Hergoth sat ensconced in "heaven," a round platform erected above the stage; thunder was simulated with stone-filled barrels. A flaming rocket launched from this firmament represented the apparition of the Savior. Unfortunately, the missile set fire to Paul's trousers, but the saint nevertheless managed to fall from his horse in panic at the miraculous sight. (One wonders if the mishap was in fact written into the script.) In any case, Felix took in every bit of the action from his perch at the home of his friend Hans Irmy, the eight-year-old son of a cloth merchant, who later went into the cloth business himself (F 82). Although a sudden downpour marred the end of the spectacle, good weather returned the next day, and the actors were treated to a joyous parade through the city. The occasion thus combined piety (Paul, the theologian of grace and faith, was one of the "patron saints" of the Reformation), urban military display, and pure burlesque typical of the late medieval and Renaissance theater.

"The Resurrection of Christ," performed at the *gymnasium* of the university, offered a similar mix of piety and clownishness (F 81). This play may have been written in Latin by Georgius von Langenfeldt, also known as Macropedius, a playwright and humanist born in the Netherlands in 1475. "The Resurrection" was one of a cycle of tragedies frequently performed in secondary schools in Switzerland and elsewhere. (Later, in the seventeenth and eighteenth centuries, the Jesuits would develop a Catholic version of the genre.) Young Heinrich Ryhiner, the twenty-year-old son of a municipal court clerk, played the Virgin Mary (it was not uncommon at the time for males to play female roles). Born in 1527, Ryhiner became a doctor after studying in Basel, Paris, Montpellier, and Avignon. In the end he converted to Catholicism and moved to Auvergne, where he was killed in 1584 while serving in the French army. For Felix, Ryhiner's indebtedness and papist marriage made him a model to avoid rather than imitate (F 128). Thomas's boarders also participated in the production, performing diabolical pranks and dances that may or may not have been part of the script: demons were an important part of these "mystery plays." Among the infernal pranksters was Jacob Truchsess von Rheinfelden, another childhood friend of Felix's, who, after a bibulous interlude as a courtier of the Comte de Montbéliard, was cured of alcoholism by his old friend, who by this time was a doctor well on his way to making his mark (F 93, 291).

* * *

"The Conversion of Saint Paul" was a favorite among mystery plays, for dramatic conversions were after all a part of contemporary history: the conversion of Basel in 1529 was in a sense a colorful "remake" of the conversion of Paul. Hence the old chestnut was periodically revived. Felix's friends put on an amateur performance at the home of the Langbaums, whose son Amandus the tattle-tale was Felix's friend and sometime enemy. Also participating were Lucas Just, aged twelve, who later served as a pastor in a number of parishes, including some in Basel, and Simon Colross, the valiant son of a poet and teacher, who died of the plague in 1552 at the age of sixteen or seventeen. He passed away in the home of yet another teacher and writer, Konrad Wolfhardt (Lycosthenes). Clearly, teachers and their children formed a distinctive social group, united in death as well as life. The Langbaum home, which Felix's youthful troupe used as a theater, would continue to play an important spiritual and cultural role in young Platter's life. In 1597 it became the home of Jacques Covet-Courtois, the deacon of the French Huguenot community in Basel.[27] (Both of Thomas Platter's sons were drawn to the French language.)

The young actors also attempted to stage another play at the Langbaums', but without much success: "The Ten Ages of Man" drew on a familiar theme of European culture (reflected in places as diverse as the friezes of the palace of Versailles, the popular images that appeared in the nineteenth century on mass-produced cards from Epinal, and the painting of the American Thomas Cole). All in all, however, "The Conversion of Saint Paul" seems to have been the favorite play of Basel audiences, to judge by the fifteen or so theatrical events that Felix mentions in his memoirs. The official staging of the play in June 1546, with its hundreds of volunteer extras,[28] apparently made quite an impression on the city's youth. Felix and his friend Roll, another of Thomas's boarders, decided to stage the play themselves in the courtyard of Zum Gejägd. Young Platter, tapped for the role of Hergoth, climbed up to the chicken roost with a log he intended to use as a thunderbolt (there seems to have been some confusion between Jehovah and Jupiter). Meanwhile, Roll, playing Paul on the road to Damascus, straddled a hoe representing the saint's horse. As the apostle passed beneath Felix's roost, Felix let go of the log, which hit Roll in the eye, drawing blood. The victim protested: "I'm a poor boy abandoned by my family, or you would never treat me so badly. You'll pay for this some day." Or words to that effect.

In fact, Roll's situation was more complex than his lament suggested. As a boarding student in Basel, he was indeed far from home, but he came from a noble (if impecunious) family. His full name was Gavin de Beaufort, Baron de Rolles, and his home on the shores of Lake Leman lay in French-speaking territory. His father, Count Amédée de Beaufort, was a war veteran who did his talking with gunpowder (F 85). Over the years, and notwithstanding young Gavin's complaints at the time of the incident with the log, a genuine affection developed between the boy known as "Roll" and the Platters. He was in fact the only boarder that Thomas kept with him when plague struck in 1551. For safety's sake all the other students were sent home, but Roll stayed on because he had no one to take care of him (*vil sich seinen nieman annam* [F 115]). Thomas even considered "adopting" Roll, and it would have been quite something if the scion of a noble family had become the "son" of a former beggar. Despite his family's neglect, Roll went on to a respectable career. Noble though he was, he became a burgher of Basel (there was no contradiction between the two conditions: the eminently proud Duke de Saint-Simon did not shrink from identifying himself at times as a *bourgeois de Paris*). In 1573 Roll married the daughter of a law professor, Gertrud Brand of Basel. It was not uncommon for the daughters of professionals to marry "above their station," taking husbands in the military nobility (the technical term for this is *hypergamy*).[29] The baron from Basel and Leman never renounced either his noble or his bourgeois status: he served as a French-Swiss nobleman on the Savoy state council while continuing to own a large house in Basel, of which he remained a citizen. Through him, the relatively low-born (though privileged) Felix made early contact with the nobility of Switzerland and Savoy.

Apart from "The Conversion of Saint Paul" (mentioned three times) and "The Resurrection" (mentioned twice), several other biblical passages figure more than once in Felix's memories of early theatrical experiences. One was the story of Zacchaeus. In Luke 19, Zacchaeus, said to be "little of stature," is the chief of the "publicans" and the man in charge of collecting taxes. His contact with money taints him.[30] Being short, Zacchaeus climbs a sycamore tree to get a better glimpse of the son of God, and Jesus, looking up, sees him and tells him to come down (Luke 19:5). Moved by the divine yet familiar way in which Jesus speaks to him, Zacchaeus promises to give half his belongings to the poor: if the Heavenly Father can convert a rich man in this way, he can do anything. The burghers of Basel—men who, like Zacchaeus, were accustomed to handling large sums of money—were not loath to see themselves represented on stage by one of their most illustrious forebears, a man who had distinguished himself in the cause of righteousness. "Zacchaeus" was performed in what had been an Augustinian monastery before the Reformation came to Basel, at which time it became either a school or part of the university (F 84). Included in the cast were the daughters of "Lepusculus" (or "little hare"), also known as Sebastian Häsli, who at the time was in his forties. He later became a professor of Greek and then a full-time Protestant ecclesiastic—yet another instance of a man who combined teaching with the ministry. Lepusculus, the Hellenist pastor, went to his eternal rest in a tomb shared with Felix's mother.

The author of "Zacchaeus," who also performed in the play, was Heinrich Pantaleon, a young man, not yet twenty-five, who wore a goatee and whose humorous expression was not without a malicious edge. A man of remarkable intellect, Pantaleon pursued his studies at the universities of Basel, Heidelberg, and Valence, the last a mediocre institution from which he received a doctorate in medicine in record time. At various times a professor of Latin, rhetoric, and physics as well as an administrator in his spare moments, he eventually became count palatine and poet laureate of the Holy Roman Empire. His "Zacchaeus," published by Cratander in Basel in 1546, was the first of a long series of his works and translations devoted to the Church and its martyrs, the knights of Rhodes, the Russians, the Franks, the Germanic heroes, and William of Tyre.

The theatrical life of the time was intense, and though many of the plays involved are forgotten today, they elicited the enthusiasm of their original audiences. Among other plays performed at the former Augustinian monastery was one about Esther, the Jewish beauty who outwits Haman, the vizier of Ahasuerus (Xerxes or Artaxerxes), and saves the Jews from slaughter. In the end, according to *midrash* (Hebrew commentary on the Bible), she even manages to cause the death of 75,000 of her enemies, would-be accomplices in the slaughter that is happily averted— at a heavy price. The episode is a religious apologia, an explanation of a miracle—yet another stroke of grace. Although the historical basis of the story turns out to be slight or nonexistent, it long served in Jewish tradition to bolster the confidence of the Jewish people in the face of persecution. The story was also exploited by the heirs to Jewish tradition: both Catholic and Protestant writers and artists identified Esther with the justice of their cause and Haman with the wickedness of the other side— Lutherans or papists. The story of Esther, well known to people of Felix's and subsequent generations, thus became a theme common to both Protestant literature (as in sixteenth-century Basel) and Catholic literature (in the work, for instance, of Lope de Vega and of Racine, who wrote to justify the Revocation of the Edict of Nantes). It also figured in a great deal of European painting: in the work of Rembrandt on the Protestant side and of Veronese, Tintoretto, Rubens, Poussin, and Lorrain in the Catholic camp.

The text used in the Basel performance was probably "Hamanus" by Thomas Naogeorgius, whose German name was Kirchmeyer or Kirchmair. This play was expressly described as a "new tragedy" based on the Bible, a tragedy that attacked the calumny and tyranny of the powerful in the hope of inspiring fear of God. It was first published in Leipzig in 1543 and reprinted in Basel in 1547 by Thomas Platter's friend Oporinus. Naogeorgius, who backed Luther and sometimes outflanked him "on the left," portrayed Mordecai in no uncertain terms as a good Protestant and Haman as a thoroughly wicked Catholic. In Basel the role of Haman was played by Cellarius (Isaac Keller), who as it happens went on to live a less than spotless life (F 169). The son of a cloth merchant, he became, at the age of eight, the stepson of Felix's godfather Simon Grynaeus. This symbolic genealogy created a spiritual kinship between the two boys, despite the fact that Isaac was six years older than Felix. Cellarius had lived in Basel for a time before continuing his studies in Strasbourg. It was while living in Basel in 1546 or 1547, at some time between his sixteenth and eighteenth birthdays, that he played Haman. Fate would later take him to England, Montpellier, Toulouse, and Valence, where he received his doctorate in medicine. Shortly thereafter, at the age of twenty-three, he was named to a chair in medicine at the University of Basel. A quarter of a century later he was implicated in a financial scandal and obliged to leave the city. He nevertheless remained a doctor and ended his career as a humble physician in Alsace.

"Hamanus," though full of Lutheran and indeed ultra-Lutheran propaganda, also had plenty of the usual tragicomic mishaps. Ludwig Hummel, a future pastor who was playing the role of executioner, was supposed to "hang" both Haman and his son, but he somehow slipped and left the actor who was playing the son hanging for real; he quickly cut the rope, however, and saved the boy, Gamaliel Gyrenfalck, a pastor's son who escaped with nothing worse than a rope burn on his neck.

Among the plays performed in Basel during Felix's childhood were also two classical Latin comedies, "Aulularia" by Plautus (the ancestor of Molière's "L'Avare") and "Phormio" by Terence (a foreshadowing of the "Fourberies de Scapin"). The themes of these plays, well known today because of their use by Molière, were thus already familiar to the urban audiences of the Renaissance.

Of the fourteen performances from the 1540s mentioned in Felix's *Tag-*

ebuch, eight were based on Bible stories, six from the Old Testament and two from the New. Six others had nonreligious themes, three based on Latin plays (including "Hypocrisin," in which Felix and the future humanist Theodor Zwinger performed) and two on "folklore": "The Ten Ages of Man" and a comedy written by Thomas Platter himself, entitled "The Innkeeper with the Dried Branch," which has not survived—a loss that we need not regret unduly. Thus 85 percent of the plays can be classed under the rubrics "humanism" or "Reformation." The directors and actors, many of them quite young, either belonged to or were descended from members of the interlocking worlds of Protestant pastors, bureaucrats, professors, historians, publishers, scholars, and printers of the city of Basel. In short, this was the local intelligentsia, the world of intellectuals and semi-intellectuals. Militant as well as learned, the theater was a spectacle that the elite staged for itself as well as for the common people. This was in no sense an authentically and totally "popular" theater, despite later stereotypes to that effect.

*   *   *

June 1546 was a high point of the theatrical season. Felix, born in October 1536, was nine years and eight months old at the time and already an occasional performer. In October 1552, when he left for Montpellier, Felix was just sixteen. The six years (or, more precisely, seventy-five months) that elapsed between the two dates, between childhood and adolescence, were shaped by family, school, and friends. They were marked by the seasons, current events, and brief journeys, as well as by history on a broad scale (viewed from afar) and, of course, by the plague and the need to choose a vocation. Felix's father is present on virtually every page of his autobiography. His mother seldom makes an appearance, but when she does her presence is strongly felt. Yet Frau Platter was not in the best of health. She was no longer a young woman. When Felix was ten, she was already in her fifties. Frequently bedridden, Anna appears to have suffered from pleurisy, which manifested itself in an irritating dry cough. Right up to the time of her death in 1572 at the age of seventy-eight, she was bothered by recurrent respiratory problems: frequent bronchopulmonary infections and asthma attacks exacerbated by the dampness of unheated rooms (only a few rooms were heated with ceramic stoves).

    She also suffered, as early as 1549, from another ailment, possibly related to her pleurisy: *roten schaden,* or hemorrhagic tenesmus (a painful contraction of the anus or bladder) . This affliction made an impression on Felix, aged twelve or thirteen at the time, who remembered that it came in the same year as the fire that destroyed the Beckhenhaus, killing the baker Claus Peyger and his wife Ursula despite the organization of a heroic bucket brigade. Corpulent Claus became trapped in a window of the burning building and was unable to escape, and Ursula died when the rope that she, together with her son or a baker's boy, was attempting to climb down broke from the excess weight.[31] Thus the blaze claimed three lives: there was danger living in close proximity to a working bread-oven (F 108).

Despite her poor physical condition, Felix's mother was a strong woman (as Thomas's mother had been). Anna Dietschi did not shrink from telling off the Strasbourg-born sculptor Hans Tobell (or Tobel), who one day took after Felix with an ax and chased him right into the kitchen of Zum Gejägd (F 105). Did he intend to carve the boy up? Tobell was not just any artist: in 1547 he did the statue of an armed man that embellished the fountain in Basel's market square. After being taken to task by the professor's wife, he confined himself to amusements of a less violent sort. One day he perusaded Felix and his friends that an execution was about to take place. The boys ran as fast as their legs could carry them to the appointed place, but it turned out that the sculptor had made the whole thing up. In 1558, however, when Tobell fell ill, he begged forgiveness of young Dr. Felix Platter, who at twenty-two had just completed his medical education; Felix assisted the dying man in his final moments.

Anna Dietschi demonstrated her usual energy in another dispute, one in which Felix became embroiled with a man who sold gingerbread men that Felix claimed had broken several of his teeth and caused his face to swell. Anna found the man, called him a scoundrel, and refused to pay for what Felix had broken in the fight. Anna's ill temper occasionally sparked quarrels at home, especially during the spring and summer of 1552 (F 124). Felix, by then close to sixteen, was better equipped to grasp his family's material and moral situation. Although Thomas owned extensive property in land and buildings, he still had large debts, and these led to quarrels between husband and wife, which Felix, who loved and wanted to remain on good terms with both, found painful. It was Anna, of course, who criticized her husband for making foolhardy investments that had led the family repeatedly into debt. But relations between Felix's parents never became as bitter as the situation in the household of the late knight von Rufach, whose tombstone Felix was able to admire when he went to Alsace with his father in 1551 to buy a new donkey. For the stone covering his grave, the knight had commissioned a bas-relief depicting himself armed from head to toe and lying on his stomach with his face pressed to the ground and his (armored) back facing the starry vault above. This unusual posture was chosen because his wife had threatened to piss on his face if the artist depicted him in the usual supine posture. *Se non è vero, è ben trovato.*

*   *   *

Ursula, Felix's sister, was the young woman of the house and the only surviving daughter. Her two elder sisters, Margret I and Margret II, born in 1530 and 1533, had died of the plague in 1531 and 1539 respectively (F 50). Born in 1534, Ursula was pampered by her father and mother as well as her little brother Felix, who was two years younger. In 1546, when she was twelve, Ursula had gone to Strasbourg to stay with Margret Erbsin, the widow of Simon Lithonius Steiner, Thomas Platter's cousin from the Valais who became the *famulus* (assistant) of the Strasbourg reformer Martin Bucer and later a professor in Alsace. In the capital of that province, Ursula found time to write charming letters to her family back in Basel, but she grew bored after her aunt remarried, choosing the Alsatian pastor Lorenz Offner, with whom she would have four daughters and a son. Thomas's only choice was to bring his daughter back home. She and her little brother had plenty to talk about: together they worried about their parents' quarrels over their debts. Concerned, Anna occasionally spoke briefly to the children about what was going on. The children's dismay about the small inheritance they were likely to receive only tightened the bonds between them.

In 1549 or 1550, Ursula, by now a young woman, attended at the bedside of her supposedly dying mother. (In fact, Frau Platter recovered "by the grace of God," *durch gottes gnodt*—again, the idea, typically Protestant, of divine grace [F 109]). Felix also stayed at his mother's bedside. The two children commiserated about their mother's affliction but above all about their fear that a stepmother would take Anna's place and surely, they believed, mistreat the children of the first marriage. This was a common refrain whenever a family was threatened with disintegration in the early modern period. Ursula was a cultivated young woman: along with her brother, she took Latin and lute lessons from Thomas's assistant, Johannes von Schallen (F 117). At age fifteen or sixteen she fell for a worthy young peasant by the name of Werlin Bur, who helped out with farm chores on Thomas Platter's country estate in Gundeldingen. He was an earnest, pious, hardworking young fellow, strong, skillful, and the son of a prosperous farmer as well as a member of the Anabaptist sect. Thomas Platter, following the lead of the tolerant Sebastian Castellion (F 89),

hoped to convert "heretics" like the Burs to the official creed of Basel as
set forth by Œcolampadius and Zwingli.

Things took an unforeseen turn when Werlin fell in love with Ursula
too. He asked Thomas for her hand, but Thomas, despite his daughter's
tears, turned him down cold. Did he refuse because of the religious difference (which in fact was relatively slight)? Or did Thomas and Anna
have bigger things in mind for their children? Ursula was the attractive,
cultivated, musical daughter of a man who was no longer poor. She had
numerous suitors despite her lack of a dowry. The Platters were unwilling
to marry their daughter to a mere peasant, even if he came from a prosperous family. In the end, the plague decided the lovers' fate. A local surgeon, Master Wolf, had indeed predicted "great misfortunes." In 1551
Ursula and Werlin succumbed almost simultaneously. Felix later renewed
his acquaintance with Werlin's two sisters, Ann and Ketterin. He was
even invited to Ann's wedding. But the newlywed treated him like a
stranger, as was customary among peasant wives. Felix was disappointed:
hadn't these pretentious farm folk ever heard of the relaxed ways of city
women? If Felix is to be believed, Ann and Ketterin lived to a ripe old age
and grew as wrinkled as withered apples (F 90).

*   *   *

Ursula had a curious influence on her brother during her brief life and
even after her death. Knowing his fetish for cleanliness, for being as
"clean as a cat" (*katzrein*), she one day made herself rings of flesh from
chicken gizzards taken from her mother's kitchen. Then she chased after
Felix and rubbed his face with the rings. The effect on Felix was extraordinary, especially when Ursula, despite her affection for her little brother,
repeated the experiment. In a panic, he ran away and collapsed in a fit of
vomiting. Although Felix was in general a well-balanced individual, the
psychological trauma of this episode was so severe that throughout his
life he could never bear to look at even a painting of a ring, and it made no
difference that the painting was of a ring of gold or silver rather than
chicken gizzard. His aversion became well known, and wherever he went
pranksters were always putting gizzard rings in his food, even in the
princely courts where the eminent physician later practiced medicine.
His reaction was always the same: disgust, flight, nausea. Never having
read Freud, Felix was able to write in all innocence that he was horrified
by anything "round and perforated" (*rundt und gelöchert* [F 101]). Here is
a symptom to be borne in mind as we seek to penetrate the depths of Felix
Platter's mind. Even the bobbins of spinning wheels filled him with hor-

ror, and he would no doubt have been dismayed by the curtain rings our great-grandmothers used.

In light of this story, it will come as no surprise that Ursula, as well educated as she was, spent most of her time working in her mother's kitchen, while Felix devoted his time to nobler, more intellectual tasks, as well as to farm chores (which he disliked) on the Gundeldingen estate.

The account of Ursula's death is one of the most moving parts of Felix's memoirs. In March 1551, the plague, which had been lurking in the city for almost a year, at last struck the Platter household. One of the boarders, Niclaus Sterien, who came from a family of seigneurial officeholders, came down with the disease and took to his bed on a Sunday morning. He died that afternoon. Ursula found him dead when she took food to his room. Her fright was her undoing: people at the time believed that the plague could be transmitted by fear or even by a mere glance. Niclaus was buried the same day in the St. Elsbethen cemetery, where he would soon be joined by many other victims of the disease. Thomas immediately put emergency measures into effect: many of the boarders had gone to Gundeldingen to make whistles out of willow bark, and Thomas sent word that they were not to return to town for Sunday evening services. Some, including Felix, were evacuated to Rötteln, in Baden, which apparently was a plague-free zone. Two months later, in May, Werlin Bur developed plague symptoms, as did Ursula Platter. Ursula, with a bubo on her thigh, lay ill for several days. Despite the contagion she piously kissed her parents, whispering: "Say goodbye to my dear little brother" (*meinen lieben bruderlin*).

Then she died. She was seventeen years old. Her parents buried her at St. Elsbethen, where her elder sister Margret II had been buried thirteen years earlier, in 1539, when she had died in her seventh year. Thomas revealed the news to Felix, still in Rötteln, only gradually. Finally, in July 1551, two months after the event, he wrote his son informing him that his sister was dead. Sixty years letter, Felix still could not read this tender, affectionate letter without crying. History ordinarily takes little notice of such fraternal devotion. An exception is the case of Louis XIII, who revealed his genuine love, tinged with sadness, for his sister when she left France for good to marry the heir to the Spanish throne in 1615: she was "such a good sister," the sovereign observed simply.[32]

*   *   *

Thus Felix's life at this stage was partly serious, partly playful, occasionally tragic. His year consisted of two distinct seasons: a snowy winter, which also included carnival time, and a lengthy summer. During the winter Thomas sometimes permitted snowball fights by the light of the moon. His son took part along with the students, who at this point ranged in age from ten to twelve. Among them were Ambrosius Frobenius, who in keeping with his family tradition became a printer, and Niklaus (or Niclaus) Kalbermatten, a strong lad from a family of seigneurial officeholders. Once, Niklaus was working in a heated room at the top of the spiral staircase when he was accidentally struck by one of Felix's snowballs, packed so hard that it had turned to ice. When there was no snow, the boys used carrots as projectiles (Anna Dietschi, who did not shrink from hard labor, dug carrots from her own garden). These scenes of boys on the loose (*meisterlos*) might have come from a painting by Brueghel.

At carnival time, the snowball fights continued. Occasionally Thomas was hit in the face by an errant snowball. The sight of blood made him angry. During one carnival season Felix made an important journey, to visit the von Andlaus, a noble family living in Neuenburg, some twenty miles north of Basel. Sigmund von Andlau was one of Thomas's boarders and a good friend of Felix's (F 87). He liked to grab Thomas's behind in the privy, and one day after playing this game he was obliged to wash his hands. Felix and Sigmund set out for Neuenburg with Balthasar Hummel, a future pharmacist who came from a modest family and would remain one of Felix's close friends. Balthasar had known Sigmund for a long time, because his father, Peter Hans Hummel, had been the von Andlaus' handyman (F 88). Although the boys were close friends, the social distance between them remained. On the journey Felix and Sigmund were allowed to ride Papa Hummel's horse, while Balthasar walked. His good humor was not diminished, however.

In this (Protestant) "evangelical" milieu, carnival meant among other things that the boys were encouraged to participate in anticlerical pranks by Sigmund's mother, née Eva von Pfirt. They made fun of the red-robed Catholic priest who ate the Eucharist at mass without sharing it with anyone (in fact he was offering communion to his flock, but Felix seems to have overlooked this "detail"; it may be that frequent communion was not the norm in "papist" circles at this time). Another time the trio of friends verbally assaulted a passing priest, thereby failing in their duty to show respect to their elders in general and clerics in particular—a corrosive consequence of religious mixing. Religious differences aside, however, the boys delighted in carnival treats, dances, and the sight of men dressed in women's clothing.[33]

The three von Andlau daughters, one of whom was married and the

mother of a baby, did not hesitate to show themselves to Felix almost naked or in their underwear (*underrock* [F 88]). Still a child, he told them
stories as they knelt before him, fascinated by his talents as a storyteller,
which manifested themselves early. Clearly Felix was a gifted child, who
spoke well and played the lute.

* * *

Felix has less to say about the summer season. He and Thomas's boarders
often went to the Platter farm in the country, where they helped out with
the heavy chores. Felix's classmates frequently blackmailed him by threatening to tell his father about his candy binges and classroom mischief.
Sometimes they beat him. Once they cut the rope of his swing while he
was swinging. Looking back on these childish pranks, Felix had no hard
feelings. In some of his mischief he took after his father: once, while playing near a pond, he killed a goose with a well-aimed stone. Thomas was
obliged to pay the bird's owner. Always a stickler for cleanliness, young
Platter liked to swim in a tributary of the Rhine. One time he was nearly
carried away by the current, but fortunately a strong swimmer was there
to save him.

* * *

In Felix's memories of his tenth to fifteenth years, the news of the day
occupies just as large a place as the routines of daily life, despite the fact
that there were as yet no newspapers or other media. And much of the
news was of a familiar sort, involving sex and violence. Living in Basel at
the time was a seamstress from Zug by the name of Regula (or Regel)
Rüttiman (F 102). Though an Anabaptist, she did not always abide by the
sect's rigid moral code. She lived alone, or at any rate she was separated
from her husband, who had been locked up as a lunatic. She did sewing
and cooking for the Platters and sometimes bathed little Felix. She also
made him shirts decorated with colorful birds and liked to banter with
the boarders. Everyone was fond of her. She fell in love with Paul
Höchstetter, who came from a notable Augsburg family that had turned
to the professions when the family business went bankrupt. This must
have happened sometime between 1544 and 1546, when Paul, approximately twenty-one at the time, was living with Thomas. But nothing
came of Regula's infatuation. When the object of her affections left Basel,
she set her sights on an older man: Franz Jeckelmann, Felix's future
father-in-law, who, well into his forties, had lost his wife in 1549. One
night at supper, while dining at Thomas's table, Regula declared: "I think

I've got a live one. He's a widower." A man, she hinted, likes to have a woman around the house who can sew. But Felix's father, no widower, did not altogether appreciate her manner. A short time later, she left the Platters to work in nobler households, where she apparently made a good deal of money—enough, at any rate, to buy herself a house in Basel, where she had decided to settle. She now had an affair with Conrad Klingenberg, the keeper of the Stork Inn (F 122). Conrad, also known as Küntz or Cunz, had a bad reputation, but no worse than that of his daughter Anne: both had been compromised in various marital and other scandals. From her liaison with Küntz, Regula gave birth to an illegitimate son, Georg Felix. Felix was one of the comely child's godfathers; the other, a tailor, was of course named Georg (F 123). Georg Felix proved to be a gifted lad, and with a good education he became a surgeon who treated Bern mercenaries for gallstones so that they could fight in France's wars of religion. He later returned to Basel, where, with support from Felix, by then an important doctor, he became a citizen. One day he decided to visit his mother, who had left Basel for Säckingen in the wake of persecution not for immorality but for Anabaptism. While there, he became drunk one night and agreed to marry the daughter of a minister in return for a promised dowry of 1,000 gold gulden. The girl was the product of an incestuous relationship between her clergyman father and his sister. Gossip had it that the randy young minister had also been to bed with his daughter. Marrying the girl off to Regula's son was a way of concealing the evidence of this presumed double incest. When Georg discovered the secret, he "died of sorrow." The girl went off with another man. The fornicating pastor, meanwhile, was strongly advised to leave town and not to stop until he reached Constance, quite a distance away. There we lose track of him (F 102, 122–23).

*   *   *

Georg Felix was the product of an extramarital affair. How common were such affairs in this segment of society? What might nowadays be called sexual harassment was tolerated: according to Felix, it was considered normal even in the most respectable households for the master to fondle the breasts of his servants at least once while they were in his employ.[34] Some people even felt that it was an honor for a girl to be treated this way. The fact that Felix underlined the qualification "even in the best households" (*firnemmen hüseren* [F 106]) suggests that in theory the dominant classes were expected to behave in a more ethical and civilized manner than others. When someone of the upper crust exceeded the tolerable limits, he was discredited in the eyes of society. Take the case of Dr. Hans Leuw: a one-time monk who became a Protestant minister and married an ex-nun, Leuw was also a doctor who treated the plague at Solothurn (F 103). Later he enjoyed a brilliant career as an anatomist and became an assistant to the great Vesalius himself in 1546. Ultimately, however, he was forced to leave Basel because of an adulterous relationship that resulted in two illegitimate children (F 105). The scandal was too great to tolerate.

* * *

There were also love affairs among Thomas's colleagues. Take for instance the teacher of lute and Latin whose name we have already encountered several times. Johannes (or Hans) von Schallen, also known as Scalerus, was born in 1525. He was the bastard son of a notary and soldier. Hans began with Thomas as a boarder at the age of thirteen and went on to become his chief assistant. He had a (legitimate) brother, a certain Niklaus, who had been a student in Basel and later became the municipal treasurer of Sion. He and Johannes engaged in bitter brawls, sometimes in the Platter house, during which they exchanged blows, hurled objects at each other, overturned tables, and grappled in the dark. Thomas tried to stop them, while Ursula and Felix howled in fear.

In any case, Johannes von Schallen at some point fell madly in love with a beautiful young woman from Basel, who belonged to the municipal oligarchy. Either she or her mother sat as a model for some of Hans Holbein's Madonnas. Johannes used Felix as a messenger to send notes to this woman, who was married. Once, Felix found her, fresh from her bath, lying naked on a sofa (*gutschen*): Cranach's nudes were not simply evocations of antiquity. The beautiful lady accepted the love note without showing the slightest embarrassment in front of Felix, who at fourteen enjoyed the spectacle. Johannes Scalerus lived with the young woman and even had a child by her, a child that her "good husband" (*gut man*) raised as his own. Later, Johannes moved to Sion, where he became a teacher and eventually mayor. His former lover, desperate after his departure, wrote him ardent letters—very much in the manner of Madame Bovary—in which she spoke of leaving her husband and children to be with him. She even cried on Thomas's shoulder, but Thomas, stern puritan that he was, warned her against such foolish thoughts. In the end she died. Of a broken heart? Felix apparently thought so. Meanwhile, Johannes, on the other side of the Alps, was stricken with guilt and confessed his sins in a letter to his former employer. He, too, died at the age of thirty-six, according to Felix at any rate. According to other sources, he did not depart this vale of tears, spitting blood, until he had reached the age of forty-five and become a church deacon after living with tuberculosis for many years.

Another much more serious affair involving crime as well as sex concerned not Thomas's servants or colleagues but his extended family. This episode demonstrates Felix's memory and powers of observation at their best. Margret Erbsin, a "cousin" of the Platters by marriage and a true friend of the family, had lived in Thomas's house for a time after the death of her husband in 1543. While there, she aroused the passion of Niklaus Petri, a teacher from Lorraine living in Basel, who had divorced his first wife after she became pregnant in an adulterous affair. Niklaus married a second time, but his new wife also died. When Margret discouraged her lonely suitor's advances, he accused Thomas of having turned her against him and actually brandished a sword with murder in mind. Meanwhile, Margret returned to Strasbourg, where in 1546 she married a pastor. (Her first husband had been a professor: once again we encounter the endogamy of the professional classes, that is, their tendency to marry within their own social group.) Not discouraged by his failure, Niklaus now turned his attentions to the eighteen-year-old sister of his late wife. A pretty girl by the name of Maria, she had shown great kindness to the widower's children. When Maria also spurned his advances, Niklaus, after attending morning services at a Protestant church, plunged a dagger into her bosom on January 13, 1546. She collapsed at the bottom of the stairs of the house that she and her killer shared, but not before telling all the world, "He killed me" (*Er hatt mich gemördet*).

Meanwhile, Niklaus got rid of the murder weapon, fled to a nearby house, and leaped into the frozen Rhine through a privy hole. A blue and white flag taken from the enemy a generation earlier in the Battle of Novara (1513) hung nearby. Some fishermen fished the fleeing killer out of the river, wrung him out, dried him off, warmed him up, and helped him to escape to a forest in Alsace north of Basel. But soldiers from the city were in hot pursuit and soon caught the escaped murderer. His quick trial ended in a sentence of death: Niklaus was to be broken on the wheel. He had time to make a will, with Thomas serving as notary, and this proved to be of great solace to the condemned man. A week after his capture, he was put to death. Felix, aged ten, would not have missed this spectacle for the world, any more than he would have missed the theatrical performances that were staged in the city a few months later. The execution was an occasion for the boy to make everyone laugh with some bad puns on *hochgericht* (gibbet) and *gericht* (meal). The torture of Niklaus Petri could not have been more odious. The condemned man was attached to the wheel and stretched with levers until his limbs snapped, causing him to scream, in Latin, "Jesus, son of David (*sic*), have mercy on me!" The final blow, on his chest, caused his tongue to protrude from his mouth. The body was secretly buried at night.

So the criminal Niklaus Petri died as a pious scholar and Latinist, crying out *Jesu filii David miserere mei!* in the midst of his torture (F 96). A common thief of less exalted station proved less relgious and more down-to-earth. When one of a gang of sneak thieves from Rötteln was driven in a cart to the execution site, he kept repeating the same words over and over again all the way to the gallows: "I'm going to hang. The crows will get me." (Had he read François Villon, or was this a commonplace of the time, known to common criminals as well as to poets?)

Petri's long and painful torture seemed harsh, even to contemporaries not noted for shedding tears over the sufferings of criminals. Some said that the Basel authorities had been compelled by the muttering of the "common" people to impose an extremely harsh sentence. Apparently that muttering was the result of an earlier episode, which took place toward the end of 1545. A huge, fat carter from Brabant who was working in Basel had raped and committed other obscene acts upon a seventy-year-old woman, the mother of a country innkeeper. The elderly woman had made the mistake of traveling alone through the Hart Forest en route to the family inn. The carter had pulled her down from her horse before subjecting her to "vile crimes."

All but caught in the act, the Brabançon had been tortured by an executioner from Basel, a strong, conceited fellow who had torn out a piece of his victim's chest with red-hot pincers before hauling him, half-dead, to the chopping block to cut off his head. The man's body had then been impaled on a pike before being placed in its grave. Thomas Platter had insisted on taking his son to see the grave before it was filled in so that the boy might carry the memory of this edifying spectacle with him to the end of his days. But many people thought that the man had been cruelly and unusually punished. And it was whispered among the common people of Basel that Niklaus Petri, who was an intellectual (*gelerter*) judged by other intellectuals (the judges), might well be let off more leniently even though he had committed a worse crime than the carter from Brabant. Indeed, "class justice" does sometimes go easy on certain well-placed academics even when they commit crimes as heinous as murdering their wives. The Basel tribunal was therefore careful to mete out a particularly harsh punishment to Petri in order to prevent public opinion, always potentially dangerous, from getting out of hand. The use of executions as a pedagogical spectacle for the edification of children and the masses would continue, of course, to the nineteenth century and beyond.

*   *   *

Note, by the way, that criminals were often seen as foreigners: Petri, though from Lorraine, was viewed as a Burgundian; another criminal, a vintner by profession, was said to be a "Welch"; and the carter was a Brabançon. Is this tendency to see criminals as foreigners a deeply rooted prejudice or an accurate reflection of a persistent reality?

*   *   *

Children did not suffer when a father was disgraced. Was this a happy byproduct of the nature of Basel society, which did not place much stock in hierarchy or ancestry and whose *Genossenschaft* mentality was rather tolerant and democratic? Niklaus Petri's three sons enjoyed respectable if modest careers despite their father's tragedy. One was a tailor who received help from the generous Myconius. Another, Israel by name, became a painter who worked for Felix before dying of plague along with his wife in 1564 (F 98). It was only after his death that Felix learned of the elder Petri's threats against his father Thomas. People in Basel were capable of respecting the law of silence as long as necessary.

*   *   *

Felix later became a great traveler, but during childhood and early adolescence he journeyed only once to Baden and twice to Alsace. Anna Dietschi took her son to Strasbourg in 1550 or shortly before to visit a "respectable" family—of social status equal to the Platters—of preachers, teachers, organists, and clerks. Then, in 1551, after the plague season (during which Felix had been sent away to Baden) but before winter set in, Thomas and his son went to Rouffach, a town dominated by a huge castle in what is now the Guebviller district of the Haut-Rhin. The purpose of their visit was to purchase an ass, an animal disdained in Basel as oldfashioned or ludicrous for riding but less expensive than a horse for carrying fruit and other produce from Gundeldingen to town. Unfortunately, the younger Platter's memories of Alsace at the height of the Renaissance are slender. Upon returning from Strasbourg he recalled that he had found his father suffering from an accidental knife wound to the arm. And after the second trip, Thomas, who this time accompanied his son, had remarked, "Felix, you're glad to be home, but I'm not, because my daughter is gone." The dead child weighed on his mind. Thomas's words plunged Felix into distress. As hard as Ursula's loss was for Thomas to bear, he appreciated his son's active presence. His erstwhile severity lived on only in Felix's memory.

Before making the journey to Rouffach to buy the ass, during the spring and summer of 1551 (the period during which Ursula died), Thomas sent Felix to Rötteln in Baden where he would be safe from the plague (F 118). Unaware of his sister's death, news of which was kept from him for some time, the adolescent used his time in Baden to practice the lute. He also observed the amorous stratagems of a medical student who was courting the wife of an absent soldier. Along with a friend Felix stole pears and apples from the orchards of the Rötteln castle. This earned him some harsh words from the local sheriff, Ulrich Müllner, who seized the opportunity to rail against the Swiss—not much appreciated by certain Germans, apparently, despite their all being *Teutschen*. Later, this sheriff was dismissed by the nobleman who employed him and emigrated to Basel, where Felix treated him for an illness. A little later, Felix returned to Rötteln to launch his medical career after completing his studies in Montpellier. Ulrich meanwhile married and had a child but later "died and rotted along with his spouse and offspring." Such was Felix's brief obituary for a former patient whom he treated despite his personal dislike for the man.[35]

Felix knew more than just what was happening in his own life. News of the wider world appears in his memoir as early as 1544, when he was just nine years old. He reports, for example, on the expulsion of Swabian peasants from Munich: Protestants, they were forced to flee papist Bavaria for Swiss territory, where they lived hand to mouth. Thomas and Felix became acquainted or, more accurately, reacquainted with one such pair of Lutheran refugees, a husband and wife who had been members of the important soapmakers' guild in Munich. Once rich, they had used what remained of their fortune to buy a small house on "tanners' alley" in Basel in 1544.

The two refugees scraped by on their knowledge of soapmaking. The husband, Hans Schräll, an elderly man, made soap in his house, which also served as his workshop. His wife, "the old lady," whose name was Margaretha or Margret, sold what her husband produced in a tiny shop next to what had been an abbey. With their Bavarian dialect, dress, and belongings, the two passed for eccentrics. Hans got himself in trouble with the authorities for racist outbursts: "The Bavarians and Swabians could cook the Baselers and Confederates and eat them for dinner." Margret, for her part, never could get rid of her Bavarian dialect, to the great

amusement of the Swiss. In all innocence she greeted Swiss children with
words that sounded like "darling whoreson." Once she told the pharmacist who had sold her a laxative for her dog that "my pooch is shitting so
much that he can't work anymore." Thomas recognized this impoverished pair as the generous couple that had saved him from starvation in
Munich years earlier, in the days when he had had to fight dogs for his
dinner and pick food out of cracks between floorboards. Hans, Margaretha, and their erstwhile protégé Thomas fell into one other's arms.
From that day until the day he died, Thomas offered the two émigrés
from southern Germany generous assistance, thus repaying them for the
kindness they had shown him thirty-five years earlier when he had fetched
up on the banks of the Isar.

*   *   *

Rumors of wars outside Switzerland also reached Basel, whose youth
avidly seized on every scrap of information. Veterans fresh from battle in
France and Germany had stories to tell or, if need be, to embellish with
reconstructed memories. Felix, all ears, soaked these up and later poured
them out in the pages of his memoirs. He was struck by the adventures of
one of his neighbors, the cobbler Hans Bart, who owned the house across
the street (F 106). Bart was a stout fellow, always ready to take up arms for
the Protestant cause. At Mühlberg (1547) and Moncontour (1569) he
came close to meeting his Maker. Through his hair-raising tales, Felix
learned about the wars of religion in Germany and France. The flood of
refugees from those wars, together with the work hastily undertaken to
shore up walls around the city of Basel, persuaded eleven-year-old Felix
Platter that his city and country were in grave danger, a conviction that
would only deepen with time. In young Felix's mind it was entirely possible that one day Charles V would arrive with his cavalry to occupy the
city and sleep with his boots on in the bürgermeister's bed.

*   *   *

Felix's fears proved groundless, but the Basel of that time was indeed a
hotbed of anti-imperial plots, which Charles's secret agents sought to
combat with whatever means were at hand, at times with ludicrous or
tragic results. The episode that created the greatest stir along the banks of
the upper Rhine was an attempt to assassinate Colonel Sebastian Schertlin, a charismatic soldier of fortune in his fifties who had amassed a fortune while serving under Charles V in the sack of Rome (1527). At
midcentury, however, his loyalties were dearly purchased by the francophile or anti-imperial camp around Henri II. The imperial administra-

tion hired a spy to keep an eye on him, a man by the name of Hans Birkling, who, like many of his ilk, enjoyed the raucous company at an inn
called Zum Blumen, which was also a favorite haunt of the "felonious"
colonel. Did Birkling really try to poison Schertlin? In any case he was
arrested, forced to "confess" under torture, sentenced to death, and beheaded. Shortly thereafter, Colonel Schertlin headed up a troop of
twenty Swiss mercenaries who rode off to reinforce the French in the
siege of Metz. These events took place in 1552, when Felix was fifteen and
already deeply interested in medicine. He would have liked to dissect the
body of the executed spy, but it was said to be rotten with pox, the
"French disease" (*voller Franzosen*), so that Felix had to give up any
thought of dissection, while handsome Niklaus, the executioner of Basel,
strutted about in the Iberian mode in the clothing that had belonged to
his victim. No profit was too small.

*   *   *

When it came to the study of anatomy, Felix had a good model (F 103).
His father, a doctor *manqué*, loved dissecting things. Early in 1546 (when
Felix was nine and a half), Thomas Platter had participated in a dissection
with the surgeon Franz Jeckelmann, Vesalius's former assistant and Fe-
lix's future father-in-law. The two men, accompanied by the apothecary
Gengenbach, whose shop adjoined the cattle market, went to Riehen,
where they met the local pastor, a strange character known as Johan Jacob
Leu, alias Hans Leuw. A pseudo-physician and pastor of the Œcolampadian persuasion, soon to be defrocked, as well as an admitted fornicator,
Leuw had taken delivery of a decapitated criminal whose body the city of
Basel had donated to science. It was snowing. As was customary, beggars
came to the rectory in search of alms. Wolves prowled nearby. Back in
Basel, far from the out-of-the-way village of Riehen, Felix trembled for
his father's life: he felt a deep affection for the old man despite the whippings he had received. But Thomas, far from being afraid, was enjoying
himself. With the help of the apothecary and the surgeon, he chopped up
the cadaver obligingly furnished by the Basel authorities. He and his
companions then showed the body parts to the beggars outside the rectory, who fled in fear that the same fate might be in store for them. The
amused anatomists enjoyed the joke until one French vagrant, more courageous or perhaps simply more shrewd than his German confederates,
threatened them with a sword and swore to make mincemeat of them as
they had made mincemeat of their victim. Note, incidentally, that this
beggar (who admittedly came from far-off France) was equipped with a
sword.

The following night Thomas had a dream about cannibalism. When he woke up, he vomited. Shortly after the dissection, the authorities in Schaffhouse, a town not far from Riehen, charged the three anatomy students with murder: the local constabulary had bought the crowd's interpretation of the event. Not long thereafter, Reverend Leuw was obliged to leave town on charges of adultery. Although the morals of the age were sometimes loose, the morals of the clergy were no laughing matter. The departed preacher left the skeleton of the dissected criminal behind: reassembled bone by bone, it remained for many years in the basement of the rectory, where it could be viewed by the faithful (F 103).

"You will be a doctor, my boy": that was Thomas's implicit message to Felix, and it was also the message of the surgeon and the apothecary who had joined Felix's father in perpetrating a rather tasteless deception. Yet the young man's medical vocation was by no means an uncomplicated matter. It was closely associated with the boy's wish to make a good marriage and rise in society, a wish fostered in part by his mother. Anna Dietschi had not forgotten that, though born poor, she came from a distinguished line, which over the centuries had included various illustrious Zurich burghers and noblemen. She did not wish to see her son endure the social purgatory that she had known as a child. In 1549, as she lay on what was thought at the time to be her deathbed (in fact she was to live for many more years), she offered this advice to her almost adolescent son: "Don't be stupid enough, son, to marry a strumpet, as boorish students do. It would ruin you. All you could hope for then would be to eke out a living as a schoolteacher like your father's assistants [the delicacy of this advice has to be admired]. Or else you'll wind up as a wretched village priest or pastor" (F 109). This sage counsel did not fall on deaf ears. Ambition, a desire for luxury, a good career, a rich marriage—all these things entered into the fourteen-year-old boy's partially formulated plans. Here, after all, was a youth not unimpressed by the ostentatious weddings common among the cream of Basel society in the year 1551. What did it matter that one of the grooms was the son of a soldier who had fought on the losing side at Marignano, or that one of the couples thus joined in matrimony would succumb shortly thereafter to the plague of 1552 (F 112)?

* * *

Felix's medical vocation stemmed above all from his family environment. Think of the medical books in ancient tongues that Thomas Platter published or at any rate stored in his home and sold, copies of which were surely available to young Felix. And recall the (sad) story of Epiphanius,

Thomas's late physician and patron, who had rekindled Thomas's youthful passion for medicine, though by then it was too late for him to do anything about it. The tale of Epiphanius, retold a hundred times by Thomas sitting beside the fire, had been a constant presence throughout the first fifteen years of Felix's life. The ghost of the Venetian physician, resurrected by an old story, thus became a model for the future.

* * *

Felix's motives for studying medicine stemmed as much from the flesh as from the spirit, however. From early childhood (when he was no more than eight or ten years old), he loved to watch butchers at work, opening beef carcasses to remove the hearts. He spoke to the animals before they were slaughtered: "Tell me what miracle the butcher will find in you." He knew everything there was to know about slaughtering and butchering hogs at the farm in Gundeldingen. He played hooky so as not to miss a trick. He overcame the disgust that his sister's practice of making rings out of chicken gizzards aroused in him. With tears in his eyes he killed small birds so that he might dig out the veins in their thighs with a small knife. He dissected maybugs, flies, and burweeds (separating out the veins in the latter, as children do with chestnut leaves today). This was the origin of Felix's *Beruf,* his calling. *Beruf,* of course, was a word that Luther liked to use to speak of God's call to man to perform some particular mission on earth.[36] In short, God spoke to Felix through the entrails of cows and pigs. A haruspex of Roman times would not have been surprised.

Felix's down-to-earth (or down-to-flesh) motives were not incompatible with more elevated considerations. As a young man, his primary goal was not really to save his fellow man from disease and suffering. At any rate this was not a goal he wrote about, although he was clearly a compassionate person, ready to help anyone who was suffering and even to care for those close to him who came down with the plague. But when it came to choosing a profession, his concerns were not fundamentally charitable; he was motivated, rather, by admiration. Felix identified in advance with the professors of medicine, the deans and rectors who treated dukes and princes, important academics whom he saw strutting the streets of Basel in their velvet costumes, followed by servants on horseback. Thomas pointed out processions of such prominent citizens in order to remind the boy of the rewards of hard work. In a Protestant city already moving toward greater democracy and self-government, a city in which the status hierarchy was by no means frozen, a talented young man could dream of every sort of social advancement, however illusory such hopes might prove in reality. His father, moreover, encouraged Felix's hopes from early on by admonishing him to do well in school and if need be by cuffing him on the ear.

*　　*　　*

Furthermore, when it came time ultimately to choose a profession, Thomas intervened. He did not conceal his joy at his son's choice of a medical career and encouraged him to read and take notes on subjects such as botany and therapeutics. Thomas (F III) also confided in his boarder Höchstetter, a future prosecutor and physician: "The boy [Felix] will by the grace of God become a doctor. He will do what I was unable to do, and that will be his vocation, his calling [*Beruf*]." At the time of this pronouncement in the best Lutheran style, Felix was eleven or twelve years old. Over the next few years he realized that his future career disgusted him in some ways. As much as he wished to be an anatomist, he despised filth and disliked handicaps. When his sick mother vomited, he was a dutiful son and held her head, but he averted his eyes, for he was afraid he might faint. His father was obliged to scold him: "If you are going to be a doctor, get used to things that may disgust you."

Felix's decision to go into medicine was reinforced by his marriage plans. On New Year's Day, 1550 (when Felix was fifteen), Thomas stopped in to see his friend and fellow dissector, the surgeon Franz Jeckelmann. While there, he noticed a pretty girl of sixteen or seventeen, Madlen, who kept house for her widowed father. (Jeckelmann had lost his wife, Chrischona, the year before.) Thomas mused to himself that the girl would make a nice wife for his son and hinted as much to Felix, who was excited by the idea, as he confided to his friend Martin Huber, the son of the great Basel physician. But when he met the girl, he blushed, stammered, and was paralyzed with shyness, Madlen did not take it amiss, however, for she had already made up her mind. Felix immediately began dressing with even more elegance than usual, and he worked harder than ever at medicine with the idea of becoming a presentable son-in-law for "old Franz" (who was actually not yet fifty).

*　　*　　*

Felix's marriage plans came up again in the summer of 1551, while he was away in Rötteln avoiding the plague. In Thomas's letters wishes became facts: Ursula was dead, so Madlen would one day become his daughter-in-law and take his daughter's place. The couple would live on Felix's earnings as a doctor. Felix's passion for Madlen preoccupied him: he wrote Latin poems to her and left them in the lining of his jacket, where a tailor found them and circulated them around town, to the amusement of all who knew him. But Thomas kept his head. He had dreamed up this marriage with God's help, and with God's help it would take place. Felix languished in Rötteln throughout the plague-ridden summer of 1551, while his father engaged in extended negotiations with Jeckelmann. The two men got on well together. Small gifts of wine and food passed from one household to the other. Nothing more needed to be spelled out. Everything was understood. The engagement became an open secret, about which Felix, far away in Baden, received news through his friends' mocking letters.

In September 1551 a new chapter opened in Felix's life: the plague was over (F 123). At any rate it was no longer a constant threat. Felix entered college as a freshman (as we would say) at age fifteen. Some of his classmates, drawn from the middle or lower-middle class of the city's intellectuals, were as young as eleven or twelve. Social classes were homogeneous, whereas school cohorts were heterogeneous. After a brief period of hazing or initiation, the young college student got down to work on Roman history, medicine, and Greek, which he studied under the aegis of Thomas, himself an excellent Hellenist. Sadness had descended on the Platter household since Ursula's death. The parents fought because Anna worried about the debts Thomas had incurred. Here was yet one more reason for Felix to work feverishly, taking assiduous notes in Johannes Huber's lectures on medicine. He also knuckled down to the study of Hippocrates, who was back in favor in the Basel region. These preliminary studies were to prepare him to study medicine at the University of Montpellier. Unlike Thomas, Felix was no self-made man, heading out into the wide world to seek his destiny. He was a well-educated boy, far better educated in his speciality than many college students are today. Felix left German territory and set out for the land of the "Welch," where he would discover French, Latin, and Languedoc culture in both the popular and academic spheres. Ursula, whom Thomas had hoped would make a grand marriage, was dead, so all his paternal hopes were now invested in his boy, on whom the future of the Platter line depended.

*   *   *

In the summer of 1552, Thomas, who had been nursing his decision for a long time, therefore made up his mind. Felix was his only surviving child;

his three daughters were all dead. Hence it would not hurt anyone if he invested everything he had in his son. Sending his boy to Montpellier, one of the world's leading medical schools and certainly the best north of the Alps, would give him the best possible start as a doctor in Basel in the shortest possible time. Once established as a physician, Felix would help his father meet expenses and pay off the debts that had hung over his household for too long.

ÆTATIS · 83 ·
1581

1. Portrait of Thomas Platter Sr. (1499–1582), in his eighties, by Hans Bock the Elder (oil on canvas). Oeffentliche Kunstsammlung, Basel, Kunstmuseum, Inv. 83. *Photo by courtesy of the museum*.

2. Portrait of Felix Platter (1536–1614). The great Basel physician is portrayed in a slightly pretentious manner among objects that reflect his passion for collecting items pertaining to natural history. This portrait is also the work of Hans Bock the Elder (oil on canvas). Oeffentliche Kunstsammlung, Basel, Kunstmuseum, Inv. 84. *Photo by courtesy of the museum.*

3. Portrait of Thomas Platter Jr. (1536–1614). To judge by this rather unflattering portrait, the youngest of the "great Platters" lacked the personal magnetism of his father and brother. The portrait is by Bartholomaüs Sarburg. Oeffentliche Kunstsammlung, Basel, Kunstmuseum, Inv. 42. *Photo by courtesy of the museum.*

4. Chrischona Jeckelmann (1577–1624), the wife of Thomas Platter Jr. and niece of Felix Platter's wife. The young woman is holding a small gold chain given to her as a gift by Felix Platter's wife, Madlen. Felix purchased the item in 1557 as a gift for Madlen, then his fiancée, from a shop in Paris located on one of the bridges across the Seine. The portrait is by Bartholomaüs Sarburg. Oeffentliche Kunstsammlung, Basel, Kunstmuseum, Inv. 43. *Photo by courtesy of the museum.*

5. Portrait by Hans Bock of Theodor Zwinger (1533–1588) surrounded by symbols of Time and Wisdom. Zwinger, a great humanist and physician, held the chair in Greek philosophy at the University of Basel and was a friend of Felix's Platter's, as well as the sixteenth-century thinker most responsible for the idea of the "scientific journey." Oeffentliche Kunstsammlung, Basel, Kunstmuseum, Inv. 1877. *Photo by courtesy of the museum.*

6. Portrait by an anonymous artist of the Anabaptist David Joris (1501?-1556). Joris, a resident of Basel, was a native of the Netherlands. The fate of this friend of the Platters is discussed in chapter 9. Oeffentliche Kunstsammlung, Basel, Kunstmuseum, Inv. 561. *Photo by courtesy of the museum.*

The following "urban" illustrations are taken from Georg Braun and Franz Hogenberg, *Civitates orbis terrarum* (Cologne, 1572) and, for later decades, from subsequent editions of the same work (more complete than the first printing), the last of which appeared in 1618.

7. Map of the city of Basel. On the right bank of the Rhine was "Little Basel," the city's "minority" suburb. *Bibliothèque nationale de France.*

8. Sion, or Sitten (*Sedunum* in Latin), was a large town in the Valais, Thomas Platter Sr.'s home territory. Thomas, Felix, and Felix's wife and father-in-law stayed here in June 1563. *Bibliothèque nationale de France.*

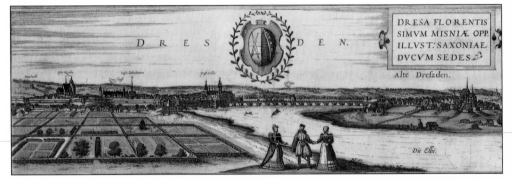

9. A pleasant, aristocratic view of Dresden. From his vagabond youth Thomas Platter remembered mainly having slept in a room here in which the straw was so full of lice that one could hear them moving. The harsh memory of the young "student" thus contrasts with the flattering image here of a "garden city," as conceived by a contemporary artist. *Bibliothèque nationale de France.*

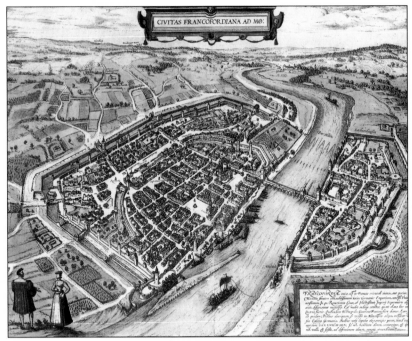

10. Thomas Platter Sr. transacted business at the Frankfurt book fairs during his years as a printer in the 1530s. *Bibliothèque nationale de France.*

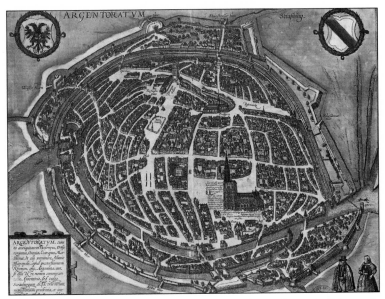

11. Thomas Sr. and Felix had frequent contacts with Strasbourg both in youth and later. The city is mentioned at least fifty times in Thomas's *Lebenbeschreibung* and especially in Felix's *Tagebuch*. For the people of Basel, then as now, Alsace was just next door. *Bibliothèque nationale de France.*

12. Thomas Sr. and Felix went to Rouffach in 1551 to buy an ass. They visited the castle and admired the tombstone of a knight, a bas-relief in which the knight is lying face down in order to shield himself from "symbolic" revenge by a shrewish wife. *Bibliothèque nationale de France.*

13. The Platter clan had frequent contacts with Colmar and other Alsatian cities and towns. Felix's good friend Thomas Schöpflin, who also traveled down the Rhone Valley with him in 1552, became the municipal physician of Colmar around 1560. *Bibliothèque nationale de France.*

14. A famous theological colloquium was held in Baden in 1526. Thomas Platter followed the proceedings assiduously. This meeting had an important impact on the religious future of German Switzerland. *Bibliothèque nationale de France.*

15. Mainz: the Platters had little direct contact with this city, but it did provide Thomas Sr. with friends in his youth and Felix with friends later on. It was also the unique birthplace of printing, despite some scholarly claims to the contrary. *Bibliothèque nationale de France.*

16. En route to Montpellier, Felix Platter stayed in Lyons from October 20 to October 23, 1552. There he met the great physician Rondelet, who, at the University of Montpellier, would later teach him about medicine and show him how to dissect bodies. *Bibliothèque nationale de France.*

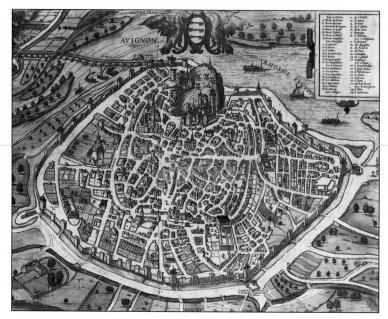

17. Felix Platter spent several days in Avignon around October 28, 1532. There he experienced fear and a brief depressive episode, but he also listened to hymns sung in a Catholic Church and began to moderate his hostility to Catholicism in his first authentic contact with the faith. *Bibliothèque nationale de France.*

18. Felix Platter passed through Nîmes on October 30, 1552. He cast an attentive eye on local antiquities. He also unwittingly came into contact for the first time with the pro-Protestant culture of Lower Languedoc. *Bibliothèque nationale de France.*

MONSPESSVLANVS, MONTPELLIER.

G. Les freres prescheurs.   O. Pour aller au
H. Le chemin de Gignac.   Chatuer.
I. Le chemin de Pecenas.   P. La petite Obervelee
K. La Palissade.   Q. S. Thomas.
L. Rue S. Guilhem.   R. La palissade
M. Les Relieuses   S. S. Sauuere.
    S. Guilhem.   T. Le chemin de Besiers.
N. La Magdaline.   V. Le grand S. Iehan.

Cum Priuileg

19. Montpellier, where Felix spent the years 1552 to 1557, remained a vivid memory when the elderly physician sat down to write his memoirs in 1608–13. His memories of the city as an attractive place were mingled with nostalgia for youth, the student life, and the pleasures of swimming in the Mediterranean. *Bibliothèque nationale de France.*

20. Felix visited Marseilles in 1555. He made detailed notes about his physical condition and appearance in this city. At the end of the sixteenth century, his brother Thomas Jr. gave a more objective account of the city and its port. *Bibliothèque nationale de France.*

21. Felix was in Bordeaux from March 11 to March 14, 1557. He viewed the Atlantic, visited Roman ruins, ate fresh fish, and participated in numerous musical activities, including small improvised concerts. *Bibliothèque nationale de France.*

22. On March 18, 1557, Felix visited Poitiers (his brother would later follow suit). He climbed a tower, visited a castle, and spoke with booksellers. *Bibliothèque nationale de France.*

23. On March 20, 1557, Felix passed through Tours, the first "jewel" of the Loire Valley, where Renaissance architecture was far more prevalent than in other regions of France. An industrial city, Tours specialized in the production of luxury goods (silk). Its fountains, marvels of city planning, and its castle made a particularly strong impression on the son of the Basel teacher. *Bibliothèque nationale de France.*

24. Orléans (March 23–25, 1557) gave Felix an opportunity to enjoy himself with the colony of German students at the local university. The student from Basel committed an egregious error of historical interpretation concerning the city's statue of Joan of Arc, however. *Bibliothèque nationale de France.*

25. In Paris, where Felix spent the first two weeks of April 1557, he visited important physicians, the Louvre, Notre-Dame, and the abbey of Saint-Denis in the northern suburbs and amused himself with shopping expeditions and revels with German and Swiss students. *Bibliothèque nationale de France.*

26. In Bourges, which Felix visited during hard times in 1557 and Thomas Jr. saw much later in the century, both Platters were drawn to the city's churches, to the "diamond-point" tower, and to the treasures bequeathed to the church by Jean de Berry. Felix also frequented the local German community, which at the time of his visit was still in mourning for a young Bavarian lord who had recently drowned while boating near the city. *Bibliothèque nationale de France.*

CHAPTER FOUR

Platter Enterprises: Thomas

Thomas's debts were long-standing. They went back to at least 1535 or 1536, when the family was reduced by plague to father, mother, and one daughter and then increased to four by the birth of Felix in 1536. The subsequent period, from 1536 to 1551 or 1552, is the one we have just examined through the inescapably youthful and often poetic gaze of Felix. "Old" Thomas offers us an adult vision of the same years—the view of a dynamic, active Renaissance man. His account is given in vivid prose, and the picture he paints contrasts with the verdant if sometimes tragic paradise described by Felix. Thomas, a man of learning, had reached a point in his life where he wanted to make money, or at any rate to earn a living, climb the so-called social ladder, and achieve a modicum of well-being, a respectable level of "comfort." His decision to take in paying boarders (*Tischgänger*) was an additional resource, a reliable if modest source of income. The regular payment of room and board by his students helped Thomas to meet his growing need for cash, for he had embarked on a plan to acquire land and buildings. The rent generated by the boarders only supplemented other sources of income, however—at least at first, for the situation would change later on. In Basel as in Lyons, the best prospect for an intellectual or semi-intellectual with a good knowledge of ancient languages like Thomas Platter—the royal road to a better life, if perhaps also a trap for the unwary—was for a brief time the printing trade, or, more accurately, the ownership of a print shop. Did printing provide Thomas with enough to live on? In any case it fed the dreams of a journeyman typographer who had not yet risen to the rank of master printer, or *Trukerr herren* (T 129). Master printers did good business and could amass a considerable amount of capital with a minimum of sweat. Such, at any rate, was what people said, and they may have embellished the truth somewhat. Wives of Gutenberg's allegedly well-compensated disciples pestered their husbands to take the books they printed to the Frankfurt book fair and sell them there, and then bring home nice cushions and pewter from the shops of that great German city (T 119). Many lived beyond their means. Even after he became the owner of a print shop, Thomas, who knew the value of a penny, contented himself with purchasing simple ironware on the banks of the Main (*ich koufft isin hä-ven*). But many printers' wives, once they were assured that their husbands' businesses would prosper, longed to move up in society, fighting their way upstream like trout or salmon desperate to reach the higher levels of the cascade of contempt.

This was the case with the wife of Andreas Hartmann, or Cratander, a native of Strasbourg who became a pious printer in Reformation Basel. The printer of Plautus, he had presented Thomas with a volume of that author's works whose printing he had overseen; this was the volume that Thomas had unstitched and hidden among the fibers in the ropemaker's shop where he worked, in the hope of combining mental with manual labor.[1] Cratander's success as a publisher proved to be brief. His ambitious wife persuaded him and their son Polycarpus to shun the scribbles and scrawls (*sudlery*) of the printing trade and take up the supposedly more respectable and certainly less grimy business of bookselling. True, Thomas did much the same thing some years later, when, his success assured, his capital amassed, his loans covered if not repaid, and his house bought and paid for, he abandoned the typesetter's chair and apron for the robes of a professor. An early mountain climber, Thomas-the-highlander inched his way up the social hierarchy by first establishing a foothold and then, with his free hand, searching the smooth rock face for the still higher protuberance, the small granite ledge that was all he needed to thrust his body up another notch: begging provided him with his first toehold, after which came literacy, and from there it was on to ropemaking, teaching, and printing and all the way to the status of boarding-school headmaster and leading pedagogue (even if his status was contested by the university).

Thomas was not only an intellectual but also a worker, a breadwinner. In the struggle for social recognition he had one big advantage: the physique of a soldier, a fighter. His son Felix knew this at first hand, having been at times the object of his father's beatings. But Thomas's combativeness, one of the many talents of this Renaissance man, was not directed solely against members of his family. In the very print shop in which he was a partner he fought a Homeric battle with Balthasar Ruch. Ruch worked for Episcopius as a typesetter until 1534, then, in 1535, joined Thomas Platter and two others to found a sort of printers' cooperative (T 118). Ruch and Platter quarreled over the financial details of the business, financial matters being something about which Thomas was always sensitive, as evidenced by his quarrels with his wife over his debts. To believe Thomas, whose version of the event portrays him, as usual, in an entirely innocent light, Ruch had attempted to bludgeon him from behind with a thick plank one night while he was reading proof, but he saw the blow coming and managed to avoid it. The two men fought, gouged each other, pulled hair, and went for the scalp. Thomas nearly lost an eye as the two exchanged blows. He then laid Ruch out with a punch to the nose. The loser's wife cried.[2] Employees of the two partners intervened: the journeymen evidently felt that their bosses had more important things to do than to put each other's eyes out. The results of this ferocious battle were as follows: Ruch was forced to wear a bandage on his nose for eight weeks, during which time he had to put in an appearance at the Frankfurt book fair, while Thomas wore a dressing on his middle finger for four weeks.

Did the two men make up after their fight? In his memoirs, at any rate, Thomas describes Ruch as a good typographer and a man capable of courage (obviously) and noble sentiments. He was also a good friend (*guttergsell* [T 118]) with an eye to social advancement: in Thomas's book this was a point in his favor. Relations between the two men were disrupted briefly by the fight but improved later on when Ruch quit the partnership and went into business for himself from 1538 to 1541. The two had certainly had a good understanding earlier, around 1535, when they had formed the partnership with two other friends. (I arrive at the date 1535 for the formation of the partnership because it occurred after the birth of Ursula in 1534 and after Ruch quit his job with Episcopius but before the birth of Felix in October 1536 and the first joint production of books by Platter and Ruch in March 1536.)

Who else was involved? There was of course the ubiquitous Oporinus, who turned up at almost every important juncture in Thomas's life following his return from Germany and Alsace. Oporinus (whose German name was Johannes Herbster, "the autumnal one") was seven or eight years younger than Thomas and the son of a well-known painter (*verriempter Maler* [T 119]). This illustrious ancestry earned him the privilege of membership in his father's guild, Zum Himmel (In Heaven): guilds in Basel recruited on a partly professional, partly familial, consciously elitist basis (the consequent contradictions apparently went unnoticed). What Arlette Farge has called the "good fortune of being included" conferred considerable advantages. With his strong connections to the Basel middle class, Oporinus good-naturedly dominated his older friend, a country boy who was still something of a bumpkin, a "hick" according to urban prejudice. Of course such snobbish distinctions were soon blurred in a city ravaged by plague and religious upheaval: hardworking, talented new arrivals quickly filled the places that became available. The taint of low birth was soon effaced in the eyes of natives.

Oporinus never suffered from any such social stigma. An excellent Latinist, he had from the age of nineteen progressed steadily in his teaching career through primary, secondary, and university ranks. What is more, he had enjoyed the signal privilege of employment as Paracelsus's medical secretary. To supplement his income, he also corrected proof, and in 1535 he joined with Platter and Ruch in their print cooperative.[3] Fascinated by the printing trade, Oporinus quit the university altogether in 1542. It was a wise decision: in 1543 he produced his most important work as a publisher, a splendid edition of Vesalius's *Humani corporis fabrica*. A first-rate artist in the "graphical" tradition of the great dissector whose fame he helped to promote, Oporinus was not much of a businessman and regularly ran himself into bankruptcy. Although Thomas owed almost everything he achieved to Oporinus's influence, he nevertheless remarks acidly on his friend's penchant for burying himself in debt. Although one of Oporinus's two wives came from a wealthy family of goldsmiths, both proved to be spendthrifts, which did nothing to improve his situation. Toward the end of his life, however, a third and then a fourth marriage put him back on his feet. But was it really necessary to run through four women in order to end one's life in comfort?

Oporinus exerted considerable influence on a whole phase of Thomas Platter's existence. The younger man adored his older friend; he gradually transformed Thomas from a mangy, cloddish highlander into a respectable burgher. When Platter was still an ill-nourished, overworked ropemaker, Oporinus had made it possible for him to teach Hebrew to a class of twenty students at Saint Leonhard's school (this was at a time when Thomas, being something of a working-class militant ultra-Protestant with iconoclastic tendencies, took a particular interest in the Old Testament). Oporinus, with his bourgeois connections, also provided Thomas with a letter of introduction (*durch brieff Kundschafft*) to Heinrich Billing, the stepson of the bürgermeister of Basel; the Billing family subsequently took the ex-Valaisian under its wing (T 95). Somewhat later, after Oporinus had become the head of a prestigious school adjacent to the cathedral and settled comfortably into quarters in the former bishop's residence (the new Protestant teachers having snapped up the best jobs and apartments), he chose Thomas as his assistant at the unheard of salary of forty pounds a year.

We can now understand more fully why Thomas, whose Protestant convictions were no doubt quite sincere, had, if he wished to get ahead, no choice but to throw in his lot with the reform faction, which was Œcolampadian in Basel just as it had been Zwinglian in Zurich. It was either join the "heretics" or resign himself to being a nobody. Oporinus disapproved when Platter, on a whim, suddenly quit his relatively com-

fortable teaching post to become the valet and student of Epiphanius, the
Bavarian-Venetian doctor, from whom Thomas had hoped to learn medicine and improve himself more rapidly (a miscalculation later redeemed
by his son's success as a physician). Not one to hold a grudge, however,
Oporinus cheerfully welcomed the disenchanted Thomas back to Basel
after Epiphanius's tragic death in 1531. The two together then copied the
precious prescriptions from the Venetian doctor's pharmacopoeia: their
complicity, if not always scrupulous, was now complete.

Cooperation led to triumph when Thomas brought his old teacher and
friend Myconius from Zurich, then under papist threat, to Basel and
found lodging for him with Oporinus (T 112). In the following year Myconius inherited nothing less than the pulpit of the late Œcolampadius,
the Protestant preacher who had converted Basel and become the city's
foremost minister. From then on, things moved quickly. The two
"scholars," Oporinus and Thomas, both taught in the city's *paedagogium*,
switching from Hebrew to Greek and accordingly from iconoclastic
(biblical) fanaticism to benevolent (Hellenic) humanism. Dissatisfied
with their teaching salaries, our "duo" continued their progress by seeking part-time work as proofreaders (*Oporinus ouch . . . in den trukeryen
corrigiert* [T 118]).

Hence there is nothing mysterious about the two men's later partnership in the printing business. Since Oporinus had for many years provided Thomas with bed, board, work, and all the rest, it is rather
shocking to note the cold tone with which Platter describes his young
friend's heavy debts, from which he escaped only by marrying a third and
ultimately a fourth time. Such ingratitude or at any rate lack of concern is
common in the writing of this successful social climber, who owed his
good fortune largely to two men, Myconius in Zurich and Oporinus in
Basel. Both were Protestants, and both—the strict preacher and the humanist aesthete—were destined to end their days as citizens of Basel: Myconius succumbed to the plague there in 1552, and Oporinus died in 1568.

There is no mystery about Thomas's two other partners in the printing
business. Balthasar Ruch, whom we encountered earlier, and Ruprecht
Winter both came out of the "stable" of Oporinus, who was not only the
deus ex machina of the group but also by far the most talented printer.
Winter was the son of a "good merchant" of Basel (T 172). He married a
goldsmith's daughter, the sister of Oporinus's second wife. Though born
wealthy, these women defied convention in their choice of marriage partners. Winter, examples of whose printwork from the middle third of the
sixteenth century have survived, also ended up bankrupt. He spent everything he earned and had no head for business.

Ruch, despite his spectacular row with Thomas, was originally a friend of his as well as of Oporinus. All four partners were highly skilled printers. Separately and collectively, they produced a number of noteworthy books, foremost among which (apart from Oporinus's edition of Vesalius mentioned earlier) was Calvin's *Christianae religionis institutio*, which came off Thomas's presses in 1536. Their shop was one of the leading presses in Basel, a city that numbered among the publishing capitals of the world at that time. Oporinus, as was mentioned earlier, was a member of the guild Zum Himmel. Winter and Ruch belonged to Zum Bären (The Bear). At their request, Thomas was invited to join the latter in 1536, shortly before Felix's birth in October. Thomas also became a burgher of the city, a status that carried with it certain rights and privileges. Although he was now a citizen of some prominence, he felt himself under no compulsion to conceal his past as a poor highland boy. On the contrary, he told his story to anyone who was willing to listen. Early modern society was evidently not as closed and snobbish as one might think, at least not in the democratic cities of Switzerland.

The new printing business needed money and equipment. Providential assistance came from Cratander (Andreas Hartmann) (T 80, 163). Already in his fifties, Cratander had retired from publishing at the urging of his wife and gone into bookselling, which was less physically taxing than printing, a trade that required not only intellect but also physical stamina. His son Polycarpus helped out in the bookshop; the boy's name, like the father's, suggests that someone in the family knew Greek.

In about 1525 Polycarpus had himself been a boarder in the home of Collinus, also known as Rudolf Ambüel (also spelled Am Biel or Am Buol [F 259]).[4] Collinus, born in 1499, was an exact contemporary of Thomas Platter. Subtle and learned (*gelehrter*), this former student at universities in Switzerland, Austria, and Italy had been obliged to quit his teaching post in the Catholic city of Lucerne because of his outspoken Zwinglianism. As a refugee in Basel, he learned the ropemaking trade in 1524 and then, in 1526, opened a ropemaking shop. Meanwhile, he taught courses in Greek at the university, while Thomas, as an apprentice ropemaker in his shop, improved his Latin by reading the copy of Plautus that Cratander had given him. (It would be pleasant if today's workers felt driven to study Latin and Greek on the job.) Collinus also took in boarders to supplement his modest income. Both he and Thomas subsequently abandoned ropemaking in favor of full- or part-time teaching. The Am Buol family, through which the Cratanders made contact with the Platters (including Felix: see F 259), is particularly interesting because another member, Kaspar Am Buol, was one of the first learned apothecaries to extol the therapeutic virtues of hot baths, in his canton at any rate—and in Switzerland such priority is no small achievement. For Thomas Platter these men were models: scholarship, teaching, manual labor, and taking in boarders were all things he would try at one point or another in his lifetime. Here we see some features of Swiss humanism at its best.

Cratander stood at the center of a network linking the worlds of culture, printing, education, and craftsmanship. Besides having given Thomas the Plautus that he took with him into the ropemaking shop, he was in contact with Balthasar Ruch, the printer-pugilist, whose notes he sometimes countersigned. Another Basel printer linked in several ways to this network was Johannes Bebel, or Bebelius, who like Cratander came from Alsace. Bebelius was a friend of Thomas's and used the familiar *du* with him (although Thomas always called him Herr); he also considered him a *lantzman,* or countryman, although the reasons for this are not clear, since Alsace is nowhere near the Valais (T123, 137). Bebelius was also connected to Ruprecht Winter, whose debts he obligingly forgave (T 122). And he was a close friend of Cratander's. When Cratander died, Bebelius bought his bookshop, saving his heirs from ruin. Clearly this was a close-knit group, almost a holding company whose investors were "outsiders" rather than Basel natives: immigration has its rewards.

When Thomas and his partners set up shop, Cratander discreetly sold the new business certain essential equipment for the sum of 800 gulden. Did the money come in part from Ruprecht Winter, who had access to cash through his father and wife? In any case it was a loan that had to be paid off within a specified period (*uff ein gwyss zyt zu betzalen*). Besides supplying the partners with needed equipment, Cratander also rented them Bear House (the animal lent its name to the shop as well as the guild).

*   *   *

The birth of Thomas's son in October 1536—the beloved only son of his first marriage—offers an opportunity to measure the strength of the ties that Thomas, a self-made man, had forged in the worlds of publishing, teaching, and the clergy in Basel. Indeed, the baby's first godfather was none other than Simon Grynaeus, or Grynaer, who grew up on the banks of the Danube and later pursued his studies along the banks of the Neckar. In Basel he taught Greek and later "biblical science." His relations with the University of Basel were stormy: the institution apparently challenged his academic credentials, or perhaps his lack of or failure to obtain such credentials (T 170). The *alma mater* had no use for autodidacts. In this respect Grynaeus held fairly radical views, which associated him with the working-class militancy or at any rate the anti-academic, "anti-prof" extremism that was shared to varying degrees by Myconius, Collinus, and Thomas Platter. Grynaer had a passion for teaching, however. It was he who, some years later, strongly advised Thomas to return to teaching, whose advantages and disadvantages he laid out in detail: "Become a schoolmaster, Thomas! No profession is more divine! None could suit me better! Ah, if only I didn't have to repeat everything I say!" The final sentence, which still rings true today, did not discourage Simon Grynaer's son Samuel (1539–99), who evidently remembered only the first part of the paternal paean. Samuel Grynaer, who became a professor of Roman law at the University of Basel (T 148 and 181; F 123), played a role similar to his father's vis-à-vis the Platters. On July 27, 1574, he become godfather to Thomas's second son, Thomas Jr., the fruit of septagenarian but still vigorous Thomas Sr.'s second marriage to a much younger woman. Thomas Jr., thirty-eight years younger than his brother Felix, would, like Felix and his father, also write his memoirs. But to get back to Felix's baptism, it was *Herr* Simon Grynaer (Thomas conferred this mark of social distinction upon him) who, upon leaving the church in which the sacrament had just been performed, remarked to Thomas that the child would indeed be *felix* (happy), "or else all my senses deceive me" (*oder all meine sin driegen mich*). Simon was not mistaken, except for the fact that Felix never fathered a child of his own. Thomas filled in for him, however, by remarrying at an advanced age and producing a second brood of sons and daughters. Apparently the name Felix was chosen primarily because Thomas's wife, who came from Zurich, respected that city's onomastic traditions: one of Myconius's sons was also baptized Felix. In this there is further evidence of Thomas Platter's fondness for his Zurich-based, "Myconian" connections, which had first allowed him to escape from the misery of his childhood.

Felix's other godfather was Johannes Walterus *typographus*. Everyone understood that this appellation referred to the typographer Johann Walter, who was active in Basel in the 1530s but has left no other trace in our sources (T 121, 173). Walter moved in the same professional circles as Thomas but at a lower social and cultural level. The fact that he came from Zurich argued in his favor, however, for Thomas continued to feel strong ties to the old Helvetic city on the banks of the Limmat and the Silh.

Ottilia Nachpur was Felix's godmother. The wife of a young and wealthy draper, Macharius Nussbaum, she evidently did not live long, for her husband soon took a second wife. The prestigious merchant lived on until 1553, long enough to offer Thomas Platter useful advice about investments in land and buildings (T 125).

*　　*　　*

Thomas's career as a printer, which extended from 1535 or 1536 to 1543 or 1544, had its ups and downs, which left their mark on him. In the summer of 1535 he paid an entry fee to join the Bear Guild, which accepted artisans in the trades of precious metals, coinage, typemaking, and printing. Oporinus, who like Thomas was also a professor and printer, remained a member of the Heaven Guild, a rather heterogeneous organization that accepted glassmakers, saddlers, and painters, including Oporinus's father, a celebrated local artist (T 119). In October 1535 Thomas also became a burgher of Basel (*ich ward burger* [T 119, 172]). Having risen in social status, he pursued his trade in partnership with his friendly enemy Balthasar Ruch until the spring of 1538, at which time he continued in business on his own. His partnership with Ruch had lasted nearly three years (from 1535–36 to 1538) and produced some two dozen books, including not only religious works but also secular humanist volumes and even medical texts, all bearing the mark of Ruch and Platter.

The peak of Thomas's career as a "typographer-intellectual" came early in his partnership with Ruch: it was nothing less than the publication of the first edition of Calvin's *Christianae religionis institutio* in March 1536. Was Thomas impressed by the mathematical precision with which the Huguenot leader set forth his thought, imposing a Cartesian clarity *avant la lettre* on the five hundred pages of the first surviving edition of his work—the masterpiece of Thomas Platter, printer?[5] Calvin takes up several subjects in succession: the law (an explanation of the Ten Commandments); faith (an elucidation of the Credo, a discussion of the importance of justification); prayer (glosses on the Lord's Prayer); and the sacraments (baptism and the Lord's Supper being the only ones that Calvin recognized, for he denied that the five other sacraments accepted by the Roman Church had any divine status). He concludes his magisterial if not always convincing work with some thoughts on Christian freedom, in which he relates the attributes of the two powers, ecclesiastic and temporal. Through many subsequent editions the thought of the "heresiarch" became considerably more ponderous, losing some of the joyfully militant simplicity of the first, "Platterian" edition of 1536. The whole work was suffused with the harsh principles of predestination, that divine forebear of royal absolutism (which had other antecedents as well): according to this formidable doctrine, the pot cannot complain to the potter (whose decision is arbitrary) of being a lowly chamber pot rather than a beautiful amphora (Romans 9:21). The artisan has power over his clay; he is the master.

More radical than Luther, Calvin rejected the mass, the real presence of Christ in the host, and the ecclesiastical hierarchy. The effect of his writing could only have been to confirm Thomas in the rather extremist attitude he had absorbed from his master, Zwingli. But Platter, unlike the Picardian theorist, was no ideologue. His fisticuffs with Ruch notwithstanding, he, like his sons after him, was throughout his life a nonviolent person in the mold of Montaigne, at least when it came to religion, politics, and intellectual discussion. One cannot help smiling at the *ad hoc* text that appears below the title of the *Institutio:* "Envisaging everything connected with the doctrine of salvation, a work worthy of being read by any student of pious subjects; with a preface addressed to the Most Christian King [Francis I] as an offering in profession of faith." In this, Thomas's first in-depth contact with French culture (albeit in its Latin form), it is also moving to read the final words of the volume: "*Basileae per Thomam Platterum et Balthasarum Lasium . . . martio 1536*" ("Basel, by Thomas Platter and Balthasar Lasius [Ruch], March 1536"). The two men were thus sanctified by the vast work whose reproduction they made possible. One suddenly finds it rather difficult to imagine them in their real lives as hardworking, hot-tempered printers exchanging blows and pulling each other's hair out by the roots. Astonishingly enough, Thomas's memoirs do indeed fail to mention the *Institutio,* a fact that suggests that the Valaisian's mystical period, which began with his conversion to Zwinglianism in 1520, was now behind him, even if he remained quite pious in his everyday life. By contrast, the memoirs deal at length, as is only to be expected, with the financial difficulties that beset the four partners, and particularly Ruch and Platter.

The partnership's business was conducted not only in Basel but also in Frankfurt, at the great book fairs that were held there. The assets of the business included the 800 gulden worth of equipment that Cratander had sold the partnership. The liabilities were increased by loans to finance the purchase of raw materials and other operating expenses. In addition, Ruprecht Winter had put up part of the partnership's assets as collateral for a loan he obtained to defray his wife's expenses. Trips to Frankfurt by one or another of the partners were also a drain on the business, and the money earned from the sale of books was often spent on trinkets and luxury items. Thomas was the only exception in this regard: of course his wife, though born a servant, harbored a few grandiose ideas, but she did not covet luxury as did the wives of Winter and Oporinus, who had been born into the Basel bourgeoisie. All in all, the partnership contracted debts of 2,000 gulden. Things got so bad that at one point it was feared that the partners would have to forgo their modest salaries, which had been set at 104 gulden annually for each of them and had at first been paid regularly (T 107). (For comparison, when Thomas became a school headmaster in 1540, he received a comfortable compensation of 200 gulden annually from the Basel authorities.)

In the spring of 1538, or more precisely sometime after the Frankfurt book fair around Easter of that year, the partnership dissolved, and Thomas became the head of his own business. Production immediately dropped off: the shop no longer turned out books as prestigious as Calvin's *Institutio,* which had been the opportunity of a lifetime. Calvin had literally launched Thomas Platter in 1536, though of course the religious leader had other things on his mind and had no idea what his book had meant to its printer. The temporary setback to Thomas's fortunes may have been more apparent than real, but the number of books produced certainly did decline: "From March 1538 to March 1543 [or perhaps 1544), the shop's imprimatur appeared on no more than thirteen or fourteen impressions," as compared with twenty-four at the peak of the Platter-Ruch collaboration (March 1536–March 1538), that is, twelve volumes annually in the peak period versus two to three volumes during the period in which Thomas was essentially on his own. At first sight, then, it would appear that Thomas was a much less substantial force in the printing trade than when he had been assisted in the management of the business by the dynamic if at times violent Ruch.

This hasty judgment is not entirely borne out by the facts, however, for it was during the second phase of his printing career that Thomas was able to buy a house and fair-sized farm in the nearby countryside. He enjoyed this prosperity, moreover, despite the fact that he was deprived, if we accept his side of the story, of one hundred gulden due him from the dissolved partnership (the money went instead to his hapless partner Ruprecht Winter). Is there something missing from his account? In fact, Platter probably made his way out of the cooperative venture with certain personal benefits about which he does not deign to inform us. His partner Ruch's desire to bash his head in may have had something to do with the anger of a shareholder and manager who felt swindled by a greedy "friend." Whatever Thomas may or may not have embezzled from the business, the fact remains that he was able to reopen the shop under his own personal management in 1538. The business was well equipped. Thomas had many friends among the city's diecasters, engravers, and manufacturers of type fonts who provided him with indispensable sets of carefully honed, aligned, and calibrated typefaces—all, he tells us, for a relatively modest price (*umb ein ring gelt*).[6] Among these benefactors, who may not have been as disinterested as Thomas maintains, was Martin Hosch, a typemaker formerly of Strasbourg who became a citizen of Basel in 1530. When he died in 1541, his widow married another typemaker, Christoph Behem: the trade was endogamous. There was also Master Utz (whose real name was Goruch Köpfle), a typemaker and engraver. Above all, there was the astonishing Peter Schöffer Jr., who owned a fabulous set of dies and whose perfectly honed typefaces nicely completed Thomas's equipment without costing him a penny. Schöffer came by his skills naturally, "for he was related to the early inventors of printing in Mainz itself" (*uss Welches gschlächt die trukery zu Mentz erfunden ist* [T 122]).[7] His father was Peter Schöffer Sr., the son-in-law and collaborator of Johannes Fust, a financier and aesthete typographer who had worked directly with Gutenberg. The three men, Gutenberg, Fust, and Schöffer Sr., collaborated on the celebrated forty-two-line Bible of 1453. Hence young Schöffer had quite an astonishing pedigree for a person in the printing trade.

After lending Thomas Platter crucial assistance in Basel, the younger Schöffer turned up in Venice in 1541, where he printed bibles and a work by Raymond Lull. By 1542 he was back in Basel, where he died in 1547. In the interim he was widowed and remarried and was accepted as a citizen of Basel.[8] In addition to a wide range of typefaces, Thomas seems to have obtained, without investing any large sums, the presses (*prässen*) essential for his business. "Young" printer though he was, he prided himself on his professionalism and his capital, both mechanical (the presses) and intellectual: his hardware and software. He never forgot that he had been a teacher (and would teach again). He therefore instructed his young apprentices (*lerbuben*) in the rudiments of Latin and even Greek (probably no more than the alphabet in the case of Greek, however), so that they could perform their daily work (*tagwerch*) under his supervision. Thomas's success in the book business was probably due to his striving for philological as well as typographical quality.

At various places Thomas alludes to the metals business and metalworking technology in typography. In fact, however, he had little detailed knowledge of metalworking techniques, for unlike Peter Schöffer or Martin Hosch he was neither a typemaker nor an engraver. Although he was a subcontractor in the world that revolved around Frobenius, he has little to say about the purchase of raw materials such as paper and ink. It has been found that centuries before the actual discovery of titanium (a metal used today in the manufacture of jet aircraft), there was titanium in the ink used by Gutenberg for his Bible. Thomas, who probably received helpful advice at the beginning from his partner Ruch, nevertheless solved many technical problems without being an expert himself. The pages of his edition of Calvin's *Christianae religionis institutio* have not yellowed after fifteen generations (see the fine specimen preserved at the Bibliothèque Nationale in Paris). Skilled workers did the rest, including members of the family: Thomas's children (Felix and Ursula) often prepared and folded paper until their fingers bled (*das inen die finger blutten*). Their mother, Anna, set an example for them to follow. Times were hard, but the business went well (*übel zyt, aber es gieng myr woll*).

*   *   *

Thomas's early experience as a printer, particularly during the time of his partnership with Ruch (1536–1538), involved substantial risk from debt. He did not lack for good advice or cautionary examples. Among those from whom he received advice was Konrad Rösch, or Resch, a Basel citizen of Swabian origin, born on the banks of the Neckar (T 174, F 436). Resch was related to Wattenschnee, alias Johannes Schabler (T 123), for whom Thomas produced books as a subcontractor. Like Schabler, Resch had been a student at Tübingen. For a long time he had also sold books— in Paris, in fact, the Swiss having switched their allegiance after the Battle of Marignano (1515) to France and its culture, radiant with triumph and later with humanism (this despite, or perhaps because of, the massacre of French enemies on the field of battle). In Basel, Resch, a member of the Saffron Guild, lived adjacent to the fish market. He had successively married two sisters, as good a way as any of integrating into a society. In lengthy conversations with Thomas he delivered sermons against indebtedness, but he also described France and his stays in Paris. Was he the person who gave Thomas the idea of one day sending his son Felix to study medicine in Montpellier? Moreover, the unfortunate Cratander, who lay on his deathbed under a crushing burden of debt, revealed his financial woes to Thomas and warned him against burdening his business with too many liabilities.

How pertinent were Cratander's reflections on the eve of his demise? Thomas was trusted in Basel as a man of skill and know-how. Because he enjoyed solid credit, he eventually decided to move his business to more convenient and imposing quarters (still in rented space, however). The move took place in 1538, the same year that the partnership with Ruch ended (F 55; T 119, 172). Felix, Thomas's son, was two years old at the time. Thomas took advantage of the exodus of Catholic priests from Basel after the city adopted Protestantism as its official and compulsory religion in 1529. Ten years later, Thomas was able to rent two houses that had belonged to the former secretary of the local chapter of canons, a man by the name of Kächtler or Kechtler, who had arrived in Basel to attend the university in 1521 (T 174). A man of substantial means who achieved success in the city as well as in the church, Kächtler in 1524 purchased three adjoining houses at 90, 92, and 94 Obere Freie Strasse (according to the numbering on an 1859 map, drawn up well after the Renaissance, but residential addresses in the city had changed little in the intervening years). These houses were close to one of the city's gates, the Inneres Aschentor. They also abutted the Gothic apse of a church, the Barfüsserkirche. Together they defined a small triangular plaza extending beyond Freie Strasse (F 48 ff., figs. 2 and 3). Kächtler's influence in Basel and his extensive real-estate purchases reflected the economic and demographic growth of his native Alsace, both Catholic and Protestant. Alsace was the base that furnished Basel with both people and the cash that fueled its financial and real-estate market. After 1529, Kächtler, like so many other Catholic priests and laymen, was driven out by the Protestant revolution and forced to emigrate. But the Republic of Basel was not vindictive: it was not yet 1793! A regime of democratic or representative immanence rather than divine or royal transcendence, it did not in most cases confiscate émigré property. Hence the printer Platter was able to rent two houses from the "canonical secretary in exodus" for the not exorbitant sum of sixteen gulden per year (as a partner in a modest printing business, Thomas had an annual salary of one hundred gulden). Here we see how far Thomas had come between 1531, when he had not hesitated to accept a job as a physician's valet in order to sustain himself and continue his studies, and 1538, when he became an independent small businessman, in debt, to be sure, but still relatively prosperous. He was now able to move into substantial quarters, though of course his first order of business was to fill the space with as many beds as possible for boarders, and to fill the one-time clerical residence, whose facade he repainted, with new equipment for printing. Three presses were brought in. The shop took on work for Frobenius, or more precisely for Frobenius-Herwagen and associates, while Thomas continued to sell books that he produced on his own. At first twenty and later as many as thirty to forty noisy boarders—elementary and secondary school students—were accommodated on closely packed beds and yielded Thomas a good income (*so hat ich mer den zwenzig tischgenger, das ich do vill gwan*). This was makeshift capitalism, pay as you go: printing provided the means to expand into the operation of a boarding house, in which Anna played an important if exhausting role. Felix and his sister Ursula enjoyed a private, heated room of their own. In the attic, Kächtler, the absentee secretary of the canonical chapter, had left a storeroom filled with old clothes, unused cassocks, and the like. The stouthearted fellow still hoped that the Catholic, Apostolic, and Roman religion would one day return to its former glory in Basel, restoring him to his former glory along with it, and he was determined to be ready when the time came. Thomas, who maintained good relations with Kächtler (mainly by letter), paid no attention to these delusions. His chief concern was to repay his debts, and by some miracle he actually managed to do so. Indeed, he was so pleased with himself that in 1539, the year after he first took the lease on his new property, he had a hunting scene depicting a hunter, his dog, and the head of a stag with antlers painted on the facade of his new residence, the house at 90, Obere Freie Strasse, closest to Barfüsserkirche. Henceforth this two-story house was known as Zum Gejägd or Zum Gejegt (At the Hunt).

Was the mural intended to depict deer hunting? Did it suggest hunting with hounds? Did Thomas harbor seigneurial ambitions (for Felix, perhaps)? In any case, if Thomas believed that to escape from debt was ultimately a desirable goal, for the time being he had other projects to contend with. He had grasped the fact that in a time of inflation, borrowing, if done judiciously, is a way of getting rich over the relatively long run. No matter how much Anna harassed him on this issue, nothing could make him change his mind. Husband and wife might throw dishes at each other, but credit was credit. God took a hand in the matter. God was often present at important moments in Thomas's life: he who had cured his servant of illness in 1538 and had given him a male child now encouraged him to buy the two houses he was renting on Obere Freie Strasse. The year was now 1540, and poor Kächtler, the former chapter secretary, knew that there was no longer any chance of returning from exile to his former residence now that papism had been pulled up from Basel root and branch. He and his "woman," Ursula Güderin (who may have been a wife, a mistress, or merely a nurse or concubine), decided to sell all three houses. "On the advice of God and several other worthy people [sic]," Thomas initially bought the two houses he was already renting and then acquired the adjoining structure: this was to prevent a farmer from purchasing the property and using the building to house his livestock, which would have allowed him to pile manure on the triangular plaza in front. This would not only have created a stinking nuisance but, even worse, would have contaminated the subsurface water with urine (Basel's water table was high), thereby preventing Thomas from sinking a well. Once the three houses were his, Thomas was able to proceed immediately to the drilling of the famous well. The work cost him one hundred gulden, not counting the cost of feeding the well-diggers. This, as we have seen, was equivalent to his annual income as a partner in a modest printing business.

In order to acquire this block of buildings, the ex-Valaisian had to go into debt once again. No doubt he needed to borrow less than would have been the case a few years earlier, for the exodus of many wealthy Catholic clergy and laymen had led to a collapse in real-estate prices as many properties were put up for auction. What is more, Thomas was seen as a good risk: the sellers, the canon and his companion in exile, chose the dynamic Platter over more prestigious but impecunious and less adaptable buyers, including a noble by the name of von Offenburg belonging to a somewhat ridiculous family with which Thomas had come into contact on a trip from Zurich to Basel, and a city official, the head of the local mint (*Müntzmeister*). Having won this contest, Thomas spent the entire year of 1540 in negotiations over the purchase and sale. The deal was finally completed at the end of January 1541, with the purchase of all three houses for a total of 950 gulden, including deposits made (or promissory notes signed) over the previous several months. The terms were similar in some ways to a rental-purchase agreement or lease with option to buy and in some ways to an installment loan. Various agents served as intermediaries in the negotiations between the Catholic party (Kächtler) and the Protestant party (Platter); by this time religious antagonisms were of relatively minor importance in such matters. Thomas's days as a fanatic were over. He was prepared to tolerate the peaceful coexistence of the Œcolampadian and Roman sects, and indeed so were most other people, although beneath the surface considerable hostility continued to smolder on both sides. The Valaisian, who now enjoyed powerful connections, received advice from highly placed friends, including such "dear old gentlemen" (*die lieben alten herren*) as Bürgermeister zum Hirtzen and the draper Nussbaum.

Debts! The accounting that Thomas gives in his memoirs may not always be strictly accurate, but it seems that he paid 750 gulden for the first two of the three houses. His rent for the previous two years was 16 gulden per year, which works out to a relatively low return on capital of just 2.1 percent. True, the Catholic absentee landlord was hardly in a position to pressure his tenant and soon-to-be buyer, who enjoyed the support of powerful city officials. Kächtler, who felt he was being swindled by the printer, lost his temper at times: "Your collateral isn't worth a bucket of ashes" (*ein züber mit äschen*), he burst out one day after Thomas proposed to use his business assets as collateral to guarantee his loan (T 125). In any case, the sum of 750 gulden included not just the buildings but certain items of furniture, for Platter had agreed to pay 50 gulden of the total in compensation for Kächtler's old beds and other white elephants (actually not worth a brass farthing). Thomas bought the furniture only because he was forced to, or because he could fob it off on his two or three dozen boarders. From Thomas's rather esoteric calculations it emerges that on the 750 gulden that he owed the seller after closing the sale of the two houses, he paid only 5 percent interest on the first 500 gulden and 20 percent on the remaining 250, for a total of 75 gulden in annual interest, or an annual rate of 10 percent. This was by no means excessive, particularly when we take into account the fact that prices were rising intermittently or steadily over the long term, so that the seller was forced to charge a higher rate of interest to cover himself against the inflation that was "in the air." (The underlying causes of this inflation are still not altogether clear: Was it the first influx of precious metals from the New World, augmenting the traditional supply from Central Europe and the Sudan? Or the growing population, which exerted inexorable pressure on supply and hence on prices?) Bear in mind, however, that while the rise in prices that afflicted the sixteenth century may have been impressive to the early modern mind, it was moderate compared with the runaway inflation that the twentieth century has seen.

Platter and Kächtler soon agreed on the sale of the third house as well. Thomas's debts now rose to a grand total of 950 gulden (the equivalent of 120,000 Swiss francs of 1975): not an inconsiderable sum but not an excessive amount either by current standards (which are considerably more tolerant of debt, to be sure, than sixteenth-century standards were). Platter, after several stormy scenes with Kächtler in Freiburg, managed to come up with the necessary cash on his return to Basel. By 1542 he was able, through obliging intermediaries, to repay 300 gulden of the 950 he owed to the secretary in exile. Within five years he had paid off the entire debt (*ich hatt in 5 jaren gar zalt*). Thus by 1546 or 1547 he owned his property outright, fulfilling the dream of so many peasants of the past, who sank their hearts into their land (T 127). Thomas Platter remained a peasant at heart, and before long he became at least a part-time peasant in actual fact. Several things made this remarkable feat possible: Thomas's good connections with the Protestant bourgeoisie of Basel; his net profit of 200 gulden per year from the print shop; and the backbreaking work of Platter, his wife, and his children to make the boardinghouse work. Business was good, in fact excellent. In 1539 the Junker von Offenburg had been willing to pay 600 gulden cash (*bar*) for at least two of the houses. Within a few years, the master of the Basel mint offered Thomas 1,200 gulden for *just one* of the three houses he now owned. Housing prices were thus rising rapidly, doubling or tripling in just a few years. Indeed, the economic climate of the 1530s and 1540s was generally favorable in German-, French-, and Romansch-speaking Switzerland (although setbacks were not uncommon in the printing business). The age was thus propitious for the kind of speculation in real estate that gladdens the hearts and lines the pockets of born calculators like Thomas Platter.

* * *

After buying his houses, Thomas went on to acquire farmland. His career plan was clear. Like so many citizens of Western cities then and later, this Basel burgher became a rural landowner. In the spring of 1549 he was still simply the owner, free of debt, of three adjacent houses on Obere Freie Strasse, but the time had come to make his move, even if that meant putting himself into the red again. In June of that year he bought several pieces of potential farmland and adjoining buildings, all close to various fortified medieval structures.[9] None of the plots was more than a quarter of an hour's walk beyond Basel's old southern ramparts (on what is now Gundeldingerstrasse). The seller, not accidentally, was one Ulrich Hugwald Mutz, known simply as Hugwald. Born in the late fifteenth century and slightly older than Thomas Platter, Hugwald came from Thurgovia. As a young man he had been an enthusiastic manual laborer and farmer: "Thou shalt toil in the fields and earn thy daily bread in the sweat of thy brow" (F 103). He had even tasted the peasant life on occasion and in the end chose it as his own. Then, bitten by the bug to teach and join the elite, he became a teacher and taught at the Burgschule until 1540, when he became a professor in the Faculty of Arts. In 1549, he published a Latin history of Germany. (Did he pay for the publication himself or with money paid or promised to him by Thomas Platter?) In Basel, once one reached a certain social status that Thomas had already moved well beyond, everyone (with few exceptions) knew everyone else. But it was surely through the Burgschule that close ties were established between Hugwald, who had taught in the school and left his mark on it, and Thomas, who became a teacher there in the 1540s.

In order to purchase land, the printer-teacher short of cash was once again forced to rely on credit, which he obtained without difficulty (T 137, 178). He borrowed 500 gulden from the innkeeper of the White Dove, possibly a man named Hans Galle, and 200 additional gulden handed to him on the spot by Jacob Kannengiesser, a draper who at the time was probably engaged to Esther Frobenia, the daughter of Frobenius, the printer and bookbinder and Thomas Platter's friend and protector (T 137, 178; F 135). Jacob would marry Esther less than two years later in the winter of 1550–51. Here we detect the useful influence of the typographical network that grew up around Frobenius, Herwagen, and Episcopius, a network in which Thomas was still a relatively minor but already influential participant. Johannes Herwagen Sr. also played a key role in arranging Thomas's loans, not without reluctance, but it was the least he could do given that Thomas had done him an important favor by arranging a reconciliation between Herwagen and his wife (*ich im wider zu siner frowen geholffen han*), one Frau Lachnerin, the widow of the late Johannes Frobenius, who was the founder of the Basel typographical dynasty to which he gave his name (F 69, 357). And it has to be said that in this case the reconciliation was not easy, since Herwagen had put his wife in high dudgeon by having an affair with the wife of Frau Lachnerin's son by her first marriage. The ensuing scandal had set tongues wagging in Basel from 1542 to 1545. It took a man with the skills of Thomas Platter to rescue poor Herwagen from his plight (T 138, 179). The ex-Valaisian borrowed considerable sums not just to buy the land in Gundeldingen but to pay the cost of planting, digging wells, and building on his new property. Tears were shed and teeth gnashed before the deal was done, and Anna Platter, as usual, dismayed by the financial risks that her husband, much more imaginative than she, was willing to take, had lost her temper more than once. In any case, Thomas refused to find a co-signer to guarantee his debt to Hugwald, for he had no desire to be beholden to anyone. He therefore worked out the same kind of arrangement he had made to purchase his property in the city. After hard bargaining, he put up the land and three houses in the city as collateral for Hugwald's loan of the purchase price of the land. With hay in his boots, Platter was now a man of substance, who could gain the confidence of would-be lenders by pointing if not to a comfortable hoard of cash then at least to holdings in real estate.

Thomas thus did business with other people's money. At this stage of his life he was not yet a long-term lender (in contrast to his son, who became a substantial lender later on) or even a short-term usurer. He was rather one of the vast number of people who used other people's money to make more money for everyone concerned. Thou shalt invest! was the commandment that Thomas put into practice in school, boardinghouse, print shop, real estate, farming, and ultimately in securing a college education for his son, his only surviving child. He invested heavily in his new farm in Gundeldingen, using whatever cash he had on hand together with loans on which he paid sixty gulden in annual interest. He owed a thousand gulden all told to practically every burgher (*alle burgshafft* [T 138]) in Basel, by which he meant his friends and acquaintances, who were not always cordial when money was at stake. These people constituted a certain elite; they were among the Protestant city's secular and civic leaders. They included printers and innkeepers. Can this group be called a "bourgeoisie"? Certainly, but not the high bourgeoisie of aristocrats and big businessmen, for whom Thomas Platter was only a minor player. And not the elite of pastors and professors who, financially speaking, held the devil by the tail, even if God was on their side when it came to the spiritual aspect of things. And of course in all this business God marched as always at Thomas's side (T 138). But God helped those who helped themselves. Thomas fixed up the existing house, barn, and stable. As he had already done with his property in the city, he sank a well on his new farm. While not stinting on his own labor, he also paid and fed others to come work for him. For all this he needed to borrow. He planted vinestock on his property and in the best Valaisian tradition began to raise livestock. He purchased (for 130 gulden) three acres of pasture from the wheelwright Lux Dersam, who was also an official in various Basel hospitals and guilds (T 139).[10]

Thomas's return to the land may seem astonishing, yet it was in many ways typical. The peasant from the highlands of the Valais became a farmer in the plains around Basel. Geographically he had moved to a lower altitude, while socially he had moved to a higher one. In neither respect was he alone. Hundreds of thousands of residents of early modern cities, small businessmen as well as professionals, bought land as soon as they had the means to do so. They cultivated that land with their own hands and with the help of their families, servants, and hired hands. Their goal was to eat what they produced themselves; to ensure a supply of food in time of scarcity or crisis; and to satisfy a deeply rooted craving to live on the soil (a craving that would prove to be much less pronounced in Felix than it was in Thomas). And then, too, there was simply a desire to invest, even if the money for investment was borrowed, and to make more money by selling what one produced. These people did not "exploit" the countryfolk or the countryside—on this point a respectable historiographical tradition needs correcting.[11] On the contrary, they invested, increased the productivity of the land, diversified crops, and speculated on potentially profitable new ventures such as vineyards and pastureland. They also responded to the demands of the city, which consumed quantities of high-priced, high-quality products such as wine, meat, milk, and vegetables. Thus the fringes of the city were turned into a kind of countryside by the proliferation of suburban vineyards, vegetable gardens, orchards, and small farms. The monotony of lowland fields and meadows and highland pastures was relieved by these new ventures.

In this respect Thomas Platter can serve as a model. His was a successful resumé, one that could be copied by other members of the social groups through which he passed in his various capacities, sometimes with the slowness of a tortoise, at other times with the speed of a hare. He was of course one of a host of citydwellers who bought, worked, and improved rural properties, one of a host who renovated Gothic farmsteads that had survived the Middle Ages and who planted vineyards in weed-choked fields. He had been a highland peasant, a beggar, an urban craftsman, and finally a burgher. He had known the life of the poor peasant and the social outcast. He had been a worker and then a small businessman in the "manufacturing sector" (printing). And he had worked in the "service sector" (teaching) before returning to "agriculture" (with his suburban farm). Yet it is well to recall that his first vocation, by now largely forgotten, was to become a priest. In all this Thomas Platter was a Renaissance man, somewhere between Lazarillo de Tormes and Guillaume Budé, the beggar and the professor.

Before long, Thomas's suburban farm was thriving, and his investments in real estate were yielding a good return. He found himself briefly torn, however, between his most recent occupation (printing) and one of his earliest and deepest vocations (teaching). The printing business was quite profitable, generating a net income of roughly 200 gulden annually. But Frau Platter and her children were working their fingers to the bone. The journeymen printers, who shared the family's meals and quarters, were often incompetent or clumsy (*ungeschikt* [T 129]). Of course not everyone was capable of proofreading or even setting type in Greek and Hebrew: non-Latin characters held pitfalls for the unwary. Worse still, the journeymen sometimes displayed arrogance (*unbescheidenheit* [T 147]). They demanded higher wages in a crude manner: this, too, was a consequence of steadily rising prices. The great Lyons printers' strike, led by French workers, was not far off.

War also had certain negative repercussions on the market. The last clash between France and the Empire in the reign of Francis I took place between 1542 and 1544. It was marked by the "immoral" alliance of France and Turkey against Charles V, and by Charles's attempts to launch a "Germanic" invasion of French territory. The Valois monarch's victory at Ceresole, won by troops under the command of François de Bourbon, prince d'Enghien, in April 1544, had impressed the people of Basel because thousands of Swiss had fought in the battle.[12] Felix, eight years old at the time, remembered this episode and the veterans' war stories for a

long time afterward. Thus various factors—the unpleasant wartime atmosphere, a restive work force, and a soft market—conspired in the end
to drive Thomas out of the printing business and into the relatively calm
world of teaching. There at least one was less likely to be disturbed.

* * *

Nothing is simple in this story. The relationship between Thomas's diverse activities, including printing, and his permanent vocation to teach
took various forms in the years between, roughly speaking, 1520 and 1555.
Platter was not simply a man with two mistresses, the printing press and
the classroom. The workaholic Sunday farmer always remained a teacher
at heart. Just before becoming an apprentice ropemaker in the 1520s, he
had taught his cousin in the Valais his *abc*'s. After that he became tutor to
the two Werdmüller boys in Zurich, where he was able to eat to his heart's
content (T 65). Later he gave private lessons in Hebrew to various
preachers around Zurich. And finally, after a stint with Collinus, the Hellenist and ropemaker, he found himself employed by the "red ropemaker" in Basel, where he studied Plautus while braiding rope and in his
off hours taught Hebrew to twenty-some students under the aegis of
Oporinus at Saint Leonhard's. Shortly after that, he became a schoolteacher (as well as a small merchant, in business with his wife) back in the
Valais (T 80). And then, after returning to Basel, he taught high school in
1531. Following the episode with Epiphanius and the death of Zwingli, he
became Oporinus's colleague in the aptly named *paedagogium,* where he
taught Greek from 1532 to 1540. Meanwhile, he and Oporinus became
proofreaders in Herwagen's print shop. There was even talk of finding
him a position once again as a schoolmaster in the Valais, but those plans
came to naught when someone denounced him to the region's bishop.

Even as he worked as a proofreader, a partner in a printing business,
and finally a self-employed printer, Thomas continued to take in boarders
and to teach. All in all, Thomas's work as a printer was, despite the impressive feat of publishing Calvin's *Institutio* in 1536, an important though
not a central episode in his life, even if it dragged on until 1555. The major
story was not printing but teaching. And a major event in that story was a
bizarre approach by a city official responsible for matters of education.
This man, Heinrich Ryhiner, was not just anybody. A graduate of the
University of Basel, he had served for a long time as the city's episcopal
procurator and imperial notary (F 157). He wrote a chronicle of the Peasant Wars for the year 1525. In 1538, he summoned Platter, whom he regarded as an expert on teaching, for a consultation: "Can you explain," he

asked, "why things at the university are not going well?" The question might well have been asked at many times in history. In any case, Thomas did not mince words: his answer, in substance, was "too many professors—more professors than there are students" (an answer that points up the minuscule size of the University of Basel at the time, at least in terms of the number of students). Thomas's advice continued: "Invite a few good teachers from Germany, no more than eight. You'll have no trouble persuading them to come because of the religious upheavals there. Pay them well, and you will attract a sufficient number [*gnug*] of students." But, the official inquired, "What will become of our local teachers [*unsren basleren*]?" His concern reflected the anxiety of a city whose academics liked to think of themselves, not entirely accurately, as an established, ingrown group and did not relish either unemployment or competition from outsiders. "If you find people from Basel, use them or keep them," Thomas concluded. "Otherwise, invite good teachers from outside for the sake of your young students." Did Thomas see himself as an outsider, someone from the Valais immune from the consequences of the treacherous advice he was giving? If so, he deceived himself. The city, having consulted his opinion, changed its tactics (but not its strategy), leaving Thomas in the lurch: he was dismissed, along with Oporinus (*gab uns urloub* [T 129]). The authorities disapproved of the way the two men divided their time between printing in the private sector and teaching in schools supported by public funds.[13] It was felt that they were neglecting their teaching duties in favor of their work as printers, which paid better. Thomas's dismissal probably occurred in the autumn of 1538, while Oporinus's came in 1539; both men bowed to the decision of the authorities, if not without grumbling. The dismissals did not become fully effective until 1540.[14] This dispute with city authorities, though vexing, was short-lived. The need for good secondary-school teachers was simply too great. Thomas now moved back from the private to the public sector, in 1541 according to his text and surely no later than December 1544. On the eve of this move, he was, of necessity, working essentially only as a printer. By midcentury he was once again a full-fledged teacher and boardinghouse keeper; he now devoted only a small part of his time to printing, while farming had become a major preoccupation, taking up much of his time when he was not with his "beloved blond students." In the meantime, the great strike in the Lyons printing industry had taken place (1539–42). Did this have repercussions among print workers in Basel, whom Thomas described as resentful and incompetent? Did they drive Thomas, whose experience as a printer was relatively recent and who was not wedded to the profession, out of the business?

The wars of the period, which choked off the market for books, did not help matters. The resurgence of conflict between France and the Empire between 1542 and 1544 has already been mentioned. And in the duchy of Cleves hostilities erupted in the same period between Charles V and the Protestants of Germany. The defeat of the German Lutherans at Mühlberg in 1547 was surely a blow to their coreligionists in Basel, and not just those in the printing business. As an experienced teacher with a knowledge of Hebrew and Greek in a time of difficulty in the book trade, Thomas decided to return to the world of education. Once again he demonstrated his old aptitude for mobility, for changing his line of work at a moment's notice. This time he benefited from the advice of friends and protectors, including Bürgermeister Adelbert Meyer zum Pfeil, now in his sixties, as well as the future bürgermeister, Theodor Brand, a man ten years older than Thomas and something of a father figure to him (T 176). Brand, the scion of a distinguished family of surgeons, was well known as a conciliator among city officials.

Felix's godfather, Simon Grynaeus, also urged Thomas to return to teaching and related lines of work, though his advice was tinged a bit more than that of some others with warnings against academic doddering. This mixed counsel had to have been offered sometime before April 1, 1541, the date of Grynaeus's death at the age of forty-nine. Joining the unanimous chorus of Thomas's admirers was the city clerk of Basel (*den herren Stadtschriber*), whom Platter, always eager to show off his illustrious acquaintances, does not fail to mention for the benefit of future readers. The only discordant voice was that of his old friend Myconius. Nevertheless, the city fathers sent Myconius to see Thomas and try to persuade him to quit the press for the lectern (T 130). Myconius, however, was only too aware of his former pupil's stubbornness: "I know that you're the best man for the job," he said. "But the thing is, I know you. You'll do just as you please [*du wirst dim kopf wellen nach gan*]. You'll quarrel with the university. They won't let you teach the way you want to."

Myconius's warning was to no avail, however. The offer was attractive. Thomas had had his fill of Gutenberg's noble art, which no longer appealed to him as a full-time occupation. What is more, becoming a professor was like the fulfillment of a dream to a man who had once thought of becoming a priest: to trade the priest's cassock he never wore for the cap and gown of a professor was an honorable transaction in the eyes of both God and man. Herr Rudolf Fry, a merchant and one of the leaders of the city council, put it this way when Thomas came to him on an errand (in addressing Thomas, Fry used the formal *Sie*): "My good man, become a teacher. You will enjoy yourself, and you will be doing a service to the city council, to God, and to your fellow man." The purpose of education at the time was twofold: to turn out young Christians while at the same time giving students the means to succeed economically and socially. The paradox was that their new secular knowledge carried with it the potential of diminishing their Christian faith.

The errand that took Thomas Platter to visit Rudolf Fry is of some interest, by the way. Hans Rudolf Fry, a native of Mellingen, had been a Basel city councillor since 1529, the year of the Protestant revolution in the city: Fry was thus a member of the group of Protestant militants who had controlled the city ever since and whose backing Thomas Platter had consistently enjoyed. Fry was a merchant who dealt in various lines, including parchment. It was precisely in order to buy parchment that Thomas had gone to see him, for he had noticed the excellent quality of the line that Fry carried, some of which came from the illuminated medieval texts that delighted little Felix Platter when he stumbled onto them in the storeroom of his father's shop. Thomas bought parchment to use as binding material for the books he printed. His boarders were pressed into service as apprentice bookbinders. Many of these adolescents sprang from the elite of the Valais and spoke Latin with Thomas, whom they adored despite his occasional severity. The twenty or thirty boarders who lived in Thomas's houses ate the produce of his farm, including vegetables, eggs, and milk. Not only did he benefit from their work as bookbinders, he absolutely depended on the money he received from their parents for room and board, money that sometimes had to be dragged out of them. Without this influx of cash, he could never have paid his bills or met his debts.[15]

* * *

Rudolf Fry the merchant thus sold vellum to Thomas, the owner of a print shop that turned out scholarly tomes. The same Fry, as a local politician in charge of funds for education, urged Thomas to become a full-time teacher and forget about printing and binding books. Indeed, a fair number of the local elite literally besieged the Valaisian immigrant with requests that he change his way of life. They were determined to make him headmaster of the Burgschule, and for the next several decades this prestigious school, attached to an important church, did indeed become his principal place of employment. The situation at the school had gotten out of hand: there had been six headmasters between 1537 and 1541. Just as governmental instability can be damaging to a country, instability of leadership can be damaging to an educational institution. To many local leaders, Thomas Platter seemed likely to be a disciplined leader and an excellent teacher. It was felt that, in a town where talented men did not grow on trees, here was someone who could put a dying school back on its feet.

But before he could close up the print shop (and set himself up in the teaching business), Thomas had to tie up loose ends and sell his remaining stock. He therefore went to Frankfurt to liquidate his remainders, which he sold by the pound for the paper they contained (*das myr Kum das papyr zalt ward*), or so he claims. The buyer was none other than Barthli Vogel of Wittenberg, who for twenty years remained an important associate of the leading Basel printers. A connection was thus established between the two men, the one a former disciple of Zwingli and the other a compatriot of Luther.

Thomas still had a substantial number of books back in Basel, which he sold to Jacques de Puys of Paris. He then unloaded his presses and other equipment on Petrus or Pietro Berna, originally of Lucca, who hoped to break into the printing business in a city where printers were not always receptive to new competition (Berna's efforts would prove successful in the second half of the sixteenth century). Pietro Berna enrolled in the University of Basel in 1542. Thomas Platter did not take up his post as headmaster of the Burgschule until the fall of 1544. Hence the sale of the presses must have taken place sometime between 1542 and 1544 (T 136, 178). The individuals involved in Thomas's farewell to publishing represented a good part of Europe, an area ranging from Wittenberg to Frankfurt to Basel to Lucca to Paris. Books published in Latin could be read anywhere on the continent, and the world of publishing was truly international: even a modest publisher like Thomas Platter was engaged in a cosmopolitan network.

*　*　*

It is astonishing to see a man about to become a teacher selling off his books. True, his teaching required only a few works by major authors: Cicero, Terence, Homer, and so on. And in any case he needed the money, because he was still hungry for land. The liquidation of his assets in Basel and Frankfurt afforded him only brief respite. By the late 1540s he was once again in debt owing to the purchase of his suburban farm in Gundeldingen. By the end of 1549, he owed a hundred crowns (*Sunnenkronen* [T 137]). Herwagen had lent him money, it will be recalled, in gratitude for Thomas's help in reconciling him with his wife. Herwagen nevertheless proved to be an insistent creditor. And such important printers as Frobenius and Episcopius flew into a rage when Platter took the side of their former friend and partner Herwagen, who was now their enemy for having made a cuckold of Frobenius's son. They stopped sending work Thomas's way in the wake of the Herwagen affair, without which, Thomas insists, there would have been enough business to keep three presses running for a decade. He would have become a rich fellow (*ein richer gsell* [T 138]). But once the big printers turned their backs on him, he had no choice but to close up shop, or at any rate to shut down gradually. Here was yet another reason for Thomas to give up printing and go into teaching. In a sense he was driven out of the business by the Herwagen scandal, which became a Platter scandal when Thomas intervened. In Thomas's retelling, however, his banishment from the profession is presented as a personal decision on his part to return to teaching.

What became of Thomas's debt to Herwagen of a hundred crowns? Herwagen being a hard man despite all that Thomas had done for him, the debtor arranged to transfer his debt to Bebelius, another printer who remained on cordial terms with him and who was much more "pliable" than Herwagen. In other words, Bebelius repaid the loan to Herwagen and in turn became Thomas's creditor. Of course Bebelius did not have anywhere near this amount, so he actually borrowed the necessary hundred crowns from Balthasar Han, a glassmaker-artist and onetime student of Holbein as well as an influential member of the city council and the guild Zum Himmel (T 137, 178; F 82). Han seems to have regarded Thomas with the same immediate sympathy as did other open-minded members of the Basel elite: they sized him up as a worthy fellow who deserved their help. And indeed, the line of credit did not end with Han, who was short of cash himself and borrowed the needed sum from a deposit of 600 crowns entrusted to him by Count Michel de Gruyère of Freiburg, who, despite his mouth-watering name, was, aside from this propitious occasion, generally in debt himself (T 137, 179).

This old-fashioned system of loans thus depended on both the credit of the city and the often volatile fortunes of the old aristocracy. For the time being, however, it was Bebelius who held Thomas's note (on which he demanded no interest payment, by the way). Bebelius, a native of Alsace whose real name was Johann Bebel, did not die until after 1550. On his deathbed, he asked Bonaventura von Brunn, a friend of Balthasar Han's and of the Platter family, to summon Thomas. Brunn, a future bürgermeister, belonged to the circle of wealthy drapers, tanners, and butchers with whom Thomas had been on good terms since the 1540s. These men of substance treated the Valaisian immigrant familiarly but with respect. Bebel told Thomas that he was transferring his note to an honorable but less indulgent creditor, namely, his son-in-law, the printer Isengrinius, who, unlike his father-in-law, required Thomas to make payments of principal and interest on this and other, subsequent loans (T 138). The change in the terms of the loan was not pleasant for Thomas, but neither, apparently, was it usurious or catastrophic. Even if pressed (*ubertriben*) from time to time, he was reliable, intelligent, and hardworking and managed to stay on good terms with people in Basel. He gradually worked his way out from under his debt so that the sheriff was never forced to come to his door to confiscate bed, breadbasket, and china.

If only all his troubles had been financial. Twice, however, Thomas's house was visited by a scourge far worse than debt: the plague. Margretlin II (1533–39), Thomas and Anna's second daughter, died in the first epidemic, which lasted from August 1538 until June 1539 (T 128), just as Margretlin I had succumbed in 1531. At the time Thomas was involved in printing and managing a boardinghouse for the several dozen boarders whose rent kept him in the black. When the plague struck in August of 1538, no thought was given to sending the boarders back to the Valais, for they would simply have carried the disease with them. Hence the Platter family together with its young boarders—some forty people in all—moved to a place three leagues from Basel, where they remained for four months, well into autumn. Their temporary quarters were in the former episcopal town of Liestal (T 128). There, Thomas and part of his nomadic entourage lived perilously close to the cemetery in an inn run by one Ulrich Wentz, a former tanner who belonged to a family of textile workers (F 54). Since the "Platter group" occupied only one room, some of the boarders must have been housed elsewhere. Felix, aged two, slept in a cradle part of the time.

The death of little Margretlin II, briefly described, plunged Thomas and his wife into deep sadness. In reserved terms Thomas describes his dead daughter as a dear child (*lieb kind*) as well as a pretty one (*hüpsch kind*). Sixteen weeks after the exodus began, Thomas was back in Basel, where he immediately resumed his activity as a printer. A decade later, in 1551, another *lieb kind* would succumb to the series of plagues that ravaged Basel from 1550 to 1553.[16] Ursula (or Urselin), Thomas and Anna's third and only surviving daughter, passed away in 1551 at the age of eighteen (her father erroneously recorded her age as sixteen and a half).[17] Ursula's death disrupted life in the Platter household. To be sure, the neighbors accompanied the girl's body to its final resting place, but the boarders scattered like a flock of sparrows. One could live with the plague in a city, but when it struck a boardinghouse, the only wise course was to get out, and quickly.

*   *   *

By the time school resumed in the fall of 1551, things had returned to normal. The plague had subsided. Thomas's school, despite his recent loss, reopened its doors. Its curriculum had at last been worked out, and the general outline of a system that would endure for thirty years was now clear. Of course Thomas had considerable experience as a teacher. As early as 1531 he had taught at the Burgschule. Over the next eight years he gave lessons in Greek at the *paedagogium*. And from 1544 on he became the most important, though not the only, figure in secondary education in Basel (1544 and not, as he misleadingly suggests, 1540, for he did not wish to lend substance to the accurate charge that he had been excluded from teaching between 1540 and 1544 on the grounds that his work as a printer conflicted with his teaching duties, and perhaps also for reasons of bad character).

Now that he was headmaster, Thomas supervised the work of three subordinates. Together, the four teachers taught four classes that met for four hours daily, two in the morning and two in the afternoon, with a period of supervised study in between. The alphabet and reading were taught in the first class; Latin authors and catechism in the second; the Bible, Cicero, grammar, the "science of fine language," and Aesop's fables in the third; and Ovid, Terence, dialectics, rhetoric, and music (in small doses) in the fourth, which also included translation into Latin. This four-grade system was less effective and less carefully designed than the Jesuit system of six or seven grades, however.[18] Hence there was room for improvement, whether one remained Catholic or converted to Protestantism.

Religious instruction, punctuated by attendance at Protestant services on Sundays and Tuesdays, was not neglected. The authors selected, including Cicero and, among modern Latinists, Erasmus and Castellion, were chosen for their humanism and tolerance. Thomas Platter had come a long way from the fanatical iconclasm of his youth, a period in which he had suffered from the infantile disorder of hysterical ultradogmatic orthodoxy. By now his religious convictions no longer blinded him or confined him to an ideological dungeon.

His students ranged in age from six to fifteen. There was a span of ages in each of the four grades. The University of Basel kept a finicky eye on

Thomas's teaching, but the oversight was tolerable and easily circum-vented. In any case, he was reputed to be one of the most reliable teachers to be found in Alsace, the Basel region, and the Valais, indeed one of the best secondary educators in all of northern Switzerland. When his stu-dents graduated, they went into various walks of life, including the crafts and commerce; some went on to the university. Thomas educated many of Basel's professionals in his time, including clergymen, teachers, jurists, and public officials.[19] Not surprisingly, his former students adored him. When they returned home, they sang his praises: Platter had friends ev-erywhere.

Thomas would not have succeeded professionally or acquired so many friends without the important contribution made by Anna, his faithful companion and hardworking helpmate. Her management of the school helped spread the former Valaisian's fame far and wide. She ran the kitchen and dining room that served the boarders whose rent helped keep the Platter household afloat. When she died on February 20, 1572, neither Thomas nor Felix was short of memories of the "little housewife" (*hussmutterlin*) who for so many years had shared the bed of the one and the childhood and youth of the other. Of noble birth but an orphan and therefore *déclassée,* Anna had worked for seven years as a servant in the home of Myconius. The marriage of reason that the latter had arranged between her and Thomas Platter had developed, not without quarrels, into a solid mutual affection, reinforced by genuine love on Thomas's part (as his letters to Felix prove) coupled with a stoic acceptance of his wife's moods: "What do you expect?" he observed in a philosophical let-ter to his son in 1553. "She has worked hard and grown old, and she is a woman."[20] By 1564 she was an old woman with a cough, no teeth, illiter-ate, and six painful buboes from the plague. She had always worked ex-tremely hard, whether in the print shop or spinning cotton to make thread, which she then sold for pocket money. Throughout her years in Basel, moreover, Anna Dietschi-Platter maintained her sense of humor. And once she even developed a crush on a boarder from the south of France with an attractive goatee, though nothing came of it.

Although she was illiterate, she dictated letters to her son when he was in medical school at Montpellier (1552–57); inspiration often eluded her, however, even if her gushing affection could hardly be concealed. She recovered her eloquence, however, when it came to urging her son not to fall for a French girl (his German-speaking fiancée Madlen was waiting for him in Basel) and not to acquire any debts. Her husband's debts were enough for one lifetime. Very ambitious for her brilliant son, she received tokens of his gratitude in the form of presents sent from Montpellier by mail, or at any rate what took the place of mail in those days. In 1555, for example, she received a crate of five dozen oranges. Felix's return to Basel in 1557 and his marriage the following year to a young woman whom Anna liked a great deal were great joys to her. Though emaciated, she continued in her fifties to sing like a girl of twenty, *ac si viginti esset annorum*.[21] Her death in 1572 came one year after her son was appointed professor of medicine.

*   *   *

In any case, to return to the fall of 1551, it was a time for a new beginning. Although the plague epidemic was not over, it had subsided. Felix began a preparatory course at the University of Basel with the idea that he would soon go to Montpellier to study medicine, fulfilling the "Aesculapian" dreams of both father and son.

To find the young student a room in the capital of Languedoc took some clever maneuvering. This was always the case when a family in those days lacked cash to pay for the upkeep of a student far from home. The arrangements made to cover Felix's expenses are worth examining in some detail (F 128). Friedrich Ryhiner, the son of a Basel bailiff and a friend (and soon ally) of the Platter family, had gone off to medical school in Montpellier, where he had found lodging with the apothecary Laurent Catalan, in exchange for which Laurent's son Jacques was given a room in the Ryhiner house in Basel. But the younger Ryhiner, whose ambitions were increasingly centered on France (he eventually became a colonel under Henri III), left Montpellier for Paris. His room in the Catalan household was not allowed to go vacant. Jacques Meier, the son of a Strasbourg jurist, took his place (F 128). Meanwhile, Jacques Catalan left Basel for Strasbourg. Moreover, Jacques's brother, Gilbert Catalan, also went to Strasbourg, trading places with Hans von Odratzheim (the son of a Strasbourg city councillor), who lived with the Catalans while studying medicine in the southern French city. Thus the two Catalan boys went to Strasbourg, while two Strasbourg boys went to Montpellier: the score was even.

Eventually, however, young Odratzheim left Montpellier and returned to Alsace. Once again there was an opening, which was filled by Felix Platter. But Gilbert Catalan no longer had a place in Strasbourg, so he moved to Basel, where he became one of Thomas's boarders, filling the niche left by Felix's departure. Everything balanced out. Laurent Catalan now had two medical students living with him, Meier from Strasbourg and Platter from Basel. And the two Catalan boys were in the north, Jacques in Strasbourg, Gilbert in Basel. The arrangements were worked out by the German physician Heinrich Wulff, a graduate of Montpellier and a friend of both the Platters and the Catalans, families that traded sons as bankers trade letters of exchange.

PART THREE

Five Years in the Land of Oc
(1552–1556)

CHAPTER FIVE

Traveling to Montpellier

The arrangements had been made; now it was time for Felix to depart. Preparations began in the late summer of 1552. The young man (he was just sixteen) needed someone to accompany him on his journey to France. Fortunately, the fairs in Frankfurt drew many merchants from Lyons, and perhaps one of them could be prevailed upon to take the boy in hand on the return trip from the banks of the Main. Of course someone else would then have to be found to accompany him the rest of the way, from the confluence of the Saône and the Rhône to Montpellier. The young student was not yet old enough to set out on such a lengthy journey alone. As luck would have it, Thomas Schöpflin, an Alsatian music teacher and (much younger) colleague of Thomas Platter's, was headed in the same direction. A friend who had taught harmony to the Platter family, Schöpflin was also about to embark on the study of medicine at Montpellier (he would later practice in France and Switzerland [F 73, 129]). His story shows how teaching could serve as a stepping-stone to other careers. Thomas Platter had started too low to make the jump to medicine, but Schöpflin succeeded. Schöpflin's background also exemplifies the close ties that linked Switzerland, Languedoc, and Alsace—a repeated refrain in Felix's memoirs.

Thomas still needed to locate a horse and other equipment for his son's travels. For seven crowns he bought the boy a small horse (*rösslin*) that turned out to be almost as sentimental as its youthful rider. The right man to serve as Felix's guide and mentor on his travels through France still had to be found, moreover. This took time. It was hoped that a printer from Lyons named Bering would pass through town, but he never turned up, perhaps because he was afraid of the plague that still lurked in the vicinity (F 129). Thomas was therefore forced to call upon the services of a certain Robert, a distinguished Parisian, possibly a jurist, who agreed to accompany Felix as far as Geneva, his own destination. After that, someone else would have to be found. In any case, the idea of stopping in Geneva appealed to Felix's father: a year earlier, when the plague was raging, he had thought of sending his son to live either in the city on Lake Leman or in Zurich.

*   *   *

As it happens, the plague returned to Basel in the summer of 1552. It was a relatively minor outbreak, but a decision had to be made. October 9 was devoted to packing, which was kept simple: the bags had to be carried, by horse to be sure, but still it was best not to overload the animal. Felix's father (and not, as one might expect, his mother) made up his bundle: he rolled two shirts and a few handkerchiefs in oilcloth. Not without anguish, Thomas parted with an écu and seven crowns, three of them gold; a part of this hoard was sewn into the boy's clothing. His mother contributed another crown: the difference between the maternal and paternal contributions reflected the respective share of each parent in the finances of the household. Whether poor or miserly, Thomas reminded his son that he had borrowed every penny of this money, including the purchase price of the horse. To Felix this was a familiar tune, but he took it to heart. "Work hard, take care." This shopworn advice was taken seriously by the young student for whom it was intended. On the evening of October 9, Thomas invited the surgeon Franz Jeckelmann and his son to dinner. The idea was still that Felix should eventually marry Jeckelmann's daughter, and the boy was only too glad to have his hand so sweetly forced. The dinner—rabbit and quail—was festive, a hunter's meal. The future nuptials were referred to often around the table, but the guests pretended not to understand what all the talk was about. At nine Jeckelmann had to leave the company: someone had come to ask if he could bleed a plague victim by the name of Batt Meier, a well-known debauchee (F 131). The quiet courage of a man ready at any hour to lance a contagious bubo elicited no particular comment from the assembled guests. Professionalism was taken for granted.

Early on the morning of October 10 two men on horseback appeared in front of the Platter house. Thomas Schöpflin and Robert from Paris were ready to go. Frau Anna Platter, who had been quite gay the night before, was in tears now. Would she ever see her son again? Although politics was not her cup of tea, she, like many others in Basel, was afraid: the emperor, Charles V, was just then marching on Metz with an army of more than 60,000 men. His objective was to reconquer the city from the French King Henri II and troops commanded by François de Guise. If successful, would the imperial army proceed to seize and destroy Basel? Such a prospect was the basis of Anna Platter's fears, which happily proved groundless when Metz held out against the besieging imperials. Nevertheless, the events of this period are important for understanding why the Platters and indeed all Basel were now Francophiles. Henri II was a Catholic, to be sure, but his alliances with the Protestant princes of

Germany made him a suitable ally for the Swiss in their struggles with the Holy Roman Empire. This latent francophilia was one of the ulterior motives behind Felix's departure for the University of Montpellier, an institution in the forefront of "Welch" medicine.

At last the young man was ready to climb onto his horse, but not before tripping over his spurs, which he was unaccustomed to wearing, and falling down the stairs. The first stage of the journey took the three travelers, accompanied by Thomas, to Liestal, the small town where Felix and his father had met Calvin some years earlier. The innkeeper, whose son was a student in Basel, offered them a free dinner. In Liestal Thomas Platter finally took leave of his son. He was so choked with emotion that he could only get out the first syllable of his Latin farewell: *Vale* became simply *Va*. At this point Felix's joy, like his mother's earlier, gave way to sadness. But young Felix had been well advised to put distance between himself and his native city: on the very day of his departure, his companion Schöpflin's maid and his father's servant, Anna Oswald, took to their beds with plague. Buboes once again erupted up and down Freie Strasse. Fortunately, Anna Oswald recovered, as she had many times before (F 131, 132). Felix heard all this bad news only afterward, in a letter from his father. After dinner the travelers rode a few more miles, and Felix suffered a minor spill from his horse but was not injured. They stopped for the night at the Stallion Inn in Langenbruck (F 132).

The next day (October 11) took the travelers as far as the "big" city of Solothurn, where they had lunch at the Lion Inn in the midst of the annual fair. Thomas Schöpflin, who ordinarily played the lute, tried his hand on the organ of the local church with the permission of the organist, Master Georgius. In the afternoon they continued past the former Abbey of Frauenbrunnen, which had been secularized since the beginning of the Reformation almost half a century earlier. In his first tourist's observation, Felix notes that in the twilight he was able, with difficulty, to decipher the medieval inscription at the top of a pillar of stone, which recorded for posterity the tribulations of a group of English soldiers in 1375. The young man was struck by this: he drew the column with its epigraph in his notebook—something he did only rarely. This is the first allusion in Felix's memoirs to "recent" history, in this case the fourteenth century. It is the only medieval notation among the miscellaneous observations collected in his traveler's *Tagebuch*. The day's ride ended after nightfall in a smoky inn that served a large peasant clientele, directly below the castle of Jegenstorf, only a mile from Bern (F 133). On October 12 the travelers stopped for dinner at the Falcon Inn in that city and visited its (now Protestant) churches, defensive walls, and bear pit. The afternoon proved diverting: along the way Felix drank from a bubbling fountain and traveled some distance in the company of a recent bride, who showed her legs when she fell from a horse. That night the men slept in Freiburg in "Welch" territory, that is, in what we would nowadays call Romansch- or French-speaking Switzerland. Crossing the linguistic boundary impressed Felix even more than the young lady's legs had done. The travelers bedded down "in the French manner." We know what this phrase means today: the French tuck in their covers, the Germans don't. Psychoanalysts have spilled a great deal of ink in their attempts to decipher the meaning of this. But what did the words mean in the sixteenth century?

*   *   *

We come now to one of the more dramatic parts of the journey, reminiscent of Thomas Platter's brushes with crime while traveling in Germany earlier in the century. October 13 started badly. It rained all morning. After a good ride, the three travelers stopped at the Lion Inn in Romont to dry out and eat lunch. The afternoon was even worse than the morning had been. It was still raining, and when Thomas Schöpflin wandered off the trail, it took his companions a good while to find him. Then all three riders became totally lost in a forest thick with thieves. After encountering some inhospitable villagers, they ended up at an unlicensed inn in a place called Mézières, where peasants and beggars drank themselves into a stupor on spiked wine while eating chestnuts and black bread. The night was difficult: tramps, soaked to the gills, snored in front of the fire, which died out. Meanwhile, the three visitors from Basel kept vigil, their swords unsheathed (this is Felix's first mention of the weapon he carried).

Three hours before daybreak, Felix and his friends made off on their already exhausted mounts. They plunged into the forest, but not before making several detours intended to throw any pursuers off the track, with the young peasant who had previously shown them the way to the despicable inn leading them. The guide, certain now of a fat tip, took them to the highway, and from there they made their way to Lausanne without further difficulty. At the inn in Lausanne they were congratulated on their narrow escape. The Jorat Forest had a very bad reputation. The men with whom the unfortunate travelers had spent the night were very likely criminals and, had the desperadoes not been drunk, might well have attacked or even murdered Felix and his friends. Apparently the area between French- and German-speaking territory was not very secure. Shortly after Felix's encounter, a bandit chieftain was put to the wheel in Bern after confessing to a number of crimes, including a plan to murder students staying in the inn in Mézières, whose keeper was apparently also a shady character. Had Felix had a brush with disaster? Or was he exaggerating the danger for the benefit of his future readers?

*   *   *

At the time Lausanne was a large, semirural town of 6,000, squeezed between the vineyards along Lake Leman and the bandit-ridden Jorat Forest to the north.[1] Savoyard and episcopal influence in the town had been quelled by the powers in Bern since 1536. In religion the city inclined to a German style of Protestantism but with a liturgy in French. Two "depapalized" churches replaced the dozen or so Catholic churches that had served Lausanne previously. The Bern authorities were represented by a sheriff assisted by several locals, who shared power with a mayor and council drawn largely from the local elite. A Protestant academy for the training of pastors boasted as many as 700 students (a large number for a small town), but in 1559 it moved most of its operations to Geneva in order to bolster the "Welch" character of the Huguenot teaching it so generously dispensed.

For Felix Platter, Lausanne was a familiar and friendly place in terms of both politics and religion, if not language. He remained there only a few hours, however, just long enough to have lunch on October 14.

*   *   *

When he arrived in Geneva from the east, Felix, as he conscientiously inspected the city's fortifications, could not help being impressed by the massiveness of the ramparts and other bastions erected in the 1530s.[2] The suburbs outside the walls had been demolished to enhance security still further. This had made it necessary to relocate 1,700 people, aggravating an already serious housing shortage within the walls. The city's defensive precautions were aimed essentially at the Savoyards. Between 1513 and 1532, Geneva had sought to divorce itself from its bishop and from the dukes of Savoy. After 1532, the combined effects of Farel's preaching and the insistent demands of Bern, a crucial ally, had transformed political emancipation into religious dissidence. When the mass was "finally" abolished in 1535 or 1536, the Genevans, or at any rate those who spoke in their name, decided to live under the law of the Gospel as interpreted and imported by Bernese reformers. The French influence became fundamental: after 1536, through thick and thin, exile and return, the destiny of Calvin was inextricably linked to Geneva.

Calvin's dominance in the city attained its doleful apogee shortly after Felix's visit with the execution of the ultra-Protestant extremist Michael Servetus: Calvin had no desire to be outflanked on his left. Geneva's population was increasing rapidly owing to an influx of Huguenot refugees not only from France but also from Italy and, briefly, from England and other countries as well. From a population of 13,000 in 1550 (the equivalent of Montpellier at the time), the city had grown to at least 22,000 by 1560. Additional stories were added to buildings, houses were divided, and new dwellings were erected in the courtyards of old ones. With the Catholic clergy barred from administering the sacraments, Protestant pastors performed marriages and baptisms as fast as they could. In the wake of the Reformation the local authorities set up German-style guilds of artisans and began regulating the grain trade, despite the fact that Geneva had previously favored a fairly liberal approach to manufacturing and food supply on the model of Lyons. The growth of the printing industry was of considerable importance for the purposes of Huguenot propaganda. Calvin's books became inspirational best-sellers. Among the new industries of the day were the drawing of gold thread and the confection of silk fabric and clocks, which required skilled artisans, many of whom, at least in the silk crafts, came from Italy. Along the northern and western banks of Lake Leman, small craft carried wood and wine to the port of Geneva.

Genevans still spoke a Savoyard dialect in reaction against both the many newcomers from France and their former Savoyard masters, who had spoken French as a language of snobbery and convenience. In Geneva Felix had the honor of meeting Calvin, with whom he was able to converse in Latin. As for French, he did not understand a single word of the sermon the great man delivered to a large congregation in the language of Ronsard. The supreme leader of the French "heretics" chose a new companion for Felix: Michel Héroard, later to be the father of Jean Héroard, Louis XIII's physician. The Parisian bookseller Dupuys (or de Puys), who had bought Thomas Platter's remainders some years earlier, also joined the group, which on October 17 set out for the Rhône and Montpellier. Clearly, Felix was going to have to learn French or else speak Latin. Before leaving Geneva he had spruced himself up with a haircut. Until then he had worn his hair long in the provincial manner of Basel. Short hair had become the custom in the cities of the Empire as well as France, but not in German Switzerland. Having shed his protective mane, he promptly caught a cold, and for several days his nose ran like a fountain.

* * *

Five people set out from Geneva on the afternoon of October 17: Felix, Schöpflin, Héroard and his valet, and Dupuys. The route took the travelers straight to Lyons by way of Collonges and Nantua, with the southern elbow of the Rhône off to their left. In Collonges Felix suffered from nocturnal diarrhea and soiled the inn's circular balcony and freshly painted white walls. (He delights in intimate revelations of this sort.) The innkeeper was livid. The travelers blamed Héroard's valet, who had left early for Nantua to arrange room and board for the others. It is always easiest to blame those not present to defend themselves.

* * *

On October 18 the travelers found themselves on the road, or rather the series of wretched trails, leading from Collonges to Cerdon by way of Nantua. The steep paths took them past many mills powered by rapidly flowing streams. Outside one small town Felix for the first time observed hanged men dangling from gibbets. There were so many of them that to his horror he almost ran into one in the dark. His astonishment suggests that there may have been a difference between French and German customs in hanging, the French displaying the victims publicly outside city limits, the Germans taking a less exhibitionist approach.

* * *

To enter the extreme northern portion of the former Savoyard state in 1552 was to enter "French" territory, though it had not been French for long. The duchy of Savoy had been annexed by Francis I in 1536. The death, in 1535, of Francesco Sforza, the ruler of the Milanese region coveted by the king of France, had incited the latter to cross the Alps and attempt to seize Milan, which had required him to trample on the territories of the legitimate ruler of the north-Alpine state of Savoy, Duke Charles III. In this the French had been aided by their allies in Bern. His Most Christian Majesty the king of France had formed the habit of relying on the aid of Protestant principalities in his perpetual struggle with Charles V, the Hapsburg emperor.

The Bernese, for their part, had advanced as far as Geneva in 1536, thereby covering the northern flank of the French invasion. Seventeen years later, in 1552, at more or less the same time that Felix was beginning his visit to the regions of the Rhône and Languedoc, the victory of French troops under the duc de Guise over Charles V's besieging army at Metz would allow Henri II's agents to consolidate their control over the defunct state of the exiled Charles III. Indeed, the French agents, by no means dogmatic in their tactics, were all the more successful because of their decision to mollify the local populace by allowing them to maintain their venerable representative institutions (the Three Estates) and granting them a brand new Parlement located in Chambéry and of course loyal to the authorities transplanted from the banks of the Seine and the Loire. This Parlement confined itself to persecuting the small handful of local Protestants sufficiently to gladden the hearts of the Catholic clergy who held all the power in this mountainous region—a clergy increasingly inclined to collaborate with the French occupiers.[3] Thus the left hand of Henri II, allied with the German Swiss "heretics," ignored the fact that the right hand did not hesitate to send the Huguenots of Savoy to the stake in the region to the south and northwest of Lake Leman. Savoy—that bastion of the Counter Reformation—was only superficially French in the middle third of the sixteenth century. Its population was growing rapidly, and unlike many invading armies the Valois troops did nothing that might have slowed it down. It had grown 50 percent since the beginning of the century; some cities had doubled in size. As was often the case at the time, human proliferation went hand in hand with misery: in a classic Malthusian "scissors," economic growth and agricultural output failed to keep pace with the increasing population (rural industry was relatively rare in Savoy). Many small farms lacked even a single cow, and country folk reduced to wage labor crowded the roads leading to the cities, especially Lyons, where Felix Platter was also headed but for very different reasons.

In many respects, however, this demographic congestion hints at the powerful vitality of Renaissance Savoy. Nothing comparable would occur in this part of Europe until the nineteenth century. Content to reap the benefits of native energies, the French occupation did no damage to Savoy in the quarter century that it lasted. In 1559 it suddenly came to an end: virtually the entire duchy was restored to the legitimate heir, young Emmanuel Philibert. In command of Spanish troops, this brilliant general had earlier, in 1557, defeated the army of Henri II and his oafish constable Anne de Montmorency near Saint-Quentin. By 1559, however, with the French Wars of Religion already looming, Felix Platter had been back in his native Basel for some time. To him it scarcely mattered whether papist Savoy belonged to the king or the duke now that he had shaken the dust from his traveling boots and settled down back home.

* * *

Felix's visit to Nantua in 1552 certainly caused less of a stir than the visit of Francis I. While passing through Bresse seventeen years earlier, the monarch had stopped in the town and stayed in the local monastery or priory.[4] François and Pierre du Breul, who served successively as priors, remained *savoisiens* at heart. They stood fast against agents of the Valois monarch dispatched by Louis de Lorraine, Cardinal de Guise, the titular possessor of the benefice and a friend of the French crown. In Nantua the Breuls' secret motto was, "Not one monk, not one *sou* for the clergy of France."[5] The town, which stood beside a fish-stocked lake, bore a silver trout upon a lake of sinople on its coat of arms; travelers from Germany, Switzerland, and Italy to the great city of Lyons passed by its gates. Owing to the ease with which brass could be imported, the townspeople had specialized in the manufacture of pins, which they exported to the south. En route, Felix passed trains of mules laden with shipments of these pins. North of Nantua he had unwittingly grazed the edge of a region in which freight transport was dominated by French carters. The narrow, bumpy trails here and elsewhere in the south were inhospitable to wagons, however, and suitable only for pack animals like the mule, or for that matter Felix's horse.

* * *

On Wednesday, October 19, 1552, Felix slowly made his way out of Savoy, at that time under Valois administration, and into the kingdom of France proper. During the morning the travelers passed through a region of steep trails and chestnut forests. In this mountainous region, where grains, the normal source of carbohydrates, were much more difficult to grow than in the endless plains of the Saône and Seine to the north, chestnuts were a useful staple. Felix thus made his first discovery of the vast "chestnut zone" of southern France, which Olivier de Serres would describe a little later as extending through "Dauphiné, Haute-Provence, and parts of Languedoc, the Vivarais, Gévaudan, and Velay. Also Auvergne, the Limousin, Périgord, Guyenne, and several parts of Gascony."[6] In other words, the Alps, the Massif Central, and the southern Jura. At noon, having emerged from the forest of "bread trees," the travelers stopped for lunch[7] in Saint-Maurice-de-Beynost at the Cardinal's Hat Inn.[8] Already the influence of the big Italian bankers of Lyons extended this far into the countryside; later, these same bankers did not consider it beneath their dignity to extend usurious operations to such remote backwaters.[9] That night, after a further journey, Felix and his friends stopped in a small town, where they slept at an inn called the Crown, kept by a drunken German.

Despite this German presence, the travelers were now truly in France, in the kingdom of the Valois, which had been ruled for almost six years by Henri II. In appearance, at any rate, the kingdom was in great shape. Its population was greater than at any time since the Hundred Years' War. In 1552, some twenty million souls were encompassed within the borders of what is now metropolitan France, and perhaps sixteen or seventeen million within the borders of France as they then existed. The wars that French sovereigns had waged since 1494 had affected mainly France's neighbors, leaving French territory largely untouched. Agricultural production, fostered by this lengthy period of internal peace and regional development, was sufficient in most years to feed the bulk of Henri's subjects. To be sure, vigorous demographic growth coupled with rising prices and falling wages had had a deleterious effect on the standard of living of the *menu peuple,* those at the very bottom of the social hierarchy. But even the poor generally "got by," except for those who succumbed in brief periods of increased mortality. Reigning over the whole society was the king, who ruled with a relatively small number of functionaries (some ten thousand *officiers*[10] for the entire country, which is a very small number compared with the millions of civil servants employed by the French state today). The top "official," King Henri II, was a cultivated man, intelligent but not brilliant. He was a competent, decisive military commander. His achievements under the circumstances were quite as impressive as those of Francis I, who, for all his undeniable merits, ultimately suffered a greater number of disastrous reverses than his successor.

Whereas Michelet regarded Henri II as a sad figure in every way,[11] English-speaking historians, as always impartial because not caught up in our Franco-French conflicts, have recently offered a generally positive assessment of this king's activities.[12] Furthermore, his accidental death in 1559, which soon plunged France into a civil war that saw the country martyred by both its liberators and their enemies, in retrospect pointed up the usefulness of a vigorous prince like Henri, who reigned from 1547 to 1559. A certain balance between rival factions—that of Montmorency, more inclined to peace, and that of the Guises, more authoritarian and bellicose, the one and the other firmly associated with the power of the monarch—was essential for keeping the peace at home. It was a precarious peace, to be sure, but infinitely precious given the disastrous bloodletting to come in the period 1560–94. The "Henrician" state was traditional in structure, dominated by the court, the high nobility who were the provincial governors, and the magistrates of *parlement* and the other sovereign courts, who to all intents and purposes owned their offices. Despite the dominance of these archaic or at any rate traditional institutions, the king took steps to modernize his government: he appointed secretaries of state, remote but already powerful forerunners of today's ministers; he also created posts for *intendants des finances,* who functioned as undersecretaries of state in matters of finance, and *intendants de généralité,* still few in number but precursors of the celebrated regional *intendants* destined to play so important a role under Richelieu and an even greater role under Louis XIV. From a literary and artistic point of view, the ongoing Renaissance did not suffer from the death of Francis I, for all his remarkable achievements. Michelet hints at a cultural decline after 1550.[13] The work of the poet Pierre de Ronsard, already in full flower, along with that of the architect Philibert de L'Orme and the painter Primaticcio, among others, should suffice to prove him wrong.

Public order was strenuously maintained in mid-sixteenth-century France, despite some notable lapses. Peasant and urban uprisings in the southwestern part of the country in 1548 were harshly repressed by the royal army. Paradoxically, the rioters achieved their goal, which was to prevent modernization of the tax system in order to facilitate the financing of military operations. Henri had hoped to do this by extending the *gabelle,* or salt tax, to the entire country, including Aquitaine. Although the leaders of the rioting were put to death, the government was forced to abandon plans to institute the *gabelle* in the area between the Loire and the Garonne. Of greater consequence was the significant growth of Protestantism in the cities and even in certain rural areas, especially in the Cévennes. Henri met the wave of "heretical" conversions with harsh repression from which his "class brothers" in the aristocracy were exempt, however. The persecution thus fell on the middle and lower classes. Though strict, the king was by nature a committed Gallican and had no intention of permitting anything like a Spanish Inquisition run by the clergy and agents of the pope on French soil. Hence there was no inquisition as such in France, for which we can only be grateful, although the civil courts were often heavy-handed in religious matters. What is more, Henri was obliged to tread carefully with the Protestant princes of Germany who, like the Zwinglians and other Swiss "heretics," were his allies in his wars with the ultra-Catholic Hapsburgs.

Militarily speaking, the start of Henri's reign was a triumph. Piedmont, Savoy, and Corsica all fell into French hands. The Valois king also extended his possessions to Metz at the expense of Charles V and to Boulogne at the expense of the Tudors. There were disappointments to come, to be sure, but never a disaster as crushing as the French defeat at Pavia in 1526. With its 450,000 square kilometers of territory, its thousand "walled cities," and its big cities with populations as large as 350,000 in the case of Paris, France was the most powerful consolidated territorial state in Western Europe, even if it was surpassed in overall influence by the heterogeneous empire of Charles V, whose far-flung possessions included, in addition to Spain, territories ranging from Germany to Italy and from the Netherlands to the Americas.

But for his unshakable character, Felix could easily have found himself divided between two loyalties: on the one hand his loyalty to the Germanic world of which he was already a distinguished member, *Teutsch* to the very depths of his soul, and on the other his growing loyalty to France, where he remained for more than five years a young man eager to learn, to observe, and to wonder.

* * *

October 20, 1552: "We reached Lyons after crossing a flat plain" (*durch ein eben landt*). The city, in which Felix would remain until the twenty-third, was large for its time and at the peak of its expansion.[14] Its population had more than tripled since the reign of Louis XI to 55,000 or 60,000 by the middle of the sixteenth cenutry, on a par with Florence, Rome, Antwerp, London, and Seville. Italian merchants kept the goods flowing, and trade was further stimulated by the expenditures of the French army as the Valois attempted to make inroads into the Italian peninsula. In printing and silk manufacturing, Lyons was the leading city in France. The bankers of this city at the crossroads of the Savoy, Saône, and Rhône regions lent money to princes bent on military adventures. And merchants, both Italians and to a lesser degree natives, ran things, occupying the highest offices in the so-called *consulat*.

The poor and, more generally, the *menu peuple* certainly did not enjoy their fair share of the growing collective wealth. Yet in the realm of social policy the consuls took the bold step, quite in keeping with the spirit of the times, of creating the Aumône générale, or General Alms, in 1531, to ensure that the poor would always have bread. The city had previously been shaken by popular protest in the *rebeyne*, or rebellion, of 1529, when confraternities of artisans had rioted against high grain prices. After that came the typographers' strike, the first important industrial conflict of modern times. The repercussions of this event, which we detected earlier in Thomas Platter's shop in Basel, were still felt in many Lyons print shops at the time of Felix Platter's brief visit.

Despite the strikes, the vigor of the local publishing industry indicates that Lyons was a city of culture, comparable in this respect to Basel but much more populous than the Swiss city. Furthermore, most artisans were literate, especially those employed in print shops. The city was also distinguished by the work of great poets, among them Louise Labé, who in 1555 published her *Elégies et sonnets,* culminating a long personal and literary journey:

> Baise m'encor, rebaise moy et baise;
> Donne m'en un de tes plus savoureux
> Donne m'en un de tes plus amoureux
> Je t'en rendray quatre plus chaus que braise.

> [Kiss me again, kiss me and kiss me;
> Give me one of your sweetest kisses
> Give me one of your most loving kisses
> And I'll return the favor with four kisses hotter than burning
>   coals.]

In this warm (and not simply puritanical) soil, Protestantism took root before and after Felix's visit. In 1546, the Pardon of Saint John, a summer festival that was at once religious and communal, was disrupted, some said polluted, by Huguenot demonstrations. In 1551, Henri issued the royal edict of Châteaubriant, intended to stamp out heresy and the sale of proscribed books. In May 1553, a half-dozen students educated in Lausanne were burned alive on the Place des Terreaux in Lyons despite appeals from the Protestant cities of Switzerland, Œcolampadian and Zwinglian alike. In the spring of 1561, the Reformation was in serious trouble up and down the valley of the Rhône.

Felix in 1552 had a front-row seat. In October, on his way to Lyons, he saw a "Christian in a shirt," that is, a Huguenot, with a huge bundle of straw tied to his back to fuel the fire in which he was to be burned to death.[15] Felix's cool eyewitness account contrasts with the descriptions of his suffering when, as a child, he heard stories of little girls being put to death in the Netherlands for the good Protestant cause. At this point he sees himself as an anatomist, a strictly objective observer. He became inured to seeing martyrs on their way to execution, just as he had overcome his fear after bumping into the hanged man on the way to Lyons (F 137, 138).

In Lyons, a great European crossroads, he also heard news of great events connected with the history of the Reformation. He learned of the victories of Colonel Schertlin, whose misadventures in Basel had kept that city amused some months earlier. With his band of anti-imperial Protestant mercenaries, Schertlin, in Picardy, had defeated a colonel from the Netherlands in the service of Charles V. The defeated soldier was named Martin Rossheim, and he had made a name for himself by laying waste to Picardy, pillaging the countryside at will and wreaking havoc in the rear of French forces. He also lined his pockets in the unscrupulous tradition of the generals and *condottieri* of the time.[16] The Rossheim-Schertlin battle was a minor episode in the vast conflict between Charles V and the Protestant princes of Germany, backed by Henri II of France. The French king had taken Metz from the Imperials a short while earlier. He now made ready to protect his conquest and in the final weeks of 1552 turned back the emperor's counteroffensive.

For Felix, Lyons was above all a stopping place, a way station on his journey southward. For lodging, he had the choice of at least fifty hotels equipped to receive numerous travelers, especially itinerant merchants who came to the city for its fairs or simply to trade.[17] The young man from Basel chose, as he often would in the course of his extended travels, to stay with a German host, with whom he felt safer. He therefore took a room, or at any rate a bed, at the sign of the Bear, an inn kept by a Swiss compatriot, Paul Herbelin of Zurich (F 138). The other guests were all German. There was even a stove, made of terra-cotta or tile, just as in Basel; such stoves were rare in France. The average price of lodging in a hotel of this caliber, neither overly luxurious nor unbearably bug-ridden, was fourteen or fifteen sous per night (for comparison, the average daily wage of a construction worker was five sous at midcentury).[18] This bears out Felix's statement that he spent fifty sous for three nights' lodging in Lyons, from October 20 to October 23, 1552. Fortunately, he had his own horse. Hiring a mount would have increased his daily outlay by half.[19]

When it came to horses, incidentally, the members of Felix's traveling party were not always lucky. One of them (Schöpflin) had purchased a mount in Basel from none other than Werner Wölflin, a draper and city council member with a good reputation among his fellow businessmen. The horse had seemed superb but soon proved to be lame and useless. Had the buyer been swindled? In any case, he was obliged to sell the horse for almost nothing in Lyons. True, horses, whether used by travelers or merchants, were often overloaded with heavy baggage in addition to their riders.[20] Schöpflin was forced to continue his journey down the Rhône by riverboat, aboard one of the countless vessels that drifted or were rowed downstream filled with donkeys, grain, and bundles of fabric. On the return trip they were hauled upriver by men or animals (horses or donkeys).

* * *

Felix's "naval" experience on the Rhône was less extensive: he had only to cross the river, not travel downstream, to visit his future teacher, Professor Rondelet of the medical school in Montpellier, who was then staying in Lyons. But after boarding a ferry he found himself threatened by the woman in charge, who promised to hurl him into the river if he did not pay an exorbitant fare for passage. He had no choice but to fork over the cash. This is all we know about the strange company of *traversières*, or female ferry operators, who made it possible to cross the Rhône; none of the other sources mentions them.[21]

Dr. Rondelet, whose presence enticed young Felix to cross the Rhône, had come up from Montpellier to treat Cardinal de Tournon, lieutenant general of the province since 1542 and archbishop of Lyons since 1551. After suffering temporary disgrace following the death of Francis I, the cardinal, in Rome, soon contrived to patch up a rift between the pope and the king of France. On his return from Italy in September of 1552, he made a triumphal entry into Lyons.[22] He was welcomed by various official bodies, including the monks and the clergy, the corporations of German, Milanese, Luccan, and Florentine merchants, and, last but not least, the consuls of the city. All wore sumptuous costumes of satin and velvet, with black the predominant color. The cardinal, however, wore red and white. But his splendor proved ephemeral: worn out by old age and diplomatic vexations, the prelate was soon forced to take to his bed. On October 14 his condition improved, but the steadfast Dr. Rondelet was reluctant to leave his bedside. Felix was therefore obliged to go to the archbishop's residence to visit the already famous professor of medicine from Montpellier.

*   *   *

Guillaume Rondelet was born in Montpellier in 1507, one of many children of a man whose business was selling fragrances, a sort of olfactory apothecary.[23] Was it because he had been put out to nurse as an infant that Guillaume had been a weak and sickly child afflicted with every disease known to man other than elephantiasis? Or so he said, with the same playful sense of humor that had landed him a part, along with his fellow medical student François Rabelais, in a comic play about a doctor and a mute woman that was performed in Montpellier in 1530. An orphan from an early age, Rondelet was educated under the supervision of an elder brother and for a time supported and housed by his sister Catherine, the well-endowed widow of a wealthy Florentine merchant who had settled years earlier in Languedoc. As the University of Montpellier's *procureur,* or student representative, Guillaume soon took up Protestant ideas, but his religious convictions did not prevent him from associating with and treating prelates of the Catholic Church.

Like the Platters, Rondelet got around. He had lived for several years in Paris, where, like many of his contemporaries among the elite of southern France, he had become steeped in Latin and indeed in French culture. He had also attended the great Italian universities in Padua, Ferrara, Bologna, and Pisa. As a young man, he had briefly earned a living practicing medicine in the small towns of the Vaucluse and the Massif Central. In the French capital he had been greatly influenced by his friend Jean Gonthier from Andernach, a native of Germany educated in the Netherlands and in France and one of the foremost anatomists of the Renaissance. An impassioned anatomist himself, Rondelet would have dissected father, mother, children, and friends had the opportunity arisen (on occasion it did arise when a close acquaintance passed away). He made efforts, at times successful, to secure the patronage of various powerful lords, lay as well as ecclesiastic, including the bishop of Montpellier and above all Cardinal de Tournon, who became his primary patron. This achievement was all the more noteworthy because Tournon, since 1527 or 1528, had been, in theory at any rate, a fierce enemy of Protestantism in France and elsewhere. Apparently the prince of the Church whom Dr. Rondelet served as physician was not greatly troubled by the medical man's heterodox views in matters of religion. In any case, Dr. Rondelet frequently left his patron to resume teaching at Montpellier. He was appointed to a chair at the university there in 1545. When the cardinal fell ill in 1552, however, the doctor left Montpellier for Lyons in order to attend at his bedside. The great physician briefly interrupted his supervision of the patient's enemas to receive Felix.[24] Evidently the interview went well on both sides, for Rondelet, the eminent botanist and dissector, became the teacher who initiated Felix into the mysteries of human anatomy and the classification of herbs.

On October 23, 1552, Felix and his friends left Lyons for Vienne. Thomas Schöpflin traveled by boat on the Rhône. Felix and Michel Héroard rode along the left bank. Their route thus took them into the Dauphiné, a region that they would come to know better as they approached the city of Vienne. It was a rich province, of course, and one in feverish expansion following the (temporary) annexation of Savoy to France in 1536. The Chartreuse mountains and the Piedmontese marquisate of Saluces (Saluzzo) thus came under the jurisdiction of the ruler of Dauphiné, who saw himself as the inheritor of the old imperialist mantle of the Allobroges.[25]

That night the travelers arrived in Vienne, where they stayed at the Auberge de Sainte-Barbe on rue de la Chèvrerie in the Est district.[26] The morning of the twenty-fourth was devoted to touring the city; there was much to see. Vienne, the second largest city in Dauphiné, with roughly

8,000 inhabitants (compared with 12,000 in Grenoble, the provincial capital), deserved better than the Basel tourist's disdainful description of it as an *alt stettlin,* or little old city (F 139).[27] In truth, Felix was not very interested in the city's churches and chapels, of which there were dozens, along with hundreds of priests—a profusion of targets for the virulent propaganda of the local Protestants. The "heretic" Michael Servetus was living in Vienne at the time, quietly drafting a text of fire and brimstone. What caught Felix's eye, in any event, were the old Roman ruins: a theater, the temple of Augustus and Livia, the portico of the baths, a temple of Cybele, an odeon, and the pyramid of the circus, not all of which were identified. Of these he was most interested in the pyramid, of which he left a fairly decent sketch and a verbal description: "It is pointed, built by the Romans, and beautiful in its antiquity." He of course had no idea that in imperial times this pyramid stood at the center of a raised area in the center of a track around which chariots raced.

*   *   *

The tour of Vienne was soon complete, and the travelers prepared to set out again later that same day, Schöpflin still traveling by boat, Felix and Héroard still on horseback. They exchanged loud greetings back and forth from towpath to river. After traveling a few miles, the two riders encountered a tributary of the Rhône that was swollen by a recent storm and impassable. Meanwhile, a "great lord" arrived en route to the south with five horses and a retinue of servants. It was Pierre Danès, tutor to the dauphin, the future Francis II (the Short). Since Danès and Felix could not communicate in French or German, they conversed in Latin. It was a stroke of good luck for the young man from Basel. Danès, born in 1497 to a family of Parisian drapers and furriers, had been a professor at the Collège Royal.[28] Now living on ecclesiastical benefices (as curé of Suresnes), he had enjoyed a long career as a humanist and royal functionary. Though he wrote little, he had produced an edition of Pliny the Elder. He knew Aristotle, Cicero, and Lucian like the back of his hand. And at one time or another he had been a disciple or friend of Budé, Dolet, Turnèbe, Marot, Oronce Finé, and many others.

Steeped in Erasmian evangelism, pre-Reformation ideas, Italian culture, and a Paduan rationalism that smacked of heresy,[29] but at the same time a zealous and obsequious servant of the kings of France, the excellent Danès was also the protégé of important prelates and cardinals such as Charles de Lorraine, Selve, Tournon, and Contarini—the elite of the conclave. The potential Huguenot in him never materialized. He rejected schism as he rejected the inconvenient rigors of the Augustinian-

Calvinist idea of grace. He was a Pelagian and friend of the Jesuits, and he ended up bishop of Lavaur and a rather hard-nosed Catholic militant. But in 1552, as he traveled in Dauphiné, he was at the midpoint of a lengthy career that had taken him as the French representative to the Council of Trent in 1546. In 1556 he would be appointed to the coveted position of confessor to his pupil the dauphin. At mid-century, however, Danès was still open-minded and tolerant and especially curious about the thinking of the young. He questioned Felix endlessly about political and religious problems in Basel, a notorious hotbed of heresy.[30] While waiting for the swollen tributary of the Rhône to subside, Pierre Danès took his new friend to see a local nobleman, a penniless petty aristocrat and gentleman farmer in the manner of Olivier de Serres, who cordially received the travelers in his humble farmhouse and served them lunch, for which he charged them—such were the straits to which the lesser nobility were reduced. After lunch the travelers returned to the river, having been informed by a servant that the waters had subsided. Danès's horse led the way across the submerged ford, and Felix followed. The caravan stopped for the night in Saint-Vallier, a small town of one or two thousand inhabitants that was one of many towns affected by the general growth in population.[31] The rising demographic tide stimulated consumption, commerce, and agriculture, strengthened local and fiscal authorities, and promoted education, all in symbiosis, in Saint-Vallier as elsewhere.[32] A population of drapers, papermakers (serving the Lyons printers), postal riders, carpenters, blacksmiths, locksmiths, masons, salt transporters (remember the *gabelle*), ferrymen, barbers, tailors, cobblers, weavers, dyers, mercers, and of course the inevitable butchers, bakers, and millers animated this tiny but lively town.[33]

Felix, not wanting to be left out of things, stammered his first words of French on the night of October 24: "*Donne-moi allons,*" he said at the inn to the servants of Pierre Danès, for he had somehow gotten the idea that the word *allons,* which he heard frequently, meant *drincken,* to drink (F 141). Sixty years later, having long since discovered his mistake, he was still laughing about it.

It was also later, sometime in the period between 1609 and 1612 when he was writing his memoirs, that Felix, then in his seventies, rounded out his account of the next stage of his journey down the Rhône in 1552 after leaving Saint-Vallier on the morning of October 25. The travelers passed close to a mountain, where they recognized, on their left, from descriptions they had heard, an old (Roman?) building known locally as the "house of Pilate." The legend that Pontius Pilate had died in the valley of the Rhône lived on in the memory of the people of Dauphiné as well as in

German scholarship. Pilate, Felix tells us, was supposed to have ended his days in misery in the house that the travelers recognized in passing. By the time the elderly physician completed his memoirs, however, he had gained further knowledge of the story of Pilate from a work published in Basel in 1610, which he read shortly thereafter. This text uses almost the exact same wording as Felix does, stating that Pilate had lived in the valley "in misery" (*ins ellendt* or *im ellendt*).[34] All of southeastern France was awash with folklore into which bits of biblical stories had been woven, so that people like Mary Magdalene and Pontius Pilate were associated with various places in the region.

Felix next crossed the Isère by ferry (*im schif*), complete with horse and baggage, and arrived in Valence on the night of October 25. The city, with its double walls and stout towers, its well-irrigated pasture to the east of the ramparts, and its grain, wool, and above all salt markets, was a sight to see. With 1,800 houses and five to six thousand inhabitants, it was much more than a *stettlin*, or small town, but rather, as Felix put it, a *statt*, or major city. A conscientious student, Felix noted the presence of a university, which was growing rapidly at the time and competing successfully with the efforts of rival intellectuals in Grenoble. Naturally the young traveler's attention was drawn by the medical teaching in Valence: by the late 1560s, when Felix's career was flourishing in Basel, Valence was awarding three to six doctorates in medicine annually.[35] In the early 1550s, however, the school was oriented more toward law than medicine owing to the influence of Italian universities in Bologna, Padua, Pavia, and Pisa.[36] At the noon meal our young traveler was approached by a servant in the inn who offered him a juicy pear in exchange for a little loving. The adolescent Felix turned red as a beet and took off. A hundred years later, in 1661, Racine had no better luck with another servant in Valence, who stuck a chafing dish under his bed in place of the chamber pot. Was this a linguistic misunderstanding, as Racine believed, or a pratical joke that the budding poet failed to grasp?

*   *   *

From Valence, Felix Platter and Michel Héroard continued on to the confluence of the Rhône and the Drôme, which joined the Rhône on its east bank. They crossed by ferry, which had its perils, but this time there was no mishap. Ferries remained in use in the area until 1789, when a bridge was completed, establishing a "veritable link between north and south."

The travelers passed Livron, a fortified city capped by a an enchanted tower complete with fairies overlooking the valley of the Drôme and the road to Marseilles; they stopped just long enough to await the ferry. Although Livron was a small town of 1,500, it boasted some twenty priests and other clergy distributed among its parish church and fourteen chapels. Apart from its walls, the town was also protected by drawbridges and massive gates. A castellan dispensed justice in the name of the bishop of Valence and monitored the activities of the consuls, who were more or less democratically elected—actually rather less than more. Felix noted the presence of a hospital, a grain market, several other markets, and a set of measuring stones. René Favier has classified sixteenth-century Livron as a "large town."[37] Nevertheless, the place made a strong impression on the visitor from Basel. When he wrote his memoirs some sixty years after his visit, he mentioned the siege of Livron, which, having been infiltrated by Huguenots, became Protestant sometime after 1560. In 1574 a royal and Catholic army under the command of the maréchal de Bellegarde laid siege to the town on behalf of Henri III. Three thousand cannonballs and numerous assaults failed to overcome the tenacity of Livron's defenders, including women who, distaffs in hand, mocked the enemy from the town walls and later avenged themselves in a deplorable way on the bodies of slain attackers. The arrival of reinforcements led by the young duc de Lesdiguières, who would go on to even greater achievements, forced the Catholics to call off the siege.[38]

* * *

After a short additional ride, the busy day of October 25 came to an end in Loriol, a town of 300 houses and 1,500 inhabitants under the jurisdiction of the bishop of Valence. There the travelers bedded down for the night at the Three Kings, an inn whose name evokes the three magi of the Gospel. An impressive town of moderate size, Loriol did not lack for protection. A wall with fifteen towers was intended to dissuade the French army, which often passed by on its way to Italy, from disporting itself within. The century's prosperity had left its mark, even if the gains were not evenly distributed. Four annual fairs and a weekly market had been authorized or confirmed by letters-patent from the king since 1535. The people, however, especially the poor, were no better off than elsewhere. Yet they did enjoy the consolation—laughable, to be sure, in the eyes of a Protestant medical student like Felix Platter—of a collegial church containing the jaw of Saint Romain de Barral still blessed with all its teeth, a relic granted to the town by divine dispensation to offer healing to those afflicted with diseases of the mouth.

On the morning of October 26, Felix left the inn in Loriol. Proceeding without haste, he arrived a few hours later for lunch in Montélimar, a city of 6,000 with winding, narrow, filthy streets. Montélimar was famous for the manufacture of "Morocco leather" (and after 1759 would be famous also for its nougat). New vineyards and fields were clustered around the city's gates, attesting here as elsewhere in the region to recent growth typical of the Renaissance. Montiliens (as the residents were known) still shuddered at the memory of the German-speaking landsknechts (mercenaries) who had plagued the region in the second decade of the century. The city claimed exemption from royal taxes, but neither the sovereign on the banks of the Seine nor the parlement in Grenoble was impressed.

Our riders, following the course of the Rhône, crossed the city from north to south almost without stopping. They entered through the Porte Saint-Martin on Montélimar's northern edge, then proceeded along rue Droite, rue Alamanderie, rue Fruiterie, rue Saunière, rue Barute, and rue Charreterie to the Porte d'Aygu. Along the way they passed, on their right, the collegiate church of Sainte-Croix, then under restoration; and also on their right the Franciscan convent, where Huguenot influence had reared its head (urban women were particularly receptive to Huguenot preaching). Finally, toward the end of their route, they passed the Commandery of Saint John of Jerusalem on their left. That same evening, October 26, Héroard and Platter reached Pierrelatte, where they stopped for the night. The *bourgade* stood at the foot of a steep cliff topped by a pair of chapels dedicated to the Holy Angels and a fortress preceded by a gateway dating from the time of the Black Plague. Eleven years later, Pierrelatte achieved a modest celebrity that it could have done without: in July 1562, the baron des Adrets, commanding a small army of Protestants and cutthroats, massacred many local residents along with a royal and Catholic garrison composed mainly of *arquebusiers* (harquebus men) from Provence.[39] Felix, always curious about herbs and trees, noticed the many olive trees already in evidence here, at the northern extreme of the olive-growing zone, as well as further south along the flat road leading from Pierrelatte to Pont Saint-Esprit. Indeed, the growth of the economy, steady in the sixteenth century and intermittent later on, led to a gradual northward extension of the olive-growing zone.[40] In October of 1552, it was in Pierrelatte that Felix, traveling down the Rhône from Lyons, first encountered olive trees laden with green, red, and black fruit, already ripe but still quite bitter for his taste. Three centuries later, Flahaut encountered olive groves ten kilometers farther north, in Viviers. On the right bank of the great river one finds a similar progression: in 1595, according to Thomas Platter Jr., the northern tip of the olive region was located in Bourg-Saint-Andéol; by 1886 it had moved thirty-three ki-lometers upstream. The olive tree thus traveled northward at the respect-able speed of one kilometer per decade, or ten kilometers per century.

In any case, it was almost time for the annual beating of the trees and gathering of olives. Meanwhile, poplar, elm, apple, pear, plum, cherry, and fruit-laden chestnut trees were beginning to shed their leaves. Beg-gars hastened to fill baskets with fallen chestnuts. The leaves on grape-vines turned yellow, but the holly remained green. Turnip-digging time had arrived. Slugs devastated freshly sown wheat fields. Many children still went barefoot despite the autumn mud. And people faced the threat of pestilential fevers.

*   *   *

On October 27, after a brief excursion through the olive groves to the eastern end of Pont Saint-Esprit, the famous bridge across the Rhône, Felix, Héroard, and Danès arrived at the walls of Orange, which Felix described as a "little old city" (*gar alt stettlin*) despite the fact that its pop-ulation stood at about 5,000—a sort of second Montélimar. Orange, ad-ministered by consuls and syndics, belonged in theory and occasionally in practice to the Dutch prince of Nassau, whose officials met with oppo-sition, at times bloody, from elements of the populace and from a pro-French faction of the elite. In 1549 the ongoing struggle between the Valois and the Hapsburgs emboldened agents of Henri II to seize con-trol. Vicissitudes of politics aside, cultural forces also propelled the city toward closer ties with France: minutes of council meetings had been kept in French rather than Latin since 1525. Some twenty years later, in 1547, the first Protestants began to emerge from a prolonged period of heretical ferment. The local bishop, Rostaing de La Baume-Suze, who had occupied the episcopal throne since 1543, responded relatively mildly, sentencing heretics, some of whom may have enjoyed the long arm of Nassau's protection, to prison terms on bread and water. During the few hours that Felix spent in Orange, he explored mainly the city's Roman antiquities, especially the triumphal arch, which was used as a target by crossbow marksmen, and the proscenium of the theater, which—progress being unstoppable—was used in a similar way by sharpshooters equipped with the more modern harquebus.[41]

On the evening of October 27 Felix and his companions reached Avig-non, which our memoirist describes as a *mechtige stat,* a large and power-ful city. Despite the departure of the popes, Avignon was still a fairly large city in 1552. Its population in the middle third of the sixteenth century numbered some fifteen or sixteen thousand, smaller, to be sure, than the thirty thousand of 1368 or the forty thousand of 1343, when the Avignon papacy was at its height. Still, in the reign of Henri II, the number of people living in the city was still almost triple the five or six thousand who had lived there when Clement V, the first pope to reside in Avignon, arrived in 1309.[42] In any case, by the time Felix visited Avignon, the human dimension of the city had shrunk owing to the papacy's return to the Vatican in the previous century, whereas the physical dimension remained as vast as it had been in the fourteenth century. By 1552 the visitor to Avignon did not feel cramped—certainly no cause to complain.

What is more, the city remained a business center for Italian merchants with connections in Lyons and Marseilles and export-import routes extending as far as the Levant. Not far from the city, mills on the Sorgue produced paper (supplying printers in Lyons, who generally drew their raw materials from the south). In the manufacture of silk and velvet for merchants in Milan and Lyons, Avignon was second only to Lyons. And money from Avignon was invested in farms throughout the Comtat Venaissin. Many people took a dim view of usury, a business in which Jews served as intermediaries—and as scapegoats.[43] Usury aside, we must be careful not to idealize this region's undeniable prosperity in the mid-sixteenth century. Hard times were frequent during and after the reign of Francis I, and falling wages imposed hardships on this Judeo-Christian community. At the time of Felix's visit, some of the most enlightened minds in Avignon were giving thought to setting up a central almshouse for the poor, a step finally taken in 1555.

Avignon did not live by silk, paper, low wages, and alms alone. The most important industry in this bustling city was still Catholicism, which drew in huge sums through the tithe and distributed equally huge sums in the form of prebends, contracts, and expenditures of all kinds, thereby exerting a tremendous influence on the local economy. The cumbersome papal bureaucracy was another source of profit: in the sixteenth century it included a cardinal legate, an archbishop, and several chapters of canons. Every year six hundred or more priests and deacons were ordained; the vast majority then left Avignon to find work (or unemployment) elsewhere. In addition, the municipal authorities subsidized frequent and impressive processions. Private devotional services created a demand for printed books of hours. In short, the religious life of the city was extraordinarily robust, even if some of the local prelates were known to keep concubines in their homes. Children's choirs were directed by well-trained singing teachers, whose efforts ensured that the musical life of the city could rival that of Basel and Nuremberg. When young Felix fell briefly into a deep depression in Avignon, he revived his spirits by visiting two suburban churches, where singing and organ music eased his pain. "God sustained me," he wrote (F 142). In this case God was not specifically either Huguenot or papist but an ecumenical Heavenly Father who presided over church music that enabled the young traveler to overcome his melancholy. When it came to religion, Felix was not a narrow-minded sectarian, as Montaigne would observe in 1580.

*   *   *

For a young man not previously troubled by adversity, the evening of October 27 and the entire following day in Avignon were painful and even depressing. Pierre Danès departed, on friendly terms to be sure, for his estate in Provence and a glorious future: within a few years he became confessor to the king's children and bishop of Lavaur. The adolescent traveler and the middle-aged humanist promised to see each other again, but their paths diverged: friendships begun while traveling are often short-lived. Felix also parted company temporarily with Michel Héroard, who advised him to find a room in Villeneuve-lès-Avignon. Accommodations there were less costly than in Avignon proper, and the churches were admirable. Héroard, meanwhile, went to comfortable quarters in the home of a friend of his, the master of the Avignon mint; a great deal of metal flowed through the city, some of it precious, some not, and much of it suitable for coinage. Héroard's friend tampered with the scales used to weigh copper for making the *billon*, a small, not very valuable coin of copper-silver alloy. Only later was this secret revealed.

At the Inn of the Cock, a second-rate hotel in the suburb of Villeneuve-lès-Avignon, Felix rubbed shoulders with rough (*rauwen*) boatmen wearing blue caps and bell-bottom trousers. Afraid of being murdered, he spent a lonely, sleepless night. He was completely miserable, and his horse, tied up in an adjoining stable, was no happier among the strange draft horses in the neighboring stalls. The next morning, Felix cried for a long time on his beloved horse's withers; he spoke to the animal in German, a language that the beast appeared to understand.[44] The clouds hanging over Felix seemed to dissipate, however, as the day wore on: the church music helped, and then he was invited to eat and sleep at the home of the mint official where Héroard was staying. Felix's "depression" was over as quickly as it began. In a good mood he set out again, at dawn on October 29, for Languedoc, accompanied by his friend Héroard. The two crossed the celebrated Pont d'Avignon and stopped at the wretched Inn of the Cock just long enough to pay Felix's bill. The hostess, a woman who knew how to do sums, totaled up the bill on a slate or board while Felix looked on: the total was twenty-one sous, two of which went for a tip. With her left hand the woman fingered her rosary. Arguing about the bill was out of the question: she spoke the *langue d'oc* (the dialect of the region), and Felix spoke German. It was the same difficulty he had faced earlier with the far more aggressive woman aboard the ferry. But the rosary is significant: it reminds us that Felix's visits to the Catholic churches of the Comtat had a radical effect on him. Henceforth, wherever he traveled as a tourist or on business, he deigned to take an interest in the churches of the Roman religion, whereas previously he had had eyes only for Protestant churches and Latin antiquities. His sensibility had evolved; his travels had made him more open-minded.

* * *

At the first rise in the trail to the west, Felix's horse began to limp. It had picked up a pebble between its shoe and hoof. With the pebble removed, the horse again moved at a good clip. The riders crossed the Gardon by ferry. At midday on October 29 they stopped at the Inn of the Angel in the large village of Sernhac (200 hearths, 1,000 inhabitants). The innkeeper's daughter attempted to greet Felix with the customary kiss, but our naive traveler spurned the girl's offer and immediately departed for Nîmes. As timid as he was, he was just beginning to learn the ways of Languedoc.[45] In general, conditions there were much the same as in Savoy and Dauphiné: demographic growth had led to crowding in many villages and towns; economic output had increased dramatically, but not enough to offset the concomitant increase in population; members of the elite had grown wealthy and cultivated; and a segment of the *menu peuple* had been reduced to poverty. At the time of Felix's visit, however, the food situation was not too bad. In October 1552, shortly before his arrival, the Provincial Estates in Nîmes had granted permission for free trade in grain between *sénéchaussées,* from Beaucaire to Carcassonne and vice versa. Export of grain outside the province was prohibited, however, which suggests that although there was a certain reserve of grain in storage, it was not sufficient to remove all worry about what might happen in future winters. War raged elsewhere, but it was not an immediate concern. Nobles did have to remain in readiness, however. In June 1552, the blue-blooded reserves of the region, the *ban* and the *arrière-ban,* had been summoned to fight the Spaniards, but in July it was learned that the Iberian galleys had withdrawn and there was nothing more to fear, even if some commoners may have felt threatened by the unruly behavior of the nobles who had responded to the call. Meanwhile, in October, came the first news of the siege of Metz, which Guise was defending against the forces of Charles V.

The progress made by the Protestant religion in Languedoc was as "worrisome" as in other regions, if not more so. A provincial council was therefore held in Narbonne in 1551; the failure of nearly all the bishops of the province to attend shows that certain abuses persisted. The council decided to prohibit the use of churches for celebrating the festival of fools and the festival of choir children, which were considered to be too profane. Dancing in churches and cemeteries was also forbidden. Priests were requested to decline invitations to so-called banquets *de fructu* at which people sang grotesque "psalms" such as *"Memento David sans truffe."* But these measures came late. In Nîmes, Felix's destination on this stage of his journey, several heretics had been burned in August of 1551 and their property confiscated. Agents appointed by the parlement of Toulouse also tracked down Huguenots in Montpellier, Montagnac, Béziers, and Pézenas. There were well-defined limits to the persecution, however, as we shall see later on.

On the night of October 29, Felix and Michel reached Nîmes, where they stayed at the Red Apple Inn. The next morning they visited the Arena and admired the statue of Romulus and Remus. This work shows the two boys with the she-wolf, one leaning against her thigh, the other at her nipples and seemingly caressed by the animal (F 143).[46] The two travelers were also interested in another statue at the Arena, this one depicting a man with three heads, two of them bearded, all three surmounted by a crown. This "Tricephalus" can be seen today at the Musée de Lyon.[47] The amphitheater also contained a trio of priapic statues, one with birds pecking at its phallus "representing the passions that cause us to suffer a thousand pains." Much later, Thomas Platter Jr. would be quite impressed by this same statue.[48]

During the first three decades of the sixteenth century, the pious agricultural laborers who inhabited Nîmes witnessed innumerable impressive miracles at the city's Holy Cross. But times had changed. A plague of paupers after 1530 persuaded a ruling class steeped in Renaissance humanism that strict regulations had to be imposed on the poor. Beggars were compelled to comply with the new rules or else be thrown into irons or sent to the galleys. The authorities closed the local brothel in 1532 to prevent the spread of venereal disease. Although the municipal government was run by lay officials, it claimed the right to reform convents and monitor the activities of nuns. "Heresy," encouraged by the moralistic bent of municipal reformers, drew numerous recruits; its future was assured.

Several bishops of Nîmes belonged to the Briçonnet family of Tours and were protégés of Marguerite de Navarre, who was favorably disposed to Erasmian humanism; these absentee bishops favored church reforms so long as they remained moderate. The spread of Protestantism was further aided by the fact that the clergy in Nîmes were less vigilant against it than were their colleagues in Avignon, where agents of the pope kept a close eye on things. In 1534 a new *collège,* or high school, began to offer quality teaching, and this, too, aided, among other things, the Huguenot "sect." In this city of six to seven thousand people, proud of its Roman monuments but marred by a haphazard maze of fetid sewers and alleyways, traditional Catholicism was on the decline. Torture and burnings slowed the progress of Protestantism, but once incidents of rioting and iconoclasm broke out in 1561, a Calvinist seizure of power seemed inevitable. The growth of the wool and especially the silk industry lay in the future, primarily in the seventeenth and eighteenth centuries. In 1552, when Felix passed through Nîmes, times were good: neither plague nor famine afflicted the city. Things would change shortly, but the peaceful interlude is worth noting.[49]

The Swiss visitor's brief passage fell among a series of events that reveal something of the flavor of life in Nîmes in 1552. Pierre d'Airebaudouze, a prominent local citizen who had been converted to Calvin's new dogma by the secret teachings of the *collège,* fled to Geneva in that year. In June, sentinels were posted atop the towers of the Dominican church and the church of Saint-Antoine to watch for a possible Spanish invasion. Kegs of wine were laid in for a meeting of the Estates of Languedoc in October 1552. The new presidial (a court of justice) was installed in December. The cattle market, which had been banished for a time to a location two leagues from the city, was returned to a new suburban site near the Carmelite convent. And in what was apparently a sign of good economic times, a commercial exchange, providing such services as currency conversion, was established on a square adjacent to the cathedral, the Calade.[50]

Felix raced through the city's antiquities early in the morning on October 30. When his brief archeological tour was complete, he and Michel left for Montpellier. They stopped for lunch in Lunel, a small town (*stettlin*) of 2,500 inhabitants located between the two larger cities.[51] The route was bordered by olive groves set among fields of barley and wheat. In Lunel Felix drank his first mug of muscatel, which was either produced locally or imported from Frontignan. Although it was late October, the weather was hot, which surprised the Swiss traveler used to Basel's cool autumns. After lunch, the two young men, acquiescing in southern custom, bedded down on straw mattresses for a siesta at a local inn. Before long, however, they were on their feet again and ready to go. A livestock town with muddy streets, Lunel stood close to broad pastures and coastal salt marshes. Many of the buildings and implements in the town and the surrounding countryside had survived from the Middle Ages, predating the years of crisis (1348–1450). The ramparts, built in the thirteenth and refurbished in the first half of the fifteenth century, traced the limits of a town almost triple the size of the old Roman *castrum,* vestiges of which could still be seen in the pattern of streets intersecting the main north-south (Sommières-Mauguio) and east-west (Nîmes-Montpellier) roads. The banner of Catholicism still flew high in Lunel in 1552, perhaps owing to the memory of Saint Gerard, who was said to have belonged to a family of local nobles. And there was also the memory of Saint Anthony of Padua, who had allegedly performed the miracle of silencing frogs whose croaking had disturbed the prayers of the local Franciscans, or so the hagiographies reported a phenomenon that may have been a consequence of the destruction of a swamp ecology by urbanization. Yet all of these vestiges of Catholicism, starting with the monastery of the Franciscans, or *cordeliers,* which had been richly endowed as recently as the time of Francis I, would be swept away within a few years by Protestantism, which surely must already have been deeply entrenched at the time of Felix's passage.

In leaving Lunel, incidentally, Héroard and Platter escaped another rather dangerous band of professional thieves who plundered travelers in the vicinity of a suburban tavern known as La Bégude Blanche. This was another of the unlicensed inns that Henri II's agents had been trying to close down for years without success. Order was not established in this regard until the seventeenth century. The two young men proceeded toward Montpellier, their ultimate destination. In this large city the presidial, established only in 1552, had just asserted jurisdiction over the barony of Lunel, which had formerly been attached to the *sénéchaussée* of Nîmes and Beaucaire. Riding westward on the afternoon of October 30, Michel Héroard was pleased to think that he would spend the night in the city of his birth. En route the two riders passed through Sambres, which Felix, in his memoirs, mistakenly refers to as Chambéry. A little farther on, at the Pont du Lez near the inn of Castelnau, the young man from Basel again saw the bodies of hanged men whose souls had departed for a better world. Although the past few weeks on the road had surely hardened him, this sight made an unpleasant impression on him and made him feel strange (*seltzam*). The "depression" he had experienced in Avignon returned. He uttered one last prayer (whether silently or out loud he does not say); it is the first time he has mentioned praying since his departure. In his prayer Felix begged God to grant him grace (*gnodt*) —he was, after all, a Protestant—in his studies and his eventual return to Switzerland. From a hillside topped by a cross the two travelers enjoyed a panoramic view of the capital of Languedoc and—an important first for Felix—the Mediterranean to the south.

At the gates of the city, Platter again felt anxious, a feeling comprehensible in an adolescent entering a strange city for the first time—in this case a city capable of disconcerting even a native Frenchman, for the cities of southern France are not like cities elsewhere. Fortunately, the first sights Felix saw inside the walls were a pleasant change after the hanged men he had seen at Castelnau, and this revived his spirits. The two riders (who remained on their horses even inside the city proper) encountered a group of distinguished citizens, possibly nobles, all dressed in white and carrying banners and stringed instruments. They held silver shells and spoons with which they made a loud racket. With these spoons they also distributed candies and sweets to the well-born young ladies they passed along the way.

The explanation for all this is that it was the day before All Saints' Day, which is followed by All Souls' Day. And October 31 is also Halloween, once a pagan festival of death and witchcraft, which has been preserved in the Anglo-Saxon world but obscured in the Latin countries by a Catholic liturgy of much later origin. On these occasions one finds, on both sides of the English Channel, young people wearing masks and costumes, dancing, collecting candy, and engaging in other activities; Felix's account suggests that what was being celebrated was more All Saints' than All Souls': the festivities were gay, elitist, and socially acceptable. There were no *danses macabres* or other unruly or anarchic manifestations.[52]

*   *   *

Felix Platter and Michel Héroard parted company in the middle of Montpellier, not far from the Catalan pharmacy where Felix was to board. The shop stood alongside the residence of its owner, Laurent Catalan, across from what would become, in the twentieth century, the prefecture of Montpellier, itself adjacent to the present-day market. Michel Héroard rode off to his father's house alone. Felix, meanwhile, spotted the pharmacist Laurent Catalan and his wife standing on their doorstep watching the noble dancers in the street. It was Sunday, a day of rest for master apothecaries and shopkeepers. Felix jumped down from his horse and addressed the pharmacist in Latin before handing him a letter of recommendation that he had brought all the way from Basel. It was from a prominent citizen of Basel whom Catalan knew well. The conversation proceeded in Latin. Catalan gave out deep sighs (*seuftzget*) at the thought of his own boys far away on the banks of the Rhine, their lodging there obtained in exchange for the room to be placed at the disposal of the new arrival. Centuries later we can still hear those paternal sighs.

Felix's horse was led away to a stable. Johann von Odratzheim, a young Alsatian of good family and Laurent Catalan's apprentice, showed the newcomer to the tiny room that had been reserved for him through negotiations conducted by mail between Montpellier and Basel (F 128). All that remained was for Catalan's servant, Béatrix, to assist Felix in removing his boots. Felix's account of Béatrix's death a few years after this scene took place is rather curt, reading almost like a coroner's report: "On December 3, 1556, Catalan's former servant, Béatrix [Bietris], who removed my boots the night I arrived in Montpellier in 1552, was hanged on the square [in front of Montpellier's city hall and Notre-Dame cathedral] from a gallows with a single arm. She was hanged and choked to death. She had left the Catalan house a year earlier [in 1555] to go to work for a young priest [*pfaff*] who got her pregnant. When the child came to term, she threw it into the toilet in the priest's house, where its little body was found. The mother was sentenced to death and executed. Her body was given to the School of Medicine for dissection. Its uterus was still swollen and enlarged, because the birth had taken place only a week earlier. The executioner wrapped his victim's remains in a sheet and hung them from a gibbet outside the city."[53] Felix's text contains not a single word of reproach for the poor woman's clerical lover (who apparently went unpunished), except that the word *pfaff* as used by a convinced Protestant like Felix Platter was a term of opprobrium.

*   *   *

Here it was, the end of October, and all that remained for Felix now that he had arrived in Montpellier was to total up his accounts (which the editors of his memoirs and I have corrected using information he provides). The trip from Basel to Montpellier took twenty-one days, sixteen of which were spent on the road and five resting in or touring cities along the way. His average expenses were eleven sous, sixteen deniers per day, compared with the average mason's daily wage of five sous. The young student, even as the son of a professor of no great fortune, was thus clearly better off than the average proletarian, as one would expect. Traveling by horseback one could cover an average of forty-five kilometers per day, with actual distances ranging from thirty to sixty kilometers depending on what there was to see, the winds, and so on. In sixteen days of actual travel, Felix covered a distance of slightly over 700 kilometers: 705 according to his own calculations, 720 if we correct his figures slightly. The distance between Basel and Montpellier if one travels by automobile today is 654 kilometers; modern roads make it possible to avoid certain detours that sixteenth-century riders were obliged to take (F 145). Thus a fairly fast driver can make the trip in a single day. Modern means of transportation accordingly reduce the length of the journey by a factor of only sixteen.

Felix thus went from a city of 16,000, Basel, to a city of 12,500, Montpellier. Once famous for its commerce, by the sixteenth century Montpellier had been displaced to some extent by Marseilles and other Mediterranean ports. Hence judges, lawyers and their clerks, and university professors and students (especially medical students) increasingly dominated daily life in the city.

CHAPTER SIX

Living in Montpellier

On November 4, 1552, Felix registered at the University of Montpellier. The night before, he had witnessed the burning in the streets of numerous secretly circulated "heretical" books and had not lifted a finger to stop the destruction. What good would it have done? Meanwhile, more prosaically, he had sold his horse for eight crowns, with which he was able to buy some clothes and a *flassada*, a type of Catalonian blanket (the November nights were already cold). His registration at the university brought him into contact with Dr. Honoré Du Chatel, a brilliant physician, womanizer, Catholic, and transplanted Parisian, who examined Felix and found his knowledge sufficient to begin a course of medical studies. Certain Marrano connections played a part in Felix's matriculation. His official academic patron, tutor, permanent advisor, and intellectual godfather (officially recognized as such by the local authorities) was Dean Antoine Saporta, a friend of Rabelais's and the grandson of Louis Saporta Sr., a Jewish doctor originally from Lerida who had been Charles VII's personal "caretaker." Louis's son, Louis Saporta Jr., the father of Antoine Saporta, had been a student at Montpellier before becoming a fashionable physician in Toulouse. Heredity in medicine? Yes, and also heresy: Antoine Saporta, a Marrano by birth, marriage, and numerous friendships, was a Protestant sympathizer. From the time Felix arrived in Montpellier, or perhaps even earlier, he was warmly recommended to Saporta by his landlord, the apothecary Laurent Catalan, also a Marrano with Lutheran sympathies (Catalan's son would later call himself a Spaniard by birth, a Frenchman by nationality, and a German—read Lutheran—at heart).[1] In Basel as well as Montpellier, in other words, there was a connection or association between Marranos and Protestants: recall that Catalan's sons were or would become boarders of Thomas Platter's and that Dean Antoine Saporta was a friend of Laurent Catalan's and in a sense a coreligionist. Catalan, moreover, was a complex individual: he had had his sons circumcised and felt drawn to Felix's Protestant, biblical, and anticlerical cultural background. Nevertheless, he paid for masses to be said in honor of the Virgin for the sake of his son Gilbert, a failure whom his father hoped to encourage through pious prayer to return to the path of righteousness and hard work. Catalan was thus triply ecumenical, joining Jewish roots and new Protestant thinking to Catholic tradition—a man who wanted to cover all the bases.

The next five years of Felix Platter's life stand apart. A man who liked to avoid complications, he shunned Sunday and midnight masses like the plague, in contrast to his younger brother, Thomas Jr., who, out of an interest in folklore and perhaps a desire to edify his readers about papist superstitions, would latter attend Catholic Christmas Eve celebrations in Montpellier. As suspicious as Felix was of the Church of Rome, he nevertheless refrained from making the slightest gesture that might be interpreted as Huguenot. Felix Platter had no taste for martyrdom. He was living in Montpellier and working within a meritocratic system in order to prepare himself for a career in medicine, period. In childhood his heart may have bled for the victims of Charles V's persecution in the Netherlands, but as a mature student he seems to have calmed down. His response to witnessing the torture of Protestants in Montpellier and its environs is rather cool. His greatest involvement in religious conflict came one day when he tried to stop the executioner's henchmen from entering the pharmacy of his master Laurent Catalan in order to buy turpentine for the purpose of reigniting a bonfire (in danger of extinction by rain) on which a southern French heretic was being burned to death (F 190). On that occasion the apothecary's assistants immediately reminded the Swiss lodger that if he failed to mind what he said and above all what he did, if he dared to rebuke the executioner's aides, he might well find himself tied to the stake himself. No fool, Felix saw the wisdom of this advice and did not make an issue of the matter. Furthermore, he never attended a clandestine Protestant service in Montpellier: such an exploit, while dangerous, was hardly inconceivable at the time. Had Felix been eager for the opportunity, he surely would have found it. In his defense, however, we may note that he never dissected a Protestant, whereas he had no compunction when it came to cutting up papist cadavers.

For the young man from Basel temporarily ensconced in Montpellier, the years 1552–1556 were thus a period of religious hibernation. This did not stop him from continuing to hold firm "heretical," and more precisely "Œcolampadian," convictions or from forming solid friendships with "papists" such as Professor Honoré Du Chatel, whom he even addressed by his first name. Typical in this respect was his love-hate relationship with Brother Bernard, a lay brother who kept Felix supplied with *coq au vin* and cadavers surreptitiously exhumed for use in clandestine anatomy lessons. Not until 1557, on the eve of his return to Basel and after years of honest and loyal service, did Felix quarrel with Bernard, who had for so long been his accomplice and almost his friend.

As a student in the faculty of medicine of the University of Montpellier, Felix Platter reaped the benefits of the institution's growth and prestige (F 258 ff.).[2] The university had developed considerably in the wake of Charles VIII's decision toward the end of the fourteenth century to create four magisterial chairs. In making this decision, the king took note of reforms already accomplished at the university between 1462 and 1485. These measures, aided by the municipality, affected the faculties of law, theology, and liberal arts. The academies of Languedoc had suffered during the wars with England, but Henri II was determined to improve the quality of education, and by 1552 the decadence of earlier years was already a distant memory. Yet the city's hospitals, as active as they were, still played only a minor role in the training of future physicians. Medical students were more interested in diseases than in patients. To be sure, Felix saw the bedridden in the flesh in Montpellier, but he owed this signal favor to his good friend Dr. Du Chatel (alias Castellan).

In the city, a system of colleges similar to the one that used to exist at the Sorbonne and that still exists at Oxford allowed penniless students, primarily from Lozère and Catalonia, to enjoy the intellectual benefits of the alma mater. Student power was no idle phrase, despite opposition orchestrated as early as 1550 by Professor Schyron (whom we shall meet again). Students, even students from German-speaking countries, could compel their professors to attend to their teaching duties by threatening to obtain reductions of academic salaries or to go on strike against offending teachers. Willingly or unwillingly, Felix would participate in one of these work stoppages in the autumn of 1556, even though he risked disappointing his teacher and patron, Professor Saporta (F258). (Saporta, as was mentioned earlier, was a Marrano, but this caused him few problems in a society where racial prejudice did not exist so long as one adopted the Christian faith.) The entire administration of the university consisted of a secretary, a porter, and a treasurer, who between them managed to keep the whole apparatus running fairly smoothly.

When it came to "intellectual geography," professors at Montpellier looked down on the "universities" of Valence and Orange. Moreover, they knew themselves to be superior to their colleagues in Paris by virtue of the academic freedom they enjoyed, but, not being fools, they of course respected the natural preeminence of the capital. A Parisian was always an elder brother. Finally, our Languedocians showed a certain respect for the teaching offered in Avignon, which drew many students from Germany. Many of the professors in that papal city came from Montpellier. As for baths and other therapeutic facilities (other than hospitals) within Montpellier's sphere of influence (facilities that might have supported the work of the university), it must be said that the baths of

Balaruc a few leagues outside "Clapas" (as Montpellier was popularly known) did not achieve success until later, at the very end of the sixteenth century, as Thomas Platter Jr.'s visit would confirm. Ocean baths, which were sometimes used as substitutes for mineral baths, were not recommended by Montpellier physicians except for the treatment, always problematic, of rabies, as well as for scabies and another skin malady known locally as *grattadis,* which caused itching.

In "Clapas," the local Pantheon or collective Aesculapius comprised four regents, the professors who occupied the magisterial chairs created in 1498 by Charles VIII and who were in theory remunerated from the royal treasury. The creation of these chairs had marked an important step in the emergence of the leading city of Languedoc; further progress was indicated by the establishment of a Chambre des Comptes in 1523, by the translation *intra muros* of the bishopric of Maguelonne in 1536, by the installation of two royal treasurers in 1542, and finally by the inauguration of the presidial in 1552. Knowledge attracted power. The four regents of medicine elected the regent-chancellor, who answered only to God in the management of the university's affairs (the regulations limiting the number of electors had been adopted only a short while earlier). In addition, owing to another "Malthusian" regulation of 1554, only four or five doctors served as supplementary instructors. The senior doctor served as dean of the university, responsible for setting course schedules and ensuring that all required subjects were taught. The four regents were exempt from taxes, which caused some muttering among less favored fellow citizens, but they did not number among the wealthiest people in the city. They merely belonged to the middle class, distinguished by knowledge rather than wealth. At midcentury all the regents were Huguenots, or at any rate Huguenots at heart, except for Dr. Du Chatel, a confirmed papist. In general, they co-opted one another, sometimes with, sometimes without, competition inside or outside the ranks; after 1550 the leadership thus rotated among Protestants, which tells us a great deal about religious persecution under Henri II: it was limited in the main to outsiders or public figures imprudent enough to be caught.

Of his various professors, whether regents or doctors, Felix had particularly unpleasant memories of Jean Schyron, a native of Anduze (in present-day Gard), who was regent-chancellor and a Huguenot but also quite reactionary (he had worked behind the scenes to shape the restrictive regulations of 1550 and 1554). Schyron was "quite elderly" (in fact in his sixties) and reputedly unable to control his sphincters when he lectured, a matter of some mirth in a city where Christian charity was not the foremost virtue. His public courses, once a first-class source of knowledge of Greek medicine, were no longer much good, if Felix is to be believed. About Rondelet, or *Rondibilis,* as he was known, a native of Languedoc with a receding hairline, thick beard, and prominent nose who succeeded Schyron as regent-chancellor, I shall have little to say here, for we saw a good deal of him earlier when Felix called on him in Lyons. The young man from Basel had boundless admiration for Rondelet owing to the latter's prodigious knowledge of zoology and especially anatomy. In emulation of this teacher, Felix even dissected dogs, whose remains he stored in Laurent Catalan's closets, to Catalan's utter dismay (F 187). After all, had not *Rondibilis* himself dissected his own sister-in-law and benefactress, his first wife, and his stillborn son, to say nothing of his public dissection of the placenta of his twin children? An ichthyologist as well as the discoverer of the mite that causes scabies, and the builder, in 1554, of a new and ultramodern anatomical amphitheater in Montpellier, Rondelet would further distinguish himself in 1564, when Charles IX visited the city, by obtaining a quadrupling of the salaries of the four regents, whose pay had been frozen since the end of the fifteenth century despite two- or three-figure inflation in the intervening years. True, the professors also saw many private patients and did not live solely on their salaries; furthermore, the salary increase reflected a trend evident throughout Languedoc, for example in the increase granted that same year to Montpellier nurses whose fees had also been frozen for almost seven decades.[3] Pay was going up across the board for everyone involved in the care of the sick. Still, pay increases had a hard time keeping up with skyrocketing prices.

Antoine Saporta, who was named dean of the medical faculty in 1556 and went from Marrano-Catholic to Protestant back to Catholic again after the Saint Bartholomew's Day massacre (one can understand why), became, as planned, Felix Platter's patron and surrogate father. But Felix's great friend was Dr. (and later Professor-Regent) Honoré Du Chatel, a Parisian of talent transplanted to Montpellier, who for a time was regularly denied promotion to a professorship because of his Catholic views—and this was well before the death of the anti-Huguenot Henri II. Du Chatel nevertheless obtained his promotion in the end: discrimination had run its course. While Felix was in Montpellier, Dr. Du Chatel often invited him to dinner and took him to see patients; once he even obtained tickets so that Felix could watch, along with many noblemen and damsels, from a window with a view on the scaffold, the execution of an anticlerical peasant sorcerer who was hanged near city hall—this, too, was an anatomy lesson. Du Chatel was firmly on the side of the priests, indeed of the heretic-burners. He was also the lover of old Dr.

Griffy's wife, and he liked to take his mistress's pulse as she languished in bed in her husband's absence.[4] Meanwhile, Felix, like old Polonius, hid behind the arras—but the young medical student was there to play the lute: this was not Shakespeare but Marivaux. The young man from Basel, after all, had come to be on a first-name basis with the very Parisian doctor who had somehow landed in deepest Occitania. In the end Du Chatel became physician to the kings of France, one of the many Montpellier graduates whose careers culminated in an appointment as chief physician to one of the crowned heads of Europe. Indeed, thirty years later, after a splendid ascent up the rungs of the social ladder, Felix would become one of them.

For the time being, however, he was simply a student. Courses in medicine were offered by the professors free of charge from Saint Luke's Day (October 18) to Easter.[5] During the summer, ordinary doctors (not regents) were authorized to teach but without compensation. Meanwhile, the regent professors could continue to give lessons if they wished and were permitted to charge students. These courses were generally mediocre, in Felix's judgment, but the same can also be said of many of the courses offered in prestigious schools today, and despite this they remain the training grounds of the young elite. Some of the teaching may have been of questionable value, but it was nonetheless fascinating and of lasting impact. Sundays, holidays, and Wednesdays (Hippocrates' day) were free; otherwise the academic schedule began at six in the morning with the courses of Professors Sabran, Saporta, and Schyron. The young Germans, who were not impressed by Schyron's senile maundering, took advantage of his hour to drink excellent muscatel (a liter and a half's worth) and eat pork with mustard (no pork was eaten where Felix was staying, because Catalan was a Marrano and kosher to the tips of his fingers [F 163]). This breakfast was consumed at the Inn of the Three Kings in the suburbs below the medical school, which was located inside the city walls on what is now the rue de l'Ecole-de-Pharmacie. At nine the students hastened back up the hill so as not to miss the lecture of Professor Rondelet, who was still quite popular. After lunch came the lectures of Professor Bocaud, a Huguenot from Montpellier, and of Drs. Guichard, Fontanon, and Griffy (Du Chatel's "rival"). Only Guichard was not a native of Montpellier. So much for medicine proper. As for "chemistry" and pharmacy, Felix learned these subjects on the job, as it were, in the shop of his landlord, the apothecary Catalan, as well as by copying manuscript recipes from various countries that circulated among the students. In anatomy, the student from Basel, an excellent judge in the matter, delighted in Rondelet's practical demonstrations, to say nothing of his own expeditions in the company of fellow students to snatch bodies from cemeteries around the city. Felix was a man for whom dissection was what breathing is to ordinary mortals.

The magisterial courses consisted essentially of more or less densely commented readings of Greek authors. By midcentury the Renaissance spirit had effectively conquered Montpellier. More and more of the teaching concerned the Greeks. First came Hippocrates, whose reputation was firmly established and whose teachings were already appreciated when Rabelais attended the university under Francis I. Then came Galen and Paul of Egina, who made dazzling posthumous appearances in the discourse of the professors after 1531 and 1545, respectively. Felix Platter himself would turn out to be a diligent student of Galen, whose bound volumes, imported from Lyons or Basel on muleback, adorned his modest library in the attic and back rooms of the Catalan home (F 186, 188). Despite the reactionary recommendations of the Grands Jours of Béziers in 1550, the books of the Arab physicians who had been so admired in the Middle Ages were finally abandoned in Mediterranean Languedoc in the middle of the sixteenth century. These disciples of Muhammad, the *toubibs* (the word has survived in contemporary French as slang for doctor), were henceforth dismissed as poor interpreters of the Greeks who obscured the purity of the original texts. One thing is certain: the reputation of the Muslim doctor Avicenna suffered a precipitous decline at Montpellier in the years 1550–55. The reputation of Razi also collapsed at about the same time; it revived somewhat after 1560 but only for a brief time, and the ensuing obscurity was all the more complete as a result.

Montpellier progressed with the Renaissance, by leaps and bounds. The revival of Hebrew and Greek learning had begun in the second half of the fifteenth century with the invention of printing and the fall of Constantinople. As a result of the latter event, the West came into possession of manuscripts from ancient Greece, medical texts among them. Charles VIII, back from Naples, encouraged French bookbinders and illuminators to emulate Italian Renaissance models after 1495.[6] Between 1520 and 1535 the energy of the Renaissance spread from Europe to the rest of the world. The conquest of Mexico and Peru, which has been described as the true discovery of the New World, or at any rate the moment when the Old World took possession of the New, spelled the end of the Middle Ages. At the same time the ideas of Luther and Zwingli spread with lightning speed, one consequence of which was that in the 1520s Thomas Platter abandoned both his Catholicism and his traditional rural heritage. The decade of the 1550s marked the triumph of Greek thought, not only in the châteaus of the Valois but also at the University of Montpellier, where medical Hellenism in all its purity scored triumph after triumph among both professors and students, Felix foremost among them.[7]

Students at the university worked extremely hard, at least if they were brilliant, conscientious, and motivated, as Felix was. They also engaged regularly in public and private debates. Felix participated in a *disputatio* every two weeks in 1556, af first among Germans but later with French students as well. Indeed, Felix was the only *Teutschen* who dared to cross the linguistic boundary to debate with the *Welches*, even though arguments were generally conducted in Latin.

Students also spent a great deal of time copying pharmaceutical formulas from Italy and Germany, which passed from hand to hand. They learned formulas for enemas, some of which were still unknown in Basel. They studied "topical" remedies such as pommades and carminatives (drugs that induce the expulsion of gas from the stomach) and wrote down mixtures of spices such as cinnamon and ginger that were said to reduce gas. At the same time they glued specimens of medicinal herbs and other plants to the pages of an herbarium. Felix also arranged for a secret copy to be made of a manuscript by Falcon, the great Marrano physician of Montpellier, who had died in 1540. Besides having amassed a fortune in his own lifetime (in this respect, too, he would be a model for Felix), this Jewish-Catholic doctor was also the author of a book about medicine and surgery that remained unpublished for some time after his death.

In preparing copies and editions of medical and pharmaceutical texts, Felix and his most diligent fellow students used a hyperanalytic method known as "isagogics," which involved compiling tables or outlines of major themes broken down into subthemes, sub-subthemes, and so on. This taxonomical method had been invented by Porphyry in Antiquity and had later been perfected and used by Raymond Lull in Catalonia, Ramus and Figon in France, and Fallope in Padua, as well as Zwinger and Platter in the German Swiss diaspora. When necessary, Felix pored over these texts by candlelight in his attic room in the Catalan house, beneath a starry sky that could be seen with great clarity through the unpolluted atmosphere of Renaissance Montpellier.

Finally, the students also engaged in practical work with patients. But one had to be careful. If caught, there was danger of being accused of treating patients by "cut and try" empirical methods and, until one had one's doctorate, of practicing medicine illegally. The punishment for breaking the law in this way was to be paraded through the city while mounted backward on an ass and to be subjected to the insults and brickbats of local ruffians. This tragi-burlesque ritual had a long history: it had been used in Rome in the year 1000 against antipopes accused of usurping papal sovereignty.[8] Felix was therefore extremely cautious about treating the sick. He chose the reasonable course of offering medical or paramedical advice only to his German friends, who he could be sure would not denounce him to the Montpellier authorities because of the language barrier if for no other reason.

All in all, the University of Montpellier resembled what would be called in France today a *grande école,* that is, an elite institution like the Ecole Normale Supérieure of Paris. In the sixteenth century the medical school served no more than 150 to 200 students at any given time, with 30 to 50 new students admitted each year. Students who had personally exercised a mechanical or artisanal trade were not accepted, moreover, although little attention was paid to the status of an applicant's father, mother, or other forebears. The bias against artisans and others of inferior social status concerned only the student's own generation.

For the purpose of comparison, it may be worth noting that the faculty of medicine of the University of Montpellier in 1950 still had only 700 students, and the course work was still as time-consuming and laborious as it had been four centuries earlier. The main difference was that instead of spending all day in lecture courses, medical students in the 1950s divided their time between the hospital in the morning and lectures in the afternoon.

Felix Platter arrived in Montpellier when the student population was at its height: in the 1550s fifty-two new students were admitted annually, compared with thirty or forty in each year of the five previous decades. After 1560, admissions again dropped to thirty or so because of the Wars of Religion and eventually to fifteen as the turmoil continued. Admissions did not return to the previous level of thirty until the end of the century when Thomas Platter Jr. came to Montpellier (1594–1600). This return to normality would not have been possible without the restoration of peace under Henri IV.

Students at the university were a cosmopolitan lot. Of 3,366 students enrolled in the sixteenth century, 692 were foreigners. Of these, 270 were Iberian, mainly Spaniards, and for a long time they lived apart from their classmates from north of the Pyrenees because the wars between France and Spain poisoned relations between the two groups. What is more, the "extreme southern" Catholicism of the countries subject to the Inquisition was different from French Catholicism. Further evidence of this split would emerge during the Wars of Religion, with the development, typically French, of the Catholic party known as *les politiques,* who were in fact moderates, unlike their Spanish coreligionists or for that matter their adversaries in the French Ligues. From Germanic regions and Central Europe came another 315 students, counting natives of the Netherlands, Scandinavia, and Poland, who can hardly be considered "Teutons." There were also 75 Italians.

One of these "East Peninsulars" was a certain "Flaminius," or Flamini, about whom we have no further information (F 191). Flamini achieved posthumous celebrity in 1554 owing to an event that caused something of a stir in Languedoc. After a wedding ball marking the marriage of the son of Professor Fontanon, whose forty-year-old mule had made him famous throughout the province, the Italian, quick with a dagger, became involved in a brawl in the course of which he rather foolishly impaled himself on the sword of one Le Beau, a (noble) medical student from Tours. Le Beau was arrested for murder after a chase across the rooftops of the city. After languishing in prison for a time, the young murderer (whose crime was almost inadvertent) was finally liberated. He went on to a medical career in Tours, where he was still doctoring in the early seventeenth century. In addition to the 75 Italians (for the whole of the sixteenth century), there were also 27 students from the British Isles (including Ireland as well as England). In general, the foreign localities most amply represented in Montpellier were Basel, Constance, Geneva, Utrecht, Liège, Tournai, and five Spanish dioceses. Clearly, Felix was a typical foreign student in two senses: he came to Montpellier in the 1550s, when the student body there was largest and the university was in fashion throughout Europe; and he came from Basel, a Swiss city with strong connections to the academic and medical institutions of urban Languedoc.

* * *

But it was not only the academic and medical institutions that interested Felix. The young man from the north was also fascinated by southern life and Mediterranean customs in general, which stood in sharp contrast to the customs of the Upper Rhine that had shaped the first fifteen years of his existence. The whole atmosphere of Montpellier and its environs was new to him, as he became acutely aware in the spring of 1553, in late March and early April, when the broom and narcissus and almond blossomed and the alder sprouted catkins and the willows grew leaves and the box trees bloomed on the limestone plateaus known as *causses;* when the big flies became annoying, and snakes and lizards emerged from the earth; and when bats filled the evening sky. Already the young thrushes were plump; the sap was up in the chestnut trees, from whose bark barefoot children made trumpets, while men in shirtsleeves hoed the vineyards. In March seeds were laid in for peas and wheat, lambs were shorn for slaughter, and one ate salads of fresh greens.

As the good weather returned, the young man from Basel longed to see the Mediterranean, which he had already glimpsed once from afar from a hilltop between Sambres and Castelnau on his way to Montpellier. The sea had been flat, stretched out like a vast bolt of fabric all aglitter with flecks of gold. His temptation was compounded by the fact that from his half-timbered room atop the Catalan house (not far from the present-day prefecture), Felix caught almost daily glimpses of the sea that filled his dreams. He claimed that on certain days he could even hear the sound of the waves in the middle of town (F 173). Unable to keep his impatience in check, he and several friends visited the shore south of Pérols (not far from present-day Palavas) on February 22. It was a beautiful, hot day. In Pérols, Felix and his friends, all German-speaking students, observed a mineral spring whose "poisoned" water had killed one of the king's lackeys as His Majesty (we do not know which one) looked on impassively (F160). Using a small boat without oars, the group of students had crossed a salt pond to reach the beach: a few pulled the boat along with ropes, while the others kept dry inside. The beach, between the salt pond and the sea, was covered with seaweed, shells, cuttlefish, and fish bones—enough to make a wagonload (F 161). The waves filled the visitors' shoes and socks with water. Without hesitation they stripped down and went swimming. To these young men from the north the water seemed fine. The tourists then covered themselves with hot sand. This was a sort of medical treatment: it made the skin dry, hard, and firm, and was indicated in cases of scabies, ringworm, and various allergies at a time when people rarely washed. The young Germans collected shells of various colors and round crabs before returning to Pérols for lunch and on to Montpellier by nightfall.

During Lent, the sea was present on every table in Montpellier, and particularly on the table of Laurent Catalan: the apothecary's windows looked out on the cramped, foul-smelling fish market in the center of town. The market lined the narrow streets in the neighborhood of the butcher shop and the flour and herb markets. Catalan, a Marrano, had no reason to offend devout Catholics, some of whom were customers, by eating meat during Lent. Hence in February and March there was dried cod at every meal, or sole or tuna (the tuna transported to the fish market for cutting measured up to fifteen feet in length). The family also ate fried mackerel and sardines; quantities of eel; lobsters up to two feet long; and occasionally shrimp by the basketful. Everything was cooked in oil (butter was never used in Montpellier). In the evening during Lent, one also ate lettuce, endives, onions, and chestnuts, but not cheese or fruit.

On April 7 Felix made another trip to the sea. In the company of other German students he traveled to Villeneuve-lès-Maguelonne, where a fortified, Roman-style church had been erected on the coast to deter corsairs from the Maghreb. This time, however, no boat was available for crossing the salt pond to Maguelonne, and the students returned to Montpellier empty-handed. The coast offered little in the way of services to would-be tourists and swimmers. Those who lived inland feared the malaria that lurked in the coastal swamps. They rarely swam more than a few times a year, if that. In Montpellier the brackish marshes were thought to be filthy and disease-ridden. Felix and his friend Melchior Rotmundt, who had studied in Tübingen and Paris and who later practiced medicine in Saint-Gall, learned this the hard way when, while wearing white trousers, they tried to cross a muddy stretch of coast on the way to the city of Aigues-Mortes, already celebrated for its walls and its lighthouse. The excellent partridges that the two friends consumed at a local inn were scant compensation for the damage done to their wardrobes.

After Lent, on May 22, Felix again returned to the sea (F 197). After emerging from the water, he decided once more to bury himself in the sand. Three days later, he came down with bronchitis and a head cold and a terribly runny nose and felt as if he might die. A purge put him back on his feet. Eventually his father became alarmed by Felix's repeated trips to the insalubrious coastal marshes. By letter from Basel he offered his son this unforgettable advice: "Felix, be careful about swimming in the sea. Remember that you almost drowned in the Rhine a few years back. And beware of any French girls who might try to lead you on" (F 185). On August 30, 1553, Felix made another excursion to the beaches, as usual in the company of other *Teutschen,* in this case students who had not yet seen the sea because they had just arrived in Montpellier (F 222). They collected herbs, shells, and seaweed and went swimming. Among the newcomers was Johann Wachtel, the son of a Strasbourg apothecary who had come to Montpellier to apprentice in pharmacy and who would soon have his own shop in the Alsatian capital at the sign of Chapelle Saint-Jacques on the rue des Piques. Felix played a rather rough game with Johann, who did not know how to swim: the two tried to dunk each other's heads in the water to the point where they were blowing sea water out of their nostrils.

Young Platter's last "beach party" was also the best. In late September 1553, two noted German writers asked him to take them to the beach at Maguelonne so that they could round out a collection they were making of zoological specimens. The principal collector was Heinrich Pantaleon, a small man with a flowing beard, a round head, and intelligent eyes set in a wrinkled face. A theologian, he had been disappointed in his hopes of becoming pastor of Saint Peter's in Basel as a result of political maneuvering. A brilliant, highly cultivated man and a Latinist in the style of Montaigne, Pantaleon had thrown himself into the study of medicine at the age of thirty. He had hastily completed his coursework in a few semesters at the mediocre University of Valence, which was a kind of diploma mill, and graduated toward the end of 1552 or the beginning of 1553. The news caused something of a stir in Basel, where it was feared that physicians already in practice would suffer from the competition (F 286). Of course Pantaleon was no newcomer to the field, for in the 1540s he had attended the lectures of his friend Alan zum Thor, the disciple and friend of the two greatest Basel physicians, Paracelsus and Vesalius.

With his new doctorate in hand, Pantaleon had gone to Languedoc in the fall of 1553 to make the acquaintance of medical authorities there, both French and German, as well as to recover an old debt owed him by a recalcitrant debtor living on the banks of the Hérault. Heinrich appreciated pretty women and bacchic songs. Though a connoisseur of partridges, he could not tell a fig from a pomegranate. Until the collectors and their guide reached Maguelonne, Pantaleon had no complaints about Felix's services as a guide. A distinguished writer of prose, he was accompanied on this journey by the German-Latin poet Peter Lotich, a talented improviser of verse. The son of a peasant, Lotich had been around any number of universities. A former soldier, he was also reputed to be a secret agent. In any case, he had earned his living for a number of years as tutor to a family of German nobles, the Stibars. He traveled with the Stibar children and accompanied them to the leading French schools, including Montpellier. Perpetually in love, Lotich sang of his doomed passions. En route to the coast he celebrated the alluring qualities of one Claudia von Wittenberg, who had been unfaithful to him, as well as Tunicata of Montpellier, alias Kallirhoe, the wife of an Auvergnat jurist, who had fallen ill and died despite the ministrations of Dr. Rondelet—she could not have expired in better hands (F 214). Nor was Lotich any more successful with the women of Italy, where he had pined after a shepherdess who had unfortunately been determined to enter a nunnery and die a virgin. On the way to Maguelonne the two writers exchanged pedantries in Latin: *Germani socii tendunt ad litora maris* (the German friends are headed for the seacoast [F 184]). Felix did not hesitate to join in. Periodically the three travelers sang the "Song of the Knight von Steurmarck," a tune that became popular in Germany in the sixteenth century. On the beach they filled huge crates with shells. Looking out at the Mediterranean from atop the church of Maguelonne, Felix thought of Africa (*Aphrika*), which he knew lay off to the south even though he could not see it (F 256). Later, Pantaleon, having had his fill of maritime scenery, continued on toward Pézenas in the hope (ultimately disappointed) of recovering the money owed to him.

After 1553, Felix's enthusiasm for the beach and swimming seems to have cooled, although he did like to watch fishermen working with the *bouliech*, a long net that required twenty people to drop into the water and then drag it back, full of fish, including the *pastinaca marina*, or *boug-nette*, which Rondelet loved, onto the beach. The bougnette is a Mediterranean fish with poisonous stingers that are dangerous to touch (F 179). Was he now tired of the sea, whose charms he had appreciated numerous times? Was he afraid of contracting malaria, a disease that modern medicine had yet to banish to the tropics? Or was it simply, now that his return to Basel loomed nearer, that he was now devoting himself primarily to his studies in order to avoid the unemployment that awaited many graduates after they received their diplomas? In any case, drownings were frequent, as he was well aware, and perhaps in the end he took all the warnings to heart. In August of 1555, moreover, the medical student in "exile" from his native Basel received a salvo of letters from Switzerland, concerning his fiancée, various musical instruments, and that mischievous scamp and indefatigable womanizer Gilbert Catalan, the son of Laurent the apothecary. And then there was also the Flemish humanist Utenhove, who had recently become a boarder in Thomas's house. One of these missives came from Albrecht Gebwiller, the bürgermeister who had given Felix a place to stay during the plague of 1551 that had killed his sister Ursula. The municipal official told his correspondent in Montpellier about the most recent drownings in the Rhine on April 5, 1555: young boys from Basel had been competing with one another by diving from the main bridge, and spectators had gathered on the bridge to watch. A railing had given way, and several dozen people had fallen into the water. The locksmith Heinrich Sprenger had "broken his back" when he landed on a raft of logs caught between bridge pilings. A little girl, sent by her parents to buy mustard, had miraculously survived. When rescuers fished her out, unconscious but still alive, she was clutching the mustard pot and the four sous she had been given for her purchases at the grocery store— obviously a well-trained child.

Despite these dissuasive object lessons, Felix risked one more swimming expedition the following year, this time in fresh water. The summer of 1556 was one of the hottest and driest that Western Europe has ever known, comparable to the summers of 1718, 1794, and 1976. Forest fires damaged woods as far north as Cotentin, usually exempt from such disasters.[9] Even pastures went up like straw mattresses. In Montpellier, which had suffered from oppressive heat (*grosse hitz*) since the end of April, a merchant's house burned down on Place Notre-Dame, not far from the cathedral of the same name (near the present-day Place Jean-Jaurès) (F 246). It was a stone house, not all that common in a city built mainly of wood and cob with many structures dating from the fifteenth century. The walls remained standing, but the whole interior of the building was destroyed. While it burned, the real show was in the street. Onlookers were enchanted; they came close to applauding as they enthusiastically watched the progress of the disaster. In Basel, where corporate solidarities were more robust than in France, citizens would have formed a bucket brigade. The authorities would have seen to it that water was hauled to the scene. During the heat wave, Felix sensibly set off for a dip in the Lez, despite his recent decision to give up swimming altogether. The poor boy just couldn't stand the heat any longer. Indeed, the ground was so hot that dogs could barely stand to run along the ridges between furrows in the freshly-plowed fields. Felix hurried across the same fields and felt the burning through the ultrathin soles of his shoes.

This torrid swim came in the midst of a desiccated harvest. The heat wave, which had begun in April, ended in a series of substantial storms, which refreshed the entire countryside (F 244). Feet no longer burned but sank into the mud. On June 15, lightning destroyed the steeple, altar, interior decoration, and door of the Saint-Hilaire church near the Dominican chapel, not far from the present-day Jardin du Peyrou. Reconstructed at the behest of the city council, Saint-Hilaire would be destroyed again by Huguenots in 1561. Another storm on June 25 unleashed hailstones the size of chickens' eggs. This was followed by an especially violent storm on July 11, 1556, which produced still further damage. Streets were turned into dangerous rapids by the runoff, and a person could easily have been swept away by the current. Felix was now afraid of drowning if he tried to swim.

Credulous citizens seized on an apocalyptic prophecy that had been making the rounds in Montpellier and elsewhere for some time.[10] The end of the world was supposed to arrive on Magdalene's Day, July 22, 1556. Feverish interpreters had a field day with a host of supposedly premonitory signs. Fortunately, however, the appointed day came and went without any notable disaster, although the heat wave did continue for a time in Switzerland, where Thomas Platter complained of losing a number of recently planted young trees (*junge beum*) (F 254).

* * *

End of the world or not, Felix, as a medical man, associated summer with death from heat stroke, fever, and even plague, which struck Toulouse, "not far from us" (F 221), in the heat of early August 1555. City-dwellers did not remain passive in the face of the annual summer ordeal: apartments in Montpellier were sprinkled with water, and leafy branches and strips of canvas were hung to shade narrow streets (F 175). The custom of shading streets and squares with fabric awnings has all but vanished from southern France today, but one still finds shaded patios in Italy and Spain. The grain harvest in the south, which began earlier than the August wheat harvest in the north, was a period of intense activity on the land. In addition to getting in the wheat, laborers also picked hemp and cut the fresh growth of alfalfa (*auzerda*); they planted turnips and dressed vines. Peasants were so busy they didn't know which way to turn. Highlanders came down from the Cévennes into the plains of lower Languedoc in search of employment. Meanwhile, sheep from the plains moved in the opposite direction, up into the Aigoual to summer in the highlands. The herds of humans and the herds of sheep crossed paths, as it were. Meanwhile, wasps grew particularly aggressive in the summer heat, as did fleas and bugs. Stalks of wheat stood out among thick weeds, while thistles blossomed and poppies faded. Raspberries and *bon-chrétien* pears ripened. With an eye to the future, vine growers gauged the size of maturing grapes: did they resemble chickpeas, peppercorns, or lead shot? Quail and locusts raised a ruckus. Young blackbirds already as big as the parent birds attracted the attention of the local nimrods.

Although Felix was aware of the rural world through his parents, his view of the harvest was rather remote: he was no Brueghel. His chief interest, whether looking down on the countryside from the ramparts or observing the scene in the suburbs of Montpellier near the church of Saint-Denis, was in the threshing of the wheat in one of the large threshing areas reserved for local grain growers (F 209). There, teams of half a dozen mules trotted around circular tracks like circus animals to crush the sheaves of grain and separate the wheat from the chaff. Thomas Jr., although less intelligent than his older brother, was also more of a geographer and quicker to generalize: he noted threshing areas next to nearly every large barn in the southern countryside. Both Platters remarked on the striking differences between French and Swiss threshing techniques: in Switzerland, threshing was done in the winter, inside the barn, with a flail, whereas along the Mediterranean the "treading out" (*dépiquage*) was done in the summer, outside on the threshing ground. An Italian-

French artist of talent, influenced by the School of Fontainebleau, later had the idea of depicting both the northern and the southern techniques on a single canvas, a masterpiece of ethnographic insight even though the painter lacked the realistic touch.[11]

*   *   *

Weeks passed. Everyone in Montpellier, residents and students alike, closely followed the progress of the grapes. Everyone kept one foot figuratively in the vineyards, which grew close to the ramparts and in some cases even within the city walls. Several years in a row, on or about August 10 (August 20 according to our modern Gregorian calendar), Felix went to help his master Laurent Catalan harvest grapes for the table (what is properly called the *vendange,* or harvest of wine grapes, took place somewhat later). The apothecary's vineyard was located in a rural suburb of Montpellier. At this time of year the nearby pastures were full of crocuses and fat white caterpillars with mottled yellow markings and no hair. Small gray grasshoppers jumped about everywhere. Peasants harvested black figs and mowed the second growth in irrigated meadows.

Besides his landlord, Felix's usual companions on these grape-picking expeditions were Balthasar Hummel and Jacob Myconius (F 175, 202). Hummel came from a Basel family of nine children, including two pastors and a supervisory teacher in the school run by Thomas Platter Sr. The father of this large brood, Peter Hans Hummel, was a native of Little Basel who had been a mercenary (F 87). A childhood friend of Felix's and longtime apprentice in various pharmacies, Balthasar Hummel went on to become an apothecary in Basel in the latter part of the century. As for Jacob Myconius, he was the adopted[12] son of Oswald Geisshüssler, also known as "Bald Head" (Myconius), a self-taught Basel pastor and the successor of Œcolampadius as the city's spiritual leader, as well as Thomas Platter Sr.'s teacher and close friend (F 51, 166). Jacob went from being a student in Montpellier to being a doctor at the mediocre University of Avignon (the papal city had nothing against young Lutherans) and later became the municipal physician (*stadtarzt*) of Mulhouse. Jacob was by nature less "puritanical" than his father. He often joined Felix and others in nocturnal drinking bouts; the young men drained kegs of wine stored in the cellars of Laurent Catalan, who did not make a fuss since his wine never lasted more than a year anyway.

During the August grape-picking, Catalan liked to pick on young Hummel, for the boy had yet to master the languages of the Welches, the *langue d'oïl* and the *langue d'oc.* The apothecary therefore addressed the Swiss student in bad Latin: "Use your sword [*gladium*] to cut the grapes." Hummel took out his dagger. "You want to fight [*vis pugnare*]?" the apothecary then asked. And then he would explain that of course he meant not a dagger but a vine knife for sawing stems and separating them from their stalks. The vines in question were not espaliered, as in Lausanne or Geneva, but allowed to run along the ground, as was customary in Languedoc. When the harvest was done, Madame Catalan hung bunches of grapes from the ceiling of Felix's room to keep the rats from eating them. Felix claimed that these grapes were so fat and juicy that one a day was enough to assuage his passion for the fruit of the vine.

The *vendange* came in September, often in the second half of the month (by the Gregorian calendar). There was much to do besides cutting and pressing grapes. Acorns had to be gathered for the hogs. The bushes were thick with blackberries. Walnuts were shaken from their trees and chestnuts knocked loose with long poles (*gaules*). The pears were excellent, so long as they were not worm-eaten. Radishes were juicy and good to eat, but aphids went after the leaves of turnips left in the ground. Pigeons and slugs battened on the freshly planted seeds of wheat. Moles left trails in fields and meadows. Spiders worked day and night. Wasps and thrushes descended upon the vines. Wolves came down from the mountains. Snakes did not yet carpet the earth. And the children, still barefoot despite the first autumn rains, continued to swim in the river.

Felix, absorbed by his schoolwork now that the new term had begun, did not participate physically in the *vendange;* the work he had done earlier, during the academic vacation in August, to gather grapes for the table was enough. He did, however, note that his landlord Laurent Catalan was very busy: "On September 13, 1552 [September 23, new style], my master harvested his grapes. The fall weather is generally quite humid. It rains a lot, considerably more than during the winter" (F 181). He also described, as his younger brother would do toward the end of the century, the process of harvesting grapes and making wine in Montpellier. Donkeys (1553) or mules (1555) were used to carry *comportes,* or tubs of grapes, two per animal, into the city. Their braying warned people to get out of the way, and since the streets were narrow and there were no sidewalks, anyone who failed to heed the warnings risked losing an eye. A naked man hanging by his arms from a beam in the wine cellar trampled the grapes in their tubs; care had to be taken lest the trampler succumb to the fumes of carbon dioxide given off by the first fermentation of the grapes. Special porters hauled wine barrels from place to place. The first wine to be drawn was the light-red *clairet,* then the dark red, and finally the poor-quality *aiguade* or *piquette,* which was served to the servants of the vintner's family.[13] The wine of Languedoc, an urban product par excellence, or, rather, a symbol of a certain urban-rural synergy, points to a characteristic type of environment. Vine-growing areas, even those like the region around Montpellier that produced a diversity of crops, relied primarily on donkeys and mules for transportation and traction, whereas the Massif Central depended on oxen for plowing and the Swiss plateau and northern France used horses.

The earth beneath medieval as well as modern Montpellier was as full of holes as a Swiss cheese owing to the many vaulted wine-cellars. In 1553, the city was one huge wine-making factory comprising many individual operations that functioned in part independently, in part collectively. A fifth of the city's population lived off of agriculture, primarily the fruit of the vine. Streets and squares were riddled with holes for manure, as Felix discovered in January 1553, when people of high society began to enjoy themselves at carnival dances. The Swiss student went to one such dance with the daughter of Professor Griffy, a Protestant, of course, and an important figure in the faculty of medicine. The girl was also the granddaughter of a former chancellor of the university. While attempting to guide his companion around a pool of manure, Felix slipped in himself, splattering the young lady with filth from head to toe. His friends joked that he had been trying to anoint the girl with holy water.

Two drinking cultures coexisted in Montpellier. The majority of the natives drank regularly but not to excess. The minority of German students drank irregularly but immoderately, without limit. In the home of Laurent Catalan, a true man of the Mediterranean, people drank substantial amounts without ever getting drunk. Red wine was always available but generally mixed with water. It did not go to one's head. The pharmacist's boarders drank to console themselves for the modest fare. They ate stew at midday, and salad and roast meat for dinner (except during Lent, when only fish was consumed). Wine was also commonly drunk at student breakfasts. Sometimes there were also midnight suppers: on one extramural grave-robbing expedition by medical students eager to perform dissections, the students' accomplice, a monk, prepared a meal of *coq au vin.*

The drinking bouts that remained most vivid in Felix's memory were strictly German affairs. In Marseilles in September 1555, Felix was introduced to two German nobles, landsknechts in Captain Reckenroth's company, which had fought alongside Henri II's troops around Siena in association with Blaise de Monluc (F 226).[14] Felix and the two men together quaffed a substantial number of flagons of wine, so much, in fact, that someone had to undress the young student from Basel and put him to bed. His head was spinning. That night, the two gentlemen pissed in their violet breeches, leaving large stains on the fabric.

The rest of the trip was filled with similar adventures, and the students (commoners) behaved themselves no better than the professional soldiers (aristocrats). On the way back to Montpellier, Felix and his friends, all medical students at the university, stopped to admire the Pont du Gard (F 230). At an inn in the village of Sernhac where they spent the night, the band of students drank each other under the table while shooting dice and playing cards. Stephan Kunz, alias Contzenus, the nephew of a Protestant reformer in Bern, who was studying medicine in Montpellier while awaiting a doctorate from Avignon that would allow him to become the municipal physician of his native city, became increasingly aggressive. He threatened to go on a rampage and shoot the place up. Tension grew between Kunz and Benedikt Burgauer (F 203). Burgauer, the son of a pastor from Schaffhouse, was also studying in Montpellier while awaiting a doctorate from Avignon and a post as municipal physician in Schaffhouse, where eventually he became justice of the peace. The two came to blows, and it proved difficult to separate them. The next morning, Kunz woke up early; in the meantime he had sobered up. Disconsolate because everyone blamed him for the fight, he left Sernhac and returned alone to Montpellier (this took place on September 25–26, 1555).

There were other monumental "drunks" as well. After a night of drinking, Johannes-Ludwig Höchstetter and Melchior Rotmundt were completely "sloshed" and decided to pull a practical joke. Melchior, a "milk face" (that is, a beardless novice), cut off Johannes-Ludwig's thick beard and stuck it inside his jacket. Without his beard Johannes-Ludwig was unrecognizable and passed himself off as a Teutonic knight who had just arrived in town. He was received with all the honors due his rank. When he revealed his true identity, everyone burst out laughing, including Felix, who laughed himself silly. It is worth noting that Höchstetter, who came from an important but bankrupt family of patrician merchants in Augsburg, had studied or would go on to study in Tübingen, Montpellier, and Heidelberg. He became the municipal physician of Esslingen but ultimately drowned in the Neckar in 1566. Rotmundt, the son of a bailiff, had studied in Basel, Tübingnen, Paris, and Montpellier. He became a justice of the peace, city councillor, and municipal physician in Saint-Gall. His brother Kaspar, for the time being in Lyons, later founded an important commercial house and dynasty (F 55, 239). These young men of "good family" were sowing their wild oats.

In that vein the ultimate was no doubt Hans Brombach, who came

from a family of gunsmiths and was a student or at any rate former student, landsknecht, and indefatigable drinker. In 1553 or 1554 he was expelled from the University of Basel for drunkenness. He then became a
bodyuguard of Antoine de Bourbon, king of Navarre (and the father of
Henri IV), a position that allowed him to rub elbows with many
Huguenot coreligionists in the king's entourage. On a visit to Montpellier on April 18, 1554, Brombach, elegantly attired in slashed breeches
and armed with halberd and sword, was welcomed by Felix and his compatriots and treated to a feast. Moved by all this hospitality, he swore to
champion the cause of the Swiss students, in exchange for which his new
friends poured a glass of wine over his head as he rode out of town (F
196).

The drinking customs of those who came from German-speaking
countries (as well as from Brittany, Normandy, England, and Poland)
contrasted sharply with native customs in the grape-growing south: the
natives were generally moderate drinkers, although excesses were by no
means unheard of. The north of Europe discovered wine much later, centuries or perhaps even millennia after the Mediterranean. Hence northerners had not learned to master it, assimilate it, or civilize it to the same
degree as southerners had done through Dionysiac or Christian cults
with their rationalizing, moderating influence. Recent studies of the geographic distribution of alcoholism in France and Europe tend to bear this
out, and so do the memoirs of the Platters. In Barcelona, according to
Thomas Platter Jr., one found hundreds of prostitutes in the dives along
the waterfront but not a single drunk. And consider what Felix has to say
about the countryside around Montpellier in 1552: "My master Laurent
Catalan owned a house and some land in the village of Vendargues [a few
miles from Montpellier]. His steward [*meier*] there was a man named
Guillem, who secretly subscribed to our religion [Protestantism]. He often spoke out against the papists as well as the Marranos, especially when
he'd had a snootful (F 166). This was behavior that Guillem had learned in
Germany [that is, in German Switzerland], for Laurent Catalan had sent
him to Basel to deliver his two sons, Gilbert and Jacques, in baskets on a
donkey's back [so that the two boys, thus conveniently transported,
could pursue their studies and complete their apprenticeship]. In fact, I
have seen very few people in Montpellier drunk on wine except for our
Germans."

This passage is worth pausing over. It is unlikely that Guillem picked
up his anti-Semitic or at any rate anti-Marrano attitudes exclusively from
his travels along the Rhine. This was simply his way (shared with other
members of the lower strata of Languedoc society) of pursuing the "class

struggle," admittedly at a rather low level, against his employer Catalan, a Marrano. Guillem's contact with German culture did, however, turn him from Protestant sympathizer into active Protestant. And his alcoholism, while not necessarily of German origin, followed a pattern that in Felix's opinion was much more prevalent in German-speaking areas than in the south of France.

Taking things a step further, let us ask whether, in the eyes of a young man from Basel studying in Montpellier, it was possible to be a good, decent, middle-class German without also being an honest-to-God drinker, an unabashed consumer of fine red wine? Felix raised the question in May 1554 in connection with the case of Hans Beat Häl, or Hel, a contemporary of his in Basel, about which he learned by letter. Hans Beat was the son of a shopkeeper and the pretty daughter of a surgeon (F 198). He had been a classmate of Felix's and had gone on to the University of Basel in 1547–48, but his behavior there soon caused problems. He was a good-looking boy with a fine voice who was an only child; for a long time people made excuses for him precisely because he was an only child. While a student, he endlessly wandered the streets of Basel playing the lute, an instrument whose intricacies he had mastered. He chased girls and got involved in all sorts of masquerades. On occasion he fought with his fellow students. Eventually, however, he beame engaged to a seamstress, the daughter of a fisherman, whose first name was Barbara and who came from a respectable family in Little Basel. The two married in January 1551, the very year in which Hans was to become a member of the Saffron Guild. Marriage did not put an end to his disorderly ways, however (F 199). In August 1553, "he was even thrown in jail for six days and six nights" for instigating a rather scandalous "mummery" (masquerade). What is more, he did not obey his parents, with whom he continued to live after his marriage. He was ordered to swear that he would avoid suspect places and boardinghouses in the future. Henceforth he was supposed to eat only at his wife's home or his parents' home. The young couple apparently got on well enough, for they produced two sons, Hans Beat Jr. and Jacob, who went on to fairly good careers: the former became a secondary school teacher and the latter a pastor. They were raised, however, by their grandfather rather than by their father, who abandoned them when they were still quite young. The erratic youth had fallen in love with Anna Bottschuh (who was seventeen at the time). Anna, or Annette (Annline to her friends), was the daughter of a deceased keg measurer and the stepdaughter of Gregor Wentz, who kept an inn at the sign of the Salmon off the grain market. Hans Beat had deceived young Anna in the time-honored if indelicate manner of promising to marry her as his first wife lay dying. He had gotten Anneline pregnant on a pile of Catalan rugs in the course of a long evening of music and dancing. The rugs were there to muffle the noise so as to spare the neighbors downstairs.

Word of the girl's pregnancy got out, however, and Hans Beat landed in prison, where he attempted suicide. In July 1554 a court banished him from Basel. Anneline also tried to do away with herself, but in vain. She (along with her mother and accomplice) were let off with a fine of fifty gulden; then she gave birth. She went on to marry two or three husbands. The first, whom she wed in 1557, was an innkeeper at the sign of the Star, in the same line of work as Gregor Wentz. In the course of her various marriages, Anneline was convicted of adultery several times. Meanwhile, Hans Beat, having left Basel, went to Lorraine. Being an incorrigible sinner but of ecumenical disposition, he there seduced a well-born nun from the convent of Remiremont, whose inmates were reputedly of noble descent but loose morals. The girl was caught first, then her lover. He was tied up and placed in a wagon. While crossing a river, he fell in and was drowned, headed feet first for a better world. His death may have been an accident, or he may have been pushed: no one ever found out for sure. There were good reasons, Felix gravely noted, to have been suspicious of this fellow for a long time, for "he did not drink wine, except for sugared wine on rare occasions." The very idea of behaving in such a way!

* * *

In Languedoc, all roads lead to wine, or start from it. Not much was exported northward, however, because wine in those days was hard to preserve. Felix, who bankrupted himself sending packages of all kinds to his parents, never included fine wine in his expensive shipments. But he did send fruits that tasted exotic to their Swiss recipients, along with his collections of plants and of animal skeletons, as well as raisins, which he had often admired as they lay drying on beds of chalk when he passed by on trips like the one to Villeneuve-lès-Maguelonne in the company of the two German nobles. His mother was particularly appreciative of these packages, especially those containing fruits. Thomas, if we are to believe his son, retained the tastes of a peasant and often left oranges and other mouthwatering deserts to his wife. But both Thomas and his wife greatly appreciated the raisins their son sent from the land of Oc.

* * *

After the grape came the olive: the olive harvest in late fall or early winter was also a sight to see, though less fraught with social symbolism than the grape harvest. In "oil season," Felix, though still a fledgling student, found himself drawn into the German community the moment the olive picking began in early November 1552. He joined a band of students that included Jacob Baldenberger, or Baldenbergius, from Saint-Gall, who had studied in Basel before coming to Montpellier and who later practiced medicine in Switzerland (F 147). There was also the Saxon Gregor Schett, who, upon completing his studies in Montpellier, easily landed a job as professor of anatomy and surgery at the University of Leipzig. Johann Vogelgang of Flanders, an old hand at medical studies in Languedoc, was also part of the group, as was Hans Odratzheim, the son of a Strasbourg city councillor and an apprentice apothecary in the shop of Laurent Catalan, as well as Felix's roommate in the Catalan house. In the wee hours of the morning of November 2, Hans jumped out of the bed he shared with Felix and told him not to worry about the Don Quixote-esque presence of warriors armed with lances in the street below the pharmacy window: these were olive pickers equipped with the long poles that were the tools of their trade. Now that the olives had changed color, these harvesters had come down from the mountains in search of work. The oil content of the olives was already 19 percent and would increase to 25 percent at maturity over the next few weeks. Following the harvest, the olives were subjected to a first pressing or grinding by means of granite millstones turned by donkeys. Then, after the pure initial juice was drained off, the pulp was scalded, and a second pressing was obtained. The oil was then stored in large terra-cotta pots for household use or poured, as in Roman times, into goatskin bottles for export on the backs of donkeys or mules.

In Montpellier, the production of olive oil in the period between Toussaint (November 1) and Easter was largely an urban affair, conducted by hurried entrepreneurs and workers who did not complain about their heavy workload. They slept little (to the astonishment of the doctors), ate constantly, and worked hard for their wages. In the off-season, olive trees served another purpose: they played an essential role in a macabre display whose objective was to deter criminals. On July 22, 1553, a handsome young man, the son of a bread baker, having been convicted of a crime, was sent for execution on the Place Notre-Dame in front of Montpellier's city hall. A wooden scaffold supported a long chopping block covered by a wooden roof. The executioner blindfolded the condemned man, had him lie down with his neck on the block, and then took from beneath his robes a large hunting knife normally used for butchering deer. With two blows to the back of the neck, he deftly removed the man's head, then cut off his arms and legs and arranged all the pieces on the floor of the scaffold, with the head set among the severed limbs. There the dismembered body was allowed to remain all night. In the morning the pieces were hung from an olive tree outside the city and allowed to rot. The whole punishment was pure Machiavelli, except for the "oil tree," a local addition.[15]

* * *

Olives, grain, vines: all of these could be drawn together, as they were, for instance, on the Catalan farm, which was not very different in principle from the *meierhof*, or suburban farm, that Thomas Platter kept in Gundeldingen. In this respect Felix was in familiar territory. In Vendargues, a village about six miles from Montpellier, Laurent Catalan owned what was called a *mas*, or diversified farm producing a number of crops as well as livestock; it also served as a country home. His two sons sometimes rode out to the property on donkeys, each with a girl riding behind—a Marrano girl, naturally. The landlord's steward (known as a *payre* or *ramonet* in the local dialect and *meier* in Felix's German) was the same Guillem whom we encountered earlier, an astonishing and alarming mix of anti-Semitism, alcoholism, sputtering antipapism, and crypto-Lutheranism.

* * *

What would the *mas* have been—the land, the olives, the vineyards, and the gardens—without the men and women who cultivated it, the Languedocian peasants and gardeners whom Felix frequently encountered? We have seen something of Guillem the steward. Thanks to Felix's *Tagebuch*, we can also become more closely acquainted with the gardener Antoine, or rather Antony. Felix generally uses Occitanian first names (Guillem, Antony) when referring to common folk while reserving the *langue d'oïl* for members of the elite (Gilbert, Laurent, Jeanne, and so on), whether Marrano or pure Christian. This bilingualism was so embedded in the soil and so spontaneous that it seemed almost natural: the young man from Basel studying in the south of France felt no need to explain himself. For him, both were "Welch" dialects: what did he care whether a first name or anything else reflected the *langue d'oïl* or the *langue d'oc*?

Antony first appears in Felix's journal on January 28 or 29, 1554. A professional gardener who worked in both urban and rural settings (a true "rurbanite," as Renaissance men so often were), he was employed at the time by Laurent Catalan, who owned *ortalisses*, or gardens, in the suburbs.[16] These gardens were useful to the apothecary both for feeding his family and for growing certain medicinal herbs from which pharmaceutical products could be prepared. In the off-season, Antony, with his employer's consent, supplemented his income by traveling back and forth between Montpellier, Switzerland, and Alsace, carrying packages and mail for German students. The postal service established by Louis XI had yet to supplant rival private services.[17] The latter would subsist until the time of Henri IV.

On his first trip to Switzerland, Antony sold his services to two young clients (F 192). The first of these was Jacob Huggelin, a student of twenty-four and the son of a Basel tailor (F 152). In the winter of 1554, Jacob found himself in need of cash. He gave Antony a message for his mother, asking her to send the money he needed. Meanwhile, Felix asked Antony to carry a package of precious pharmaceutical products to his father. The most important of these was a universal antidote and antiplague formula prepared by Rondelet himself from powdered viper, vipers being more plentiful in the *garrigue* (scrub) around Montpellier than in Basel. The package also contained tincture of violet prepared from violets grown in Antony's gardens.

The gardener-messenger took four long weeks to make the round trip to Basel and back on foot. Felix, anxious for his return, took late afternoon walks after class but before dinner along the road to Nîmes, as far as the olive groves in the suburban village of Castelnau (olives were ubiquitous in southern France in the sixteenth century). This was the route by which Antony surely must return. Finally, on February 26, Felix could just make out Antony's stout silhouette in the distance as he returned safe and sound from his trip to German-speaking lands. In Basel the emissary from Montpellier had been welcomed with open arms by Felix's parents and their friends. The visit was celebrated with red wine, but Antony managed to avoid drinking to excess, unlike his colleague Guillem, who apparently contracted the German national "vices" in the course of his northern travels. The gardener returned from Basel with a thick packet of letters, but good manners prevented the boarders in the Catalan house from opening their mail during dinner. *No reading at the dinner table.* But Laurent Catalan, the master of the household, did not deprive himself of the pleasure of opening letters from his sons, both of whom were studying in Basel. Felix rushed through dinner so that he could at last set eyes on the news from his family, which proved to be good. But Huggelin's mother had not sent him one sou. It was therefore decided that the "traveling gardener" should be sent to Basel one more time to extract the needed cash from the coffers of Frau Huggelin.

The summer of 1554 passed without mention of Antony. There is nothing surprising about this: it was the growing season, and he was too busy with farm or garden work. He reappears in our source on November 14. On that day, Felix sent his father a crate of "exotic" fruits (oranges, figs, and pomegranates), together with a crayfish without pincers and a large crab shell to use as a dish. He also sent a cactus from America that had reached him by way of Spain and Italy (Felix mentions only Italy, but the rest of the route can be inferred), and with it the skeleton of a mouse and a letter. Antony contributed several pomegranates from his garden (*uss seim garten*). He was good with trees as well as vegetables. Was the gardener himself assigned to accompany this crate, loaded on the back of a donkey or mule, on its journey to the northeast? A letter from Thomas to his son suggests that this was the case. In any event, Antony left Montpellier on November 16, bound for Strasbourg (perhaps by way of Basel) on a mission for another German student, who as usual needed money. The loyal Antony wore himself out with the burden of so much traveling with so much freight; Thomas, who welcomed him warmly whenever he came to Switzerland, never failed to sing the gardener's praises in his letters. It was through a letter from Felix that Antony delivered to Basel in late 1554 that the elder Platters learned of the presence of forty or so Turkish galleys (allied with France) at Frontignan and Aigues-Mortes. Henri II's Ottoman alliances were of course destined to counter the power of the Hapsburgs of Austria as well as Spain.

Antony returned from Alsace (via Switzerland) around Christmas of 1554. The journey from Basel to Montpellier took him two weeks (F 211). He brought letters from Felix's friends as well as from the humanist Castellion and from Thomas himself (Thomas's letter was dated December 10, 1554). Lengthy journeys remained possible for Antony so long as the weather stayed cold so that there was little gardening to do. On February 28, 1555, the gardener again departed for Strasbourg, with a stop in Basel. He returned in April, carrying a letter from Thomas dated March 28 (this time it took him twelve days to walk from Basel to Montpellier). In addition to this letter, Antony brought Felix two beautiful pieces of hide, from which the student had two pairs of trousers made (F 214). These earned him the admiration of the young nobles of the region with whom he went dancing. Nothing like these pants had ever been seen in Montpellier. Unfortunately they were too tight for Felix, for the thoughtless tailor had taken part of the skins to make a stunning bag (*seckel*) for his wife (F 217), which meant that he cut Felix's trousers closer than he should have.

Antony's last trip, or at any rate the last excursion of which we have any knowledge, began on November 1, 1555, when he was once again sent to Strasbourg by a German (*Teutsch*), as Felix calls him, or, as we would say,

214

FIVE YEARS IN THE LAND OF OC

an Alsatian (F 233). On his way north, he delivered to Thomas a letter from Felix concerning the fall term just under way at the University of Montpellier. The gardener returned on December 13 after visits to Basel and Strasbourg (F 236). He carried with him a long letter from Thomas to his son, bound in leather: Thomas expressed pleasure at the relatively tolerant attitude toward German Lutheran students in Montpellier and also discussed his confidential and rather promising negotiations with the family of Felix's intended, Madlen Jeckelmann. These discussions were carried on through an intermediary, Frau Frön, Franz Jeckelmann's godmother, a blind woman probably in her seventies.

We have enough information to attempt a portrait of Antony as he was in life. A peasant (*buren*), he was also a highly qualified urban artisan and a skilled gardener capable of performing grafts and cultivating fruit trees like the pomegranate. An affable fellow, he was also as strong as an ox, capable of walking more than thirty-five miles a day to cover the distance between Basel and Montpellier in thirteen or fourteen days (for comparison, it took Felix sixteen full days to cover the same distance on horseback). He was not only a cultivator of the soil but an active participant in the pharmaceutical industry of the day. Although not gifted in foreign languages (he needed an interpreter to converse in German or Latin with Thomas Platter), he acquired a remarkable knowledge of the geography of southern France, Alsace, and Switzerland. Although he was a sturdy man, we have Thomas Platter's word for it that he did tire after his long journeys. Despite being illiterate, he was in his way a Renaissance man of the "lower classes."

* * *

Felix knew the world of the peasant mainly through people such as Guillem and Antony. He was familiar with the major crops—grains, grapes, olive trees, and vegetables—but has little to say about farm animals or, for that matter, about plants and animals considered individually, unless they differed from what he was accustomed to in Switzerland. For example, he frequently remarks on donkeys and mules, which were rare in Switzerland (although his father kept donkeys) but common in southern France. Conversely, he was struck by the relative absence of cows in Languedoc. At the Catalan farm in Vendargues he saw many goats of a type quite common in this region known as *cabrils*, distinguished by long, floppy ears—a trait unheard of in the northern goat. In Marseilles he saw another exotic species, this one from Africa: Barbary rams with plaited tails (which he describes, rather implausibly, as being several yards long), intertwined horns, and thick body hair that hung down to the ground. He also saw ostriches; Arabian horses capable of lifting building blocks; and pieces of intricately ramified coral.

*　*　*

Still more exotic were the turkeys of Vendargues, which fed on grass and made their way to market on their own, almost without supervision (F 166). These fowl, whose presence in Languedoc at such an early date was not known until the Platter memoirs were published, had only recently been imported from America. So had the Indian cactus of which Felix sent cuttings to Basel and the wood from Brazil that Felix must have seen because he says that the wine he used to write his journal (*biechlin*) on a trip to Provence was "redder than Brazil wood" (April 1555). Last but not least, all young men were aware of one poisoned gift from the New World: the treponema of syphilis, which Felix mentions in passing in connection with the death of Captain Niklaus Irmy (May 1553). Irmy, who succumbed to the new disease "in a secret part of his body," was a merchant's son and city councillor who had married beautiful Anna Meyer, the daughter of a Basel bürgermeister, whom Hans Holbein had painted in a kneeling posture when she was sixteen as the "Madonna of Darmstadt." The widow, apparently uncontaminated (Niklaus having contracted the "French disease" in Paris), did not have much trouble finding another man: Captain Wilhelm Hebedening married the former madonna but left her a widow a second time when he succumbed to a more honorable death in battle five years later (F 107, 168, 223). Turkey, treponema, cactus, Brazil wood: America is present in Felix's text mainly by way of its biological imports, both animal and vegetable. Neither the influx of precious metals from Mexico nor the growing Spanish power over the West Indies captured the memoirist's attention.

*　*　*

Wild animals figure only incidentally in Felix's prose. A visit in 1553 to one corner of the garrigue with its typical vegetation of holm oak and rock-rose provided him with an opportunity to sketch the many rabbits that scampered about at his feet as he walked. The flesh of these rabbits, which fed on fragrant herbs, was considered a delicacy, but hunting them was a privilege reserved for the "priestlings" (*pfaffen*) of a small nearby monastery. By 1596, when Thomas Platter Jr. visited this same spot, known as Grammont, between Montpellier and Pérols, the priestlings had fallen victim to the Wars of Religion and disappeared; the monastery had been deconsecrated and now served as a storage shed where peasants from the area kept plows and other implements; but the rabbits were still there, more active and tastier than ever. Partridges were also abundant, as well as excellent, and were often served for dinner, particularly in the villages of the plains that were located close to swamps (F 184, 256).

Penniless German students such as Sigmund Weisel from Breslau, who arrived in Montepellier on August 26, 1555, often poached herons and other shore birds commonly found in the coastal marshes. Weisel, who hadn't a sou to his name, was a real lout (*grob*) but an excellent shot who bagged a good haul of waterfowl with the aid of his dog Fasan. The other *teutschen* students in Montpellier took up a collection to help him out, and he ended up practicing medicine in Silesia. While living there in the early seventeenth century, he liked to spend winter evenings telling the Germans and Poles of the region stories about his past exploits as a hunter on the shores of the Gulf of the Lion.

$$* \quad * \quad *$$

When Sigmund Weisel arrived in Montpellier in 1555, Felix was beginning to ask himself if the time had not come for him to leave. He was fed up with the teaching available at the university, most of which he found mediocre. In any case, he had overcome his first hurdle: on May 28, 1556, in the midst of a severe drought, Felix Platter passed his final examination for the baccalaureate in medicine (F 245). His patron (*praeses*), Antoine Saporta, had lost his wife the year before, and Felix, together with a few friends, had accompanied her remains to their final resting place. During the examination, Professors Schyron, Griffy, Fontanon, and Feynes had challenged young Platter's views. The exam had lasted three hours, from six in the morning until nine. Afterwards, Felix put on a red gown. He recited a speech and some doggerel of his own composition in Latin, in which he included a few thoughts for his German classmates at the university. He disbursed the sum of eleven livres three sous to cover the cost of his examination and received in return a diploma with an enormous seal and writing in Latin done by an Alsatian calligrapher by the name of Johann Sporer, who had been a student at Montpellier since May 1555.

The seal was affixed to this parchment in the church of Saint-Firmin, where the seals of the university were kept. This symbolic act was a reminder of the nominal authority of the Catholic clergy over the medical school, an authority that was in fact much diminished in comparison with the past. With his diploma in hand, Felix briefly considered making a pilgrimage to Santiago de Compostela in Spain—purely as a tourist of course, but one never knows what can happen. This idea had come to him in late April, when he had encountered five pilgrims of Saint James from deepest Switzerland—in fact, from the rural, old-Catholic canton of Zug. One of them, Caspar Fry, a man with only one arm, was actually a professional pilgrim. He had already made the round trip from Switzerland to Spain and back fifteen times for the purpose of expiating the sins of people who did not wish to make the journey themselves and who paid him to take their place. The five nomads all sported beards and were covered with medals and cockle shells (symbols of Saint James). They were traveling at the time with five pious old hags, also beggars, who gave the Welches unfortunate ideas about the beauty of Swiss women. But Felix's plans to travel to Spain came to naught. The extended heat wave of 1556 discouraged him, and so, perhaps, did fears of the Spanish Inquisition, whose harshness stood in sharp contrast to the tolerance of the French toward German Protestant students (F 236). In the end he decided to forgo the trip across the Pyrenees. In any case his thoughts were turning more and more toward Basel, where his young and virtuous fiancée awaited him.

PART FOUR

The Year 1557

CHAPTER SEVEN

Going to Paris (Spring 1557)

Months passed: it was now January 1557. Felix's spirits revived. Many signs, not all of them favorable, indicated that the moment of departure was near. On January 12, during the winter dance season that preceded the Carnival, the young man from Basel was invited with a few friends from the local nobility to a masked ball at the home of a socially prominent family. This ball was to be the culmination of several masquerades, otherwise known as "mummeries" (*mumerien*). In the course of the evening, the mistress of the house, reputedly a lady of no great virtue, lost a precious rosary. Felix was suspected of having stolen it, a charge that filled him with revulsion. In fact (or so Felix alleges), the lady had secretly given the sacred object to her lover, a "priestling." She was merely trying to pull the wool over her husband's eyes by diverting suspicion from herself. Disgusted by the whole affair, Felix decided not to attend any more balls as long as he remained in Montpellier. He bluntly dismissed an emissary from the lady in question, a sort of monk, who came with the intention of searching him (in fact the so-called monk was the lay brother Bernard, the grave robber who had supplied Felix with anatomical specimens).

Before departing, Felix had letters to write and a few last packages to send off to Basel by cart or mule, including a crate crammed with books together with some skeletons of fish and land animals. The young man understood his father's psychology. Knowing that Thomas was anxious that he might not find work after returning home, he sent a letter with the crate: "I am now twenty years old and full of experience. I shall find a way to treat the city of Basel with Montpellier's excellent pharmaceutical remedies, which are vastly superior to those of my Swiss homeland." The young man calculated that he would be home by May at the latest. And indeed, he did reach Basel on May 9, 1557, after traveling through Aquitaine, the Loire Valley, Ile-de-France, Burgundy, and Franche-Comté. He knew, however, that he would need financial assistance en route. He therefore asked Thomas to arrange from Basel for an agent in Paris by the name of Martin Betschart to provide him with the funds he would need when he reached that city.

Felix also wrote to his father on behalf of Laurent Catalan to arrange for Jacques Catalan, Laurent's son, to return home to Montpellier for Easter. He also suggested that Jacques travel with the son of a friend of the Platters, a defrocked canon from Basel who eventually married and had a son, Sigmund von Pfirt, who was about to begin medical studies in Montpellier. Felix found a Montpellier businessman who was willing to give Sigmund lodging and return his horse to Basel (using it on the way). By this time, Montpellier's networks of exchange, which Thomas had exploited in 1552, held no further secrets for Felix.

Felix's final weeks in Montpellier were marked by several incidents that left a bad taste. On January 18 the city was treated to the spectacle of a pregnant woman walking a high tightrope (F 262). On the evening of January 21, Felix's German classmates stood him to a round of drinks to wish him farewell and treated him to a rabbit pâté—which turned out to be not rabbit but cat. The butt of this practical joke was none too happy about it.

On January 26 Felix received Thomas's final letter, which had been dispatched almost a month earlier, on December 29. He learned that three of his classmates had been appointed "municipal physicians" in Bern, Mulhouse, and Colmar (such posts were more common in Germany than in France). All three had studied in Montpellier, but two, Stephan Kunz and Jacob Myconius, had received their doctorates from Avignon. The third laureate, Schopefius or Schöpflin, was the former schoolteacher who had accompanied Felix from Basel to Montpellier in 1552; his doctorate was merely from the University of Valence. Thus the signs were good for Felix, whose Montpellier degree was more prestigious than these degrees from Avignon and Valence and therefore likely to win him a better reception back in Switzerland. (What is more, Felix later received a second doctorate from the University of Basel, in 1557.)

All that remained was to find a traveling companion for the journey from Montpellier to Basel by way of Toulouse, Bordeaux, and Paris. Such a decision deserved to be weighed carefully. Fortunately, Felix chose Theodor Birkmann, a young man who was completing a two-year stay in Montpellier (F 218). Theodor came from Cologne, from a family of printers of markedly higher status than the Platters; for all his youth, he was a man of learning steeped in the traditions of Greek medicine as well as a highly accomplished musician. Felix, anticipating the kinds of distractions that his coming journey would require, expected a great deal of such a friend.

An even more important choice was that of a mount. As it happened, a horse was up for sale not far from the Catalan residence. It belonged to a neighbor of the Marrano pharmacist, the noble Simon de Sandre, who had bought it from a young pharmacy student from Strasbourg who was apprenticed to Catalan. The sturdy animal thus began its life in Alsace, spent several years in Languedoc, and would ultimately end up in Basel.

With traveling companion and horse both lined up, it was time for Felix to sell his lute, which pained him greatly. Then came a farewell dinner with classmates, most likely of German extraction. He also said goodbye to his teachers (*doctoribus*) and good French friends from both the north and the south. And he bade farewell to a couple of young ladies, passing fancies, apparently, about whom we have no other information.

At about ten in the morning on February 27, the caravan left Montpellier. It included Birkmann, Gilbert Catalan, Felix, and several German friends who came to escort the travelers a part of the way before bidding them a final adieu. The preliminary farewells were lengthy and heartrending: Laurent Catalan stood on his doorstep and cried, flanked by his wife and his entire family, including the servants. Felix was "heartbroken" at the thought that he might never again see the city he loved so well (*geliepten statt* [F 263]). The first half-day's journey, to the southwest along the Pézenas road, took the youthful travelers to Fabrègues, an old *circulade*, or circular village, of a few hundred inhabitants. This embryonic Protestant community cultivated a variety of crops on the fringes of the garrigue.[1] After lunch at the inn, the group continued on to Loupian, a parish of roughly the same size as Fabrègues located near coastal marshes and the "mountain" of Sète. The next day they covered the final stretch of the ancient Roman road known as the *via Domitia*, arriving on Sunday, February 28, in Béziers right in the middle of carnival season. Located in the heart of a plain that in those days was devoted primarily to wheat, Béziers had benefited from the broad economic upturn of the 1550s. The year before Felix's visit a weekly market had been established or confirmed there: every Friday merchants came to the city from a radius of more than sixty miles.[2] The city was controlled by the local bishop (who belonged to a prestigious Italian family), by royal agents (who maintained a discreet presence), and by the consulate (which kept minutes in French from 1540 on).

As in other cities, the magistrates of Béziers had recently gained control of the consulate and asserted their priority over the merchants, who, despite their energy, were relegated to a secondary place in the common body. The "*bonne ville*" in which businessmen had once claimed seniority was gone. In the small world of local officialdom, the recently established *présidial* snapped up what had been the functions of the *sénéchaussée*. The presidial thus created a judicial core of some fifty officeholders of modest to high rank in a city of fewer than ten thousand people. Out of this group grew several new lineages of nobles who owed their nobility to the law or to royal office. Did this create a certain climate of conformity? Although Huguenot tendencies were not unknown in Béziers, the city lay outside the central area of Protestant influence, which included the Cévennes, Nîmes, and Montpellier. Felix found nothing to compare with this zone until he had traveled further west and northwest, to Montauban and the mid-Garonne, and even there the Protestantism was relatively attenuated.

In Béziers, Felix and his friends, young Germans from Alsace, Switzerland, and the like, were greeted by masked carnival dancers. These were young Jews, or rather Marranos, belonging to the family of Isabelle Catalan, the daughter of Felix's former landlord. Isabelle had married one of the dancers, the son of a Marrano merchant of Béziers, who that night held a banquet and ball. Gilbert Catalan, the black sheep of his family, who accompanied Felix on this first stage of his journey, danced with his Béziers cousins, who also encouraged the attentions of the Alsatians in the group. Felix spent a pleasant evening almost alone in a corner by the fire with a Marrano girl who wore yellow silk trousers. In those days yellow was a Lutheran color in Languedoc.[3] The girl teased her Swiss companion about abandoning the young ladies of France. She did not think of herself primarily as Jewish (though her remote ancestors were Jews) or Occitanian but rather as French, or at any rate "Welch," that is, part of the community of Romance-language speakers, probably with Huguenot sympathies. Between lunch at the inn and the evening banquet, Felix had had time, as was his custom, to make a brief tour of Béziers. As so often, he was interested primarily in the *Antiquitäten* of the city.

He expresses no admiration at all for the cathedral of Saint-Nazaire, even though the place was known as the site of an all too famous massacre.[4] The cathedral sits on a spur of land overlooking the Orb, standing as a bulwark against invasion from Spain by land or by river. By contrast, he was fascinated, as all Béziers had been fascinated for a thousand years, by an ancient statue, unfortunately mutilated, of Emperor Augustus, alias Pépézuc [*sic*]. In the Baroque Era this colossal marble torso served as a pretext for comic plays in the vernacular, including one featuring funeral orations by Pépézuc's ambassador.[5]

Before leaving Béziers, we should mention a minor but irritating incident, which Felix, who like Montaigne is always keen to impart news of intimate physical matters, duly reports. In the course of his conversation with the girl in yellow trousers, the young man from Basel broke a small piece off one of his back teeth (*ein kleinem sticklin von einem hindesten zan*

[F 264]). This frightened him, and he began to worry about further injuries to his jaw. Was Felix's habit of consuming large quantities of sugar to blame for his decaying teeth? Was it sugar from Spain or Sicily? Or, more likely, Iberian sugar from a more remote source such as Madeira, the Azores, the Canary Islands, Cape Verde, or even São Tomé in the Gulf of Guinea? The range of possibilities is broad, for this was a time when sugar from Spanish-Portuguese or offshore African sources accounted for 2 percent of French imports.[6] One thing is certain: the sugar could not yet have been Brazilian.[7] At this date only small quantities of Brazilian sugar had yet appeared on southern European markets.

On the morning of March 1, 1557, the group of travelers left Béziers. All were now German speakers, Gilbert Catalan having chosen to stay behind and spend a few more days with his cousins. At around noon, after a quick ride of almost thirteen miles to the southeast, the travelers reached the walls of Narbonne.

In 1557 Narbonne was only a modest or even small city of six thousand, governed by a consulate. Elections to this body had been held most recently in February 1557, and everything had proceeded normally, as it had in previous elections and would in subsequent ones. In order of precedence, the consuls were a doctor of law, two bourgeois, an apothecary, and two merchants.[8] Like Avignon, Narbonne had been decimated by the plague: the present population was a far cry from the thirty to forty thousand people who had lived during the "pre-plague" period from 1300 to 1340 in prodigiously crowded conditions in what was then one of the largest textile centers of medieval Europe. The sixteenth century, with its usual contradictions, had left an indelible mark on the large Languedocian town, really a frontier city holding the key to Roussillon and Spain. Between 1490 and 1560 Narbonne surrounded itself with impressive modern fortifications in "the Italian style."[9] These cost a fortune and were paid for out of the *gabelle,* or salt tax, hence ultimately by taxpayers. The new fortifications were the material embodiment of a largely harmonious collaboration between the agents of the kings of France and the consuls of Narbonne. The consuls, in the years since 1537, had accomplished the kind of municipal "revolution" that one finds everywhere in southern France during the Renaissance. Nobles, notaries, and magistrates loyal to the monarchy supplanted the merchants and textile manufacturers who had long constituted the cream of the local elite. The sixteenth century also did much to restore the city's prosperity, though the population never returned to the levels achieved two centuries earlier. It did increase but peaked at a relatively modest height. New dwellings rose on land that had gone vacant a century or more earlier under Charles VI and Charles VII, the monarchs who reigned over the difficult years.

The "merchant's bridge" across the Roubine, which linked the two parts of Narbonne known as *le bourg* and *la cité,* had been filled with merchants' houses since the time of Louis XII. The city had tamed the waters, equipping itself with an aqueduct, fountains, and mills. Immigrants from the Massif Central, eastern Aquitaine, and even northern France had swollen the population. By contrast, the Spanish presence was negligible, apart from a few "outside" nobles from nearby Catalonia. This lack of a Spanish influx reflected the fact that relations between France and Spain were not good and would not improve for some time. Intensive cultivation of the flat land around the city supported the revival of the urban center. Olive groves spread rapidly, as they did all along the Mediterranean. Wheat, which remained the principal export crop of the Narbonne region in the early modern era, flourished. Villages in the area kept faith with the civilization of the *agora,* in which the spoken word played a key role. The use of the written word for administrative and other purposes was largely confined to the principal town in each region. Exploitation of the local salt marshes was at its height, rivaling that of the marshes of Camargue. The proceeds from the salt tax paid for the city's fortifications. Urban aristocrats owned vast stretches of these profitable marshlands. At this point Narbonne was cut out of direct trade with the Levant, which had been responsible for its prosperity as a textile center in the thirteenth century. But it was an integral part of a vast network of coastal trade dominated by Provençal (and especially Marseilles) shippers, a network that extended from the Andalusian coast to the Roman *campania* and included Barcelona, Aigues-Mortes, Genoa, and Livorno. Woad (a plant from which a blue indigo dye was obtained) from Toulouse was one of the principal export goods, along with iron, linen, broadcloth, honey, and wine. In the city a new aristocracy emerged, composed of natives together with a handful of Iberians and Italians; many of the latter were former merchants or sons of merchants who had come as part of the entourage of Florentines whom the Valois monarchs had chosen to serve as bishops of Narbonne and Béziers.

In many respects the city in the Aude developed a reputation for an Italian-style *dolce vita,* a reputation reflected in Italian Renaissance literature by writers who visited lower Languedoc to see for themselves. Tuscan touches can still be seen in the marble ornaments and moldings on fountains and facades. At this distance from Geneva and the Cévennes, Protestantism had little chance of establishing a permanent foothold. It had largely run its course, hindered from further progress by a vigorous

Catholicism that was buttressed by devout Spain and, as in Carcassonne and Toulouse, was stubbornly resistant to the new faith.[10]

* * *

Felix and his German friends stayed in Narbonne for one day and one night, March 1–2, 1557, a Monday night and the following morning, which happened to be Mardi Gras. Upon arriving at the city walls at noon on March 1, they had been greeted rather coolly. The sentinels, guarding the gateway to France, refused to allow the German quartet to enter on the grounds that they were subjects of the Hapsburgs (France was at war) and therefore accomplices of the Spanish enemy. Felix pointed out that he was Swiss. Indeed, this was the first time since his arrival in France that he had boasted of his Swiss identity. Among his Welch friends he usually identified himself as *Teutsch,* or German, which in a sense he was. In the present situation, however, it was better to be a Confederate (*Eidgenosse*), because the Swiss Confederation and France had signed a treaty of perpetual peace in 1516. Felix's protests succeeded in assuaging the sentinels' fears, and the travelers were allowed to enter the city, where the governor, a man of Italian descent by the name of Fourquevaux, personally arranged for lodging at an inn. Once again they enjoyed the carnival festivities, which as it happens were presided over by a masked German nobleman living in Narbonne.

The traveler from Basel was once again attracted by the city's Roman antiquities. Vestiges of ancient white marble had recently been incorporated into the gray Renaissance masonry of the renovated city walls. Felix even had time to visit the cathedral of Saint-Just. Papist though it was, it was well worth the detour. The student went into ecstasies over giant candles so high that one had to climb a ladder to light or extinguish their flames (he was not so ecstatic, however, that he failed to add ironic afterthoughts to his commentary). By contrast, he did not so much as glance at (or at any rate record having glanced at) Sebastiano del Piombo's *Resurrection of Lazarus* (today in London's National Gallery), which, some forty years later, his younger brother Thomas Jr. would admire down to such details as the hands and hair of the figures portrayed. On Tuesday morning, as the last fires of the "fat days" waned, Felix burst into tears in his bed, just as he had done before in Avignon.[11] This time, however, the tears flowed at the thought that he might never again see Montpellier, a city that had come to occupy an important place in his heart. He was also worried about the dangerous journey ahead of him through southwestern and western France. He and Theodor Birkmann left Narbonne alone, the other Germans having turned back. Felix and Theodor took the right fork toward Toulouse; the left fork would have taken them toward Spain.

The first stage of the journey took place on the morning of Mardi Gras (March 2), but there was nothing festive about it as far as the two young travelers were concerned. By noon they had reached Moux, a small parish (population 300) typical of a border region, for while it lay in the diocese of Narbonne, it was "positioned" in what would later become the district of Carcassonne.[12] It being early March, the broom had sprouted new shoots and the cherry buds were about to open. Plenty of bees were in evidence, along with flies, ants, and butterflies, some lemon yellow, others orange spotted with black. Mushrooms were ready to be gathered, the apricot trees were in flower, the peach trees showed new leaves, rushes had returned to the meadows, and new leaves had appeared on blackberry bushes. Lilies of the valley were up more than an inch. In Moux, Theodor and Felix replenished themselves at an inn, for the younger Platter was one of those people who, when traveling, prefer to dine only in restaurants if they can afford it. The picnics in the country that nineteenth-century landscape painters were so fond of depicting held little appeal for our Renaissance traveler. After lunch, the two *Teutschen* continued on to Carcassonne, where they arrived late in the afternoon and remained for the night.

Carcassonne in 1557 was a busy textile town. Indeed, business was so good that there had been talk as early as 1547 of opening a third mint[13] there to supplement the two already in existence in Montpellier and Toulouse.[14] Carcassonne was not an intellectual center. Its gifted students left at an early age to pursue their studies and careers in Toulouse and its environs. By the late 1550s the city had only barely been touched by the Reformation: Huguenot propaganda had been spread among the local artisans by ex-monks and other emissaries from the entourage of Marguerite de Navarre, who had set up headquarters first in Nérac and later in the Béarn. The clergy of Carcassonne were quite fond of missions, miracles, and other syndromes of religious "panic" and not at all fond of the queen of Navarre even though she was the king's sister. When she visited Carcassonne in 1537, the only gifts she received from the consuls were a few cases of candles, preserves, and refreshments, whereas not only the king and queen of France but the merest seneschal or governor of Languedoc who visited the city in this period were likely to be heaped with expensive gold and silver drinking vessels and dinnerware.[15]

The consuls of Carcassonne, long suspicious of heresy, were also "royalized." It was the same story as in other cities: the power of the monarchy had long allied itself with local magistrates, who championed their cities' affirmation of a new identity. By 1547, the magistrates, with their flair for statecraft, had pushed the merchants aside as they had done throughout the Midi and seized the post of first consul. The "community" of Carcassonne was in fact not much of a community: it had been ravaged by persistent conflict between the natives of the "High Town" (*la Cité*) and the residents of the "Low Town" (*le Bourg*), whose population was less clerical and less "Ancien Régime" than that of *la Cité*. In the period 1555–65 *la Cité* was conformist; it counted few Huguenots among its residents, even fewer than in *le Bourg*. The two parts of the city also fought over the location of important institutions, especially new ones: the presidial, which was created in Carcassonne as in other southern cities in 1552, became a political football to be kicked back and forth between High Town and Low Town.[16] At first it seemed natural to locate it in the fortified High Town, the noble quarter and the normal location of anything bearing the hallmark of official state business. But by May 1553 the new court had been moved to the Low Town.[17] In September a council decree ordered it moved back to the High Town. In December, that order was reversed by letters patent. In February 1554 a new decree again ordered that the presidial be moved to *la Cité*. Then, in the month of May, a royal edict reversed that order. In September the King's Council sent the court back up to the heights while initiating an investigation into the *commodo et incommodo* of the affair. In December, new letters patent authorized yet another move to the "*bourg neuf*," or Low Town. The struggle continued for three generations (though not all of these orders were actually carried out).

Felix in his own way took note of Carcassonne's obviously schizophrenic identity. The city, he wrote, "lies partly on low ground, partly on the hill" (*liegt zum theil im boden, zum theil auf den Berg* [F 266]). He also recorded that his journey from Narbonne by horseback had covered eight leagues (Felix had his own notion of what a league was). He left Carcassonne on March 3. Eight months later, a plague struck the city and continued to rage until Lent of 1558. It was said to have caused 2,500 deaths, probably a good third of the total population. For once, Low Town and High Town were fraternally united in disaster.

* * *

At dawn on Ash Wednesday, March 3, 1557, Felix and Theodor left Carcassonne. Lent had begun (F 266). For the next forty days, until the two young men reached Paris in the first fortnight of April, they would eat no

more meat (*kein fleisch mer*). People along the way seemed to observe
Lent properly, even in towns touched by Huguenot influence. *La France
toute catholique* was no myth, at least not on the surface.

The first stretch of the trip to Toulouse proceeded over bad road. In
Castelnaudary, where the two riders stopped for the night, Felix hit his
head against an iron hook projecting from the wall of a butcher shop as
he rode down a narrow street in the dark. His blood ran down a side of
beef hanging from the hook. The next day, west of Castelnaudary, the
travelers bade farewell to the last stretch of lower Languedoc and
glimpsed Aquitaine just ahead. The countryside was unquestionably
making rapid strides as diversified farming took hold, although some
smallholders suffered cruelly as a result of the change.[18] Farmers grew
woad (for dye, but in small amounts), grains, and grapes. There were of
course no olive groves, because the local climate was too damp and subject to frequent frosts. Forests survived but suffered from excessive land-
clearing. The growth of the population was not always compatible with
ecological sensitivity: in extreme cases, peasants short of wood (because
of overcutting of the forests) were forced to burn straw in order to bake
bread.

The valley of the Ariège lay just ahead: there, mines and forges catered
to the needs of the north, both civilian and military. Gunpowder was produced at Le Mas-d'Azil downstream from Ariège, where there were caves
filled with saltpeter. Huguenots, encouraged by the local dynasty of Marguerite de Navarre and later Jeanne d'Albret, were not uncommon
among the people. There was no shortage of silver. Attempts were made
to extract it from "foxholes" (supposedly mineshafts) in the county of
Foix, but after 1549 and the "silver rush" in the north of Mexico, most
silver came from the south. The precious metal traveled across the Atlantic through Spain and into Aquitaine by way of Narbonne, Bayonne, and
the passes of the Pyrenees.[19] At first Felix noticed little of the vitality of
southwestern France. Shortly after leaving Castelnaudary with his companion, he deviated from his route to escape the ominous attentions of a
pair of highway robbers. Later, while galloping once more along the
road to Toulouse, the two students met up with a compatriot who
seemed friendly (F 267). The man was a German, part highwayman and
part tramp, and accompanied by a puppy on a leash; while carrying a
sword on his shoulder, he sang at the top of his lungs. His name was Samuel Hertenstein, and he was the son of Dr. Philipp Hertenstein of Lucerne. Samuel had been a student of Thomas Platter's in Basel from 1546
to 1549 and had known Felix as a small child. Later he had practiced "empirical" medicine in Toulouse, where he was well known in all the gam-

bling dens. After that he had fought in the Piedmont. Now, dressed in tatters, he was on his way back to Toulouse, where he hoped to earn enough money to pay for his return to Basel. After stops in various taverns in which Samuel joked with the innkeepers, the three travelers entered Toulouse during the evening of March 4 and rented a room at the Saint-Pierre inn.

Toulouse, with a population of 30,000 or more (the exact figure is unknown), was at this point probably the fourth or fifth largest city in France after Paris, Lyons, Orléans, and Rouen. In the 1550s the economic influence of the capital of Aquitaine extended over an area of some 15,000 square kilometers, roughly the size of three French *départements* today.[20] To get an idea of the material progress the city had made, a brief look at the history of the grocery (and cookware) trade is worth more than a long-winded description. In the second half of the fifteenth century, the leading staples were somewhat different from what they are today. The most important items were such basic ingredients as olive oil and sea salt from lower Languedoc and salted fish from the Atlantic. Spices and nonferrous metals were still of minor importance. Things changed somewhat in the second half of the second decade of the sixteenth century, however: there was increased commerce in copper from Central Europe, tin from the British Isles, and wax (for candles, a sign of "enlightenment" in a university town). There was also increased trade in dyestuffs and related substances such as Flemish madder and alum. Sales of spices increased, as did the consumption of Portuguese sugar. The years from 1527 to 1531 were crucial in a number of respects: the issue of how to deal with the poor came to the fore, and southern France began to feel the first rumblings of the Reformation. On the other hand, consumer society was just getting off to a modest start, limited primarily (though not exclusively) to the elite: the influx of wax from Germany, salted fish from the Atlantic, and wood from Brazil increased, as did trade in sugar and dried fruit.

Between 1540 and 1560 Toulouse consolidated its position as an exporter of agricultural products, such as prunes, goose feathers, and above all woad (the source of indigo), which formed the basis of many fortunes. Trade was encouraged by the fact that Toulouse enjoyed substantial tax privileges. In 1558, the year after Felix's visit, the residents of Languedoc paid 562,282 *livres tournois* of the tax known as the *taille*, but Toulouse, one of the province's leading cities, contributed not a *denier* of that total because it had been exempt from taxes since the great conflagration of 1463. The flames had been a blessing. The city paid the king only one small tax of 2,500 livres.[21]

Felix's visit to Toulouse on March 5, 1557, concentrated on theological and military matters. He toured the city's ramparts of brick, or "baked stones" (*bachenen steinen*), and inspected the recently reconstructed walls, equipped by engineers from Italy with defensive structures known as demilunes or ravelins. In the construction of defensive fortifications, the great French military architect Sébastien Le Prestre de Vauban (1633–1707) was, to judge by the many cities already fortified in the mid-sixteenth century, more of a continuator or end of a line than he was an innovator. Felix spent most of his time in Toulouse visiting churches. In these pages of his memoirs he "softpedals" his anticlericalism, although it never altogether disappears. Despite the presence of eight hundred actual or potential Huguenots within its walls, the city remained a bastion of Catholicism thanks to its parlement, which countered the influence of a municipal government sympathetic to Protestantism.22 The young man from Basel was particularly interested in *la Daurade* (from *deaurata*, the "gilded temple"). This was an unusually well-preserved Visigothic or Frankish monument in the shape of a regular decagon with a central altar "topped by a cupola with an opening in the center."23 The structure stood close to the river, virtually with its feet in the water, as it were, between the court known as the *viguerie* and the fish market.

The inside of *la Daurade* was notable for its mosaics interspersed with marble columns. Dating back to Merovingian times, these mosaics, which stretched from floor to ceiling, were composed of small silvered and gilt stones and offered a compendium of Judeo-Christian theology, ranging from Abraham and Moses to the Archangels and the Apostles and the Virgin and Child. The whole church was dedicated to the cult of Mary, which held little attraction for a convinced Protestant like Felix. What is more, the future doctor, interested as always in Gallo-Roman and neo-pagan archaeology even when he toured churches, confidently maintained that *la Daurade* was originally a non-Christian construction, a temple of Isis. (Thomas Platter Jr. would later call it a temple of Jupiter [T2 409]). Anything but Catholic, in short: not for nothing was our author a Swiss humanist and Protestant. On the eve of the Wars of Religion *la Daurade* was occupied by a Benedictine community, which the Cluniac chapter had tried to reform by proposing a new set of statutes in 1535.24 Under Richelieu, it would host a group of Benedictines from Saint-Maur, who supplanted the order of Cluny and who became noted for their scholarly researches. In the eighteenth century, unfortunately, *la Daurade* was destroyed, thus depriving France of a rare jewel of late antique or very early medieval religious art. Felix's account focuses mainly on the mosaics. He reports an oral tradition that he picked up in Toulouse in 1557: if one pressed one of the small colored stones into the walls or floor, it would make its way back to the surface in the space of a single night, returning infallibly to its appointed place in the intricate and sacred puzzle.

Even more impressive to the traveler from Basel—who had become a decided fancier of churches, if not of the papist religion—was the immense basilica of Saint-Sernin, the model of a whole tradition of Romanesque architecture in southern France. In the sixteenth century Saint-Sernin was still an important financial and religious power. Felix, focusing on the essential, went straight to the crypt, which contained twelve silver sarcophagi in which were preserved, supposedly, the bodies of the twelve apostles, including the decapitated skeleton of Saint James. Accordingly, Felix reports, pilgrims on their way to Santiago de Compostela still marched in procession through Saint-Sernin, just like their medieval predecessors, who, having been gouged on prices for wine and oats provided by crooked horse dealers who also sold them blind and decrepit animals, nevertheless passed through the church, content, their eyes fixed on a faraway tomb.

Felix's tour of Toulouse was concluded with breakneck speed. His memoirs make no mention of the *parlementaires* of the city, despite their important role, or of the highly militant local Huguenots (who were in the minority, however, and soon marginalized). Nor does he mention the University of Toulouse, where intellectual life was intense. Following the lead of Coras, learned jurists were there putting the finishing touches on theories of legislative sovereignty in the monarchical state, theories that would soon be taken up by Bodin.[25] The university of the "pink city" specialized in law, counterbalancing the University of Avignon, which was dedicated to theology. All that Felix later remembered, however, was that he had visited a print shop in Toulouse where there was a typographer who had once worked as an apprentice and messenger for his father. He also casts a brief glance at the mills on the Bazacle with their stone pillars, wooden frames, and tile roofs. These mills were kept supplied by endless trains of mules, which brought wheat in and carried flour out.

If we believe Thomas Platter Jr., this "factory" was capable of feeding 100,000 people in the city and surrounding plain (T2 422). While this figure may be exaggerated, Toulouse's future as a flour producer was foreshadowed as early as 1557. But none of this seemed important at the time. There were more pressing matters to be considered: the ground was burning beneath our travelers' feet, because the city had been stricken by plague. Four hundred fifty houses were already infected.[26] On March 6, 1557, after the noon meal, Felix and Theodor left Toulouse for Montauban. They had previously paid the innkeeper at the inn of Saint-Pierre.

Generous but penniless Samuel Hertenstein bade the two travelers a heartfelt farewell after signing Felix's remembrance book. Felix never saw the paramedical tramp again; he died in France without ever returning to Switzerland.

*   *   *

The usual route from Toulouse to Agen and Bordeaux passed through Montauban, which meant leaving the towpath along the Garonne and making a small detour to the north. In Montauban a sixteenth-century bridge with seven pointed brick arches made it easy to cross the Tarn.

The route in general turned out to be secure, which would not have been the case a century earlier, when brigands set loose by the Hundred Years' War still roamed the area. In all his travels in francophone territory, Felix had encountered truly dangerous criminals only rarely: once north of Lausanne in 1552, a second time at an inn in the Comtat Venaissin, and a third time after leaving Castelnaudary. Each time he was frightened but not hurt. On the whole, the France of Henri II was not overly plagued with crime, particularly in view of the weak constabulary. Montauban, which had grown rapidly in the twelfth century, had long since recovered from the afflictions of the late Middle Ages, when the community, practically ruined, had been little more than a support base for the English forces of the prince of Wales in fourteenth-century Aquitaine.

In the age of Henri II, the city, refurbished from top to bottom, still surrounded by impressive ramparts, and embellished by a new pilastered square in the Florentine manner, served as a port of transit for wine and wheat being shipped to the lower Garonne by way of the Tarn.[27] Manufacturing of common textiles and coarse fabrics such as burlap and caddis developed around the center of town in the middle of the sixteenth century. The work force grew, replenished from such "demographic reservoirs" as the Massif Central, the Rouergue, and the dioceses of Mende and Saint-Flour. From the time of Louis XII on, Renaissance architecture left its indelible mark on the *hôtels particuliers* of Montauban in the form of "basket handle" motifs over doorways in place of the traditional ogee lintels typical of late Gothic architecture and once quite common in the south of France.

Control of the city was divided among three powers: the bishop, the *quercynol*, or seneschal's lieutenant, and the consuls. The latter were the most active, and as in other cities magistrates were more influential than merchants. The consuls formed a republic of minor municipal sovereigns, micro-potentates whose principal merit was to be present in the street whenever anything happened.

The consular authorities took a favorable attitude toward Protestantism in Montauban, all the more so since Bishop Jean de Lettes, the
nephew of the previous prelate, Jean des Prés, and uncle of the subsequent diocesan Jacques des Prés, was involved in a romantic idyll with a
young noblewoman. He married her in 1556 and spent the last quarter of
his honeymoon between Geneva and Lausanne. Had it not been for the
ever-vigilant parlement of Toulouse, "heresy" would have found few im-
pediments in Montauban. It had deep roots among the city's artisans,
having first gained a foothold through teachers in the excellent local
schools with support from the middle-ranking clergy of the diocese, including a clerical judge, an "administrator of episcopal property," and a
preacher in the mold of Savonarola.

Felix thus came into contact with the ribbon-like Huguenot stronghold of the central Garonne region. The contrast between this and the
area between Béziers and Toulouse, where heresy lacked vitality, was astonishing. In Montauban Felix found himself once again in reformed territory such as he had known in Nîmes in 1552 and suspected in
Montpellier in subsequent years. Just outside Montauban, in the suburban church of Saint-Jacques, a dog named Poclès who had been following Felix for months staged a sort of pro-Protestant demonstration. The
Lutheran animal somehow got the idea that the ciborium on the altar
cloth contained food and tried to wolf it down. On its first attempt the
dog was beaten by a sacristan who happened to be present. As a result of
this experience, Poclès conceived a holy horror of the papist cult. The dog
never missed an opportunity to yap loudly at Catholic altars and ciboria
in France and Switzerland. It thus boldly proclaimed the reformed opinions of its master Felix. The dog was truly a *bouffe-curé,* or priest-eater.

Felix and Theodor spent March 7 and part of March 8 in Moissac, a
town notable for the astonishing doorway of its Cluniac abbey, its houses
with dovecotes, and its old bridge of brick and wood. The travelers then
crossed an ecological divide: cows (of which Felix had seen few for years)
suddenly became plentiful and the countryside became moister and
greener as they traveled toward the northwest. On the afternoon of
March 8, the two riders, accompanied by Poclès, reached Agen (F 270). A
flourishing town with a population of 14,000 (6,000 of whom were
Huguenots), Agen, with its cathedral of Saint-Etienne whose radiating
chapels had just been vaulted, rivaled Montpellier despite the lack of a
university. The city's new quarters, with their recently built houses of red
brick and exposed framing, gave evidence of a flourishing commercial vocation: Agen exported prunes and *minots* (barrels filled with flour) by
way of the Garonne.

Numerous colonies of Italian merchants lived cheek by jowl with a variety of immigrants from Poitou, Brittany, and southwestern France. Agen, important as the site of one of sixteen tax collection centers (*recettes générales des finances*) throughout France,28 stood at the crossroads of two principal transportation routes: the Garonne river and the land route linking the Swiss cantons to the Basque region by way of Auvergne and Gascony. Not only merchants but to an even greater degree prelates from Italy had opened the way for the Italian intelligentsia: "A monk approached us in the street and asked us if we wanted to meet Julius Scaliger, an illustrious resident of Agen. But this was a joke [*spot*] directed at us, and we dropped the subject" (F 270). It may well have been a joke, but the monk was indeed correct that Scaliger, a gladiator of humanism, was an active member of an important and creative network of literary figures. Born in Riva del Garda, Julius Caesar Scaliger, erstwhile soldier of Italy and former monk as well as a great collector, had followed the bishop Della Rovere to Agen. Scaliger took a wife in the city and became a consul. In 1561 he published *Poetics,* one of the works that later inspired the classicism of Boileau. He was the best known of a whole constellation of writers associated to one degree or another with Agen. Among them were Julius Scaliger's son Joseph Scaliger (all of Julius's children went on to brilliant careers in the nobility, magistracy, or commerce), Bernard Palissy, and the two Marguerites, Marguerite de Navarre (who played a crucial role in the Huguenot politics of the central Garonne) and Marguerite de Valois. Others included Monluc, Nostradamus, Belleforest, and above all Bandello.

Matteo Bandello, a writer of tales and friend of Scaliger, enjoyed the protection of the Fregosos, a family with episcopal claims that came originally from Genoa but had been living in gilded exile in Agen since 1542. During the twenty years Bandello spent in Agen (1542–61), he wrote and published the best of his fiction, the *Novelle,* or tales, one of which inspired Shakespeare's *Romeo and Juliet*. In 1554, shortly before Felix's visit, Bandello had just completed six years of conscientious service as bishop of Agen—an astonishing performance for an outspoken advocate of ribald hedonism, a man closer in spirit to Alfred de Musset than to Bishop Bossuet. Of course the writer had merely been keeping the episcopal throne warm until the titular bishop, a Fregoso of tender age, was old enough to succeed him. When Bandello tired of the job, a second place-warmer by the name of Corniolio replaced him as bishop from 1555 to 1558, a period that spanned the time of Felix's visit.

On March 9 and 10 the itinerant students covered the distance from Agen to Bordeaux in two stretches. While crossing the Garonne, Felix came close to drowning, along with horse and baggage, when the boat carrying the travelers capsized, fortunately close to shore. In Aiguillon near the mouth of the Lot, the travelers had to swear that they had not come from Toulouse, where the plague was raging. Their false oath was accepted all the more readily because they stated, as they had already done once before, that the were Swiss and therefore allies of the French. At the inn in Aiguillon they had ample time to appreciate the plumage of an immigrant from the tropics: a parrot. They also had a new linguistic experience: their first contact with the French of the "masses," which took place near Marmande, in an area recently repopulated by *"gavaches d'oïl"* (southern dialect for "skunks" from the north) from Saintonge and Anjou. They then passed through the heavily fortified town of La Réole; after that came Saint-Macaire, one of the few communities that had refused to join in the first anti-salt-tax revolts in the 1540s.[29] Between Saint-Macaire and Bordeaux they had to pass through the Cap de l'Homme forest, which was apparently a den of thieves. In Felix's mind, forests (not only this one near Bordeaux but others outside Basel, Lausanne, Lunel, and Toulouse) posed a threat of violence, whether real or imaginary we cannot say. Did cutting down trees therefore mean greater security? In any case, Felix's fears of the Cap de l'Homme proved as groundless as most of his earlier fears.

When the two students reached the walls of Bordeaux on the night of March 10, they were forbidden to enter the city. It was nighttime and the gates were closed. Security was of paramount consideration. Felix and his companion dined at a suburban inn. The menu included squid (*sepia*) and spider crabs (*merspinnen*): they were close to the ocean. On the morning of March 11 the travelers entered Bordeaux. There was no shortage of hotels: the new arrivals were free to choose among the Quatre Mendiants and the Ecu de Bretagne, the cosmopolitan Monde qui tourne, and the rustic Autruche, Cheval Blanc and Trois Lapins.[30] But the lure of the harbor drew them to an inn on the waterfront: the Chapeau Rouge, also known as the Chapeau de Cardinal, which stood adjacent to a forest of masts and hulls. In the 1550s, the mouth of the Garonne, as vast as it is, was crowded with ships, and collisions were inevitable. There were good reasons for this crowding of the harbor. It was easy to transport wine from throughout Aquitaine to Bordeaux by river, and from there it was carried to the thirsty drinkers of northern Europe by ship via the Atlantic. Felix watched barrels of wine being loaded aboard an English ship. Other export commodities included woad, hemp, honey, and tar from the moors; foreign sales of all these items were soaring. Imports (from the Netherlands) included furniture, paintings, tapestries, and copper kitchenware (from Flanders). From the British Isles came fabrics, tin, lead, and alabaster. Other imports included salted and smoked fish rich in iodine (hence a remedy for goiter); oats and salt from Saintonge; and, from the Basque region and Spain, smaller amounts of iron, weapons, anchors, pottery, bundled wool, barrels of sardines and whale meat, and Portuguese silver.[31] From the more or less recently discovered colonies came sugar (from Madeira), wood (from Brazil), and above all cod from Newfoundland. Cod, imported since 1517, arrived in substantial amounts, especially in the decade and a half after 1546.

During the reign of Henri II high-risk loans sustained the Newfoundland shippers, who in good years sent twenty or more vessels across the Atlantic. Trade rose substantially under the last five Valois kings. Exports exceeded imports in both weight and value, to the benefit of the Atlantic port. As a result, the docks were soon covered with piles of ballast, and no one knew what to do with it all. With the increase in business the port tended to expand beyond the ramparts into the area downriver around the port of Les Chartreux. Inside the city Felix rubbed elbows with substantial numbers of northerners who mingled with the 45,000 native inhabitants.[32] To be sure, there were also large numbers of visitors from the south, Basques and Bayonnais and Spaniards. But they were eclipsed by Normans, Bretons especially, and Englishmen. By 1550, moreover, there was a noticeable influx of people from Germany and the Netherlands, especially Flanders, as more and more of the city's trade was with the Low Countries (this trend would continue into the next century). Drinkers in Amsterdam were fond of their *brandwein* (brandy), which had been exported from Bordeaux since 1513. Aquitaine thus had a lead of a century and a half over lower Languedoc, whose glorious career in distilling did not begin until the age of Colbert. Historians are always quick to refer to "Marignano, 1515." But other dates also have their importance in the history of Bordeaux: the first local production of brandy in 1513;[33] the first Lutheran book in a canon's library, 1521; the first case of clerical syphilis in 1514; and the first cod from Newfoundland in 1517. These last two dates are the first signs of American influence for good and for ill.

The host of ships crowding the harbor included countless small "tramps," or coastal vessels of forty-five tons or less. These, according to Felix, were simply allowed to rest on the bottom at low tide; their keels suffered less than would have been the case with large ships weighed down by ballast and cargo and moved about by the shifting tides.[34] These smaller vessels carried diverse cargoes and could sail just as easily over shallow lobster beds as they could on the deep sea. Most ships' captains, or "masters," made do with very little specialized equipment: a compass (in common use in Bordeaux since 1500), a chronometer, and a sounding line; marine charts were virtually nonexistent. The Bordelais themselves were not great navigators and let foreign sailors take the lead in shipping even in their own port. There were no more than six hundred ablebodied seamen and mates in the substantial population of this port city—a very small number indeed. And half of these were freshwater sailors who piloted barges along the river or fishermen who went after lamprey, a river fish in season in the spring. During his three days in Bordeaux, Felix ate lamprey for lunch and dinner at the Chapeau Rouge. The Garonne, unpolluted in those days, was as well stocked with fish as anyone could wish. Those Bordeaux sailors who had direct experience of the sea belonged to religious confraternities rather than to the trade guilds that were common in northern Europe. Bordeaux merchants were wine shippers, just as their counterparts in Toulouse shipped woad and those in England shipped fabrics and fish.[35] Speed of travel depended on whether one was a sailor, rider, or spirochete. It took Felix five days to ride from Toulouse to Bordeaux on horseback. The same trip by river would have taken him four days going downstream but eleven days going upstream. Biological journeys were not as rapid. It took syphilis twenty years to reach Bordeaux from Naples (1494–1514).[36]

Owing to chance encounters and Felix's personal predilections, his seventy-two hours in Bordeaux were largely taken up with music (*wir musicierten* [F 272]). A shopkeeper from Berne who dealt in stringed instruments kept the two young travelers company. He lent Felix a harp and Theodor a lute. The Swiss trio spent much of their stay giving modest concerts that attracted crowds of natives. There is nothing surprising about the musical interests of the Bordelais: under Louis XII and Francis I, Bordeaux had been the residence of Clément Janequin, who, under the patronage of the archbishop, had composed twenty-odd polyphonic songs, 80 percent of which were devoted to themes of love and the remainder to war.[37]

In Bordeaux, a community open to currents from the four corners of the earth, Latin literature provided a shared culture, a frame of reference that loomed large in the minds of men like Etienne de La Boétie and Michel de Montaigne, who, still young in 1557, was just beginning a new term in the parlement of Bordeaux. The Swiss visitor was well aware of the depth of Bordeaux's Latin culture. He made an excursion outside the walls in the company of a guide from Bern to visit the Palais Gallien, a stadium in the shape of a vast oval—Thomas Jr. would later describe it as an elongated egg (T2 411). Built in the time of the Severi (after 193 C.E.), the amphitheater sat atop an underground prison. Originally it could accommodate 15,000 spectators for gladiatorial combats.[38] By the time of

Felix's visit, the still majestic and well-preserved ruins had become a sort of lover's lane. Amorous couples barely moved when riders, barrel-laden ox carts, or curious visitors passed by.

Forty years apart, Felix and Thomas Jr. also visited the "guardian pillars," another impressive relic of Gallo-Roman times that had become a destination for curious tourists and moonstruck couples. The two brothers independently counted seventeen or eighteen columns still standing, complete with acanthus-leaf capitals, architrave, and caryatids. In the sixteenth century a square garden (replacing the old imperial forum) in the center of the open area enclosed by the columns covered a series of vast wine cellars. Small houses with tiled roofs stood nearby. The great architect and jack-of-all-trades Claude Perrault observed the "guardian pillars" still standing in the time of Colbert, but they were destroyed under Louis XIV after a major local rebellion in 1675 so as to discourage future rebels by extending the defensive glacis of the Château-Trompette. To the Sun King's way of thinking—and dismay—Bordeaux was indeed a city of "powder and saltpeter," prone to rebellion and therefore to be taken firmly in hand. This was already the case in the "time of Platter," that is, during the reign of Henri II, who took a rather repressive attitude toward the people of Bordeaux.

* * *

Apart from the monuments of Antiquity, which lay outside the city proper, Felix explored the city thoroughly (*überal*) in the company of his guide from Bern. He inspected the building in which the parlement of Bordeaux met (*das haus do das Parlament wird gehalten* [F 272]), the old Palais de l'Ombrière, where there is today a street of the same name, at the southeastern corner of the old Roman *castrum*.[39]

L'Ombrière, a medieval building ensconced in an ancient setting, was none other than the palace of the dukes of Aquitaine, which in the thirteenth century became the headquarters of the pro-British seneschals of Gascony. It stood at the southeastern entrance to a first line of fortifications, which followed the boundaries of the *castrum*. In the sixteenth century, the decrepit former palace became the home of the parlement of Bordeaux. The magistrates of parlement, wealthy vineyard owners, resided in the vicinity of the high court, whose filthy appearance set off their splendid houses. Felix noted the poor repair of the prestigious symbolic building, the structural defects, and the "filth" of the court chambers. Yet lucid observers, Thomas Platter Jr. among them, were not deceived by the wretched appearance of the place. The parlement had certainly suffered from the popular anti-tax rebellions of 1548 in the Gironde, in the wake of which a furious Henri II had temporarily suspended its normal judicial functions. But after 1550, things resumed their normal course.

The sovereign court (which had tripled the number of its magistrates in response to demographic, economic, and governmental growth between Louis XI and Francis I) was still the arbiter of justice in Bordeaux and Aquitaine. The magistrates were highly cultivated men. Parlement dealt with the royal governor and his lieutenant general as peers. It set the tone for other official institutions of the municipal and royal government: the *jurade* (aldermen), the *amirauté* (admiralty), and *les finances* (fiscal authorities). Despite the growing influence of Protestantism among intellectuals and aristocrats, parlement kept the city and the port, with its ships named for the Virgin and the saints, obediently Catholic, much as the parlement of Toulouse did in that city, where Papism was even more firmly ensconced than in the lower Garonne. Thus Bordeaux, which willingly or unwillingly kept faith with the traditional religion, experienced none of the Calvinist upheaval that occurred at this time in places like Nîmes and Agen, two among many communities in the Cévennes and central Garonne region where, in the absence of a sufficient institutional counterweight, the propaganda of a few preachers ultimately sufficed to win a majority of the population and personnel in key institutions over to the "heretical" cause. Nevertheless, the durable, persistent Catholicism of certainly highly placed people in Bordeaux remained open-minded and evangelical, even if it was tainted by the tortures inflicted on a number of Calvinists in Guyenne. Despite such bloody stains on its escutcheon, Bordeaux's "papism" was closer to the thinking of Montaigne than to that of the papists of Toulouse or to the fanaticism of the followers of the Duc de Guise or Cardinal de Lorraine. The humanist Platter was in his element among the men of letters of Bordeaux even if he was not aware of it. Later, in 1580, he would actually meet the author of the *Essais* during Montaigne's pilgrimage to Basel and Italy.

*   *   *

On March 14, Felix, accompanied by Theodor (F 272), boarded the ship *Aquilon* (or *Aiguillon:* for once, a ship from Bordeaux had a name having nothing to do with the Virgin or a saint). They embarked near the Chapeau Rouge, which simplified matters. At around noon, after an untroubled crossing, the ship landed at Blaye, a small town on the right bank of the Gironde estuary consisting of a city proper, a fortress, and a suburb, all controlling an extraordinarily profitable customs post where duties were levied on ships sailing to or from Bordeaux. Felix located Blaye incorrectly as lying midway between Bordeaux and La Rochelle; in fact, it is close to Bordeaux and relatively far from La Rochelle. When Thomas Platter Jr. visited Blaye at the end of the century, he was less close-mouthed about it than his brother and more informative about local legends. He reports, for example, that locals believed, rightly or wrongly, that their town was the site of the tomb of Roland, the hero of the famous *Chanson,* who, with Herculean might, had supposedly hurled a heavy lance into the middle of the Garonne, which was in fact quite broad at the site of the fortified toll station (T2 449). After a stop at a tavern in Blaye for the inevitable noon meal, Felix and his friend crossed the border between Guyenne and Saintonge and headed for Mirambeau, where they arrived by early evening and spent the night.

In passing from Guyenne into Saintonge, moreover, the two travelers also crossed, apparently without noticing it, the linguistic boundary between the *langue d'oc* and the *langue d'oïl.* Indeed, this was the first time that Felix had really set foot in "France" (that is, in the France *d'oïl*), but of course Saintonge had still been "English" little more than a century earlier. The road north took the student past almost new Saintonge-style manors distinguished by their circular or polygonal towers with pointed roofs—a signature of the reconstruction of the region in the wake of the Hundred Years' War. Saintonge had also recovered from the more recent ordeal of the rebellions that had erupted against the salt tax in 1542 and 1548 in Charente as well as Bordeaux.

*   *   *

On the morning of March 15, as Felix and Theodor rode north, they witnessed a genre scene: a *prévôt* (sheriff) accompanied by a squadron of mounted police captured an alleged criminal before the very eyes of our travelers. The prisoner was tied to a horse and taken off to an unknown destination (F 272). The arresting officer was one of a number of provincial and special *prévôts* whose posts were created under Charles VIII and Francis I. They patrolled the highways, collared suspects, and meted out summary justice, which may have been effective but drew much criticism from the regular courts. The question of whether judicial powers should be granted to policemen was an old one. The *prévôts* were still active in 1557 in Saintonge and elsewhere. There were not very many of them (Felix had not seen one since Montpellier, or for that matter since Lyons). Henri II had made a move to eliminate the office a few years earlier. Perhaps he meant his order to be enforced, perhaps not, but in any case it had no effect. The *prévôts* continued their itinerant, provincial careers under the royal aegis.[40]

On March 15 the two students passed Pons, an important stop on the way to Santiago de Compostela. Pilgrims traveling from north to south could find food and shelter in a vaulted hospice built in the town between 1157 and 1192. Felix and Theodor had just enough time to cast an eye on an imposing keep that dated from around 1185. This rectangular fortress, thirty meters high, was augmented by a tower built on its north face in the fifteenth century.[41]

Shortly after noon that same day, the two travelers approached Saintes, a city of four to five thousand people on the banks of the Charente. As they drew near the ramparts, they passed on their left an amphitheater built in the time of Tiberius—a perfect oval that adorned the Valley of Arenas. To the west they saw the suburban church of Saint-Eutrope, a sanctuary for pilgrims in transit.[42] Saint-Eutrope featured a flamboyant steeple barely a century old—the Gothic work still looked new. The two young men now crossed the five-meter-wide moat around the city, whose fortified walls followed the contours of the old Roman *castrum* everywhere except for an enlargement by the river. Passing through the Porte-Evêque, situated in the jurisdiction of the local prelate, they proceeded along narrow streets, rutted by iron-clad cart wheels. The streets were flanked by houses with sculpted beams, double-gabled facades, mullioned windows, and turrets with spiral staircases.[43] The students' route, though sinuous, corresponded more or less to the old *decumanus maximus,* which divided the Roman *castrum* along a north-south axis. They passed a stone's throw from the residence of the bishop, the astonishing Tristan de Bizet.[44] The bishop displayed a certain laxity (perhaps owing to lack of zeal) toward local Huguenots, among whom dynamic artisans played a leading role.[45] He was on hostile terms, however, with the various local authorities, both civil and ecclesiastic, on account of certain dark tales of murder involving his nephew. Felix's route, and for that matter the entire bishopric, lay in the shadows of the cathedral of Saint-Pierre, a vast forest of Gothic arches that had been entirely rebuilt in the time of Louis XI and his successors. Although almost new, the cathedral had only a dozen more years to live: it was largely destroyed when Protestants seized the city in 1568.

The two *Teutschen* also passed close to some of the community's defining structures on their right: there was the great bridge designed in the late twelfth century by Isambert, the head of the cathedral school, and dominated by the thirty-meter-high Tour Mausifrote (whose name alludes to the motto of Louis XI, "Qui s'y frotte s'y pique," touch here and be stung). A chapel of the Virgin stood nearby. On the other bank of the Charente stood a triumphal arch from the time of Tiberius. As an amateur archaeologist, Felix normally would have been interested in this two-bay arch, but on this day he was in too much of a hurry. On both sides of the bridge were landings for barges, which traveled upstream laden with salt and downstream with wheat, wine, tiles, ceramics, and wood for barrels. Immediately north of the Tour Mausifrote stood one of the towers in the city wall. This tower, with its views of Gothic and ancient architecture and aquatic scenery, contained the studio of an illustrious Huguenot, Bernard Palissy, who on this very spot had recently discovered the secrets first of white enamel and later of colored enamels. The riverside fish market a short distance away inspired the pisciform reliefs of Palissy's colorful dinner plates. What is more, "Master Bernard" was at the heart of an active circle of Calvinist intellectuals.[46] To exit the city one passed by the communal building, where in 1557 Antoine Ogier (by profession a *receveur de la gendarmerie et des aides,* that is, a sort of tax collector) became the latest in a series of mayors, all of whom had been, since 1492 and probably much earlier, nobles or magistrates.[47] Here as elsewhere, merchants had been driven out of the highest offices. They did not lose their rights, however: city hall stood adjacent to a series of long market buildings in which meat, bread, and textiles were sold beneath the walls of a machicolated keep, the Capitole, which anchored the western wall of the ramparts. Now that Felix had made his way from one end of Saintes to the other, he had only to exit the city through its northern gate, the Porte Aiguière, beyond which lay the road to Poitiers.[48]

Soon the travelers would be in Poitou. But for the time being they were still in Saintonge. Along the way, the two friends ran into an amiable fellow, a citizen of Saint-Jean-d'Angély (their next stop), who waxed ecstatic about Felix's good looks: "You have a handsome nose," he told the young man, who was flattered by the remark (F 273). Felix, after all, was from Basel, where between 1517 and 1532 Hans Holbein the Younger had painted portraits of Erasmus and the bürgermeister Jacob Meyer in which the promontory of the nose became what André Chastel called "the decisive argument of the face."[49]

This episode also gives us a rare record of a dialogue between Switzerland and Saintonge on the road to Poitou: the pleasant acquaintance described various particularities of the region for the two wandering students. His account made them regret that they did not have time to visit the free port of La Rochelle, a city of twenty thousand. It lay to the left of their route as they deliberately headed inland toward the Loire Valley and Paris, thus bidding farewell to the shimmering image of a city already in contact with America, a city whose new and renovated streets were lined with passageways, arcades, and houses of stone that replaced the shanties of the previous century, as well as with fine aristocratic *hôtels* adorned by Doric columns and bucranium friezes. The port exported brandy (already), wine, salt, and wheat and imported spices (which now arrived via the Cape rather than by way of Venice), drugs, sugar, textiles, and salted fish.[50] The Catholic priests in La Rochelle were at this point not particularly well educated (things would improve in the future), and they found it difficult to hold their own in argument with Huguenot militants whose propaganda was readily received in this economically bustling, highly religious city.

By the time Felix reached Saint-Jean-d'Angély he had crossed not only a linguistic but also a juridical boundary separating the south of France, where written law prevailed, from the north, which had long been governed by customary law. Indeed, it was only in 1520 that the three orders of Saintonge, convoked by *commissaires* of the parlement, had met in Saint-Jean to cast the customary laws of the province into the titles and articles of a written legal code.[51] Saint-Jean was also the place to which another Felix, a monk by profession, had brought the head of Saint John the Baptist, which he had stolen in Egypt, to the site of a future monastery; this was in the time of Pepin the Short. Other illustrious heads of the decapitated (Saint Reverend, known in local folklore, and Saint Mark) were eventually added to the collection.

In Toulouse Felix had shown an interest in reliquaries, but in Saint-Jean he ignored the skulls of Reverend, Mark, and John the Baptist. They were soon gone, in any case, destroyed five years later by Huguenots. Was the loss irreparable? Actually, remains of holy personages were so abundant in Saint-Jean that in 1539 the local monks did not hesitate to trade in holy relics, much to the horror of the parlement of Bordeaux.

March 16, 1557: the travelers covered a long (sixty kilometers) and not very interesting stretch of road, with a stop for lunch at Villedieu (twenty-two kilometers north of Saint-Jean-d'Angély) before continuing on (another thirty-eight kilometers) to Chenet, where they spent the night. This dreary day had nothing but the fatigue of travel in common with the next, a brilliant March 17, which took our travelers to Lusignan, the home, as Felix noted, of the fairy Melusina. Indeed, he was so impressed by this fact that he miscalculated the distances he had traveled and misrecorded the places he had passed through.

Lusignan, a fortress that dated back to the tenth or eleventh century and that would soon become a target of Huguenot attacks, had once belonged to the noble Lusignan family. In the late Middle Ages it had fallen to the English before finally being captured by the French crown. Felix had a good view of the huge castle perched on a hill (*uf dem Berg*).[52] The fairy Melusina had supposedly lived in this fortress (*gewont soll haben* [F 273]). That illustrious tourist Charles V had visited Lusignan seventeen years earlier and heard the old-wives' tales about Melusina, the fairy-serpent, stories that many people took to be literally true.[53] At the end of the century, Thomas Platter Jr. also described a part of the Loire Valley near Poitou where the nobility and country people alike took the Melusina stories absolutely seriously (T2 490ff.). At Cinq-Mars-la-Pile,[54] Thomas Jr. gazed at length on a castle so imposing that only *phées*, or fairies (the spirits or ghosts of gods), could have built it. Even the largest cannon was of no avail against these indestructible walls. One of the towers of this fortress was indeed supposed to have been the refuge or prison of a fairy, again named Melusina: the same Magical Woman about whom, according to the Platters, so much had been written, published, and printed in German as well as French since the last quarter of the fifteenth century (these publications were based on much earlier manuscripts). The two brothers took a keen interest in this body of fairy tales because they were aware of Melusina's role as patron of the building trades (T2 471). She herself was supposedly a mason capable of building walls stout enough to withstand artillery barrages—an indication that Melusina was a modern and not simply a medieval legend. In Poitou, moreover, she was reputed to have imported the green bean from America: in other words, this legendary figure was not scrapped in the sixteenth and seventeenth centuries but recycled in new myths that continued to depict her as a servant to the people of the region.

The Platters were not unaware of Melusina's totemic role.[55] Flying in the face of the Church, which held that man had been created in God's image, Melusina was part reptile, part human mother. She gave birth to quite a number of vigorous male offspring, who became the founders of aristocratic lineages for which she stood as totem, among them the Lusignans (Poitou) and the Sassenages (Dauphiné). Because the Platters were interested in Christian and pagan myths generally, they occasionally mention various other totemic mother figures. In addition to Melusina, Thomas Jr. discusses the Porcelets of Camargue, an astonishing family of aristocrats celebrated in Lorraine as well as in Provence: this noble lineage, while not actually descended from a sow (T2 134), did trace its origins back to a medieval lady whose vile behavior had led to her being compared to the "female of the boar." Her offspring, all nobles of good stock and illustrious lineage, were therefore referred to as *porcelets*, or piglets. Similar fantastic matriarchies figured in the foklore of Lorraine, a region with which the Platters had many connections.[56]

The travelers covered the distance from Lusignan to Poitiers on the afternoon of March 17. Along the way they encountered ironic peasants (did this mark the end of a certain southern cordiality?), peasants not quick to give directions but always ready to ask questions—"Oh, you want to go there? It's pretty there, I've been there. You must be foreigners. Where do you come from? The weather's nice. The road is nice. Why are you alone?"—and similar foolishness before telling the visitors what they wanted to know. The poorer peasants tilled the soil by hand, the wealthier ones with oxen. Most were armed with sticks, a few with rusty swords or *braquemarts* (short, double-bladed swords). Felix and Theodor (and Thomas Jr. later on) expressed their pleasure at the huge numbers of barely tamed donkeys, the poor man's stallions, which were bred with mares to produce Poitou mules for export as far away as Spain.

According to Thomas Jr., moreover, these donkeys earned good money, for at the rate of four or five daily matings they could make as much as four or five crowns a day, whereas their market value as reproductive males was only 120 crowns. The return on capital was therefore quite good. The two *Teutschen* also expressed surprise at the extraordinary number of birds and rabbits that the locals caught with snares or ferrets. They were entering game-rich northern France. There was no shortage of protein in the wild, although at a time of overall prosperity and demographic growth the poverty of a portion of the lower class was becoming a problem. Our travelers passed small castles that, with the king's permission, had been fortified in the fifteenth century through the addition of machicolations, watch towers, turrets, stairs, loopholes, and moldings.[57]

The years around 1557 were something of a golden age in Renaissance Poitou. By then, the Hundred Years' War was almost forgotten, but the Wars of Religion and the capture of La Rochelle in 1628 had not yet cast a dark pall over the brilliant successes of the sixteenth century. A three-year crop rotation cycle was generally observed in Poitou. This was no longer the sunny south, although the travelers did see numerous almond trees, a sign of a slightly warmer climate, perhaps, than today. Natives of the region spoke a bizarre dialect, definitely not Occitanian but not quite Parisian French. Death was still an obsession, and the old Romanesque churches in the villages were flanked by new funerary chapels built by the elite. Imperceptible but powerful transformations affected the environment: *Champagne* (open fields) gave way to *bocage* (fields enclosed by hedgerows). Noble landlords pieced together estates through entail-

ments (*retraits lignagers*) on tenant titles. They also turned recently reclaimed heath and gorse barrens into additional enclosed fields. The
manor system had substituted a contractual (though not yet capitalist)
relationship for the whole feudal system.[58]

On the morning of March 18 our travelers were ready for a brief tour
of Poitiers. Felix climbed the towers and admired the city's gardens. It
was a large city, of fifteen to twenty thousand inhabitants, a population
that, following the painful hiatus of the Wars of Religion, would not be
equalled again until the beginning of the seventeenth century. In 1557 the
demographic pressure was apparently strong: landlords in the region
were therefore able to rack temporary tenants with high rents. Paradoxically, however, the city, which lacked an adequate building strategy and
was badly paved to boot, floated in the midst of its vast fortified enclosure: gardens and empty and cultivated fields occupied as much space
inside the walls under Henri IV as under Henri II. As for the urban landscape proper, although much of it was quite filthy, the city had been reju-
venated by the construction of *hôtels particuliers* with new facades in the
Renaissance style, with oblique windows following the turns of spiral
staircases. The city was surrounded by thick ramparts some seven kilometers in circumference and flanked by seventy towers or "turrets." Here as
elsewhere, the protective walls were paid for by local taxes on wine
known as *souquets* or *chiquets*. The protective walls were also protection-
ist, serving to enforce the payment of customs duties as much as to discourage would-be attackers. The city was strong, hence its *pucelage* (or
chastity, as the contemporary expression had it) was guaranteed. Thirteen years after Felix's visit, in 1569, the city held out against a siege by
Coligny, despite the admiral's establishment of bridgeheads on the left
bank of the Clain River. Thanks to this successful resistance, Poitiers
gained prestige as a Catholic stronghold.

No Platter could visit a city like Poitiers without contemplating at least
once the vestiges of Roman monuments. Felix probably and Thomas Jr.
certainly cast a ritual glance at the local amphitheater, which dated from
the end of the second century c.e. and was one of the most important
amphitheaters in ancient Gaul.[59] The two Platters might also have seen
sections of sewer and the crumbling arches of aqueducts that once supplied the city with water. In the sixteenth century, however, the job of
carrying water was assigned to donkeys rather than to the lead pipe of
Gallo-Roman times; the city lacked fountains and cisterns, and the water
hauled in by endless trains of donkeys had to be purchased from sup-
pliers. Indeed, one of the Platters stayed at an inn called At the Fountain,
a sign that such an obviously useful public source of water inside the city
walls was a remarkable rarity.

To jump from Antiquity to the Middle Ages and from amphitheater to princely palace, the Platters also showed great interest in the triangular castle that Jean, the duc de Berry and brother of Charles V, had built in the late fourteenth century on the edge of town, where it formed an integral part of Poitier's ramparts. Soon thereafter, the castle was immortalized by the illuminations in *Les Très Riches Heures,* a book of hours prepared at the duke's request. Jean de Berry had planned his *hôtel* to house the two hundred eighty persons of his retinue; by the time Felix visited, only a porter remained on the premises. Castles were no longer what they once had been, but the book business was booming. Felix looked up one bookseller, whose shop bore the arms of Basel on its sign; this man had once provided lodging to an old friend of the Platter family, none other than the law professor Bernhard Brand. This surgeon's son had connections with the best families among the municipal and corporate elite of Basel and Alsace. Six years earlier, Brand had temporarily left his young Swiss wife to do combat on French soil. Later, he returned to Switzerland to pursue a brilliant career, which culminated in his ennoblement by the emperor. In Poitiers, Sir Brand had been able to choose among any number of erudite hosts: in the 1550s there were three print shops in the city and twenty-three bookstores. Such a flourishing book trade was perfectly normal in an academic city boasting some two thousand students of all ages, or 12 percent of the total population. The schools were a training ground for future local officials.

While a segment of the lower class wallowed in misery, the city's officials, prosecutors, and attorneys prospered. Poitiers was primarily an administrative center, hence a city that consumed rather than produced, and a place where money was easy to come by, at least for members of the elite. To the Platters it seemed a lot like Montpellier: in the capital of Poitou the rich danced in the winter and the poor in the summer, marking, respectively, the end of cold weather with the Carnival and the happy conclusion of the harvest. Poitou's dances easily found their way to court and became the rage throughout France. And yet this city, charming in so many ways, was not ripe for antipapism. The view from here was very different from the view in Niort, a lesser regional center, where the Calvinist Reformation would soon become hegemonic. In Poitiers, clerical, judicial, and state institutions (such as the *sénéchaussée,* the *présidial,* the tax collecting and disbursing *élection,* and the *hôtel des monnaies,* or mint) had been growing since the fifteenth century and were much too strong, as in Toulouse and Bordeaux, for Protestant influence to overcome. Calvin seldom if ever prevailed in the major cities of either the north or the south of France. In Poitou, Huguenots would never be more than an influential and active minority. All in all, the local intellectuals, who included magistrates and other jurists, chose to devote themselves to belles-lettres rather than to the stringent rigors of heresy.

* * *

En 1599, Thomas Jr. departed Poitiers to the northeast, crossing the Clain by way of the Pont-à-Jaubert, a skillful construction capped by a pointed rectangular turret. Once outside the city walls the rider passed through the suburbs of Montbernage and Saint-Saturnin, the traditional home of the city's poorest residents (the average tax paid in these villages in 1552 ranged from six to twenty-five sous, compared with more than a hundred sous in the better sections of the city of magistrates on the left bank of the river). Felix's younger half-brother would later wax ecstatic over the huge neolithic dolmen that the Melusinian Saint Radegund, known like her sisters in Camarge and Anjou for her prodigious ability to move rocks, had dropped here before going on to build a church for herself inside the walls. At the end of the century, Thomas Jr. would proceed from the site of the dolmen to the Loire Valley. When Felix left Poitiers on March 19, 1557, he most likely followed a similar route. On first leaving the city, Felix and Theodor were fortunate enough to be accompanied by a third man, who would remain with them part of the way, thus affording the travelers an additional "security" they had not enjoyed since leaving Narbonne.

Later that day, the three travelers reached Châtellerault, a surprising city, which had benefited in the first half of the century from the installation of a sensechal's court and from work done to improve the navigability of the Vienne downstream.[60] In 1549 Henri II had pledged the duchy of Châtellerault to the Scot James Hamilton, count of Arran, as a reward for his important services to France in connection with the marriage of Mary Stuart. The young count of Arran, heir apparent to the new holder of the title, spared no effort to convert his new ducal city to Protestantism. Henri II thus involuntarily continued his perpetual double-dealing: with one hand he persecuted the Protestants, while with the other hand he encouraged them with sometimes ill-considered support for his "faithful nobility," whether Scottish or French, which included many people sympathetic to the new thinking.[61]

* * *

En route from Châtellerault to Tours, the three travelers stopped, as everyone must, to visit one of the famous "chateaus of the Loire" (or in this case, almost of the Loire). The château in question was Candé, a fine early sixteenth-century residence located between Montbazon and Tours.[62]

This manor belonged to a marquis, who had an impressive collection of helmets and shields (F 274). This collection reminds us that a substantial armaments industry, inspired by Italian examples, had grown up in Tours, not far away, in the time of Jacques Coeur and, later, of Louis XI. In 1557 important vestiges of that industry remained, and samples of its past ended up in the chateaus of the region, which functioned as museums of armament.[63] The château also had its rural aspect: the trio climbed up to a dovecote in a large turret adjacent to the castle's farm. The dovecote was of course one of the classic feudal edifices of northern France: the pigeon's guano, which after all began as seed snatched from the fields of wheat surrounding the manor, officially belonged to the lord of the land. In the course of a single day Felix thus visited the farm and the manor, both typical of the land tenure system of the Loire Valley. Such was feudalism between the Loire and the Meuse.[64]

On the afternoon of March 20, the three men drew near Tours. The (rather poor) road from Châtellerault first traversed a swampy area known as "Les Boyres" and then continued on to Tours proper. The city sat on a sort of mesa some fifteen to thirty feet above the Loire, which paralleled the river over a distance of a mile and a quarter. Standing thus between the river and the alluvial plain, it was beyond the reach of high waters. Late March marked a time of transition in this industrial city: winter, with its short evenings (owing to the expense of candles) was over, hence so was the season of low wages and unemployment.[65] "October to May was the busy season only for shippers" on the Loire, who carried wheat and wine downstream from the Beauce (on a river whose current had become stronger during the Renaissance) and then returned upstream with slate and salt, a primary source of income for the social and fiscal elite. Freshwater fish such as pike, carp, bass, barbel, eel, bream, plaice, and lamprey were on many tables, and not just during Lent.[66]

When it came to the choice of a hostelry, Felix once again had many options: a city accustomed to royal visits, Tours boasted more than fifty inns. It was the sixth largest city in France, after Paris, Lyons, Rouen, Bordeaux, and Toulouse, with a population of twenty thousand in 1557 compared with around ten thousand at the beginning of the fourteenth century. By the time of Henri II, Tours was not nearly as prosperous as it had been at its peak, but no major upheaval had accompanied its decline. For eighty years, from 1444 to 1524 (with high points and low points in between), the Valois kings had made this one of their favorite stopping places. Lately, however, they had abandoned it in favor of other cities in the vicinity and in the Paris region: *centralisation oblige*. Lovely vestiges remained, however, at the confluence of the Loire and the Cher. Of all the cities that Felix had visited, except Lyons, Tours was one of the few that deserved to be called an industrial bastion: a third of the population depended on the silk industry; embroiderers, tapestry makers, goldsmiths, and deluxe armorers also flourished. The châteaus of the Loire were the work of a distinguished elite, including the Berthelots of Azay-le-Rideau and the Bohiers of Chenonceaux. Tours was the very prototype of the good city warmed by the rays of the monarchic sun while its buildings and ramparts looked down on the peasant frogs croaking in the nearby marshlands.

In Tours, Felix briefly visited the royal castle ensconced in the northeastern corner of the old city at the southern terminus of the bridge across the Loire, which had been rebuilt at the beginning of the sixteenth century. The purpose of the reconstruction was to replace the old beams and planks that had spanned the bridge's vaulted stone arches, for these wooden components had been vulnerable to damage from floods. The château, a rectangular structure with four massive towers, dated from the end of the thirteenth century and the reign of Philip the Bold. Kings Charles VII and Louis XI had not been terribly fond of the ponderous old castle, which they used only for brief stays. According to a "Trojan" legend, the old fortress was supposed to contain the tomb of Turnus, Aeneas's unfortunate rival. This story did not displease Felix, who had a weakness for Latin pedantry. The visitor from Basel also had time to inspect the city's beautiful fountains (*die schön brunnen*). These were worth a detour: in 1506, Mayor Bohier, who belonged to one of the most illustrious local families, had decided to pipe water into the city from the Saint-Avertin spring.[67] Thanks to the construction of an underground aqueduct and a siphon beneath the Cher, it proved possible to supply four fountains inside the city walls, and the best artists of the province, including the painter Bourdichon, were summoned to work on them. One of these fountains, underwritten by Jacques de Beaune-Semblançay, still exists.

At the same time, the fish market and slaughterhouse were moved outside the space enclosed by the ramparts. Because the authorities in Montpellier had not been able to accomplish this feat, Felix's nostrils had been offended by odors from the fish market for the nearly five years that he had been a student there.

On March 21, Felix and Theodor left Tours for Amboise. By this time the travelers were in the heart of the French breadbasket, a long way from the *pays d'oc*. They marveled at the many caves they saw in the region. These were of course very ancient, but increases in agricultural output and population had bestowed a new significance on them: people were now living in them. "Riding [along the left bank of the Loire], we passed close to many cliffs pierced by cave entrances. With rocky ceilings for roofs, these caves were being used as dwellings and sealed against the elements. There were many of this type" (F 274). Some caves were also used for wine storage. The very soft subsoil could be worked easily with a pick. Vinestocks grew out of the rock around doors and windows, and smoke from fires was vented through soft chalky slopes.

The limestone hills were riddled with caves of this sort, which were not very healthy to live in. But clearly they were lived in during the reign of the Valois, as certain architectural motifs indicate. Felix's text corroborates this physical evidence, showing that the Loire Valley was comparable in this respect to various sites in Aquitaine, Scotland, Camargue, and Cornwall.[68] On the eve of the Wars of Religion, in a time of economic prosperity, people who lived in caves should not be thought of as survivals of prehistoric troglodytes. The silk trimmers of the Tours suburbs and the peasants of the surrounding countryside were simply coping with rapid economic expansion in a perfectly reasonable if not entirely comfortable manner.

In 1599, the youngest of the three Platters was curious enough about these cave dwellers to visit their homes. "In this region," Thomas Jr. wrote, "I saw countless dwellings hollowed out of rock. I went inside a number of them. People live in these places like foxes in their lairs. Most of the residents of these wretched hovels are poor peasants [arme bauren]. The cave openings, situated either along the road or part way up the slopes, are generally no farther than a harquebus shot apart" (T2 498). In writing these lines, had Thomas Jr. forgotten that his own father had also been a "poor peasant?"[69]

The agricultural Loire Valley, which Felix would follow upstream toward Orléans, was a little like the Comtat Venaissin of the popes, another region exploited by a growing population (population growth led, in classic fashion, to an increase in the number of farms at the expense of common lands).[70] Here, however, planting became increasingly sophisticated, as the royal court insisted on a variety of luxury products such as melons and asparagus. From Tours to Amboise and beyond, Felix, riding along the south bank of the Loire from west to east, could see the great earthen levee of 1480 along the right bank.[71] In fact, the word levée was of recent coinage: in the Middle Ages the river had been lined not with levees but with turcies, dikes constructed of pilings and gravel and planted with trees to protect the farmland while occasionally allowing water laden with fertilizing silt to pass through. After the end of the Hundred Years' War, these were gradually replaced by levees made entirely of earth, without stones, trees, or pilings. The new structures were tall enough to be insubmersible. They constituted a modern, rigid form of embankment whose purpose was to channel the Loire, facilitate navigation, and provide a commercially useful roadway along the levee's crest. In short, the *turcies* were the work of peasant artisans, whereas the levees were designed by the royal engineer. The purpose of the levees was to boost the economies of the cities, where the demand for them originated, rather than to assist in the fertilization of fields. The definitive change in vocabulary from *turcie* to *levée,* from countryside to city, occurred in the 1550s, during Felix's visit to France.

On the subject of urbanization, of such obvious importance to the prewar Valois reign, it is worth noting that the Loire Valley contained a string of cities of which Felix was able to visit only a few. The section of the valley from Tours to Orléans through which he traveled between the twenty-first and the twenty-sixth of March boasted a number of sizeable cities: among them were Gien, Sully, Jargeau, Orléans, Meung, Beaugency, Blois, and Amboise.[72] Several of these were river ports controlled by a company of merchants. Half-a-dozen of them had built stone bridges across the river. These cities were the hubs of a network of roads linked to the central axis of the river, a network whose northern and southern extremities were, respectively, Chartres and Bourges. The Loire was a royal avenue, a vehicle of Italian influences, which brought silk workshops to Tours and, before long, ceramic workshops to Nevers.[73] It was also a vehicle for Protestant ideas, which passed through the royal court. Calvin came to the University of Orléans in 1530. Extremist antipapist placards were posted in Amboise in 1534, triggering repression of Huguenots. The peasants of the Blois region refused to pay the tithe in 1542. Duc Antoine de Bourbon "infected" his duchy of Vendôme with the spirit of the Reformation. And many converts to heresy were drawn from the ranks of urban nobles, priests, professionals, artisans and merchants, lackeys and domestics. Protestant churches, or more precisely communities, were "established" in Angers in 1555, Tours and Blois in 1556, Orléans in 1557 (the year of Felix's visit), and Beaugency in 1559.[74]

On March 21, Felix and Theodor traveled from Tours to Amboise. The "road" between the two cities, along the left bank of the Loire, was mediocre, despite a cash gift from the king in 1552 for the purpose of improving the roadways in this portion of the Loire Valley. Felix approached Amboise through the area around the church of Saint-Denis, which was situated to the west of town, outside the walls, near the Hôtel-Dieu. The church, built in the twelfth century, had recently been completed by the addition of a highly ornate collateral wing, justified by the recent growth of the city's population. Adjacent to the church was a cemetery, which served not only as a place to bury the dead but also as a source of trees for the local timber industry. Felix probably stopped for lunch in the faubourg Saint-Denis, in the square of the same name, where a number of regional highways converged.

Entering the city through the Porte Saint-Denis, Felix eyed one section of the city's fortifications. Well maintained, the walls were equipped with cannon, culverins, harquebuses, and sentry boxes, which made Amboise, a city dominated by an imposing castle, one of the staunchest fortresses in the Valois kingdom.

In 1557 Amboise had a population of fifteen or sixteen hundred. It began as an island between the Loire to the north and the two branches of a southern tributary, the Amasse, at a point where the great river narrowed sufficiently to facilitate crossing by those headed from far-off Paris to Spain; the east-west route along the left bank of the river intersected the north-south route here. Inside the walls, hogs, geese, and pigeons roamed the streets. Public buildings were built of white stone and covered with slate roofs. Private houses were built of wood and had tile roofs. Thatched roofs were not allowed in the city because of the fire hazard. Amboise boasted a primary school but no *collège*, or secondary school. A print shop is mentioned in 1557, the year in which, with encouragement from Henri II, the city gave itself a mayor, who in theory was supposed to be a gentleman of *robe courte*, that is, a nobleman.

Following the course of the Loire from southwest to northeast, Felix proceeded from the Porte Saint-Denis toward the center of town along Amboise's principal thoroughfare (what is today the Rue Nationale). He passed by the Tour de l'Horloge (Clock Tower), flanked by smelly tanneries. Then, as if wandering through a ghost town, he made his way among vestiges of the early Middle Ages and even Late Antiquity, which had been refurbished during the Renaissance: he had already seen the *ecclesia* (the church of Saint-Denis); now he discovered the *vicus*, or burg, extended along the river upstream of the gate; and finally, dominating this fortified town, was the *oppidum* or *castellum*, the high château that had become, since the time of Charles VII and Charles VIII, a powerful royal palace perched on its spur of rock.

Along the way he passed the great bridge across the Loire on his left, adjacent to which stood Notre-Dame-de-Grâce (1521), one of the many new churches that Amboise owed to the artistic, religious, and demographic Renaissance. Off to the right lay the *varennes*, land that had been drained since the Hundred Years' War and made good for farming; comestibles from the Cher valley reached the city through this former wasteland, which now sported gardens and orchards producing apricots, pears, cherries, morellos, carnations, and apples. Farther east, the young man came upon the port of Petit-Fort, squeezed between the river and the castle. This was a district of recently constructed buildings: the salt warehouse and the city hall. The memoirist mentions the château, which, with its casemates, deep moats, towers, arsenal, and thick walls, was still impregnable. But Felix left it to his younger brother to elucidate, some forty years later, the intertwined philosophies of the city and the fortress: at an inn in the city Thomas Jr. saw a deck of tarot cards depicting the pope (offering his blessing), a judge (deciding a case), a woman (being unfaithful to her husband), a peasant (providing food for others), death, and, last but not least, the king, guarding and protecting all (*ich verwahre und beschirm euch alle*) by means of his monarchical power, which was both "coactive" and military. As depicted in Amboise, then, the function of defense, or, if need be, of making war, was no longer assigned exclusively to the nobles, whose role was at most to defend the city hall, but to the sovereign, the heir to the military and protective powers once reserved to the nobility. The king and his (standing) army controlled access to that "mega-casemate," the city and castle of Amboise. The deck of tarot cards thus illustrated one aspect of the "birth of the modern state," namely, the transfer of the monopoly of the means of violence from the nobility to the monarchy.

French kings before and after Charles VIII were fond of hunting in the forests of the Loire region, and signs of this predilection were abundant throughout Amboise, from the castle above to the city below. Adjacent to the esplanade of the fortress, an elevated parade ground large enough to accommodate three hundred soldiers in formation, Thomas Jr. discovered, in the balcony of the castle church, a set of stag's antlers fifteen feet long (?) and six feet wide. The antlers had twelve points and were as thick at the root as a man's thigh. The animal that had sported this marvelous headdress had been killed during the reign of Louis XI in the the the Lutzelbourg wood of the Ardenne forest.[75] The giant stag allegedly wore a golden collar on which was inscribed the name of Julius Caesar!

Thomas Jr. also had a chance to feed sugared almonds to a tame stag that he found wandering on the castle heights. The "cult of the stag" was thus firmly established in Amboise. After the death of Louis XI, Charles VIII, also a great hunter, ordered a chapel built adjacent to the esplanade in honor of Saint Hubert, the patron saint of hunters.[76] Today one can still see a Renaissance bas-relief on a door lintel depicting a stag whose antlers are adorned with a glowing cross: the animal is an avatar of Jesus. This Christianized theme was borrowed, however, from a body of not very Catholic folklore from India or perhaps Armenia. Meanwhile, another chapel in honor of Saint Hubert was erected, also in the time of Charles VIII, outside the castle in the faubourgs of Amboise, across the bridge on the right bank of the river. This is a fairly large church, with a single nave of five bays, twenty-three meters long and nineteen meters wide.

What a convergence of influences: ultramodern sugared almonds fed to a live deer; pagan legends Christianized and embodied in chapels and churches; Germanic folklore from the Ardenne combined with Christian tales of miracle-working stags associated with Saint Hubert; and, on top of all that, remembrances of ancient times in the form of a collar supposedly bearing the name of Julius Caesar, who also knew a thing or two about the secrets of the Ardenne. Amboise's memorial to the great stag and its royal hunter surely fascinated the traveling Platters, who always showed a keen interest in cultural syncretism.[77]

On the afternoon of March 21, the travelers left for Blois, which they reached that evening. As they crossed the great bridge at Blois from south to north, they witnessed something quite rare in the sixteenth century: a suicide. To be sure, in Blois, a large city of almost 20,000, this rather "modern" form of self-destructive behavior was less infrequent than in smaller towns and villages.[78] The bridge was a constant temptation in this respect. As Felix watched, a woman jumped over the guard rail and into the river (F 274). The unfortunate woman was carried downstream by the current before rescuers could fish her out. Felix jumped from his horse and ran to the victim to offer his assistance. She was still breathing. An apothecary stuffed some pills into her mouth, but she could not chew or swallow them. The "therapeutic" lozenges stuck to her throat. The woman gagged and died. Felix was outraged.

He crossed the bridge from the right bank, passing first through the southern gate, next proceeding across the central span, which was lined with sentry boxes, mills, and tripe stands, then passing through the bridge's northern gate, flanked by two towers, and continuing on into the city. Veering off to the west, he entered a section of shops, grouped by occupation: first cobblers, then money changers, then butchers.[79] Blois, the central town of an important vineyard region, was also a major livestock center, and many buildings were devoted to the processing of meat and hides. Sporadic royal visits sustained a number of luxury craftsmen: there were a dozen goldsmiths in the city, for example, along with potters, tapestry makers, enamelers, glovemakers, cutlers, cabinetmakers, and ceramicists. The city was also noted for artisans in all the latest fields: clockmaking, for example, was represented by only one craftsman in 1528 (the first of this profession to be recorded), but by 1535 there were three or four horologists in Blois, then seven under Henri II, and ultimately seventeen under Henri III.[80]

Civil architecture: the route followed by our travelers took them past Gothic edifices with turrets for stairways on the facade. In the cramped city, which lacked public spaces and abounded in culs-de-sac, these still recent buildings stood among new noble and bourgeois dwellings that reflected the stylistic evolution of the Loire châteaus: regular facades, horizontal moldings, medallions, superimposed pilasters, and "ornamental lozenges and disks."

At the base of the château (which stood in the middle of the city), Felix discovered some of the new realities of power[81] as redefined by Louis XII some sixty years earlier in accordance with Machiavelli's idea that the best fortress for a king is the affection of his people.[82] Without being too sentimental about it, we can say that Louis XII, who commanded considerable authority and a strong army and no longer had to contend with the civil wars that had hampered his immediate predecessors, was able to afford the "luxury" of razing the manorial or castellar fortifications that had separated him from his subjects in Blois. For the first time in European history, he had (to the dismay of some observers) gutted or knocked down the ramparts of his manor and surrounded it with gardens, thereby transforming the old fortress into a glorious facility for receiving foreign princes. In this vast new dwelling, largely open to the outside world, and its immediate vicinity, he had made room for hundreds of servants and thousands of soldiers, who constituted a court that surrounded, glorified, protected, and ran the apparatus of state.

From the memoirs it would appear that Felix Platter mainly contemplated the loggias of the main facade, which dated from the time of Francis I. He described the royal château of Blois as powerful (*gwaltig*), meaning not impregnable (for it no longer was) but stunning, for the sight of such impressive architecture truly amazed the visitor from Switzerland. Amboise was a place that provided military security as well as room to house a growing court. Blois now met only the second of these two criteria. On the subject of the relation of castle and city to the central power of the king, Thomas Jr. was even more outspoken than Felix: "They say that when the king prepares to go to Blois, the women of the city laugh and scratch the fronts of their bellies (*das vordertheil des bauchs*), saying, 'My goodwife, the king is coming.' And when His Majesty leaves, they change their tune and say, in all sadness, while scratching their behinds, 'My goodwife, the king is going.'"[83]

On March 22, 1557, in the early morning hours, Felix left Blois.[84] He again crossed the bridge to the south, then headed toward Orléans along the right bank of the Loire. As the afternoon wore on, the two young men, having stopped for lunch in Saint-Laurent des Eaux, reached Cléry after a ride of almost thirty miles (F 275). This was a town of 154 houses (and roughly 700 inhabitants), 97 on the south side of the main street and 57 on the north side, with rudimentary fortifications.[85] At the center of town was the church of Notre-Dame, dedicated to the Mother of God, whose heavenly grace redounded to the prosperity of the local townspeople. Felix was always careful to record details about important pilgrimage sites (*grosse wallfarten*). Of this one, he notes that a statue of the Madonna with Child had allegedly been unearthed in the vicinity in about 1280 by local peasants; similar miracles were associated with many other pilgrimage sites. This statue, carved in rustic style from a rough-hewn log, was still drawing a Brueghelesque assortment of humanity to the site in 1557: among them, the ill and the mute, devout shepherds, hermits, and devotees of divine interventions of all sorts, including maritime miracles. Indeed, the Virgin of Cléry was credited with miraculous rescues of the victims of shipwrecks, even though she was located hundreds of kilometers from the coast.

Notre-Dame de Cléry was, to believe our two Teutonic travelers, something like a great, glowing ship in the night, with hundreds of tapers and candles burning in the radiant windows of its oversized nave. The walls of the church were literally lined, according to Felix, with mementoes of miracles: wooden legs, devotional objects in wax, silver arms; relics of Louis XI and Dunois, the latter emblazoned with armorial bearings in copper; the heart of Charles VIII in a box with epitaph; stained glass, paintings, gilt objects, statues, and sculpted plaques of bronze, marble, and alabaster. Vault intersections and pillars were covered with grotesque animals. There were images of an eagle snatching a sheep, canons playing the bagpipes, four-leafed roses, acorns, teeth, pearls, spindles, scalloped niches, leafy moldings, and carved pews donated by Henri II. There were also statues of Saint Sebastian, Saint James with a pilgrim's staff, and Saint Andrew.[86] Our two Protestants turned their backs on all these marvels, just a short distance from their path, and spurred their horses on to Orléans, only fifteen kilometers away. By the time they reached the city, it was pitch-dark.

Felix and his friend spent March 23, 24, and 25 in Orléans, They stayed at the Auberge du Lansquenet, a favorite of German students. Orléans was a large city, one of the largest that Felix had visited since leaving home. Its population was by now almost thirty thousand, compared with twelve to fifteen thousand in the time of Charles VII. On the eve of the Wars of

Religion, things had been peaceful in the region since 1429, when the city was saved by Joan of Arc; the capture of Calais in 1558 and the Treaty of Cateau-Cambrésis in 1559 ended a long war that had raged elsewhere without affecting the Loire Valley. From Louis XI on, the last Valois kings had collaborated in extending the city's fortifications, doubling the developed or developable area. Streets were relatively broad. Planning far in advance of other cities had endowed Orléans with numerous squares, including the *places du Martroi, de l'Etape,* and *de la Porte-Renard,* which became marketplaces for wheat, wine, and vegetables.

Orléans was one city that Felix felt he had to visit. It was home to a substantial group of his compatriots, some two or three hundred Swiss and German students. Most of these were law students who had arrived in town with a knowledge of Greek and Latin. Except for two from Saxony, all of the twenty or so students from beyond the Vosges and the Rhine whose birthplace or original residence Felix mentions came from the western part of German-speaking Europe: from Alsace, Zurich, Augsburg, Zweibrücken, and Bavaria—the Platters' regular haunts (F 276). A few were noble or on the way to becoming noble. Others had itinerant pasts typical of the Renaissance: Johannes Achilles Yllisung, from Augsburg, had been a student at the Universities of Padua in 1552, Freiburg in 1555, and Orléans in 1557. In 1572 he became an imperial councillor and bailiff in Swabia.

In Orléans, moreover, Felix was reunited with his childhood friend Sigmund von Andlau, now twenty-one years old. Felix had known Sigmund as a boarder in the Platter household twelve years earlier, at a time when both boys were intoning Latin verses (F 86, 87, 275). As a temporary resident of Orléans, Sigmund did not hesitate to spend money to "roll out the red carpet" for his friend. It was no more than Felix was due: as a student in Montpellier, he had always seen to it that Swiss visitors were received properly and had spent lavishly to keep his guests in drink. In Orléans, Sigmund arranged a splendid banquet (*panquet*) with other Germans, "who came from various social estates, high and low" (*von hoch und nider standts*). The meal included all sorts of preserves, a favorite of the time and the subject of a substantial portion of Olivier de Serres's *Théâtre d'agriculture*. Felix washed these sweets down with excessive amounts of an Orléans wine of which he thought quite highly (the city and nearby farmland were full of vineyards that produced quality wines, and vintners from the surrounding plains came to learn how it was done). There was a further "digestive" complication, however: it was Lent, and von Andlau's lavish banquet featured seafood that had gone bad. Felix had already consumed more than his share of spoiled fish during his long weeks of travel, which coincided with the forty-day Lenten fasts prescribed by the Catholic Church. The visitor spent the night of March 23–24 puking his guts out. By morning he was suffering the tortures of a martyr.[87] His German friends whispered that he might not survive. But the prospect of a midday meal put him back on his feet. Later, his illness forgotten, he went dancing at the home of German students. Before an audience of admiring Teutons he performed a series of typical French (*welsche*) dances. In gratitude the German colony lavished still further attentions on the travelers, to whom they lent harps. With these instruments the visitors became, for the next forty-eight hours, the official musicians of the German contingent in a city noted for its strolling fiddlers' guild. Foreigners though they were, the German students were an integral part of the University of Orléans, one of the foremost institutions of higher learning in France; they constituted one of its "nations."

The university depended on a network of print shops and libraries. It also relied on official and unofficial groups of legal specialists, scholars in various fields, and neo-Latin poets. In a city where the Reformation was the almost legitimate offspring of humanism, Calvin and Théodore de Bèze made brief appearances. Orléans, an intellectual way station between Paris and Lyons, was home to many cultivated men, and humanism's raucous squabbles with scholasticism continued throughout the century. A figure like Thomas Platter Sr., who taught courses in Hebrew and Greek for so much a head in Basel, would not have been out of place in Orléans, where one found many itinerant Hellenists competing for pupils and living on what they earned by giving private or group lessons. German-speaking Lutheran students felt at home among the native Huguenots, who were firmly ensconced in Orléans (but remained discreet about their presence, since it was still possible for Protestants to be burned at the stake).

The local German community squired Felix about the city's major tourist sites. Foremost among them was the summer meeting place of nude swimmers: the bridge across the Loire, with its statue of Joan of Arc. In fact, this was not a single statue but a group of several figures installed between 1502 and 1508. The ensemble contained a crucified Christ, a Virgin, a king (probably Louis XII), and the Maid of Orléans with her hair down and decked out with sword, spurs, lance, helmet, and plume. Felix had little time for the patriotism of the French, however; his primary interest was in ancient art objects. He therefore described the heroic young woman (about whom he knew nothing) as an "antiquity" carved in stone. He was mistaken on two counts: this image of Joan had actually been cast in bronze relatively recently, at the beginning of the sixteenth century.

From the bridge the city could be taken in at a single glance: in the center loomed the Tour Neuve, overlooking the ramparts; on the far right, the Tour de la Brebis, which commanded the southeastern section of wall; in the distance, toward the northeast, the church of Notre-Dame-du-Chemin, near the Porte de Bourgogne, which controlled access from the east; and finally, in the center background, loomed the Sainte-Croix cathedral, which had been renovated at the end of the fifteenth century. With Felix in the forefront, the group of young Germans visited the cathedral and were entranced by the sight of a holy measuring rod, which indicated the exact size of Christ's body and was revered as if it were a relic of Christ himself. As always when it came to relics, this elicited from Felix a brief outburst of Platterian (or Calvinist or pre-Voltairian) irony, after which he and his new friends climbed the stairs of the cathedral's bell tower, a sturdy structure completed relatively recently, in 1511. After a dizzying climb to the base of the lead-clad spire, the young man from Basel faced a shaky ladder leading to the very pinnacle. Some of his companions made the ascent, but the ladder swayed disconcertingly back and forth. Felix, looking down, saw the narrow alleyways of the cathedral quarter filled with people. A man accustomed to gentle terrain, he was gripped by panic. He climbed back down, unscathed by the taunts of his comrades.

*　*　*

On the morning of March 26, Felix left Orléans and headed straight north through the forest of Orléans, where hogs were raised on acorns.[88] Before departing, he had purchased a new saddle for his horse, the old one having rotted (F 277). Like their compatriots in Languedoc, the Germans from the university formed an escort (*gleit*) and accompanied the travelers on the first twenty miles of their journey, until they stopped for lunch. Before setting out, they had signed Felix's notebook (*stamm-biechlin*), which was filled with signatures of people he had met, sayings, inscriptions, and dedications.

*　*　*

On leaving the forest, still headed north, the travelers discovered a region that was densely populated, or rather repopulated after having been reduced to near wasteland in the 1440s by war with England. In 1557, the rural population density increased, as one approached Paris, from 65 or 70 per square kilometer to 120 on the immediate outskirts of the capital.

These densities declined somewhat in the seventeenth century. Along the way Felix did not see a single donkey, but he did notice four-wheeled wagons with axles made of metal rather than, as in the past, of wood. Toward the end of the century, Thomas Jr. would follow the same route in a carriage traveling on paved road. On both sides of the road, peasants were busy with the spring planting, primarily of oats, as well as with various chores connected with fallow land. Fallow fields were not particularly demanding and could be maintained by allowing sheep to graze at the rate of one or two per hectare. The travelers also saw cows, mostly brown and black, some with light spots. Near Etampes, the grain fields (of winter wheat and spring oats) were separated by plots of garlic and onion. And there were some notable absences: no field beans or lentils and not even any sainfoin (yet), despite the market for horses in the capital. The slopes, covered with vinestocks, offered a sampling of the wines of the Paris region, which at the time was one of the most important wine-producing regions in the world (these vineyards have since vanished). The 350,000 residents of the capital had to be kept supplied. There were a few vast, open fields, but farming on this scale was still rare. Other fields were much smaller: some plots were in the shape of long, narrow strips, eighty meters long by five meters wide, and laid out like a parquet. Others were little more than small beds of wheat or vines, endlessly repeated. The mediocre wine produced by these vineyards rarely lasted more than a few months, and the yield was apparently miserable (ten to twenty liters per hectare).[89]

The villages of the region, composed of blocks of houses built close together, had replenished their population to the point where small, isolated farms began to spring up on the land between villages from the middle of the sixteenth century on. Rural churches had been restored or rebuilt over the previous century; the ogival and flamboyant styles still dominated. Local sculptors had carved countless altar tables and tombstones in these modest sanctuaries, a sign of the relative prosperity of a generation of farmers now dead; these were peasants who had enriched themselves under Francis I, when the rural economy was thriving. Clear glass windows flooded church interiors with light, helping those parishioners who could read to decipher the prayers in the relatively inexpensive missals that were Gutenberg's gift to the people of the Beauce and the Ile-de-France. Many of these peasants were devout Catholics, despite some Protestant influence in the region. Memories of the great drought of 1556 remained vivid; amid a forest of crosses under leaden skies, men from the villages had gone in procession to the Parisian shrine of Saint Geneviève to pray for rain.

In March of 1557 the road was crowded with prosperous peasant couples on foot, on horseback, and in wagons. The farmer "wore a great-coat that hung down to the middle of the leg" while allowing his carefully buttoned doublet to show through; his wife "wore a flat hood or bonnet tied at the neck," a rosary on her belt, and a gown and bodice adorned "with gorget and velvet trim." He was on his way to Paris to sell a load of grain and hay after making his way to market through traffic jams on the rue Saint-Jacques. His wife had many things on her mind: "cows, chickens, dairy, oven, cellar, bedroom, linen, sheep, garden, clothing, kitchen utensils." Such farmers formed what was almost a hereditary caste; they were nearly totally endogamous and lived on substantial two-plow farms of roughly seventy hectares per household. These entrepreneurs of the land were a prolific group: the women married young, were well fed, and lived longer than did female workers or "manual laborers."

In social terms, these well-to-do farmers rented their land from a class of landlords, including *grands seigneurs* such as the abbots of monasteries, illustrious magistrates, and other public officials—in short, the *Who's Who?* of Paris—together with a certain number of rural nobles with substantial landholdings.

Eager to reach Paris, Felix temporarily set aside the curiosity that had led him to spend several days with the humanist *grand seigneur* Pierre Danès when both men were traveling down the Rhône Valley. Only a week before his arrival in the Beauce, this same curiosity had impelled him to visit the Château de Candé, a veritable museum of modern weaponry. Between Orléans and Paris, however, Felix did not stop at a single one of the unpretentious manors that dotted his route, manors that housed the *hobereaux,* or country squires, of Ile-de-France, who either cultivated their fields *par valets* (that is, with hired hands) or leased their land to tenant farmers. Had he visited one of these lesser aristocratic manors, he would not have found the décor any different from that of a "substantial" farmer's farmhouse. In both he would have found two bedrooms, a downstairs room, and furniture of oak or walnut: "beds, tables, chests, benches, stools, and a buffet or sideboard." The real social distance between the "commoner" and the "man of privilege" revealed itself in the stable: a commoner might own four horses averaging seven to eight years of age, whereas the squire might own seven horses: as in the thirteenth century, every noble wanted to be a *chevalier,* or horseman (knight).

On March 27 the travelers reached Etampes. They passed through this long "street-village," actually a city of four thousand, repopulated in the period 1480–1520 by immigrants from both the north and the south (Au-

vergne, Limousin). Since 1514 or 1517 the city had had a dynamic municipal council, which took the lead in building new schools and hospitals.
Having achieved official status toward the end of the reign of the Louis
XII, the community sought and obtained designation as a *bonne ville*, a
recently created status that bestowed the privilege of electing aldermen
(from the beginning of the reign of Francis I) and a mayor, chosen as
usual from the ranks of the *noblesse de robe*, the royal magistrates and officeholders. Felix and Theodor followed the Orléans-Paris or Bordeaux-
Paris road through Etampes, the same route that pilgrims on their way to
Santiago de Compostela followed in the other direction. At the Porte
Saint-Martin, where northbound tourists entered the old city, the two
young men paid the traditional *droit de barrage*, or toll levied on riders as
well as merchandise. After that, they simply followed the city's traditional
central axis (their passage was marred by a few spills from their mounts):
first the especially tortuous ruelle d'Enfer, then the rue des Cordeliers,
which passed by the thirteenth-century Franciscan monastery. From
there, through the intersection with the rue de la Manivelle, they entered
the rue basse de la Foulerie (the name evokes textile manufacturing), then
rues Saint-Santoine, de la Juiverie, and de la Tannerie, and finally rue
Evezard, which led to the "exit," the Porte Evezard, flanked by two pep-
permill towers with loopholes for cannons. Were these ancient popguns
intended to ward off potential British or imperial attackers from the
north? Once outside the walls, Felix and his companion rode along the
port of Etampes, which had been growing since 1490, reflecting the prosperity of the new century. Barges that drew as much as three feet of water
and were all too prone to running aground in poorly dredged channels
choked with mud, filth, and sand (the famous sand of Etampes, prized by
glassmakers) stopped here to take on hundreds of sacks of grain for Paris.
Occasionally one saw an intellectual perched atop these sacks, taking advantage of the calmness of the voyage to finish a book. After passing the
leper colony, which by this time actually held only a few inmates, most of
whom were shamming, Felix, with a good lunch in his belly, was on his
way to Paris.

Etampes left our young man above all with the memory of a dozen
churches and bell towers carefully restored over the previous two generations. He also remembered (on his left as he rode through the city) a large
tile-roofed castle with a projecting keep known as La Guinette, which
appears in *Les Très Riches Heures* painted by the Limbourg brothers in the
previous century. Felix actually caught only a brief glimpse of "downtown" Etampes and the new residences erected there for the royal mistresses of Francis I and Henri II.[90]

After leaving Etampes and riding through forests and vineyards, our travelers came to the populous farming region around Arpajon (which at the time was called Châtres). To the east of their route lay plains planted with wheat or oats, and just to the right stood a leper house known as Saint-Blaise, close to but outside of Arpajon. This was similar to the leprosarium they had passed on the way out of Etampes. Châtres offered the new arrivals the spectacle of a city whose ramparts had been refurbished over the past thirty years through the addition of new walls, towers, moats, gates, and drawbridges. It was a small town of at most 1,200 to 1,500 people, short of the 3,000 needed to qualify as a *bonne ville*. The influence of the municipal authorities, if any, seems to have been negligible. By contrast, that of the great lords, powerful investors, and rebuilders was apparently considerable in the eyes of the Eternal: among them were not only court aristocrats like Malet de Graville, who came from the *noblesse d'épée,* but also men like the Villeroys, typical of the new elite of *secrétaires d'Etat.*

Châtres gave these families a great deal and also owed them a great deal. Entering the city through a gate called, logically enough, the Porte d'Etampes, our travelers simply had to follow the one major street, which led (regional centralism *oblige*) to the Porte de Paris. The street was flanked by houses, including many inns (owing to the proximity of the capital). Even though these buildings were situated inside the walls of the fortified city, they were surrounded by shrubs, flowers, and vegetable gardens. Proceeding north past the almost new market shed, built after urban fairs were authorized in 1490 with a roof supported by twelve chestnut pillars, the two men crossed the bridge over the Orge. They glanced briefly at the urban castle of the Malet de Graville family, patrons of the local clergy as well as the wine market. The château looked out on a park of no less than seven hectares, as large as the courtyard of the Palais-Royal in Paris today. There was no shortage of green space in Châtres-Arpajon. Finally, close to the Porte de Paris stood the church of Saint-Clément. Once Romanesque, the church had been turned into a charnel house by the English (who burned nearly a thousand people alive inside it in 1360, much as the Nazis did in Oradour in the 1940s). In 1510 the church was rebuilt in the late Gothic style at the behest of the local lords.

Heading due north out of the city, Felix and Theodor rode along the park of the château de Chanteloup, a gift from Francis I in 1518 to Nicolas de Neuville, *seigneur de* Villeroy and *secrétaire des Finances,* in exchange for another house whose salubrious climate suited the king's mother, Louise de Savoie. Felix did not have time to visit Chanteloup, but his younger brother Thomas Jr. was in less of a hurry: on his way to the capital later in the century, he found a few hours to visit the splendid gardens adjacent to the manor. The youngest of the Platters admired the multi-colored depictions of myths from Ovid's *Loves* that were created with flowering and leafy plants on the park's walls and in its flower beds. He especially enjoyed the walkways covered with thick sand from the quarries of Etampes. This made it possible to tour the garden even on a rainy day without muddying one's soles or heels (*man auch regenwetterszeit gar trocken darinnen gehen kan* [T2 543]). Thus the sandy walkways, which were carefully raked to remove all footprints, were a favorite with early modern gardeners not only because they were pleasant to look at but also because they were convenient for visitors.[91]

* * *

On the afternoon of March 27, after riding for a time past vineyards to his right and the edge of a forest to his left,[92] Felix arrived in Montlhéry, a community of a thousand to twelve hundred people situated on a truncated spur of land dominated by a castle spread out along the northern slope of a vine-covered hill and equipped with a series of four enclosures culminating in a hundred-foot-high keep with a conical roof of slate and lead. The two riders entered the city through the Porte Baudry and then followed the Grand-Rue and the rue de la Chapelle, lined with inns and a dozen or so bakeries, to the Porte de Paris at the other end of town. The shops along the rue aux Juifs and the rue du Soulier-de-Judas, populated by drapers, corn chandlers, weavers, and grocers who shared a network of interconnected underground storage cellars, held little appeal for Felix. A city of fairs and markets that received a good deal of Paris traffic, Montlhéry in the mid-sixteenth century was afflicted by numerous "ills, robberies and larcenies by bad fellows," bold as brass, "men deliberately abiding in the fields," vagrants "who frequently assaulted, robbed, beat, and insulted" the natives.[93] Although this description may have been exaggerated, it gives us an idea of the state of mind that led the residents of Montlhéry to ask the king in 1540 for permission to spend their own money to enclose the city with a system of walls and barbicans—yet another enclosure. Despite the vigorous efforts of the local *prévôté*, crime was not entirely a myth. Late in the century, Thomas Platter Jr. would complain that one night as he lay sleeping not far from Montlhéry, he was robbed by a roving fiddler (T2 546).

CHAPTER EIGHT

The Spring of 1557: Anabasis

On the afternoon of March 27, the two friends left Montlhéry and proceeded to Paris along the interminable rue Saint-Jacques (*durch S. Jacob Stross* [F 278]). Along the way they passed through Longjumeau and Berny and followed the triumphal route through the vineyards, a road that followed the same course as today's suburban rapid transit line, the Ligne de Sceaux. This brought them to the heart of the largest city on the continent, the "Great Beast," which had only recently displaced the Loire Valley as the seat of the Capetian kingdom.

From southern Paris the two visitors gazed upon the distant hill (*berg*) of Montmartre, atop which stood a Benedictine convent (*Kloster*) housing some sixty nuns, who had once (before 1503) been a subject of scandal but were now "reformed" in the Catholic sense of the word. This convent looked out over a large vineyard, beside which, halfway up the hill, stood the humble chapel in which Ignatius Loyola founded the Society of Jesus in 1534.[1] The big city seemed to be surrounded by windmills (*windt mülenen*). These were administered by a highly diverse group of millers dominated by a handful of wealthy flour wholesalers.[2] These businessmen played an essential role in feeding the capital's 350,000 people. Paris, already the most populous city in Christendom, was still growing. The two young men rode quickly through the rapidly expanding faubourg Saint-Jacques. Laid out in a thin line from north to south, the faubourg followed the street from which it took its name (like many another suburb or single-street village).[3] The travelers passed the chapel of Saint-Jacques-du-Haut-Pas on their left and proceeded on through the Porte Saint-Jacques adjacent to the recently rebuilt Convent of the Jacobins, which housed several dozen monks; a steady stream of new vocations kept the ranks replenished. The rue Saint-Jacques followed the route of the ancient Roman road from Paris to Orléans. This "vital artery" was lined with tall buildings crowded close together, along with bookstores and print shops. The inhabitants of the *faubourg* were people of modest station. Upon passing through the gate, Felix and Theodor found themselves in the university quarter on the south bank of the river. The Sainte-

Geneviève *quartier*—the Latin Quarter par excellence—stood off to their right; the Saint-Séverin *quartier* to their left. In between, still on the rue Saint-Jacques, they registered at the Auberge de la Croix, which they, translating into German, referred to as *Zum Kreutz*.

At this inn our travelers met the first of a long series of *Teutschen*, a certain Jochum, who was in fact a prominent citizen of Strasbourg by the name of Johann von Mundolsheim (F 278). That night (March 27) they looked around the city for the first time, just to get a feel for its "ambiance." Paris thrived, of course, on the centralized administrative apparatus of the monarchy. France was an *Etat d'offices*, or state of offices, typified by the Parlement and Chambre des Comptes, whose size, in terms of number of offices, increased steadily under Henri II.[4] It was also an *Etat de finance*, embodied in the coffers of the Royal Treasury at the Louvre, coffers that were empty more often than they ought to have been. His Majesty, in flesh and blood, might, if it pleased him, make war in the northeast or go hunting in the forests of the Loire, yet Paris could still say: *L'Etat, c'est moi*. This was especially true since the return from captivity in Spain of Francis I, who spent more and more of his time residing along the banks of the Seine in and around the capital, a choice symbolized by the commencement, in 1528, of work on the Château de Madrid in the game-rich forests of the Bois du Boulogne; in this Francis was followed by his son Henri. In the 1520s the whole system of royal finance was restructured; the decade was also decisive for Paris in other ways. The first serious plans for the capital were drawn up in these years: the celebrated woodcut by Truschet and Hoyau, an excellent map conserved among the papers of the University of Basel, has survived as a later reflection of these early plans; it has been dated, *a posteriori, circa* 1550. The resumption of economic and demographic growth in Paris probably began in the second half of the 1440s. By 1500 the city boasted a population of 200,000. By the time of Felix's visit, it had grown to 350,000: the pre-plague, pre-war high-water mark of the fourteenth century had been surpassed once and for all. Paris also left the cities of Italy in its dust: Naples had a population of 212,000 in 1547; Venice, 150,000 in 1557; Milan, 180,000 after 1550. And forget London, whose population rose from 60,000 in 1520 to 200,000 in 1600 but still, despite an extraordinary rate of growth, lagged far behind the capital of France.[5]

"Peace" had a major impact on the specific form that the growth of Paris took—this despite the fact that France was in fact perpetually at war. Its conflicts were modest ones, however, relegated to the borders of Italy, Lorraine, and "Belgium" and involving smaller armies than would be engaged in the next century. Between the Treaty of Crépy-en-Laonnois (1544) and the French debacle at Saint-Quentin (August 1557, not long after Felix's visit), Paris had nothing to fear from foreign invaders. In March and April of 1557, however, the city was still quite tranquil: no one had an inkling of the catastrophe looming on the horizon (the magnitude of which should not be exaggerated, however).

On the evening of his arrival (March 27), Felix took his first stroll along the banks of the Seine and was struck by the extraordinary array of boats of every description. Paris in those days looked more like Bordeaux than like Limoges or Clermont. The sea was not far off. Fish from the ocean made the journey posthaste, within twenty-four hours if possible; seafood was rarely spoiled when it reached the market stalls of the capital. The streets and quays along the river were a vital, almost tumultuous place, with some 5,000 porters, longshoremen, and warehousemen and some 10,000 water carriers to keep things moving. Poverty was everywhere; it spread as rapidly as wealth (at times fabulous), as wages in some trades went into sharp decline after the turn of the sixteenth century. The government had a hand in this: if the Renaissance monarchy took a relatively relaxed attitude toward assemblies of its provincial estates, it kept a close watch on the activities of the capital's aldermen.[6] In 1533, moreover, the monarchy initiated work on a major public project in the Italian style, with the construction of the Hôtel de Ville. Such public works would continue to the end of the century.

The *prévôt de marchands,* equivalent to a mayor, was generally (despite a 1547 edict to the contrary) a man of the *robe,* for the municipal government of Paris, like that of Montpellier and Béziers, was dominated by royal officeholders. The king kept a close watch on this official: since the days of Etienne Marcel (1315–58), the agents of the central government looked upon Paris as a potential powderkeg. The *prévôt* was elected, not without royal interference, by extremely limited bodies of electors. He presided over representatives of the city's sixteen *quartiers,* the famous "Seize" [Sixteen], who took on real political importance only in the last two decades of the sixteenth century (during the Wars of Religion). For the time being, the Sixteen were on their best behavior. The big problem of the moment was the growing Protestant influence among the citizens, *robins,* and nobles of the city. This would cause something of a stir five months after Felix's visit, in early September 1557, when 350 Protestants gathered on the rue Saint-Jacques, not far from the inn where Felix had stayed, behind the Sorbonne. They were arrested in the early morning hours of September 5 by the royal prosecutor of the Châtelet following a night of unpleasantness that might be likened to a minor pogrom. Among those imprisoned were several Swiss, who were soon released at the request of the Swiss cantons; some of them had spent time with Felix during his visit.

On the morning of March 28, Felix Jr., always ready to move on, decided to leave the Auberge de la Croix. Perhaps it was too expensive for him. In any case, he and his friend moved to the Mortier d'Or, a boarding house of dubious reputation on the rue Saint-Jacques. Despite the sonorous name, the reality was sordid. The two young men shared a minuscule room with one bed above a pharmacy (the *mortier*, or mortar, of the name referred to the pharmacist's mortar and pestle). There they remained for the next three weeks, until April 21. From this convenient base they fanned out to explore the various quarters of Paris, on the Left Bank, the Right Bank, and the Ile de la Cité. They soon made a new acquaintance: Carl Utenhove, originally from Flanders but German-Swiss by adoption (the visitors remained in the German orbit). Utenhove came from a good humanist family in Ghent. He called frequently on his two friends at the Mortier d'Or. To do so, he had to climb the spiral staircase to their room. Utenhove's family had connections to Erasmus as well as to the University of Montpellier.[7] The young man flirted with the neo-Latin muse. The Platters knew him well, because he had been a boarder in Thomas Sr.'s Gymnasium in Basel. Later, he continued his studies in England, where he prepared himself for a career in teaching and the study of Greek, which eventually took him to Cologne. Thus, in the person of Utenhove, the Flemish diaspora with its British and German offshoots touched the life of Felix Platter. The Flemish presence in Paris was even greater than in Montpellier.

At the Mortier d'Or, our Swiss traveler saw yet another (temporarily) uprooted countryman: Balthasar Krug, the son of the bailiff and half-brother of a future bürgermeister, also a Krug—the megalomaniac mayor who would become an important associate of the Platter family in years to come. Balthasar was an odd fellow, sociable and resourceful, with more friends in Paris than financial resources. Felix also met the French king's Swiss guards, whose undoubted Protestantism apparently bothered no one. The guards' headquarters when it came to reveling was the Auberge du Mouton, it, too, on the rue Saint-Jacques. One of the guards, from Zurich, had married a Frenchwoman, who invited Felix for an evening of drink. Another, a tall, slender fellow from Basel by the name of Jockel, had a pain in his groin about which he consulted with the traveling medical man, who offered his sage advice. Was this the same man who died of a groin problem a few days later?

Did Felix meet only Germans and their associates in Paris? Not exactly: he did also see Frenchmen, but, as was often the case with him, they were doctors, people who had things to teach him or who might be of use to him professionally. This was true in Montpellier and even in Lyons, where, shortly after arriving in France, Felix had been received by Dr. Rondelet. In Paris his first "medical" visit was to Jacques Goupyl, known as Gubillus, a Hellenist from the Poitou and professor at the Collège Royal who was responsible for translations of ancient Latin and Greek texts on medicine, botany, and zoology, including works of Alexander of Tralles, Aretaeus of Cappadocia, Dioscorides, Galen, and Paul of Egina, as well as Ausonius from the literary realm and Alessandro Piccolomini from the Italian. Most of these translations, particularly those on medical subjects, appeared prior to 1557, so that Felix would have known them. Even more important, Goupyl had the wisdom to publish, in 1554, a convenient student handbook containing the works of Rufus of Ephesus on the various parts of the body, the kidneys, the bladder, purgations, and menstruation in women.[8] Felix found this compendium quite handy seven years letter when a plague struck Basel in 1564: on July 26 of that year, Thomas Platter discovered a bubo on his right knee, as well as a boil, which Felix noted when he removed, without shame, his father's pants (F 435). He treated the older man with pills based on one of Rufus's formulas, a mixture of two-thirds aloe and one-third myrrh dissolved in wine. His brother-in-law, the surgeon Daniel Jeckelmann, lanced the boil without fear of contagion. Thanks to the ministrations of his son and his son's wife's brother, Thomas Platter was back on his feet a few weeks later.

Felix also met Louis Duret, a student of philosophy who hailed originally from the valley of the Loire and was destined for a brilliant career as physician to kings and professor at the Collège Royal. A good speaker who was popular with students as well as a competent specialist in the works of Hippocrates and Arab medicine, Duret was reputedly a traditionalist.[9] The same could not be said of Jean Fernel, a man of modernity, or, more precisely, of Antiquity, and therefore hostile to the intermediary glosses of Muslim physicians, to which he referred as "Arabic garbage" (*sic*). Felix's encounter with Fernel, a Parisian by predilection who became, in the year of Felix's visit, Henri II's personal physician, would prove crucial. It supplied Felix with arguments that he would use against the academics of Basel a few months later, when he defended his thesis on the controversial issue of native heat.[10] The fact that Felix was received without difficulty by three of Paris's most prominent physicians (Duret, Goupyl, and Fernel) suggests that he arrived on the banks of the Seine with a certain reputation, which persuaded his older colleagues to open their doors to him. Perhaps he carried letters from Dr. Saporta, his patron in Montpellier, who was well-known in medical circles in France and throughout Europe. Be that as it may, the religious scrutiny of the *sorbon-nard* theologians weighed heavily on the University of Paris, including the faculty of medicine. Felix was unable to find the climate of free research, open to Jews and Huguenots and ready to engage when necessary in dissections, that he had experienced during his five years in Montpellier. For any Protestant worthy of the name, the Sorbonne could only be the devil's own synagogue, an abominable intellectual bordello, the gateway to hell.[11] But Felix seemed not to care.

Dr. Jean Fernel, Welch though he was, had a Swiss cousin, Andreas Wechel, a bookseller and printer, who agreed to show Felix the interesting sites of the *Université, Cité,* and *Ville.* Andreas was the son of Christian (or Chrétien) Wechel, a Swiss native who had set up in business as a printer in the Ile-de-France and who had published, during the reign of Francis I, hundreds of scholarly works for the French market.[12] As successor to his father (who had himself succeeded Conrad Rosch, a Swiss-Parisian bookseller "*à l'écu de Bâle*" from 1515 to 1526),[13] Andreas continued a long Parisian publishing tradition. He liked to welcome foreigners to the city. His house was a meeting place for visiting Protestants from across the Vosges and the Rhine. Though a notorious Huguenot, the younger Wechel escaped persecution for a time, but in the end his luck ran out: his inventory of books was burned in 1569; in 1572, after the Saint Bartholomew's Day massacre, he was forced to flee to Frankfurt, where he lived out his days as a bookseller. In 1557, with this adoptive Parisian as a guide, Felix explored the vicinity of the rue Saint-Jacques and the banks of the Seine. One of their first excursions took the two men to the Louvre: King Henri II was absent that day because he was off visiting his estate at Villers-Cotterêts (which Felix in his *Tagebuch* spelled Ville-Accoustrée).

Henri II loved his grand château at Villers-Cotterêts. Although of recent construction, the castle was quite traditional, rectangular in shape with a long interior corridor, slanted roof, tall rectangular chimney stacks, park with evergreen shrubbery, and lanes lined with hazelnut trees, complemented by an *orangerie* and a wooded area for hunting.[14] The king had not gone to his palace in the northeast just to relax. He also wanted to keep an eye on the work of his masons (the château was still under construction). Most of all, he wanted to inspect for himself the next likely theater of military operations, where his prospects did not look good. The Truce of Vaucelles (February 1556) had just been denounced, and France had lightheartedly declared war once again on the Spanish Hapsburg Philip II, the son and partial heir of Charles V—that

ever-troublesome House of Burgundy again! Having made a rather bizarre marriage with Mary Tudor, Philip II had secured the paradoxical
support of the English for several years. This was a sobering prospect for
Henri II, for in the face of the Madrid-Brussels-London axis that was
thus created, France's northern borders were virtually undefended: François de Guise had just marched off to Italy with an army of thirteen thousand men, leaving the heartland vulnerable to attack. The remainder of
the French army numbered only twenty to twenty-five thousand men,
concentrated in Attigny (now Ardennes) and commanded by the not
very capable Montmorency. This rump of an army was not up to the task
of fending off Philip II's horde of forty-four thousand men under the able
Emmanuel Philibert of Savoy. To make matters worse, the Hapsburg
commander had it in for the French, who in 1536 had stripped him of his
hereditary duchy in the northern Alps and Piedmont. Here was an opportunity for revenge. Philip II, sure of himself, took up a position in
Cambrai and bided his time.[15]

In Villers-Cotterêts it was easier for Henri II to prepare to meet the
peril than it was in Paris. The French disaster at Saint-Quentin in August
would show how inadequate his preparations were, however. In early
June, Henri held a council of war at Villers-Cotterêts to consider the
British problem.[16] Although the whole situation was already clear by
March, Felix does not breathe a word of it in his diary, which contains
observations he wrote down at the time and recopied half a century later.
Was this ignorance? Certainly. But it was also, no doubt, indifference,
silence, and prudence.

Regardless of the king's absence, the Swiss visitor took an interest in
the Louvre. Since 1528, when Francis I made a definitive decision to return to Paris, this palace had become a significant center of power; what is
more, it was close to the Parlement of Paris, which did nothing to diminish its importance. The authorities reacted accordingly. The huge central
keep was razed and replaced by a paved courtyard, now the Cour carrée.
Like Blois before it, the Louvre began to shed its fortresslike character. It
became a relatively open palace, more or less integrated into the city's
ramparts and taking the friendly disposition of the capital's population
for granted. The quays along the Seine had recently been straightened,
paved with stone, and made fit for wagons. They ran along the edge of
the palace, where horses once drank from troughs in the berm bordering
the muddy towpath. Pierre Lescot and Jean Goujon were at work on the
nascent Cour carrée, whose west wing was just being completed at the
time of Felix's visit.[17]

On his way to and from the palace, the young man mingled with the population of the *quartier:* washerwomen, goldsmiths, leather workers, fishmongers, and courtiers with pointy mustaches and plumed hats. Despite the fact that the king was frequently out of Paris, the Louvre in its new form was by mid-century a major component of the machinery of power. Its transformation came after the Forbidden City of Peking and the Kremlin, two enclosed palaces that dated from the fifteenth century, but before the Escorial, a semi-abbatial residence that would be partly open to the public, as Henri II's palace already was.

After touring the seat of government embodied in the long building along the Seine, Felix went on to inspect the colleges of the university and the city's churches (*vil colegia, vil kilchen*). His German-speaking friend Wechel made up for his lack of a tourist guidebook. Their round of churches was purely for touristic purposes, since neither man cared for the papist atmosphere of these religious edifices. The tour sites ranged from the brand-new rood-screen of Saint-Etienne-du-Mont to the vast construction site at Saint-Eustache, where work was proceeding on the choir chapels and the final bays of the nave. The pace of construction matched the growing animation of the surrounding market district, Les Halles. Our tourists also visited Notre-Dame in the heart of the wealthy clerical and judicial quarter on the Ile-de-la-Cité. In order to reach the cathedral, Felix had to pass the Hôtel-Dieu on his right (the access was different from what it is today) and the church of Saint-Christophe, which had been entirely rebuilt in 1500, on his left. Once inside, he found the elite of the clergy, a class of priests far superior to those he had known as a student in Montpellier.

Visiting Notre-Dame later in the century, Felix's brother Thomas Jr., a confirmed anticlerical, insisted that the cathedral's choir was full of roving pimps and madams offering their services (*Diensten*) to anyone who happened by (T2 560). Around the pillars of the sanctuary, he also saw beds crowded with foundlings. As for prostitution, it is true that a *quartier chaud* (literally, hot quarter) had developed over the centuries on the Ile-de-la-Cité around the rue Glatigny and extending all the way to the Pont Notre-Dame, "even adjacent to the cathedral."[18] Some of this debauchery had apparently spilled over into the interior of the huge Gothic structure at a time when sacred and profane activities were less distinct than they are now. Felix mentions only that, as in Orléans, he climbed the bell tower so as to enjoy the spectacle of the huge bells and the lead roofs below. The entry, nave, and screen of the sanctuary were at this point much as the builder Jean Le Bouteiller had left them when the last major work was done on the cathedral in 1351. Overall, Notre-Dame did not change much from the time Felix saw it until the late seventeenth century,

when certain architectural changes were made at behest of Louis XIV.
The pure art of the Gothic arch, embodied in Notre-Dame, was thus fro-
zen for three centuries, from 1360 to 1660, long enough for Felix and
Thomas Jr. to appreciate it.

From Notre-Dame to the Pont au Change, which Felix calls the Pont
aux Orfèvres, was but a short distance. Felix walked quickly because his
purpose now was not to see the sights but to purchase gifts for his fiancée,
Madlen Jeckelmann. The wooden Pont au Change, built at the end of the
thirteenth century, was the oldest bridge in Paris as well as the most solidly built, to judge by the way it withstood time and the elements. To be
sure, the low houses that lined both sides of the bridge were refurbished
fairly regularly, every half century or so (*vast alle so jahr*).[19] Its sturdy architecture is confirmed by the fact that the structure bore their weight.
Aligned with a major north-south thoroughfare (the rue Saint-Denis),
the Pont au Change faced the threshing mills of the Pont aux Meuniers to
the west. Some years before Felix's visit, there had even been a rather far-
fetched proposal to install mills on the Pont au Change itself. Joining the
wealthier quarters of the capital, the bridge passed close to some of the
major sights of the Right Bank, among them the church of Saint-Jacques-
de-la-Boucherie with its famous tower of the 1510s, a masterpiece of flamboyant Gothic architecture, and the stalls of the (dying) Grande-
Boucherie; the fortress of the Châtelet, the headquarters of the *prévôté* of
Paris and other regional authorities and thus the seat of power in the Ile-
de-France; and the stone quays of the Right Bank, which Felix had seen
earlier while visiting the Louvre. Built between 1528 and 1538, the quays
served as conduits for long lines of wagons that stretched along the Seine
westward from the bridges of the Ile-de-la-Cité to the royal residence and
the site of the present and future Tuileries.[20]

The Pont au Change had once been an obligatory passage for joyous
royal entries, but it had lost that role to the Pont Notre-Dame in 1515. It
nevertheless remained a mecca for goldsmiths, a place to buy reliquaries,
showpieces, monstrances, and even golden ship models.[21] Felix went
"shopping" there for jewelry in the well-placed studio of Hans Jacob
David, who came from a leading Basel family that included city coun-
cillors, exchange agents, and more or less noble knights. Hans, however,
had gone to Paris to seek his fortune.

At a special price for friends and fellow Germans, Felix bought Madlen
a gold chain, which eventually became a family heirloom: Madlen, by
then the elderly Frau Platterin, gave it one day to Chrischona, the wife of
Thomas Jr., a pretty woman whose portrait would be painted in the early
seventeenth century with Felix's gold chain hanging from her belt. At

Hans David's studio our student met another young man of about his own age named Felix Keller. Keller, from Zurich, had come to the Pont au Change to apprentice before returning to his birthplace, where he became a jeweler, city councillor, and member of the leading municipal guilds (F 280). The city of Paris, with its deep traditions of craftsmanship extending back to the thirteenth century, was a remarkable school for training specialists in the fashioning of precious metals, some of whom went on to settle in the French heartland, while others returned to exercise their French-perfected talents in their native lands. Our tourist shoppers on the Pont au Change also enjoyed visiting the studios of the bookbinders, whose art reached a pinnacle of perfection under Henri II.[22] Felix, in the mood for gifts, purchased a pocket Bible (actually a half-Bible, a *Testamentum,* probably the New Testament) for his fiancée, whose name he had inscribed in gold letters on the handsomely bound volume. Was it the Latin Vulgate, that is, a Catholic Bible, or a German translation by Luther that had escaped the notice of royal censors unable to decipher the language of France's neighbor?

Felix's anticlerical tendencies made themselves felt in one way or another, even if the Bible he purchased was not a very Catholic one. A few days after his visit to the bookbinder, the young Helvetian visited the Cimetière des Innocents on the rue Saint-Denis, six or seven "blocks" north of the Pont au Change and the Châtelet. Somewhat further north along the same street was the Cimetière de la Trinité, where the dead from the Hôtel-Dieu were buried until 1554, when a royal decree put an end to the practice on hygienic grounds.[23]

Hygiene, or more accurately the lack of it, was in the forefront of Felix's mind as he walked to the cemetery. During the plague of 1531, the Cimetière des Innocents was literally gorged with the dead and gave off a pestilential odor that was seen as a danger to the public. The stench was almost as strong when Felix visited the cemetery a quarter of a century later. The surfeit of cadavers was greater than ever in this place haunted by the Angel of Death. The neighbors had made their peace with it: the *quartier* had its share of prostitution but was dominated by the textile trade (mercers, dyers, shearers, drapers). At the Innocents there was something for every taste, outside the walls as well as inside. Felix discovered various artifacts of late-medieval taste: an alabaster skeleton of Death from the early sixteenth century and a charnel-house gallery illustrated by scenes of the *danse macabre.*[24] The Renaissance was also present in the form of bas-reliefs of Seine nymphs and fluted arcades and pilasters on the new Fontaine des Innocents (1549), which was designed by Jean Goujon to resemble a royal tribune. The transition from the funerary alabaster of the early 1500s to the time of Henri II in mid-century dramatized the cultural transformation that had taken place. Yet a certain clerical presence remained, hence an anticlerical presence as well: Felix witnessed a procession of monks and "priestlings" (*pfaffen*) that went on for an hour and a quarter. Felix meant the word "priestlings" to be as disagreeable as possible: he despised these sovereign clerics whose word would soon be law for the Parisians of the League (the Wars of Religion were only a few decades away).[25]

Of course the man in the street in those days was still accustomed to religious processions, especially when there were funerals. In March, shortly before Felix arrived in Paris, the city had witnessed the funeral of Cardinal de Bourbon, which had resulted in disputes over priority leading to fisticuffs between the canons of Notre-Dame and those of Saint-Germain-l'Auxerrois.[26] As the persecution of Protestants continued (Parlement recently having requested that the bishop provide information against suspect preachers), Henri II, reacting to this and other scandals associated with ecclesiastical processions, issued an order establishing the priority of various official bodies: Parlement came first, followed by the Chambre des Comptes, the Cour des Aides, the Chambre des Monnaies, the provost of Paris, the Châtelet, and finally the Hôtel de Ville.

One Sunday morning (was it March 28 or April 4?), Felix faced the problem of what to do with his time. Attending mass was of course out of the question. His dog Poclès, more Calvinist even than its master, would have forbidden it. From dawn until noon Felix therefore made a quick tour of the circumference of Paris, which approximated the shape of a pumpkin.

The German community in Paris was a city within a city, or, more precisely, a village, a very lively village. Felix rarely left the company of this gregarious group, except when he called on the three leading French physicians at the beginning of his visit, which otherwise remained "ethnocentric." A German injured himself on the inside of his knee, and the young Swiss doctor was summoned. He found the wound still fresh (*ziemlich frisch*). The next day, the man was dead: was it an embolism, a hemorrhage, or a rapid infection? Everyone was overcome (*was uns allen leidt*). The burial took place at night, by torchlight, with torches held aloft at arm's length to illuminate the dead man's coat of arms, which was displayed along with the body, for he was a noble. The German community of students and shopkeepers turned out for the burial, Felix among them, even though he was only a migratory bird on a brief visit, an Alsatian stork ready to take flight at a moment's notice. Still, his compatriots, well established in the Ile-de-France, adopted the young Swiss for the duration of his visit.

The Germans' communal sentiments extended, moreover, to the countries of Central Europe without regard for boundaries, just as in the time of Thomas Platter Sr. When a Polish nobleman died in Paris in the spring of 1557, "we accompanied him to his final resting place," wrote Felix, who was always fascinated by burials so long as the deceased hailed from "the other side of the Rhine," a geographical expression that has to be understood in the broadest possible terms as extending all the way to the Vistula.

Crédit Suisse: when Felix's money began to run out, he was obliged to call on a rather strange countryman, Martin Betschart, a native of Lucerne and former resident of Basel who had chosen Paris as his place of business: he was a pawnbroker and perhaps also a usurer. From 1557 to 1559 he served as agent or broker in northern France for a Zurich printer. In the time of Henri II he lived on a small street noted for its prostitutes (*gmeine wiber*) in a horseshoe- or crescent-shaped block of buildings known as Champ-Gaillard, situated between Saint-Nicolas-du-Chardonnet and rue Bordelle and between rue d'Arras, rue Saint-Victor, and rue Clopin. Champ-Gaillard had a bad reputation; the Parlement of Paris complained about it as early as 1555.[27] Betschart himself was a curious fellow, whose facial scars and the spicy stories they seemed to suggest made him famous among German visitors. Among other things, he was always rubbing his nose with saliva in the vain hope of getting rid of the striking scars that disfigured his face.

Betschart had previously tried his hand at various trades, including those of proofreader and musical copyist. Later, he moved up a notch to become the representative of the German nation in the French capital. From 1529 until his death in 1569, he served first as *procureur,* then as *questeur,* and finally as *doyen* of the Germans of Paris. One can readily imagine him as a secret agent of the Swiss. He did his best to find rooms at reasonable rents for students from the Alps and the Jura. He complained in his letters that the morals of young people were easily corrupted in Paris (and especially in Champ-Gaillard), while French husbands were tyrannized by their wives. He bailed Felix out by lending him twelve crowns on his father's credit. The young visitor was astonished by Betschart's house, a treasure trove filled with furniture, jewelry, and even food left in pawn by his clients. The Betschart pawnshop forged a kind of bond between the Rhine and the Seine.[28]

In early April Felix went to see the great abbey in Saint-Denis, a small town of two thousand that had come down quite a bit since the fourteenth century, when its population was said to have been ten thousand before the Black Plague. In letters patent issued in November of 1556, Henri II had only recently authorized the town to resume holding the Lendit fair within its walls, but this privilege could not compensate for the failure to thrive.[29] The declining population was reflected in the presence of large green spaces (cultivated fields, forests, and gardens as well as uncultivated land) within the fortified enclosure. The route from Paris to Saint-Denis had long been marked by the peregrinations of the saint himself (dead as well as alive); he was often depicted holding his severed head in his hands and washing it as he went, just as he was supposed to have done when he continued on his way to Saint-Denis after being decapitated in Montmartre. The road from the capital to the monastery was also the customary route of the *hanouars,* who in ordinary times hauled salt but who, when a king died, were charged with the mission of bearing the royal corpse to its final resting place.[30] Their last occasion to do so had been in 1547, on the death of Francis I. Felix and Theodor entered Saint-Denis through the woad market, then proceeded down rue Cordonnerie and rue Boulangerie, passing the Hôtel-Dieu on their right. From there they went to the abbey church of Saint-Denis. Since it was late, they took a room at the Auberge du Maure.

That evening they had time for a rousing tennis match at a local court. All the Platters took an interest in the game. Thomas Jr. counted eight tennis courts in Montpellier in 1595, seven in the city and one in the *vorstatt,* or suburb. In Montpellier recreation halls were frequented mainly by court officers and soldiers, bachelors fond of dancing, horses, and sports. In Paris, Thomas Jr. counted no fewer than 1,100 tennis courts (other sources report only 600, which still comes to one court for every four hundred people or one hundred households). Courts were so popular and so profitable that when the faubourgs of Paris were partially destroyed by cannon fire in the siege of 1590, damaged buildings were replaced by tennis courts, which yielded a better return on investment.

Felix, by now an accomplished tourist completing a long and educational journey, leapt out of bed the next morning and hastened off to see the sacred works and treasures on display at Saint-Denis, a stone's throw from the Auberge du Maure. He described and admired what he saw, distinguishing among three types of artifacts: religious and cultural objects (reliquaries and antiquities); funerary sculptures (such as tombstones); and precious objects, valuable in the world here below (*kostlichen Sachen*).

For once he looked at relics without his customary Protestant irony. He mentions the crucifixes of gold and silver containing fragments of the

True Cross, part of a gift from Jean de Berry, as well as a nail from the Crucifixion kept in a gilt vermillion reliquary that had been given to Charlemagne by Constantine (or so Felix quite astonishingly believed—yet another Donation of Constantine!). Saint Denis's head with its jewel-encrusted miter is supported by two gilt angels, while a third angel holds up a many-faceted reliquary containing the saint's jawbone. The reliquary bust of Saint Benedict, weighing more than a hundred and thirty pounds, contains pieces of the skull and arms of the founder of the Benedictine Order. The bust is covered with ancient cameos, including a Victory, a left profile of Domitian, and two galloping horses, all given to the abbey in 1401 by the same Jean, duc de Berry. (Later, in 1804, some of these cameos were transferred for the anointment of Napoleon to the counterfeit "crown of Charlemagne" with which the emperor was crowned.)

A golden reliquary containing a hand of the apostle Thomas, also flanked by a pair of angels, was yet another gift from the Maecenas of Berry. Thomas's finger, which had once explored the wound in Jesus's side, "was covered with gold and wore a ring with a set stone."[31] Felix also reports finding a tooth of Saint John the Baptist (more "scholarly" sources speak only of a reliquary of John the Baptist containing part of the saint's shoulder along with a tooth from Saint Pancras Martyr, as well as two walrus tusks given by King David of Scotland). There was also the money that Judas had received for betraying Christ and the lantern that Judas had been holding when Christ was arrested. Antiquities constituted a second facet of a certain Renaissance "ensemble" (ancient culture after Christian culture): in this case, according to Felix, there were cameos of Cleopatra, Antony, and Nero. These identifications are rather fanciful, because the actual cameos in the crypt of Saint-Denis would more likely have depicted emperors such as Claudius, Augustus, and Caracalla. The last "antiquity" that Felix mentions is the "jawbone" or tusk of an "elephant": to judge from the surviving inventories, this can only have been the *olifant de Roland,* Roland's horn, actually an eleventh-century Hispano-Moorish ivory hunting horn, or perhaps another horn in the Saint-Denis collection, a fifteenth-century horn decorated with an ape emerging from a chalice to preach to an audience of birds arranged in two rows.[32]

Felix turns next to mortuary objects: the celebrated tombstones of Saint-Denis, which played a part in the royal funerals of the Renaissance. No monk disturbed the young man's thanatological explorations or inquired in an inquisitorial voice as he peered at some funerary tile whether he was a Huguenot or a Papist. The two German tourists first visited the sepulchre of Charles VIII with its bronze mausoleum, which was destroyed in the course of the repugnant exhumations carried out in 1793. They went next to the tomb of Louis XII and Anne of Brittany. There, the Gothic arches of the dais were juxtaposed with ancient-style *tempietto*.[33] The young Helvetian saw the old theme of the king's two bodies brought to life in a striking new way: the sovereigns' naked cadavers, depicted with striking realism, are contrasted with images of them kneeling as they were in life. When the sepulchres were violated at the end of the eighteenth century, two crowns of gilt copper were found on the sarcophagus of the Franco-Breton couple.[34] Francis I could well have placed a solid gold crown on the tomb had he wanted to; in this instance he showed himself to be miserly. His prodigality was lavished, of course, on the visible structures rather than the hidden depths of the sepulchre, as Felix and his companion discovered when they inspected the white marble statues around the monument to Louis XII representing the mirror and serpent of Prudence, the sword and orb of Justice, the lionskin of Strength, and the clock and bridle of Temperance. As for the (mortuary) arch of triumph dedicated to Queen Claude and Francis I, whose figures were enveloped in a shroud of stone and carved into the stylobate, work was still in progress in the spring of 1557 (*doran man noch werckt* [F 281]).

Felix also mentions that attached to the cenotaph of Francis were statues of his mother, Louise of Savoy, and Charlotte, Louise's granddaughter. The modeling and realism of the figures, whether erect or recumbent, delighted our traveler. These cadavers were full of life. Felix's sensibility responded to the art of the Renaissance, which was being created all around him. But "medieval" sculpture did not leave him cold either: he noted the tomb of a fourteenth-century constable, possibly that of Louis de Sancerre, with its brutal expression, or Bertrand du Guesclin. In the abbey Felix marveled at the open book of French history, transformed into a heroic cemetery bristling with columns and statuary.

Leaving piety, classicism, and death behind, he next moved on to a more traditional sort of museum, filled with regalia, or symbols of sovereignty that played a role in the royal anointment ceremony, mingled with miscellaneous treasures. Among the regalia Felix mentions a golden scepter with a hand[35] on top made of "unicorn horn" (actually a hand of justice).[36] The visitor also saw three royal crowns that no longer exist: a Gothic "king's crown" with a bonnet "topped by the huge ruby of John the Good"; a queen's crown dating from 1250–1300 and encrusted with gold, precious gems, and *fleurs de lys;* and finally, a holy crown, contemporary with the queen's crown and embellished with a hundred and fifty large pearls as well as a sliver of the Crown of Thorns and hairs from the

Savior's head—still more relics. Of these three crowns, one vanished in 1590, when it was confiscated and melted down by agents of the League. The two others met the same fate in 1793–94. Among the other regalia in the abbey in the sixteenth century were three swords: that of Charles VII; Charlemagne's sword, the so-called *Joyeuse*, today in the Louvre; and, most important of all, the sword of Saint Louis, which vanished during the Revolution. Of these three weapons, Felix saw or at any rate mentioned only one, that of Saint Louis, about which he tells us only that he saw it.[37]

Felix also marveled at a plate or tablet (*tafel*) covered with precious gems, probably the red and white ornamental clasp with heraldic emblems that Charles V had made for his son to wear to his anointing; it was encrusted with forty pearls, nine red rubies, and four cut diamonds.[38] The Swiss visitor also mentions certain royal garments that were essential pieces of the regalia: pants and shoes (*Hosen und Schuh*) were a basic part of the anointing costume. In fact these "pants" were sumptuous breeches, decorated with pearls,[39] and the shoes were boots with spurs bearing dragons' and lions' heads (one of which was reworked in 1547, ten years before Felix's visit). Last but not least were two real conversation pieces. The first was a "unicorn horn" six feet long (*ein einhorn 6 schu lang*) preserved in a basin of water behind the altar. The water was to be ingested for therapeutic purposes. The horn was in fact one of the finest narwhal tusks in France. The second conversation piece Felix referred to simply as "Solomon's cup" (*Soll des Künigs Salomons gwesen sein*). It was in fact a Sassanian rock crystal cup with gold stem dating from the sixth or seventh century and either a gift of Charles the Bald or booty from a raid by Charlemagne: "This goblet was made of pure gold together with fine emeralds and garnets and beautifully wrought," according to the author of the *Grandes Chroniques de France* in the fourteenth century.[40]

Felix spent only about thirty hours in the abbatial town of Saint-Denis.[41] By mid-April he was back in Paris. Shortly after arriving, he made a brief excursion to Les Tournelles, the site of the royal stables. He thus explored two perpendicular tourist axes: an east-west axis running from the Louvre to Les Tournelles, the axis of (royal) power, and a north-south religious axis running from the Sorbonne to Notre-Dame to the Innocents to Saint-Denis. The two intersected at the Pont au Change, a place for shopping and buying presents.

Les Tournelles belonged to a vast ensemble of royal residences on the eastern fringes of the capital's circumference. Among these was the Hôtel Saint-Paul, which had not been used since the reign of Francis I or perhaps before. In this huge building, Charles V had allegedly lived such a democratic life, so close to the common people, that Louis-Sébastien Mercier, writing in the time of Louis XVI, was able to refer to his reign retrospectively as the "Popular Front" of medieval monarchy.[42] As for Les Tournelles, the shift of fashion toward the west end, a phenomenon observed in many cities over the preceding centuries, had gradually diminished the palace's value. In 1519 Louise of Savoy abandoned it, having found its stench unbearable. The royal family continued to reside here during the winter, but during the high season there was competition from Fontainebleau, Saint-Germain, and the Louvre.

Les Tournelles continued to be useful, however, as a site for equestrian exercises and military maneuvers. Its park, though inside the walls of Paris, was extensive and well suited to military drill. When Felix visited in the spring of 1557, he saw two figures silhouetted in an upper-story window of the big house: the dauphin François (the future Francis II) and Charles II, duc de Lorraine.[43] In the following year, 1558, Charles married Claude de France, the second daughter of Catherine de Médicis. But for now, as Felix looked on in April 1557, the dauphin picked up a dog and hurled it through the window at a page galloping past, who adroitly caught the animal as he rode (F 283). Forty-five years later, Felix would relate this memory to Duke Charles, whose official physician and friend he had meanwhile become.

Felix wrote about his reminiscences of Paris during the reigns of Henri IV and Louis XIII. But in 1557, when he was still only twenty-one, he faced a decision. Although Paris was by no means boring, it was time to move on. His financial resources were running low, and the presents he had purchased were costly. The longer the young man from Switzerland dawdled in Ile-de-France, the more likely it was that Madlen, his fiancée, would wind up in the arms of another man. Better get a move on! Before that, however, there was time for a dinner among *Teutschen,* a regular occurrence whenever it came time for one of them to head home. A group of twenty young tourists from Switzerland attended the banquet. They had just come through central and eastern France, hoping to see something of the kingdom and visit the great city. And since they happened to be in Paris, why not meet Felix, who, because of his long stay abroad, had become, *in absentia,* an almost legendary figure in his native city? Among the guests was also a part-time soldier named Hans. As luck would have it, he decided to accompany Felix on his journey home. And of course the cream of Basel's itinerant typographers and humanists also turned up. Among them was Basilius Amerbach, aged twenty-three, at one time a student in Germany, France, and Italy, the son of a jurist, and himself a humanist and soon to be professor and rector in Basel. His visit to Paris in 1557–58 is of historical importance because he returned home with the only surviving copy of the map by Truschet and Hoyau, which eventually became the jewel of the Basel University Library collection. Amerbach allegedly lent the map to his friend Theodor Zwinger for the printing of a work entitled *Methodus Apodemica*.[44]

Seated beside Amerbach at Felix's dinner was Caspar Herwagen, whose name calls to mind one of the leading families of Basel printers. This particular Herwagen belonged, however, to a bastard offshoot of the illustrious line: he was the illegitimate son of a Herwagen who had become a priest. Caspar, having distinguished himself as a student in France and Germany, served first a Catholic bishop and later a Protestant prince. Also present was Aurelius Erasmus Frobenius, whose name alone speaks volumes: he was the son of a printer (the publisher of Erasmus), the brother of another printer, and a printer himself. And soon he would father a brood from which would come yet another printer. Next to him was Eusebius Bischof, also a printer's son who grew up to be a printer and who, in his forties, would be ennobled by the emperor. Then there was Bernhard Burckhardt, aged twelve, who came from a family of drapers and aldermen and who would soon become a draper and silk merchant. It may seem surprising that Bernhard's parents allowed him to travel to Paris at such a tender age, but he was surrounded by staunch friends. Finally, to round out the guest list, let us mention the iron-monger's son Hans Jacob Ruedin, who, over the next few days, would make Felix a disagreeable companion on the road from Paris to Basel. Our banquet of humanists thus included a fair sampling of gilded or semi-gilded youth, friends and professional colleagues of the guest of honor who temporarily found themselves traveling abroad. This dinner capped Felix's weeks in Paris, one of the high points of his life. On April 22, having shilly-shallied for some time (Ruedin had injured his eye in a ball game), three men set out for Etampes, from which they would proceed, not without detours, to Orléans, Bourges, and Basel: Felix was joined by the mercenary Hans, armed to the teeth, and by Herr Ruedin, who wore a patch over his left eye. They looked like a Renaissance engraving of a trio of landsknechts—almost a Dürer.

The road from Paris took the three travelers first to Etampes (April 24), then to Orléans (two days later). Felix spent the night of April 26 at an inn in Pierrefitte, between Orléans and Bourges. Plague lurked in the vicinity, and the next day, after a hasty lunch, the three Swiss departed for Bourges, which they reached that evening. They had traveled through a region of hedged fields, heath, and vineyards before coming to the area of open grain fields interspersed with vineyards just north of the capital of

Berry. The revival of the countryside over the previous century leapt to
the travelers' eyes. In the absence of other criteria, we can use the "white
cloak" of new manors as a test: of 123 chateaus inventoried in Berry[45] (the
list is incomplete), we "find 72 that had been enlarged or renovated between 1430 and 1550; of these 72, 62 had been entirely rebuilt." In other
words, half of all noble dwellings were new in 1557. These sported Italian
facades with medallioned loggias and finely wrought towers "with windows capped by stepped gables."[46]

The city of Bourges was not totally unknown to Felix. A year earlier, he
had heard through the German grapevine about the disaster that had occurred there in early July: the duke of Bavaria, aged fifteen, a student in
Bourges, had drowned while boating on the Auron river just outside of
town. His accidental death had touched the people of Berry as well as
German students all over France.

The young duke's drowning tells us something about the topography
of the region: around Bourges one found, in addition to cultivated land,
any number of swamps and small streams. Owing to the density of the
hydrographic network, the moats surrounding the fortified walls were
almost always filled with water even in times of drought, thus improving
the city's defensive position. The heath and fallow land in the surrounding countryside provided good pasture for sheep, whose wool supplied
the mills and studios that produced a much-prized woolen fabric. Solemn processions marked the importance of the local textile industry: in
January 1544, when the future Francis II was born, Bourges celebrated
not only with bonfires but also with a procession including (in order)
students, officers of the courts, and vintners followed immediately by car-
ders, fullers, and weavers. Bourges hosted half a dozen fairs annually, or
so Felix reported in his memoirs, unaware that some of these fairs may
have dwindled to a pale shadow of the splendid future envisioned for
them by the Estates General convoked in 1484 by Anne de Beaujeu.

In 1487 a huge fire had destroyed half the city, seriously diminishing the
size of its fairs and their likelihood of success. When Thomas Jr. visited
Bourges in 1599, he counted eighty imposing towers along the ramparts
(a 1567 map shows only fifty or so).[47] Felix, forty-two years earlier, approached the city from the north, crossing countless streams whose
banks were dotted with grain and textile mills. Beyond the gate he passed
a relatively new hospital on his right. Built in the 1520s, the Hôtel-Dieu
attested to the city's thriving population and spirit of initiative. Bourges,
having been designated a *bonne ville* in 1492, had enjoyed the privilege of a
municipal government since that time. Demographic growth had also led
to an increase in pauperism, however, especially after 1520. Veering to-

ward the east, Felix headed up the rue du Bourbonnou, not far from the gate of the same name with its two slender towers. On this street, which skirted a section of monuments, Felix found lodging at the Auberge du Boeuf Couronné, where he stayed for several days.

His first venture out was for a meeting with German students, the elite of the University of Bourges, founded in 1463 by Louis XI and among that king's many successes. In 1517 the university moved to improve its legal and other faculties by recruiting teachers from abroad at the city's expense. Among the scholars lured to the banks of the Auron were Ferrandina from Portugal, Wolmar from Germany, Jacques Amyot from France, and above all the Italian Alciati, a fist-rate jurist and theorist of royal sovereignty. After a period of decline around 1530, order was restored early in the reign of Henri II: students were no longer allowed to participate in the election of the rector, and new faculty were recruited, including Le Duaren of Brittany, Cujas of Toulouse, and the "German-Parisian" Hotman. Representing two successive generations, these teachers trained such prodigious students as Calvin, Beza, and De Thou. A few scapegoats were sent to the stake in anti-Protestant persecutions, but the leading heretics were left untouched in their academic chairs or *hôtels particuliers*. In the 1550s, even before the death of Henri II, the University of Bourges, like that of Montpellier, went over to the Reformation bag and baggage. What is more, royal princesses extended their protection to the city's intellectuals. They contributed to the university's development and saw to it that its faculty and students were spared by rampaging inquisitors. The princesses in question were of course Marguerite de Navarre, the sister of Francis I, and Marguerite de Valois, the sister of Henri II, who took up residence in her duchy of Berry in the middle of the sixteenth century. It is easy to understand why German students would have felt "comfortable" in Bourges: many of them were Lutherans, hence all the more pleased to rub shoulders with their French-speaking Huguenot classmates and colleagues.

This religious tolerance did not keep the Teutons from attending papist ceremonies, however, as in 1556, when the young duke of Bavaria drowned just outside of Bourges. This was one of the rare occasions when the "German nation" (as the students from the east were collectively called) marched as a group. Felix reports some details of this occasion: a group of a hundred to a hundred and twenty Germans preceded the body of the prince, which was carried in great pomp to the church of the Jacobins in the center of town, west of the cathedral, which stood adjacent to the ramparts. Each of the marchers carried a torch bearing the victim's coat of arms. Behind them marched another German carrying a

long lance, from the end of which flew black streamers bearing mottoes
and encomia to the illustrious genealogy of the deceased. The prince's
horse, draped in black cloth, was led by two young Germans; it carried
the heart of the dead duke, escorted by two German noblemen, one on
each side. Finally, the duke's body rested on the shoulders of eight or ten
Germans dressed in mourning garb. This all-German part of the procession was followed by a substantial number of Frenchmen representing
the municipality and the university. The size of the German contingent
reveals the importance of the German influence in Bourges in the time of
Henri II and young Felix Platter.[48] Note, too, that the contingent of visitors from the east was itself divided according to age and social hierarchy.

Felix's visits with the students of Bourges took place three hundred
days after this funeral, on April 27, 1557. The next day was given over to
visiting churches and chapels. The "great schools," as the faculties of the
university were known, stood in a building adjacent to the cathedral of
Saint-Etienne. Thomas Jr., who followed in his elder brother's footsteps
forty years later, gives us some idea of what Felix must have seen when
he visited the local churches. At Saint-Etienne—"the greatest French
church," according to our author, who is exaggerating a bit—Renaissance architects were still at work in 1557, embroidering on Gothic structures inherited from the thirteenth century. The student from Montpellier enjoyed a fleeting glimpse of the tall, lead-encased spire topped by
a twelve-foot bronze cross, which was still being installed high above the
great nave.[49] Plunging right in, Thomas Jr. entered through the new portal of Saint-Guillaume with its hagiographic sculptures. The portal had
been cut into the base of the massive Tour de Beurre, also built after 1506
and distinguished by a series of balustrades and interwoven blind arches
marking the upper stories. The two brothers liked the windows of the
huge edifice with their brilliant, sun-concealing stained glass. The colorful windows of the small Tellier chapel were just twenty-five years old in
1557 and still radiant; their painted figures illustrated the exploits of various members of the Tellier family, which had contributed six canons to
the clergy of Bourges.

At the Sainte Chapelle, close to the cathedral, Felix and later Thomas
Jr. retraced the princely path of the ubiquitous Jean, duc de Berry, who
long after his death seemed to dog the two brothers' footsteps as they
traveled from Tours to Etampes to Saint-Denis to Bourges. In the
"princely" crypt of the Sainte Chapelle, which was consecrated in 1405
and modeled after the Sainte Chapelle of Paris, Thomas Jr. marveled at a
priceless crucifix encrusted with rubies, turquoises, emeralds, and pearls
as big as hazel nuts and covered with cameos, among them a veiled aristo-

crat in profile crowned in oak leaves that had been made for the duke.[50]
He also noted the presence of historiated chasubles, a gold crown donated by Jean de Berry, and a goblet carved out of a giant emerald. The
"museum rules" of the time were fairly liberal: these precious objects
were kept in locked chests in the crypt's vaults and displayed to any visitor
deemed worthy of viewing them. The Platters enjoyed a glimpse into the
ecclesiastical history of Bourges: the architecture of the Tour de Beurre
showed off the influence of the Renaissance; the treasures in the crypt
revealed the fifteenth century; and, to round out the tour of French history, the crypt itself dated from the twelfth century. The younger of the
two brothers paid tribute to the airiness and lightness of this underground church, whose capitals, like those of Notre-Dame of Paris, are
adorned with leaves of fern, water lily, and acanthus.

Students, priests, and finally soldiers: upon leaving the cathedral, Felix
headed south. He ignored the archepiscopal palace, a long building with
high gables and mullioned windows. Beyond Notre-Dame-de-Sales he
came to the ramparts, dominated by the Grosse Tour, which housed a
sort of siege engine. The tower was decorated with rustic protuberances
pretentiously dubbed "diamond points" (*wie die spitzen diamant* [T2
519]). It had been built in 1188 at the behest of Philip Augustus. The great
tower was still a considerable dissuasive force, with its walls eighteen feet
thick at their base (*Die wändt seyen 18 Schu dick,* according to Thomas Jr.'s
accurate observation). This fortress had been used to store arms and munitions, especially crossbow projectiles, since the thirteenth century.[51]
Behind one of the doors, Felix discovered an old crossbow, as tall and
broad as a man (*eins mans lang und gross*). Louis XI, who took an interest
in the Grosse Tour, had ordered an iron cell installed in the arms room
"above the first joists."[52] The cell was a square roughly three and a half
feet on a side, for a total living area of twelve square feet: prisoners were
definitely not indulged. The walls were of ironclad wood. This minuscule
prison did not escape Felix's notice; he claimed that a king had been incar-
cerated there for a lengthy period. As usual, his notions of French
history—even recent French history—are quite vague.[53] His brother
Thomas Jr., more scrupulous as to his sources, states that the unfortunate
prisoner was named *Sforcia;* in fact, it was Cardinal Ascanio Sforza,
brother of the Milanese Ludovico Il Moro, who had been a prisoner of
Louis XII at Saint-Encize in Lyons and later in the Grosse Tour of
Bourges.[54]

Thomas Jr. tells us little about the economy of Bourges, and Felix tells
us even less. Both confine themselves mainly to empty generalities. There
is one exception to this rule, however: Thomas was struck, during his

brief stay in Bourges, by the bell founders he saw at work in the street. Bell-casting was and is a sophisticated business; its techniques have been passed down through the ages largely unchanged to this day. Making bells was a current matter in 1599 because a decision had been made to replace those removed, destroyed, or melted down by Huguenots after 1562. Thomas noted that many onlookers tossed counterfeit or retired coins into the molten metal being prepared for casting. This was one not very scrupulous way of "contributing" to the common effort. Despite such indelicacies, the clergy did not hesitate to baptize (*tauffen*) the new bell a few days later, after the metal had cooled and the mold had been removed. Thomas, who was given to caricaturing the ways of the Catholic clergy, reports that this baptism was performed in highly ceremonious fashion. In fact, he was echoing his brother's sentiments, because as a young man he had carefully read the first draft of Felix's diary, and Felix had indeed been struck by the large bells (*gröste glocken*) of Saint-Etienne in 1557.

The two Platters' vision of Bourges is ultimately eclectic, even "impressionistic" in the best sense of the word, although it is not always profound or comprehensive. Felix missed one point entirely: 1557 was a difficult year for the city's "lower classes." From the journal kept by Father Jean Glaumeau, a rather odd Bourges priest who kept a concubine and ultimately became, logically enough, a Protestant, we know that the drought of 1556 had led to food shortages in Bourges and its environs in the spring of the following year: "This year, for eight or ten months running, corn was very dear, so dear that a bushel of wheat went for XVII to XVIII *soulz*. Oats, five *soulz*. The poor suffered a great deal, so much that, according to the elders, never in living memory had corn been dearer. Yet society [in the past] did not suffer as much, because other things were all less dear. This year, however, all things were dear, hence when August, September, and October came, the poor were afflicted with countless maladies, pestilential fevers and other incurable diseases, and many died."[55]

Father Glaumeau's analysis of the way in which a dangerous rise in grain prices, long-term inflation, and increased pauperization combined to cause suffering among the "little people" is quite astute. Notice that our tourist's financial resources, though modest, were sufficient to allow him to get by, while the plight of the poorest inhabitants of the places he visited eluded him. As a young man, Felix's father had shared the distress of the poor, but the old man's son now belonged to a sheltered segment of society. Felix does, however, allude briefly to an outbreak of plague in the village of Neuvy, just before Bourges; he seems to have been aware of the grain shortage and its connection with disease, the very connection that would later alarm Father Glaumeau. But let us not be too hard on Felix. As the municipal physician of Basel some years later, he did his best to cope with the epidemics that afflicted his fellow citizens. The good doctor's zeal would go a long way to make up for the tourist's inattentiveness.

* * *

On April 29 Felix left Bourges, where the first covered tennis court in the city was under construction.[56] Our traveler avoided the normal route to the east, which led to Burgundy through Nevers. This road passed too close to the Massif Central, known to be a lair of criminals; in particular, it passed through the dangerous forest of Frétoy. Perhaps the drought and the ensuing food shortage made this route particularly hazardous in 1557. Hard times had driven more than one highwayman into the woods to prey upon unlucky travelers. Felix decided to head more to the northeast along the "big old road" or "high road" (*chemin de la chaussée*) that led through Sancerre, Clamecy, and Vézelay to Dijon. The first stage of the journey, on the afternoon of April 29, took him to Sancerre. This was an old *ville champignon,* or "mushroom city," of the tenth and eleventh centuries, which had grown into an oval-shaped town of three thousand perched on high ground a quarter of a league from Saint-Thibaut, a small port on the Loire that was inhabited by about fifty people. Sancerre contained approximately five hundred houses, half of which had been built or rebuilt in the Renaissance; these were arranged on the hillside in rows, as in an amphitheater. The place was dominated by a more or less rectangular citadel over three hundred feet long. Perched at the edge of a precipice, this castle was protected by an "iron gate" that opened onto the rabbit-ridden countryside: sentinels amused themselves by pelting rabbits with stones from the battlements. Ramparts, reinforced at intervals by nine towers, encircled the town, which could be entered through any of four separate gates. The approach took Felix through hedgehog-filled vineyards laid out on a gently sloping hillside; donkeys were used to work the ground. The fashionable grapes of the moment were the *chardonnay* (for white wine) and the *pinot noir* (for red). Both red and white wines were exported to Paris, Flanders, and Normandy, where they appeared on noble and bourgeois tables.[57] Felix entered the city through the Porte de Bourges, also known as Porte Vieille or Portevieil; this was also the outlet through which the town's waste water was discharged. He exited to the east through the Porte Oyson, probably a deformation of the word *portillon* or *porteson;* or perhaps he took the scenic route, which actually skirted the walls of the city from the Portevieil to the Porte Oyson. In "normal" times Sancerre had little use for its walls. The ramparts did, however, continue to have a function in peacetime under Henri II: they kept wolves out of the center of town. Without adequate walls, the wolves would soon have made their way into the city by night, attracted by the meat in the butcher shops.

The function of the walls would change after 1561, when Sancerre, which had long been full of neophyte Huguenots and had recently begun to welcome refugees of the same stripe, became one of the strongholds of the Reformed Church. Accordingly, the city was "predestined" to become the target of a terrible siege by royal and Catholic troops in 1573, as celebrated in its day as La Rochelle would be later on. In old age, Felix telescoped his own experience of Sancerre as a young man in 1557 with impressions he had gathered subsequently from reading the gazettes and listening to rumors. In his memoirs he mentions the harsh famine (*hungersnöthe*) that the papist siege produced in Sancerre's *annus horribilis,* 1573.[58]

On April 29, Felix crossed the Loire and headed north toward the city of Cosne. This was a small, rectangular town of 2,500 to 3,000 inhabitants adjacent to a château surrounded by ramparts from which at most four or five towers protruded. Felix, arriving from the south, crossed the Saint-Aignan bridge and then entered the city through the gate and along the street of the same name. Atop the gate was a conical tower and possibly a cross. Felix crossed the city in a northeasterly direction along the rue d'En-bas, rue Jean-d'Or, rue des Chapelains, and rue Bourgeoise. On his right he passed the church of Saint-Jacques with its corbelled facade. To his left he glanced at signs of recent construction reflecting Renaissance tastes in ecclesiastical and official buildings. These were especially evident in the chapel of Notre-Dame-de-Galles, whose almost new stained-glass windows bore the arms of a bishop of Auxerre, framed by dragons with silver banners.

The salt warehouse, adjacent to the chapel, had also been refurbished under Louis XI. Thus the two buildings maintained an architectural dialogue that paralleled the heraldic dialogue between the escutcheon of the canons of Notre-Dame-de-Galles (vert and sable—i.e., green and black—separated by a diagonal silver bar, or tiercé in bend) and that of their neighbors the *gabelous,* or salt tax collectors (gules and or—i.e., red and gold—also separated by a diagonal bar of silver). Cosne collected considerable tolls from traffic on the Loire, which supplemented its income from the salt tax. The city could boast of its social accomplishments: the transition, characteristic of the early modern period, from the medieval leprosarium to the modern hospital was already well under way. Religious turmoil was also in evidence: the quasi-public wedding of a priest caused a scandal in Cosne toward the end of Francis I's reign. This eventually led to the erection of a stake, followed by a public burning that reduced the unfortunate clerical bridegroom to ashes, but not before he had been strangled to death—a humanitarian gesture that the temper of the times demanded. A year before Felix's visit, the *maréchaussée,* or magistrate's court, had been obliged to hold hearings in Cosne to "root out the wicked," that is, to punish religious dissidents, despite the judge's evident inability to sort out doctrinal issues; the repression was not very successful. Felix does not deign to tell us which inn he slept in. The next morning, he and his companions left Cosne via the Porte d'Auxerre, headed for Clamecy.[59]

They passed through Donzy, where the local barony, a possession of François de Clèves, the first duke of Nevers, was transformed into a *duché-pairie* at midcentury.[60] From there they proceeded to Clamecy, a city of 2,500 on the Yonne, where all the teachers and students of a thriving school would be wiped out by plague in 1582.[61] Clamecy was a timbering center from which logs were floated downstream either singly or bound together in rafts. The destination was Paris, whose feverish growth was stoked by huge quantities of fuel from the forests of the Morvan and elsewhere.[62]

On May 1, after leaving Clamecy, Felix and friends passed below the former monastery of Vézelay, perched on top of a hill (*uf dem berg* [F 288]). This former Benedictine abbey with its tympanum bearing a huge image of Christ, high Romanesque nave, and linden-shaded gardens was by 1557 no more than a shadow of its former self, despite or perhaps because of its vast property-holdings and constant flow of pilgrims. With backing from Francis I, the erstwhile monks had secured Pope Paul III's approval for their secularization, that is, their transformation into a college of no more than a dozen purely secular canons, whose leader, the *abbé commendataire,* was appointed by the king.

In the community around the abbey, moreover, all roads led, however briefly, to Protestantism. A small Huguenot community had developed in the town in 1555. "Trouble" never comes alone: in 1560, Cardinal Odet of Châtillon, Coligny's brother, became *abbé commendataire* of Vézelay. He soon went over to Protestantism, with the incidental benefit that he was able to marry Isabelle de Hauteville, a woman half his age. Felix followed a street "under the walls" south of the abbey and at the foot of the hill. He crossed the Yonne and headed for Dijon. In the memoirs he wrote in 1612 from notes hastily jotted down in a notebook, he mentions his visit to Vézelay only in passing; he spells the name of the town "Verde-let," a slip no doubt linked to the word *verdet,* verdigris, with which he was familiar because of the custom among women of the bourgeoisie and common people in Languedoc of making small copper plaques, of which Felix had seen thousands during his stay in southern France.[63]

On May 2 Felix, while traveling from Précy-sous-Thil to Fleury-sur-Ouche, had a brush with danger (*ein grosse gfor*). Riding through moist terrain, he guided his horse onto a narrow high road that formed a sort of dike between two ponds (F 288). Eventually the path narrowed to the point where the horse could neither proceed nor turn around, and its rider could not dismount. Felix was afraid that he might fall into the water with his horse and all his belongings. He somehow managed to back the horse out without dismounting and then made a detour around the bad patch of road.

On Monday, May 3, Felix reached Dijon, a city built on marl and pudding stone from the Oligocene as well as on recent alluvial deposits lying at the base of vine-covered hills where, Thomas Jr. tells us, Gallo-Roman coins were still frequently unearthed (T2 906). The city offered a jagged skyline of tall monuments, mostly churches. The biggest were Saint-Philibert, Saint-Jean, and Notre-Dame, in whose belltower with skylight sentinels were posted. There was also Saint-Bénigne, where the kings of France stopped on their rounds of the country to swear that they would respect the privileges and liberties (*privilegien und freyheiten*) of the people of Dijon. And last but not least, there was the remarkable Tour de Philippe. The days when Brussels and Mechelen were the capitals of the dukes of Burgundy and Dijon was their official necropolis lay in the not-so-distant past. The population of Dijon, comprising Huguenot artisans and Catholic vintners, was roughly fifteen thousand in the time of Henri II, perhaps as many as twenty thousand, and conditions in the city had been fairly crowded since 1513, when the Swiss infantry, well equipped with cannon, had feigned a siege after a brief expedition. In preparation for such an attack, the local authorities had razed a number of suburbs in order to give the city's defenders a clear field of fire. As in Geneva, the population of these suburbs had had to be relocated inside the city, which had led to a housing shortage and to new residential construction.

There was also a certain poverty within what was apparently a thriving community. More than a thousand people, almost a tenth of the population, were officially listed as below the poverty line. Their care was entrusted to a *chambre des pauvres,* or poorhouse, that dated back to the famine of 1529, as in Lyons. Together with the parlement, municipal officials, and the *vicomte majeur*, the poorhouse administered alms and other funds collected for the poor.

The Swiss emergency of 1513 only increased Dijon's innate tendency to erect impressive ramparts and then hunker down behind them. Under the terms of the Treaty of Senlis (1493), the Burgundian capital remained a frontier city within reach of imperial (and later Spanish) outposts. The walls of the city were therefore strengthened through the addition of ten imposing towers with far greater dissuasive power than the medieval tur- rets punctuating the walls of many other cities. From these towers Felix enjoyed a view of Dijon almost equivalent to that of a print offering a bird's-eye view of the city that Edouard Bredin created in 1574 for Belle- forest's *Cosmographie universelle*, which came out the following year.

The thick walls were backed up by a militarized city. The conical- roofed towers of the royal castle adjacent to the walls near the point where Felix made his discreet entry were manned by no more than eight or ten of the king's soldiers, but the local authorities could if necessary muster some eight to ten thousand men in arms, counting reinforce- ments from the surrounding plains. There was reason to fear, however, that this municipal militarism, coupled with Burgundian tradition, might some day pose a threat to the power of the French king. But al- ready, only three-quarters of a century after the death of Charles the Bold, the memory of the "Great Duke of the West" was fading. Loyalty to France outweighed any nostalgia for an independent Burgundy.

The city of Dijon stood first and foremost for judicial power, which had grown steadily over the half century preceding Felix's visit. In 1511 the provincial parlement had moved into a palace of its own. In 1533 the Es- tates of Burgundy were depicted as a series of concentric circles, with fi- nancial institutions and the *chambres des comptes* in the center surrounded by city mayors, nobility, and clergy. In 1535 a complex system of municipal elections was established based partly on genuine elections, partly on municipal cooptation. In 1536–38, Francis I's ephemeral conquests in Sa- voy made it possible to expand the (scanty) jurisdiction of the parlement of Dijon as far as Bresse and Bugey. In 1537 the same parlement, accus- tomed to steady growth, added an additional chamber, the so-called Chambre Criminelle de la Tournelle. In 1542, Burgundy, along with its capital Dijon, was integrated into the system of *généralités*, remote ances- tors of the provincial *intendances*; other *généralités* were set up at the same time throughout France. In 1553 the city's mayor and aldermen took ad- vantage of the monarchy's war debt to purchase the local and royal *pré- vôté*, which exercised general police functions.

These developments were of interest to Felix only incidentally, insofar as they had already begun to give Dijon its distinctive character as a judicial city, a character that it would retain throughout the Ancien Régime. A clique of magistrates from parlement owned most of the surrounding flatland and dominated the peasantry, in enlightened fashion to be sure.[64] Felix had his own concerns. On May 3 he immersed himself in the past. Early in the morning, even before entering Dijon, he had visited the Carthusian monastery at Champmol, on the western edge of the ramparts. He had sincerely admired the tombs of the dukes of Burgundy (*schöne begräbnissen*) and appreciated the cenotaph of Philip the Bold, portrayed as a recumbent figure, almost life-sized, wrapped in an ermine-lined azure mantle and resting on the lion of Flanders—a typical product of the union of Capetian ancestry (the *fleur de lys*) with Flemish energy. Felix was struck by the sculpted figures of monks encircling a miniature cloister at the base of Philip's tomb. The monks' hoods revealed or concealed a wide range of personalities from preacher to dandy, ascetic to intellectual.

Felix also enjoyed a privilege we can no longer share: he was able to contemplate the entirety of the Carthusian calvary, a destination of countless pilgrims and source of innumerable indulgences, which had been built in the late fourteenth and early fifteenth century under the supervision of Claus Sluter. Here, a crucified Christ, man's intercessor with the hereafter, stands next to a Saint John, preaching the faith, a dolorous Virgin, and a sinful but repentant Magdalene. Felix, who knew his Gospels, nevertheless mistook this Golgotha for a Mount of Olives carved in stone (*gehuwener ölberg*). This error reveals the young Swiss traveler's devotion to the Last Supper and the anguish of Christ, for which the Mount of Olives served as a stage or witness in the time of the Gospel.

Of course one couldn't expect a "heretic" like Felix to express enthusiasm for the cult of the Virgin. When Georges Lengherand, the mayor of Mons (in present-day Belgium), visited Champmol in 1486, he noted that the Carthusian church contained "a gold and silver table marking the death of the Virgin Mary, a chapel of the Annunciation to the Virgin, quite beautiful . . . and a number of beautiful reliquaries, including one containing Our Lady's arm." Felix mentions none of these things. A full-fledged citizen of Basel, he had banished veneration of the Virgin from his mind. Yet when he mentions the monks, or rather the sculptured images of monks, he spares us for once his constant jibes at "priestlings," whether regular or secular. Perhaps the funereal grandeur of Champmol had touched him deeply.

At the end of this full day in May 1557, Felix may have spent the night at an inn in Dijon, a city whose textile and pewter industries had prospered, attracting new clients to local hostels. After all, the Rouen-Paris-Lyons-Dijon axis was a major trade route, further stimulated by France's annexation of Burgundy in the 1480s. The number of inns in the city had increased steadily, from thirty or so in 1530 to sixty-six in 1593; there must have been about fifty at the time of Felix's visit. Following the example of Lyons, the municipal authorities adopted a laissez-faire, antiguild economic policy. They could only approve of the consequent increase in the number of inns. Of course *hôtel* rhymes with *bordel* (bordello), and the disorderly conduct that frequently went along with such rapid growth triggered certain puritanical reflexes in Renaissance Burgundy. These were in part a response to the increase in veneral disease, one concrete result of which was an attempt to establish a home for repentant prostitutes on rue de la Poulaillerie in 1538.

Felix, however, was in no mood to linger in Dijon. Basel lay within reach. He stayed just long enough to have lunch with his young friend Caspar Krug, who was living in Dijon at the time. Caspar was just fifteen, as Felix had been in 1552 when he first went to Montpellier. He was the son of Caspar Krug Sr., himself the son of a locksmith and by trade an iron-monger who became a guild leader and bürgermeister of Basel. Krug Sr. was also a Latinist, and in 1563 he was ennobled by Emperor Ferdinand I during a stay in the Rhineland (F 299). About the great man's son we know only that he was raised in the splendor of his father's house, Spalen-hof (which later became a theater), and that he had been in Dijon for some time (*ein zeit lang*), so long that he had practically forgotten his German (*Teutsch vergessen*), a circumstance that made conversation with Felix difficult. It is highly unlikely that Caspar Jr. was a student in the Burgundian capital. Francis I's efforts to found a university in Dijon in 1516 had not borne fruit, and the best the city could boast of was a *collège*, or secondary school, which had been in operation since the 1530s, having replaced a school headed by Pierre Turel, the Burgundian Nostradamus and author in 1523 of a work entitled *Grant pronostication*.

On the afternoon of May 3, Felix bade farewell to young Krug and left Dijon. His route took him near the old church of Saint-Michel: partially rebuilt, its triumphal facade, decorated with a Last Judgment in the latest Renaissance style, depicted a recent execution, which had taken place some time between 1547 and 1551. He also passed Saint-Pierre, a powerful if oddly round bastion which stood as a defense against attack from Franche-Comté. This fortress had been built in 1515 along the southern ramparts in conjunction with repairs to the city's walls. From there the two young men proceeded along the road to Auxonne and Dole. But first they had to cross the Ouche, which was well stocked with fish (*sehr fischreich wasser*).[65] They stopped for the night in Genlis, a few leagues from Dijon.

On May 4, Felix crossed the Saône. The bridge made an impression on him. Underneath its arches, traveling upstream and down, passed lines of vessels loaded with iron, wheat, wine, glass and wood from Lorraine, bundles of hide and wool, oil, and herring. That afternoon and evening he visited Dole, a city of 3,000 to 3,500 inhabitants. He briefly inspected the irregular, polygonal enclosure consisting of seven winged bastions connected by curtains "in the Genoese style," whose construction Charles V had ordered in 1541 as a defensive measure against a possible French attack from the west. Continuing along the logical route, Felix headed toward the center of town, passing Notre-Dame, a collegiate church in a heavy late-Gothic style on which construction had begun in 1509 and would end in 1557, the year of Felix's visit. The porch tower of this church, topped by a belfry and lookout post manned round-the-clock by a sentry, was not yet finished.[66] Dole lived in fear of French invasion, although in this era of regional peace that fear was seldom fulfilled. This small community could muster nearly a thousand men to defend it, including active soldiers and reservists, militiamen and arquebusiers, and residents of both the town itself and its adjoining suburbs and countryside.

The porch of the church faced a line of forty-eight shops. Next door stood the parlement, the seat of collective government, whose twenty magistrates, grouped in two chambers, represented the local elite of the Comté, or Franche-Comté as it was also known. The parlement of Dole embodied—constitutional patriotism *oblige*—the ideal of a government of judges, an ideal that the Paris parlement would never achieve despite its desire to do so in the period between the Fronde and the Revolution. Felix Platter paid a brief visit to the University of Dole, where he probably felt at home. The university dispensed knowledge to a hundred or so students from Flanders, the Tyrol, Saxony, and Pomerania—that is, to *Teutschen*, hence Felix's compatriots in the broad sense, many of whom retained their folk ways and were not terribly serious students.[67]

On the morning of May 5, Felix made his way on horseback across Franche-Comté from Dole to Besançon (which was not a French city at the time). In the countryside he saw houses with pointed gables and thick stone walls pierced by tiny windows; vast haylofts stored the land's produce. Towns were surrounded by ramparts of red brick lapped by a muddy stream or extended by a system of moats. After spending the night of May 5 at the Auberge du Bois de Cerf, Felix entered Besançon on May 6 via the Porte des Arènes, which involved passing through a double partition and a sort of obstacle course. Along the way he passed extensive vineyards both outside and inside the walls; these stretched north, south, west, and northwest of the city. In the streets Felix and his companion encountered vintners carrying sacks and two-tined pitchforks on their shoulders and picks or pruning knives in their hands as well as small kegs fastened to their belts.

Felix spent the entire day of May 6 in Besançon (population 10,000), where a statue of Charles V stood in front of the city hall. The emperor, revered by the local populace, was poised astride an eagle soaring off on the north wind. Hans Ruedin, the son of a Basel ironmonger and Felix's disagreeable companion ever since Paris, had lived near Besançon as an adolescent and had learned French there. Although the city's schools functioned only intermittently, they were not bad. A partially secularized *collège* had been in operation for a decade, offering courses in reading and writing, grammar, rhetoric, and Greek. Ruedin, a convivial fellow, took Felix to see his former landlords, who owned a house (*hus*) in town. The two young men spent the day dancing, playing the lute, chatting, and flirting with the daughter of the house, a certain Barbel. Forty-three years later, while traveling in Franche-Comté, Professor Felix Platter would again meet this same Barbel. Now past sixty, his former dance partner had grown old and ugly in Felix's eyes; no doubt he hadn't looked at himself in the mirror recently. In the interim she had given birth to two illegitimate sons, now grown men.

After supper, Felix and Hans, having left young Barbel, went for a walk with some young nobles who, in the course of their revels, tried to pass themselves off as peasants (*buren*). These aristocratic youths stemmed from a part of the Franche-Comté elite whose nobility was of recent date. They followed in the footsteps of two illustrious Franche-Comtois, Nicolas Perrenot and his son, Cardinal Grandvelle, in the sense that their roots were in the judicial bourgeoisie, which had supplanted the older noble lineages that once dominated the region. Felix joined his new friends in raising a ruckus in front of the houses of Italian merchants (from Genoa, Milan, and Florence) whose business had brought them to reside in Besançon, where they rubbed shoulders with German businessmen from Strasbourg, Wurtemberg, and Basel and with traders from Geneva. These businessmen were not averse to investing their capital in local vineyards. The presence of the Italians was due in part to a decision by the Republic of Genoa in 1535 to organize exchange fairs in Besançon. This fledgling financial market did not last long, however, because the Genoese soon came to feel that the Besançon arrangement was cumbersome and perhaps even harmful to their interests.

Still, the 1535 decision remained important: the term *bizensone* was still applied to foreign exchange fairs even when held in other places such as Poligny and Chambéry. The fact that the name stuck shows how significant the event was in people's minds as well as in the fortunes of the city on the Doubs. As for the confrontation between the young French-speaking nobles and the local foreign colony, whether from Italy or elsewhere, this was a common occurrence, not at all unusual in a city of any size, and not only in Franche-Comté. Sometimes students of different "nations" clashed, and at other times there were confrontations that were partly ethnic, partly social in origin. In this case it was local nobles versus merchants from across the Alps.

*   *   *

During his stay in Besançon, Felix was greatly concerned about the behavior of his friend Hans Ruedin.[68] After celebrating with the group of young nobles, Ruedin had become so drunk that he had collapsed fully clothed on the bed the two travelers were sharing at the inn. Annoyed at the prospect of a sleepless night, Felix undressed and placed his naked behind on his sleeping friend's face (F 290). Although he doesn't tell us what ensued, we shall refrain from making any diagnosis of latent homosexuality, that perennial favorite of psychoanalysts who pose as historians.

This scabrous incident temporarily put an end to two weeks of intense and very difficult relations with Hans Ruedin, from whom Felix had expected great things but who had in fact caused him no end of trouble since leaving Paris. The two had fought constantly on the journey home. We have only Felix's side of the story. Hans, who used the familiar *du* with Felix, was, according to young Platter, rich, pretentious, and much given to practical jokes, only some of which were funny. All in all, he lacked maturity and was woefully ignorant. At the beginning of their trip together, he had tricked Felix into contributing to the support of the mercenary who was traveling with them, a soldier of fortune who continually embarrassed the son of the old printer-pedagogue. Hans Ruedin also did not hesitate to mock the professional hopes of the recent graduate of the University of Montpellier by predicting that when Felix became a doctor he would have difficulty finding a job.

Furthermore, Ruedin coldly discussed the possibility of killing the dog that had followed young Platter all the way from Languedoc. Felix was especially disappointed in his friend because relations between them had been good when they had first met back in Paris. Still, Felix was not one to hold a grudge. Ruedin had an eye ailment that was slow to heal, and his companion, despite their differences, changed the dressings on the bad eye every night. In the end the treatment proved effective. Back in Switzerland, the two youths eventually made up. Ruedin, soon after arriving, married Rosina Irmy, the daughter of a Basel burgher. When Felix married Madlen Jeckelmann, Hans and Rosina gave the couple a rather handsome goblet in gratitude for the ophthalmological treatment Felix had dispensed on the road from Paris (F 290, 329). Hans died young, of plague, in 1564.

On May 7 and 8, 1557, Hans and Felix rode hard to cover the long distance between Besançon and Montbéliard. For a while they followed the Doubs Valley; they came close to the abbey of Baume-les-Dames but did not stop. On the morning of May 8, they took a room at the Auberge de la Tête de Maure. Montbéliard (population 2,000–3,000) was at this time the capital of a county in which both French and Romansch were spoken. Henriette, the countess of Montbéliard, had married Eberhard von Wurtemberg early in the fifteenth century, transforming her fief south of the Vosges into a possession of the Wurtemberg dynasty for several generations. In May 1553, Duke Kristof von Wurtemberg, preoccupied with his duchy, had ceded possession of the county of Montbéliard to his uncle, Georg von Wurtemberg. Two years later, in 1555, Georg, aged fifty-seven, married Barbe, daughter of Philip the Magnanimous, the landgrave of Hesse; Barbe was nineteen, thirty-eight years younger than her husband.

From this marriage was born Count Friedrich, who was destined to succeed his father. On the whole, Georg was an enlightened sovereign. He tried, without much success, to make the Doubs navigable; given the means available at the time, the job was impossible. As conflict gradually diminished, he respected the liberties of the city of Montbéliard, which enjoyed the privilege of self-government through its aldermen, while Georg retained responsibility for governing the vast county of which the city was the capital. The count's religious policy was of even greater importance. The county of Montbéliard, which lay in "Welch" territory, was the only non-German region to adhere to a fairly strict variety of Lutheranism. In 1550 the two religions, Catholic and Protestant, coexisted in Montbéliard on an "interim" basis decreed by Charles V. Soon, however, Duke Kristof and later Count Georg prohibited "papist" practices, abolished the mass, and banished priests. In 1552, the priests of Montbéliard were described in an official document as "animals, asses, public embarrassments, drunkards, blasphemers, and murderers who are only after their poor lambs' lips and fleece." Texts such as these tell us a great deal about a certain form of sixteenth-century intolerance. The logical culmination of such attitudes came in October 1556, a few months before Felix's visit, when Count Georg outright prohibited pilgrimages, masses, baptisms, confessions, prayers for the dead, holy water, the ringing of bells to ward off bad weather, the use of blessed candles and branches by clerics, and other "superstitions." In contrast, listening to the word of God was prescribed, and one version of Christianity was granted a monopoly.[69]

Exclusionary measures against the papists did not necessarily lead to intolerance among Protestants: Georg and his friend Toussain, chief pastor of the county of Montbéliard, steered a middle course between the Lutheran orthodoxy advocated by Wurtemberg and the Calvinist rigidity that had taken hold in Geneva. They deplored Calvin's excesses, including his execution of Michael Servetus (whose path Felix had crossed in Vienne in 1552, when the Jewish-born heresiarch was secretly preparing his great treatise on unitarian, anti-trinitarian, pre-Socinian theology, a theology that would come into its own in the twentieth century long after its author had perished at the stake in 1553).[70] In this respect, the ideas of the Protestant humanist Castellion in Basel clearly had a calming influence on Count Georg and Reverend Toussain, as well as on the Platters, both father and son. Calvin accordingly nursed a certain suspicion of the authorities in Montbéliard. This made no difference to Count Georg: his authority as "Protestant prince" gave him full power in religious matters, and his response was to insist on the education of the young within his principality. His hope was that this would not only contribute to their earthly well-being but also familiarize them with the texts of the Gospels and the Old Testament and those of their Protestant interpreters. Meanwhile, relations between the county of Montbéliard and the France of Henri II remained friendly, insofar as Henri, while persecuting Huguenots at home, sought alliances with Protestant princes to the east, especially when those princes controlled territories in which Romance languages were spoken, as was the case with the Wurtemberg dukes and counts.[71]

We have two versions of Montbéliard, one from Felix, the other from Thomas Jr. The younger Platter wrote his account in February 1600, shortly after his visit to the region. He correctly noted the growth of the population, not only in recent years but also over the past century and more. Both city and county had gained in size, buildings, people, and wealth (grösse, gebeüwen, volck und reichtumb). New mills had sprung up, as well as botanical gardens and zoos in which deer gamboled inside city walls. A new palace had been built next to the old château. All of this, moreover, had taken place in a stimulating climate of bilingual Protestantism, which left it up to the individual to choose between Welch and Teutonic traditions (T2 923). Although Felix's text concerned his exploration of Montbéliard in the spring of 1557, he wrote it much later, in 1612, and it was far more "existential" and personal than his younger brother's account.

At the inn where he was staying on May 8, Felix ran into a childhood friend, Jacob Truchsess, who came from a noble family in Basel, perhaps the most illustrious family in the city. Jacob had in the meantime been appointed to an important post as *Hofmeister* at Count Georg's court. He had made a good marriage, in 1555, to Salomé von Andlau, the daughter of Arbogast von Andlau and Eva von Pfirt—a whole series of *vons* that augured well for the young couple's future. The Hofmeister, a compliant courtier, decided to escort the young Swiss travelers out of the city on the last leg of their journey. He began by getting drunk at the inn (the Platters, as upstanding burghers, invariably poured scorn in their memoirs on the bibulous habits of the nobility). Already intoxicated, Jacob pulled on his boots with some difficulty and then got up to accompany his friends, who had not asked for an escort. At the first ford, Truchsess, unsteady on his feet, came close to drowning (F 291). Once again, we see the German penchant for drunkenness (from which Hans Ruedin himself was not exempt) in contrast to the relative moderation of the "Welches."

Fortunately, Count Georg had foreseen the difficulty. Well aware of his Hofmeister's chronic drinking, he had sent a small escort after him. The soldiers fished the drunken courtier out of the stream and carried him home, soaking wet and fully sobered up. Hans and Felix continued without stopping all the way to Seppois, the gateway to Alsace, between Montbéliard and Basel. Seppois marked the limit of the Romance-language zone, and Felix was well aware of having crossed a linguistic boundary the minute he set foot in Germanic territory. In contrast, his earlier passage from Catholic into Protestant territory (Besançon to Montbéliard) had not made any particular impression on him, Protestant though he was. The last stage of the journey, on May 9 (with a lunch stop at Waldighofen), was marked by yet another dispute between Felix and Hans, whose tattered felt cloak made him look like a beggar. Hans insisted on borrowing Felix's cloak and threatened to throw it in the mud if Felix refused. Felix wanted no part of this, but to mollify his companion he took from his bag, and risked soiling, the new Spanish cape that he had been keeping pristine for the imminent reunion with his family and fiancée. Did this quarrel spoil the homecoming? No, for Basel lay just ahead, beckoning to her prodigal sons.

At the first sight of the Basel cathedral, Felix felt himself bursting with joy, to which he gave vent by firing his harquebus. In his excitement he fired two shots into a garden gate. Spitting fire, the quarreling travelers thus arrived at the monumental Spalentor, the city's main gates. Along the walls were three rows of towers, rebuilt in the second half of the fourteenth century when the ramparts were repaired after an earthquake in 1356.[72] The Spalentor was the entrance to Basel for travelers from France and Alsace, and Felix's arrival marked the end of his Tour de France. On this trip from Montpellier through southwestern France and Paris and on to Basel, he had averaged more than thirty miles a day, roughly the same as on his trip from Basel to Montpellier five years earlier, in 1552. *O Basilea finis mea:* O Basel! End of my journey.

CHAPTER NINE

Summer and Fall: Thesis and Wedding

After passing through the Spalentor, Felix parted company with Hans at Gens ("Goose House"), the house that Hans's father, Jacob Ruedin, had enlarged and renovated. This construction work reflected Jacob's success in his career, which within a few years would take him to Paris as the official representative of the Swiss Leagues at the court of the Valois. Goose House would continue to occupy an important place in Hans's life. Even after his marriage, he came often to see his father and his eleven brothers and sisters (children of his own mother or of Jacob's three subsequent wives) as well as his forty-odd nephews and nieces. A good comrade who held no grudges, Felix walked a short way with his other companion, the annoying mercenary who had been with him since Paris. (To be sure, Felix and the two Hanses had made a well-armed trio, a daunting enough presence to discourage any French highwayman with larceny in mind). When it came time to part, Felix gave the mercenary his cloak. At last he was alone. But then he ran into Georg von Brück, still wearing mourning for his father, David Joris, who had died in late August 1556 and whose real name was Johann von Brück. A wealthy refugee from Holland, Johann had secretly subscribed to the ultimate heresy, Anabaptism, of which Protestant officialdom in Basel took a dim view. He had had eleven children, counting Georg, and had been a great friend of the Platters. Two years later, Felix looked on unflinchingly when the cadaver of Johann von Brück, freshly exhumed for the purpose, was consigned to the flames in a posthumous "execution" imposed by the Basel authorities for the grave crime of "Anabaptism."[1] The "condemned" man had successfully kept his heresy hidden until after his death. Despite the deplorable public incineration of his corpse, Johann's many descendants were not barred from pursuing successful careers in Basel once they had made their peace with the local religious authorities. The burning of the corpse was forgotten.

From Tanners' Alley to Zum Gejägd, the home of the Platters, Felix was tempted to take a direct route, which would have taken him past the home of his fiancée, Madlen Jeckelmann, in the middle section of Freie Strasse at the corner of Rüdengasse (F 294). But he chose a detour instead, for he knew that Madlen, a frightened doe of a girl if ever there was one, was modest and reserved. Perhaps he also wanted his own family to be the first to experience the joy of his homecoming. At last the not very prodigal son came to Obere Freie Strasse and stood before his father's house, where he found only a man carrying a urine pot and obviously in search of a doctor—possibly a good omen (*tütnus*).

Felix rang the bell, but the house was empty. It was Sunday, and his father was off working on his suburban farm. The servant was at church. Felix's mother, who had been gossiping with neighbors, ran over, burst into tears, and hugged her son. Thinner, older, and more wrinkled than Felix remembered, she wore a green cloak and fashionable white shoes. Eventually his father returned, accompanied by Castellion, the tolerant humanist. Thomas exclaimed at how much his son had grown. Indeed, in almost six years in Montpellier, he had grown taller by a head and a neck (*kopf und halss*).

By late afternoon Felix's homecoming had turned into a block party. The neighbors came—the same neighbors who would turn up six months later at the younger Platter's wedding. Dorly (or Dorothea), the servant, ran over to the Jeckelmanns to tell Madlen that her beau had returned. She made such a fuss that Felix's presumptive fiancée almost fainted. The young man's friends were invited that night for dinner. Among them was Balthasar Hummel, the son of the mercenary from Little Basel, a childhood companion of Felix's and a staunch friend during the Montpellier years. He had recently gone into business as an apothecary, and his shop, after struggling at first, was at last showing signs of life. Also present was Theodor Bempelford (Theodorus Pempelfurdus), a native of Düsseldorf and a student in Basel since 1556, after having been a proofreader in Lyons, Paris, and Basel. In April, Theodorus had carried letters home to Basel from Felix in Paris (F 285). Such favors could not go unrewarded. After supper, all the young people, including Felix, left to escort Theodor back to his rooms at the inn Zur Kronen. On Freie Strasse (Fryenstros) they ran into Madlen Jeckelmann. She recognized Felix in his Spanish cape and took off as usual like a frightened lark. During his six years in Montpellier, Felix had apparently remained faithful to his nervous young lady, preferring the prospect of a lifetime of happiness to the pleasures of a Mediterranean night. Madlen's skittishness did not offend him. Time had opened up before him: the future redeemed the present. At Zur Kronen the group of young men accepted a *drunck*, or round of drinks, from the innkeeper, Emmanuel Bomhart, who had taken over the inn from his father and had once been a classmate of Felix's. Unlike some of his colleagues in the tavern trade,

Emmanuel "had culture": he had received a bachelor's degree from the University of Basel in 1552 and a master's degree a short time later. The informal celebration at the inn was moving for Felix, because the guests included his future brother-in-law, Franz Jeckelmann Jr., and Franz's brother-in-law, Daniel Wielandt of Alsace, the son of a municipal official in Mulhouse who would soon succeed his father in office. Franz and Daniel had married the Schoelly sisters, Mergelin and Sophie, the daughters of a master saddlemaker. And they were not the only connection with Alsace and Mulhouse, a region and a city with which the Platters had deep affinities. The host, Emmanuel Bomhart, had married a wealthy Mulhouse heiress, Anna Wächter, in 1557. Other marriages subsequently united the pair's siblings, creating still further ties between the Wächter and Bomhart clans and hence between Mulhouse and Basel. Emmanuel Bomhart had been a suitor of Madlen Jeckelmann but had been rejected in favor of Felix. He did not pass up the opportunity to have some fun at Felix's expense. The younger Platter's "secret" if promising idyll with the Jeckelmann girl was hardly a secret any more. No one talked about anything else. Around midnight, Felix returned home, where his parents were still celebrating his safe return, which of course they owed to the grace of God.

From Monday, May 10, to Saturday, May 15, Felix paid courtesy calls, accepted dinner invitations, and made various arrangements. He repaired his father's harp and the cypress lute that he had received long ago as a gift from his music teacher Thiebold Schoenauer. He also took long walks with Thomas to the family estate in Gundeldingen. Thomas reminded him of the need to put first things first: his doctorate and his marriage, his thesis and his wife. Thomas also asked him to speak more slowly, for Felix had picked up the southern French habit of chattering at a rapid rate. There were inevitable encounters with Madlen in the streets of Basel. The most notable of these took place near the Marktplatz, just outside the huge Schol slaughterhouse. Felix, on his way home from church, was wearing a velvet cap and a dagger at his side, as was the custom among students at the time, even non-noble students of modest background such as the Platters. Madlen was standing in line to buy meat. When she spotted the fashionably dressed young man in the distance, she ran into the slaughterhouse and hid among the beef carcasses and pork bellies. For a long time thereafter she refused to set foot in the Schol, where all the butcher's boys were now on to her romance and wouldn't let her forget it.

Other encounters were more wrenching. When Felix went to the cathedral with Balthasar Hummel on Monday morning, he immediately ran into a Junker named Ludwig von Reischach. A German aristocrat in his seventies, Reischach had become a burgher of Basel because of his conversion to Protestantism. He gave Felix the cold shoulder and pretended not to recognize him because he took the young man's velvet cap and dagger to be aristocratic pretensions—a usurpation of the noble identity. On the plaza in front of the cathedral the former Montpellier student also encountered a trio of university professors, including his former teacher Hans Huber, to whom he presented a work of Clément Marot bound in Paris, where the bookbinding craft had reached a pinnacle of aesthetic perfection under Henri II. This work of Marot's was one of Felix's few contacts with the "Welch" literature of his time. It was of course a work by a Protestant author, and Felix in any case served only as an intermediary between author and reader. Was he perhaps more of a man of science than a man of letters? In any case, Huber continued to represent the francophone community of Basel, as he had done for many years.

Meanwhile, Felix devoted some effort to fixing up a small room for himself in his father's house, because he needed an agreeable place to study. This room was his father's, but since Thomas was busy with his teaching and with managing his boardinghouse, he let Felix use it during the day. Felix painted the bookshelves and turned wood under the supervision of a carpenter, whose wife taught him the art of mixing strong glues, though as the lesson proceeded she became totally confused. But Felix's major problems remained his thesis and his bride-to-be. The two were not independent: no doctorate, no wife. Jeckelmann would never give his daughter's hand to a man who was not a doctor, a good-for-nothing.

Felix took the first big step: he began courting Madlen. It was expected that courtship would lead quickly to a formal proposal to marry, after which the betrothed couple would be allowed to visit more frequently until the time of the wedding. To screw up his courage, Felix first went on May 10 to see his friend Jacob Huggelin, who, at twenty-seven, was older than Felix and already a doctor. Jacob had set up in practice in Basel. He lived with his father-in-law, not far from where Felix lived on the upper part of Freie Strasse, toward the center of town. The son of a tailor, Jacob had married a weaver's daughter (endogamy in the textile trade). For Felix he was a role model: married, in practice, and moving up in society. Huggelin had studied Greek, philosophy, and medicine in Basel and Montpellier and perhaps also in Paris and Valence. With strong backing from the Basel city council, he had embarked on a successful career and would soon go on to become official physician to the margrave of Baden.

Seven years later, however, in 1564, his remarkable career would be cut short by the plague, which claimed him and so many others. Tragically, the young made way for the younger. In 1557 Jacob Huggelin was already famous in Basel for his elegant dress and especially for his Polish leather shoes, known locally as "horned pumps." Once, when he slipped and fell flat on his back, the "horns" on his shoes protruding upward made a nice effect (F 308). After leaving Huggelin's office, Felix went to lunch with Sigmund von Pfirt. A noble and former Catholic priest, von Pfirt had married a woman of the aristocracy and become a burgher of Basel. He had been made a canon and been given a sinecure that the Protestants had taken over from the Catholics. In his sixties, he had hopes that Felix might marry his daughter Susanna. Unfortunately, the "pretty person" (*schön mensch*) was out of reach, boarding with a countess near Colmar, and in any case she was not long for this world. The beauty's brothers Sigmund Jr. and Solon had both been good friends of Felix's since childhood, when they had been part-time boarders at Thomas's Gymnasium. The elder von Pfirt was beyond prejudice: though born noble, he was willing to allow his daughter to marry Felix, the son of a man who was not only a commoner but had spent his early years in grinding poverty. Basel was a democratic place.

Von Pfirt and Huggelin were not the main issue, however; Madlen was. The campaign to win her can be divided into three phases: the introduction, the marriage proposal, and the romance. The introduction was in a sense an artificial rite of passage, since the two young people already knew each other. It was decided, however, to make a ceremony of the occasion: an official introduction would serve as a kind of initiation. Thomas Platter therefore proposed a luncheon for May 16, during which the couple would be formally "introduced." The guests were to include Felix and the young woman dearest to his (and his father's) heart, Madlen's father and brother, and the brother's fiancée, a woman named Dorothea, a lively girl who was the daughter of a leading blacksmith. The setting chosen for this ceremonious occasion was the Platter estate in Gundeldingen. To start things off, the guests took an invigorating walk around the grounds. Then came "luncheon," which was actually a formal dinner. Afterwards there was music and dancing, and Felix distinguished himself by playing the lute and dancing a very French dance, the *gaillarde*. Finally, the whole company returned to Basel on foot: the two prospective fathers-in-law, the teacher and the surgeon, walked in front, while the young people brought up the rear, kept in good spirits by Dorothea's indefatigable conversation. Her practical advice to the lovelorn brought a blush to modest Madlen's cheeks: "When two young people are fond of each other and see each other frequently," the blacksmith's daughter remarked, "they mustn't wait too long, for there can easily be a mishap [*unglick*]."[2] That night, when he went to bed, Felix felt strange, "like stone." Was something he had been dreaming about for years soon to come true? Madlen, though still reserved, had shown herself not just cooperative but quite happy. The introduction was one hurdle out of the way. Now he could make an official proposal of marriage. It would be no less complex than the sort of proposal a powerful family might make when negotiating a dynastic marriage. Time was of the essence, because the young couple, their appetites whetted, had agreed to meet, chaperoned only by the ubiquitous Dorothea and Frau Frön, an elderly, blind matchmaker and godmother of Jeckelmann the surgeon. Frau Frön had Madlen's full confidence; indeed, the old woman and the young maiden sometimes shared the same bed. On May 25, the three young people and the old lady went cherry picking just outside the Spalentor. Increasingly amorous, Felix lavished ardent words on his intended, who received them warmly, albeit with her customary modesty. When Felix pressed her, she readily acknowledged that his affection did not displease her. She had nothing against it. Thus she returned tenderness for tenderness, even if the reflection was but a pale copy of the original.

The consent of Madlen's father, Franz Jeckelmann, still had to be obtained, however. Good friends from various segments of Basel society urged the surgeon to award his daughter's hand to Felix. Caspar Krug, one of the city's leading metal dealers, played an important role. The son of a locksmith, well known in town and enormously proud of his prominence, Krug, in his sixties, did not shrink from envisioning a rather grandiose epitaph for himself, inspired by the Latin poet Ennius: "What a small sepulchre for such a great man!" In 1557, Caspar Krug held high positions in various local guilds. The guilds enforced strict professional rules and facilitated social relations among the elite in a sort of freemasonry without the secret rituals and rigamarole. Before long, Krug would be mayor of Basel and would represent the city at international meetings, at the imperial court, at gatherings of the Swiss Confederation, and at royal courts, including that of Henri II. He held Felix in high esteem because his wife, Anna Nussbaum, had recently suffered from exhaustion after giving birth to twins, and the young doctor had treated her. Felix prescribed slices of marzipan concocted of sugar, egg whites, lemon juice, and orange blossom in accordance with a recipe he had brought back from Montpellier. Within a few days, Anna was back on her feet. Felix's "gentle medicine" had worked. What is more, Krug had sounded out the young pharmacist Balthasar Hummel about Felix, and he had passed on the favorable report he had received. Thus the modest shop-keeper (Hummel) and the distinguished merchant (Krug) had joined hands to bestow their blessing on the future doctor of medicine. Felix, they told Jeckelmann, would make a suitable son-in-law.

Equally positive reports reached Jeckelmann via his friends and noble protectors, the Reich zu Reichensteins, a family of Catholic aristocrats. The head of the family, Jacob Reich Jr., known as "the Old Man" (*der Alt*), had one eye askew and sported a well-trimmed beard. He presided over a family of ten children. He was also Dr. Jeckelmann's spiritual kin, because Jeckelmann had been godfather to the old man's son, Jacob Reich III. The surgeon was always visiting the Reichs in their rural for-tress with its deep moats, where great celebrations were often held. A horse from the Reich stables had been placed at Dr. Jeckelmann's dis-posal. At the time, moreover, the Jeckelmanns and the Reichs were in particularly close contact because one of the Old Man's sons, stricken with the pox, was being cared for in a heated room just off the street in Dr. Jeckelmann's surgery. Among the Reichs, Felix found ardent cham-pions of his marriage proposal. What is more, the noble clan enjoyed par-ticular prestige in Basel despite the city's Protestantism, because one of the Reich children had been miraculously healed by the Virgin Mary after a fall in the mountains. Over the next few years, the Reichs of Basel and Alsace would become loyal clients of Dr. Felix Platter.

Krug and Reich, the bourgeoisie and the nobility: all the best people in Basel urged Jeckelmann to consent to his daughter's wedding. The sur-geon still held out. Was Felix's marriage to become an affair of state? The unanimous chorus of burgraves, constituting the upper crust of Basel so-ciety, lacked only the favorable opinion of the high magistrates invested with *auctoritas*—magistrates who, in Basel, tended to be clerics and pas-tors, doctors, politicians, and administrators rather than jurists. The judgment from this quarter would also prove to Felix's advantage, thanks to Professor Dr. Hans Huber, who, with Thomas Platter's consent, was charged with delivering the official proposal of marriage, and also thanks to Franz Jeckelmann himself. Hans Huber, in his fifties, was the son of an innkeeper from Ravensburg.[3] He had gone on to study in a *collège* and then at universities in Sélestat, Paris, Montpellier, and Toulouse. Huber was an extremely active and busy person, much like the man Felix Platter would become. Since 1543 he had been professor of both practical medi-cine and physics at the University of Basel, at times holding both posi-tions simultaneously. He was also the city's *Stadtarzt*, or municipal physician, and rector. A handsome man with a tapered mustache and vel-vety eyes, he had seventeen children by his second wife. Keen for innovation, Huber was for Felix the very embodiment of the good teacher and benign elder, the best and most trustworthy of friends, and a man who could always be counted on to be optimistic and joyful (F 110, 299). Taking it upon himself to convey Felix's proposal of marriage to Jeckelmann, Huber one morning invited the surgeon to the cathedral. With the peremptoriness of the invitation, he stressed his social superiority, as a university professor, to a mere practitioner with lancet and scalpel. When he had heard Huber's requests beneath the sacred arches of the cathedral, did Jeckelmann still need convincing? He raised objections, beginning with Thomas Platter's heavy debts. Huber responded that Platter's land and houses constituted assets at least equal to his liabilities. Jeckelmann then expressed the fear that the din raised by Thomas's boarders on the school playground next to his house might offend his daughter's tender ears. Huber accordingly conveyed Thomas's promise that he would close his boardinghouse, a promise that Thomas had no intention of keeping and in fact did not keep. The final objection was one that the widower Jeckelmann did not voice out loud: he needed his daughter, a good worker, as long as he could have her to keep house for him. This hurdle was easily overcome: for the first years of her married life, Madlen Jeckelmann would manage two households, her husband's and her father's. Hans Huber had an answer for everything, and in any case it was Madlen, not Huber, who would have to bear the exhausting burden.

The time had come to take the fateful step. Jeckelmann gave Professor Huber his tentative agreement. The accord was to remain secret, however, until Felix had obtained his doctorate, the key to all his plans for the future. Over the coming weeks, the young couple were permitted to see a great deal of each other. Felix spent every afternoon and many evenings at the home of his intended. He chatted with her about a thousand and one frivolous things, while she listened in indulgent silence. The couple were never left alone: chaperones were always present, often Jeckelmann himself, who pretended not to notice anything. The indulgent Frau Frön was part of the furniture: though blind, she didn't stuff cotton in her ears. Dorothea, Madlen's good friend and future sister-in-law, could not have been more discreet. And of course, in the next room, we mustn't forget the Junker Mark Reich zu Reichenstein III. The truth is that he heard none of the young lovers' mainly verbal wooing because he was too busy trying to bake or sweat away his pox in front of a fireplace stoked with guaiacum, a harsh treatment that was coupled with strict fasting on bread and water and impressive sweating.

Madlen and Felix were by now on quite good terms at home, but since their engagement was not yet official, "secrecy" still had to be maintained in public, or else people would talk. So once, for example, in early summer, when Felix and Dr. Huber were on their way to Hummel's pharmacy for a friendly chat, they ran into Madlen, who wore ribbons in her hair and a green apron (*griener schuben*). Following Jeckelmann's orders, she did not so much as glance at Felix, who stared at her without embarrassment from the other side of the street (F 301).

There was a similar lack of response when Felix, accompanied by his friend Schoenauer, the post-rider Bempelford, and the jeweler Hagenbach, a weaver's son and professional whistler, staged a nocturnal serenade in furtherance of the marriage plans of Thomas Guérin, a Helvetized Walloon printer, who hoped to marry Elisabeth Isengrien, the daughter of a printer with a shop on Freie Strasse. The concert was held in front of the Isengrien house, Zum Falcken. The players played stringed instruments—two lutes, a viola, and a harp—while Hagenbach accompanied with whistles, his specialty. The Isengriens then regaled the musicians with a *Schlofdrunck,* or nightcap, which was served with a variety of preserves. The party ended quite late, late enough so that the night watch checked the revelers' identity before allowing them to pass. Meanwhile, Felix had persuaded his fellow musicians to repeat their performance beneath Madlen's windows. Killing two birds with one stone, he thus transformed a cordial evening with his friends from Freie Strasse into a concert for his beloved. But the always haughty Jeckelmann kept a watchful eye on the proceedings. No door was opened to welcome the musicians and repay them for their efforts with food and drink. They considered themselves fortunate that no one had poured a bucket of water (or worse) on their heads. The musicians went home disappointed and empty-handed. Every man was king in his own castle, and the surgeon's household was almost puritanical in its ways.

Such amorous premarital secrecy had its share of bizarre consequences. Felix's intended received him warmly in the privacy of her home, but his evening visits eventually came to the attention of the local defenders of public morality, who treated the young man as if he were a criminal and unrepentant seducer. One night, as he was making his discreet exit from the Jeckelmann home, two zealots of virtue spotted him and took out after him with the intention of administering a shellacking (*gesteubt*). He escaped only because he was fleet of foot.

*   *   *

"There is no such thing as love, only proofs of love." When a girl of rather chilly temperament such as Madlen became jealous, was her jealousy, in the absence of more concrete signs of passion, a sign of attachment, of possessiveness toward her beloved? Consider the case of Cleopha Baer, a widow of forty-six and a woman of easy virtue, or so people said—but then people will say anything. She was the daughter of Hans Baer, a man with three claims to fame, for he had been a draper, a court officer, and an ensign at the battle of Marignano, where he had died for Switzerland in 1515. Cleopha was a free woman, that is, a woman not under the tutelage of father or spouse: her husband, a local castellan of noble extraction, had died in 1552. And she had a crush on Felix. During the summer of 1557, she invited him to her house to play the lute at a sort of breakfast or brunch known as *morgen sup* (literally, "morning soup"). And she invited herself to Thomas's house, despite the cool welcome she received from both the master and his son. Madlen, who soon learned of these contacts, gave the man to whom she was now all but officially engaged a hard time about them. Felix was no fool, and certainly not fool enough to try to run down two hares at once. He quickly broke off his dalliance with Cleopha, and Madlen's attitude improved immediately. What Felix omits to tell us is that Cleopha died later that same year, thus putting an end once and for all to any further testing of Felix's affections for his fiancée. Cleopha's son Jonas went on to an administrative career in Innsbruck, where he became a member of the nobility, thus continuing the rise in society that his mother had begun, from textile bourgeoisie to aristocracy.

*   *   *

Felix's preparations for the doctorate, the last hurdle he had to overcome before he could marry, began with an explicit reconciliation between the Platter family and the faculty of arts of the University of Basel (F 301). The professors of the faculty had long been on bad terms with Thomas, who had balked at granting them even a modicum of control over his Gymnasium. But Felix was a promising young man, and, impressed by his return, the professors threw in the towel. They invited him to come have a drink with them on June 10 at Zur Kronen, the inn kept by Felix's friend Emmanuel Bomhart, where they heaped him with presents (*schankten*), congratulated him, and declared their readiness to help him obtain his doctorate in medicine, which, however, it was not in their power to grant, their province being arts and letters, not the art of Aesculapius. Young Felix was delighted by this stroke of good fortune, not only for himself but also for his father, whose eminent contribution to education in the city had at last been granted a deserved seal of approval by the leading lights of the Basel intelligentsia.

The triumph with the faculty of arts merely whetted Felix's appetite, however. What remained was to win the absolutely indispensable backing of the faculty of medicine, which would grant him his doctorate. He lost no time in proposing his services as a junior lecturer, and his offer was accepted. Between June 10 and July 21, Felix diligently revised his notes. Then, on July 21, he gave his "maiden speech," as it were, an inaugural lesson that was attended by all the professors of medicine—a sort of dress rehearsal for a future thesis defense. Practically no one attended his next lecture, except for two Dutch students whom Felix now took on as private students, meeting with them four times a week starting at eight in the morning. In order to win their loyalty, he invited them to his father's home and authorized them to climb a fruit tree in the yard and eat the fruit. As a further demonstration of his trust, he showed them the curiosities in his personal museum. From his travels Felix had returned with an amateur's collection of stuffed lizards, shells from around Montpellier, fish from Palavas-les-Flots, and similar specimens. During these months of intensive study, Felix rarely lifted his nose from his books. He sold his horse for half what the noble animal had cost him. Worse luck, his father pocketed the money, much to the dismay of Felix, who was perpetually broke. Thomas's behavior seemed at odds with his natural obligations. Nevertheless, Felix consoled himself with music, his faithful companion throughout his life. He played the lute with two friends in one of the cottages on the Rhine that give the old houses of Basel their charm. Joining him were his old friend Thiebold Schönhauer and a new acquaintance, also a music lover, named Johann Jacob Wecker. Born in Basel eight years before Felix, Wecker was a universal man who had studied at universities in Saxony and Italy. Back in his home town, he would soon become a professor of Latin and dialectics and later a professor of medicine and dean of the medical faculty. Ultimately, gripped once again by wanderlust, he would set off for Colmar, where he became *Stadtarzt*. Wecker was interested in ways to make noble women look more beautiful than nature intended. In 1557 his wedding was still recent: he had married the widow Anna Keller, the sister of Professor Isaac Keller of the faculty of medicine. She was the author of a cookbook that attracted some notice in the German-speaking world, culinary backwater that it was. A woman by the name of Platter, also a noted cook, would score a similar success in the seventeenth century, in the time of Louis XIV.

Felix also saw Hans Ruedin occasionaly. Ruedin was still rather unpleasant, much as he had been on the trip from Paris to Montbéliard. Young Platter also saw Ruedin's brother-in-law, Ambrosius Frobenius, a member of the famous dynasty of humanist printers and publishers. At the time Ambrosius was still living in his family's beautiful house at 18, Bäumleingasse, where Erasmus had once stayed. All these young men— Ruedin, Frobenius, and Hummel—were now married, and Felix, for the time being still a lonely hunter and bachelor, burned to follow in their footsteps.

*   *   *

There were five hurdles to overcome in short order before Felix could receive his doctorate: the petition, the *tentamen* (or preliminary examination), the examination, the disputation, and the promotion. The petition began with a petition to make a petition (*sic*), a sort of petition squared, that is, an application to apply for the doctorate in medicine: formalities beget formalities. On Saturday, August 14, 1557, Felix went to the home of Professor Dr. Oswald Baer, dean of the faculty of medicine. Baer, aged seventy-five at the time and originally from the Tyrol, was another Schyron: a preening, pretentious nonentity, a village peacock spreading his feathers at every opportunity, a vain opportunist, the very type of the low academic intriguer and professorial parvenu. He redeemed himself to some extent with a decided passion for music, an ever-smiling good humor, an unshakable affability, and a demonstration of authentic courage in confronting the plague. His remarkable pliability at various junctures had propelled him to the highest posts in Basel medicine, around which he had fluttered for forty years. He was professor, rector, dean, and municipal physician. His very mediocrity had allowed him to replace the extraordinary Paracelsus as *Stadtarzt,* for Paracelsus had, without apparent effort, succeeded in alienating nearly all the city's officials, who were jealous of a genius that often provoked hostility and left no one indifferent. True, Baer, even after he had arrived, sometimes suffered for his lack of scruples, as well as for his practice of splitting fees with his pharmacist first wife, which shocked many people in Basel and many graduates of the university. Still, Oswald Baer was clever enough to escape from more than one bad pass. After his first wife died, he married twice more, each marriage more brilliant than the last. He even managed to survive the religious and cultural upheavals of 1529–32, when Œcolampadian Protestantism captured the city. The revolution somehow spared Baer even as it destroyed the careers of other, less tenacious men. In any case, Professor Baer received Felix in a conciliatory manner because the young man posed no threat to him. Their meeting on August 14 took place in a house near the cathedral, one of several houses placed at the elderly teacher's disposal. Felix easily obtained Baer's approval to petition for the doctorate. The next day, he was summoned again to present his formal petition: once this compulsory ritual was out of the way, he would be officially a candidate for the doctorate.

Accordingly, on Sunday afternoon, Felix once again set out for the Baer house behind the cathedral. In theory this was a private home, but given the professor's position, it also served as a sort of semiofficial dean's office. Felix was well acquainted with the Baer real-estate holdings, since one of the buildings the professor owned was located at the sign of the Great Red Lion on Freie Strasse, not far from the Platters' house.

At Baer's residence Felix was greeted by two other old acquaintances: Professor Huber, who had already lent him a hand in presenting his marriage proposal to Madlen Jeckelmann, and Professor Isaac Keller (Cellarius), a man seven years older than Felix and, since 1552, professor of theoretical medicine. Keller would continue to enjoy a brilliant career in Basel until the day, a quarter of a century later, when he became involved up to his neck in a financial scandal that forced him to start over as *Stadtarzt* of Sélestat.

Felix showed this magisterial trio his Montpellier degrees, bachelor's and master's. The capital of Languedoc enjoyed the utmost prestige in Basel, a "gallophile" city without a trace of anti-French feeling. With a speech prepared for the occasion, Felix asked for permission to seek the doctorate. Things seemed to be going well when all of a sudden one of the examiners asked his age. Felix, it turned out, would only turn twenty-one that fall. Baer's reaction to this news was hostile: to become a doctor one had to be twenty-four. Dumbfounded, Felix took his leave. He felt as though he was walking on hot coals. That night, Madlen's father unveiled his friendly firepower for the first time, launching this salvo in support of his prospective son-in-law: "If they don't want you here, I'll give you my horse [*gib ich euch mein ross*], and you can go pass your doctorate in Montpellier" (F 305). In addressing Felix, Jeckelmann used the formal form of the second-person pronoun.

The alarm soon proved unwarranted, however. Baer's hostility was actually a sort of initiation ritual: in any thesis defense, objections must be raised, no matter how absurd. The rules of the game demand it. The professors were as upset as Felix because of his brusque departure. By the next day, however, August 16, the whole scene was forgotten, and the candidate was summoned by the university beadle to sit for the *tentamen*, or preliminary examination. His *ad hoc* jury was composed of the same three professors, Minos, Aeacus, and Rhadamanthus, which is to say, Baer, Keller, and Huber, once again gathered in Baer's residence. For several hours they bombarded the young man with questions about their respective specialties. Felix's answers were cordial, respectful, and correct. Then they asked him, in Latin of course, to prepare two presentations for the next day on assigned topics as part of his formal examination, which was scheduled for August 17.

When the *tentamen* was over, Margret Baer, the professor's daughter, served pastry and liqueurs. Felix paid for these refreshments, which put everyone in a good mood, including Margret, who was not particularly happy in her marriage into a family of seigneurial bailiffs. The tradition according to which the doctoral candidate pays for refreshments for the jury has a long history, but in Basel this tradition had a life of its own: Felix, as was customary, would lay out considerable sums throughout the extended doctoral process to entertain not only the members of the jury but also his friends, his friends' friends, his thesis referees, and even, as was only fitting, his enemies.

The examination proper took place on Tuesday, August 17, once again at Baer's residence. The two subjects that Felix had been assigned the day before at the conclusion of the *tentamen* are remarkable for their lack of intellectual interest. One was an aphorism of Hippocrates': "Changes in the weather produce diseases." The other was a saying of Galen's: "Medicine is the science of remedies." It would be difficult to come up with more tired topics than these. When Felix himself became a professor a few years later, he would modernize this age-old exercise. Meanwhile, however, he had to play by the rules, as usual. For more than an hour, therefore, he recited the text he had written and memorized the night before. He pretended, ritually, to be delivering a magisterial lecture, a sort of sermon learned by heart. The three judges who composed his audience then turned the tables on him for the next three hours: it was their turn to shine, echoing the brilliance of the candidate, while Felix listened with bated breath. Oswald Baer, who regarded himself as a philosopher of distinction (*so ein grosser philosophus sein wolt*), took an aggressive attitude and once again succeeded only in making himself look ridiculous. He was definitely a character from a play by Labiche. After enduring the dean's pedantry, the members of the jury asked Felix to withdraw while they deliberated. Then as now, this was a purely formal ritual, because the result was foreordained (although nowadays a candidate may of course succeed in winning an honorable—or dishonorable—mention with his performance on "orals"). Felix was summoned almost immediately and told to prepare for the disputation, the one great moment of public drama in the whole process. So far he had jumped every hurdle and seemed well on his way to finishing the race in style. Once again Felix stood the jury to a round of drinks, served by Margret Baer. Three days later, he paid for a supper at Zur Kronen, which put his three examiners in an excellent mood. Thus Felix was out of pocket for three rounds of refreshment in the space of a week.

During the last ten days of August, Felix girded himself with science for the ultimate test, the disputation. Professor Baer assigned the young candidate two subjects for public debate at the beginning of September. Privately, Felix regarded both subjects as ridiculous. But he was still playing by the accepted rules. He "crammed" for the test he had been assigned. In principle the disputation was open to the public, and in particular to the *doctoribus et professoribus* of the city. Not many medical students would attend this portion of the defense, for their numbers were greatly diminished: there were scarcely more students than professors— a pedagogical ideal. Only in the last third of the century, under the influence of a Felix Platter grown older and more powerful, were the doors of the medical school opened more widely. In 1557 the prevailing attitude was still one of limiting competition for scarce resources—academic Malthusianism, if you will. In August, the candidate paid for the printing of a public notice listing the scientific agenda of the meeting. This notice was to be posted outside the city's four parish churches (the parish, in Basel as in Paris, was still one of the primary geographical units in terms of which communal life was organized).

The Baer-Platter *themata* were thus printed on placards on August 29 and sent to all the *doctoribus et professoribus* of the city in advance of the disputation, scheduled for September 2. In France, this acme or culmination of the doctoral trial later came to be called the *thèse,* or thesis. According to Furetière's seventeenth-century *Dictionnaire universel,* "a *thèse,* in academic parlance, is a placard on which a number of theses, or propositions, are recorded for public display. On the appointed day, these theses in philosophy or medicine are to be defended against all comers. . . . Invitations are issued to attend theses."[4]

*   *   *

Medicine, or rather disease, reasssserted its rights, however, just when it was least expected. The candidate's preparations were briefly interrupted by uncontrollable fits of coughing, the result of a catarrh or perhaps of whooping cough. Some sort of late-summer epidemic seems to have swept a vast stretch of Europe from the scrub around Montpellier to the Swiss plateau in 1557.

On Thursday, September 2, the official disputation for the doctorate was held. For such an occasion the Baer residence was no longer suitable, despite its quasi-official status. The size of the audience and the ceremonial importance of the event required the use of the Medical Hall (*aula medicorum*) of the faculty of medicine, itself located in the *Obere Collegium*, which was none other than a former monastery once occupied by Augustinian monks, who, now that the Reformation had come to Basel, had lost their raison d'être. Felix's *disputatio* began at seven in the morning and continued until the noon meal—three hundred minutes by the clock. In the audience that morning were the handful of students who regularly attended the courses given by Professors Huber and Keller. Baer, trusting to his fifty years of "experience" (half a century of stupidity does not make an intelligent man), brandished the texts of Avicenna to confront Felix on the matter of natural heat. At Montpellier in the middle third of the sixteenth century, Avicenna's star had paled considerably, along with the stars of other Arab physicians once renowned in Languedoc. Felix would not back down, however. Compared with his Basel colleagues, he had the immense advantage of knowing his French (and Greek) medicine like the back of his hand. He crushed Baer with the arguments of Fernel, the illustrious scholar he had recently met in Paris and whose *De naturali parte medicinae* he had read along with other works. On the subject of natural heat, Fernel distinguished, in highly scientific fashion, between plants, which are cold, and animals, especially humans, which stand closer to heat and fire. Bread, meat, wine, pepper, mustard, blood, sperm, spirit, heart, liver, and spleen can be classed with the hot; the brain is cold and moist; some specifics are cool, others warm (in essence), depending on the part of the body to be treated. Fernel, an out-and-out Galenist, described the concepts, causes, and symptoms of diseases in the spirit of ancient medicine. Felix, having no desire to outdo his teacher, simply followed Fernel's lead in his oral thesis defense. Later, however, a time would come when groups of symptoms could at last be correlated with lesions revealed by pathological anatomy; Professor Platter would then base his practice and even his theory on more realistic notions than those imparted to him by Fernel.[5]

By this point in the defense, Baer had sufficiently demonstrated his brilliance, and a new quartet of physicians—Pantaleon, Keller, Huggelin, and Philip Bächi, known as Bechius—proceeded to attack Felix's positions. We are already familiar with Huggelin and the eminent Pantaleon, whose mere presence in the *aula medicorum* shows what an important academic event Felix's disputation was. Bächi is a newcomer to our tale, however. A native of Baden, aged thirty-six, he had studied at Lutheran universities in Saxony and was a Hellenist, Latinist, poet, physician, and, coming from Saxony, an expert on mines; he was also pious, a lover of fine wines, and afflicted with a malady of the lungs. Despite Bächi's many qualities, Felix could not stand him and had an even lower opinion of his wife, a remarried widow whom he accused of inventing stupid practical jokes such as placing a nail-studded board in the bed of a servant by the name of Heidegger whom she happened to fancy, thus running the risk of injuring the man.[6] In the debate, however, Bächi proved to be a worthy adversary for Felix. In this phase of the disputation, he and Huggelin concentrated their criticism on the issue of natural heat previously raised by Baer. The two examiners drew some of their arguments from a work by Pietro d'Albano, a bizarre thirteenth-century Italian philosopher and physician. The son of a notary, Albano was a Hellenist, astrologer, traveler (who had been as far as Byzantium and Scotland), self-styled sorcerer, and possibly atheist; his book was entitled *Conciliator*.[7] Fortunately, Felix knew the work of "Petrus de Abanus" intimately and had no difficulty routing his adversaries. The candidate, no mean student, had acquired considerable book learning in Montpellier, along with his practical study of the anatomy of cadavers.

The *disputatio* (called *Disputatz* in Basel) thus ended well, and Felix's last task was to entertain professors and friends one more time at Zur Kronen, where everyone gathered for a somewhat delayed noon meal. Having depleted the family savings a little further, Felix, now almost a laureate, followed dessert with a brief visit to his fiancée, who worried that a stubborn cold and runny nose might have impaired his oratory. Felix took her by the hands and reassured her. She must have been even more reassured when, four days later, on Monday, September 6, the doctors of the faculty finally informed him that he had been accepted (*zuglossen*) for the doctorate. In the meantime, a second deliberation had taken place, but we know nothing about it other than that its outcome was favorable.

The "promotion," or final, purely ceremonial stage of the doctoral process, was set for Sunday, September 20. This ceremony marked the culmination of Felix's dreams and perhaps the beginning of an even more brilliant future for the recent graduate of the University of Montpellier. In the third week of September, he prepared and memorized the speeches he would deliver a few days later. He also prepared invitations to the event. Small notices were hung on parish bulletin boards. Meanwhile, the university beadle (*pedellus*) took charge of inviting Basel's former and current mayors, high guild officials, professors in various branches of learning, and friends. Guests were invited from as far away as the Black Forest: invitations went out to Peter Gebwiller, the clerk of Rötteln, an old friend who had given Felix a place to stay during the plague epidemic of 1551, and his stepson, Michael Rappenberger, whose wealthy marriages had rapidly transformed him into a castellan living in a newly rebuilt manor. Felix clearly wanted to invite upwardly mobile people. It may come as a surprise that the mayor, aldermen, and other political dignitaries would participate in such a doctoral celebration, which nowadays would be a purely academic affair unless the participation of some elite figure drew in the upper crust. Bear in mind that between 1550 and 1567 only four doctoral theses in medicine were defended in Basel, or roughly one every four to five years. Doctoral candidates preferred to take their degrees elsewhere, in France or Italy,[8] rather like younger scholars today who return to Europe with a master's degree or a Ph.D. from Berkeley or Yale. The presence of the mayor at this scientific gathering was intended to encourage the bold native of the city who had returned home full of learning and knowledge of the world to defend his thesis after a long journey.[9]

Felix's first stop on September 20 was at Professor Baer's house, where he bolstered his courage with several glasses of Greek wine. Then he, along with Professors Baer and Huber, left for the *aula medicorum*. The place could hardly be recognized on account of the huge crowd and the tapestries covering the walls—all for young Platter, who couldn't believe his eyes. Neither could his father. The ceremony lasted four hours. There was a concert of trumpets. Professor Keller gave a speech. Then Felix spoke interminably, in theory on subjects that had come up in the course of the proceedings but in fact known to the candidate in advance. Some additional oratory followed. Then came the procession: the bearded beadle marched in front, wearing a flowing cape, ribbons below his knees and on his shoes, and in his right hand carrying a scepter, a symbol of sovereignty. Behind this representative of order came Felix, smiling vacantly, looking cherubic and almost childish in his red pants, red silk doublet, and wrapped in two feet of velvet over his black doctoral gown. Dean Baer brought up the rear. Everyone climbed onto the podium, where Baer placed the velvet doctor's cap on Felix's head. He also placed a ring on Felix's finger, triggering a reaction of disgust: the new doctor could dissect any cadaver, even one that had begun to stink, but he could not bear to wear a ring, whether of flesh or metal.[10] Finally, Felix gave two speeches, neither of them "spontaneous." Then everyone went back out into the street, with the beadle and a brass band leading the way. Alongside Felix marched Rector Wolfgang Wissenberger, who wore a sword at his side as if he were a noble even though he was the son of a weaver—upward mobility once again. The entourage was no longer strictly medical: Wissenberger was a professor of mathematics and theology, close to Œcolampadius. And Bonifacius Amerbach, who marched beside Felix, was a jurist, humanist, and former rector. Seventy invited guests joined Felix at Zur Kronen, around seven tables, reminiscent of a Brueghel. All this cost the Platters some fifty florins, five of which were provided by Dr. Jeckelmann, Felix's future father-in-law, stingy as usual. The meal lasted until three in the afternoon. The day ended with an *Obendrunck,* a sort of late-afternoon cocktail party, at Michael Rappenberger's house in the suburbs of Basel. Felix's friends were with him through thick and thin: Rappenberger's stepfather had given Felix a place to stay during the plague, and now the stepson conscientiously drank a toast to the new doctor.

Only a short while before, Felix had witnessed a similar doctoral procession and ritual in Montpellier, where the style was much the same. The parade included horses, trumpets, and flutes (T2 69). Everyone wore gloves, there were lots of candles, and candy was distributed. Such parades honored new doctors whom everyone already saw as future professors, whether because of their own genius or thanks to the influence of powerful backers.

*   *   *

The thesis was like the eucharist: if nothing else it effected a transsubstantiation. Dr. Felix Platter was no longer just plain Felix Platter. Young local artisans now looked upon him as someone worthy to be godfather to their newborn children. Within a few weeks of his doctoral triumph, he had held five children over the baptismal font virtually one after another. Among them were the sons of a typographer, a constable, and a hatter, as well as little Margret, the daughter of his friend Hummel the pharmacist.

In 1557 the Platters still moved chiefly within the artisanal milieu. Felix served as godfather to the babies of artisans, while he dealt professionally with physicians, professors, and intellectuals who were themselves upwardly mobile sons of artisans. Sociologists have developed theories of social reproduction that may (or may not) be valid for late-twentieth-century Western societies but that seem much less useful for understanding urban societies in a period of rapid (and not unproblematic) economic and demographic growth like the Renaissance. The ruling strata in these cities had to be replaced periodically owing simply to death from the plague and other causes. They were profoundly shaken, moreover, by the fruitful trauma of the Protestant Reformation, which led to a sweeping renewal of elites in many fields: the religious, of course, but also the political, intellectual, and academic. In the Swiss Confederation in the second third of the sixteenth century, individuals and families apparently had a good chance to improve their status. The Platter family was not the only one to take advantage of this situation.

* * *

Now that Felix had his doctorate in hand, what about the wedding? Dr. Jeckelmann, who held the young couple's future happiness in his hands, continued to stall throughout the month of October. Basically, the widower was still reluctant to give up his incomparable pearl of a daughter, who was also his housekeeper. He kept putting Thomas off, if not indefinitely then at least until early November, when the Basel fairs would be over. There was no choice but to be patient, especially since Jeckelmann was not entirely negative: he opened his house to Felix (the door was never locked, for people may have been afraid of crime but not of robbery—the streets of Basel were not like the thick forests of France and Switzerland). Under Madlen's direction, Felix put up preserves for the surgeon's kitchen (his love of sugar had stayed with him). Sometimes he told his fiancée jokes or played tricks on her. He entertained her by enumerating her charms and the debts he had contracted in Montpellier. He also discussed the loves of Daniel Jeckelmann, his future brother-in-law. He went so far as to offer her a bracelet, which she refused for the time being for fear of what people might say, although she accepted a handsomely bound Bible that Felix had bought for her in Paris. Such a gift was hardly compromising, for it spoke of the engaged couple's deep religious convictions.

* * *

When the fairs were over, a wedding date was finally set. Jeckelmann made all the decisions. The marriage contract would be signed on November 18; the wedding itself would take place on November 22.

On November 18, 1557, the parties gathered at the surgeon's house in a room off the kitchen (*Kuchi*). Madlen's father was flanked by four colleagues drawn from among the city's merchants and distinguished artisans: Caspar Krug, the powerful ironmonger and future bürgermeister; Martin Fickler, an Alsatian draper from a textile family and a naturalized citizen of Basel; Batt Hug, a master fishmonger and the son of a freshwater fisherman, one of those wealthy boatmen of Alsace and Switzerland who went out on the upper Rhine early enough to meet the herons and took several hundred pounds of fish daily using broad-gauge nets for tench, trout, and pike and narrow nets for miraculous draughts of fishes, to say nothing of well-endowed daughters; and, fourth in the group, Gorius Schieli, a butcher, innkeeper, hospital administrator, court clerk, and former police captain. Schieli was a stout fellow and a good organizer; all he lacked was intelligence.

On Thomas's side, the witnesses were comparable to the foregoing in financial status but could boast of more prestigious intellectual credentials or "symbolic capital."[11] Among them was Professor Hans Huber, a leading physician, convinced Protestant, and close friend of Felix's. Huber could be unpredictable: once, while treating the superior of a Catholic abbey near Basel, he had attached his patient's coat of arms to the wall above his private toilet; when the monks learned of the joke, Huber cried copiously and made abject excuses to the abbot. The second Platter witness was Mathis Bomhart, a seventeen-year-old apprentice goldsmith, brother of the owner of Zur Kronen, and ally of the family of Myconius, Thomas Platter's longtime protector. The third and final witness was Henric Petri, an elderly printer whose father had also been a printer and who was a high official in various local guilds and a member of the city council; once married to an ex-nun who had quit her order in 1529 (the year of Basel's religious revolution), he had since remarried, taking the widow of a Frobenius for his second wife.

Both Thomas and Felix would come away from the signing of the marriage contract with bitter memories. Jeckelmann, punctilious as usual, offered a dowry of four hundred gulden, of which one hundred were to be paid in cash, the rest in the form of a trousseau. Did he keep his word (any more than Thomas did)? In any case, Thomas was obliged to acknowledge that he hadn't a penny to put on the table and that all his son could contribute to the new household was the shirt on his back (and of course his thesis), a humiliating confession for both the old teacher and the new doctor. The discussion with Jeckelmann turned bitter, and the parties came close to parting in anger.

In the end, his back to the wall, Thomas promised to contribute four hundred gulden, not a cent of which he could actually lay hands on. He would pay his share gradually by allowing the young couple to share his hearth and table and live at Zum Gejägd at his expense. What a delightful prospect! The schoolmaster further promised, with crossed fingers, to send his boarders elsewhere so as to spare his prospective daughter-in-law the distress of having to put up with their dreadful racket. With this the two fathers more or less patched things up, but there was little joy in the conciliatory supper that followed the negotiations. Felix was dismayed by the absence of any musical accompaniment. Meanwhile, Madlen, who had had her ear glued to the wall during the painful row over finances, was left speechless. To top off this black Thursday, Madlen's brother, Daniel Jeckelmann, got himself completely drunk and, while walking Felix back to Zum Gejägd, said horrible things about his sister. It

was a wretched way to end the day, and the future bridegroom went to
bed in a foul mood.

* * *

On Saturday, November 20, invitations to the wedding were sent out
to a total of one hundred fifty people, counting wives and children.
Only forty guests were invited to the Norman wedding described in
Flaubert's *Madame Bovary*, a minuscule affair compared with the Platter
nuptials. Among the guests, of eighty-five family heads whose professions are known, fifty-five were merchants or artisans (including a few
artists). In other words, this was a largely middle-class or petit-
bourgeois crowd, for this was where the Platters and Jeckelmanns had
their roots. Of these fifty-five, the textile trade accounted for eleven;
leather for seven; the metal business for eight; and the grocery trade for
sixteen. At the top of this commercial group were five goldsmiths and
moneychangers; four typographers or printers; and four artists (including a glassblower, a glass painter, and a sculptor). There were also fourteen individuals associated with the medical profession (including four
university professors along with various surgeons, physicians, and
apothecaries), plus six members of the Protestant clergy and half a
dozen minor city officials (clerks, a constable, etc.). Finally, there were
four nobles or castellans and of course, as always, a few guests who cannot be assigned to any group.

When we break down the guest list still further, it is clear that the
guests invited by Felix and Thomas were, as a group, of higher status than
those invited by Madlen's surgeon father. There were many more intellectuals and nobles on the Platters' list than on the Jeckelmanns'. Felix in
fact boasts of this superiority, noting that his father invited not only a
large number of his Freie Strasse neighbors but also representatives of
the guilds, the city council, the university, and the nobility. Of course,
since the Platters were relative newcomers to Basel, they had no family in
the city. To compensate for this, they honored their neighbors with invitations and made a show of their connections in intellectual circles, connections that would continue to proliferate as Felix pursued his career.

* * *

Sunday, November 21, was not a much more cheerful occasion than the
preceding Thursday had been. To be sure, the marriage was announced at
the cathedral, and tables for the wedding banquet were set up at
Thomas's house under the direction of Batt Oesy, the innkeeper and cook

at Zum Engel, a suburban inn. An old friend of the Platters, the alchemist Hans Rust, arrived at the house with a giant wheel of Gruyère in honor of the young couple. But nothing went right, and Thomas was in high dudgeon because he felt that all the work of preparing for the wedding had fallen to him. To hear him tell it, his only son was a lazy fellow in thrall to his fiancée, with whom he spent all his time instead of helping his own father. Having to face hostility from three sides—his father-in-law over questions of money, his brother-in-law with his scathing remarks about his bride, and his father, overwhelmed by the preparations for the celebration—Felix felt quite low. Sharing a house and meals with his parents could easily turn into a nightmare. November 21 was a black day indeed. Thomas was rarely in bad humor, but when he was, it was a terrible thing to behold. Perhaps Felix was feeling the onset of a fifth bout of "depression" (having already suffered depressive episodes in Avignon, Montpellier twice, and Narbonne).

By Monday morning, however, things looked brighter. Thomas woke up ready to resume his tirades of the day before, but nothing was amiss. The sideboards groaned with food for the afternoon feast. Before Thomas could spew out a new stream of invective, the kitchen maid Dorothea Schenk lit into him so sharply that he was left speechless. Dorothea, who came from a local family of metallurgists, was a take-charge woman. We have seen several examples of powerful women who knew how to knock an aggressive old man down a peg or two. Frau Platter herself had once put Thomas in his place for being too hard on Felix. And Surgeon Jeckelmann frequently sided with his daughter (whom he adored) against his son.

With calm restored, Felix was able to dress for the wedding: he wore a red silk doublet, flesh-colored breeches, a wedding shirt with short ruff, gold pins, and gilt collar, and a velvet doctoral cap with a braid of pearls and flowers encircling the base where it rested on the groom's head. The bride wore a flesh-colored blouse that matched the groom's breeches. The red in Felix's doublet was matched by Professor Baer's scarlet gown. Despite his seventy-five years, the good professor did not hesitate to wear camlet and a slashed silk doublet. Age differences more or less evaporated when it came time to celebrate. On such occasions no one was afraid of looking ridiculous. Young girls put ribbons in their hair and wore pearls and gold jewelry. The wedding procession, led by the printer Petri, ended at the big church, where a sermon was delivered, rings were exchanged, and bride and groom pledged to have and to hold each other until death did them part. Then it was back to Zum Gejägd for apéritifs and sumptuous gifts for the bride in anticipation of the midday meal.

*   *   *

For this occasion, fifteen well-stocked tables had been set up throughout the house to accommodate the 150 guests. Servants, male and female, kept glasses and plates filled. Jowly, buxom old women with bare arms carried huge wooden trays laden with comestibles. At the end of the meal, the servants were invited to share in the dessert of fruit and cheese. All told, somewhere between 150 and 200 people took part in the dinner. Friends and relatives of the young couple were seated according to a rather "puritanical" notion of segregation by sex. Basel was not like Brueghel's rural Flanders, where men and women rubbed elbows and laughed heartily around the banquet table. Recall that Zum Gejägd, the Platter residence, actually comprised three houses arrayed around a common square. Two large rooms were reserved for male guests: one, off the garden, was kept warm by the stove in the adjacent print shop (the wedding took place on a cool day in late autumn); the other, reserved for the less distinguished male guests, was in the *Mittelhus,* or middle house, and could be reached via a spiral staircase. The more elite women guests were seated in the print shop, where the oppressive heat left them soaked with sweat. Another room was set aside for women of the more "common" sort and still another for unmarried girls. Felix sat with the men of substance, alongside Bürgermeister Theodor Brand, the celebrated surgeon of Ox Street. Felix's new bride, now Frau Platter, presided over the gathering of elite women. Little Madlen Hug, a fishmonger's daughter, aged ten, wore a pearl headpiece that made her one of the ornaments of the younger girls' dining room.

The food was served in four courses (*vier mol uf*): appetizers, fish, roast, and dessert.[12] The same standard order was observed for the evening meal, which followed an interlude of dancing. Indeed, this was the standard order for wedding dinners throughout German Switzerland, where sumptuary excess was frowned upon. On several occasions, and as late as 1628, the city, hoping to encourage frugality, promulgated sumptuary laws governing what could be served at wedding banquets. The Platters offered an impressive variety of dishes: various kinds of fowl, beef, pork, and game, along with several varieties of freshwater fish. Among patricians and aspiring patricians in Basel, marriage was thus an occasion to survey the whole spectrum of social groups (all represented in the guest list), sexes (men, women, and maidens), and comestible fauna (including primarily domestic animals but also wild animals living on land or in the water). (See the chart below)

	Felix Platter's Wedding, November 1557, Midday Meal	*Felix Platter's Wedding, November 1557, Evening Meal*	*Basel sumptuary regulation of 1628 for weddings*
First Course: Appetizer (*voressen*)	Chopped fish Soup Meat Chicken	Chicken Liver Tripe "Meat" soup Chicken	Chopped fish Soup Smoked meat Chicken
Second Course: Fish	Boiled pike	Boiled carp	Fish (unspecified)
Third Course: Roast	Roast Pigeon, Cock, Goose Boiled Rice Liver slices in aspic	Roast as earlier Black Forest game stew Fish cakes	Roast Pigeon, Chicken, Goose Boiled Rice Pieces of fish in aspic
Fourth Course: Dessert	Cheese Fruit	Pastries	Cheese Fruit

On a comparative note, Flaubert, in his description of Madame Bovary's wedding, favored beef, lamb, and pork (sirloin, veal casserole, leg of lamb, roast suckling pig, and pork sausages with sorrel) over fish and chicken (in contrast to the Platter dinner, the Bovary banquet included no fowl other than a chicken fricassee).[13] But the Norman affair offered greater diversity of drink: the guests at the Bovary wedding drank both red wine and sparkling sweet cider. Felix, on the other hand, was a man of one faith, one woman, and one vintage: he served all his guests a generous quantity of Rang wine from the vineyards of the Thann "mountain" in Alsace, near Engelburg Castle. According to Sebastian Munster's *Cosmographie,* this beverage from the west bank of the Rhine was much appreciated in sixteenth-century Basel. The German saying *"Dass dich der Rang anstoss"* (Let the Rang hit you) referred to the wallop this wine packed. It went down as easily as milk, but a single glass could lay a man out.[14]

This time there was no question of Jeckelmann's vetoing the musical entertainment as he had done to Felix's dismay the Thursday before. The tedium of a lengthy four-course dinner in the middle of the day was relieved by a choral recital, featuring a choir of students from the Platter

Gymnasium accompanied by trumpets and violas under the baton of Roman Winmann, who had recently become the school's assistant headmaster (his predecessor having married and moved to another city to pursue
his teaching career [F 325]). Winmann (also known as Oenander) was a
native of Basel, an intelligent, moderate man, loyal and unassuming. In
1550 he had been a poor student in Wittenberg, reduced to begging for his
dinner. For the past few years he had earned his living as a teacher (*provisor*) in the Platter Gymnasium. After failing in his first appointment as a
Protestant minister, he became pastor to a rural community two leagues
from Basel, where he remained until 1610. His stint at the Gymnasium
served him well in his later career, for it allowed him to perfect not only
his Latin but also his skills as choirmaster, both useful in his later church
work.[15]

At the wedding banquet the student choir performed, among other
things, the "spoon song," a musical setting of a long, tedious poem for
which Felix was partly responsible. The poem concerned the classification of spoons, revealing a mania for taxonomy that Felix had already
demonstrated in his grouping of guests by sex and social status and in his
choice of meat and fish courses.

Between the afternoon and evening meals there was dancing in the
presence of a distinguished audience gathered in the large reception hall
on the first floor of Professor Baer's residence. Lorentz Richart, a bachelor surgeon whose father was also a surgeon, played the lute. A man
named Christellin put down his trumpet and strolled about with a fiddle
instead. Felix received the customary applause for his solo performance
of a French-style *gaillarde,* but his timid wife refused to accompany him.

These festivities, which had gone on since dawn, might seem lavish
and impressive, but they can hardly hold a candle to the absurdly ostentatious displays through which Basel patricians of later generations
sought to demonstrate their power and prestige.[16]

When supper was over and the last grateful speeches had been delivered, the family gathered for a discreet and private farewell. Discretion
was essential, for there was always a danger that mischievous young men,
and especially Thomas's boarders, might attempt some tasteless
wedding-night tomfoolery at the newlyweds' expense. Felix and Madlen
therefore slipped out to Thomas's bedroom for a private adieu. Astonishingly enough, Jeckelmann was there to shed a tear, even though he
lived only a short distance away and could visit his beloved daughter
whenever he wished. Madlen also feigned a tear or two. The ever-ready
Felix punctuated parting's sweet sorrow by serving sugared claret from
his private cask to the godmothers and other matrons who had gathered

in certainty that the tearful young bride would crave consolation and a few last words of advice before facing the agitated night ahead.

Finally, the newlyweds once more slipped off to an attic room under the rafters just behind the maid's room and overlooking the garden. It was a lot like the room Felix had occupied as a student in Montpellier. For a short while he and Madlen sat shivering on the edge of the bed—it was November, after all. Finally, unable to hold out any longer, if only because it was so cold, they slipped under the covers. Unlike Thomas, they did not put the moment off for several weeks. A humorous note was struck by Anna Dietschi, Thomas's wife, about whom we have heard little over the past several days even though she had borne much of the burden of the wedding reception. Now that it was all over and her son was safely married, Anna was exultant. With a heavy step she climbed the narrow staircase and entered the privy adjacent to the nuptial chamber, where, venting her joy, she sang at the top of her lungs without regard for the proprieties or her relatively advanced age. At the sound of her voice, Madlen, in bed, recovered her high spirits of the past few weeks and burst out laughing. And so the curtain falls on Felix and Madlen's wedding night. Did the couple start off on the right foot?

PART FIVE

Boy or Girl?

CHAPTER TEN

Gredlin

More than sixteen years had passed since Felix's marriage. The year was 1573 or 1574, and times were hard in northern France and German Switzerland. The harsh winter of 1572–73, "strange and impetuous,"[1] had greatly diminished the grain harvest.[2] During an abbreviated week of the academic year 1573–74, Professor Felix Platter went as usual to the family estate in Gundeldingen, not far from Basel. His career, subsequent to the childhood and youth we have traced in detail, as in a *Bildungsroman,* through 1557, had been brilliant. By 1561, his income from medical and other sources had increased sufficiently to allow him to move out of Zum Gejägd, where he and his wife had lived since their marriage in sometimes stormy proximity to Felix's parents. The two couples parted company without acrimony when Felix bought a house of his own, Zum Rotenfluh (F 17). He also bought a horse, an acquisition comparable to the purchase of an automobile by a young doctor today. He and Madlen could now afford a maid. With substantial honoraria flowing in from a growing number of patients, supplemented perhaps by income from moneylending and usury, Felix could look forward to better days ahead. He liked to travel in neighboring regions, particularly where German was spoken, for pleasure and profit.

By 1559, many people in Basel, professionals and laymen alike, had remarked on the young doctor's skill as an anatomist, a skill enhanced by his collaboration with his father-in-law, Surgeon Jeckelmann. Honors and positions accumulated at an impressive rate: in 1562, Felix, just over twenty-five at the time, was appointed dean of the faculty of medicine (success came early then); in 1570 he was named rector; and in 1571 he succeeded his teacher Hans Huber as *Stadtarzt,* or municipal physician, and professor of practical medicine. For the next four decades, this Montpellier graduate would lord it over the medical profession of Basel. Since his student days he had amassed more than a thousand observations of cases of individual morbidity, and the rector's *Observationes* became a landmark in medical history when published in 1614. To be sure, Dr. Platter was not a medical eminence of the first rank, but he was a top-notch physician. His discoveries concerning retinal vision attracted the attention of one of the leading scientists of the day, Johannes Kepler.[3] And his fellow citizens never forgot the courageous devotion he demonstrated during the regional plague of 1563–64, which killed 4,000 people in Basel, a quarter of the city's population.

As mentioned earlier, the period 1573–74 was also difficult, not because of plague, but because food was in short supply. At Gundeldingen Felix had his father for company: Thomas, of peasant stock, often went to the farm to tend his cattle, hunt fox, fish in the pond, chop wood, and plant trees or make grafts in his orchard. Felix, however, was a city boy, not at all a farmer though drawn at times to gardening. He had no attachment to the countryside, much less to the mountains, which continued to exert a powerful hold on his father. After Thomas died in 1582, Professor Platter's first order of business was to sell off the Gundeldingen estate. (His younger brother Thomas Jr., more faithful to family tradition, would purchase a nearby farm in 1622, however.)

In 1573–74, though, Thomas Sr. was still very much alive, and Felix, as always a dutiful son, visited him on the "country estate" that was the old man's proudest acquisition. It was a period of near famine, and typhus and other diseases raged in the city as well as in the plains and mountains. Basel, ensconced within its walls, shunned outsiders: the city's constables turned away wretched beggars from the surrounding region. With nowhere to go, these unfortunates descended on places like Gundeldingen, which had no high walls to defend it. Felix was rather unhappy about the presence of such vagabonds, or "rabble," on his property; his father's *Meyer,* or steward, a decent fellow, allowed them to sleep in the sheds and stables (F 451). Among the refugees was a married couple: Benedict Simon was French, or at any rate "romanophone," and a native of Pontarlier;[4] his wife, Elsbeth Shärin, was Swiss, from a town near Zurich. Both had worked as agricultural laborers at Bartenheim in Haute-Alsace. Elsbeth was gravely ill, probably with typhus. She was most likely on her way home, hoping to have sufficient strength to make it back to the Zurich region. The pair had a small child with them, a girl not yet one year old. Felix spoke bluntly to the steward: "You shouldn't have allowed people of that sort to stay here. I am greatly displeased [*missfiel mir*]."

* * *

Of course Thomas was still the owner of the property and should have dealt personally with a matter such as whether or not to accommodate paupers. On this particular day, however, he happened to be away. He had gone off for two days of fishing with a professional fisherman, Jacob Jüppen, and another friend, the wife of a Protestant "canon." When the trio returned, still laden with fishnets, they went to look in on Elsbeth Shärin, the dying woman from Zurich, who lay in agony in one of the bedrooms. Her husband, also ill by now, seemed likely to pull through. At the sight of this couple in distress, Thomas was inevitably reminded of his own youth, which had been so hard. A conscientious physician, Felix treated the suffering woman with various potions that had little effect. He peered through a window at the scene inside, glancing also at the child, who lay sleeping outdoors in case her mother was contagious. The child gestured with its little hands (*hendlin*) and bruised its neck on the hard wood of a cradle that was in fact little more than a crate.

Felix and the others who witnessed this affecting scene were moved by it. They felt pity (*bedauren*) for the child, thus casting doubt on the alleged indifference to childhood that Philippe Ariès claimed to find in this period but for which he offered no real proof (F 411).[5] Elsbeth Schärin died. Her body was loaded onto a donkey (a real curiosity in the region) and transported to the St. Margreten cemetery in Gundeldingen. Felix's sister, who died of plague in 1551, was buried in the same cemetery.

Night fell. Felix and Madlen both had dreams (nightmares?) about children. Felix awoke with a start and roused his sleeping wife. His dream had been frightening, but it was also more than that: a child had fallen upon him from heaven.[6] It's raining swaddled babies, ladies, hold out your red aprons! In his dream, Felix stretched out his long professorial gown to break the baby's fall and prevent it from smashing into the ground. Did this dream stem from Felix's having noticed the bruise on the little girl's neck the day before? In any case, one sad fact could not be denied: Felix and his wife were childless. For sixteen years their marriage had remained barren. Felix loved his wife but never really accepted the situation, and Madlen was sorely afflicted by it. She still remembered the futile pilgrimage to the mineral baths of Valais in 1563, to waters that were supposed to have made her fertile.

*   *   *

The next morning was a time for sad farewells: Benedict placed the baby in a basket (*auf einer hurt*) and lifted it onto his back. He returned Felix's jars of medicine and thanked him from the bottom of his heart. Madlen bent down to kiss the child. Everyone was in tears. The two paupers, father and daughter, vanished into the distance, bound who knows where? One wonders if they knew themselves. Benedict took with him a small amount of cash, a gift from the Platters. Death seemed to be the little girl's inevitable fate. How could her father, poor as he was, possibly feed her?

Was this the end of it? The Platters sat down to lunch in a wretched mood. Their consciences would not let them alone. At the table were Felix and Madlen and Thomas and his young wife Hester (Anna Dietschi, Felix's mother, had died in February 1572, and Thomas, a restless widower, had remarried in April). Although Hester was ten years younger than Felix, the good doctor did not hesitate to call her "mother" (*Mutti*). The remaining guests came from various classes of society: they included the fisherman Jüppen and perhaps the seamstress Krössel, although she may have remained standing in order to wait on the others. When the appetizers were served, Felix and Madlen tried to lighten the atmosphere by recounting their dreams. The fisherman, Felix noted, reacted immediately: "Why didn't you keep the baby? You have no child of your own." With characteristic understatement, Madlen said that would have been all right with her, but then she added that she would gladly bring up the child if only she could retrieve her. "If that's what you want, Madlen," Felix replied.[7] The seamstress, putting in her two cents, said that she would knit caps for the baby if the men succeeded in bringing it home. Thomas and his young wife added their voices to the chorus. Everyone was in favor of going after Benedict in the hope of persuading him to give up his daughter, but no one was sure where he had gone. After an interval of silence, Felix wholeheartedly agreed with the idea of searching for the pair, which had now become his wish (*begirt*), as it was also the express wish of Thomas, the family patriarch. A dutiful son is a dutiful son. All that remained now was to find the lost infant.

Thomas took charge. He sent two of his students in hot pursuit, one to the northwest (toward Mulhouse), the other to the southeast. Wherever they went, they were instructed to ask the same question: "Have you seen a man carrying a baby on his back?"

That first night there was no news. The next morning, the scout returned from the southeast empty-handed. Felix had already returned to the university. At midday he went to the student cafeteria, whose hours were strictly regulated.[8] In the middle of his meal, a message arrived: the girl had been found. She and her father were in Bartenheim, almost midway between Basel and Mulhouse, on the same farm where Benedict and Elsbeth had been employed as laborers. Informed of the Platters' offer, Benedict returned to Gundeldingen at once, carrying his child and escorted by the student from Thomas's Gymnasium. The moment they arrived, Madlen began to lavish on the child the treasures of maternal devotion she had been hoarding up for years. She took the infant girl out of her basket and peeled away her swaddling, leaving her entirely naked, without even a cap on her head, then bathed her, wrapped her in fur, and put her to sleep.

Felix, meanwhile, talked things over with Benedict, who cried tears of joy. He would gladly allow the professor to raise, educate, and arrange a marriage for the child. Having obtained what he wanted, Felix dismissed the tramp rather curtly, but not before scheduling a meeting in Basel one week hence for the signing of a contract, which was to be not a formal adoption but rather, if one can put it this way, a long-term loan or lease. A week later, the two men met as planned at Thomas's Gymnasium. Naturally, Thomas kept an eye on the business, which, after all, was being transacted in his house. He had been married to Hester for only a short time, and this adoption was another way of perpetuating his line, even if it involved an external "graft." Present to certify the legality of the arrangement was the notary Ubelin, at thirty soon to become a man of property and already in the early stages of a successful career. It was Felix who drafted the contract, however. Benedict was officially recognized as the child's father and granted visiting rights, but nothing more. Felix, for his part, promised in writing to raise the girl and provide her with trousseau and dowry. He kept his word.

"Thanks to me," the good doctor observed in retrospect, Benedict's daughter "was brought up through childhood and adolescence. She learned to sew, to embroider, [and] to play musical instruments." Did Felix teach the little girl to play the lute? It was common at the time for girls to be given music lessons (F 453). She was also given a name: Margret Simon or Simonin, also known as Margareta Platterin and familiarly called Gredlin. For Thomas, of course, the name evoked memories of the two Margrets he had lost to the plague. Gredlin, a charming child, inspired affection well beyond the narrow circle of the "nuclear family." Hester and old Thomas doted on her. Her relations with Benedict Simon, her natural father, proved to be difficult, however. Simon became a soldier of fortune serving, like other Swiss mercenaries, under foreign princes, a profession in which he no doubt earned a better living than he had commanded as an agricultural laborer. He called on Gredlin from time to time and never forgot her. She found him hard to tolerate, however. He frightened her with his military uniform and swaggering ways.

Gredlin was a happy child, but there was one sad episode in her otherwise sunny existence (the date of this incident is unknown, but it certainly occurred before 1604): certain "nasty people" took it upon themselves to inform her that she was not really the Platters' daughter.[9] She suffered greatly from this revelation, but it did not spoil her good relations with the "parents" who had treated her so well. In the patrician home of the Basel physician, Gredlin was a ray of sunshine. She filled the role of daughter of the house, assuming all or part of the responsibility of running the household, just as Madlen had done for her father, Surgeon Jeckelmann.

Gredlin was getting on in years: she was twenty-seven at the turn of the seventeenth century. To complicate matters still further, she had taken a lover. Her "parents" adored her. They would have liked her to grow old with them, for she had served them faithfully. Perhaps they could have made a better match for her than she made for herself. Felix seems to have reproached himself to a certain extent on this score. In any event, Gredlin settled her own fate: she expressed her desire to marry Michel Ruedin, by whom she was pregnant. Felix and Madlen gave their consent in a joint decision that shows how important a role the doctor's wife had come to play in the family. In short, Gredlin's "mother and father," by this time almost seventy, agreed, in 1604, to a marriage of which they did not disapprove, even if it was not exactly what they would have wished. Michel Ruedin was of rural background and a tailor by trade. He took the Platters back to their peasant and artisan roots. The wedding took place in September 1604: Michel Ruedin married "Margret Simonin" at St. Peter's Church. Ruedin went on to a successful career, rising from tailor to cloth merchant. He was elected a member not only of the tailors' guild but also of the Saffron and the Key, the city's elite organizations. His father-in-law's influence may have had something to do with this, but Felix was already dead by the time the latter two nominations were made, and Ruedin's personal merits certainly played a part.

Michel and Gredlin had six children, all boys, in eight years. The first was of course already conceived at the time of the wedding, proof that the marriage was one of passion and perhaps part of the explanation for Felix's strangely reserved tone in writing about it. The Platters' relations with Gredlin remained warm, even though Hester Gross, who, after Thomas's death, had taken a tile- and brick-maker as her second husband, was apparently shocked by the "misbehavior" of a young woman of whom she had previously been so fond. Felix, however, remained as fond of the girl as ever, so fond, in fact, that he left her more than a thousand gulden in his will, an amount considerably larger than the dowry his wife had brought him in 1557. Even when we allow for the inflation of the intervening years and the considerable increase in the doctor's wealth, this was a substantial gift. What is more, Felix allowed Gredlin's eldest son to be named Felix, despite the fact that he was a love child. In forty years of medical practice, the great doctor had seen more than a few of those. His brother Thomas Jr. would even serve as godfather to another of Gredlin's sons, Michael, who became a surgeon like his "grandfather" Jeckelmann.

CHAPTER ELEVEN

Tomilin

T homas Jr. offered the Platters a second solution, another answer to
their irrepressible wish to have a child. Thomas Sr., widowed in
February 1572, married again in April. His new wife was Hester
Gross, aged twenty-five, the daughter of a Protestant pastor (from the
Valais, like Thomas himself) and of a schoolteacher from Little Basel by
the name of Maria Küeffer. Because her profession was the same as
Thomas's, Maria, recently widowed, had been invited to Felix's wedding
in November 1557. Thomas, in his seventies, had a number of children by
his second wife. Did this upset Felix, who could easily have worried
about being deprived of a portion of his father's inheritance? If so, he
soon got over it. Thomas, a rumbustious old fellow, fathered six children
in eight years: Magdalena Platter (born 1573), Thomas Jr. (1574), who, like
his father before him, was known as Tomilin, or "little Thomas," Ursula
(1575), Niklaus (1577), Anna (1579), and Elsbeth (1580). Finally, his demographic mission accomplished, Thomas Sr. was free to pass on, which he
did on January 26, 1582, at the age of eighty-two. The wedding torch became a funeral torch. Three of his daughters by his second marriage—
Ursula, Anna, and Elsbeth—followed him almost immediately into the
grave, victims of the plague that raged in Basel between June and October 1582. The eldest daughter, Magdalena, married a judge and lived to
the age of seventy-eight. When she died in 1661, she left a cookbook written in her own firm hand. Thomas and Hester's two sons, Thomas Jr. and
Niklaus, were respectively eight and five in 1582. The plague threatened
them too, of course. The prospect of losing two male Platters horrified
Felix: "May it please God to let some of the Platters live" (*Cuperem aliquos
Plateros conservari, si Deo placeret*).[1] In fairly blunt language the great doctor therefore wrote to his young stepmother, Hester, whom he called
Mutti, or "mother," urging her to send the boys to him for safekeeping.
She reluctantly complied, sending not only the boys but also their books
and clothing. She had good reason to accede, no matter how unwillingly,
to Felix's wishes, for she, too, was about to remarry. Shortly after the
death of her venerable husband, Hester left the enormous Platter home
on Freie Strasse, which henceforth stood empty and forlorn. She found

refuge in Little Basel, where she may have cared for her elderly mother, the schoolteacher. After only a few months of widowhood, she married Hans Lützelmann, a manufacturer of tile and bricks. With him she had a first child in the summer of 1583. Having soared for a time among the Basel intelligentsia (her father having being a clergyman and her mother and first husband both teachers), Hester returned to earth with her second marriage to a man who, as a brickmaker with his own business, belonged to a less prestigious but still prosperous group of artisans. As we have seen, she gave up her two sons from her first marriage to her stepson, the illustrious Basel physician, who cited the plague as a convenient pretext for asserting his authority over these scions of the Platter line. Felix gave the two boys rooms in his house and sent them to stay for brief periods at the home of a private tutor. Hester Lützelmann, as she was now called, kept up sporadic contact with her sons through the first decade of the seventeenth century, after which communication dwindled. Trampling on her rights as mother, Felix, who lacked a male heir, thus solved the problem in his own high-handed fashion. Who could resist such a powerful personage, a *pontifex maximus* of the University of Basel? Hester chose to cut her losses.

The good doctor was in fact bound and determined to transfer his double legacy—wealth and professional status—to one of his half-brothers, since he had no son. He had two choices: Thomas, thirty-eight years younger than Felix, and Niklaus, forty-one years younger. Felix's surrogate sons were young enough to have been his grandsons. In the matter of succession, Felix had something in common with the kings of France: after Louis X ("the Headstrong"), the crown went first to his brother Philip V ("the Long") and then to his other brother, Charles IV ("the Fair"); in the sixteenth century, Francis II was followed by Charles IX and Henri III, all three sons of Henri II. Much later, Louis XVI was eventually succeeded by his brothers Louis XVIII and Charles X. Three brothers thus succeeded one another three times in half a millennium of French monarchy: the third occurrence (Louis XVI to Charles X) was not, as it turned out, the lucky one.

Felix knew what he was doing, however. In 1590, he arranged for Thomas Jr., the heir apparent, to enter the University of Basel. Six years later, Thomas followed in his older brother's footsteps: in 1595 he went to study medicine at the University of Montpellier. Meanwhile, young Niklaus, Thomas's last surviving son, was kept in reserve. In 1595, using his influence as rector, Felix easily arranged for Niklaus to enroll at the university, just as he had done for Thomas Jr. His carefully laid plans soon went astray, however: Niklaus died of bloody diarrhea in 1597. Thomas

Jr., genuinely pained by the loss of his little brother, was now the only son still in the running to succeed Felix.

Thus for fifteen years, from 1582 to 1597, there were in effect three children in Dr. Platter's household: Gredlin, Thomas Jr., and Niklaus. Not bad for a couple with no children of their own! And for icing on the cake, yet another child transformed this trio into a quartet. In 1580, Felix lost his brother-in-law Daniel Jeckelmann, Madlen's brother. Like his father before him, Daniel had been a surgeon, as had his brother, Franz Jeckelmann Jr., who had died prematurely in 1565. Felix had always found Daniel a rather disagreeable relative, but he could commiserate when the surgeon lost two small daughters, Madelin and Esterlin, to the plague in 1563 (F 70). When Daniel died at a relatively early age in 1580, he was survived by two other children, one of whom was a daughter named Chrischona, named for her grandmother, Chrischona Jeckelmann, née Harscher, the wife of Franz Jeckelmann Sr.. The elder Chrischona also died young, in 1549. Obviously the Jeckelmanns were a conservative family when it came to the choice of a profession (all those surgeons) or a name (two Chrischonas, two Franzes, etc.).

When his brother-in-law died in 1580, Felix proved both generous and calculating. He took in little Chrischona, who was now practically an orphan, probably with the secret hope of marrying her off one day to Thomas Jr. Felix may not have had his father's surefootedness in the mountains, but he remained a Valaisian in his soul. Arranging marriages in the cradle had long been the custom in the Valais. The calculations of our provident Aesculapius[2] would ultimately turn out to have been quite shrewd. From the outset Chrischona got along famously with Madlen, now her de facto mother. Frau Platter, who took it upon herself to raise Chrischona, was of course actually the girl's aunt (the sister of the child's late father Daniel Jeckelmann). This foster-parenting arrangement also harked back to an old Valaisian custom, a response to the high adult mortality rate: Thomas Sr., whose father died when he was still quite young, had been raised by his aunt. Madlen, moreover, had nothing but praise for her young charge Chrischona, who honored, cherished, and obeyed her foster mother from 1580 to 1600. All that affection earned Chrischona a substantial bequest in Madlen's will. When Thomas Jr., soon to become a doctor of medicine, returned from Montpellier in 1602, he married his former playmate, a superb creature, as pleasant to look at as her husband was not. A portrait of her in the Dutch style has survived: it depicts her as a young Juno of radiant complexion with a ruff around her neck and a gold chain in her hands, the same chain that Felix had given his fiancée Madlen back in 1557, passed on from one couple to the next.

Thus Thomas Jr. followed almost exactly in his brother's footsteps a half century later. In both cases a young physician, soon to become a professor, married the daughter of a surgeon, and the surgeon's daughter in the second instance happened to be the niece (and ward) of the physician in the first. There was a family strategy at work here, to be sure, but also a professional strategy. Both marriages were made partly for love and partly by arrangement, and both joined the two key medical disciplines, the theoretical medicine of Hippocrates and Galen read in the original Greek (Platter) and the resolutely modern surgical anatomy of the great Vesalius (Jeckelmann).

* * *

From, broadly speaking, 1580 to 1600, Felix and Madlen thus enjoyed the privilege of four children in the house, two boys and two girls. Thomas Jr. and Gredlin were the oldest, Niklaus and Chrischona the youngest. The Platter children, being relatively close in age—their birth dates ranged from 1573 to 1577—formed a real community. Because of the high mortality rate in the early modern period, many families were broken up as children moved from foster home to foster home. But sometimes whole families were created out of fragments: in the best of cases, such as the one that interests us here, new families arose where death seemed to have left things in a shambles. In the case of Thomas Jr. and Chrischona, it was all the more remarkable that children could be so close yet not have a drop of blood in common, so that they could marry without concern for their future offspring, who proved to be healthy and numerous.

* * *

Surrounded by children and sumptuously housed at Zum Samson, the imposing residence that Felix acquired in 1574 and turned into one of the finest natural history museums in Europe, Madlen Platter should have been happy despite her inability to conceive children of her own. She had family, possessions, and wealth to compensate her for her loss. Felix had become one of the richest and most fashionable men in Basel. Her father-in-law, Thomas Sr., loved her as if she were his own daughter. And yet she suffered because she had no child that was physically hers. Her visit to the baths at Leuk in 1563 accomplished nothing, despite the reputed ability of the waters there to work miracles for women who wished to become pregnant.

Felix, though discreet on the subject, blamed his wife's frigidity: she was a sea of ice rather than a volcano. In his mind, the two afflictions were

related: his wife could not give birth, and she could not experience pleasure. It was widely believed at the time that the female orgasm was a guarantee of fertility. No one seems even to have entertained the possibility
that Felix might have been the cause of the couple's inability to conceive.
One wonders if he had any affairs and whether, on one of his medical
visits, he impregnated a mistress or fathered an illegitimate child. If we
knew, we could say with confidence that he was not the cause of the
couple's sterility, but we do not know. Nevertheless, the simple truth is
that Madlen blamed herself and suffered for it. She was an avid reader,
day and night, of the Lutheran Bible, of which she kept her own personal
copy. She identified with Sarah, Abraham's "barren" wife. Over and over
again she read the biblical passages describing Sarah's suffering (Genesis
16–23). Abraham blames Sarah for failing to produce children. He lies
with his servant Hagar, a Bedouin. Nature reasserts its dominion. Sarah,
jealous, drives Hagar into the desert, where she and her son Ishmael (the
ancestor of the Arabs) are aided by an angel. Later, Sarah, already old, is
visited by an incarnation of Yahweh in the form of three visitors who (in
Christian exegesis) prefigure the Holy Trinity. Subsequently, she too
gives birth to a son, in the fourth age (of the works of Abraham), a legitimate son, Isaac, whom the Lord uses to test Abraham's faith: the patriarch is about to obey an order to sacrifice his son when an angel stops
him. Between 1591 and 1594, Madlen, assisted by her ward and niece
Chrischona (both women being skilled embroiderers), created two tapestries illustrating the main themes of this biblical tale: the quarrel between Sarah and Hagar, the expulsion of Hagar, Hagar in the desert,
Ishmael saved by the angel, Abraham visited by the three "messengers
from God," and, finally, the aborted sacrifice of Isaac.

The reference to Genesis was explicitly indicated at the bottom of these
tapestries. The four evangelists appear in the corners of these works, thus
establishing a link between the Old and the New Testaments. Two *putti*
are depicted playing lutes, Felix's cherished instrument. The two tapestries reflect a whole aspect of Madlen's life, that of the dutiful wife subject
to the authority of the patriarch (1 Peter 3:6) and living in intimacy with
children not her own. Frau Platter's fears and jealousies were also evoked:
might not Felix, like Abraham, have taken a mistress in some nearby town
on one of his medical visits? The years during which the tapestries were
completed, 1591–94, coincided roughly with the time when Thomas Jr.,
the "outsider's" child added to the family in the manner of Ishmael, registered at the university (1591), took his baccalaureate (1593), and began
work on his master's degree (awarded in July 1595), all leading up to his
departure for Montpellier in September 1595. Toward the end of her life,

Madlen, who had been a "vivacious" (F 327) girl in the 1550s, returned, as
a bedridden matron, to the same biblical story of Abraham and his wife
and servant: she listened as a reader read the Bible and a minister sat by
the bedside to comfort her now that she could no longer go to the church
where, when her health was better, she had been active in the work of the
parish. And Frau Platter's obsession with the Old Testament tale did not
end there: at Madlen's express request, the eulogy pronounced over her
grave in 1613 compared her to Sarah and Felix to Abraham.

* * *

So Madlen, identified with Sarah, had lived a melancholy life. But what
about Felix-Abraham? He was the very embodiment of social success,
which for him was not very far from true happiness. The professor's life,
like that of his father before him, had placed him at the heart of the Renaissance and Reformation. The origins of the journey went all the way
back to the first decade of the sixteenth century, when Thomas, Felix's
father, was still an illiterate, "medieval" mountain lad in the Valais. With
remarkable zeal, however, he had immersed himself in the renascent cultures of Latin, Greek, and Hebrew. He had simultaneously discovered
Protestantism in its more brutal—iconoclastic and Zwinglian and later,
in Basel, Œcolampadian—forms. Although the identity crisis had been
short-lived, father and son never wavered from the path Luther had
blazed, even though both men, and especially Felix, considerably muted
the more aggressive aspects of the Swiss Reformation that had marked
them in youth. Felix saw a great deal of the humanist Castellion, an excellent conciliator, and he had visited the great "papist" churches of France
as if they were so many museums. Later, he paid medical visits to charming abbesses in the Rhineland, gracious women full of good humor.
These experiences left him anything but a fierce sectarian. He was, rather,
a man open to the varied lessons of an unprejudiced Christianity (and
even of Marrano Judaism). Yet at the center of his being he remained a
believer, rooted in the certitudes of the Protestant faith and the Lutheran
Bible.[3]

Did the Renaissance come to outweigh the Reformation in Felix's life?
It is not implausible to think so, if only because of the way he turned his
new house into a prodigious museum, filled with animals, minerals,
plants, and a whole host of ingredients that went into the medications he
prescribed for his patients. A student of Rondelet in Montpellier, himself
a disciple of the Italian naturalists, Felix began, as was only proper, with
the study of anatomy, which revealed a new inner universe, a prefigura-

tion of the intimate exploration of the body, human as well as animal, that became such a prominent feature of the Renaissance mentality. Felix prepared mouse skeletons for display (which greatly impressed his father-in-law Jeckelmann, by the way), and his exhibits included mammoth bones that he mistook for relics of a monstrous man nearly twenty feet tall. He also displayed the skeleton of a man who had been executed, whose cadaver Felix had personally dissected. The dead man's mother came from time to time to sit in sadness and contemplate her son's bones: it was a merciless century. Felix's museum also contained an herbarium of many volumes, whose pages displayed carefully selected specimens of plants from the Valais, Languedoc, and the Basel region. Thus Felix continued the ancient tradition of the herbalist Dioscorides, which had come down to him through the monks and apothecaries of the Middle Ages. His magnificently rich collections, amassed by an amateur but in many ways worthy of a professional, contained many other things as well: stones, both precious and nonprecious; seeds; insects; antiquities; stuffed crocodiles; guaiacum for "sweating out the pox"; moccasins and ponchos from the New World; Turkish, Chinese, and Japanese objects; antique vases; a large library; a garden of tulips and hyacinths; a lemon orchard, whose fruits were sold at good prices to German princes; American beans and corn; rabbits; pigeons, silkworms; a live elk, that kept the grass mowed and from which Felix derived medicines that amazed scientific Europe.

As a man of the Reformation (prudent despite his anticlericalism) and herald if not hero of the Renaissance, Felix also contributed to the Platter discovery of Europe. His father had explored Germany and Switzerland, the western part of Poland, and perhaps Hungary. Felix was more focused on western Germany and was also an indefatigable explorer of "Welch" territory. He became not only a francophile but also a francophone and even an "occitanophone," which only increased the pleasure he took in visiting France. His choices, freely made, thus ratified the anti-imperial, pro-German, and above all pro-Protestant foreign policy of the Valois monarchs. That policy had been conceived by Francis I, who, after Marignano, had been quick to negotiate a perpetual peace with the Swiss and to ally himself with Lutheran princes against the Hapsburgs. The first "contact" of this sort was in 1528 with Philip of Hesse, who became the French king's friend. Later, Henri II "positioned" himself to follow a similar line of action and thought. Henri, who was well respected in Basel, tried to involve German Protestant principalities in a system of alliances.

From Francis I to Louis XVI, in fact, a very "Platterian," very "Protestantophile" policy snakes its way like a giant sea serpent through the

murky history of the Ancien Régime. The objectives of this policy included not only the Germanic world but also the Netherlands and Great
Britain. After Henri II, it was carried on by Sully, Henri IV, and the
cardinal-ministers Richelieu, Mazarin, Dubois, and Fleury; Louis XIV,
of course, stands out as a major and unfortunate exception. This long-
standing positive French attitude toward Protestantism, this olive branch
held out to heresy, was something of which Thomas Platter Jr. could only
approve. His travels in Elizabeth's England and Henri IV's France in 1595
were in part a product of this cultural and diplomatic ecumenicism.

Benevolent spirits emanating from the Renaissance, the Reformation,
and an open, tolerant pan-European attitude toward education thus
watched over the destiny of the Platter clan. Those spirits rescued the
family from the Middle Ages or, at any rate, from what Marx not very
charitably called "the idiocy of rural life."[4] Beyond those benevolent
spirits, the positive genius of upward social mobility was also at work,
tugging at the shoulder of the printer-pedagogue and his son the doctor. Financially speaking, the transformation was palpable: Thomas Sr.
was buried in debt, whereas Felix, whose budgets were always in the
black, sometimes substantially so, lent far more than he borrowed. In
three-quarters of a century, the family went from misery in the Valais to
opulence in Basel. Even at the height of his success in northern Switzerland, Thomas the schoolmaster never recruited students beyond the
Swiss Alps and Upper Alsace. But Herr Professor Doktor Platter belonged to the medical elite that gathered around the dukes and princes of
Renaissance Germany. Such a remarkable ascent in so brief a time was
nothing short of miraculous. But it was an ascent with one indispensable
prerequisite: each generation had to produce an heir. In continuing the
Platter line, the great doctor was thus essentially a surrogate father. He
served as parent to a quartet of children: two boys young enough to be
his grandsons; Gredlin, almost a foundling; and Chrischona Jeckelmann,
his very affectionate homebody of a niece. His wife, Madlen, suffered in
the paradoxical role of "barren mother." Felix played the hand he was
dealt. He did indeed act as father to this brood, far more of a father than
some men whose only claim to the title is chromosomal. Gredlin, in particular, looked upon Felix as her authentic parent, an honor she long refused to bestow on Benedict Simon, the peasant-soldier who was her
biological progenitor.

In 1544, in the city of Bourges, which Thomas Sr.'s son would visit a
few years later, residents cast themselves in the surrogate father role when
they hailed the birth of their future king, Francis II, with a triumphal
festival of bonfires, Corpus-Christi-like processions, high masses,

chanted prayers, *Te Deums,* farces, morality plays, pastry, drinking, and cannonades. To justify their claim to collective paternity, the citizens of Bourges quoted a verse from Isaiah (9:6) in the Latin of the Vulgate: *Puer natus est nobis et filius datus est nobis.*[5] As an avid reader of the Old Testament, Felix had had many occasions to meditate upon the question of nongenetic filiation. How could he not have thought of this passage from Isaiah when he took Thomas Jr. and Niklaus into his house? Or again in 1595, when Thomas Jr. left for Montpellier, spreading his wings in a way that made his older brother—his "father" if you will—proud?[6] Or yet again, in 1605, when another Felix, the aptly named love child and firstborn of Gredlin, came into the world, soon followed, one after another, by five little brothers born between 1607 and 1613? Or in 1602, 1605, *et cetera,* when the marriage of Thomas Jr. to Chrischona produced Felix Platter Jr., Felix Platter III, Thomas Platter III, and Franz Platter? (Neither the Platters nor the Jeckelmanns had much imagination when it came to first names. Like many other people at the time, they generally drew on the two previous generations' "onomastic stock.")

All these "blessed events" preceded the death of Dr. Felix Platter in 1614. The family's continued presence in the medical profession was now assured for more than a century.[7] Just as the passage from Isaiah had come immediately to the minds of the citizens of Bourges in 1544, it had also occurred to Felix on each of these happy occasions. He found it easily in Luther's translation of the Bible, which he always kept within reach: *Denn uns ist ein Kind geboren, ein Sohn ist uns gegeben . . . Und er heisst wunderbar . . . Ewigvater.* (The King James version is: "For unto us a child is born, unto us a son is given . . . and his name shall be called Wonderful . . . The Everlasting Father.") Now, as the reign of Henri IV, the Swiss cantons' cordial neighbor to the west, drew to a close, the Platter trajectory—now in the seventeenth century no longer astonishing, as it had been in the Renaissance, but simply noteworthy—was firmly mapped out: the baton had been passed, through Felix, from Thomas Sr. to Thomas Jr., from true father to true son. And so, now visible but as through a glass darkly, the long sixteenth century drew to a close: a century of folly and glory, of imbecility and greatness, in love with darkness but even more in love with light.

NOTES

CHAPTER ONE

1. Cf. the claim that mineral waters can make women "fertile": Janine Garrisson, *Marguerite de Valois* (Paris: Fayard, 1994), p. 228.

2. The Platters used the term "Welches" to refer to Latins generally, whether Venetians or French, north or south European.

3. In the Valais and in French Switzerland as in east-central and southern France in the fourteenth to sixteenth centuries, a "castellan" was often only an officer of low to high rank charged by local authorities with keeping watch, in a military or nonmilitary sense, on a castle, for the purpose of ensuring the security of the surrounding countryside. Hence the word "castellan" should not necessarily be taken to be imply any sense of aristocratic grandeur.

4. Grächen was a highland hamlet of a few dozen houses on the north slope of the southern chain of Upper Valaisian Alps, more than an hour's walk from Saint-Niclaus, a village also situated above the valley of the Mattervisp (1,121 meters altitude).

5. The German *Stein* (stone) is *lithos* in Greek.

CHAPTER TWO

1. The use of horns for nursing was common in this "remote" era. See the catalogue of the show "L'enfance au Moyen Age" at the Bibliothèque Nationale (Autumn-Winter 1994).

2. Matthaëus Schiner (1465–1522) had been bishop of Sitten (Sion) since 1499. He was elevated to cardinal in 1511.

3. Emmanuel Le Roy Ladurie and Orest Ranum, eds., *Pierre Prion, scribe. Mémoires d'un écrivain de campagne au XVIIIe siècle* (Paris: Gallimard, 1985), p. 48.

4. Emmanuel Le Roy Ladurie, "Gavet," *L'Histoire* (March 1979), no. 10.

5. Matthäus Schwarz of Augsburg, though of bourgeois background, also took to the road for several seasons while he was still a small child: see Philippe Braunstein, ed., *Un banquier mis à nu* (Paris: Gallimard, 1992).

6. Norman Davies, *God's Playground: A History of Poland* (New York: Columbia University Press, 1982).

7. A city that would belong to Saxony and later to Prussia.

8. Ernest Lavisse, *Histoire générale* (Paris: Armand Colin, 1894), vol. 4, p. 398.

9. On what follows, see Philippe Dollinger, *Documents sur l'Histoire de l'Alsace* (Toulouse: Privat, 1972), pp. 176ff., and, more generally, the chapters on the Renaissance in Jean-Jacques Hatt, *Histoire de l'Alsace* (Toulouse: Privat, 1970), pp. 190 ff.

10. Jean Châtillon and Pierre Debongnie, *"Devotio moderna,"* in M. Viller and

Charles Baumgartner, eds., *Dictionnaire de spiritualité* (Paris: Beauchesne, 1957), vol. 2, pp. 714–747.

11. Hatt, *Histoire de l'Alsace*, pp. 190 ff.

12. François Furet and Jacques Ozouf, *Lire et écrire* (Paris: Editions de Minuit, 1977), vol. 1, pp. 199 ff.

13. Michel Fize, *La Démocratie familiale, évolution des relations parents-adolescents* (Paris: Presses de la Renaissance, 1990). The quoted passage is taken from advertising for the book, in which the author summarizes one of its central themes.

14. On these controversial matters, see J.-V. Pollet, *Huldrych Zwingli* (Paris: Vrin, 1988), pp. 15 ff., 341, and passim.

15. Peter Brown, *The Cult of the Saints* (Chicago: The University of Chicago Press, 1981).

16. On iconoclasm, see Olivier Christin, *Une révolution symbolique, l'iconoclasme huguenot et la reconstruction catholique* (Paris: Editions de Minuit, 1991); Robert Sauzet, in *Revue d'histoire de l'Eglise de France*, vol. 66 (1980), pp. 5–15; and Solange Deyon and Alain Lottin, *Les Casseurs de l'été 1566. L'iconoclasme dans le Nord* (Paris: Hachette, 1981). For a general overview, see the brilliant and profound book of Alain Besançon, *L'Image interdite* (Paris: Fayard, 1994).

17. See the catalogue from the major show at the Louvre, *Sculptures allemandes de la fin du Moyen Age* (Paris: RMN, 1992).

18. This was shortly before the Baden conference (see below), which took place in May 1526 (T 159).

19. Thomas pinpoints the exact moment (T 74, 161) when he emerged from poverty (*armut*) to the point where he was able to count on eating a snack (*zuymbiss*) every day: it coincides with the period described here, when he became the tutor of the two sons of the Zwinglian miller and city councillor Heinrich Werdmüller; the boys later went on to careers in religion and teaching. For some time thereafter, Thomas still occasionally ate "sick meat" with a certain rope-maker, but on the whole his life of poverty was over. This change marks a major psychological and existential turning point in the biography of the boy from the Valais.

20. Alain Belmont, in his recent (unpublished) thesis on "L'Artisanat à Grenoble du XVIe au XVIIIe siècle," gives abundant details concerning such problems of apprenticeship in Alpine and sub-Alpine regions.

21. Stähelin was a native of Swabia (a German province), and Swabians had the reputation of being rather crude.

22. See T 80 and Dollinger, *Histoire d'Alsace*, p. 194.

23. Emile G. Leonard, *Histoire générale du protestantisme* (Paris: Presses Universitaires de France, 1961), vol. 1, p. 140; and *Basler Chronik*, first published 1765, reprinted in 1883, pp. 396–418 (see bibliography).

24. S. Coignard, "Scènes de ménage," *Le Point*, 7 (December 1991).

25. The same "dreamlike or miraculous savior" occurs in the folklore of other mountainous regions in Scotland, the Chartreuse, and the Belledonne.

26. The first was at the time of his initial "schooling," the second when he was staying with the mother of Rudolfus Gwalterus.

27. And not in 1529 as stated in F 50.

28. Andreae Vesalii, *De humani corporis fabrica libri septem* (Basel: [Oporinus],

1543). For a recent edition, see *La Fabrique du corps humain* (Paris: IN-SERM/Actes Sud, 1987); Pierre Huard published a selected iconography with R. Dacosta in 1980.

29. This Cellarius is not to be confused with another Cellarius, Professor Isaac Keller (F 169, and below, chap. 10).

30. Hence she must have been born in the spring of 1530. A recent edition of Felix Platter's memoirs erroneously put her birth in 1529 (F 50). The same edition correctly fixes the time of Thomas and Anna's marriage, however, in the summer of 1529.

31. The epidemic of 1531 is not mentioned in Jean-Noël Biraben, *Les Hommes et la peste* (Paris: Mouton, 1975), vol. 1, p. 411. But Biraben notes that the "disease that sows terror" did afflict Geneva in 1528, 1529, and 1530. The outbreak of the disease in 1531 was probably a vestige of these earlier epidemics, whose germs still lurked on Swiss soil.

32. Yves-Marie Bercé, *Histoire des croquants. Etude des soulèvements populaires en France au XVIIe siècle* (Geneva: Droz, 1974).

33. Biraben, *Les Hommes et la peste,* vol. 1, chronological tables for 1538.

Chapter Three

1. R. J. Knecht, *Francis the First* (Cambridge, England: Cambridge University Press, 1982), pp. 224–25.

2. Playing with wooden or other "mock" horses had been a major recreation of children since the Middle Ages. Did this interest in horses suggest a fascination with the "equestrian" life of the nobility? See the Bibliothèque Nationale exhibition on childhood in the Middle Ages, cited earlier.

3. Lucien Febvre would have found interesting material here for understanding the irrational outlook of certain sixteenth-century writers: see his *Problème de l'incroyance au XVIe siècle: La religion de Rabelais,* 1942 (reprinted Paris: Albin Michel, 1968), p. 408, translated by Beatrice Gottlieb as *The Problem of Unbelief in the Sixteenth Century: The Religion of Rabelais* (Cambridge, Mass.: Harvard University Press, 1982).

4. Many cities in Western Europe had proud military traditions. This old Swiss tradition of crossbow competitions was later revived in the federal shooting matches.

5. The second Margretlin. Recall that the first died in 1531, before Felix was born.

6. Recall that Felix was also told that snow flakes were really old women. On the question of adoption, see the penultimate chapter of this book.

7. Duc d'Aumale (Henri d'Orléans), *Histoire des princes de Condé* (Paris: Lévy, 1863), vol. 2, p. 112.

8. For more of the same, see F 64, 295, 379.

9. Thomas uses the word *Sod* for well, and Felix (F 69) uses *Sodtbrunnen,* both of which imply that the water was slightly carbonated.

10. Income from interest accounted for 29,296 of the 118,669 pounds of monetary income he received from all sources, including his medical practice, between 1558 and 1612 (F 531–533).

11. Felix's memoirs are more chronologically precise than Thomas's. Felix, educated from early childhood, was in the habit of writing down dates. He also

marked calendars, which have been intelligently studied by the editor of his memoirs, Valentin Lötscher, who has been able to provide important dates concerning his relatives and friends.

12. "La musicologie au CNRS," *CNRS-Info,* June 1991.

13. Anne Chattaway, "La Musique dans le journal intime et les écrits de H. F. Amiel," master's thesis presented to the UER de Lettres Modernes of the Université de Toulouse-Le-Mirail, October 1985.

14. Hartmut Boockmann, Michael Stürmer et al., *Mitten in Europa. Deutsche Geschichte* (Berlin: Siedler, 1984), pp. 132 ff.

15. Ibid., p. 135.

16. Ibid.

17. *Limes:* the northern and eastern border of the Roman Empire, where it came into contact with the territory of the Germanic tribes.

18. F. Mote and Dennis Twitchett, *The Ming Dynasty,* vol. 7 of Dennis Twitchett and John K. Fairbank, eds., *The Cambridge History of China* (Cambridge, England: Cambridge University Press, 1988), chap. 8.

19. Olivier de Serres, *Théâtre d'agriculture* (Grenoble: Dardelet, 1973), book 8, chap. 2.

20. Fernand Braudel, *Civilisation matérielle, économie et capitalisme* (Paris: Armand Colin, 1979), vol. 1, p. 192.

21. When the Platters visited Thomas's native village in June 1563, they were greeted with the same (purely conventional) invocation of the devil, signifying an unwelcome guest (see above, chap. 1).

22. *In partibus* because she actually died in 1549, several years before Felix's marriage to her daughter Madlen in 1557.

23. Madeleine Foisil, *Le Journal de Jean Héroard* (Paris: Fayard, 1989), vol. 1, pp. 75 ff.

24. Olivier de Serres, *Théâtre d'agriculture* (Grenoble: Dardelet, 1973), book 1, chap. 6, p. 47.

25. On this sort of "typological" interpretation, see Catherine Maire, "La trajectoire janséniste au XVIIIe siècle," *Annales ESC* (September–October 1991), pp. 1177–1205; and idem, *Les Convulsionnaires de Saint-Médard* (Paris: Gallimard, 1985).

26. See the catalogue of the Louvre exhibition *Art allemand de la fin du Moyen Age,* November 1991–January 1992 (Paris: RMN, 1992).

27. Felix refers in his memoirs to Covet's heirs, hence he must have written this passage after Covet died in January 1608 (F 86).

28. On this practice, common in both Catholic and Protestant cities at the time, see Ulysse Chevalier, *Mystère des Trois Doms, du chanoine Pra, [joué] en 1509 à Romans* (Lyons, 1887).

29. See Emmanuel Le Roy Ladurie and Jean-François Fitou, "Notes sur la population saint-simonienne," in *Résumé des cours et travaux du Collège de France* (Paris: Collège de France, 1989–1990), pp. 699–728.

30. On the impure and even scatological connotations of money according to certain (Freudian) theories, see Serge Viderman, *De l'argent en psychanalyse et au-delà* (Paris: Presses Universitaires de France, 1992), pp. 7 ff.; and Saint-Simon, *Mémoires,* ed. Boislile (Paris, 1885), vol. 5, pp. 422–23.

31. When a similar fire broke out in Montpellier (see below, chap. 6), Felix

seized the opportunity to compare the corporate solidarity of the citizens of Basel to the extreme individualism of the people of Montpellier.

32. Pierre Chevallier, *Louis XIII* (Paris: Fayard, 1979), p. 98.

33. On the Carnival as an implicit Christian holiday, a "burial of pagan life" in preparation for Lent and a festival marked by dancing, feasting, and satire, see my *Carnaval in Romans,* trans. Mary Feeney (New York: Braziller, 1979), and Michel Feuillet, *Le Carnaval* (Paris: Editions du Cerf, 1991). Feuillet's analyses are quite intelligent despite his minimal bibliography. Evidently the Protestant assault on the Carnival as a pagan festival had not yet begun in this region north of Basel. Indeed, the tenacious festival was thought of as a satirical weapon against the Roman Church, which remained powerful in the region. The Basel Carnival is still an important event to this day.

34. See, for example, the diary of Samuel Pepys, passim.

35. We saw earlier that he once treated a sculptor who had been his enemy.

36. The word *Beruf* in this sense appears for the first time in German in Luther's biblical translation of Ecclesiasticus, chap. 11: *beharre in deinem Beruf, bleib in deinem Beruf.* See also Max Weber, *The Protestant Ethic and the Spirit of Capitalism,* chap. 1, part 3.

CHAPTER FOUR

1. Cratander's Plautus was printed in September 1523, hence Thomas could not have worked in the rope shop before that date.

2. The touchingly possessive words of Ruch's wife upon learning of Thomas's knockout punch are worth quoting: *O we, du hast mier min man zu todt geschlagen!* (Woe is me! You've beaten my husband to death!)

3. Platter (T 122) calls Ruch and his other partner, Winter, by their first names, Balthasar and Ruprecht, but he always respectfully refers to Johannes Herbster using the Greco-Latin honorific "Oporinus."

4. The period 1524–26 is important for an accurate chronology of Thomas Platter's years of apprenticeship. Collinus became an apprentice ropemaker on May 23, 1524 (T 162). Then, after a brief stint of military service in Wurtemberg, he opened a ropemaking shop on February 23, 1526. Hence Thomas's apprenticeship with Collinus must have begun after that date.

5. A copy of the first edition, in Latin and printed by Thomas Platter with a date of 1536, can be found in the Bibliothèque Nationale.

6. *Ring = gering* (T 123).

7. This text should finally convince skeptics reluctant to admit that Mainz was the birthplace of printing.

8. This information is taken from Albert Brückner, *Schweizer Stempelschneider und Schriftgiesser* (Basel, 1943), p. 42 and passim.

9. Much of this is based on Valentin Lötscher, "Felix Platter und seine Familie," *Helbing, Basler Nejahrsblatt* 153(1975):63 ff.

10. The reader may wish to compare Platter's activities with those of his contemporary, the Sire de Gouberville: see Robillard de Beaurepaire, ed., *Le Journal [rural] du sire de Gouberville* (Caen: Delesques, 1892).

11. *Histoire de la France urbaine* (Paris: Seuil, 1980), vol. 1, pp. 15–16.

12. Knecht, *Francis the First,* p. 367.

13. Felix Platter also split his time later on, indeed more so than Thomas and

Oporinus, devoting part of each day to work as a physician, pharmacist, and surgeon.

14. Lötscher, "Felix Platter und seine Familie," p. 26.

15. Ibid., pp. 82–83.

16. Ibid., pp. 46 ff.

17. Thomas's moving letter about his daughter's death was published by Alfred Hartmann in *Basilea latina* (Basel, 1931). See T 139, 179.

18. See also Lötscher, "Felix Platter und seine Familie," pp. 27 ff.

19. Ibid., pp. 81 ff.

20. Ibid., p. 40.

21. At times Anna Dietschi-Platter could also be quite mean-spirited: "After our return home [to the Valais for a brief visit prior to the birth of Margretlin I], Anna was delighted [*fro*]," Thomas tells us, "because the priest had come down with the plague" (T 92). Was the difference of religion the only reason for her jubilation?

CHAPTER FIVE

1. Danielle Anex-Cabanis et al., *Histoire de Laussane* (Toulouse: Privat, 1982).

2. Paul Guichonnet et al., *Histoire de Genève* (Toulouse: Privat, 1974). See also René Guerdan, *Genève au temps de Calvin* (Geneva: Editions du Mont-Blanc, 1977); idem, *Histoire de Genève* (Paris: Mazarine, 1981); and idem, *La Vie quotidienne à Genève au temps de Calvin* (Paris: Hachette, 1973); Anne-Marie Piuz, *L'Éco-nomie genevoise de la Réforme* (Geneva: Georg, 1990); and above all J.-F. Bergier, *Les Foires de Genève: Genève et l'économie européenne de la Renaissance* (Paris: SEVPEN, 1963).

3. The history of Savoy has been treated in many works, some of them quite remarkable. Among those I have used, let me mention works by Roland Edighoffer (Paris: Presses Universitaires de France, 1992) and especially Paul Guichonnet (Toulouse: Privat, 1973); J.-P. Leguay (Rennes: Ouest-France, 1983); Henri Menabréa (Chambéry: IRC, 1970); V. de Saint-Genis (Marseilles: Lafitte, 1978); A. Perrin (Chambéry, 1900); and of course the important thesis of Jean Nicolas, *La Savoie* (Paris: Maloine, 1978), 2 vols.

4. A Guilbert, *Histoire des villes de France* (Paris: Furne et Perrotin, 1848), vol. 5, p. 122.

5. G. de Bombourg, *Histoire de Nantua et de son abbaye* (Nantua, 1858), p. 156.

6. Olivier de Serres, *Théâtre d'agriculture* (Grenoble: Dardelet, 1973), book 6, chap. 26.

7. I use this word in its modern sense to mean the midday meal.

8. This town is located in the Bourg-en-Bresse district of the canton of Montluel in the department of the Ain.

9. Richard Gascon, *Lyon et ses marchands* (Paris-The Hague: Mouton, 1971), vol. 2, p. 838.

10. In those days *officiers* (or officeholders) were mainly civilian, with a smaller number of military officers.

11. Jules Michelet, *Histoire de France, Renaissance et Réforme,* book 2, chap. 12, and book 3, chap. 2.

12. Frederic J. Baumgartner, *Henri II, King of France* (Duke: Duke University Press, 1988). In French, there is Ivan Cloulas, *Henri II* (Paris: Fayard, 1985).

13. Michelet, *Histoire de France,* book 3: *Guerres de Religion,* chap. 3. The truth of Michelet's assertions, often dubious, is inversely proportional to the remarkable quality of his style, at least so far as Henri II is concerned.

14. See A. Kleinclausz, *Histoire de Lyon* (Marseilles: Laffitte Reprints, 1978); J. Rossiaud, F. Bayard et al., *Histoire de Lyon* (Saint-Etienne: Horvath, 1990); and A. Latreille, ed., *Histoire de Lyon et du Lyonnais* (Toulouse: Privat, 1975). See also Guillaume Paradin, *Histoire de Lyon* (1573), reprinted (Roanne: Horvath, 1973), and the amusing Françoise Bayard, *Histoire de Lyon en bande dessinée* (Roanne: Horvath, 1978). And do not forget the admirable Richard Gascon, *Lyon et ses marchands,* which was cited earlier.

15. Frank Lestringant, the eminent Renaissance historian, sees this march to execution as an allusion to Christ's climb up Calvary Hill.

16. See Heinrich Pantaleon, *Heldenbuch, Prosopographiae heroum* (Basel, 1565–70), vol. 3, pp. 326–29.

17. Gascon, *Lyon,* vol. 1, p. 385.

18. Ibid., vol. 1, p. 186.

19. Ibid. and F 146.

20. Gascon, *Lyon,* vol. 1, p. 170.

21. An enlargement of a later (seventeenth- or eighteenth-century) engraving of these boatwomen is displayed on the main staircase of the Ecole Supérieure des Bibliothèques near Lyons.

22. Michel François, *Le Cardinal François de Tournon* (Paris: Editions De Boccard, 1951), p. 288.

23. Louis Dulieu, "Guillaume Rondelet," *Clio medica* (1966), vol. 1, pp. 89–111.

24. BN, ms. lat. 8647, fol. 15.

25. B. Bligny, *Histoire du Dauphiné* (Toulouse: Privat, 1973), p. 200. See also Jean Boudon, *Histoire du Dauphiné* (Lyons: Horvath, 1992), and Paul Dreyfus, *Histoire du Dauphiné* (Paris: Presses Universitaires de France, 1972).

26. See the map of sixteenth-century Vienne, with various detail views, in Pierre Cavard, *Le Procès de Michel Servet à Vienne* (Vienne: Blanchard, 1953); Thomas Mermet, *Histoire de Vienne* (Paris: Res Universis, 1992); André Pelletier, *Histoire de Vienne* (Roanne: Horvath, 1980).

27. René Favrier, *Les Villes du Dauphiné aux XVIIe et XVIIIe siècles* (Grenoble: Presses Universitaires de Grenoble, 1993).

28. Now the Collège de France.

29. Henri Busson, *Les Sources et le développement du rationalisme dans la littérature française de la Renaissance* (Paris: Letouzey, 1920), pp. 70–94.

30. On Pierre Danès, see Mireille Forget, *Humanisme et Renaissance,* 1936, pp. 365 ff., and 1937, pp. 59 ff. In addition to the works of Danès, who was an apologist for Valois foreign policy, the reader may wish to consult the biography written by his great-grandnephew Pierre-Hilaire Danès, *Abrégé de la vie de Pierre Danès* (Paris: Quillau, 1731).

31. Favier, *Les Villes du Dauphine,* part 1; Albert Caise, "Le registre baptistaire de Saint-Vallier, 1568–1575," *Bulletin de la Société d'archéologie et de statistique de la Drôme* (Valence, 1892), pp. 5 ff.

32. E. Fayard, *Notice historique sur Saint-Vallier* (Lyons: Georg, 1894); see also Albert Caise, *Cartulaire de Saint-Vallier* (Paris-Valence, 1870), pp. 73 (on the influence of Diane de Poitiers, who was born into a family from the region).

33. Caise, "Le registre," pp. 14–15. See also H.-E. Martin, *Paroisses et communes de France. Drôme* (Paris: Centre National de Recherche Scientifique, 1981), p. 494.

34. See T 2–47; see also Catherine Velay-Vallantin, *L'Histoire des contes* (Paris: Fayard, 1992), pp. 30–59.

35. Dominique Julia and Jacques Revel, eds., *Les Universités européennes du XVIe siècle au XVIIIe siècle. Histoire sociale des populations étudiantes* (Paris: Ecole des Hautes Etudes en Sciences Sociales, 1989), vol. 2, p. 486.

36. Abbé Joseph-Cyprien Nadal, *Histoire de l'université de Valence* (Valence: Marc-Aurel, 1861).

37. René Favier, *Les Villes du Dauphiné aux XVIIe et XVIIIe siècles* (Grenoble: Presses Universitaires de Grenoble, 1993); see also Abbé A. Vincent, *Notice historique sur Livron* (Valence: Marc-Aurel, 1853), pp. 24 and passim.

38. Victor Cassien and Alexandre Debelle, *Album du Dauphiné* (Grenoble: Editions des Quatre Seigneurs, 1978), vol. 4, p. 78.

39. Cassien and Debelle, *Album du Dauphiné,* vol. 4, p. 126; Rodolphe Bringer, "Le siège de Pierrelatte," *Le Bassin du Rhône* (Montélimar, 1910), no. 10, pp. 231–35; A. Lacroix, *L'Arrondissement de Montélimar* (Valence: Combier et Nivoche, 1888), vol. 7, pp. 74 ff.; Adolphe Rochas, *L'Abbaye joyeuse de Pierrelatte* (Grenoble: Drevet, 1881), pp. 13 ff.

40. Emmanuel Le Roy Ladurie, *Les Paysans de Languedoc* (Paris: SEVPEN, 1966), pp. 201–3, and *Histoire de Montélimar* (Toulouse: Privat, 1993).

41. Joseph-Antoine Bastet, *Histoire de la ville et de la principauté d'Orange* (Orange: Raphel, 1856), reprinted (Marseilles: Lafitte, 1977), and idem, *Essai historique sur les évêques du diocèse d'Orange* (Orange: Escoffier, 1837), and *Notice historique sur Orange,* 1840; Roland Sicard, *Paroisses et communes de France. Vaucluse* (Paris: Centre National de Recherche Scientifique, 1987), p. 183.

42. Sylvain Ganière et al., *Histoire d'Avignon* (La Calade: Edisud, 1979); Henri Dubled, *Histoire du Comtat Venaissin* (Villelaure: Credel, 1982); and especially the essential work by Marc Venard, *Réforme protestante, Réforme catholique dans la province d'Avignon au XVIe siècle* (Paris: Cerf, 1993).

43. On the general phenomenon of scapegoating as it relates to the particular phenomenon of anti-Semitism, see the important work of Yves Chevalier, *L'Antisémitisme* (Paris: Cerf, 1988), pp. 99–182.

44. See Emmanuel Le Roy Ladurie, *Paris-Montpellier* (Paris: Gallimard, 1982).

45. See C. Devic and J. Vaissette, *Histoire générale de Languedoc* (Toulouse: Privat, 1889), vol. 11, pp. 294 ff., and, in Emmanuel Le Roy Ladurie, *Paysans de Languedoc* (Paris: SEVPEN, 1966), the chapters dealing with the sixteenth century.

46. Hubert Gautier, *Histoire de la ville de Nîmes* (Paris-Nîmes, 1724), p. 59; a modern (1991) reprint is available from C. Lacour in Nîmes.

47. Gautier, *Histoire,* p. 61.

48. T2 106 and Gautier, *Histoire,* p. 61.

49. Raymond Huard, ed., *Histoire de Nîmes* (Aix-en-Provence: Edisud, 1992).

50. Léon Ménard, *Histoire civile, ecclésiastique et littéraire de la ville de Nîmes* (Paris: Ch. Aubert, 1753), vol. 4, pp. 205–23, reprinted in Marseilles in 1975 by Lafitte.

51. There were 5,000 inhabitants in the first half of the fourteenth century; 1370: 725 hearths; 1693: 540 hearths; 1698: 624 hearths; 1709: 664 hearths; 1740: 2,400

residents; 1766: 664 hearths. These figures are taken from Claude Motte et al., *Paroisses et communes de France. Hérault* (Paris: Centre National de Recherche Scientifique, 1989), p. 257; Roger Imbert and Jean Baille, *Lunel et son passé* (Lunel: Peis, 1989): Th. Millerot, *Histoire de la ville de Lunel depuis son origine jusqu'en 1789* (Montpellier, 1881); Abbé A. Rouet, *Notice sur la ville de Lunel au Moyen Age et vie de saint Gérard, seigneur de cette ville au XIIIe siècle* (Montpellier, 1878); E. Rouet, *Essai sur la topographie physique et médicale de Lunel* (Montpellier, 1822) (thesis in medicine).

52. Of course these young people wearing white masks and costumes may have represented or symbolized a procession of ghosts from the Land of the Dead connected with Toussaint or the Day of the Dead. See Carlo Ginzburg, *The Night Battles: Witchcraft and Agrarian Cults in the Sixteenth and Seventeenth Centuries,* trans. John and Anne Tedesch: (Baltimore: Johns Hopkins University Press, 1983). But this would be hard to prove, and in any case this flirtatious, elitist procession shows that what may originally have been a macabre event had been tamed by the forces of social integration, just as the more unbridled aspects of the Carnival were tamed: see Maria Isaura Pereira de Queiroz, *Carnaval brésilien* (Paris: Gallimard, 1992). On all this, see Arnold Van Gennep, *Manuel de folklore français contemporain* (Paris: A. and J. Picard), tome 1, vol. 6, part 4, pp. 2808 ff. Compare D. Fabre, *Carnaval* (Paris: Gallimard, 1992).

53. The bibliography at the end of this volume contains a list of works on Montpellier in the sixteenth century.

CHAPTER SIX

1. Felix Platter's Montpellier publisher (Coulet, 1892, p. 34) confused Marranos with Moors! The same egregious error can be found in Mark Musa's "bilingual" edition of Machiavelli's *Prince* (New York: St. Martin's Press, 1964), chap. 24, pp. 184–85, where *Marrani* is translated as "Moors."

2. Louis Dulieu, *La Médecine à Montpellier,* vols. 1 and 2 (Lille: Presses Universelles, 1975 and 1979). See also the bibliography concerning Montpellier at the end of this volume.

3. See Le Roy Ladurie, *Paysans de Languedoc,* 1966 edition, vol. 3, graphs on p. 1020.

4. Du Chatel's reputation as a womanizer would follow him, for good reason, all the way to the court of the Valois, where he served, at the height of his career, as royal physician. See Brantôme, *Recueil des Dames* (Paris: Gallimard, 1991), p. 480.

5. Recall that Saint Luke, whose feast day is October 18, is the patron saint of physicians. See Benedictines of Paris, *Vie des saints et des bienheureux* (Paris: Letouzey, 1952), pp. 594–600, for the month of October.

6. See the catalogue of the exhibition at the Bibliothèque Nationale entitled *Des livres et des rois,* edited by M.-P. Laffitte and Ursula Baurmeister (Paris: Editions du Quai Voltaire and Bibliothèque Nationale, 1992), a fundamental work.

7. Dulieu, *La Médecine à Montpellier,* vol. 2; Charles Lichtenthaeler, *Histoire de la médecine* (Paris: Fayard, 1978).

8. Pierre Riché, *Gerbert d'aurillac, pape de l'an mil* (Paris: Fayard, 1987), p. 192.

9. Gilles de Gouberville, *Journal,* ed. Bricquebosz (Pont de Neuville: Les Editions des Champs, 1993), vol. 2, pp. 281 ff., July 16 and July 18–22, 1556.

10. On apocalyptic beliefs among French Catholics in the sixteenth century, see Denis Crouzet, *Les Guerriers de Dieu* (Champ-Vallon: Seyssel, 1990), part 1.

11. This painting was on display at the show "Paysages, paysans" at the Bibliothèque Nationale in the spring of 1994. See the reproduction in the show catalogue, Emmanuel Le Roy Ladurie, ed., *Paysages, paysans* (Paris: Bibliothèque Nationale-RMN, 1994). See also Emmanuel Le Roy Ladurie, *Etat royal* (Paris: Hachette, 1987), pp. 56–57.

12. This adoption was de facto, not necessarily de jure.

13. Lötscher, the editor of Felix Platter's memoirs, misinterprets the words *deigade* and *aiguade,* which for some reason he confuses with the French for "decant."

14. Blaise de Monluc, *Commentaires* (Paris: Renouard, 1872), vol. 1, pp. 440, 466; vol. 2, pp. 66, 67; vol. 4, p. 43. Here the leader of the landsknechts is referred to as Rinckrock.

15. Machiavelli, *The Prince,* chap. 7: execution of Remirro de Orca.

16. The word *ortalisse* or *ourtalis* was commonly used for garden on sixteenth-century Languedocian cadasters. See Frédéric Mistral, *Trésor du félibrige,* art. *ourtalis.*

17. See Didier Gazagnadou, *La Poste à relais* (Paris: Kimé, 1994).

Chapter Seven

1. G. Saumade, *Fabrègues* (Montpellier: L'Abeille Workers' Cooperative, 1908).

2. Jean Sagnes, *Histoire de Béziers* (Toulouse: Privat, 1986).

3. See Alain Molinier, "De la religion des oeuvres à la réformation dans les Cévennes," *Revue d'histoire de l'Eglise de France,* vol. 72, 1986, pp. 258–59.

4. Sagnes, *Histoire de Béziers,* p. 106.

5. Ibid., pp. 42, 64, 203.

6. Gilles Caster, *Le Commerce du pastel et de l'épicerie à Toulouse de 1450 environ à 1561* (Toulouse: Privat, 1962).

7. The first black slaves destined for sugar and other plantations were exported from Portugal to Brazil in 1559. See Katia M. de Queiros Mattoso, *Etre esclave au Brésil, XVIe-XIXe siècle* (Paris: Hachette, 1979), p. 32, translated by Arthur Goldhammer as *To Be a Slave in Brazil* (New Brunswick: Rutgers University Press, 1985).

8. Germain Mouynes, *Ville de Narbonne. Inventaire des Archives communales antérieures à 1790* (Narbonne: E. Caillard, 1871–79), subseries BB, pp. 1–2 (BB1, February 1557).

9. Anne Blanchard in André Corvisier, ed., *Histoire militaire de la France* (Paris: Presses Universitaires de France, 1992), pp. 263–68.

10. On Narbonne in the sixteenth century, see the admirable thesis on the history of this city from the Middle Ages to the nineteenth century which Gilbert Larguier recently defended at the University of Paris VII. While awaiting publication of this "great work," one can also consult Jacques Michaud, *Histoire de Narbonne* (Privat: Toulouse, 1988), or Paul Carbonel, *Histoire de Narbonne* (Narbonne: Caillard, 1956; reprinted Marseilles: Lafitte, 1988).

11. This is the third depressive episode mentioned in Felix's *Tagebuch,* following two earlier incidents in Avignon and one just after his arrival in Montpellier.

12. Marie-Caroline Roederer, Michel Mollat, and Jean-Pierre Bardet, *Paroisses*

et communes de France, Aude (Paris: Centre National de Recherche Scientifique, 1979), p. 357.

13. Fathers Claude Devic and J. Vaissette, *Histoire générale de Languedoc* (Toulouse: Privat, 1879), vol. II, p. 285.

14. See the maps in the appendix to Frank C. Spooner, *L'Economie mondiale et les frappes monétaires en France* (Paris: Armand Colin, 1956).

15. Father Thomas Bouges, *Histoire ecclésiastique et civile de Carcassonne* (Paris: Gandouin, 1741).

16. Devic and Vaissette, *Histoire générale de Languedoc.*

17. For all that follows concerning the location of the presidial, see Jean Guilaine, *Histoire de Carcassonne* (Toulouse: Privat, 1984), p. 116.

18. Claudine Pailhès, *D'or et de sang. Le XVIe siècle ariégeois* (Foix: Editions des Archives Départementales, 1992).

19. Ibid., on Ariège. As for silver from Mexico after 1549, see Henry Bamford Parkes, *A History of Mexico* (Boston: Houghton Mifflin, 1960), pp. 59–79.

20. Gilles Caster, *Le Commerce du pastel et de l'épicerie à Toulouse de 1450 à 1560* (Toulouse: Privat, 1962), pp. 269–372.

21. Philippe Wolff, Bartolomé Bennassar, et al., *Histoire de Toulouse* (Toulouse: Privat, 1974), p. 232.

22. Charles Higounet, *Histoire de Bordeaux,* vol. 4 (Bordeaux: Fédération Historique du Sud-Ouest, 1966), p. 243, n. 171.

23. Wolff, Bennassar et al., *Histoire de Toulouse,* p. 47.

24. Ibid., p. 222.

25. On the cultural climate in Toulouse in the sixteenth century, see the remarkable work of A. London Fell, *Origins of Legislative Sovereignty and the Legislative State* (Westport, Conn.: Greenwood, 1983–1991). This essential work deserves to be rescued from the almost total obscurity in which it is shrouded today, at least in France.

26. Devic and Vaissette, *Histoire générale de Languedoc,* vol. II, p. 317. On the population of Toulouse, see Wolff, Bennassar et al., *Histoire de Toulouse,* p. 294 and passim: in 1335, 35,000; 1398, 24,000; 1405, 22,500; 1550, 30–40,000; 1640, 42,000; 1695, 43,000.

27. Henry Le Bret, *Histoire de Montauban* (Montauban, 1841; reprinted Marseilles: Lafitte, 1976); Daniel Ligou, *Histoire de Montauban* (Toulouse: Privat, 1984), pp. 205–6.

28. Charles Higounet, *Histoire de Bordeaux* (Bordeaux: Fédération historique du Sud-Ouest, 1962), vol. 4 (on the sixteenth century), p. 287. This particular *recette* moved to Bordeaux in 1566.

29. Guilbert, *Histoire des villes de France,* vol. 2, p. 399.

30. Higounet, *Histoire de Bordeaux,* vol. 4, p. 181.

31. Jacques Bernard, *Navires et gens de mer à Bordeaux (vers 1400–vers 1550)* (Paris: SEVPEN, 1968), p. 520 and passim; Higounet, *Histoire de Bordeaux,* p. 277.

32. Higounet, *Histoire de Bordeaux,* p. 153.

33. A similar date in Fécamp: the local liqueur, a stronger ancestor of today's Benedictine, was supposedly produced by a "Normanized" Italian monk in 1510. See Laurence Haloche, *Bénédictine, histoire d'une liqueur* (Lausanne: Conti, 1991), p. 29; see also Hugues et Alfred Le Roux, *La Bénédictine de l'ancienne abbaye de Fécamp* (Rouen: Le Cerf, 1905), pp. 13–14.

34. Higounet, *Histoire de Bordeaux,* pp. 126–28, 163.

35. Ibid.

36. These figures are taken from Jacques Bernard's thesis.

37. Clément Janequin, *Chansons polyphoniques* (Monaco: Lesure, 1965), vol. 1 ("Bordeaux period"), Oiseau Lyre and Les Remparts labels.

38. Robert Etienne, *Histoire de Bordeaux* (Toulouse: Privat, 1990), pp. 40–41.

39. Ibid., pp. 42, 102.

40. R. Doucet, *Les Institutions de la France au XVIe siècle* (Paris: Picard, 1948), vol. 1, pp. 275 ff.

41. Jean-Noël Luc, *La Charente-Maritime, Aunis et Saintonge* (Saint-Jean-d'Angély: Bordessoules, 1981), p. 170. See also G. and J. Musset, *Pons* (La Rochelle: Bergevin, 1926), p. 9 and passim.

42. Alain Michaud, *Histoire de Saintes* (Toulouse: Privat, 1989), p. 120.

43. Ibid., p. 110.

44. Ibid., p. 136.

45. André Baudrit, "Saintes au XVIe siècle," thesis, Faculty of Letters, University of Bordeaux, 1957, vol. 1, pp. 194 ff. I was able to consult a copy of this thesis made available by the Bibliothèque Municipale of Saintes.

46. Higounet, *Histoire de Bordeaux,* vol. 4, p. 131; Eutrope-Louis Dangibeaud, *Etudes historiques: Saintes au XVI siècle* (Evreux: Hérissey, 1863), pp. 53–64.

47. Baron Eschassériaux, *Etudes, documents . . . relatifs à la ville de Saintes* (Saintes: Orliaguet, 1876), p. 33 and passim.

48. Michaud, *Histoire de Saintes,* p. 103.

49. André Chastel, *Le Présent des oeuvres* (Paris: De Fallois, 1993), p. 219.

50. Marcel Delafossse, *Histoire de La Rochelle* (Toulouse: Privat, 1985), pp. 73 ff.

51. On this and what follows, see Louis-Claude Saudau, *Saint-Jean-d'Angély* (Saint-Jean-d'Angély: J.-B. Ollivier, 1886).

52. *Discours des choses les plus remarquables advenues . . . durant le siège de Lusignan en 1574* (Poitiers, 1577), pp. 62 ff., B. N., anonymous, L 634–93.

53. Brantôme, *Oeuvres complètes,* ed. L. Lalanne (Paris: Renouard, 1869), vol. 5, p. 19.

54. Chinon district, canton of Langeais.

55. Jacques Le Goff and Emmanuel Le Roy Ladurie, "Mélusine maternelle et défricheuse," *Annales* (May–October 1971), pp. 587 ff.; Jean Tarrade, *La Vienne, de la Préhistoire à nos jours* (Saint-Jean-d'Angély: Bordessoules, 1986), pp. 108, 377, and passim; Edmond-René Labande, *Histoire du Poitou* (Toulouse: Privat, 1976), pp. 108 ff.

56. Gédéon Tallemant des Réaux, *Historiettes* (Paris: Gallimard, 1967), vol. 1, p. 594.

57. René Crozet, *Histoire du Poitou* (Paris: Presses Universitaires de France, 1970), p. 61.

58. On the history of Poitou in the sixteenth century, see Crozet, *Histoire de Poitou;* Georges Bordonove, *Histoire du Poitou* (Paris: Hachette, 1973); Tarrade, *La Vienne, de la Préhistoire à nos jours;* Labande, *Histoire du Poitou;* Dr. Louis Merle, *La Métairie et l'évolution agraire de la Gâtine poitevine de la fin du Moyen Age à la Révolution* (Paris: SEVPEN, 1958). See also the works of Paul Raveau on Poitou in the sixteenth century for information on agriculture, the peasantry, aristo-

cratic life, and social and economic conditions (Raveau's works were published by Rivière in Paris in 1926 and 1931 and in Poitiers in 1917 and 1935).

59. The vestiges of this amphitheater gradually disappeared in the centuries following the Platters' visits.

60. Labande, *Histoire du Poitou*, pp. 218–21.

61. *Mémoires chronologiques pour servir à l'histoire de Châtellerault*, collected and arranged in 1788 by Roffay des Pallus and published by Camille Page (Châtellerault: Rivière, 1909), p. 71; and Alfred Hérault, *Histoire de Châtellerault* (Châtellerault: Videau, 1926), pp. 11 ff.

62. Karl Baedeker, *Le Centre de la France* (Leipzig-Paris: Ollendorf, 1889), p. 22.

63. Bernard Chevalier, *Tours, ville royale* (Louvain-Paris, 1975), pp. 258, 347; and idem, *Histoire de Tours* (Toulouse: Privat, 1985), p. 136.

64. Georges Duby, *L'Economie rurale et la vie des campagnes dans l'Occident médiéval* (Paris: Aubier, 1962), pp. 171–76; and F. L. Gansho, *Qu'est-ce que la féodalité?* (Paris: Tallandier, 1982).

65. Chevalier, *Tours*, pp. 122–52.

66. Ibid., pp. 130–52.

67. Ibid., pp. 528 ff.

68. Sabine Baring-Gould, *Cliff Castles and Cave Dwellings in Europe* (London: Seeley, 1911; reprinted Detroit: Singing Tree Press, 1968), chap. 2.

69. Patrick Saletta, *Voyage dans la France des troglodytes* (Antony: Sides, 1991), pp. 145, 153, 161, 167, 185, 201.

70. C. Croubois, *Le Loir-et-Cher* (Saint-Jean-d'Angély: Bordessoules, 1985), p. 191.

71. Roger Dion, *Val de Loire* (Tours: Arrault, 1934), vol. 1, p. 418, reprinted Marseilles: Lafitte, 1978.

72. Ibid., pp. 357–58, for all that follows.

73. Madeleine Chabrolin et al., *Histoire de Nevers* (Saint-Etienne: Le Coteau, Horvath, 1984), p. 171.

74. François Lebrun et al., *Histoire des pays de la Loire* (Toulouse: Privat, 1972), pp. 219 ff.; Claude Croubois, ed., *Le Loir-et-Cher de la préhistoire à nos jours* (Saint-Jean-d'Angély: Bordessoules, 1985), pp. 193 ff.; Philippe Mantellier, *Histoire de la communauté des marchands fréquentant la rivière de Loire et fleuves descendant en icelle,* vol. 2 (Orléans: Jacob, 1864).

75. In the département of the Moselle, Sarrebourg district, Phalsbourg canton.

76. Yvonne Labande-Mailfert, *Charles VIII et son milieu (1477–1498)* (Paris: Klincksiec, 1975), p. 580 (with many references).

77. On Amboise: Léon-Auguste Bosseboeuf, *Amboise, le château, la ville et le canton* (Tours: Pericat, 1897); Abbé Casimir Chevalier, *Inventaire analytique des archives communales d'Amboise, 1421–1789* (Tours: Georges-Joubert, 1874); Jacqueline Melet, *Le Développement historique de la ville d'Amboise des origines jusqu'au XVIIIe siècle,* reviewed in *Positions des thèses soutenues par les élèves de la promotion de 1972* (Paris: Ecole des chartes, 1972), pp. 107–13; Jacqueline Melet-Samson, "La ville d'Amboise aux XVe et XVIe siècles," *Bulletin de la Société archéologique de Touraine* (1973), pp. 263–68; idem, "Provenance des matériaux utilisés pour la construction des édifices publics de la ville d'Amboise aux XVe et XVIe siècles," *Congrès national des sociétés savantes* (Saint-Etienne, 1973), pp. 225–34.

78. Exhaustive searches of thousands of death certificates over a period of two centuries have turned up only one or two cases of suicide: see Alain Croix, *La Bretagne aux XVIe siècles* (Paris: Maloine, 1980), 2 vols.; and Alain Molinier, *Stagnation et croissance. Le Vivarais aux XVIIe et XVIIIe siècles* (Paris: EHESS/Touzot, 1985).

79. Yves Denis, *Histoire de Blois et de sa région* (Toulouse: Privat, 1988), pp. 65–67, 95.

80. Ibid., p. 95.

81. Michel Melot, article in *Gazette des Beaux-Arts* (December 1967), p. 326 (fundamental).

82. Machiavelli, *The Prince,* chap. 20.

83. See also Jean Bernier, *Histoire de Blois* (Paris: Muguet, 1682), pp. 21–22.

84. On Blois, see Ursula Baurmeister and M.-P. Lafitte, *Des livres et des rois* (Paris: Bibliothèque Nationale, 1992); Dr. Frédéric Lesueur, *Le Château de Blois, tel qu'il fut* (Paris: A. et J. Picard, 1970); Louis Bergevin and Alexandre Dupré, *Histoire de Blois* (Marseilles: Laffitte, 1977, reproduced from an earlier edition: Blois: E. Dezairs, 1846–1847); Jean Caplat, *Histoire de Blois depuis les origines jusqu'à nos jours* (Blois: Caplat, 1968).

85. These figures do not include a small number of houses reserved for clerics.

86. On the great church at Cléry, see Canon Lucien Millet, *Notre Dame de Cléry* (Paris: Lethielleux, 1961); Jean Mercier, *Notre-Dame de Cléry* (Cléry: Paroisse Notre-Dame, 1988); Michel Caffin de Mérouville, *Notre-Dame de Cléry* (Paris: Plon, 1963); Louis Jarry, *Histoire de Cléry et de l'église collégiale et chapelle royale de Notre-Dame de Cléry* (Cléry: Editions de l'Association des Amis de Cléry, 1984), facsimile of the Orléans edition of 1899.

87. See Saint-Simon, *Mémoires,* ed. Boislisle (Paris: Hachette), vol. 8, p. 239.

88. On Orléans, see Louis d'Illiers, *Histoire d'Orléans* (Marseille: Laffitte, 1977; reprinted from the second edition, Orléans: Ruddé, 1954); Jacques Debal, *Histoire d'Orléans et de son terroir,* vol. 1 (Roanne: Horvath, 1983); Jean de Viguerie, ed., *Histoire religieuse de l'Orléannais* (Chambray: CLD, 1983); J. de La Martinière, "Le monument de la Pucelle sur le pont d'Orléans," *Mémoires de la Société archéologique et historique de l'Orléannais,* vol. 37 (1936), pp. 109 ff.; François Lebrun, ed., *Histoire des Pays de la Loire, Orléannais, Touraine* (Toulouse: Privat, 1972).

89. Jean-Marc Moriceau, *Les Fermiers de l'Ile-de-France* (Paris: Fayard, 1994).

90. See Michel Billard, *Voyages à travers l'histoire d'Etampes* (Etampes: Editions du Soleil 1985); idem, *A la découverte d'Etampes. Sur les pas des pèlerins de Saint-Jacques* (Etampes: Editions du Soleil, 1987); idem, *Eglises et chapelles d'Etampes, autour de Notre-dame* (Etrechy: Editions du Soleil, 1988); Maxime Legrand, *Histoire d'Etampes* (Res Universis; a facsimile of the 1902 edition was published under the title *Etampes pittoresque* in Paris in 1991); Justin Bourgeois, *Quelques recherches sur le port d'Etampes* (Etampes: A. Allier, 1860); Basile Fleureau, *Les Antiquités de la ville et du duché d'Etampes* (Marseilles: Laffitte reprints, 1977; reproduction of the 1683 Paris edition published by J.-B. Coignard); Léon Guibourgé, *Etampes, ville royale* (Etampes, 1958); Liliana Klein, *Etampes d'hier et d'aujourd'hui* (Etampes: Editions du Soleil, 1988); Maxime de Montrond, *Essais historiques sur la ville d'Etampes* (Etampes: Fortin, 1836); *Les Très Riches Heures du duc de Berry,* with an introduction by Jean Longnon (Paris: Vilo, 1969); Charles Forteau,

"Comptes de recettes et de dépenses de la maladrerie d'Etampes," *Annales de la Société historique et archéologique du Gâtinais,* vol. 21, pp. 100 ff.; Joseph Délivré, "L'immigration dans le doyenné d'Etampes après la guerre de Cent Ans," *Mémoires et documents de la Société historique et archéologique de Corbeil, de l'Essonne et du Hurepoix,* vol. 14, 1988, and, in the same volume, the article by Joseph Crocy on "L'Hôtel-Dieu d'Etampes."

91. Abel Cornaton, Jean Burtin, et al., *Arpajon, les grandes étapes de son histoire* (Arpajon, 1968); Abbé J.-M. Alliot, *Les Curés d'Arpajon* (Arpajon: Lamouche, 1889); *Histoire de pays de Châtres. Chronologie des principaux événements de l'histore d'Arpajon et de sa région* (Etampes: Editions Soleil, 1988); Jean-Joseph Beaugrand, *Notes historiques sur Arpajon* (Paris, 1833); Jacques Dupâquier et al., *Paroisses et communes de France. Dictionnaire d'histoire administrative et démographique. Région parisienne* (Paris: Centre National de Recherche Scientifique, 1974), article "Arpajon."

92. Jean Jacquart, *La Crise rurale en Ile-de-France* (Paris: Armand Colin, 1974).

93. André Jouanen, *Montlhéry, douze siècles d'histoire* (Etampes: Editions du Soleil, 1989), and idem, *Montlhéry et son histoire* (Ballainvilliers: Association Renaissance et Culture, 1983).

CHAPTER EIGHT

1. Jean-Pierre Babelon, *Nouvelle histoire de Paris au XVIe siècle* (Paris: Hachette, 1986), pp. 247–259 and passim.

2. Jean-Marc Moriceau, *Les Fermiers de l'Ile-de-France* (Paris: Fayard, 1994), part 1, as well as p. 645 and passim. Moriceau's remarkable book helps us to understand the countryside of the Ile-de-France at the time of Felix's visit.

3. Babelon, *Nouvelle histoire,* pp. 247–53.

4. This is according to Jean-François Pernot, who is currently writing a book on the Chambre des Comptes of Paris under the Ancien Régime.

5. K.-P. Poussou, "Les métropoles, parasites ou stimulants?" in Jacqueline Beaujeu-Garnier, ed., *La Grande Ville, enjeu du XXIe siècle,* texts in honor of Jean Bastié (Paris: Presses Universitaires de France, 1991), pp. 17–29.

6. It is not always easy to accept the characterization of the Valois kings, and especially Francis I, as "absolute monarchs": see Philippe Hamon, *L'Histoire,* no. 183, December 1994. The American historian Russell Major has given a much less absolutist picture of "Renaissance monarchy." See his *Representative Institutions in Renaissance France* (Madison: University of Wisconsin Press, 1960), a work of fundamental importance.

7. A member of Utenhove's family was a boarder in Erasmus's house in 1528–29 according to Alfred Hartmann, ed., *Die Amerbach-Korrespondenz* (Basel: Editions de la Bibliothèque Universitaire de Bâle, 1942), vol. 4, p. 418, note 1.

8. August Hirsch, *Biographisches Lexicon aller hervorragenden Ärzten aller Zeiten,* new edition (Munich-Berlin: Urban, 1962), vol. 4, art. "Rufus."

9. J. Karcher, *Felix Platter, Lebensbild des Basler Stadtarztes* (Basel: Helbing, 1949), p. 23; Hirsh, *Biographisches Lexicon,* vol. 2, art. "Duret."

10. Karcher, *Felix Platter,* p. 23. On Fernel, see also Jean Goulin, *Mémoires littéraires, critiques . . . pour servir à l'histoire ancienne et moderne de la médecine* (Paris: Bastien, 1777), pp. 286–408.

11. J. Maritain, *Trois réformateurs* (Paris: Plon, 1925), p. 44.

12. In the period 1531–35 alone, Wechel published 148 different works, mostly in Latin and Greek. For the titles of these works, see Brigitte Moreau, *Inventaire chronologique des éditions parisiennes du XVIe siècle*, based on the manuscripts of Philippe Renouard, vol. 4, 1531–1535 (Abbeville: Imprimerie Paillar, 1992).

13. *Amerbach-Korrespondenz*, vol. 6, p. 312.

14. Christiane Riboulleau, *Villers-Cotterêts, un château royal en forêt de Retz* (Amiens: Association pour la généralisation de l'Inventaire général en Picardie, 1991).

15. Ferdinand Lot, *Recherches sur les effectifs des armées françaises, 1494–1562* (Paris: SEVPEN, 1982), chap. 10.

16. Ivan Cloulas, *Henri II* (Paris: Fayard, 1985), p. 460.

17. Jean-Marie Pérouse de Montclos, *Le Guide du Patrimoine* (Paris: Hachette, 1987), p. 291.

18. Babelon, *Nouvelle histoire,* p. 192.

19. T2 599; see also Babelon, *Nouvelle histoire,* pp. 223–24 and passim, for all that follows.

20. Babelon, *Nouvelle histoire,* pp. 226–282.

21. Ibid., pp. 148–49.

22. On bookbinding in France under Henri II, "the greatest French bibliophile of his time," see L.-M. Michon, *La Reliure française* (Paris: Larousse, 1951), chap. 5.

23. Babelon, *Nouvelle histoire,* p. 232.

24. Ibid., pp. 390–442.

25. *La Ligue* was the confederation of French Catholics that played an essential role in the Wars of Religion after 1576.—Trans.

26. Michel Félibien, *Histoire de l'abbaye royale de Saint-Denis en France* (Paris, 1973), pp. 105 ff.

27. J. B. M. Jaillot, *Recherches critiques sur la ville de Paris* (Paris: Lottin, 1774), XVIe quartier, place Maubert, p. 6. Lötscher (in F 281, note 141) confuses the rue d'Arras with the rue d'Assas.

28. *Amerbach-Korrespondenz,* vol. 6, p. 422; and Emile Châtelain, *Les Etudiants suisses de Paris, aux Xve et XVIe siècles* (Paris: Emile Bouillon, 1891), p. xlviii.

29. Félibien, *Histoire de l'abbaye royale de Saint-Denis en France,* for the year 1556.

30. R. Giesey, "Cérémonial et puissance souveraine," *Cahiers des Annales* (Paris: Armand Colin, 1987), p. 26, and idem, *Le roi ne meurt jamais* (Paris: Flammarion, 1987), pp. 102–10.

31. D. Gaborit and M.-P. Laffitte, *Le Trésor de Saint-Denis* (Dijon: Faton, 1992), p. 99.

32. Ibid., pp. 20, 74.

33. Alain Erlande-Brandenburg, *L'Eglise abbatiale de Saint-Denis* (Paris, 1976).

34. The Convention ordered the violation of the royal tombs in the summer of 1793, but its decision was scarcely legal, for although it was in theory a body chosen in free elections to represent the Nation, it had in fact been purged several months earlier by a very Parisian, anti-Girondin "putsch" on May 31, 1793. On the event itself in Saint-Denis, see Alain Boureau, *Le Simple Corps du roi* (Paris: Editions de Paris, 1988), *in fine*.

35. And not a horn, as Felix's editor erroneously transcribes [F 282].

36. Monin, *Histoire de la ville de Saint-Denis* (Saint-Denis, 1928; reprinted Marseilles: Laffitte, 1977), p. 239.

37. Gaborit and Laffitte, *Le Trésor de Saint-Denis,* p. 204; see also Monin, *Histoire,* p. 237.

38. Ibid., pp. 272 ff.

39. Ibid., p. 198.

40. Ibid., p. 80.

41. Sylvie Chaber d'Hières, *Que lire sur l'histoire de la Seine-Saint-Denis* (Seine-Saint-Denis: Archives Départementales, 1986); Roger Bourderon and Pierre de Perreti, *Histoire de Saint-Denis* (Toulouse: Privat, 1988); Alain Erlande-Brandeburg and Georges Chassé, *L'Eglise abbatiale de Saint-Denis* (Paris: Librairie de la Nouvelle Faculté, 1976), especially "Historique et visite. Les tombeaux royaux"; Michel Félibien, *Histoire de l'abbaye royale de Saint-Denis en France* (Paris: Editions du Palais-Royal, 1973); Henry Monin, *Histoire de la ville de Saint-Denis et de la basilique* (Marseilles: Lafitte, 1977); Ralph E. Giesey, *Le roi ne meurt jamais* (Paris: Flammarion, 1987), pp. 102–10, and idem, *Cérémonial et puissance souveraine* (Paris: Armand Colin, 1987); Fernand Bournon, *Histoire de la ville et du canton de Saint-Denis* (Paris, 1892); and the fundamental work of D. Gaborit and M.-P. Laffitte, *Le Trésor de Saint-Denis* (Dijon: Faton, 1992), as well as B. de Montesquiou-Fezensac and D. Gaborit, *Trésor de Saint-Denis* (Paris: Picard, 1973).

42. Louis-Sébastien Mercier, *Tableau de Paris* (Paris: Mercure de France, 1994), vol. 1, chap. 178, pp. 429, 1618.

43. Chalres II, who is usually (and mistakenly) referred to as Charles III, duc de Lorraine (1543–1608), had been duke of Lorraine since 1545. On him and his family, see Saint-Simon, *Mémoires,* ed. Boislisle (Paris: Hachette, 1901), vol. 15, pp. 24–25 and notes.

44. Babelon, *Nouvelle histoire,* p. 40.

45. The area traditionally known as "Berry" corresponds to what is today included in the *départements* of Indre and Cher.

46. On all of this, see G. Devailly, *Histoire du Berry* (Toulouse: Privat, 1987), p. 168.

47. Emile Meslé, *Histoire de Bourges* (Roanne: Horvath, 1988), p. 6. Can the difference between the two figures be explained by efforts between 1567 and 1599 to bolster the city's security in the face of the interminable Wars of Religion?

48. This is taken from Father Jean Glaumeau, *Journal* (Bourges and Paris: Editions Hiver, 1867), p. 86.

49. Ibid., p. 7.

50. Meslé, *Histoire de Bourges,* p. 113.

51 Ibid., p. 65.

52. Buhot de Kersers, *Statistique départementale du Cher* (Bourges: Tripault, 1883, vol. 2, p. 94; reprinted Marseilles: Laffitte, 1977).

53. We encountered his vagueness about Joan of Arc earlier, at the time of his visit to Orléans.

54. Bernard Quilliet, *Louis XII «père du peuple»* (Paris: Fayard, 1986), p. 258.

55. Glaumeau, *Journal,* notes for 1555–58.

56. On Bourges, see Meslé, *Histoire de Bourges;* Jean Chaumeau, seigneur de

Lassay, *Histoire du Berry* (Lyons: Gryphe, 1566; reprinted 1985 by the Cercle d'histoire d'Argenton); A. Buhot de Kersers, *Histoire et statistique monumentale du départment du Cher*, vol. 2 (canton of Bourges) (Bourges, 1883); Pierre Pradel, *La Cathédrale de Bourges* (Paris: Tel, 1939); *Journal de Jehan Glaumeau de Bourges, 1541–1562* (Bourges: Just-Bernard, 1867); Guy Devailly, ed., *Histoire du Berry* (Toulouse: Privat, 1987).

57. Gérald Jack Gilbank, *Les Vignobles de qualité du sud-est du bassin de Paris* (Paris: by the author, 1981), p. 380.

58. On Sancerre, see Gérald Nakam, *Au lendemain de la Saint-Barthélemy: l'Histoire mémorable du siège de Sancerre (1573) de Jean de Léry* (Paris: Anthropos, 1972), p. 100 and passim; Abbé Camille-Marie Charpentier, *Le Beffroi de Sancerre dans l'Histoire des beffrois* (Sancerre: Société de Presse Berrichonne, 1956); idem, *Sancerre et Saint-Satur dans l'histoire de France* (Sancerre: Société Coopérative Ouvrière d'Imprimerie, 1951); *Histoire de la ville de Sancerre* (BN, anonymous) (Cosne: Gourdet, 1826); Vincent Poupard, *Histoire de Sancerre* (Bourges: J. Bernard, 1858; reprinted Marseilles: Laffitte, 1975); A. Buhot de Kersers, *Statistique monumentale du département du cher*, vol. 7 (Bourges, 1895); Gilbank, *Les Vignobles de qualité*.

59. *Alfred Faivre, Cosne à travers les âges. Essai historique et archéologique* (Horvath: Le Coteau, 1986), a reprint of the 1895 edition with important maps and engravings; the same work has also been published under a different title: *Histoire de Cosne* (Paris: Res Universis, 1990).

60. Guilbert, *Histoire des villes de France*, vol. 4, p. 252.

61. G. Gauthier, "La peste à Clamecy au XVIe siècle," *L'Echo de Clamecy*, April 30, 1905.

62. Guibert, *Histoire des villes*, vol. 4, p. 268; Paul Cornu, *Les Forêts du Nivernais* (Nevers: Editions de la Société Académique du Nivernais, 1981), pp. 99ff. For our purposes there is little of interest in Charles P. Milandre, *Vieilleries clamecycoises* (Clamecy: Editions de la Société Scientifique et Artistique de Clamecy, 1938).

63. M. Gally, *Voyage dans l'Avallonnais. Vézelay monastique* (Tonnerre: Bailly, 1887), pp. 87–110; and the review *Zodiaque*, nos. 12–13, 1953, especially the appendix with map; Claude Jean-Nesmy, *Le Pèlerinage et la Cité. Inventaire de Vézelay* (Zodiaque, 1970), esp. pp. 8–16; Nicolas-Léonard Martin, *Précis historique sur la ville et l'ancienne abbaye de Vézelay* (Auxerre: Gallot-Fournier, 1832), pp. 192–213; Joseph Calmette, *Les Grandes Heures de Vézelay* (Paris: Sfelt, 1951), pp. 184–87; Pierre Meunier, *Iconographie de l'église de Vézelay* (Avallon: Odobé, 1862) (a very detailed work). On the verdigris of Montpellier, see F 178.

64. Gaston Roupnel, *La Ville et la campagne au XVIIe siècle. Etude sur les populations du pays dijonnais* (Paris: Armand Colin, 1955), pp. 354ff.

65. On Dijon and the Carthusian monastery of Champmol, see BN-Estampes, *Topographie de la France* (Côte-d'Or, Dijon, la chartreuse de Champmol), H. 117.442 to H.117.577; Pierre Gras, ed., *Histoire de Dijon* (Toulouse: Privat, 1987); Jean Richard, *Histoire de la Bourgogne* (Toulouse: Privat, 1978), reprinted 1988; Cyprien Monget, *La Chartreuse de Dijon* (Montreuil-sur-Mer: Imprimerie Notre-Dame-des-Prés, 1898); Kathleen Morand, *Claus Sluter, Artist at the Court of Burgundy*, with photographs by D. Finn (London: Harvey Miller, 1991); Pierre Quarré, *La Chartreuse de Champmol, foyer d'art au temps des ducs Valois* (Musée de Dijon, Palais des Ducs de Bourgogne, 1960); idem., *La Chartreuse de Champmol,*

centre d'art européen (Dijon: Publication du Centre Européen d'Etudes Burgondes), no. 3, 1961 (Rencontres d'Utrecht, 4 and 5 November 1960); Laurence Blondaux, "Le puits des prophètes de la chartreuse de Champmol: conservation et restaurations depuis le Moyen Age," *Gothiques*, no. 27, 1991, pp. 17–29; Christian de Mérindol, "Nouvelles observations sur la symbolique royale à la fin du Moyen Age. La chartreuse de Champmol," *Bulletin de la Société nationale des antiquaires de France*, 1988, pp. 288ff.; Georges Lengherand, *Voyages de Georges Lengherand, 1485–1486,* with an introduction by the marquis de Godefroy-Menilglaise (Mons: Imprimer de Masquillier et Dequesne, 1861) (Société des Bibliographes de Mons); also cited by J. Chipps Smith in "The Chartreuse de Champmol in 1486: The Earliest Visitor's Account," *Gazette des Beaux-Arts,* vol. 106, July-August 1985.

66. J. Theurot, p. 71.

67. Jacky Theurot, Daniel Bienmiller, et al., *Histoire de Dole* (Roanne: Horvath, 1982); Jacky Theurot, *Dole, évolution d'un espace urbain: du Moyen Age à nos jours,* 1981; Annie Gay and Jacky Theurot, *Dole pas à pas* (Roanne: Horvath, 1985); idem, *Essor et apogée d'une capitale provinciale, 1274–1674* idem, *Dole au comté de Bourgogne;* Jules Gauthier, *Les Fortifications de Dole* (Caen, 1894), excerpt from a paper read to the Fifty-Eighth French Archeological Congress at Besançon in 1891; Elie Puffeney, *Histoire de Dole* (Besançon, 1882; reprinted Marseilles: Laffitte, 1975).

68. Claude Fohlen, *Histoire de Besançon, des origines à la fin du XVIe siècle* (Paris: Nouvelle Librairie de France, 1964), reprinted 1981; José Gentil Da Silva, *Banque et crédit en Italie au XVIIe siècle* (Paris: Klincksieck, 1969).

69. Rev. John Viénot, who rightly championed tolerance toward his coreligionists, does not appear to have expressed much outrage in his great works (see below) on Protestantism in the Montbéliard region about this intolerant decree of the Lutheran authorities against local Catholics.

70. After Servetus, Socinius became one of the leading opponents of the dogma of the Trinity in the second half of the sixteenth century.

71. On Montbéliard and Franche-Comté in general, see Johen Viénot, *Histoire de la Réforme dans le pays de Montbéliard, depuis les origines jusqu'à la mort de P. Toussain, 1524–1573* (Montbéliard: Imprimerie Montéliardaise, 1900), and idem, *Histoire du pays de Montbéliard à l'usage de la jeunesse et des familles* (Audincourt: Villard, 1904); Charles Duvernoy, *Ephémérides de l'ancien comté de Montbéliard* (Besançon: Deis, 1832), reprinted by Blaise Mériot, 2 vols. (Montbéliard: Société d'Emulation de Montbéliard, 1953–1959); R.-E. Tuefferd, "Histoire des comtes souverains de Montbéliard," *Mémoires de la Socété d'émulation de Montbéliard,* 1877, pp. 380ff.; Michel Billerey, "La principauté de Montbéliard et l'évêché de Bâle, introduction à leur histoire comparée," *Mémoires de la Société pour l'histoire du droit,* 21st fascicule (Dijon, 1960), pp. 103–9; *Le Pays de Montbéliard et l'ancien évêché de Bâle dans l'histoire* (Société d'émulation de Montbéliard and the Société jurassienne d'émulation, 1984); Guy J. Michel, *La Franche-Comté sous les Habsbourg, 1413–1678* (Wettolsheim-Colmar: Editions Mars et Mercure, 1978); Roland Fiétier, ed., *Histoire de la Franche-Comté* (Toulouse: Privat, 1977); Jean-Etienne Caire and Christian Deloche, *Histoire des Franc-Comtois* (Paris: Nathan, 1981); Lucien Febvre, *Histoire de Franche-Comté* (Paris, 1922; reprinted Marseilles: Laffitte, 1983); Lucien Febvre, *Philippe II et la Franche-Comté* (Paris: Champion,

1912), reprinted, unfortunately without notes (Paris: Flammarion, 1970 and 1984); Jean-Marc Debard, *Le Pays de Montbéliard, du Wurtemberg à la France, 1793. Bicentenaire du rattachement de la principauté de Montbéliard à la France* (Montbéliard: Société d'émulation de Montbéliard, 1992).

72. Carl Roth, *Basler Jahrbuch,* 1936, pp. 1–30.

CHAPTER NINE

1. See Alain Boureau, *Le Simple Corps du roi* (Paris: Editions de Paris, 1988), on revolutionary exhumations at the end of the eighteenth century.

2. Such a mishap did indeed happen to Felix's "adopted" daughter Gredlin at the beginning of the seventeenth century. We can understand why he would have been struck by Dorothea's remark, made in 1557, when he began working on the fair copy of his *Tagebuch* in 1609 and especially after 1612 (when Louis XIII was king of France).

3. In Baden-Wurtemberg today. Upward social mobility in sixteenth-century Basel seems to have been considerable, owing largely to repeated plague epidemics and to the effects of the Protestant Reformation. From tavern or inn to the professions was often but one step, or, more precisely, one generation.

4. Furetière, *Dictionnaire universel,* 1690, art. "thèse," reprinted in facsimile edition (Paris: Robert, 1978).

5. On Jean Fernel, see L. Figard, *Un médecin philosophe au XVIe siècle* (Paris: Alcan, 1903); Dr. Alexandre Herpin, *Jean Fernel, médecin et philosophe* (Paris: Vrin, 1949); Jacques Roger, *Jean Fernel et les problèmes de la médecine de la Renaissance* (Paris: Editions du Palais de la Découverte, 1960); and above all Jean Goulin, *Mémoires pour servir à l'histoire de la médecine* (Paris: Bastien, 1777), a remarkable monograph on Fernel.

6. F 363ff. and *Amerbach-Korrespondenz,* vol. 7, pp. 273–79.

7. *Conciliator, Petri Aponensis . . . liber* (Venice, 1521), fol. 83 and passim (on heat). Pietro d'Albano figures in the printed catalogue of the BNF, at letter P, under the name Petrus de Abanus. There were at least four editions of his *Conciliator* between 1472 and 1548. Felix Platter had certainly studied one of them. The reference given by Valentin Lötscher (F 308, n. 18) on this point is, for once, completely off the mark, because he uses the dictionary of medicine published by B. Mayrhofer, *Wörterbuch* (Jena, 1937), whose article on *conciliator* is inept and only adds to the stockpile of human ignorance. It is astonishing that Lötscher sought the advice of two of Basel's greatest physicians only to reproduce Mayrhofer's absurd article, whose publication in 1937, at the height of the Nazi period, cannot excuse its imbecility. Lötscher, usually so competent, would have done better to use Goulin, *Mémoires littéraires, critiques . . . pour servir à l'histoire . . . de la médecine* (Paris: Bastien, 1777), pp. 30ff. (translation by Goulin of an Italian note on Albano by G. M. Mazzuchelli).

8. Edgar Bonjour, *Die Universität Basel* (Basel: Helbing, 1960), p. 172.

9. Joachim Du Bellay, *Regrets,* sonnet 31, "Heureux qui comme Ulysse" (Paris: Gallimard, 1975).

10. See above, chap. 3, for the origin of this phobia.

11. The term "symbolic capital" was first proposed by Pierre Bourdieu.

12. The corresponding French (royal) order during the Ancien Régime would

have been: hors-d'oeuvres and soups, entrées, roast meat or game, entremets and desserts.

13. Gustave Flaubert, *Madame Bovary* (Paris: Gallimard/Pléiade, 1983), vol. 1, p. 350.

14. Abbé Adolphe Mosschenross, *Thann à travers son passé* (Rixheim: Sutter, 1947), pp. 7–8, n. 2; and Max Rieple, *Maierisches Elsass* (Bern: Hallweg, 1964), p. 25.

15. F 325 and *Amerbach-Korrespondenz*, vol. 8, p. 10, no. 2.

16. Still, the wedding expenses were considerable. Besides the usual reasons for ostentatious consumption, it was basically a matter of making marriage indissoluble on account of the considerable financial investment that its staging required. A couple would have to think twice before separating. Wedding celebrations also brought unmarried young people together and thus paved the way for future marriages. As for other major expenditures alluded to previously, such as the expenses that Felix incurred in obtaining his doctorate, the investment required obviously tended to exclude clever sons of the poorer classes. Felix no longer belonged to this category, since his father, though born poor, now enjoyed a certain wealth and a "decent" social status. Thus upward mobility from the artisan or peasant class to the status of physician theoretically took at least two generations.

Chapter Ten

1. On this subject, see my *Paysans de Languedoc* (Paris: SEVPEN, 1966), vol. 1, p. 48.

2. Lötscher is inclined to place the Gredlin story in 1572. Since Felix does not give a precise date, there is room for disagreement on this point.

3. See H. M. Koelbing, "L'apport suisse à la renaissance de l'ophthalmologie," *Médecine et hygiène* (Geneva), vol. 22, no. 637, 1964, p. 5.

4. The period from December 1572 to December 1573 was a time of serious famine in Franche-Comté: see Lucien Febvre, *Philippe II et la Franche-Comté* (Paris: Champion, 1911), p. 766. The fact that the baby's father was from Franche-Comté tends to confirm the chronology I proposed at the beginning of this chapter.

5. An exposition on childhood in the Middle Ages at the Bibliothèque Nationale in November 1994 under the direction of Pierre Riché cast a judicious eye on Ariès's celebrated thesis, which, though ingenious and correct in some respects, can also be highly misleading.

6. Was there, in this new dream, a remembrance of earlier childhood dreams? See chap. 2 above.

7. This is the actual dialogue as recorded in Felix Platter's text (F 452).

8. Edgar Bonjour, *Die Universität Basel* (Basel: Helbing, 1960), pp. 75 ff.

9. When Gredlin married in 1604 at the age of thirty, she freely recorded her name in the parish register as Margret *Simonin* (daughter of Benedict Simon) (F 453). Hence the painful revelation of her birth had to have occurred before this date. She had already survived the psychological shock.

Chapter Eleven

1. Valentin Lötscher, "Felix Platter und seine Familie," *Basler Neujahrsblatt*, no. 153, 1975, p. 155.

2. "Felix Platter, Aesculapius of his city and of the entire world," was Thomas Jr.'s epitaph for Felix Platter, quoted in Lötscher, "Felix Platter und seine Familie," p. 176.

3. A few words on Biblicism and Hellenism in Basel generally and more particularly in the Platters: at the time of the Swiss cultural revolution in the third and fourth decades of the sixteenth century, Thomas Sr. knew Latin and Greek, but he was also a Hebrew scholar steeped in Joshua-style Old Testament iconoclasm and fanaticism. Later, however, Hebrew seems to have played a much smaller role in the Platters' cultural milieu, where it was supplanted by Greek, a language that many of Felix's friends taught and that he himself knew well. This change reflects a transition to Erasmian and, by definition, Hellenizing New-Testament style evangelism. It also reflects a shift to a more tolerant and scholarly humanism as exemplified by a "man of letters" like Castellion. At the same time, medical scholars also became humanists as they turned back to the classical medical works of Antiquity in the manner of the late-sixteenth-century and increasingly "Platterized" University of Basel.

4. See two articles with incredible titles, "Rural Idiocy" and "Peasant Idiocy," in Josef Wilczynsky, *An Encyclopedic Dictionary of Marxism* (Berlin-New York: De Gruyter, 1981), pp. 424 and 501. Marx's uncharitable remarks on rural life, the "barbaric countryside," and troglodyte peasants can be found primarily in *The German Ideology, Capital,* and *The Eighteenth Brumaire of Louis Napoleon.* Fernand Braudel, in private conversations on this subject, told me that these Marxian texts had greatly impressed him. See also Robert C. Tucker, *The Marx-Engels Reader* (New York: Norton, 1978), pp. 176, 608–9.

5. Glaumeau, *Journal,* p. 13 and passim.

6. When Felix died in 1614, Thomas Jr. referred to him as my "brother or, rather, father." See Lötscher, "Felix Platter und seine Familie," p. 176.

7. Ibid., p. 172.

BIBLIOGRAPHY

Manuscripts
(from the catalogue of the University of Basel)
Platter, Thomas Sr. *Lebensbeschreibung*, 1572, A λ II la, 1b, 1c, 2a, 31a, 31a *bis*.
Platter, Felix. *Der Stadt Basel Beschreibung*, 1610, A λ III 3 Nr 6b.
———. *Brief an Heinrich Strübin*, Januar 1609, A A II 2a, Beilage hinten.
———. *Historie vom Gredli*, A λ III 3 Nr 9b.
———. *Kaiser Ferdinand kommt gen Basel*, 1562, A λ III 3 Nr 8.
———. *Gedichte*, A GV 30.
———. *Lebensbeschreibung und Biographisches*, A λ III 3 Nr 1–3.
———. *Sieben regierende Pestilenzen*, 1539–1611, A λ Ill 5a.
———. *Rechnung über seine Einnahmen*, 1558–1612, A λ III 3 Nr 5.
———. *Reis Markgrafen Georg Friedrich zu Baden und Hochberg etc. nach Hochingen [. . .] auf die Hochzeit, so zwischen Graf Johann Georg von Zollern mit Fraülein Franziska Wild- und Rheingräfin gehalten worden*, 1598, A λ III 3 Nr 7c.
———. *Reis Markgrafen Georg Friedrichen zu Baden und Hochburg gon Stuttgarten [. . .] zu der Kindstaufen des Herzogen v. Würtemburg Suns Augustigennant [. . .]*, 1596, A λ III Nr 7b.
———. *Reis gen Simringen auf Graf Christoph von Zollern Hochzeit*, 1577, A λ III 3 Nr 7a
———. *Verzeichnis der Personen, so in dem Königreich auf der Kindtaufcn gewesen*, 1600, A λ III 3 Nr 7cc.
———. *Autographischer Eintrag*, 1609, A λ II 2a, Beilage vorn.
———. *Ex libris* (von Hans Heinrich Glaser), 1618, A λ II 31a, Bl. IVr.
———. *Beschreibung von Basel, aus den Pestschriften*, V. B. mscr P 15 no 14.
———. *Selbstbiographie*, V. B. mscr P 42 e Nr 1
Platter, Thomas Jr. *Beschreibung der Reisen durch Frankreich, Spanien, England und die Niederlande*, 1595–1600, A λ V 7.8.
———. *Brief an Heinrich Strübin*, 1609, A λ II 2a, Beilage hinten.
———. *Hauptbuch, mit Testamenten und Inventaren*, 1615, A λ V 9.
———. *Inventarium und Register über [. . .] liegende and fahrende Hab und Güter*, 1622, A 6 V9, 491.
———. *Autographischer Eintrag*, 1609, A λ II 2a, Beilage vorn.
———. *Schreiber*, A λ III 3, *passim*.

ON THE PLATTER FAMILY
Epitaphia Basiliensia Platterorum, A λ II 1b Anhang.
Epitaphia Basiliensia Platterorum, A λ II 1c Anhang.
Genealogia Platteriana, A λ II 1a Beilage.
Genealogia Platteriana, A λ II 31a Beilage VII.

The Library of the University of Basel has preserved approximately five hundred letters of Thomas Platter Sr., Felix Platter, and Thomas Platter Jr., the vast majority of which are written in Latin and for the most part unpublished.

Platteriana
Bibliography of printed texts, in chronological order

THOMAS PLATTER SR.

Historiae vitae Thomae Platteri. Zurich, 1724.
Lebensbeschreibung, ed. M. Lutz. Basel, 1790.
Thomas Platters Leben, ed. E. G. Baldinger. Marburg, 1793.
Lebensbeschreibung, ed. J. F. Franz, in *Leben berühmter Gelehrter.* Saint-Gall, 1812.
Thomas Platter and Felix Platter, zwei Autobiographien, ein Beitrag zur Sittengeschichte des XVI Jahrhunderts, ed. D. A. Fechter. Basel, Seul und Mast, 1840.
The Autobiography of Thomas Platter, a Schoolmaster of the Sixteenth Century, trans. E. A. MacCaul, 3rd ed. London, 1847.
"Ein fahrender Schüler," in *Bilder aus der deutschen Vergangenheit,* ed. G. Freytag. Leipzig, 1852.
La Vie de Thomas Platter, écrite par lui-même, trans. E. Fick. Geneva, Impr. J. G. Frick, 1862.
Zur Sittengeschichte des 16 Jahrhunderts, ed. H. Boos. Leipzig, 1878.
Thomas Platters Selbstbiographie. Gütersloh, 1882.
Thomas Platters Leben, ed. H. Düntzer. Stuttgart, Spemann, 1882.
Thomas Platters Briefe an seinen Sohn Felix, ed. A. Burckhardt. Basel, Detloff, 1890.
Thomas Platters Lebensgeschichte. Zurich, 1891.
Vie de Thomas Platter (1499–1582). Suivie d'extraits des Mémoires de Felix Platter (1536–1614), trans. E. Fick. Lausanne, Bridel, 1895.
Avtobiografija Fomi Plattera, trans. N. V. Speranskij. Ocerki po narodnoj skoly, Moscow, 1896.
Thomas Platters Selbstbiographie, Frankfurt, 1910.
Lebensbeschreibung. Munich, 1911.
Thomas Platter. Geisshirt, Seiler, Professor, Buchdrucker. Rektor. Leipzig, 1912.
Lebensbeschreibung. ed. A. Hartmann, preface by W. Muschig. Basel, Schwabe, 1944 (fundamental).
Lebenserinnerungen. Zurich, 1955.
Autobiographie, ed. and trans. Marie Helmer, *Cahier des Annales,* no. 22. Paris, A. Colin, 1964.
Lebenserinnerungen. Basel, 1969.
Ma vie, trans. E. Fick. Lausanne, L'Age d'Homme, 1982
Autobiographia, F Cichi e L. de Venuto, eds. Rome and Salerno, E. Campi, 1988.
La mia vita (1505–1585), ed. G. O. Bravi. Bergamo, P. Lubrina, 1988.

There are many editions of the writings of the three Platters in modern German for a broad audience and sometimes fictionalized. See the bibliography given by Valentin Lötscher in his edition of Felix Platter's Beschreibung der Stadt Basel (see below). There is also a Japanese edition, translated by K. Abe (Tokyo, 1984). The works of the Platters are therefore known to an extensive read-

ership in Germany, Switzerland, and indeed throughout Europe. The more
recent editions are available to interested readers in libraries and bookstores.

FELIX PLATTER (SEE ALSO THOMAS PLATTER SR.)
De corporis humani structura et usu. Basileae, 1583; reprinted in 1603 (with illustrations by Vesalius).
De mulierum partibus generationi dicatis. Basileae. 1586 ; reprinted Argentinae, 1597.
De feribus liber. Francofurti, 1595.
Praxeos seu de cognescendis. praedicendis. Basileae, Waldkirch, 1603 ; reprinted twice in 1609.
Observationes in hominis affectibus plerisque corpori et animo functionum laesione, dolore aliave molestia et vitio incommodantibus, libri tres. Basileae, 1614; reprinted in 1641 et 1688.
Praxis medica. Basileae, 1602–1608; reprinted in 1625, 1656, 1666, 1680 and 1736.
Quaestionum medicarum paradoxarum et eudoxarum centuria, posthuma. Basileae, 1625.
Thomas Platter und Felix Platter. Zwei Autabiographien, ed. D. A Fechter. Basel, 1840.
"Eines jungen Gelehrten Hochzeit und Haushalt," in *Bilder aus der deutschen Vergangenheit,* ed. G. Freytag. Leipzig, 1852.
Mémoires de Felix Platter, trans. E. Fick, Geneva, J. G. Fick, 1866; 2nd edition, Lausanne, 1895.
Felix und Thomas Platter, ein Beitrag zur Sittengeschichte des 16. Jahrhunderts. Leipzig, 1878.
Aus Felix Platters Bericht über die Pest zu Basel in den Jahren 1609–1611. Basel, 1880.
Briefe. Basel, 1880.
Felix Platters Erinnerungsblätter. Gütersloh. 1882.
Felix Platters Reisen an die Höfe der Grafen van Hohenzollern-Sigmaringen und Hechingen, 1575 und 1598. Basel, 1890.
"Die Historie vom Gredlin," ed. H. A. Gessler. *Basler Jahrbuch,* 1893.
Felix et Thomas Platter à Montpellier (1552–1557 et 1595–1599), travel notes of two students from Basel based on original manuscripts belonging to the Library of the University of Basel, trans. M. Kieffer. Montpellier, Coulet, 1892 ; reprinted Marseilles, Laffitte, 1979.
"Extraits, relatifs à la Provence, des Mémoires de Felix et Thomas Platter," in Ludovic Legré, *La Botanique en Provence au XVIe siècle.* Marseilles, 1900.
Aufzeichnungen. Munich, 1911.
Tagebuchblätter aus dem Jugendleben eines deutschen Arztes. Leipzig, 1913.
Felix Platters Ungdoms-Erindringer, trans. T. Gertz. Copenhagen, 1915.
Felix Platters Reisen an die Höfe der Grafen von Hohenzollern-Sigmaringen und Hechingen, 1575 und 1598. Hechingen, 1927.
Thomas und Felix Platter. Zurich, 1935.
Tagebuchblätter. Zurich, 1955.
Beloved Son Felix. The Journal of Felix Platter, a Medical Student in Montpellier in the 16th Century, trans. S. Jennett. London, 1961.
"Little-known English versions of the *Praxis and Observationes* of Felix Platter (1662 and 1664) ," *Journal of the History of Medicine,* no. 17, 1962.
Observationes I, trans. G. Goldschmidt, ed. H. Buess. Bern, Huber, 1963. (*Obser-*

vationes II and *III* were not published, but the manuscript of the translation is preserved at Basel's Library for the History of Medicine.)

Funktionnelle Störungen des Sinnes und der Bewegung. Bern, 1963.

Tagebuchblätter. Basel, 1969.

Tagebuch, ed. V Lötscher. Basel, Schwabe. 1976 (the text and footnotes are of fundamental importance).

Lebenserinnerungen und Tagebuchblätter, ed. Rosa Schudel-Benz. Basel, GS-Verlag, 1977.

Beschreibung der Stadt Basel 1610 und Pestbericht 1610/1611, ed. V. Lötscher. Basel, Schwabe, 1987.

THOMAS PLATTER JR. (SEE ALSO FELIX PLATTER)

Huit jours à Genève en 1595, trans. C. Le Fort, *Mémoires et documents de la Société d'histoire de Genève,* no. 20, 1934.

Un étudiant bâlois à Orléans en 1599, trans. P. de Félice. Orléans, H. Herluison, 1879.

Visite de Thomas Platter à Nîmes et au pont du Gard (février 1596), trans. A. Alioth. Nîmes, Peyrot-Tinel, 1880.

Voyage à Rouen (1599), trans. M. Keittinger. Montpellier, Impr. J. Martel aîné, 1890.

Thomas Platter et les Juifs d'Avignon, trans. S. Kahn. Paris, Société des études juives, 1892.

Description de Paris (1599), trans. L. Sieber and M. Weibel, *Memoires de la Société de l'histoire de Paris et de l'Ile-de-France,* vol. 23. Paris, 1896.

Une description de Bruges. trans. M. Letts. Bruges, 1924.

Thomas Platter des Jüngeren Englandfahrt in Jahre 1599, ed. U. Hecht, Halle, 1929.

Visite à Bourges de deux étudtants bâlois, trans. R. Gandilhon. Bourges, 1934.

Travels in England, 1599, trans. C. Williams. London, 1937.

Journal of a Younger Brother, The Life of Thomas Platter, a Medical Student in Montpellier, trans. S. Jennet. London, 1963.

Beschreibung der Reisen durch Frankreich, Spanien, England und den Niederlanden, ed. Rut Keiser. Basel, Schwabe, 1968 (fundamental).

"Hausbuch oder Hauptbuch, enthaltend Testamente und Inventare der Familie, geschrieben 1615 von Thomas Platter," ed. V. Lötscher. *Basler Neujahrsblatt.* no. 153, 1975.

CONTEMPORARY TEXTS

Ramus, Petrus. *La Basilea ad senatum populumque basiliensem,* n.p., 1571.

Zwinger, Theodor. *Theatrum vitae humanae,* preface by Felix Platter. Basileae, Froben, 1565.

———. *Methodus apodemica in eorum gratiam qui cum fructu in quocumque tandem vitae genere peregrinari cupiunt.* Basileae, Hervag, 1577.

Wurstisen, Christian. *Baszler Chronicken.* Basel, Henric Petri, 1580 (reprinted in 1765, 1883).

Burckhardt, Jacob. *Oratio funebris de vita et obitti celeberrimi Felicis Plateri.* Basileae, 1614.

Gast, Johannes. *Tagebuch (1531–1552),* ed. P. Burckhardt, Basler Chroniken, vol. 8, Basel, l945.

Montaigne, Michel de. *Journal de voyage en Italie.* in *Oeuvres complètes.* Paris, Gallimard. 1980.

Amerbach, Bonifacius, *Amerbach-Korrespondenz,* ed. A Hartmann et B. R. Jenny. Basel, Verlag der Universitätsbibliothek, 1991. 10 vols.

Secondary Works on the Platters
(in alphabetical order)

"Vom Anfang neuer Zeit. Drei Selbstbiographien aus dem Jahrhundert der Glaubenskämpfe. Thomas und Felix Platter und Théodore Agrippa d'Aubigné," in *Erlebnis und Bekenntnis,* ed. O. Fischer, vol. 1. Munich, 1911.

Bruckner, Albert. "Drei Briefe von Anna Platter-Dietschi an ihren Sohn Felix," *Basler Nachrichten,* no. 32, 7 August 1932.

Buess, Heinrich. "Gynäkologie und Geburtshilfe bei Felix Platter," in *Festschrift für A. Labhardt.* Basel, 1941.

———. "Schweizer Arzte als Forscher," *Entdecker und Erfinder.* Basel, 1945.

———. "Ein Basler Gedenktag," *National-Zeitung,* no. 405, 3 septembre 1964.

———. "Der Einfluss Vesals auf die praktische Anatomie am Beispiel Felix Platters," *Med. Monatsschrift.* no. 18, 1964.

Burckhardt, Albrecht. *Die medizinische Fakultät zu Basel.* Basel, 1917.

Buxtorf-Falkeisen, Karl. "Blicke in das Privatleben Dr. Felix Platters," *Basler Taschenbuch,* 1850, pp. 88–105.

———. *Baslerische Stadt- und Landgeschichten aus dam 16. Jahrhundert.* Basel, 1868.

Carlen, Louis. "Rechtsgeschichtliches aus Frankreich, Spanien, England und den Niederlanden in einem Reisebericht von 1595–1600," Brig, in *Schriften des Stockalperarchivs,* Heft 22, 1971.

Christoffel, Hans. "Psychiatrie und Psychologie bei Felix Platter," *Monatsschrift für Psychiatrie und Neurochirurgie,* no. 127, Basel, 1954.

———. "Eine systematische Psychiatrie des Barock, Felix Platters *Laesiones mentis,*" *Schw. Archiv für Neurologie und Psychiatrie,* vol. 77, 1956.

Ernst, Felix. "Die beiden Platter," *Neue Schweizer Rundschau,* no. 20, Zurich, 1927.

Fehlmann, Hans-Rudolf. *Der Einfluss der Pharmazie in Montpellier auf den Basler Arzt Felix Platter.* Stuttgatt, 1975.

Felix Platter (1536–1614) in seiner Zeit. Proceedings of the Basel Colloquium, 8 November 1986, ed. H- Buess and U. Trohler. Basel, Schwabe, 1991.

Gorsse, Pierre de. *Toulouse au XVIe siècle vue par deux étudiants bâlois.* Toulouse. 1940.

Häfliger, Joseph. *Felix Platters sogenannte Hausapotheke.* Zurich, 1936.

Hunziger, Rose. *Felix Platter als Arzt und Stadtrat in Basel.* Zurich, 1938.

———. (Under the name Reiman). "Felix Platters Abhandlungen über die Zustände und Krankheiten des Geistes," *Schweizer Archiv für Neurologie und Psychiatrie,* no. 62, 1948.

Jenny, Ernst. "Goethe und Thomas Platter," *Basler Jahrbuch,* 1902.

Karcher, Felix. *Felix Platter, Professor, praxeos und Stadtarzt von Basel.* Basel, 1943.

———. *Felix Platter. Lebensbild des basler Stadtarztes.* Basel, 1949.

———. *Theodor Zwinger und seine Zeitgenossen.* Basel, 1956.

Koelbing, Huldrych M. "Felix Platter als Ophtalmologe," *Ophtalmolgica,* no. 133, 1957.

————. "Felix Platters Stellung in der Medizin seiner Zeit," *Gesnerus*, no. 22, Aarau, 1965.

————. *Renaissance der Augenheilkunde, 1540–1630*. Berne, Stuttgart, 1967.

————. "Diagnose und Aetiologie bei Felix Platter," in *Festschrift für H. Goerke*. Munich, 1978.

————. "Felix Platter als Augenarzt," *Gesnerus*, no. 47, 1990.

Kölner, Paul. "Das Gelehrtengeschlecht Platter ," *Basler Nachrichten*, no. 33, 19 August 1956.

Landolt, Elisabeth. "Materialien zu Felix Platter als Sammler und Kunstfreund," *Basler Zeitschrift*, no. 72, 1972.

Liebenau, Theodor von. "Felix Platter von Basel und Rennward Cysat von Luzern," *Basler Jahrbuch*, 1900.

Liechtenhan, Francine-Dominique. "Theodor Zwinger, théoricien du voyage," *Littérales*, no. 7, 1990

Lötscher, Valentin. "Felix Platter und seine Familie ," *Basler Neujahrsblatt*, no. 153, 1975.

————. *Gedächtnisausstellung zum 400. Todestag von Thomas Platter*. Gemeindehaus zu Grächen, 1982.

————. "Thomas Platter, Bürger zu Basel, zum 400. Todestag," *Basler Zeitung*, 30 January 1982.

Merlan, Peter. "Nachrichten über Felix Platters Naturaliensammlung," *Berichte der Verhandlungen der Naturforschenden Gesellschaft*, 1833–1840, vol. 4. Basel, 1840.

Merian, Wilhelm, "Felix Platter als Musiker," *Sammelbände der Internat. Musikgesellschaft*, XIII, Jg. 2. Leipzig, 1912.

Miescher, Friedrich. *Die medizinische Fakultät*. Basel, 1860.

Rytz, Walter. *Geschichte eines Herbars*. Bern, 1931.

————. "Das Herbarium Felix Platters," *Berichte der Verhandlungen der Naturforschenden Gesellschaft*, vol. 44. Basel, 1932.

Schnidrig, Aloys. *Die Platterfamilie rehabilitiert*. Pratteln, 1972.

————. "Rehabilitation der Platterfamilie," *Basellandschaftliche Zeitung*, 1966, no. 294.

Schiewek, Ingrid. "Zur Autobiographie des Stadtarztes Felix Platter," *Forschungen und Fortschritte*, no. 39, 1964.

Skerlak, Vladimir. *Felix Platter und seine Zeit. Eine Ausstellung zu seinem 450. Geburtstag, Diss. Med.* Basel, 1989.

Stähelin, Margrit. "Felix Platter, der Basler Stadtarzt," *Basler Jahrbuch*, 1909.

Steiner, Gustav. "Arzte and Wundärzte, Chirurgenzunft and medizinische Fakultlät in Basel," *Basler Jahrbuch*, 1954.

Stoll, Clemens "Zum Basler Apothekerwesen im 16. Jahrhundert, der Briefwechsel von Balthasar Hummel and Felix Platter zwischen 1555 und 1557," in *Zur Geschichte des schweizer Apothekerwesens*. Zurich, Juris-Verlag, 1988.

Das Thomas Platter Haus. Basel, 1966.

Vortisch, Christian Martin. "Felix Platter als Pestarzt," in *Das Marrkgräflerland*. Schopfheim, 1989.

Voyager à la Renaissance. Proceedings of the Tours Colloquium of 1983, H. Céard and J.-C. Margolin, eds. Maisonneuve et Larose, 1987.

Despite their many similarities, the memoirs of the three Platters (the best modern editions of which are the 1944 for Thomas Sr., the 1976 for Felix, and the 1968 for Thomas Jr.) represent three distinct intellectual generations (not the same as biological generations). In describing a virtuous hero (himself) and his struggles against adverse fortune, Thomas Sr. was working in the Renaissance tradition of Petrarch's *Epistolae familiares,* a work that as a teacher and publisher he knew fairly well and more or less at first hand. Thomas Jr., though the youngest of the three Platters, was the second to write his memoirs, at the turn of the seventeenth century, and his writing reflects the ideal of the humanist travel diary—scholarly, objective, and at times pedantic, à la Theodore Zwinger. Felix was the last of the three to write, shortly after either 1608 or 1611. Though much older than Thomas Jr, Felix is also the most modern of the three, writing in a tradition that was still new in 1610 but destined to become dominant: the modern travel account. The modern travel writer is at once extroverted and, to an even greater degree, introverted. The modern tradition was begun by Montaigne and continued, after Felix Platter, by Jean-Jacques Rousseau, Frédéric Amiel, and many others. (See Francine-Dominique Liechtenhan, "Autobiographie et voyage entre la Renaissance et le Baroque: l'exemple de la famille Platter," *Revue de Synthèse,* nos. 3–4, July-December 1993, pp. 455–71.)

OTHER SECONDARY WORKS

Most but not all of the works listed below concern the history of Montpellier in the sixteenth century.

Archives municipales de Montpellier (Tour des Pins). BB 393. Manuscript record of the deliberations of the city council in the 1550s.

Archives de la ville de Montpellier. *Inventaires et documents,* vol. 6: Inventaire de Joffre, Archives du greffe de 1a maison consulaire, Armoires A et B (compoix), ed. M. Oudot de Dainville. Montpellier, L'Abeille, 1934.

Archives de la ville de Montpellier. *Inventaires et documents,* vol. 7: Inventaire de Joffre, Archives du greffe de la maison consulaire, Armoire C (sous-série BB), municipal deliberations, ed. M. Oudot de Dainville. Montpellier, L'Abeille, 1939.

Archives communales de Nîmes, registre LL8 (manuscript), municipal deliberations for the 1550s (subsequent to 21 August 1552).

Barral, Marcel. *Les Noms de rues à Montpellier du Moyen Age à nos jours.* Montpellier, P. Clerc, Espace Sud, 1989.

Baumel, Jean. *Vie, moeurs et traditions populaires à Montpellier et dans ses environs au cours de la deuxième moitié du XVe siècle, d'après les frères Platter.* Montpellier, Dehan, 1974.

———. *Montpellier au cours des XVIe et XVIIe , siècles. Les guerres de religion (1510–1685).* Montpellier, Causse, 1970.

Beloved Son Felix. The Journal of Felix Platter, trans. Seán Jennett. London, Muller, 1961. (Contains important maps of Montpellier and the Platters' world in the sixteenth century.)

Benedict, Philip, ed. *Cities and Social Change in Early Modern France.* London, Unwin Hyman, 1989. (Especially the chapters on Montpellier, Paris, Dijon, Aix-en-Provence, and Toulouse in the sixteenth century.).

Benedict, Philip. *Rouen during the Wars of Religion.* Cambridge, Cambridge University Press, 1981. (For comparative purposes.).

Bosc, Henri. *Les Grandes Heures du protestantisme à Montpellier.* Montpellier, Reschly, 1957.

Braudel, Fernand, *La Méditerrannée et le monde méditerranéen au temps de Philippe II.* Paris, Armand Colin, 1966 (2 volumes).

Cholvy, Gerard. *Histoire de Montpellier.* Toulouse, Privat, 1984.

Darmon, Pierre. *Les Cellules folles.* Paris, Plon, 1993 (especially chap. 2.).

Darnton, Robert. "A Bourgeois Puts His World in Order: The City as Text," in *The Great Cat Massacre.* New York, Basic Books, 1984, pp. 107–44.

Delormeau, Charles. "Les circonscriptions ecclésiastiques protestantes du Languedoc méditerranéen aux XVIe et XVIIe siècles," in *Actes du XXXVIIe Congrès de la Fédération historique du Languedoc méditerranéen et du Roussillon.* Limoux, 1964, p. 63 ff.

[Delormeau, Charles]. Catalogue of exhibition "Coligny et la Réforme à Montpellier au XVIe siècle" at the Salle Pétrarque in Montpellier, 16–30 November 1974. Documents and information by Charles Delormeau. Montpellier, 1974.

————. "Les débuts de la Réforme à Montpellier," in *Hommage à Jacques Fabre de Morlhon. Mélanges historiques et généalogiques, Rouergue-Bas-Languedoc,* ed. Jean-Denis Bergasse. Albi, Ateliers professionnels de l'OSJ, 1978, pp. 239–48.

Dulieu, Louis. "Les locaux médicaux de l'enseignement à Montpellier à travers les âges," *Monspeliensis Hippocrates,* no. 4 (1959).

————. "Une famille médicale à la Renaissance: les Saporta," *Languedoc médical,* no. 2, 1963.

————. "Quelques aspects des relations médicales entre Bâle et Montpellier à l'époque de la Renaissance," in *XIXe Congrès international d'histoire de la médecine.* Basel, 1964.

————. "Les Étudiants en médecine de Montpellier à i'époque de la Renaissance," *Monspeliensis Hippocrates,* no. 38 (1967).

————. "La chirurgie à Montpellier au XVIe siècle," in *Medizingeschichte in unserer Zeit,* Festgabe für Edith Heischkel-Artelt und Walter Artelt zum 65. Geburtstag, ed. Hans-Heinz Lamer. Stuttgart, Ferdinand Enke Verlag, 1971, pp. 145–59.

————. *La Médecine à Montpellier,* vol. 2: *La Renaissance.* Avignon, Les Presses Universelles, 1979 (important).

————. *La Médecine à Montpellier du XIIe siècle au XXe siècle.* Paris, Hervas, 1990.

Fabre, Jean-Henri. *Souvenirs entomologiques.* Paris, Robert Laffont, 1989, II, pp. 890–91. (A remarkable work on the diet of peasants in Mediterranean France in times past.)

Freedman, Joseph S. "Aristotle and the Content of Philosophy Instruction at Central European Schools and Universities during the Reformation Era (1500–1650)," *Proceedings of the American Philosophical Society,* vol. 137, no. 2, June 1993, pp. 213–53. (Interesting on the use of taxonomic categories for the refinement of knowledge, a technique used by the Platters.)

Gariel, Pierre. *Idée de la ville de Montpellier.* Montpellier, P. Pech, 1665 (facsimile by Editions de la Tour Gile, Péronnas, 1993).

Germain, Alexandre C. "La Renaissance à Montpellier," *Publications de la Société archéologique de Montpellier,* 1re série, section des lettres, vol. 6. Montpellier, Martel, 1870–71, pp. 9–64 (important).

————. "Les étudiants de l'école de médecine de Montpellier au XVIe siècle. Etude historique sur le *liber procuratoris studiosorum*," *Revue historique*, 1877.

Grasset-Morel, Louis. Montpellier. ses sixains, ses îles . . ." Montpellier, L Valat, 1908 (facsimile by C. Lacour, Nîmes, 1989).

Grmek, Mirko D. *Les Maladies à l'aube de la civilisation occidentale.* Paris, Payot, 1944, pp. 199–225. (On venereal diseases in the sixteenth century.)

Guiraud, Louise, *Histoire du culte at des miracles de Notre-Dame des Tables.* Montpellier, 1885. (All of Louise Guiraud's work is essential for understanding Montpellier in the Renaissance.)

————. *La Paroisse Saint-Denis de Montpellier.* Montpellier, Martel, 1887.

————. *Les Fondations d'Urbain V à Montpellier*, vol. 1: *Le collège des Douze Médecins ou collège de Mende.* Montpellier. J. Martel aîné, 1889; vol. 2: *Le collège Saint-Benoît, le collège Saint-Pierre, le collège du Pape.* Montpellier, J. Martel aîné, 1890; vol. 3: *Le monastère Saint-Benoît et ses diverses transformations depuis son érection en cathédrale en 1536.* Montpellier, J. Martel, 1891.

————. *Recherches topographiques sur Montpellier au Moyen Age.* Montpellier, Coulet, 1895.

————. *Le Procès de Guillaume Pellicier, évêque de Maguelone-Montpellier (1527-1567).* Paris, Picard fils, 1907.

————. *Etudes sur la Réforme à Montpellier.* Mémoires de la société archéologique de Montpellier, vols. 6 and 7. Montpellier, 1918 (fundamental).

————. "Un registre inconnu de l'université de droit de Montpellier (1536-1570)," *Bulletin philologique et historique (jusqu'à 1715)*, year 1913, nos. 1 and 2. Paris, Imprimerie nationale, 1913.

————. "Plans successifs de la cathédrale Saint-Pierre de Montpellier," Société archéologique de Montpellier (after 1905).

Hauser, Henri. *La Modernité du XVIe siècle.* Paris, PUF, Alcan, 1930.

Hébert, Brigitte. "Le lansquenet dans les contes drolatiques Allemands au XVe siècle," in *L'Homme de guerre au XVIe siècle.* Publications de l'Université de Saint-Etienne, 1992, pp. 244–56.

Hyrvoix, Albert, "François Ier et la première guerre de religion en Suisse," *Revue des questions historiques*, 1902, pp. 465–537 (on the limited pro-Helvetic philo-Protestantism of the French monarchy, chiefly after 1530).

Imbert, Jean. *Le Droit hospitalier de l'Ancien Régime.* Paris, Presses Universitaires de France, 1993.

Irvine, Fred. "Social Structure, Social Mobility and Social Change In Sixteenth-Century Montpellier: From Renaissance City-State to Ancien-Régime Capital," Ph. D. thesis, University of Toronto (Department of History), 1979.

Jouanna, Arlette. "La première domination des Réformés à Montpellier (1561-1563)," in *Les Réformés, enracinement socio-culturel*, XXVe Colloque international des humanistes, Tours, 1–13 July 1982, Etudes réunies par Bernard Chevalier et Robert Sauzet. Paris, Editions de La Maisnie, 1985.

Koelbing, Huldrych. "Montpellier, vu par Felix Platter, étudiant en médecine (1552-1557)," in *110e Congrès national des sociétés savantes*, Montpellier, 1985.

Le Roy Ladurie, Emmanuel. "Sur Montpellier et sa campagne aux XVI et XVIIe siècles," *Annales ESC*, 1957, pp. 223–30. I also deal with the Platters in my *Paysans de Languedoc* (Paris: SEVPEN, 1966); in Philippe Wolff, ed., *L'Histoire du Languedoc* (Toulouse: Privat, 1988), chap. 8; and in my *Histoire du Languedoc* (Paris: Presses Universitaires de France, 1962), where I coined the phrase *le beau XVIe siècle* that has since been taken up by many other French historians.

Leboutte, René. "Offense against family order: infanticide . . . from the fifteenth through the early twentieth centuries," *Journal of the History of Sexuality,* 1991, vol. 2, no. 2.

Léry, Jean de. *Indiens de la Renaissance. Histoire d'un voyage fait en la terre du Brésil, 1557,* with an introduction by Anne-Marie Chartier. Paris, Ed. Epi, 1972. (Léry made his ocean voyage in the same year that Felix Platter traveled in France, 1557.)

Lichtenthaeler, Charles. *Histoire de la médecine.* Paris, Fayard, 1978.

Mademoiselle [sic] *Louise Guiraud* (Bio-bibliography of). Montpellier, Roumégous et Dehan, 1920 (important).

Mallary Masters, G. "L'humanisme montpelliérain au service des sciences naturelles: quelques préfaces littéraires de textes médicaux de la Renaissance," *Bulletin de l'Académie des sciences et lettres de Montpellier,* vol. 22, 1991, pp. 323–37.

Marques, Corinne. "Les Guidons da taille montpelliérains de 1549, 1565, 1576, 1581, 1591 et 1599. Démographie historique et géographie sociale (aspects statistiques)." Master's thesis directed by Mme Arlene Jouanna. Université Paul-Valéry de Montpellier, June 1990.

Michau, Françoise. "Montpellier, son consulat, ses consuls, 1550–1558." Master's thesis directed by Mme Arlene Jouanna. Université Paul-Valéry de Montpellier, June 1985.

Michon, Louis M. *La Reliure française.* Paris, Larousse, 1951 (especially the sections concerning the reign of Henri II).

Muchembled, Robert. "Les jeunes, les jeux et la violence . . . au XVIe siècle," in *Les Jeux à la Renaissance.* Paris, Vrin, 1982 (for comparative purposes).

Otis, Leah Lydia. *Prostitution in Medieval Society. The History of an Urban Institution in Languedoc.* Chicago, University of Chicago Press, 1985.

Pomian, Krzysztof. *Collectionneurs, amateurs et curieux. Paris, Venise: XVIe-XVIIIe siècle.* Paris, Gallimard, 1987 (important for understanding Felix Platter's outlook as a collector).

Rabelais et son temps. Exhibition at the Cour de Cassation, Paris, June–July 1994, Catalogue edited by Annick Tillier. Paris, Cour de cassation, 1994 (especially pp. 25ff. on medicine in Montpellier in the sixteenth century).

Revillout, Charles. "Les promoteurs de la Renaissance à Montpellier," *Mémoires de la Société archéologique de Montpellier,* 2e série, vol. 2, 1re fascicule. Montpellier, Martel, 1900, pp. 14–383 (fundamental).

Rey, Roseline. *Histoire de la douleur.* Paris, La Découverte, 1993, pp. 70ff. (on "Vesalian" anatomy).

Schneider, Robert A. *Public Life in Toulouse, 1463–1789: From Municipal Republic to Cosmopolitan City.* Ithaca, Cornell University Press, 1989 (important).

Serres. Pierre. *Abrégé de l'histoire du calvinisme dans la ville de Montpellier,* ed. Marcel Banal and Michel Péronnet. Montpellier, Editions de l'Entente bibliophile, Tour de la Babote, 1977.

Sournia, Bernard et al. *Montpellier, la demeure médiévale. Inventaire général des Monuments.* Paris, Imprimerie nationale, 1991.

Spooner, F. *Economie mondiale et frappes monétaires en France (1493–1680).* Paris, SEVPEN, 1956.

Teissier, M.-F. "Documents sur Montpellier au XVIe siècle d'après les [premiers] registres d'état civil huguenot," Société de l'histoire du protestantisme français, *Bulletin historique et littéraire*, 48e année, 8e année de la 4e série, no. 1, 15 January 1899.

Thomas, Louis J. *Montpellier, ville marchande*. Montpellier, Valat, Coulet, 1936.

Villa, Robert. "Montpellier à l'heure de l'«Union», 1574–1577." Master's thesis, directed by Mme Arlette Jouanna, Université Paul-Valéry de Montpellier, June 1983.

Wolfe, Martin. *The Fiscal System of Renaissance France*. New Haven, Yale University Press, 1972.

Further bibliographic information can be found in the notes, in particular concerning Felix Platter's travels in France. Finally, I wish to express my gratitude to the authors of the various unpublished master's theses cited above, as well as to Professor Arlette Jouanna, who directed their work; their scholarship was most valuable.

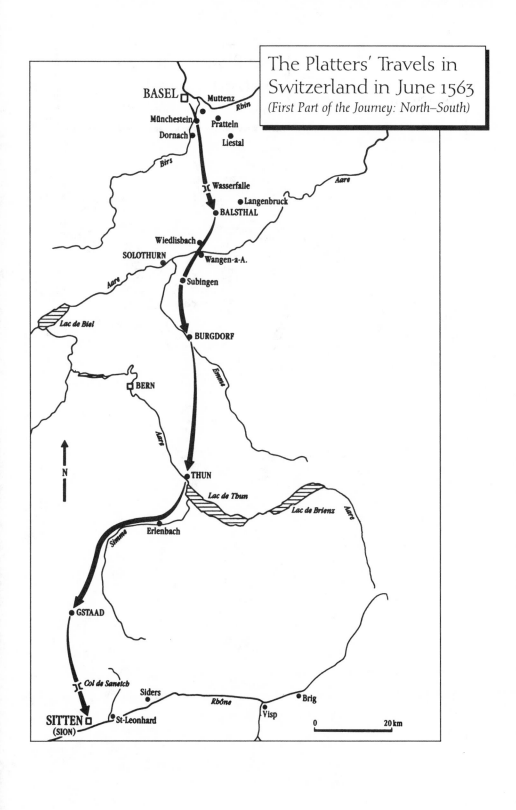

The Platters' Travels in
Switzerland in June 1563
(First Part of the Journey: North–South)

BASEL · Muttenz
Rhin
Münchestein · Pratteln
Dornach · Liestal
Birs
Aare
)(Wasserfalle
· Langenbruck
· BALSTHAL
Wiedlisbach
SOLOTHURN · Wangen-a-A.
Aare
· Subingen
Lac de Biel
· BURGDORF
Emme
□ BERN
Aare
↑
N
· THUN
Lac de Thun
Lac de Brienz
Aare
Simme
· Erlenbach
· GSTAAD
)(Col de Sanetch
· Siders
Rhône · Brig
· Visp
SITTEN □ · St-Leonhard
(SION)
0   20 km

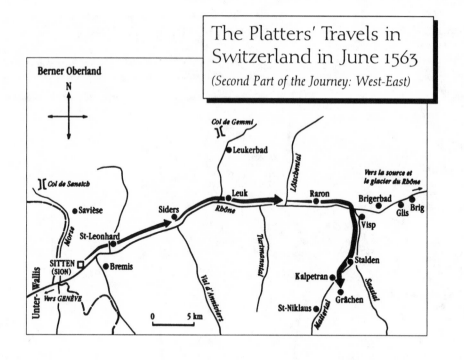

The Platters' Travels in
Switzerland in June 1563
(Second Part of the Journey: West-East)

Berner Oberland

N

Col de Gemmi

Leukerbad

Col de Sanetch

Savièse

Siders

Leuk

Rhône

Raron

Brigerbad

Brig

Glis

Vers la source et
le glacier du Rhône

St-Leonhard

SITTEN
(SION)

Bremis

Morge

Unter-Wallis

Vers GENÈVE

Val d'Anniviers

Turtmanntal

Lötschental

Visp

Stalden

Kalpetran

Grächen

St-Niklaus

Saastal

Mattertal

0   5 km

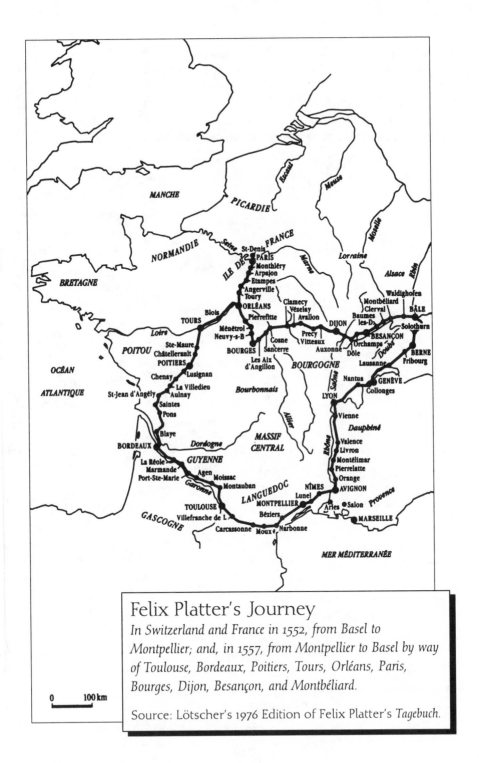

MANCHE

PICARDIE

NORMANDIE

BRETAGNE

OCÉAN
ATLANTIQUE

Seine FRANCE
St-Denis
PARIS
ÎLE DE Monthléry
Arpajon
Étampes
Angerville
Toury
ORLÉANS
Blois Pierrefitte
TOURS
Loire Ménétrol
Neuvy-s-B
Ste-Maure
Châtellerault
POITOU POITIERS
Chenay Lusignan
La Villedieu
St-Jean-d'Angély Aulnay
Saintes
Pons
Blaye
BORDEAUX
La Réole Dordogne GUYENNE
Marmande
Port-Ste-Marie Agen Moissac
Garonne Montauban
LANGUEDOC
TOULOUSE
GASCOGNE Villefranche de L.
Carcassonne Moux

Lorraine Meuse
Alsace Rhin
Moselle

Waldighofen
Montbéliard
Clervał
Baumes
les-D.
Clamecy BÂLE
Vézelay
Avallon DIJON Orchamps Solothurn
Précy BESANÇON
Cosne Vitteaux
Sancerre Auxonne Dôle Doubs BERNE
Les Aix BOURGES Fribourg
d'Angillon BOURGOGNE Lausanne

MASSIF
CENTRAL Bourbonnais
Allier Nantua GENÈVE
Collonges
LYON

Rhône
Vienne
Dauphiné
Valence
Livron
Montélimar
Pierrelatte
Orange
NÎMES AVIGNON
Lunel
MONTPELLIER Arles Salon Provence
Béziers MARSEILLE
Narbonne

MER MÉDITERRANÊE

Felix Platter's Journey

*In Switzerland and France in 1552, from Basel to
Montpellier; and, in 1557, from Montpellier to Basel by way
of Toulouse, Bordeaux, Poitiers, Tours, Orléans, Paris,
Bourges, Dijon, Besançon, and Montbéliard.*

Source: Lötscher's 1976 Edition of Felix Platter's *Tagebuch*.

0   100 km

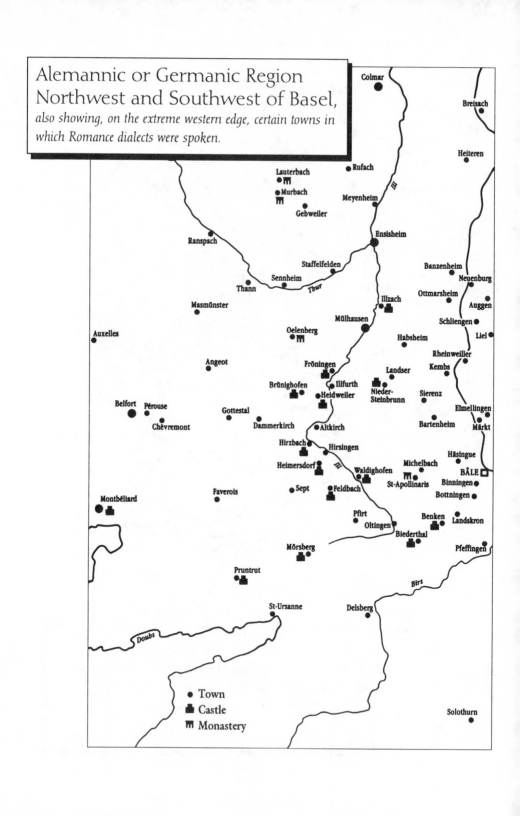

Alemannic or Germanic Region
Northwest and Southwest of Basel,
also showing, on the extreme western edge, certain towns in
which Romance dialects were spoken.

Colmar

Breisach

Heiteren

Rufach

Lauterbach
ₘ
Murbach
ₘ

Meyenheim

Ill

Gebweiler

Ensisheim

Ranspach

Staffelfelden

Banzenheim

Neuenburg

Sennheim
Thann

Thur

Ottmarsheim

Auggen

Masmünster

Illzach

Schliengen

Liel

Oelenberg
ₘ

Mülhausen

Habsheim

Rheinweiller

Auxelles

Angeot

Fröningen

Landser

Kembs

Brünighofen
Heidweiler

Illfurth

Nieder-
Steinbrunn

Sierenz

Elmellingen

Belfort
Pérouse

Gottestal

Chèvremont

Dammerkirch

Altkirch

Bartenheim

Märkt

Hirzbach

Hirsingen

Häsingue

Heimersdorf

Ill

Waldighofen

Michelbach
ₘ
St-Apollinaris

BÂLE □

Faverois

Sept

Feldbach

Binningen

Bottningen

Montbéliard

Pfirt
Oltingen

Benken

Landskron

Biederthal

Mörsberg

Pfeffingen

Pruntrut

Birs

St-Ursanne

Delsberg

Doubs

● Town
🏰 Castle
ₘ Monastery

Solothurn

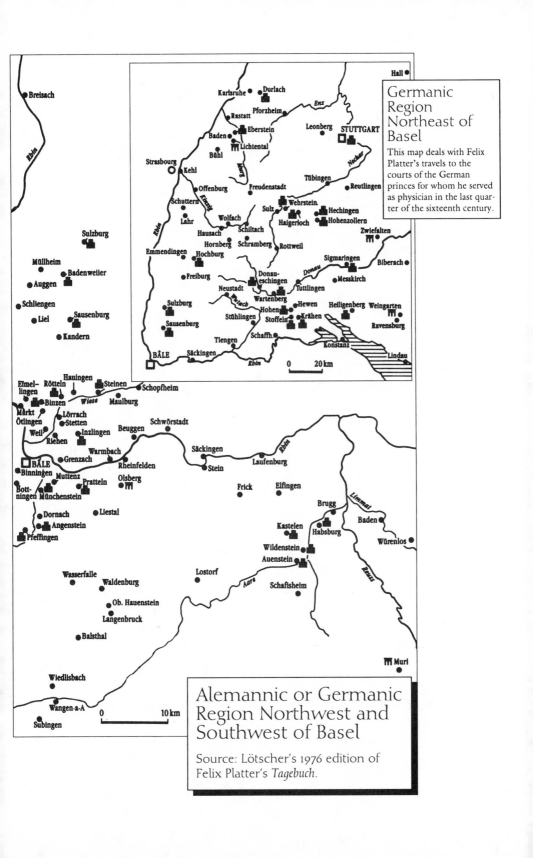

Breisach

Sulzburg
Müllheim
• Badenweiler
• Auggen
• Schliengen   Sausenburg
• Liel
• Kandern

Germanic
Region
Northeast of
Basel

This map deals with Felix
Platter's travels to the
courts of the German
princes for whom he served
as physician in the last quarter of the sixteenth century.

Hall •

Karlsruhe •   • Durlach
           Pforzheim
   Rastatt
Baden •   • Eberstein   Leonberg   STUTTGART
      Lichtental
   Bühl

Strasbourg
        Kehl
   • Offenburg   Freudenstadt   Tübingen   • Reutlingen
Schuttern
      Wolfach   Sulz   • Wehrstein   Hechingen
   Lahr   Haigerloch   Hohenzollern
      Hausach   Schiltach   Zwiefalten
      Hornberg   Schramberg   Rottweil
Emmendingen   Hochburg
                  Sigmaringen   Biberach •
   • Freiburg   Donau
      Donau-   Messkirch
      eschingen   Tuttlingen
   Neustadt   Wartenberg   Heiligenberg   Weingarten
      Sulzburg   Hewen
         Hohen
      Sausenburg   Stühlingen Stoffeln Krähen   Ravensburg
            Schaffh.
   Tiengen   Konstanz
BÂLE   Säckingen   Lindau
            Rhin   0   20 km

Elmel-   Hauingen
lingen Rötteln Steinen   Schopfheim
Binzen   Wiese Maulburg
Märkt   Lörrach
Ötlingen Stetten
   Weil   Riehen   Inzlingen   Beuggen   Schwörstadt
BÂLE   Grenzach   Warmbach   Säckingen
Binningen   Rheinfelden   Laufenburg   Rhin
   Muttenz   Prattein   Olsberg   Stein
Bott-   Münchenstein   Frick   Elfingen
ningen
• Dornach   • Liestal   Brugg   Limmat
   Angenstein   Kastelen   Baden •
Pfeffingen   Habsburg   Würenlos
                  Wildenstein
                  Auenstein
   Wasserfalle   Lostorf
      Waldenburg   Aare   Schafisheim
         Ob. Hauenstein
      Langenbruck   Reuss
   • Balsthal

                              Muri

Wiedlisbach

Wangen-a-A   0   10 km
• Subingen

Alemannic or Germanic
Region Northwest and
Southwest of Basel

Source: Lötscher's 1976 edition of
Felix Platter's Tagebuch.

INDEX

395

INDEX

Catalan, Laurent: bids farewell to Felix Platter, 223; drinking in house of, 205; farm of, 211; gardens of, 211–12; harvesting grapes, 203–4; keeping kosher, 192; Felix Platter arrives at home of, 183–84; Platter storing dissected dogs with, 191; religious practices of, 187–88; seafood served by, 197; students boarding with, 151

cave dwellers, 252–53

Cellarius (Martin Borrhaus), 49, 69–70, 355 n.29

Cellarius (Isaac Keller), 99, 317, 319, 322, 324, 355 n.29

Ceporinus (Jacob Wiesendanger), 62

Ceresole Alba, Battle of, 74, 83, 141

Champ-Gaillard (Paris), 280

Champol, 297, 370 n.65

Chanteloup, château de, 266–67

Charles II, duc de Lorraine, 285, 369 n.43

Charles III, Duke of Savoy, 161

Charles V (Holy Roman Emperor): Basel as center of anti-imperial plots, 113; conflict with Francis I, 74; decade of the emperor, 86; extent of empire of, 166; fortress in Dole built by, 299; France enlarged at expense of, 165; Francis I and Turkey ally against, 84, 141; Henri II defeats, 168; march on Metz, 156, 161, 180; 1542–44 as turning point in imperial lands, 85; Protestants sent to the stake by, 93; statue in Besançon, 300

Charles V of France, 285–86

Charles VIII of France, 189, 193, 242, 256, 257, 259, 283

Charles IX of France, 191

Chastel, André, 244

"Chaste Susanna" (Birk), 94

château de Candé, 250–51

château de Chanteloup, 266–67

château de Villers-Cotterêts, 274, 275

chateaus of the Loire, 250–51

Châtellerault, 250

Châtres (Arpajon), 266

chestnut zone of France, 163

children: changes in attitudes toward, 18, 339, 373 n.5; Thomas Platter's memoirs of his childhood, 25; punishment of, 90

China, 87

Christianae religionis institutio (*Institutes of the Christian Religion;* Calvin), 65, 68–69, 126, 129–30, 142

Christmas customs, 68

Cimetière des Innocents, 278

Clamecy, 294

Cléry, 259

cod, 238

Coignet, Captain, 25

Collinus (Rudolf Ambüel; Rudolf Am Buol), 126, 128, 142, 357 n.4

Colmar, 222, *Plate 13*

Colross, Simon, 96

Condé, Prince Henri de, 74, 77

Contzenus (Stephan Kunz), 206, 222

"Conversion of Saint Paul, The" (Boltz), 94–95, 96

Copernicus, 20, 88

Cosne, 293–94

Council of Trent, 84

Covet-Courtois, Jacques, 96

Cratander (Andreas Hartmann), 37, 71, 98, 122, 126, 127, 133

Crato, Johannes, 76

Crépy, Treaty of, 86

criminals: execution of, 109–10, 161, 184, 210–11; as foreigners, 111; in the France of Henri II, 234; in Massif Central, 292; Felix Platter attacked near Montlhéry, 267; Thomas Platter attacked near Nuremberg, 21; *prévôts* for combating, 242; in Silesia, 20; thieves outside Lunel, 182; torture of, 109–10

cult of the stag, 256

D

Danès, Pierre, 171–72, 176, 178, 359 n.30

Daurade, la (Toulouse), 232

David, Hans Jacob, 277

decade of the Emperor, 86

Dersam, Lux, 140

devotio moderna, 26

Dialogues (Lucian), 61

Diesbach, Ludwig von, 77

Dietschi, Anna. *See* Platter, Anna Dietschi

Dijon, 295–98, 370 n.65

disputations, 194

Dole, 299

Dolet, Etienne, 84

Donatus, Aelius, 26, 27

Donzy, 294

Dorly (servant of Thomas Platter, Sr.), 308, 329

Dorn, Ambrosius, 82

Dorn, Gerhard, 82

Dorn, Peter, 82

INDEX

W9-CCB-485

THE GREATEST TREASURE HUNT IN HISTORY

The Story of the Monuments Men

ALSO BY ROBERT M. EDSEL

SAVING ITALY
The Race to Rescue a Nation's Treasures
from the Nazis

THE MONUMENTS MEN
Allied Heroes, Nazi Thieves, and
the Greatest Treasure Hunt in History

RESCUING DA VINCI
Hitler and the Nazis Stole Europe's Great Art,
America and Her Allies Recovered It

Monuments Man Lieutenant James Rorimer (center) at the castle of Neuschwanstein supervising the removal of paintings stolen by the Nazis.

THE GREATEST TREASURE HUNT IN HISTORY

The Story of the Monuments Men

by

ROBERT M. EDSEL

SCHOLASTIC
FOCUS

NEW YORK

If you purchased this book without a cover, you should be aware that this book is stolen property. It was reported as "unsold and destroyed" to the publisher, and neither the author nor the publisher has received any payment for this "stripped book."

Copyright © 2019 by Robert M. Edsel

All rights reserved. Published by Scholastic Focus, a division of Scholastic Inc., *Publishers since 1920*. SCHOLASTIC, SCHOLASTIC FOCUS, and associated logos are trademarks and/or registered trademarks of Scholastic Inc.

This book was originally published by Scholastic Focus, an imprint of Scholastic Inc., in 2019.

The publisher does not have any control over and does not assume any responsibility for author or third-party websites or their content.

No part of this publication may be reproduced, stored in a retrieval system, or transmitted in any form or by any means, electronic, mechanical, photocopying, recording, or otherwise, without written permission of the publisher. For information regarding permission, write to Scholastic Inc., Attention: Permissions Department, 557 Broadway, New York, NY 10012.

ISBN 978-1-338-25124-1

10 9 8 7 6 5 4 3 2 1   21 22 23 24 25

Printed in the U.S.A.   40
This edition first printing 2021

Book design by Abby Dening

To my wife and soulmate, Anna, whose unwavering support guided me in writing this book, as it does all that I do; and to our beautiful sons, Francesco and Rodney

CONTENTS

CAST OF CHARACTERS

WESTERN ALLIES

Serving in Italy

CAPTAIN DEANE KELLER
Age as of June 1944: 42.
Born: New Haven,
Connecticut.
Portrait painter; professor
of art at Yale University.

SECOND LIEUTENANT FRED HARTT
Age: 30.
Born: Boston,
Massachusetts.
Art historian.

Serving in Northern Europe

LIEUTENANT GEORGE L. STOUT
Age: 46. Born: Winterset,
Iowa. Art conservator at the
Fogg Museum, Harvard
University.

CAPTAIN WALKER HANCOCK
Age: 43. Born: St. Louis,
Missouri. Award-winning
sculptor.

CAPTAIN ROBERT POSEY
Age: 40. Born: Morris,
Alabama. Architect.

PRIVATE FIRST CLASS LINCOLN KIRSTEIN
Age: 37. Born: Rochester,
New York. Cofounder of
the New York City Ballet
(originally known as the
American Ballet
Company).

SECOND LIEUTENANT JAMES J. RORIMER
Age: 38. Born: Cleveland,
Ohio. Curator at The
Metropolitan Museum of
Art and The Cloisters.

ROSE VALLAND
Age: 45. Born: Saint-
Étienne-de-Saint-Geoirs,
France. Custodian of the
Jeu de Paume Museum
in Paris.

MAJOR RONALD EDMUND BALFOUR
Age: 40. Born: Oxfordshire,
England. Lecturer in
history at Cambridge
University.

CAPTAIN WALTER "HUTCH" HUCHTHAUSEN
Age: 39. Born: Perry,
Oklahoma. Architect.

PRIVATE HARRY ETTLINGER
Age: 18. Born: Karlsruhe,
Germany. Immigrated to
the United States when he
was thirteen years old.

AXIS POWERS

Leader of Fascist Italy

BENITO MUSSOLINI
Age: 60. Born: Dovia di
Predappio, Italy.
Dictator.

Leaders of Nazi Germany

ADOLF HITLER
Age: 55. Born: Braunau
am Inn, Austria. Dictator.

HERMANN GÖRING
Age: 51. Born:
Rosenheim, Germany.
Reichsmarschall.

Serving in Italy

GENERAL KARL WOLFF
Age: 44. Born:
Darmstadt, Germany.
Supreme leader of all SS
troops and police
in Italy.

ALEXANDER LANGSDORFF
Age: 45. Born: Alsfeld,
Germany. Accomplished
archaeologist.

Serving in Northern Europe

ALFRED ERNST ROSENBERG
Age: 51. Born: Reval,
Russia. Leader of the
ERR, the chief Nazi
looting organization.

COLONEL KURT VON BEHR
Age: 54. Born: Hanover,
Germany. Head of the
ERR in Paris, France.

BRUNO LOHSE
Age: 32. Born: Buer,
Germany. Deputy Chief
of the ERR in Paris,
France.

HERMANN BUNJES
Age: 32. Born: Bramsche,
Germany. Göring's
personal art agent in
France.

ABOUT THE
MONUMENTS MEN

T he Monuments Men were a group of American and British men and women—accomplished museum curators, art scholars and educators, architects, archivists, and artists—who volunteered for military service during World War II combat operations to preserve works of art, monuments, and other cultural treasures from the destruction of war and theft by Adolf Hitler and the Nazis. Together, they made up the Monuments, Fine Arts, and Archives section, or MFAA, part of the Civil Affairs division of the Western Allied armies.

The MFAA was an extraordinary experiment. It marked the first time an army fought a war while comprehensively attempting to mitigate damage to cultural treasures. Those who served in the MFAA, known as the Monuments Men, were a new kind of soldier, charged with saving rather than destroying. Initially, they consulted with Allied air commanders to direct bombing away from cultural sites. As they entered the battered cities of Europe alongside combat troops, the Monuments Men, working without adequate transportation, supplies, or personnel, effected temporary repairs to hundreds of churches and monuments.

During the final months of the war, as the extent of Nazi looting became known, the Monuments Men served in harm's way as art detectives engaged in the greatest treasure hunt in history.

Prior to this war, no army had thought of protecting the monuments of the country in which and with which it was at war, and there were no precedents to follow . . . All this was changed by a General Order issued by the Supreme Commander-in-Chief [General Eisenhower] just before he left Algiers, an order accompanied by a personal letter to all Commanders . . . the good name of the Army depended in great measure on the respect which it showed to the art heritage of the modern world.

MONUMENTS MAN LIEUTENANT COLONEL
SIR LEONARD WOOLLEY, 1952

Dennis Posey, son of Monuments Man Captain Robert Posey, on the family horse.

Dear Dennis: Germany started this war by invading one small country after another until finally France and England had to declare war on her. We helped France and England but didn't start fighting. Then suddenly Japan attacked us and Germany declared war on us at the same time. And so we had to fight, painfully at first for we were unprepared. Now we are strong; England is strong; Russia, who was attacked by Germany is strong; Italy who fought with Germany has been defeated by us and has swung over to our side; France who was defeated by Germany but liberated by us is building a powerful army . . . And so, these are the reasons that I think we will soon defeat Germany and Japan and teach them such a lesson that when you and other little boys like you grow up you will not have to fight them all over again. And I hope no other country will start a fight to get its way for wars are bad.

MONUMENTS MAN CAPTAIN ROBERT POSEY,
IN A LETTER TO HIS SEVEN-YEAR-OLD SON

PRELUDE

In 1907, an eighteen-year-old aspiring artist named Adolf Hitler applied for admission to the Academy of Fine Arts in Vienna, Austria. He felt humiliated when a group of jurors, whom he believed were Jews, rejected his application. The memory of this experience never left him. It fanned the flames of an already burning desire to seek revenge against people who he believed had wronged him. For the remaining thirty-eight years of his life, Hitler continued to see himself as a gifted artist and architect, a creator, with an unyielding determination to prove his genius to the world.

As the leader of Nazism, Hitler used art as a weapon of propaganda to instill a sense of superiority in the German people at the expense of those he termed subhuman, particularly Jews. German

Aspiring artist Adolf Hitler.

Watercolor painted by Adolf Hitler in 1914.

art through the nineteenth century—"true art" in Hitler's view—
was easy to comprehend, often depicting scenes of everyday life.
Renderings of the human form evoked youth, strength, heroism,
and sacrifice, the qualities of the "master race" that Hitler wanted to
project at home and abroad.

Hitler believed that modern art, with its bold colors and distorted figures, could only be the product of sick minds. The Nazis
labeled these works and the artists who created them "degenerate."
In their view, such interpretive paintings and sculpture destroyed
the more traditional concept of beauty and were incomprehensible
to the viewer.

To avoid spoiling the minds of the nation's citizens, Nazi
leaders ordered German museum directors to remove from their
walls some sixteen thousand "degenerate" works of art by greats,
including Pablo Picasso, Henri Matisse, Edgar Degas, Paul

Gauguin, and Vincent van Gogh. Some of these artworks were traded. Almost five thousand were destroyed in a Berlin bonfire as part of a fire department training exercise. Others were sold on the international art market. As one high-ranking Nazi Party official reasoned, "In so doing we hope at least to make some money from this garbage."

In May 1938, Hitler made his first official state visit to Italy. The trip began in Naples, where the people welcomed him with hundred-foot-long banners bearing Nazi swastikas hung from balconies overlooking the path of his motorcade. In Rome, he and other senior Nazi leaders walked through the Colosseum, retracing the steps of Roman rulers and gladiators. But it was the beauty of Florence, jewel of the Renaissance, with its extraordinary churches, bridges, and museums, that Hitler most wanted to see.

The German leader spent two hours walking through the art-filled rooms of the Pitti Palace and Uffizi Gallery, past masterpieces of the Renaissance, enjoying the splendor and richness of the collections. Hitler saw himself as an artist among artists. During his tour, an idea took hold, one with far-reaching consequences: Hitler, the visionary, decided to build a museum in his hometown of Linz, Austria, and assemble a collection of art and cultural objects that he believed would rival some of the world's most respected museums.

It had a formal name—Gemäldegalerie Linz—but it quickly became known as the Führermuseum. His idea had a major obstacle: Many of the masterpieces and other cultural objects that he would need for his Führermuseum were already in Europe's most important museums and private collections. That would soon change.

Hitler and Italian dictator Benito Mussolini (to Hitler's left, wearing cap) visiting the Florence museums in May 1938.

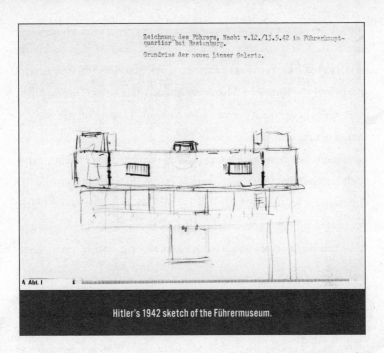

Zeichnung des Führers, Nacht v.12./13.5.42 im Führerhaupt-
quartier bei Rastenburg.

Grundriss der neuen Linzer Galerie.

A Abt. I

Hitler's 1942 sketch of the Führermuseum.

Nazi Germany invaded Poland on September 1, 1939, marking the formal beginning of World War II. The invasion also
sounded the starter gun for the most premeditated looting operation the world had ever seen. Thefts are normally associated with
speed—get in and get out quickly. However, the Nazi looting
operation continued without interruption for nearly six years.

The occupation of Poland alone provided Hitler and his
museum with treasures of immense rarity and value. Cracow, one
of the most picturesque cities in all of Europe, suffered irreplaceable losses. From the Czartoryski Museum, the Nazis stole the
only painting by Leonardo da Vinci in Poland, one of just sixteen
paintings by Leonardo known to exist in the world. From Saint
Mary's Basilica, they looted the most important object in all of
Poland, the Veit Stoss Altarpiece. With these priceless pieces and

riches from the private collections of Austrian Jews that had been confiscated the previous year, in particular from the Austrian branch of the Rothschild banking dynasty, Hitler and his art advisors quickly amassed a treasure that rivaled many of the world's major art museums.

Nazi Germany's invasion of the Netherlands, France, and Belgium in May 1940 pried open Western Europe's treasure chest. In contrast to their brazen looting of Eastern Europe, the Nazis wanted to pillage under a veil of legality in the West, so they simply changed the laws of conquered nations to strip Jews of their rights

Nazi Reichsmarschall Göring and Hitler admiring a painting.

to own private property. This created an avalanche of opportunities for Hitler and his agents, and also for the number two man in the Nazi Party, Reichsmarschall Hermann Göring, an art collector with an insatiable appetite.

The greatest theft in history was underway.

JUNE 26, 1939

Letter from Hitler directing Dr. Hans Posse to supervise the construction of the Führermuseum in Linz.

ADOLF HITLER'

OBERSALZBERG, den 26. Juni 1939

Ich beauftrage Herrn Galeriedirektor Dr.Hans Posse, Dresden, mit dem Aufbau des neuen Kunstmuseums für die Stadt Linz/Donau.

Alle Partei- und Staatsdienststellen sind verpflichtet, Herrn Dr.Posse bei Erfüllung seiner Aufgabe zu unterstützen.

"I commission Dr. Hans Posse, director of the Dresden Gallery, to build up the new art museum for Linz Donau. All Party and State services are ordered to assist Dr. Posse in fulfillment of his mission."
—Adolf Hitler.

NOVEMBER 5, 1940

Reichsmarschall Hermann Göring's order concerning distribution of Jewish art treasures.

In carrying out the measures taken to date for the safeguarding of Jewish art property by the Chief of Military Administration in Paris and the Einsatzstab Rosenberg (Chef OKW. 2 f 28.14. W. Z. Nr 3812/ 40 g), the categories of art objects moved to the Louvre will be established as follows:

1. Those art objects for the further disposition of which the Führer has reserved for himself the right of decision;

2. Those art objects which will serve to complete the collection of the Reichsmarschall;

3. Those art objects and library material which appear useful for building up the Hohe Schule and for the task of Reichsleiter Rosenberg;

4. Those art objects that are appropriate for
   turning over to German museums . . . will
   immediately be inventoried, packed and
   transported to Germany by the Einsatzstab
   with all due care and with the assistance of
   the Luftwaffe.

5. Those art objects which are appropriate for
   transfer to French museums and to the
   French and German art trade will be sold at
   auction at a date yet to be fixed; and the
   proceeds will be assigned to the French
   State for benefit of the French dependents
   of war casualties.

6. Further seizure of Jewish art property in
   France will be effected in the heretofore
   efficient manner by the Einsatzstab
   Rosenberg, in co-operation with the Chief of
   the Military Administration Paris.

Paris, 5 November 1940

I shall submit this suggestion to the Führer,
pending whose approval this procedure will remain
effective.

Signed: GÖRING

★ SECTION I ★

Hitler sketching preliminary concepts for the Führermuseum in Linz.

MAJOR BATTLE LINES AND ART REPOSITORIES IN ITALY

Gene Thorp

CHAPTER 1

LETTERS HOME

Palestrina, Italy: June 1944

The army jeep crept along the hillside road leading to Palestrina, a small Italian town about twenty miles east of Rome. Captain Deane Keller—artist, professor, husband, father, and newly assigned Monuments Man for U.S. Fifth Army—knew the path from his student days, when his painting and drawing talents had earned him the opportunity to study at the American Academy in Rome. No one was shooting at him then, but that was eighteen years ago. Recent reports detailing how German troops were using elevation and blind turns as part of their ambush-and-retreat tactics caused great concern. Determined to serve his country and return home to his wife, Kathy, and their three-year-old son, Dino, Keller and Giuseppe de Gregorio, an officer of the Carabinieri and also his driver, continued advancing up the hill, cautiously.

After rounding a bend in the road, Keller grabbed Giuseppe's arm and told him to stop. He was out of the jeep before it came to a halt. About one hundred feet ahead, lying facedown in the road, was the body of an American soldier. As Keller approached, he thought of a phrase he had once heard used to describe a corpse: "sweetish smell." There was nothing sweet in the air on this hot

Deane Keller and his son, Dino.

June day. Despite the overpowering and nauseating stench, he continued walking.

Those one hundred feet felt like a mile. With each step Keller thought about "the boys," as he referred to them in his letters to Kathy. They had been fighting their way up the Italian peninsula since landing at Salerno in September 1943, taking one hill after another. Some were the age of his art students at Yale University. He wasn't sure why he felt such paternal feelings of pride for them. Maybe it was a consequence of being forty-two years old. Maybe it was being five thousand miles away from his own son, unable to be the father that he had envisioned. Seeing the young men in uniform—"the boys" driving the tanks, the infantry soldiers crouching behind them, and this brave warrior lying in the road—reminded him of Dino.

As he knelt beside the young man's body, Keller noticed something in the overturned helmet. Wedged inside the helmet liner was an airmail envelope addressed to the soldier's mother. Keller wiggled the envelope out of the webbing. As best he could tell, the letter had been hurriedly written, perhaps before or even during battle. All he could do at this point was make sure it was posted.

Keller, like all the soldiers he'd met, relished receiving mail from home. Letters were the sole connective tissue—a lifeline of hope—for soldiers separated by time and distance from family and close friends. Even those containing the most dreaded news were preferred to the heartache and gnawing pain of no news at all.

Keller recalled a letter he'd received from his mother before beginning his assignment as a Monuments Man that filled him with pride and emboldened him for the difficult days he knew were ahead. Standing next to the body of this American soldier, caressing a letter to a mother that contained the last earthly thoughts of her son, was just such a day.

Military service "is a big sacrifice for you," he remembered his mother writing, "but I am thankful you can see beyond that to realize the great need for good men to help. I believe you will never regret it for your own sake and the sake of Dino. He says proudly now—'My Daddy's a sojer.' I don't know who told him that—but I suppose he saw you in that first uniform."

On the long dust-filled drive back to headquarters, with the dead soldier's letter inside his shirt pocket pressed against his chest, Keller closed his eyes for what seemed like just a few minutes, lost in thought about all that had happened since leaving his teaching position at Yale to get into the fight.

New Haven, Connecticut: May 1943

In May 1943, as the end of the semester approached, Keller finally received a reply from the Marine Corps. "Rejected: poor eyesight," or so they said. Admittedly, at 5 feet 7 and 170 pounds, with a grayish tint to his hair and the stereotypical wire-rimmed glasses of a professor, he was hardly the strapping figure of youth that so frequently passed through the recruiting office. Then a well-timed letter from a colleague, Tubby Sizer, the former director of the Yale University Art Gallery, mentioned a newly created art protection unit that would comprise soldiers charged with saving rather than destroying. In Keller's mind, that sounded just right. At the end of his letter, Tubby tried to preempt Keller's natural tendency. "Don't be so damned MODEST," he wrote. "Put it on thick." Keller did, and it worked.

By the time Keller reported to Fort Myer, Virginia, for active duty in late September 1943, circumstances in Italy had changed dramatically. Operation Husky, the successful invasion of Sicily by U.S., British, and Canadian forces that began on July 10, resulted in the removal from office of Benito Mussolini, known as "Il Duce," the leader of Fascist Italy and Adolf Hitler's most important ally.

The battlefield then shifted to the Italian mainland, and within days, Italy signed an armistice agreement with the Allies. Hitler was enraged that his former ally had surrendered. He immediately transferred one million German soldiers to Italy to build a series of defensive lines that stretched across the Italian peninsula between Rome and Naples, intended to slow the Allied advance and make it as costly and bloody as possible. The war was now going to be fought in a country that contained millions of works of art, monuments, and churches, placing some of the greatest masterpieces of Western civilization at risk of being destroyed. It was a recipe for disaster.

Following a month of orientation and training at Fort Myer, Captain Deane Keller boarded a Liberty ship bound for North Africa. Like his 550 shipmates, including many young soldiers headed into combat, he felt proud, excited, and scared. On December 2, 1943, after more than three weeks at sea, he reached his temporary home, an army Civil Affairs training school in the remote hillside town of Tizi Ouzou, Algeria.

The kaleidoscope of fall color of the Virginia countryside was just a memory now. Standing in this desolate Algerian town, all Keller could see were colorless clusters of half-finished buildings and an abundance of braying donkeys and bleating goats. The sound of a familiar voice over his shoulder caught him by surprise.

He turned around, shaking his head in disbelief, and smiled: Standing before him was Major Tubby Sizer, the man who had encouraged him to join the new art protection unit and become a Monuments Man.

Sizer had been among the first selected to serve as a Monuments Man. The army had created the Civil Affairs school, where Keller now found himself, to educate American and British officers about military government and how to run a town once combat troops moved on. With their training now complete, Sizer, fellow American Captain Norman Newton, and British Monuments Man Captain Teddy Croft-Murray were on their way to Naples, Italy.

Despite the obvious good intentions of leaders in Washington and the Monuments Men at Tizi Ouzou, everyone questioned whether the mission could succeed. Would Allied commanders listen to the recommendations of middle-aged art history professors or architects to direct artillery fire *away from* a church or monument when being fired upon? Would Allied troops respect signs the Monuments Men posted making churches and historical buildings off-limits, even if it meant sleeping outside in the rain? And how could just eight Monuments Men, in an army of more than two hundred thousand soldiers, protect even a portion of the works of art and monuments in culturally rich Italy? After eight weeks of training, Keller was on his way to Naples to find out.

Keller's initial duties involved inspections of nearby towns and villages. These experiences left him feeling sad, not because of the extent of destruction, but out of sympathy for what the Italian people had endured. As an artist, he had always admired the country's beauty and boundless creative achievements, but it was the

Italian people who had won his heart so many years earlier. "'*Buona gente, buonissima gente, ma bisogna saperla prendere.*' Good people, very good people," he always told his students and the soldiers he met, "but you have to know how to take them."

During one inspection, Keller visited a hospital where he saw a man without a nose. In its place were two holes. Before the war, had he seen someone in such sad condition, he would have looked away. But sights such as this were all too common during war. Now, each wounded child, destroyed home, and damaged town made him realize how sheltered and privileged his life had been.

The severity of fighting at the town of Cassino, about seventy miles northwest of their headquarters in Naples, had Allied forces pinned down and the Monuments Men waiting until the battle was over. The only practical route into central Italy, and the big prize, Rome, required passage through the Liri Valley. That meant contending with an impregnable mountain bastion overlooking the entire valley, the Abbey of Monte Cassino—and the Germans knew it.

Every effort had been made to avoid damage to the abbey, but General Dwight D. Eisenhower's December 29, 1943, order concerning the protection of cultural treasures made it clear: "If we have to choose between destroying a famous building and sacrificing our own men, then our men's lives count infinitely more and the buildings must go." On the morning of February 15, waves of Allied bombers severely damaged the abbey, but the fighting continued for three more bloody months.

Norman Newton was the first Monuments Man to reach the heavily mined and booby-trapped abbey, still under fire from enemy mortars, just hours after the remaining Germans had been

DECLASSIFIED
Authority
NND 7 60210
By A NARA Date 8/11/05

C O P Y

~~CONFIDENTIAL~~

ALLIED FORCE HEADQUARTERS

Office of The Commander-in-Chief

AG 000.4-1

29 December 1943

SUBJECT: Historical Monuments

TO : All Commanders

Today we are fighting in a country which has contributed a great deal to our cultural inheritance, a country rich in monuments which by their creation helped and now in their old age illustrate the growth of the civilization which is ours. We are bound to respect those monuments so far as war allows.

If we have to choose between destroying a famous building and sacrificing our own men, then our men's lives count infinitely more and the buildings must go. But the choice is not always so clear-cut as that. In many cases the monuments can be spared without any detriment to operational needs. Nothing can stand against the argument of military necessity. That is an accepted principle. But the phrase "military necessity" is sometimes used where it would be more truthful to speak of military convenience or even of personal convenience. I do not want it to cloak slackness or indifference.

It is a responsibility of higher commanders to determine through A.M.G. Officers the locations of historical monuments whether they be immediately ahead of our front lines or in areas occupied by us. This information passed to lower echelons through normal channels places the responsibility on all Commanders of complying with the spirit of this letter.

/s/ Dwight D. Eisenhower

DWIGHT D. EISENHOWER,
General, U. S. Army,
Commander-in-Chief.

DISTRIBUTION:
"C"

CLASSIFICATION CHANGED
TO RESTRICTED
By authority of CALA
By J. F. PAISLEY AGD
Date 4 AUG 1945

Restricted Classification
Removed

1   189

driven out. His damage assessment report painted a grim picture: "Reconstruction of entire Abbey is possible although much is now only heap of pulverized rubble and dust."

The far greater tragedy was the body count. Four months of fighting in grueling weather conditions had exacted a toll so great it hardly seemed believable: fifty-five thousand Allied soldiers dead, wounded, or missing; twenty thousand dead or wounded

Monuments Men approach the remains of the Abbey of Monte Cassino.

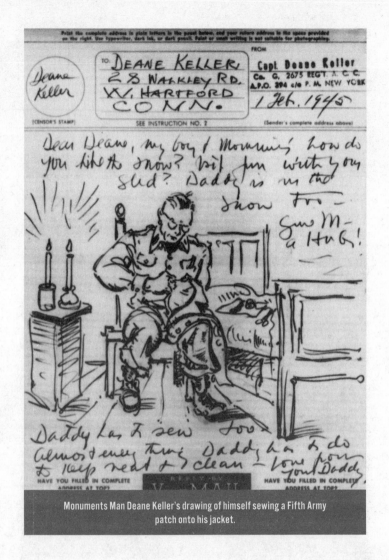

Dear Deane, my boy! Mornin', how do you like the snow? Will fun with your sled? Daddy is in the snow too — Give M— a Hug!

Daddy has to sew too almost every thing Daddy has to do to keep neat & clean — Love from your Daddy

TO: DEANE KELLER,
28 WALKLEY RD.
W. HARTFORD
CONN.

FROM
Capt. Deane Keller
Co. G, 2675 REGT. A.C.C.
A.P.O. 394 c/o P.M. NEW YORK
1 Feb. 1945

Monuments Man Deane Keller's drawing of himself sewing a Fifth Army patch onto his jacket.

Germans; and one historic but largely destroyed fourteenth-century Benedictine abbey.

With the stalemate at Cassino ended, Allied forces and the Monuments Men began their advance toward Rome. Several received new assignments. Keller's exceeded all expectations: He would be the first Monuments Officer attached to Fifth Army and its fighting force of eighty thousand soldiers.

On his last night in Naples, Keller held up the sleeve of his uniform to the small, dim lamp near his bunk. Needle and thread in hand, he began sewing onto his uniform the shoulder patch for Fifth Army, which he had purchased earlier in the day from a street vendor. "I haven't worn my ribbon or shoulder patch yet. Don't know when I will," he had written Kathy. "I feel the boys at [the] front are the ones to wear the stuff. Maybe some day I'll feel I earned it." That day had finally come.

About one week into his new assignment, things were going well for Monuments Man Captain Deane Keller. He had the job he wanted—a position of enormous responsibility—and a jeep, a rarity for the Monuments Men. He swelled with pride serving his country and helping the Italian people, but it came at a high cost. The bloodbath at the Battle of Monte Cassino served as a painful reminder to Keller and his family that he might not see them again, ever. Most of all, he missed being the dad that he had promised to be when Dino was born.

For now, he resigned himself to writing letters, lots of letters. Each letter to Kathy had a message for Dino, right up until the time he realized that his three-year-old boy couldn't yet read. A few weeks later, or perhaps months—war was like that, the blurring of time—he realized that the solution to communicating with his son wasn't through words but images. Every boy liked looking at cartoons, and after all, Keller was an artist and an art teacher.

One of Monuments Man Deane Keller's early drawings to Dino summarizing his experiences as a soldier.

One of Keller's earliest drawings summarized his journey, step by step, from his trip to North Africa and training at Tizi Ouzou—"Toozy Woozy," as he jokingly referred to it—to his work in Italy.

With Keller's assignment as a Monuments Man now underway, Dino would be receiving many more drawings.

Near Palestrina, Italy: June 1944

Somewhere on the road back to headquarters, Keller awakened and quickly checked the pocket of his shirt. The letter from the dead American soldier was still there. It prompted him to write to Kathy as soon as he reached his tent. He began his June 25 letter by recounting some of the experiences of his first few weeks as a Monuments Man. With the death of the young soldier fresh on his mind, the tone of his letter changed. He wanted to share with Kathy something he'd been thinking about. "The life of one American boy is worth infinitely more to me than any monument I know." Keller thought of it as a personal manifesto of sorts, one that would guide him in his work as a Monuments Man.

Rome, Italy: June 1944

Monuments Men Lieutenant Perry Cott, British Captain Humphrey Brooke, and Lieutenant Fred Hartt, who had joined the operation in late April, couldn't believe they were in Rome, not under these conditions. Like Keller, Cott and Hartt had each visited the city during their time as students, but those experiences couldn't compare with the exhilaration of accompanying Fifth Army troops into the Eternal City.

It had taken the Western Allies six months to blast through Monte Cassino before sprinting north to Rome. The first units fought their way into the city on the morning of June 4, liberating it by late afternoon. The sound of the deliriously happy throngs of people cheering as the tank column of a modern army motored past the almost nineteen-hundred-year-old Colosseum left Hartt, Cott, and Brooke speechless. But the appearance of the Arch of Constantine and Trajan's Column, and many of the city's other landmarks, wrapped in protective casing made of brick, sandbags, and scaffolding brought them back to the reality of the war—and their mission.

While Brooke and Hartt set out to conduct damage assessments, Cott began gathering information on the status of works of art. The Vatican and its collection, one of the most comprehensive and important holdings of art in the world, were safe. So, too, were the treasures of the Brera Picture Gallery in Milan, the Accademia in Venice, the Borghese Gallery in Rome, and those from many of the nation's most important churches, which Pope Pius XII had allowed to be stored for safekeeping within the Vatican's walls. Cott, a seasoned museum curator and art scholar, was astonished at the thought that, with these combined holdings, the Vatican was the richest museum in the world, at least for the moment.

Monuments Man Lieutenant Colonel Ernest DeWald, director of the MFAA in Italy, reached Rome several days later. After presenting his credentials to the Holy Father and explaining the purpose of the Monuments operation, he and Cott gained access to the Vatican storage areas. On June 26, they began their investigation into works of art belonging to museums in Naples that the

Hermann Göring Tank Division had delivered to Rome for safe-keeping. Suspicions abounded.

The media spectacle surrounding the Hermann Göring Tank Division's arrival was Nazi propaganda at its best—they seldom missed a chance to promote a good deed done. But when two trucks of this elite fighting unit mysteriously disappeared on the way to Rome with the artwork, it greatly concerned Italian art officials, especially since it involved a division named after Hermann Göring, the Nazi Party's second-most powerful man and the most prolific art collector in the world.

After a quick look at the crates that the Hermann Göring Division had delivered to Rome in January, DeWald and Cott began inventorying the contents, starting with crate number 1. A few minutes passed before DeWald looked at Cott, puzzled. Crate number 1, which according to their inventory schedule had been packed with three paintings, was completely missing. That hardly

Pieter Bruegel the Elder, *The Blind Leading the Blind*, 1568.

seemed an accident. Later they opened crate number 29, relieved to find one of the paintings that belonged in the missing crate number 1. A second of the missing paintings appeared in crate number 58. But they never found the third and most important painting: the world-famous masterpiece by Pieter Bruegel the Elder, *The Blind Leading the Blind*.

"There can be no doubt that the paintings were stolen by persons who knew just what they wanted," DeWald told Cott in disbelief. The thieves clearly had a shopping list. What else could explain that in several instances they had left behind paintings of far greater importance? Hiding the works that they didn't want in crates with extra space was a cover-up attempt as clumsy as the theft itself.

DeWald and Cott were gobsmacked by the audacity of the theft. In all, seventeen works of art from Naples and the ancient site of Pompeii were missing, a few of which were among the most recognizable works of art in the world. The Hermann Göring Division soldiers might as well have driven to Naples, backed up their trucks to the doors of the Museo Nazionale in broad daylight, and lifted the masterpieces off the wall. Both DeWald and Cott believed that the works of art were in Nazi Germany, probably recent additions to the ever-growing collection of Reichsmarschall Hermann Göring.

Reports of Nazi looting throughout Europe were hardly new, but the Vatican inventory provided the Monuments Men with their first hard evidence that the Nazis had looted art treasures in Italy. With German troops now retreating north toward Florence, the Monuments Men feared that this was just the beginning.

CHAPTER 2

INDEPENDENCE DAY

English Channel: July 4, 1944

George Stout loved being on the water. The ocean air reminded him of the summer he spent working with his uncle in Corpus Christi, Texas. One day each week, he would paddle a small wooden boat over the shallow waters of the Gulf of Mexico and spend the day fishing. For a young boy from landlocked Iowa, the vastness of the ocean created a fascination that never left him. But those carefree days were long ago. Now he was aboard the Liberty ship SS *Joseph Story* with hundreds of other soldiers, steaming from Southampton, England, to the bloodied beaches of Normandy, France.

Four weeks earlier, on June 6, 1944—"D-Day"—American, British, and Canadian forces had mounted the largest seaborne invasion in history. Almost 156,000 men crossed the English Channel that day, from safety into hell. With the British coastline now only faintly visible on the early-morning horizon, Stout closed his eyes and tried to picture the unimaginable: 7,000 ships crossing these same waters, all at the same time, headed into battle.

The D-Day landings proved successful, but the casualty figures were staggering. Enemy fortifications on the coastal ridgeline provided a clear killing field for German machine gunners on

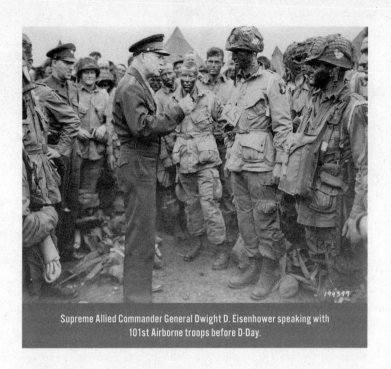

Supreme Allied Commander General Dwight D. Eisenhower speaking with 101st Airborne troops before D-Day.

beaches increasingly pockmarked by mortar and artillery shells. Many Allied soldiers never made it onto the beach; many who did never made it off. By the end of the initial operation, some twelve thousand American, British, and Canadian soldiers were dead, wounded, or missing.

In the thirty days of fighting that followed, Western Allied forces had their foothold in Europe, but progress proved agonizingly slow. Savage German resistance had limited the Allied advance to just seven miles inland. Berlin, the capital of Nazi Germany, was still 778 miles away. On the Eastern Front, the Wehrmacht was reeling. Just weeks earlier, the Soviets had hurled over one million Red Army soldiers at the center of the German line, inflicting catastrophic damage to Hitler's forces. The fall of

Rome to U.S. Fifth Army pressured German forces to the south. Now, with the successful landing of Western Allied forces on French soil, Hitler and his military commanders were fighting a three-front war.

Stout, like the other men on board, nervously wondered what he would confront once he reached France and beyond, and, of far greater concern, if he would be returning home. Those same thoughts had filled his mind when he crossed this stretch of water as a young U.S. Army private to fight in World War I, back when no one ever thought they would have to number them. Stout reminded himself that he had survived the carnage of that war; he was determined to survive this one, too.

June 6, 1944: D-Day landings at Omaha Beach.

Standing on deck, Stout gently swayed to the rhythmic motion of the ship. Being on the ocean was like being locked in a room with just your thoughts. The crossing would take about five hours—plenty of time to ponder how an idea of his had landed on the desk of the president of the United States, and, in turn, how he and a much too small group of men were going to save hundreds of thousands of the world's most precious art and cultural objects from the destruction of war.

Stout had only himself to blame for being on this troop transport in the first place. Had it not been for his idea to create teams of cultural preservation officers, he would have been in the safety of his conservation lab at Harvard University wearing a white overcoat instead of an army uniform. But President Franklin D. Roosevelt had approved his "brain child," as friend and former boss Paul Sachs, associate director of Harvard University's Fogg Museum, referred to it. As a member of the Roberts Commission, charged with the selection of Monuments Officers, Sachs had written him expressing hope that he would volunteer to become a Monuments Man, "because not only is this commission the result of your great thinking and clear statements at the time of the Metropolitan [Museum] meeting just after Pearl Harbor, but in a very true sense you seem to me the real father of the whole show . . . It is my deliberate opinion that the appointment of this Commission is due to your initiative, imagination and energy."

At forty-six years of age, Stout knew enough to be suspicious of such laudatory praise, even from someone he trusted. "You are kind to give me so much credit in getting this work under way," he remembered telling Sachs, "but you magnify it one hell of a lot. Something far below the average set of brains is needed to figure out what ought to be done. Getting it done is what counts." George Leslie Stout had defined his life by getting things done.

Paul Sachs had made a correct assessment, and Stout couldn't deny it. He possessed exactly the right qualities to lead the Monuments Men operation in northern Europe. He was unflappable under pressure. His methodical and reasoned approach would prove essential to solving problems. Everyone knew there would be plenty of those. He was a naturally charismatic man and a confident leader, the kind that men want to believe and follow. He even looked the part, with his pencil-thin mustache, combed-back black hair, and movie star good looks.

No person in the United States had spent more time pondering how to protect works of art and other cultural treasures during war than George Stout. Years of experiments and research at the Fogg Museum led him to develop a set of scientific principles for the evaluation and preservation of cultural treasures. He was an avid believer in sharing information with fellow conservators. Gradually, Stout and his colleagues had guided the profession of conservation from an art form to a science.

Stout watched as the storm clouds of war gathered over Europe once again. Technological developments introduced during the Spanish Civil War added a sense of urgency. In October 1936, incendiary bombs landed near El Escorial, the imposing monastery-museum thirty miles northwest of Madrid. Two weeks later, high-explosive bombs blew out the windows of Spain's national museum, the Prado. The implications were clear: Massive aerial bombardment and the consequent fires instantly created a new threat to museums, libraries, and other monuments that would require a whole new way of thinking about how to protect them.

By the time of America's entry into World War II, following the December 7, 1941, Japanese sneak attack on Pearl Harbor, Hawaii, Stout was ready. Acting on his own initiative, he had prepared instructional pamphlets addressing the need he had anticipated years earlier. More important, he made an eloquent and compelling case for why the governments of the United Nations had a responsibility to take every measure possible to protect the world's shared cultural heritage. He argued why the work had to be done. He wrote the book on how to do it. Then he put his career on hold and volunteered for military service, leaving his wife, Margie, and their two boys behind.

The Monuments operation had begun in earnest in 1943, when President Roosevelt ordered Captain Mason Hammond, a classics professor at Harvard—and the first Monuments Man—to Sicily, but not until three weeks *after* the invasion of Italy had commenced. An army of one Monuments Officer was better than none at all. While Paul Sachs and other officials in the United States and England scrambled to get more Monuments Men into treasure-laden Italy, Hammond hitchhiked his way from town to town conducting inspections and posting OUT OF BOUNDS signs. Somehow, working without a jeep, and on his own for four weeks before other Monuments Men began arriving, Hammond found a way to get the job done.

Stout arrived in Shrivenham, England, at the United States–British Civil Affairs training center in March 1944, now a lieutenant in the U.S. Naval Reserve. Others soon followed . . . very

~~RESTRICTED~~

TO ALLIED FORCES

NATIONAL MONUMENT

OUT OF BOUNDS
OFF LIMITS

IT IS STRICTLY FORBIDDEN TO REMOVE STONE OR
ANY OTHER MATERIAL FROM THIS SITE

SOUVENIR HUNTING, WRITING ON WALLS OR
DAMAGE IN ANY FORM WILL BE DEALT WITH AS

MILITARY OFFENCES

DWIGHT D. EISENHOWER,
GENERAL,
Supreme Commander,
Allied Expeditionary Force

By order of
J. E. DIXON-SPAIN
Sqdn Ldr.,
MFA - A. Spec. offr.

~~RESTRICTED~~

DECLASSIFIED
Authority NND 750148
By QM NARA, Date 4/3/81
21st Army Group.

An OUT OF BOUNDS sign posted by the Monuments Men.

few others. His original plan had called for a new class of specially trained conservators who would be attached to each of the U.S. Army's three army groups in Europe. Each conservator would have a minimum staff of ten people that would include skilled packers, movers, taxidermists, secretaries, drivers, and photographers. They would be provided with jeeps, covered trucks, field radios, crates, boxes, packing materials, rope, cameras with film (the army was notorious for providing one without the other), aerometers to check air quality, and hygrometers to check humidity levels. But army bureaucracy had slowed the approval process to a crawl. Stout realized he would be lucky to begin the operation with ten Monuments Men total. Staff support per his recommendation? Not a chance.

Several British Monuments Men had already begun their training at Shrivenham, including Stout's roommate, Captain Ronald Balfour, a historian at King's College in Cambridge, whose pride and joy was his personal library containing some eight thousand volumes. Balfour was a slightly balding forty-year-old bachelor who had dedicated his life to history and ecclesiastical studies. Stout took an instant liking to Balfour. His expertise with books, archives, and religious objects would make him a valuable addition to the team; so, too, would his military upbringing.

Others in the British contingent included Lieutenant Colonel Geoffrey Webb, one of England's most distinguished art scholars, and the senior ranking officer among the initial group of Monuments Men in northern Europe; Major Lord Methuen, an accomplished artist; and Squadron Leader Dixon-Spain, a noted architect. The latter two were veterans of World War I.

The American side included Captain Marvin Ross, a Harvard graduate and expert on Byzantine art, who was second in command to Webb. Captain Ralph Hammett and Captain Bancel LaFarge, both renowned architects, would be immensely important to the operation in determining which damaged buildings could be salvaged and which were beyond repair. Captain Walker Hancock, the most decorated member of the group, was a forty-three-year-old award-winning sculptor. His knowledge of Europe and expertise with languages would be an invaluable asset. More than that, Stout admired Hancock's relentlessly optimistic and easygoing demeanor, prized personal attributes at any time, but doubly so during periods of stress.

Second Lieutenant James Rorimer, at just thirty-eight years of age, had risen through the ranks of the museum world to become curator of medieval art at The Metropolitan Museum of Art in New York City and its newly opened Cloisters Museum. Rorimer, a true Francophile, spoke the language fluently. He was an ambitious man, a hard charger. Nothing and no one was going to get in his way. The Monuments Men would need those skills in the months ahead. Sachs had made a great choice selecting him.

Then there was Captain Robert Posey, an outsider to the group of art scholars and museum men, but very much an insider when it came to the military. Posey loved soldiering; it was in his blood. Stout didn't know much about him other than he wasn't a member of Paul Sachs's Harvard circle. Posey was an architect, however, and that skill plus his military training made him invaluable to the group. Stout did know that they shared one very important thing: young sons at home whom they missed very much.

Stout had retraced the situation in his mind countless times. There were just eleven men, including him—at least initially, and for who knew how long—responsible for protecting the accumulated artistic and cultural wealth of Western civilization located in northern Europe from the destruction of war and theft by the Nazis. But the "brain child" he had envisioned and what the army provided him were worlds apart. With eleven men—one Monuments Man for every eighty thousand U.S. Army soldiers—how were they going to get it done? *Could* it even be done? Stout didn't want to use the word "impossible," but "unlikely" seemed about right.

For the operation to have any success, they would certainly need some breaks along the way, especially from combat commanders in the field. Three early assets provided hope. First, the Monuments Men went to war with a priority list of what needed to be saved. Volunteers in the United States, skilled in the arts, had compiled a Monuments, Fine Arts, and Archives List of Protected Monuments for each western European country, with maps indicating the locations, which were then forwarded to the Monuments Men serving in Italy and those training at Shrivenham. They had also overlaid this information onto aerial reconnaissance photographs, providing pilots with critical imagery that would hopefully spare those sites from damage.

The second asset wasn't a thing but a person: Captain Mason Hammond, the very first Monuments Man. Hammond's five months of experience in Sicily and the Italian mainland supplied insightful examples for General Eisenhower and his staff on what worked and what hadn't. Adjustments had already been made to the invasion plans for northern Europe that they hoped would provide a critical edge for Stout and his team, assets that Hammond did not have in Italy. With Hammond in London, attached to Eisenhower's staff, the Monuments Men in the field had someone in their corner who was reliable, trustworthy, and experienced in what they were about to do.

General Eisenhower himself was the third source of encouragement. "Ike," like Hammond, had struggled with how to fight a war in a country that, for all practical purposes, was a museum.

Initially, Eisenhower did not believe that the Monuments Men needed any special endorsement of their mission from the senior commander. By December 1943, he realized he had been wrong. The order that he issued on December 29, 1943, transformed the Monuments operation in Italy from that point forward by providing the explicit backing of the senior military commander, but it came late, after six months of combat. Not wanting to repeat the same mistake, and no doubt a consequence of Mason Hammond's admonitions, Eisenhower issued a similar order to all commanders eleven days *before* D-Day.

Beads of saltwater dripping off the rim of his helmet awakened him. George Stout wasn't sure how long he had been dozing, but he remembered thinking about Eisenhower and his order. Reaching into his leather jacket pocket, he pulled out the order and, with a great sense of pride in their mission, read the first paragraph again:

Shortly we will be fighting our way across the Continent of Europe in battles designed to preserve our civilization. Inevitably, in the path of our advance will be found historical monuments and cultural centers which symbolize to the world all that we are fighting to preserve. It is the responsibility of every commander to protect and respect these symbols whenever possible . . .

The sight of hundreds of anchored ships with a canopy of protective barrage balloons overhead confirmed for Stout and the others on board that they had reached their destination, Utah Beach. Getting ashore involved more waiting. Since being in the army, he had taken to heart a soldier's saying: "Hurry up and wait." Around 11:00 a.m., Stout stood on deck and watched as vessels at anchor began a makeshift fireworks display. Even war wasn't going to interrupt the chance to celebrate the Fourth of July. After all, the navy had plenty of explosives.

The Normandy landing beaches.

A Rhino barge carried them the rest of the way. Not once did Stout take his eyes off the sand wall overlooking the exposed beaches. Like everyone who set foot on any one of the D-Day landing beaches, Stout felt anguish for the soldiers who had made this same journey on June 6 into a torrent of gunfire. He couldn't imagine what it must have been like on Omaha Beach, where Germans high above on cliffs could shoot down on the American soldiers scrambling to safety. It reminded him of the nightmarish trench warfare and the scenes of carnage he had witnessed during World War I.

Lieutenant George Wilson, who had reached Normandy the same week as Stout, made observations universal to the soldiers who had seen those beaches:

> *I'm sure much of the horrific results of that battle had been cleared away, and all the dead and wounded were gone. Still, the terrible scars of war seemed to shout at us. Burned-out vehicles, sunken landing craft, ships, tanks, guns, pillboxes lay twisted and still. It hardly seemed possible anyone could have survived, yet men had waded in and driven the Germans back, now some seven or eight miles inland in most places.*

Like many arriving soldiers, Wilson had freedom of movement the first few days and used them to wander around the battle area. What he saw sickened him:

> *The ghastly stories we had heard about the fierceness of the fighting were true. German war prisoners were*

digging up the partially decomposed bodies of their own
dead—buried in neat rows in mass graves about three
feet deep—for movement to a new location. Working
with shovels and bare hands, the prisoners stuffed the
corpses into mattress covers and piled them on trucks in
rows, like cordwood. Some of the bodies were badly
mangled and very difficult to pick up. Stern-faced men
turned white, and many had to turn away to vomit at
the sight and smell.

Later that evening, after reporting to First Army headquarters, after laying out his bedroll on the sand of Utah Beach under a star-filled sky, and after the excitement of a German plane passing overhead spraying the beach with machine-gun fire, Stout thought about the irony of his day. This was the second time he had set foot on French soil during war. It happened on the 168th anniversary of the day when 13 American colonies renounced British rule and declared their independence as a newly formed nation. Now, those two nations, once at war with each other, were united in their determination to defeat Nazi Germany. And France, the nation that had provided early critical support to those united states, would at some point be the first country in northern Europe to be liberated and regain its own independence with their assistance.

With first light at 6:00 a.m., Stout needed to get what sleep he could. It would be one of many precious commodities in the busy days ahead.

CHAPTER 3

"LITTLE SAINTS, HELP US!"

On the road to Siena, Italy: July 4, 1944

As his jeep made its way north from Rome to Siena, Deane Keller marveled at the beauty of the Tuscan countryside. Vast golden wheat fields accented by groves of green cypress trees covered undulating hills as far as the eye could see. Six-hundred-year-old bell towers emerged from the distant ridgelines, set against an endless blue sky. The tranquility of the drive made it easy for him to forget about the war, but it was always just one gunshot, one destroyed building, one dead American boy away from smothering any other thought.

Keller entered Siena on the Fourth of July, one day after the city's liberation by Fifth Army troops, who had been charging north since taking Rome. To avoid a catastrophic fight in the center of a medieval art–filled town, the German commander, Generalfeldmarschall Albert "Smiling Al" Kesselring, so called because of his effortless and ever-present grin, had declared Siena an "open city." Under this arrangement, Allied troops refrained from attacking while German forces withdrew. Only two hours separated the opposing armies. Keller pulled out his field journal and noted that despite minor damage, Siena had been "artistically bypassed."

After making sure OUT OF BOUNDS signs had been posted on the fifty buildings and churches on the MFAA List of Protected Monuments, Keller wanted to check the status of the city's legendary works of art. First he had to figure out where they were.

Just one week earlier, Monuments Officers DeWald and Cott had conducted their inspection of the Naples treasures. During their walk through the Vatican storage area they saw thousands of crates from museums in Milan, Venice, and Rome, but none from the art-rich cities of Tuscany, in particular Florence and Siena. Officials in Rome did have lists indicating the locations of the various Tuscan repositories, but they considered them outdated. No cause for worry, they said. Superintendent of Florentine Galleries Giovanni Poggi had no doubt relocated the art treasures back into the cities out of the way of the coming ground battle.

On July 8, Keller and his Carabinieri driver, Giuseppe, pulled up to the Bishop's Palace in Mensanello—the most important of the three major Sienese art repositories—caked in dust. Tuscany was beautiful, but driving on the roads was a punishing experience, like wading through talcum powder. While the "open city" declaration had spared Siena from war, it hadn't extended as far as Mensanello, about eighteen miles outside the city. Allied forces had just wrenched control of the area from German troops. French-manned artillery batteries, part of Fifth Army forces, pounded German positions nearby.

After dusting himself off and trying to adjust for the deafening boom and vibration of the howitzer cannon, Keller entered the palace to discover a makeshift first aid station. Boom! A French military doctor was treating three wounded French colonial soldiers. Keller attempted to make an introduction and explain why he was there, but continuous artillery fire drowned out his words. He could barely hear himself. Boom! Sizing up the scholarly middle-aged Fifth Army officer standing before him, the French doctor assumed it had something to do with the two large crates leaning against the wall, so he pointed to them. Boom!

Keller walked over to the crates for a closer look. Someone had cut helmet-sized holes in the sides of both crates and then removed the packing material and flannel wrapping to see what was inside. What person wouldn't have been curious, he thought; he certainly was. For a moment, as he crouched down on one knee to peer inside the hole, Keller was oblivious to the sound of the artillery, the blood on the floor, and even the injured soldiers. His eyes needed a few seconds to adjust to the diminished light, and then time stopped. Staring back at him was an old friend—the Madonna and Child panel of the *Maestà*, Siena Cathedral's high altarpiece and the city's most iconic work of art. He'd last seen the seven-by-thirteen-foot double-sided wood panel painting, now disassembled, as a student almost two decades earlier.

The Sienese artist Duccio di Buoninsegna created the exquisitely refined painting of the Madonna and Child, surrounded by angels and saints, between 1308 and 1311. Duccio used vivid colors to paint his figures with delicacy and tenderness, a style that influenced two centuries of artists who followed. And now Keller had found it, 633 years later, in the middle of a war zone. The altarpiece appeared safe and, from what he could see, undamaged.

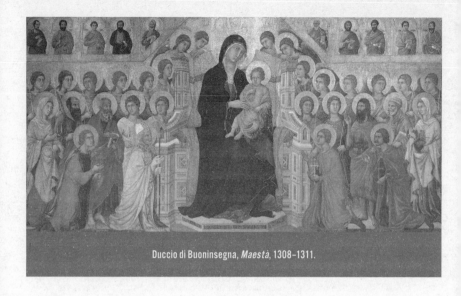

Duccio di Buoninsegna, *Maestà*, 1308–1311.

Other smaller paintings, about forty in all, lay hidden inside the palace chapel. Keller examined each one before individually wrapping them in blankets to create a measure of protection against the constant vibration. Nearby he noticed a protected-monuments sign posted by order of the German commander Kesselring. In this instance, it appeared that German troops had respected it. For now, unable to post guards, all Keller could do was notify art officials in Siena that the *Maestà* had come through the battle safely.

Florence, Italy: late July 1944

With Fifth Army giving chase, German forces continued their strategic retreat north to the Gothic Line, intending to make a stand in the Apennine Mountains. Directly in their path lay Florence, the capital city of Tuscany—and the single greatest concentration of art in the world. Siena and Rome had been lucky. Would Florence, with its magnificent churches, beautiful bridges, and irreplaceable works of art, be so fortunate? And where were the city's paintings, sculptures, and other artistic treasures? Had they been moved back into the city as officials in Rome believed, or were they still in the various countryside villas surrounding Florence, at risk of being stolen, or worse, destroyed?

Second Lieutenant Fred Hartt, Regional Monuments Officer for Tuscany, was determined to find the answer.

Hartt was an impassioned, at times impetuous, and immensely talented art historian who had spent more than half of his life studying Italian artists and their works. His gift for the arts was apparent from an early age. While most of his schoolmates longed

Monuments Man Second Lieutenant Fred Hartt.

to be on the athletic fields, Hartt was lost in a world of French Gothic cathedrals, Italian Renaissance sculpture, and Oriental silk screens. At thirty years of age, he was at least ten years younger than the other Monuments Men, which spoke to the level of respect for his ability. His gangling appearance, accented by dark, heavy-rimmed glasses, masked a brilliant scholar with a photographic memory and boundless energy.

The obliterated courtyard of Santa
The Last Supper is covered by

When he arrived in Italy in mid-January 1944, Hartt had been assigned to a photographic interpretation unit assessing collateral damage to nearby monuments caused by Allied bombing. He hated his job. Volunteering for military service had been a personal quest to help save the art of Italy. Instead, he found himself confirming its destruction. Restless and impatient, he looked for ways to wrangle a transfer into the Monuments section. On April 6, he

Maria delle Grazie Church in Milan.
wooden scaffolding (center left).

wrote Ernest DeWald, director of the MFAA in Italy, pleading for a transfer. His orders came through two weeks later.

Shortly before departing for his new assignment as a Monuments Man, Hartt prepared a report summarizing bomb damage in sixteen Italian cities. After checking and rechecking one of the photographs, adjusting the overhead lamp with one hand while repositioning his magnifying glass with the other, he was sure. On the night of August 15, 1943, a British high-explosive bomb had completely obliterated the courtyard of the Santa Maria delle Grazie Church in Milan, and all but the northwest corner of its dining hall. Hartt couldn't be certain, but as best as he could tell, given the resolution of the photograph, the wall containing Leonardo da Vinci's greatest masterpiece, *The Last Supper*, may have been reduced to rubble. It was a bitter realization that he and the other Monuments Men feared might be repeated in the Tuscan capital.

On July 27, Hartt pulled up to British Eighth Army headquarters in a battered army jeep with worn tires, defective shock absorbers, and a shattered windshield. Unlike most military vehicles, his had a name. At some point in its storied existence, whether in North Africa or Sicily, no one knew, someone had painted "Lucky 13" across the metal riser that once contained a windshield. Hartt knew that just having a vehicle was a stroke of luck, even one as beat up as his. Like Keller, he guarded his jeep like a cowboy did his horse—it was that important.

Hartt and the other officers and soldiers of Eighth Army were eager to get into Florence and begin inspections. He'd first visited Italy in 1936 and dreamed of returning ever since. The thought that German forces would use his beloved city as a defensive fortification, risking damage to hundreds of years of beauty, sickened him.

Several days later, while eating breakfast in the officers' mess at British Eighth Army headquarters, Hartt heard a stunning announcement broadcast by BBC Radio. Wynford Vaughan-Thomas, a veteran correspondent, accompanied by Major Eric Linklater of the British Royal Engineers, had stumbled upon an art repository in the middle of a major battle zone just outside Florence. It contained masterpieces from two of the city's most important museums, the Uffizi Gallery and the Palatine Gallery, housed inside the Pitti Palace. Rome officials had been grievously wrong: The Florentine treasures had not been moved back into the city. Hartt felt exhilaration and horror, all at once. Mind-jarring images of unprotected, art-filled villas dotting the Tuscan countryside filled his head.

Castle of Montegufoni.

Never one to sit still, Hartt immediately sought authorization to drive to the art repository—the Castle of Montegufoni—to secure it and report back as quickly as possible. Permission in hand, Hartt, "armed and helmeted," jumped into Lucky 13 and headed out. Heavy artillery fire blocked portions of the route, forcing him onto alternate roads so small they didn't appear on his maps. Stops at numerous military checkpoints chewed up more time. Throughout the journey, the night sky flickered from the constant flashes of artillery. Exhausted after spending almost twelve hours driving a mere eighty-three miles, Hartt decided to spend the night at Eighth Army press camp at San Donato in Poggio.

That evening Hartt met with Vaughan-Thomas and Major Linklater, who had just returned to camp after spending the day checking on three additional art repositories nearby. Did they ever have a story to tell! Linklater, who had been commissioned to write the official history of the Eighth Army campaign, had been eager to visit the 8th Indian Infantry Division, just one of the many multinational components of British Eighth Army. He and Vaughan-Thomas had arrived at the Castle of Montegufoni on the afternoon of July 30. Enemy forward positions were now just a little more than a mile away from the castle. While waiting to interview the senior commander, Linklater and Vaughan-Thomas had wandered through the cavernous building and noticed various groups of panel paintings leaning against the wall. Hartt couldn't believe what he was hearing, especially the fact that the paintings were not in crates and that the painted surface was visible rather than facing the wall as an added measure of protection.

Hartt found these paintings from the Florence museums inside the Castle of Montegufoni.

"But they're very good! They must be copies!" one of the men recalled saying. Then Linklater told Hartt how he had entered another room filled with paintings—a few crated, most not—and heard Vaughan-Thomas shout, "The whole house is full of pictures. They've come from the Uffizi and Pitti Palace!"

Fred Hartt sat stunned, speechless at what he'd just heard. The two men ran down a list of the paintings they had seen. Hartt shook his head in disbelief. Some of the most important works of art in the world, each priceless, lying on the floor of a villa, unprotected, covered in dust, in a war zone . . . It seemed too incredible to believe.

The following day, August 1, Hartt, accompanied by Linklater and Vaughan-Thomas, drove the short distance to Montegufoni. Cesare Fasola, librarian of the Uffizi Gallery, who had walked seventeen miles from Florence through a combat zone to watch over the collection, greeted them. British artillery encircling the castle continued firing their thunderous rounds. Enemy shells passed overhead and exploded in the distance, but not far enough away to be of any comfort to the four men.

The scene inside the castle was no less bizarre. Hartt immediately recognized each painting, a mind-jarring assembly of works by world-class artists of the Renaissance, including Raphael, Rubens, Giotto, Cimabue, Andrea del Sarto, Pontormo, and Uccello. It wasn't just the importance of the artists whose works had been stored there; many of these paintings were the most famous and important work ever created by the artist. Botticelli's tour de force, *Primavera*, the sight of which stunned Vaughan-Thomas, was just one example. Seeing so many works of art that he had studied and admired, leaning against the walls of the castle, unprotected, left Fred Hartt feeling overwhelmed.

Deane Keller standing beside Botticelli's masterpiece, *Primavera*.

While Hartt tried to gather himself, Fasola described recent events. After leaving Florence ten days earlier, he'd stopped at another repository, the Villa Bossi-Pucci in the tiny town of Montagnana. German troops had already taken 291 masterpieces belonging to the Uffizi and Pitti Palace museums. Only those objects too large to fit in their trucks were left behind. The villa was a mess: doors pried off their hinges, windows left wide open, and books tossed from the library strewn about the grounds, many bearing soldiers' boot marks.

With nothing more to do at Villa Bossi-Pucci, Fasola then walked to the Castle of Montegufoni, fearful he would discover a similar scene. While those paintings were still inside the castle, German troops were, too. "The packing cases had all been opened, the pictures taken out and flung about," he explained to Hartt. As the days passed, he tried to befriend the soldiers to keep them away from the paintings, especially after discovering that they were using a dark corridor containing eight fifteenth-century paintings by Fra Angelico as a latrine. When Fasola pleaded for them to remove their bottles and glasses from the surface of *Adoration of the Magi*, a fifteenth-century tondo by Ghirlandaio, a German soldier pulled out a knife and threw it at the wooden panel, piercing an area of the sky.

Lacking any authority, Fasola defensively told Hartt that all he could do was accompany the castle custodian on his nightly rounds. It was a helpless feeling, but not hopeless. One evening, Fasola recalled, he watched as the custodian stared at a group of religious paintings and whispered to himself, "Little Saints, help us!" It was an incredible story, Hartt thought, by a man who had done more than anyone could have expected to preserve objects that in so many ways defined the history of Florence—a man who was a true hero.

It took several hours, but when finished, Hartt confirmed that the inventory count was correct. All 246 paintings that Florentine officials had placed at the castle were accounted for and undamaged. But the Castle of Montegufoni was just one of the art repositories housing treasures from Florence. Many others were located behind enemy lines. The Allies could only wonder about their fate.

Hartt sounded the alarm in a blunt and to-the-point cable to Ernest DeWald: "Five deposits located. Reference BBC broadcast. Situation in hand. All safe save for damage to Pontormo *Visitation* and Bronzino *Portrait*." He then prepared a memo to Lieutenant General Oliver Leese, commander of British Eighth Army, marked SECRET, which contained map references, a list of twelve other deposits, and a terse summation of the situation: "The fate of these priceless treasures lies in the hands of the Eighth Army."

CHAPTER 4

THE MEETING

Saint-Lô, France: August 1944

George Stout entered the town of Saint-Lô in a state of disbelief. Exactly one month had passed since setting foot on Utah Beach, and in that time, he'd visited dozens of small villages and towns on daily inspections and witnessed every kind of damage possible, including some that seemed impossible. But nothing compared with the panorama of devastation that now lay before him.

All that remained of the skyline of Saint-Lô, a thousand-year-old walled town about thirty-five miles from the Normandy landing beaches, was a series of saw-toothed structures that resembled fields of densely packed stalagmites. No building had escaped damage. Rubble piles reached twenty feet high. Most streets—if you could even locate where the street had once been—were impassable. Stout couldn't find an unbroken piece of glass in any building or home. Fully mature trees in bloom had been decimated, leaving lonely twigs, void of any greenery, rising to the sky. War had killed the town of Saint-Lô, and perhaps as many as twelve hundred of its twelve thousand inhabitants.

It wasn't intended to be this way. On the evening of the D-Day landings, in an effort to create transport bottlenecks and cut off German reinforcements, Allied naval guns and air forces

The smashed French town of Saint-Lô.

relentlessly pummeled the Saint-Lô rail station and power plant. Leaflets dropped the day before warning townspeople that a raid was imminent were blown off course. The strikes hit their targets, but they also killed innocent people, shattered historic buildings, and pulverized the entire town. Ten days later, a fierce ground battle began for control of the ruins, but not before yet more bombers dropped their payloads over the city in support of the assault forces. Once American boys of the 29th Infantry Division entered Saint-Lô, the Germans returned the favor and began raining shells down on them, smashing the rubble into dust. Twice the number of American boys were killed taking Saint-Lô than during the carnage of the D-Day landings. Fire consumed the Hôtel de Ville—the city's town hall—along with its library of rare manuscripts. The eight-hundred-year-old Church of Sainte-Croix survived largely intact, but almost nothing was left of the town museum.

Stout maneuvered his way around piles of stone fragments to inspect the heavily damaged fifteenth-century Gothic-style Church of Notre-Dame, one of the few buildings still standing, but military police refused to let him enter. After explaining his orders—to conduct inspections of historic structures, place OUT OF BOUNDS signs, and effect temporary repairs where possible—the MPs explained theirs: No one was to enter the church by order of British Monuments Officer Dixon-Spain, who had already inspected the church and posted the MPs. Stout knew that Dixon-Spain was in the Normandy area, but without field radios, one Monuments Man had no idea what a fellow officer had inspected, or where he might be headed next. That was a major problem.

The MPs shared one other piece of news: The Germans had mined the church pulpit and altar, and they had also connected a stick of dynamite to a piece of stone near the entry, which an unsuspecting priest or soldier was sure to move and trigger an explosion. Stout flipped the page of his field diary and added it to a growing list of booby traps he'd come across in other inspections.

The Monuments Men were supposed to stay behind combat troops, but in the Normandy area, Allied and German soldiers were so densely packed together that it was tough to tell where the lines of one side ended and the other's began. Like a summer storm that suddenly appears and just as quickly vanishes, the war came to small towns and then moved on, only to reappear. Proximity to the fighting lines, added to the countless number of booby traps hidden near altars, underneath dead animals, and behind doors, meant that the Monuments Men were in constant danger.

Standing in the rubble of Saint-Lô, Stout realized that a meeting with the other Monuments Men was now urgent. Inefficiencies were irritations in civilian life, but Stout knew that they could lead to deadly mistakes during war. The likelihood that one or more of his group might not make it home—perhaps even he himself—was something he'd considered while at Shrivenham, and each day since. But tempting fate by driving through combat zones for an inspection that another Monuments Officer had already conducted was negligent. Mistakes like that had to end immediately.

The Monuments Men were doing their jobs, but they weren't working in a coordinated manner. In fairness, without field radios, how could they? They were already woefully understaffed and largely on their own. Without command authority, they had to assess each situation and consult with each combat commander before using the only weapon they had—the power of persuasion. That took time. Stout had to hand it to his friend Paul Sachs, whose selection of middle-aged Monuments Men with extensive life experiences and teaching backgrounds had proven a stroke of genius. Still, despite their expertise and planning, the Monuments Men were frustrated about the lack of army support.

Stout took a moment to look down the list of the men he'd trained with at Shrivenham. Webb and Ross were always destined to spend most of their time in London advising General Eisenhower's command staff. Balfour, the lifelong historian, and Hancock, the award-winning sculptor, were, much to his frustration, victims of army bureaucracy, stuck in England waiting on orders just when he needed them most. Trying to get the two World War I veterans—British Monuments Men Lord Methuen and Dixon-Spain—across zones for a meeting would involve even more army red tape and delay. Better to just gather the Americans: Rorimer, the hard-charging curator; distinguished architects LaFarge and Hammett; and Posey, the dedicated soldier.

Near Saint-Lô, France: August 13, 1944

The meeting took place on August 13, at a First Army supply center just outside the ruined city of Saint-Lô. It had taken a few days, but Stout managed to get confirmations from everyone. Rorimer, who had walked ashore on Utah Beach just nine days earlier, hitched a ride from headquarters with Hammett, and the two arrived first. LaFarge followed in a small British vehicle. Some minutes passed before Stout pulled up, to everyone's great surprise, in a captured German Volkswagen Kübelwagen, which he had been assigned just a few days earlier. It was a wreck of a car, without a top or windshield. But bad as it was, it was his. He was grateful to not be dependent on cargo trucks and other military vehicles to do his job. Wheels meant independence.

The fifth American, Monuments Man Robert Posey, was unable to secure a ride, so they had to begin the meeting without him. Stout chuckled. Long ago he'd learned to find the humor in difficult situations, even if just a wince—part of his unflappable approach to life. After all, who couldn't appreciate the irony of this situation: The lack of transportation prevented all the Monuments Men from meeting to solve, among other problems, the lack of transportation.

Even though LaFarge, the first Monuments Man to set foot in France, outranked the others, everyone deferred to George Stout and his quiet confidence. Besides, five weeks in and out of the front lines conducting inspections had earned him seniority in the field. Far from being a complaint session, the purpose of the meeting was to share their individual experiences, then apply their collective resourcefulness to find solutions to each problem. Stout repeated what he had said so many times in letters to Paul Sachs, and to each of the men at Shrivenham: What matters—all that matters—is getting the job done.

Jim Rorimer, the determined curator who had impressed Stout from the outset of their training at Shrivenham, quickly spoke up. "There's so much to do it's difficult to know where to begin. Trying to cover my sector is like trying to clear the woods of acorns." With so many historic churches and monuments in the Normandy region of France, any "attempt to record this damage effort amid the many gaping craters and fire-swept hulks of buildings would be like trying to scoop up wine from a broken keg." Stout agreed; Rorimer's metaphors aptly described what he had seen in Saint-Lô, Caen, and many other destroyed towns along the Normandy coast.

Rorimer then recounted how German soldiers had made a mockery of the Hague Convention's rules of land warfare by regularly using church steeples as observation posts and sniper nests. Allied forces overcame the problem by firing an artillery round at the steeple: no more German observer or sniper, but also no more steeple. The others all nodded, somewhat impatiently: They had each seen plenty of damaged churches.

Of course you have, Rorimer acknowledged, but that's not the point. Whether or not Allied commanders were looking at the MFAA List of Protected Monuments he couldn't be sure, but somehow they instinctively knew that if it was possible to kill the enemy and only damage but not destroy a church or other historic landmark, that was the right choice. It then fell to the Monuments Men to determine if the damage could be repaired or if it was so great that the building was at risk of collapse. In those situations, combat commanders ordered the precious remains of the churches, hundreds of years old, scooped up for use as road base to keep their heavily mechanized armies on the move. Rorimer described several confrontations with citizens who had begged for their churches to be spared. But when he explained that there was no other way, that this was the price of freedom, they usually understood.

On his visit to the severely damaged Abbey of Saint-Sauveur-le-Vicomte, Rorimer found American GIs sharing their rations with the children and nuns who had miraculously survived the Allied air raids. At the Abbey of Cerisy-la-Forêt, an American general had ordered his troops to vacate their dry quarters and head outdoors, well aware of the cultural importance of the building. Right actions like that were going to win the respect of the French, and, Rorimer believed, the war.

"How are we supposed to know what one another are doing without field radios?" someone asked. That would have to be presented to the higher-ups, Stout replied. It was no easy task getting someone to listen. Twelfth Army Group, after all, had over one million men. Until then, everyone should provide duplicate copies of their daily field reports to Advance Section headquarters and circulate them among the group, including the two British World War I veterans, Lord Methuen and Dixon-Spain.

"What about the shortage of OFF LIMITS signs?" Stout had an answer for that, too: The army has commandeered a printing press in Cherbourg. Stout looked at Rorimer and asked him to arrange for five hundred signs to be printed immediately. Until then, they would improvise and make them by hand. If that didn't work, they would wrap white engineering tape around important locations. They knew that no soldier, no matter how curious, would wander into a site marked DANGER: MINES!

Transportation—as in, "There isn't any!"—was the most pressing problem. LaFarge had his beaten-up car and Stout his topless Volkswagen, which had already broken down once. But Rorimer and presumably Posey were wasting precious hours hitching rides. This, too, was on the list of needs that Hammett and Stout would discuss at their meeting with the duty officers of Twelfth Army Group on August 16.

Many things had indeed gone wrong, but Stout paused for a minute to focus on all that had gone right. He didn't need to reach for his notebook for prompts; that list he had memorized. There were the close calls, including the bombing of his encampment outside the town of Valognes, when a bomb landed just three hundred feet from his tent. Only in the morning did he learn that a medical corpsman had been killed. Yet, as exposed as they all were, especially to booby traps, no one in their small army of seven had been injured or killed. They had inspected hundreds of structures on the MFAA List of Protected Monuments and had posted many more OUT OF BOUNDS signs. Somehow they had also managed to dislodge American and British troops and French citizens from the comfort of being indoors in protected buildings without making enemies. In fact, Stout believed that the respect they had shown for these old structures had in some instances won over the support of the local people and even some Allied troops, despite the added hardship.

Even acknowledging that they had been lucky a time or two, Stout considered their mission thus far a success. Army bureaucracy was an impediment, but the commanders on the ground had been largely respectful of their work, so far at least. This came as a welcome surprise. The reports from Rorimer, LaFarge, and Hammett, and his meeting with Posey several weeks earlier, confirmed what Stout believed from the outset: With so little help from the army, the only way this mission had a chance of working was by winning over Allied commanders and the troops in the field, face-to-face, one by one.

CHAPTER 5

PRICELESS DUST

Florence, Italy: August 1944

On August 13, the same day that the American Monuments Men in France—all five of them—were meeting near the gutted city of Saint-Lô, Monuments Man Fred Hartt was making his way into Florence. Sporadic gunfire, perhaps from snipers, crackled ahead. Shellfire reverberated in the distance. Hartt's driver, Franco Ruggenini, maneuvered Lucky 13 through Porta Romana, the southern entrance to the city, past the Boboli Gardens, before turning left toward Villa Torrigiani, Allied Military Government (AMG) headquarters. But Hartt was oblivious to the sounds and the chaos, lost in thought about a city he considered his own.

Florence had in some ways saved his life; at least that's how Hartt saw it. His passionate study of the Renaissance provided an escape from memories of an unhappy childhood. Understanding the greatness of Michelangelo, Giotto, Masaccio, Botticelli, Donatello, Leonardo da Vinci, Raphael, and others who lived and worked in Florence required a thorough knowledge of the city's history. Hartt specialized in it.

The origin of Florence stretches back to the first century BCE, when the well-developed Etruscan society began to move down to the Arno River, which in time became the lifeblood of the city. The

Romans arrived during the time of Julius Caesar. By the 1400s, Florence had emerged as a center of international commerce. Its currency, the gold florin, and the banking dynasty it produced, the Medici family, became European powerhouses. The Medici wealth funded the artists of the Italian Renaissance, Western civilization's most prolific period of artistic achievement since the days of Greek democracy in Athens.

Hartt marveled at the genius of Filippo Brunelleschi, who applied mathematics to ancient architecture in order to design and construct the world's largest cupola atop the Florence cathedral, the Church of Santa Maria del Fiore. He admired the tenderness of Lorenzo Ghiberti's work, which magically wrought from bronze perfect expressions of human anatomy to produce for the cathedral's baptistery doors panels so beautiful that Michelangelo admiringly referred to them as the "Gates of Paradise." And now, filled with anguish, Hartt worried about how many of these things of beauty had survived.

A fortuitous meeting at AMG headquarters with Professor Filippo Rossi, Director of the Galleries of Florence, provided Hartt with an escort for his meeting with city art officials. Hartt and Rossi jumped into Lucky 13 for the short drive to the Pitti Palace, once home to the Medici family. Hartt knew the elegant palace and its stunning collection of art so well that a person could be forgiven for thinking he had once lived there himself. But the grandeur of *that* Pitti Palace and its expansive Boboli Gardens had given way to the emergencies of war. Now it provided refuge for more than six thousand Florentines who had been dislodged from their homes by German forces. From a distance, Hartt thought it resembled a crowded slum in Naples more than a royal palace. Clothing hung from nearly every balcony.

The engine of Lucky 13 moaned as it made the steep approach. Hundreds of people filled the sun-soaked piazza, including what turned out to be an informal welcoming committee of art superintendents and museum officials excited to meet the American Monuments Man. As he entered the building, Hartt could see people wandering aimlessly; others sat on the ground huddled in groups. Babies were crying. A few injured people nearby were moaning. But he also heard laughter and could see children at play. Try as they might, Hartt thought, the Nazis didn't break the spirit of the Florentines. These people were tired, filthy, hungry, and thirsty, but they were still alive.

The Florentine superintendent, Giovanni Poggi, and Dr. Ugo Procacci, an art official of the Tuscan museums, had, like the other citizens, been trapped in their city for nine days, worried about the fate of the treasures stashed in villas around the Tuscan countryside and eager for information. Hartt had precious details to share. He had just completed inspections of the Castle of Montegufoni, with its priceless paintings; the Villa Bossi-Pucci in Montagnana, which German troops had thoroughly looted; and several other Florentine repositories.

As the officials listened to Hartt explain the mission of the Monuments Men and discuss what he had discovered on his inspections, they couldn't believe their good fortune. The American had military authority, a jeep, and extraordinary knowledge of the city's monuments and works of art. The best chance of protecting the other repositories, Hartt explained, depended on him having a complete list of all the Tuscan repositories and their locations. Poggi and Procacci quickly complied.

Hartt took a moment and hurriedly scanned the list, making a running tally in his head of the number of art repositories. When he reached the last page, the magnitude of the problem nearly knocked him off his feet. Thirty-eight villas in all, located amid constantly shifting battle lines, housed many of the world's greatest art masterpieces. Making matters worse, about one-third of the works had no protective crates or wrapping. Hartt was frustrated— and angry. His most dreaded nightmare had now become a reality. How many masterpieces had already been destroyed in battles or stolen by fleeing German forces, he wondered. He could and would inspect the remaining repositories in Allied-controlled areas, but there wasn't a thing he could do about those located behind enemy lines other than wait. Hartt abhorred waiting.

Their meeting at an end, Hartt asked Dr. Procacci to show him how to reach the most damaged portions of the city. As they set out on foot, moving very slowly over smashed stone and broken glass in the direction of the Ponte Vecchio, Procacci began recounting the dying days of the beautiful city.

Toward the end of July, German commanders had issued a proclamation ordering everyone living along the Arno to evacuate their homes. On July 31, civilians were prohibited from crossing any of the city's six main bridges. This divided Florence into northern and southern halves. While German sappers laid their cables and explosive devices beneath the bridges, soldiers went house to house along the Arno, ensuring that everyone had complied with the evacuation order. When they found a locked door, they used grenades to open it.

Several days passed, followed by a new decree ordering all citizens to remain in the lower floors of their homes, away from all windows. Clearly the German commanders didn't want any witnesses to the Wehrmacht's evil deeds. By this time, thousands of people had crammed themselves into the Pitti Palace, seeking any safety they could find. The first in a series of thunderous explosions came on the evening of August 3, each so forceful that the ground shook. Terror seized the crowd, then someone cried out, "The bridges, the bridges!"

The destroyed bridges of Florence.

Explosions continued until dawn, when an eerie quiet descended upon the city. Under the cover of darkness German forces had retreated north, to the relative safety of the Gothic Line, leaving behind smoldering ruins. Five of the six bridges no longer crossed the Arno but lay in it. In an absurd effort to spare the Ponte Vecchio—Hitler's favorite bridge, Procacci pointed out—German forces deliberately destroyed entire city blocks of buildings and medieval towers hoping to create impassable rubble piles.

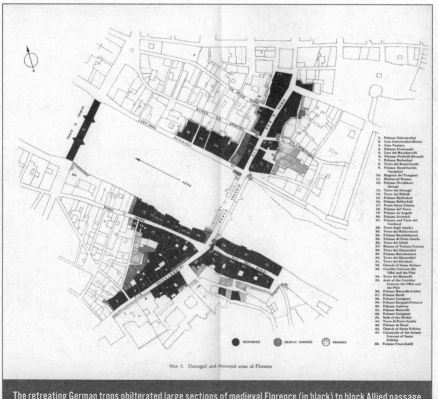

MAP 3. Damaged and destroyed areas of Florence

The retreating German trops obliterated large sections of medieval Florence (in black) to block Allied passage across Hitler's favorite bridge, the Ponte Vecchio (center).

By the time Hartt and the superintendent reached a small piazza near the Arno, Hartt no longer needed anyone to describe the destruction; he could see it for himself. It was worse than anything he could ever have imagined, "one gigantic trash pile together, spilling into the Arno." In an instant, centuries of beauty and history had been reduced to priceless dust.

Conditions elsewhere in the city were abysmal. The intense heat of August had cooked human waste from the broken sewers and decaying corpses buried under collapsed buildings to create a suffocating smell. Hartt pulled out his handkerchief, but it did little good. Barefoot women stood shoulder to shoulder preparing spartan meals on outdoor stoves. Children sat in circles on the ground, devouring their meager suppers. No one indulged in vanity. Young women looked thirty years older, with their once well-coifed hair

Rubble piles are all that remained of the medieval towers that once flanked the Ponte Vecchio.

standing on end, caked with grayish dust. Men patched and repatched their ragged clothes.

There were shortages of everything except dust, bullets, and the dead. Snipers randomly picked off civilians. German artillery shells intermittently rained down on the city, claiming even more lives. Men, armed with picks and shovels, hacked away at the thirty-foot-high mounds of medieval stone to clear paths so workers could begin rebuilding. Women searched through the pieces for heirlooms. A cluster of people usually indicated the location of one of the city's temporary clean water supplies. Such oases were rather easy to discover by following someone carrying straw-covered wine jugs or gasoline cans in each hand. It was a pitiful sight. All the destruction would take months to clean up and years to repair, and even then, Hartt sighed, the city would never look the same.

With the complete list of repositories in hand, Hartt wanted to resume his inspections, but the situation in the city center was desperate. Florence needed as many Monuments Men as possible to protect the remains of historic buildings that had any chance of being salvaged and to recover what they could of rare books and works of art buried in the debris. The search for the stolen Florentine treasures would have to wait.

Near Pisa, Italy: September 1944

Hunkered down on the outskirts of another destroyed Italian town, Deane Keller flipped through the pages of his field diary and made some calculations in his head. Maybe he was off by a few hundred miles here or there, but in the nearly four months since becoming a Monuments Man, Keller figured he'd driven about eight thousand miles, over dusty, bomb-cratered roads, inspecting hundreds of damaged towns. The scenes of misery and hardship were always similar; only the names of the places changed. But from what he was hearing from the boys of Fifth Army, the situation in the city of Pisa might be the worst of all. Compounding matters, half of Fifth Army's strength had been depleted in just a couple of months, partly the result of combat losses, but mostly because General Eisenhower had siphoned units for an invasion of southern France, called Operation Dragoon, which began in August.

As German shells continued to fall, Keller pulled out his regional map, its folded edges now as soft as tissue paper. Pisa was located fifty miles west of Florence, and as the seagulls overhead confirmed, just eight miles inland from the Tyrrhenian Sea. The ancient city owed its early development to the Romans, who understood the importance of its strategically positioned port. The Arno River, flowing east to west, divided the city center just as it did in Florence. This fate of geography also meant the river was a barrier the Allies would have to cross in their offensive that continued to grind north.

Allied leaders had declared Florence off-limits to bombing due to its historic, art-rich city center. But Pisa, a city with a rich artistic and cultural history of its own, had no such exemption and was subjected to continuous punishing bombing raids that caused immense destruction. Fifth Army artillery then targeted any German-occupied buildings that the bombers had missed. After six grueling weeks of battle, Keller hoped there was still something left to liberate.

The following day, September 2, Keller and a small team of AMG specialists entered the south side of the city and crept along in their jeeps until the volume of debris forced them to abandon their vehicles and walk. They climbed over ruins, jumping at the occasional rat in the rubble, all the while looking for mines. With four months of experience walking through destroyed Italian towns, Keller instinctively assumed that German forces had booby-trapped every building and pathway. After walking just a few blocks in Pisa, he was sure of it.

The going was slow and tedious, but by the end of the day he and the other officers finally reached the old city hall near the banks of the Arno. To celebrate their harrowing journey, Keller and Captain McCallum, the engineer on his reconnaissance team, decided to hang the Stars and Stripes and the Union Jack from a balcony that overlooked the river. As he looked out over the destroyed city and its demolished bridges, Keller realized that he had gone the entire day and seen just two citizens in a city with a prewar population of seventy-two thousand people.

Early the next morning, Keller had to use the remains of a narrow streetcar track like a jungle gym just to cross the Arno on his way to inspect the heart of the city, the Piazza dei Miracoli—Square of Miracles. The growth and prosperity of Pisa from the eleventh through the thirteenth centuries had funded construction of the piazza and its duomo (cathedral), *battistero* (baptistery), campanile (bell tower—known as the Leaning Tower of Pisa), and *camposanto* (cemetery). But a cruel siege in 1406 by Pisa's most fierce rival, Florence, signaled an end to the maritime republic's power. Pisa had lived in the shadow of the Tuscan capital ever since.

Piazza dei Miracoli in Pisa. The Camposanto Monumentale, with its missing roof, can be seen at the upper right.

Entering the piazza, Keller noticed that the baptistery had sustained hits. He could see several holes in the roof of the Duomo and one on a facade column, but none looked too serious. A quick glance to his right confirmed that the Leaning Tower of Pisa was undamaged . . . and still leaning. But as he emerged from between the baptistery and the Duomo, he froze. The roof of the city's famed cemetery, the Camposanto Monumentale, was gone. Keller could see a few stubs of charred timber emerging above its walls, but nothing more. In this war, even the cemeteries were dying.

The architectural curiosity of the Leaning Tower of Pisa had for centuries drawn steady crowds, but Keller knew that the real jewel of the Piazza dei Miracoli was the Camposanto, constructed in 1278. The building consisted of two rectangles, one inside the other. The outer rectangle, about the size of an American football field, was covered; the interior rectangle, which contained a grass courtyard in the style of a cloister, was not. Separating the two rectangular spaces were Gothic marble arcades open to the grass courtyard from all four sides. The exterior walls and the Gothic marble arcades supported a wooden A-frame roof covered with lead.

Keller knew that the Camposanto glorified local memory stretching back to the medieval era. The marble pavement was interspersed with tombs, each marking the burial spot of a city luminary. Adding to the veneration, fourteenth- and fifteenth-century artists had then blanketed the interior walls with vibrantly colored frescoes. The Camposanto contained more painted surface than the entire Sistine Chapel at the Vatican, twenty thousand square feet in all. But Keller's overriding memory as a student wasn't of the building's frescoes, tombs, or history: It was the serenity of the space, a welcoming respite for the living, a solemn resting place for the dead.

Keller reached into his pocket and pulled out his field diary and, like a pathologist preparing to conduct an autopsy, started recording the damage:

> *On the floor next to the walls [are] thousands of pieces of fresco which have fallen to the ground either from the heat [or] the concussion from the jarring of the great beams as they fell to the floor. These [are] mingled with myriads of pieces of broken roof tiles, carved chunks of all sizes from the tombs, blackened embers and nails. All the*

sculptures [are] covered on the upper sides thoroughly
with the molten lead from heat and the running lead [is]
to be found on tombs and paintings alike.

"Thousands of pieces" wildly understated the volume of fragments. As Keller thought about it, they numbered into the millions. The floor of the Camposanto was now the world's largest jigsaw puzzle.

Out of the corner of his eye, Keller saw a man rushing toward him speaking Italian so hurriedly that it took a few minutes to calm him down before asking him to begin again. Bruno Farnesi, technical assistant—and witness to the fire—had quite a story to tell.

The roofless Camposanto Monumentale.

Five weeks earlier, on July 27, a violent artillery barrage had shaken the Piazza dei Miracoli. A few shells hit the massive structure. The Americans seemed to be aiming at a German observation post in the bell tower, Farnesi explained, but he doubted the Allies were trying to destroy it. German soldiers had established a position there to call in target coordinates to artillery batteries located far away from the Square of Miracles. Several other rounds struck the Duomo. Farnesi knew the cathedral was strong. It could take a dozen blows. But when the shelling stopped and the sky cleared, he saw a thin column of smoke rising from the Camposanto.

Even from the ground, flames were clearly visible on the northern side of the roof. Farnesi said he would have doused them, but the city had been without water for days. The only weapon to fight the fire was a tall ladder, which he had placed inside the Camposanto two months earlier.

A small group of volunteers, armed with nothing more than shovels, clubs, and poles, followed him up the ladder, but the wind off the Tyrrhenian Sea was pushing the fire across the roof faster than the men could fight it. The day was dying, but the fire was gathering strength. Farnesi watched as it ran along the great wooden support beams and wrapped its fingers around the lead roof. The beams snapped and crashed to the ground, causing the lead to run in rivulets down the walls. Farnesi urged the men forward, despite the blistering heat.

A shell whistled in, hitting the Duomo, but the great building held. Soon a volley of shells was raining down on the complex. The crowd scattered. The men struggled down the ladder and huddled behind the walls of the Camposanto. The shellfire seemed to be coming from the south, where the Americans were encamped. While the wall offered no protection from artillery, it was the only spot sheltered from the heat of the flames. Another explosion less than one hundred feet away knocked one of the men to the ground. This time, the small group ran for the safety of the cathedral.

Sometime later, maybe ten minutes or an hour—it was impossible for Farnesi to determine—the artillery fire stopped. Farnesi told Keller what happened next:

> *In the night, the Piazza dei Miracoli seemed to bleed in the vermilion color of the flames; the Duomo, the Baptistery, and the Campanile . . . were there, solemn, almost tinted with blood, to witness the tragic destiny of their brother, minor in age but not in beauty, who was perishing and was irredeemably consumed.*

It was a sad story, Keller admitted, and he'd heard plenty of them from all the Bruno Farnesis in each town that he had inspected.

Without another word, Keller turned and walked away, his head dropped and shoulders slumped. As he slowly crossed the lawn, his mind raced through a jumbled mix of memories . . . of Kathy and Dino, who never left his thoughts . . . of driving eight thousand miles inspecting dead cities . . . of the women in Naples, carrying buckets of rubble while their babies sat in the ruins . . . of San Miniato, on the hills outside of Florence, where twenty-seven civilians were killed when a mine detonated inside the cathedral into which they had been herded by the Germans . . . of Fred Hartt's preliminary report on Florence, with its bridges and medieval towers now reduced to dust and hundreds of its master-pieces stolen.

And during those four months, he wondered, what meaningful thing had he done other than inspections and advising others? "My assignment is MFAA officer, AMG Fifth Army," he had written his parents just weeks earlier. "I am not supposed to step out of my role. I would have no authority at all. The way I help is to talk with people, serve as interpreter—give help to any of the others who need it, and once in a while interject something in a meeting."

His thoughts drifted again, to the first dead American soldier he'd seen, and the letter the GI had tucked in the lining of his helmet for his mother. That American boy had become every soldier. That village had become every place he'd visited. But Keller also recalled other memories besides death and destruction, moments that had provided him with encouragement to go to the next place, and the next, like his time in Sezze Romano, where fifty towns-people had followed him to his jeep, offering prayers and thanks; and his stop in Monte Oliveto Maggiore, where the monks had hidden Allied personnel amid the artwork of Siena.

He also remembered the joy of hearing that Rome had been liberated virtually unharmed, and the excitement of finding Siena's most prized painting, Duccio's *Maestà*, safely inside its wooden crates. But this situation in Pisa was different, a chance to actually *do* something, something good, something permanent. Keller knew that Fifth Army didn't have the resources for the exhaustive and time-consuming project that he had in mind, but ignoring the problem would draw the scorn of the press and alienate Italians. One rainstorm would wash away the remains of centuries of history. Something had to be done. Keller was convinced that if the Monuments Men operation ever stood for anything, this was the moment to prove it.

A few minutes later, his body stiffened, and with a bounce to his step, he started back across the lawn of the piazza toward Farnesi and instructed him to bar entry to anyone who had not first obtained his permission. He then wandered off again, looking for a unit with a field radio; he had to make an emergency call.

CHAPTER 6

OBJECTIVES

Paris, France: late August to September 1944

The convoy of Allied troops lumbered into the outskirts of Paris—the City of Light—on August 25, snaking around barricades and an occasional burning vehicle. Sporadic gunfire crackled along the route. After four years of Nazi tyranny, the day of liberation had arrived and Monuments Man Jim Rorimer, part of the advance team entering the city, was in the thick of it.

German forces were fighting a desperate retreat everywhere. On the Eastern Front, the Soviets routed another Wehrmacht army group—five hundred thousand soldiers—in Ukraine and eastern Poland. While the Germans weren't hemorrhaging as much territory in Western Europe, the loss of Paris was a symbolic blow. German General Dietrich von Choltitz had surrendered his forces just hours earlier, but danger still lurked. Enemy snipers crouched in their hiding places, taking aim at the approaching military vehicles and curious civilians emerging to feel freedom once again. Rorimer could see signs of the fight for the city everywhere, including pickets and barbed wire on the streets, sandbag barricades in front of buildings, abandoned tanks and other military vehicles scattered about, smoldering embers of fires recently extinguished, and German artillery pieces still warm to the touch.

After spending the night in a hotel room that some German officer had occupied just twenty-four hours earlier, Rorimer put on his chocolate OD shirt (which was really dark green in color), fastened the buckles on his once-brown suede combat boots, grabbed his garrison cap, and walked across the Tuileries Garden to the cultural heart of the city, the Louvre Museum. Second Lieutenant—and former museum curator—Jim Rorimer knew practically every inch of the Louvre, one of the largest and most frequently visited art museums in the world. The paintings and sculpture that covered the walls and filled its rooms were as recognizable to him as his oldest friends. But that was a different time. War had a way of making familiar ground feel unfamiliar.

An unsettling silence had replaced the hustle and bustle of tourists. As Rorimer ascended the grand entry stairwell, he was shocked by the absence of one of the Louvre's signature pieces, a work that for decades had towered over all who climbed the steps: *The Winged Victory of Samothrace*, a second-century BCE Greek sculpture. At the top of the staircase he turned right, then right again into the main gallery. The paintings were also gone. In their place, someone had handwritten in chalk the names of artists and inventory numbers of their work. The Louvre was empty: no visitors, no works of art, just a lone Monuments Man armed with dozens of questions, striding with purpose—Rorimer always walked with purpose—down the Grande Galerie of the museum on his way to an appointment.

As he approached the museum's offices, Rorimer glanced out the window. U.S. Army soldiers were herding hundreds of German prisoners into the courtyard. In the distance, more GIs were

Empty frames that held Louvre masterpieces before their evacuation.

positioning antiaircraft guns around the perimeter. Nothing about this visit to the Louvre was normal until he rounded a corner and saw Jacques Jaujard, Director of the National Museums of France.

Being in the Louvre with a valued colleague provided a brief but welcome return to the world of normal. Rorimer admired Jaujard for helping museum colleagues in Madrid relocate to Switzerland art masterpieces at risk of being damaged during the Spanish Civil War. Jaujard's role in protecting the Louvre treasures bordered on magical. *How* he had done it was a mystery Rorimer wanted his friend to explain.

The experience in Spain contributed, Jaujard said, but it was advance planning that won the day. Rorimer leaned forward in his chair like a young boy eager to hear a great tale. When the Louvre, like other museums across Western Europe, closed in late August

1939, staff and volunteers worked around the clock to protect France's cultural heritage. Paintings, drawings, sculpture, and other precious objects, requiring thirty-seven convoys of five to eight trucks each, were taken to countryside châteaux. Vast quantities of centuries-old stained glass were removed from cathedrals in Paris, Chartres, and other cities, then packed and stored. The concern at that stage was getting everything to the countryside to protect it from bombing and the consequent fires. Rorimer, having walked through the ruins of fire-damaged cities in Normandy, recognized all too well what would have happened to the Louvre treasures had Paris suffered the same fate.

Knowing *The Winged Victory of Samothrace* weighed several tons, and, contrary to appearances, was not one solid piece of marble but thousands of shards painstakingly reassembled, Rorimer was eager to learn how Jaujard and his team moved it down the stairwell. Simple, Jaujard explained. They built a pulley that enabled them to mount the sculpture on wooden skids, then lowered it down the steps like a skier on a downhill slope—but at a snail's pace.

Rorimer also wanted to know the fate of the *Mona Lisa*, the most famous painting in the world. "*La Joconde*," Jaujard sighed with a smile, using the French name of Leonardo's masterpiece. With great satisfaction, he explained how his team had evacuated it on an ambulance stretcher in the dead of night, into a waiting van. A museum curator accompanied the masterpiece on its journey. To maintain a stable climate for the painting, the doors of the van were sealed. The painting arrived at its destination safely, but the curator had nearly suffocated. This was just the first of five moves. In the end, it found safety lying on a floor in Château de

Evacuation of *The Winged Victory of Samothrace*, second century BCE, from the Louvre Museum.

Montal, in southwestern France, inside its custom-made red-velvet-lined wooden case, next to the bed of a fifteen-year-old girl.

The conversation took on a more serious tone when Jaujard began describing the challenges of protecting other treasures from the French museums during the four-year-long Nazi occupation. Realizing the importance the Nazis placed on creating an appearance of legality in their transactions, Jaujard had converted French

Monuments Man James Rorimer (right) in front of the wall where Leonardo da Vinci's most famous work, *Mona Lisa*, once hung.

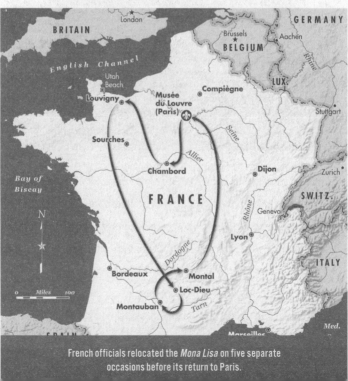

French officials relocated the *Mona Lisa* on five separate occasions before its return to Paris.

bureaucracy into a weapon by waging a paper war to prevent, or at least slow to a crawl, any effort to steal works of art from the national collections. The strategy for the most part worked. Covert connections with the French Resistance, his virtual eyes and ears when tracking German activity, also proved important.

But there were notable failings, Jaujard lamented. While the French museum collections had largely been saved, the Nazis' premeditated and systematic looting of Jewish-owned collections, especially the preeminent dealer-collector dynasties, was a loss of immeasurable proportion. Jaujard estimated that one-third of the French private collections—perhaps as many as twenty thousand works of art—were now in Germany. Rorimer listened as his friend ran down the list of prominent collectors who had been looted, including Rothschild, Rosenberg, and David-Weill. He knew them all. Unfortunately, so did the Nazis. These enormously rich, museum-quality private collections contained treasures by Old Master artists, including Johannes Vermeer and Rembrandt van Rijn, the great Postimpressionist painter Vincent van Gogh, and twentieth-century master Pablo Picasso. Museum directors hoped someday to acquire them. The Nazis had a simple and more certain plan: just steal them.

This initial visit with Jaujard was meant to be more of a social call than a briefing session, but Rorimer considered it a welcome beginning to his first day of duty as the MFAA Specialist Officer for Paris. As Rorimer said his goodbyes, he realized that perhaps only a fellow museum man could fully appreciate Jaujard's herculean achievements during the Nazi occupation. Rorimer knew that his friend was far too modest to ever lay claim to an act of bravery, but there was no question that Jacques Jaujard was a hero, not just to France, but to all those who loved the arts.

Exiting the museum, Rorimer passed several U.S. Army tanks parked in the Tuileries Garden, a Paris landmark that he believed as worthy of protection as any historic building. The tankers gathered around small fires where they were preparing a hot breakfast and coffee. Others were shaving.

Rorimer wasn't focused on the tanks, or the soldiers, or possible billeting violations; his thoughts centered on opportunity. Jacques Jaujard had provided the Monuments Men with key information about priceless paintings that the Nazis had stolen from French collectors and then shipped to Germany. *He did say one-third of the private collections in France, right?* Someone had to find those treasures and return them to France, but where to begin? Jaujard mentioned that some museum employees had lists of what was stolen and some idea of where it had been taken, but Berlin was still 655 miles away and Rorimer clearly had his hands full of work in Paris. Still, it wouldn't hurt to dig deeper. Perhaps Jaujard would be willing to arrange a meeting with his museum employees?

Bruges, Belgium: mid-September 1944

On September 16, three weeks after the liberation of Paris, British Major Ronald Balfour, George Stout's roommate at Shrivenham, reached the Belgian town of Bruges. Four days earlier, the First Canadian Army had taken the city in a dash along the Channel coast. Army bureaucracy had delayed his departure from England until the last week of August, but now, attached to First Canadian

Army, he was finally at work as a Monuments Man, following leads on a brazen theft by the Nazis.

Sitting on a pew inside the Church of Our Lady, with a few minutes to spare before his meeting with the dean, Balfour reached into his field pack, pulled out a stack of typed notes, and began shuffling through the pages. He was constantly revising his thoughts about how to explain to the fighting men why cultural preservation mattered. As he scanned the pages he found the paragraph of interest.

"We do not want to destroy unnecessarily what men spent so much time and care and skill in making," he whispered. "These examples of craftsmanship tell us so much about our ancestors." The echo of footsteps caused him to look up from the page, but it was just a parishioner. After watching the local woman light a candle, he resumed. "If these things are lost or broken or destroyed, we lose a valuable part of our knowledge about our forefathers. No age lives entirely alone; every civilisation is formed not merely by its own achievements but by what it has inherited from the past. If these things are destroyed, we have lost a part of our past, and we shall be the poorer for it." He'd found the right words; of that he was sure. Now he needed to find more opportunities to share them with the men.

Moments later the church sacristan tapped him on the shoulder. The dean, Reverend René Deschepper, was ready to meet with him. As they walked past parishioners on the way to Deschepper's office, Balfour could see that the euphoria of two days earlier, when British troops liberated the city, had already given way to the reality of the

difficult road ahead. The hardships of Nazi rule had created shortages of everything. Despite that, the dean had thoughtfully arranged
for his assistant to bring them tea. Field journal in hand, Balfour
began taking notes as the dean shared the events of September 7.

Sometime around midnight, two German officers appeared at
the locked doors of the church demanding entry. In the street behind
them were twenty or more armed sailors from the local barracks and,
curiously, several trucks marked with Red Cross insignias. "We're
taking the Michelangelo. To protect it from the Americans," one of
them said. Reverend Deschepper, anguished from just recounting
the story, explained to Balfour, almost defensively, that there was

Michelangelo, Bruges *Madonna*,
1501–1504.

nothing he could do to stop them. He
then handed the British Monuments
Man a postcard containing a photograph of what the Germans had stolen.

Even before taking it, Balfour knew
that the dean was speaking about the
Bruges *Madonna*. It was priceless,
famous for being the only sculpture by
Michelangelo to leave Italy during his
lifetime. The nearly life-sized masterpiece, carved out of white marble in
1504, when the Florentine master was
twenty-nine years old, depicted the tenderness between a very young virgin
mother and her Christ child. As he
looked at the image, Balfour marveled
at how Michelangelo had transformed a

rigid, heavy piece of stone into a work that revealed the softness of human skin and the lightness of fabric folds. His genius had breathed life into both figures. Beyond the protective pose of a young boy standing between his mother's legs and her flowing robes, their fingers interlocked, Michelangelo subtly foreshadowed the painful fate of Christ. Balfour put down the postcard, adjusted his glasses, and asked the dean to continue.

The two German officers posted several sailors at the doors and ordered others to the north aisle of the church, where the sculpture had been placed in 1940 as a protective measure. In near darkness, using only flashlights to continue their nefarious operation, they positioned a bed mattress on the floor in front of the sculpture. And this, the dean said with emphasis, revealed the true evil of their actions.

Four days earlier, a Dr. Rosemann had personally delivered the mattresses, offering them as additional protection from Allied bombing. Rosemann was the senior official in Belgium of the German art protection unit, known as the Kunstschutz. When the two German commanders in charge of the looting operation specifically asked for the mattresses, the dean realized that far from being a last-minute thought, the Germans had devised a plan to loot the church of the Michelangelo sculpture long before the actual theft. The only spontaneous aspect of their operation was the theft of eleven valuable paintings that had hung inside the church for centuries.

The dean and sacristan watched as a group of sailors inched the sculpture forward and then tilted it toward the mattress on the floor. It took nearly a dozen sailors to lift and carry it toward the door. Once there, they laid a second mattress on top of the sculpture, tied it into place, then loaded it into one of the Red Cross trucks. The paintings were put in the second truck. The two German officers and remaining sailors departed in the third. It took them five hours, but when done, the Germans had looted a work of art that had been in Bruges for 440 years. The Church of Our Lady was missing its centerpiece; Belgium was missing a national treasure.

Reverend Deschepper had no idea where the sculpture was, or how the Germans intended to transport it, presumably back to Nazi Germany. But he pleaded with Balfour to find it and see that it was returned to its home in Bruges. He then handed him the stack of postcards on the off chance that someone who might have seen the sculpture would come forward with information. It seemed unlikely, but that—and prayer—were his only hope.

After thanking the dean for his good wishes and the stack of postcards, Balfour exited the church, positioned his beret, and found a nearby bench to supplement his interview notes. That the Germans had looted was hardly news. But the fact that they were *still* looting, at a time when Allied soldiers were less than a week away from Bruges, when human nature should be screaming for a person to flee, not hang around and steal something as iconic as Michelangelo's Bruges *Madonna*, indeed *was* news. He reached into his field pack once more, pulled out one of the postcards the dean had given him, and took a long look. Reverend Deschepper was certainly right about one thing: Someone somewhere knew something about the whereabouts of the Michelangelo. Balfour was determined to find him.

Near Verdun, France: late September 1944

Robert Posey, the lone American Monuments Man unable to attend the August 13 meeting near Saint-Lô, pushed the most recent package from Supreme Headquarters Allied Expeditionary Force (SHAEF) out of the way, trying to find the calendar in his pup tent. With a towel wrapped around his neck and dog tags, he was about to take his first hot shower in two months, in a captured German barracks no less. The timing of it made him laugh. Just days earlier, he had written his wife, Alice, pointing out how "things that seem luxuries in the field would seem to be the most meager of items" in civilian life. The "meager" items—a home-cooked meal; a bed, preferably indoors; and yes, even a hot shower—were always things to savor, but not knowing when the next opportunity to experience them might come made Posey all the more appreciative.

As Monuments Officer for General George S. Patton's U.S. Third Army—well, it wasn't really Patton's army, but try and convince anyone serving under him of that—Posey was sure he had the best assignment in the whole army. For a guy from a poor family, raised on a dirt farm outside the small town of Morris, Alabama, population five hundred, he'd done well for himself. Besides, what he and his family lacked in money they more than made up for in patriotism.

Serving in the military was in his blood. A Posey had fought for the British crown during the colonial period, in the French and Indian War; served as a minuteman in the South Carolina militia during the Revolutionary War; and battled against the Creek

Nation in the War of 1812. Eight Posey brothers fought in the Civil War; only one survived. Now, Robert Posey was in eastern France, a captain in the U.S. Army, continuing that proud tradition of service to the nation.

Family tradition wasn't the only reason he'd joined the military. The army's Reserve Officers' Training Corps—the ROTC—was his ticket out of Morris, Alabama, and into Auburn University. With scant family finances, there was no other way he could have attended college. Architecture became his interest, and that, in turn, helped him get a job and provide for his family. He figured he owed the army a lot.

After his shower, back in his tent and dressed, he opened the package from SHAEF. Reports . . . directives . . . those were the norm . . . but the inclusion of photographs of works of art? They looked interesting! A detailed description of each work of art accompanied the photographs, all Belgian treasures, and summary information about their history right up until the time they went missing. Missing? They haven't gone missing, he thought. The Nazis have stolen them.

Two of the objects were so iconic he recognized them immediately: Michelangelo's Bruges *Madonna*, whose theft had been reported by Monuments Man Ronald Balfour one week earlier, and the Ghent Altarpiece, certainly the most important painting in Belgium and perhaps among the five most important works of art in the world. The sculpture by Michelangelo was valuable, but the Ghent Altarpiece dwarfed it in importance. With no further obligations that afternoon, Posey lay down on his cot and started reading through the materials.

The Adoration of the Mystic Lamb—its formal name—belonged in Saint Bavo's Cathedral in the town of Ghent, about thirty miles east of Bruges. The double-sided wood panel painting, measuring twelve feet high and sixteen feet wide, was completed in 1432 by Jan van Eyck and his brother, Hubert. From the outset, the painting was considered a towering achievement in the development of art. The use of oil-based paint to create lifelike renderings of people, not the idealized forms of centuries past, astonished viewers. The minute attention to detail—whiskers and beards, fabric on gowns, brightly illuminated landscapes, jeweled embroidery, and even individual strands of hair—demonstrated an artistic ability unlike anything anyone had ever seen.

Jan and Hubert van Eyck, Ghent Altarpiece, 1432.

To Adolf Hitler and the Nazis, the Ghent Altarpiece was Germanic in style and therefore belonged in Germany. Six of the twenty-four panels had been owned by a German museum for nearly one hundred years, until 1919, when the surrender terms of the Treaty of Versailles that ended World War I forced Germany to relinquish them as war reparations. Those six panels were taken to Belgium and united with the other panels, leaving Germans, and Adolf Hitler, with a bitter, festering wound.

Germany's invasion of Western Europe in May 1940 provided Hitler with a chance to get even and right the perceived historic wrongs of Versailles. Belgian officials knew exactly what that meant. While German Wehrmacht troops were advancing west into France, three trucks carrying the Ghent Altarpiece were on the road to Italy, desperately hoping to reach the Vatican and safety. By the time the trucks approached the border, Italy had declared war on France. Closed borders forced the drivers to change direction. They headed west, eventually finding an art repository at the foot of the Pyrenees, in the southwestern French town of Pau. At that point the safety of the Ghent Altarpiece became the responsibility of the French government.

German officials knew where the Belgian treasure had been hidden, but why rush to take it? By 1942, Hitler, unable to resist temptation any longer, ordered a secret delegation to France with instructions not to return to Germany without the van Eycks' masterpiece. French art officials, including Jacques Jaujard, protested vigorously; so did Belgian officials. But it was all too little, too late. The painting disappeared into Nazi Germany and had not been seen since.

After finishing the report, Posey dropped it on the wood pole floor of his tent and grabbed his map. He figured that, at the speed of Third Army's advance, they should be crossing the border into Germany, now less than sixty miles away, in no time at all. It was anyone's guess what they would find on enemy soil, but hiding something that important without anyone knowing about it seemed unlikely. Posey felt sure of one thing: If the Ghent Altarpiece was hidden somewhere in Third Army's area of operations, it was as good as found—assuming the Nazis hadn't destroyed it.

With his work duties complete, Posey poked around in his field pack for some writing paper and a pen. Each envelope he mailed home contained a letter for his wife, Alice, and a separate one for his seven-year-old son, Dennis, whom he often called "Woogie." Army censors limited what he could say about his work and forbade any reference to where he was, or where he was headed. But he always made sure to let Alice know how much he missed her and Woogie, and that his time away from them, though painful, was worth it. He was happy in his job and honored by what he was doing. Letters to Woogie always asked about "the Zoo," a growing menagerie of animals that were part of their family. Most recently Woogie had added a bunny rabbit. His son didn't just love animals; he was a born zookeeper.

There wasn't much Posey didn't like about the army other than missed opportunities with his son, like seeing his first ride on a horse and being at his side to comfort him when he got the measles. But coming from such a poor family, Posey knew the value of the little things he seldom had as a child and made a point of surprising Woogie by including souvenirs with his letters. Sometimes it was a postcard from one of the cities Third Army had liberated, or foreign stamps and currency. Occasionally he sent home some war booty like a Nazi swastika belt buckle.

This night, as he thought about what to write his boy, he remembered that Alice had mentioned some problems Dennis was having with bullies. Pen in hand, he got out a piece of U.S. Army stationery and started writing:

> *Dear Dennis: I am sorry that you have so much trouble with the kids fighting around town. That is the price one pays for being a bit more civilized than the people about him. I think the best way to handle it is to develop a good uppercut. When you get a bit older you can take boxing lessons . . . Until you learn some fist fighting ways it is probably better to avoid them.*

After rereading what he'd written, Posey realized it likely wouldn't be much help. Advice was always a distant second to the magic of a hug. Trying to be an engaged dad from afar was the toughest part of war.

CHAPTER 7

RESURRECTION
AND TREACHERY

Pisa, Italy: September to October 1944

Monuments Man Deane Keller knew there was risk in making the call. The office of Brigadier General Edgar Hume, commander of Allied Military Government in Italy, was already being bombarded with requests for help, made worse by the devastation to medieval Florence being reported by Fred Hartt. It would be easy for the general's staff to ignore his request and write off the Camposanto as another casualty of war. But Keller knew that Hume, who had served on General Eisenhower's command staff in North Africa, had spent one year of graduate school in Rome. Perhaps the general's knowledge of Italy and its cultural heritage would work in his favor.

The following morning, September 4, a small convoy of military jeeps pulled into the Piazza dei Miracoli. Keller could barely contain his smile. His call had worked. General Hume hadn't just sent his staff—he'd come himself, accompanied by the archbishop of Pisa. It was a hopeful beginning. As they approached the medieval structure, Keller, serving as translator, pulled some tourist postcards of the Piazza dei Miracoli out of his pocket and passed them to General Hume and the archbishop. The two stood outside the entrance holding the photographs of the undamaged Camposanto, with its lead-lined timber roof, at arm's length, juxtaposed against the now-bare cemetery walls.

Seeing that the postcards were having the desired effect, Keller led the small group into the burial site. Even five weeks after the inferno, the smell of smoke lingered in the air. The crackling sound of shoes crushing tiny fragments of hundreds-of-years-old plaster and debris jolted his visitors. Millions of pieces of fresco fragments blanketed the floor of the Camposanto. Ancient tombs and urns, shattered by the intensity of the fire, lined the interior walls. Charred remains of frescoes still affixed to the wall had the consistency of dust after being baked by thirty-eight days of exposure to the intense Tuscan sun. The sight and smell of so much fire-damaged beauty created a somber but fitting mood. After all, Keller thought, they were in a cemetery.

As the visitors emerged from the remains back into the Piazza dei Miracoli, Keller realized his gamble had paid off. The presence of the archbishop of Pisa pleading the case for emergency intervention had certainly helped. But providing General Hume with an opportunity to see and feel the damage to this once-great monument proved the decisive factor. Something could be done, the general told Keller. Something *must* be done.

Seven days later, Keller walked the floors of the Camposanto, cleared of most of the fresco remains and debris. Overseeing a small army of engineers, Italian military personnel, and fresco specialists from Florence and Rome that General Hume's staff had somehow located and transported to Pisa, provided a sense of accomplishment not present in his previous inspection work. Each day presented new challenges, but he loved the opportunity to be "doing" something. No lumber? No problem, Keller told his team. A midnight "requisition" from an overstocked ship in nearby Livorno would suffice. All the while, German shells rained down on the area, killing one woman in a nearby building.

By October 12, the job was complete. Army engineers and Italian volunteers put the finishing touches on a temporary roof made of tarpaulin and tarpaper. The interior walls of the Camposanto and what remained of the once-great fresco cycle would now be safe until a new roof could be constructed. Keller had used much of that time to supervise the gathering and storage of the detached pieces of frescoed plaster that had littered the floor of the cemetery when he first arrived, in anticipation of the day when the tedious work of reassembling the pieces could begin. The Camposanto would get the second chance that so many damaged churches and historic structures in Italy would not.

Exhausted but proud, Keller returned to his tent to write Kathy and share the good news. "The job is done, works perfectly. The frescoes were dry as a 15th-century tibia in the last downpour." In another letter he put the achievement into perspective. "This is the biggest job I have had of its kind," he told Kathy. "It has been interesting all through, though fraught with unforeseen troubles. I wonder if this whole story will ever come out for people to know about and to realize—I doubt it."

Florence, Italy: September to October 1944

Fred Hartt scrolled another piece of paper into his typewriter to complete his initial damage assessment report on Florence.

Deane Keller "supporting" the Leaning Tower of Pisa.

Michelangelo's towering achievement, the sculpture *David*, had come through the battle unscathed, but the images of other cultural treasures far less fortunate paraded across his mind, leaving him feeling like a grief-stricken family member identifying a deceased loved one.

The sweltering heat of August had not helped his mood.

Having addressed the destruction of five of the city's six bridges and made mention of the one that had survived, the Ponte Vecchio, another thought came to mind. "The destruction may not have held up the war in Italy five minutes," he typed, "but it paralyzed the city. This had been the heart of Dante's Florence. These were the streets and squares scarcely altered since Giotto and Masaccio walked them." Now everything Hartt saw, "houses, towers, palaces with all they contained and with all their glorious memories, lay collapsed in mountainous heaps of rubble."

Flipping the pages of his field journal, the name of a church that he'd inspected caught his eye. It didn't have the importance of the city's duomo, or the beauty of Santa Maria Novella, but something notable had taken place there that Hartt wanted to add to his typed report.

> *Santo Stefano is gravely damaged. The 13th-century*
> *facade is split from top to portal, the roof tiles are gone,*
> *and the interior full of rubble. The 93-year-old parish*
> *priest, Padre Veneziani, refused to leave his church, and*
> *died from the concussion of the mines. His body was*
> *removed only 18 August, from the sacristy where it had*
> *lain since 3 August.*

Michelangelo, *David*, 1501–1504.

Florentine craftsmen entombed the *David* (background)
and other Michelangelo sculptures (foreground) to protect them from Allied bombing.

The death of the parish priest put a face to his mission, but more than that, it reminded him of something Deane Keller had said several months earlier. Hartt couldn't remember Keller's exact words, but the point of his remark was this: Being a Monuments Man required balancing the dramatic with the mundane. Saving works of art or a building was important, but so were the essential tasks of securing supplies and writing reports. Despite the focus on *things*, the job existed to help *people*.

By early September, with Fifth and Eighth Armies' long-awaited assault on the Gothic Line underway, Hartt resumed his inspections of the other repositories on the list provided by Florentine art officials Poggi and Procacci. Shifting battle lines still prevented access to some of the villas used to store art, but on September 5, Hartt and his driver were able to reach a royal villa in the small town of Poggio a Caiano. Days earlier, the Allies had received a bizarre telegram from Swiss officials conveying a German request that Allied forces *not* bomb Poggio a Caiano because of the art treasures being stored there. The message explicitly stated that there were no German troops in that particular area. Something didn't add up, Hartt thought. Was it a trick of some kind? Had German forces laid booby traps throughout the villa expecting the Allies to rush to the scene? Without a firsthand inspection it remained a mystery.

Gaining access to Poggio a Caiano was not easy. The destruction of a key bridge forced Hartt and his driver, Ruggenini, to take a back route, then wade across a canal before inching up a steep embankment. Hartt wanted to laugh at how goofy they must have looked, crawling hand over foot like two children mimicking monkeys, but he was too winded to spare the extra breath. They emerged from the gully to be greeted as liberators by villagers excited to see their first Allied officer.

Hartt found the custodian and wasted no time in getting to the bottom of what had taken place. Had German soldiers been here? Did they take any of the works of art that had been stored in the villa? The custodian, although nervous, seemed relieved for a chance to share what he'd seen with somebody of authority.

A Major Reidemeister, a representative of the Kunstschutz, the German art protection unit, had arrived toward the end of August, the custodian explained. He had with him trucks, men, and an order to remove certain items. Determined to prevent the removals, the custodian had informed the German major that the villa and its contents were under the protection of the Holy See in Rome, and that Generalfeldmarschall Kesselring, the senior German military commander in Italy, had also issued a protective order for the works of art.

Hartt, increasingly anxious, pressed again. The details were important, but what he wanted was a yes or no to his question. Did the Germans take any of the works of art that had been stored in the villa? Yes, the custodian replied.

Overwhelmed by anger and impatience, Hartt barked more than asked: What precisely *did* the Germans take? Flustered, the custodian sputtered, "Bargello Museum!" Hartt wanted to cry out in pain. The Bargello housed the most important collection of Gothic and Renaissance sculpture in the world, including masterpieces by Michelangelo and Donatello that had, over centuries, come to define the city.

The dates of the theft corresponded precisely to the German government's message to Swiss officials. Clearly the request for the Allies to avoid bombing Poggio a Caiano was a feint to buy time for German troops to empty the villa. Speechless at the involvement of German government officials and the deceptiveness of the theft, Hartt immediately wrote Ernest DeWald, director of the MFAA in Italy:

> Dear Ernest, This is what they stole. I retain the original hand written document which the custode [sic] made out . . . They started stealing the stuff two days before they broadcast to us not to bomb it. God knows where it is now. If I were you I would call in the correspondents & make a big story out of this. Maybe that will save other stuff from being stolen.

In early October, with the inspections of all but one of the thirty-eight Tuscan repositories now complete, Hartt gathered his interview notes and field journal to write a summary report of his findings. The thieves had acted on specific orders from the German military commander of Florence, Colonel Metzner, and SS Colonel Alexander Langsdorff, recently appointed head of the Kunstschutz operation in Italy. General Karl Wolff, the SS commander for all of Italy, had issued orders that provided Langsdorff with the trucks and gasoline that he needed for the operation. Each theft involved either subterfuge or threat. At least one—the looting of Palazzo Pretorio in the town of Poppi—took place at gunpoint.

Michelangelo, *Bacchus*, 1496–1497.

Typing what had been stolen left Hartt feeling like a father listing the names of his missing children. There were masterpieces by foreign artists acquired by the Medicis hundreds of years earlier: the pioneering Dutch and Flemish painters Rembrandt and Rubens; German masters Dürer and Cranach; and the greatest Spanish painter to ever hold a paintbrush, Diego Velázquez. The Italian artists that Hartt had long studied and dearly loved followed, including Michelangelo, Raphael, Caravaggio, Titian, Botticelli, and Donatello.

Looking over the list of missing masterpieces, Hartt felt sick to his stomach, like he had six months earlier when he realized the

Donatello, *Saint George*, 1417.

peril to Leonardo da Vinci's bomb-damaged masterpiece, *The Last Supper*. But as he quieted his emotions, he started thinking about what the Germans could have stolen but didn't. Two of Leonardo's paintings, the *Annunciation* and the *Adoration of the Magi*, had been left behind along with Michelangelo's *Doni Madonna*, one of only four known paintings by the Florentine master and certainly his most important. While there was no masking the loss to Florence, and to all those who loved art, plenty of masterpieces had survived the German looting operation and were now safe.

Hartt tallied what the Germans had stolen and then resumed typing. "A grand total of 529 paintings, 162 works of sculpture and minor arts, 6 large cartoon drawings, and 38 pieces of medieval and Renaissance textiles have been taken from the public collections of Florence, in all 735 objects." He stumbled for a few minutes trying to find the right words and then they came to him: Florence "had suffered a robbery on a scale to dwarf the depredations of Napoleon."

Writing reports wasn't going to get the Florence treasures back home, though. Waiting for something to happen wasn't an acceptable alternative, either, not for a restless art historian. Determined to act, Hartt ran down his list of the most influential people in Florence. One name came to mind: the archbishop of Florence, Cardinal Elia Dalla Costa. Perhaps he would be willing to use his extensive connections with the Vatican to make inquiries about the whereabouts of the stolen masterpieces.

CHAPTER 8

SEARCHING FOR CLUES

Outside Aachen, Germany: October 1944

Walker Hancock, the award-winning sculptor, appreciated the irony. He'd spent most of his forty-three years as an artist creating beauty. Now, as the Monuments Officer for First Army, he passed each dreadful day watching beauty—entire cities—be destroyed. Aachen was under siege, the first German city to experience the wrath of Allied ground forces. Plumes of dense smoke by day and the glow of fires on the horizon at night served as marker beacons for a battle that still raged after nearly ten days of house-to-house fighting.

First Army's task was to break through Aachen and drive into Germany's industrial heartland, the Ruhr Valley. Since the city was part of the Siegfried Line, the defensive fortifications that protected Germany's western border, Hitler knew that a breach there would quickly be filled with Western Allied forces steamrolling their way to Berlin. Aachen had to hold or Nazi Germany was doomed.

As the wind picked up carrying the first blast of winter chill, Hancock lifted the collar on his field jacket and thought about all that had happened since leaving the comfort of his art studio in the village of Lanesville, Massachusetts. News of the Japanese sneak attack on Pearl Harbor had rearranged his priorities, like it had for so many millions of Americans. The decision to volunteer for U.S. Army Air Forces Intelligence had come easily, but he failed the physical examination and was rejected. Determined to serve, he signed up for Naval Intelligence and passed their physical, only to be drafted by the army and sent to basic training. Hancock considered it a near-perfect lesson in the ways of the military: Sometimes nothing made sense.

Hancock crossed the English Channel on September 26, the last of the group who trained together at Shrivenham to set foot on the European continent. He spent his first night in Paris, in a comfortable apartment with fellow Monuments Man Jim Rorimer. Neither of them slept much as Rorimer passed the hours recounting many of his experiences since landing on Utah Beach six weeks earlier. Hancock listened closely, treating each of Rorimer's stories as a tutorial for Monuments work. "Safeguarding" came up several times in conversation, a word the Nazis regularly used to describe their good deeds removing cultural treasures from war zones. But Jacques Jaujard, Director of the National Museums of France, had counseled Rorimer not to be fooled. "Safeguarding" was nothing more than a Nazi synonym for "theft."

From Paris, Hancock hitched a ride to his first official assignment inspecting monuments near the rear of First Army territory, only to discover that George Stout had already inspected many of the sites. With sun-drenched skies and beautiful countryside, Hancock felt more like a tourist on holiday than a soldier during war, but that began to change after reaching First Army headquarters in Verviers, Belgium, just twenty-five miles from the dark storm clouds of war gathering over Aachen.

The early skirmishes around Aachen had begun in mid-September. Hancock knew that the city had very little military value, but what it lacked in industry it made up for in historical importance. It had been the capital of Charlemagne, the first ruler in nearly three centuries to unite much of Europe. On Christmas Eve in the year 800, Pope Leo III crowned Charlemagne the Holy Roman Emperor. Over the next six hundred years, the Palatine Chapel, part of Aachen Cathedral, served as the coronation hall for more than thirty kings. In Hitler's view, a German city so rich in history and so important in symbolism had to be defended to the death.

A forced evacuation of the city sent all but 20,000 of the 165,000 inhabitants fleeing east. German troops then fought a desperate battle, using every nook and cranny, including the sewer system, to defend the city. The Allies responded with flamethrowers, igniting everything and everyone inside. Allied tanks flattened any target that bombing and long-range artillery had missed. The sturdiness of hundreds-of-years-old stone buildings frustrated U.S. commanders. Aggrieved at the loss of their troops, they wheeled artillery into position and fired point-blank at the defiant walls. Periodically, dazed citizens who had ignored the evacuation notice rushed out of hiding, pushing baby carts and wheelbarrows overflowing with personal belongings. The casualty figures on both sides were horrendous.

Wehrmacht troops surrendered at noon on October 21. The

The gutted streets of Aachen, Germany.

following morning, Hancock and Monuments Man George Stout hitchhiked their way to Aachen in a jeep with war correspondents. On the way into town they passed minefields, defensive fortifications made of concrete pylons, pillboxes outfitted with machine guns, and barbed wire. The city was deathly quiet. The smell of battle still hung in the air. Most street markers were missing. Mangled vehicles, twisted trolley lines, and craters the size of small buses had turned the streets into an obstacle course. Bombs had sheared off entire sides of buildings. Hancock caught a glimpse of one, six stories in height, with the kitchens on each floor exposed to view.

Aware the city had been conquered, German military commanders unleashed a barrage of artillery fire that sent Hancock racing from one doorway to another seeking cover. Inspections would have to wait, Hancock thought. This day was going to be spent just trying to survive. Maneuvering through the city center, Hancock heard a rhythmical but out-of-place sound. Looking over his shoulder he did a double take as a U.S. soldier wearing a Native American headdress atop a horse galloped down the cobblestone street. The whistle of another incoming artillery shell and the near-simultaneous explosion sent him dashing for yet another doorway. He had to laugh at the absurdity of it all, the American Old West meeting medieval Germany, all in the middle of a war zone.

The oldest part of Aachen was a labyrinth of narrow streets that never seemed to meet at right angles, which made it difficult to get a line of sight on his objective, the Palatine Chapel. Suddenly, as the smoke from another round of artillery faded, the chapel appeared, undamaged. Surprisingly, the double doors were wide open. One sprint later, Hancock felt the safety of the chapel's large Byzantine-influenced octagonal space that for centuries had provided peace and refuge for pilgrims and worshippers. The stone construction of Charlemagne's time, now more than eleven hundred years old, felt more like a blast-proof bunker than a chapel. Hancock paused and gave thanks for both.

As his eyes adjusted to the darkness, his other senses compensated. Glass crackled as he stepped on it. The stench of soiled mattresses and blankets strewn on the floor wafted in the stale air. The refugees who had occupied this space had obviously left in a hurry, perhaps when the Allied bomb, which he could see resting beneath one of the vaults of the apse, came crashing down through the ceiling. While the impact of the bomb had demolished the

Inside the battle-damaged Aachen Cathedral.

high altar, it miraculously had not exploded. Providence had looked with favor on the cathedral that day.

A nearby voice startled Hancock, causing him to crouch as he swung around. The figure motioned him forward with one hand; the other held a small lantern. The young man's face didn't appear threatening—more worried than anything else. One by one they climbed a narrow spiral staircase. When they reached the top step, the man turned and introduced himself. "I am Father Erich Stephany, the church vicar." The man trembled constantly. Hancock pitied him. Shelling and confinement indoors had taken a visible toll on his health.

Hancock quickly explained his mission. The Aachen Cathedral, famed for its treasury, contained one of the rarest collections of late-medieval art objects in the world, including a Gothic silver-gilt bust of Charlemagne and the eleventh-century jewel-encrusted processional Cross of Lothair. Hancock wanted to see the treasury objects and confirm that they were safe.

Father Stephany also had a request for Hancock. American GIs had detained six boys, ages fifteen to twenty, all members of the church fire brigade. Together, these boys had successfully extinguished five separate fires caused by incendiary bombs. The church is defenseless without them, the vicar explained. No one else is able to operate the pumps and hose should disaster strike again. They are good boys, the vicar pleaded, who in their adolescent enthusiasm joined the Hitler Youth even though they didn't feel it in their hearts. The vicar asked if Hancock could take civilian clothes to the boys and have them released and brought back to the church. Hancock looked at the vicar and saw a face consumed with worry. Clearly he feared that some GI might mistake the Hitler Youths for Wehrmacht soldiers because of the similarity in uniforms and shoot them.

After writing down the names in his field diary, Hancock promised to do what he could to find the boys. Having responded to the vicar's request, he returned to his own. Where are the objects that belong in the treasury? The vicar said he didn't know; the last time he saw them, German soldiers had packed the most important

Bust of Charlemagne, 14th century.

Cross of Lothair, 11th century.

Fire Guard for Cathedral

		approximate age
Hans	Dürnholz	20
Helmut	Jansen	17
Georg	Stockem	17
Nikolaus	Geurten	17
Karl	Pirotti	19
Willi	Minartz	15

Monuments Man Captain Walker Hancock's list of the fire brigade boys.

items, including the two Hancock had specifically asked about—the Bust of Charlemagne and the Cross of Lothair—and taken them deeper into Germany.

Paris, France: late November 1944

Three days after Thanksgiving, Jim Rorimer crossed the sixteenth-century Tuileries Garden. With the war now on Germany's doorstep, more than 150 miles away from Paris, some semblance of normal life had returned with people strolling through the gardens enjoying a brisk November afternoon. Rorimer smiled. Just two months earlier, he'd prevented the army from converting the Jeu de Paume Museum into a post office. That turned out to be relatively easy. Then he'd managed to get the army to remove hundreds of jeeps, troop carriers, and ten-ton trucks from the historic garden. That had proved the greater challenge.

Seeing the citizens of Paris resume some semblance of normal life following four years of Nazi occupation and knowing he had played a part left Rorimer feeling good, but now he feared progress had stalled. The urgency in the Parisian air during those initial weeks of liberation had faded. French bureaucracy mixed with army regulations slowed everything down even further, adding to his frustration.

As he neared the Louvre Museum, Rorimer zeroed in on what was bothering him the most. If Jacques Jaujard was correct, and more than twenty thousand works of art had indeed been stolen from French private collectors and dealers, where was the paper trail? Where were the leads? After weeks of digging, he had found only dead ends. Someone knew something, but clearly he hadn't identified who that "someone" was, not yet at least. Parisians just wanted to put the horrible memories of occupation behind them and move on with their lives. That greatly impeded his efforts.

The scene inside the Louvre looked very different than it had when Rorimer first visited in late August. Visitors! Noise! Paintings hanging on the walls! Rorimer paused to take it all in and smiled. The Louvre had reopened several weeks earlier, but Rorimer thought only of the twenty thousand works of art still missing—and the fact that he had no leads to pursue.

He arrived in Jaujard's office as a friend in need. When Rorimer began to ask for information, the director rose from his desk, went to his office door, and shut it. Jaujard intended for this to be a private conversation between two trusted friends and colleagues who shared a common objective. Rorimer began by expressing his frustration, almost disbelief, about the lack of leads, especially given the size of the theft. He knew that the French museum establishment had formed the Commission for the Recovery of Works of Art to address this problem, but that was two months ago, at the end of September. As far as Rorimer knew, the commission hadn't made much progress.

Jaujard, seeing an opportunity, looked at his friend and said just two words: Rose Valland. Sensing confusion, Jaujard reminded him that he'd met Valland in passing during one of his previous visits to the director's office. Rorimer apologized; he hadn't really paid her much attention. Jaujard smiled: neither had the Germans.

As Rorimer leaned forward in his chair, Jaujard opened up with details and descriptions that sent the Monuments Man hurriedly flipping through his notepad to find a blank page. He wanted to take down every detail.

Soon after occupation, the Einsatzstab Reichsleiter Rosenberg, or ERR, the Nazi looting organization dedicated to the confiscation of Jewish-owned property, converted the Jeu de Paume Museum into its looting operation headquarters. The museum's central location and proximity to the Louvre made it the ideal clearinghouse for thousands of works of art that the Nazis were stealing from Jews and other private collectors. They informed Jaujard that they needed one person familiar with the facility who could keep the building operational. He had asked Mademoiselle Valland, the custodian and, for all practical purposes, the curator of the museum, to remain at her position to assist the Germans— and to spy for him.

Hearing the word "spy" stunned Rorimer. He knew that Jaujard had performed heroically to save the national museum collections from the Nazis, but the risks he must have taken, not to mention those of his spy, Rose Valland, exceeded anything he had imagined.

The risks were quite real, Jaujard acknowledged, but the opportunity to have someone trusted inside the Nazi looting headquarters, someone who also understood German, was too great to ignore. In October 1940, shortly after the Nazis took control of the Jeu de Paume, Jaujard had taken Valland aside and ordered her to remain at her post, "no matter what." She accepted this new responsibility without hesitation; in fact, she considered it an honor to have been asked. Take my word on this, Jaujard implored his friend: Valland's commitment to saving the art of France should be questioned by no one.

While Jaujard described the forty-six-year-old Valland, Rorimer furiously scribbled down bullet points of his comments. "Middle-age; simplicity in her manners; self-reliant [*sic*]; independent; strong willed manner; indefatigable; never complained about her own personal grievances or discomforts."

All this information fascinated Rorimer, but his characteristic impatience got the better of him. With a heavy tone of skepticism in his voice, he asked Jaujard why, if Valland had all this information, had she not turned it over to the French commission? And why was Jaujard being so forthcoming with an American? Both were good questions, Jaujard said. Valland *had* turned over to the commission important lists of locations used by Nazi officials and warehouses where they had stored stolen objects in Paris until

Middle age

simplicity in her

manners

self - relient independent

feminine charms as the

as inscrutable cat & mouse play

sense of humor

sighs before speaking in

never anything but

cheerful

Strong willed manner

feminine charms

wanted to carry her own

suit case

Rorimer's notes about Rose Valland. [Please note: The typed annotations have been added by the author.]

shipment to Germany. But of course the Nazi officials, like the stolen objects, were no longer there. However, Valland had not provided other essential information to the commission about where the objects might be now. Jaujard acknowledged that Albert Henraux, head of the French commission, had asked him to encourage Rorimer to speak with Valland. Perhaps by getting to know her he could earn her trust and find out more details about what she knew.

Rorimer wanted to know why this woman, a complete stranger, would trust *him*, when she wouldn't trust her own countrymen on the commission? He also had another concern: Suppose she didn't really have what Jaujard thought she had. Maybe her information, if any, was worthless. The wily museum director reasoned that Valland would trust Rorimer precisely because he was *not* French. The problem of collaboration with the Nazis did not end with their departure. One of the city's newspapers, *Le Figaro*, printed a daily feature titled "Les arrestations et l'épuration" (Arrests and purges) that detailed the previous day's developments in the pursuit of collaborators. Beneath the article appeared two lists: *les exécutions capitales* (death sentences) and *les exécutions sommaires* (summary executions). Not certain who could be trusted, Valland was reluctant to turn over all of her information to the French commission, or anyone else. Seen in that light, her hesitation made sense to Rorimer.

It is true, Jaujard continued, that many people do not believe that Valland has any information of substance. He knew otherwise. She had confided some of it to him; much she had not, though, and he agreed with her decision because even he could not guarantee that her information would remain confidential. Rorimer, it seemed, was in the best position to gain access to the valuable information gathered by Rose Valland and use it to find France's stolen treasures.

Jaujard, seeing that his friend didn't appear entirely convinced, reminded him that when the U.S. Army had wanted to convert the Jeu de Paume Museum into a post office, it was Rorimer who had taken action to prevent it. Valland was never one to say much, but she didn't miss anything. In her mind, Rorimer had saved "her" museum from suffering through yet another occupation. That had made quite an impression on her, and indeed on everyone in the Paris museum community.

At that moment Rorimer's head was spinning with thoughts, doubts, possibilities. Suppose Jaujard was right? Valland certainly was in a position to have gathered critical information. Somehow she had managed to avoid being caught or killed. And if she did have lists of what was stolen and where it was . . . twenty thousand works of art? There really wasn't anything to think about. If Jaujard or others on the French commission would help with another introduction, he would of course be pleased to meet with her.

CHAPTER 9

GETTING HELP

Florence, Italy: November 1944

Throughout a wet Tuscan fall, Fred Hartt continued salvaging all he could of his beloved Florence. Nearly every building in the city center needed terra-cotta roof tiles at a time when torrential rains created a new threat to the city's cultural heritage. Each day brought progress, but Hartt felt frustrated that it was always measured in increments, not giant leaps. The same was true for the boys up in the mountains north of Florence, who were fighting relentless rain and boot-sucking mud as much as they were the German defenders they often could not see. Although preoccupied with his work addressing problems in the city, Hartt never stopped thinking about the 735 missing Florentine masterpieces. In mid-November, he received news that sent his spirits soaring.

Two months had passed since he and Giovanni Poggi, Superintendent of Florentine Galleries, had met with Archbishop of Florence Cardinal Elia Dalla Costa to seek the Vatican's assistance in locating the works stolen by German troops. Hartt had hoped for a quick reply, but with the passing of days, then weeks, he assumed that Vatican officials had decided not to use their extensive network of contacts to pursue the matter. A phone call from Poggi rekindled his hopes. The archbishop had finally received a reply from the Vatican.

Hartt nearly burst with excitement. If Vatican officials knew nothing, they probably wouldn't have wasted time writing a letter, or responding at all. They must know something! He wanted Poggi to blurt it out, and he did. According to the Vatican secretariat of state, "the works of art were stored in the [Alto] Adige, in a place called 'Neumelans in Sand.'" Finally, a name! A place!

Hartt quickly grabbed a map of northern Italy. The Alto Adige region, a mountainous German-speaking portion of Italy that shared borders with Switzerland and Austria, was a perfect hiding spot. At a moment's notice the works could be spirited across the Italian border into Nazi-controlled Austria. But despite his best effort, Hartt couldn't find "Neumelans in Sand" on the map, or in any Italian guidebook, which meant the Monuments Men were right back where they had started.

Five days later Hartt received new information from an Italian freedom fighter. At the end of July, two German trucks loaded with the stolen works of art taken from Florence arrived at a villa near the town of Modena. Wehrmacht troops offloaded many of the paintings and used them to decorate the villa for a large party that German military officials had hosted in early August. Mid-month, they reloaded their war booty back onto the trucks and headed north, destination unknown.

Hartt's emotions were a roller coaster of news: one minute hopeful that someone would at least confirm the works were safe, regardless of where they were located, the next dejected at not knowing anything. He slept only slightly better on December 9, when Nazi-sympathetic Italian officials announced that they had been allowed to inspect the works of art. But for slight damage, the works of art were safe. They made no mention of where the stolen art was hidden. For all Hartt knew, it might very well be in Nazi Germany.

With the Allied armies digging in for winter, mired in the central mountains hundreds of miles from northern Italy, there wasn't much Hartt could do about it anyway. Finding the Florentine treasures, to Hartt's great frustration, would have to wait until spring, when offensive operations resumed.

Brussels, Belgium: November 1944

The British Monuments Man for First Canadian Army, Ronald Balfour, spent much of October and November at various harbors along the Belgian coast searching for clues about the whereabouts of Michelangelo's masterpiece the Bruges *Madonna*. The concentration of Allied troops on the ground and Allied superiority in the sky would have made an overland route far too risky. The sailors who stole the priceless sculpture and paintings at gunpoint must have loaded it onto a ship that then steamed through the North Sea to reach Germany. If the ship hadn't departed from a Belgian port, it must have sailed from one in the Netherlands.

Balfour never made it, though. On November 29, disaster struck when his vehicle crashed. He suffered a broken ankle and other cuts and bruises. Doctors at the hospital in Eindhoven insisted that he be sent back to England for care, but he refused. He would be of no use to the MFAA there, so he finagled a transfer to a Brussels hospital instead. Being hospital-bound meant suspending his search for the Bruges *Madonna*, but it didn't prevent the search from continuing. Each day for three weeks, British Captain George Willmot, a recent addition to the expanding group of Monuments Officers, stopped by the hospital to see Balfour, not as a visitor, but as a student.

Working from his bed, Balfour shared his field experiences with Willmot, including details about the theft of the Bruges *Madonna*. On that last day, he reached into his field pack, rummaged around for a few seconds, pulled out one of the postcards given to him by Reverend Deschepper at the church in Bruges, and handed it to Willmot—just in case the newcomer needed it.

Aachen, Germany: November 1944

In late October, Monuments Men Walker Hancock and George Stout began their search for the six boys in the fire brigade in Brand, a suburb of Aachen. Walking door-to-door making inquiries seemed fruitless until an old woman pointed to a nearby home. Hancock pulled the list of names out of his pocket as he approached the residence, then knocked on the door and asked to see Helmut Jansen. After a bit of commotion, a frightened but composed boy came to the door. Hancock thought he looked about seventeen years old. One by one the other boys appeared.

Hancock introduced himself and told the boys that they were needed in Aachen to resume their work protecting the cathedral. With that, he handed them the civilian clothes Father Stephany had provided and told them to change. The local combat commander who had accompanied the two Monuments Officers watched in disbelief. "Well, I'll be damned," he said to himself as much as to Hancock and Stout. "Here they are, at least safe, and when you tell them they can go back into that hell-hole they act as if you'd given 'em a thousand dollars apiece. I can't figure it out." But the two Monuments Men understood perfectly well. The cathedral, Aachen's most important monument, had defined the city since its construction. It hadn't survived centuries of war and turmoil by accident. The fire brigade boys proudly continued the tradition of preserving it for future generations, even at the risk of their lives. In fact, they considered it an honor.

In early November, a new threat emerged that Stout believed would marginalize his skills and disrupt the MFAA at a time when it was gaining traction. Some army planner had issued new orders transferring him out of First Army to a new position with army groups fighting in the Netherlands. In the four months since arriving in France, Stout had survived bombs and booby traps. He wasn't about to succumb to the army's bureaucracy.

Stout didn't complain; he never complained. Instead, he immediately went to work using army regulations to press his case. He formally requested reconsideration of the order. The response came back quickly: request denied on grounds he was specifically qualified for the assignment. Stout agreed that he was qualified, but he believed that his present assignment with First Army in Germany, where most of the stolen objects would likely be found, was the optimal use of his skills.

First Army's Acting Chief of Staff for Civil Affairs concurred and forwarded Stout's request up the chain of command all the way to General Omar Bradley's headquarters at Twelfth Army

Group. On November 6, Stout received new orders containing another surprise. The previous orders transferring him to the Netherlands mission were rescinded; Stout would now be the emergency inspector for Twelfth Army Group (which included First, Third, Ninth, and Fifteenth Armies). Monuments Officers assigned to these armies would be in the lead with the combat troops, identifying situations needing special attention, including, everyone anticipated, discoveries of stolen works of art. Stout would be the man "on call," like a trauma doctor ready to respond to emergencies.

Despite the distraction caused by the series of orders, Stout continued his inspections. He also made a day-trip to Paris, where local authorities discussed information indicating that much of what had been stolen from France had been shipped to southern Germany. Stout found this only mildly helpful. Southern Germany covered a vast amount of territory with extensive mountainous areas. What he and the other Monuments Men needed were detailed leads, captured German documents, and luck if they were to find the loot.

On November 18, Stout met Hancock in Aachen, still under bombardment by German artillery, to resume their search for treasures missing from the city's major art museum. The battle for Aachen had been waged from the air, in the streets, and from room to room. Every building had some battle scar. While the facade of the Suermondt Museum building had suffered minor damage, the interior spaces had been trashed. Shattered glass and debris littered the floors. Soldiers, or perhaps displaced persons, had rifled through the museum records. The place was a wreck.

Sifting through the records looking for clues was painstaking work, even for a sculptor and artist like Hancock who measured progress over months and years. Too little light and too much dust forced him to use his flashlight, but reading documents through the floating silvery particles illuminated by the beam strained his eyes. He coughed constantly. Then came a breakthrough.

Hancock found a list of schools and courthouses where the Suermondt's less valuable holdings had been stored for safety. Further digging led to a copy of the official museum catalogue. A note on the cover explained that objects marked in red had been moved a second time for safety to Siegen, a town about 110 miles east of Aachen. Hancock quickly unfolded his map while pondering a new problem. Somewhere in the town of Siegen, 104 paintings and 48 pieces of sculpture—and who knew what else—belonging to the Suermondt Museum in Aachen lay in hiding, but where? And when would U.S. troops force a German retreat sufficient to allow the Monuments Men to enter Siegen?

Hancock felt certain about one thing: If the ferocity of the battle for Aachen was indicative of the fight ahead, any art repository in Siegen might not survive, even if they could find it. But at last, their detective work had paid a dividend. The Monuments Men had a name, a target: Siegen, Germany.

Near Aachen, Germany: early December 1944

Captain Walter Huchthausen, one of two new additions to the Monuments Men, reported for duty to Ninth Army in early December. Army bureaucracy was only partly to blame for the six-month delay in getting him into service. In mid-June 1944, just

Monuments Man Captain Walter Huchthausen.

days after arriving in London, Huchthausen was seriously injured during a V-1 rocket attack, German retaliation for the successful D-Day landings at Normandy. Even while recuperating, he worked each day preparing a glossary of commonly used German terms for English-speaking soldiers.

Having studied in prewar Germany, Huchthausen knew the country and the language, both valuable attributes for the challenges ahead. His experience as an architect was an essential skill to aid in the salvation of damaged but repairable buildings, especially as the amount of enemy territory under Allied control increased. The Monuments Men who had met with him—Rorimer over dinner in Paris, Stout during a field inspection, and Hancock when First Army turned over responsibility for Aachen to Ninth

Army—all liked this handsome, boyish-looking thirty-nine-year-old architect. To the man, they considered Huchthausen a great addition to their small army, with just one caveat. Everyone had a difficult time pronouncing "HUCK-towzen" correctly, so they immediately gave him the nickname "Hutch."

Even in the early weeks of his first assignment in Aachen, Hutch demonstrated the kind of initiative that earned the respect of his more experienced peers by converting the Suermondt Museum into a safe house for works of art being found in dozens of locations in and around the city. Hancock couldn't figure out if Hutch's popularity with soldiers or some magical touch was responsible for his ability to procure transportation, but it was certainly a skill that he admired.

Near Nancy, France: December 1944

In December, after six months of waiting in London, Lincoln Kirstein, another new recruit to the Monuments Men, finally arrived in Europe, none too happy about all the delays. Most of the Monuments Men knew Kirstein, a towering figure in the arts. He'd authored six books; cofounded the American Ballet Company, Harvard Society for Contemporary Art, and *Hound & Horn* literary magazine; and been a successful art critic, all before his thirty-seventh birthday. Simply put, Kirstein was a polymath, exceptionally gifted in multiple fields.

George Stout had instructed Kirstein when he was a graduate student at Harvard. Jim Rorimer, the hard-charging curator, had befriended him when they both lived and worked in New York City. In Germany, Kirstein was just another soldier in uniform, at

Monuments Man Private First Class
Lincoln Kirstein.

least to Robert Posey. Like any new soldier, he would have to prove himself.

As Posey looked over the new man's résumé and thought about what he'd heard others say about Kirstein, he realized just how different they both were, an odd-couple pairing extraordinaire. Posey loved being a soldier and understood life in the military; Kirstein found the experience dreadful. Posey knew the rules and followed them; Kirstein preferred to write his own. Posey approached problems logically; Kirstein trusted his instinct and liked to improvise. Posey tended to be stable in demeanor; Kirstein was manic-depressive.

The Posey family had been so poor that Robert's mother gave his sister to an aunt after his father died because there wasn't enough food for three children. Kirstein, the son of a wealthy self-made businessman, never experienced poverty. Posey knew a lot about architecture, but not a great deal about works of art, and it was at that moment that he realized why someone, probably Stout, had paired the two of them. Kirstein knew a lot about everything, including art and architecture. No wonder Stout, Rorimer, and other Monuments Officers had pleaded with the Roberts Commission and the army to get Kirstein into the MFAA.

One other distinction couldn't be missed. Every Monuments Man in northern Europe served as an officer but one, Lincoln Kirstein, who held one of the lowest ranks in the army, private first class. Some arcane army rule prohibited privates from serving in the MFAA. Only repeated pleadings by the Roberts Commission resulted in the army relenting and making this exception.

Kirstein wouldn't officially begin his position until January. Until then, Posey had plenty of reports to write, including an update on the Ghent Altarpiece. That's a laugh, he thought. With no leads of any sort, that particular report will be a blank page. Posey also had letters to write, especially with Christmas fast approaching. A rather large package from home, marked "with love from your family," had arrived a few weeks earlier. He'd wanted to save it for Christmas Day, but on December 16, a mixture of excitement, curiosity, and loneliness prevailed.

Alice had really packed this box well, far better than all the others, he noticed, which forced him to slow down and savor the moment. There seemed no end to the material she used. Finally he reached something firm—a package within a package—that he pulled out of the box. Snuggly taped between two protective layers of cardboard he found a phonograph record. The absence of a note made him even more curious. With his helmet in one hand and the record in the other, he dashed out of his tent to Special Services, where a sergeant manning the radios motioned Posey into an adjacent room while he put the disc on the record player.

After an agonizingly slow few moments, he heard something, not music, but a voice—one absent from his life for more than a year—emerge from the nearby speaker. Alice spoke first, prompting Woogie to "say anything you want." As Posey thought about it, speaking into a microphone to your dad when you can't see him must have been a weird experience for a seven-year-old boy. Then came his son's voice, and Christmas greetings, and more comments from them both, followed by a song. During war, surprises were rarely welcomed. Posey considered this an extraordinary exception, a single moment that would sustain him as long as necessary and serve as a lifelong reminder of the importance of family.

That evening, still basking in the glow of the Christmas greeting from his family, Posey heard a radio report about a new German offensive in the Ardennes Forest. U.S. troops had tried to absorb the blow but were falling back. First reports were often suspect, so Posey decided to hang around Special Services to find out more.

CHAPTER 10

LONGINGS

Paris, France: Christmastime 1944

Blowing wind mixed with record low temperatures did nothing to dampen Jim Rorimer's enthusiasm. Jacques Jaujard had wanted him to meet with Rose Valland. Now, just a few days before Christmas, this matronly-looking woman wearing small wire-rimmed glasses was standing next to him, chain-smoking, while they shivered outside waiting for the manager of the Warehouse for Enemy Property to arrive with the keys.

The process of earning Valland's trust began six days earlier with Rorimer's discovery of several paintings and engravings inside a U.S. military facility. Following protocol, he promptly delivered them to the Jeu de Paume Museum, now the headquarters of the French Commission for the Recovery of Works of Art, and its secretary, Rose Valland. The artworks weren't terribly important, but the act of turning them over to the commission surprised Valland. "Thank you," she had told him. "Too often, your fellow liberators give us the painful impression they have landed in a country whose inhabitants no longer matter."

Being at the Jeu de Paume Museum that day provided Rorimer with a chance to visit with the leader of the commission, Albert Henraux, who, like Jaujard, suggested Rorimer and Valland cooperate to find France's stolen treasures. But Henraux had gone one step further, handing Rorimer a list containing the addresses of nine buildings in Paris, mostly apartments and one warehouse, used by the ERR. After scanning the list, Rorimer wondered aloud who had compiled the information. Henraux smiled: "Mademoiselle Valland, of course." Henraux then nudged the persistent curator, suggesting that he enlist the help of Valland to inspect each address.

Rorimer and Valland visited six of the nine locations several days later. Their search produced little, but the time they spent together proved invaluable. Over coffee between stops at the ERR apartments, Valland gradually revealed some of what she had seen during her four years as Jaujard's spy. Rorimer soon had no doubt that Jaujard and Henraux's suspicions were true. Rose Valland *did* know much more than she had told the commission.

It all made sense. Every day for four years, Valland had entered the den of thieves, observed their operation, and compiled secret notes about the day's activities. With German soldiers watching her by day and the Gestapo trailing her at night, she somehow avoided being caught. It was hardly surprising that she guarded her notes so closely. More than just pieces of paper, they defined her life.

Since arriving in Paris, Rorimer had gathered every piece of information he could about the Nazi looting operation. Although the ERR took its name from Nazi Party ideologue Alfred Rosenberg, it was Nazi Reichsmarschall Hermann Göring, the second-most powerful man in all of Germany, who quickly commandeered the operation. ERR operatives served as dealmakers loyal to him and his burgeoning art collection. Now Rorimer had an opportunity to hear from the only person who could describe these events as they had happened. Rose Valland had much to say.

Within months of the invasion of France in May 1940, the Nazis had converted the Jeu de Paume Museum into a concentration camp for works of art. "The atmosphere around me changed immediately with the arrival of the German trucks loaded with stolen works of art," Valland explained to Rorimer.

> *The rooms and offices were immediately occupied. The Luftwaffe soldiers carried in the crates that they had been escorting . . . The unpacking started the next morning. Paintings by Old Masters were passed from hand to hand until the human chain ended at a support wall. Some of them were dropped and ended up underneath the boots, but the order was to proceed as quickly as possible.*

The sheer volume of paintings, sculpture, drawings, and furniture that passed through the doors of the museum was one thing; the quality of it was different. Valland, with her nearly photographic memory, made mental lists of incoming masterpieces by some of the most famous Old Master painters, including Vermeer, Raphael, and Velázquez. Hours later, German troops would barge through the door with another group of priceless paintings by the most revered Impressionist artists, such as Monet, Renoir, and Degas. Although Hitler had declared works by the Impressionists "degenerate," they might still prove valuable in trades. With her teeth gritted in anger, she watched Nazi officials mishandle these degenerate works and place them in a rear area of the museum, a room Valland referred to as the "room of martyrs."

After a long drag on a cigarette, Valland looked at Rorimer and summed up the scale of the problem. "France and its art world represented for the Nazi leaders a vast and inexhaustible hunting reserve, jealously guarded and managed." When Rorimer mentioned that Jaujard had estimated, during one of their visits, that the Nazi looters stole more than twenty thousand works of art from private collectors in France, Valland responded with a wry smile. They took far more than twenty thousand objects, she said. France was powerless to stop them from taking all that they wanted. What more could the French have done? What could anyone have done when the Nazis issued decrees stripping French Jews of their right to own private property? How do you protect private collections from the greed of Reichsmarschall Göring, who is willing to use his position and influence to do anything to add to his personal art collection? *C'était une situation impossible.* Rorimer agreed; it was an impossible situation.

Each time Bruno Lohse, one of Göring's art buyers; Hermann Bunjes, a corrupt Kunstschutz official; and Colonel Kurt von Behr, commandant of the Jeu de Paume and local leader of the ERR, appeared at the museum, a flurry of activity quickly followed. They began by displaying the most recent arrivals—paintings, furniture, and tapestries that had been seized from Jewish collectors. Chilled champagne and hand-rolled cigars were at the ready. A period of calm followed. Everyone waited.

The sound of car tires crushing gravel, the squeal of brakes, car doors opening and closing, and the echo of heavy boots confirmed

Göring's arrival. While his Luftwaffe was flying nightly bombing missions over London, trying to knock Britain out of the war, Göring decided to add to his art collection. The scene was repeated with slight variation on each of his subsequent nineteen visits. Rorimer shook his head in disbelief. Twenty visits by the master thief, and Rose Valland had been there to witness each one of them.

Göring would slowly approach each work of art with the arrogance of an emperor, sometimes jingling loose emeralds in his pocket as normal people do coins, speaking in hushed tones to his group. Occasionally a painting or piece of furniture was so famous, such as Vermeer's masterpiece *The Astronomer*—assigned the ERR inventory code "R-1," the first object stolen from the Rothschild collection—that Göring had no choice but to reserve it for Hitler and the Führermuseum. The next best he took for himself. Once he made his choices, the items were crated, packed on trucks, and driven to his personal train to accompany him back to the Fatherland.

A final spasm of looting occurred in August 1944, during the final days of Nazi occupation, with the loading of 148 cases of stolen art onto 5 railway boxcars. Each day, the departure of the art train was postponed because of delays in loading 46 other boxcars filled with furniture and personal belongings stolen from the homes of Paris's Jews as part of a separate looting project known as M-Aktion. As the Allies approached Paris, Valland secretly met with Jaujard. With the train number, destination of the art crates, and their contents all in hand, she pleaded with Jaujard for French Resistance fighters to sabotage the train engines, or simply reroute

Nazi Reichsmarschall Göring
examines a painting.

Johannes Vermeer, *The Astronomer*, 1668.

Göring admires two stolen paintings by Henri Matisse during one of his visits to the Jeu de Paume. Bruno Lohse, one of the Reichsmarschall's art buyers, is holding the paintings.

it. The Resistance did their job well. Train number 40044 and its contents remained trapped in Paris.

The 5 boxcars containing the 148 crates of art were unloaded and taken to the Louvre and the Jeu de Paume museums. But the contents of the other 46 boxcars, eventually offloaded and stored at the Warehouse for Enemy Property, went largely ignored. Now Rorimer and Valland had come to inspect it.

After a brief introduction, the manager invited them inside the warehouse. Within the cavernous space, wooden crates, one stacked upon another, towered forty feet into the air, as far as they could see. Uncrated chairs and tables rested on top, taken in such haste that the thieves hadn't had time to pack them. As they walked

Inside the Warehouse for Enemy Property, Paris.

through the warehouse, they saw pianos, radiators, mirrors, pots, pans, children's toys—even ladies' nightgowns—all that remained of Paris's once-vibrant Jewish community.

Rorimer felt gut-punched. The Nazi theft of priceless works of art had involved stealing from the rich, for the most part. This discovery evidenced quite the opposite; petty thievery of personal belongings on an industrial scale, priceless in their intrinsic value, looted from thousands of France's most vulnerable citizens. But the sick feeling in the pit of his stomach went deeper than just his role as a Monuments Officer. Decades earlier, his father had changed the spelling of the family name from "Rorheimer" because of his concerns about anti-Semitism in American life. Like the people whose possessions were stacked in rows before him, Jim Rorimer was also a Jew.

The warehouse was a likely place to find at least a few of the works of art stolen from France. Finding none, Rorimer felt disappointed. He struggled to make sense of not finding anything. Valland's lack of surprise convinced him that she'd known all along what was inside the warehouse—and what was not. Then another realization hit him: While he had been inspecting the nine apartments and one warehouse, Valland had been inspecting and watching him. What was this cat-and-mouse game she seemed to be playing?

As they exited the building, Rorimer decided to press Valland for specific information about where the Nazis had taken the art masterpieces, even as she quietly walked ahead of him. When she didn't respond, he asked again, this time with an edge to his voice that caused her to stop. Slowly she turned, faced him, and curtly said, "I'll tell you where, when the time is right."

Near Metz, France: Christmastime 1944

It didn't take long for Robert Posey, and everyone else who heard that first radio report, to realize that the German incursion into the Ardennes Forest was a major offensive. The attack succeeded in catching General Eisenhower and his commanders by surprise. Hitler had gambled that his troops could split two of Eisenhower's armies and mount a lightning-fast charge to the Belgian port of Antwerp, a crucial source of supplies for U.S. and British forces. Horrific fighting in the harshest possible winter conditions created mounting losses and a need for additional forces and replacement troops. Robert Posey immediately volunteered. His instructions were simple: "Keep firing until you can't fire anymore." And that's exactly what he did, right up until the time he stepped in a snow-covered hole and broke the arches on both of his feet.

Liège, Belgium: Christmastime 1944

Walker Hancock spent Christmas Day in Liège, Belgium, trying to enjoy a bath. War respected no holidays though. When a nearby explosion shook the building, he leapt out of the hot water, got dressed in record time, and hurried toward the bomb shelter, but by then the attack had ended. Dressed for the day, he decided to attend Mass in Saint Paul's Cathedral. Another bomb attack cut the service short. He did manage to get a haircut without interruption and catch a quick meal before heading to the bomb shelter to try and sleep. Despite the danger and disruptions, Hancock knew he had it far better than the boys on the front line, trying to find safety from German bullets, and winter weather just as lethal, in some shallow, rock-hard foxhole.

As he shifted back and forth trying to get comfortable on the cold, hard floor, Hancock's thoughts drifted to his wife, Saima, as they did every night. It seemed impossible to believe that they had been apart for more than eleven months, especially after twenty years of friendship. Then he thought about the Polish soldier bunked next to him days earlier. That poor fellow hadn't seen his family for *six* Christmases. "He's discouraged," Hancock had written Saima, "but we are guaranteeing him this will be the last away from home." Hancock hoped that would prove true, but who knew?

Florence, Italy: Christmastime 1944

After more than fifteen months away from home, Deane Keller needed a friend. While standing in line for mail in Florence, he found one. T/5 Charley Bernholz had just completed an assignment as driver for a senior officer relieved of duty. Keller liked his easygoing manner and considered his experience driving on Italian roads an asset. Within days, he arranged for Bernholz to become his driver.

Bernholz had another quality that Keller admired: He was a quiet hero, one of the boys. Before becoming a Monuments Man, Bernholz had pulled a severely wounded soldier from a burning truck filled with ammunition. He could have called it quits after dragging the man to safety. Instead, he went back to the truck again to check for other survivors. It was all there in his personnel file, along with a copy of his Bronze Star citation signed by Lieutenant General Mark Clark.

As Christmas neared, Keller and Bernholz used their jeep to

Deane Keller and his friend and driver, T/5 Charley Bernholz.

transport the poor children of Florence and their parents to the Allied Forces Christmas program. Each trip pulled at Keller's heartstrings; each little boy reminded him of Dino. But the program provided a temporary escape from the hardships of war for the people of Florence and the soldiers helping to rebuild the city, and for that he was grateful.

Reading in *Stars and Stripes*, the American military newspaper, about the tough fight the boys were having in the Ardennes Forest tempered any holiday celebration. Keller tried to compensate for his second Christmas away from Kathy and Dino by drawing scenes of Santa Claus delivering gifts and Dino, his face alight, opening them on Christmas morning. Somehow, seeing an image of Dino holding an oversized present made him feel a bit closer to home, even if it was a sketch of a make-believe scene that he had drawn.

On Christmas Day, Keller sat down to write Kathy and their son. He spent a while searching for the right words. Allaying her concern about his safety was always at the top of the list, especially with the news of the Ardennes Offensive filling the headlines. Censors limited what he could say about his work. A thought crossed his mind, one that seemed just right, and he began to write:

> *Today is Christmas and my first thoughts are with you and Deane . . . As I write the roar of tanks and heavy vehicles is in the air . . . Some boys will eat a turkey leg in a pup tent or in a foxhole. Some will die this day . . . Downstairs the radio has just come on and someone is singing a Carol . . . This is my Christmas—a big one filled with the highest ideals man is capable of . . .*

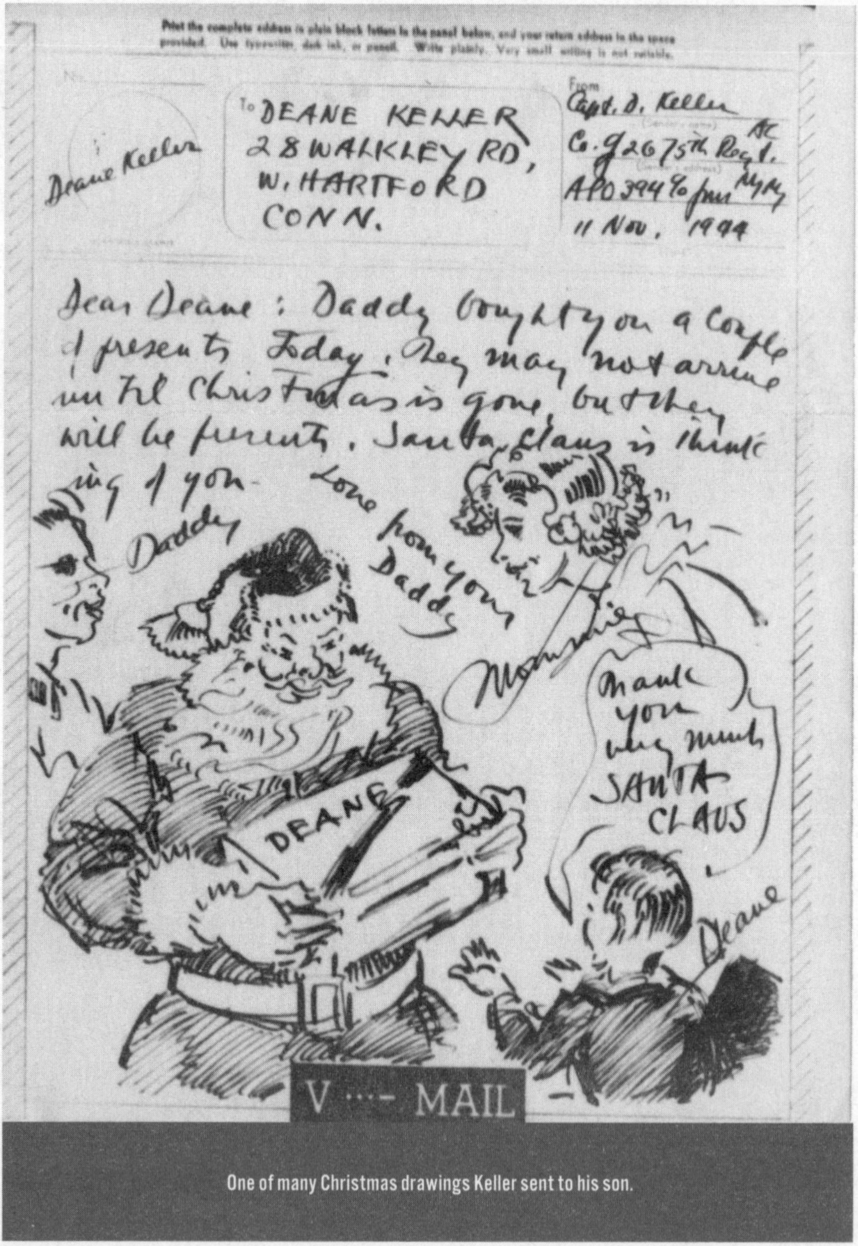

One of many Christmas drawings Keller sent to his son.

CHAPTER 11

SMALL VICTORIES

Near Givet, France: January 1945

By the end of January, the fight in the Ardennes Forest, dubbed the "Battle of the Bulge," had ended. Hitler had gambled that in one bold move he could force the Western Allies out of the war. If only he could blast through the Allied line and then get behind them, he would surround enough of Eisenhower's forces to convince American and British leaders to negotiate a peace. If he could do that, it would free his hands in Western Europe and allow him to concentrate on the Soviets in the east.

German forces did push a large bulge in the front line, but Western Allied forces quickly recovered, ending Nazi Germany's offensive capability. The cost was horrifying. Almost twenty thousand American boys lay dead; perhaps as many as eighty thousand were wounded or missing. Casualties meant the fighting armies needed replacements, and that's where nineteen-year-old Private Harry Ettlinger and twenty-five hundred other American soldiers were headed.

The trucks filled with replacement troops provided no real protection from the record cold temperatures. Only the bodily warmth of twenty-five soldiers crammed shoulder to shoulder inside each of the one hundred trucks made any difference, and even then, it was slight. But the bitter weather concerned Harry far less than figuring out how to stay alive. Soon they would be in battle on German soil, where the speed of the previous month's advances had ground to a crawl and every yard gained would cost some Allied soldier his life. Harry had been born in Germany, but he certainly didn't want to die there.

For centuries, Ettlingers had lived in the town of Karlsruhe, in southwest Germany. In fact, their last name derived from the nearby town of Ettlingen, where Harry's ancestors had been born. Harry grew up in a prominent family of retail and wholesale merchants who had built successful businesses despite anti-Semitic laws that prevented Jews from owning farmland and barred them from trade guilds.

Harry didn't see himself as being different from other boys until he was banned from the local sports association in 1933, the year Adolf Hitler rose to power as chancellor of Germany. Even then, the politics of hate and intolerance didn't mean much to a seven-year-old boy. But that changed two years later, at the start of fifth grade, when Harry's grades dropped precipitously. One of only two Jews in his class of forty-five students, Harry had been forced to sit in the back of the classroom, not because of some new regulation, but due to the prejudice of his teachers.

In 1937, a nationwide boycott of Jewish-owned enterprises, which had started four years earlier, finally forced the Ettlinger family business into bankruptcy. Harry didn't understand a lot about business, but he certainly remembered the time he had a bicycle accident and reached the hospital only to be denied admission. Even nine-year-old boys couldn't escape the hatred of the times. Nazi Germany had effectively declared war on its own people if they were Jews, immigrants, gay, or mentally ill. Harry's parents, like so many of their family friends, realized the time had come to leave their homeland, but where could they go? Many countries did not welcome the sudden increase in immigration requests from German Jews. Switzerland, Great Britain, France, and the United States had each denied the Ettlingers' applications. Still they tried again. In early May 1938, Harry's parents received notification that their second request to immigrate to the United States had been approved. But before leaving, Harry had to celebrate his bar mitzvah, a rite of passage ceremony for thirteen-year-old Jewish boys when they publicly become accountable for their actions.

With the drums of war beating more loudly, waiting until their son's thirteenth birthday presented too great a risk, so Harry's parents advanced the date of his bar mitzvah several times. At the end of September 1938, Harry entered adulthood in Karlsruhe's beautiful Kronenstrasse Synagogue. The family departed Germany for the United States the following day, and just in time. In less than two months, the Nazis used the assassination of a German diplomat as an excuse to declare open war on Germany's Jews. On November 9, *Kristallnacht*—the "Night of Broken Glass"—stormtroopers and Hitler Youth destroyed seven thousand Jewish-owned businesses and two hundred synagogues, including the one in Karlsruhe that had welcomed Harry Ettlinger into adulthood, the last bar mitzvah celebrated in the city during the Nazi era.

A Jewish-owned storefront, one of thousands damaged during *Kristallnacht*.

Before Hitler's rise to power, the Ettlingers were a well-to-do and respected family in their hometown. In America, a country with unfamiliar language and customs, they entered the growing ranks of poor immigrant families seeking little more than a chance to begin anew. Life was difficult. Harry's father spent three years looking for work before securing a job as a night watchman in a luggage factory. Harry learned to speak English, but with a thick German accent that made him stand out from the other boys in his class. Each day he took a commuter bus from his home in Newark, New Jersey, to his high school downtown. After school, he worked in a factory to help support his family.

Once America entered World War II, more and more boys joined the fight. By late spring 1944, only one-third of Harry's classmates attended graduation ceremonies because the other two-thirds either had volunteered for military service or had been drafted. Harry's draft notice arrived shortly after graduation. In mid-August, he joined a long line of army recruits headed off to basic training at Camp Wheeler in Macon, Georgia. Day after day, they drilled, marched, and disassembled and reassembled their M1 rifles until they could do it in their sleep.

In mid-October, near the end of training, a drill sergeant barked Harry's last name during morning roll call and pulled him aside.

"Private Ettlinger, are you a citizen of the United States?" he asked.

"No, sir. I'm a German Jew."

"Not for long. Come with me."

Harry found himself standing before a local judge, swearing an oath of allegiance to his new country, the United States of America.

Two months later, the warm feeling he felt the day he became an American citizen was a distant memory in the bone-chilling cold of France. The rumble of a hundred idling truck engines created a trail of exhaust that wafted in the freezing air and infiltrated the back of the deuce and a half's cargo area where Harry and the other replacement soldiers were sitting on benches. Let's get going, he thought. The smell was sickening. Waiting just created more anxiety. But get going to where? Harry didn't know. He looked at each of the eight buddies in his unit; none of them knew either. All anyone did seem to know was that the convoy of new recruits would link up with the mauled 99th Division, jokingly nicknamed the "Battle Babies," somewhere along the front lines.

Muffled voices and whistles outside, followed by the sound of engines revving, signaled the convoy was underway. The truck carrying Harry and his buddies lurched forward. This is it, Harry thought, a German-born American Jew on his way into battle.

Suddenly, Harry and the others heard someone running past their truck yelling "Stop, stop!" It took a minute for the convoy to grind to a halt, but once it did and the noise died down, they could hear the sound of crunching snow as someone marched by each truck yelling the same message over and over: "The following three men get your gear and come with me." Harry sat there trying to stay warm until one of his buddies elbowed him and said, "Hey dummy, that's you!"

After tossing his gear out of the truck and climbing down, the shouting started again. "Okay, let's get going!" someone yelled. Harry barely had time to turn and wave goodbye to the eight men who had been with him from the start, the guys who had become his family all the way through boot camp.

Harry had no idea why he and the other two soldiers had been ordered off the convoy or where they were headed, other than it wasn't to the front. But this much he knew for certain: Being pulled off that truck on January 28, 1945, his nineteenth birthday, was the best gift ever.

Spa, Belgium: February 1945

Walker Hancock had studied the situation map at First Army headquarters in the Belgian town of Spa so frequently that he knew it as well as the area back home. Although the German offensive in the Ardennes had failed, it did penetrate Allied-controlled territory, including towns Hancock and George Stout had already inspected. These places would have to be inspected again.

Hancock was particularly interested in the tiny village of La Gleize, Belgium, which he had visited just seventeen days before the Battle of the Bulge. The kindness of a young lady, Mademoiselle Geenen, and the beauty of a late-fourteenth-century sculpture of a Madonna had been on his mind ever since. Advance reports described the village as a "complete wreck," including the church housing the Madonna, but somehow the statue survived. Armed with a letter from the Bishop of Liège offering to provide shelter for the Madonna, Hancock arranged for a car and driver and set out for La Gleize on February 1.

Icy roads to the hilltop village turned a simple eight-mile drive into an adventure. The early reports proved correct; the village was in shambles. Hancock entered the church through a gaping shell hole in the wall near the front doors, which, strangely, were locked. The sight inside the church was a microcosm of war: overturned pews used as barricades by the German defenders, ammunition and shell casings, empty food ration cans, and shredded uniforms that in desperation had become makeshift bandages. Freezing cold weather mercifully muted what would otherwise have caused wretched smells. Hancock suspected that snowdrifts hid corpses of the defenders.

Despite the destruction and gruesome scene, the Madonna of La Gleize stood exactly where she had been when Hancock first visited the church in early December. The three-foot-high wooden

The Madonna of La Gleize, 14th century, inside the shell-damaged church.

sculpture lacked a certain refinement, but its grace and beauty overshadowed any shortcomings of the unknown artist. The Madonna, with her left hand resting across her heart and the right raised as if to offer a blessing, was mounted on a stone pedestal in the center of the church.

Hancock couldn't find the curé—the parish priest—but a Monsieur George offered to help. Monsieur George's bandaged head and weary look made Hancock think he might be in greater need of assistance than the Madonna. Upon hearing Hancock's intent and reading the bishop's letter, Monsieur George resolutely stated that the Madonna was going nowhere. The battle had passed and the sculpture had survived. It was safe inside the church, he insisted, and that's where it would remain.

In an effort to appease the Monuments Man, Monsieur George convened a meeting of the dozen or so villagers in what remained of his home and proposed that the sculpture be relocated to his cellar. Two men objected to that idea. The village mason stated with certainty that moving the sculpture was a physical impossibility. He had personally cemented the wooden sculpture to its stone base in such a way that the two were inseparable. After taking all this in, Hancock raised the possibility that perhaps the sculpture and stone base could together be freed from the wooden floorboards. The mason nodded; yes, perhaps that could be done. Then the village notary, with his steely eyes, spoke softly but authoritatively, stating that the sculpture would remain exactly where it was. Period. No need for further discussion.

Realizing that emotions had overwhelmed reason, Hancock had an idea. Perhaps a new solution might emerge if they continued the discussion in the church, where they could all see the Madonna. The small group walked the short distance to the front door of the mangled church. Hancock started to step through the shell hole, but hearing the sound of keys, he turned and followed the villagers using the main entrance. The motley crew gathered in a circle around the statue, waiting for someone to resume the discussion. Snow had started falling through the gaping hole in the roof, lightly dusting the Madonna. A gust of wind shifted one of the already loosened pieces of timber overhead, releasing a chunk of plaster that narrowly missed the Madonna—and the head of the village notary.

Mustering all the diplomacy he could, Hancock looked at the notary but asked the group if they still thought it a good idea to leave the Madonna inside the church. For a moment, all anyone could hear was the howl of the wind overhead, the squeak of a roof beam rocking back and forth, some loose papers and leaves rustling, and the almost imperceptible sound of snow gently landing. Just as Hancock had hoped, the notary spoke first. "I propose that the statue be moved to the cellar of the house of Monsieur George." Everyone nodded.

The mason had not exaggerated one bit. Separating the statue from the base was impossible. It took the collective effort of everyone, using two timber planks, to rock the pedestal loose. They then placed the Madonna and its stone base atop the boards and

Monuments Man Captain Walker Hancock (with helmet) leads the procession of townspeople as they relocate the Madonna of La Gleize.

used them like a battlefield litter. Moving it out the doorway of the church and down the icy path to Monsieur George's cellar required the balance of a ballet dancer and the brute strength of a wrestler. No one in the procession exerted more of himself than the village notary.

On the drive back to First Army headquarters, Hancock replayed the day's events over and over in his head. Working with local townspeople to protect the Madonna—their most revered cultural treasure—was a fundamental element of being a Monuments Officer. While salvaging a work of art was of course important, it was the act of demonstrating respect for the cultural treasures of others that filled him with a sense of mission accomplished. The whole experience provided encouragement for what he knew would be difficult days ahead.

Near Florence, Italy: February 1945

The bitter cold winter that gripped all of Europe validated the decision of Allied leaders in Italy to rest their troops and prepare for an offensive in the spring. Fifth and British Eighth Armies had tried in vain to blow through the Gothic Line and link up at Bologna, where they would then drive into the Po River Valley together to take northern Italy. The rainy autumn and a stubbornly entrenched Wehrmacht defense unraveled the plan. Now German troops continued work reinforcing their positions, well aware of the battle that was coming. In the interim, the two sides still skirmished from time to time where their lines met, adding to the casualties being moved back from the front.

Deane Keller and Fred Hartt spent their time supervising temporary repairs in some of the many damaged towns they had inspected. Their concern about the missing Florentine treasures continued, but with German forces in control of northern Italy, there wasn't anything they could do about it, even if they knew the precise location.

In mid-February, Keller had to figure out how to move a massive 350-year-old bronze statue of Cosimo I de' Medici, the great Florentine ruler, and his horse from a Tuscan villa fourteen miles back to its original location in Florence. The task seemed simple: Florentine art officials had moved the eight-ton sculpture to the countryside on an ox-drawn cart in August 1943. But passage was threatened by pending repairs to a railroad bridge damaged during combat, adding to the urgency of Keller's assignment.

After several days of planning and preparation, working in some of the muddiest conditions he had experienced, Keller arranged for a crane to hoist Cosimo onto the back of a truck. Moving the far larger and heavier horse, which was standing in a trotting position atop a wooden skid, with its front and rear legs astride a crisscrossed stack of logs for stability, proved far more difficult. It took three and a half hours to pull the skid into position on the tank trailer using a primitive moving technique Keller likened to "a Maine back countryman moving a house with pulleys and tackle and a horse for the power," but it worked.

Keller's driver and friend, Charley Bernholz, acted as traffic warden for the convoy, but Keller still needed a volunteer to ride atop the horse and lift the telephone and telegraph wires along the

Keller (center left with cap and overcoat) supervises the positioning of Cosimo's horse atop wooden skids.

route into the city. A boisterous GI named Smokey eagerly mounted Cosimo's horse and straddled the hole where the Florentine ruler and his saddle would normally be joined. As they approached the town, the driver of a horse-drawn carriage pulled even with the truck, raised his hat, and beaming ear to ear, shouted to Smokey and Keller, "Cosimo, welcome back!" Soon they reached the Piazza della Signoria in the center of Florence, where Fred Hartt, in Lucky 13, Superintendent of Florentine Galleries Giovanni Poggi, and a few hundred curious citizens braving the rain greeted them.

Keller knew that returning the statue to the city wasn't going to shorten the war even one second, but it was a victory for the people of Florence to see something they had cherished for more than three centuries restored to its prewar position. It demonstrated a respect for their culture and heritage that German troops had destroyed. But the joy of the achievement proved short-lived. One week later, Keller learned that Smokey had been killed in action.

Monuments Man Lieutenant Fred Hartt (standing left of Lucky 13) greets Keller and the return of Cosimo's horse to Florence.

CHAPTER 12

TREASURE MAPS

Paris, France: March 1945

Riding a bicycle through the streets of Paris, even on a frigid mid-March evening, was one of the joyful consequences of his assignment. Some of the city was still without electricity, but from Jim Rorimer's point of view, nothing could detract from the beauty of Paris, especially at such a hopeful moment. Just days earlier, he had received his new assignment as Monuments Man for Seventh Army. A phone call from Rose Valland inviting him to her apartment for dinner could mean only one thing: The courageous curator was finally ready to share her secrets. At the Warehouse for Enemy Property, where Rorimer had pressed Valland for the locations of the stolen art, she had walked away, telling him, "I'll tell you where, when the time is right." With orders in hand that would soon have him on the road to Germany, Rorimer hoped that moment had finally come.

A gust of wind passing through the Pont de la Concorde almost knocked Rorimer off his bicycle. After crossing the River Seine, he veered left at the National Assembly onto Boulevard Saint-Germain. The ride to Valland's apartment in the 5th arrondissement would take about twenty minutes more, just enough time to run through his checklist of questions.

The sting of the abrupt parting with Valland following their December inspection of the Warehouse for Enemy Property had long since faded. Rorimer knew he had pushed too hard, too fast, all but demanding that Valland turn over information she had risked her life to gather. Of course, his approach had offended her. But in the days that followed, he learned that Valland had experienced her own regrets about being so dismissive of a man who had done much to help Paris get back on its feet in the early days of liberation.

Sending a bottle of champagne to his apartment days later changed the dynamic of their relationship. Rorimer had returned the gesture by inviting Valland to his apartment for a Christmas dinner. It didn't take long for him to realize that she had come that evening to deliver a very important message. Valland, Jaujard, and Henraux wanted him reassigned. They believed he had surpassed his usefulness stationed in Paris. Having demonstrated his commitment to the preservation of the culture of France, they needed him in Germany at the very earliest moment to help find and return the tens of thousands of works of art stolen from their country.

The events that followed unfolded rapidly. His request for a transfer had been well received. In fact, as his superior officer noted, someone in the French mission had suggested the idea already. Rorimer remembered smiling upon hearing that. Clearly, Jaujard and Valland had been hard at work behind the scenes, and just in time.

The Allied victory at the Battle of the Bulge on January 17, and the Soviet crossing of the Oder River on January 31, which put the

Red Army just fifty miles east of Berlin, had the enemy in a vise. The fall of the German city Cologne to U.S. 3rd Armored Division just one week earlier left no doubt that Nazi Germany's days were numbered. Allied forces knew that soon they would find dozens of hiding places, if not more, containing thousands of stolen works of art—if the Nazis didn't first destroy them.

Valland's greeting alone confirmed Rorimer's hopes. The two were already on a first-name basis, but the warmth of her reception told him this visit was going to be different. Rorimer hardly felt surprise when Valland congratulated him on his new assignment with Seventh Army. She, too, had a checklist to discuss with him and wasted no time getting to it.

Rorimer had barely taken a seat before Valland reached into a small box, pulled out a stack of photographs, and placed them on the table. He felt a chill run down his spine at the sight of the first image: Nazi Reichsmarschall Hermann Göring. Valland painted the number two man in the Nazi Party as a person consumed with greed who used the Jeu de Paume Museum as a private hunting ground to add to his collection. A photograph of Alfred Rosenberg, the anti-Semite and namesake of the Nazi looting organization, the ERR, followed.

The men in the next three images at first appeared unfamiliar until Valland matched their faces with names that Rorimer knew well. Colonel Kurt von Behr, commandant of the Jeu de Paume and local leader of the ERR, whose officer's cap cast a shadow that covered his glass eye, was a social climber who thrived on his position of power. Bruno Lohse, one of Göring's chief art buyers, loved money and everything it could purchase. Young, tall, athletic, and with considerable power, he was popular with the ladies of Paris. Finally, there was Hermann Bunjes, a thirty-three-year-old art historian. As a consultant and middleman to the Göring theft ring and the Paris art scene, Bunjes had traded his career as a minor art scholar for rapid advancement as a corrupt official in the Kunstschutz, the German art protection unit.

Valland had group photographs as well: Göring, wearing a hat, overcoat, and scarf on one of his shopping expeditions with Lohse

Göring departs the Jeu de Paume Museum.
Art buyer Bruno Lohse is standing in the doorway, on the left; Kurt von Behr, leader of the ERR in Paris, is in the right foreground.

and Walter Andreas Hofer, his art curator, in tow; von Behr inspecting stolen property in one photo, and in his office surrounded by his staff in another; and Rosenberg parading through the Jeu de Paume in civilian clothes, personally inspecting the looting operation.

On the handful of occasions Rorimer and Valland had seen each other during January and February, Valland's stories about the activities at the Jeu de Paume were always sprinkled with the names of Göring, Rosenberg, von Behr, Lohse, and Bunjes. These photos were confirmation of all she had told him, and more—it struck Rorimer that these images were actually mug shots of the people he hoped to find, arrest, and bring to justice once he got to Germany. Valland was counting on it.

ERR namesake, Alfred Rosenberg, arrives at the Jeu de Paume Museum for an inspection.

While Rorimer studied each photograph, Valland disappeared into the bedroom and quickly returned carrying another larger box. Having started with photos of the thieves, Valland now wanted him to see images of what they had stolen. Most were world-famous works of art that Rorimer recognized instantly, like *The Astronomer*, by Johannes Vermeer, one of only thirty-four works painted by the seventeenth-century Dutch master. Valland explained how the Nazis had stolen the painting off the wall of the famed Parisian banker and renowned art collector Édouard de Rothschild.

Rorimer saw photographs of more paintings, by Rembrandt, Rubens, Cranach, and other Old Master painters, but there were also images of Renaissance jewelry, Flemish tapestries, and rare furniture. These objects alone would have constituted one of the most important and comprehensive museums in the world. The breadth and quality of what the Nazis had stolen was staggering.

Valland then reached into the box to retrieve documents that she had transcribed or found in wastepaper baskets, including train manifests, shipping receipts, and the prize Rorimer most wanted to see: a list of where the stolen objects had been hidden—a treasure map. Valland had it all. Names, photos, and objects taken. It all added up to years' worth of work. Up to that moment, the Monuments Men had only dreamed of such an intelligence coup. Now, he was holding everything he needed.

Having the information was all that really mattered, but Rorimer couldn't help but wonder how Valland had gathered so many details and lived to tell about it. He recalled Jaujard's comments in late November about her unobtrusiveness, and how she'd used her knowledge of German without her captors being aware that she could understand all they were saying. But that alone couldn't possibly account for the information that filled the boxes on her dining room table.

After a long pause, Valland explained how circumstances demanded that she transform her shy personality into one that engaged others in small talk to earn their confidence and trust. Important details soon followed, in particular from Alexandre, the head packer, who monitored the movement of what the Nazis had confiscated. One of the chauffeurs used by the ERR to transport stolen works provided Valland with information about the loading of trains. Rorimer could only imagine the sense of relief she was feeling from sharing all of this after keeping it secret for five years.

Every few days, Valland walked the short distance to the Louvre for regular meetings with Jaujard or his secretary. Those visits provided her with a place where she could always count on receiving sound advice and encouragement from the few people, in fact the *only* people, she could trust. But those visits also ratcheted up the pressure by reminding her that mistakes would prove deadly to her, Jaujard, his secretary, and others.

There had been several close calls, but only once, in February 1944, did the Nazi lackeys catch her red-handed trying to read addresses on shipping documents. Bruno Lohse, Göring's art buyer, confronted Valland, warning that she could be shot for such indiscretions. But she sloughed it off, telling him, "No one here is stupid enough to ignore the risk," before walking away. Luck had favored her that day, but with the Allied landings at Normandy, threats became more frequent and menacing. Lohse and von Behr both considered her an embarrassing witness to be eliminated before the end of hostilities. She expected that they would send her to Germany with some of the stolen works of art and then shoot her once the train crossed the border.

None of that mattered now, she told Rorimer. All the risks taken, all the years of worry, would amount to nothing if Hitler, in a fit of rage, ordered his henchmen to destroy the works of art, the furniture, the tapestries—everything! Valland moved some of the documents aside to find the list that had so excited Rorimer, the treasure map of where the stolen objects had been taken. Some of the names on the list he had heard mentioned in their prior conversations, including Heilbronn, Buxheim, Hohenschwangau, and the one Valland urged him to get to first—Neuschwanstein Castle. There, she told him, you will find the works of art stolen from France and the ERR documents that evidence the work of the thieves.

The urgency in her voice revealed a genuine fear that Hitler or other Nazis might destroy the works stolen from France. Hitler hadn't hesitated to order the destruction of all but one of the bridges in Florence. Had General von Choltitz, his military commander in Paris, followed orders, the Allies would have entered the French capital to find only smoldering ruins. Then, as if to underscore the urgency and validate her concern, Valland told Rorimer another story.

On July 23, 1944, a German military truck delivered to the interior garden of the Jeu de Paume Museum five to six hundred paintings by Picasso, Dali, Léger, Miró, Klee, and others that the Nazis considered "degenerate" and unsuitable even for sale or trade. German soldiers then tossed them, one by one, onto a flaming bonfire. With a mixed look of anger and sorrow, she added, "Nothing could be saved."

The lightness of being that Rorimer had experienced riding his bicycle to Valland's apartment had changed in a matter of hours. His ride home felt completely different. Valland, no doubt with Jaujard's encouragement, hadn't just entrusted her information to Rorimer—she handed it over to him. He now had the weight of the world on his shoulders. The Nazi hiding places on Valland's list were all located in what would become Seventh Army territory—his army, his territory, and now his responsibility.

Fighting a war against an enemy was one thing; fighting a war against a madman was something entirely different. Would Hitler, a man who had professed his love of art and desire to be recognized as an artist, really order the destruction of the very thing he so revered? Valland had no doubt that he would; Rorimer agreed. And that added even more urgency to the mission of the Monuments Men. Now, it was a race against time.

Cleve, Germany: March 10, 1945

After two months in a hospital, British Monuments Man Ronald Balfour felt as though he could survive anything. At any other time in his life he would have praised the heavens to have so much uninterrupted time for reading. Being stuck on the sidelines at a time when an epic fight to the death was taking place at the Battle of the Bulge pained him more than the truck accident that broke his ankle. The Allied armies already had a shortage of Monuments Officers. His unavailability just made things worse.

Balfour eagerly returned to action in February, making inquiries about the missing Bruges *Madonna* in the southwestern town of Vlissingen, Netherlands. Rumors continued to circulate that the thieves had loaded the Madonna onto a Red Cross ship that passed through the historic port before sailing the North Sea to Germany, but Balfour concluded that they were just rumors. Five months had passed since the theft with no sightings or substantiated leads. In all likelihood, Michelangelo's masterpiece had already been stashed somewhere in Germany. That suited Balfour, because First Canadian Army was now *in* Germany, which put him one step closer to finding it.

By early March, many German towns along the Lower Rhine River were in Allied hands, the result of Operations Veritable and Blockbuster, but the immensity of destruction from Allied bombing was astonishing. Estimates of damage to the town of Cleve, birthplace of Henry VIII's fourth wife, Anne, approached 90 percent. A dozen Monuments Men would have had a difficult time keeping up with all the work—First Canadian Army had just one.

Less than one mile from the front, under constant shelling, Balfour spent his days inspecting historic buildings, city archives, and churches, salvaging documents and objects, even fragments, of value. On March 3, during a lull in the fighting, he found time to write his friend Lieutenant Colonel Geoffrey Webb, the senior ranking Monuments Officer. Webb looked forward to Balfour's field reports more than those of any other Monuments Officer. Balfour's sense of humor and keen insights made them a good read. "It was a splendid week for my job—certainly the best since I came over," Balfour wrote. "On the one hand there is the tragedy of real destruction, much of it completely unnecessary; on the other the comforting feeling of having done something solid myself."

Looting by Allied troops was an unending problem. When OFF LIMITS signs proved ineffective, Balfour improvised and began confiscating objects himself as a measure of last resort. That created a new problem: Where to put them? Always up for a challenge, Balfour created a makeshift repository in the attic of a building in Cleve. Although occupied by troops and refugees, with no proper protection, the building had what most other buildings in town did not: a roof, doors, and windows. Inside the attic's locked doors, Balfour stored medieval town records, statues, and church vestments salvaged from various ruins. He even befriended a local monk who watched over the place when he was away on inspections.

On March 10, at 9:30 a.m. sharp, Balfour arrived at Allied Military Government headquarters in Cleve for a meeting with the sexton of Christus König Kirche, Christ the King Church, and four German workers who were going to assist with the removal of its treasures. Lack of transportation, bomb-cratered streets, and a relatively short distance made a handcart suitable for the job, which the four workers had positioned in front of the building. All present, Balfour signaled them to start. With any luck, they should cover the two-mile distance to the church in well under an hour.

They set out in a southwesterly direction, toward the train station, which lay about half the distance to their destination. Balfour walked on the left side of the road; the four German workers with the cart walked on the right, followed by the sexton. With the train station in view, Balfour started to cross the street, when the deafening swoosh of an artillery round, moving at the rate of twenty-seven hundred feet per second, slammed into the street. The violent, disorienting impact shook the ground, creating a plume of dust between Balfour and the group of five on the right side of the street. When it cleared, the sexton could see the cart up ahead, but the four German workers had fled the scene. Splayed by the blast against the sidewalk railing was the blood-covered body of Monuments Officer Major Ronald Balfour.

A death in their ranks stunned the other Monuments Men. Each of them had experienced their own close calls from booby traps, aircraft strafing, firefights, and artillery strikes. They all considered it something of a miracle that, up to this point, no one on their small team had been severely wounded or killed. Now that dreaded threshold had been crossed.

The sorrowful task of notifying Balfour's family fell on his superior officer and friend, Lieutenant Colonel Webb. With Balfour's March 3 letter nearby, Webb gathered his thoughts and began writing:

> I want very much to tell you how much Ronald was
> appreciated by all the officers who knew him in their
> work. He had a quality of clear headedness and practical
> common sense and a knowledge of the army combined
> with the obvious distinction of his mind that gave him a
> special position among the monuments officers. Both
> British and Americans felt that if they talked things over
> with him they would get help in their problems, and were
> always going to him for advice. I was in the same case as
> others, only more so, for Ronald was not only a friend of

long standing, but a stand by in difficulties, for I could
go to him and know that I would get something that for
fairness and a real understanding of a situation I could
get nowhere else. There are never very many men who
have got the combination of really penetrating
intelligence combined with fairmindedness and real
humourous appreciation of their fellow men that
Ronald had.

Trier, Germany: March 1945

The odd couple, Captain Robert Posey and Private First Class Lincoln Kirstein, didn't prove to be very odd at all. Far from pushing them apart, the demands of war had threaded their differences into a tightly woven team. The pace at which General Patton's Third Army was liberating cities created plenty of work for the two Monuments Men, but they still made time to identify people they believed might know something—anything—about the whereabouts of the Ghent Altarpiece.

In the French town of Metz, they had spoken with a civilian who had worked with the Kunstschutz. The man had only heard rumors, but word had it that the Ghent Altarpiece could be found in an underground bunker at the nearby fortress of Ehrenbreitstein. Or possibly inside one of Göring's homes. Or even the Führer's home in Berchtesgaden, the Berghof. It might even have been taken to Switzerland, or some other neutral country. It was difficult to say. That sobering conversation provided just a sampling of the challenges the two Monuments Men faced in trying to find a single object in such a vast amount of space during war.

Passing through Luxembourg, they sought out and asked local museum directors if they knew the location of the Ghent Altarpiece. One of the directors indicated that, indeed, he did know. "It's in a salt mine somewhere, possibly in the South. Or perhaps in a subterranean vault in the Berlin Reichsbank." In other words, he, too, had no idea where it was hidden.

The same could be said for the people and places Posey and Kirstein saw during the rest of March. When they reached Third Army base in the German town of Trier, perhaps the oldest city in Europe and one of the largest in the Roman Empire, they couldn't believe the level of destruction. Kirstein, with a great appreciation for the city's storied history and its early Christian, Romanesque, and Baroque architecture, recorded the scene in a letter back home:

> *The desolation is frozen, as if the moment of combustion*
> *was suddenly arrested, and the air had lost its power to*
> *hold atoms together and various centers of gravity had a*
> *dogfight for matter, and matter lost.*

Only two thousand of the ninety thousand inhabitants remained in Trier, and most of them lived a bare existence, seeking shelter in a series of wine cellars. "Certainly St. Lô was worse, but it didn't have anything of importance," Kirstein added. "Here everything was early Christian, or roman or Romanesque or marvelous baroque."

By March 29, after overseeing protection programs in Trier, Posey had to address a toothache that he had been ignoring for several weeks. With very limited German-speaking skills, Kirstein sought help from a young blond boy they passed in the street, using three sticks of Pep-O-Mint gum and a few humorous moments pantomiming a sore tooth—and it worked. Hand in hand, the boy and Kirstein led Posey to a dentist's office just a few blocks away.

Their luck continued inside as the friendly, old dentist spoke English. Question followed question, even while treating Posey's impacted wisdom tooth. The dentist wanted to know where Posey and Kirstein were from, what they did in civilian life, and all about their mission as Monuments Men. Kirstein had to turn away at the sight of what followed, but Posey's scream told all. A few moments later, without missing a beat, the dentist insisted they speak with his son-in-law, an art scholar who had been in Paris during the occupation. The dentist didn't have a car, and his son-in-law lived in a remote valley, but he offered to accompany the Monuments Men and serve as their guide.

The trip took twice the time it should have due to stops the dentist insisted on making along the way. When he returned to the jeep with vegetables and bottles of wine instead of information, Kirstein and Posey, whose head felt like it was going to explode, began to suspect it was a trap. More than twelve miles from Trier, with fewer and fewer white pillowcases and sheets indicating surrender flying from homes, the two Monuments Men considered turning around. Suddenly the old dentist tapped Posey on the shoulder and pointed to a small weekend cottage sitting on a low hill. The smile on his face told them they had arrived.

A man in his midthirties greeted them speaking French and introduced his mother, wife, and their two children. His name was Hermann Bunjes. They entered the modest home to find bookshelves filled with scholarly tomes, walls lined with photographs of many of Paris's most famous sites, and small vases filled with flowers from the early blossoms of spring. For a moment, all thoughts of war vanished.

After exchanging pleasantries, the four men took a seat around the family table. Before Posey or Kirstein could ask their first question, Bunjes started recounting his experience in Paris working for Reichsmarschall Hermann Göring. Without revealing their surprise, the two Monuments Men sat in stunned silence and listened. Yes, it was true he had joined the Nazi Party in 1938, but he resigned the following year when he entered service in the Wehrmacht. As to his service to Göring, Alfred Rosenberg, and the Nazi looting organization, the ERR, it had but one purpose: the protection of art. Posey and Kirstein quickly realized that this was a man eager to tell a story, one that sounded rehearsed, as if Bunjes had prepared it for the day of reckoning he surely knew would come.

Without breaking stride, Bunjes continued. When he advised the Reichsmarschall on February 5, 1941, that the confiscation of Jewish property violated the Hague Convention's rules of land warfare, Göring simply raised his hand and said, "First, it is *my* orders that you have to follow. You will act directly according to my orders." Bunjes didn't let it go, pointing out that the German military commanders in France probably wouldn't agree with the Reichsmarschall. "Dear Bunjes," Göring replied, "let me worry about that; I am the highest Jurist in the State."

Possessing considerable knowledge of the looting operation and those involved, Bunjes now wanted to offer his services to the

Allies. He promised to share his information, including what was taken and where it could be found, in return for the chance to resume his life as an art scholar and live in peace. Posey and Kirstein looked at each other, both wanting to blurt out, "Where is the Ghent Altarpiece?" Posey chose to push back a little to gauge the reaction by informing Bunjes that he did not have the authority to offer any deals or assurances.

After a long pause, Bunjes slid his chair away from the table, stood up, and walked out of the room. Posey, despite his stone face, worried that he'd gone too far. What felt like minutes of awkward silence followed. When Bunjes reappeared, he had a large bound album in his hands that he placed on top of the table in front of the Monuments Men. As he opened the album, Posey and Kirstein looked on in disbelief. Catalogued on each page were works of art stolen from France. Beside each object was the name of the artist, title of the work, its size, the price paid and the exchange rate, and the name of the victim from whom it had been stolen, page after page after page.

Far from done, Bunjes asked the two men to spread their maps on the table. He then started pointing to the places where the stolen works of art could be found—if they hadn't since been moved. The SS art scholar knew that Göring's immense collection had been moved from Carinhall, outside Berlin, to another of his homes, called Veldenstein, in the southern state of Bavaria, but he added that it might have been relocated again. Names of art dealers in Berlin who were actively dealing in looted works followed.

"What about the Ghent Altarpiece?" Posey asked in such a manner as if to suggest that *he* knew the answer but wanted to see what Bunjes might say. Bunjes adjusted the map, placed his fore-finger on it, and began moving it around, searching for a particular spot. "It is here, in the salt mine in Altaussee, Austria, with the other works in Hitler's collection."

After more than seven months of dead ends, the Monuments Men had, by persistence and luck, hit the jackpot. But getting to Altaussee, 450 miles away, seemed like a pipe dream. Any route to the mountainous mining town passed through Bavaria, where U.S. Army intelligence officials believed Hitler's most die-hard fol-lowers would certainly fight to the death. By that time, the works of art might have been moved again. At this stage of the war, no one knew if Third Army and its two Monuments Men would be assigned that area, not even General Patton himself and certainly not Posey and Kirstein. But they had the information they needed, and much more—a veritable treasure map.

CHAPTER 13

GAINS AND LOSSES

Siegen, Germany: first week of April 1945

Walker Hancock and George Stout, accompanied by two American GIs and their guide, Father Stephany—the guardian angel of the six boys in the Aachen Cathedral fire brigade—entered Siegen's ghostlike ruins late on the afternoon of April 2 to the sound of sporadic gunfire. The helmet of a GI caught Hancock's eye, as did the pool of blood nearby, another horrible reminder that many men, like their friend and colleague Ronald Balfour, would never return home. Debris littered the streets, forcing them to continue by foot.

Almost five months had passed since Hancock discovered a key clue when digging through dust-laden documents: a museum catalogue with the name "Siegen" written inside. Only now, with the Allied advance more than one hundred miles inside Nazi Germany, were he and Stout able to reach Siegen. The long, frustrating wait to locate their first art repository neared an end.

First Army had taken Bonn and Cologne one month earlier, then swung north and west to link up with Ninth Army, capturing three hundred thousand prisoners and trapping the last effective enemy fighting force in northwestern Germany. Being in those German cities had provided Hancock with an opportunity to gather more information to determine the precise location of the Siegen repository. A well-placed German source informed him that the Suermondt Museum treasures could be found in a copper mine inside a hill beneath the city's medieval quarter. But another piece of information proved even more surprising. Contrary to what he had been told by Father Stephany months earlier, the Aachen Cathedral treasures and those of the cathedral in Cologne were also inside the mine.

Father Stephany, still embarrassed that he had been unwilling to trust Hancock with the truth, soon found one of the two entrances to the Siegen repository teeming with people. Stout was convinced that he had seen just about everything possible since setting foot on Utah Beach nine months earlier, but even he had a difficult time processing all that his senses were experiencing:

> Around a hole in the steep hill stood some twenty people. They fell back and we went in. The tunnel—an old mineshaft—was about six feet wide and eight high, arched and rough. Once away from the light of the entrance, the passage was thick with vapor and our flashlights made only faint spots in the gloom. There were people inside. I thought we must soon pass them and that they were a few stragglers sheltered there for safety. But we did not pass them. It was a hard place to judge distance. We walked more than a quarter mile, probably less than a half a mile through that passage. Other shafts branched from it. In places it had been cut out to a width of about twenty feet.

Throughout we walked in a path not more than a
foot and a half. The rest was compressed humanity. They
stood, they sat on branches and on stones. They lay on cots
or stretchers. This was the population of the city, all that
could not get away. At one time the priest had to stop and
speak to a woman who was ill. Many must have been ill.
There was a stench in the humid air. Babies cried
fretfully.

We were the first Americans they had seen. They had
no doubt been told that we were savages. The pale grimy
faces caught in our flashlights were full of fear and hate.
Children were snatched out of our path. And ahead of us
went the fearful word, halfway between sound and
whisper—'Amerikaner.' That was the strange part of the
occurrence, the impact of hate and fear in hundreds of
hearts close about us and we the targets of it all.

Hancock felt it, too. He heard awed whispers as they walked deeper into the mine. In front of them, mothers called for their children in fear. The vicar, sensing the two men's discomfort, said, "They are afraid that you will kill the children." To think that was one thing, but to hear someone confirm it out loud saddened both men, especially Stout, father of two boys. Seeking to put his statement in context, the vicar added, "The radio threatened that recently. Anything to keep them fighting."

There was some indifference, though. Stout noticed a boy about ten years old blowing on a cup, trying to cool its contents. There was something else in that fetid air, something Stout could only sense—until he felt a touch on his hand. Shining his flashlight, he saw a boy about seven years old. The boy looked up and smiled, took Stout's hand, and began walking. I shouldn't let him do this, Stout thought. Yet he didn't pull his hand away. He didn't feel any sense of regret.

The experience stuck with Stout. Later, he wondered why the boy was so trusting. With the horror of war that the seven-year-old had experienced in his town, and the propaganda that he had undoubtedly heard, Stout would always wonder how the boy sensed that he was not a monster.

After walking more than a quarter of a mile into the hill, Father Stephany reached a locked door and knocked. A short but muscular man, Herr Etzkorn, the guardian, opened the door and greeted the vicar by name. The guardian's demeanor changed quickly at the sight of four American soldiers standing behind him. After passing through several more doors, the group reached a hollowed-out chamber more than thirty feet long, containing wooden racks filled with paintings and sculpture rising to the ceiling.

It didn't require a detailed inspection for Stout and Hancock to realize that they had found what they were looking for—and more. Paintings by Rembrandt, Fragonard, van Gogh, Gauguin, Cézanne, and Cranach filled the chamber. Even works painted by Siegen's favorite son, the prolific Flemish artist Peter Paul Rubens, were there. In all, over four hundred paintings were jammed into fourteen wooden bays constructed inside the old mineshaft. The two Monuments Men quickly determined that the Siegen repository didn't house just the Aachen museum collection, but also those of Bonn, Cologne, Essen, and several other Rhineland cities.

A GI looks at racks of paintings and sculpture hidden inside the Siegen art repository.

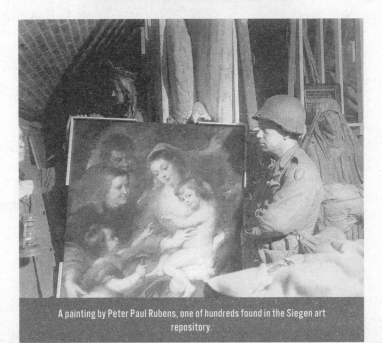

A painting by Peter Paul Rubens, one of hundreds found in the Siegen art repository.

Of greatest interest to Father Stephany were the Aachen Cathedral treasures, safe inside their heavy cases, wax seals untouched.

As Hancock and Stout turned to leave, Herr Etzkorn pointed to a stack of crates, forty in all, and said they belonged to the Beethoven house in Bonn, birthplace of the genius composer and pianist. One of the crates contained the manuscript of his famous Sixth Symphony. Nearby were two ornately carved eleventh-century oak doors removed from Cologne's Saint Maria im Kapitol, a Romanesque church that had suffered gravely from the continual bombing of the city. The artist in Hancock admired the crafts-manship of the unknown sculptor who used his carving chisels and knives to make scenes from the life and death of Christ come alive.

A section of the eleventh-century carved oak doors from a church in Cologne that Walker Hancock so greatly admired.

Stout lamented the storage conditions. The heating system was not operational and, as a consequence, the air was filled with moisture, made worse by dripping water from the ceiling. Some canvas paintings had mold damage; wood panels had flaking paint. But all in all, Stout believed that the Siegen repository was the safest place for the objects until arrangements could be made to move them to a better storage facility.

The number of German cities falling to Allied forces increased each day. In the north, the British were bearing down on Hanover. Patton and his Third Army were leading the charge into the heart of Nazi Germany at an ever-increasing pace. To the east, the Soviets had amassed 2.5 million troops outside Berlin, poised for the final showdown. With more conquered territory, though, came more requests for inspections by the Monuments Men. Stout and Hancock were needed elsewhere. For now, all they could do was post guards at the Siegen copper mine until they could return. No one had any idea when that might be.

In transit to Recklinghausen, Germany: April 4, 1945

While Hancock and Stout were in Siegen inspecting the repository, Captain Walter "Hutch" Huchthausen and his new assistant and driver, Monuments Man T/5 Sheldon Keck, were investigating reports of a looted altarpiece.

After stopping at Ninth Army forward headquarters to check the situation map, Hutch and Keck headed to the town of Recklinghausen, about eighty miles northwest of Siegen.

Hutch thrived in his assignment to Ninth Army. His work at the Aachen Cathedral, overseeing repairs to the roof, shoring up

Monuments Men T/5 Sheldon Keck (kneeling) and Lieutenant Lamont Moore.

the choir buttresses, and covering empty window frames had drawn the attention of a reporter who was curious about the motivation of an American soldier determined to preserve a German landmark. Hutch, welcoming the question, smiled and said:

> It may seem strange to some people that while we are still
> fighting the Germans we should be restoring their
> monuments. But Pilgrims from all over the world came
> to Aachen cathedral in the Middle Ages. Thirty kings
> were crowned there. It has survived every European war

since the seventh century and has an historical
significance which transcends political and economic
difference. It is architecturally unique and it is our duty
to preserve it for generations to come.

Then he thought about his answer for a couple of seconds and realized that there was an even simpler response. Looking the reporter in the eye, he added: "Aachen Cathedral belongs to the world and if we can prevent it from falling in ruins among the rest of Aachen's rubble then we are doing a service to the world."

The February arrival of Keck, an accomplished art restorer who had studied under George Stout at Harvard's Fogg Museum, and the availability—finally—of a jeep, enabled Hutch to make dozens of inspections in Dutch towns and villages along the border as well as inside western Germany, even while Allied forces continued their advance. Gradually, the character of his work shifted. Rather than initiating inspections, Hutch found himself more frequently responding to requests for assistance, like the one he and Keck were on their way to investigate.

Reaching Recklinghausen around 3:00 p.m., Hutch and Keck were unable to locate a passable road north. While stubbornly backpedaling, Wehrmacht troops had been executing the Führer's scorched-earth policy, destroying German bridges, roads, and all other infrastructure that might slow the Allied advance. Seeking an alternative route north, the two Monuments Men headed south out of town until they reached the autobahn, the world's first freeway network. There they turned left, hoping to use the high-speed road to find a northbound route not blocked by rubble or debris.

The sudden absence of U.S. Army markers on the highway indicated they were in an area where combat operations had recently ended, or might still be underway.

On the smooth road, the jeep's engine roared as the duo passed under three overhead bridges, hoping to find one that might lead them north to XIX Corps territory. Farther ahead, although difficult to make out, something appeared to be blocking their path. As they got closer, Keck slowed to a crawl. Wehrmacht troops had detonated the bridge, making the highway impassable. Keck started to make a U-turn left when he noticed the helmets of U.S. troops, who were peering at them over the northern embankment.

Seeking directions, Keck stopped. At that moment, machine-gun fire from enemy troops hiding near the bridge sprayed the right side of the jeep, perforating the hood. "They are firing at us!" Keck screamed. Out of the corner of his eye, as he instinctively jumped from the vehicle, Keck saw Hutch shift in his seat, as if he, too, were preparing to jump. Two infantrymen in a nearby foxhole pulled Keck into their defensive position while simultaneously firing in the direction of the overpass rubble. "Captain!" he yelled, "Captain!" but there was no reply.

All Keck could see from the foxhole was a column of black smoke rising above the jeep. However, an infantryman in the foxhole farther east could see what Keck could not: the right side of the burning vehicle, with Captain Huchthausen still in his seat, motionless, bleeding from the ear. Amid the danger and chaos of bullets flying back and forth, acrid smoke belching out of the jeep, and incoming enemy artillery fire now that their position had been spotted, the infantryman crawled the distance to Keck. "Your captain is dead, corporal," the soldier shouted over the sound of the German buzz saw. "Head wound. He's white as snow."

Incoming artillery fire and the location of the jeep rendered medical assistance impossible, even if medics had been standing by. After about forty-five minutes, the artillery fire diminished enough for Keck to make his way to the company command post, where he requested medical assistance for Huchthausen and filed his report, but by that time medics had arrived and removed the body. Thirty-six excruciating hours passed before Keck received confirmation that his captain—and friend—was indeed dead, plenty of time to replay the dramatic and tragic events in his head over and over again. It had all happened in an instant, with such fury and confusion, but this much Keck knew for certain: By inadvertently shielding him from enemy fire, Walter Huchthausen had saved his life.

The news of a second death among the Monuments Men serving in northern Europe—two out of an initial nine—spread slowly to the other men in the field, to Keller and Hartt preparing for the start of the spring offensive in Italy, to Mason Hammond and the other senior officers at SHAEF headquarters in London, and finally, to Paul Sachs and the members of the Roberts Commission, who had approved Huchthausen's selection. Some nights later, Walker Hancock took out pen and paper to share the news with his wife, Saima:

> The buildings that Huchthausen hoped, as a young
> architect, to build will never exist . . . but the few people
> who saw him at his job—friend and enemy—must think
> more of the human race because of him.

CHAPTER 14

SURPRISES

Frankfurt, Germany: first half of April 1945

After crossing the Rhine River, U.S. 4th Armored Division sprinted across Germany, capturing Mainz, Frankfurt, and then . . . they just disappeared. Posey and Kirstein made a point of checking the wall-sized map at headquarters each evening, where spotters posted the day's advance onto transparent acetate overlays using a red crayon. The 4th Armored was General Patton's lead unit, so wherever it was, the other four divisions in Third Army would be heading next, including the two Monuments Men.

The map did indicate that the 90th Infantry Division had established a command post in the town of Kieselbach. That meant Third Army was moving away from, not closer to, Altaussee, Austria, and the repository containing Hitler's art collection and the Ghent Altarpiece. Some dumb luck, the two Monuments Men thought. All those months had passed without a clue on the whereabouts of the Ghent Altarpiece or Hitler's art hoard. Now, because of something as fluky as Posey's dental needs, they knew exactly where both were hidden—and their army was headed elsewhere.

Posey and Kirstein checked the wall map once again on the evening of April 4. The 4th Armored Division had reappeared and, along with soldiers of the 89th Infantry, neared the town of

Gotha, just two hundred miles southwest of Berlin. Rumors about some big discovery had been circulating since late afternoon. The following day brought firsthand accounts that left Posey and Kirstein, and every other soldier, seething.

Early that cold and rainy morning, April 4, Private Ralph G. Rush, part of an intelligence and reconnaissance platoon of the 89th Infantry, sighted a double-fenced barbed-wire enclosure. Seeing empty guard towers, he and his scout squad cautiously approached the front gate. A dozen dead bodies littered the ground in front of them, including three GIs, shot in the back of the neck

U.S. Third Army soldiers discovered this ghastly scene of death at Ohrdruf, where Nazi guards had executed prisoners before fleeing.

while kneeling, hands bound behind their backs. Their bodies were still warm to the touch. Emaciated prisoners, little more than skeletons tightly wrapped in skin with what remained of their ragged striped uniforms draped over them, sat in bed or on the ground, with barely the energy to die.

These Third Army advance units had by chance found Ohrdruf, a forced labor camp that once held thousands of prisoners from Russia, Poland, Hungary, and other European countries. It was the first Nazi camp liberated by American forces. Private Rush, and most every other soldier on or near the front lines, had seen the horror of death far too frequently, but the gruesome scenes he and the other scouts witnessed defined inhumanity:

> *It seemed that dead bodies were everywhere—a large shed contained 50 or more naked bodies with parchment like skin, stacked like cordwood, with lye sprinkled on them to keep down the smell. We passed what appeared to be a torture apparatus—we later learned it was a whipping table . . . We also saw a gallows that we were told was used for prisoners who had attempted to escape . . . Further on we came upon a crude crematorium or burning pit—a long pit had been dug with a mound at each end and railroad rails laid about 3 feet apart from mound to mound. A fire was still smoldering in the pit and partially destroyed bodies remained on the rails and burnt parts were in the pit. The stench was overwhelming.*

Two days later, Posey received a telegram ordering him and Kirstein to report immediately to the town of Merkers, forty miles west of Ohrdruf. Third Army had made another major discovery. Word had come down from the man himself, General Patton: TOP SECRET. NO PRESS.

The two Monuments Men reached the Merkers salt mine on the afternoon of April 8. Security was unlike anything Posey had ever seen. Tank battalions, infantry regiments, and military police—more than a thousand soldiers in all, with more reporting for duty each hour—surrounded the mine and its five primary entrances. Getting past the numerous sentry posts and maze of tanks, machine gun–mounted jeeps, and other military vehicles took time, but eventually the two Monuments Men reached the mine entrance, where they were quickly briefed.

Posey and Kirstein heard an impossible story. Two days earlier, MPs stopped two women, one of whom was pregnant, walking along a dusty road past curfew. Their explanation seemed simple enough: Both were French displaced persons on their way to visit a midwife. After confirming their story, MPs provided the women with a ride. Passing the Merkers mine, the MPs asked about the facility. One of the women said that the mine contained gold and valuable works of art, which local civilians and displaced persons had been forced to help unload. Within hours, Lieutenant Colonel William Russell of the 90th Infantry Division corroborated the woman's statement and ordered the first of multiple security detachments to guard the mine entrances.

The lieutenant colonel and his team had already descended

into the mine the day before, the two Monuments Men learned. At the bottom of the elevator shaft, just outside the cage, they found 550 bags of Reichsmarks stacked against the wall. They also found the room that reportedly contained the gold, but multiple attempts to open the steel door failed.

It wasn't until engineers used half a stick of dynamite to blow a hole in the wall that the gold was revealed—tons of it. Posey and Kirstein couldn't wait to see it for themselves. Their assignment was clear: They were to make a quick inspection of the gold and currency, assess the importance and quantity of the art, then report back with their findings.

Before stepping onto an elevator large enough to transport a jeep with room to spare, someone tossed the two Monuments Men a few rags to wipe the highly corrosive salt from their leather boots. The elevator then began its descent into total darkness. Kirstein hoped that the German operator wasn't one of the "stay-behind SS men" they'd been hearing about, intent on causing destruction behind the lines. It took several minutes for the elevator to reach the base of the mine, twenty-one hundred feet beneath the surface.

They stepped out of the elevator into a subterranean beehive of activity, with heavily armed soldiers, MPs, and army photographers all running about. Finely pulverized salt blanketed the mine floor, irritating both sinus and throat. A large but still shut bank-type steel door, with combination lock and a hole in the brick wall next to it, made finding Room No. 8—and the gold—easy. Kirstein stepped through the opening, one leg at a time, just as an officer was playfully having his photograph taken staring at a helmet filled with gold coins.

Even 2,100 feet below ground, security was tight inside the Merkers mine.

Posey and Kirstein could see that Room No. 8 was nothing more than a walled-up cavern with large storage areas on either side of a mine cart track running down the center. The space measured about 75 feet wide, 150 feet long, and 12 feet high, illuminated by a string of floodlights that hung above the track. Thousands of canvas bags in knee-high piles lined the right side of the cavern, from the vault door to as far as they could see. Each bag had been stenciled with the word "Reichsbank." Nearby, bales of currency stacked in chest-high rows stretched to the back of the cavern.

The seal had already been broken on one of the bags, exposing a gold bar stamped with the weight of the ingot, the purity of the gold, and an eagle atop a swastika, the emblem of the Nazi Party.

The discovery at Merkers included bags of gold bars and coins worth $250 million (about $8.5 billion at today's gold price).

Now all the security aboveground made sense, Posey thought. Third Army had just discovered the entirety of Nazi Germany's gold reserves.

While others continued their analysis of the discovery in Room No. 8, Posey and Kirstein made their way to the art, which was no simple task. The mine complex had thirty-five miles of tunnels. The gold rush had drawn all attention away from the art. But upon seeing thousands of crates containing many of the riches of Berlin's world-class museums, the duo knew that the value of the art was no less stunning. Gold could be appraised at face value; one-of-a-kind works of art like the Bust of Nefertiti, which was more than thirty-two hundred years old, were truly priceless.

For a brief while, Kirstein felt transported to another world, one he knew intimately well, far from the horror and destruction of war. Walking among so many beautiful treasures, studying photographs that curators had clipped from museum catalogues and then pasted onto the crates to identify contents, provided a joyful escape. Almost every period of civilization was represented: Egyptian, ancient Greek and Roman, Gothic, Renaissance, Baroque, and the nineteenth and twentieth centuries. The crates contained paintings, drawings, sculpture, tapestries, rugs, prints, and rare books—even eight lead boxes filled with Egyptian papyri. In their haste to evacuate bomb-ravaged Berlin, curators had also

Monuments Man Sergeant Kenneth C. Lindsay poses
with the Bust of Nefertiti, one of many museum
treasures found inside the Merkers mine.

brought four hundred additional loose paintings, some master-pieces, which were standing in racks, back-to-back.

Posey reached two conclusions quickly: The art in the Merkers mine belonged to German museums. None of it appeared stolen. The second conclusion took but an instant. For the art to safely be moved out of the mine, they needed George Stout.

After returning to the surface and sharing their findings with Lieutenant Colonel Russell, the two Monuments Men and a Civil Affairs officer drove back to Third Army headquarters in Frankfurt to deliver their reports. The Civil Affairs officer's report on the gold stole the show. The preliminary tally of Reichsbank assets inside Room No. 8 included 8,189 gold bars, 711 bags of American twenty-dollar gold pieces, and more than 1,300 bags of other gold coins, in all worth more than 250 million dollars. That figure did not include hundreds of millions of dollars in assorted foreign currencies, and bundles of Reichsmarks totaling about 2.76 billion dollars at face value.

Posey called Stout the following morning and told him that he was urgently needed in Merkers. Having just learned of Huchthausen's death, Stout was busy lining up a Monuments Officer to fill the vacancy at Ninth Army. By the time Stout arrived on the afternoon of April 11, he heard that General Eisenhower had made the decision to relocate the contents of Merkers to a safer location. He wanted the now almost two thousand soldiers guarding the mine, and all their equipment, released from guard duty and returned to the front as quickly as possible. Eisenhower hoped that with the enemy's primary source of war funding now in the hands of the Western Allies, the war might be one step closer to ending.

At 10:30 on the morning of April 12, Generals Patton, Bradley, and Eisenhower visited the Merkers mine, their first stop on a day-long inspection tour. As the generals descended into the darkness on the rickety single-cable elevator, with a German operator at the controls, Patton quipped, "If that clothesline should part, promotions in the United States Army would be greatly stimulated."

"Okay, George, that's enough." Even in complete darkness, all those on the elevator instantly recognized Eisenhower's voice. "No more cracks until we are above ground again."

The generals entered Room No. 8 in awe. Slowly they walked alongside the mine cart track the entire distance of the cavern, past the bags of gold bars and coins and the bundled currency. In the farthest reach of the mine, almost two hundred common suitcases containing gold and silver household items—forks and knives,

General Eisenhower examining one of the two hundred suitcases overflowing with gold and silver objects stolen by the Nazis from Jews and other victims of the Holocaust.

watch bands, cigarette cases, and cups—had been lined up, side by side. Sacks containing gold tooth fillings and rings taken from concentration camp victims were nearby. Unable to smelt their loot into gold and silver bars, the SS had simply delivered the objects, including the gold fillings, to the German Reichsbank for safe-keeping. With the other generals looking on, Eisenhower reached down to one of the open suitcases and brushed his hand across the top of all that remained of thousands of people, as if to confirm the whole experience wasn't some horrific nightmare.

April 12, 1945, Generals Bradley, Patton, and Eisenhower (left to right) inspecting paintings in the Merkers mine.

GIs placed this painting by French artist Édouard Manet atop one of the mine carts.

Before departing, the group passed through the chamber containing some of the crated art objects and racks of loose paintings from Berlin, which included a masterpiece by the French painter Édouard Manet. The mine had been cleared of nonessential personnel for the duration of the generals' visit, but Monuments Man George Stout, deemed absolutely essential, continued his evacuation planning nearby.

Weimar, Germany: mid-April 1945

Several days later, at First Army headquarters in Weimar, Walker Hancock had a rare moment of calm to catch up on developments outside his small part of the war. Leafing through an edition of *Stars and Stripes* newspaper, he read updates about all that had happened on April 12: the generals' inspection of the Merkers mine, their trip later in the day to see firsthand the horrors at Ohrdruf, the forced labor camp that Third Army forces had liberated eight days earlier, and the sudden death of the thirty-second president of the United States, Franklin D. Roosevelt. Any one of those events would have dominated the news, Hancock thought, but for all three of them to happen on the same day?

Stout's evacuation of the Merkers mine had, like everything else involving the leader of the Monuments Men, come off exactly as planned. The art convoy, code name Task Force Hansen, departed the mine for Frankfurt on the morning of April 17, escorted by hundreds of infantry soldiers, military police, machine-gun platoons, an antiaircraft platoon with mobile antiaircraft guns, wreckers, an ambulance, and air cover from a P-51 Mustang fighter. Hancock marveled at Stout's organizational ability. No one else could have pulled off a move of that magnitude in such a short period of time.

Ohrdruf, where the generals had just been, was thirty miles west of the town of Weimar. Hancock stared out the window of his office, trying to imagine what it must have felt like to see an underground complex filled with Nazi treasure and, only hours later, witness something that went far beyond the savagery of war. The scene of dead and emaciated bodies at Ohrdruf had clearly gut-punched the generals. Even battle-hardened General Patton refused to enter a room containing the stacked bodies of twenty to thirty

General Eisenhower and his commanders visited Ohrdruf on the afternoon of April 12, 1945, and were sickened to see the partially charred remains of inmates murdered by the Nazi guards.

naked men, killed by starvation, fearful it would make him sick. General Eisenhower, disgusted that anyone, even an enemy, could systematically behave so cruelly, had ordered every nearby unit not on the fighting lines to tour Ohrdruf. He was incensed. "We are told that the American soldier does not know what he is fighting for. Now, at least, he will know what he is fighting against."

But the discovery of the Buchenwald concentration camp, on a hill just five miles from where First Army and Hancock were headquartered at Weimar, dwarfed what Eisenhower had seen at

Ohrdruf, or at least Hancock heard that it did. Fellow officers who had traveled the short distance returned with stories of murdered men and boys, some lying where they had fallen and died, the charred remains of others found inside industrial-sized ovens.

Hancock knew that his job as a Monuments Man depended on maintaining goodwill with German civilians. Would seeing such atrocities destroy his ability to remain committed to his mission, or sear into his mind sights of such ugliness that he might never create anything beautiful again? Possibly, he thought, and for that reason he decided against going. Besides, as an artist who had made a living studying the human form, Hancock needed to do no more than look into the hollow faces of the emaciated men, survivors of Buchenwald, wandering the streets of Weimar, barefoot, wearing their soiled striped garments, to have a sense of the inhumanity they had somehow survived.

For all the barbarity that had taken place on that hill and at Ohrdruf, an opportunity for a moment of grace appeared one day, and Hancock seized it. His friend, a Jewish chaplain, visited him after conducting the first religious service for Buchenwald survivors since its liberation. Emotionally drained, the chaplain described the experience. If only he had had a Torah, he lamented. Alas, where in Nazi Germany would someone find the most important Jewish religious object?

Hancock broke into a wide smile and said, "I have one here." Just hours earlier, Hancock had come into his office to discover a Torah sitting on his desk, which had been found at the local SS headquarters. Soldiers regularly stopped by his office when they found works of art or other cultural objects and didn't know what else to do with them. None had ever been so well-timed or more greatly appreciated. The chaplain returned to Buchenwald carrying the Torah, an experience he described days later to his friend: "The people weeping, reaching for it, kissing it, overcome with joy at the sight of the symbol of their faith."

Army Chaplain Samuel Blinder examines one of hundreds of Torah scrolls stolen by the ERR.

CHAPTER 15

ON THE MOVE

Near Worms, Germany: last half of April 1945

By the third week in April, word had come down from the top concerning the final push to end the war in Europe. General Eisenhower intended for his armies to cut off and destroy the enemy's fighting forces. The Soviet Red Army, not the Western Allies, would get the prize of encircling and crushing Berlin. And Private Harry Ettlinger would continue his walks in the countryside outside Worms, Germany, reading *Stars and Stripes*, chatting with other soldiers about news from the front, and playing an occasional game of craps—or at least, that's how it looked to him.

Three months had passed since Harry's nineteenth birthday, when he was pulled out of the convoy of replacement troops headed into battle. When he jumped off the tailgate of that truck with his gear and waved goodbye to the eight buddies in his squad, Harry figured some new assignment awaited him. But the only new assignment that came his way was to repack his gear and move to a new location—and then do it all over again, and again. Then came the news that three of his eight friends had been killed in action, and four seriously wounded. A cloud of guilt had hovered over him ever since.

Between the scuttlebutt floating around and what Harry could find in the newspapers, he learned that First Army had reached the Elbe River, just eighty-five miles from Berlin. Rather than push on farther east, or north toward Berlin, Eisenhower sent his armies, lumbering formations of one hundred thousand to one hundred fifty thousand soldiers each, to the remaining borders of Germany: the British 21st Army to the north, the French First Army to the southwest, and the U.S. Sixth and Twelfth Armies to the southeast. First, Third, and Seventh Armies marched south to form a backward L, blocking German forces from retreating southeast into neighboring Czechoslovakia, or south to Austria or Switzerland. With the spring offensive in Italy underway, and Fifth and British Eighth Armies on the move north of Florence, German troops had to choose: fight and die, or surrender. They had nowhere to run.

Now assigned to Seventh Army, all Harry could do was hope that these new orders south, toward Munich, would provide him with an assignment that might in some way make sense for having been spared the fate of his friends.

Outside Worms, Germany: last half of April 1945

Rorimer reported for duty near Worms, Germany, in mid-April as Monuments Officer for Seventh Army. Before Rorimer departed Paris for his new assignment, Valland had warned him: Get to the castle of Neuschwanstein quickly or run the risk of Bruno Lohse, or one of the other Nazi ERR gangsters, destroying the evidence of their looting operation. Even worse, they might destroy the works of art.

Eisenhower's orders removed one obstacle. The hiding places that Valland had identified, including Neuschwanstein, now fell squarely into his area of operations. But with each passing day in his new job, overwhelmed with work, Rorimer worried about getting there in time. Flooding inside a salt mine in Heilbronn, the first repository on Valland's list, threatened to destroy thousands of museum treasures from German cities, along with stained-glass windows, some dating from the twelfth century, stolen from Strasbourg Cathedral in France. Getting the pumps restarted would take days he could not afford with Seventh Army on the move.

The Heilbronn mine.

Stained-glass windows from the cathedral in Strasbourg, France, found among thousands of cultural objects inside Heilbronn mine.

Dozens of known repositories, and hundreds of leads on others, all needed to be checked by Seventh Army's lone Monuments Man. War crimes investigators wanted information and captured documents. Rorimer had plenty of both, but no spare time to assess any of it. Accusations of looting by American soldiers were on the rise and had to be followed up and reported on. Rorimer had cringed when the owner of Castle Warsberg described how an army sergeant had forced her, at rifle point, to turn over the keys to the safe before taking her jewelry and two paintings.

Jim Rorimer intended on fulfilling his duty as a Monuments Officer. He would go to his grave before disappointing Rose Valland for trusting him with her secrets. But in less than two weeks on the job, he grew increasingly concerned that a shortage of manpower placed both commitments in jeopardy.

Paris, France: last half of April 1945

The speed of the Western Allied advance into Germany, and behind-the-scenes prodding by French museum leaders Jacques Jaujard and Albert Henraux, had prompted French First Army to issue an urgent request for volunteers—men or women—to serve as Monuments Officers. Valland applied immediately. Each morning since, with a cigarette in one hand and a cup of espresso in the other, she scanned the pages of *Le Figaro*, tracking the progress of the various armies, especially U.S. Seventh and her friend Jim Rorimer. Soon she hoped to be in uniform and in Germany, engaged in the hunt for tens of thousands of treasures stolen from France, and the Nazi thieves who had threatened to kill her.

Hungen, Germany: last half of April 1945

Since learning about Altaussee, Austria, and its possible treasures from Hermann Bunjes, the corrupt Kunstschutz official, Posey and Kirstein expected that the prized target would fall outside their area of operations. Instead, General Eisenhower's order for Third Army to head southeast, deep into Austria, actually charted a direct path in that direction. Because the remote mountaintop village had no particular military value, Posey had to request Third Army tactical commanders to make the area a priority for occupation.

While Third Army troops plunged deeper into the heart of Nazi Germany, Posey and Kirstein continued their inspections. Entering the town of Hungen, they found eight large buildings filled with Jewish archives, religious items, and nearly 1.5 million books. Why torture and murder Jews at places like Ohrdruf and Buchenwald while at the same time preserving sacred objects that defined their history and faith? Initially, Posey couldn't figure it out; neither could the polymath Kirstein, himself a Jew. Both men listened in disbelief as a custodian explained that the materials had in fact been gathered for the Institut zur Erforschung der Judenfrage—Institute for the Research of the Jewish Question—a pet project of Nazi Party ideologue Alfred Rosenberg.

Acting on a hunch, the two Monuments Men decided to return to Trier and question Hermann Bunjes a second time. Now desperate for any sort of assurance of safe passage for him and his family, Bunjes eagerly revealed more. At Schloss Ellmann, owned by Nazi Reichsmarschall Göring, Posey and Kirstein would find masterpieces from the Naples museums that the Hermann Göring Tank Division had stolen from the Abbey of Monte Cassino to give to their leader on his birthday.

Bunjes also named names. A sketch of the looting operation, along with the names of Nazi officials and art dealers, like Karl Haberstock and Hildebrand Gurlitt, would certainly be helpful to war crimes investigators. With the size of Nazi Germany continuing to shrink, chances were good that the Monuments Men would be the ones to find, arrest, and interrogate some of Hitler and Göring's art henchmen. For a second time, Posey and Kirstein left Bunjes with nothing more than a goodbye, adding Schloss Ellmann and other repositories he had mentioned to their list of stops on the way to Altaussee.

Weimar, Germany: last half of April 1945

Walker Hancock pinpointed the last of the repositories on his list and circled it on the map. After a few hours of work stooped over his desk, he paused to admire his handiwork. The map looked like an utter mess, as if it had developed the measles, with hundreds of little circles around small towns, castles, churches, and mines throughout central Germany. The list of known repositories in First Army's area of operation alone now numbered 230, with more being reported daily.

During his first six months as a Monuments Man, Hancock had struggled to identify even one hiding place containing Nazi loot. Now, in a matter of weeks, the speed of the Allied advance into Germany was yielding repositories faster than they could be inspected and protected. One Monuments Man in all of First Army responsible for checking 230 locations? Impossible. Hancock knew that Posey and Kirstein in Third Army and Rorimer in Seventh Army faced similar challenges, but that in no way diminished his frustration. Nothing about the Monuments operation was more upsetting than knowing that the shortage of manpower made it a certainty that preventable damage would occur.

In the initial months of his job, Hancock, like Posey, Rorimer, Balfour, and Huchthausen, found creative solutions to overcome the chronic lack of transportation. But a soldier hitchhiking with a duffel bag was one thing; trying to move thousands of works of art on a moment's notice was something entirely different. No amount of creativity or resourcefulness could change the fact that getting to the repositories required wheels. Relocating the contents required fleets. The Monuments Men had neither.

Lack of transportation wasn't the only problem. Tens of thousands of displaced persons were wandering all over Germany, seeking any kind of shelter possible, looking for anything of value that might help them survive another day. Hiding places containing valuable works of art were, for some, a prayer twice answered. The Monuments Men needed security teams to guard the repositories, at least until they could get there and inspect them. But during combat operations, spare troops simply weren't available.

Sometimes the storage conditions inside a repository were adequate. Hancock remembered how, despite mold growing on some of the paintings in the copper mine at Siegen, George Stout had judged the overall conditions tolerable until the objects could be relocated. But relocated where? As Hancock took another look at his map, he realized that no one, not even Stout, had anticipated discovering such vast quantities of priceless treasure in so many bizarre and oftentimes remote locations.

One other thing had changed, and it sickened Hancock's artistic roots just as much as it did his sense of mission protecting cultural treasures from the destruction of war. Following the discoveries of Ohrdruf and Buchenwald, compassion for the enemy was in short supply. In the minds of some soldiers, German-owned works of art were looked at no differently than the men and women who had constructed and operated the concentration camps. As their thinking went, these cultural objects belonged to German citizens, so many of whom had stood by watching it snow during the warmth of summer, pretending they didn't know that the grayish ashes were all that remained of Jews and others judged unworthy of life by the Nazis. Or perhaps the works of art had once belonged to the family of a Wehrmacht soldier who had killed a buddy or wounded a comrade. Anything considered German was fair game for retribution.

For the time being, all Hancock could do—all any of the Monuments Men could do—was triage each reported repository, continue pleading for transportation and security, and be on the lookout for temporary shelters to relocate the priceless objects they were finding.

Frankfurt, Germany: last half of April 1945

George Stout understood the immense stress on his fellow officers. The demands on each Monuments Man serving on or near the front were increasing, but their numbers were not. The job had become even more dangerous, as the deaths of Balfour and Huchthausen confirmed. Stout shared his colleagues' frustrations about the lack of army resources and support. He remembered the loneliness of the job from his early months setting up the operation in France. Those days seemed easy compared to the enormity of what they now faced. A trickle of hidden works of art had become a flood, with no place to move them, and oftentimes no one to guard them.

On April 20, while visiting Third Army headquarters, Stout received a call from Hancock, who was "desperate for need of help." Having worked with Hancock so closely in Aachen and at the discovery in Siegen, Stout knew his friend was in trouble.

When Hancock called back three days later and reported "repos out of hand," Stout was sure of it. Posey at least had Kirstein's help. Rorimer had just received temporary support from Monuments Man Charles Kuhn, a superior officer who recognized that the need in the field was greater than in his office. But Hancock was entirely on his own.

Florence, Italy: last half of April 1945

The start of the spring offensive in Italy—Operation Grapeshot— put a very restless Deane Keller and Fred Hartt back in the hunt for the priceless treasures, 735 objects in all, belonging to the Florence museums and churches. Keller accompanied Fifth Army troops north, who were racing to beat German forces to the Po River before they could escape across the border into Nazi Austria. Hartt remained in Florence, removing the protective coverings on various monuments while scrounging for information about the missing masterpieces.

Eight months had passed since the theft by Wehrmacht troops of paintings and sculpture from a handful of Tuscan repositories. During that time, all efforts to identify the location of the missing masterpieces, including Hartt's overture to the Vatican through Cardinal Elia Dalla Costa, the archbishop of Florence, had met with dead ends. Ernest DeWald, director of the MFAA in Italy, thought the Germans might move the trove of paintings and sculpture across the border into Switzerland "when the stampede begins." But Hartt, filled with anxiety, envisioned a far worse scenario: In a last desperate act, some German commander might order the works of art destroyed. With the U.S. Fifth Army and British Eighth Army now fighting their way north toward Nazi Germany, the Monuments Men were running out of time.

Hartt had squeezed every one of his contacts in Florence hoping for a fresh lead. Major Alessandro Cagiati, an American intelligence officer whom Hartt had befriended one month earlier, had provided a break of sorts. The Florentine treasures, thought to be in a "good state," could be found in the Alto Adige region. Cagiati's operatives didn't know the actual location. Hartt grabbed his map of Italy, quickly unfolded it on the table, and followed his finger up the map, stopping at the regional capital, Bolzano. The Alto Adige, located more than 250 miles north of Florence, shared a long border with Austria, which meant the works of art were already in Nazi territory, as far as Hartt was concerned. Another message from Cagiati soon followed. Hartt read it, shaking his head in horror: "It is feared by the Germans themselves (those who are friends of the arts) that these works of art will be at the last minute removed or ruined in the haste of removing them by the SS . . ."

Bologna, Italy: last half of April 1945

Deane Keller, Charley Bernholz, and British Monuments Man Teddy Croft-Murray entered Bologna on the evening of its liberation, April 21. The sixty-seven-mile drive from Florence took eight hours as traffic crawled along blacked-out roads jammed with vehicles. Keller had seen his share of how war visited small Italian towns. "Coming into town late at night," he wrote to his parents, he saw "houses on fire, mines exploded by engineers." All around was the "smell of death, dead animals, a couple of German soldiers, one in two pieces, another headless." It all left him wondering if the destruction—and the war—would ever end.

The rapid advance meant Fifth Army needed its Monuments Officer, so Keller departed, leaving the task of locating and questioning the art superintendents of Bologna and other nearby towns to someone else. Finding anyone amid such destruction involved a fair bit of luck, but soon enough the British Monuments Officer located Dr. Pietro Zampetti, Director of Galleries in Modena. Wasting no time, with notebook in hand, Croft-Murray asked Zampetti what he knew about the Florentine treasures. The museum director answered in a very matter-of-fact manner: The works of art taken by German forces could be found in two small villages in the Alto Adige, San Leonardo in Passiria and Campo Tures.

CHAPTER 16

THE BEGINNING
OF THE END

Verdun, France: end of April through
the first week of May 1945

George Stout walked into his office at Twelfth Army headquarters in
Verdun, France, on April 29 to find another message from Walker
Hancock, his third in nine days. This one was different. "Very urgent
matter ... request inspection ... earliest possible opportunity."
Stout knew that Hancock didn't panic, and he didn't use words like
"urgent" carelessly. If he said something was "urgent," that meant
urgent! Efforts to find out more by telephone proved fruitless.

Bitter winds combined with a lingering winter chill made the
daylong, three-hundred-mile drive miserable. Stout wondered
what would end sooner, the cold weather or the war. But the
following morning, May 1, a hot cup of coffee at First Army headquarters in Weimar and a warm welcome from Hancock worked
wonders. After several brief meetings, the two Monuments Officers
and an army photographer made their way ninety miles north to
Bernterode, a salt mine in the Thuringian Forest, and the reason
for Hancock's urgent call.

With Stout at the wheel, Hancock filled in the details of how
this latest bizarre episode had begun. Two days earlier, an army

captain had walked into the chief of staff's office and laid on his desk a jeweled scepter and orb, both made of gold, which he'd removed from the mine. This made quite an impression on the boss, General Hodges, who promptly ordered Hancock to substantiate the young captain's fantastic story and report back. Having been inside the copper mine in Siegen, surrounded by priceless works of art and the Aachen Cathedral treasures, Hancock believed anything was possible in this war. Still, he drove to Bernterode with a certain degree of skepticism.

Bernterode wasn't a town as much as it was a camp for two thousand displaced men and women, Italian, French, and Russian slave laborers, who for nine years had worked in the munitions plant and storage depot deep inside the mine. A squad of GIs searching for stockpiles of ammunition reached Bernterode, made the eighteen-hundred-foot descent, and discovered the mother lode: more than four hundred thousand tons of explosives, a staggering quantity equal to the weight of about twelve thousand Sherman tanks.

As the squad searched the mine's fourteen miles of tunnels, they came upon a freshly plastered wall. Curiosity got the better of them. Six feet of rubble later, they discovered a padlocked door, which they promptly dispensed with, and entered the subterranean chamber. The room, a long rectangle measuring seventeen feet wide by forty-five feet long, had been partitioned, using salt blocks and mortar, into a series of bays, each containing paintings, military banners, tapestries, crates—and four caskets. Draped across the top of one of the three wooden boxes was a wreath and broad red silk ribbons bearing a swastika and the name "Adolf Hitler."

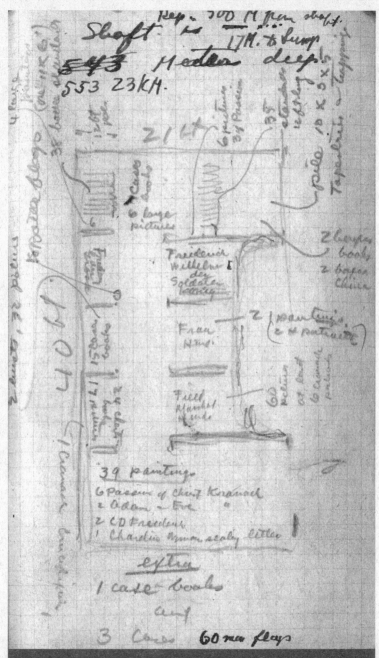

Hancock's diagram of the Nazi shrine at Bernterode.
The four caskets are indicated in the center of his sketch.

Thinking they had found the body of the leader of Nazi Germany, the sergeant posted guards, then hightailed it back to his command post to report the stunning news to his commanding officer, Captain Greenspan. The following day, the captain returned to conduct his own inspection, astonished to see exactly what the squad sergeant had described. Knowing his credibility would be on the line, and not wanting to submit such an outlandish report without some proof, the young captain departed for First Army headquarters, taking the scepter and orb with him.

Stout, Hancock, and an army Signal Corps photographer soon reached the mine and made the descent into darkness. Bernterode wasn't quite as deep as the Merkers mine, nor was its tunnel

U.S. soldiers initially believed this coffin contained Hitler's remains.

complex as vast, but Stout knew that the danger of entering a powder keg primed to explode made this, his third major repository in as many weeks, by far the most dangerous.

After crawling through the opening, it took just seconds for Stout, as it had for Hancock, to realize that Bernterode was far more than just another art repository. The two Monuments Men had entered a shrine to German military tradition to be preserved for future generations. Regimental banners, 225 in all, hung in rows over caskets containing the remains of 3 of the most important German leaders of the previous 250 years: Frederick William I, known as the "soldier-king"; his son, Frederick the Great, a champion of the arts; and Field Marshal Paul von Hindenburg. A fourth casket contained the remains of the field marshal's wife.

Stout looked at the casket that bore Hitler's name, then looked quizzically at Hancock. It's not him, Hancock said with a shake of his head. The ordnance men had thought that it was Hitler, but it's not. Someone had hastily written each of the names in reddish crayon on small strips of paper and fastened them to the respective caskets using tape, but two had become detached, causing much confusion. The wreath and red silk ribbons bearing Hitler's name rested atop the wooden casket of Frederick William I.

More than 270 priceless paintings, mounds of tapestries, and chests of books filled other spaces inside the chamber. Stout and Hancock also found three cases containing treasures from the Hohenzollern Museum in Berlin, including swords, crowns, and other coronation items—minus the jeweled scepter and orb, which Captain Greenspan had presented to General Hodges two days earlier. Taking no chances, the two Monuments Officers decided to immediately evacuate the gold and silver objects. That night they developed their plan: Hancock would deliver the three cases of coronation treasures to General Hodges at First Army headquarters while Stout scoured the mine buildings at Bernterode for packing materials. Hancock would then return and assist Stout with the removal of the remaining objects.

The following morning brought long-awaited yet shocking news. Overnight, German radio had announced that the leader of Nazi Germany, "fighting till his last breath against Bolshevism,"

PARIS EDITION

EXTRA THE STARS AND STRIPES **EXTRA**
Daily Newspaper of U.S. Armed Forces in the European Theater of Operations

Vol. 1—No. 279 · 1 Fr. · 1 Fr. · Wednesday, May 2, 1945

HITLER DEAD

Fuehrer Fell at CP, German Radio Says; Doenitz at Helm, Vows War Will Continue

German radio announced last night that Adolf Hitler had died. Adm. Karl Doenitz, former commander-in-chief of the German Navy, has succeeded him as ruler of the Reich, the radio announcement said.

Doenitz made a radio speech immediately after the announcement, Reuter said, and declared that Germany would continue to wage war. His statement spiked peace rumors which had been prevalent for more than a week in all world capitals.

Churchill Hints Peace Is at Hand

Winston Churchill indicated in a brief address to Commons yesterday that peace in Europe might come before long. Although he declined to give any details on the reported opening negotiations, the Prime Minister acknowledged that an important announcement was possible before the House adjourned Friday night. The statement was regarded as a confirmation that the negotiations are now well under way. London newspaper correspondents heard of the function. Red Cross, cross rumors denied it a more conclusive that he was losing all patience in a long...

Pope Prepares Speech

ROME, May 1 (UP)—Details of the Pope's address were not released. Vatican sources said today that the Pope specified that only prayers for an imminent worldwide happiness in the address is expected to be broadcast within his own end of the European war.

The announcement did not give any details of how the Reich dictator died. The news was broadcast after solemn Wagnerian music, including "Twilight of the Gods," was played.

"Achtung, achtung," a voice said. "In a few minutes you will hear a serious and important message to the German people. We are now going

Hitler's obituary and text of Doenitz speech on Page 4.

to play a movement of Bruckner's Seventh Symphony." Finally, the report of Hitler's death was given.

Hitler's death came three days after his brother-dictator, Benito Mussolini of Italy, was killed by Italian partisans near the village of Dongo on Lake Como.

Doenitz, in his speech, said that Hitler "had fallen at his command post," while Hamburg radio said that he died in the Reich Chancellery in Berlin yesterday afternoon. Red Army troops fighting in Ber-

(Continued on Page 8)

had fallen. Adolf Hitler was dead, but the fighting—and the dying—continued. For how long, neither Stout nor Hancock knew. But this much was certain: The dangers to cultural treasures in the hands of a desperate enemy added even greater urgency to finding the remaining hidden repositories before Nazi fanatics and other opportunists could loot or destroy them.

On the road to Modena, Italy: first week of May 1945

On May 2, after eleven exhausting days of inspections, Deane Keller and Charley Bernholz finally headed back to Fifth Army base camp in Modena. Since departing Bologna on April 21, they had driven through bitter cold, rain showers, and mud as thick as pudding, assessing damage to monuments and other cultural treasures in dozens of towns and villages in northern Italy. Now they just wanted to get home, as much as base camp could ever be called "home," and regroup before heading out again.

Seeing another military checkpoint up ahead, Bernholz slowed the jeep to a crawl and then stopped. Passing their documents to the MP, he noticed that the mood of the soldiers seemed jovial. Never one to miss out on a good joke, Bernholz asked what was up. "Haven't you heard, corporal? The war in Italy is over!" The two Monuments Men had heard that partisans had killed the Italian dictator, Benito Mussolini, and other leaders of the Fascist regime, just a few days earlier. That news, like the radio announcement of Hitler's death, had spread like wildfire. But word that all German forces in Italy had surrendered caught them by surprise.

By the time Bernholz pulled the jeep into base camp, the place was abuzz with rumors. Keller wanted facts. After speaking with a military intelligence officer, a much clearer picture emerged. Earlier in the day, representatives of Nazi SS General Karl Wolff had signed an agreement involving the surrender of one million German soldiers stationed in Italy. The war in Italy was officially over. At that moment, the Allied armies extended from the Po Valley north to the Alps, and from the port cities of Genoa on the Ligurian Sea east to Venice on the Adriatic. Troops of Fifth Army were racing north to link up with lead elements of Seventh Army pushing south, through Germany and Austria, to seal the Brenner Pass and trap enemy forces, especially high-ranking Nazis suspected of war crimes.

The sudden collapse of German forces had taken everyone by surprise. Keller walked to his tent feeling numb. Like many other officers, what excitement he felt was muted out of respect for the men still fighting to end the war in Europe. At least more of the boys in Italy would be spared and could go home to their families, he thought. But the danger of booby traps continued, and so did his work.

Before lights out, Keller started a letter to Kathy and sketched a drawing for Dino. Thoughts of home prompted him to reach for his field journal. From Fort Myer, Virginia, to Tizi Ouzou, Algeria, to Naples, Italy, and all the way up the peninsula, Keller had been away from his family 584 days. He'd missed one of his son's birthdays, and with the amount of work remaining, he was certain to miss another. Soon the combat troops would begin returning home to their families, but the work of the Monuments Men was increasing. Going home still seemed a long way off.

On May 4, while loading gear into the jeep for an inspection trip to Milan, a private came running up to Keller with an urgent telegram. The message, from Monuments Man Major Norman Newton with British Eighth Army, was short and to the point: The missing treasures from Florence were missing no longer. They could be found in the Alto Adige region, in the villages of San Leonardo in Passiria and Campo Tures. Newton's message lacked any details about the condition of the repositories or the works of art, but Keller knew that time was of the essence.

As much as he wanted to hop in the jeep with Bernholz and drive those 150 miles north, Keller had to be in Milan to hand over responsibility for the Lombardy region to Monuments Officer Lieutenant Perry Cott. For the time being, all he could do was notify Monuments Officer Lieutenant Colonel Ward-Perkins of the discovery and ask him to head north as soon as possible. Keller also sent a message to Fred Hartt ordering him to depart Florence for the Alto Adige region. Hartt had more knowledge than anyone about what had been stolen. He also had the all-important inventory lists, which they would need to check the contents and determine if anything was missing. With any luck, Keller hoped he could wrap up his work in Milan and still get to the two repositories in time to greet Ward-Perkins and Hartt.

Near Darmstadt, Germany: first week of May 1945

When Rorimer first heard the news, he immediately cabled SHAEF headquarters, but what he wanted to do was call Rose Valland. Colonel Kurt von Behr, the Nazi commandant of the Jeu de Paume who, along with Bruno Lohse, had threatened to kill her, had been found dead. In full dress uniform, the once-powerful head of the ERR in Paris had opened a 1918 vintage bottle of champagne, pouring one glass for his wife and one for himself, added a touch of cyanide to both, and cheated the hangman's noose.

The chain of events that followed were as sudden as they were dramatic. Mussolini's capture and grisly death at the hands of partisans, the news of Hitler's death in Berlin, and the German surrender in Italy all occurred in a matter of just four days. Something else happened during that period that made Rorimer's heart race: Lead elements of Seventh Army had captured Neuschwanstein Castle, apparently intact, and were awaiting his arrival.

Valland's pleas that he get to the castle with all due haste never left his thoughts. Taking no chances, Rorimer had forwarded that information to his commanders weeks earlier, making certain they knew the importance of the repository. Finally, the obstacles to getting to the castle were out of the way. Primed and full of excitement, Rorimer raced to the transport depot only to be informed that no vehicles were available.

After nine months of work as a Monuments Officer, crossing seven hundred war-torn miles, from Utah Beach in France to small towns deep in the heart of Nazi Germany, Rorimer wasn't about to let a lack of transportation stop him. Soon the war would be over; he was sure of it. Finding the remaining repositories was now more urgent than ever. Rorimer quickly cornered a Red Cross worker in a nearby office and, after explaining his predicament, talked him into lending one of their jeeps.

One of the other repositories on Valland's list happened to be on the way to Neuschwanstein Castle, so Rorimer decided to stop and inspect it. According to her notes, the Nazis were using a Carthusian monastery in the town of Buxheim, near Memmingen, just fifty miles north of the castle, to store overflow items and as a studio for the restoration of damaged works of art. A detachment of Seventh Army soldiers had already arrived and was busy securing the monastery from looting by displaced persons.

Rorimer quickly found what Valland had assured him was there. Looted Renaissance and eighteenth-century furniture filled the corridors. Some rooms were in shambles, with pottery and paintings lying about; others contained shelving with sculpture and art objects neatly stacked. Every space had something that belonged to someone else.

Wooden crates in an adjacent room, each bearing black stencil marks on the side, caught his eye. As he got closer, the lettering came into focus: D.W., the Nazi ERR inventory code for objects stolen from Pierre David-Weill, one of the world's most prominent collectors of art. Rorimer counted seventy-two crates in that one room alone. Upon entering the chapel, Rorimer stopped dead in his tracks. The Nazis had converted this place of worship into a storage facility for rugs and tapestries, all ERR loot stolen from the Rothschild family and other Jewish collectors. Every piece he had seen up to this point had passed through the Jeu de Paume Museum under the watchful eye of Rose Valland.

Rorimer barely had time to catch his breath when he found the ERR restoration studio and more than 150 paintings by some of the most admired artists in the world, including Goya, Watteau, Fragonard, Murillo, and Renoir. Few museum collections in the world could rival what filled just this one room. Valland had tried to prepare him for sights such as this; Jacques Jaujard had, too. But hearing about it couldn't compare with finally seeing it. "Works of art could no longer be thought of in ordinary terms—a roomful, a carload, a castle full, were the quantities we had to reckon with." If this was just the ERR overflow, what awaited him at Neuschwanstein Castle?

The sudden death of Walter Huchthausen one month earlier served as a constant reminder of the dangers of driving on the roads in Nazi Germany, even with vastly superior forces. After a restless night filled with anticipation of what he might find, Rorimer completed the journey to Füssen, a small town at the foot of the mountaintop castle, the following morning. Troops of the 20th Armored Division, which just days earlier had participated in the liberation of Dachau, the first concentration camp constructed by the Nazis, had acted on Rorimer's tip and secured the castle.

Local guidebooks described the castle of Neuschwanstein, built on a rugged cliff against a picturesque mountain backdrop, as the fairy-tale castle of King Ludwig II of Bavaria. But from Rorimer's point of view, it was nothing more than a "romantic and

Rorimer found stolen paintings inside the Nazi restoration studio at the Buxheim monastery.

Neuschwanstein Castle.

remote setting for a gangster crowd to carry on its art looting activities." Driving up the forested winding road in the crisp mountain air brought Rorimer and Major Duncan, of the 20th Armored Division, to the castle entrance. The cannon-mounted armored cars parked on either side of its great iron doors made quite an impression, even on Rorimer.

Christoph Wiesend, custodian of the castle for fourteen years, served as their guide and led them through the lower court entry and up the first of many steep flights of steps. At each door Wiesend stopped, reached for a large ring with dozens of skeleton keys, unlocked the door for all to enter, then turned and locked it behind him. The first room they entered contained crates stacked to the ceiling, each stenciled with an ERR inventory code that identified the Jewish collector from whom it had been stolen.

The small group continued ascending a spiral stairwell, stopping for the custodian to perform his door unlocking and locking ritual, only to find another room filled with more crates of art objects stolen from France, many with the shipping labels still intact. They also came across thirteen hundred paintings that belonged to German museums in Bavaria, including those in Munich. Some rooms contained rare furniture belonging to Paris collectors, while others had sculpture and art objects. Rorimer felt like he was in a trance seeing so many important art objects stored in such a place. Delving further would have to wait for another day.

The next room required two keys to open a concealed steel door. Valland's voice echoed in Rorimer's mind: "Get to the castle of Neuschwanstein quickly or run the risk of Bruno Lohse, or one of the other Nazi ERR gangsters, destroying the evidence of their looting operation." Had he made it in time? The room—more like a vault—didn't contain the ERR records as Rorimer had hoped, but instead was filled with thousands of pieces of silver from the David-Weill and other collections, along with two large chests of priceless medieval jewelry belonging to the Rothschild family.

Their mind-boggling tour moved on to the *Kemenate*, a room in the castle containing two coal stoves and proof that the Nazis had at least started if not completed the destruction of evidence. Rorimer grabbed a poker and pulled out what remained of a Nazi uniform. The sight of charred documents, including one with the signature of Adolf Hitler, made his heart sink.

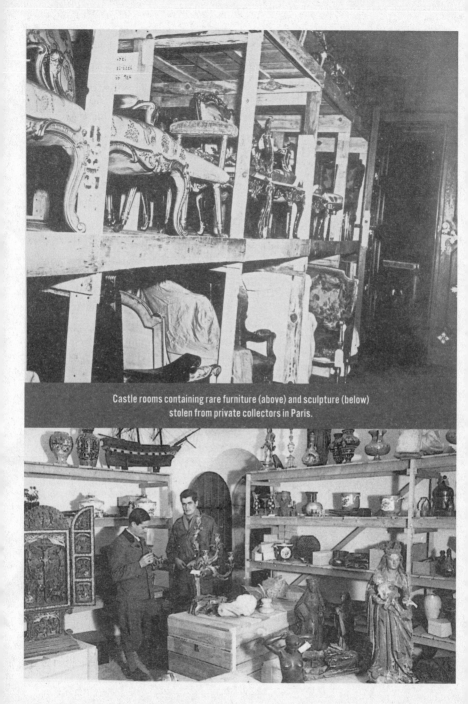

Castle rooms containing rare furniture (above) and sculpture (below) stolen from private collectors in Paris.

Rorimer holds a priceless piece of jewelry stolen from the Rothschild family in Paris.

Moments later, the custodian ushered them into yet another room. In an instant, Rorimer knew his search for the documents had come to an end. It was all there: file cabinets containing more than eight thousand photo negatives of stolen objects, individual catalogue cards of what had been taken and from whom, and thirty-nine brown leather albums containing photographs of the most important and valuable stolen works, a gift for the Führer from the head of the ERR, Alfred Rosenberg. This one room contained documents that not only proved the guilt of those involved but provided a road map of the ERR looting operation, which would enable the Monuments Men to run the theft in reverse and get the stolen items back to their rightful owners.

Rorimer discovered these file cabinets containing records documenting the Nazi looting operation in Paris.

While making plans to return to the castle the following day, Rorimer casually flipped through the security logbook until the sight of a familiar name caught his eye: Dr. Bruno Lohse. The custodian confirmed that Lohse had indeed been at the castle just one week earlier. To bag all the ERR records *and* possibly one of the most notorious thieves, all in a day? The very idea seemed too good to be true. After a few more questions, Rorimer learned that Lohse was hiding in a nearby village. Before departing, he ordered the sentry to deny admission to anyone who tried to enter—no exceptions.

Several hours later, with very little daylight left, Rorimer, accompanied by an army counterintelligence officer, pulled up to a Methodist nursing home. A short conversation with the mother

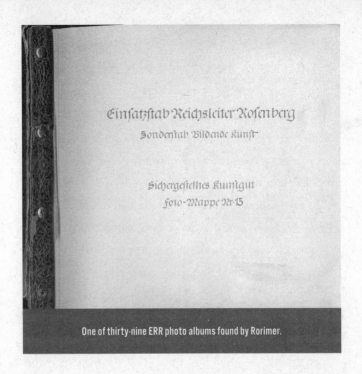

Einſatzſtab Reichsleiter Roſenberg

Sonderſtab Bildende Kunſt

Sichergeſtelltes Kunſtgut
Foto-Mappe Nr 15

One of thirty-nine ERR photo albums found by Rorimer.

superior confirmed that Lohse and Dr. Günther Schiedlausky, another ERR figure, were in residence. She hadn't wanted to admit them, but as they insisted, she figured that taking in "dogs and fiends" was a reasonable price to pay for liberation.

By 7:00 p.m., Dr. Bruno Lohse, successor to Colonel Kurt von Behr as chief of staff of the western division of the ERR, had a new temporary residence: the local jail. Thousands of paintings, drawings, sculpture, and pieces of furniture and jewelry belonging to private collectors in France had been found safe. Evidence of the Nazi looting operation in France had been secured. And the remaining living figure who had threatened to kill Rose Valland was under arrest. Rorimer considered it a pretty good day.

Near Munich, Germany: first week of May 1945

Three days later, a disconsolate Private Harry Ettlinger found himself sitting in a German military barracks on the outskirts of Munich. The war would end soon—everyone knew it—and he had yet to make a single meaningful contribution. Lost in thought, the sound of a nearby voice startled him.

"I hear you speak German," the voice said.

"Yes, sir," Private Ettlinger replied, almost saluting before noticing that the soldier speaking to him was also a private.

"I've been translating for the last two days. It's interesting work, but it's not for me. Perhaps you'd be interested in taking the job?"

Ettlinger jumped at the chance to do something, anything, while there was still something to be done. Following the directions the private had given him, he crossed the parade ground in front of the barracks and went to the second floor of the building that housed Seventh Army headquarters. Inside a small office he found two men working at their desks. A third man standing in the middle was asking questions rapid-fire.

"Are you the new translator?" asked the standing man, a lieutenant.

"Yes, sir. Private Harry Ettlinger, sir."

"You sound German, Ettlinger."

"American, sir. But born a German Jew. From Karlsruhe."

"Are you assigned to a unit, Ettlinger?"

"Not that I know of, sir."

The lieutenant reached for a stack of papers and handed them to Ettlinger. "Read these documents and tell us what's in them.

Just the gist, and anything specific: names, locations, works of art." And just that quickly, the lieutenant turned and hurried out the door.

"What a wheeler-dealer," Harry said to one of the men sitting at his desk.

"You don't know the half of it," the man replied. "He's trying to secure the two most sought-after buildings in Munich, Hitler's office and the former Nazi Party headquarters. Patton wants them for his regional headquarters, but knowing our lieutenant they'll soon be the MFAA collecting points for all the stolen art that's been found."

Seeing that Ettlinger looked a bit confused, the man laughed and introduced himself. "Welcome to Monuments work. I'm Lieutenant Charles Parkhurst, from Princeton University."

"Harry Ettlinger, from Newark. And who was *that*?"

"That was Lieutenant James Rorimer. Your new boss."

CHAPTER 17

SALT MINES
AND JAIL CELLS

Bernterode, Germany: first week of May 1945

After delivering the three cases of jewel-encrusted gold and silver
coronation items removed from Bernterode to the Reichsbank
vault in Frankfurt, Walker Hancock hurried back to the mine to
assist George Stout. Packing the rare books, paintings, tapestries,
and military banners and preparing them for removal to the surface started on May 4. Over the next three days, wet conditions
inside the mine, along with power outages that made it seem like

Monuments Men George Stout, Walter Hancock, and Steve Kovalyak, with an
unidentified soldier (second from left), at the Bernterode mine.

the darkness had swallowed them up, complicated an already exhausting process.

With Hitler dead and the war near an end, Hancock's mind periodically drifted to thoughts of seeing his wife, Saima, again. Another power outage threw the mine into total darkness, which brought work to a halt. Until the generators could be restarted, Hancock took advantage of the moment and reached for his flash-light—and a four-hundred-year-old painting by German master Lucas Cranach. Using the back of the wood-panel masterpiece as a writing desk, Hancock aimed the flashlight beam and began writing:

> *Dear Saima, You could never imagine what strange circumstances this is being written under. I can't tell you now, but I do want you to have a line actually written in one of the most unbelievable places . . . Geo. Stout is here to give me an urgently needed boost. He really is a friend in need.*

By the time the two packing crews finished work on the night of May 6, everything but the four caskets had been wrapped, water-proofed, transported to the surface, and placed in a shed at ground level. The following morning, Hancock directed the men, fifteen in all, as they strained to lift the casket containing Frau von Hindenburg, to carry it through the narrow chamber passageway, around a tight corner, and down the dimly lit corridor to the mine-shaft elevator fifteen hundred feet away. Maneuvering the lightest of the four caskets into the limited space of the elevator took some time, but soon it was on its way. The mortal remains of Frederick William I, the "soldier-king," followed hours later.

With more than half the day gone, Hancock decided to end his subterranean existence and rode to the surface atop the third casket, containing Field Marshal von Hindenburg. Only the massive steel chest with Frederick the Great remained. It took the underground evacuation team an hour to load the twelve-hundred-pound casket into the elevator. After four days of constant use, everyone hoped that the groaning elevator would survive the journey and make it to the surface.

A radio installed in the mine office next to the elevator landing was blaring in the background, but Stout and Hancock focused all their attention on the elevator and its cargo. The trip up normally took about six minutes, but rising at the slowest possible pace would more than double that time. Around 11:00 p.m., the sound of the elevator engines signaled that the eighteen-hundred-foot journey had started. At that moment, the unmistakable melody of "The Star-Spangled Banner" blared out from the radio. Upward Frederick the Great's remains rose toward the surface. His casket emerged when yet another well-known song began playing: "God Save the King." The war in Europe was over.

Altaussee, Austria: second week of May 1945

The German surrender brought an end to the fighting, but with hundreds of repositories to check and the big prize of Hitler's collection still missing, Posey and Kirstein hardly felt like celebrating. That changed quickly on May 12, however, when they learned that

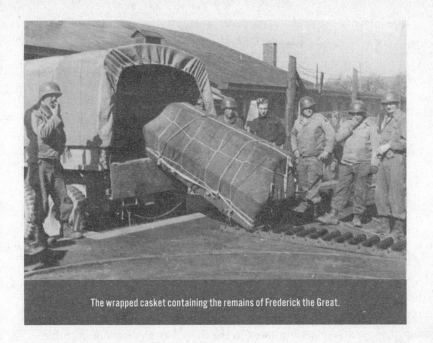

The wrapped casket containing the remains of Frederick the Great.

troops of the 80th Infantry Division had reached Altaussee. They set out immediately.

With Kirstein at the wheel and Posey serving as navigator, they headed south. In towns, it seemed like every piece of white cloth available was hanging out of windows. On the highways, they passed columns of surrendered German forces, still armed, which made a far greater and more ominous impression. Constantly outnumbered, Posey and Kirstein at times felt as if *they* were the prisoners. By the time they reached the border and crossed into Austria, the steady stream of defeated troops and displaced persons, including women and the wounded, had become a flood.

The sight of snowcapped mountains in the distance confirmed that they had entered the Salzkammergut, a mountainous region of Austria containing vast reserves of salt, which locals had mined for thousands of years. Winding hairpin roads took them up forested hills that opened into a series of valleys dotted with Alpine lakes and villages, each seemingly untouched by war. Soon they reached the tiny and picturesque hamlet of Altaussee, where an SS unit had just surrendered to U.S. forces. After a brief stop, they returned to their jeep to drive the short distance to the mine entrance, nervous and excited about what they would find.

On the last stretch of gravel-covered road, the two Monuments Men spotted a two-story rectangular building that housed the mine administration offices. Several days earlier, commanding officer Major Ralph Pearson and a truckload of GIs had captured the building and mine without a fight. Dozens of soldiers and miners were now milling about in the cleared area in front of the mine offices, awaiting orders.

After brief introductions, Major Pearson summarized the situation. The mine had been blown. Hearing the words they had feared most, Posey stared straight ahead, wanting more information. Kirstein, shoulders slumped, shook his head in disgust. Seeing their reactions, Pearson quickly clarified: It was the miners, not the Nazis, who had set off the detonations in the hopes of blocking the salt mine passageways. After entering the administration office building, which housed the Steinberg mine entrance to Altaussee, Pearson continued recounting what he knew.

Weeks earlier, August Eigruber, a Nazi fanatic loyal to the Führer, delivered to the mine for storage eight wooden cases marked "*Vorsicht—Marmor—nicht stürtzen*": "Attention—Marble—Do Not Drop." The miners assumed the contents were more statues

Monuments Man Captain Robert Posey (center) outside the Steinberg mine at Altaussee.

being shipped to the mine for storage. But the cases didn't contain statues. Inside each crate was a fifteen-hundred-pound high-explosive bomb, essential components of Eigruber's plan to destroy the mine and all its priceless contents.

Soon the miners discovered the contents of the crates. Fearful of seeing their livelihood destroyed along with the works of art, mining executives prevailed upon a high-ranking SS officer hiding nearby to order Eigruber to remove the bombs. The mining executives then immediately enacted their own plan to prevent Eigruber's men from entering the mine: They detonated 6 tons of explosives, sealing 137 tunnels.

Passageways providing access to the mine chambers were now blocked by rubble. The extent of damage to the works of art was

Gauleiter August Eigruber (far left) meeting with Hitler, years before his hastily arranged plan to destroy the works of art stored at Altaussee.

unknown. Standing in front of a pair of wooden doors on either side of a mine cart track, like the one they had seen at Merkers, Pearson handed Posey and Kirstein small acetylene lamps and encouraged them to have a look.

Unlike Merkers, the Altaussee mine contained a maze of horizontal shafts that ran for miles inside the Sandling Mountain, each branching off to some hollowed-out cavern. Timber lined the narrow upside-down-U-shaped passageways to protect against the immense pressure of the mountain. Holding the lamp in front of him, Posey bent his head slightly and stepped into the cold darkness. After months of searching for clues, the time had come to find out what remained of the Ghent Altarpiece and the rest of Hitler's hoard.

Slowly the two men proceeded in single file, rhythmically swinging their lamps side to side, unable to see more than a few feet in front of them. The mine was deathly silent but for the crunching of gravel beneath combat boots, an occasional trickle of water, and then a *yelp!* Kirstein inadvertently bumped his hand against the stone wall, scraping an exposed live electrical wire. The surprise of it startled him more than hurt him. The frigid air helped by partially numbing his hand. A few feet ahead they had to stop again, this time to crawl over debris, and that's when they noticed it: Someone had drilled a hole in a block of stone and inserted a stick of dynamite, which, for whatever reason, had not detonated. More exposed electrical wires, and now sticks of dynamite—Posey wondered what was next.

Taking a few more steps forward, Posey stopped so suddenly that Kirstein almost bumped into him. Standing shoulder to shoulder, they suspended their lamps to see a wall of rubble. Not even two thousand feet into the mine, they had reached a dead end. Posey wondered if the rubble from the explosions had damaged or destroyed whatever was hidden beyond the debris. Did the force of the explosions blast a path for water to flood the chambers and their contents? Until they could get on the other side, there was no way for Posey and Kirstein to know.

After exiting the mine, Posey hastily arranged a meeting with Major Pearson, an army combat engineer, and several of the miners. "How long will it take the workmen to clear the blocked passageways so we can get in?" he asked. The Austrian mine workers estimated seven to fifteen days at best. Posey, convinced the work could be done with the help of the army engineer within a week, perhaps even in just a couple of days, ordered the miners to start immediately and work around the clock. Each day of work meant a sleepless night for the two Monuments Men, wondering what they would find.

Milan, Italy: second week of May 1945

On May 11, with Fred Hartt in transit to the German art repositories at San Leonardo in Passiria and Campo Tures, Deane Keller was still in Milan, and none too happy about it. An army clerical error had prevented Lieutenant Perry Cott, the new Monuments Officer for the Lombardy region, from reporting for duty on time, so Keller had no choice but to extend his stay. At best, he hoped to meet Hartt the following evening in San Leonardo in Passiria.

Most of the cultural landmarks in Milan had sustained some degree of damage from Allied bombing, but the one that worried Keller the most was the church of Santa Maria delle Grazie and its refectory, housing Leonardo da Vinci's greatest artistic achievement, *The Last Supper*. The scene of devastation took his breath away:

> *Bomb hit of August 1943 in the cloister destroyed the right [east] wall of the refectory facing Leonardo's Last Supper. The roof was hit and collapsed when the wall fell. The painting had been sandbagged for protection, plus wood planks and iron scaffolding . . . The roof is nearing completion and the [east] wall has been reconstructed. Until there is no danger from the elements, or danger from what is left of the vaults, which is little, the painting will not be uncovered . . . Its fate is not known.*

For a fleeting moment, standing inside the long rectangular room, with the sound of workmen overhead hammering away, Keller thought about the Camposanto in Pisa and how close its frescoes had come to being lost forever. Had an incendiary instead of high-explosive bomb landed in the courtyard of Santa Maria delle Grazie, the wooden scaffolding would have ignited. The resulting fire would have baked Leonardo's masterpiece to the wall. After his experience in Pisa, Keller knew all too well how that would have turned out. But for the protective bracing installed by local art officials, the high-explosive detonation that destroyed the east wall and roof would have taken the north wall and the painting with it.

Inside the Santa Maria delle Grazie refectory, with its newly constructed east wall and roof, just weeks before the removal of the scaffolding covering *The Last Supper*.

A miracle had taken place inside this space on August 15, 1943; of that Keller was sure. All he could do now—all anyone could do—was hope that Leonardo's *The Last Supper* would emerge intact from behind the scaffolding. In his judgment, for that to happen, they needed a second miracle.

On the road to the Alto Adige region, Italy: second week of May 1945

With orders in hand, and an inventory of what had been stolen from the Florentine art repositories, a very excited Fred Hartt departed for San Leonardo and Campo Tures on May 10. He was accompanied by his driver, Franco Ruggenini, and Professor Filippo Rossi, Director of the Galleries of Florence. They drove two full days, covering 240 miles, through the vast countryside. Everywhere they looked, they saw

> shell holes, and mountainsides showing more shell holes
> than grass. The trees were shaved into spikes by the
> passing shells, the farmhouses reduced to sand heaps, the
> roads torn by artillery and mines, the villages smashed
> and tottering, reeking sharply of death in the warm air of
> a spring morning . . . Mass raids of Flying Fortresses had
> altered the very landscape, plowing it into craters twenty
> feet deep, leaving freight and passenger trains dangling
> into the muddy stream like bunches of grapes.

Lucky 13 and its passengers stopped in Bolzano on May 11. Hartt desperately wanted to continue, but darkness argued against it. Just thirty-five miles and a few lousy hours of sleep separated him from the Florentine treasures. Finding a hotel in Bolzano proved nearly impossible. Armed and arrogant, lingering German officers occupied all the best lodging in the city. SS generals drove through town in cars loaded with women. Drivers of German staff cars and armored personnel carriers took delight in running U.S. Army vehicles off the road. The sudden end to the war resulted in Allied forces being greatly outnumbered, perhaps ten-to-one or more, by German military personnel in the Alto Adige region. Until reinforcements arrived, Hartt had orders: Avoid incidents and keep a low profile.

The following morning, arriving to the sound of honking geese and screaming children, Franco pulled Lucky 13 up to a three-story building that had once served as the town jail, and stopped. Only iron bars on the ground-floor windows provided a

The jail in San Leonardo in Passiria, Italy.

hint of the building's previous use. After identifying himself to the security detachment from the 88th Infantry Division—known as the "Blue Devils"—that had arrived several days earlier, Hartt waited while a GI fumbled through a massive ring of keys. Impatience quickly changed to excitement as Hartt entered the dark and damp ground floor hallway. Then another delay: The individual jail cells had to be unlocked.

With the jingling of forty skeleton keys, it took what for Hartt felt like an eternity for the nervous GI to find the right one. When he finally opened the door, Hartt nearly fainted. Inside the damp, narrow cell, leaning one against the other, painted sides exposed, were some of the masterpieces stolen from the repository in Montagnana the previous summer.

The first cell alone left him speechless. He immediately recognized Caravaggio's painting *Bacchus*, and other paintings by Rubens, Titian, and Dosso Dossi, propped against the wall like prisoners from the pages of his art history books. Moments later, Hartt jumped when Rossi let out a shriek of joy. There before them were the two fifteenth-century paintings by German master Lucas Cranach, *Adam* and *Eve*, stolen by SS Colonel Langsdorff nine months earlier.

Hartt found other paintings by Botticelli, Andrea del Sarto, Signorelli, and Lorenzo Monaco stacked every which way on the wood plank floors of another cell. The overcrowding of paintings inside such small spaces prevented him from seeing everything that the Germans had stashed inside the jail. Conducting an inventory would have to wait for another day.

He tried to take it all in, but his mind was racing. Cell after

Professor Filippo Rossi standing next to a painting of *Eve*, by German master Lucas Cranach.

This painting by Italian artist Filippino Lippi, was one of more than three hundred found inside the San Leonardo jail by Fred Hartt.

cell, floor upon floor, three hundred paintings—more than half of them among the most important in the world—had survived being transported hundreds of miles over bombed-out roads, stacked side by side on open trucks, many with no more protection than a few blankets and strands of straw. Miraculously, aside from one painting that suffered a split down the entire length of the panel, most of the damage consisted of relatively minor scratches to the paintings and frames from handling and transportation.

It was late, so the three men returned to Bolzano hoping to find Deane Keller and to prepare for the next day's trip to the second art repository, in Campo Tures. Hartt knew that they had been extremely lucky their first day out. With hundreds of works of art still unaccounted for, including all the sculpture, plenty could still go wrong.

CHAPTER 18

CLOSURE

Campo Tures, Italy: May 13, 1945

Early in the morning on May 13, Hartt and Rossi departed Bolzano for the two-hour drive to Campo Tures. The engine of Lucky 13 moaned as it made the gradual climb through the mountainous valley. Snowmelt-filled streams and verdant meadows sprinkled with gingerbread cottages provided a beautiful distraction from war, but Hartt thought only of the hundreds of Florentine treasures that he hadn't found the day before inside the San Leonardo jail.

Months of investigative work during the winter lull had paid dividends. More than just arriving to the Alto Adige region with the inventory of stolen objects, Hartt had also gathered extensive details about the German art looting operation. Florentine superintendent Giovanni Poggi recounted how SS Colonel Alexander Langsdorff, head of the Kunstschutz in Italy, had personally assured him that not a single work of art would be removed from any of the thirty-eight Florentine repositories unless they were in immediate danger. What he didn't tell Poggi was at that very moment, German troops were already loading paintings and sculpture onto trucks for the trip north. And now, just a few miles up the road, Hartt hoped to confront the man whom he believed was responsible for executing the "greatest single art-looting operation in recorded history."

At the end of the V-shaped valley, Hartt could see two prominent castles set against snow-covered Alpine peaks. The larger of the two, Taufers Castle, was nestled on a hill behind the small town of Campo Tures. Neumelans Castle, which reportedly housed the Florentine treasures, marked the beginning of the town and was constructed on the valley floor. A curious mix of GIs from the 85th—the "Custer" Division—Italian partisans, and German soldiers had been guarding Neumelans, a sixteenth-century Tyrolean castle, for about one week while waiting on the Monuments Men to arrive.

As Franco slowed Lucky 13 to a stop in front of the stone wall perimeter, Hartt peered through the metal gate and noticed a very irritated-looking German officer standing in front of the castle door. Rossi recognized him immediately as the man who had promised to protect the cultural treasures of Florence when, in fact, he had facilitated their theft, SS Colonel Langsdorff. The introductions were strained. When the SS colonel criticized Hartt for the delay in getting to the two repositories—after all, he explained,

British Monuments Officer John Bryan Ward-Perkins (far right) supervises SS Colonel Alexander Langsdorff (second from right) and others at the Campo Tures art repository.

he had been on location since April 30 on direct orders from SS General Wolff—and sought credit for his role in protecting the works from Florence, Hartt snapped. After giving Langsdorff a brief tongue-lashing, Hartt entered the castle hoping to find the remaining stolen masterpieces.

In contrast to the damp jail cells at San Leonardo, the dry, airy, high-ceilinged rooms here made Neumelans Castle an ideal storage facility, to Hartt and Rossi's initial relief. They quickly found some of the less important paintings from the Florence museums and works belonging to private collectors. Another room contained small bronzes, ceramics, and tapestries, but still no sculpture. "Where are the works by Michelangelo and Donatello?" Hartt

SS General Karl Wolff.

demanded to know. When someone mentioned the nearby carriage house, Hartt bolted out the front door.

The Gothic stone carriage house had long since been converted into a garage with two large wooden double doors. Hartt wanted them unlocked and opened immediately. A couple of GIs peeled back the creaky doors while everyone watched in rapt anticipation. The darkness of the interior made it difficult for Hartt and Rossi to make out the contents, but once their eyes adjusted, they smiled with glee. The carriage house was packed, wall-to-wall, with crates containing the Florentine treasures. Hartt squeezed in between the tight spaces and found Donatello's sculpture *Saint George* and Michelangelo's *Bacchus*, signature pieces he once feared might be lost forever.

Until Hartt, Rossi, and Keller could inventory the contents of both repositories and check the results against the list that Hartt had brought from Florence, there was no way to know for certain that they had found everything. Transporting a group of the most important works of art in the world nearly three hundred war-torn miles back to Florence presented another obstacle. But those would be challenges for another day. For now, with the cultural and artistic treasures of Florence safe, and Langsdorff and several other members of the Kunstschutz under detention, Hartt felt elation—and relief.

Altaussee, Austria: May 13, 1945

Less than 140 miles away, Posey and Kirstein entered the Steinberg mine at Altaussee for a second time, accompanied by two Austrian miners. Laboring through the night, mine workers had cleared enough rubble for one man at a time to squeeze through the opening. They followed the two miners down the main passageway they had walked the previous day until a pile of sledgehammers and shovels leaning up against the walls told them that this was the spot. At the top of a fifteen-foot-high rubble pile Posey could see a narrow crawl space illuminated by the glow of one of the miner's lamps.

Feeling a mixture of fear and excitement about what he might find, Posey climbed the forty-five-degree slope of debris using his hands and feet, grabbed an acetylene lamp from the lead miner, and disappeared through the opening. Kirstein did the same and followed. From the other side, Posey could see that the miners had done their job well. The detonation had blocked a single short passageway but caused no other apparent damage. Most important, Posey didn't see any sign of flooding.

The two Monuments Men and one of the miners soon reached an iron door with two padlocks, which they ordered removed. The narrow path opened into a small hollowed-out chamber. Ducking down, they entered and saw resting on four empty cardboard boxes eight of the twelve panels of the Ghent Altarpiece.

Eight months had passed since Posey received his first briefing package photo of the van Eyck brothers' masterpiece, and three years since its theft, and now the "odd couple," Captain Robert Posey and Private First Class Lincoln Kirstein, had found it. For a fleeting moment, its beauty seemed to wash away all the ugliness they had seen since setting foot on the beaches of Normandy.

Posey and Kirstein slid over this rubble pile to access the Steinberg mine chambers.

"By our flickering acetylene lamps," Kirstein wrote, "the miraculous jewels of the Crowned Virgin seemed to attract this light. Calm and beautiful, the altarpiece was, quite simply, there."

With their hearts racing, Posey and Kirstein maneuvered around another blocked passageway that took them deeper into the dark, frigid mine. Soon the narrow path opened into a much larger cavern that vaulted nearly three stories high. The floor of the mine had been covered with wooden boards. Heavy beams supported racks filled with hundreds of paintings. Off to the side, almost as a castaway, lying on her shoulder with her son firmly embraced between her legs, was Michelangelo's Bruges *Madonna*, still wrapped in the mattress mentioned in the reports of British Monuments Man Ronald Balfour.

The Monuments Men found these disassembled panels from the Ghent Altarpiece inside the Steinberg mine.

Overwhelmed by what they had seen and unable to reach other chambers, Posey and Kirstein called it a day and followed the lead miner back to the surface. Realizing that much, if not all, of what Hermann Bunjes had told them was true—that somewhere in the Altaussee mine they would find thousands of objects destined for Hitler's Führermuseum—Posey stepped up security.

One major problem emerged after another. The mountain had many access points besides the main mine tunnel entrance Posey and Kirstein had been using. By entering through one of the abandoned mine chambers that had not flooded from use, a person could gain access to the caverns that Posey was desperately trying to secure. Then Posey learned that an ex–mine foreman had a duplicate set of keys to all the security doors. When two gunmen

George Stout hoists the Bruges *Madonna*, still wrapped in the mattress German soldiers used when stealing it.

sent by someone in one of the offices of Nazi ERR leader Alfred Rosenberg arrived at the mine in an empty truck, no doubt unaware that U.S. forces had taken control, Posey had them arrested.

Within three days, the Austrian miners had cleared enough debris that Posey and Kirstein were able to reenter the mine to inspect several other chambers. The two Monuments Men entered a cavern known as a *Mineralienkammer*, which contained various crystal samples found in the mine—and the remaining panels of the Ghent Altarpiece. They also found many other valuable paintings, including "R-1," Vermeer's *The Astronomer*, the first object stolen by the Nazis from the Paris branch of the Rothschild family. Keeping track of all the riches they had seen was becoming increasingly difficult.

Another cavern used as a memorial chamber contained rare gold coins and medals as well as valuable collections of military guns, swords, and other weapons. In the *Springerwerke* chamber, they found all eleven paintings that Balfour had reported stolen from the church in Bruges the night the sailors came for the Michelangelo, and hundreds of paintings looted from thirty Jewish Viennese private collectors.

The extensive network of tunnels that connected different levels of the mine complicated the inspection process. Then there was the temperature. Working inside a mountain that functioned like

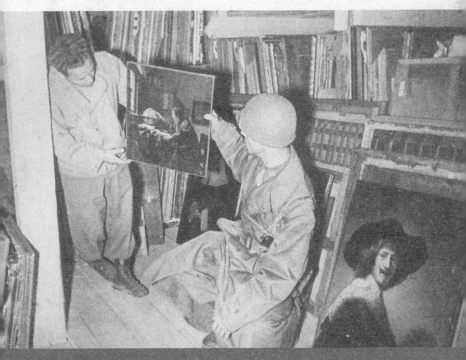

Monuments Men holding Vermeer's *The Astronomer*,
perhaps the single work of art that Hitler coveted most.

a giant refrigerator set at forty-six degrees chilled one to the bone, especially for newcomers like Posey and Kirstein. Soon enough they reached the *Kammergrafe*, a huge cavern that housed rack after rack of paintings and other art objects that made it a museum unto itself. Kirstein, who had lived a life surrounded by the arts, felt overwhelmed with the variety of what each bin contained, including drawings, prints, etchings, rare books, a theatrical collection, armor, sculpture, tapestries, and furniture.

While Posey added to his inspection notes, Kirstein began flipping through some of the paintings stacked in a different area of the cavern. These were masterpieces of the very highest quality, including Pieter Bruegel the Elder's *The Blind Leading the Blind*, Titian's painting *Danaë*, and other stellar works by Botticelli, El Greco, and Raphael. After a little more digging, Kirstein discovered bronze sculpture from the ancient site of Pompeii. When he saw the words "Monte Cassino" written in crayon on the

The Monuments Men found thousands of stolen paintings stored inside this hollowed-out mine chamber.

temporary frame of one of the paintings, he realized that these were the treasures from the National Museum in Naples that had been stored at the Abbey of Monte Cassino and later stolen by the Hermann Göring Tank Division.

Posey knew right away that conducting any kind of inventory was a job for George Stout and a team of people that he and Kirstein didn't presently have. To prepare for Stout's arrival, Posey ordered the miners to work around-the-clock shifts clearing rubble from the passageways of the Steinberg mine at Altaussee, the closest anyone would ever come to finding Aladdin's magic treasure cave.

A painting by Italian master Bernardino Luini, one of the treasures stolen by the Hermann Göring Tank Division from the Abbey of Monte Cassino.

CHAPTER 19

GOING HOME

Altaussee, Austria: late May to mid-July 1945

By the time word of the discovery at Altaussee reached George Stout, he and Walker Hancock had already relocated the treasures—and four coffins—from the Bernterode mine to a temporary collecting point in Marburg and were in the process of evacuating the contents of the Siegen discovery. Leaving Hancock behind to supervise the remaining work, Stout departed on May 21 for Altaussee.

With the miners still at work clearing the passageways, Stout used the time to develop a preliminary removal and transfer plan. Having worked with him at the Merkers mine, Posey knew that Stout would need to see summary reports of the mine contents to make those calculations. He had them ready.

Sitting inside the mine administration office, beneath an annoyingly dim bulb, Stout strained his eyes as he scanned the mine logbook. After studying just a few pages, he realized that emptying Altaussee of its contents wasn't going to take days or weeks, but months. The quantity of what Hitler had accumulated inside this one mine was staggering. According to the logbook, the various chambers of the Steinberg mine at Altaussee contained:

6,577 paintings

230 drawings or watercolors

954 prints

137 pieces of sculpture

129 pieces of arms and armor

79 baskets of objects

484 cases of objects thought to be archives

78 pieces of furniture

122 tapestries

181 cases of books

1,200–1,700 cases of books or similar

283 cases of contents completely unknown

Clearing the mine passageways was agonizingly slow work, but in mid-June, Stout commenced the first shipment of Hitler's hoard to a central collecting point that Jim Rorimer had established in Munich. A shortage of food, sleeping quarters, and power had everyone in a cranky mood. Incessant rain added to the complications, but still the work continued. Day after day, Stout and his small team loaded trucks with works of art stolen by Hitler's lackeys and watched as they descended the hazardous mountain road bound for Munich.

On the morning of July 10, Stout gathered his team for a short announcement. "This looks like a good day for the gold-seal products," he said. His understated manner caught no one by surprise. The team had spent days crating each separate panel of the Ghent Altarpiece and wrapping the Bruges *Madonna* expecting that they would soon be on their way. That day had now come.

George Stout (center, wearing helmet) crating the central panel of the Ghent Altarpiece.

Using a specially designed rope and pulley system, Stout carefully elevated Michelangelo's marble sculpture about four feet off the ground, then gently lowered it a few inches onto one of the mine carts that had been positioned beneath it. "I think we could bounce her from Alp to Alp, all the way to Munich, without doing her any harm," Stout confidently told one of his coworkers.

Slowly Stout walked alongside the mine cart, his hand gently resting on the Madonna that his friend Ronald Balfour had so desperately hoped to find. Down the dark and narrow passageway, the miners pushed the cart past several chambers that Stout and his team had already emptied. After a bend in the track, it was a straight shot to the mine entrance doors. They offloaded the Bruges *Madonna* and returned for the crates containing the panels of the Ghent Altarpiece.

The following morning, after double-checking that the precious cargo in each truck was firmly secured in place, Stout boarded the lead vehicle and gave the signal to head out. The time had come for the Ghent Altarpiece and Bruges *Madonna*, two of the most important and beautiful works of art in Western civilization, to begin their journey home.

Campo Tures, Italy: late May to late July 1945

Deane Keller finally connected with Fred Hartt for his first visit to the Alto Adige art repositories on May 14. They began at Campo Tures, then drove to San Leonardo the following day. While Hartt rejoiced about finding the masterpieces intact, Keller was already focused on logistics: hundreds of paintings lying about uncrated, persistent shortages of packing materials, roads to Florence that were pulverized, and a railway system that didn't function because Allied aircraft had destroyed it.

Keller initially hoped to transport the works to Florence in a truck convoy that would conclude with a prominent ceremony, allowing Florentines to bear witness to the return of their art. For his plan to succeed, he needed fifty trucks. The only person he knew with that kind of authority was the man who had come to the rescue of the Camposanto, General Hume. "Remember how crowded the Piazza della Signoria was when they put up Michelangelo's David?" he quipped in his request to the general. "You don't, and neither do I, but that's the idea." Alas, the trucks were not available; the army had a duty to feed the starving populations of Milan and other northern Italian cities. He would have to find another solution.

Keller's drawing of one of his interrogations of a German officer.

Dusting off old plans, Keller realized that it might be possible to return the Florentine treasures by rail now that the bridge crossing the Po River neared completion. With Keller at Campo Tures and Hartt at San Leonardo, the two Monuments Men set to work inventorying and packing the art. Hartt soon discovered that ten paintings from the Florence repository at Montagnana, including several of immense value and importance, never made it to the Alto Adige. German soldiers had stolen them en route.

On July 20, Keller watched as 109 crates of paintings from San Leonardo and 46 crates of mostly sculpture from Campo Tures were loaded onto the art train at Bolzano. In filling out a freight

Keller (center, back turned) supervises the removal of sculpture from the carriage house in Campo Tures, Italy.

waybill for the shipment, Keller noted the contents as "art treasures." Under remarks, he wrote simply, "Extreme care necessary." The form also had a space to declare the value of the shipment. After conferring with Professor Rossi, Keller adjusted his glasses, took a deep breath, and wrote in the blank, "$500,000,000."

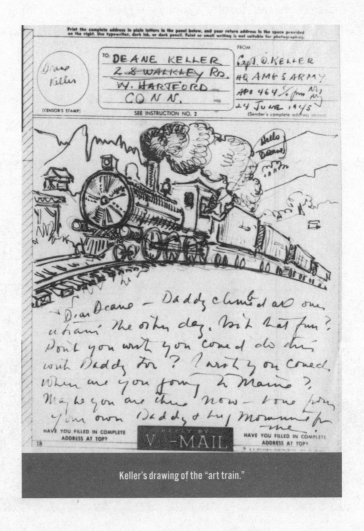

Keller's drawing of the "art train."

The art train arrived in Florence in just under twenty-four hours without incident. The following day, a small convoy, headed by a jeep loaded with MPs, then followed by Hartt in Lucky 13, Keller and Bernholz in their jeep, and six Fifth Army trucks containing some of the art treasures, rolled into the Piazza della Signoria, where thousands of cheering Florentines had gathered. The trucks parked within a few feet of where Nazi leader Adolf Hitler and Italian dictator Benito Mussolini had shared their twisted vision of a new world order seven years earlier. A banner attached to the side of one of the Fifth Army trucks had an inscription in Italian, which, translated, read plainly, "The Florentine works of art return from the Alto Adige to their home."

The triumphant return of the Tuscan treasures to Florence.

Bavaria, Germany: last half of May 1945

After four years of watching Nazi Reichsmarschall Hermann Göring and his SS henchmen use her country like a piggy bank, Rose Valland finally had a chance to do something about it. Being commissioned into the French First Army provided her with a uniform and transportation. Captain Rose Valland headed straight for the Neuschwanstein Castle.

Valland reached the castle in mid-May, just ten days after Rorimer's astonishing discovery. Driving up the same winding road, she got as far as the great iron doors of the castle before a

French First Army Captain Rose Valland.

young GI on guard duty, having no idea who she was, denied her entry. Even through her disappointment, Valland felt a measure of satisfaction. By going to such lengths to protect the stolen works inside the castle, Rorimer had proven to be the ally and friend that France needed.

Hoping to connect with Rorimer and let him know about her new position, Valland turned the jeep around and headed for the MFAA office in Munich. This was just the beginning of her mission in Germany hunting for stolen objects. A visit inside the castle would have to wait for another day.

Rorimer and his new translator, nineteen-year-old Private Harry Ettlinger, moved from place to place at a breakneck pace, rarely setting foot inside his Munich office. After four months of sitting around doing nothing, that suited Harry just fine. Working alongside such a "wheeler-dealer" was exciting. One day he found himself translating for Rorimer as he interrogated a high-level Nazi; the next they were on their way to investigate the discovery of some new art repository.

Toward the end of May, Harry accompanied Rorimer to Neuschwanstein Castle, a place he had grown up hearing about but had never seen. Walking through the iron gates was like stepping into a fairy tale from his childhood, but the fairy tale became a nightmare when he entered the first of dozens of rooms bulging with objects stolen from Jewish collectors in France. Harry couldn't help but wonder how many of the Jewish owners were still alive to claim their belongings.

Because the objects inside the castle had come from France, Rorimer saw no reason to send them to one of the Allied collecting points for processing. Better to ship them back directly. Organizing the trains and emptying the castle might take several months, but until then, everything inside was safe.

The arrest of Nazi Reichsmarschall Hermann Göring on May 9 created quite a stir. His wife was found carrying stolen paintings in her handbag. His trains, which had been abandoned, were overflowing with loot. Then troops of the 101st Airborne found a freshly plastered cave containing hundreds of gold and silver objects, paintings, and sculpture. While Rorimer investigated, Harry hitched a ride to Hitler's mountain chalet, the Berghof. British bombing had damaged portions of the home. Retreating SS troops had tried but failed to burn down what remained. And now

Part of the Göring loot found in a hidden bunker by troops of the 101st Airborne.

Monuments Man Harry Ettlinger, an American, and the last Jewish boy in his hometown of Karlsruhe to celebrate a bar mitzvah before the Nazis unleashed their reign of terror, stood in the expansive windowsill of the home of Adolf Hitler, overlooking a free Germany.

The grand window inside the fire-damaged remains of Adolf Hitler's mountain home, the Berghof.

EPILOGUE

World War II was the most destructive conflict in history, claiming sixty-five million lives, including six million Jews systematically persecuted and murdered by the Nazi regime. The study of this war often focuses on the motivations and actions of the dictators who set these cataclysmic events into motion. The story of the Monuments Men instead highlights the actions of a few good men who, with established careers and families and no reason to volunteer for military service, risked their lives to preserve our shared cultural heritage. In a break with civilizations past—and a victory for the rule of law—it was the policy of the Western Allies to return stolen objects to the countries from which they had been taken for ultimate restitution to the rightful owner. The last Monuments Man didn't depart Europe for home until 1951. By that time, the Monuments Men had overseen the return of nearly four million stolen objects. Good had triumphed over evil.

While this book focuses on the wartime experiences of ten Monuments Men and Rose Valland, there were in fact about 350 or so Monuments Men and Women from 14 nations who served from 1943 to 1951. Initially, the operation comprised Americans and citizens of the British Commonwealth, but the liberation of Western European nations expanded the participation as

Monuments Officers from France, Holland, Belgium, and other European nations volunteered.

Rose Valland remained in Germany for several years after the war, tracking down thousands of stolen works of art. Finding household belongings and personal items taken from the homes of Paris's Jews, which filled 29,436 German railroad cars—in most cases all that remained of the more than 70,000 French Jews who perished in Nazi concentration camps—proved exceedingly difficult. Far from being a shy and timid curator, Valland was bold, strong-minded, intelligent, and courageous. She was a tireless and vocal advocate for the restitution of stolen art until her death in 1980. For her efforts, Rose Valland received the French Legion of Honor and the Medal of Resistance and was made a Commander of the Order of Arts and Letters, making her the most decorated French woman of her time.

Ronald Balfour is buried in the British cemetery outside Cleve, Germany, not too far from where he was killed in action. In 1954, his photograph was placed in the Cleve archive building beside a plaque that reads, in part, "This gentleman saved as a British Monuments Officer precious medieval archives and items of lower Rhine towns. Honor to his memory."

Walter Huchthausen is buried in the Netherlands American Cemetery in Margraten, Holland, among more than eighty-three hundred fallen comrades. His death was a devastating blow to the van Schaïk family, who had befriended Hutch when he was stationed near their home in Maastricht, Holland, several months before he departed on his fateful mission. Frieda van Schaïk was

The author and Monuments Man Harry Ettlinger at the Netherlands American Cemetery, visiting the grave of Monuments Man Captain Walter Huchthausen.

among the first to care for his grave, a tradition that continues through the Foundation for Adopting Graves program and its adopters. Huub, Marlie, and Peter Schouteten care for Walter's grave today. They are the most recent, living proof of the eternal commitment of the people of Holland to honor those who made the ultimate sacrifice for their freedom.

Walker Hancock returned home to his wife, Saima, at the end of 1945. Soon they became parents to a daughter, Deanie. Hancock continued to be a sought-after sculptor and teacher. His most enduring work is the Pennsylvania Railroad War Memorial, located in the 30th Street train station in Philadelphia, a tribute to the thirteen

Walker Hancock's towering sculpture *Angel of the Resurrection*, at the 30th Street train station in Philadelphia.

hundred railroad employees who died during World War II. He received the National Medal of Arts and the Presidential Medal of Freedom from President George H. W. Bush. Walker Hancock died in 1998, beloved to his last day by all who knew him.

Robert Posey accompanied the Ghent Altarpiece to Belgium in August 1945, the very first work of stolen art restituted after the end of the war in Europe. He returned home to Alice, "Woogie," and the Zoo in September 1945 and resumed his career as an architect, working on such notable projects as Sears Tower in Chicago and the Lever House skyscraper in New York. He received the

President George H. W. Bush enjoys the unveiling of his bust alongside sculptor Walker Hancock.

Order of Leopold, one of the highest honors in Belgium, and the French Legion of Honor. Robert Posey died in 1977.

Lincoln Kirstein also returned home in September 1945. The following year, he and his business partner, choreographer George Balanchine, established a new dance troupe, the Ballet Society (renamed the New York City Ballet in 1948), one of the most influential dance companies of the twentieth century. By the end of his life, Kirstein was widely considered one of the major cultural figures of his generation. He received the National Medal of Arts and the Presidential Medal of Freedom from President Ronald Reagan. Lincoln Kirstein died in 1996.

Fred Hartt returned home in 1946 to begin a lifelong teaching career as one of the foremost experts on art of the Renaissance, but only after being made an honorary citizen by the city of Florence for his service during the war. In 1966, he traveled back to Florence to help combat raging floodwaters that threatened much of the city. During his prolific career, he published eighteen books, including *The History of Italian Renaissance Art*, still a widely used textbook on the subject. Fred Hartt died in 1993. He is buried in Florence, Italy, adjacent to the eleventh-century San Miniato al Monte Church, overlooking the only city he ever considered home.

Jim Rorimer was the first of several Monuments Men to receive the French Legion of Honor. He continued work as a Monuments Officer until 1946, when he returned to New York City to become the director of The Cloisters, home of The Metropolitan Museum's medieval art collection. In 1955, he became the sixth director of The Metropolitan Museum of Art. Extremely proud of his military service, Rorimer wore his army combat boots to work almost every day. His sudden death in 1966 cut short a brilliant career. When asked his formula for success, Rorimer offered, "A good start, a willingness—even eagerness—to work beyond the call of duty, a sense of fair play, and a recognition of opportunities before and when they arrive. In other words, it is important to find a course and steer it." He might as well have been describing the MFAA and his role within it.

George Stout, the father of the MFAA operation, returned to the United States in late July 1945, but not for long. By October, he was in Japan setting up the Arts and Monuments Division in the Pacific Theater. After his deployment to Japan, Stout accepted a position as the director of the Worcester Art Museum, and later the Isabella Stewart Gardner Museum in Boston. Like the other Monuments Men, and World War II veterans in general, he seldom discussed his military service. George Stout died in 1978. Monuments Officer Craig Hugh Smyth, who worked with Stout near the end of his tour of duty in Europe, described Stout as "a leader—quiet, unselfish, modest, yet very strong, very thoughtful and remarkably innovative . . . One believed what he said; one wanted to do what he proposed." Perhaps Lincoln Kirstein put it best: "George Stout was the greatest war hero of all time—he actually saved all the art that everybody else talked about."

Deane Keller didn't return home until May 1946, after two and a half years of military service overseas. In addition to the Order of the Crown of Italy and the U.S. Legion of Merit, Keller was made a member of the Order of Saint John Lateran by the Vatican and awarded the British Empire Medal. He resumed his teaching career at Yale, where his uniform hung proudly in a corner of his classroom. One of his students, also a World War II veteran, noted that "Keller tried to hide his humanity and soul with gruffness, but those of us who had served in uniform could see he was a pussycat underneath." During the 1950s he became the unofficial portrait painter at Yale. One of his most prized subjects was a portrait of his friend and driver, Charley Bernholz. Deane Keller died in 1992. Portions of his ashes are interred on the north side of the Camposanto in Pisa, Italy, the only non-Italian to be so honored.

Harry Ettlinger was discharged in August 1946 and returned to New Jersey to attend college on the GI Bill. With a degree in mechanical engineering, Harry worked for Singer, overseeing the manufacture of sewing machine motors. He later changed careers and accepted a position in the defense industry. In his last position,

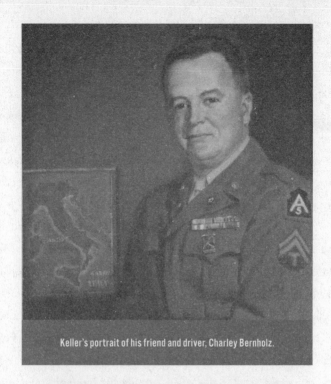

Keller's portrait of his friend and driver, Charley Bernholz.

DEANE KELLER
PITTORE
14 XII 1901 12 IV 1992

UFFICIALE DELLA V ARMATA STATONITENSE
NEL SETTEMBRE · OTTOBRE 1944
INCOMBENTE ANCORA LA MINACCIA NEMICA
PROCURO' MATERIALI E MEZZI
PERCHE' QUESTO CAMPOSANTO
QUASI DISTRUTTO DALLA GUERRA
FOSSE PRESERVATO DALL'ESTREMA ROVINA

AMICISSIMUS AD AMICOS
MAGGIO 2000

The tombstone honoring the resting place of Monuments Man
Deane Keller at the Camposanto in Pisa.

he served as deputy program director in the development and production of the guidance system for the submarine-launched Trident missile. Harry has remained active in veterans' groups and Jewish causes and is a lifelong supporter of the Raoul Wallenberg Foundation. In October 2015, speaking in the halls of Congress, he accepted on behalf of the Monuments Men and Women of all fourteen nations the Congressional Gold Medal, the highest civilian honor bestowed by the United States.

And what of the murderers and thieves? Nazi leader Adolf Hitler did not die "fighting till his last breath against Bolshevism," as the May 1 radio announcement proclaimed. The father of the Holocaust committed suicide in an underground bunker, but only after leading his nation and its people to utter ruin.

Harry Ettlinger accepting the Congressional Gold Medal on behalf of the Monuments Men and Women of all fourteen nations.

U.S. forces arrested Nazi Reichsmarschall Hermann Göring on May 9, 1945. At first, he denied his role in the Holocaust, proclaiming, "I revere women and I think it unsportsmanlike to kill children . . . For myself I feel quite free of responsibility for the mass murders." In a private interview during the Nuremberg trials, Göring noted, "They tried to paint a picture of me as a looter of art treasures . . . However, none of my so-called looting was illegal . . . I always paid for them or they were delivered through the Hermann Göring Division, which, together with the Rosenberg Commission [ERR] supplied me with my art collection." On October 15, 1946, the night before his scheduled hanging, Göring, like Hitler, cheated the hangman's noose and committed suicide.

Alfred Rosenberg, leader of the ERR and Hitler's chief racial theorist, denied complicity in any wrongdoing. He was tried, found guilty of war crimes, and hanged on October 16, 1946.

August Eigruber, the Nazi fanatic who ordered bombs placed inside the Altaussee mine, was arrested in May 1945. He was tried and found guilty of war crimes committed at Mauthausen concentration camp. Unrepentant to the bitter end, his last words before the trapdoor of the gallows opened were "Heil Hitler!"

Hermann Bunjes, the art scholar who sold his soul in Paris to Göring and the ERR, and later tried to buy it back by telling what he knew to Monuments Men Robert Posey and Lincoln Kirstein, hanged himself from the window of his prison cell on July 25, 1945. He left his family penniless and starving in a broken Germany.

Bruno Lohse, who as Göring's representative to the ERR in Paris threatened to kill Rose Valland, later admitted that he had been involved with the looting operation in Paris, but he insisted that he had done nothing wrong. In exchange for leniency, Lohse testified against some fellow looters and helped French authorities locate several caches of stolen art. He was released from prison in 1950 and resumed his art dealing activities, insisting he was a legitimate art dealer who had been a victim of the Nazis. Lohse died in March 2007 at the age of ninety-five. Within two months of his death, a safety deposit box he controlled was discovered in a Zurich, Switzerland, bank. Inside were tens of millions of dollars in paintings stolen during the war.

Alexander Langsdorff, whom Monuments Man Fred Hartt believed was responsible for the theft of the Florentine treasures, was arrested and interrogated by Monuments Man Deane Keller, but the will to prosecute such crimes in Italy quickly faded at war's end. Langsdorff returned to Germany, where he died of ill health in 1946.

SS General Karl Wolff, who authorized Langsdorff to take the Florentine treasures and ordered that they be brought to the Alto Adige region of Italy, was, incredibly, not tried for war crimes, at least not initially. Wolff was later found guilty as a "minor offender" and released. In 1964, the German government tried Wolff a second time and found him guilty of complicity in genocide. He was sentenced to fifteen years in prison, but released after serving less than five due to ill health. Maintaining his innocence to the end, Wolff lived another fifteen years before his death in 1984.

"Who owns art?" Nazi leader Adolf Hitler, like many conquerors before him, believed that to the victor belong the spoils of war.

Hitler went one step further, defining what, in his view, constituted "good" art, while destroying those objects that he judged inferior. The Monuments Men had a simple answer to this question that explained why they believed so strongly in their mission. Their answer: "Everyone." Works of art are part of our shared cultural heritage, no matter where in the world the art is located. Consequently, the Monuments Men believed that it was incumbent on everyone to protect it.

"Is art worth a life?" This question was also central to the mission of the Monuments Men. The image of a person running into a burning building to save a work of art is certainly dramatic. But would it be worth risking or even sacrificing a human life for an object, no matter its importance?

Monuments Man—and artist—Deane Keller answered this question by making an important distinction: dying to save an object versus dying to defend a cause. Neither Ronald Balfour nor Walter Huchthausen wanted to lose their lives, but both men accepted the risks because they believed in the cause.

During World War II, the United States and Britain, under the leadership of President Franklin D. Roosevelt and British Prime Minister Winston Churchill, fought to preserve democracy, freedom of speech, freedom of religion—in fact, our very way of life. The Monuments Men believed that fighting to preserve our cultural heritage was no less important. They could not imagine living in a dark and ugly world without these things of importance and beauty that have for centuries defined who we are as a civilization.

★

No one person spent more of his life thinking about the importance of protecting cultural treasures during times of conflict and then doing something about it than Monuments Man George Stout. His words serve not only as a reminder but as a call to action for world leaders, military commanders, and each one of us.

In areas torn by bombardment and fire are monuments cherished by the people of those countrysides or towns: churches, shrines, statues, pictures, many kinds of works. Some may be destroyed; some damaged. All risk further injury, looting or destruction . . .

To safeguard these things will not effect [sic] the course of battles, but it will affect the relations of invading armies with those peoples and their governments . . .

To safeguard these things will show respect for the beliefs and customs of all men and will bear witness that these things belong not only to a particular people but also to the heritage of mankind. To safeguard these things is part of the responsibility that lies on the governments of the United Nations. These monuments are not merely pretty things, not merely valued signs of man's creative power. They are expressions of faith, and they stand for man's struggle to relate himself to his past and to his God.

GLOSSARY

ALLIED NATIONS
A coalition led by the United States, Great Britain, France, and the Soviet Union formed in opposition to the Axis Powers.

AMG
Allied Military Government, the governing body put in place to ensure public order and safety during the Allied occupation of Germany.

ANTI-SEMITE
A person who is hostile to, prejudiced, or discriminatory against Jews.

AXIS POWERS
A coalition led by Germany, Italy, and Japan formed in opposition to the Allied Nations.

BBC
British Broadcasting Corporation.

CARABINIERI
The military police for the Italian armed forces that also functions as the state police.

ERR
Abbreviation for Einsatzstab Reichsleiter Rosenberg, a special task force that Nazi Germany established to plunder cultural valuables in occupied countries.

FATHERLAND

German term for homeland, used primarily in the Nazi era to refer to the state, often in a nationalist sense.

FLYING FORTRESS

Name for the Boeing B-17, a four-engine heavy bomber the U.S. Army Air Forces flew during World War II.

GESTAPO

Abbreviation of Geheime Staatspolizei, Nazi Germany's secret police.

GI

A nickname given to U.S. Army soldiers during World War II.

GOTHIC LINE

A series of fortifications two hundred miles long that the Germans built into the northern range of Italy's Apennine Mountains as a last line of defense against the Allied armies.

GUSTAV LINE

Also called the Winter Line, it was the first formidable German tripwire for the Allies in Italy, located at the skinniest part of the peninsula, south of Rome.

HAGUE CONVENTION

A series of international treaties that dictate the laws of war. These treaties were negotiated during two international peace conferences in 1899 and 1907.

HITLER YOUTH

State organization established in 1926 to educate young boys in the Nazi worldview and train them for eventual service in the armed forces.

HOLY SEE

Originating from *Sancta Sedes*, Latin for "Holy Chair," it is the authority of the pope in Rome to serve as the sovereign head of the Catholic Church.

KUNSTSCHUTZ

A German term for the policy of preserving cultural objects during armed conflict. Those in opposition to Nazi Germany saw the policy as veiled looting.

MFAA

Monuments, Fine Arts, and Archives Sections of the Civil Affairs Division of the U.S. Army. Tasked with safeguarding works of art and other cultural objects in war zones, the members of this special program were more commonly known as the Monuments Men.

MP

Military police.

NAZISM

Common term for the political ideology of the National Socialist German Workers' Party, which governed Germany from 1933 to 1945. Defined by extreme racism and authoritarian views.

OD

Olive drab, the color of the standard uniform for U.S. GIs and military vehicles during World War II.

RHINELAND

Region in western Germany along both banks of the Rhine River.

RHINO BARGE

A flat, rectangular deck with outboard engines used to ferry troops and equipment short distances.

ROBERTS COMMISSION

Established by President Franklin D. Roosevelt on June 23, 1943, the commission provided lists and reports on cultural treasures to military units and proposed the establishment of the MFAA.

ROTC

Reserve Officers' Training Corps, a leadership program that prepares college students to become officers in the U.S. military.

SCUTTLEBUTT

Slang term for gossip.

SHAEF

Supreme Headquarters Allied Expeditionary Force, led by General Dwight D. Eisenhower, exercised command over the armed forces of eleven nations that contributed men and materiel to operations against Nazi Germany.

STORMTROOPERS

Term used for members of the Sturmabteilung, the Nazi Party's semimilitarized force.

V-1

Guided missiles the Germans launched primarily at Britain from the French and Dutch coastlines.

BIBLIOGRAPHY

BOOKS

Aksenov, Vitali. *Favorite Museum of the Führer, Stolen Discoveries*. St. Petersburg: Publishing House Neva, 2003.

Atkinson, Rick. *The Guns at Last Light: The War in Western Europe, 1944–1945*. New York: Henry Holt and Company, 2013.

Blumenson, Martin. *U.S. Army in World War II, European Theater of Operations: Breakout and Pursuit*. Washington, DC: Center of Military History, 1961.

Caddick-Adams, Peter. *Monte Cassino: Ten Armies in Hell*. New York: Oxford University Press, 2013.

D'Este, Carlo. *Eisenhower: A Soldier's Life*. New York: Henry Holt and Company, 2002.

Downing, David. *The Nazi Death Camps*. New York: Gareth Stevens Publishing, 2006.

Duberman, Martin. *The Worlds of Lincoln Kirstein*. New York: Alfred A. Knopf, 2007.

Dulles, Allen W. *The Secret Surrender: The Classic Insider's Account of the Secret Plot to Surrender Northern Italy During WWII*. Guilford: Lyons Press, 2006.

Edsel, Robert M. *Saving Italy: The Race to Rescue a Nation's Treasures from the Nazis*. New York: Norton, 2013.

Edsel, Robert M., with Bret Witter. *The Monuments Men: Allied Heroes, Nazi Thieves, and the Greatest Treasure Hunt in History*. New York: Center Street, 2009.

Fasola, Cesare. *The Florence Galleries and the War: History and Records*. Florence: Casa Editrice Monsalvato, 1945.

Feliciano, Hector. *The Lost Museum: The Nazi Conspiracy to Steal the World's Greatest Works of Art*. New York: Basic Books, 1997.

Fowler, Michelle. "A Biography of Major Ronald Edmond Balfour." Included in Geoffrey Hayes, Mike Bechthold, and Matt Symes, eds.

Canada and the Second World War: Essays in Honour of Terry Copp.
Waterloo: Wilfrid Laurier University Press, 2012.

Fröhlich, Elke, ed. *Die Tagebücher von Joseph Goebbels.* Vol. 3, part 1.
Munich: K. G. Saur Verlag, 1987.

Gilbert, Martin. *Kristallnacht: Prelude to Destruction.* New York: Harper
Collins, 2007.

Goldensohn, Leon. *The Nuremberg Interviews: An American Psychiatrist's
Conversations with the Defendants and Witnesses.* New York: Alfred A.
Knopf, 2004.

Hancock, Walker, with Edward Connery Lathem. *A Sculptor's Fortunes.*
Gloucester: Cape Ann Historical Association, 1997.

Hartt, Frederick. *Florentine Art Under Fire.* Princeton: Princeton
University Press, 1949.

Hoving, Thomas. *Making the Mummies Dance: Inside the Metropolitan
Museum of Art.* New York: Simon & Schuster, 1994.

Howe, Jr., Thomas Carr. *Salt Mines and Castles.* New York: Bobbs-
Merrill, 1946.

Il Führer in Italia. S.1., Agenzia Stefani, Milano: Alfieri & Lacroix,
1938.

Kesselring, Albert. *The Memoirs of Field-Marshal Kesselring.* London:
Greenhill Books, 2007.

Kirstein, Lincoln. *The Poems of Lincoln Kirstein.* New York: Antheneum,
1987.

Linklater, Eric. *The Art of Adventure.* London: Macmillan and Co.,
1947.

MacDonald, Charles B. *United States Army in World War II, European
Theater of Operations: The Last Offensive.* Washington, DC: Center
of Military History, 1973.

———. *United States Army in World War II, European Theater of
Operations: The Siegfried Line Campaign.* Washington, DC: Center
of Military History, 1990.

Methuen, Lord. *Normandy Diary: Being a Record of Survivals and Losses
of Historical Monuments in North-Western France, together with
those in the Island of Walcheren and in that Part of Belgium
traversed by 21st Army Group in 1944–45.* London: Robert Hale
Limited, 1952.

Nazi Conspiracy and Aggression. Vol. 3. Washington, DC: U.S. Government Printing Office, 1946.

Nicholas, Lynn. *The Rape of Europa: The Fate of Europe's Treasures in the Third Reich and the Second World War.* New York: Vintage Books, 1995.

Petropolous, Jonathan. *Art as Politics in the Third Reich.* Chapel Hill: University of North Carolina Press, 1996.

Piña, Leslie A. *Louis Rorimer: A Man of Style.* Kent, OH: Kent State University Press, 1990.

Report of the American Commission for the Protection and Salvage of Artistic and Historic Monuments in War Areas. Washington, DC: U.S. Government Printing Office, 1946.

Rorimer, James J. *Survival: The Salvage and Protection of Art in War.* New York: Abelard Press, 1950.

Sigal-Klagsbald, Laurence and Isabelle le Masne de Chermont. "*À qui appartenaient ces tableaux?: La politique françaises de recherche de provenance, de garde et de restitution des oeuvres d'art pillées durant la Seconde Guerre mondiale.*" Exhibition catalogue. France, 2008.

Simon, Matila. *The Battle of the Louvre: The Struggle to Save French Art in World War II.* New York: Hawthorne Books, 1971.

Smyth, Craig Hugh. *Repatriation of Art from the Collecting Point in Munich after World War II.* Montclair, NJ: Abner Schram, 1988.

Trial of the Major War Criminals before the International Military Tribunal. Vol. 9. Nuremberg, 1947.

Valland, Rose. *Le Front de l'art: Défense des collections françaises, 1939–1945.* Paris: Réunion des Musées Nationaux–Grand Palais, 2014.

War Department Historical Division. *American Forces in Action Series: St-Lô (7 July–19 July 1944).* Washington, DC: Center of Military History, United States Army, 1946.

Wilson, George. *If You Survive: From Normandy to the Battle of the Bulge to the End of World War II—One American Officer's Riveting True Story.* New York: Ballantine Books, 1987.

Woolley, Sir Leonard. *The Protection of the Treasures of Art and History in War Areas.* London: His Majesty's Stationery Office, 1947.

Yeide, Nancy H., Konstantin Akinsha, and Amy L. Walsh. *The AAM Guide to Provenance Research.* Washington, DC: American Association of Museums, 2001.

Ziemke, Earl F. *The U.S. Army in the Occupation of Germany, 1944–1946.* Washington, DC: Center of Military History, United States Army, 2003.

UNPUBLISHED WORKS

Ettlinger, Harry. *Ein Amerikaner: Anecdotes from the Life of Harry Ettlinger* (New Jersey, 2002).

ARTICLES

Bigart, Homer. "12 Old Masters in Loot from Naples Museum: Nazis Will Be Billed for Two Titians, a Raphael and Other Paintings." *New York Herald Tribune*, 4A (July 12, 1944). ProQuest Historical Newspapers: *New York Tribune / Herald Tribune* (1282911536).

Bradsher, Greg. "Nazi Gold: The Merkers Mine Treasure." *Prologue: Quarterly of the National Archives and Records Administration* 31, no. 1 (Spring 1999): n.p. www.archives.gov/publications/prologue/1999/spring/nazi-gold-merkers-mine-treasure.html.

_____. "Monuments Men and Nazi Treasures: U.S. Occupation Forces Faced a Myriad of Problems in Sorting Out Riches Hidden by the Third Reich." *Prologue: Quarterly of the National Archives and Records Administration* 45, no. 2 (Summer 2013): 13–21.

_____. "The Monuments Men and the Recovery of the Art in the Merkers Salt Mine April 1945." *The Text Message Blog*, National Archives. January 27, 2014, https://text-message.blogs.archives.gov/2014/01/27/the-monuments-men-and-the-recovery-of-the-art-in-the-merkers-salt-mine-april-1945/.

Churchill, Rhona. "Elderly Germans Being Used to Restore Aachen." March 12, 1945, n.p. *The Journal News.* Newspapers.com (162391017).

Hancock, Walker. "Experiences of a Monuments Officer in Germany." *College Art Journal* 5, no. 4 (May 1946): 271–311.

Houghton, Jr., Arthur A. "James J. Rorimer." *The Metropolitan Museum of Art Bulletin* (Summer 1966, Part Two).

Kirstein, Lincoln. "The Quest for the Golden Lamb." *Town and Country* 100, no. 428 (Sept. 1945): 115, 182–86, 189, 198.

von Lingen, Kerstin. "Conspiracy of Silence." *Holocaust and Genocide Studies*, 22, no. 1 (Spring 2008): 74–109. http://hgs.oxfordjournals.org.

PUBLIC COLLECTIONS

Archives des Musées Nationaux, Paris, France

    Rose Valland Papers

Archivio Catalogo Beni Storico-Artistici, Florence, Italy

    Giovanni Poggi Archive

British School at Rome, Rome, Italy

    John Bryan Ward-Perkins Papers

Dokumentationsarchiv des österreichischen Widerstandes, Vienna, Austria

    Max Eder Papers, DÖW 10610

Harvard University Archives, Harvard University, Cambridge, Massachusetts

Imperial War Museum, London, United Kingdom

King's College Archive Centre, University of Cambridge, Cambridge, United Kingdom

    Papers of Ronald Edmond Balfour

Monuments Men Foundation for the Preservation of Art, Dallas, Texas

    Robert K. Posey Papers

National Archives and Records Administration (NARA), Washington, DC

    OSS Art Looting Investigation Unit Reports, 1945–46, M1782

    MFA&A: Personnel: Officers—U.S.: Personal Histories

    Record Group 239

    Record Group 260

    Record Group 331

    A3380: Microfilm Copies of Reports from the Mediterranean and European Theaters of Operations Received from the Allied Military Government, 1943–1946

    DN1924: Records relating to the administration and operation of the Foreign Exchange Depository Group within the Office of the Finance Advisor, OMGUS, 1944–1950

    M1941: Records Concerning the Central Collecting Points ("Ardelia Hall Collection"): OMGUS Headquarters Records, 1938–1951

M1944: Records of the American Commission for the Protection and Salvage of Artistic and Historic Monuments in War Areas (The Roberts Commission), 1943–1946

M1946: Records Concerning the Central Collection Points ("Ardelia Hall Collection"): Munich Central Collecting Point, 1945–1951

M1949: Records of the Monuments, Fine Arts, and Archives (MFAA) Section of the Reparations and Restitution Branch, OMGUS, 1945–1951

Gallery Archives, National Gallery of Art, Washington, DC

Frederick Hartt Papers

James J. Rorimer Papers

New York Public Library for the Performing Arts, Jerome Robbins Dance Division, Archives, New York, NY:

Lincoln Kirstein Papers, c. 1914–1991 MGZMD 97

[Writings by Lincoln Kirstein are © 2019 by the New York Public Library (Astor, Lenox and Tilden Foundations) and may not be reproduced without written permission.]

Princeton University Archives, Princeton University, Princeton, New Jersey

Ernest Theodore DeWald Papers

Smithsonian Archives of American Art, Washington, DC

W. G. Constable Papers

Walker Hancock Papers

George Leslie Stout Papers

Manuscripts and Archives, Yale University Library, Yale University, New Haven, Connecticut

Deane Keller Papers

PRIVATE COLLECTIONS

Charles Bernholz Papers

ONLINE SOURCES

"Death of Hitler in the Berlin Chancellery." May 2, 1945. *Guardian*. https://www.theguardian.com/world/1945/may/02/secondworldwar .germany.

Italian National Institute for Statistics

Opera della Primaziale Pisana

Rush, Ralph G. "Holocaust: Confirmation and Some Retribution." www.89infdivww2.org/memories/pstory2.htm.

Stato della Città del Vaticano

AUTHOR INTERVIEWS AND CONVERSATIONS

Harry Ettlinger

Leonard Fisher

Thomas Gibbs

James Huchthausen

Robert M. Posey

Marlie Schouteten

Thomas Stout

Judy Thompson

INTERVIEWS COURTESY OF ACTUAL FILMS

Frédérique Hébrard

SOURCE NOTES

BACK COVER

"Works of art" "Preservation of Works of Art in Italy," May 8, 1944. NARA, RG 239, M1944: Records of the American Commission for the Protection and Salvage of Artistic and Historic Monuments in War Areas (The Roberts Commission), 1943–1946, Roll 63.

EPIGRAPH

Prior to this war Lord Methuen, *Normandy Diary: Being a Record of Survivals and Losses of Historical Monuments in North-Western France, together with those in the Island of Walcheren and in that Part of Belgium traversed by 21st Army Group in 1944–45* (London: Robert Hale Limited, 1952), xv–xvi.

Dear Dennis Posey to Dennis, November 29, 1944, Robert K. Posey Papers, Monuments Men Foundation for the Preservation of Art, Dallas, TX.

PRELUDE

sixteen thousand "degenerate" works Jonathan Petropolous, *Art as Politics in the Third Reich* (Chapel Hill: University of North Carolina Press, 1996), 52.

Almost five thousand were destroyed Lynn Nicholas, *The Rape of Europa: The Fate of Europe's Treasures in the Third Reich and the Second World War* (New York: Vintage Books, 1995), 25.

"In so doing" Elke Fröhlich, ed., *Die Tagebücher von Joseph Goebbels* (Munich: K. G. Saur Verlag, 1987), vol. 3, part 1, entry for July 29, 1938.

spent two hours *Il Führer in Italia* (Agenzia Stefani, Milano: Alfieri & Lacroix, 1938).

veil of legality Petropolous, *Art as Politics in the Third Reich*, 80.

The document on p. xxvi is reproduced from Vitali Aksenov, *Favorite Museum of the Führer, Stolen Discoveries*, photo p. 3; the caption is drawn from Art Looting Investigation Unit, "Consolidated Interrogation Report #4: Linz," Attachment 1, NARA.

The document on p. xxvii is drawn from *Nazi Conspiracy and Aggression*, vol. 3, 188–189.

SECTION I

CHAPTER 1: LETTERS HOME

lying face down in the road Deane Keller, "Letter to the Editor," April 1, 1948, *The Hamden Chronicle*, Deane Keller Papers, MS 1685, Manuscripts & Archives, Yale University Library, Yale University, New Haven, CT, Box 2, Folder 18.

"the boys" Keller to Kathy, March 18, 1944, Deane Keller Papers, Box 7, Folder 45.

As he knelt beside Keller, "Letter to the Editor," April 1, 1948, *The Hamden Chronicle*, Deane Keller Papers, Box 2, Folder 18.

"is a big sacrifice"... "but I am thankful" Mother to Keller, October 7, 1943, Deane Keller Papers, Box 5, Folder 30.

"Rejected: poor eyesight" Keller to Parents, n.d., Deane Keller Papers, Box 5, Folder 24.

"Don't be so damned MODEST"... "Put it on thick" Theodore Sizer to Keller, May 30, 1943, Deane Keller Papers, Box 12, Folder 99.

Keller reported to Fort Myer, Virginia "Status of Officer," January 4, 1945, Deane Keller Papers, Box 21, Folder 33.

among the first *Report of the American Commission for the Protection and Salvage of Artistic and Historic Monuments in War Areas* (Washington, DC: U.S. Government Printing Office, 1946), 51.

"Buona gente" Deane Keller, "American Impressions of Italians and Italian Customs," NARA, RG 331, 10000 / 145, 1.

Keller visited a hospital Keller to Kathy, December 18, 1944, Deane Keller Papers, Box 7, Folder 51.

impregnable mountain bastion Gen. Harold Alexander, Companion of the Order of the Bath citation speech, Polish Institute and Sikorski Museum, cited in Peter Caddick-Adams, *Monte Cassino: Ten Armies in Hell* (New York: Oxford University Press, 2013), n.p.

"If we have to choose" Sir Leonard Woolley, *The Protection of the Treasures of Art and History in War Areas* (London: His Majesty's Stationery Office, 1947), 22.

first Monuments Man to reach Norman Newton, "Inspection of Abbey of Montecassino," May 19, 1944, NARA, RG 331, 10000 / 145 / 45.

"Reconstruction of entire Abbey" Norman Newton, "Montecassino Abbey," May 18, 1944, NARA, RG 331, 10000 / 145 / 45.

fifty-five thousand Allied soldiers dead... twenty thousand dead Thomas Gibbs (Historian, The National World War II Museum), in discussion with the author via email correspondence, June 18, 2012.

which he had purchased Keller, handwritten account, Deane Keller Papers, Box 22, Folder 39, 4.

"I haven't worn my ribbon"... "I feel the boys" Keller to Kathy, March 18, 1944, Deane Keller Papers, Box 7, Folder 45.

"Toozy Woozy" Keller, "Dear Deane: This is Daddy's History," Deane Keller Papers, Box 6, Folder 33.

"The life of one American boy" Keller to Kathy, June 25, 1944, Deane Keller Papers, Box 7, Folder 47.

were the treasures "MFAA Inventory No. 31: Art Objects from Carpegna, Sassocorvaro, Urbino actually in the Vatican," John Bryan Ward-Perkins Papers, British School at Rome, Rome, Italy, Inventories of Art Deposits.

After presenting his credentials H. C. Newton, "Report on Status of Monuments, Fine Arts, and Archives in the Mediterranean Theater of Operations," August 20, 1944, NARA, RG 331, 10000 / 145 / 203, 17.

The media spectacle Robert M. Edsel, *Saving Italy: The Race to Rescue a Nation's Treasures from the Nazis* (New York: Norton, 2013), 89–90.

two trucks Ernest DeWald, "Works of Art Formerly Stored at Montecassino and Later Transferred to the Vatican," July 20, 1944, NARA, RG 331, 10000 / 145 / 400, 1.

Crate number 1 Ibid., 2.

"There can be no doubt" Homer Bigart, "12 Old Masters in Loot from Naples Museum: Nazis Will Be Billed for Two Titians, a Raphael and Other Paintings," *New York Herald Tribune*, July 12, 1944, 4A. ProQuest Historical Newspapers: *New York Tribune / Herald Tribune* (1282911536).

seventeen works of art DeWald, "Works of Art Formerly Stored at Montecassino and Later Transferred to the Vatican," July 20 1944, NARA, RG 331, 10000 / 145 / 400, 1–2.

were in Nazi Germany *Report of the American Commission for the Protection and Salvage of Artistic and Historic Monuments in War Areas*, 75.

CHAPTER 2: INDEPENDENCE DAY

the summer he spent Thomas Stout (George Stout's son), in an interview with the author, 2008.

aboard the Liberty ship SS *Joseph Story* George Stout daily journal, entry July 4, 1944, George Leslie Stout Papers, Smithsonian Archives of American Art, Washington, DC.

Almost 156,000 men . . . 7,000 ships crossing Rick Atkinson, *The Guns at Last Light: The War in Western Europe, 1944–1945* (New York: Henry Holt, 2013), 29, 84.

twelve thousand American, British, and Canadian soldiers Ibid., 85.

just seven miles inland George Wilson, *If You Survive: From Normandy to the Battle of the Bulge to the End of World War II—One American Officer's Riveting True Story* (New York: Ballantine Books, 1987), 7.

about five hours George Stout daily journal, entry July 4, 1944, George Leslie Stout Papers.

"brain child" . . . "because not only is this commission" Craig Hugh Smyth, *Repatriation of Art from the Collecting Point in Munich after World War II* (Montclair, NJ: Abner Schram, 1988), 77–78.

"You are kind" . . . "but you magnify it" Stout to Paul Sachs, September 13, 1943, NARA, RG 239, M1944, Roll 57.

In October 1936 Nicholas, *The Rape of Europa*, 50.

on his own for four weeks Mason Hammond to David Finley, NARA, RG 239, M1944, Roll 14.

His original plan Smyth, *Repatriation of Art from the Collecting Point in Munich after World War II*, 81–82.

his personal library finding aid, Papers of Ronald Edmond Balfour, King's College Archive Centre, University of Cambridge, Cambridge, United Kingdom, https://janus.lib.cam.ac.uk/db/node.xsp?id=EAD%2FGBR%2F0272%2FPP%2FREB.

Volunteers in the United States *Report of the American Commission for the Protection and Salvage of Artistic and Historic Monuments in War Areas*, 2.

overlaid this information Ibid.

"Shortly we will be fighting" Ibid., 102.

a makeshift fireworks display George Stout daily journal, entry July 4, 1944, George Leslie Stout Papers.

"I'm sure much of the horrific results" Wilson, *If You Survive*, 7–9.

"The ghastly stories we had heard" Ibid.

after laying out his bedroll George Stout daily journal, entry July 5, 1944, George Leslie Stout Papers.

CHAPTER 3: "LITTLE SAINTS, HELP US!"

"open city" Albert Kesselring, *The Memoirs of Field-Marshal Kesselring* (London: Greenhill Books, 2007), 309.

"artistically bypassed" "Fine Arts Section," Deane Keller Papers, Box 19, Folder 10, 27.

Officials in Rome Frederick Hartt, *Florentine Art Under Fire* (Princeton: Princeton University Press, 1949), 16.

Keller entered the palace . . . Keller walked over Field Report, June 11, 1944, Deane Keller Papers, Box 21, Folder 31.

Other smaller paintings Ibid.

he wrote Ernest DeWald Hartt to DeWald, April 6, 1942 [sic], Ernest Theodore DeWald Papers, Princeton University Archives, Princeton University, Princeton, NJ, Box 4.

On the night of August 15, 1943 Hartt, "Notes on Bomb Damage to Cultural Monuments in Enemy-Occupied Italy," NARA, RG 331, 10000 / 145 / 7.

battered army jeep Hartt, *Florentine Art Under Fire*, 9.

He'd first visited Italy Eddie DeMarco, "After 17 years as professor, Hartt reflects on art, life," Frederick Hartt Papers, RG 28, Gallery Archives, National Gallery of Art, Washington, DC, Box 23, Folder 1.

while eating breakfast Hartt, *Florentine Art Under Fire*, 16.

"armed and helmeted" Ibid.

Linklater, who had been commissioned Eric Linklater, *The Art of Adventure* (London: Macmillan and Co., 1947), 255–57.

"But they're very good!" Ibid., 257.

"The whole house" Ibid., 258.

Cesare Fasola, librarian of the Uffizi Cesare Fasola, *The Florence Galleries and the War: History and Records* (Florence: Casa Editrice Monsalvato, 1945), 57.

After leaving Florence . . . With nothing more . . . "The packing cases" Ibid., 57–59.

"Little Saints, help us!" Ibid., 60.

All 246 paintings Hartt, *Florentine Art Under Fire*, 19.

"Five deposits located." Hartt, telegram, July 31, 1944, NARA, RG 331, 10000 / 145 / 362.

He then prepared a memo . . . "The fate of" Hartt, memo, "Secret," Frederick Hartt Papers, Box 3, Folder 8.

CHAPTER 4: THE MEETING

twelve hundred of its twelve thousand inhabitants George Stout daily journal, entry August 12, 1944, George Leslie Stout Papers.

On the evening of the D-Day landings Martin Blumenson, *U.S. Army in World War II, European Theater of Operations: Breakout and Pursuit* (Washington, DC: Center of Military History, 1961), 146–48.

Twice the number War Department Historical Division, *American Forces in Action Series: St-Lô (7 July–19 July 1944)* (Washington, DC: Center of Military History, United States Army, 1946).

No one was to enter George Stout daily journal, entry August 4, 1944, George Leslie Stout Papers.

the Germans had mined James J. Rorimer, *Survival: The Salvage and Protection of Art in War* (New York: Abelard Press, 1950), 15.

The meeting took place George Stout daily journal, entry August 13, 1944, George Leslie Stout Papers.

What matters Stout to Sachs, September 13, 1943, NARA, RG 239, M1944, Roll 57.

"There's so much to do" Rorimer, *Survival*, 9.

"attempt to record" Ibid., 2.

American GIs sharing their rations Ibid., 11.

American general had ordered Ibid., 10.

commandeered a printing press Ralph Hammett, "Meeting of Monuments, Fine Arts and Archives Specialist Officers 13 August—Master Supply," August 14, 1944, James J. Rorimer Papers, Gallery Archives, National Gallery of Art, Washington, DC, Box 3, Folder 2.

the bombing of his encampment George Stout daily journal, entry July 11, 1944, George Leslie Stout Papers.

CHAPTER 5: PRICELESS DUST

A fortuitous meeting Hartt, *Florentine Art Under Fire*, 37.

Now it provided refuge Ibid., 38.

Toward the end of July . . . Several days passed . . . "The bridges, the bridges!" Ibid., 39–43.

"one gigantic trash pile" Ibid., 45.

The intense heat Ibid., 48.

Barefoot women . . . There were shortages *Il Martirio di Firenze*, archival film, Imperial War Museum, London, United Kingdom, CO153; Edsel, *Saving Italy*, 189.

in the nearly four months Keller to Kathy, October 3, 1944, Deane Keller Papers, Box 7, Folder 49.

Keller and a small team "Fine Arts Section," Deane Keller Papers, Box 19, Folders 10, 36-37; Edsel, *Saving Italy*, 179.

hang the Stars and Stripes and the Union Jack Ibid.; Field Report, September 7, 1944, Deane Keller Papers, Box 21, Folder 32.

prewar population of seventy-two thousand people This data comes from ISTAT, the Italian National Institute for Statistics. The census of the population in Pisa was taken in 1936 and registered precisely 72,468 people living in the city.

Entering the piazza Field Report, September 7, 1944, Deane Keller Papers, Box 21, Folder 32.

contained more painted surface The painted area of the Camposanto was 16,145 sq. feet, whereas the painted area of the Sistine Chapel is slightly more than 12,972 sq. feet. "Affreschi del Camposanto," in Opera della Primaziale Pisana, 2003–2007, http://www.opapisa.it/it/attivita/cantieri-e-restauri /affreschi-del-camposanto.html; "Cappella Sistina," Stato della Città del Vaticano, http://www .vaticanstate.va/content/vaticanstate/en/monumenti/musei-vaticani/cappella-sistina.paginate.1.html.

"On the floor next to the walls" "Fine Arts Section," Deane Keller Papers, Box 19, Folder 10, 42.

Five weeks earlier . . . Even from the ground . . . A small group of volunteers . . . A shell whistled in Bruno Farnesi, "Cronaca della distruzione dell'incomparabile gioiello d'arte che era il/celebre Camposanto Monumentale di Pisa, Avvenuta il 27 Luglio 44 a causa di una granata di artiglieria," July 28, 1944, Frederick Hartt Papers, Box 4, Folder 6.

"in the night, the Piazza dei Miracoli" Ibid.

of San Miniato Field Report, August 24, 1944, Deane Keller Papers, Box 21, Folder 32.

"My assignment is MFAA officer" . . . **"I am not supposed to"** Keller to Parents, July 24, 1944, Deane Keller Papers, Box 5, Folder 26.

his time in Sezze Romano Edsel, *Saving Italy*, 185.

his stop in Monte Oliveto Ibid.

instructed him to bar entry Field Report, September 7, 1944, Deane Keller Papers, Box 21, Folder 32.

CHAPTER 6: OBJECTIVES

German artillery pieces still warm Rorimer, *Survival*, 46–47.

After spending the night Rorimer to Rockefeller, September 25, 1944, James J. Rorimer Papers.

U.S. Army soldiers Rorimer, *Survival*, 50.

requiring thirty-seven convoys Matila Simon, *The Battle of the Louvre: The Struggle to Save French Art in World War II* (New York: Hawthorne Books, 1971), 23.

his team had evacuated Ibid., 26.

it found safety Frédérique Hébrard, interview courtesy of Actual Films, n.d.

Jaujard estimated Rorimer, *Survival*, 51.

The tankers gathered around Ibid., 49.

"We do not want to destroy" . . . **"These examples"** . . . **"If these things are lost"** "Draft Lecture," Papers of Ronald Edmond Balfour, Misc. 5, 9.

Sometime around midnight . . . **"We're taking the Michelangelo."** "Removal of Works of Art from the Church of Notre-Dame at Bruges," September 24, 1944, Papers of Ronald Edmond Balfour, Misc. 5.

The two German officers . . . **Four days earlier** . . . **The dean and sacristan** Ibid.

With a towel wrapped around his neck Posey to Alice, September 23, 1944, Robert K. Posey Papers.

"things that seem luxuries" Posey to Alice, September 5, 1944, Robert K. Posey Papers.

A Posey had fought Robert M. Posey (Robert K. Posey's son), in an interview with the author, February 29, 2008.

A detailed description Lincoln Kirstein, "The Quest for the Golden Lamb," *Town and Country* 100, no. 428 (Sept. 1945): 182.

three trucks carrying the Ghent Altarpiece Nicholas, *The Rape of Europa*, 85.

"the Zoo" Posey to Alice, November 1, 1944, Robert K. Posey Papers.

added a bunny rabbit Posey to Dennis, April 5, 1944, Ibid.

his first ride Posey to Dennis, August 9, 1944, Ibid.

being at his side Posey to Dennis, April 22, 1944, Ibid.

"Dear Dennis" Posey to Dennis, October 3, 1944, Ibid.

CHAPTER 7: RESURRECTION AND TREACHERY

he'd come himself "Fine Arts Section," Deane Keller Papers, Box 19, Folder 10, 42–43.

Overseeing a small army Ibid.

A midnight "requisition" Leonard Fisher (friend of Deane Keller), in an interview with the author, December 23, 2010.

"The job is done" Letter, October 12, 1944, Deane Keller Papers, Box 21, Folder 32.

"This is the biggest job" . . . **"It has been interesting"** Keller to Kathy, October 9, 1944, Deane Keller Papers, Box 7, Folder 49.

"The destruction" . . . **"but it paralyzed the city"** . . . **"houses, towers, palaces"** Hartt, *Florentine Art Under Fire*, 45-46.

"Santo Stefano" "Damage to Monuments in Florence," August 20, 1944, Frederick Hartt Papers, Box 3, Folder 8.

had received a bizarre telegram Hartt, *Florentine Art Under Fire*, 68.

greeted as liberators Ibid., 69.

the dates of the theft "Report on German Removals of Works of Art from Deposits in Tuscany," October 8, 1944, Frederick Hartt Papers, Box 3, Folder 10; Edsel, *Saving Italy*, 196.

"Dear Ernest" Hartt to DeWald, September 7, 1944, NARA, RG 331, 10000 / 145 / 71.

took place at gunpoint Hartt, *Florentine Art Under Fire*, 72.

"A grand total of 529 paintings" . . . **"had suffered a robbery"** Ibid., 76.

CHAPTER 8: SEARCHING FOR CLUES

he failed the physical examination Walker Hancock with Edward Connery Lathem, *A Sculptor's Fortunes* (Gloucester: Cape Ann Historical Association, 1997), 122.

Hancock crossed the English Channel handwritten note, Walker Hancock Papers, Smithsonian Archives of American Art, Washington, DC.

his first night in Paris Hancock with Lathem, *A Sculptor's Fortunes*, 135.

A forced evacuation Charles B. MacDonald, *United States Army in World War II, European Theater of Operations: The Siegfried Line Campaign* (Washington, DC: Center of Military History, 1990), 307.

they wheeled artillery into position MacDonald, Ibid., 311–12.

hitchhiked their way Walker Hancock, "Experiences of a Monuments Officer in Germany," *College Art Journal* 5, no. 4 (May 1946): 273.

twisted trolley lines Ibid., 272.

unleashed a barrage Ibid., 273.

Native American headdress Ibid., 272.

the double doors Ibid., 273.

stench of soiled mattresses Ibid.

"I am Father Erich Stephany" . . . **Shelling and confinement** Ibid., 274.

American GIs had detained Ibid.

he'd prevented the army from converting James Rorimer typescript journal, entry September 3, 1944, James J. Rorimer Papers, 28MFAA-J1 Wartime Journals and Reports, 1944–1945, Box 1-1.

he'd managed to get the army to remove Rorimer, *Survival*, 63–64.

"no matter what" Jacques Jaujard, Introduction, Rapports de Mademoiselle R. Valland, Rose Valland Papers, Archives des Musées Nationaux, Paris, France.

"Middle-age" handwritten note, James J. Rorimer Papers, 28MFAA-J2 Survival Research Files, 1940–1989, Box 2-12 Paris [1944–1945].

Le Figaro Robert M. Edsel with Bret Witter, *The Monuments Men: Allied Heroes, Nazi Thieves, and the Greatest Treasure Hunt in History* (New York: Center Street, 2009), 121.

That had made quite an impression Rose Valland, *Le Front de l'art: Défense des collections françaises, 1939–1945* (Paris: Réunion des Musées Nationaux–Grand Palais, 2014), 218.

CHAPTER 9: GETTING HELP

Nearly every building Hartt to Walter W. S. Cook, November 24, 1944, NARA, RG 239, M1944, Roll 23.

"the works of art" Poggi, "Memo," November 11, 1944, Giovanni Poggi Archive, Archivio Catalogo Beni Storico-Artistici, Florence, Italy, Serie VIII, n. 155, 5.

Hartt couldn't find Hartt, *Florentine Art Under Fire*, 96.

Hartt received new information Fasola to Hartt, November 20, 1944, NARA, RG 239, M1949: Records of the Monuments, Fine Arts, and Archives (MFAA) Section of the Reparations and Restitution Branch, OMGUS, 1945–1951, Roll 4.

Nazi-sympathetic Italian officials announced Fascist Radio, "Messaggio sull'ispezione fatta dal Direttore Generale delle Arti, prof. Carlo Anti," December 11, 1944, Giovanni Poggi Archive, Serie VIII, n. 155, 5.

disaster struck when his vehicle crashed Balfour, "Sixth Report—Dec 44 and Jan 45," February 1, 1945, NARA, RG 239, M1944, Roll 70.

British Captain George Willmot L. Bancel LaFarge, "Progress Report, MFA&A, for fortnight of 29th Dec 44 to 11th Jan 45," January 12, 1945, NARA, RG 239, A3380: Microfilm Copies of Reports from the Mediterranean and European Theaters of Operations Received from the Allied Military Government, 1943–1946, Roll 1, 114.

Walking door-to-door Hancock, "Experiences of a Monuments Officer in Germany," 275.

"Well, I'll be damned" . . . "Here they are" Ibid., 276.

request denied George Stout daily journal, entry October 29, 1944, George Leslie Stout Papers.

Stout would now be George Stout daily journal, entry November 6, 1944, George Leslie Stout Papers.

Shattered glass Hancock, "Experiences of a Monuments Officer in Germany," 279.

Hancock found Ibid., 279–80.

Huchthausen was seriously injured Judy Thompson and James Huchthausen, in discussion with the author, n.d.

Stout had instructed Kirstein Martin Duberman, *The Worlds of Lincoln Kirstein* (New York: Alfred A. Knopf, 2007), 393.

had been so poor Robert M. Posey (Robert K. Posey's son), in discussion with the author, n.d.

Some arcane army rule Duberman, *The Worlds of Lincoln Kirstein*, 389.

Snuggly taped between . . . After an agonizingly . . . "say anything you want" Posey to Alice, December 16, 1944, Robert K. Posey Papers.

CHAPTER 10: LONGINGS

was standing next to him Rorimer, *Survival*, 109–10.

"Too often" Valland, *Le Front de l'art*, 218.

visited six of the nine locations Rorimer, *Survival*, 114–16.

into a concentration camp Valland, *Le Front de l'art*, 96.

"The atmosphere around me" . . . "The rooms and offices" Valland, *Le Front de l'art*, 81–82.

"room of martyrs" Hector Feliciano, *The Lost Museum: The Nazi Conspiracy to Steal the World's Greatest Works of Art* (New York: Basic Books, 1997), 107–08.

"France and its art" Valland, *Le Front de l'art*, 122.

Twenty visits J. S. Plaut, "Consolidated Interrogation Report No. 1: the ERR," August 15, 1945, OSS Art Looting Investigation Unit Reports, 1946-46, M1782, NARA, 6.

sometimes jingling loose emeralds Valland, *Le Front de l'art*, 98.

"R-1" "2609/Aussee 1953/1," Ardelia Hall Collection: Munich Property Cards, NARA, RG 260, M1946: Records Concerning the Central Collecting Points ("Ardelia Hall Collection"): Munich Central Collecting Point, 1945–1951, Roll 170.

A final spasm Rorimer, *Survival*, 109.

Train number 40044 Laurence Sigal-Klagsbald and Isabelle le Masne de Chermont, *"À qui appartenaient ces tableaux?: La politique françaises de recherche de provenance, de garde et de restitution des oeuvres d'art pillées durant la Seconde Guerre mondiale,"* exhibition catalogue (France, 2008), 217.

As they walked through Rorimer, *Survival*, 110.

"Rorheimer" Leslie A. Piña, *Louis Rorimer: A Man of Style* (Kent, OH: Kent State University Press, 1990), 123.

"Keep firing" . . . And that's exactly what he did Robert M. Posey (Robert K. Posey's son), in an interview with the author, February 29, 2008.

Walker Hancock spent Christmas Day Hancock with Lathem, *A Sculptor's Fortunes*, 146.

"He's discouraged" . . . "but we are guaranteeing" Hancock to Saima, December 4, 1944, Walker Hancock Papers.

Bernholz had pulled Mark Clark, "Award of Bronze Star Medal," May 21, 1944, Charles Bernholz Papers, Private Collection.

to transport the poor children T. Parr to Keller, December 30, 1944, Deane Keller Papers, Box 21, Folder 32.

"Today is Christmas" Letter to Kathy, December 25, 1944, Deane Keller Papers, Box 7, Folder 51.

SECTION II

CHAPTER 11: SMALL VICTORIES

Almost twenty thousand American boys lay dead Charles MacDonald, *United States Army in World War II, European Theater of Operations: The Last Offensive* (Washington, DC: Center of Military History, 1973), 53.

Harry didn't see himself . . . In 1937 Harry Ettlinger, *Ein Amerikaner: Anecdotes from the Life of Harry Ettlinger* (unpublished, New Jersey, 2002), 9, 11–14, 17.

seven thousand Jewish-owned businesses Martin Gilbert, *Kristallnacht: Prelude to Destruction* (New York: Harper Collins, 2007), n.p.

the last bar mitzvah Monuments Man Harry Ettlinger, in an interview with the author, 2008.

Harry's father spent . . . Once America entered World War II . . . In mid-October . . . Harry found himself Ettlinger, *Ein Amerikaner*, 26–28, 43.

the eight buddies Ibid., 44.

"The following three men" Ibid.

Being pulled off that truck Ibid.

Hancock entered the church Hancock with Lathem, *A Sculptor's Fortunes*, 149.

Hancock couldn't find the curé . . . In an effort to appease . . . Realizing that emotions . . . Mustering all the diplomacy . . . "I propose" . . . The mason Ibid., 149–50.

Florentine art officials Poggi, "Relazione sui Monumenti e le Opere d'Arte di Firenze durante la Guerra 1940–1945," June 5, 1945, Giovanni Poggi Archive, Serie VIII, n. 157, 12; Field Report, February 17, 1945, Deane Keller Papers, Box 21, Folder 33; "Bronze Statue di Cosimo I," February 21, 1945, Frederick Hartt Papers, Box 3, Folder 14.

After several days of planning . . . "a Maine back countryman" Field Report, February 17, 1945, Deane Keller Papers, Box 21, Folder 33.

"Cosimo, welcome back!" Ibid.

Smokey had been killed photo, Deane Keller Papers, Box 36, Folder 222.

CHAPTER 12: TREASURE MAPS

A phone call Rorimer, *Survival*, 111.

Sending a bottle of champagne Ibid., 110.

wanted him reassigned Valland, *Le Front de l'art*, 222.

pulled out a stack of photographs Rorimer, *Survival*, 113.

another larger box Ibid., 113–14.

in particular from Alexandre Valland, *Le Front de l'art*, 104–105.

One of the chauffeurs Ibid., 105.

the Nazi lackeys . . . "no one here is stupid enough" Valland note, February 1944, R 32-1, Rose Valland Papers.

She expected Valland, *Le Front de l'art*, 105.

you will find Rorimer, *Survival*, 114.

delivered . . . five to six hundred paintings Valland, *Le Front de l'art*, 187. The date of the burning of these artworks is drawn from notes by Rose Valland of her eyewitness account, July 23, 1943, Rose Valland Papers.

"Nothing could be saved" Rapports de Mademoiselle R. Valland, entry July 23, 1943, Rose Valland Papers.

the thieves had loaded Michelle Fowler, "A Biography of Major Ronald Edmond Balfour," included in Geoffrey Hayes, Mike Bechthold, and Matt Symes, eds., *Canada and the Second World War: Essays in Honour of Terry Copp* (Waterloo, Canada: Wilfrid Laurier University Press, 2012), n.p.

"It was a splendid week" . . . "On the one hand" Translation of article in *Rheinpost*, September 12, 1985, Hachmann, "The Sexton, Eyewitness of Major Balfour's Death," Papers of Ronald Edmond Balfour, Misc. 5.

created a makeshift repository Fowler, "A Biography of Major Ronald Edmond Balfour," included in Hayes, Bechthold, and Symes, eds., *Canada and the Second World War: Essays in Honour of Terry Copp*, n.p.

On March 10, at 9:30 a.m. sharp . . . They set out Translation of article in *Rheinpost*, September 12, 1985, Hachmann, "The Sexton, Eyewitness of Major Balfour's Death," Papers of Ronald Edmond Balfour, Misc. 5.

"I want very much to" handwritten letter excerpt, Webb to Balfour's Mother, Papers of Ronald Edmond Balfour, Misc. 5.

but word had it Kirstein, "The Quest for the Golden Lamb," 182.

"It's in a salt mine" Ibid.

"The desolation is frozen" Kirstein to Groozle, March 24, 1945, Lincoln Kirstein Papers MGZMD 97, New York Public Library for the Performing Arts, Jerome Robbins Dance Division, Archives, New York City, NY, Box 2–25.

Only two thousand Ibid.

"Certainly St. Lô was worse" . . . "Here everything" Ibid.

Kirstein sought help Lincoln Kirstein, *The Poems of Lincoln Kirstein* (New York: Antheneum, 1987), 264.

the dentist insisted . . . The trip took twice the time . . . A man in his midthirties . . . After exchanging pleasantries Kirstein, "The Quest for the Golden Lamb," 182–83.

he had joined the Nazi Party in 1938 . . . RG 260, M1941: Records Concerning the Central Collecting Points ("Ardelia Hall Collection"): OMGUS Headquarters Records, 1938–1951, Roll 31.

"First, it is *my* orders" . . . "Dear Bunjes" . . . "let me worry about that" Bunjes letter presented at Nuremberg trials, March 20, 1946, in *Trial of the Major War Criminals before the International Military Tribunal*, vol. 9 (Nuremberg, 1947): 547–49.

Posey chose to push back Kirstein, "The Quest for the Golden Lamb," 183.

a large bound album Kirstein, *The Poems of Lincoln Kirstein*, 265.

He then started pointing Ibid., 265–66.

"It is here" Ibid., 266–67.

CHAPTER 13: GAINS AND LOSSES

entered Siegen's ghostlike ruins Hancock, "Experiences of a Monuments Officer in Germany," 291.

A well-placed German source Ibid., 290.

"Around a hole" . . . "Throughout we walked" . . . "We were the first" Stout to Margie, April 4, 1945, George Leslie Stout Papers.

"They are afraid" . . . "The radio threatened" Hancock, "Experiences of a Monuments Officer in Germany," 291.

Stout noticed a boy Ibid.

Herr Etzkorn George Stout daily journal, entry April 2, 1945, George Leslie Stout Papers.

over four hundred paintings Hancock, "Experiences of a Monuments Officer in Germany," 292.

a stack of crates, forty in all Ibid.

Stout believed George Stout daily journal, entry April 2, 1945, George Leslie Stout Papers.

His work at the Aachen Cathedral Rhona Churchill, "Elderly Germans Being Used to Restore Aachen," March 12, 1945, n.p. *The Journal News*, Newspapers.com (162391017).

"It may seem strange" Ibid.

"Aachen Cathedral belongs" Ibid.

Reaching Recklinghausen around 3:00 p.m . . . On the smooth road . . . Seeking directions . . . All Keck could see . . . "Your captain is dead" . . . "Head wound" . . . "He's white as snow" Sheldon Keck, handwritten memo, "Statement Regarding the Incident Involving the Decease of Captain Walter J. Huchthausen, AC," NARA, MFA&A: Personnel: Officers—U.S.: Personal Histories.

After about forty-five minutes Ibid.

"The buildings that Huchthausen hoped" Hancock to Saima, November 25, 1945, Walker Hancock Papers.

CHAPTER 14: SURPRISES

Early that cold and rainy morning Ralph G. Rush, "Holocaust: Confirmation and Some Retribution," http://www.89infdivww2.org/memories/pstory2.htm.

"It seemed that" Ibid.

TOP SECRET. NO PRESS. Carlo D'Este, *Eisenhower: A Soldier's Life* (New York: Henry Holt, 2002), 685–86.

more than a thousand soldiers in all Lincoln Kirstein, "The Mine at Merkers," Robert K. Posey Papers.

Two days earlier, MPs stopped two women "Report covering the discovery, removal, transporting and storage of gold, silver, platinum and currency, fine arts treasures and German patent records from salt mines in the Merkers and Heringen area," April 1945, NARA, RG260, DN1924: Records relating to the administration and operation of the Foreign Exchange Depository Group within the Office of the Finance Advisor, OMGUS, 1944–1950, Roll DN1924_0140.

550 bags of Reichsmarks Greg Bradsher, "Nazi Gold: The Merkers Mine Treasure," *Prologue: Quarterly of the National Archives and Records Administration* 31, no. 1 (Spring 1999): n.p., www.archives.gov/publications/prologue/1999/spring/nazi-gold-merkers-mine-treasure.html.

It wasn't until engineers . . . Before stepping Ibid.

"stay-behind SS men" Kirstein, "The Mine at Merkers," Robert K. Posey Papers, n.p.

Kirstein stepped through the opening Ibid.

The space measured Bradsher, "Nazi Gold: The Merkers Mine Treasure," n.p.

Almost every period of civilization Kirstein, "The Mine at Merkers," Robert K. Posey Papers, n.p.

After returning to the surface Bradsher, "Nazi Gold: The Merkers Mine Treasure," n.p.

"If that clothesline should part" . . . "Okay, George" . . . "No more cracks" D'Este, *Eisenhower*, 686.

two hundred common suitcases Bradsher, "Nazi Gold: The Merkers Mine Treasure," n.p.

code name Task Force Hansen Greg Bradsher, "The Monuments Men and the Recovery of the Art in the Merkers Salt Mine April 1945," *The Text Message Blog*, National Archives, January 27, 2014, https://text-message.blogs.archives.gov/2014/01/27/the-monuments-men-and-the-recovery-of-the-art-in-the-merkers-salt-mine-april-1945/.

General Patton refused D'Este, *Eisenhower*, 686.

"We are told" Ibid.

His friend, a Jewish chaplain Hancock with Lathem, *Sculptor's Fortunes*, 158.

"I have one here" Ibid.

"the people weeping" Ibid.

CHAPTER 15: ON THE MOVE

walks in the countryside Ettlinger, *Ein Amerikaner*, 44.

three of his eight friends Ibid.

the owner of Castle Warsberg Rorimer, *Survival*, 240.

had prompted French First Army Valland, *Le Front de l'art*, 222.

eight large buildings Robert Posey, "Semi-Monthly Report on Monuments, Fine Arts and Archives, Period Ending 15 April, 1945," April 17, 1945, NARA, RG 260, M1941, Roll 31.

At Schloss Ellmann Robert Posey, "Semi-Monthly Report on Monuments, Fine Arts and Archives, Period Ending 30 April, 1945," April 30, 1945, NARA, RG 260, M1941, Roll 31.

Bunjes also named names Ibid.

Tens of thousands Earl F. Ziemke, *The U.S. Army in the Occupation of Germany, 1944–1946* (Washington, DC: Center of Military History, United States Army, 2003), 52–53.

despite mold growing Hancock to Saima, April 4, 1945, Walker Hancock Papers.

"desperate for need of help" George Stout daily journal, entry April 20, 1945, George Leslie Stout Papers.

"repos out of hand" George Stout daily journal, entry April 23, 1945, George Leslie Stout Papers.

"when the stampede begins" "Visit to Switzerland," March 26, 1945, NARA RG 331, 10000 / 145 / 297.

"good state" Alessandro Cagiati to Hartt, "Removal of Works of Art by Germans," April 3, 1945, Frederick Hartt Papers, Box 3, Folder 16.

"It is feared by the Germans" Pietro Ferraro, "Memo," signed Antonio, April 10, 1945, Giovanni Poggi Archive, Serie VIII, n. 155, 5.

"Coming into town" . . . "houses on fire" . . . "smell of death" Keller to Parents, April 25, 1945, Deane Keller Papers, Box 5, Folder 27.

the works of art Teddy Croft-Murray, "Displaced Works of Art from Florence," April 27, 1945, NARA, RG 331, 10000 / 145 / 401.

CHAPTER 16: THE BEGINNING OF THE END

"Very urgent matter" George Stout daily journal, entry April 29, 1945, George Leslie Stout Papers.

an army captain Hancock with Lathem, *A Sculptor's Fortunes*, 158.

four hundred thousand tons of explosives George Stout daily journal, entry May 1, 1945, George Leslie Stout Papers.

As the squad searched George Stout daily journal, entry May 2, 1945, George Leslie Stout Papers; Greg Bradsher, "Monuments Men and Nazi Treasures: U.S. Occupation Forces Faced a Myriad of Problems in Sorting Out Riches Hidden by the Third Reich," *Prologue: Quarterly of the National Archives and Records Administration* 45, no. 2 (Summer 2013): 14.

Regimental banners Hancock with Lathem, *A Sculptor's Fortunes*, 159–60.

Someone had hastily written Ibid., 160.

More than 270 priceless paintings Bradsher, "Monuments Men and Nazi Treasures: U.S. Occupation Forces Faced a Myriad of Problems in Sorting Out Riches Hidden by the Third Reich," 14.

"fighting till his last breath" radio broadcast transcript, "Death of Hitler in the Berlin Chancellery," May 2, 1945, *Guardian*, https://www.theguardian.com/world/1945/may/02/secondworldwar.germany.

representatives of Nazi SS Allen W. Dulles, *The Secret Surrender: The Classic Insider's Account of the Secret Plot to Surrender Northern Italy during WWII* (Guilford: Lyons Press, 2006), 176–77.

On May 4 Field Report, May 12, 1945, Deane Keller Papers, Box 21, Folder 33.

The message Memo from Newton, May 4, 1945, NARA, RG 331, 10000 / 145 / 401.

For the time being Field Report, May 12, 1945, Deane Keller Papers, Box 21, Folder 33.

In full dress uniform Nicholas, *Rape of Europa*, 379.

Rorimer quickly cornered Rorimer, *Survival*, 163.

According to her notes Ibid.

Looted Renaissance and eighteenth-century furniture Ibid., 164.

D.W. Ibid., 163–64; Nancy H. Yeide, Konstantin Akinsha, and Amy L. Walsh, *The AAM Guide to Provenance Research* (Washington, DC: American Association of Museums, 2001), 300.

more than 150 paintings Rorimer, *Survival*, 182.

"Works of art" Ibid., 115, 182.

"romantic and remote" Ibid., 183.

Christoph Wiesend Ibid., 184.

thirteen hundred paintings Ibid.,185.

The room—more like a vault Ibid., 185–86.

Rorimer grabbed a poker Ibid., 186.

file cabinets containing Ibid.

The custodian confirmed Ibid., 186–87.

Several hours later . . . "dogs and fiends" . . . By 7:00 p.m. James Rorimer typescript journal, entry May 4, 1945, James J. Rorimer Papers, Box 1-1, 183.

"I hear you speak German" Monuments Man Harry Ettlinger, in an interview with the author, 2008.

"Are you the new translator?" Ibid.

"What a wheeler-dealer" Ibid.

CHAPTER 17: SALT MINES AND JAIL CELLS

Over the next three days Hancock with Lathem, *A Sculptor's Fortunes*, 162.

Using the back Hancock to Saima, May 4, 1945, Walker Hancock Papers.

"Dear Saima" Ibid.

Hancock directed the men . . . With more than half the day gone . . . A radio installed in the mine office Hancock with Lathem, *A Sculptor's Fortunes*, 162–164.

felt as if *they* were the prisoners Kirstein, "The Quest for the Golden Lamb," 183–84.

Weeks earlier . . . Soon the miners Ibid., 184–85.

Kirstein inadvertently bumped Ibid., 184.

"How long will it take" Ibid.

An army clerical error Field Report, May 12, 1945, Deane Keller Papers, Box 21, Folder 33.

"Bomb hit of August 1943" Ibid.

"shell holes, and mountainsides" Hartt, *Florentine Art Under Fire*, 103.

Finding a hotel . . . The following morning . . . With the jingling Ibid, 103, 105.

three hundred paintings Edsel, *Saving Italy*, 289.

aside from one painting Field Report, May 22, 1945, Deane Keller Papers, Box 21, Folder 33; Hartt, *Florentine Art Under Fire*, 104.

CHAPTER 18: CLOSURE

Poggi recounted how Poggi, "Relazione sui Monumenti e le Opere d'Arte di Firenze durante la Guerra 1940–1945," 12.

"greatest single art-looting operation" Hartt, *Florentine Art Under Fire*, 105.

A curious mix Ibid.

When the SS colonel Ibid.

The carriage house was packed Ibid.

Laboring through the night Kirstein, "The Quest for the Golden Lamb," 184.

From the other side . . . The two Monuments Men Ibid.

"By our flickering acetylene lamps" . . . "the miraculous jewels" Ibid., 186.

Off to the side Kirstein, "The Quest for the Golden Lamb," 186; Thomas Carr Howe, Jr., *Salt Mines and Castles* (New York: Bobbs-Merrill, 1946), 159.

Then Posey learned Ibid., 186.

Mineralienkammer Ibid., 189.

Springerwerke Ibid.

Kammergrafe Ibid., 198.

"Monte Cassino" Ibid.

To prepare for Stout's arrival Ibid., 184.

CHAPTER 19: GOING HOME

According to the logbook Max Eder, Zusammenfassung der mir bekannten Einlegerungen im Salzbergwerk Altaussee, Max Eder Papers, DÖW 10610, Dokumentationsarchiv des österreichischen Widerstandes, Vienna, Austria, 4.

"This looks like a good day" Howe, Jr., *Salt Mines and Castles*, 159.

"I think we could bounce her" Ibid.

"Remember how crowded" . . . "You don't" Memo to Col. Arthur Sutherland, May 16, 1945, Deane Keller Papers, Box 21, Folder 33.

ten paintings "Inventory Check of Works of Art Removed by Germans," May 31, 1945, NARA, RG 331, 10000 / 145 / 401.

109 crates of paintings "Fine Arts Section," Deane Keller Papers, Box 19, Folder 10, 74.

"art treasures" . . . "Extreme care necessary" Freight Waybill, Frederick Hartt Papers, Box 3, Folder 19.

"$500,000,000" "Fine Arts Section," Deane Keller Papers, Box 19, Folder 10, 72.

The following day Hartt, *Florentine Art Under Fire*, 109–10.

Driving up the same winding road Valland, *Le Front de l'art*, 225; Rorimer, *Survival*, 190.

EPILOGUE

29,436 railroad cars Nicholas, *The Rape of Europa*, 139.

more than 70,000 French Jews David Downing, *The Nazi Death Camps* (New York: Gareth Stevens Publishing, 2006), 11.

"This gentleman saved" Letter to Mr. Kenneth Balfour, October 1, 1954, Papers of Ronald Edmond Balfour, Misc. 5.

Frieda van Schaïk van Schaïk to "Cambridge University," October 16, 1945, Harvard University Archives, Harvard University, Cambridge, MA; Marlie Schouteten (grave caretaker) in discussion with the Monuments Men Foundation, 2017.

Extremely proud of his military service Thomas Hoving, *Making the Mummies Dance: Inside the Metropolitan Museum of Art* (New York: Simon & Schuster, 1994), 19.

"a good start" Arthur A. Houghton, Jr., "James J. Rorimer," *The Metropolitan Museum of Art Bulletin* (Summer 1966, Part Two): 39.

"a leader" Smyth, *Repatriation of Art from the Collecting Point in Munich after World War II*, 16.

"George Stout was the greatest war hero" Duberman, *The Worlds of Lincoln Kirstein*, 403.

"Keller tried to hide his humanity" Leonard Fisher (friend of Deane Keller) in an interview with the author, December 23, 2010.

"I revere women" Leon Goldensohn, *The Nuremberg Interviews: An American Psychiatrist's Conversations with the Defendants and Witnesses* (New York: Alfred A. Knopf, 2004), 132.

"They tried to paint" Ibid., 128–29.

"Heil Hitler" Edsel with Witter, *The Monuments Men*, 404.

"minor offender" Kerstin von Lingen, "Conspiracy of Silence," *Holocaust and Genocide Studies* 22, no. 1 (Spring 2008): 93, http://hgs.oxfordjournals.org.

Deane Keller answered Edsel, *Saving Italy*, 340; Keller, "Sectional History—Fine Arts," Deane Keller Papers, Box 23, Folder 56, 30, 32, 38.

"in areas torn" ... **"To safeguard"** ... **"To safeguard"** ... George Stout, "Protection of Monuments: A Proposal for Consideration during War and Rehabilitation," n.d., W. G. Constable Papers, Smithsonian Archives of American Art, Washington, DC, Section 6a.

PHOTOGRAPH AND MAP CREDITS

COVER

Cover photos ©: cover top left: National Archives and Records Administration; cover top right: Paul Almasy/akg-images; cover bottom: Arianna and Elisa Magrini/Edizioni Polistampa, Firenze; back cover: PR Archive/Alamy Stock Photo.

BOOK

Photos ©: cover top left: National Archives and Records Administration; cover top right: Paul Almasy/akg-images; cover bottom: Arianna and Elisa Magrini/Edizioni Polistampa, Firenze; back cover: PR Archive/Alamy Stock Photo; iv: National Archives and Records Administration; xi Keller: Robert M. Edsel Collection; xi Hartt: Robert M. Edsel Collection; xi Stout: National Archives and Records Administration; xi Hancock: Archives of American Art, Smithsonian Institution, Hancock Collection; xi Posey: Robert Posey Collection/Monuments Men Foundation; xi Kirstein: Lincoln Kirstein © 2019 by the New York Public Library (Astor, Lenox and Tilden Foundations); xi Rorimer: National Archives and Records Administration; xi Valland: Archives diplomatiques du Ministère de l'Europe et des Affaires étrangères; xi Balfour: King's College, Archive Centre; xi Huchthausen: Frieda van Schaïk Gumn Collection/Monuments Men Foundation; xi Ettlinger: Harry Ettlinger Collection/Monuments Men Foundation; xii Mussolini: ullstein bild Dtl./Getty Images; xii Hitler: ullstein bild Dtl./Getty Images; xii Goering: REX/Shutterstock; xii Wolff: Walter Frentz Collection; xii Langsdorff: Mareile Langsdorff Claus Collection; xii Ronsenberg: Harvard Law School Library/Wikimedia; xii Behr: Archives diplomatiques du Ministère de l'Europe et des Affaires étrangères; xii Lohse: Landesarchiv Berlin; xii Bunjes: Rheinische Friedrich-Wilhelms-Universität Bonn Archiv; xvi: Robert Posey Private Collection; xix: Library of Congress; xx: Photo 12/Getty Images; xxii: Arianna and Elisa Magrini/Edizioni Polistampa, Firenze; xxiii: Bayerisches Hauptstaatsarchiv; xxiv: Library of Congress; xxvi: Monuments Men Foundation; 1: Monuments Men Foundation; 2: Robert M. Edsel Collection; 4: William Keller Collection; 10, 11: National Archives and Records Administration; 12, 14: DeaneKeller Papers (MS 1685). Manuscripts and Archives, Yale University Library; 17: Wellcome Collection; 20: Library of Congress; 21, 25, 30: National Archives and Records Administration; 36: Antonio Quattrone/age fotostock; 37: Frederick Hartt Papers. National Gallery of Art, Washington, D.C., Gallery Archives. 28MFAA-D8_13994_002; 38, 39: Civico Archivio Fotografico Milano; 41, 43: A. S. Pennoyer Collection, Department of Art and Archaeology, Princeton University; 44: DeaneKeller Papers (MS 1685). Manuscripts and Archives, Yale University Library; 48: Hulton Archive/Getty Images; 60: A. S. Pennoyer Collection, Department of Art and Archaeology, Princeton University; 61: Eugene Markowski Collection; 62: Ministero per i Beni e le Attività Culturali; 66, 68: National Archives and Records Administration; 75: Paul Almasy/akg-images; 77: Ministère de la Culture/Médiathèque du Patrimoine, Dist. RMN-Grand Palais/Art Resource, NY; 78 top: National Archives and Records Administration; 78 bottom: Robert M. Edsel Collection; 82: Roberto Cerruti/Shutterstock; 87: Erich Lessing/Art Resource, NY; 94: DeaneKeller Papers (MS 1685). Manuscripts and Archives, Yale University Library; 96 top and bottom: Ministero per i Beni e le Attività Culturali; 100: Vincenzo Fontana/Getty Images; 101: Wikimedia; 106, 108: National Archives and Records Administration; 110 top: Wikimedia; 110 bottom: CEphoto, Uwe

Aranas/Wikimedia; 111: Walker Hancock Papers/Monuments Men Foundation; 115: James J. Rorimer Papers. National Gallery of Art, Washington, D.C., Gallery Archives; 125: Frieda van Schaïk Gumn Collection/Monuments Men Foundation; 127: Lincoln Kirstein © 2019 by the New York Public Library (Astor, Lenox and Tilden Foundations); 135 top: Bayerische Staatsbibliothek München/Bildarchiv; 135 bottom: A. Burkatovski/Fine Art Images/Superstock, Inc.; 136: Archives diplomatiques du Ministère de l'Europe et des Affaires étrangères; 137: James J. Rorimer Papers. National Gallery of Art, Washington, D.C., Gallery Archives. 28MFAA-J9_17269_I14F; 140: Eric Bernholz Private Collection; 142, 143: DeaneKeller Papers (MS 1685). Manuscripts and Archives, Yale University Library; 148, 152, 154: National Archives and Records Administration; 157, 158: DeaneKeller Papers (MS 1685). Manuscripts and Archives, Yale University Library; 162: Library of Congress; 163: Archives diplomatiques du Ministère de l'Europe et des Affaires étrangères; 181 top and bottom: National Archives and Records Administration; 182: Florian Monheim/age fotostock; 184, 189, 193, 194: National Archives and Records Administration; 195: Walter I. Farmer Papers. National Gallery of Art, Washington, D.C., Gallery Archives. 28MFAA-C7_13670_001; 197, 198, 199, 201, 203: National Archives and Records Administration; 206: Dale Ford Collection/ Monuments Men Foundation; 207: National Archives and Records Administration; 218: Archives of American Art, Smithsonian Institution, Hancock Collection; 219: Archives of American Art, Smithsonian Institution, Hancock Collection; 221: Peter Horree/Alamy Stock Photo; 227: Charles Parkhurst Papers. National Gallery of Art, Washington, D.C., Gallery Archives. 28MFAA-F8_14255_2; 228, 230 top and bottom, 231, 232: National Archives and Records Administration; 233: Monuments Men Foundation; 236: Archives of American Art, Smithsonian Institution, Hancock Collection; 239: National Archives and Records Administration; 241: Robert Posey Private Collection; 242: Walter Frentz Collection; 245: DeaneKeller Papers (MS 1685). Manuscripts and Archives, Yale University Library; 247: National Archives and Records Administration; 249 top: Frederick Hartt Papers. National Gallery of Art, Washington, D.C., Gallery Archives. 28MFAA-D8_13990_013; 249 bottom: Frederick Hartt Papers. National Gallery of Art, Washington, D.C., Gallery Archives. 28MFAA-D8_13992_011; 252: Frederick Hartt Papers. National Gallery of Art, Washington, D.C., Gallery Archives. 28MFAA-D8_13990_014; 253: Bundesarchiv, Berlin, Bild R 58/9362; 256: Robert Posey Private Collection; 257: TopFoto/The Image Works; 258: Craig Hugh Smyth Papers. National Gallery of Art, Washington, D.C., Gallery Archives. 28MFAA-G7_14427_02; 259: Documentation Archive of the Austrian Resistance; 260: Topham/The Image Works; 261: Archives of American Art, Smithsonian Institution, Thomas Howe Collection; 264: National Archives and Records Administration; 266, 267, 268: DeaneKeller Papers (MS 1685). Manuscripts and Archives, Yale University Library; 269: National Archives and Records Administration; 270: Archives diplomatiques du Ministère de l'Europe et des Affaires étrangères; 272: William Vandivert/Getty Images; 273: G. R. and G. A. Walden Collection; 277: Robert M. Edsel Collection; 278: Wikimedia; 279: George Bush Presidential Library and Museum; 282 top: Eric Bernholz Private Collection; 282 bottom: Robert M. Edsel Collection; 283: Monuments Men Foundation.

INDEX

Note: Page numbers in *italics* refer to illustrations.

ACKNOWLEDGMENTS

Writing a book requires a tremendous commitment of time. Like any undertaking of excellence, it demands discipline and sacrifice, and in this instance on the part of not just the author but also his wife and two young sons. Anna shared my excitement about introducing the story of the Monuments Men to young readers. Without her understanding, support, and encouragement, I could not have written this book. Whatever success attends this effort belongs in equal measure to her.

In 1996, while crossing the Ponte Vecchio in Florence, I wondered how so many of the works of art and cultural monuments of Europe survived the most destructive war in history, and who were the people who saved them. Driven by curiosity, I located and interviewed twenty-one Monuments Men and Women. I thank each of them, and their family members, for entrusting me with their legacy, in particular S. Lane Faison, Jr., and my dear friend Harry Ettlinger. Gathering their stories, a journey that has now consumed more than twenty years, has been the privilege of my life.

While my name alone appears on this book as author, others helped me along the way. Dr. Seth Givens, a gifted military historian and teacher, has been invaluable to me throughout the writing process. This is a much better book because of his involvement. My wife and lead researcher, Anna Bottinelli, helped assemble the many photographs and read the manuscript throughout the writing process. The candor of her counsel and her thorough knowledge of the material helped me beyond measure. Casey Shelton has done an outstanding job sorting through my extensive files at the Monuments Men Foundation for the Preservation of Art to stay ahead of my research needs. Her meticulous work has been essential to a project of this scope and magnitude. Finally, the day-to-day support of Michele Brown, my executive assistant, in handling many of the business and personal matters that constantly threaten the completion of a writer's task enabled me to finish the book on time. Thank you, Michele.

I am particularly pleased to have had the opportunity to tell these heroes' wartime experience in Italy and northern Europe in one book. It is a new telling of the Monuments Men story made possible by more than fifteen years of research. For that reason, I want to recognize and thank members of my previous research teams, including Bryce McWhinnie, Dorothee Schneider, Christy Fox, and Elizabeth Hudson. I also want to tip my hat and thank Bret Witter, coauthor of my second book, *The Monuments Men*. Special thanks also to Michelle Rapkin and Tom Mayer, both of whom helped me become a better writer.

Lisa Sandell and her team at Scholastic have been enthusiastic supporters of this project from the outset. An author benefits greatly from an engaged editor; Lisa has been that and more. Our frank exchanges of views benefited this book in many ways. And I would like to thank the rest of the Scholastic team: Jael Fogle, Keirsten Geise, Olivia Valcarce, Crystal McCoy, Emily Heddleson, Jasmine Miranda, Matthew Poulter, Lizette Serrano, Danielle Yadao, Tracy van Straaten, Rachel Feld, Isa Caban, Vaishali Nayak, Mindy Stockfield, David Levithan, Ellie Berger, the entire Sales force, and the Scholastic Book Clubs and Book Fairs.

Finally, I want to express my appreciation to some of the people whose work behind the scenes has enabled me to remain focused on bringing visibility to the Monuments Men and their remarkable legacy. Robert and Patty Hayes have been longstanding supporters of my efforts to honor these men and women. No amount of praise for their assistance would be too great. Similarly, I want to thank the generous donors who have sustained the Monuments Men Foundation in ways both large and small. My attorney and friend, Michael Friedman, has been with me from the start of my career as an author. I continue to benefit from his wise counsel. Thanks also to my agent, Richard Abate.

The Archivist of the United States, David Ferriero, and his outstanding team at the National Archives in College Park, Maryland, in particular Greg Bradsher, have been an important part of my success. They continue to share my commitment to see this important part of our nation's history broadly known. The National WWII Museum and its cofounder Dr. Nick Mueller, now president and CEO emeritus, recognized the importance of the Monuments Men story at an early stage. With the backing of its dedicated trustees, the Museum will soon begin construction of a permanent exhibition honoring the Monuments Men and Women that will preserve these scholar-soldiers' contribution to civilization for all time.

This is my fourth book about the Monuments Men, but my first book for young readers. I have long wanted to share this exciting and noble story with a young audience, the Monuments Men and Women of tomorrow. Preserving our shared cultural heritage for future generations depends on them.

ABOUT THE AUTHOR

A former nationally ranked tennis player and pioneer in the oil and gas exploration business, Robert M. Edsel is recognized as one of the world's foremost advocates for art preservation and the recovery of cultural treasures missing since World War II.

Mr. Edsel is the author of three other books about the Monuments Men, including the number one *New York Times* bestseller *The Monuments Men*, which Academy Award recipient George Clooney adapted into a feature film, and *Saving Italy*, also a *New York Times* bestseller. He is also the coproducer of the Emmy-nominated documentary film *The Rape of Europa*. In 2007 he founded the Monuments Men Foundation for the Preservation of Art, recipient of the National Humanities Medal, the United States' highest honor for work in the humanities.

Mr. Edsel has received numerous awards, including the Anne Frank Human Writes Award from the Anne Frank Center; the Texas Medal of Arts; the Hope for Humanity Award, presented by the Dallas Holocaust Museum; and the Records of Achievement Award from the Foundation for the National Archives, which recognizes an individual whose work has fostered a broader national awareness of the history and identity of the United States through the use of original records. Previous recipients have included Tom Hanks, Ken Burns, David McCullough, and Steven Spielberg.

Mr. Edsel has served as a trustee on numerous not-for-profit organizations, including the National WWII Museum and St. Mark's School of Texas.

He lives in Dallas, Texas, with his family.

Robert M. Edsel is a dynamic and passionate public speaker who has introduced the Monuments Men to audiences throughout the United States and worldwide. Using a mix of photographs and film clips, Mr. Edsel shares his experiences locating and interviewing some twenty Monuments Men and Women, working with George Clooney to bring these heroes' legacy to film, and the ongoing discoveries by the Monuments Men Foundation of priceless works of art and other treasures missing since the end of World War II. He has educated and inspired sold-out audiences at schools and community centers, and many of our nation's most prominent universities and museums.

To inquire about inviting Mr. Edsel to your school or organization, please contact David Buchalter at David.Buchalter @unitedtalent.com.

SCHOLASTIC
FOCUS

An inspiring line of narrative nonfiction books that will change the way you read the world.

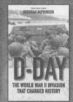

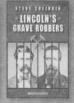

Bring Your World Into
FOCUS

scholastic.com/ScholasticFocus

■ SCHOLASTIC

SCHOLASTIC and associated logos are trademarks and/or registered trademarks of Scholastic Inc.   FOCUSSPR21

W9-CCU-047

PRAISE FOR STEPHEN KING AND
HEARTS IN ATLANTIS

"This is wonde fiction. . . . [King's] take on the including effects Vietnam—is scarily

—*Entertainment Weekly*

"[A] spellbinding of literature. . . . New char—
acters become old as the reader struggles with
them through e and trial (some of which are
classically King ing to survive in the end."

—*Library Journal*

"King *nails the '60s* legacy."

—*Publishers Weekly*

"An overtly autobiocal and heartfelt work."

—*The Village Voice*

"Page after page, a mature King does everything right and de some kind of literary
rosette. His masterpie

—*Kirkus Reviews*

"You will see Stephen King in a new light. Read this
moving, heartfelt modern tragedy and weep—weep
for our lost conscience."

—*BookPage*

THE GIRL WHO LOVED TOM GORDON

"An absorbing tale. . . . *Girl* sure is big."

—*People*

"A delightful read, a jaunty walkabout . . . not just for backpackers . . ."

"**Impressive**. . . . A wonder of courage, faith, and hope. . . . It is mesmerizing and difficult to put down."
—*The Wall Street Journal*

"A fast, scary read. . . . blasts a homer. . . . [He] expertly stirs the majients of the American psyche—our spiritual love of children, passion for baseball, and the fear of the bad thing we know lurks on the ry of life."
—New York *Daily News*

"King paints a masterfterrifying picture of every child's (and maybe adultorst fear. . . . King uses that creepy-crawly paranoo perfection."
—*St. Louis Post-Dispatch*

"Plenty of thrills. . . . [King's] an elegant writer and a master of pacing."
—*Entertainment Weekly*

BAG OF BONES

"A rare blend of luminous prose, thought-provoking themes, and masterful storytelling."
—*The San Diego Union-Tribune*

"What I admire most about *Bag of Bones* is its intelligence of voice, not only the craftsmanship—the indelible sense of place, the well-fleshed characters, the unstoppable story line—but the witty and obsessive voice of King's powerful imagination."
—Amy Tan

"*Bag of Bones* is, hands down, King's most narratively subversive fiction. Whenever you're positive—just positive!—you know where this ghost story is heading, that's exactly when it gallops off in some jaw-dropping new direction."
—*Entertainment Weekly*

"This is King at his clever, terrifying best."
—*Mademoiselle*

"Contains some of [King's] best writing. . . . This is King's most romantic book, and ghosts are up and about from the get-go. . . . The big surprise here is the emotional wallop the story packs."
—*Newsweek*

STEPHEN KING

The Shining

POCKET BOOKS

New York   London   Toronto   Sydney

For information regarding special discounts for bulk purchases,
please contact Simon & Schuster Special Sales at 1-800-456-6798 or
business@simonandschuster.com

The sale of this book without its cover is unauthorized. If you purchased
this book without a cover, you should be aware that it was reported to
the publisher as "unsold and destroyed." Neither the author nor the
publisher has received payment for the sale of this "stripped book."

Lyrics from "Call Me," © 1973 by Jec Music Publishing Co. and Al Green Music, Inc.
for the world. All rights for Canada controlled by Felsted Music of Canada Ltd. All rights
for world except the United States and Canada controlled by Burlington Music Co. Ltd.,
London, England.

"Your Cheatin' Heart," by Hank Williams. Copyright 1952 by Fred Rose Music, Inc.
Used by permission of the publisher, Fred Rose Music, Inc., 2510 Franklin Road,
Nashville, Tennessee 37204. All rights reserved.

Lyrics from "Twenty Flight Rock" by Ned Fairchild. Copyright © 1957 by Hill and
Range Songs, Inc. Noma Music, Inc. and Elvis Presley Music. International Copyright
Secured. ALL RIGHTS RESERVED. Used by permission of Unichappell Music, Inc.

"Bad Moon Rising" by John C. Fogerty, © 1969 Jondora Music, Berkeley, Calif. Used
by permission. All rights reserved. International copyright secured.

This book is a work of fiction. Names, characters, places, and incidents are products of the
author's imagination or are used fictitiously. Any resemblance to actual events or locales or
persons, living or dead, is entirely coincidental.

POCKET BOOKS, a division of Simon & Schuster, Inc.
1230 Avenue of the Americas, New York, NY 10020

Copyright © 1977 by Stephen King
Introduction copyright © 2001 by Stephen King

Published by arrangement with Doubleday,
a division of Bantam Doubleday Dell Publishing Group, Inc.

All rights reserved, including the right to reproduce
this book or portions thereof in any form whatsoever.
For information address Doubleday, a division of
Bantam Doubleday Dell Publishing Group, Inc.
1540 Broadway, New York, NY 10036
ISBN -13: 978-0-7434-2442-4
ISBN -10: 0-7434-2442-5
First Pocket Books printing September 2001

20 19 18

POCKET and colophon are registered trademarks of
Simon & Schuster, Inc.

Cover art by Lisa Litwack, photo by Gavin R. Wilson/Photonica

Printed in the U.S.A.

This is for Joe Hill King, who shines on.

My editor on this book, as on the previous two, was Mr. William G. Thompson, a man of wit and good sense. His contribution to this book has been large, and for it, my thanks.

—S.K.

Some of the most beautiful resort hotels in the world are located in Colorado, but the hotel in these pages is based on none of them. The Overlook and the people associated with it exist wholly within the author's imagination.

It was in this apartment, also, that there stood . . . a gigantic clock of ebony. Its pendulum swung to and fro with a dull, heavy, monotonous clang; and when . . . the hour was to be stricken, there came from the brazen lungs of the clock a sound which was clear and loud and deep and exceedingly musical, but of so peculiar a note and emphasis that, at each lapse of an hour, the musicians of the orchestra were constrained to pause . . . to hearken to the sound; and thus the waltzers perforce ceased their evolutions; and there was a brief disconcert of the whole gay company; and, while the chimes of the clock yet rang, it was observed that the giddiest grew pale, and the more aged and sedate passed their hands over their brows as if in confused reverie or meditation. But when the echoes had fully ceased, a light laughter at once pervaded the assembly . . . and [they] smiled as if at their own nervousness . . . and made whispering vows, each to the other, that the next chiming of the clock should produce in them no similar emotion; and then, after the lapse of sixty minutes . . . there came yet another chiming of the clock, and then were the same disconcert and tremulousness and meditation as before.

But in spite of these things, it was a gay and magnificent revel . . .

—E. A. POE
"The Masque of the Red Death"

The sleep of reason breeds monsters.

—GOYA

It'll shine when it shines.

—Folk saying

INTRODUCTION

Introduction

STEPHEN KING

I think that in every writer's career—usually early
in it—there comes a "crossroads novel," where the
writer is presented with a choice: either do what
you have done before, or try to reach a little higher.
What you realize only in retrospect is how important that choice is. Sometimes the moment comes
only once. For me, the crossroads novel was *The
Shining*, and I did decide to reach. I can even
remember the exact moment the choice came: It
was when Jack Torrance, *The Shining*'s flawed pro-
tagonist, is remembering his father, a drunken
brute who abused his son mentally, physically and
emotionally . . . all the ways it can be done, in other
words.

Part of me wanted to describe the father's brutal-
ity and leave it at that. Surely, I thought, the book's
readers would make the connection between Jack's
relationship with his father and Jack's relationship
with his own son, Danny, who is, of course, *The
Shining*'s psychic focal point.

Another part of me wanted to go deeper—to admit Jack's love of his father in spite of (perhaps even *because* of) his father's unpredictable and often brutal nature. That was the part I listened to, and it made a big difference to the novel as a whole. Instead of changing from a relatively nice guy into a two-dimensional villain driven by supernatural forces to kill his wife and son, Jack Torrance became a more realistic (and therefore more frightening) figure. A killer motivated to his crimes by supernatural forces was, it seemed to me, almost comforting once you got below the surface thrills provided by any halfway competent ghost story. A killer that might be doing it because of childhood abuse *as well as* those ghostly forces . . . ah, that seemed genuinely disturbing. Furthermore, it offered a chance to blur the line between the supernatural and the psychotic, to take my story into that I-hope-this-is-only-a-dream territory where the merely scary becomes outright horrifying. My single conversation with the late Stanley Kubrick, about six months before he commenced filming his version of *The Shining,* suggested that it was this quality about the story that appealed to him: What, exactly, is impelling Jack Torrance toward murder in the winter-isolated rooms and hallways of the Overlook Hotel? Is it undead people, or undead memories? Mr. Kubrick and I came to different conclusions (I *always* thought there were malevolent ghosts in the Overlook, driving Jack to the precipice), but perhaps those different conclusions are, in fact, the same. For aren't memories the true ghosts of our lives? Do they not drive all of us to words and acts we regret from time to time?

The decision I made to try and make Jack's father a real person, one who was loved as well as hated by his flawed son, took me a long way down the road to my current beliefs concerning what is so blithely dismissed as "the horror novel." I believe these stories exist because we sometimes need to create unreal monsters and bogies to stand in for all the things we fear in our real lives: the parent who punches instead of kissing, the auto accident that takes a loved one, the cancer we one day discover living in our own bodies. If such terrible occurrences were acts of darkness, they might actually be easier to cope with. But instead of being dark, they have their own terrible brilliance, it seems to me, and none shine so bright as the acts of cruelty we sometimes perpetrate in our own families. To look directly at such brilliance is to be blinded, and so we create any number of filters. The ghost story, the horror story, the uncanny tale— all of these are such filters. The man or woman who insists there are no ghosts is only ignoring the whispers of his or her own heart, and how cruel that seems to me. Surely even the most malignant ghost is a lonely thing, left out in the dark, desperate to be heard.

None of these things occurred to me in coherent or even semi-coherent form when I was writing *The Shining* in my little study looking out toward the Flatirons; I had a story to write, my daily goal of

3,000 words to meet (I'm lucky if I can manage 1,800 a day in my sixth decade). All I knew was that I had a choice, either to make little Jacky's father a flat-out bad guy (which I could do in my sleep) or to try for something a little more difficult and complex: in a word, reality.

If I had been less well-fixed financially, I might well have opted for choice number one. But my first two books, *Carrie* and *'Salem's Lot*, had been successful, and we Kings were doing okay in that regard. And I didn't want to settle for less when I sensed I could up the book's emotional ante considerably by making Jack Torrance a real character instead of just the Overlook's boogeyman.

The result wasn't perfect, and there is a cocky quality to some of *The Shining*'s prose that has come to grate on me in later years, but I still like the book enormously, and recognize the importance of the choice it forced on me: between the safe unreality of the amusement park funhouse and the much more dangerous truths that lurk between the lines of the fantasy genre's more successful works. That truth is that monsters are real, and ghosts are real, too. They live inside us, and sometimes they win.

That our better angels sometimes—often!—win instead, in spite of all odds, is another truth of *The Shining*. And thank God it is.

New York City
February 8, 2001

PART ONE

Prefatory
Matters

1

Job Interview

Jack Torrance thought: *Officious little prick.*

Ullman stood five-five, and when he moved, it was with the prissy speed that seems to be the exclusive domain of all small plump men. The part in his hair was exact, and his dark suit was sober but comforting. I am a man you can bring your problems to, that suit said to the paying customer. To the hired help it spoke more curtly: This had better be good, you. There was a red carnation in the lapel, perhaps so that no one on the street would mistake Stuart Ullman for the local undertaker.

As he listened to Ullman speak, Jack admitted to himself that he probably could not have liked any man on that side of the desk—under the circumstances.

Ullman had asked a question he hadn't caught. That was bad; Ullman was the type of man who would file such lapses away in a mental Rolodex for later consideration.

"I'm sorry?"

"I asked if your wife fully understood what you would be taking on here. And there's your son, of course." He glanced down at the application in front of him. "Daniel. Your wife isn't a bit intimidated by the idea?"

"Wendy is an extraordinary woman."

"And your son is also extraordinary?"

Jack smiled, a big wide PR smile. "We like to think so, I suppose. He's quite self-reliant for a five-year-old."

No returning smile from Ullman. He slipped Jack's application back into a file. The file went into a drawer. The desk top was now completely bare except for a blotter, a telephone, a Tensor lamp, and an in/out basket. Both sides of the in/out were empty, too.

Ullman stood up and went to the file cabinet in the corner. "Step around the desk, if you will, Mr. Torrance. We'll look at the hotel floor plans."

He brought back five large sheets and set them down on the glossy walnut plain of the desk. Jack stood by his shoulder, very much aware of the scent of Ullman's cologne. *All my men wear English Leather or they wear nothing at all* came into his mind for no reason at all, and he had to clamp his tongue between his teeth to keep in a bray of laughter. Beyond the wall, faintly, came the sounds of the Overlook Hotel's kitchen, gearing down from lunch.

"Top floor," Ullman said briskly. "The attic. Absolutely nothing up there now but bric-a-brac. The Overlook has changed hands several times since World War II and it seems that each successive manager has put everything they don't want up in the attic. I want rattraps and poison bait sowed around in it. Some of the third-floor chambermaids say they have heard rustling noises. I don't believe it, not for a moment, but there mustn't even be that one-in-a-hundred chance that a single rat inhabits the Overlook Hotel."

Jack, who suspected that every hotel in the world had a rat or two, held his tongue.

"Of course you wouldn't allow your son up in the attic under any circumstances."

"No," Jack said, and flashed the big PR smile again. Humiliating situation. Did this officious little prick actually think he would allow his son to goof around in a rattrap attic full of junk furniture and God knew what else?

Ullman whisked away the attic floor plan and put it on the bottom of the pile.

"The Overlook has one hundred and ten guest quarters," he said in a scholarly voice. "Thirty of them, all suites, are here on the third floor. Ten in the west wing (including the Presidential Suite), ten in the center, ten more in the east wing. All of them command magnificent views."

Could you at least spare the salestalk?

But he kept quiet. He needed the job.

Ullman put the third floor on the bottom of the pile and they studied the second floor.

"Forty rooms," Ullman said, "thirty doubles and ten singles. And on the first floor, twenty of each. Plus three linen closets on each floor, and a storeroom which is at the extreme east end of the hotel on the second floor and the extreme west end on the first. Questions?"

Jack shook his head. Ullman whisked the second and first floors away.

"Now. Lobby level. Here in the center is the registration desk. Behind it are the offices. The lobby runs for eighty feet in either direction from the desk. Over here in the west wing is the Overlook Dining Room and the Colorado Lounge. The banquet and ballroom facility is in the east wing. Questions?"

"Only about the basement," Jack said. "For the winter caretaker, that's the most important level of all. Where the action is, so to speak."

"Watson will show you all that. The basement floor plan is on the boiler room wall." He frowned impressively, perhaps to show that as manager, he did not concern himself with such mundane aspects of the Overlook's operation as the boiler and the plumbing. "Might not be a bad idea to put some traps down there too. Just a minute . . ."

He scrawled a note on a pad he took from his inner coat pocket (each sheet bore the legend *From the Desk of Stuart Ullman* in bold black script), tore it off, and dropped it into the out basket. It sat there looking lonesome. The pad disappeared back into Ullman's jacket pocket like the conclusion of a magician's trick. Now you see it, Jacky-boy, now you don't. This guy is a real heavyweight.

They had resumed their original positions, Ullman behind the desk and Jack in front of it, interviewer and interviewee, supplicant and reluctant patron. Ullman folded his neat little hands on the desk blotter and looked directly at Jack, a small, balding man in a banker's suit and a quiet gray tie. The flower in his lapel was balanced off by a small lapel pin on the other side. It read simply STAFF in small gold letters.

"I'll be perfectly frank with you, Mr. Torrance. Albert Shockley is a powerful man with a large interest in the Overlook, which showed a profit this season for the first time in its history. Mr. Shockley also sits on the Board of Directors, but he is not a hotel man and he would be the first to admit this. But he has made his wishes in this caretaking matter quite obvious. He wants you hired. I will do so. But if I had been given a free hand in this matter, I would not have taken you on."

Jack's hands were clenched tightly in his lap, working against each other, sweating. *Officious little prick, officious little prick, officious—*

"I don't believe you care much for me, Mr. Torrance. I don't care. Certainly your feelings toward me play no part in my own belief that you are not right for the job. During the season that runs from May fifteenth to September thirtieth, the Overlook employs one hundred and ten people full-time; one for every room in the hotel, you might say. I don't think many of them like me and I suspect that some of them think I'm a bit of a bastard. They would be correct in their judgment of my character. I have to be a bit of a bastard to run this hotel in the manner it deserves."

He looked at Jack for comment, and Jack flashed the PR smile again, large and insultingly toothy.

Ullman said: "The Overlook was built in the years 1907 to 1909. The closest town is Sidewinder, forty miles east of here over roads that are closed from sometime in late October or November until sometime in April. A man named Robert Townley Watson built it, the grandfather of our present maintenance man. Vanderbilts have stayed here, and Rockefellers, and Astors, and Du Ponts. Four Presidents have stayed in the Presidential Suite, Wilson, Harding, Roosevelt, and Nixon."

"I wouldn't be too proud of Harding and Nixon," Jack murmured.

Ullman frowned but went on regardless. "It proved too much for Mr. Watson, and he sold the hotel in 1915. It was sold again in 1922, in 1929, in 1936. It stood vacant until the end of World War II, when it was purchased and completely renovated by Horace Derwent, millionaire inventor, pilot, film producer, and entrepreneur."

"I know the name," Jack said.

"Yes. Everything he touched seemed to turn to gold . . . except the Overlook. He funneled over a million dollars into it before the first postwar guest ever stepped through its doors, turning a decrepit relic into a showplace. It was Derwent who added the roque court I saw you admiring when you arrived."

"Roque?"

"A British forebear of our croquet, Mr. Torrance. Croquet is bastardized roque. According to legend,

Derwent learned the game from his social secretary and fell completely in love with it. Ours may be the finest roque court in America."

"I wouldn't doubt it," Jack said gravely. A roque court, a topiary full of hedge animals out front, what next? A life-sized Uncle Wiggily game behind the equipment shed? He was getting very tired of Mr. Stuart Ullman, but he could see that Ullman wasn't done. Ullman was going to have his say, every last word of it.

"When he had lost three million, Derwent sold it to a group of California investors. Their experience with the Overlook was equally bad. Just not hotel people.

"In 1970, Mr. Shockley and a group of his associates bought the hotel and turned its management over to me. We have also run in the red for several years, but I'm happy to say that the trust of the present owners in me has never wavered. Last year we broke even. And this year the Overlook's accounts were written in black ink for the first time in almost seven decades."

Jack supposed that this fussy little man's pride was justified, and then his original dislike washed over him again in a wave.

He said: "I see no connection between the Overlook's admittedly colorful history and your feeling that I'm wrong for the post, Mr. Ullman."

"One reason that the Overlook has lost so much money lies in the depreciation that occurs each winter. It shortens the profit margin a great deal more than you might believe, Mr. Torrance. The winters are fantastically cruel. In order to cope with the problem, I've installed a full-time winter caretaker to run the boiler and to heat different parts of the hotel on a daily rotating basis. To repair breakage as it occurs and to do repairs, so the elements can't get a foothold. To be constantly alert to any and every contingency. During our first winter I hired a family instead of a single man. There was a tragedy. A horrible tragedy."

Ullman looked at Jack coolly and appraisingly.

"I made a mistake. I admit it freely. The man was a drunk."

Jack felt a slow, hot grin—the total antithesis of the toothy PR grin—stretch across his mouth. "Is that it? I'm surprised Al didn't tell you. I've retired."

"Yes, Mr. Shockley told me you no longer drink. He also told me about your last job . . . your last position of trust, shall we say? You were teaching English in a Vermont prep school. You lost your temper, I don't believe I need to be any more specific than that. But I do happen to believe that Grady's case has a bearing, and that is why I have brought the matter of your . . . uh, previous history into the conversation. During the winter of 1970–71, after we had refurbished the Overlook but before our first season, I hired this . . . this unfortunate named Delbert Grady. He moved into the quarters you and your wife and son will be sharing. He had a wife and two daughters. I had reservations, the main ones being the harshness of the winter season and the fact that the Gradys would be cut off from the outside world for five to six months."

"But that's not really true, is it? There are telephones here, and probably a citizen's band radio as well. And the Rocky Mountain National Park is within helicopter range and surely a piece of ground that big must have a chopper or two."

"I wouldn't know about that," Ullman said. "The hotel does have a two-way radio that Mr. Watson will show you, along with a list of the correct frequencies to broadcast on if you need help. The telephone lines between here and Sidewinder are still aboveground, and they go down almost every winter at some point or other and are apt to stay down for three weeks to a month and a half. There is a snowmobile in the equipment shed also."

"Then the place really isn't cut off."

Mr. Ullman looked pained. "Suppose your son or your wife tripped on the stairs and fractured his or her skull, Mr. Torrance. Would you think the place was cut off then?"

Jack saw the point. A snowmobile running at top speed could get you down to Sidewinder in an hour and a half . . . maybe. A helicopter from the Parks Rescue Service could get up here in three hours . . . under optimum conditions. In a blizzard it would never even be able to lift off and you couldn't hope to run a snowmobile at top speed, even if you dared take a seriously injured person out into temperatures that might be twenty-five below—or forty-five below, if you added in the wind chill factor.

"In the case of Grady," Ullman said, "I reasoned much as Mr. Shockley seems to have done in your case. Solitude can be damaging in itself. Better for the man to have his family with him. If there was trouble, I thought, the odds were very high that it would be something less urgent than a fractured skull or an accident with one of the power tools or some sort of convulsion. A serious case of the flu, pneumonia, a broken arm, even appendicitis. Any of those things would have left enough time.

"I suspect that what happened came as a result of too much cheap whiskey, of which Grady had laid in a generous supply, unbeknownst to me, and a curious condition which the old-timers call cabin fever. Do you know the term?" Ullman offered a patronizing little smile, ready to explain as soon as Jack admitted his ignorance, and Jack was happy to respond quickly and crisply.

"It's a slang term for the claustrophobic reaction that can occur when people are shut in together over long periods of time. The feeling of claustrophobia is externalized as dislike for the people you happen to be shut in with. In extreme cases it can result in hallucinations and violence—murder has been done over such minor things as a burned meal or an argument about whose turn it is to do the dishes."

Ullman looked rather nonplussed, which did Jack a world of good. He decided to press a little further, but silently promised Wendy he would stay cool.

"I suspect you did make a mistake at that. Did he hurt them?"

"He killed them, Mr. Torrance, and then committed suicide. He murdered the little girls with a hatchet, his wife with a shotgun, and himself the same way. His leg was broken. Undoubtedly so drunk he fell downstairs."

Ullman spread his hands and looked at Jack self-righteously.

"Was he a high school graduate?"

"As a matter of fact, he wasn't," Ullman said a little stiffly. "I thought a, shall we say, less imaginative individual would be less susceptible to the rigors, the loneliness——"

"That was your mistake," Jack said. "A stupid man is more prone to cabin fever just as he's more prone to shoot someone over a card game or commit a spur-of-the-moment robbery. He gets bored. When the snow comes, there's nothing to do but watch TV or play solitaire and cheat when he can't get all the aces out. Nothing to do but bitch at his wife and nag at the kids and drink. It gets hard to sleep because there's nothing to hear. So he drinks himself to sleep and wakes up with a hangover. He gets edgy. And maybe the telephone goes out and the TV aerial blows down and there's nothing to do but think and cheat at solitaire and get edgier and edgier. Finally . . . boom, boom, boom."

"Whereas a more educated man, such as yourself?"

"My wife and I both like to read. I have a play to work on, as Al Shockley probably told you. Danny has his puzzles, his coloring books, and his crystal radio. I plan to teach him to read, and I also want to teach him to snowshoe. Wendy would like to learn how, too. Oh yes, I think we can keep busy and out of each other's hair if the TV goes on the fritz." He paused. "And Al was telling the truth when he told you I no longer drink. I did once, and it got to be serious. But I haven't had so much as a glass of beer in the last fourteen months. I don't intend to bring any alcohol up here, and I don't think there will be an opportunity to get any after the snow flies."

"In that you would be quite correct," Ullman said. "But as long as the three of you are up here, the potential for problems is multiplied. I have told Mr. Shockley this, and he told me he would take the responsibility. Now I've told you, and apparently you are also willing to take the responsibility—"

"I am."

"All right. I'll accept that, since I have little choice. But I would still rather have an unattached college boy taking a year off. Well, perhaps you'll do. Now I'll turn you over to Mr. Watson, who will take you through the basement and around the grounds. Unless you have further questions?"

"No. None at all."

Ullman stood. "I hope there are no hard feelings, Mr. Torrance. There is nothing personal in the things I have said to you. I only want what's best for the Overlook. It is a great hotel. I want it to stay that way."

"No. No hard feelings." Jack flashed the PR grin again, but he was glad Ullman didn't offer to shake hands. There were hard feelings. All kinds of them.

Boulder

She looked out the kitchen window and saw him just sitting there on the curb, not playing with his trucks or the wagon or even the balsa glider that had pleased him so much all the last week since Jack had brought it home. He was just sitting there, watching for their shopworn VW, his elbows planted on his thighs and his chin propped in his hands, a five-year-old kid waiting for his daddy.

Wendy suddenly felt bad, almost crying bad.

She hung the dish towel over the bar by the sink and went downstairs, buttoning the top two buttons of her house dress. Jack and his pride! *Hey no, Al, I don't need an advance. I'm okay for a while.* The hallway walls were gouged and marked with crayons, grease pencil, spray paint. The stairs were steep and splintery. The whole building smelled of sour age, and what sort of place was this for Danny after the small neat brick house in Stovington? The people living above them on the third floor weren't married, and while that didn't bother her, their constant, rancorous fighting did. It scared her. The guy up there was Tom, and after the bars had closed and they had returned home, the fights would start in earnest—the rest of the week was just a prelim in comparison. The Friday Night Fights, Jack called them, but it wasn't funny. The woman—her name was Elaine—would at last be reduced to tears and to repeating over and over again: "Don't, Tom. Please don't. Please don't." And he would shout at her. Once they had even awakened Danny, and Danny slept like a corpse. The next morning Jack caught Tom going out and had spoken to him on the sidewalk at some length. Tom started to bluster and Jack had said something else to him, too quietly for Wendy to hear, and Tom had only shaken his head sullenly and walked away. That had been a week ago and for a few days things had been better, but since the weekend things had been working back to normal—excuse me, abnormal. It was bad for the boy.

Her sense of grief washed over her again but she was on the walk now and she smothered it. Sweeping her dress under her and sitting down on the curb beside him, she said: "What's up, doc?"

He smiled at her but it was perfunctory. "Hi, Mom."

The glider was between his sneakered feet, and she saw that one of the wings had started to splinter.

"Want me to see what I can do with that, honey?"

Danny had gone back to staring up the street. "No. Dad will fix it."

"Your daddy may not be back until suppertime, doc. It's a long drive up into those mountains."

"Do you think the bug will break down?"

"No, I don't think so." But he had just given her something new to worry about. *Thanks, Danny. I needed that.*

"Dad said it might," Danny said in a matter-of-fact, almost bored manner. "He said the fuel pump was all shot to shit."

"Don't say that, Danny."

"Fuel pump?" he asked her with honest surprise.

She sighed. "No, 'All shot to shit.' Don't say that."

"Why?"

"It's vulgar."

"What's vulgar, Mom?"

"Like when you pick your nose at the table or pee with the bathroom door open. Or saying things like 'All shot to shit.' Shit is a vulgar word. Nice people don't say it."

"Dad says it. When he was looking at the bugmotor he said, 'Christ this fuel pump's all shot to shit.' Isn't Dad nice?"

How do you get into these things, Winnifred? Do you practice?

"He's nice, but he's also a grown-up. And he's very careful not to say things like that in front of people who wouldn't understand."

"You mean like Uncle Al?"

"Yes, that's right."

"Can I say it when I'm grown-up?"

"I suppose you will, whether I like it or not."

"How old?"

"How does twenty sound, doc?"

"That's a long time to have to wait."

"I guess it is, but will you try?"

"Hokay."

He went back to staring up the street. He flexed a little, as if to rise, but the beetle coming was much newer, and much brighter red. He relaxed again. She wondered just how hard this move to Colorado had been on Danny. He was close-mouthed about it, but it bothered her to see him spending so much time by himself. In Vermont three of Jack's fellow faculty members had had children about Danny's age—and there had been the preschool—but in this neighborhood there was no one for him to play with. Most of the apartments were occupied by students attending CU, and of the few married couples here on Arapahoe Street, only a tiny percentage had children. She had spotted perhaps a dozen of high school or junior high school age, three infants, and that was all.

"Mommy, why did Daddy lose his job?"

She was jolted out of her reverie and floundering for an answer. She and Jack had discussed ways they might handle just such a question from Danny, ways that had varied from evasion to the plain truth with no varnish on it. But Danny had never asked. Not until now, when she was feeling low and least prepared for such a question. Yet he was looking at her, maybe reading the confusion on her face and forming his own ideas about that. She thought that to children adult motives and actions must seem as bulking and ominous as dangerous animals seen in the shadows of a dark forest. They were jerked about like puppets, having only the vaguest notions why. The thought brought her dangerously close to tears again, and while she fought them off she leaned over, picked up the disabled glider, and turned it over in her hands.

"Your daddy was coaching the debate team, Danny. Do you remember that?"

"Sure," he said. "Arguments for fun, right?"

"Right." She turned the glider over and over, looking at the trade name (SPEEDOGLIDE) and the blue star decals on the wings, and found herself telling the exact truth to her son.

"There was a boy named George Hatfield that Daddy had to cut from the team. That means he wasn't as good as some of the others. George said your daddy cut him because he didn't like him and not because he wasn't good enough. Then George did a bad thing. I think you know about that."

"Was he the one who put holes in our bug's tires?"

"Yes, he was. It was after school and your daddy caught him doing it." Now she hesitated again, but there was no question of evasion now; it was reduced to tell the truth or tell a lie.

"Your daddy . . . sometimes he does things he's sorry for later. Sometimes he doesn't think the way he should. That doesn't happen very often, but sometimes it does."

"Did he hurt George Hatfield like the time I spilled all his papers?"

Sometimes—

(Danny with his arm in a cast)

—he does things he's sorry for later.

Wendy blinked her eyes savagely hard, driving her tears all the way back.

"Something like that, honey. Your daddy hit George to make him stop cutting the tires and George hit his head. Then the men who are in charge of the school said that George couldn't go there anymore and your daddy couldn't teach there anymore." She stopped, out of words, and waited in dread for the deluge of questions.

"Oh," Danny said, and went back to looking up the street. Apparently the subject was closed. If only it could be closed that easily for her—

She stood up. "I'm going upstairs for a cup of tea, doc. Want a couple of cookies and a glass of milk?"

"I think I'll watch for Dad."

"I don't think he'll be home much before five."

"Maybe he'll be early."

"Maybe," she agreed. "Maybe he will."

She was halfway up the walk when he called, "Mommy?"

"What, Danny?"

"Do you want to go and live in that hotel for the winter?"

Now, which of five thousand answers should she give to that one? The way she had felt yesterday or last night or this morning? They were all different, they crossed the spectrum from rosy pink to dead black.

She said: "If it's what your father wants, it's what I want." She paused. "What about you?"

"I guess I do," he said finally. "Nobody much to play with around here."

"You miss your friends, don't you?"

"Sometimes I miss Scott and Andy. That's about all."

She went back to him and kissed him, rumpled his light-colored hair that was just losing its baby-fineness. He was such a solemn little boy, and sometimes she wondered just how he was supposed to survive with her and Jack for parents. The high hopes they had begun with came down to this unpleasant apartment building in a city they didn't know. The image of Danny in his cast rose up before her again. Somebody in the Divine Placement Service had made a mistake, one she sometimes feared could never be corrected and which only the most innocent bystander could pay for.

"Stay out of the road, doc," she said, and hugged him tight.

"Sure, Mom."

She went upstairs and into the kitchen. She put on the teapot and laid a couple of Oreos on a plate for Danny in case he decided to come up while she was lying down. Sitting at the table with her big pottery cup in front of her, she looked out the window at him, still sitting on the curb in his bluejeans and his over-sized dark green Stovington Prep sweatshirt, the glider now lying beside him. The tears which had threatened all day now came in a cloudburst and she leaned into the fragrant, curling steam of the tea and wept. In grief and loss for the past, and terror of the future.

Watson

You lost your temper, Ullman had said.

"Okay, here's your furnace," Watson said, turning on a light in the dark, musty-smelling room. He was a beefy man with fluffy popcorn hair, white shirt, and dark green chinos. He swung open a small square grating in the furnace's belly and he and Jack peered in together. "This here's the pilot light." A steady blue-white jet hissing steadily upward channeled destructive force, but the key word, Jack thought, was *destructive* and not *channeled*: if you stuck your hand in there, the barbecue would happen in three quick seconds.

Lost your temper.

(Danny, are you all right?)

The furnace filled the entire room, by far the biggest and oldest Jack had ever seen.

"The pilot's got a fail-safe," Watson told him. "Little sensor in there measures heat. If the heat falls below a certain point, it sets off a buzzer in your quarters. Boiler's on the other side of the wall. I'll take you around." He slammed the grating shut and

led Jack behind the iron bulk of the furnace toward
another door. The iron radiated a stuporous heat at
them, and for some reason Jack thought of a large,
dozing cat. Watson jingled his keys and whistled.

Lost your—

(When he went back into his study and saw
Danny standing there, wearing nothing but his training pants and a grin, a slow, red cloud of rage had
eclipsed Jack's reason. It had seemed slow subjec-
tively, inside his head, but it must have all happened
in less than a minute. It only seemed slow the way
some dreams seem slow. The bad ones. Every door
and drawer in his study seemed to have been ran-
sacked in the time he had been gone. Closet, cupboards, the sliding bookcase. Every desk drawer
yanked out to the stop. His manuscript, the three-act
play he had been slowly developing from a novelette
he had written seven years ago as an undergraduate,
was scattered all over the floor. He had been drinking
a beer and doing the Act II corrections when Wendy
said the phone was for him, and Danny had poured
the can of beer all over the pages. Probably to see it
foam. *See it foam, see it foam,* the words played over and
over in his mind like a single sick chord on an out-of-
tune piano, completing the circuit of his rage. He
stepped deliberately toward his three-year-old son,
who was looking up at him with that pleased grin, his
pleasure at the job of work so successfully and recently
completed in Daddy's study; Danny began to say
something and that was when he had grabbed Danny's
hand and bent it to make him drop the typewriter

eraser and the mechanical pencil he was clenching in it. Danny had cried out a little . . . no . . . no . . . tell the truth . . . he screamed. It was all hard to remember through the fog of anger, the sick single thump of that one Spike Jones chord. Wendy somewhere, asking what was wrong. Her voice faint, damped by the inner mist. This was between the two of them. He had whirled Danny around to spank him, his big adult fingers digging into the scant meat of the boy's forearm, meeting around it in a closed fist, and the snap of the breaking bone had not been loud, not loud but it had been *very* loud, *HUGE,* but not loud. Just enough of a sound to slit through the red fog like an arrow—but instead of letting in sunlight, that sound let in the dark clouds of shame and remorse, the terror, the agonizing convulsion of the spirit. A clean sound with the past on one side of it and all the future on the other, a sound like a breaking pencil lead or a small piece of kindling when you brought it down over your knee. A moment of utter silence on the other side, in respect to the beginning future maybe, all the rest of his life. Seeing Danny's face drain of color until it was like cheese, seeing his eyes, always large, grow larger still, and glassy, Jack sure the boy was going to faint dead away into the puddle of beer and papers; his own voice, weak and drunk, slurry, trying to take it all back, to find *a way* around that not too loud sound of bone cracking and into the past—is there a status quo in the house?—saying: *Danny, are you all right?* Danny's answering shriek, then Wendy's shocked gasp as she came around them and saw the peculiar angle Danny's forearm had to his elbow; no arm was meant to hang quite that way in a world of normal families. Her own scream as she swept him into her arms, and a nonsense babble: *Oh God Danny oh dear God oh sweet God your poor sweet arm;* and Jack was standing there, stunned and stupid, trying to understand how a thing like this could have happened. He was standing there and his eyes met the eyes of his wife and he saw that Wendy hated him. It did not occur to him what the hate might mean in practical terms; it was only later that he realized she might have left him that night, gone to a motel, gotten a divorce lawyer in the morning; or called the police. He saw only that his wife hated him and he felt staggered by it, all alone. He felt awful. This was what oncoming death felt like. Then she fled for the telephone and dialed the hospital with their screaming boy wedged in the crook of her arm and Jack did not go after her, he only stood in the ruins of his office, smelling beer and thinking—)

You lost your temper.

He rubbed his hand harshly across his lips and followed Watson into the boiler room. It was humid in here, but it was more than the humidity that brought the sick and slimy sweat onto his brow and stomach and legs. The remembering did that, it was a total thing that made that night two years ago seem like two hours ago. There was no lag. It brought the shame and revulsion back, the sense of having no worth at all, and that feeling always made him want to have a drink, and the wanting of a drink brought still blacker despair—would he ever have an hour, not a week or even a day, mind you, but just one waking hour when the craving for a drink wouldn't surprise him like this?

"The boiler," Watson announced. He pulled a red and blue bandanna from his back pocket, blew his nose with a decisive honk, and thrust it back out of sight after a short peek into it to see if he had gotten anything interesting.

The boiler stood on four cement blocks, a long and cylindrical metal tank, copper-jacketed and often patched. It squatted beneath a confusion of pipes and ducts which zigzagged upward into the high, cob-web-festooned basement ceiling. To Jack's right, two large heating pipes came through the wall from the furnace in the adjoining room.

"Pressure gauge is here." Watson tapped it. "Pounds per square inch, psi. I guess you'd know that. I got her up to a hundred now, and the rooms get a little chilly at night. Few guests complain, what the fuck. They're crazy to come up here in September anyway. Besides, this is an old baby. Got more patches on her than a pair of welfare overalls." Out came the bandanna. A honk. A peek. Back it went.

"I got me a fuckin cold," Watson said conversationally. "I get one every September. I be tinkering down here with this old whore, then I be out cuttin the grass, or rakin that roque court. Get a chill and catch a cold, my old mum used to say. God bless her, she been dead six year. The cancer got her. Once the cancer gets you, you might as well make your will.

"You'll want to keep your press up to no more than fifty, maybe sixty. Mr. Ullman, he says to heat the west wing one day, central wing the next, east wing the day after that. Ain't he a crazyman? I hate that little fucker. Yap-yap-yap, all the livelong day, he's just like one a those little dogs that bites you on the ankle then run around an pee all over the rug. If brains was black powder, he couldn't blow his own nose. It's a pity the things you see when you ain't got a gun.

"Look here. You open an close these ducks by pullin these rings. I got em all marked for you. The blue tags all go to the rooms in the east wing. Red tags is the middle. Yellow is the west wing. When you go to heat the west wing, you got to remember that's the side of the hotel that really catches the weather. When it whoops, those rooms get as cold as a frigid woman with an ice cube up her works. You can run your press all the way to eighty on west wing days. I would, anyway."

"The thermostats upstairs—" Jack began.

Watson shook his head vehemently, making his fluffy hair bounce on his skull. "They ain't hooked. up. They're just there for show. Some of these people from California, they don't think things is right unless they got it hot enough to grow a palm tree in their fuckin bedroom. All the heat comes from down here. Got to watch the press, though. See her creep?"

He tapped the main dial, which had crept from a hundred pounds per square inch to a hundred and two as Watson soliloquized. Jack felt a sudden shiver cross his back in a hurry and thought: *The goose just walked over my grave.* Then Watson gave the pressure wheel a spin and dumped the boiler off. There was a great hissing, and the needle dropped back to ninety-one. Watson twisted the valve shut and the hissing died reluctantly.

"She creeps," Watson said. "You tell that fat little peckerwood Ullman, he drags out the account books and spends three hours showing how he can't afford a new one until 1982. I tell you, this whole place is gonna go sky-high someday, and I just hope that fat fuck's here to ride the rocket. God, I wish I could be as charitable as my mother was. She could see the good in everyone. Me, I'm just as mean as a snake with the shingles. What the fuck, a man can't help his nature.

"Now you got to remember to come down here twice a day and once at night before you rack in. You got to check the press. If you forget, it'll just creep and creep and like as not you an your fambly'll wake up on the fuckin moon. You just dump her off a little and you'll have no trouble."

"What's top end?"

"Oh, she's rated for two-fifty, but she'd blow long before that now. You couldn't get me to come down an stand next to her when that dial was up to one hundred and eighty."

"There's no automatic shutdown?"

"No, there ain't. This was built before such things were required. Federal government's into everything these days, ain't it? FBI openin mail, CIA buggin the

goddam phones . . . and look what happened to that
Nixon. Wasn't that a sorry sight?

"But if you just come down here regular an check
the press, you'll be fine. An remember to switch those
ducks around like he wants. Won't none of the rooms
get much above forty-five unless we have an amazin
warm winter. And you'll have your own apartment
just as warm as you like it."

"What about the plumbing?"

"Okay, I was just getting to that. Over here
through this arch."

They walked into a long, rectangular room that
seemed to stretch for miles. Watson pulled a cord and a
single seventy-five-watt bulb cast a sickish, swinging
glow over the area they were standing in. Straight ahead
was the bottom of the elevator shaft, heavy greased
cables descending to pulleys twenty feet in diameter
and a huge, grease-clogged motor. Newspapers were
everywhere, bundled and banded and boxed. Other cartons were marked *Records* or *Invoices* or *Receipts*—SAVE!
The smell was yellow and moldy. Some of the cartons
were falling apart, spilling yellow flimsy sheets that
might have been twenty years old out onto the floor.
Jack stared around, fascinated. The Overlook's entire
history might be here, buried in these rotting cartons.

"That elevator's a bitch to keep runnin," Watson
said, jerking his thumb at it. "I *know* Ullman's buying
the state elevator inspector a few fancy dinners to
keep the repairman away from that fucker.

"Now, here's your central plumbin core." In front
of them five large pipes, each of them wrapped in

insulation and cinched with steel bands, rose into the shadows and out of sight.

Watson pointed to a cobwebby shelf beside the utility shaft. There were a number of greasy rags on it, and a loose-leaf binder. "That there is all your plumbin schematics," he said. "I don't think you'll have any trouble with leaks—never has been—but sometimes the pipes freeze up. Only way to stop that is to run the faucets a little bit durin the nights, but there's over four hundred taps in this fuckin palace. That fat fairy upstairs would scream all the way to Denver when he saw the water bill. Ain't that right?"

"I'd say that's a remarkably astute analysis."

Watson looked at him admiringly. "Say, you really are a college fella, aren't you? Talk just like a book. I admire that, as long as the fella ain't one of those fairy-boys. Lots of em are. You know who stirred up all those college riots a few years ago? The homma-sexshuls, that's who. They get frustrated an have to cut loose. Comin out of the closet, they call it. Holy shit, I don't know what the world's comin to.

"Now, if she freezes, she most likely gonna freeze right up in this shaft. No heat, you see. If it happens, use this." He reached into a broken orange crate and produced a small gas torch.

"You just unstrap the insulation when you find the ice plug and put the heat right to her. Get it?"

"Yes. But what if a pipe freezes outside the utility core?"

"That won't happen if you're doin your job and keepin the place heated. You can't get to the other pipes anyway. Don't you fret about it. You'll have no trouble. Beastly place down here. Cobwebby. Gives me the horrors, it does."

"Ullman said the first winter caretaker killed his family and himself."

"Yeah, that guy Grady. He was a bad actor, I knew that the minute I saw him. Always grinnin like an egg-suck dog. That was when they were just startin out here and that fat fuck Ullman, he woulda hired the Boston Strangler if he'd've worked for minimum wage. Was a ranger from the National Park that found em; the phone was out. All of em up in the west wing on the third floor, froze solid. Too bad about the little girls. Eight and six, they was. Cute as cut-buttons. Oh, that was a hell of a mess. That Ullman, he manages some honky-tonky resort place down in Florida in the off-season, and he caught a plane up to Denver and hired a sleigh to take him up here from Sidewinder because the roads were closed—a *sleigh,* can you believe that? He about split a gut tryin to keep it out of the papers. Did pretty well, I got to give him that. There was an item in the Denver *Post,* and of course the bituary in that pissant little rag they have down in Estes Park, but that was just about all. Pretty good, considerin the reputation this place has got. I expected some reporter would dig it all up again and just sorta put Grady in it as an excuse to rake over the scandals."

"What scandals?"

Watson shrugged. "Any big hotels have got scandals," he said. "Just like every big hotel has got a ghost. Why? Hell, people come and go. Sometimes one of em will pop off in his room, heart attack or stroke or something like that. Hotels are superstitious places. No thirteenth floor or room thirteen, no mirrors on the back of the door you come in through, stuff like that. Why, we lost a lady just this last July. Ullman had to take care of that, and you can bet your ass he did. That's what they pay him twenty-two thousand bucks a season for, and as much as I dislike the little prick, he earns it. It's like some people just come here to throw up and they hire a guy like Ullman to clean up the messes. Here's this woman, must be sixty fuckin years old—my age!—and her hair's dyed just as red as a whore's stoplight, tits saggin just about down to her belly button on account of she ain't wearin no brassy-ear, big varycoarse veins all up and down her legs so they look like a couple of goddam roadmaps, the jools drippin off her neck and arms an hangin out her ears. And she's got this kid with her, he can't be no more than seventeen, with hair down to his asshole and his crotch bulgin like he stuffed it with the funnypages. So they're here a week, ten days maybe, and every night it's the same drill. Down in the Colorado Lounge from five to seven, her suckin up singapore slings like they're gonna outlaw em tomorrow and him with just the one bottle of Olympia, suckin it, makin it last. And she'd be makin jokes and sayin all these witty things, and every time she said one he'd grin just like a fuckin ape, like she had strings tied to the corners of his mouth. Only after a few days you could see it was gettin harder an harder for him to grin, and God knows what he had to think about to get his pump primed by bedtime. Well, they'd go in for dinner, him walkin and her staggerin, drunk as a coot, you know, and he'd be pinchin the waitresses and grinnin at em when she wasn't lookin. Hell, we even had bets on how long he'd last."

Watson shrugged.

"Then he comes down one night around ten, sayin his 'wife' is 'indisposed'—which meant she was passed out again like every other night they was there—and he's goin to get her some stomach medicine. So off he goes in the little Porsche they come in, and that's the last we see of him. Next morning she comes down and tries to put on this big act, but all day she's gettin paler an paler, and Mr. Ullman asks her, sorta diplomatic-like, would she like him to notify the state cops, just in case maybe he had a little accident or something. She's on him like a cat. No-no-no, he's a fine driver, she isn't worried, everything's under control, he'll be back for dinner. So that afternoon she steps into the Colorado around three and never has no dinner at all. She goes up to her room around ten-thirty, and that's the last time anybody saw her alive."

"What happened?"

"County coroner said she took about thirty sleepin pills on top of all the booze. Her husband showed up the next day, some big-shot lawyer from New York. He gave old Ullman four different shades of holy hell. I'll sue this an I'll sue that an when I'm through you won't even be able to find a clean pair of underwear, stuff like that. But Ullman's good, the sucker. Ullman got him quieted down. Probably asked that bigshot how he'd like to see his wife splashed all over the New York papers: Wife of Prominent New York Blah Blah Found Dead With Bellyful of Sleeping Pills. After playing hide-the-salami with a kid young enough to be her grandson.

"The state cops found the Porsche in the back of this all-night burger joint down in Lyons, and Ullman pulled a few strings to get it released to that lawyer. Then both of them ganged up on old Archer Houghton, which is the county coroner, and got him to change the verdict to accidental death. Heart attack. Now ole Archer's driving a Chrysler. I don't begrudge him. A man's got to take it where he finds it, especially when he starts gettin along in years."

Out came the bandanna. Honk. Peek. Out of sight.

"So what happens? About a week later this stupid cunt of a chambermaid, Delores Vickery by name, she gives out with a helluva shriek while she's makin up the room where those two stayed, and she faints dead away. When she comes to she says she seen the dead woman in the bathroom, layin naked in the tub. 'Her face was all purple an puffy,' she says, 'an she was grinnin at me.' So Ullman gave her two weeks' worth of walking papers and told her to get lost. I figure there's maybe forty-fifty people died in this hotel since my grandfather opened it for business in 1910."

He looked shrewdly at Jack.

"You know how most of em go? Heart attack or stroke, while they're bangin the lady they're with. That's what these resorts get a lot of, old types that want one last fling. They come up here to the mountains to pretend they're twenty again. Sometimes somethin gives, and not all the guys who ran this place was as good as Ullman is at keepin it out of the papers. So the Overlook's got a reputation, yeah. I'll bet the fuckin Biltmore in New York City has got a reputation, if you ask the right people."

"But no ghosts?"

"Mr. Torrance, I've worked here all my life. I played here when I was a kid no older'n your boy in that wallet snapshot you showed me. I never seen a ghost yet. You want to come out back with me, I'll show you the equipment shed."

"Fine."

As Watson reached up to turn off the light, Jack said, "There sure are a lot of papers down here."

"Oh, you're not kiddin. Seems like they go back a thousand years. Newspapers and old invoices and bills of lading and Christ knows what else. My dad used to keep up with them pretty good when we had the old wood-burning furnace, but now they've got all out of hand. Some year I got to get a boy to haul them down to Sidewinder and burn em. If Ullman will stand the expense. I guess he will if I holler 'rat' loud enough."

"Then there are rats?"

"Yeah, I guess there's some. I got the traps and the poison Mr. Ullman wants you to use up in the attic and down here. You keep a good eye on your boy, Mr. Torrance. You wouldn't want nothing to happen to him."

"No, I sure wouldn't." Coming from Watson the advice didn't sting.

They went to the stairs and paused there for a moment while Watson blew his nose again.

"You'll find all the tools you need out there and some you don't, I guess. And there's the shingles. Did Ullman tell you about that?"

"Yes, he wants part of the west roof reshingled."

"He'll get all the for-free out of you that he can, the fat little prick, and then whine around in the spring about how you didn't do the job half right. I told him once right to his face, I said . . ."

Watson's words faded away to a comforting drone as they mounted the stairs. Jack Torrance looked back over his shoulder once into the impenetrable, musty-smelling darkness and thought that if there was ever a place that should have ghosts, this was it. He thought of Grady, locked in by the soft, implacable snow, going quietly berserk and committing his atrocity. Did they scream? he wondered. Poor Grady, feeling it close in on him more every day, and knowing at last that for him spring would never come. He shouldn't have been here. And he shouldn't have lost his temper.

As he followed Watson through the door, the words echoed back to him like a knell, accompanied by a sharp snap—like a breaking pencil lead. Dear God, he could use a drink. Or a thousand of them.

4

Shadowland

Danny weakened and went up for his milk and cookies at quarter past four. He gobbled them while looking out the window, then went in to kiss his mother, who was lying down. She suggested that he stay in and watch "Sesame Street"—the time would pass faster—but he shook his head firmly and went back to his place on the curb.

Now it was five o'clock, and although he didn't have a watch and couldn't tell time too well yet anyway, he was aware of passing time by the lengthening of the shadows, and by the golden cast that now tinged the afternoon light.

Turning the glider over in his hands, he sang under his breath: "Skip to m Lou, n I don't care . . . skip to m Lou, n I don't care . . . my master's gone away . . . Lou, Lou, skip to m Lou . . ."

They had sung that song all together at the Jack and Jill Nursery School he had gone to back in Stovington. He didn't go to nursery school out here because Daddy couldn't afford to send him anymore.

He knew his mother and father worried about that, worried that it was adding to his loneliness (and even more deeply, unspoken between them, that Danny blamed them), but he didn't really want to go to that old Jack and Jill anymore. It was for babies. He wasn't quite a big kid yet, but he wasn't a baby anymore. Big kids went to the big school and got a hot lunch. First grade. Next year. This year was someplace between being a baby and a real kid. It was all right. He did miss Scott and Andy—mostly Scott—but it was still all right. It seemed best to wait alone for whatever might happen next.

He understood a great many things about his parents, and he knew that many times they didn't like his understandings and many other times refused to believe them. But someday they would have to believe. He was content to wait.

It was too bad they couldn't believe more, though, especially at times like now. Mommy was lying on her bed in the apartment, just about crying she was so worried about Daddy. Some of the things she was worried about were too grown-up for Danny to understand—vague things that had to do with security, with Daddy's *selfimage*, feelings of guilt and anger and the fear of what was to become of them—but the two main things on her mind right now were that Daddy had had a breakdown in the mountains (*then why doesn't he call?*) or that Daddy had gone off to do the Bad Thing. Danny knew perfectly well what the Bad Thing was since Scotty Aaronson, who was six months older, had explained it to him. Scotty knew because his daddy did the Bad Thing, too. Once, Scotty told him, his daddy had punched his mom right in the eye and knocked her down. Finally, Scotty's dad and mom had gotten a DIVORCE over the Bad Thing, and when Danny had known him, Scotty lived with his mother and only saw his daddy on weekends. The greatest terror of Danny's life was DIVORCE, a word that always appeared in his mind as a sign painted in red letters which were covered with hissing, poisonous snakes. In DIVORCE, your parents no longer lived together. They had a tug of war over you in a court (tennis court? badminton court? Danny wasn't sure which or if it was some other, but Mommy and Daddy had played both tennis and badminton at Stovington, so he assumed it could be either) and you had to go with one of them and you practically never saw the other one, and the one you were with could marry somebody you didn't even know if the urge came on them. The most terrifying thing about DIVORCE was that he had sensed the word—or concept, or whatever it was that came to him in his understandings—floating around in his own parents' heads, sometimes diffuse and relatively distant, sometimes as thick and obscuring and frightening as thunderheads. It had been that way after Daddy punished him for messing the papers up in his study and the doctor had to put his arm in a cast. That memory was already faded, but the memory of the DIVORCE thoughts was clear and terrifying. It had mostly been around his mommy that time, and he had been in constant terror that she would pluck the word from her brain and drag it out of her mouth, making it real. DIVORCE. It was a constant undercurrent in their thoughts, one of the few he could always pick up, like the beat of simple music. But like a beat, the central thought formed only the spine of more complex thoughts, thoughts he could not as yet even begin to interpret. They came to him only as colors and moods. Mommy's DIVORCE thoughts centered around what Daddy had done to his arm, and what had happened at Stovington when Daddy lost his job. That boy. That George Hatfield who got pissed off at Daddy and put the holes in their bug's feet. Daddy's DIVORCE thoughts were more complex, colored dark violet and shot through with frightening veins of pure black. He seemed to think they would be better off if he left. That things would stop hurting. His daddy hurt almost all the time, mostly about the Bad Thing. Danny could almost always pick that up too: Daddy's constant craving to go into a dark place and watch a color TV and eat peanuts out of a bowl and do the Bad Thing until his brain would be quiet and leave him alone

But this afternoon his mother had no need to worry and he wished he could go to her and tell her that. The bug had not broken down. Daddy was not off somewhere doing the Bad Thing. He was almost home now, put-putting along the highway between Lyons and Boulder. For the moment his daddy wasn't even thinking about the Bad Thing. He was thinking about . . . about . . .

Danny looked furtively behind him at the kitchen window. Sometimes thinking very hard made something happen to him. It made things—real things—go away, and then he saw things that weren't there. Once, not long after they put the cast on his arm, this had happened at the supper table. They weren't talking much to each other then. But they were thinking. Oh yes. The thoughts of DIVORCE hung over the kitchen table like a cloud full of black rain, pregnant, ready to burst. It was so bad he couldn't eat. The thought of eating with all that black DIVORCE around made him want to throw up. And because it had seemed desperately important, he had thrown himself fully into concentration and something had happened. When he came back to real things, he was lying on the floor with beans and mashed potatoes in his lap and his mommy was holding him and crying and Daddy had been on the phone. He had been frightened, had tried to explain to them that there was nothing wrong, that this sometimes happened to him when he concentrated on understanding more than what normally came to him. He tried to explain about Tony, who they called his "invisible playmate."

His father had said: "He's having a Ha Loo Sin Nation. He seems okay, but I want the doctor to look at him anyway."

After the doctor left, Mommy had made him promise to never do that again, to *never* scare them that way, and Danny had agreed. He was frightened himself. Because when he had concentrated his mind, it had flown out to his daddy, and for just a moment, before Tony had appeared (far away, as he always did, calling distantly) and the strange things had blotted out their kitchen and the carved roast on the blue plate, for just a moment his own consciousness had plunged through his daddy's darkness to an incomprehensible word much more frightening than DIVORCE, and that word was SUICIDE. Danny had never come across it again in his daddy's mind, and he had certainly not gone looking for it. He didn't care if he never found out exactly what that word meant.

But he did like to concentrate, because sometimes Tony would come. Not every time. Sometimes things just got woozy and swimmy for a minute and then cleared—most times, in fact—but at other times Tony would appear at the very limit of his vision, calling distantly and beckoning . . . .

It had happened twice since they moved to Boulder, and he remembered how surprised and pleased he had been to find Tony had followed him all the way from Vermont. So all his friends hadn't been left behind after all.

The first time he had been out in the back yard and nothing much had happened. Just Tony beckoning and then darkness and a few minutes later he had come back to real things with a few vague fragments of memory, like a jumbled dream. The second time, two weeks ago, had been more interesting. Tony, beckoning, calling from four yards over: *"Danny . . . come see . . ."* It seemed that he was getting up, then falling into a deep hole, like Alice into Wonderland. Then he had been in the basement of the apartment house and Tony had been beside him, pointing into the shadows at the trunk his daddy carried all his important papers in, especially "THE PLAY."

"See?" Tony had said in his distant, musical voice. "It's under the stairs. Right under the stairs. The movers put it right . . . under . . . the stairs."

Danny had stepped forward to look more closely at this marvel and then he was falling again, this time out of the back-yard swing, where he had been sitting all along. He had gotten the wind knocked out of himself, too.

Three or four days later his daddy had been stomping around, telling Mommy furiously that he had been all over the goddam basement and the trunk wasn't there and he was going to sue the goddam movers who had left it somewhere between Vermont and Colorado. How was he supposed to be able to finish "THE PLAY" if things like this kept cropping up?

Danny said, "No, Daddy. It's under the stairs. The movers put it right under the stairs."

Daddy had given him a strange look and had gone down to see. The trunk had been there, just where Tony had shown him. Daddy had taken him aside, had sat him on his lap, and had asked Danny who let him down cellar. Had it been Tom from upstairs? The cellar was dangerous, Daddy said. That was why the landlord kept it locked. If someone was leaving it unlocked, Daddy wanted to know. He was glad to have his papers and his "PLAY" but it wouldn't be worth it to him, he said, if Danny fell down the stairs and broke his . . . his leg. Danny told his father earnestly that he hadn't been down in the cellar. That door was always locked. And Mommy agreed. Danny never went down in the back hall, she said, because it was damp and dark and spidery. And he didn't tell lies.

"Then how did you know, doc?" Daddy asked.

"Tony showed me."

His mother and father had exchanged a look over his head. This had happened before, from time to time. Because it was frightening, they swept it quickly from their minds. But he knew they worried about Tony, Mommy especially, and he was careful about thinking the way that could make Tony come where she might see. But now he thought she was lying down, not moving about in the kitchen yet, and so he concentrated hard to see if he could understand what Daddy was thinking about.

His brow furrowed and his slightly grimy hands clenched into tight fists on his jeans. He did not close his eyes—that wasn't necessary—but he squinched them down to slits and imagined Daddy's voice, Jack's voice, John Daniel Torrance's voice, deep and steady, sometimes quirking up with amusement or deepening even more with anger or just staying steady because he was thinking. Thinking of. Thinking about. Thinking . . .

(thinking)

Danny sighed quietly and his body slumped on the curb as if all the muscles had gone out of it. He was fully conscious; he saw the street and the girl and boy walking up the sidewalk on the other side, holding hands because they were

(?in love?)

so happy about the day and themselves together in the day. He saw autumn leaves blowing along the gutter, yellow cartwheels of irregular shape. He saw the house they were passing and noticed how the roof was covered with

(*shingles. i guess it'll be no problem if the flashing's ok yeah that'll be all right. that watson. christ what a character. wish there was a place for him in "THE PLAY." i'll end up with the whole fucking human race in it if i don't watch out. yeah. shingles. are there nails out there? oh shit forgot to ask him well they're simple to get. sidewinder hardware store. wasps. they're nesting this time of year. i might want to get one of those bug bombs in case they're there when i rip up the old shingles. new shingles. old*)

shingles. So that's what he was thinking about. He had gotten the job and was thinking about shingles. Danny didn't know who Watson was, but everything else seemed clear enough. And he might get to see a wasps' nest. Just as sure as his name was

"Danny . . . Dannee . . ."

He looked up and there was Tony, far up the street, standing by a stop sign and waving. Danny, as always, felt a warm burst of pleasure at seeing his old friend, but this time he seemed to feel a prick of fear, too, as if Tony had come with some darkness hidden behind his back. A jar of wasps which when released would sting deeply.

But there was no question of not going.

He slumped further down on the curb, his hands sliding laxly from his thighs and dangling below the fork of his crotch. His chin sank onto his chest. Then there was a dim, painless tug as part of him got up and ran after Tony into funneling darkness.

"Dannee—"

Now the darkness was shot with swirling whiteness. A coughing, whooping sound and bending, tortured shadows that resolved themselves into fir trees at night being pushed by a screaming gale. Snow swirled and danced. Snow everywhere.

"Too deep," Tony said from the darkness, and there was a sadness in his voice that terrified Danny. "Too deep to get out."

Another shape, looming, rearing. Huge and rectangular. A sloping roof. Whiteness that was blurred in the stormy darkness. Many windows. A long building with a shingled roof. Some of the shingles were greener, newer. His daddy put them on. With nails from the Sidewinder hardware store. Now the snow was covering the shingles. It was covering everything.

A green witchlight glowed into being on the front of the building, flickered, and became a giant, grinning skull over two crossed bones.

"Poison," Tony said from the floating darkness. "Poison."

Other signs flickered past his eyes, some in green letters, some of them on boards stuck at leaning angles into the snowdrifts. NO SWIMMING. DANGER! LIVE WIRES. THIS PROPERTY CONDEMNED. HIGH VOLTAGE. THIRD RAIL. DANGER OF DEATH. KEEP OFF. KEEP OUT. NO TRESPASSING, VIOLATORS WILL BE SHOT ON SIGHT. He understood none of them completely—he couldn't read!—but got a sense of all, and a dreamy terror floated into the dark hollows of his body like light brown spores that would die in sunlight.

They faded. Now he was in a room filled with strange furniture, a room that was dark. Snow spattered against the windows like thrown sand. His mouth was dry, his eyes like hot marbles, his heart triphammering in his chest. Outside there was a hollow booming noise, like a dreadful door being thrown wide. Footfalls. Across the room was a mirror, and deep down in its silver bubble a single word appeared in green fire and that word was: REDRUM.

The room faded. Another room. He knew
(would know)
this one. An overturned chair. A broken window with snow swirling in; already it had frosted the edge of the rug. The drapes had been pulled free and hung on their broken rod at an angle. A low cabinet lying on his face.

More hollow booming noises, steady, rhythmic, horrible. Smashing glass. Approaching destruction. A hoarse voice, the voice of a madman, made the more terrible by its familiarity:

Come out! Come out, you little shit! Take your medicine!

Crash. Crash. Crash. Splintering wood. A bellow of rage and satisfaction. REDRUM. Coming.

Drifting across the room. Pictures torn off the walls. A record player
(?Mommy's record player?)
overturned on the floor. Her records, Grieg, Handel, the Beatles, Art Garfunkel, Bach, Liszt,

thrown everywhere, Broken into jagged black pie wedges. A shaft of light coming from another room, the bathroom, harsh white light and a word flickering on and off in the medicine cabinet mirror like a red eye, REDRUM, REDRUM, REDRUM—

"No," he whispered. "No, Tony please—"

And, dangling over the white porcelain lip of the bathtub, a hand. Limp. A slow trickle of blood (REDRUM) trickling down one of the fingers, the third, dripping onto the tile from the carefully shaped nail—

No oh no oh no—

(oh please, Tony, you're scaring me)

REDRUM REDRUM REDRUM

(stop it, Tony, stop it)

Fading.

In the darkness the booming noises grew louder, louder still, echoing, everywhere, all around.

And now he was crouched in a dark hallway, crouched on a blue rug with a riot of twisting black shapes woven into its pile, listening to the booming noises approach, and now a Shape turned the corner and began to come toward him, lurching, smelling of blood and doom. It had a mallet in one hand and it was swinging it (REDRUM) from side to side in vicious arcs, slamming it into the walls, cutting the silk wallpaper and knocking out ghostly bursts of plasterdust:

Come on and take your medicine! Take it like a man!

The Shape advancing on him, reeking of that sweet-sour odor, gigantic, the mallet head cutting across the air with a wicked hissing whisper, then the great hollow boom as it crashed into the wall, sending the dust out in a puff you could smell, dry and itchy. Tiny red eyes glowed in the dark. The monster was upon him, it had discovered him, cowering here with a blank wall at his back. And the trapdoor in the ceiling was locked.

Darkness. Drifting.

"Tony, please take me back, please, please—"

And he *was* back, sitting on the curb of Arapahoe Street, his shirt sticking damply to his back, his body bathed in sweat. In his ears he could still hear that huge, contrapuntal booming sound and smell his own urine as he voided himself in the extremity of his terror. He could see that limp hand dangling over the edge of the tub with blood running down one finger, the third, and that inexplicable word so much more horrible than any of the others: REDRUM.

And now sunshine. Real things. Except for Tony, now six blocks up, only a speck, standing on the corner, his voice faint and high and sweet. "Be careful, doc . . ."

Then, in the next instant, Tony was gone and Daddy's battered red bug was turning the corner and chattering up the street, farting blue smoke behind it. Danny was off the curb in a second, waving, jiving from one foot to the other, yelling: "Daddy! Hey, Dad! Hi! Hi!"

His daddy swung the VW into the curb, killed the engine, and opened the door. Danny ran toward him and then froze, his eyes widening. His heart crawled up into the middle of his throat and froze solid. Beside his daddy, in the other front seat, was a short-handled mallet, its head clotted with blood and hair.

Then it was just a bag of groceries.

"Danny . . . you okay, doc?"

"Yeah. I'm okay." He went to his daddy and buried his face in Daddy's sheepskin-lined denim jacket and hugged him tight tight tight. Jack hugged him back, slightly bewildered.

"Hey, you don't want to sit in the sun like that, doc. You're drippin sweat."

"I guess I fell asleep a little. I love you, Daddy. I been waiting."

"I love you too, Dan. I brought home some stuff. Think you're big enough to carry it upstairs?"

"Sure am!"

"Doc Torrance, the world's strongest man," Jack said, and ruffled his hair. "Whose hobby is falling asleep on street corners."

Then they were walking up to the door and Mommy had come down to the porch to meet them and he stood on the second step and watched them kiss. They were glad to see each other. Love came out of them the way love had come out of the boy and girl walking up the street and holding hands. Danny was glad.

The bag of groceries—*just* a bag of groceries—crackled in his arms. Everything was all right. Daddy was home. Mommy was loving him. There were no bad things. And not everything Tony showed him always happened.

But fear had settled around his heart, deep and dreadful, around his heart and around that indecipherable word he had seen in his spirit's mirror.

5

Phonebooth

Jack parked the VW in front of the Rexall in the Table
Mesa shopping center and let the engine die. He wondered again if he shouldn't go ahead and get the fuel
pump replaced, and told himself again that they
couldn't afford it. If the little car could keep running
until November, it could retire with full honors anyway.
By November the snow up there in the mountains
would be higher than the beetle's roof . . . maybe higher
than three beetles stacked on top of each other.

"Want you to stay in this car, doc. I'll bring you a
candy bar."

"Why can't I come in?"

"I have to make a phone call. It's private stuff."

"Is that why you didn't make it at home?"

"Check."

Wendy had insisted on a phone in spite of their
unraveling finances. She had argued that with a small
child—especially a boy like Danny, who sometimes
suffered from fainting spells—they couldn't afford not
to have one. So Jack had forked over the thirty-dollar

installation fee, bad enough, and a ninety-dollar security deposit, which really hurt. And so far the phone had been mute except for two wrong numbers.

"Can I have a Baby Ruth, Daddy?"

"Yes. You sit still and don't play with the gearshift, right?"

"Right. I'll look at the maps."

"You do that."

As Jack got out, Danny opened the bug's glovebox and took out the five battered gas station maps: Colorado, Nebraska, Utah, Wyoming, New Mexico. He loved road maps, loved to trace where the roads went with his finger. As far as he was concerned, new maps were the best part of moving West.

Jack went to the drugstore counter, got Danny's candy bar, a newspaper, and a copy of the October *Writer's Digest.* He gave the girl a five and asked for his change in quarters. With the silver in his hand he walked over to the telephone booth by the key-making machine and slipped inside. From here he could see Danny in the bug through three sets of glass. The boy's head was bent studiously over his maps. Jack felt a wave of nearly desperate love for the boy. The emotion showed on his face as a stony grimness.

He supposed he could have made his obligatory thank-you call to Al from home; he certainly wasn't going to say anything Wendy would object to. It was his pride that said no. These days he almost always listened to what his pride told him to do, because along with his wife and son, six hundred dollars in a checking account, and one weary 1968 Volkswagen, his pride was all that was left. The only thing that was his. Even the checking account was joint. A year ago he had been teaching English in one of the finest prep schools in New England. There had been friends—although not exactly the same ones he'd had before going on the wagon—some laughs, fellow faculty members who admired his deft touch in the classroom and his private dedication to writing. Things had been very good six months ago. All at once there was enough money left over at the end of each two-week pay period to start a little savings account. In his drinking days there had never been a penny left over, even though Al Shockley had stood a great many of the rounds. He and Wendy had begun to talk cautiously about finding a house and making a down payment in a year or so. A farmhouse in the country, take six or eight years to renovate it completely, what the hell, they were young, they had time.

Then he had lost his temper.

George Hatfield.

The smell of hope had turned to the smell of old leather in Crommert's office, the whole thing like some scene from his own play: the old prints of previous Stovington headmasters on the walls, steel engravings of the school as it had been in 1879, when it was first built, and in 1895, when Vanderbilt money had enabled them to build the field house that still stood at the west end of the soccer field, squat, immense, dressed in ivy. April ivy had been rustling outside Crommert's slit window and the drowsy sound of steam heat came from the radiator. It was no set, he remembered thinking. It was real. His life. How could he have fucked it up so badly?

"This is a serious situation, Jack. Terribly serious. The Board has asked me to convey its decision to you."

The Board wanted Jack's resignation and Jack had given it to them. Under different circumstances, he would have gotten tenure that June.

What had followed that interview in Crommert's office had been the darkest, most dreadful night of his life. The wanting, the *needing* to get drunk had never been so bad. His hands shook. He knocked things over. And he kept wanting to take it out on Wendy and Danny. His temper was like a vicious animal on a frayed leash. He had left the house in terror that he might strike them. Had ended up outside a bar, and the only thing that had kept him from going in was the knowledge that if he did, Wendy would leave him at last, and take Danny with her. He would be dead from the day they left.

Instead of going into the bar, where dark shadows sat sampling the tasty waters of oblivion, he had gone to Al Shockley's house. The Board's vote had been six to one. Al had been the one.

Now he dialed the operator and she told him that for a dollar eighty-five he could be put in touch with Al two thousand miles away for three minutes. Time is relative, baby, he thought, and stuck in eight quarters. Faintly he could hear the electronic boops and beeps of his connection sniffing its way eastward.

Al's father had been Arthur Longley Shockley, the steel baron. He had left his only son, Albert, a fortune and a huge range of investments and directorships and chairs on various boards. One of these had been on the Board of Directors for Stovington Preparatory Academy, the old man's favorite charity. Both Arthur and Albert Shockley were alumni and Al lived in Barre, close enough to take a personal interest in the school's affairs. For several years Al had been Stovington's tennis coach.

Jack and Al had become friends in a completely natural and uncoincidental way: at the many school and faculty functions they attended together, they were always the two drunkest people there. Shockley was separated from his wife, and Jack's own marriage was skidding slowly downhill, although he still loved Wendy and had promised sincerely (and frequently) to reform, for her sake and for baby Danny's.

The two of them went on from many faculty parties, hitting the bars until they closed, then stopping at some mom 'n' pop store for a case of beer they would drink parked at the end of some back road. There were mornings when Jack would stumble into their leased house with dawn seeping into the sky and find Wendy and the baby asleep on the couch, Danny always on the inside, a tiny fist curled under the shelf of Wendy's jaw. He would look at them and the self-loathing would back up his throat in a bitter wave, even stronger than the taste of beer and cigarettes and martinis—martians, as Al called them. Those were the times that his mind would turn thoughtfully and sanely to the gun or the rope or the razor blade.

If the bender had occurred on a weeknight, he would sleep for three hours, get up, dress, chew four

Excedrins, and go off to teach his nine o'clock American Poets still drunk. Good morning, kids, today the Red-Eyed Wonder is going to tell you about how Longfellow lost his wife in the big fire.

He hadn't believed he was an alcoholic, Jack thought as Al's telephone began ringing in his ear. The classes he had missed or taught unshaven, still reeking of last night's martians. Not me, I can stop anytime. The nights he and Wendy had passed in separate beds. Listen, I'm fine. Mashed fenders. Sure I'm okay to drive. The tears she always shed in the bathroom. Cautious looks from his colleagues at any party where alcohol was served, even wine. The slowly dawning realization that he was being talked about. The knowledge that he was producing nothing at his Underwood but balls of mostly blank paper that ended up in the wastebasket. He had been something of a catch for Stovington, a slowly blooming American writer perhaps, and certainly a man well qualified to teach that great mystery, creative writing. He had published two dozen short stories. He was working on a play, and thought there might be a novel incubating in some mental back room. But now he was not producing and his teaching had become erratic.

It had finally ended one night less than a month after Jack had broken his son's arm. That, it seemed to him, had ended his marriage. All that remained was for Wendy to gather her will . . . if her mother hadn't been such a grade A bitch, he knew, Wendy would have taken a bus back to New Hampshire as soon as Danny had been okay to travel. It was over.

It had been a little past midnight. Jack and Al were coming into Barre on U.S. 31, Al behind the wheel of his Jag, shifting fancily on the curves, sometimes crossing the double yellow line. They were both very drunk; the martians had landed that night in force. They came around the last curve before the bridge at seventy, and there was a kid's bike in the road, and then the sharp, hurt squealing as rubber shredded from the Jag's tires and Jack remembered seeing Al's face looming over the steering wheel like a round white moon. Then the jingling crashing sound as they hit the bike at forty, and it had flown up like a bent and twisted bird, the handlebars striking the windshield, and then it was in the air again, leaving the starred safety glass in front of Jack's bulging eyes. A moment later he heard the final dreadful smash as it landed on the road behind them. Something thumped underneath them as the tires passed over it. The Jag drifted around broadside, Al still jockeying the wheel, and from far away Jack heard himself saying: "Jesus, Al. We ran him down. I felt it."

In his ear the phone kept ringing. *Come on, Al. Be home. Let me get this over with.*

Al had brought the car to a smoking halt not more than three feet from a bridge stanchion. Two of the Jag's tires were flat. They had left zigzagging loops of burned rubber for a hundred and thirty feet. They looked at each other for a moment and then ran back in the cold darkness.

The bike was completely ruined. One wheel was gone, and looking back over his shoulder Al had seen it lying in the middle of the road, half a dozen spokes sticking up like piano wire. Al had said hesitantly: "I think that's what we ran over, Jacky-boy."

"Then where's the kid?"

"Did you *see* a kid?"

Jack frowned. It had all happened with such crazy speed. Coming around the corner. The bike looming in the Jag's headlights. Al yelling something. Then the collision and the long skid.

They moved the bike to one shoulder of the road. Al went back to the Jag and put on its four-way flashers. For the next two hours they searched the sides of the road, using a powerful four-cell flashlight. Nothing. Although it was late, several cars passed the beached Jaguar and the two men with the bobbing flashlight. None of them stopped. Jack thought later that some queer providence, bent on giving them both a last chance, had kept the cops away, had kept any of the passers-by from calling them.

At quarter past two they returned to the Jag, sober but queasy. "If there was nobody riding it, what was it doing in the middle of the road?" Al demanded. "It wasn't parked on the side; it was right in the fucking *middle*!"

Jack could only shake his head.

"Your party does not answer," the operator said. "Would you like me to keep on trying?"

"A couple more rings, operator. Do you mind?"

"No, sir," the voice said dutifully.

Come on, Al!

Al had hiked across the bridge to the nearest pay phone, called a bachelor friend and told him it would be worth fifty dollars if the friend would get the Jag's snow tires out of the garage and bring them down to the Highway 31 bridge outside of Barre. The friend showed up twenty minutes later, wearing a pair of jeans and his pajama top. He surveyed the scene.

"Kill anybody?" he asked.

Al was already jacking up the back of the car and Jack was loosening lug nuts. "Providentially, no one," Al said.

"I think I'll just head on back anyway. Pay me in the morning."

"Fine," Al said without looking up.

The two of them had gotten the tires on without incident, and together they drove back to Al Shockley's house. Al put the Jag in the garage and killed the motor.

In the dark quiet he said: "I'm off drinking, Jacky-boy. It's all over. I've slain my last martian."

And now, sweating in this phonebooth, it occurred to Jack that he had never doubted Al's ability to carry through. He had driven back to his own house in the VW with the radio turned up, and some disco group chanted over and over again, talismanic in the house before dawn: *Do it anyway . . . you wanta do it . . . do it anyway you want . . .* No matter how loud he heard the squealing tires, the crash. When he blinked his eyes shut, he saw that single crushed wheel with its broken spokes pointing at the sky.

When he got in, Wendy was asleep on the couch. He looked in Danny's room and Danny was in his crib on his back, sleeping deeply, his arm still buried in the cast. In the softly filtered glow from the street-light outside he could see the dark lines on its plastered whiteness where all the doctors and nurses in pediatrics had signed it.

It was an accident. He fell down the stairs.

(o you dirty liar)

It was an accident. I lost my temper.

(you fucking drunken waste god wiped snot out of his nose and that was you)

Listen, hey, come on, please, just an accident—

But the last plea was driven away by the image of that bobbing flashlight as they hunted through the dry late November weeds, looking for the sprawled body that by all good rights should have been there, waiting for the police. It didn't matter that Al had been driving. There had been other nights when he had been driving.

He pulled the covers up over Danny, went into their bedroom, and took the Spanish Llama .38 down from the top shelf of the closet. It was in a shoe box. He sat on the bed with it for nearly an hour, looking at it, fascinated by its deadly shine.

It was dawn when he put it back in the box and put the box back in the closet.

That morning he had called Bruckner, the department head, and told him to please post his classes. He had the flu. Bruckner agreed, with less good grace than was common. Jack Torrance had been extremely susceptible to the flu in the last year.

Wendy made him scrambled eggs and coffee. They ate in silence. The only sound came from the back yard, where Danny was gleefully running his trucks across the sand pile with his good hand.

She went to do the dishes. Her back to him, she said: "Jack. I've been thinking."

"Have you?" He lit a cigarette with trembling hands. No hangover this morning, oddly enough. Only the shakes. He blinked. In the instant's darkness the bike flew up against the windshield, starring the glass. The tires shrieked. The flashlight bobbed.

"I want to talk to you about . . . about what's best for me and Danny. For you too, maybe. I don't know. We should have talked about it before, I guess."

"Would you do something for me?" he asked, looking at the wavering tip of his cigarette. "Would you do me a favor?"

"What?" Her voice was dull and neutral. He looked at her back.

"Let's talk about it a week from today. If you still want to."

Now she turned to him, her hands lacy with suds, her pretty face pale and disillusioned. "Jack, promises don't work with you. You just go right on with—"

She stopped, looking in his eyes, fascinated, suddenly uncertain.

"In a week," he said. His voice had lost all its strength and dropped to a whisper. "Please. I'm not promising anything. If you still want to talk then, we'll talk. About anything you want."

They looked across the sunny kitchen at each other for a long time, and when she turned back to the dishes without saying anything more, he began to

shudder. God, he needed a drink. Just a little pick-
me-up to put things in their true perspective—

"Danny said he dreamed you had a car accident,"
she said abruptly. "He has funny dreams sometimes.
He said it this morning, when I got him dressed. Did
you, Jack? Did you have an accident?"

"No."

By noon the craving for a drink had become a low-
grade fever. He went to Al's.

"You dry?" Al asked before letting him in. Al
looked horrible.

"Bone dry. You look like Lon Chaney in *Phantom of
the Opera*."

"Come on in."

They played two-handed whist all afternoon. They
didn't drink.

A week passed. He and Wendy didn't speak much.
But he knew she was watching, not believing. He
drank coffee black and endless cans of Coca-Cola. One
night he drank a whole six-pack of Coke and then ran
into the bathroom and vomited it up. The level of the
bottles in the liquor cabinet did not go down. After his
classes he went over to Al Shockley's—she hated Al
Shockley worse than she had ever hated anyone—and
when he came home she would swear she smelled
scotch or gin on his breath, but he would talk lucidly
to her before supper, drink coffee, play with Danny
after supper, sharing a Coke with him, read him a bedtime story, then sit and correct themes with cup after
cup of black coffee by his hand, and she would have to
admit to herself that she had been wrong.

Weeks passed and the unspoken word retreated further from the back of her lips. Jack sensed its retirement but knew it would never retire completely. Things began to get a little easier. Then George Hatfield. He had lost his temper again, this time stone sober.

"Sir, your party still doesn't—"

"Hello?" Al's voice, out of breath.

"Go ahead," the operator said dourly.

"Al, this is Jack Torrance."

"Jacky-boy!" Genuine pleasure. "How are you?"

"Good. I just called to say thanks. I got the job. It's perfect. If I can't finish that goddam play snowed in all winter, I'll never finish it."

"You'll finish."

"How are things?" Jack asked hesitantly.

"Dry," Al responded. "You?"

"As a bone."

"Miss it much?"

"Every day."

Al laughed. "I know that scene. But I don't know how you stayed dry after that Hatfield thing, Jack. That was above and beyond."

"I really bitched things up for myself," he said evenly.

"Oh, hell. I'll have the Board around by spring. Effinger's already saying they might have been too hasty. And if that play comes to something—"

"Yes. Listen, my boy's out in the car, Al. He looks like he might be getting restless—"

"Sure. Understand. You have a good winter up there, Jack. Glad to help."

"Thanks again, Al." He hung up, closed his eyes in the hot booth, and again saw the crashing bike, the bobbing flashlight. There had been a squib in the paper the next day, no more than a space-filler really, but the owner had not been named. Why it had been out there in the night would always be a mystery to them, and perhaps that was as it should be.

He went back out to the car and gave Danny his slightly melted Baby Ruth.

"Daddy?"

"What, doc?"

Danny hesitated, looking at his father's abstracted face.

"When I was waiting for you to come back from that hotel, I had a bad dream. Do you remember? When I fell asleep?"

"Um-hm."

But it was no good. Daddy's mind was someplace else, not with him. Thinking about the Bad Thing again.

(I dreamed that you hurt me, Daddy)

"What was the dream, doc?"

"Nothing," Danny said as they pulled out into the parking lot. He put the maps back into the glove compartment.

"You sure?"

"Yes."

Jack gave his son a faint, troubled glance, and then his mind turned to his play.

6

Night Thoughts

Love was over, and her man was sleeping beside her.

Her man.

She smiled a little in the darkness, his seed still trickling with slow warmth from between her slightly parted thighs, and her smile was both rueful and pleased, because the phrase *her man* summoned up a hundred feelings. Each feeling examined alone was a bewilderment. Together, in this darkness floating to sleep, they were like a distant blues tune heard in an almost deserted night club, melancholy but pleasing.

> *Lovin' you baby, is just like rollin' off a log,*
> *But if I can't be your woman, I sure ain't goin' to be*
> *your dog.*

Had that been Billie Holiday? Or someone more prosaic like Peggy Lee? Didn't matter. It was low and torchy, and in the silence of her head it played mellowly, as if issuing from one of those old-fashioned jukeboxes, a Wurlitzer, perhaps, half an hour before closing.

Now, moving away from her consciousness, she wondered how many beds she had slept in with this man beside her. They had met in college and had first made love in his apartment . . . that had been less than three months after her mother drove her from the house, told her never to come back, that if she wanted to go somewhere she could go to her father since she had been responsible for the divorce. That had been in 1970. So long ago? A semester later they had moved in together, had found jobs for the summer, and had kept the apartment when their senior year began. She remembered that bed the most clearly, a big double that sagged in the middle. When they made love, the rusty box spring had counted the beats. That fall she had finally managed to break from her mother. Jack had helped her. She wants to keep beating you, Jack had said. The more times you phone her, the more times you crawl back begging forgiveness, the more she can beat you with your father. It's good for her, Wendy, because she can go on making believe it was your fault. But it's not good for you. They had talked it over again and again in that bed, that year.

(Jack sitting up with the covers pooled around his waist, a cigarette burning between his fingers, looking her in the eye—he had a half-humorous, half-scowling way of doing that—telling her: *She told you never to come back, right? Never to darken her door again, right? Then why doesn't she hang up the phone when she knows it's you? Why does she only tell you that you can't come in if I'm with you? Because she thinks I might cramp her style a little bit. She wants to keep putting the thumbscrews right to you, baby. You're a fool if you keep letting her do it. She told you never to come back, so why don't you take her at her word? Give it a rest.* And at last she'd seen it his way.)

It had been Jack's idea to separate for a while—to get perspective on the relationship, he said. She had been afraid he had become interested in someone else. Later she found it wasn't so. They were together again in the spring and he asked her if she had been to see her father. She had jumped as if he'd struck her with a quirt.

How did you know that?

The Shadow knows.

Have you been spying on me?

And his impatient laughter, which had always made her feel so awkward—as if she were eight and he was able to see her motivations more clearly than she.

You needed time, Wendy.

For what?

I guess . . . to see which one of us you wanted to marry.

Jack, what are you saying?

I think I'm proposing marriage.

The wedding. Her father had been there, her mother had not been. She discovered she could live with that, if she had Jack. Then Danny had come, her fine son.

That had been the best year, the best bed. After Danny was born, Jack had gotten her a job typing for half a dozen English Department profs—quizzes, exams, class syllabi, study notes, reading lists. She ended up typing a novel for one of them, a novel that never got published . . . much to Jack's very irreverent and very private glee. The job was good for forty a week, and skyrocketed all the way up to sixty during the two months she spent typing the unsuccessful novel. They had their first car, a five-year-old Buick with a baby seat in the middle. Bright, upwardly mobile young marrieds. Danny forced a reconciliation between her and her mother, a reconciliation that was always tense and never happy, but a reconciliation all the same. When she took Danny to the house, she went without Jack. And she didn't tell Jack that her mother always remade Danny's diapers, frowned over his formula, could always spot the accusatory first signs of a rash on the baby's bottom or privates. Her mother never said anything overtly, but the message came through anyway: the price she had begun to pay (and maybe always would) for the reconciliation was the feeling that she was an inadequate mother. It was her mother's way of keeping the thumbscrews handy.

During the days Wendy would stay home and housewife, feeding Danny his bottles in the sun-washed kitchen of the four-room second-story apartment, playing her records on the battered portable stereo she had had since high school. Jack would come home at three (or at two if he felt he could cut his last class), and while Danny slept he would lead her into the bedroom and fears of inadequacy would be erased.

At night while she typed, he would do his writing and his assignments. In those days she sometimes came out of the bedroom where the typewriter was to find both of them asleep on the studio couch, Jack wearing nothing but his underpants, Danny sprawled comfortably on her husband's chest with his thumb in his mouth. She would put Danny in his crib, then read whatever Jack had written that night before waking him up enough to come to bed.

The best bed, the best year.

Sun gonna shine in my backyard someday . . .

In those days, Jack's drinking had still been well in hand. On Saturday nights a bunch of his fellow students would drop over and there would be a case of beer and discussions in which she seldom took part because her field had been sociology and his was English: arguments over whether Pepys's diaries were literature or history; discussions of Charles Olson's poetry; sometimes the reading of works in progress. Those and a hundred others. No, a thousand. She felt no real urge to take part; it was enough to sit in her rocking chair beside Jack, who sat cross-legged on the floor, one hand holding a beer, the other gently cupping her calf or braceleting her ankle.

The competition at UNH had been fierce, and Jack carried an extra burden in his writing. He put in at least an hour at it every night. It was his routine. The Saturday sessions were necessary therapy. They let something out of him that might otherwise have swelled and swelled until he burst.

At the end of his grad work he had landed the job at Stovington, mostly on the strength of his stories—four of them published at that time, one of them in *Esquire*. She remembered that day clearly enough; it would take more than three years to forget it. She had almost thrown the envelope away, thinking it was a subscription offer. Opening it, she had found instead that it was a letter saying that *Esquire* would like to use Jack's story "Concerning the Black Holes" early the following year. They would pay nine hundred dollars, not on publication but on acceptance. That was nearly half a year's take typing papers and she had flown to the telephone, leaving Danny in his high chair to goggle comically after her, his face lathered with creamed peas and beef purée.

Jack had arrived from the university forty-five minutes later, the Buick weighted down with seven friends and a keg of beer. After a ceremonial toast (Wendy also had a glass, although she ordinarily had no taste for beer), Jack had signed the acceptance letter, put it in the return envelope, and went down the block to drop it in the letter box. When he came back he stood gravely in the door and said, *"Veni, vidi, vici."* There were cheers and applause. When the keg was empty at eleven that night, Jack and the only two others who were still ambulatory went on to hit a few bars.

She had gotten him aside in the downstairs hallway. The other two were already out in the car, drunkenly singing the New Hampshire fight song. Jack was down on one knee, owlishly fumbling with the lacings of his moccasins.

"Jack," she said, "you shouldn't. You can't even tie your shoes, let alone drive."

He stood up and put his hands calmly on her shoulders. "Tonight I could fly to the moon if I wanted to."

"No," she said. "Not for all the *Esquire* stories in the world."

"I'll be home early."

But he hadn't been home until four in the morning, stumbling and mumbling his way up the stairs, waking Danny up when he came in. He had tried to soothe the baby and dropped him on the floor. Wendy had rushed out, thinking of what her mother would think if she saw the bruise before she thought of anything else—God help her, God help them both—and then picked Danny up, sat in the rocking chair with him, soothed him. She had been thinking of her mother for most of the five hours Jack had been gone, her mother's prophecy that Jack would never come to anything. *Big ideas,* her mother had said. *Sure. The welfare lines are full of educated fools with big ideas.* Did the *Esquire* story make her mother wrong or right? *Winnifred, you're not holding that baby right. Give him to me.* And was she not holding her husband right? Why else would he take his joy out of the house? A helpless kind of terror had risen up in her and it never occurred to her that he had gone out for reasons that had nothing to do with her.

"Congratulations," she said, rocking Danny—he was almost asleep again. "Maybe you gave him a concussion."

"It's just a bruise." He sounded sulky, wanting to be repentant: a little boy. For an instant she hated him.

"Maybe," she said tightly. "Maybe not." She heard so much of her mother talking to her departed father in her own voice that she was sickened and afraid.

"Like mother like daughter," Jack muttered.

"Go to bed!" she cried, her fear coming out sounding like anger. "Go to bed, you're drunk!"

"Don't tell me what to do."

"Jack . . . please, we shouldn't . . . it . . ." There were no words.

"Don't tell me what to do," he repeated sullenly, and then went into the bedroom. She was left alone in the rocking chair with Danny, who was sleeping again. Five minutes later Jack's snores came floating out to the living room. That had been the first night she had slept on the couch.

Now she turned restlessly on the bed, already dozing. Her mind, freed of any linear order by encroaching sleep, floated past the first year at Stovington, past the steadily worsening times that had reached low ebb when her husband had broken Danny's arm, to that morning in the breakfast nook.

Danny outside playing trucks in the sandpile, his arm still in the cast. Jack sitting at the table, pallid and grizzled, a cigarette jittering between his fingers. She had decided to ask him for a divorce. She had pondered the question from a hundred different angles, had been pondering it in fact for the six months before the broken arm. She told herself she would have made the decision long ago if it hadn't been for Danny, but not even that was necessarily true. She dreamed on the long nights when Jack was out, and her dreams were always of her mother's face and of her own wedding.

(*Who giveth this woman*? Her father standing in his best suit which was none too good—he was a traveling salesman for a line of canned goods that even then was going broke—and his tired face, how old he looked, how pale: *I do*.)

Even after the accident—if you could call it an accident—she had not been able to bring it all the way out, to admit that her marriage was a lopsided defeat. She had waited, dumbly hoping that a miracle would occur and Jack would see what was happening, not only to him but to her. But there had been no slowdown. A drink before going off to the Academy. Two or three beers with lunch at the Stovington House. Three or four martinis before dinner. Five or six more while grading papers. The weekends were worse. The nights out with Al Shockley were worse still. She had never dreamed there could be so much pain in a life when there was nothing physically wrong. She hurt all the time. How much of it was her fault? That question haunted her. She felt like her mother. Like her father. Sometimes, when she felt like herself she wondered what it would be like for Danny, and she dreaded the day when he grew old enough to lay blame. And she wondered where they would go. She had no doubt her mother would take her in, and no doubt that after a year of watching her diapers remade, Danny's meals recooked and/or redistributed, of coming home to find his clothes changed or his hair cut or the books her mother found unsuitable spirited away to some limbo in the attic . . . after half a year of that, she would have a complete nervous breakdown. And her mother would pat her hand and say comfortingly, *Although it's not your fault, it's all your own fault. You were never ready. You showed your true colors when you came between your father and me.*

My father, Danny's father. Mine, his.

(*Who giveth this women? I do.* Dead of a heart attack six months later.)

The night before that morning she had lain awake almost until he came in, thinking, coming to her decision.

The divorce was necessary, she told herself. Her mother and father didn't belong in the decision. Neither did her feelings of guilt over their marriage nor her feelings of inadequacy over her own. It was necessary for her son's sake, and for herself, if she was to salvage anything at all from her early adulthood. The handwriting on the wall was brutal but clear. Her husband was a lush. He had a bad temper, one he could no longer keep wholly under control now that he was drinking so heavily and his writing was going so badly. Accidentally or not accidentally, he had broken Danny's arm. He was going to lose his job, if not this year then the year after. Already she had noticed the sympathetic looks from the other faculty wives. She told herself that she had stuck with the messy job of her marriage for as long as she could. Now she would have to leave it. Jack could have full visitation rights, and she would want support from him only until she could find something and get on her feet—and that would have to be fairly rapidly because she didn't know how long Jack would be able to pay support money. She would do it with as little bitterness as possible. But it had to end.

So thinking, she had fallen off into her own thin and unrestful sleep, haunted by the faces of her own mother and father. *You're nothing but a home-wrecker,* her mother said. *Who giveth this woman?* the minister said. *I do,* her father said. But in the bright and sunny morning she felt the same. Her back to him, her hands plunged in warm dishwater up to the wrists, she had commenced with the unpleasantness.

"I want to talk to you about something that might be best for Danny and I. For you too, maybe. We should have talked about it before, I guess."

And then he had said an odd thing. She had expected to discover his anger, to provoke the bitterness, the recriminations. She had expected a mad dash for the liquor cabinet. But not this soft, almost toneless reply that was so unlike him. It was almost as though the Jack she had lived with for six years had never come back last night—as if he had been replaced by some unearthly doppelgänger that she would never know or be quite sure of.

"Would you do something for me? A favor?"

"What?" She had to discipline her voice strictly to keep it from trembling.

"Let's talk about it in a week. If you still want to."

And she had agreed. It remained unspoken between them. During that week he had seen Al Shockley more than ever, but he came home early and there was no liquor on his breath. She imagined she smelled it, but knew it wasn't so. Another week. And another.

Divorce went back to committee, unvoted on.

What had happened? She still wondered and still had not the slightest idea. The subject was taboo between them. He was like a man who had leaned around a corner and had seen an unexpected monster lying in wait, crouching among the dried bones of its old kills. The liquor remained in the cabinet, but he didn't touch it. She had considered throwing them out a dozen times but in the end always backed away from the idea, as if some unknown charm would be broken by the act.

And there was Danny's part in it to consider.

If she felt she didn't know her husband, then she was in awe of her child—awe in the strict meaning of that word: a kind of undefined superstitious dread.

Dozing lightly, the image of the instant of his birth was presented to her. She was again lying on the delivery table, bathed in sweat, her hair in strings, her feet splayed out in the stirrups

(and a little high from the gas they kept giving her whiffs of; at one point she had muttered that she felt like an advertisement for gang rape, and the nurse, an old bird who had assisted at the births of enough children to populate a high school, found that extremely funny) the doctor between her legs, the nurse off to one side, arranging instruments and humming. The sharp, glassy pains had been coming at steadily shortening intervals, and several times she had screamed in spite of her shame.

Then the doctor told her quite sternly that she must *PUSH,* and she did, and then she felt something being taken from her. It was a clear and distinct feeling, one she would never forget—the thing *taken.* Then the doctor held her son up by the legs—she had seen his tiny sex and known he was a boy immediately—and as the doctor groped for the airmask, she had seen something else, something so horrible that she found the strength to scream again after she had thought all screams were used up:

He has no face!

But of course there had been a face, Danny's own sweet face, and the caul that had covered it at birth now resided in a small jar which she had kept, almost shamefully. She did not hold with old superstition, but she had kept the caul nevertheless. She did not hold with wives' tales, but the boy had been unusual from the first. She did not believe in second sight but—

Did Daddy have an accident? I dreamed Daddy had an accident.

Something had changed him. She didn't believe it was just her getting ready to ask for a divorce that had done it. Something had happened before that morning. Something that had happened while she slept uneasily. Al Shockley said that nothing had happened, nothing at all, but he had averted his eyes when he said it, and if you believed faculty gossip, Al had also climbed aboard the fabled wagon.

Did Daddy have an accident?

Maybe a chance collision with fate, surely nothing much more concrete. She had read that day's paper and the next day's with a closer eye than usual, but she saw nothing she could connect with Jack. God help her, she had been looking for a hit-and-run accident or a barroom brawl that had resulted in serious injuries or . . . who knew? Who wanted to? But no policeman came to call, either to ask questions or with a warrant empowering him to take paint scrapings from the VW's bumpers. Nothing. Only her husband's one hundred and eighty degree change and her son's sleepy question on waking:

Did Daddy have an accident? I dreamed . . .

She had stuck with Jack more for Danny's sake than she would admit in her waking hours, but now, sleeping lightly, she could admit it: Danny had been Jack's for the asking, almost from the first. Just as she had been her father's, almost from the first. She couldn't remember Danny ever spitting a bottle back on Jack's shirt. Jack could get him to eat after she had given up in disgust, even when Danny was teething and it gave him visible pain to chew. When Danny had a stomachache, she would rock him for an hour before he began to quiet; Jack had only to pick him up, walk twice around the room with him, and Danny would be asleep on Jack's shoulder, his thumb securely corked in his mouth.

He hadn't minded changing diapers, even those he called the special deliveries. He sat with Danny for hours on end, bouncing him on his lap, playing finger games with him, making faces at him while Danny poked at his nose and then collapsed with the giggles. He made formulas and administered them faultlessly, getting up every last burp afterward. He would take Danny with him in the car to get the paper or a bottle of milk or nails at the hardware store even when their son was still an infant. He had taken Danny to a Stovington-Keene soccer match when Danny was only six months old, and Danny had sat motionlessly on his father's lap through the whole game, wrapped in a blanket, a small Stovington pennant clutched in one chubby fist.

He loved his mother but he was his father's boy.

And hadn't she felt, time and time again, her son's wordless opposition to the whole idea of divorce? She would be thinking about it in the kitchen, turning it over in her mind as she turned the potatoes for supper over in her hands for the peeler's blade. And she would turn around to see him sitting cross-legged in a kitchen chair, looking at her with eyes that seemed both frightened and accusatory. Walking with him in the park, he would suddenly seize both her hands and say—almost demand: "Do you love me? Do you love daddy?" And, confused, she would nod or say, "Of course I do, honey." Then he would run to the duck pond, sending them squawking and scared to the other end, flapping their wings in a panic before the small ferocity of his charge, leaving her to stare after him and wonder.

There were even times when it seemed that her determination to at least discuss the matter with Jack dissolved, not out of her own weakness, but under the determination of her son's will.

I don't believe such things.

But in sleep she did believe them, and in sleep, with her husband's seed still drying on her thighs, she felt that the three of them had been permanently welded together—that if their three/oneness was to be destroyed, it would not be destroyed by any of them but from outside.

Most of what she believed centered around her love for Jack. She had never stopped loving him, except maybe for that dark period immediately following Danny's "accident." And she loved her son. Most of all she loved them together, walking or riding or only sitting. Jack's large head and Danny's small one poised alertly over the fans of old maid hands, sharing a bottle of Coke, looking at the funnies. She loved having them with her, and she hoped to dear God that this hotel caretaking job Al had gotten for Jack would be the beginning of good times again.

And the wind gonna rise up, baby,
and blow my blues away . . .

Soft and sweet and mellow, the song came back and lingered, following her down into a deeper sleep where thought ceased and the faces that came in dreams went unremembered.

7

In Another Bedroom

Danny awoke with the booming still loud in his ears, and the drunk, savagely pettish voice crying hoarsely: *Come out here and take your medicine! I'll find you! I'll find you!*

But now the booming was only his racing heart, and the only voice in the night was the faraway sound of a police siren.

He lay in bed motionlessly, looking up at the wind-stirred shadows of the leaves on his bedroom ceiling. They twined sinuously together, making shapes like the vines and creepers in a jungle, like patterns woven into the nap of a thick carpet. He was clad in Doctor Denton pajamas, but between the pajama suit and his skin he had grown a more closely fitting singlet of perspiration.

"Tony?" he whispered. "You there?"

No answer.

He slipped out of bed and padded silently across to the window and looked out on Arapahoe Street, now still and silent. It was two in the morning. There was nothing out there but empty sidewalks drifted with fallen leaves, parked cars, and the long-necked streetlight on the corner across from the Cliff Brice gas station. With its hooded top and motionless stance, the streetlight looked like a monster in a space show.

He looked up the street both ways, straining his eyes for Tony's slight, beckoning form, but there was no one there.

The wind sighed through the trees, and the fallen leaves rattled up the deserted walks and around the hubcaps of parked cars. It was a faint and sorrowful sound, and the boy thought that he might be the only one in Boulder awake enough to hear it. The only human being, at least. There was no way of knowing what else might be out in the night, slinking hungrily through the shadows, watching and scenting the breeze.

I'll find you! I'll find you!

"Tony?" he whispered again, but without much hope.

Only the wind spoke back, gusting more strongly this time, scattering leaves across the sloping roof below his window. Some of them slipped into the raingutter and came to rest there like tired dancers.

Danny . . . Danneee . . .

He started at the sound of that familiar voice and craned out the window, his small hands on the sill. With the sound of Tony's voice the whole night seemed to have come silently and secretly alive, whispering even when the wind quieted again and the leaves were still and the shadows had stopped moving. He thought he saw a darker shadow standing by the bus stop a block down, but it was hard to tell if it was a real thing or an eye-trick.

Don't go, Danny . . .

Then the wind gusted again, making him squint, and the shadow by the bus stop was gone . . . if it had ever been there at all. He stood by his window for

(a minute? an hour?)

some time longer, but there was no more. At last he crept back into his bed and pulled the blankets up and watched the shadows thrown by the alien streetlight turn into a sinuous jungle filled with flesh-eating plants that wanted only to slip around him, squeeze the life out of him, and drag him down into a blackness where one sinister word flashed in red:

REDRUM.

PART TWO

Closing Day

8

A View of the Overlook

Mommy was worried.

She was afraid the bug wouldn't make it up and down all these mountains and that they would get stranded by the side of the road where somebody might come ripping along and hit them. Danny himself was more sanguine; if Daddy thought the bug would make this one last trip, then probably it would.

"We're just about there," Jack said.

Wendy brushed her hair back from her temples. "Thank God."

She was sitting in the right-hand bucket, a Victoria Holt paperback open but face down in her lap. She was wearing her blue dress, the one Danny thought was her prettiest. It had a sailor collar and made her look very young, like a girl just getting ready to graduate from high school. Daddy kept putting his hand high up on her leg and she kept laughing and brushing it off, saying Get away, fly.

Danny was impressed with the mountains. One day Daddy had taken them up in the ones near

Boulder, the ones they called the Flatirons, but these were much bigger, and on the tallest of them you could see a fine dusting of snow, which Daddy said was often there year-round.

And they were actually *in* the mountains, no goofing around. Sheer rock faces rose all around them, so high you could barely see their tops even by craning your neck out the window. When they left Boulder, the temperature had been in the high seventies. Now, just after noon, the air up here felt crisp and cold like November back in Vermont and Daddy had the heater going . . . not that it worked all that well. They had passed several signs that said FALLING ROCK ZONE (Mommy read each one to him), and although Danny had waited anxiously to see some rock fall, none had. At least not yet.

Half an hour ago they had passed another sign that Daddy said was very important. This sign said ENTERING SIDEWINDER PASS, and Daddy said that sign was as far as the snowplows went in the wintertime. After that the road got too steep. In the winter the road was closed from the little town of Sidewinder, which they had gone through just before they got to that sign, all the way to Buckland, Utah.

Now they were passing another sign.

"What's that one, Mom?"

"That one says SLOWER VEHICLES USE RIGHT LANE. That means us."

"The bug will make it," Danny said.

"Please, God," Mommy said, and crossed her fingers. Danny looked down at her open-toed sandals and saw that she had crossed her toes as well. He giggled. She smiled back, but he knew that she was still worried.

The road wound up and up in a series of slow S curves, and Jack dropped the bug's stick shift from fourth gear to third, then into second. The bug wheezed and protested, and Wendy's eye fixed on the speedometer needle, which sank from forty to thirty to twenty, where it hovered reluctantly.

"The fuel pump . . ." she began timidly.

"The fuel pump will go another three miles," Jack said shortly.

The rock wall fell away on their right, disclosing a slash valley that seemed to go down forever, lined a dark green with Rocky Mountain pine and spruce. The pines fell away to gray cliffs of rock that dropped for hundreds of feet before smoothing out. She saw a waterfall spilling over one of them, the early afternoon sun sparkling in it like a golden fish snared in a blue net. They were beautiful mountains but they were hard. She did not think they would forgive many mistakes. An unhappy foreboding rose in her throat. Further west in the Sierra Nevada the Donner Party had become snowbound and had resorted to cannibalism to stay alive. The mountains did not forgive many mistakes.

With a punch of the clutch and a jerk, Jack shifted down to first gear and they labored upward, the bug's engine thumping gamely.

"You know," she said, "I don't think we've seen five cars since we came through Sidewinder. And one of them was the hotel limousine."

Jack nodded. "It goes right to Stapleton Airport in Denver. There's already some icy patches up beyond the hotel, Watson says, and they're forecasting more snow for tomorrow up higher. Anybody going through the mountains now wants to be on one of the main roads, just in case. That goddam Ullman better still be up there. I guess he will be."

"You're sure the larder is fully stocked?" she asked, still thinking of the Donners.

"He said so. He wanted Hallorann to go over it with you. Hallorann's the cook."

"Oh," she said faintly, looking at the speedometer. It had dropped from fifteen to ten miles an hour.

"There's the top," Jack said, pointing three hundred yards ahead. "There's a scenic turnout and you can see the Overlook from there. I'm going to pull off the road and give the bug a chance to rest." He craned over his shoulder at Danny, who was sitting on a pile of blankets. "What do you think, doc? We might see some deer. Or caribou."

"Sure, Dad."

The VW labored up and up. The speedometer dropped to just above the five-mile-an-hour hash-mark and was beginning to hitch when Jack pulled off the road

("What's that sign, Mommy?" "SCENIC TURNOUT," she read dutifully.)

and stepped on the emergency brake and let the VW run in neutral.

"Come on," he said, and got out.

They walked to the guardrail together.

"That's it," Jack said, and pointed at eleven o'clock.

For Wendy, it was discovering truth in a cliché: her breath was taken away. For a moment she was unable to breathe at all; the view had knocked the wind from her. They were standing near the top of one peak. Across from them—who knew how far?—an even taller mountain reared into the sky, its jagged tip only a silhouette that was now nimbused by the sun, which was beginning its decline. The whole valley floor was spread out below them, the slopes that they had climbed in the laboring bug falling away with such dizzying suddenness that she knew to look down there for too long would bring on nausea and eventual vomiting. The imagination seemed to spring to full life in the clear air, beyond the rein of reason, and to look was to helplessly see one's self plunging down and down and down, sky and slopes changing places in slow cartwheels, the scream drifting from your mouth like a lazy balloon as your hair and your dress billowed out . . .

She jerked her gaze away from the drop almost by force and followed Jack's finger. She could see the highway clinging to the side of this cathedral spire, switching back on itself but always tending northwest, still climbing but at a more gentle angle. Further up, seemingly set directly into the slope itself, she saw the grimly clinging pines give way to a wide square of green lawn and standing in the middle of it, overlooking all this, the hotel. The Overlook. Seeing it, she found breath and voice again.

"Oh, Jack, it's gorgeous!"

"Yes, it is," he said. "Ullman says he thinks it's the single most beautiful location in America. I don't care much for him, but I think he might be . . . Danny! Danny, are you all right?"

She looked around for him and her sudden fear for him blotted out everything else, stupendous or not. She darted toward him. He was holding onto the guardrail and looking up at the hotel, his face a pasty gray color. His eyes had the blank look of someone on the verge of fainting.

She knelt beside him and put steadying hands on his shoulders. "Danny, what's—"

Jack was beside her. "You okay, doc?" He gave Danny a brisk little shake and his eyes cleared.

"I'm okay, Daddy. I'm fine."

"What was it, Danny?" she asked. "Were you dizzy, honey?"

"No, I was just . . . thinking. I'm sorry. I didn't mean to scare you." He looked at his parents, kneeling in front of him, and offered them a small puzzled smile. "Maybe it was the sun. The sun got in my eyes."

"We'll get you up to the hotel and give you a drink of water," Daddy said.

"Okay."

And in the bug, which moved upward more surely on the gentler grade, he kept looking out between them as the road unwound, affording occasional glimpses of the Overlook Hotel, its massive bank of westward-looking windows reflecting back the sun.

It was the place he had seen in the midst of the blizzard, the dark and booming place where some hideously familiar figure sought him down long corridors carpeted with jungle. The place Tony had warned him against. It was here. It was here. Whatever Redrum was, it was here.

9

Checking It Out

Ullman was waiting for them just inside the wide, old-fashioned front doors. He shook hands with Jack and nodded coolly at Wendy, perhaps noticing the way heads turned when she came through into the lobby, her golden hair spilling across the shoulders of the simple navy dress. The hem of the dress stopped a modest two inches above the knee, but you didn't have to see more to know they were good legs.

Ullman seemed truly warm toward Danny only, but Wendy had experienced that before. Danny seemed to be a child for people who ordinarily held W. C. Fields' sentiments about children. He bent a little from the waist and offered Danny his hand. Danny shook it formally, without a smile.

"My son Danny," Jack said. "And my wife Winnifred."

"I'm happy to meet you both," Ullman said. "How old are you, Danny?"

"Five, sir."

"*Sir,* yet." Ullman smiled and glanced at Jack. "He's well mannered."

"Of course he is," Jack said.

"And Mrs. Torrance." He offered the same little bow, and for a bemused instant Wendy thought he would kiss her hand. She half-offered it and he did take it, but only for a moment, clasped in both of his. His hands were small and dry and smooth, and she guessed that he powdered them.

The lobby was a bustle of activity. Almost every one of the old-fashioned high-backed chairs was taken. Bellboys shuttled in and out with suitcases and there was a line at the desk, which was dominated by a huge brass cash register. The BankAmericard and Master Charge decals on it seemed jarringly anachronistic.

To their right, down toward a pair of tall double doors that were pulled closed and roped off, there was an old-fashioned fireplace now blazing with birch logs. Three nuns sat on a sofa that was drawn up almost to the hearth itself. They were talking and smiling with their bags stacked up to either side, waiting for the check-out line to thin a little. As Wendy watched them they burst into a chord of tinkling, girlish laughter. She felt a smile touch her own lips; not one of them could be under sixty.

In the background was the constant hum of conversation, the muted *ding!* of the silver-plated bell beside the cash register as one of the two clerks on duty struck it, the slightly impatient call of "Front, please!" It brought back strong, warm memories of her honeymoon in New York with Jack, at the

Beekman Tower. For the first time she let herself believe that this might be exactly what the three of them needed: a season together away from the world, a sort of family honeymoon. She smiled affectionately down at Danny, who was goggling around frankly at everything. Another limo, as gray as a banker's vest, had pulled up out front.

"The last day of the season," Ullman was saying. "Closing day. Always hectic. I had expected you more around three, Mr. Torrance."

"I wanted to give the Volks time for a nervous breakdown if it decided to have one," Jack said. "It didn't."

"How fortunate," Ullman said. "I'd like to take the three of you on a tour of the place a little later, and of course Dick Hallorann wants to show Mrs. Torrance the Overlook's kitchen. But I'm afraid—"

One of the clerks came over and almost tugged his forelock.

"Excuse me, Mr. Ullman—"

"Well? What is it?"

"It's Mrs. Brant," the clerk said uncomfortably. "She refuses to pay her bill with anything but her American Express card. I told her we stopped taking American Express at the end of the season last year, but she won't . . ." His eyes shifted to the Torrance family, then back to Ullman. He shrugged.

"I'll take care of it."

"Thank you, Mr. Ullman." The clerk crossed back to the desk, where a dreadnought of a woman bundled into a long fur coat and what looked like a black feather boa was remonstrating loudly.

"I have been coming to the Overlook Hotel since 1955," she was telling the smiling, shrugging clerk. "I continued to come even after my second husband died of a stroke on that tiresome roque court—I told him the sun was too hot that day—and I have *never* . . . I repeat: *never* . . . paid with anything but my American Express credit card. Call the police if you like! Have them drag me away! I will still refuse to pay with anything but my American Express credit card. I repeat: . . ."

"Excuse me," Mr. Ullman said.

They watched him cross the lobby, touch Mrs. Brant's elbow deferentially, and spread his hands and nod when she turned her tirade on him. He listened sympathetically, nodded again, and said something in return. Mrs. Brant smiled triumphantly, turned to the unhappy desk clerk, and said loudly: "Thank God there is one employee of this hotel who hasn't become an utter Philistine!"

She allowed Ullman, who barely came to the bulky shoulder of her fur coat, to take her arm and lead her away, presumably to his inner office.

"Whooo!" Wendy said, smiling. "There's a dude who earns his money."

"But he didn't like that lady," Danny said immediately. "He was just pretending to like her."

Jack grinned down at him. "I'm sure that's true, doc. But flattery is the stuff that greases the wheels of the world."

"What's flattery?"

"Flattery," Wendy told him, "is when your daddy says he likes my new yellow slacks even if he doesn't or when he says I don't need to take off five pounds."

"Oh. Is it lying for fun?"

"Something very like that."

He had been looking at her closely and now said: "You're pretty, Mommy." He frowned in confusion when they exchanged a glance and then burst into laughter.

"Ullman didn't waste much flattery on me," Jack said. "Come on over by the window, you guys. I feel conspicuous standing out here in the middle with my denim jacket on. I honest to God didn't think there'd be anybody much here on closing day. Guess I was wrong."

"You look very handsome," she said, and then they laughed again, Wendy putting a hand over her mouth. Danny still didn't understand, but it was okay. They were loving each other. Danny thought this place reminded her of somewhere else

(the beak-man place)

where she had been happy. He wished he liked it as well as she did, but he kept telling himself over and over that the things Tony showed him didn't always come true. He would be careful. He would watch for something called Redrum. But he would not say anything unless he absolutely had to. Because they were happy, they had been laughing, and there were no bad thoughts.

"Look at this view," Jack said.

"Oh, it's gorgeous! Danny, look!"

But Danny didn't think it was particularly gorgeous. He didn't like heights; they made him dizzy. Beyond the wide front porch, which ran the length of the hotel, a beautifully manicured lawn (there was a putting green on the right) sloped away to a long, rectangular swimming pool. A CLOSED sign stood on a little tripod at one end of the pool; *closed* was one sign he could read by himself, along with *Stop, Exit, Pizza,* and a few others.

Beyond the pool a graveled path wound off through baby pines and spruces and aspens. Here was a small sign he didn't know: ROQUE. There was an arrow below it.

"What's R-O-Q-U-E, Daddy?"

"A game," Daddy said. "It's a little bit like croquet, only you play it on a gravel court that has sides like a big billiard table instead of grass. It's a very old game, Danny. Sometimes they have tournaments here."

"Do you play it with a croquet mallet?"

"Like that," Jack agreed. "Only the handle's a little shorter and the head has two sides. One side is hard rubber and the other side is wood."

(Come out, you little shit!)

"It's pronounced *roke*," Daddy was saying. "I'll teach you how to play, if you want."

"Maybe," Danny said in an odd colorless little voice that made his parents exchange a puzzled look over his head. "I might not like it, though."

"Well if you don't like it, doc, you don't have to play. All right?"

"Sure."

"Do you like the animals?" Wendy asked. "That's called a topiary." Beyond the path leading to *roque* there were hedges clipped into the shapes of various animals. Danny, whose eyes were sharp, made out a rabbit, a dog, a horse, a cow, and a trio of bigger ones that looked like frolicking lions.

"Those animals were what made Uncle Al think of me for the job," Jack told him. "He knew that when I was in college I used to work for a landscaping company. That's a business that fixes people's lawns and bushes and hedges. I used to trim a lady's topiary."

Wendy put a hand over her mouth and snickered. Looking at her, Jack said, "Yes, I used to trim her topiary at least once a week."

"Get away, fly," Wendy said, and snickered again.

"Did she have nice hedges, Dad?" Danny asked, and at this they both stifled great bursts of laughter. Wendy laughed so hard that tears streamed down her cheeks and she had to get a Kleenex out of her handbag.

"They weren't animals, Danny," Jack said when he had control of himself. "They were playing cards. Spades and hearts and clubs and diamonds. But the hedges grow, you see—"

(*They creep*, Watson had said . . . no, not the hedges, the boiler. *You have to watch it all the time or you and your fambly will end up on the fuckin moon.*)

They looked at him, puzzled. The smile had faded off his face.

"Dad?" Danny asked.

He blinked at them, as if coming back from far away. "They grow, Danny, and lose their shape. So I'll have to give them a haircut once or twice a week until it gets so cold they stop growing for the year."

"And a playground, too." Wendy said. "My lucky boy."

The playground was beyond the *topiary*. Two slides, a big swing set with half a dozen swings set at varying heights, a jungle gym, a tunnel made of cement rings, a sandbox, and a playhouse that was an exact replica of the Overlook itself.

"Do you like it, Danny?" Wendy asked.

"I sure do," he said, hoping he sounded more enthused than he felt. "It's neat."

Beyond the playground there was an inconspicuous chain link security fence, beyond that the wide, macadamized drive that led up to the hotel, and beyond that the valley itself, dropping away into the bright blue haze of afternoon. Danny didn't know the word *isolation,* but if someone had explained it to him he would have seized on it. Far below, lying in the sun like a long black snake that had decided to snooze for a while, was the road that led back through Sidewinder Pass and eventually to Boulder. The road that would be closed all winter long. He felt a little suffocated at the thought, and almost jumped when Daddy dropped his hand on his shoulder.

"I'll get you that drink as soon as I can, doc. They're a little busy right now."

"Sure, Dad."

Mrs. Brant came out of the inner office looking vindicated. A few moments later two bellboys, struggling with eight suitcases between them, followed her as best they could as she strode triumphantly out the door. Danny watched through the window as a man in a gray uniform and a hat like a captain in the Army brought her long silver car around to the door and got out. He tipped his cap to her and ran around to open the trunk.

And in one of those flashes that sometimes came, he got a complete thought from her, one that floated above the confused, low-pitched babble of emotions and colors that he usually got in crowded places.

(i'd like to get into his pants)

Danny's brow wrinkled as he watched the bellboys put her cases into the trunk. She was looking rather sharply at the man in the gray uniform, who was supervising the loading. Why would she want to get that man's pants? Was she cold, even with that long fur coat on? And if she was that cold, why hadn't she just put on some pants of her own? His mommy wore pants just about all winter.

The man in the gray uniform closed the trunk and walked back to help her into the car. Danny watched closely to see if she would say anything about his pants, but she only smiled and gave him a dollar bill—a tip. A moment later she was guiding the big silver car down the driveway.

He thought about asking his mother why Mrs. Brant might want the car-man's pants, and decided against it. Sometimes questions could get you in a whole lot of trouble. It had happened to him before.

So instead he squeezed in between them on the small sofa they were sharing and watched all the people check out at the desk. He was glad his mommy and daddy were happy and loving each other, but he couldn't help being a little worried. He couldn't help it.

10

Hallorann

The cook didn't conform to Wendy's image of the typical resort hotel kitchen personage at all. To begin with, such a personage was called a *chef*, nothing so mundane as a cook—cooking was what she did in her apartment kitchen when she threw all the leftovers into a greased Pyrex casserole dish and added noodles. Further, the culinary wizard of such a place as the Overlook, which advertised in the resort section of the New York Sunday *Times*, should be small, rotund, and pasty-faced (rather like the Pillsbury Dough-Boy); he should have a thin pencil-line mustache like a forties musical comedy star, dark eyes, a French accent, and a detestable personality.

Hallorann had the dark eyes and that was all. He was a tall black man with a modest afro that was beginning to powder white. He had a soft southern accent and he laughed a lot, disclosing teeth too white and too even to be anything but 1950-vintage Sears and Roebuck dentures. Her own father had had a pair, which he called Roebuckers, and from time to time he would push them out at her comically at the supper table . . . always, Wendy remembered now, when her mother was out in the kitchen getting something else or on the telephone.

Danny had stared up at this black giant in blue serge, and then had smiled when Hallorann picked him up easily, set him in the crook of his elbow, and said: "You ain't gonna stay up here all winter."

"Yes I am," Danny said with a shy grin.

"No, you're gonna come down to St. Pete's with me and learn to cook and go out on the beach every damn evenin watchin for crabs. Right?"

Danny giggled delightedly and shook his head no. Hallorann set him down.

"If you're gonna change your mind," Hallorann said, bending over him gravely, "you better do it quick. Thirty minutes from now and I'm in my car. Two and a half hours after that, I'm sitting at Gate 32, Concourse B, Stapleton International Airport, in the mile-high city of Denver, Colorado. Three hours after *that,* I'm rentin a car at the Miama Airport and on my way to sunny St. Pete's, waiting to get inta my swimtrunks and just laaafin up my sleeve at anybody stuck and caught in the snow. Can you dig it, my boy?"

"Yes, sir," Danny said, smiling.

Hallorann turned to Jack and Wendy. "Looks like a fine boy there."

"We think he'll do," Jack said, and offered his hand. Hallorann took it. "I'm Jack Torrance. My wife Winnifred. Danny you've met."

"And a pleasure it was. Ma'am, are you a Winnie or a Freddie?"

"I'm a Wendy," she said, smiling.

"Okay. That's better than the other two, I think. Right this way. Mr. Ullman wants you to have the tour, the tour you'll get." He shook his head and said under his breath: "And won't I be glad to see the last of *him*."

Hallorann commenced to tour them around the most immense kitchen Wendy had ever seen in her life. It was sparkling clean. Every surface was coaxed to a high gloss. It was more than just big; it was intimidating. She walked at Hallorann's side while Jack, wholly out of his element, hung back a little with Danny. A long wallboard hung with cutting instruments which went all the way from paring knives to two-handed cleavers hung beside a four-basin sink. There was a breadboard as big as their Boulder apartment's kitchen table. An amazing array of stainless-steel pots and pans hung from floor to ceiling, covering one whole wall.

"I think I'll have to leave a trail of breadcrumbs every time I come in," she said.

"Don't let it get you down," Hallorann said. "It's big, but it's still only a kitchen. Most of this stuff you'll never even have to touch. Keep it clean, that's all I ask. Here's the stove I'd be using, if I was you. There are three of them in all, but this is the smallest."

Smallest, she thought dismally, looking at it. There were twelve burners, two regular ovens and a Dutch oven, a heated well on top in which you could simmer sauces or bake beans, a broiler, and a warmer—plus a million dials and temperature gauges.

"All gas," Hallorann said. "You've cooked with gas before, Wendy?"

"Yes . . ."

"I love gas," he said, and turned on one of the burners. Blue flame popped into life and he adjusted it down to a faint glow with a delicate touch. "I like to be able to see the flame you're cookin with. You see where all the surface burner switches are?"

"Yes."

"And the oven dials are all marked. Myself, I favor the middle one because it seems to heat the most even, but you use whichever one you like—or all three, for that matter."

"A TV dinner in each one," Wendy said, and laughed weakly.

Hallorann roared. "Go right ahead, if you like. I left a list of everything edible over by the sink. You see it?"

"Here it is, Mommy!" Danny brought over two sheets of paper, written closely on both sides.

"Good boy," Hallorann said, taking it from him and ruffling his hair. "You sure you don't want to come to Florida with me, my boy? Learn to cook the sweetest shrimp creole this side of paradise?"

Danny put his hands over his mouth and giggled and retreated to his father's side.

"You three folks could eat up here for a year, I guess," Hallorann said. "We got a cold-pantry, a walk-in freezer, all sorts of vegetable bins, and two refrigerators. Come on and let me show you."

For the next ten minutes Hallorann opened bins and doors, disclosing food in such amounts as Wendy had never seen before. The food supplies amazed her but did not reassure her as much as she might have thought: the Donner Party kept recurring to her, not with thoughts of cannibalism (with all this food it would indeed be a long time before they were reduced to such poor rations as each other), but with the reinforced idea that this was indeed a serious business: when snow fell, getting out of here would not be a matter of an hour's drive to Sidewinder but a major operation. They would sit up here in this deserted grand hotel, eating the food that had been left them like creatures in a fairy tale and listening to the bitter wind around their snowbound eaves. In Vermont, when Danny had broken his arm

(when *Jack* broke Danny's arm)

she had called the emergency Medix squad, dialing the number from the little card attached to the phone. They had been at the house only ten minutes later. There were other numbers written on that little card. You could have a police car in five minutes and a fire truck in even less time than that, because the fire station was only three blocks away and one block over. There was a man to call if the lights went out, a man to call if the shower stopped up, a man to call if the TV went on the fritz. But what would happen up here if Danny had one of his fainting spells and swallowed his tongue?

(oh God what a thought!)

What if the place caught on fire? If Jack fell down the elevator shaft and fractured his skull? What if—?

(what if we have a wonderful time now stop it, Winnifred!)

Halloran showed them into the walk-in freezer first, where their breath puffed out like comic strip balloons. In the freezer it was as if winter had already come.

Hamburger in big plastic bags, ten pounds in each bag, a dozen bags. Forty whole chickens hanging from a row of hooks in the wood-planked walls. Canned hams stacked up like poker chips, a dozen of them. Below the chickens, ten roasts of beef, ten roasts of pork, and a huge leg of lamb.

"You like lamb, doc?" Hallorann asked, grinning.

"I love it." Danny said immediately. He had never had it.

"I knew you did. There's nothin like two good slices of lamb on a cold night, with some mint jelly on the side. You got the mint jelly here, too. Lamb eases the belly. It's a noncontentious sort of meat."

From behind them Jack said curiously: "How did you know we called him doc?"

Hallorann turned around. "Pardon?"

"Danny. We call him doc sometimes. Like in the Bugs Bunny cartoons."

"Looks sort of like a doc, doesn't he?" He wrinkled his nose at Danny, smacked his lips, and said, "Ehhhh, what's up, doc?"

Danny giggled and then Hallorann said something

(Sure you don't want to go to Florida, doc?)

to him, very clearly. He heard every word. He looked at Hallorann, startled and a little scared. Hallorann winked solemnly and turned back to the food.

Wendy looked from the cook's broad, serge-clad back to her son. She had the oddest feeling that something had passed between them, something she could not quite follow.

"You got twelve packages of sausage, twelve packages of bacon," Hallorann said. "So much for the pig. In this drawer, twenty pounds of butter."

"*Real* butter?" Jack asked.

"The A-number-one."

"I don't think I've had real butter since I was a kid back in Berlin, New Hampshire."

"Well, you'll eat it up here until oleo seems a treat," Hallorann said, and laughed. "Over in this bin you got your bread—thirty loaves of white, twenty of dark. We try to keep racial balance at the Overlook, don't you know. Now I know fifty loaves won't take you through, but there's plenty of makings and fresh is better than frozen any day of the week.

"Down here you got your fish. Brain food, right, doc?"

"Is it, Mom?"

"If Mr. Hallorann says so, honey." She smiled.

Danny wrinkled his nose. "I don't like fish."

"You're dead wrong," Hallorann said. "You just never had any fish that liked *you*. This fish here will like you fine. Five pounds of rainbow trout, ten pounds of turbot, fifteen cans of tuna fish—"

"Oh yeah, I like tuna."

"and five pounds of the sweetest-tasting sole that ever swam in the sea. My boy, when next spring rolls around, you're gonna thank old . . ." He snapped his fingers as if he had forgotten something. "What's my name, now? I guess it just slipped my mind."

"Mr. Hallorann," Danny said, grinning. "Dick, to your friends."

"That's right! And you bein a friend, you make it Dick."

As he led them into the far corner, Jack and Wendy exchanged a puzzled glance, both of them trying to remember if Hallorann had told them his first name.

"And this here I put in special," Hallorann said. "Hope you folks enjoy it."

"Oh really, you shouldn't have," Wendy said, touched. It was a twenty-pound turkey wrapped in a wide scarlet ribbon with a bow on top.

"You got to have your turkey on Thanksgiving, Wendy," Hallorann said gravely. "I believe there's a capon back here somewhere for Christmas. Doubtless you'll stumble on it. Let's come on out of here now before we all catch the pee-numonia. Right, doc?"

"Right!"

There were more wonders in the cold-pantry. A hundred boxes of dried milk (Hallorann advised her gravely to buy fresh milk for the boy in Sidewinder as long as it was feasible), five twelve-pound bags of sugar, a gallon jug of blackstrap molasses, cereals, glass jugs of rice, macaroni, spaghetti; ranked cans of fruit and fruit salad; a bushel of fresh apples that scented the whole room with autumn; dried raisins, prunes, and apricots ("You got to be regular if you want to be happy," Hallorann said, and pealed laughter at the cold-pantry ceiling, where one old-fashioned light globe hung down on an iron chain); a deep bin filled with potatoes; and smaller caches of tomatoes, onions, turnips, squashes, and cabbages.

"My word," Wendy said as they came out. But seeing all that fresh food after her thirty-dollar-a-week grocery budget so stunned her that she was unable to say just what her word was.

"I'm runnin a bit late," Hallorann said, checking his watch, "so I'll just let you go through the cabinets and the fridges as you get settled in. There's cheeses, canned milk, sweetened condensed milk, yeast, bakin soda, a whole bagful of those Table Talk pies, a few bunches of bananas that ain't even near to ripe yet—"

"Stop," she said, holding up a hand and laughing. "I'll never remember it all. It's super. And I promise to leave the place clean."

"That's all I ask." He turned to Jack. "Did Mr. Ullman give you the rundown on the rats in his belfry?"

Jack grinned. "He said there were possibly some in the attic, and Mr. Watson said there might be some more down in the basement. There must be two tons of paper down there, but I didn't see any shredded, as if they'd been using it to make nests."

"That Watson," Hallorann said, shaking his head in mock sorrow. "Ain't he the foulest-talking man you ever ran on?"

"He's quite a character," Jack agreed. His own father had been the foulest-talking man Jack had ever run on.

"It's sort of a pity," Hallorann said, leading them back toward the wide swinging doors that gave on the Overlook dining room. "There was money in that family, long ago. It was Watson's granddad or great-granddad—I can't remember which—that built this place."

"So I was told," Jack said.

"What happened?" Wendy asked.

"Well, they couldn't make it go," Hallorann said. "Watson will tell you the whole story—twice a day, if you let him. The old man got a bee in his bonnet about the place. He let it drag him down, I guess. He had two boys and one of them was killed in a riding accident on the grounds while the hotel was still a-building. That would have been 1908 or '09. The old man's wife died of the flu, and then it was just the old man and his youngest son. They ended up getting took back on as caretakers in the same hotel the old man had built."

"It is sort of a pity," Wendy said.

"What happened to him? The old man?" Jack asked.

"He plugged his finger into a light socket by mistake and that was the end of him," Hallorann said. "Sometime in the early thirties before the Depression closed this place down for ten years.

"Anyway, Jack, I'd appreciate it if you and your wife would keep an eye out for rats in the kitchen, as well. If you should see them . . . traps, not poison."

Jack blinked. "Of course. Who'd want to put rat poison in the kitchen?"

Hallorann laughed derisively. "Mr. Ullman, that's who. That was his bright idea last fall. I put it to him, I said: 'What if we all get up here next May, Mr. Ullman, and I serve the traditional opening night dinner'—which just happens to be salmon in a very nice sauce—'and everybody gits sick and the doctor comes and says to you, "Ullman, what have you been doing up here? You've got eighty of the richest folks in America suffering from rat poisoning!" ' "

Jack threw his head back and bellowed laughter. "What did Ullman say?"

Hallorann tucked his tongue into his cheek as if feeling for a bit of food in there. "He said: 'Get some traps, Hallorann.' "

This time they all laughed, even Danny, although he was not completely sure what the joke was, except it had something to do with Mr. Ullman, who didn't know everything after all.

The four of them passed through the dining room, empty and silent now, with its fabulous western exposure on the snow-dusted peaks. Each of the white linen tablecloths had been covered with a sheet of tough clear plastic. The rug, now rolled up for the season, stood in one corner like a sentinel on guard duty.

Across the wide room was a double set of batwing doors, and over them an old-fashioned sign lettered in gilt script: *The Colorado Lounge.*

Following his gaze, Hallorann said, "If you're a drinkin man, I hope you brought your own supplies.

That place is picked clean. Employee's party last night, you know. Every maid and bellhop in the place is goin around with a headache today, me included."

"I don't drink," Jack said shortly. They went back to the lobby.

It had cleared greatly during the half hour they'd spent in the kitchen. The long main room was beginning to take on the quiet, deserted look that Jack supposed they would become familiar with soon enough. The high-backed chairs were empty. The nuns who had been sitting by the fire were gone, and the fire itself was down to a bed of comfortably glowing coals. Wendy glanced out into the parking lot and saw that all but a dozen cars had disappeared.

She found herself wishing they could get back in the VW and go back to Boulder . . . or anywhere else.

Jack was looking around for Ullman, but he wasn't in the lobby.

A young maid with her ash-blond hair pinned up on her neck came over. "Your luggage is out on the porch, Dick."

"Thank you, Sally." He gave her a peck on the forehead. "You have yourself a good winter. Getting married, I hear."

He turned to the Torrances as she strolled away, backside twitching pertly. "I've got to hurry along if I'm going to make that plane. I want to wish you all the best. Know you'll have it."

"Thanks," Jack said. "You've been very kind."

"I'll take good care of your kitchen," Wendy promised again. "Enjoy Florida."

"I always do," Hallorann said. He put his hands on his knees and bent down to Danny. "Last chance, guy. Want to come to Florida?"

"I guess not," Danny said, smiling.

"Okay. Like to give me a hand out to my car with my bags?"

"If my mommy says I can."

"You can," Wendy said, "but you'll have to have that jacket buttoned." She leaned forward to do it but Hallorann was ahead of her, his large brown fingers moving with smooth dexterity.

"I'll send him right back in," Hallorann said.

"Fine," Wendy said, and followed them to the door. Jack was still looking around for Ullman. The last of the Overlook's guests were checking out at the desk.

11

The Shining

There were four bags in a pile just outside the door. Three of them were giant, battered old suitcases covered with black imitation alligator hide. The last was an oversized zipper bag with a faded tartan skin.

"Guess you can handle that one, can't you?" Hallorann asked him. He picked up two of the big cases in one hand and hoisted the other under his arm.

"Sure," Danny said. He got a grip on it with both hands and followed the cook down the porch steps, trying manfully not to grunt and give away how heavy it was.

A sharp and cutting fall wind had come up since they had arrived; it whistled across the parking lot, making Danny wince his eyes down to slits as he carried the zipper bag in front of him, bumping on his knees. A few errant aspen leaves rattled and turned across the now mostly deserted asphalt, making Danny think momentarily of that night last week when he had wakened out of his nightmare and had heard—or thought he heard, at least—Tony telling him not to go.

Hallorann set his bags down by the trunk of a beige Plymouth Fury. "This ain't much car," he confided to Danny, "just a rental job. My Bessie's on the other end. She's a car. 1950 Cadillac, and does she run sweet? I'll tell the world. I keep her in Florida because she's too old for all this mountain climbing. You need a hand with that?"

"No, sir," Danny said. He managed to carry it the last ten or twelve steps without grunting and set it down with a large sigh of relief.

"Good boy," Hallorann said. He produced a large key ring from the pocket of his blue serge jacket and unlocked the trunk. As he lifted the bags in he said: "You shine on, boy. Harder than anyone I ever met in my life. And I'm sixty years old this January."

"Huh?"

"You got a knack," Hallorann said, turning to him. "Me, I've always called it shining. That's what my grandmother called it, too. She had it. We used to sit in the kitchen when I was a boy no older than you and have long talks without even openin our mouths."

"Really?"

Hallorann smiled at Danny's openmouthed, almost hungry expression and said, "Come on up and sit in the car with me for a few minutes. Want to talk to you." He slammed the trunk.

In the lobby of the Overlook, Wendy Torrance saw her son get into the passenger side of Hallorann's car as the big black cook slid in behind the wheel. A sharp pang of fear struck her and she opened her mouth to tell Jack that Hallorann had not been lying about taking their son to Florida—there was a kidnaping afoot. But they were only sitting there. She could barely see the small silhouette of her son's head, turned attentively toward Hallorann's big one. Even at this distance that small head had a set to it that she recognized—it was the way her son looked when there was something on the TV that particularly fascinated him, or when he and his father were playing old maid or idiot cribbage. Jack, who was still looking around for Ullman, hadn't noticed. Wendy kept silent, watching Hallorann's car nervously, wondering what they could possibly be talking about that would make Danny cock his head that way.

In the car Hallorann was saying: "Get you kinda lonely, thinkin you were the only one?"

Danny, who had been frightened as well as lonely sometimes, nodded. "Am I the only one you ever met?" he asked.

Hallorann laughed and shook his head. "No, child, no. But you shine the hardest."

"Are there lots, then?"

"No," Hallorann said, "but you do run across them. A lot of folks, they got a little bit of shine to them. They don't even know it. But they always seem to show up with flowers when their wives are feelin blue with the monthlies, they do good on school tests they don't even study for, they got a good idea how people are feelin as soon as they walk into a room. I come across fifty or sixty like that. But maybe only a dozen, countin my gram, that *knew* they was shinin."

"Wow," Danny said, and thought about it. Then: "Do you know Mrs. Brant?"

"Her?" Hallorann asked scornfully. "She don't shine. Just sends her supper back two-three times every night."

"I know she doesn't," Danny said earnestly. "But do you know the man in the gray uniform that gets the cars?"

"Mike? Sure, I know Mike. What about him?"

"Mr. Hallorann, why would she want his pants?"

"What are you talking about, boy?"

"Well, when she was watching him, she was thinking she would sure like to get into his pants and I just wondered why——"

But he got no further. Hallorann had thrown his head back, and rich, dark laughter issued from his chest, rolling around in the car like cannonfire. The seat shook with the force of it. Danny smiled, puzzled, and at last the storm subsided by fits and starts. Hallorann produced a large silk handkerchief from his breast pocket like a white flag of surrender and wiped his streaming eyes.

"Boy," he said, still snorting a little, "you are gonna know everything there is to know about the human condition before you make ten. I dunno if to envy you or not."

"But Mrs. Brant——"

"You never mind her," he said. "And don't go askin your mom, either. You'd only upset her, dig what I'm sayin?"

"Yes, sir," Danny said. He dug it perfectly well. He had upset his mother that way in the past.

"That Mrs. Brant is just a dirty old woman with an itch, that's all you have to know." He looked at Danny speculatively. "How hard can you hit, doc?"

"Huh?"

"Give me a blast. Think at me. I want to know if you got as much as I think you do."

"What do you want me to think?"

"Anything. Just think it *hard*."

"Okay," Danny said. He considered it for a moment, then gathered his concentration and flung it out at Hallorann. He had never done anything precisely like this before, and at the last instant some instinctive part of him rose up and blunted some of the thought's raw force—he didn't want to hurt Mr. Hallorann. Still the thought arrowed out of him with a force he never would have believed. It went like a Nolan Ryan fastball with a little extra on it.

(Gee I hope I don't hurt him)

And the thought was:

(*!!! HI, DICK!!!*)

Hallorann winced and jerked backward on the seat. His teeth came together with a hard click, drawing blood from his lower lip in a thin trickle. His hands flew up involuntarily from his lap to the level of his chest and then settled back again. For a moment his eyelids fluttered limply, with no conscious control, and Danny was frightened.

"Mr. Hallorann? Dick? Are you okay?"

"I don't know," Hallorann said, and laughed weakly. "I honest to God don't. My God, boy, you're a pistol."

"I'm sorry," Danny said, more alarmed. "Should I get my daddy? I'll run and get him."

"No, here I come. I'm okay, Danny. You just sit right there. I feel a little scrambled, that's all."

"I didn't go as hard as I could," Danny confessed. "I was scared to, at the last minute."

"Probably my good luck you did . . . my brains would be leakin out my ears." He saw the alarm on Danny's face and smiled. "No harm done. What did it feel like to you?"

"Like I was Nolan Ryan throwing a fastball," he replied promptly.

"You like baseball, do you?" Hallorann was rubbing his temples gingerly.

"Daddy and me like the Angels," Danny said. "The Red Sox in the American League East and the Angels in the West. We saw the Red Sox against Cincinnati in the World Series. I was a lot littler then. And Daddy was . . ." Danny's face went dark and troubled.

"Was what, Dan?"

"I forget," Danny said. He started to put his thumb in his mouth to suck it, but that was a baby trick. He put his hand back in his lap.

"Can you tell what your mom and dad are thinking, Danny?" Hallorann was watching him closely.

"Most times, if I want to. But usually I don't try."

"Why not?"

"Well . . ." He paused a moment, troubled. "It would be like peeking into the bedroom and watching while they're doing the thing that makes babies. Do you know that thing?"

"I have had acquaintance with it," Hallorann said gravely.

"They wouldn't like that. And they wouldn't like me peeking at their thinks. It would be dirty."

"I see."

"But I know how they're feeling," Danny said. "I can't help that. I know how you're feeling, too. I hurt you. I'm sorry."

"It's just a headache. I've had hangovers that were worse. Can you read other people, Danny?"

"I can't read yet at all," Danny said, "except a few words. But Daddy's going to teach me this winter. My daddy used to teach reading and writing in a big school. Mostly writing, but he knows reading, too."

"I mean, can you tell what anybody is thinking?"

Danny thought about it.

"I can if it's *loud*," he said finally. "Like Mrs. Brant and the pants. Or like once, when me and Mommy were in this big store to get me some shoes, there was this big kid looking at radios, and he was thinking about taking one without buying it. Then he'd think, what if I get caught? Then he'd think, I really want it. Then he'd think about getting caught again. He was making himself sick about it, and he was making *me* sick. Mommy was talking to the man who sells the shoes so I went over and said, 'Kid, don't take that radio. Go away.' And he got really scared. He went away fast."

Hallorann was grinning broadly. "I bet he did. Can you do anything else, Danny? Is it only thoughts and feelings, or is there more?"

Cautiously: "Is there more for you?"

"Sometimes," Hallorann said. "Not often. Sometimes . . . sometimes there are dreams. Do you dream, Danny?"

"Sometimes," Danny said, "I dream when I'm awake. After Tony comes." His thumb wanted to go into his mouth again. He had never told anyone but Mommy and Daddy about Tony. He made his thumb-sucking hand go back into his lap.

"Who's Tony?"

And suddenly Danny had one of those flashes of understanding that frightened him most of all; it was like a sudden glimpse of some incomprehensible machine that might be safe or might be deadly dangerous. He was too young to know which. He was too young to understand.

"What's wrong?" he cried. "You're asking me all this because you're worried, aren't you? Why are you worried about me? Why are you worried about *us*?"

Hallorann put his large dark hands on the small boy's shoulders. "Stop," he said. "It's probably nothin. But if it is somethin . . . well, you've got a large thing in your head, Danny. You'll have to do a lot of growin yet before you catch up to it, I guess. You got to be brave about it."

"But I don't *understand* things!" Danny burst out. "I *do* but I *don't!* People . . . they feel things and I feel them, but I don't know what I'm feeling!" He looked down at his lap wretchedly. "I wish I could read. Sometimes Tony shows me signs and I can hardly read any of them."

"Who's Tony?" Hallorann asked again.

"Mommy and Daddy call him my 'invisible playmate,' " Danny said, reciting the words carefully. "But he's really real. At least, I think he is. Sometimes, when I try real hard to understand things, he comes. He says, 'Danny, I want to show you something.' And it's like I pass out. Only . . . there are dreams, like you said." He looked at Hallorann and swallowed. "They used to be nice. But now . . . I can't remember the word for dreams that scare you and make you cry."

"Nightmares?" Hallorann asked.

"Yes. That's right. Nightmares."

"About this place? About the Overlook?"

Danny looked down at his thumb-sucking hand again. "Yes," he whispered. Then he spoke shrilly, looking up into Hallorann's face: "But I can't tell my daddy, and you can't, either! He has to have this job because it's the only one Uncle Al could get for him and he has to finish his play or he might start doing the Bad Thing again and I know what that is, it's getting *drunk,* that's what it is, it's when he used to always be *drunk* and that was a Bad Thing to do!" He stopped, on the verge of tears.

"Shh," Hallorann said, and pulled Danny's face against the rough serge of his jacket. It smelled

faintly of mothballs. "That's all right, son. And if that
thumb likes your mouth, let it go where it wants."
But his face was troubled.

He said: "What you got, son, I call it shinin on,
the Bible calls it having visions, and there's scientists
that call it precognition. I've read up on it, son. I've
studied on it. They all mean seeing the future. Do
you understand that?"

Danny nodded against Hallorann's coat.

"I remember the strongest shine I ever had that
way . . . I'm not liable to forget. It was 1955. I was
still in the Army then, stationed overseas in West
Germany. It was an hour before supper, and I was
standin by the sink, givin one of the KPs hell for
takin too much of the potato along with the peel. I
says, 'Here, lemme show you how that's done.' He
held out the potato and the peeler and then the
whole kitchen was gone. Bang, just like that. You say
you see this guy Tony before . . . before you have
dreams?"

Danny nodded.

Hallorann put an arm around him. "With me it's
smellin oranges. All that afternoon I'd been smellin
them and thinkin nothin of it, because they were on
the menu for that night—we had thirty crates of
Valencias. Everybody in the damn kitchen was
smellin oranges that night.

"For a minute it was like I had just passed out.
And then I heard an explosion and saw flames. There
were people screaming. Sirens. And I heard this hissin
noise that could only be steam. Then it seemed like I

got a little closer to whatever it was and I saw a railroad car off the tracks and laying on its side with *Georgia and South Carolina Railroad* written on it, and I knew like a flash that my brother Carl was on that train and it jumped the tracks and Carl was dead. Just like that. Then it was gone and here's this scared, stupid little KP in front of me, still holdin out that potato and the peeler. He says, 'Are you okay, Sarge?' And I says, 'No. My brother's just been killed down in Georgia.' And when I finally got my momma on the overseas telephone, she told me how it was.

"But see, boy, I already knew how it was."

He shook his head slowly, as if dismissing the memory, and looked down at the wide-eyed boy.

"But the thing you got to remember, my boy, is this: *Those things don't always come true.* I remember just four years ago I had a job cookin at a boys' camp up in Maine on Long Lake. So I am sittin by the boarding gate at Logan Airport in Boston, just waiting to get on my flight, and I start to smell oranges. For the first time in maybe five years. So I say to myself, 'My God, what's comin on this crazy late show now?' and I got down to the bathroom and sat on one of the toilets to be private. I never did black out, but I started to get this feelin, stronger and stronger, that my plane was gonna crash. Then the feeling went away, and the smell of oranges, and I knew it was over. I went back to the Delta Airlines desk and changed my flight to one three hours later. And do you know what happened?"

"What?" Danny whispered.

"*Nothin!*" Halloran said, and laughed. He was relieved to see the boy smile a little, too. "Not one single thing! That old plane landed right on time and without a single bump or bruise. So you see . . . sometimes those feelins don't come to anything."

"Oh," Danny said.

"Or you take the race track. I go a lot, and I usually do pretty well. I stand by the rail when they go by the starting gate, and sometimes I get a little shine about this horse or that one. Usually those feelins help me get real well. I always tell myself that someday I'm gonna get three at once on three long shots and make enough on the trifecta to retire early. It ain't happened yet. But there's plenty of times I've come home from the track on shank's mare instead of in a taxicab with my wallet swollen up. Nobody shines on all the time, except maybe for God up in heaven."

"Yes, sir," Danny said, thinking of the time almost a year ago when Tony had showed him a new baby lying in a crib at their house in Stovington. He had been very excited about that, and had waited, knowing that it took time, but there had been no new baby.

"Now you listen," Halloran said, and took both of Danny's hands in his own. "I've had some bad dreams here, and I've had some bad feelins. I've worked here two seasons now and maybe a dozen times I've had . . . well, nightmares. And maybe half a dozen times I've thought I've seen things. No, I won't say what. It ain't for a little boy like you. Just nasty things. Once it had something to do with those damn hedges clipped to look like animals. Another time there was a maid, Delores Vickery her name was, and she had a little shine to her, but I don't think she knew it. Mr. Ullman fired her . . . do you know what that is, doc?"

"Yes, sir," Danny said candidly, "my daddy got fired from his teaching job and that's why we're in Colorado, I guess."

"Well, Ullman fired her on account of her saying she'd seen something in one of the rooms where . . . well, where a bad thing happened. That was in Room 217, and I want you to promise me you won't go in there, Danny. Not all winter. Steer right clear."

"All right," Danny said. "Did the lady—the maiden—did she ask you to go look?"

"Yes, she did. And there was a bad thing there. But . . . I don't think it was a bad thing that could *hurt* anyone, Danny, that's what I'm tryin to say. People who shine can sometimes see things that are *gonna* happen, and I think sometimes they can see things that *did* happen. But they're just like pictures in a book. Did you ever see a picture in a book that scared you, Danny?"

"Yes," he said, thinking of the story of *Bluebeard* and the picture where *Bluebeard*'s new wife opens the door and sees all the heads.

"But you knew it couldn't hurt you, didn't you?"

"Ye—ess . . ." Danny said, a little dubious.

"Well, that's how it is in this hotel. I don't know why, but it seems that all the bad things that ever happened here, there's little pieces of those things still layin around like fingernail clippins or the boogers that somebody nasty just wiped under a chair. I don't know why it should just be here, there's bad goings-on in just about every hotel in the world, I guess, and I've worked in a lot of them and had no trouble. Only here. But Danny, I don't think those things can hurt anybody." He emphasized each word in the sentence with a mild shake of the boy's shoulders. "So if you should see something, in a hallway or a room or outside by those hedges . . . just look the other way and when you look back, it'll be gone. Are you diggin me?"

"Yes," Danny said. He felt much better, soothed. He got up on his knees, kissed Hallorann's cheek, and gave him a big hard hug. Hallorann hugged him back.

When he released the boy he asked: "Your folks, they don't shine, do they?"

"No, I don't think so."

"I tried them like I did you," Hallorann said. "Your momma jumped the tiniest bit. I think all mothers shine a little, you know, at least until their kids grow up enough to watch out for themselves. Your dad . . ."

Hallorann paused momentarily. He had probed at the boy's father and he just didn't know. It wasn't like meeting someone who had the shine, or someone who definitely did not. Poking at Danny's father had been . . . strange, as if Jack Torrance had something—*something*—that he was hiding. Or something he was holding in so deeply submerged in himself that it was impossible to get to.

"I don't think he shines at all," Hallorann finished. "So you don't worry about them. You just take care of you. *I don't think there's anything here that can hurt you.* So just be cool, okay?"

"Okay."

"Danny! Hey, doc!"

Danny looked around. "That's Mom. She wants me. I have to go."

"I know you do," Hallorann said. "You have a good time here, Danny. Best you can, anyway."

"I will. Thanks, Mr. Hallorann. I feel a lot better."

The smiling thought came in his mind:

(Dick, to my friends)

(Yes, Dick, okay)

Their eyes met, and Dick Hallorann winked.

Danny scrambled across the seat of the car and opened the passenger side door. As he was getting out, Hallorann said, "Danny?"

"What?"

"If there *is* trouble . . . you give a call. A big loud holler like the one you gave a few minutes ago. I might hear you even way down in Florida. And if I do, I'll come on the run."

"Okay," Danny said, and smiled.

"You take care, big boy."

"I will."

Danny slammed the door and ran across the parking lot toward the porch, where Wendy stood holding her elbows against the chill wind. Hallorann watched, the big grin slowly fading.

I don't think there's anything here that can hurt you.

I don't *think*.

But what if he was wrong? He had known that this was his last season at the Overlook ever since he had seen that thing in the bathtub of Room 217. It had been worse than any picture in any book, and from here the boy running to his mother looked so *small* . . .

I don't *think*—

His eyes drifted down to the topiary animals.

Abruptly he started the car and put it in gear and drove away, trying not to look back. And of course he did, and of course the porch was empty. They had gone back inside. It was as if the Overlook had swallowed them.

12

The Grand Tour

"What were you talking about, hon?" Wendy asked him as they went back inside.

"Oh, nothing much."

"For nothing much it sure was a long talk."

He shrugged and Wendy saw Danny's paternity in the gesture; Jack could hardly have done it better himself. She would get no more out of Danny. She felt strong exasperation mixed with an even stronger love: the love was helpless, the exasperation came from a feeling that she was deliberately being excluded. With the two of them around she sometimes felt like an outsider, a bit player who had accidentally wandered back onstage while the main action was taking place. Well, they wouldn't be able to exclude her this winter, her two exasperating males; quarters were going to be a little too close for that. She suddenly realized she was feeling jealous of the closeness between her husband and her son, and felt ashamed. That was too close to the way her own mother might have felt   . too close for comfort

The lobby was now empty except for Ullman and the head desk clerk (they were at the register, cashing up), a couple of maids who had changed to warm slacks and sweaters, standing by the front door and looking out with their luggage pooled around them, and Watson, the maintenance man. He caught her looking at him and gave her a wink . . . a decidedly lecherous one. She looked away hurriedly. Jack was over by the window just outside the restaurant, studying the view. He looked rapt and dreamy.

The cash register apparently checked out, because now Ullman ran it shut with an authoritative snap. He initialed the tape and put it in a small zipper case. Wendy silently applauded the head clerk, who looked greatly relieved. Ullman looked like the type of man who might take any shortage out of the head clerk's hide . . . without ever spilling a drop of blood. Wendy didn't much care for Ullman or his officious, ostentatiously bustling manner. He was like every boss she'd ever had, male or female. He would be saccharin sweet with the guests, a petty tyrant when he was backstage with the help. But now school was out and the head clerk's pleasure was written large on his face. It was out for everyone but she and Jack and Danny, anyway.

"Mr. Torrance," Ullman called peremptorily. "Would you come over here, please?"

Jack walked over, nodding to Wendy and Danny that they were to come too.

The clerk, who had gone into the back, now came out again wearing an overcoat. "Have a pleasant winter, Mr. Ullman."

"I doubt it," Ullman said distantly. "May twelfth, Braddock. Not a day earlier. Not a day later."

"Yes, sir."

Braddock walked around the desk, his face sober and dignified, as befitted his position, but when his back was entirely to Ullman, he grinned like a schoolboy. He spoke briefly to the two girls still waiting by the door for their ride, and he was followed out by a brief burst of stifled laughter.

Now Wendy began to notice the silence of the place. It had fallen over the hotel like a heavy blanket muffling everything but the faint pulse of the afternoon wind outside. From where she stood she could look through the inner office, now neat to the point of sterility with its two bare desks and two sets of gray filing cabinets. Beyond that she could see Hallorann's spotless kitchen, the big portholed double doors propped open by rubber wedges.

"I thought I would take a few extra minutes and show you through the Hotel," Ullman said, and Wendy reflected that you could always hear that capital *H* in Ullman's voice. You were supposed to hear it. "I'm sure your husband will get to know the ins and outs of the Overlook quite well, Mrs. Torrance, but you and your son will doubtless keep more to the lobby level and the first floor, where your quarters are."

"Doubtless," Wendy murmured demurely, and Jack shot her a private glance.

"It's a beautiful place," Ullman said expansively. "I rather enjoy showing it off."

I'll bet you do, Wendy thought.

"Let's go up to third and work our way down," Ullman said. He sounded positively enthused.

"If we're keeping you—" Jack began.

"Not at all," Ullman said. "The shop is shut. *Tout fini,* for this season, at least. And I plan to overnight in Boulder—at the Boulderado, of course. Only decent hotel this side of Denver . . . except for the Overlook itself, of course. This way."

They stepped into the elevator together. It was ornately scrolled in copper and brass, but it settled appreciably before Ullman pulled the gate across. Danny stirred a little uneasily, and Ullman smiled down at him. Danny tried to smile back without notable success.

"Don't you worry, little man," Ullman said. "Safe as houses."

"So was the *Titanic,*" Jack said, looking up at the cut-glass globe in the center of the elevator ceiling. Wendy bit the inside of her cheek to keep the smile away.

Ullman was not amused. He slid the inner gate across with a rattle and a bang. "The *Titanic* made only one voyage, Mr. Torrance. This elevator has made thousands of them since it was installed in 1926."

"That's reassuring," Jack said. He ruffled Danny's hair. "The plane ain't gonna crash, doc."

Ullman threw the lever over, and for a moment there was nothing but a shuddering beneath their feet and the tortured whine of the motor below them.

Wendy had a vision of the four of them being trapped between floors like flies in a bottle and found in the spring . . . with little bits and pieces gone . . . like the Donner Party . . .

(*Stop it!*)

The elevator began to rise, with some vibration and clashing and banging from below at first. Then the ride smoothed out. At the third floor Ullman brought them to a bumpy stop, retracted the gate, and opened the door. The elevator car was still six inches below floor level. Danny gazed at the difference in height between the third-floor hall and the elevator floor as if he had just sensed the universe was not as sane as he had been told. Ullman cleared his throat and raised the car a little, brought it to a stop with a jerk (still two inches low), and they all climbed out. With their weight gone the car rebounded almost to floor level, something Wendy did not find reassuring at all. Safe as houses or not, she resolved to take the stairs when she had to go up or down in this place. And under no conditions would she allow the three of them to get into the rickety thing together.

"What are you looking at, doc?" Jack inquired humorously. "See any spots there?"

"Of course not," Ullman said, nettled. "All the rugs were shampooed just two days ago."

Wendy glanced down at the hall runner herself. Pretty, but definitely not anything she would choose for her own home, if the day ever came when she had one. Deep blue pile, it was entwined with what seemed to be a surrealistic jungle scene full of ropes and vines and trees filled with exotic birds. It was hard to tell just what sort of birds, because all the interweaving was done in unshaded black, giving only silhouettes.

"Do you like the rug?" Wendy asked Danny.

"Yes, Mom," he said colorlessly.

They walked down the hall, which was comfortably wide. The wallpaper was silk, a lighter blue to go against the rug. Electric flambeaux stood at ten-foot intervals at a height of about seven feet. Fashioned to look like London gas lamps, the bulbs were masked behind cloudy, cream-hued glass that was bound with crisscrossing iron strips.

"I like those very much," she said.

Ullman nodded, pleased. "Mr. Derwent had those installed throughout the Hotel after the war—number Two, I mean. In fact most—although not all—of the third-floor decorating scheme was his idea. This is 300, the Presidential Suite."

He twisted his key in the lock of the mahogany double doors and swung them wide. The sitting room's wide western exposure made them all gasp, which had probably been Ullman's intention. He smiled. "Quite a view, isn't it?"

"It sure is," Jack said.

The window ran nearly the length of the sitting room, and beyond it the sun was poised directly between two sawtoothed peaks, casting golden light across the rock faces and the sugared snow on the high tips. The clouds around and behind this picture-postcard view were also tinted gold, and a sunbeam glinted duskily down into the darkly pooled firs below the timberline.

Jack and Wendy were so absorbed in the view that they didn't look down at Danny, who was staring not out the window but at the red-and-white-striped silk wallpaper to the left, where a door opened into an interior bedroom. And his gasp, which had been mingled with theirs, had nothing to do with beauty.

Great splashes of dried blood, flecked with tiny bits of grayish-white tissue, clotted the wallpaper. It made Danny feel sick. It was like a crazy picture drawn in blood, a surrealistic etching of a man's face drawn back in terror and pain, the mouth yawning and half the head pulverized—

(*So if you should see something . . . just look the other way and when you look back, it'll be gone. Are you diggin me?*)

He deliberately looked out the window, being careful to show no expression on his face, and when his mommy's hand closed over his own he took it, being careful not to squeeze it or give her a signal of any kind.

The manager was saying something to his daddy about making sure to shutter that big window so a strong wind wouldn't blow it in. Jack was nodding. Danny looked cautiously back at the wall. The big dried bloodstain was gone. Those little gray-white flecks that had been scattered all through it, they were gone, too.

Then Ullman was leading them out. Mommy asked him if he thought the mountains were pretty. Danny said he did, although he didn't really care for the mountains, one way or the other. As Ullman was closing the door behind them, Danny looked back over his shoulder. The bloodstain had returned, only now it was fresh. It was running. Ullman, looking directly at it, went on with his running commentary about the famous men who had stayed here. Danny discovered that he had bitten his lip hard enough to make it bleed, and he had never even felt it. As they walked on down the corridor, he fell a little bit behind the others and wiped the blood away with the back of his hand and thought about

(blood)

(Did Mr. Hallorann see blood or was it something worse?)

(*I don't think those things can hurt you.*)

There was an iron scream behind his lips, but he would not let it out. His mommy and daddy could not see such things; they never had. He would keep quiet. His mommy and daddy were loving each other, and that was a real thing. The other things were just like pictures in a book. Some pictures were scary, but they couldn't hurt you. *They . . . couldn't . . . hurt you.*

Mr. Ullman showed them some other rooms on the third floor, leading them through corridors that twisted and turned like a maze. They were all sweets up here, Mr. Ullman said, although Danny didn't see any candy. He showed them some rooms where a lady named Marilyn Monroe once stayed when she was married to a man named Arthur Miller (Danny got a vague understanding that Marilyn and Arthur had gotten a DIVORCE not long after they were in the Overlook Hotel).

"Mommy?"

"What, honey?"

"If they were married, why did they have different names? You and Daddy have the same names."

"Yes, but we're not famous, Danny," Jack said. "Famous women keep their same names even after they get married because their names are their bread and butter."

"Bread and butter," Danny said, completely mystified.

"What Daddy means is that people used to like to go to the movies and see Marilyn Monroe," Wendy said, "but they might not like to go to see Marilyn Miller."

"Why not? She'd still be the same lady. Wouldn't everyone know that?"

"Yes, but—" She looked at Jack helplessly.

"Truman Capote once stayed in this room," Ullman interrupted impatiently. He opened the door. "That was in my time. An awfully nice man. Continental manners."

There was nothing remarkable in any of these rooms (except for the absence of sweets, which Mr. Ullman kept calling them), nothing that Danny was afraid of. In fact, there was only one other thing on the third floor that bothered Danny, and he could not have said why. It was the fire extinguisher on the wall just before they turned the corner and went back to the elevator, which stood open and waiting like a mouthful of gold teeth.

It was an old-fashioned extinguisher, a flat hose folded back a dozen times upon itself, one end attached to a large red valve, the other ending in a brass nozzle. The folds of the hose were secured with a red steel slat on a hinge. In case of a fire you could knock the steel slat up and out of the way with one hard push and the hose was yours. Danny could see that much; he was good at seeing how things worked. By the time he was two and a half he had been unlocking the protective gate his father had installed at the top of the stairs in the Stovington house. He had seen how the lock worked. His daddy said it was a NACK. Some people had the NACK and some people didn't.

This fire extinguisher was a little older than others he had seen—the one in the nursery school, for instance—but that was not so unusual. Nonetheless it filled him with faint unease, curled up there against the light blue wallpaper like a sleeping snake. And he was glad when it was out of sight around the corner.

"Of course all the windows have to be shuttered," Mr. Ullman said as they stepped back into the elevator. Once again the car sank queasily beneath their feet. "But I'm particularly concerned about the one in the Presidential Suite. The original bill on that window was four hundred and twenty dollars, and that was over thirty years ago. It would cost eight times that to replace today."

"I'll shutter it," Jack said.

They went down to the second floor where there were more rooms and even more twists and turns in the corridor. The light from the windows had begun to fade appreciably now as the sun went behind the mountains. Mr. Ullman showed them one or two rooms and that was all. He walked past 217, the one Dick Hallorann had warned him about, without slowing. Danny looked at the bland number-plate on the door with uneasy fascination.

Then down to the first floor. Mr. Ullman didn't show them into any rooms here until they had almost reached the thickly carpeted staircase that led down into the lobby again. "Here are your quarters," he said. "I think you'll find them adequate."

They went in. Danny was braced for whatever might be there. There was nothing.

Wendy Torrance felt a strong surge of relief. The Presidential Suite, with its cold elegance, had made her feel awkward and clumsy—it was all very well to visit some restored historical building with a bedroom plaque that announced Abraham Lincoln or Franklin D. Roosevelt had slept there, but another thing entirely to imagine you and your husband lying beneath acreages of linen and perhaps making love where the greatest men in the world had once lain (the most powerful, anyway, she amended). But this apartment was simpler, homier, almost inviting. She thought she could abide this place for a season with no great difficulty.

"It's very pleasant," she said to Ullman, and heard the gratitude in her voice.

Ullman nodded. "Simple but adequate. During the season, this suite quarters the cook and his wife, or the cook and his apprentice."

"Mr. Hallorann lived here?" Danny broke in.

Mr. Ullman inclined his head to Danny conde-scendingly. "Quite so. He and Mr. Nevers." He turned back to Jack and Wendy. "This is the sitting room."

There were several chairs that looked comfortable but not expensive, a coffee table that had once been expensive but now had a long chip gone from the side, two bookcases (stuffed full of Reader's Digest Condensed Books and Detective Book Club trilogies from the forties, Wendy saw with some amusement), and an anonymous hotel TV that looked much less elegant than the buffed wood consoles in the rooms.

"No kitchen, of course," Ullman said, "but there is a dumb-waiter. This apartment is directly over the kitchen." He slid aside a square of paneling and dis-closed a wide, square tray. He gave it a push and it disappeared, trailing rope behind it.

"It's a secret passage!" Danny said excitedly to his mother, momentarily forgetting all fears in favor of that intoxicating shaft behind the wall. "Just like in *Abbott and Costello Meet the Monsters*!"

Mr. Ullman frowned but Wendy smiled indul-gently. Danny ran over to the dumb-waiter and peered down the shaft.

"This way, please."

He opened the door on the far side of the living room. It gave on the bedroom, which was spacious and airy. There were twin beds. Wendy looked at her husband, smiled, shrugged.

"No problem," Jack said. "We'll push them together."

Mr. Ullman looked over his shoulder, honestly puzzled. "Beg pardon?"

"The beds," Jack said pleasantly. "We can push them together."

"Oh, quite," Ullman said, momentarily confused. Then his face cleared and a red flush began to creep up from the collar of his shirt. "Whatever you like."

He led them back into the sitting room, where a second door opened on a second bedroom, this one equipped with bunk beds. A radiator clanked in one corner, and the rug on the floor was a hideous embroidery of western sage and cactus—Danny had already fallen in love with it, Wendy saw. The walls of this smaller room were paneled in real pine.

"Think you can stand it in here, doc?" Jack asked.

"Sure I can. I'm going to sleep in the top bunk. Okay?"

"If that's what you want."

"I like the rug, too. Mr. Ullman, why don't you have all the rugs like that?"

Mr. Ullman looked for a moment as if he had sunk his teeth into a lemon. Then he smiled and patted Danny's head. "Those are your quarters," he said, "except for the bath, which opens off the main bedroom. It's not a huge apartment, but of course you'll have the rest of the hotel to spread out in. The lobby fireplace is in good working order, or so Watson tells me, and you must feel free to eat in the dining room if the spirit moves you to do so." He spoke in the tone of a man conferring a great favor.

"All right," Jack said.

"Shall we go down?" Mr. Ullman asked.

"Fine," Wendy said.

They went downstairs in the elevator, and now the lobby was wholly deserted except for Watson, who was leaning against the main doors in a rawhide jacket, a toothpick between his lips.

"I would have thought you'd be miles from here by now," Mr. Ullman said, his voice slightly chill.

"Just stuck around to remind Mr. Torrance here about the boiler," Watson said, straightening up. "Keep your good weather eye on her, fella, and she'll be fine. Knock the press down a couple of times a day. She creeps."

She creeps, Danny thought, and the words echoed down a long and silent corridor in his mind, a corridor lined with mirrors where people seldom looked.

"I will," his daddy said.

"You'll be fine," Watson said, and offered Jack his hand. Jack shook it. Watson turned to Wendy and inclined his head. "Ma'am," he said.

"I'm pleased," Wendy said, and thought it would sound absurd. It didn't. She had come out here from New England, where she had spent her life, and it seemed to her that in a few short sentences this man Watson, with his fluffy fringe of hair, had epitomized what the West was supposed to be all about. And never mind the lecherous wink earlier.

"Young master Torrance," Watson said gravely, and put out his hand. Danny, who had known all about handshaking for almost a year now, put his own hand out gingerly and felt it swallowed up. "You take good care of em, Dan."

"Yes, sir."

Watson let go of Danny's hand and straightened up fully. He looked at Ullman. "Until next year, I guess," he said, and held his hand out.

Ullman touched it bloodlessly. His pinky ring caught the lobby's electric lights in a baleful sort of wink. "May twelfth, Watson," he said. "Not a day earlier or later."

"Yes, sir," Watson said, and Jack could almost read the codicil in Watson's mind: . . . *you fucking little faggot.*

"Have a good winter, Mr. Ullman."

"Oh, I doubt it," Ullman said remotely.

Watson opened one of the two big main doors; the wind whined louder and began to flutter the collar of his jacket. "You folks take care now," he said.

It was Danny who answered. "Yes, sir, we will."

Watson, whose not-so-distant ancestor had owned this place, slipped humbly through the door. It closed behind him, muffling the wind. Together they watched him clop down the porch's broad front steps in his battered black cowboy boots. Brittle yellow aspen leaves tumbled around his heels as he crossed the lot to his International Harvester pickup and climbed in. Blue smoke jetted from the rusted exhaust pipe as he started it up. The spell of silence held among them as he backed, then pulled out of the parking lot. His truck disappeared over the brow of the hill and then reappeared, smaller, on the main road, heading west.

For a moment Danny felt more lonely than he ever had in his life.

13

The Front Porch

The Torrance family stood together on the long front porch of the Overlook Hotel as if posing for a family portrait, Danny in the middle, zippered into last year's fall jacket which was now too small and starting to come out at the elbow, Wendy behind him with one hand on his shoulder, and Jack to his left, his own hand resting lightly on his son's head.

Mr. Ullman was a step below them, buttoned into an expensive-looking brown mohair overcoat. The sun was entirely behind the mountains now, edging them with gold fire, making the shadows around things look long and purple. The only three vehicles left in the parking lots were the hotel truck, Ullman's Lincoln Continental, and the battered Torrance VW.

"You've got your keys, then," Ullman said to Jack, "and you understand fully about the furnace and the boiler?"

Jack nodded, feeling some real sympathy for Ullman. Everything was done for the season, the ball of string was neatly wrapped up until next May 12—

not a day earlier or later—and Ullman, who was responsible for all of it and who referred to the hotel in the unmistakable tones of infatuation, could not help looking for loose ends.

"I think everything is well in hand," Jack said.

"Good. I'll be in touch." But he still lingered for a moment, as if waiting for the wind to take a hand and perhaps gust him down to his car. He sighed. "All right. Have a good winter, Mr. Torrance, Mrs. Torrance. You too, Danny."

"Thank you, sir," Danny said. "I hope you do, too."

"I doubt it," Ullman repeated, and he sounded sad. "The place in Florida is a dump, if the out-and-out truth is to be spoken. Busywork. The Overlook is my real job. Take good care of it for me, Mr. Torrance."

"I think it will be here when you get back next spring," Jack said, and a thought flashed through Danny's mind

(but will we?)

and was gone.

"Of course. Of course it will."

Ullman looked out toward the playground where the hedge animals were clattering in the wind. Then he nodded once more in a businesslike way.

"Good-by, then."

He walked quickly and prissily across to his car—a ridiculously big one for such a little man—and tucked himself into it. The Lincoln's motor purred into life and the taillights flashed as he pulled out of his parking stall. As the car moved away, Jack could read the small sign at the head of the stall: RESERVED FOR MR. ULLMAN, MGR.

"Right," Jack said softly.

They watched until the car was out of sight, headed down the eastern slope. When it was gone, the three of them looked at each other for a silent, almost frightened moment. They were alone. Aspen leaves whirled and skittered in aimless packs across the lawn that was now neatly mowed and tended for no guest's eyes. There was no one to see the autumn leaves steal across the grass but the three of them. It gave Jack a curious shrinking feeling, as if his life force had dwindled to a mere spark while the hotel and the grounds had suddenly doubled in size and become sinister, dwarfing them with sullen, inanimate power.

Then Wendy said: "Look at you, doc. Your nose is running like a fire hose. Let's get inside."

And they did, closing the door firmly behind them against the restless whine of the wind.

PART THREE

The Wasps' Nest

14

Up on the Roof

"Oh you goddam fucking son of a bitch!"

Jack Torrance cried these words out in both surprise and agony as he slapped his right hand
against his blue chambray workshirt, dislodging
the big, slow-moving wasp that had stung him.
Then he was scrambling up the roof as fast as he
could, looking back over his shoulder to see if the
wasp's brothers and sisters were rising from the
nest he had uncovered to do battle. If they were, it
could be bad; the nest was between him and his
ladder, and the trapdoor leading down into the
attic was locked from the inside. The drop was seventy feet from the roof to the cement patio between
the hotel and the lawn.

The clear air above the nest was still and undisturbed.

Jack whistled disgustedly between his teeth, sat
straddling the peak of the roof, and examined his
right index finger. It was swelling already, and he
supposed he would have to try and creep past that

nest to his ladder so he could go down and put some ice on it.

It was October 20. Wendy and Danny had gone down to Sidewinder in the hotel truck (an elderly, rattling Dodge that was still more trustworthy than the VW, which was now wheezing gravely and seemed terminal) to get three gallons of milk and do some Christmas shopping. It was early to shop, but there was no telling when the snow would come to stay. There had already been flurries, and in some places the road down from the Overlook was slick with patch ice.

So far the fall had been almost preternaturally beautiful. In the three weeks they had been here, golden day had followed golden day. Crisp, thirty-degree mornings gave way to afternoon temperatures in the low sixties, the perfect temperature for climbing around on the Overlook's gently sloping western roof and doing the shingling. Jack had admitted freely to Wendy that he could have finished the job four days ago, but he felt no real urge to hurry. The view from up here was spectacular, even putting the vista from the Presidential Suite in the shade. More important, the work itself was soothing. On the roof he felt himself healing from the troubled wounds of the last three years. On the roof he felt at peace. Those three years began to seem like a turbulent nightmare.

The shingles had been badly rotted, some of them blown entirely away by last winter's storms. He had ripped them all up, yelling "Bombs away!" as he dropped them over the side, not wanting Danny to get hit in case he had wandered over. He had been pulling out bad flashing when the wasp had gotten him.

The ironic part was that he warned himself each time he climbed onto the roof to keep an eye out for nests; he had gotten that bug bomb just in case. But this morning the stillness and peace had been so complete that his watchfulness had lapsed. He had been back in the world of the play he was slowly creating, roughing out whatever scene he would be working on that evening in his head. The play was going very well, and although Wendy had said little, he knew she was pleased. He had been roadblocked on the crucial scene between Denker, the sadistic headmaster, and Gary Benson, his young hero, during the last unhappy six months at Stovington, months when the craving for a drink had been so bad that he could barely concentrate on his in-class lectures, let alone his extracurricular literary ambitions.

But in the last twelve evenings, as he actually sat down in front of the office-model Underwood he had borrowed from the main office downstairs, the roadblock had disappeared under his fingers as magically as cotton candy dissolves on the lips. He had come up almost effortlessly with the insights into Denker's character that had always been lacking, and he had rewritten most of the second act accordingly, making it revolve around the new scene. And the progress of the third act, which he had been turning over in his mind when the wasp put an end to cogitation, was coming clearer all the time. He thought he could rough it out in two weeks, and have a clean copy of the whole damned play by New Year's.

He had an agent in New York, a tough red-headed woman named Phyllis Sandler who smoked Herbert Tareytons, drank Jim Beam from a paper cup, and thought the literary sun rose and set on Sean O'Casey. She had marketed three of Jack's short stories, including the *Esquire* piece. He had written her about the play, which was called *The Little School,* describing the basic conflict between Denker, a gifted student who had failed into becoming the brutal and brutalizing headmaster of a turn-of-the-century New England prep school, and Gary Benson, the student he sees as a younger version of himself. Phyllis had written back expressing interest and admonishing him to read O'Casey before sitting down to it. She had written again earlier that year asking where the hell was the play? He had written back wryly that *The Little School* had been indefinitely—and perhaps infinitely— delayed between hand and page "in that interesting intellectual Gobi known as the writer's block." Now it looked as if she might actually get the play. Whether or not it was any good or if it would ever see actual production was another matter. And he didn't seem to care a great deal about those things. He felt in a way that the play itself, the whole thing, was the roadblock, a colossal symbol of the bad years at Stovington Prep, the marriage he had almost totaled like a nutty kid behind the wheel of an old jalopy, the monstrous assault on his son, the incident in the parking lot with George Hatfield, an incident he could no longer view as just another sudden and destructive flare of temper. He now thought that part of his drinking problem had stemmed from an unconscious desire to be free of Stovington and the security he felt was stifling whatever creative urge he had. He had stopped drinking, but the need to be free had been just as great. Hence George Hatfield. Now all that remained of those days was the play on the desk in his and Wendy's bedroom, and when it was done and sent off to Phyllis's hole-in-the-wall New York agency, he could turn to other things. Not a novel, he was not ready to stumble into the swamp of another three-year undertaking, but surely more short stories. Perhaps a book of them.

Moving warily, he scrambled back down the slope of the roof on his hands and knees, past the line of demarcation where the fresh green Bird shingles gave way to the section of roof he had just finished clearing. He came to the edge on the left of the wasps' nest he had uncovered and moved gingerly toward it, ready to backtrack and bolt down his ladder to the ground if things looked too hot.

He leaned over the section of pulled-out flashing and looked in.

The nest was in there, tucked into the space between the old flashing and the final roof undercoating of three-by-fives. It was a damn big one. The grayish paper ball looked to Jack as if it might be nearly two feet through the center. Its shape was not perfect because the space between the flashing and the boards was too narrow, but he thought the little buggers had still done a pretty respectable job. The surface of the nest was acrawl with the lumbering, slow-moving insects. They were the big mean ones, not yellow jackets, which are smaller and calmer, but wall wasps. They had been rendered sludgy and stupid by the fall temperatures, but Jack, who knew about wasps from his childhood, counted himself lucky that he had been stung only once. And, he thought, if Ullman had hired the job done in the height of summer, the workman who tore up that particular section of the flashing would have gotten one hell of a surprise. Yes indeedy. When a dozen wall wasps land on you all at once and start stinging your face and hands and arms, stinging your legs right through your pants, it would be entirely possible to forget you were seventy feet up. You might just charge right off the edge of the roof while you were trying to get away from them. All from those little things, the biggest of them only half the length of a pencil stub.

He had read someplace—in a Sunday supplement piece or a back-of-the-book newsmagazine article— that 7 per cent of all automobile fatalities go unexplained. No mechanical failure, no excessive speed, no booze, no bad weather. Simply one-car crashes on deserted sections of road, one dead occupant, the driver, unable to explain what had happened to him. The article had included an interview with a state trooper who theorized that many of these so-called "foo crashes" resulted from insects in the car. Wasps, a bee, possibly even a spider or moth. The driver gets panicky, tries to swat it or unroll a window to let it out. Possibly the insect stings him. Maybe the driver just loses control. Either way it's bang! . . . all over. And the insect, usually completely unharmed, would buzz merrily out of the smoking wreck, looking for greener pastures. The trooper had been in favor of having pathologists look for insect venom while autopsying such victims, Jack recalled.

Now, looking down into the nest, it seemed to him that it could serve as both a workable symbol for what he had been through (and what he had dragged his hostages to fortune through) and an omen for a better future. How else could you explain the things that had happened to him? For he still felt that the whole range of unhappy Stovington experiences had to be looked at with Jack Torrance in the passive mode. He had not done things; things had been done to him. He had known plenty of people on the Stovington faculty, two of them right in the English Department, who were hard drinkers. Zack Tunney was in the habit of picking up a full keg of beer on Saturday afternoon, plonking it in a backyard snowbank overnight, and then killing damn near all of it on Sunday watching football games and old movies. Yet through the week Zack was as sober as a judge— a weak cocktail with lunch was an occasion.

He and Al Shockley had been alcoholics. They had sought each other out like two castoffs who were still social enough to prefer drowning together to doing it alone. The sea had been whole-grain instead of salt, that was all. Looking down at the wasps, as they slowly went about their instinctual business before winter closed down to kill all but their hibernating queen, he would go further. He was *still* an alcoholic, always would be, perhaps had been since Sophomore Class Night in high school when he had taken his first drink. It had nothing to do with willpower, or the morality of drinking, or the weakness or strength of his own character. There was a broken switch somewhere inside, or a circuit breaker that didn't work, and he had been propelled down the chute willy-nilly, slowly at first, then accelerating as Stovington applied its pressures on him. A big greased slide and at the bottom had been a shattered, owner-less bicycle and a son with a broken arm. Jack Torrance in the passive mode. And his temper, same thing. All his life he had been trying unsuccessfully to control it. He could remember himself at seven, spanked by a neighbor lady for playing with matches. He had gone out and hurled a rock at a passing car. His father had seen that, and he had descended on little Jacky, roaring. He had reddened Jack's behind . . . and then blacked his eye. And when his father had gone into the house, muttering, to see what was on television, Jack had come upon a stray dog and had kicked it into the gutter. There had been two dozen fights in grammar school, even more of them in high school, warranting two suspensions and uncounted detentions in spite of his good grades. Football had provided a partial safety valve, although he remembered perfectly well that he had spent almost every minute of every game in a state of high piss-off, taking every opposing block and tackle personally. He had been a fine player, making All-Conference in his junior and senior years, and he knew perfectly well that he had his own bad temper to thank . . . or to blame. He had not enjoyed football. Every game was a grudge match.

And yet, through it all, he hadn't *felt* like a son of a bitch. He hadn't felt mean. He had always regarded himself as Jack Torrance, a really nice guy who was just going to have to learn how to cope with his temper someday before it got him in trouble. The same way he was going to have to learn how to cope with his drinking. But he had been an emotional alcoholic just as surely as he had been a physical one——the two of them were no doubt tied together somewhere deep inside him, where you'd just as soon not look. But it didn't much matter to him if the root causes were interrelated or separate, sociological or psychological or physiological. He had had to deal with the results: the spankings, the beatings from his old man, the suspensions, with trying to explain the school clothes torn in playground brawls, and later the hangovers, the slowly dissolving glue of his marriage, the single bicycle wheel with its bent spokes pointing into the sky, Danny's broken arm. And George Hatfield, of course.

He felt that he had unwittingly stuck his hand into The Great Wasps' Nest of Life. As an image it stank. As a cameo of reality, he felt it was serviceable. He had stuck his hand through some rotted flashing in high summer and that hand and his whole arm had been consumed in holy, righteous fire, destroying conscious thought, making the concept of civilized behavior obsolete. Could you be expected to behave as a thinking human being when your hand was being impaled on red-hot darning needles? Could you be expected to live in the love of your nearest and dearest when the brown, furious cloud rose out of the hole in the fabric of things (the fabric you thought was so innocent) and arrowed straight at you? Could you be held responsible for your own actions as you ran crazily about on the sloping roof seventy feet above the ground, not knowing where you were going, not remembering that your panicky, stumbling feet could lead you crashing and blundering right over the rain gutter and down to your death on the concrete seventy feet below? Jack didn't think you could. When you unwittingly stuck your hand into the wasps' nest, you hadn't made a covenant with the devil to give up your civilized self with its trappings of love and respect and honor. It just happened to you. Passively, with no say, you ceased to be a creature of the mind and became a creature of the nerve endings; from college-educated man to wailing ape in five easy seconds.

He thought about George Hatfield.

Tall and shaggily blond, George had been an almost insolently beautiful boy. In his tight faded jeans and Stovington sweatshirt with the sleeves carelessly pushed up to the elbows to disclose his tanned forearms, he had reminded Jack of a young Robert

Redford, and he doubted that George had much trouble scoring—no more than that young football-playing devil Jack Torrance had ten years earlier. He could say that he honestly didn't feel jealous of George, or envy him his good looks; in fact, he had almost unconsciously begun to visualize George as the physical incarnation of his play hero, Gary Benson—the perfect foil for the dark, slumped, and aging Denker, who grew to hate Gary so much. But he, Jack Torrance, had never felt that way about George. If he had, he would have known it. He was quite sure of that.

George had floated through his classes at Stovington. A soccer and baseball star, his academic program had been fairly undemanding and he had been content with C's and an occasional B in history or botany. He was a fierce field contender but a lackadaisical, amused sort of student in the classroom. Jack was familiar with the type, more from his own days as a high school and college student than from his teaching experience, which was at second hand. George Hatfield was a jock. He could be a calm, undemanding figure in the classroom, but when the right set of competitive stimuli was applied (like electrodes to the temples of Frankenstein's monster, Jack thought wryly), he could become a juggernaut.

In January, George had tried out with two dozen others for the debate team. He had been quite frank with Jack. His father was a corporation lawyer, and he wanted his son to follow in his footsteps. George, who felt no burning call to do anything else, was willing.

His grades were not top end, but this was, after all, only prep school and it was still early times. If should be came to must be, his father could pull some strings. George's own athletic ability would open still other doors. But Brian Hatfield thought his son should get on the debate team. It was good practice, and it was something that law-school admissions boards always looked for. So George went out for debate, and in late March Jack cut him from the team.

The late winter inter-squad debates had fired George Hatfield's competitive soul. He became a grimly determined debater, prepping his pro or con position fiercely. It didn't matter if the subject was legalization of marijuana, reinstating the death penalty, or the oil-depletion allowance. George became conversant, and he was just jingoist enough to honestly not care which side he was on—a rare and valuable trait even in high-level debaters, Jack knew. The souls of a true carpetbagger and a true debater were not far removed from each other; they were both passionately interested in the main chance. So far, so good.

But George Hatfield stuttered.

This was not a handicap that had even shown up in the classroom, where George was always cool and collected (whether he had done his homework or not), and certainly not on the Stovington playing fields, where talk was not a virtue and they some-times even threw you out of the game for too much discussion.

When George got tightly wound up in a debate, the stutter would come out. The more eager he became, the worse it was. And when he felt he had an opponent dead in his sights, an intellectual sort of buck fever seemed to take place between his speech centers and his mouth and he would freeze solid while the clock ran out. It was painful to watch.

"S-S-So I th-th-think we have to say that the fuh-fuh-facts in the c-case Mr. D-D-D-Dorsky cites are ren-ren-rendered obsolete by the ruh-recent duh-duh-decision handed down in-in-in . . ."

The buzzer would go off and George would whirl around to stare furiously at Jack, who sat beside it. George's face at those moments would be flushed, his notes crumpled spasmodically in one hand.

Jack had held on to George long after he had cut most of the obvious flat tires, hoping George would work out. He remembered one late afternoon about a week before he had reluctantly dropped the ax. George had stayed after the others had filed out, and then had confronted Jack angrily.

"You s-set the timer ahead."

Jack looked up from the papers he was putting back into his briefcase.

"George, what are you talking about?"

"I d-didn't get my whole five mih-minutes. You set it ahead. I was wuh-watching the clock."

"The clock and the timer may keep slightly different times, George, but I never touched the dial on the damned thing. Scout's honor."

"Yuh-yuh-you *did!*"

The belligerent, I'm-sticking-up-for-my-rights way George was looking at him had sparked Jack's own temper. He had been off the sauce for two months, two months too long, and he was ragged. He made one last effort to hold himself in. "I assure you I did not, George. It's your stutter. Do you have any idea what causes it? You don't stutter in class."

"I duh-duh-don't s-s-st-st-stutter!"

"Lower your voice."

"You w-want to g-get me! You duh-don't w-want me on your g-g-goddam team!"

"Lower your voice, I said. Let's discuss this rationally."

"F-fuh-fuck th-that!"

"George, if you control your stutter, I'd be glad to have you. You're well prepped for every practice and you're good at the background stuff, which means you're rarely surprised. But all that doesn't mean much if you can't control that—"

"I've neh-neh-never stuttered!" he cried out. "It's yuh-you! I-i-if suh-someone else had the d-d-deb-debate t-team, I could—"

Jack's temper slipped another notch.

"George, you're never going to make much of a lawyer, corporation or otherwise, if you can't control that. Law isn't like soccer. Two hours of practice every night won't cut it. What are you going to do, stand up in front of a board meeting and say, 'Nuh-nuh-now, g-gentlemen, about this t-t-tort'?"

He suddenly flushed, not with anger but with shame at his own cruelty. This was not a man in front of him but a seventeen-year-old boy who was facing the first major defeat of his life, and maybe asking in the only way he could for Jack to help him find a way to cope with it.

George gave him a final, furious glance, his lips twisting and bucking as the words bottled up behind them struggled to find their way out.

"Yuh-yuh-you s-s-set it ahead! You huh-hate me b-because you nuh-nuh-nuh-know . . . you know . . . nuh-nuh—"

With an inarticulate cry he had rushed out of the classroom, slamming the door hard enough to make the wire-reinforced glass rattle in its frame. Jack had stood there, feeling, rather than hearing, the echo of George's Adidas in the empty hall. Still in the grip of his temper and his shame at mocking George's stutter, his first thought had been a sick sort of exultation: For the first time in his life George Hatfield had wanted something he could not have. For the first time there was something wrong that all of Daddy's money could not fix. You couldn't bribe a speech center. You couldn't offer a tongue an extra fifty a week and a bonus at Christmas if it would agree to stop flapping like a record needle in a defective groove. Then the exultation was simply buried in shame, and he felt the way he had after he had broken Danny's arm.

Dear God, I am not a son of a bitch. Please.

That sick happiness at George's retreat was more typical of Denker in the play than of Jack Torrance the playwright.

You hate me because you know . . .
Because he knew what?

What could he possibly know about George Hatfield that would make him hate him? That his whole future lay ahead of him? That he looked a little bit like Robert Redford and all conversation among the girls stopped when he did a double gainer from the pool diving board? That he played soccer and baseball with a natural, unlearned grace?

Ridiculous. Absolutely absurd. He envied George Hatfield nothing. If the truth was known, he felt worse about George's unfortunate stutter than George himself, because George really would have made an excellent debater. And if Jack had set the timer ahead—and of course he hadn't—it would have been because both he and the other members of the squad were embarrassed for George's struggle, they had agonized over it the way you agonize when the Class Night speaker forgets some of his lines. If he had set the timer ahead, it would have been just to . . . to put George out of his misery.

But he hadn't set the timer ahead. He was quite sure of it.

A week later he had cut him, and that time he had kept his temper. The shouts and the threats had all been on George's side. A week after that he had gone out to the parking lot halfway through practice to get a pile of sourcebooks that he had left in the trunk of the VW and there had been George, down on one knee with his long blond hair swinging in his face, a hunting knife in one hand. He was sawing through the VW's right front tire. The back tires were already shredded, and the bug sat on the flats like a small, tired dog.

Jack had seen red, and remembered very little of the encounter that followed. He remembered a thick growl that seemed to issue from his own throat: "All right, George. If that's how you want it, just come here and take your medicine."

He remembered George looking up, startled and fearful. He had said: "Mr. Torrance——" as if to explain how all this was just a mistake, the tires had been flat when he got there and he was just cleaning dirt out of the front treads with the tip of this gutting knife he just happened to have with him and——

Jack had waded in, his fists held up in front of him, and it seemed that he had been grinning. But he wasn't sure of that.

The last thing he remembered was George holding up the knife and saying: "You better not come any closer——"

And the next thing was Miss Strong, the French teacher, holding Jack's arms, crying, screaming: "Stop it, Jack! Stop it! You're going to kill him!"

He had blinked around stupidly. There was the hunting knife, glittering harmlessly on the parking lot asphalt four yards away. There was his Volkswagen, his poor old battered bug, veteran of many wild midnight drunken rides, sitting on three flat shoes. There was a new dent in the right front fender, he saw, and there was something in the middle of the dent that was either red paint or blood. For a moment he had been confused, his thoughts

(jesus christ al we hit him after all)

of that other night. Then his eyes had shifted to George, George lying dazed and blinking on the asphalt. His debate group had come out and they were huddled together by the door, staring at George. There was blood on his face from a scalp laceration that looked minor, but there was also blood running out of one of George's ears and that probably meant a concussion. When George tried to get up, Jack shook free of Miss Strong and went to him. George cringed.

Jack put his hands on George's chest and pushed him back down. "Lie still," he said. "Don't try to move." He turned to Miss Strong, who was staring at them both with horror.

"Please go call the school doctor, Miss Strong," he told her. She turned and fled toward the office. He looked at his debate class then, looked them right in the eye because he was in charge again, fully himself, and when he was himself there wasn't a nicer guy in the whole state of Vermont. Surely they knew that.

"You can go home now," he told them quietly. "We'll meet again tomorrow."

But by the end of that week six of his debaters had dropped out, two of them the class of the act, but of course it didn't matter much because he had been informed by then that he would be dropping out himself.

Yet somehow he had stayed off the bottle, and he supposed that was something.

And he had not hated George Hatfield. He was sure of that. He had not acted but had been acted upon.

You hate me because you know . . .

But he had known nothing. *Nothing.* He would swear that before the Throne of Almighty God, just as he would swear that he had set the timer ahead no more than a minute. And not out of hate but out of pity.

Two wasps were crawling sluggishly about on the roof beside the hole in the flashing.

He watched them until they spread their aerodynamically unsound but strangely efficient wings and lumbered off into the October sunshine, perchance to sting someone else. God had seen fit to give them stingers and Jack supposed they had to use them on somebody.

How long had he been sitting there, looking at that hole with its unpleasant surprise down inside, raking over old coals? He looked at his watch. Almost half an hour.

He let himself down to the edge of the roof, dropped one leg over, and felt around until his foot found the top rung of the ladder just below the overhang. He would go down to the equipment shed where he had stored the bug bomb on a high shelf out of Danny's reach. He would get it, come back up, and then they would be the ones surprised. You could be stung, but you could also sting back. He believed that sincerely. Two hours from now the nest would be just so much chewed paper and Danny could have it

in his room if he wanted to—Jack had had one in his
room when he was just a kid, it had always smelled
faintly of woodsmoke and gasoline. He could have it
right by the head of his bed. It wouldn't hurt him.

"I'm getting better."

The sound of his own voice, confident in the silent
afternoon, reassured him even though he hadn't
meant to speak aloud. He *was* getting better. It was
possible to graduate from passive to active, to take
the thing that had once driven you nearly to madness
as a neutral prize of no more than occasional academic interest. And if there was a place where the thing
could be done, this was surely it.

He went down the ladder to get the bug bomb.
They would pay. They would pay for stinging him.

15

Down in the Front Yard

Jack had found a huge white-painted wicker chair in the back of the equipment shed two weeks ago, and had dragged it around to the porch over Wendy's objections that it was really the ugliest thing she had ever seen in her whole life. He was sitting in it now, amusing himself with a copy of E. L. Doctorow's *Welcome to Hard Times,* when his wife and son rattled up the driveway in the hotel truck.

Wendy parked it in the turn-around, raced the engine sportily, and then turned it off. The truck's single taillight died. The engine rumbled grumpily with post-ignition and finally stopped. Jack got out of his chair and ambled down to meet them.

"Hi, Dad!" Danny called, and raced up the hill. He had a box in one hand. "Look what Mommy bought me!"

Jack picked his son up, swung him around twice, and kissed him heartily on the mouth.

"Jack Torrance, the Eugene O'Neill of his generation, the American Shakespeare!" Wendy said, smiling. "Fancy meeting you here, so far up in the mountains."

"The common ruck became too much for me, dear lady," he said, and slipped his arms around her. They kissed. "How was your trip?"

"Very good. Danny complains that I keep jerking him but I didn't stall the truck once and . . . oh, Jack, you finished it!"

She was looking at the roof, and Danny followed her gaze. A faint frown touched his face as he looked at the wide swatch of fresh shingles atop the Overlook's west wing, a lighter green than the rest of the roof. Then he looked down at the box in his hand and his face cleared again. At night the pictures Tony had showed him came back to haunt in all their original clarity, but in sunny daylight they were easier to disregard.

"Look, Daddy, look!"

Jack took the box from his son. It was a model car, one of the Big Daddy Roth caricatures that Danny had expressed an admiration for in the past. This one was the Violent Violet Volkswagen, and the picture on the box showed a huge purple VW with long '59 Cadillac Coupe de Ville taillights burning up a dirt track. The VW had a sunroof, and poking up through it, clawed hands on the wheel down below, was a gigantic warty monster with popping bloodshot eyes, a maniacal grin, and a gigantic English racing cap turned around backward.

Wendy was smiling at him, and Jack winked at her.

"That's what I like about you, doc," Jack said, handing the box back. "Your taste runs to the quiet, the sober, the introspective. You are definitely the child of my loins."

"Mommy said you'd help me put it together as soon as I could read all of the first Dick and Jane."

"That ought to be by the end of the week," Jack said. "What else have you got in that fine-looking truck, ma'am?"

"Uh-uh." She grabbed his arm and pulled him back. "No peeking. Some of that stuff is for you. Danny and I will take it in. You can get the milk. It's on the floor of the cab."

"That's all I am to you," Jack cried, clapping a hand to his forehead. "Just a dray horse, a common beast of the field. Dray here, dray there, dray everywhere."

"Just dray that milk right into the kitchen, mister."

"It's too much!" he cried, and threw himself on the ground while Danny stood over him and giggled.

"Get up, you ox," Wendy said, and prodded him with the toe of her sneaker.

"See?" he said to Danny. "She called me an ox. You're a witness."

"Witness, witness!" Danny concurred gleefully, and broad-jumped his prone father.

Jack sat up. "That reminds me, chumly. I've got something for you, too. On the porch by my ashtray."

"What is it?"

"Forgot. Go and see."

Jack got up and the two of them stood together, watching Danny charge up the lawn and then take the steps to the porch two by two. He put an arm around Wendy's waist.

"You happy, babe?"

She looked up at him solemnly. "This is the happiest I've been since we were married."

"Is that the truth?"

"God's honest."

He squeezed her tightly. "I love you."

She squeezed him back, touched. Those had never been cheap words with John Torrance; she could count the number of times he had said them to her, both before and after marriage, on both her hands.

"I love you too."

"Mommy! Mommy!" Danny was on the porch now, shrill and excited. "Come and see! Wow! It's neat!"

"What is it?" Wendy asked him as they walked up from the parking lot, hand in hand.

"Forgot," Jack said.

"Oh, you'll get yours," she said, and elbowed him. "See if you don't."

"I was hoping I'd get it tonight," he remarked, and she laughed. A moment later he asked, "Is Danny happy, do you think?"

"You ought to know. You're the one who has a long talk with him every night before bed."

"That's usually about what he wants to be when he grows up or if Santa Claus is really real. That's getting to be a big thing with him. I think his old buddy Scott let some pennies drop on that one. No, he hasn't said much of anything about the Overlook to me."

"Me either," she said. They were climbing the porch steps now. "But he's very quiet a lot of the time. And I think he's lost weight, Jack, I really do."

"He's just getting tall."

Danny's back was to them. He was examining something on the table by Jack's chair, but Wendy couldn't see what it was.

"He's not eating as well, either. He used to be the original steam shovel. Remember last year?"

"They taper off," he said vaguely. "I think I read that in Spock. He'll be using two forks again by the time he's seven."

They had stopped on the top step.

"He's pushing awfully hard on those readers, too," she said. "I know he wants to learn how, to please us . . . to please you," she added reluctantly.

"To please himself most of all," Jack said. "I haven't been pushing him on that at all. In fact, I do wish he wouldn't go quite so hard."

"Would you think I was foolish if I made an appointment for him to have a physical? There's a G.P. in Sidewinder, a young man from what the checker in the market said—"

"You're a little nervous about the snow coming, aren't you?"

She shrugged. "I suppose. If you think it's foolish—"

"I don't. In fact, you can make appointments for all three of us. We'll get our clean bills of health and then we can sleep easy at night."

"I'll make the appointments this afternoon," she said.

"Mom! Look, Mommy!"

He came running to her with a large gray thing in his hands, and for one comic-horrible moment Wendy thought it was a brain. She saw what it really was and recoiled instinctively.

Jack put an arm around her. "It's all right. The tenants who didn't fly away have been shaken out. I used the bug bomb."

She looked at the large wasps' nest her son was holding but would not touch it. "Are you sure it's safe?"

"Positive. I had one in my room when I was a kid. My dad gave it to me. Want to put it in your room, Danny?"

"Yeah! Right now!"

He turned around and raced through the double doors. They could hear his muffled, running feet on the main stairs.

"There *were* wasps up there," she said. "Did you get stung?"

"Where's my purple heart?" he asked, and displayed his finger. The swelling had already begun to go down, but she ooohed over it satisfyingly and gave it a small, gentle kiss.

"Did you pull the stinger out?"

"Wasps don't leave them in. That's bees. They have barbed stingers. Wasp stingers are smooth. That's what makes them so dangerous. They can sting again and again."

"Jack, are you sure that's safe for him to have?"

"I followed the directions on the bomb. The stuff is guaranteed to kill every single bug in two hours' time and then dissipate with no residue."

"I hate them," she said.

"What . . . wasps?"

"Anything that stings," she said. Her hands went to her elbows and cupped them, her arms crossed over her breasts.

"I do too," he said, and hugged her.

16

Danny

Down the hall, in the bedroom, Wendy could hear the typewriter Jack had carried up from downstairs burst into life for thirty seconds, fall silent for a minute or two, and then rattle briefly again. It was like listening to machine-gun fire from an isolated pillbox. The sound was music to her ears; Jack had not been writing so steadily since the second year of their marriage, when he wrote the story that *Esquire* had purchased. He said he thought the play would be done by the end of the year, for better or worse, and he would be moving on to something new. He said he didn't care if *The Little School* stirred any excitement when Phyllis showed it around, didn't care if it sank without a trace, and Wendy believed that, too. The actual act of his writing made her immensely hopeful, not because she expected great things from the play but because her husband seemed to be slowly closing a huge door on a roomful of monsters. He had had his shoulder to that door for a long time now, but at last it was swinging shut.

Every key typed closed it a little more.

"Look, Dick, look."

Danny was hunched over the first of the five battered primers Jack had dug up by culling mercilessly through Boulder's myriad secondhand bookshops. They would take Danny right up to the second-grade reading level, a program she had told Jack she thought was much too ambitious. Their son was intelligent, they knew that, but it would be a mistake to push him too far too fast. Jack had agreed. There would be no pushing involved. But if the kid caught on fast, they would be prepared. And now she wondered if Jack hadn't been right about that, too.

Danny, prepared by four years of "Sesame Street" and three years of "Electric Company," seemed to be catching on with almost scary speed. It bothered her. He hunched over the innocuous little books, his crystal radio and balsa glider on the shelf above him, as though his life depended on learning to read. His small face was more tense and paler than she liked in the close and cozy glow of the goosenecked lamp they had put in his room. He was taking it very seriously, both the reading and the workbook pages his father made up for him every afternoon. Picture of an apple and a peach. The word *apple* written beneath in Jack's large, neatly made printing. Circle the right picture, the one that went with the word. And their son would stare from the word to the pictures, his lips moving, sounding out, actually *sweating* it out. And with his double-sized red pencil curled into his pudgy right fist, he could now write about three dozen words on his own.

His finger traced slowly under the words in the reader. Above them was a picture Wendy half-remembered from her own grammar school days, nineteen years before. A laughing boy with brown curly hair. A girl in a short dress, her hair in blond ringlets, one hand holding a jump rope. A prancing dog running after a large red rubber ball. The first-grade trinity. Dick, Jane, and Jip.

"See Jip run," Danny read slowly. "Run, Jip, run. Run, run, run." He paused, dropping his finger down a line. "See the . . ." He bent closer, his nose almost touching the page now. "See the . . ."

"Not so close, doc," Wendy said quietly. "You'll hurt your eyes. It's—"

"Don't tell me!" he said, sitting up with a jerk. His voice was alarmed. "Don't tell me, Mommy, I can get it!"

"All right, honey," she said. "But it's not a big thing. Really it's not."

Unheeding, Danny bent forward again. On his face was an expression that might be more commonly seen hovering over a graduate record exam in a college gym somewhere. She liked it less and less.

"See the . . . buh. Aw. El. El. See the buhaw-el-el? See the buhawl. *Ball!*" Suddenly triumphant. Fierce. The fierceness in his voice scared her. *"See the ball!"*

"That's right," she said. "Honey, I think that's enough for tonight."

"A couple more pages, Mommy? Please?"

"No, doc." She closed the red-bound book firmly. "It's bedtime."

"Please?"

"Don't tease me about it, Danny. Mommy's tired."

"Okay." But he looked longingly at the primer.

"Go kiss your father and then wash up. Don't forget to brush."

"Yeah."

He slouched out, a small boy in pajama bottoms with feet and a large flannel top with a football on the front and NEW ENGLAND PATRIOTS written on the back.

Jack's typewriter stopped, and she heard Danny's hearty smack, "Night, Daddy."

"Goodnight, doc. How'd you do?"

"Okay, I guess. Mommy made me stop."

"Mommy was right. It's past eight-thirty. Going to the bathroom?"

"Yeah."

"Good. There's potatoes growing out of your ears. And onions and carrots and chives and—"

Danny's giggle, fading, then cut off by the firm click of the bathroom door. He was private about his bathroom functions, while both she and Jack were pretty much catch-as-catch-can. Another sign—and they were multiplying all the time—that there was another human being in the place, not just a carbon copy of one of them or a combination of both. It made her a little sad. Someday her child would be a stranger to her, and she would be strange to him . . . but not as strange as her own mother had become to her. Please don't let it be that way, God. Let him grow up and still love his mother.

Jack's typewriter began its irregular bursts again.

Still sitting in the chair beside Danny's reading
table, she let her eyes wander around her son's room.
The glider's wing had been neatly mended. His desk
was piled high with picture books, coloring books, old
Spiderman comic books with the covers half torn off,
Crayolas, and an untidy pile of Lincoln Logs. The VW
model was neatly placed above these lesser things, its
shrink-wrap still undisturbed. He and his father would
be putting it together tomorrow night or the night
after if Danny went on at this rate, and never mind the
end of the week. His pictures of Pooh and Eeyore and
Christopher Robin were tacked neatly to the wall, soon
enough to be replaced with pin-ups and photographs
of dope-smoking rock singers, she supposed. Innocence to experience. Human nature, baby. Grab it and
growl. Still it made her sad. Next year he would be in
school and she would lose at least half of him, maybe
more, to his friends. She and Jack had tried to have
another one for a while when things had seemed to be
going well at Stovington, but she was on the pill again
now. Things were too uncertain. God knew where they
would be in nine months.

Her eyes fell on the wasps' nest.

It held the ultimate high place in Danny's room,
resting on a large plastic plate on the table by his
bed. She didn't like it, even if it was empty. She wondered vaguely if it might have germs, thought to ask
Jack, then decided he would laugh at her. But she
would ask the doctor tomorrow, if she could catch
him with Jack out of the room. She didn't like the
idea of that thing, constructed from the chewings and

saliva of so many alien creatures, lying within a foot of her sleeping son's head.

The water in the bathroom was still running, and she got up and went into the big bedroom to make sure everything was okay. Jack didn't look up; he was lost in the world he was making, staring at the typewriter, a filter cigarette clamped in his teeth.

She knocked lightly on the closed bathroom room. "You okay, doc? You awake?"

No answer.

"Danny?"

No answer. She tried the door. It was locked.

"Danny?" She was worried now. The lack of any sound beneath the steadily running water made her uneasy. "Danny? Open the door, honey."

No answer.

"Danny!"

"Jesus Christ, Wendy, I can't think if you're going to pound on the door all night."

"Danny's locked himself in the bathroom and he doesn't answer me!"

Jack came around the desk, looking put out. He knocked on the door once, hard. "Open up, Danny. No games."

No answer.

Jack knocked harder. "Stop fooling, doc. Bedtime's bedtime. Spanking if you don't open up."

He's losing his temper, she thought, and was more afraid. He had not touched Danny in anger since that evening two years ago, but at this moment he sounded angry enough to do it.

"Danny, honey—" she began.

No answer. Only running water.

"Danny, if you make me break this lock I can guarantee you you'll spend the night sleeping on your belly," Jack warned.

Nothing.

"Break it," she said, and suddenly it was hard to talk. "Quick."

He raised one foot and brought it down hard against the door to the right of the knob. The lock was a poor thing; it gave immediately and the door shuddered open, banging the tiled bathroom wall and rebounding halfway.

"Danny!" she screamed.

The water was running full force in the basin. Beside it, a tube of Crest with the cap off. Danny was sitting on the rim of the bathtub across the room, his toothbrush clasped limply in his left hand, a thin foam of toothpaste around his mouth. He was staring, trancelike, into the mirror on the front of the medicine cabinet above the washbasin. The expression on his face was one of drugged horror, and her first thought was that he was having some sort of epileptic seizure, that he might have swallowed his tongue.

"Danny!"

Danny didn't answer. Guttural sounds came from his throat.

Then she was pushed aside so hard that she crashed into the towel rack, and Jack was kneeling in front of the boy

"Danny," he said. "Danny, Danny!" He snapped his fingers in front of Danny's blank eyes.

"Ah-sure," Danny said. "Tournament play. Stroke. Nurrrrr . . ."

"Danny—"

"Roque!" Danny said, his voice suddenly deep, almost manlike. "Roque. Stroke. The roque mallet . . . has two sides. *Gaaaaaa—*"

"Oh Jack my God *what's wrong with him?*"

Jack grabbed the boy's elbows and shook him hard. Danny's head rolled limply backward and then snapped forward like a balloon on a stick.

"Roque. Stroke. Redrum."

Jack shook him again, and Danny's eyes suddenly cleared. His toothbrush fell out of his hand and onto the tiled floor with a small click.

"What?" he asked, looking around. He saw his father kneeling before him, Wendy standing by the wall. "What?" Danny asked again, with rising alarm. "W-W-Wuh-What's wr-r-r—"

"Don't stutter!" Jack suddenly screamed into his face. Danny cried out in shock, his body going tense, trying to draw away from his father, and then he collapsed into tears. Stricken, Jack pulled him close. "Oh, honey, I'm sorry. I'm sorry, doc. Please. Don't cry. I'm sorry. Everything's okay."

The water ran ceaselessly in the basin, and Wendy felt that she had suddenly stepped into some grinding nightmare where time ran backward, backward to the time when her drunken husband had broken her son's arm and had then mewled over him in almost the exact same words.

(Oh honey. I'm sorry. I'm sorry, doc. Please. So sorry.)

She ran to them both, pried Danny out of Jack's arms somehow (she saw the look of angry reproach on his face but filed it away for later consideration), and lifted him up. She walked him back into the small bedroom, Danny's arms clasped around her neck, Jack trailing them.

She sat down on Danny's bed and rocked him back and forth, soothing him with nonsensical words repeated over and over. She looked up at Jack and there was only worry in his eyes now. He raised questioning eyebrows at her. She shook her head faintly.

"Danny," she said. "Danny, Danny, Danny. 'S okay, doc. 'S fine."

At last Danny was quiet, only faintly trembling in her arms. Yet it was Jack he spoke to first, Jack who was now sitting beside them on the bed, and she felt the old faint pang

(It's him first and it's always been him first)

of jealousy. Jack had shouted at him, she had comforted him, yet it was to his father that Danny said,

"I'm sorry if I was bad."

"Nothing to be sorry for, doc." Jack ruffled his hair. "What the hell happened in there?"

Danny shook his head slowly, dazedly. "I . . . I don't know. Why did you tell me to stop stuttering, Daddy? I don't stutter."

"Of course not," Jack said heartily, but Wendy felt a cold finger touch her heart. Jack suddenly looked scared, as if he'd seen something that might just have been a ghost.

"Something about the timer . . ." Danny muttered.

"*What?*" Jack was leaning forward, and Danny flinched in her arms.

"Jack, you're scaring him!" she said, and her voice was high, accusatory. It suddenly came to her that they were all scared. But of what?

"I don't know, I don't know," Danny was saying to his father. "What . . . what did I say, Daddy?"

"Nothing," Jack muttered. He took his handkerchief from his back pocket and wiped his mouth with it. Wendy had a moment of that sickening time-is-running-backward feeling again. It was a gesture she remembered well from his drinking days.

"Why did you lock the door, Danny?" she asked gently. "Why did you do that?"

"Tony," he said. "Tony told me to."

They exchanged a glance over the top of his head.

"Did Tony say why, son?" Jack asked quietly.

"I was brushing my teeth and I was thinking about my reading," Danny said. "Thinking real hard. And . . . and I saw Tony way down in the mirror. He said he had to show me again."

"You mean he was behind you?" Wendy asked.

"No, he was *in* the mirror." Danny was very emphatic on this point. "Way down deep. And then I went through the mirror. The next thing I remember Daddy was shaking me and I thought I was being bad again."

Jack winced as if struck.

"No, doc," he said quietly.

"Tony told you to lock the door?" Wendy asked, brushing his hair.

"Yes."

"And what did he want to show you?"

Danny tensed in her arms; it was as if the muscles in his body had turned into something like piano wire. "I don't remember," he said, distraught. "I don't remember. Don't ask me. I . . . *I don't remember nothing!*"

"Shh," Wendy said, alarmed. She began to rock him again. "It's all right if you don't remember, hon. Sure it is."

At last Danny began to relax again.

"Do you want me to stay a little while? Read you a story?"

"No. Just the night light." He looked shyly at his father. "Would you stay, Daddy? For a minute?"

"Sure, doc."

Wendy sighed. "I'll be in the living room, Jack."

"Okay."

She got up and watched as Danny slid under the covers. He seemed very small.

"Are you sure you're okay, Danny?"

"I'm okay. Just plug in Snoopy, Mom."

"Sure."

She plugged in the night light, which showed Snoopy lying fast asleep on top of his doghouse. He had never wanted a night light until they moved into the Overlook, and then he had specifically requested one. She turned off the lamp and the overhead and looked back at them, the small white circle of

Danny's face, and Jack's above it. She hesitated a moment

(*and then I went through the mirror*)

and then left them quietly.

"You sleepy?" Jack asked, brushing Danny's hair off his forehead.

"Yeah."

"Want a drink of water?"

"No . . ."

There was silence for five minutes. Danny was still beneath his hand. Thinking the boy had dropped off, he was about to get up and leave quietly when Danny said from the brink of sleep:

"Roque."

Jack turned back, all zero at the bone.

"Danny—?"

"You'd never hurt Mommy, would you, Daddy?"

"No."

"Or me?"

"No."

Silence again, spinning out.

"Daddy?"

"What?"

"Tony came and told me about roque."

"Did he, doc? What did he say?"

"I don't remember much. Except he said it was in innings. Like baseball. Isn't that funny?"

"Yes." Jack's heart was thudding dully in his chest. How could the boy possibly know a thing like that? Roque was played by innings, not like baseball but like cricket.

"Daddy . . . ?" He was almost asleep now.

"What?"

"What's redrum?"

"Red drum? Sounds like something an Indian might take on the warpath."

Silence.

"Hey, doc?"

But Danny was alseep, breathing in long, slow strokes. Jack sat looking down at him for a moment, and a rush of love pushed through him like tidal water. Why had he yelled at the boy like that? It was perfectly normal for him to stutter a little. He had been coming out of a daze or some weird kind of trance, and stuttering was perfectly normal under those circumstances. Perfectly. And he hadn't said *timer* at all. It had been something else, nonsense, gibberish.

How had he known roque was played in innings? Had someone told him? Ullman? Hallorann?

He looked down at his hands. They were made into tight, clenched fists of tension

(*god how i need a drink*)

and the nails were digging into his palms like tiny brands. Slowly he forced them to open.

"I love you, Danny," he whispered. "God knows I do."

He left the room. He had lost his temper again, only a little, but enough to make him feel sick and afraid. A drink would blunt that feeling, oh yes. It would blunt that

(Something about the timer)

and everything else. There was no mistake about those words at all. None. Each had come out clear as a bell. He paused in the hallway, looking back, and automatically wiped his lips with his handkerchief.

Their shapes were only dark silhouettes in the glow of the night light. Wendy, wearing only panties, went to his bed and tucked him in again; he had kicked the covers back. Jack stood in the doorway, watching as she put her inner wrist against his forehead.

"Is he feverish?"

"No." She kissed his cheek.

"Thank God you made that appointment," he said as she came back to the doorway. "You think that guy knows his stuff?"

"The checker said he was very good. That's all I know."

"If there's something wrong, I'm going to send you and him to your mother's, Wendy."

"No."

"I know," he said, putting an arm around her, "how you feel."

"You don't know how I feel at all about her."

"Wendy, there's no place else I can send you. You know that."

"If you came—"

"Without this job we're done," he said simply. "You know that."

Her silhouette nodded slowly. She knew it.

"When I had that interview with Ullman, I thought he was just blowing off his bazoo. Now I'm not so sure. Maybe I really shouldn't have tried this with you two along. Forty miles from nowhere."

"I love you," she said. "And Danny loves you even more, if that's possible. He would have been heartbroken, Jack. He will be, if you send us away."

"Don't make it sound that way."

"If the doctor says there's something wrong, I'll look for a job in Sidewinder," she said. "If I can't get one in Sidewinder, Danny and I will go to Boulder. I can't go to my mother, Jack. Not on those terms. Don't ask me. I . . . I just can't."

"I guess I know that. Cheer up. Maybe it's nothing."

"Maybe."

"The appointment's at two?"

"Yes."

"Let's leave the bedroom door open, Wendy."

"I want to. But I think he'll sleep through now."

But he didn't.

Boom . . . boom . . . boomboomBOOMBOOM—

He fled the heavy, crashing, echoing sounds through twisting, mazelike corridors, his bare feet whispering over a deep-pile jungle of blue and black. Each time he heard the roque mallet smash into the wall somewhere behind him he wanted to scream aloud. But he mustn't. He mustn't. A scream would give him away and then

(then *REDRUM*)

(*Come out here and take your medicine, you fucking crybaby!*)

Oh and he could hear the owner of that voice coming, coming for him, charging up the hall like a tiger in an alien blue-black jungle. A man-eater.

(*Come out here, you little son of a bitch!*)

If he could get to the stairs going down, if he could get off this third floor, he might be all right. Even the elevator. If he could remember what had been forgotten. But it was dark and in his terror he had lost his orientation. He had turned down one corridor and then another, his heart leaping into his mouth like a hot lump of ice, fearing that each turn would bring him face to face with the human tiger in these halls.

The booming was right behind him now, the awful hoarse shouting.

The whistle the head of the mallet made cutting through the air

(*roque . . . stroke . . . roque . . . stroke . . . REDRUM*)

before it crashed into the wall. The soft whisper of feet on the jungle carpet. Panic squirting in his mouth like bitter juice.

(*You will remember what was forgotten* . . . but would he? What was it?)

He fled around another corner and saw with creeping, utter horror that he was in a cul-de-sac. Locked doors frowned down at him from three sides. The west wing. He was in the west wing and outside he could hear the storm whooping and screaming, seeming to choke on its own dark throat filled with snow.

He backed up against the wall, weeping with terror now, his heart racing like the heart of a rabbit caught in a snare. When his back was against the light blue silk wallpaper with the embossed pattern of wavy lines, his legs gave way and he collapsed to the carpet, hands splayed on the jungle of woven vines and creepers, the breath whistling in and out of his throat.

Louder. Louder.

There was a tiger in the hall, and now the tiger was just around the corner, still crying out in that shrill and petulant and lunatic rage, the roque mallet slamming, because this tiger walked on two legs and it was—

He woke with a sudden indrawn gasp, sitting bolt upright in bed, eyes wide and staring into the darkness, hands crossed in front of his face.

Something on one hand. Crawling.

Wasps. Three of them.

They stung him then, seeming to needle all at once, and that was when all the images broke apart and fell on him in a dark flood and he began to shriek into the dark, the wasps clinging to his left hand, stinging again and again.

The lights went on and Daddy was standing there in his shorts, his eyes glaring. Mommy behind him, sleepy and scared.

"Get them off me!" Danny screamed.

"Oh my God," Jack said. He saw.

"Jack, what's wrong with him? *What's wrong?*"

He didn't answer her. He ran to the bed, scooped up Danny's pillow, and slapped Danny's thrashing left hand with it. Again. Again. Wendy saw lumbering, insectile forms rise into the air, droning.

"Get a magazine!" he yelled over his shoulder. "Kill them!"

"Wasps?" she said, and for a moment she was inside herself, almost detached in her realization. Then her mind cross-patched, and knowledge was connected to emotion. "Wasps, oh Jesus, Jack, you said—"

"*Shut the fuck up and kill them!*" he roared. "*Will you do what I say!*"

One of them had landed on Danny's reading desk. She took a coloring book off his worktable and slammed it down on the wasp. It left a viscous brown smear.

"There's another one on the curtain," he said, and ran out past her with Danny in his arms.

He took the boy into their bedroom and put him on Wendy's side of the makeshift double. "Lie right there, Danny. Don't come back until I tell you. Understand?"

His face puffed and streaked with tears, Danny nodded.

"That's my brave boy."

Jack ran back down the hall to the stairs. Behind him he heard the coloring book slap twice, and then his wife screamed in pain. He didn't slow but went down the stairs two by two into the darkened lobby. He went through Ullman's office into the kitchen, slamming the heavy part of his thigh into the corner of Ullman's oak desk, barely feeling it. He slapped on the kitchen overheads and crossed to the sink. The washed dishes from supper were still heaped up in the drainer, where Wendy had left them to drip-dry. He snatched the big Pyrex bowl off the top. A dish fell to the floor and exploded. Ignoring it, he turned and ran back through the office and up the stairs.

Wendy was standing outside Danny's door, breathing hard. Her face was the color of table linen. Her eyes were shiny and flat; her hair hung damply against her neck. "I got all of them," she said dully, "but one stung me. Jack, you said they were all dead." She began to cry.

He slipped past her without answering and carried the Pyrex bowl over to the nest by Danny's bed. It was still. Nothing there. On the outside, anyway. He slammed the bowl down over the nest.

"There," he said. "Come on."

They went back into their bedroom.

"Where did it get you?" he asked her.

"My . . . on my wrist."

"Let's see."

She showed it to him. Just above the bracelet of lines between wrist and palm, there was a small circular hole. The flesh around it was puffing up.

"Are you allergic to stings?" he asked. "Think hard! If you are, Danny might be. The fucking little bastards got him five or six times."

"No," she said, more calmly. "I . . . I just hate them, that's all. *Hate* them."

Danny was sitting on the foot of the bed, holding his left hand and looking at them. His eyes, circled with the white of shock, looked at Jack reproachfully.

"Daddy, you said you killed them all. My hand . . . it really hurts."

"Let's see it, doc . . . no, I'm not going to touch it. That would make it hurt even more. Just hold it out."

He did and Wendy moaned. "Oh Danny . . . oh, your poor hand!"

Later the doctor would count eleven separate stings. Now all they saw was a dotting of small holes, as if his palm and fingers had been sprinkled with grains of red pepper. The swelling was bad. His hand had begun to look like one of those cartoon images where Bugs Bunny or Daffy Duck had just slammed himself with a hammer.

"Wendy, go get that spray stuff in the bathroom," he said.

She went after it, and he sat down next to Danny and slipped an arm around his shoulders.

"After we spray your hand, I want to take some Polaroids of it, doc. Then you sleep the rest of the night with us, 'kay?"

"Sure," Danny said. "But why are you going to take pictures?"

"So maybe we can sue the ass out of some people."

Wendy came back with a spray tube in the shape of a chemical fire extinguisher.

"This won't hurt, honey," she said, taking off the cap.

Danny held out his hand and she sprayed both sides until it gleamed. He let out a long, shuddery sigh.

"Does it smart?" she asked.

"No. Feels better."

"Now these. Crunch them up." She held out five orange-flavored baby aspirin. Danny took them and popped them into his mouth one by one.

"Isn't that a lot of aspirin?" Jack asked.

"It's a lot of stings," she snapped at him angrily. "You go and get rid of that nest, John Torrance. Right now."

"Just a minute."

He went to the dresser and took his Polaroid Square Shooter out of the top drawer. He rummaged deeper and found some flashcubes.

"Jack, what are you doing?" she asked, a little hysterically.

"He's gonna take some pictures of my hand," Danny said gravely, "and then we're gonna sue the ass out of some people. Right, Dad?"

"Right," Jack said grimly. He had found the flash attachment, and he jabbed it onto the camera. "Hold it out, son. I figure about five thousand dollars a sting."

"What are you *talking* about?" Wendy nearly screamed.

"I'll tell you what," he said. "I followed the directions on that fucking bug bomb. We're going to sue them. The damn thing was defective. Had to have been. How else can you explain this?"

"Oh," she said in a small voice.

He took four pictures, pulling out each covered print for Wendy to time on the small locket watch she wore around her neck. Danny, fascinated with the idea that his stung hand might be worth thousands and thousands of dollars, began to lose some of his fright and take an active interest. The hand throbbed dully, and he had a small headache.

When Jack had put the camera away and spread the prints out on top of the dresser to dry, Wendy said: "Should we take him to the doctor tonight?"

"Not unless he's really in pain," Jack said. "If a person has a strong allergy to wasp venom, it hits within thirty seconds."

"Hits? What do you—"

"A coma. Or convulsions."

"Oh. Oh my Jesus." She cupped her hands over her elbows and hugged herself, looking pale and wan.

"How do you feel, son? Think you could sleep?"

Danny blinked at them. The nightmare had faded to a dull, featureless background in his mind, but he was still frightened.

"If I can sleep with you."

"Of course," Wendy said. "Oh honey, I'm so sorry."

"It's okay, Mommy."

She began to cry again, and Jack put his hands on her shoulders. "Wendy, I swear to you that I followed the directions."

"Will you get rid of it in the morning? Please?"

"Of course I will."

The three of them got in bed together, and Jack was about to snap off the light over the bed when he paused and pushed the covers back instead. "Want a picture of the nest, too."

"Come right back."

"I will."

He went to the dresser, got the camera and the last flashcube, and gave Danny a closed thumb-and-forefinger circle. Danny smiled and gave it back with his good hand.

Quite a kid, he thought as he walked down to Danny's room. *All of that and then some.*

The overhead was still on. Jack crossed to the bunk setup, and as he glanced at the table beside it, his skin crawled into goose flesh. The short hairs on his neck prickled and tried to stand erect.

He could hardly see the nest through the clear Pyrex bowl. The inside of the glass was crawling with wasps. It was hard to tell how many. Fifty at least. Maybe a hundred.

His heart thudding slowly in his chest, he took his pictures and then set the camera down to wait for them to develop. He wiped his lips with the palm of his hand. One thought played over and over in his mind, echoing with

(You lost your temper. You lost your temper. You lost your temper.)

an almost superstitious dread. They had come back. He had killed the wasps but they had come back.

In his mind he heard himself screaming into his frightened, crying son's face: *Don't stutter!*

He wiped his lips again.

He went to Danny's worktable, rummaged in its drawers, and came up with a big jigsaw puzzle with a fiberboard backing. He took it over to the bedtable and carefully slid the bowl and the nest onto it. The wasps buzzed angrily inside their prison. Then, putting his hand firmly on top of the bowl so it wouldn't slip, he went out into the hall.

"Coming to bed, Jack?" Wendy asked.

"Coming to bed, Daddy?"

"Have to go downstairs for a minute," he said, making his voice light.

How had it happened? How in God's name?

The bomb sure hadn't been a dud. He had seen the thick white smoke start to puff out of it when he had pulled the ring. And when he had gone up two hours later, he had shaken a drift of small dead bodies out of the hole in the top.

Then how? Spontaneous regeneration?

That was crazy. Seventeenth-century bullshit. Insects didn't regenerate. And even if wasp eggs could mature full-grown insects in twelve hours, this wasn't the season in which the queen laid. That happened in April or May. Fall was their dying time.

A living contradiction, the wasps buzzed furiously under the bowl.

He took them downstairs and through the kitchen. In back there was a door which gave on the outside. A cold night wind blew against his nearly naked body, and his feet went numb almost instantly against the cold concrete of the platform he was standing on, the platform where milk deliveries were made during the hotel's operating season. He put the puzzle and the bowl down carefully, and when he stood up he looked at the thermometer nailed outside the door. FRESH UP WITH 7-UP, the thermometer said, and the mercury stood at an even twenty-five degrees. The cold would kill them by morning. He went in and shut the door firmly. After a moment's thought he locked it, too.

He crossed the kitchen again and shut off the lights. He stood in the darkness for a moment, thinking, wanting a drink. Suddenly the hotel seemed full of a thousand stealthy sounds: creakings and groans and the sly sniff of the wind under the eaves where more wasps' nests might be hanging like deadly fruit.

They had come back.

And suddenly he found that he didn't like the Overlook so well anymore, as if it wasn't wasps that had stung his son, wasps that had miraculously lived through the bug bomb assault, but the hotel itself.

His last thought before going upstairs to his wife and son

(*from now on you will hold your temper. No Matter What.*)

was firm and hard and sure.

As he went down the hall to them he wiped his lips with the back of his hand.

17

The Doctor's Office

Stripped to his underpants, lying on the examination table, Danny Torrance looked very small. He was looking up at Dr. ("Just call me Bill") Edmonds, who was wheeling a large black machine up beside him. Danny rolled his eyes to get a better look at it.

"Don't let it scare you, guy," Bill Edmonds said. "It's an electroencephalograph, and it doesn't hurt."

"Electro—"

"We call it EEG for short. I'm going to hook a bunch of wires to your head—no, not stick them in, only tape them—and the pens in this part of the gadget will record your brain waves."

"Like on 'The Six Million Dollar Man'?"

"About the same. Would you like to be like Steve Austin when you grow up?"

"No way," Danny said as the nurse began to tape the wires to a number of tiny shaved spots on his scalp. "My daddy says that someday he'll get a short circuit and then he'll be up sh . . . he'll be up the creek."

"I know that creek well," Dr. Edmonds said amiably. "I've been up it a few times myself, *sans* paddle. An EEG can tell us lots of things, Danny."

"Like what?"

"Like for instance if you have epilepsy. That's a little problem where—"

"Yeah, I know what epilepsy is."

"Really?"

"Sure. There was a kid in my nursery school back in Vermont—I went to nursery school when I was a little kid—and he had it. He wasn't supposed to use the flashboard."

"What was that, Dan?" He had turned on the machine. Thin lines began to trace their way across graph paper.

"It had all these lights, all different colors. And when you turned it on, some colors would flash but not all. And you had to count the colors and if you pushed the right button, you could turn it off. Brent couldn't use that."

"That's because bright flashing lights sometimes cause an epileptic seizure."

"You mean using the flashboard might've made Brent pitch a fit?"

Edmonds and the nurse exchanged a brief, amused glance. "Inelegantly but accurately put, Danny."

"What?"

"I said you're right, except you should say 'seizure' instead of 'pitch a fit.' That's not nice . . . okay, lie just as still as a mouse now."

"Okay."

"Danny, when you have these . . . whatever they ares, do you ever recall seeing bright flashing lights before?"

"No."

"Funny noises? Ringing? Or chimes like a doorbell?"

"Huh-uh."

"How about a funny smell, maybe like oranges or sawdust? Or a smell like something rotten?"

"No, sir."

"Sometimes do you feel like crying before you pass out? Even though you don't feel sad?"

"No way."

"That's fine, then."

"Have I got epilepsy, Dr. Bill?"

"I don't think so, Danny. Just lie still. Almost done."

The machine hummed and scratched for another five minutes and then Dr. Edmonds shut it off.

"All done, guy," Edmonds said briskly. "Let Sally get those electrodes off you and then come into the next room. I want to have a little talk with you. Okay?"

"Sure."

"Sally, you go ahead and give him a tine test before he comes in."

"All right."

Edmonds ripped off the long curl of paper the machine had extruded and went into the next room, looking at it.

"I'm going to prick your arm just a little," the nurse said after Danny had pulled up his pants. "It's to make sure you don't have TB."

"They gave me that at my school just last year," Danny said without much hope.

"But that was a long time ago and you're a big boy now, right?"

"I guess so," Danny sighed, and offered his arm up for sacrifice.

When he had his shirt and shoes on, he went through the sliding door and into Dr. Edmonds's office. Edmonds was sitting on the edge of his desk, swinging his legs thoughtfully.

"Hi, Danny."

"Hi."

"How's that hand now?" He pointed at Danny's left hand, which was lightly bandaged.

"Pretty good."

"Good. I looked at your EEG and it seems fine. But I'm going to send it to a friend of mine in Denver who makes his living reading those things. I just want to make sure."

"Yes, sir."

"Tell me about Tony, Dan."

Danny shuffled his feet. "He's just an invisible friend," he said. "I made him up. To keep me company."

Edmonds laughed and put his hands on Danny's shoulders. "Now that's what your Mom and Dad say. But this is just between us, guy. I'm your doctor. Tell me the truth and I'll promise not to tell them unless you say I can."

Danny thought about it. He looked at Edmonds and then, with a small effort of concentration, he tried to catch Edmonds's thoughts or at least the color of his mood. And suddenly he got an oddly comforting image in his head: file cabinets, their doors sliding shut one after another, locking with a click. Written on the small tabs in the center of each door was: A–C, SECRET; D–G, SECRET; and so on. This made Danny feel a little easier.

Cautiously he said: "I don't know who Tony is."

"Is he your age?"

"No. He's at least eleven. I think he might be even older. I've never seen him right up close. He might be old enough to drive a car."

"You just see him at a distance, huh?"

"Yes, sir."

"And he always comes just before you pass out?"

"Well, I don't pass out. It's like I go with him. And he shows me things."

"What kind of things?"

"Well . . ." Danny debated for a moment and then told Edmonds about Daddy's trunk with all his writing in it, and about how the movers hadn't lost it between Vermont and Colorado after all. It had been right under the stairs all along.

"And your daddy found it where Tony said he would?"

"Oh yes, sir. Only Tony didn't *tell* me. He showed me."

"I understand. Danny, what did Tony show you last night? When you locked yourself in the bathroom?"

"I don't remember," Danny said quickly.

"Are you sure?"

"Yes, sir."

"A moment ago I said *you* locked the bathroom door. But that wasn't right, was it? *Tony* locked the door."

"No, sir. Tony couldn't lock the door because he isn't real. He wanted me to do it, so I did. I locked it."

"Does Tony always show you where lost things are?"

"No, sir. Sometimes he shows me things that are going to happen."

"Really?"

"Sure. Like one time Tony showed me the amusements and wild animal park in Great Barrington. Tony said Daddy was going to take me there for my birthday. He did, too."

"What else does he show you?"

Danny frowned. "Signs. He's always showing me stupid old *signs*. And I can't read them, hardly ever."

"Why do you suppose Tony would do that, Danny?"

"I don't know." Danny brightened. "But my daddy and mommy are teaching me to read, and I'm trying real hard."

"So you can read Tony's signs."

"Well, I really want to learn. But that too, yeah."

"Do you like Tony, Danny?"

Danny looked at the tile floor and said nothing.

"Danny?"

"It's hard to tell," Danny said. "I used to. I used to hope he'd come every day, because he always showed me good things, especially since Mommy and Daddy don't think about DIVORCE anymore." Dr. Edmonds's gaze sharpened, but Danny didn't notice. He was looking hard at the floor, concentrating on expressing himself. "But now whenever he comes he shows me bad things. *Awful* things. Like in the bathroom last night. The things he shows me, they sting me like those wasps stung me. Only Tony's things sting me up here." He cocked a finger gravely at his temple, a small boy unconsciously burlesquing suicide.

"What things, Danny?"

"I can't remember!" Danny cried out, agonized. "I'd tell you if I could! It's like I can't remember because it's so bad I don't *want* to remember. All I can remember when I wake up is REDRUM."

"Red *drum* or red *rum*?"

"Rum."

"What's that, Danny?"

"I don't know."

"Danny?"

"Yes, sir?"

"Can you make Tony come now?"

"I don't know. He doesn't always come. I don't even know if I want him to come anymore."

"Try, Danny. I'll be right here."

Danny looked at Edmonds doubtfully. Edmonds nodded encouragement.

Danny let out a long, sighing breath and nodded. "But I don't know if it will work. I never did it with anyone looking at me before. And Tony doesn't always come, anyway."

"If he doesn't, he doesn't," Edmonds said. "I just want you to try."

"Okay."

He dropped his gaze to Edmonds's slowly swinging loafers and cast his mind outward toward his mommy and daddy. They were here someplace . . . right beyond that wall with the picture on it, as a matter of fact. In the waiting room where they had come in. Sitting side by side but not talking. Leafing through magazines. Worried. About him.

He concentrated harder, his brow furrowing, trying to get into the feeling of his mommy's thoughts. It was always harder when they weren't right there in the room with him. Then he began to get it. Mommy was thinking about a sister. Her sister. The sister was dead. His mommy was thinking that was the main thing that turned her mommy into such a

(*bitch?*)

into such an old biddy. Because her sister had died. As a little girl she was

(*hit by a car oh god i could never stand anything like that again like aileen but what if he's sick really sick cancer spinal meningitis leukemia brain tumor like john gunther's son or muscular dystrophy oh jeez kids his age get leukemia all the time radium treatments chemotherapy we couldn't afford anything like that but of course they just can't turn you out to die on the street can they and anyway he's all right all right all right you really shouldn't let yourself think*)

(*Danny—*)

(*about aileen and*)

(*Dannee—*)

(*that car*)

(*Dannee—*)

But Tony wasn't there. Only his voice. And as it faded, Danny followed it down into darkness, falling and tumbling down some magic hole between Dr. Bill's swinging loafers, past a loud knocking sound, further, a bathtub cruised silently by in the darkness with some horrible thing lolling in it, past a sound like sweetly chiming church bells, past a clock under a dome of glass.

Then the dark was pierced feebly by a single light, festooned with cobwebs. The weak glow disclosed a stone floor that looked damp and unpleasant. Somewhere not far distant was a steady mechanical roaring sound, but muted, not frightening. Soporific. It was the thing that would be forgotten, Danny thought with dreamy surprise.

As his eyes adjusted to the gloom he could see Tony just ahead of him, a silhouette. Tony was looking at something and Danny strained his eyes to see what it was.

(*Your daddy. See your daddy?*)

Of course he did. How could he have missed him, even in the basement light's feeble glow? Daddy was kneeling on the floor, casting the beam of a flashlight over old cardboard boxes and wooden crates. The cardboard boxes were mushy and old; some of them had split open and spilled drifts of paper onto the floor. Newspapers, books, printed pieces of paper that looked like bills. His daddy was examining them with great interest. And then Daddy looked up and shone his flashlight in another direction. Its beam of light impaled another book, a large white one bound with gold string. The cover looked like white leather. It was a scrapbook. Danny suddenly needed to cry out to his daddy, to tell him to leave that book alone, that some books should not be opened. But his daddy was climbing toward it.

The mechanical roaring sound, which he now recognized as the boiler at the Overlook which Daddy checked three or four times every day, had developed an ominous, rhythmic hitching. It began to sound like . . . like pounding. And the smell of mildew and wet, rotting paper was changing to something else— the high, junipery smell of the Bad Stuff. It hung around his daddy like a vapor as he reached for the book . . . and grasped it.

Tony was somewhere in the darkness.

(*This inhuman place makes human monsters. This inhuman place*)

repeating the same incomprehensible thing over and over.

(*makes human monsters.*)

Falling through darkness again, now accompanied by the heavy, pounding thunder that was no longer the boiler but the sound of a whistling mallet striking silk-papered walls, knocking out whiffs of plaster dust. Crouching helplessly on the blue-black woven jungle rug.

(*Come out*)

(*This inhuman place*)

(*and take your medicine!*)

(*makes human monsters.*)

With a gasp that echoed in his own head he jerked himself out of the darkness. Hands were on him and at first he shrank back, thinking that the dark thing in the Overlook of Tony's world had somehow followed him back into the world of real things—and then Dr. Edmonds was saying: "You're all right, Danny. You're all right. Everything is fine."

Danny recognized the doctor, then his surroundings in the office. He began to shudder helplessly. Edmonds held him.

When the reaction began to subside, Edmonds asked, "You said something about monsters, Danny—what was it?"

"This inhuman place," he said gutturally. "Tony told me . . . this inhuman place . . . makes . . makes . . ." He shook his head. "Can't remember."

"Try!"

"I can't."

"Did Tony come?"

"Yes."

"What did he show you?"

"Dark. Pounding. I don't remember."

"Where were you?"

"*Leave me alone! I don't remember! Leave me alone!*" He began to sob helplessly in fear and frustration. It was all gone, dissolved into a sticky mess like a wet bundle of paper, the memory unreadable.

Edmonds went to the water cooler and got him a paper cup of water. Danny drank it and Edmonds got him another one.

"Better?"

"Yes."

"Danny, I don't want to badger you . . . tease you about this, I mean. But can you remember anything about *before* Tony came?"

"My mommy," Danny said slowly. "She's worried about me."

"Mothers always are, guy."

"No . . . she had a sister that died when she was a little girl. Aileen. She was thinking about how Aileen got hit by a car and that made her worried about me. I don't remember anything else."

Edmonds was looking at him sharply. "Just now she was thinking that? Out in the waiting room?"

"Yes, sir."

"Danny, how would you know that?"

"I don't know," Danny said wanly. "The shining, I guess."

"The what?"

Danny shook his head very slowly. "I'm awful tired. Can't I go see my mommy and daddy? I don't want to answer any more questions. I'm tired. And my stomach hurts."

"Are you going to throw up?"

"No, sir. I just want to go see my mommy and daddy."

"Okay, Dan." Edmonds stood up. "You go on out and see them for a minute, then send them in so I can talk to them. Okay?"

"Yes, sir."

"There are books out there to look at. You like books, don't you?"

"Yes, sir," Danny said dutifully.

"You're a good boy, Danny."

Danny gave him a faint smile.

"I can't find a thing wrong with him," Dr. Edmonds said to the Torrances. "Not physically. Mentally, he's bright and rather too imaginative. It happens. Children have to grow into their imaginations like a pair of oversized shoes. Danny's is still way too big for him. Ever had his IQ tested?"

"I don't believe in them," Jack said. "They strait-jacket the expectations of both parents and teachers."

Dr. Edmonds nodded. "That may be. But if you did test him, I think you'd find he's right off the scale for his age group. His verbal ability, for a boy who is five going on six, is amazing."

"We don't talk down to him," Jack said with a trace of pride.

"I doubt if you've ever had to in order to make yourself understood." Edmonds paused, fiddling with a pen. "He went into a trance while I was with him. At my request. Exactly as you described him in the bathroom last night. All his muscles went lax, his body slumped, his eyeballs rotated outward. Text-book auto-hypnosis. I was amazed. I still am."

The Torrances sat forward. "What happened?" Wendy asked tensely, and Edmonds carefully related Danny's trance, the muttered phrase from which Edmonds had only been able to pluck the word "monsters," the "dark," the "pounding." The after-math of tears, near-hysteria, and nervous stomach.

"Tony again," Jack said.

"What does it mean?" Wendy asked. "Have you any idea?"

"A few. You might not like them."

"Go ahead anyway," Jack told him.

"From what Danny told me, his 'invisible friend' was truly a friend until you folks moved out here from New England. Tony has only become a threatening figure since that move. The pleasant interludes have become nightmarish, even more frightening to your son because he can't remember exactly what the nightmares are about. That's common enough. We all remember our pleasant dreams more clearly than the scary ones. There seems to be a buffer somewhere between the conscious and the subconscious, and one hell of a bluenose lives in there. This censor only lets through a small amount, and often what does come through is only symbolic. That's oversimplified Freud, but it does pretty much describe what we know of the mind's interaction with itself."

"You think moving has upset Danny that badly?" Wendy asked.

"It may have, if the move took place under traumatic circumstances," Edmonds said. "Did it?"

Wendy and Jack exchanged a glance.

"I was teaching at a prep school," Jack said slowly. "I lost my job."

"I see," Edmonds said. He put the pen he had been playing with firmly back in its holder. "There's more here, I'm afraid. It may be painful to you. Your son seems to believe you two have seriously contemplated divorce. He spoke of it in an off-hand way, but only because he believes you are no longer considering it."

Jack's mouth dropped open, and Wendy recoiled as if slapped. The blood drained from her face.

"We never even discussed it!" she said. "Not in front of him, not even in front of each other! We—"

"I think it's best if you understand everything, Doctor," Jack said. "Shortly after Danny was born, I became an alcoholic. I'd had a drinking problem all the way through college, it subsided a little after Wendy and I met, cropped up worse than ever after Danny was born and the writing I consider to be my real work was going badly. When Danny was three and a half, he spilled some beer on a bunch of papers I was working on . . . papers I was shuffling around, anyway . . . and I . . . well . . . oh shit." His voice broke, but his eyes remained dry and unflinching. "It sounds so goddam beastly said out loud. I broke his arm turning him around to spank him. Three months later I gave up drinking. I haven't touched it since."

"I see," Edmonds said neutrally. "I knew the arm had been broken, of course. It was set well." He pushed back from his desk a little and crossed his legs. "If I may be frank, it's obvious that he's been in no way abused since then. Other than the stings, there's nothing on him but the normal bruises and scabs that any kid has in abundance."

"Of course not," Wendy said hotly. "Jack didn't mean—"

"No, Wendy," Jack said. "I meant to do it. I guess someplace inside I really did mean to do that to him.

Or something even worse." He looked back at Edmonds again. "You know something, Doctor? This is the first time the word divorce has been mentioned between us. And alcoholism. And child-beating. Three firsts in five minutes."

"That may be at the root of the problem," Edmonds said. "I am not a psychiatrist. If you want Danny to see a child psychiatrist, I can recommend a good one who works out of the Mission Ridge Medical Center in Boulder. But I am fairly confident of my diagnosis. Danny is an intelligent, imaginative, perceptive boy. I don't believe he would have been as upset by your marital problems as you believed. Small children are great accepters. They don't understand shame, or the need to hide things."

Jack was studying his hands. Wendy took one of them and squeezed it.

"But he sensed the things that were wrong. Chief among them from his point of view was not the broken arm but the broken—or breaking—link between you two. He mentioned divorce to me, but not the broken arm. When my nurse mentioned the set to him, he simply shrugged it off. It was no pressure thing. 'It happened a long time ago' is what I think he said."

"That kid," Jack muttered. His jaws were clamped together, the muscles in the cheeks standing out. "We don't deserve him."

"You have him, all the same," Edmonds said dryly. "At any rate, he retires into a fantasy world from time to time. Nothing unusual about that; lots of kids do. As I recall, I had my own invisible friend when I was Danny's age, a talking rooster named Chug-Chug. Of course no one could see Chug-Chug but me. I had two older brothers who often left me behind, and in such a situation Chug-Chug came in mighty handy. And of course you two must understand why Danny's invisible friend is named Tony instead of Mike or Hal or Dutch."

"Yes," Wendy said.

"Have you ever pointed it out to him?"

"No," Jack said. "Should we?"

"Why bother? Let him realize it in his own time, by his own logic. You see, Danny's fantasies were considerably deeper than those that grow around the ordinary invisible friend syndrome, but he felt he needed Tony that much more. Tony would come and show him pleasant things. Sometimes amazing things. Always good things. Once Tony showed him where Daddy's lost trunk was . . . under the stairs. Another time Tony showed him that Mommy and Daddy were going to take him to an amusement park for his birthday—"

"At Great Barrington!" Wendy cried. "But how could he *know* those things? It's eerie, the things he comes out with sometimes. Almost as if—"

"He had second sight?" Edmonds asked, smiling.

"He was born with a caul," Wendy said weakly.

Edmonds's smile became a good hearty laugh. Jack and Wendy exchanged a glance and then also smiled, both of them amazed at how easy it was.

Danny's occasional "lucky guesses" about things was something else they had not discussed much.

"Next you'll be telling me he can levitate," Edmonds said, still smiling. "No, no, no, I'm afraid not. It's not extrasensory but good old human perception, which in Danny's case is unusually keen. Mr. Torrance, he knew your trunk was under the stairs because you had looked everywhere else. Process of elimination, what? It's so simple Ellery Queen would laugh at it. Sooner or later you would have thought of it yourself.

"As for the amusement park at Great Barrington, whose idea was that originally? Yours or his?"

"His, of course," Wendy said. "They advertised on all the morning children's programs. He was wild to go. But the thing is, Doctor, we couldn't afford to take him. And we had told him so."

"Then a men's magazine I'd sold a story to back in 1971 sent a check for fifty dollars," Jack said. "They were reprinting the story in an annual, or something. So we decided to spend it on Danny."

Edmonds shrugged. "Wish fulfillment plus a lucky coincidence."

"Goddammit, I bet that's just right," Jack said.

Edmonds smiled a little. "And Danny himself told me that Tony often showed him things that never occurred. Visions based on faulty perception, that's all. Danny is doing subconsciously what these so-called mystics and mind readers do quite consciously and cynically. I admire him for it. If life doesn't cause him to retract his antennae, I think he'll be quite a man."

Wendy nodded—of course she thought Danny would be quite a man—but the doctor's explanation struck her as glib. It tasted more like margarine than butter. Edmonds had not lived with them. He had not been there when Danny found lost buttons, told her that maybe the *TV Guide* was under the bed, that he thought he better wear his rubbers to nursery school even though the sun was out . . . and later that day they had walked home under her umbrella through the pouring rain. Edmonds couldn't know of the curious way Danny had of preguessing them both. She would decide to have an unusual evening cup of tea, go out in the kitchen and find her cup out with a tea bag in it. She would remember that the books were due at the library and find them all neatly piled up on the hall table, her library card on top. Or Jack would take it into his head to wax the Volkswagen and find Danny already out there, listening to tinny top-forty music on his crystal radio as he sat on the curb to watch.

Aloud she said, "Then why the nightmares now? Why did Tony tell him to lock the bathroom door?"

"I believe it's because Tony has outlived his usefulness," Edmonds said. "He was born—Tony, not Danny—at a time when you and your husband were straining to keep your marriage together. Your husband was drinking too much. There was the incident of the broken arm. The ominous quiet between you."

Ominous quiet, yes, that phrase was the real thing, anyway. The stiff, tense meals where the only conversation had been please pass the butter or

Danny, eat the rest of your carrots or may I be excused, please. The nights when Jack was gone and she had lain down, dry-eyed, on the couch while Danny watched TV. The mornings when she and Jack had stalked around each other like two angry cats with a quivering, frightened mouse between them. It all rang true;

(dear God, do old scars ever stop hurting?)

horribly, horribly true.

Edmonds resumed, "But things have changed. You know, schizoid behavior is a pretty common thing in children. It's accepted, because all we adults have this unspoken agreement that children are lunatics. They have invisible friends. They may go and sit in the closet when they're depressed, withdrawing from the world. They attach talismanic importance to a special blanket, or a teddy bear, or a stuffed tiger. They suck their thumbs. When an adult sees things that aren't there, we consider him ready for the rubber room. When a child says he's seen a troll in his bedroom or a vampire outside the window, we simply smile indulgently. We have a one-sentence explanation that explains the whole range of such phenomena in children—"

"He'll grow out of it," Jack said.

Edmonds blinked. "My very words," he said. "Yes. Now I would guess that Danny was in a pretty good position to develop a full-fledged psychosis. Unhappy home life, a big imagination, the invisible friend who was so real to him that he nearly became real to you. Instead of 'growing out of' his childhood schizophrenia, he might well have grown into it."

"And become autistic?" Wendy asked. She had read about autism. The word itself frightened her; it sounded like dread and white silence.

"Possible but not necessarily. He might simply have entered Tony's world someday and never come back to what he calls 'real things.'"

"God," Jack said.

"But now the basic situation has changed drastically. Mr. Torrance no longer drinks. You are in a new place where conditions have forced the three of you into a tighter family unit than ever before—certainly tighter than my own, where my wife and kids may see me for only two or three hours a day. To my mind, he is in the perfect healing situation. And I think the very fact that he is able to differentiate so sharply between Tony's world and 'real things' says a lot about the fundamentally healthy state of his mind. He says that you two are no longer considering divorce. Is he as right as I think he is?"

"Yes," Wendy said, and Jack squeezed her hand tightly, almost painfully. She squeezed back.

Edmonds nodded. "He really doesn't need Tony anymore. Danny is flushing him out of his system. Tony no longer brings pleasant visions but hostile nightmares that are too frightening for him to remember except fragmentally. He internalized Tony during a difficult—desperate—life situation, and Tony is not leaving easily. But he *is* leaving. Your son is a little like a junkie kicking the habit."

He stood up, and the Torrances stood also.

"As I said, I'm not a psychiatrist. If the nightmares are still continuing when your job at the Overlook ends next spring, Mr. Torrance, I would strongly urge you to take him to this man in Boulder."

"I will."

"Well, let's go out and tell him he can go home," Edmonds said.

"I want to thank you," Jack told him painfully. "I feel better about all this than I have in a very long time."

"So do I," Wendy said.

At the door, Edmonds paused and looked at Wendy. "Do you or did you have a sister, Mrs. Torrance? Named Aileen?"

Wendy looked at him, surprised. "Yes, I did. She was killed outside our home in Somersworth, New Hampshire, when she was six and I was ten. She chased a ball into the street and was struck by a delivery van."

"Does Danny know that?"

"I don't know. I don't think so."

"He says you were thinking about her in the waiting room."

"I was," Wendy said slowly. "For the first time in . . . oh, I don't know how long."

"Does the word 'redrum' mean anything to either of you?"

Wendy shook her head but Jack said, "He mentioned that word last night, just before he went to sleep. Red drum."

"No, *rum*," Edmonds corrected. "He was quite emphatic about that. *Rum*. As in the drink. The alcoholic drink."

"Oh," Jack said. "It fits in, doesn't it?" He took his handkerchief out of his back pocket and wiped his lips with it.

"Does the phrase 'the shining' mean anything to you?"

This time they both shook their heads.

"Doesn't matter, I guess," Edmonds said. He opened the door into the waiting room. "Anybody here named Danny Torrance that would like to go home?"

"Hi, Daddy! Hi, Mommy!" He stood up from the small table where he had been leafing slowly through a copy of *Where the Wild Things Are* and muttering the words he knew aloud.

He ran to Jack, who scooped him up. Wendy ruffled his hair.

Edmonds peered at him. "If you don't love your mommy and daddy, you can stay with good old Bill."

"No, sir!" Danny said emphatically. He slung one arm around Jack's neck, one arm around Wendy's, and looked radiantly happy.

"Okay," Edmonds said, smiling. He looked at Wendy. "You call if you have any problems."

"Yes."

"I don't think you will," Edmonds said, smiling.

18

The Scrapbook

Jack found the scrapbook on the first of November,
while his wife and son were hiking up the rutted old
road that ran from behind the roque court to a
deserted sawmill two miles further up. The fine
weather still held, and all three of them had acquired
improbable autumn suntans.

He had gone down in the basement to knock the
press down on the boiler and then, on impulse, he
had taken the flashlight from the shelf where the
plumbing schematics were and decided to look at
some of the old papers. He was also looking for good
places to set his traps, although he didn't plan to do
that for another month——I want them all to be home
from vacation, he had told Wendy.

Shining the flashlight ahead of him, he stepped
past the elevator shaft (at Wendy's insistence they
hadn't used the elevator since they moved in) and
through the small stone arch. His nose wrinkled at the
smell of rotting paper. Behind him the boiler kicked
on with a thundering *whoosh*, making him jump.

He flickered the light around, whistling tunelessly between his teeth. There was a scale-model Andes range down here: dozens of boxes and crates stuffed with papers, most of them white and shapeless with age and damp. Others had broken open and spilled yellowed sheaves of paper onto the stone floor. There were bales of newspaper tied up with hayrope. Some boxes contained what looked like ledgers, and others contained invoices bound with rubber bands. Jack pulled one out and put the flashlight beam on it.

ROCKY MOUNTAIN EXPRESS, INC.
To: OVERLOOK HOTEL
From: SIDEY'S WAREHOUSE,
    1210 16th Street, Denver, CO.
Via: CANADIAN PACIFIC RR
Contents: 400 CASES DELSEY TOILET TISSUE,
    1 GROSS/CASE

Signed *D E F*
Date *August 24, 1954*

Smiling, Jack let the paper drop back into the box.

He flashed the light above it and it speared a hanging lightbulb, almost buried in cobwebs. There was no chain pull.

He stood on tiptoe and tried screwing the bulb in. It lit weakly. He picked up the toilet paper invoice again and used it to wipe off some of the cobwebs. The glow didn't brighten much.

Still using the flashlight, he wandered through the boxes and bales of paper, looking for rat spoor. They had been here, but not for quite a long time . . .

maybe years. He found some droppings that were powdery with age, and several nests of neatly shredded paper that were old and unused.

Jack pulled a newspaper from one of the bundles and glanced down at the headline.

JOHNSON PROMISES
ORDERLY TRANSITION
Says Work Begun by JFK Will Go
Forward in Coming Year

The paper was the *Rocky Mountain News*, dated December 19, 1963. He dropped it back onto its pile.

He supposed he was fascinated by that commonplace sense of history that anyone can feel glancing through the fresh news of ten or twenty years ago. He found gaps in the piled newspapers and records; nothing from 1937 to 1945, from 1957 to 1960, from 1962 to 1963. Periods when the hotel had been closed, he guessed. When it had been between suckers grabbing for the brass ring.

Ullman's explanations of the Overlook's checkered career still didn't ring quite true to him. It seemed that the Overlook's spectacular location alone should have guaranteed its continuing success. There had always been an American jet-set, even before jets were invented, and it seemed to Jack that the Overlook should have been one of the bases they touched in their migrations. It even sounded right. The Waldorf in May, the Bar Harbor House in June and July, the Overlook in August and early September, before moving on to Bermuda, Havana, Rio, wherever. He found a pile of old desk registers and they bore him out. Nelson Rockefeller in 1950. Henry Ford & Fam. in 1927. Jean Harlow in 1930. Clark Gable and Carole Lombard. In 1956 the whole top floor had been taken for a week by "Darryl F. Zanuck & Party." The money must have rolled down the corridors and into the cash registers like a twentieth-century Comstock Lode. The management must have been spectacularly bad.

There was history here, all right, and not just in newspaper headlines. It was buried between the entries in these ledgers and account books and room-service chits where you couldn't quite see it. In 1922 Warren G. Harding had ordered a whole salmon at ten o'clock in the evening, and a case of Coors beer. But whom had he been eating and drinking with? Had it been a poker game? A strategy session? What?

Jack glanced at his watch and was surprised to see that forty-five minutes had somehow slipped by since he had come down here. His hands and arms were grimy, and he probably smelled bad. He decided to go up and take a shower before Wendy and Danny got back.

He walked slowly between the mountains of paper, his mind alive and ticking over possibilities in a speedy way that was exhilarating. He hadn't felt this way in years. It suddenly seemed that the book he had semijokingly promised himself might really happen. It might even be right here, buried in these untidy heaps of paper. It could be a work of fiction, or history, or both——a long book exploding out of this central place in a hundred directions.

He stood beneath the cobwebby light, took his handkerchief from his back pocket without thinking, and scrubbed at his lips with it. And that was when he saw the scrapbook.

A pile of five boxes stood on his left like some tottering Pisa. The one on top was stuffed with more invoices and ledgers. Balanced on top of those, keeping its angle of repose for who knew how many years, was a thick scrapbook with white leather covers, its pages bound with two hanks of gold string that had been tied along the binding in gaudy bows.

Curious, he went over and took it down. The top cover was thick with dust. He held it on a plane at lip level, blew the dust off in a cloud, and opened it. As he did so a card fluttered out and he grabbed it in mid-air before it could fall to the stone floor. It was rich and creamy, dominated by a raised engraving of the Overlook with every window alight. The lawn and playground were decorated with glowing Japanese lanterns. It looked almost as though you could step right into it, an Overlook Hotel that had existed thirty years ago.

Horace M. Derwent Requests
The Pleasure of Your Company
At a Masked Ball to Celebrate
The Grand Opening of

THE OVERLOOK HOTEL

Dinner Will Be Served At 8 P.M.
Unmasking And Dancing At Midnight
August 29, 1945 RSVP

Dinner at eight! Unmasking at midnight!

He could almost see them in the dining room, the richest men in America and their women. Tuxedos and glimmering starched shirts; evening gowns; the band playing; gleaming high-heeled pumps. The clink of glasses, the jocund pop of champagne corks. The war was over, or almost over. The future lay ahead, clean and shining. America was the colossus of the world and at last she knew it and accepted it.

And later, at midnight, Derwent himself crying: "Unmask! Unmask!" The masks coming off and . . .

(*The Red Death held sway over all!*)

He frowned. What left field had that come out of? That was Poe, the Great American Hack. And surely the Overlook—this shining, glowing Overlook on the invitation he held in his hands—was the farthest cry from E. A. Poe imaginable.

He put the invitation back and turned to the next page. A paste-up from one of the Denver papers, and scratched beneath it the date: May 15, 1947.

POSH MOUNTAIN RESORT REOPENS
WITH STELLAR GUEST REGISTER
Derwent Says Overlook Will Be
"Showplace of the World"

By David Felton, Features Editor

The Overlook Hotel has been opened and reopened in its thirty-eight-year history, but rarely with such style and dash as that promised by Horace Derwent,

the mysterious California millionaire who is the latest
owner of the hostelry.

Derwent, who makes no secret of having sunk
more than one million dollars into his newest venture—and some say the figure is closer to three million—says that "The new Overlook will be one of the
world's showplaces, the kind of hotel you will
remember overnighting in thirty years later."

When Derwent, who is rumored to have substantial Las Vegas holdings, was asked if his purchase and
refurbishing of the Overlook signaled the opening
gun in a battle to legalize casino-style gambling in
Colorado, the aircraft, movie, munitions, and shipping magnate denied it . . . with a smile. "The Overlook would be cheapened by gambling," he said,
"and don't think I'm knocking Vegas! They've got
too many of my markers out there for me to do that!
I have no interest in lobbying for legalized gambling
in Colorado. It would be spitting into the wind."

When the Overlook opens officially (there was a
gigantic and hugely successful party there some
time ago when the actual work was finished), the
newly painted, papered, and decorated rooms will
be occupied by a stellar guest list, ranging from chic
designer Corbat Stani to . . .

Smiling bemusedly, Jack turned the page. Now he
was looking at a full-page ad from the New York
Sunday *Times* travel section. On the page after that a
story on Derwent himself, a balding man with eyes
that pierced you even from an old newsprint photo.

He was wearing rimless spectacles and a forties-style pencil-line mustache that did nothing at all to make him look like Errol Flynn. His face was that of an accountant. It was the eyes that made him look like someone or something else.

Jack skimmed the article rapidly. He knew most of the information from a *Newsweek* story on Derwent the year before. Born poor in St. Paul, never finished high school, joined the Navy instead. Rose rapidly, then left in a bitter wrangle over the patent on a new type of propeller that he had designed. In the tug of war between the Navy and an unknown young man named Horace Derwent, Uncle Sam came off the predictable winner. But Uncle Sam had never gotten another patent, and there had been a lot of them.

In the late twenties and early thirties, Derwent turned to aviation. He bought out a bankrupt crop-dusting company, turned it into an airmail service, and prospered. More patents followed: a new mono-plane wing design, a bomb carriage used on the Flying Fortresses that had rained fire on Hamburg and Dresden and Berlin, a machine gun that was cooled by alcohol, a prototype of the ejection seat later used in United States jets.

And along the line, the accountant who lived in the same skin as the inventor kept piling up the investments. A piddling string of munition factories in New York and New Jersey. Five textile mills in New England. Chemical factories in the bankrupt and groaning South. At the end of the Depression his wealth had been nothing but a handful of controlling interests, bought at abysmally low prices, salable only at lower prices still. At one point Derwent boasted that he could liquidate completely and realize the price of a three-year-old Chevrolet.

There had been rumors, Jack recalled, that some of the means employed by Derwent to keep his head above water were less than savory. Involvement with bootlegging. Prostitution in the Midwest. Smuggling in the coastal areas of the South where his fertilizer factories were. Finally an association with the nascent western gambling interests.

Probably Derwent's most famous investment was the purchase of the foundering Top Mark Studios, which had not had a hit since their child star, Little Margery Morris, had died of a heroin overdose in 1934. She was fourteen. Little Margery, who had specialized in sweet seven-year-olds who saved marriages and the lives of dogs unjustly accused of killing chickens, had been given the biggest Hollywood funeral in history by Top Mark—the official story was that Little Margery had contracted a "wasting disease" while entertaining at a New York orphanage—and some cynics suggested the studio had laid out all that long green because it knew it was burying itself.

Derwent hired a keen businessman and raging sex maniac named Henry Finkel to run Top Mark, and in the two years before Pearl Harbor the studio ground out sixty movies, fifty-five of which glided right into the face of the Hayes Office and spit on its large blue nose. The other five were government training films. The feature films were huge successes. During one of them an unnamed costume designer had jury-rigged a strapless bra for the heroine to appear in during the Grand Ball scene, where she revealed everything except possibly the birthmark just below the cleft of her buttocks. Derwent received credit for this invention as well, and his reputation—or notoriety—grew.

The war had made him rich and he was still rich. Living in Chicago, seldom seen except for Derwent Enterprises board meetings (which he ran with an iron hand), it was rumored that he owned United Air Lines, Las Vegas (where he was known to have controlling interests in four hotel-casinos and some involvement in at least six others), Los Angeles, and the U.S.A. itself. Reputed to be a friend of royalty, presidents, and underworld kingpins, it was supposed by many that he was the richest man in the world.

But he had not been able to make a go of the Overlook, Jack thought. He put the scrapbook down for a moment and took the small notebook and mechanical pencil he always kept with him out of his breast pocket. He jotted "Look into H. Derwent, Sidwndr lbry?" He put the notebook back and picked up the scrapbook again. His face was preoccupied, his eyes distant. He wiped his mouth constantly with his hand as he turned the pages.

He skimmed the material that followed, making a mental note to read it more closely later. Press releases were pasted into many of the pages. So-and-so was expected at the Overlook next week, thus-and-such would be entertaining in the lounge (in Derwent's time it had been the Red-Eye Lounge). Many of the entertainers were Vegas names, and many of the guests were Top Mark executives and stars.

Then, in a clipping marked February 1, 1952:

MILLIONAIRE EXEC TO SELL COLORADO INVESTMENTS
Deal Made with California Investors on Overlook, Other Investments, Derwent Reveals

By Rodney Conklin, Financial Editor

In a terse communique yesterday from the Chicago offices of the monolithic Derwent Enterprises, it was revealed that millionaire (perhaps billionaire) Horace Derwent has sold out of Colorado in a stunning financial power play that will be completed by October 1, 1954. Derwent's investments include natural gas, coal, hydroelectric power, and a land development company called Colorado Sunshine, Inc., which owns or holds options on better than 500,000 acres of Colorado land.

The most famous Derwent holding in Colorado, the Overlook Hotel, has already been sold, Derwent revealed in a rare interview yesterday. The buyer was a California group of investors headed by Charles Grondin, a former director of the California Land Development Corporation. While Derwent refused to discuss price, informed sources . . .

He had sold out everything, lock, stock, and barrel. It wasn't just the Overlook. But somehow . . . somehow . . .

He wiped his lips with his hand and wished he had a drink. This would go better with a drink. He turned more pages.

The California group had opened the hotel for two seasons, and then sold it to a Colorado group called Mountainview Resorts. Mountainview went bankrupt in 1957 amid charges of corruption, nest-feathering, and cheating the stockholders. The president of the company shot himself two days after being subpoenaed to appear before a grand jury.

The hotel had been closed for the rest of the decade. There was a single story about it, a Sunday feature headlined FORMER GRAND HOTEL SINKING INTO DECAY. The accompanying photos wrenched at Jack's heart: the paint on the front porch peeling, the lawn a bald and scabrous mess, windows broken by storms and stones. This would be a part of the book, if he actually wrote it, too—the phoenix going down into the ashes to be reborn. He promised himself he would take care of the place, very good care. It seemed that before today he had never really understood the breadth of his responsibility to the Overlook. It was almost like having a responsibility to history.

In 1961 four writers, two of them Pulitzer Prize winners, had leased the Overlook and reopened it as a writers' school. That had lasted one year. One of the students had gotten drunk in his third-floor room, crashed out of the window somehow, and fell to his death on the cement terrace below. The paper hinted that it might have been suicide.

Any big hotels have got scandals, Watson had said, *just like every big hotel has got a ghost. Why? Hell, people come and go . . .*

Suddenly it seemed that he could almost feel the weight of the Overlook bearing down on him from above, one hundred and ten guest rooms, the storage rooms, kitchen, pantry, freezer, lounge, ballroom, dining room . . .

(In the room the women come and go)

(. . . and the Red Death held sway over all.)

He rubbed his lips and turned to the next page in the scrapbook. He was in the last third of it now, and for the first time he wondered consciously whose book this was, left atop the highest pile of records in the cellar.

A new headline, this one dated April 10, 1963.

LAS VEGAS GROUP BUYS FAMED
COLORADO HOTEL
Scenic Overlook to Become Key Club

Robert T. Leffing, spokesman for a group of investors going under the name of High Country Investments, announced today in Las Vegas that High Country has negotiated a deal for the famous Overlook Hotel, a resort located high in the Rockies. Leffing declined to mention the names of specific investors, but said the hotel would be turned into an exclusive "key club." He said that the group he represents hopes to sell membership to high-echelon executives in American and foreign companies.

    High Country also owns hotels in Montana, Wyoming, and Utah.

    The Overlook became world-known in the years 1946 to 1952 when it was owned by elusive mega-millionaire Horace Derwent, who . . .

The item on the next page was a mere squib, dated four months later. The Overlook had opened under its new management. Apparently the paper hadn't been able to find out or wasn't interested in who the key holders were, because no name was mentioned but High Country Investments—the most anonymous-sounding company name Jack had ever heard except for a chain of bike and appliance shops in western New England that went under the name of Business, Inc.

He turned the page and blinked down at the clipping pasted there.

MILLIONAIRE DERWENT BACK IN
COLORADO VIA BACK DOOR?
High Country Exec Revealed to be Charles Grondin

By Rodney Conklin, Financial Editor

The Overlook Hotel, a scenic pleasure palace in the Colorado high country and once the private plaything of millionaire Horace Derwent, is at the center of a financial tangle which is only now beginning to come to light.

    On April 10 of last year the hotel was purchased by a Las Vegas firm, High Country Investments, as a key club for wealthy executives of both foreign and domestic breeds. Now informed sources say that High Country is headed by Charles Grondin, 53, who was the head of California Land Development Corp. until 1959, when he resigned to take the position of executive veep in the Chicago home office of Derwent Enterprises.

This has led to speculation that High Country Investments may be controlled by Derwent, who may have acquired the Overlook for the second time, and under decidedly peculiar circumstances.

Grondin, who was indicted and acquitted on charges of tax evasion in 1960, could not be reached for comment, and Horace Derwent, who guards his own privacy jealously, had no comment when reached by telephone. State Representative Dick Bows of Golden has called for a complete investigation into . . .

That clipping was dated July 27, 1964. The next was a column from a Sunday paper that September. The byline belonged to Josh Brannigar, a muck-raking investigator of the Jack Anderson breed. Jack vaguely recalled that Brannigar had died in 1968 or '69.

MAFIA FREE-ZONE IN COLORADO?

By Josh Brannigar

It now seems possible that the newest r&r spot of Organization overlords in the U.S. is located at an out-of-the-way hotel nestled in the center of the

Rockies. The Overlook Hotel, a white elephant that has been run lucklessly by almost a dozen different groups and individuals since it first opened its doors in 1910, is now being operated as a security-jacketed "key club," ostensibly for unwinding businessmen. The question is, what business are the Overlook's key holders *really* in?

The members present during the week of August 16–23 may give us an idea. The list below was obtained by a former employee of High Country Investments, a company first believed to be a dummy company owned by Derwent Enterprises. It now seems more likely that Derwent's interest in High Country (if any) is outweighed by those of several Las Vegas gambling barons. And these same gaming honchos have been linked in the past to both suspected and convicted underworld kingpins.

Present at the Overlook during that sunny week in August were:

Charles Grondin, President of High Country Investments. When it became known in July of this year that he was running the High Country ship it was announced—considerably after the fact—that he had resigned his position in Derwent Enterprises previously. The silver-maned Grondin, who refused to talk to me for this column, has been tried once and acquitted on tax evasion charges (1960).

Charles "Baby Charlie" Battaglia, a 60-year-old Vegas impresario (controlling interests in The Greenback and The Lucky Bones on the Strip). Battaglia is a close personal friend of Grondin. His arrest record stretches back to 1932, when he was tried and acquitted in the gangland-style murder of Jack "Dutchy" Morgan. Federal authorities suspect his involvement in the drug traffic, prostitution, and murder for hire, but "Baby Charlie" has only been behind bars once, for income tax evasion in 1955–56.

Richard Scarne, the principal stockholder of Fun Time Automatic Machines. Fun Time makes slot machines for the Nevada crowd, pinball machines, and jukeboxes (Melody-Coin) for the rest of the country. He has done time for assault with a deadly weapon (1940), carrying a concealed weapon (1948), and conspiracy to commit tax fraud (1961).

Peter Zeiss, a Miami-based importer, now nearing 70. For the last five years Zeiss has been fighting deportation as an undesirable person. He has been convicted on charges of receiving and concealing stolen property (1958), and conspiracy to commit tax fraud (1954). Charming, distinguished, and courtly, Pete Zeiss is called "Poppa" by his intimates and has been tried on charges of murder and accessory to murder. A large stockholder in Scarne's Fun Time company, he also has known interests in four Las Vegas casinos.

Vittorio Gienelli, also known as "Vito the Chopper," tried twice for gangland-style murders, one of them the ax-murder of Boston vice overlord Frank Scoffy. Gienelli has been indicted twenty-three times, tried fourteen times, and convicted only once, for shoplifting in 1940. It has been said that in recent years Gienelli has become a power in the

organization's western operation, which is centered
in Las Vegas.

Carl "Jimmy-Ricks" Prashkin, a San Francisco
investor, reputed to be the heir apparent of the power
Gienelli now wields. Prashkin owns large blocks of
stock in Derwent Enterprises, High Country Investments, Fun Time Automatic Machines, and three
Vegas casinos. Prashkin is clean in America, but was
indicted in Mexico on fraud charges that were
dropped quickly three weeks after they were
brought. It has been suggested that Prashkin may be
in charge of laundering money skimmed from Vegas
casino operations and funneling the big bucks back
into the organization's legitimate western operations.
And such operations may now include the Overlook
Hotel in Colorado.

Other visitors during the current season
include . . .

There was more but Jack only skimmed it, constantly wiping his lips with his hand. A banker with
Las Vegas connections. Men from New York who
were apparently doing more in the Garment District
than making clothes. Men reputed to be involved
with drugs, vice, robbery, murder.

God, what a story! And they had all been here,
right above him, in those empty rooms. Screwing
expensive whores on the third floor, maybe. Drinking
magnums of champagne. Making deals that would
turn over millions of dollars, maybe in the very suite
of rooms where Presidents had stayed. There was a

story, all right. One hell of a story. A little frantically, he took out his notebook and jotted down another memo to check all of these people out at the library in Denver when the caretaking job was over. Every hotel has its ghost? The Overlook had a whole coven of them. First suicide, then the Mafia, what next?

The next clipping was an angry denial of Brannigar's charges by Charles Grondin. Jack smirked at it.

The clipping on the next page was so large that it had been folded. Jack unfolded it and gasped harshly. The picture there seemed to leap out at him: the wallpaper had been changed since June of 1966, but he knew that window and the view perfectly well. It was the western exposure of the Presidential Suite. Murder came next. The sitting room wall by the door leading into the bedroom was splashed with blood and what could only be white flecks of brain matter. A blank-faced cop was standing over a corpse hidden by a blanket. Jack stared, fascinated, and then his eyes moved up to the headline.

GANGLAND-STYLE SHOOTING
AT COLORADO HOTEL
Reputed Crime Overlord Shot at Mountain Key Club
Two Others Dead

SIDEWINDER, COLO (UPI)—Forty miles from this sleepy Colorado town, a gangland-style execution has occurred in the heart of the Rocky Mountains. The Overlook Hotel, purchased three years ago as an exclusive key club by a Las Vegas firm, was the site of a triple shotgun slaying. Two of the men were either the companions or bodyguards of Vittorio Gienelli, also known as "The Chopper" for his reputed involvement in a Boston slaying twenty years ago.

Police were summoned by Robert Norman, manager of the Overlook, who said he heard shots and that some of the guests reported two men wearing stockings on their faces and carrying guns had fled down the fire escape and driven off in a late-model tan convertible.

State Trooper Benjamin Moorer discovered two dead men, later identified as Victor T. Boorman and Roger Macassi, both of Las Vegas, outside the door of the Presidential Suite where two American Presidents have stayed. Inside, Moorer found the body of Gienelli sprawled on the floor. Gienelli was apparently fleeing his attackers when he was cut down. Moorer said Gienelli had been shot with heavy-gauge shotguns at close range.

Charles Grondin, the representative of the company which now owns the Overlook, could not be reached for . . .

Below the clipping, in heavy strokes of a ball-point pen, someone had written: *They took his balls along with them.* Jack stared at that for a long time, feeling cold. Whose book was this?

He turned the page at last, swallowing a click in his throat. Another column from Josh Brannigar, this one dated early 1967. He only read the headline:

NOTORIOUS HOTEL SOLD FOLLOWING MURDER OF
UNDERWORLD FIGURE.

The sheets following that clipping were blank.

(*They took his balls along with them.*)

He flipped back to the beginning, looking for a
name or address. Even a room number. Because he
felt quite sure that whoever had kept this little book
of memories had stayed at the hotel. But there was
nothing.

He was getting ready to go through all the clip-
pings, more closely this time, when a voice called
down the stairs: "Jack? Hon?"

Wendy.

He started, almost guiltily, as if he had been drinking secretly and she would smell the fumes on him.
Ridiculous. He scrubbed his lips with his hand and
called back, "Yeah, babe. Lookin for rats."

She was coming down. He heard her on the stairs,
then crossing the boiler room. Quickly, without
thinking why he might be doing it, he stuffed the
scrapbook under a pile of bills and invoices. He stood
up as she came through the arch.

"What in the world have you been doing down
here? It's almost three o'clock!"

He smiled. "Is it that late? I got rooting around
through all this stuff. Trying to find out where the
bodies are buried, I guess."

The words clanged back viciously in his mind.

She came closer, looking at him, and he unconsciously retreated a step, unable to help himself. He
knew what she was doing. She was trying to smell

liquor on him. Probably she wasn't even aware of it herself, but he was, and it made him feel both guilty and angry.

"Your mouth is bleeding," she said in a curiously flat tone.

"Huh?" He put his hand to his lips and winced at the thin stinging. His index finger came away bloody. His guilt increased.

"You've been rubbing your mouth again," she said.

He looked down and shrugged. "Yeah, I guess I have."

"It's been hell for you, hasn't it?"

"No, not so bad."

"Has it gotten any easier?"

He looked up at her and made his feet start moving. Once they were actually in motion it was easier. He crossed to his wife and slipped an arm around her waist. He brushed aside a sheaf of her blond hair and kissed her neck. "Yes," he said. "Where's Danny?"

"Oh, he's around somewhere. It's started to cloud up outside. Hungry?"

He slipped a hand over her taut, jeans-clad bottom with counterfeit lechery. "Like ze bear, madame."

"Watch out, slugger. Don't start something you can't finish."

"Fig-fig, madame?" he asked, still rubbing. "Dirty peectures? Unnatural positions?" As they went through the arch, he threw one glance back at the box where the scrapbook

(whose?)

was hidden. With the light out it was only a shadow. He was relieved that he had gotten Wendy away. His lust became less acted, more natural, as they approached the stairs.

"Maybe," she said. "After we get you a sandwich— *yeek!*" She twisted away from him, giggling. "That tickles!"

"It teekles nozzing like Jock Torrance would like to teekle you, madame."

"Lay off, Jock. How about a ham and cheese . . . for the first course?"

They went up the stairs together, and Jack didn't look over his shoulder again. But he thought of Watson's words:

Every big hotel has got a ghost. Why? Hell, people come and go . . .

Then Wendy shut the basement door behind them, closing it into darkness.

19

Outside 217

Danny was remembering the words of someone else who had worked at the Overlook during the season:

Her saying she'd seen something in one of the rooms where . . . a bad thing happened. That was in Room 217 and I want you to promise me you won't go in there, Danny . . . steer right clear . . .

It was a perfectly ordinary door, no different from any other door on the first two floors of the hotel. It was dark gray, halfway down a corridor that ran at right angles to the main second-floor hallway. The numbers on the door looked no different from the house numbers on the Boulder apartment building they had lived in. A 2, a 1, and a 7. Big deal. Just below them was a tiny glass circle, a peephole. Danny had tried several of them. From the inside you got a wide, fish-eye view of the corridor. From outside you could screw up your eye seven ways to Sunday and still not see a thing. A dirty gyp.

(Why are you here?)

After the walk behind the Overlook, he and Mommy had come back and she had fixed him his favorite lunch, a cheese and bologna sandwich plus Campbell's Bean Soup. They ate in Dick's kitchen and talked. The radio was on, getting thin and crackly music from the Estes Park station. The kitchen was his favorite place in the hotel, and he guessed that Mommy and Daddy must feel the same way, because after trying their meals in the dining room for three days or so, they had begun eating in the kitchen by mutual consent, setting up chairs around Dick Hallorann's butcher block, which was almost as big as their dining room table back in Stovington, anyway. The dining room had been too depressing, even with the lights on and the music playing from the tape cassette system in the office. You were still just one of three people sitting at a table surrounded by dozens of other tables, all empty, all covered with those transparent plastic dustcloths. Mommy said it was like having dinner in the middle of a Horace Walpole novel, and Daddy had laughed and agreed. Danny had no idea who Horace Walpole was, but he did know that Mommy's cooking had begun to taste better as soon as they began to eat it in the kitchen. He kept discovering little flashes of Dick Hallorann's personality lying around, and they reassured him like a warm touch.

Mommy had eaten half a sandwich, no soup. She said Daddy must have gone out for a walk of his own since both the VW and the hotel truck were in the parking lot. She said she was tired and might lie down for an hour or so, if he thought he could amuse himself and not get into trouble. Danny told her around a mouthful of cheese and bologna that he thought he could.

"Why don't you go out into the playground?" she asked him. "I thought you'd love that place, with a sandbox for your trucks and all."

He swallowed and the food went down his throat in a lump that was dry and hard. "Maybe I will," he said, turning to the radio and fiddling with it.

"And all those neat hedge animals," she said, taking his empty plate. "Your father's got to get out and trim them pretty soon."

"Yeah," he said.

(Just nasty things . . . once it had to do with those damn hedges clipped to look like animals . . .)

"If you see your father before I do, tell him I'm lying down."

"Sure, Mom."

She put the dirty dishes in the sink and came back over to him. "Are you happy here, Danny?"

He looked at her guilelessly, a milk mustache on his lip. "Uh-huh."

"No more bad dreams?"

"No." Tony had come to him once, one night while he was lying in bed, calling his name faintly and from far away. Danny had squeezed his eyes tightly shut until Tony had gone.

"You sure?"

"Yes, Mom."

She seemed satisfied. "How's your hand?"

He flexed it for her. "All better."

She nodded. Jack had taken the nest under the Pyrex bowl, full of frozen wasps, out to the incinerator in back of the equipment shed and burned it. They had seen no more wasps since. He had written to a lawyer in Boulder, enclosing the snaps of Danny's hand, and the lawyer had called back two days ago—that had put Jack in a foul temper all afternoon. The lawyer doubted if the company that had manufactured the bug bomb could be sued successfully because there was only Jack to testify that he had followed directions printed on the package. Jack had asked the lawyer if they couldn't purchase some others and test them for the same defect. Yes, the lawyer said, but the results were highly doubtful even if all the test bombs malfunctioned. He told Jack of a case that involved an extension ladder company and a man who had broken his back. Wendy had commiserated with Jack, but privately she had just been glad that Danny had gotten off as cheaply as he had. It was best to leave lawsuits to people who understood them, and that did not include the Torrances. And they had seen no more wasps since.

"Go and play, doc. Have fun."

But he hadn't had fun. He had wandered aimlessly around the hotel, poking into the maids' closets and the janitor's rooms, looking for something interesting, not finding it, a small boy padding along a dark blue carpet woven with twisting black lines. He had tried a room door from time to time, but of course they were all locked. The passkey was hanging down in the office, he knew where, but Daddy had told him he shouldn't touch that. And he didn't want to. Did he?

(*Why are you here?*)

There was nothing aimless about it after all. He had been drawn to Room 217 by a morbid kind of curiosity. He remembered a story Daddy had read to him once when he was drunk. That had been a long time ago, but the story was just as vivid now as when Daddy had read it to him. Mommy had scolded Daddy and asked what he was doing, reading a three-year-old baby something so horrible. The name of the story was *Bluebeard.* That was clear in his mind too, because he had thought at first Daddy was saying *Bluebird,* and there were no bluebirds in the story, or birds of any kind for that matter. Actually the story was about *Bluebeard*'s wife, a pretty lady that had corn-colored hair like Mommy. After *Bluebeard* married her, they lived in a big and ominous castle that was not unlike the Overlook. And every day *Bluebeard* went off to work and every day he would tell his pretty little wife not to look in a certain room, although the key to that room was hanging right on a hook, just like the passkey was hanging on the office wall downstairs. *Bluebeard*'s wife had gotten more and more curious about the locked room. She tried to peep through the keyhole the way Danny had tried to look through Room 217's peephole with similar unsatisfying results. There was even a picture of her getting down on her knees and trying to look *under* the door, but the crack wasn't wide enough. The door swung wide and . . .

The old fairy tale book had depicted her discovery in ghastly, loving detail. The image was burned on Danny's mind. The severed heads of *Bluebeard*'s seven previous wives were in the room, each one on its own pedestal, the eyes turned up to whites, the mouths unhinged and gaping in silent screams. They were somehow balanced on necks ragged from the broadsword's decapitating swing, and there was blood running down the pedestals.

Terrified, she had turned to flee from the room and the castle, only to discover *Bluebeard* standing in the doorway, his terrible eyes blazing. "I told you not to enter this room," *Bluebeard* said, unsheathing his sword. "Alas, in your curiosity you are like the other seven, and though I loved you best of all, your ending shall be as was theirs. Prepare to die, wretched woman!"

It seemed vaguely to Danny that the story had had a happy ending, but that had paled to insignificance beside the two dominant images: the taunting, maddening locked door with some great secret behind it, and the grisly secret itself, repeated more than half a dozen times. The locked door and behind it the heads, the severed heads.

His hand reached out and stroked the room's doorknob, almost furtively. He had no idea how long he had been here, standing hypnotized before the bland gray locked door.

(*And maybe three times I've thought I've seen things . . . nasty things . . .*)

But Mr. Hallorann—Dick—had also said he didn't think those things could hurt you. They were like scary pictures in a book, that was all. And maybe he wouldn't see anything. On the other hand . . .

He plunged his left hand into his pocket and it came out holding the passkey. It had been there all along, of course.

He held it by the square metal tab on the end which had OFFICE printed on it in Magic Marker. He twirled the key on its chain, watching it go around and around. After several minutes of this he stopped and slipped the passkey into the lock. It slid in smoothly, with no hitch, as if it had wanted to be there all along.

(*I've thought I've seen things . . . nasty things . . . promise me you won't go in there.*)

(*I promise.*)

And a promise was, of course, very important. Still, his curiosity itched at him as maddeningly as poison ivy in a place you aren't supposed to scratch. But it was a dreadful kind of curiosity, the kind that makes you peek through your fingers during the scariest parts of a scary movie. What was beyond that door would be no movie.

(*I don't think those things can hurt you . . . like scary pictures in a book . . .*)

Suddenly he reached out with his left hand, not sure of what it was going to do until it had removed the passkey and stuffed it back into his pocket. He stared at the door a moment longer, blue-gray eyes wide, then turned quickly and walked back down the corridor toward the main hallway that ran at right angles to the corridor he was in.

Something made him pause there and he wasn't sure what for a moment. Then he remembered that directly around this corner, on the way back to the stairs, there was one of those old-fashioned fire extinguishers curled up against the wall. Curled there like a dozing snake.

They weren't chemical-type extinguishers at all, Daddy said, although there were several of those in the kitchen. These were the forerunner of the modern sprinkler systems. The long canvas hoses hooked directly into the Overlook's plumbing system, and by turning a single valve you could become a one-man fire department. Daddy said that the chemical extinguishers, which sprayed foam or CO_2, were much better. The chemicals smothered fires, took away the oxygen they needed to burn, while a high-pressure spray might just spread the flames around. Daddy said that Mr. Ullman should replace the old-fashioned hoses right along with the old-fashioned boiler, but Mr. Ullman would probably do neither because he was a CHEAP PRICK. Danny knew that this was one of the worst epithets his father could summon. It was applied to certain doctors, dentists, and appliance repairmen, and also to the head of his English Department at Stovington, who had disallowed some of Daddy's book orders because he said the books would put them over budget. "Over budget, hell," he had fumed to Wendy—Danny had been listening from his bedroom where he was supposed to be asleep. "He's just saving the last five hundred bucks for himself, the CHEAP PRICK."

Danny looked around the corner.

The extinguisher was there, a flat hose folded back a dozen times on itself, the red tank attached to the wall. Above it was an ax in a glass case like a museum exhibit, with white words printed on a red background: IN CASE OF EMERGENCY, BREAK GLASS. Danny could read the word EMERGENCY, which was also the name of one of his favorite TV shows, but was unsure of the rest. But he didn't like the way the word was used in connection with that long flat hose. EMERGENCY was fire, explosions, car crashes, hospitals, sometimes death. And he didn't like the way that hose hung so blandly on the wall. When he was alone, he always skittered past these extinguishers as fast as he could. No particular reason. It just felt better to go fast. It felt safer.

Now, heart thumping loudly in his chest, he came around the corner and looked down the hall past the extinguisher to the stairs. Mommy was down there, sleeping. And if Daddy was back from his walk, he would probably be sitting in the kitchen, eating a sandwich and reading a book. He would just walk right past that old extinguisher and go downstairs.

He started toward it, moving closer to the far wall until his right arm was brushing the expensive silk paper. Twenty steps away. Fifteen. A dozen.

When he was ten steps away, the brass nozzle suddenly rolled off the fat loop it had been lying

(sleeping?)

on and fell to the hall carpet with a dull thump. It lay there, the dark bore of its muzzle pointing at

Danny. He stopped immediately, his shoulders twitching forward with the suddenness of his scare. His blood thumped thickly in his ears and temples. His mouth had gone dry and sour, his hands curled into fists. Yet the nozzle of the hose only lay there, its brass casing glowing mellowly, a loop of flat canvas leading back up to the red-painted frame bolted to the wall.

So it had fallen off, so what? It was only a fire extinguisher, nothing else. It was stupid to think that it looked like some poison snake from "Wide World of Animals" that had heard him and woken up. Even if the stitched canvas did look a little bit like scales. He would just step over it and go down the hall to the stairs, walking a little bit fast, maybe, to make sure it didn't snap out after him and curl around his foot . . .

He wiped his lips with his left hand, in unconscious imitation of his father, and took a step forward. No movement from the hose. Another step. Nothing. There, see how stupid you are? You got all worked up thinking about that dumb room and that dumb *Bluebeard* story and that hose was probably ready to fall off for the last five years. That's all.

Danny stared at the hose on the floor and thought of wasps.

Eight steps away, the nozzle of the hose gleamed peacefully at him from the rug as if to say: *Don't worry. I'm just a hose, that's all. And even if that isn't all, what I do to you won't be much worse than a bee sting. Or a wasp sting. What would I want to do to a nice little boy like you . . . except bite . . . and bite . . . and bite?*

Danny took another step, and another. His breath was dry and harsh in his throat. Panic was close now. He began to wish the hose *would* move, then at last he would know, he would be sure. He took another step and now he was within striking distance. But it's not going to *strike* at you, he thought hysterically. How can it *strike* at you, *bite* at you, when it's just a hose?

Maybe it's full of wasps.

His internal temperature plummeted to ten below zero. He stared at the black bore in the center of the nozzle, nearly hypnotized. Maybe it *was* full of wasps, secret wasps, their brown bodies bloated with poison, so full of autumn poison that it dripped from their stingers in clear drops of fluid.

Suddenly he knew that he was nearly frozen with terror; if he did not make his feet go now, they would become locked to the carpet and he would stay here, staring at the black hole in the center of the brass nozzle like a bird staring at a snake, he would stay here until his daddy found him and then what would happen?

With a high moan, he made himself run. As he reached the hose, some trick of the light made the nozzle seem to move, to revolve as if to strike, and he leaped high in the air above it; in his panicky state it seemed that his legs pushed him nearly all the way to the ceiling, that he could feel the stiff back hairs that formed his cowlick brushing the hallway's plaster ceiling, although later he knew that couldn't have been so.

He came down on the other side of the hose and ran, and suddenly he heard it behind him, coming for him, the soft dry whicker of that brass snake's head as it slithered rapidly along the carpet after him like a rattlesnake moving swiftly through a dry field of grass. It was coming for him, and suddenly the stairs seemed very far away; they seemed to retreat a running step into the distance for each running step he took toward them.

Daddy! he tried to scream, but his closed throat would not allow a word to pass. He was on his own. Behind him the sound grew louder, the dry sliding sound of the snake slipping swiftly over the carpet's dry hackles. At his heels now, perhaps rising up with clear poison dribbling from its brass snout.

Danny reached the stairs and had to pinwheel his arms crazily for balance. For one moment it seemed sure that he would cartwheel over and go head-for-heels to the bottom.

He threw a glance back over his shoulder.

The hose had not moved. It lay as it had lain, one loop off the frame, the brass nozzle on the hall floor, the nozzle pointing disinterestedly away from him. *You see, stupid?* he berated himself. *You made it all up, scaredy-cat. It was all your imagination, scaredy-cat, scaredy-cat.*

He clung to the stairway railing, his legs trembling in reaction.

(*It never chased you*)

his mind told him, and seized on that thought, and played it back.

(*never chased you, never chased you, never did, never did*)

It was nothing to be afraid of. Why, he could go back and put that hose right into its frame, if he wanted to. He could, but he didn't think he would. Because what if it had chased him and had gone back when it saw that it couldn't . . . quite . . . catch him?

The hose lay on the carpet, almost seeming to ask him if he would like to come back and try again.

Panting, Danny ran downstairs.

20

Talking to Mr. Ullman

The Sidewinder Public Library was a small, retiring building one block down from the town's business area. It was a modest, vine-covered building, and the wide concrete walk up to the door was lined with the corpses of last summer's flowers. On the lawn was a large bronze statue of a Civil War general Jack had never heard of, although he had been something of a Civil War buff in his teenage years.

The newspaper files were kept downstairs. They consisted of the Sidewinder *Gazette* that had gone bust in 1963, the Estes Park daily, and the Boulder *Camera*. No Denver papers at all.

Sighing, Jack settled for the *Camera*.

When the files reached 1965, the actual newspapers were replaced by spools of microfilm ("A federal grant," the librarian told him brightly. "We hope to do 1958 to '64 when the next check comes through, but they're so slow, aren't they? You will be careful, won't you? I just know you will. Call if you need me."). The only reading machine had a lens that had somehow gotten warped, and by the time Wendy put her hand on his shoulder some forty-five minutes after he had switched from the actual papers, he had a juicy thumper of a headache.

"Danny's in the park," she said, "but I don't want him outside too long. How much longer do you think you'll be?"

"Ten minutes," he said. Actually he had traced down the last of the Overlook's fascinating history—the years between the gangland shooting and the takeover by Stuart Ullman & Co. But he felt the same reticence about telling Wendy.

"What are you up to, anyway?" she asked. She ruffled his hair as she said it, but her voice was only half-teasing.

"Looking up some old Overlook history," he said.

"Any particular reason?"

"No,
(and why the hell are you so interested anyway?)
just curiosity."

"Find anything interesting?"

"Not much," he said, having to strive to keep his voice pleasant now. She was prying, just the way she had always pried and poked at him when they had been at Stovington and Danny was still a crib-infant. *Where are you going, Jack? When will you be back? How much money do you have with you? Are you going to take the car? Is Al going to be with you? Will one of you stay sober?* On and on. She had, pardon the expression, driven him to drink. Maybe that hadn't been the only reason, but by Christ let's tell the truth here and admit it was one of them. Nag and nag and nag until you wanted to clout her one just to shut her up and stop the

(*Where? When? How? Are you? Will you?*)

endless flow of questions. It could give you a real

(*headache? hangover?*)

headache. The reader. The damned reader with its distorted print. That was why he had such a cunt of a headache.

"Jack, are you all right? You look pale—"

He snapped his head away from her fingers. "*I am fine!*"

She recoiled from his hot eyes and tried on a smile that was a size too small. "Well . . . if you are . . . I'll just go and wait in the park with Danny . . ." She was starting away now, her smile dissolving into a bewildered expression of hurt.

He called to her: "Wendy?"

She looked back from the foot of the stairs. "What, Jack?"

He got up and went over to her. "I'm sorry, babe. I guess I'm really not all right. That machine . . . the lens is distorted. I've got a really bad headache. Got any aspirin?"

"Sure." She pawed in her purse and came up with a tin of Anacin. "You keep them."

He took the tin. "No Excedrin?" He saw the small recoil on her face and understood. It had been a bitter sort of joke between them at first, before the drinking had gotten too bad for jokes. He had claimed that Excedrin was the only nonprescription drug ever invented that could stop a hangover dead in its tracks. Absolutely the only one. He had begun to think of his morning-after thumpers as Excedrin Headache Number Vat 69.

"No Excedrin," she said. "Sorry."

"That's okay," he said, "these'll do just fine." But of course they wouldn't, and she should have known it, too. At times she could be the stupidest bitch . . .

"Want some water?" she asked brightly.

(*No I just want you to GET THE FUCK OUT OF HERE!*)

"I'll get some at the drinking fountain when I go up. Thanks."

"Okay." She started up the stairs, good legs moving gracefully under a short tan wool skirt. "We'll be in the park."

"Right." He slipped the tin of Anacin absently into his pocket, went back to the reader, and turned it off. When he was sure she was gone, he went upstairs himself. God, but it was a lousy headache. If you were going to have a vise-gripper like this one, you ought to at least be allowed the pleasure of a few drinks to balance it off.

He tried to put the thought from his mind, more ill tempered than ever. He went to the main desk, fingering a matchbook cover with a telephone number on it.

"Ma'am, do you have a pay telephone?"

"No, sir, but you can use mine if it's local."

"It's long-distance, sorry."

"Well then, I guess the drugstore would be your best bet. They have a booth."

"Thanks."

He went out and down the walk, past the anonymous Civil War general. He began to walk toward the business block, hands stuffed in his pockets, head thudding like a leaden bell. The sky was also leaden; it was November 7, and with the new month the weather had become threatening. There had been a number of snow flurries. There had been snow in October too, but that had melted. The new flurries had stayed, a light frosting over everything—it sparkled in the sunlight like fine crystal. But there had been no sunlight today, and even as he reached the drugstore it began to spit snow again.

The phone booth was at the back of the building and he was halfway down an aisle of patent medicines, jingling his change in his pocket, when his eyes fell on the white boxes with their green print. He took one of them to the cashier, paid, and went back to the telephone booth. He pulled the door closed, put his change and matchbook cover on the counter, and dialed O.

"Your call, please?"

"Fort Lauderdale, Florida, operator." He gave her the number there and the number in the booth. When she told him it would be a dollar ninety for the first three minutes, he dropped eight quarters into the slot, wincing each time the bell bonged in his ear.

Then, left in limbo with only the faraway clickings and gabblings of connection-making, he took the green bottle of Excedrin out of its box, pried up the white cap, and dropped the wad of cotton batting to the floor of the booth. Cradling the phone receiver between his ear and shoulder, he shook out three of the white tablets and lined them up on the counter beside his remaining change. He recapped the bottle and put it in his pocket.

At the other end, the phone was picked up on the first ring.

"Surf-Sand Resort, how may we help you?" the perky female voice asked.

"I'd like to speak with the manager, please."

"Do you mean Mr. Trent or—"

"I mean Mr. Ullman."

"I believe Mr. Ullman is busy, but if you would like me to check—"

"I would. Tell him it's Jack Torrance calling from Colorado."

"One moment, please." She put him on hold.

Jack's dislike for that cheap, self-important little prick Ullman came flooding back. He took one of the Excedrins from the counter, regarded it for a moment, then put it into his mouth and began to chew it, slowly and with relish. The taste flooded back like memory, making his saliva squirt in mingled pleasure and unhappiness. A dry, bitter taste, but a compelling one. He swallowed with a grimace. Chewing aspirin had been a habit with him in his drinking days; he hadn't done it at all since then. But when your headache was bad enough, a hangover headache or one like this one, chewing them seemed to make them get to work quicker. He had read somewhere that chewing aspirin could become addictive. Where had he read that, anyway? Frowning, he tried to think. And then Ullman came on the line.

"Torrance? What's the trouble?"

"No trouble," he said. "The boiler's okay and I haven't even gotten around to murdering my wife yet. I'm saving that until after the holidays, when things get dull."

"Very funny. Why are you calling? I'm a busy—"

"Busy man, yes, I understand that. I'm calling about some things that you didn't tell me during your history of the Overlook's great and honorable past. Like how Horace Derwent sold it to a bunch of Las Vegas sharpies who dealt it through so many dummy corporations that not even the IRS knew who really owned it. About how they waited until the time was right and then turned it into a playground for Mafia bigwigs, and about how it had to be shut down in 1966 when one of them got a little bit dead. Along with his bodyguards, who were standing outside the door to the Presidential Suite. Great place, the Overlook's Presidential Suite. Wilson, Harding, Roosevelt, Nixon, and Vito the Chopper, right?"

There was a moment of surprised silence on the other end of the line, and then Ullman said quietly: "I don't see how that can have any bearing on your job, Mr. Torrance. It—"

"The best part happened after Gienelli was shot, though, don't you think? Two more quick shuffles, now you see it and now you don't, and then the Overlook is suddenly owned by a private citizen, a woman named Sylvia Hunter . . . who just happened to be Sylvia Hunter Derwent from 1942 to 1948."

"Your three minutes are up," the operator said, "Signal when through."

"My dear Mr. Torrance, all of this is public knowledge . . . and ancient history."

"It formed no part of my knowledge," Jack said. "I doubt if many other people know it, either. Not all of it. They remember the Gienelli shooting, maybe, but I doubt if anybody has put together all the wondrous and strange shuffles the Overlook has been through since 1945. And it always seems like Derwent or a Derwent associate comes up with the door prize. What was Sylvia Hunter running up there in '67 and '68, Mr. Ullman? It was a whorehouse, wasn't it?"

"Torrance!" His shock crackled across two thousand miles of telephone cable without losing a thing.

Smiling, Jack popped another Excedrin into his mouth and chewed it.

"She sold out after a rather well known U.S. senator died of a heart attack up there. There were rumors that he was found naked except for black nylon stockings and a garter belt and a pair of high-heeled pumps. Patent-leather pumps, as a matter of fact."

"That's a vicious, damnable lie!" Ullman cried.

"Is it?" Jack asked. He was beginning to feel better. The headache was draining away. He took the last Excedrin and chewed it up, enjoying the bitter, powdery taste as the tablet shredded in his mouth.

"It was a very unfortunate occurrence," Ullman said. "Now what is the point, Torrance? If you're planning to write some ugly smear article . . . if this is some ill-conceived, stupid blackmail idea . . ."

"Nothing of the sort," Jack said. "I called because I didn't think you played square with me. And because——"

"Didn't play *square*?" Ullman cried. "My God, did you think I was going to share a large pile of dirty laundry with the hotel's *caretaker*? Who in heaven's name do you think you are? And how could those old stories possibly affect you anyway? Or do you think there are ghosts parading up and down the halls of the west wing wearing bedsheets and crying 'Woe!'?"

"No, I don't think there are any ghosts. But you raked up a lot of my personal history before you gave me the job. You had me on the carpet, quizzing me about my ability to take care of your hotel like a little boy in front of the teacher's desk for peeing in the coatroom. You embarrassed me."

"I just do not believe your cheek, your bloody damned impertinence," Ullman said. He sounded as if he might be choking. "I'd like to sack you. And perhaps I will."

"I think Al Shockley might object. Strenuously."

"And I think you may have finally overestimated Mr. Shockley's commitment to you, Mr. Torrance."

For a moment Jack's headache came back in all its thudding glory, and he closed his eyes against the pain. As if from a distance away he heard himself ask: "Who owns the Overlook now? Is it still Derwent Enterprises? Or are you too smallfry to know?"

"I think that will do, Mr. Torrance. You are an employee of the hotel, no different from a busboy or a kitchen pot scrubber. I have no intention of—"

"Okay, I'll write Al," Jack said. "He'll know; after all, he's on the Board of Directors. And I might just add a little P.S. to the effect that—"

"Derwent doesn't own it."

"What? I couldn't quite make that out."

"I said Derwent doesn't own it. The stockholders are all Easterners. Your friend Mr. Shockley owns the largest block of stock himself, better than thirty-five per cent. You would know better than I if he has any ties to Derwent."

"Who else?"

"I have no intention of divulging the names of the other stockholders to you, Mr. Torrance. I intend to bring this whole matter to the attention of—"

"One other question."

"I am under no obligation to you."

"Most of the Overlook's history—savory and unsavory alike—I found in a scrapbook that was in the cellar. Big thing with white leather covers. Gold thread for binding. Do you have any idea whose scrapbook that might be?"

"None at all."

"Is it possible it could have belonged to Grady? The caretaker who killed himself?"

"Mr. Torrance," Ullman said in tones of deepest frost, "I am by no means sure that Mr. Grady could read, let alone dig out the rotten apples you have been wasting my time with."

"I'm thinking of writing a book about the Overlook Hotel. I thought if I actually got through it, the owner of the scrapbook would like to have an acknowledgment at the front."

"I think writing a book about the Overlook would be very unwise," Ullman said. "Especially a book done from your . . . uh, point of view."

"Your opinion doesn't surprise me." His headache was all gone now. There had been that one flash of pain, and that was all. His mind felt sharp and accurate, all the way down to millimeters. It was the way he usually felt only when the writing was going extremely well or when he had a three-drink buzz on. That was another thing he had forgotten about Excedrin; he didn't know if it worked for others, but for him crunching three tablets was like an instant high.

Now he said: "What you'd like is some sort of commissioned guidebook that you could hand out free to the guests when they checked in. Something with a lot of glossy photos of the mountains at sunrise and sunset and a lemon-meringue text to go with it. Also a section on the colorful people who have stayed there, of course excluding the really colorful ones like Gienelli and his friends."

"If I felt I could fire you and be a hundred per cent certain of my own job instead of just ninety-five per cent," Ullman said in clipped, strangled tones, "I would fire you right this minute, over the telephone. But since I feel that five per cent of uncertainty, I intend to call Mr. Shockley the moment you're off the line . . . which will be soon, or so I devoutly hope."

Jack said, "There isn't going to be anything in the book that isn't true, you know. There's no need to dress it up."

(*Why are you baiting him? Do you want to be fired?*)

"I don't care if Chapter Five is about the Pope of Rome screwing the shade of the Virgin Mary," Ullman said, his voice rising. "I want you out of my hotel!"

"*It's not your hotel!*" Jack screamed, and slammed the receiver into its cradle.

He sat on the stool breathing hard, a little scared now,

(a little? hell, a lot)

wondering why in the name of God he had called Ullman in the first place.

(*You lost your temper again, Jack.*)

Yes. Yes, he had. No sense trying to deny it. And the hell of it was, he had no idea how much influence that cheap little prick had over Al, no more than he knew how much bullshit Al would take from him in the name of auld lang syne. If Ullman was as good as he claimed to be, and if he gave Al a he-goes-or-I-go ultimatum, might not Al be forced to take it? He closed his eyes and tried to imagine telling Wendy. Guess what, babe? I lost another job. This time I had to go through two thousand miles of Bell Telephone cable to find someone to punch out, but I managed it.

He opened his eyes and wiped his mouth with his handkerchief. He wanted a drink. Hell, he *needed* one. There was a café just down the street, surely he had time for a quick beer on his way up to the park, just one to lay the dust . . .

He clenched his hands together helplessly.

The question recurred: Why had he called Ullman in the first place? The number of the Surf-Sand in Lauderdale had been written in a small notebook by the phone and the CB radio in the office—plumbers' numbers, carpenters, glaziers, electricians, others. Jack had copied it onto the matchbook cover shortly after getting out of bed, the idea of calling Ullman full-blown and gleeful in his mind. But to what purpose? Once, during the drinking phase, Wendy had accused him of desiring his own destruction but not possessing the necessary moral fiber to support a full-blown deathwish. So he manufactured ways in which other people could do it, lopping a piece at a time off himself and their family. Could it be true? Was he afraid somewhere inside that the Overlook might be just what he needed to finish his play and generally collect up his shit and get it together? Was he blowing the whistle on himself? Please God no, don't let it be that way. Please.

He closed his eyes and an image immediately arose on the darkened screen of his inner lids: sticking his hand through that hole in the shingles to pull out the rotted flashing, the sudden needling sting, his own agonized, startled cry in the still and unheeding air: *Oh you goddamn fucking son of a bitch* . . .

Replaced with an image two years earlier, himself stumbling into the house at three in the morning, drunk, falling over a table and sprawling full-length on the floor, cursing, waking Wendy up on the couch. Wendy turning on the light, seeing his clothes ripped

and smeared from some cloudy parking-lot scuffle that
had occurred at a vaguely remembered honky-tonk just
over the New Hampshire border hours before, crusted
blood under his nose, now looking up at his wife, blinking stupidly in the light like a mole in the sunshine, and
Wendy saying dully, *You son of a bitch, you woke Danny up.
If you don't care about yourself, can't you care a little bit about
us? Oh, why do I even bother talking to you?*

The telephone rang, making him jump. He
snatched it off the cradle, illogically sure it must be
either Ullman or Al Shockley. "What?" he barked.

"Your overtime, sir. Three dollars and fifty cents."

"I'll have to break some ones," he said. "Wait a
minute."

He put the phone on the shelf, deposited his last
six quarters, then went out to the cashier to get more.
He performed the transaction automatically, his mind
running in a single closed circle like a squirrel on an
exercise wheel.

Why had he called Ullman?

Because Ullman had embarrassed him? He had
been embarrassed before, and by real masters—the
Grand Master, of course, being himself. Simply to
crow at the man, expose his hypocrisy? Jack didn't
think he was that petty. His mind tried to seize on
the scrapbook as a valid reason, but that wouldn't
hold water either. The chances of Ullman knowing
who the owner was were no more than two in a thousand. At the interview, he had treated the cellar as
another country—a nasty underdeveloped one at
that. If he had really wanted to know, he would have

called Watson, whose winter number was also in the office notebook. Even Watson would not have been a sure thing, but surer than Ullman.

And telling him about the book idea, that had been another stupid thing. Incredibly stupid. Besides jeopardizing his job, he could be closing off wide channels of information once Ullman called around and told people to beware of New Englanders bearing questions about the Overlook Hotel. He could have done his researches quietly, mailing off polite letters, perhaps even arranging some interviews in the spring . . . and then laughed up his sleeve at Ullman's rage when the book came out and he was safely away—The Masked Author Strikes Again. Instead he had made that damned senseless call, lost his temper, antagonized Ullman, and brought out all of the hotel manager's Little Caesar tendencies. Why? If it wasn't an effort to get himself thrown out of the good job Al had snagged for him, then what was it?

He deposited the rest of the money in the slots and hung up the phone. It really was the senseless kind of thing he might have done if he had been drunk. But he had been sober; dead cold sober.

Walking out of the drugstore he crunched another Excedrin into his mouth, grimacing yet relishing the bitter taste.

On the walk outside he met Wendy and Danny.

"Hey, we were just coming after you," Wendy said. "Snowing, don't you know."

Jack blinked up. "So it is." It was snowing hard. Sidewinder's main street was already heavily powdered, the center line obscured. Danny had his head tilted up to the white sky, his mouth open and his tongue out to catch some of the fat flakes drifting down.

"Do you think this is it?" Wendy asked.

Jack shrugged. "I don't know. I was hoping for another week or two of grace. We still might get it."

Grace, that was it.

(*I'm sorry, Al. Grace, your mercy. For your mercy. One more chance. I am heartily sorry—*)

How many times, over how many years, had he—a grown man—asked for the mercy of another chance? He was suddenly so sick of himself, so revolted, that he could have groaned aloud.

"How's your headache?" she asked, studying him closely.

He put an arm around her and hugged her tight. "Better. Come on, you two, let's go home while we still can."

They walked back to where the hotel truck was slant-parked against the curb, Jack in the middle, his left arm around Wendy's shoulders, his right hand holding Danny's hand. He had called it home for the first time, for better or worse.

As he got behind the truck's wheel it occurred to him that while he was fascinated by the Overlook, he didn't much like it. He wasn't sure it was good for either his wife or his son or himself. Maybe that was why he had called Ullman.

To be fired while there was still time.

He backed the truck out of its parking space and headed them out of town and up into the mountains.

21

Night Thoughts

It was ten o'clock. Their quarters were filled with counterfeit sleep.

Jack lay on his side facing the wall, eyes open, listening to Wendy's slow and regular breathing. The taste of dissolved aspirin was still on his tongue, making it feel rough and slightly numb. Al Shockley had called at quarter of six, quarter of eight back East. Wendy had been downstairs with Danny, sitting in front of the lobby fireplace and reading.

"Person to person," the operator said, "for Mr. Jack Torrance."

"Speaking." He had switched the phone to his right hand, had dug his handkerchief out of his back pocket with his left, and had wiped his tender lips with it. Then he lit a cigarette.

Al's voice then, strong in his ear: "Jacky-boy, what in the name of God are you up to?"

"Hi, Al." He snuffed the cigarette and groped for the Excedrin bottle.

"What's going on, Jack? I got this *weird* phone call from Stuart Ullman this afternoon. And when Stu Ullman calls long-distance out of his own pocket, you know the shit has hit the fan."

"Ullman has nothing to worry about, Al. Neither do you."

"What exactly is the nothing we don't have to worry about? Stu made it sound like a cross between blackmail and a *National Enquirer* feature on the Overlook. Talk to me, boy."

"I wanted to poke him a little," Jack said. "When I came up here to be interviewed, he had to drag out all my dirty laundry. Drinking problem. Lost your last job for racking over a student. Wonder if you're the right man for this. Et cetera. The thing that bugged me was that he was bringing all this up because he loved the goddam hotel so much. The beautiful Overlook. The traditional Overlook. The bloody sacred Overlook. Well, I found a scrapbook in the basement. Somebody had put together all the less savory aspects of Ullman's cathedral, and it looked to me like a little black mass had been going on after hours."

"I hope that's metaphorical, Jack." Al's voice sounded frighteningly cold.

"It is. But I did find out—"

"I know the hotel's history."

Jack ran a hand through his hair. "So I called him up and poked him with it. I admit it wasn't very bright, and I sure wouldn't do it again. End of story."

"Stu says you're planning to do a little dirty-laun-dry-airing yourself."

"Stu is an asshole!" he barked into the phone. "I told him I had an idea of writing about the Overlook, yes. I do. I think this place forms an index of the whole post-World War II American character. That sounds like an inflated claim, stated so baldly . . . I know it does . . . but it's all here, Al! My God, it could be a *great* book. But it's far in the future, I can promise you that, I've got more on my plate right now than I can eat, and—"

"Jack, that's not good enough."

He found himself gaping at the black receiver of the phone, unable to believe what he had surely heard. "What? Al, did you say—?"

"I said what I said. How long is far in the future, Jack? For you it may be two years, maybe five. For me it's thirty or forty, because I expect to be associated with the Overlook for a long time. The thought of you doing some sort of a scum-job on my hotel and passing it off as a great piece of American writing, that makes me sick."

Jack was speechless.

"I tried to help you, Jacky-boy. We went through the war together, and I thought I owed you some help. You remember the war?"

"I remember it," he muttered, but the coals of resentment had begun to glow around his heart. First Ullman, then Wendy, now Al. What was this? National Let's Pick Jack Torrance Apart Week? He clamped his lips more tightly together, reached for his cigarettes, and knocked them off onto the floor. Had he ever liked this cheap prick talking to him from his mahogany-lined den in Vermont? Had he really?

"Before you hit that Hatfield kid," Al was saying, "I had talked the Board out of letting you go and even had them swung around to considering tenure. You blew that one for yourself. I got you this hotel thing, a nice quiet place for you to get yourself together, finish your play, and wait it out until Harry Effinger and I could convince the rest of those guys that they made a big mistake. Now it looks like you want to chew my arm off on your way to a bigger killing. Is that the way you say thanks to your friends, Jack?"

"No," he whispered.

He didn't dare say more. His head was throbbing with the hot, acid-etched words that wanted to get out. He tried desperately to think of Danny and Wendy, depending on him, Danny and Wendy sitting peacefully downstairs in front of the fire and working on the first of the second-grade reading primers, thinking everything was A-OK. If he lost this job, what then? Off to California in that tired old VW with the disintegrating fuel pump like a family of dustbowl Okies? He told himself he would get down on his knees and beg Al before he let that happen, but still the words struggled to pour out, and the hand holding the hot wires of his rage felt greased.

"What?" Al said sharply.

"No," he said. "That is not the way I treat my friends. And you know it."

"How do I know it? At the worst, you're planning to smear my hotel by digging up bodies that were decently buried years ago. At the best, you call up my temperamental but extremely competent hotel manager and work him into a frenzy as part of some . . . some stupid kid's game."

"It was more than a game, Al. It's easier for you. You don't have to take some rich friend's charity. You don't need a friend in court because you *are* the court. The fact that you were one step from a brown-bag lush goes pretty much unmentioned, doesn't it?"

"I suppose it does," Al said. His voice had dropped a notch and he sounded tired of the whole thing. "But Jack, Jack . . . I can't help that. I can't change that."

"I know," Jack said emptily. "Am I fired? I guess you better tell me if I am."

"Not if you'll do two things for me."

"All right."

"Hadn't you better hear the conditions before you accept them?"

"No. Give me your deal and I'll take it. There's Wendy and Danny to think about. If you want my balls, I'll send them airmail."

"Are you sure self-pity is a luxury you can afford, Jack?"

He had closed his eyes and slid an Excedrin between his dry lips. "At this point I feel it's the only one I can afford. Fire away . . . no pun intended."

Al was silent for a moment. Then he said: "First, no more calls to Ullman. Not even if the place burns down. If that happens, call the maintenance man, that guy who swears all the time, you know who I mean . . ."

"Watson."

"Yes."

"Okay. Done."

"Second, you promise me, Jack. Word of honor. No book about a famous Colorado mountain hotel with a history."

For a moment his rage was so great that he literally could not speak. The blood beat loudly in his ears. It was like getting a call from some twentieth-century Medici prince . . . no portraits of my family with their warts showing, please, or back to the rabble you'll go. I subsidize no pictures but pretty pictures. When you paint the daughter of my good friend and business partner, please omit birthmark or back to the rabble you'll go. Of course we're friends . . . we are both civilized men, aren't we? We've shared bed and board and bottle. We'll always be friends, and the dog collar I have on you will always be ignored by mutual consent, and I'll take good and benevolent care of you. All I ask in return is your soul. Small item. We can even ignore the fact that you've handed it over, the way we ignore the dog collar. Remember, my talented friend, there are Michelangelos begging everywhere in the streets of Rome . . .

"Jack? You there?"

He made a strangled noise that was intended to be the word yes.

Al's voice was firm and very sure of itself. "I really don't think I'm asking so much, Jack. And there will be other books. You just can't expect me to subsidize you while you . . ."

"All right, agreed."

"I don't want you to think I'm trying to control your artistic life, Jack. You know me better than that. It's just that—"

"Al?"

"What?"

"Is Derwent still involved with the Overlook? Somehow?"

"I don't see how that can possibly be any concern of yours, Jack."

"No," he said distantly. "I suppose it isn't. Listen, Al, I think I hear Wendy calling me for something. I'll get back to you."

"Sure thing, Jacky-boy. We'll have a good talk. How are things? Dry?"

(YOU'VE GOT YOUR POUND OF FLESH BLOOD AND ALL NOW CAN'T YOU LEAVE ME ALONE?)

"As a bone."

"Here too. I'm actually beginning to enjoy sobriety. If—"

"I'll get back, Al. Wendy—"

"Sure. Okay."

And so he had hung up and that was when the cramps had come, hitting him like lightning bolts, making him curl up in front of the telephone like a penitent, hands over his belly, head throbbing like a monstrous bladder.

The moving wasp, having stung, moves on . . .

It had passed a little when Wendy came upstairs and asked him who had been on the phone.

"Al," he said. "He called to ask how things were going. I said they were fine."

"Jack, you look terrible. Are you sick?"

"Headache's back. I'm going to bed early. No sense trying to write."

"Can I get you some warm milk?"

He smiled wanly. "That would be nice."

And now he lay beside her, feeling her warm and sleeping thigh against his own. Thinking of the conversation with Al, how he had groveled, still made him hot and cold by turns. Someday there would be a reckoning. Someday there would be a book, not the soft and thoughtful thing he had first considered, but a gem-hard work of research, photo section and all, and he would pull apart the entire Overlook history, nasty, incestuous ownership deals and all. He would spread it all out for the reader like a dissected crayfish. And if Al Shockley had connections with the Derwent empire, then God help him.

Strung up like piano wire, he lay staring into the dark, knowing it might be hours yet before he could sleep.

Wendy Torrance lay on her back, eyes closed, listening to the sound of her husband's slumber—the long inhale, the brief hold, the slightly guttural exhale. Where did he go when he slept, she wondered. To some amusement park, a Great Barrington of dreams where all the rides were free and there was no wife-mother along to tell them they'd had enough hotdogs or that they'd better be going if they wanted to get home by dark? Or was it some fathoms-deep bar where the drinking never stopped and the batwings were always propped open and all the old companions were gathered around the electronic hockey game, glasses in hand, Al Shockley prominent among them with his tie loosened and the top button of his shirt undone? A place where both she and Danny were excluded and the boogie went on endlessly?

Wendy was worried about him, the old, helpless worry that she had hoped was behind her forever in Vermont, as if worry could somehow not cross state lines. She didn't like what the Overlook seemed to be doing to Jack and Danny.

The most frightening thing, vaporous and unmentioned, perhaps unmentionable, was that all of Jack's drinking symptoms had come back, one by one . . . all but the drink itself. The constant wiping of the lips with hand or handkerchief, as if to rid them of excess moisture. Long pauses at the typewriter, more balls of paper in the wastebasket. There had been a bottle of Excedrin on the telephone table tonight after Al had called him, but no water glass. He had been chewing them again. He got irritated over little things. He would unconsciously start snapping his fingers in a nervous rhythm when things got too quiet. Increased profanity. She had begun to worry about his temper, too. It would almost come as a relief if he would lose it, blow off steam, in much the same way that he went down to the basement first thing in the morning and last thing at night to dump the press on the boiler. It would almost be good to see him curse and kick a chair across the room or slam a door. But those things, always an integral part of his temperament, had almost wholly ceased. Yet she had the feeling that Jack was more and more often angry with her or Danny, but was refusing to let it out. The boiler had a pressure gauge: old, cracked, clotted with grease, but still workable. Jack had none. She had never been able to read him very well. Danny could, but Danny wasn't talking.

And the call from Al. At about the same time it had come, Danny had lost all interest in the story they had been reading. He left her to sit by the fire and crossed to the main desk where Jack had constructed a roadway for his matchbox cars and trucks. The Violent Violet Volkswagen was there and Danny had begun to push it rapidly back and forth. Pretending to read her own book but actually looking at Danny over the top of it, she had seen an odd amalgam of the ways she and Jack expressed anxiety. The wiping of the lips. Running both hands nervously through his hair, as she had done while waiting for Jack to come home from his round of the bars. She couldn't believe Al had called just to "ask how things were going." If you wanted to shoot the bull, you called Al. When Al called you, that was business.

Later, when she had come back downstairs, she had found Danny curled up by the fire again, reading the second-grade-primer adventures of Joe and Rachel at the circus with their daddy in complete, absorbed attention. The fidgety distraction had completely disappeared. Watching him, she had been struck again by the eerie certainty that Danny knew more and understood more than there was room for in Dr. ("Just call me Bill") Edmonds's philosophy.

"Hey, time for bed, doc," she'd said.

"Yeah, okay." He marked his place in the book and stood up.

"Wash up and brush your teeth."

"Okay."

"Don't forget to use the floss."

"I won't."

They stood side by side for a moment, watching the wax and wane of the coals of the fire. Most of the lobby was chilly and drafty, but this circle around the fireplace was magically warm, and hard to leave.

"It was Uncle Al on the phone," she said casually.

"Oh yeah?" Totally unsurprised.

"I wonder if Uncle Al was mad at Daddy," she said, still casually.

"Yeah, he sure was," Danny said, still watching the fire. "He didn't want Daddy to write the book."

"What book, Danny?"

"About the hotel."

The question framed on her lips was one she and Jack had asked Danny a thousand times: *How do you know that?* She hadn't asked him. She didn't want to upset him before bed, or make him aware that they were casually discussing his knowledge of things he had no way of knowing at all. And he *did* know, she was convinced of that. Dr. Edmonds's patter about inductive reasoning and subconscious logic was just that: patter. Her sister . . . how had Danny known she was thinking about Aileen in the waiting room that day? And

(*I dreamed Daddy had an accident.*)

She shook her head, as if to clear it. "Go wash up, doc."

"Okay." He ran up the stairs toward their quarters. Frowning, she had gone into the kitchen to warm Jack's milk in a saucepan.

And now, lying wakeful in her bed and listening to her husband's breathing and the wind outside (miraculously, they'd had only another flurry that afternoon; still no heavy snow), she let her mind turn fully to her lovely, troubling son, born with a caul over his face, a simple tissue of membrane that doctors saw perhaps once in every seven hundred births, a tissue that the old wives' tales said betokened the second sight.

She decided that it was time to talk to Danny about the Overlook . . . and high time she tried to get Danny to talk to her. Tomorrow. For sure. The two of them would be going down to the Sidewinder Public Library to see if they could get him some second-grade-level books on an extended loan through the winter, and she would talk to him. And frankly. With that thought she felt a little easier, and at last began to drift toward sleep.

Danny lay awake in his bedroom, eyes open, left arm encircling his aged and slightly worse-for-wear Pooh (Pooh had lost one shoe-button eye and was oozing stuffing from half a dozen sprung seams), listening to his parents sleep in their bedroom. He felt as if he were standing unwilling guard over them. The nights were the worst of all. He hated the nights and the constant howl of the wind around the west side of the hotel.

His glider floated overhead from a string. On his bureau the VW model, brought up from the roadway setup downstairs, glowed a dimly fluorescent purple. His books were in the bookcase, his coloring books on the desk. *A place for everything and everything in its place,* Mommy said. *Then you know where it is when you want it.* But now things had been misplaced. Things were missing. Worse still, things had been *added,* things you couldn't quite see, like in one of those pictures that said CAN YOU SEE THE INDIANS? And if you strained and squinted, you could see some of them— the thing you had taken for a cactus at first glance was really a brave with a knife clamped in his teeth, and there were others hiding in the rocks, and you could even see one of their evil, merciless faces peering through the spokes of a covered wagon wheel. But you could never see all of them, and that was what made you uneasy. Because it was the ones you couldn't see that would sneak up behind you, a toma-hawk in one hand and a scalping knife in the other . . .

He shifted uneasily in his bed, his eyes searching out the comforting glow of the night light. Things were worse here. He knew that much for sure. At first they hadn't been so bad, but little by little . . . his daddy thought about drinking a lot more. Sometimes he was angry at Mommy and didn't know why. He went around wiping his lips with his handkerchief and his eyes were far away and cloudy. Mommy was worried about him and Danny, too. He didn't have to shine into her to know that; it had been in the anxious way she had questioned him on the day the fire hose had seemed to turn into a snake. Mr. Hallorann said he thought all mothers could shine a little bit, and she had known on that day that something had happened. But not what.

He had almost told her, but a couple of things had held him back. He knew that the doctor in Sidewinder had dismissed Tony and the things that Tony showed him as perfectly

(well almost)

normal. His mother might not believe him if he told her about the hose. Worse, she might believe him in the wrong way, might think he was LOSING HIS MARBLES. He understood a little about LOSING YOUR MARBLES, not as much as he did about GETTING A BABY, which his mommy had explained to him the year before at some length, but enough.

Once, at nursery school, his friend Scott had pointed out a boy named Robin Stenger, who was moping around the swings with a face almost long enough to step on. Robin's father taught arithmetic at Daddy's school, and Scott's daddy taught history there. Most of the kids at the nursery school were associated either with Stovington Prep or with the small IBM plant just outside of town. The prep kids chummed in one group, the IBM kids in another. There were cross-friendships, of course, but it was natural enough for the kids whose fathers knew each other to more or less stick together. When there was an adult scandal in one group, it almost always filtered down to the children in some wildly mutated form or other, but it rarely jumped to the other group.

He and Scotty were sitting in the play rocketship when Scotty jerked his thumb at Robin and said: "You know that kid?"

"Yeah," Danny said.

Scott leaned forward. "His dad LOST HIS MARBLES last night. They took him away."

"Yeah? Just for losing some marbles?"

Scotty looked disgusted. "He went crazy. You know." Scott crossed his eyes, flopped out his tongue, and twirled his index fingers in large elliptical orbits around his ears. "They took him to THE BUGHOUSE."

"Wow," Danny said. "When will they let him come back?"

"Never-never-never," Scotty said darkly.

In the course of that day and the next, Danny heard that

a.) Mr. Stenger had tried to kill everybody in his family, including Robin, with his World War II souvenir pistol;

b.) Mr. Stenger ripped the house to pieces while he was STINKO;

c.) Mr. Stenger had been discovered eating a bowl of dead bugs and grass like they were cereal and milk and crying while he did it;

d.) Mr. Stenger had tried to strangle his wife with a stocking when the Red Sox lost a big ball game.

Finally, too troubled to keep it to himself, he had asked Daddy about Mr. Stenger. His daddy had taken him on his lap and had explained that Mr. Stenger had been under a great deal of strain, some of it about his family and some about his job and some of it about things that nobody but doctors could understand. He had been having crying fits, and three nights ago he had gotten crying and couldn't stop it and had broken a lot of things in the Stenger home. It wasn't LOSING YOUR MARBLES, Daddy said, it was HAVING A BREAKDOWN, and Mr. Stenger wasn't in a BUGHOUSE, but in a SANNY-TARIUM. But despite Daddy's careful explanations, Danny was scared. There didn't seem to be any difference at all between LOSING YOUR MARBLES and HAVING A BREAKDOWN, and whether you called it a BUGHOUSE or a SANNY-TARIUM, there were still bars on the windows and they wouldn't let you out if you wanted to go. And his father, quite innocently, had confirmed another of Scotty's phrases unchanged, one that filled Danny with a vague and unformed dread. In the place where Mr. Stenger now lived, there were THE MEN IN THE WHITE COATS. They came to get you in a truck with no windows, a truck that was gravestone gray. It rolled up to the curb in front of your house and THE MEN IN THE WHITE COATS got out and took you away from your family and made you live in a room with soft walls. And if you wanted to write home, you had to do it with Crayolas.

"When will they let him come back?" Danny asked his father.

"Just as soon as he's better, doc."

"But when will that be?" Danny had persisted.

"Dan," Jack said, "NO ONE KNOWS."

And that was the worst of all. It was another way of saying never-never-never. A month later, Robin's mother took him out of nursery school and they moved away from Stovington without Mr. Stenger.

That had been over a year ago, after Daddy stopped taking the Bad Stuff but before he had lost his job. Danny still thought about it often. Sometimes when he fell down or bumped his head or had a bellyache, he would begin to cry and the memory would flash over him, accompanied by the fear that he would not be able to stop crying, that he would just go on and on, weeping and wailing, until his daddy went to the phone, dialed it, and said: "Hello? This is Jack Torrance at 149 Mapleline Way. My son here can't stop crying. Please send THE MEN IN THE WHITE COATS to take him to the SANNY-TARIUM. That's right, he's LOST HIS MARBLES. Thank you." And the gray truck with no windows would come rolling up to *his* door, they would load him in, still weeping hysterically, and take him away. When would he see his mommy and daddy again? NO ONE KNOWS.

It was this fear that had kept him silent. A year older, he was quite sure that his daddy and mommy wouldn't let him be taken away for thinking a fire hose was a snake, his *rational* mind was sure of that, but still, when he thought of telling them, that old memory rose up like a stone filling his mouth and blocking words. It wasn't like Tony; Tony had always seemed perfectly natural (until the bad dreams, of course), and his parents had also seemed to accept Tony as a more or less natural phenomenon. Things like Tony came from being BRIGHT, which they both assumed he was (the same way they assumed they were BRIGHT), but a fire hose that turned into a snake, or seeing blood and brains on the wall of the Presidential Sweet when no one else could, those things would not be natural. They had already taken him to see a regular doctor. Was it not reasonable to assume that THE MEN IN THE WHITE COATS might come next?

Still he might have told them except he was sure, sooner or later, that they would want to take him away from the hotel. And he wanted desperately to get away from the Overlook. But he also knew that this was his daddy's last chance, that he was here at the Overlook to do more than take care of the place. He was here to work on his papers. To get over losing his job. To love Mommy/Wendy. And until very recently, it had seemed that all those things were happening. It was only lately that Daddy had begun to have trouble. Since he found those papers.

(*This inhuman place makes human monsters.*)

What did that mean? He had prayed to God, but God hadn't told him. And what would Daddy do if he stopped working here? He had tried to find out from Daddy's mind, and had become more and more convinced that Daddy didn't know. The strongest proof had come earlier this evening when Uncle Al had called his daddy up on the phone and said mean things and Daddy didn't dare say anything back because Uncle Al could fire him from this job just the way that Mr. Crommert, the Stovington headmaster, and the Board of Directors had fired him from his schoolteaching job. And Daddy was scared to death of that, for him and Mommy as well as himself.

So he didn't dare say anything. He could only watch helplessly and hope that there really weren't any Indians at all, or if there were that they would be content to wait for bigger game and let their little three-wagon train pass unmolested.

But he couldn't believe it, no matter how hard he tried.

Things were worse at the Overlook now.

The snow was coming, and when it did, any poor options he had would be abrogated. And after the snow, what? What then, when they were shut in and at the mercy of whatever might have only been toying with them before?

(*Come out here and take your medicine!*)

What then? REDRUM.

He shivered in his bed and turned over again. He could read more now. Tomorrow maybe he would try to call Tony, he would try to make Tony show him exactly what REDRUM was and if there was any way he could prevent it. He would risk the nightmares. He had to *know*.

Danny was still awake long after his parents' false sleep had become the real thing. He rolled in his bed, twisting the sheets, grappling with a problem years too big for him, awake in the night like a single sentinel on picket. And sometime after midnight, he slept too and then only the wind was awake, prying at the hotel and hooting in its gables under the bright gimlet gaze of the stars.

22

In the Truck

I see a bad moon a-rising.
I see trouble on the way.
I see earthquakes and lightnin'.
I see bad times today.
Don't go 'round tonight,
It's bound to take your life,
*There's a bad moon on the rise.**

Someone had added a very old Buick car radio under the hotel truck's dashboard, and now, tinny and choked with static, the distinctive sound of John Fogerty's Creedence Clearwater Revival band came out of the speaker. Wendy and Danny were on their way down to Sidewinder. The day was clear and bright. Danny was turning Jack's orange library card over and over in his hands and seemed cheerful enough, but Wendy thought he looked drawn and

*"Bad Moon Rising," by J. C. Fogerty, © 1969 Jondora Music, Berkeley, California. Used by permission. All rights reserved. International copyright secured.

tired, as if he hadn't been sleeping enough and was
going on nervous energy alone.

The song ended and the disc jockey came on.
"Yeah, that's Creedence. And speakin of bad moon, it
looks like it may be risin over the KMTX listening
area before long, hard as it is to believe with the beautiful, springlike weather we've enjoyed for the last
couple-three days. The KMTX Fearless Forecaster
says high pressure will give way by one o'clock this
afternoon to a widespread low-pressure area which is
just gonna grind to a stop in our KMTX area, up
where the air is rare. Temperatures will fall rapidly,
and precipitation should start around dusk. Elevations
under seven thousand feet, including the metro-
Denver area, can expect a mixture of sleet and snow,
perhaps freezing on some roads, and nothin but snow
up here, cuz. We're lookin at one to three inches
below seven thousand and possible accumulations of
six to ten inches in Central Colorado and on the Slope.
The Highway Advisory Board says that if you're plan-
nin to tour the mountains in your car this afternoon or
tonight, you should remember that the chain law will
be in effect. And don't go nowhere unless you have to.
Remember," the announcer added jocularly, "that's
how the Donners got into trouble. They just weren't
as close to the nearest Seven-Eleven as they thought."

A Clairol commercial came on, and Wendy
reached down and snapped the radio off. "You mind?"

"Huh-uh, that's okay." He glanced out at the sky,
which was bright blue. "Guess Daddy picked just the
right day to trim those hedge animals, didn't he?"

"I guess he did," Wendy said.

"Sure doesn't look much like snow, though," Danny added hopefully.

"Getting cold feet?" Wendy asked. She was still thinking about that crack the disc jockey had made about the Donner Party.

"Nah, I guess not."

Well, she thought, this is the time. If you're going to bring it up, do it now or forever hold your peace.

"Danny," she said, making her voice as casual as possible, "would you be happier if we went away from the Overlook? If we didn't stay the winter?"

Danny looked down at his hands. "I guess so," he said. "Yeah. But it's Daddy's job."

"Sometimes," she said carefully, "I get the idea that Daddy might be happier away from the Overlook, too." They passed a sign which read SIDEWINDER 18 MI. and then she took the truck cautiously around a hairpin and shifted up into second. She took no chances on these downgrades; they scared her silly.

"Do you really think so?" Danny asked. He looked at her with interest for a moment and then shook his head. "No, I don't think so."

"Why not?"

"Because he's worried about us," Danny said, choosing his words carefully. It was hard to explain, he understood so little of it himself. He found himself harking back to an incident he had told Mr. Hallorann about, the big kid looking at department store TV sets and wanting to steal one. That had been distressing, but at least it had been clear what was going on, even to Danny, then little more than an infant. But grownups were always in a turmoil, every possible action muddied over by thoughts of the consequences, by self-doubt, by *selfimage*, by feelings of love and responsibility. Every possible choice seemed to have drawbacks, and sometimes he didn't understand why the drawbacks *were* drawbacks. It was very hard.

"He thinks . . ." Danny began again, and then looked at his mother quickly. She was watching the road, not looking at him, and he felt he could go on.

"He thinks maybe we'll be lonely. And then he thinks that he likes it here and it's a good place for us. He loves us and doesn't want us to be lonely . . . or sad . . . but he thinks even if we are, it might be okay in the LONGRUN. Do you know LONGRUN?"

She nodded. "Yes, dear. I do."

"He's worried that if we left he couldn't get another job. That we'd have to beg, or something."

"Is that all?"

"No, but the rest is all mixed up. Because he's different now."

"Yes," she said, almost sighing. The grade eased a little and she shifted cautiously back to third gear.

"I'm not making this up, Mommy. Honest to God."

"I know that," she said, and smiled. "Did Tony tell you?"

"No," he said. "I just know. That doctor didn't believe in Tony, did he?"

"Never mind that doctor," she said. "I believe in Tony. I don't know what he is or who he is, if he's a part of you that's special or if he comes from . . . somewhere outside, but I do believe in him, Danny. And if you . . . he . . . think we should go, we will. The two of us will go and be together with Daddy again in the spring."

He looked at her with sharp hope. "Where? A motel?"

"Hon, we couldn't afford a motel. It would have to be at my mother's."

The hope in Danny's face died out. "I know—" he said, and stopped.

"What?"

"Nothing," he muttered.

She shifted back to second as the grade steepened again. "No, doc, please don't say that. This talk is something we should have had weeks ago, I think. So please. What is it you know? I won't be mad. I can't be mad, because this is too important. Talk straight to me."

"I know how you feel about her," Danny said, and sighed.

"How do I feel?"

"Bad," Danny said, and then rhyming, singsong, frightening her: "Bad. Sad. Mad. It's like she wasn't your mommy at all. Like she wanted to eat you." He looked at her, frightened. "And I don't like it there. She's always thinking about how she would be better for me than you. And how she could get me away from you. Mommy, I don't want to go there. I'd rather be at the Overlook than there."

Wendy was shaken. Was it that bad between her and her mother? God, what hell for the boy if it was and he could really read their thoughts for each other. She suddenly felt more naked than naked, as if she had been caught in an obscene act.

"All right," she said. "All right, Danny."

"You're mad at me," he said in a small, near-to-tears voice.

"No, I'm not. Really I'm not. I'm just sort of shook up." They were passing a SIDEWINDER 15 MI. sign, and Wendy relaxed a little. From here on in the road was better.

"I want to ask you one more question, Danny. I want you to answer it as truthfully as you can. Will you do that?"

"Yes, Mommy," he said, almost whispering.

"Has your daddy been drinking again?"

"No," he said, and smothered the two words that rose behind his lips after that simple negative: *Not yet.*

Wendy relaxed a little more. She put a hand on Danny's jeans-clad leg and squeezed it. "Your daddy has tried very hard," she said softly. "Because he loves us. And we love him, don't we?"

He nodded gravely.

Speaking almost to herself she went on: "He's not a perfect man, but he has tried . . . Danny, he's tried so hard! When he . . . stopped . . . he went through a kind of hell. He's still going through it. I think if it hadn't been for us, he would have just let go. I want to do what's right. And I don't know. Should we go? Stay? It's like a choice between the fat and the fire."

"I know."

"Would you do something for me, doc?"

"What?"

"Try to make Tony come. Right now. Ask him if we're safe at the Overlook."

"I already tried," Danny said slowly. "This morning."

"What happened?" Wendy asked. "What did he say?"

"He didn't come," Danny said. "Tony didn't come." And he suddenly burst into tears.

"Danny," she said, alarmed. "Honey, don't do that. Please—" The truck swerved across the double yellow line and she pulled it back, scared.

"Don't take me to Gramma's," Danny said through his tears. "Please, Mommy, I don't want to go there, I want to stay with Daddy—"

"All right," she said softly. "All right, that's what we'll do." She took a Kleenex out of the pocket of her Western-style shirt and handed it to him. "We'll stay. And everything will be fine. Just fine."

23

In the Playground

Jack came out onto the porch, tugging the tab of his zipper up under his chin, blinking into the bright air. In his left hand he was holding a battery-powered hedge-clipper. He tugged a fresh handkerchief out of his back pocket with his right hand, swiped his lips with it, and tucked it away. Snow, they had said on the radio. It was hard to believe, even though he could see the clouds building up on the far horizon.

He started down the path to the topiary, switching the hedge-clipper over to the other hand. It wouldn't be a long job, he thought; a little touch-up would do it. The cold nights had surely stunted their growth. The rabbit's ears looked a little fuzzy, and two of the dog's legs had grown fuzzy green bonespurs, but the lions and the buffalo looked fine. Just a little haircut would do the trick, and then let the snow come.

The concrete path ended as abruptly as a diving board. He stepped off it and walked past the drained pool to the gravel path which wound through the hedge sculptures and into the playground itself. He

walked over to the rabbit and pushed the button on
the handle of the clippers. It hummed into quiet life.

"Hi, Br'er Rabbit," Jack said. "How are you
today? A little off the top and get some of the extra
off your ears? Fine. Say, did you hear the one about
the traveling salesman and the old lady with a pet
poodle?"

His voice sounded unnatural and stupid in his
ears, and he stopped. It occurred to him that he
didn't care much for these hedge animals. It had
always seemed slightly perverted to him to clip and
torture a plain old hedge into something that it wasn't.
Along one of the highways in Vermont there had
been a hedge billboard on a high slope overlooking
the road, advertising some kind of ice cream. Making
nature peddle ice cream, that was just wrong. It was
grotesque.

(*You weren't hired to philosophize, Torrance.*)

Ah, that was true. So true. He clipped along the
rabbit's ears, brushing a small litter of sticks and
twigs off onto the grass. The hedge-clipper hummed
in that low and rather disgustingly metallic way that
all battery-powered appliances seem to have. The sun
was brilliant but it held no warmth, and now it wasn't
so hard to believe that snow was coming.

Working quickly, knowing that to stop and think
when you were at this kind of a task usually meant
making a mistake, Jack touched up the rabbit's
"face" (up this close it didn't look like a face at all,
but he knew that at a distance of twenty paces or so
light and shadow would seem to suggest one; that,

and the viewer's imagination) and then zipped the clippers along its belly.

That done, he shut the clippers off, walked down toward the playground, and then turned back abruptly to get it all at once, the entire rabbit. Yes, it looked all right. Well, he would do the dog next.

"But if it was my hotel," he said, "I'd cut the whole damn bunch of you down." He would, too. Just cut them down and resod the lawn where they'd been and put in half a dozen small metal tables with gaily colored umbrellas. People could have cocktails on the Overlook's lawn in the summer sun. Sloe gin fizzes and margaritas and pink ladies and all those sweet tourist drinks. A rum and tonic, maybe. Jack took his handkerchief out of his back pocket and slowly rubbed his lips with it.

"Come on, come on," he said softly. That was nothing to be thinking about.

He was going to start back, and then some impulse made him change his mind and he went down to the playground instead. It was funny how you never knew kids, he thought. He and Wendy had expected Danny would love the playground; it had everything a kid could want. But Jack didn't think the boy had been down half a dozen times, if that. He supposed if there had been another kid to play with, it would have been different.

The gate squeaked slightly as he let himself in, and then there was crushed gravel crunching under his feet. He went first to the playhouse, the perfect scale model of the Overlook itself. It came up to his lower thigh, just about Danny's height when he was standing up. Jack hunkered down and looked in the third-floor windows.

"The giant has come to eat you all up in your beds," he said hollowly. "Kiss your Triple A rating goodbye." But that wasn't funny, either. You could open the house simply by pulling it apart—it opened on a hidden hinge. The inside was a disappointment. The walls were painted, but the place was mostly hollow. But of course it would have to be, he told himself, or how else could the kids get inside? What play furniture might go with the place in the summer was gone, probably packed away in the equipment shed. He closed it up and heard the small click as the latch closed.

He walked over to the slide, set the hedge-clipper down, and after a glance back at the driveway to make sure Wendy and Danny hadn't returned, he climbed to the top and sat down. This was the big kids' slide, but the fit was still uncomfortably tight for his grownup ass. How long had it been since he had been on a slide? Twenty years? It didn't seem possible it could be that long, it didn't *feel* that long, but it had to be that, or more. He could remember his old man taking him to the park in Berlin when he had been Danny's age, and he had done the whole bit—slide, swings, teeter-totters, everything. He and the old man would have a hotdog lunch and buy peanuts from the man with the cart afterward. They would sit on a bench to eat them and dusky clouds of pigeons would flock around their feet.

"Goddam scavenger birds," his dad would say, "don't you feed them, Jacky." But they would both end up feeding them, and giggling at the way they ran after the nuts, the greedy way they ran after the nuts. Jack didn't think the old man had ever taken his brothers to the park. Jack had been his favorite, and even so Jack had taken his lumps when the old man was drunk, which was a lot of the time. But Jack had loved him for as long as he was able, long after the rest of the family could only hate and fear him.

He pushed off with his hands and went to the bottom, but the trip was unsatisfying. The slide, unused, had too much friction and no really pleasant speed could be built up. And his ass was just too big. His adult feet thumped into the slight dip where thousands of children's feet had landed before him. He stood up, brushed at the seat of his pants, and looked at the hedge-clipper. But instead of going back to it he went to the swings, which were also a disappointment. The chains had built up rust since the close of the season, and they squealed like things in pain. Jack promised himself he would oil them in the spring.

You better stop it, he advised himself. You're not a kid anymore. You don't need this place to prove it.

But he went on to the cement rings—they were too small for him and he passed them up—and then to the security fence which marked the edge of the grounds. He curled his fingers through the links and looked through, the sun crosshatching shadow-lines on his face like a man behind bars. He recognized the similarity himself and he shook the chain link, put a harried expression on his face, and whispered: "Lemme outta here! Lemme outta here!" But for the third time, not funny. It was time to get back to work.

That was when he heard the sound behind him.

He turned around quickly, frowning, embarrassed, wondering if someone had seen him fooling around down here in kiddie country. His eyes ticked off the slides, the opposing angles of the seesaws, the swings in which only the wind sat. Beyond all that to the gate and the low fence that divided the playground from the lawn and the topiary—the lions gathered protectively around the path, the rabbit bent over as if to crop grass, the buffalo ready to charge, the crouching dog. Beyond them, the putting green and the hotel itself. From here he could even see the raised lip of the roque court on the Overlook's western side.

Everything was just as it had been. So why had the flesh of his face and hands begun to creep, and why had the hair along the back of his neck begun to stand up, as if the flesh back there had suddenly tightened?

He squinted up at the hotel again, but that was no answer. It simply stood there, its windows dark, a tiny thread of smoke curling from the chimney, coming from the banked fire in the lobby.

(Buster, you better get going or they're going to come back and wonder if you were doing anything all the while.)

Sure, get going. Because the snow was coming and he had to get the damn hedges trimmed. It was part of the agreement. Besides, they wouldn't dare—

(Who wouldn't? What wouldn't? Dare do what?)

He began to walk back toward the hedge-clipper at the foot of the big kids' slide, and the sound of his feet crunching on the crushed stone seemed abnormally loud. Now the flesh on his testicles had begun to creep too, and his buttocks felt hard and heavy, like stone.

(*Jesus, what is this?*)

He stopped by the hedge-clipper, but made no move to pick it up. Yes, there was something different. In the topiary. And it was so simple, so easy to see, that he just wasn't picking it up. Come on, he scolded himself, you just trimmed the fucking rabbit, so what's the

(that's it)

His breath stopped in his throat.

The rabbit was down on all fours, cropping grass. Its belly was against the ground. But not ten minutes ago it had been up on its hind legs, of course it had been, he had trimmed its ears . . . and its belly.

His eyes darted to the dog. When he had come down the path it had been sitting up, as if begging for a sweet. Now it was crouched, head tilted, the clipped wedge of mouth seeming to snarl silently. And the lions—

(oh no, baby, oh no, uh-uh, no way)

the lions were closer to the path. The two on his right had subtly changed positions, had drawn closer together. The tail of the one on the left now almost jutted out over the path. When he had come past them and through the gate, that lion had been on the right and he was quite sure its tail had been curled around it.

They were no longer protecting the path; they were blocking it.

Jack put his hand suddenly over his eyes and then took it away. The picture didn't change. A soft sigh, too quiet to be a groan, escaped him. In his drinking days he had always been afraid of something like this happening. But when you were a heavy drinker you called it the DTs—good old Ray Milland in *Lost Weekend,* seeing the bugs coming out of the walls.

What did you call it when you were cold sober?

The question was meant to be rhetorical, but his mind answered it

(you call it insanity)

nevertheless.

Staring at the hedge animals, he realized something *had* changed while he had his hand over his eyes. The dog had moved closer. No longer crouching, it seemed to be in a running posture, haunches flexed, one front leg forward, the other back. The hedge mouth yawned wider, the pruned sticks looked sharp and vicious. And now he fancied he could see faint eye indentations in the greenery as well. Looking at him.

Why do they have to be trimmed? he thought hysterically. *They're perfect.*

Another soft sound. He involuntarily backed up a step when he looked at the lions. One of the two on the right seemed to have drawn slightly ahead of the other. Its head was lowered. One paw had stolen almost all the way to the low fence. Dear God, what next?

(*next it leaps over and gobbles you up like something in an evil nursery fable*)

It was like that game they had played when they were kids, red light. One person was "it," and while he turned his back and counted to ten, the other players crept forward. When "it" got to ten, he whirled around and if he caught anyone moving, they were out of the game. The others remained frozen in statue postures until "it" turned his back and counted again. They got closer and closer, and at last, somewhere between five and ten, you would feel a hand on your back . . .

Gravel rattled on the path.

He jerked his head around to look at the dog and it was halfway down the pathway, just behind the lions now, its mouth wide and yawning. Before, it had only been a hedge clipped in the general shape of a dog, something that lost all definition when you got up close to it. But now Jack could see that it had been clipped to look like a German shepherd, and shepherds could be mean. You could train shepherds to kill.

A low rustling sound.

The lion on the left had advanced all the way to the fence now; its muzzle was touching the boards. It seemed to be grinning at him. Jack backed up another two steps. His head was thudding crazily and he could feel the dry rasp of his breath in his throat. Now the buffalo had moved, circling to the right, behind and around the rabbit. The head was lowered, the green hedge horns pointing at him. The thing was, you couldn't watch all of them. Not all at once.

He began to make a whining sound, unaware in his locked concentration that he was making any sound at all. His eyes darted from one hedge creature to the next, trying to *see* them move. The wind gusted, making a hungry rattling sound in the close-matted branches. What kind of sound would there be if they got him? But of course he knew. A snapping, rending, breaking sound. It would be—

(no no NO NO I WILL NOT BELIEVE THIS   NOT AT   ALL!)

He clapped his hands over his eyes, clutching at his hair, his forehead, his throbbing temples. And he stood like that for a long time, dread building until he could stand it no longer and he pulled his hands away with a cry.

By the putting green the dog was sitting up, as if begging for a scrap. The buffalo was gazing with disinterest back toward the roque court, as it had been when Jack had come down with the clippers. The rabbit stood on its hind legs, ears up to catch the faintest sound, freshly clipped belly exposed. The lions, rooted into place, stood beside the path.

He stood frozen for a long time, the harsh breath in his throat finally slowing. He reached for his cigarettes and shook four of them out onto the gravel. He stooped down and picked them up, groped for them, never taking his eyes from the topiary for fear the animals would begin to move again. He picked them up, stuffed three carelessly back into the pack, and lit the fourth. After two deep drags he dropped it and crushed it out. He went to the hedge-clipper and picked it up.

"I'm very tired," he said, and now it seemed okay to talk out loud. It didn't seem crazy at all. "I've been under a strain. The wasps . . . the play . . . Al calling me like that. But it's all right."

He began to trudge back up to the hotel. Part of his mind tugged fretfully at him, tried to make him detour around the hedge animals, but he went directly up the gravel path, through them. A faint breeze rattled through them, that was all. He had imagined the whole thing. He had had a bad scare but it was over now.

In the Overlook's kitchen he paused to take two Excedrin and then went downstairs and looked at papers until he heard the dim sound of the hotel truck rattling into the driveway. He went up to meet them. He felt all right. He saw no need to mention his hallucination. He'd had a bad scare but it was over now.

24

Snow

It was dusk.

They stood on the porch in the fading light, Jack in the middle, his left arm around Danny's shoulders and his right arm around Wendy's waist. Together they watched as the decision was taken out of their hands.

The sky had been completely clouded over by two-thirty and it had begun to snow an hour later, and this time you didn't need a weatherman to tell you it was serious snow, no flurry that was going to melt or blow away when the evening wind started to whoop. At first it had fallen in perfectly straight lines, building up a snowcover that coated everything evenly, but now, an hour after it had started, the wind had begun to blow from the northwest and the snow had begun to drift against the porch and the sides of the Overlook's driveway. Beyond the grounds the highway had disappeared under an even blanket of white. The hedge animals were also gone, but when Wendy and Danny had gotten home, she had commended him on the good job he had done. Do you think so? he had asked, and said no more. Now the hedges were buried under amorphous white cloaks.

Curiously, all of them were thinking different thoughts but feeling the same emotion: relief. The bridge had been crossed.

"Will it ever be spring?" Wendy murmured.

Jack squeezed her tighter. "Before you know it. What do you say we go in and have some supper? It's cold out here."

She smiled. All afternoon Jack had seemed distant and . . . well, odd. Now he sounded more like his normal self. "Fine by me. How about you, Danny?"

"Sure."

So they went in together, leaving the wind to build to the low-pitched scream that would go on all night—a sound they would get to know well. Flakes of snow swirled and danced across the porch. The Overlook faced it as it had for nearly three quarters of a century, its darkened windows now bearded with snow, indifferent to the fact that it was now cut off from the world. Or possibly it was pleased with the prospect. Inside its shell the three of them went about their early evening routine, like microbes trapped in the intestine of a monster.

25

Inside 217

A week and a half later two feet of snow lay white and crisp and even on the grounds of the Overlook Hotel. The hedge menagerie was buried up to its haunches; the rabbit, frozen on its hind legs, seemed to be rising from a white pool. Some of the drifts were over five feet deep. The wind was constantly changing them, sculpting them into sinuous, dunelike shapes. Twice Jack had snowshoed clumsily around to the equipment shed for his shovel to clear the porch, the third time he shrugged, simply cleared a path through the towering drift lying against the door, and let Danny amuse himself by sledding to the right and left of the path. The truly heroic drifts lay against the Overlook's west side; some of them towered to a height of twenty feet, and beyond them the ground was scoured bare to the grass by the constant wind-flow. The first-floor windows were covered, and the view from the dining room which Jack had so admired on closing day was now no more exciting than a view of a blank movie screen. Their phone had been out for the last eight days, and the CB radio in Ullman's office was now their only communications link with the outside world.

It snowed every day now, sometimes only brief flurries that powdered the glittering snow crust, sometimes for real, the low whistle of the wind cranking up to a womanish shriek that made the old hotel rock and groan alarmingly even in its deep cradle of snow. Night temperatures had not gotten above 10°, and although the thermometer by the kitchen service entrance sometimes got as high as 25° in the early afternoons, the steady knife edge of the wind made it uncomfortable to go out without a ski mask. But they all did go out on the days when the sun shone, usually wearing two sets of clothing and mittens on over their gloves. Getting out was almost a compulsive thing; the hotel was circled with the double track of Danny's Flexible Flyer. The permutations were nearly endless: Danny riding while his parents pulled; Daddy riding and laughing while Wendy and Danny tried to pull (it was just possible for them to pull him on the icy crust, and flatly impossible when powder covered it); Danny and Mommy riding; Wendy riding by herself while her menfolk pulled and puffed white vapor like drayhorses, pretending she was heavier than she was. They laughed a great deal on these sled excursions around the house, but the whooping and impersonal voice of the wind, so huge and hollowly sincere, made their laughter seem tinny and forced.

They had seen caribou tracks in the snow and once the caribou themselves, a group of five standing motionlessly below the security fence. They had all taken turns with Jack's Zeiss-Ikon binoculars to see them better, and looking at them had given Wendy a weird, unreal feeling: they were standing leg-deep in the snow that covered the highway, and it came to her that between now and the spring thaw, the road belonged more to the caribou than it did to them. Now the things that men had made up here were neutralized. The caribou understood that, she believed. She had put the binoculars down and had said something about starting lunch and in the kitchen she had cried a little, trying to rid herself of the awful pent-up feeling that sometimes fell on her like a large, pressing hand over her heart. She thought of the caribou. She thought of the wasps Jack had put out on the service entrance platform, under the Pyrex bowl, to freeze.

There were plenty of snowshoes hung from nails in the equipment shed, and Jack found a pair to fit each of them, although Danny's pair was quite a bit out-sized. Jack did well with them. Although he had not snowshoed since his boyhood in Berlin, New Hampshire, he retaught himself quickly. Wendy didn't care much for it—even fifteen minutes of tramping around on the outsized laced paddles made her legs and ankles ache outrageously—but Danny was intrigued and working hard to pick up the knack. He still fell often, but Jack was pleased with his progress. He said that by February Danny would be skipping circles around both of them.

*   *   *

This day was overcast, and by noon the sky had already begun to spit snow. The radio was promising another eight to twelve inches and chanting hosannas to Precipitation, that great god of Colorado skiers. Wendy, sitting in the bedroom and knitting a scarf, thought to herself that she knew exactly what the skiers could do with all that snow. She knew exactly where they could put it.

Jack was in the cellar. He had gone down to check the furnace and boiler—such checks had become a ritual with him since the snow had closed them in—and after satisfying himself that everything was going well he had wandered through the arch, screwed the light-bulb on, and had seated himself in an old and cob-webby camp chair he had found. He was leafing through the old records and papers, constantly wiping his mouth with his handkerchief as he did so. Confinement had leached his skin of its autumn tan, and as he sat hunched over the yellowed, crackling sheets, his reddish-blond hair tumbling untidily over his forehead, he looked slightly lunatic. He had found some odd things tucked in among the invoices, bills of lading, receipts. Disquieting things. A bloody strip of sheeting. A dismembered teddy bear that seemed to have been slashed to pieces. A crumpled sheet of violet ladies' stationery, a ghost of perfume still clinging to it beneath the musk of age, a note begun and left unfinished in faded blue ink: "*Dearest Tommy, I can't think so well up here as I'd hoped, about us I mean, of course, who else? Ha. Ha. Things keep getting in the way. I've had strange dreams about things going bump in the night, can you believe that and*" That was all. The note was dated June 27, 1934. He found a hand puppet that seemed to be either a witch or a warlock . . . something with long teeth and a pointy hat, at any rate. It had been improbably tucked between a bundle of natural-gas receipts and a bundle of receipts for Vichy water. And something that seemed to be a poem, scribbled on the back of a menu in dark pencil: "*Medoc/are you here?/I've been sleepwalking again, my dear./The plants are moving under the rug.*" No date on the menu, and no name on the poem, if it was a poem. Elusive, but fascinating. It seemed to him that these things were like pieces in a jigsaw, things that would eventually fit together if he could find the right linking pieces. And so he kept looking, jumping and wiping his lips every time the furnace roared into life behind him.

Danny was standing outside Room 217 again.

The passkey was in his pocket. He was staring at the door with a kind of drugged avidity, and his upper body seemed to twitch and jiggle beneath his flannel shirt. He was humming softly and tunelessly.

He hadn't wanted to come here, not after the fire hose. He was scared to come here. He was scared that he had taken the passkey again, disobeying his father.

He *had* wanted to come here. Curiosity

(killed the cat; satisfaction brought him back)

was like a constant fishhook in his brain, a kind of nagging siren song that would not be appeased. And hadn't Mr. Hallorann said, "I don't think there's anything here that can hurt you"?

(You promised.)

(*Promises were made to be broken.*)

He jumped at that. It was as if that thought had come from outside, insectile, buzzing, softly cajoling.

(*Promises were made to be broken my dear redrum, to be broken. splintered. shattered. hammered apart. FORE!*)

His nervous humming broke into low, atonal song: "Lou, Lou, skip to m'Lou, skip to m'Lou my daaarlin . . ."

Hadn't Mr. Hallorann been right? Hadn't that been, in the end, the reason why he had kept silent and allowed the snow to close them in?

Just close your eyes and it will be gone.

What he had seen in the Presidential Sweet had gone away. And the snake had only been a fire hose that had fallen onto the rug. Yes, even the blood in the Presidential Sweet had been harmless, something old, something that had happened long before he was born or even thought of, something that was done with. Like a movie that only he could see. There was nothing, really nothing, in this hotel that could hurt him, and if he had to prove that to himself by going into this room, shouldn't he do so?

"Lou, Lou, skip to m'Lou . . ."

(*Curiosity killed the cat my dear redrum, redrum my dear, satisfaction brought him back safe and sound, from toes to crown; from head to ground he was safe and sound. He knew that those things*)

(*are like scary pictures, they can't hurt you, but oh my god*)

(*what big teeth you have grandma and is that a wolf in a BLUEBEARD suit or a BLUEBEARD in a wolf suit and i'm so*)

(glad you asked because curiosity killed that cat and it was the HOPE of satisfaction that brought him)

up the hall, treading softly over the blue and twisting jungle carpet. He had stopped by the fire extinguisher, had put the brass nozzle back in the frame, and then had poked it repeatedly with his finger, heart thumping, whispering: "Come on and hurt me. Come on and hurt me, you cheap prick. Can't do it, can you? Huh? You're nothing but a cheap fire hose. Can't do nothin but lie there. Come on, come on!" He had felt insane with bravado. And nothing had happened. It was only a hose after all, only canvas and brass, you could hack it to pieces and it would never complain, never twist and jerk and bleed green slime all over the blue carpet, because it was only a hose, not a nose and not a rose, not glass buttons or satin bows, not a snake in a sleepy doze . . . and he had hurried on, had hurried on because he was

("late, I'm late," said the white rabbit.)

the white rabbit. Yes. Now there was a white rabbit out by the playground, once it had been green but now it was white, as if something had shocked it repeatedly on the snowy, windy nights and turned it old . . .

Danny took the passkey from his pocket and slid it into the lock.

"Lou, Lou . . ."

(the white rabbit had been on its way to a croquet party to the Red Queen's croquet party storks for mallets hedgehogs for balls)

He touched the key, let his fingers wander over it.

His head felt dry and sick. He turned the key and the
tumblers thumped back smoothly.

(*OFF WITH HIS HEAD! OFF WITH HIS HEAD!
OFF WITH HIS HEAD!*)

(*this game isn't croquet though the mallets are too short
this game is*)

(*WHACK-BOOM! Straight through the wicket.*)

(*OFF WITH HIS HEEEEEAAAAAAAD—*)

Danny pushed the door open. It swung smoothly,
without a creak. He was standing just outside a large
combination bed-sitting room, and although the
snow had not reached up this far—the highest drifts
were still a foot below the second-floor windows—
the room was dark because Daddy had closed all the
shutters on the western exposure two weeks ago.

He stood in the doorway, fumbled to his right, and
found the switch plate. Two bulbs in an overhead cut-
glass fixture came on. Danny stepped further in and
looked around. The rug was deep and soft, a quiet
rose color. Soothing. A double bed with a white cov-
erlet. A writing desk

(*Pray tell me: Why is a raven like a writing desk?*)

by the large shuttered window. During the season
the Constant Writer

(*having a wonderful time, wish you were fear*)

would have a pretty view of the mountains to
describe to the folks back home.

He stepped further in. Nothing here, nothing at
all. Only an empty room, cold because Daddy was
heating the east wing today. A bureau. A closet, its
door open to reveal a clutch of hotel hangers, the

kind you can't steal. A Gideon Bible on an endtable.
To his left was the bathroom door, a full-length mirror on it reflecting his own white-faced image. That
door was ajar and—

He watched his double nod slowly.

Yes, that's where it was, whatever it was. In there.
In the bathroom. His double walked forward, as if to
escape the glass. It put its hand out, pressed it against
his own. Then it fell away at an angle as the bathroom door swung open. He looked in.

A long room, old-fashioned, like a Pullman car.
Tiny white hexagonal tiles on the floor. At the far
end, a toilet with the lid up. At the right, a washbasin and another mirror above it, the kind that
hides a medicine cabinet. To the left, a huge white
tub on claw feet, the shower curtain pulled closed.
Danny stepped into the bathroom and walked
toward the tub dreamily, as if propelled from outside himself, as if this whole thing were one of the
dreams Tony had brought him, that he would perhaps see something nice when he pulled the shower
curtain back, something Daddy had forgotten or
Mommy had lost, something that would make them
both happy—

So he pulled the shower curtain back.

The woman in the tub had been dead for a long
time. She was bloated and purple, her gas-filled belly
rising out of the cold, ice-rimmed water like some
fleshy island. Her eyes were fixed on Danny's, glassy
and huge, like marbles. She was grinning, her purple
lips pulled back in a grimace. Her breasts lolled. Her

pubic hair floated. Her hands were frozen on the knurled porcelain sides of the tub like crab claws.

Danny shrieked. But the sound never escaped his lips; turning inward and inward, it fell down in his darkness like a stone in a well. He took a single blundering step backward, hearing his heels clack on the white hexagonal tiles, and at the same moment his urine broke, spilling effortlessly out of him.

The woman was sitting up.

Still grinning, her huge marble eyes fixed on him, she was sitting up. Her dead palms made squittering noises on the porcelain. Her breasts swayed like ancient cracked punching bags. There was the minute sound of breaking ice shards. She was not breathing. She was a corpse, and dead long years.

Danny turned and ran. Bolting through the bathroom door, his eyes starting from their sockets, his hair on end like the hair of a hedgehog about to be turned into a sacrificial

(croquet? or roque?)

ball, his mouth open and soundless. He ran full-tilt into the outside door of 217, which was now closed. He began hammering on it, far beyond realizing that it was unlocked, and he had only to turn the knob to let himself out. His mouth pealed forth deafening screams that were beyond human auditory range. He could only hammer on the door and hear the dead woman coming for him, bloated belly, dry hair, outstretched hands—something that had lain slain in that tub for perhaps years, embalmed there in magic.

The door would not open, would not, would not, would not.

And then the voice of Dick Halloran came to him, so sudden and unexpected, so calm, that his locked vocal cords opened and he began to cry weakly—not with fear but with blessed relief.

(*I don't think they can hurt you . . . they're like pictures in a book . . . close your eyes and they'll be gone.*)

His eyelids snapped down. His hands curled into balls. His shoulders hunched with the effort of his concentration:

(*Nothing there nothing there not there at all NOTHING THERE THERE IS NOTHING!*)

Time passed. And he was just beginning to relax, just beginning to realize that the door must be unlocked and he could go, when the years-damp, bloated, fish-smelling hands closed softly around his throat and he was turned implacably around to stare into that dead and purple face.

PART FOUR

Snowbound

26

Dreamland

Knitting made her sleepy. Today even Bartók would have made her sleepy, and it wasn't Bartók on the little phonograph, it was Bach. Her hands grew slower and slower, and at the time her son was making the acquaintance of Room 217's long-term resident, Wendy was asleep with her knitting on her lap. The yarn and needles rose in the slow time of her breathing. Her sleep was deep and she did not dream.

Jack Torrance had fallen asleep too, but his sleep was light and uneasy, populated by dreams that seemed too vivid to be mere dreams—they were certainly more vivid than any dreams he had ever had before.

His eyes had begun to get heavy as he leafed through packets of milk bills, a hundred to a packet, seemingly tens of thousands all together. Yet he gave each one a cursory glance, afraid that by not being thorough he might miss exactly the piece of Overlookiana he needed to make the mystic connection that he was sure must be here somewhere. He felt like a man with a power cord in one hand, groping around a dark and unfamiliar room for a socket. If he could find it he would be rewarded with a view of wonders.

He had come to grips with Al Shockley's phone call and his request; his strange experience in the playground had helped him to do that. That had been too damned close to some kind of breakdown, and he was convinced that it was his mind in revolt against Al's high-goddam-handed request that he chuck his book project. It had maybe been a signal that his own sense of self-respect could only be pushed so far before disintegrating entirely. He would write the book. If it meant the end of his association with Al Shockley, that would have to be. He would write the hotel's biography, write it straight from the shoulder, and the introduction would be his hallucination that the topiary animals had moved. The title would be uninspired but workable: *Strange Resort, The Story of the Overlook Hotel.* Straight from the shoulder, yes, but it would not be written vindictively, in any effort to get back at Al or Stuart Ullman or George Hatfield or his father (miserable, bullying drunk that he had been) or anyone else, for that matter. He would write it because the Overlook had enchanted him—could any other explanation be so simple or so true? He would write it for the reason he felt that all great literature, fiction and nonfiction, was written: truth comes out, in the end it always comes out. He would write it because he felt he had to.

Five hundred gals whole milk. One hundred gals skim milk. Pd. Billed to acc't. Three hundred pts orange juice. Pd.

He slipped down further in his chair, still holding a clutch of the receipts, but his eyes no longer looking at what was printed there. They had come unfocused. His lids were slow and heavy. His mind had slipped from the Overlook to his father, who had been a male nurse at the Berlin Community Hospital. Big man. A fat man who had towered to six feet two inches, he had been taller than Jack even when Jack got his full growth of six feet even—not that the old man had still been around then. "Runt of the litter," he would say, and then cuff Jack lovingly and laugh. There had been two other brothers, both taller than their father, and Becky, who at five-ten had only been two inches shorter than Jack and taller than he for most of their childhood.

His relationship with his father had been like the unfurling of some flower of beautiful potential, which, when wholly opened, turned out to be blighted inside. Until he had been seven he had loved the tall, big-bellied man uncritically and strongly in spite of the spankings, the black-and-blues, the occasional black eye.

He could remember velvet summer nights, the house quiet, oldest brother Brett out with his girl, middle brother Mike studying something, Becky and their mother in the living room, watching something on the balky old TV; and he would sit in the hall dressed in a pajama singlet and nothing else, ostensibly playing with his trucks, actually waiting for the moment when the silence would be broken by the door swinging open with a large bang, the bellow of his father's welcome when he saw Jacky was waiting, his own happy squeal in answer as this big man came down the hall, his pink scalp glowing beneath his crewcut in the glow of the hall light. In that light he always looked like some soft and flapping oversized ghost in his hospital whites, the shirt always untucked (and sometimes bloody), the pants cuffs drooping down over the black shoes.

His father would sweep him into his arms and Jacky would be propelled deliriously upward, so fast it seemed he could feel air pressure settling against his skull like a cap made out of lead, up and up, both of them crying "Elevator! Elevator!"; and there had been nights when his father in his drunkenness had not stopped the upward lift of his slabmuscled arms soon enough and Jacky had gone right over his father's flattopped head like a human projectile to crash-land on the hall floor behind his dad. But on other nights his father would only sweep him into a giggling ecstasy, through the zone of air where beer hung around his father's face like a mist of raindrops, to be twisted and turned and shaken like a laughing rag, and finally to be set down on his feet, hiccupping with reaction.

The receipts slipped from his relaxing hand and seesawed down through the air to land lazily on the floor; his eyelids, which had settled shut with his father's image tattooed on their backs like stereopticon images, opened a little bit and then slipped back

down again. He twitched a little. Consciousness, like
the receipts, like autumn aspen leaves, seesawed
lazily downward.

That had been the first phase of his relationship
with his father, and as it was drawing to its end he
had become aware that Becky and his brothers, all of
them older, hated the father and that their mother, a
nondescript woman who rarely spoke above a mutter,
only suffered him because her Catholic upbringing
said that she must. In those days it had not seemed
strange to Jack that the father won all his arguments
with his children by use of his fists, and it had not
seemed strange that his own love should go hand-in-
hand with his fear: fear of the elevator game which
might end in a splintering crash on any given night;
fear that his father's bearish good humor on his day
off might suddenly change to boarish bellowing and
the smack of his "*good right hand*"; and sometimes, he
remembered, he had even been afraid that his father's
shadow might fall over him while he was at play. It
was near the end of this phase that he began to notice
that Brett never brought his dates home, or Mike and
Becky their chums.

Love began to curdle at nine, when his father put
his mother into the hospital with his cane. He had
begun to carry the cane a year earlier, when a car accident had left him lame. After that he was never without it, long and black and thick and gold-headed.
Now, dozing, Jack's body twitched in a remembered
cringe at the sound it made in the air, a murderous
swish, and its heavy crack against the wall . . . or

against flesh. He had beaten their mother for no good
reason at all, suddenly and without warning. They
had been at the supper table. The cane had been
standing by his chair. It was a Sunday night, the end
of a three-day weekend for Daddy, a weekend which
he had boozed away in his usual inimitable style.
Roast chicken. Peas. Mashed potatoes. Daddy at the
head of the table, his plate heaped high, snoozing or
nearly snoozing. His mother passing plates. And suddenly Daddy had been wide awake, his eyes set
deeply into their fat eyesockets, glittering with a kind
of stupid, evil petulance. They flickered from one
member of the family to the next, and the vein in the
center of his forehead was standing out prominently,
always a bad sign. One of his large freckled hands
had dropped to the gold knob of his cane, caressing
it. He said something about coffee—to this day Jack
was sure it had been "coffee" that his father said.
Momma had opened her mouth to answer and then
the cane was whickering through the air, smashing
against her face. Blood spurted from her nose. Becky
screamed. Momma's spectacles dropped into her
gravy. The cane had been drawn back, had come
down again, this time on top of her head, splitting
the scalp. Momma had dropped to the floor. He had
been out of his chair and around to where she lay
dazed on the carpet, brandishing the cane, moving
with a fat man's grotesque speed and agility, little
eyes flashing, jowls quivering as he spoke to her just
as he had always spoken to his children during such
outbursts. "Now. Now by Christ. I guess you'll take

your medicine now. Goddam puppy. Whelp. Come on and take your medicine." The cane had gone up and down on her seven more times before Brett and Mike got hold of him, dragged him away, wrestled the cane out of his hand. Jack

(little Jacky now he was little Jacky now dozing and mumbling on a cobwebby camp chair while the furnace roared into hollow life behind him)

knew exactly how many blows it had been because each soft *whump* against his mother's body had been engraved on his memory like the irrational swipe of a chisel on stone. Seven *whumps*. No more, no less. He and Becky crying, unbelieving, looking at their mother's spectacles lying in her mashed potatoes, one cracked lens smeared with gravy. Brett shouting at Daddy from the back hall, telling him he'd kill him if he moved. And Daddy saying over and over: "Damn little puppy. Damn little whelp. Give me my cane, you damn little pup. Give it to me." Brett brandishing it hysterically, saying yes, yes, I'll give it to you, just you move a little bit and I'll give you all you want and two extra. I'll give you *plenty*. Momma getting slowly to her feet, dazed, her face already puffed and swelling like an old tire with too much air in it, bleeding in four or five different places, and she had said a terrible thing, perhaps the only thing Momma had ever said which Jacky could recall word for word: "Who's got the newspaper? Your daddy wants the funnies. Is it raining yet?" And then she sank to her knees again, her hair hanging in her puffed and bleeding face. Mike calling the doctor, babbling into

the phone. Could he come right away? It was their
mother. No, he couldn't say what the trouble was,
not over the phone, not over a party line he couldn't.
Just *come*. The doctor came and took Momma away to
the hospital where Daddy had worked all of his adult
life. Daddy, sobered up some (or perhaps only with
the stupid cunning of any hard-pressed animal), told
the doctor she had fallen downstairs. There was blood
on the tablecloth because he had tried to wipe her
dear face with it. Had her glasses flown all the way
through the living room and into the dining room to
land in her mashed potatoes and gravy? the doctor
asked with a kind of horrid, grinning sarcasm. Is that
what happened, Mark? I have heard of folks who can
get a radio station on their gold fillings and I have
seen a man get shot between the eyes and live to tell
about it, but that is a new one on me. Daddy had
merely shook his head and said he didn't know; they
must have fallen off her face when he brought her
through the dining room. The four children had been
stunned to silence by the calm stupendousness of the
lie. Four days later Brett quit his job in the mill and
joined the Army. Jack had always felt it was not just
the sudden and irrational beating his father had
administered at the dinner table but the fact that, in
the hospital, their mother had corroborated their
father's story while holding the hand of the parish
priest. Revolted, Brett had left them to whatever
might come. He had been killed in Dong Ho
province in 1965, the year when Jack Torrance,
undergraduate, had joined the active college agita-

tion to end the war. He had waved his brother's bloody shirt at rallies that were increasingly well attended, but it was not Brett's face that hung before his eyes when he spoke—it was the face of his mother, a dazed, uncomprehending face, his mother saying: "Who's got the newspaper?"

Mike escaped three years later when Jack was twelve—he went to UNH on a hefty Merit Scholarship. A year after that their father died of a sudden, massive stroke which occurred while he was prepping a patient for surgery. He had collapsed in his flapping and untucked hospital whites, dead possibly even before he hit the industrial black-and-red hospital tiles, and three days later the man who had dominated Jacky's life, the irrational white ghost-god, was under ground.

The stone read *Mark Anthony Torrance, Loving Father.* To that Jack would have added one line: *He Knew How to Play Elevator.*

There had been a great lot of insurance money. There are people who collect insurance as compulsively as others collect coins and stamps, and Mark Torrance had been that type. The insurance money came in at the same time the monthly policy payments and liquor bills stopped. For five years they had been rich. Nearly rich . . .

In his shallow, uneasy sleep his face rose before him as if in a glass, his face but not his face, the wide eyes and innocent bowed mouth of a boy sitting in the hall with his trucks, waiting for his daddy, waiting for the white ghost-god, waiting for the elevator to rise up with dizzying, exhilarating speed through the salt-and-sawdust mist of exhaled taverns, waiting perhaps for it to go crashing down, spilling old clocksprings out of his ears while his daddy roared with laughter, and it

(transformed into Danny's face, so much like his own had been, his eyes had been light blue while Danny's were cloudy gray, but the lips still made a bow and the complexion was fair; Danny in his study, wearing training pants, all his papers soggy and the fine misty smell of beer rising . . . a dreadful batter all in ferment, rising on the wings of yeast, the breath of taverns . . . snap of bone . . . his own voice, mewling drunkenly *Danny, you okay doc? . . . Oh God oh God your poor sweet arm . . .* and that face transformed into)

(momma's dazed face rising up from below the table, punched and bleeding, and momma was saying)

("*—from your father. I repeat, an enormously important announcement from your father. Please stay tuned or tune immediately to the Happy Jack frequency. Repeat tune immediately to the Happy Hour frequency. I repeat—*")

A slow dissolve. Disembodied voices echoing up to him as if along an endless, cloudy hallway.

(*Things keep getting in the way, dear Tommy . . .*)

(*Medoc, are you here? I've been sleepwalking again, my dear. It's the inhuman monsters that I fear . . .*)

("*Excuse me, Mr. Ullman, but isn't this the . . .*")

. . . office, with its file cabinets, Ullman's big desk, a blank reservations book for next year already in place—never misses a trick, that Ullman—all the keys hanging neatly on their hooks

(except for one, which one, which key, passkey—
passkey, passkey, who's got the passkey? if we went
upstairs perhaps we'd see)

and the big two-way radio on its shelf.

He snapped it on. CB transmissions coming in
short, crackly bursts. He switched the band and
dialed across bursts of music, news, a preacher
haranguing a softly moaning congregation, a weather
report. And another voice which he dialed back to. It
was his father's voice.

"—kill him. You have to kill him, Jacky, and her,
too. Because a real artist must suffer. Because each
man kills the thing he loves. Because they'll always
be conspiring against you, trying to hold you back
and drag you down. Right this minute that boy of
yours is in where he shouldn't be. Trespassing. That's
what he's doing. He's a goddam little pup. Cane him
for it, Jacky, cane him within an inch of his life. Have
a drink, Jacky my boy, and we'll play the elevator
game. Then I'll go with you while you give him his
medicine. I know you can do it, of course you can.
You must kill him. You have to kill him, Jacky, and
her, too. Because a real artist must suffer. Because
each man—"

His father's voice, going up higher and higher,
becoming something maddening, not human at all,
something squealing and petulant and maddening,
the voice of the Ghost-God, the Pig-God, coming
dead at him out of the radio and

"*No!*" he screamed back. "You're *dead*, you're in
your *grave*, you're not in me at all!" Because he had

cut all the father out of him and it was not right that
he should come back, creeping through this hotel two
thousand miles from the New England town where
his father had lived and died.

He raised the radio up and brought it down, and it
smashed on the floor spilling old clocksprings and
tubes like the result of some crazy elevator game
gone awry, making his father's voice gone, leaving
only his voice, Jack's voice, Jacky's voice, chanting in
the cold reality of the office:

"—dead, you're dead, you're dead!"

And the startled sound of Wendy's feet hitting the
floor over his head, and Wendy's startled, frightened
voice: "Jack? Jack!"

He stood, blinking down at the shattered radio.
Now there was only the snowmobile in the equipment shed to link them to the outside world.

He put his hands over his eyes and clutched at his
temples. He was getting a headache.

27

Catatonic

Wendy ran down the hall in her stocking feet and ran down the main stairs to the lobby two at a time. She didn't look up at the carpeted flight that led to the second floor, but if she had, she would have seen Danny standing at the top of them, still and silent, his unfocused eyes directed out into indifferent space, his thumb in his mouth, the collar and shoulders of his shirt damp. There were puffy bruises on his neck and just below his chin.

Jack's cries had ceased, but that did nothing to ease her fear. Ripped out of her sleep by his voice, raised in that old hectoring pitch she remembered so well, she still felt that she was dreaming—but another part knew she was awake, and that terrified her more. She half expected to burst into the office and find him standing over Danny's sprawled-out body, drunk and confused.

She pushed through the door and Jack was standing there, rubbing at his temples with his fingers. His face was ghost-white. The two-way CB radio lay at his feet in a sprinkling of broken glass.

"Wendy?" he asked uncertainly. "Wendy——?"

The bewilderment seemed to grow and for a moment she saw his true face, the one he ordinarily kept so well hidden, and it was a face of desperate unhappiness, the face of an animal caught in a snare beyond its ability to decipher and render harmless. Then the muscles began to work, began to writhe under the skin, the mouth began to tremble infirmly, the Adam's apple began to rise and fall.

Her own bewilderment and surprise were overlaid by shock: he was going to cry. She had seen him cry before, but never since he stopped drinking . . . and never in those days unless he was very drunk and pathetically remorseful. He was a tight man, drum-tight, and his loss of control frightened her all over again.

He came toward her, the tears brimming over his lower lids now, his head shaking involuntarily as if in a fruitless effort to ward off this emotional storm, and his chest drew in a convulsive gasp that was expelled in a huge, racking sob. His feet, clad in Hush Puppies, stumbled over the wreck of the radio and he almost fell into her arms, making her stagger back with his weight. His breath blew into her face and there was no smell of liquor on it. Of course not; there was no liquor up here.

"What's wrong?" She held him as best she could. "Jack, what is it?"

But he could do nothing at first but sob, clinging to her, almost crushing the wind from her, his head turning on her shoulder in that helpless, shaking, warding-off gesture. His sobs were heavy and fierce.

He was shuddering all over, his muscles jerking beneath his plaid shirt and jeans.

"Jack? What? Tell me what's wrong!"

At last the sobs began to change themselves into words, most of them incoherent at first, but coming clearer as his tears began to spread themselves.

". . . dream, I guess it was a dream, but it was so real, I . . . it was my mother saying that Daddy was going to be on the radio and I . . . he was . . . he was telling me to . . . I don't know, he was *yelling* at me . . . and so I broke the radio . . . to shut him up. To shut him up. He's dead. I don't even want to dream about him. He's dead. My God, Wendy, my God. I never had a nightmare like that. I never want to have another one. Christ! It was awful."

"You just fell asleep in the office?"

"No . . . not here. Downstairs." He was straightening a little now, his weight coming off her, and the steady back-and-forth motion of his head first slowed and then stopped.

"I was looking through those old papers. Sitting on a chair I set up down there. Milk receipts. Dull stuff. And I guess I just drowsed off. That's when I started to dream. I must have sleepwalked up here." He essayed a shaky little laugh against her neck. "Another first."

"Where is Danny, Jack?"

"I don't know. Isn't he with you?"

"He wasn't . . . downstairs with you?"

He looked over his shoulder and his face tightened at what he saw on her face.

"Never going to let me forget that, are you, Wendy?"

"Jack—"

"When I'm on my deathbed you'll lean over and say, 'It serves you right, remember the time you broke Danny's arm?' "

"Jack!"

"Jack what?" he asked hotly, and jumped to his feet. "Are you denying that's what you're thinking? That I hurt him? That I hurt him once before and I could hurt him again?"

"I want to know where he is, that's all!"

"Go ahead, yell your fucking head off, that'll make everything okay, won't it?"

She turned and walked out the door.

He watched her go, frozen for a moment, a blotter covered with fragments of broken glass in one hand. Then he dropped it into the wastebasket, went after her, and caught her by the lobby desk. He put his hands on her shoulders and turned her around. Her face was carefully set.

"Wendy, I'm sorry. It was the dream. I'm upset. Forgive?"

"Of course," she said, her face not changing expression. Her wooden shoulders slipped out of his hands. She walked to the middle of the lobby and called: *"Hey, doc! Where are you?"*

Silence came back. She walked toward the double lobby doors, opened one of them, and stepped out onto the path Jack had shoveled. It was more like a trench; the packed and drifted snow through which the path was cut came to her shoulders. She called him again, her breath coming out in a white plume. When she came back in she had begun to look scared.

Controlling his irritation with her, he said reasonably: "Are you *sure* he's not sleeping in his room?"

"I told you, he was playing somewhere when I was knitting. I could hear him downstairs."

"Did you fall asleep?"

"What's that got to do with it? Yes. *Danny?*"

"Did you look in his room when you came downstairs just now?"

"I—" She stopped.

He nodded. "I didn't really think so."

He started up the stairs without waiting for her. She followed him, half-running, but he was taking the risers two at a time. She almost crashed into his back when he came to a dead stop on the first-floor landing. He was rooted there, looking up, his eyes wide.

"What—?" she began, and followed his gaze.

Danny still stood there, his eyes blank, sucking his thumb. The marks on his throat were cruelly visible in the light of the hall's electric flambeaux.

"Danny!" she shrieked.

It broke Jack's paralysis and they rushed up the stairs together to where he stood. Wendy fell on her knees beside him and swept the boy into her arms. Danny came pliantly enough, but he did not hug her back. It was like hugging a padded stick, and the sweet taste of horror flooded her mouth. He only sucked his thumb and stared with indifferent blankness out into the stairwell beyond both of them.

"Danny, what happened?" Jack asked. He put out his hand to touch the puffy side of Danny's neck. "Who did this to y—"

"Don't you touch him!" Wendy hissed. She clutched Danny in her arms, lifted him, and had retreated halfway down the stairs before Jack could do more than stand up, confused.

"What? Wendy, what the hell are you t—"

"Don't you touch him! I'll kill you if you lay your hands on him again!"

"Wendy—"

"You bastard!"

She turned and ran down the rest of the stairs to the first floor. Danny's head jounced mildly up and down as she ran. His thumb was lodged securely in his mouth. His eyes were soaped windows. She turned right at the foot of the stairs, and Jack heard her feet retreat to the end of it. Their bedroom door slammed. The bolt was run home. The lock turned. Brief silence. Then the soft, muttered sounds of comforting.

He stood for an unknown length of time, literally paralyzed by all that had happened in such a short space of time. His dream was still with him, painting everything a slightly unreal shade. It was as if he had taken a very mild mescaline hit. Had he maybe hurt Danny as Wendy thought? Tried to strangle his son at his dead father's request? No. He would never hurt Danny.

(*He fell down the stairs, Doctor.*)

He would never hurt Danny *now*.

(*How could I know the bug bomb was defective?*)

Never in his life had he been willfully vicious when he was sober.

(*Except when you almost killed George Hatfield.*)

"No!" he cried into the darkness. He brought both fists crashing down on his legs, again and again and again.

Wendy sat in the overstuffed chair by the window with Danny on her lap, holding him, crooning the old meaningless words, the ones you never remember afterward no matter how a thing turns out. He had folded onto her lap with neither protest nor gladness, like a paper cutout of himself, and his eyes didn't even shift toward the door when Jack cried out "No!" somewhere in the hallway.

The confusion had receded a little bit in her mind, but she now discovered something even worse behind it. Panic.

Jack had done this, she had no doubt of it. His denials meant nothing to her. She thought it was perfectly possible that Jack had tried to throttle Danny in his sleep just as he had smashed the CB radio in his sleep. He was having a breakdown of some kind. But what was she going to do about it? She couldn't stay locked in here forever. They would have to eat.

There was really only one question, and it was asked in a mental voice of utter coldness and pragmatism, the voice of her maternity, a cold and passionless voice

once it was directed away from the closed circle of
mother and child and out toward Jack. It was a voice
that spoke of self-preservation only after son-preser-
vation and its question was:

(*Exactly how dangerous is he?*)

He had denied doing it. He had been horrified at
the bruises, at Danny's soft and implacable discon-
nection. If he had done it, a separate section of himself had been responsible. The fact that he had done it
when he was asleep was—in a terrible, twisted way—
encouraging. Wasn't it possible that he could be
trusted to get them out of here? To get them down
and away. And after that . . .

But she could see no further than she and Danny
arriving safe at Dr. Edmonds's office in Sidewinder.
She had no particular need to see further. The present
crisis was more than enough to keep her occupied.

She crooned to Danny, rocking him on her breasts.
Her fingers, on his shoulder, had noticed that his T-shirt
was damp, but they had not bothered reporting the
information to her brain in more than a cursory way. If
it had been reported, she might have remembered that
Jack's hands, as he had hugged her in the office and
sobbed against her neck, had been dry. It might have
given her pause. But her mind was still on other things.
The decision had to be made—to approach Jack or not?

Actually it was not much of a decision. There was
nothing she could do alone, not even carry Danny
down to the office and call for help on the CB radio.
He had suffered a great shock. He ought to be taken
out quickly before any permanent damage could be

done. She refused to let herself believe that permanent damage might already have been done.

And still she agonized over it, looking for another alternative. She did not want to put Danny back within Jack's reach. She was aware now that she had made one bad decision when she had gone against her feelings (and Danny's) and allowed the snow to close them in . . . for Jack's sake. Another bad decision when she had shelved the idea of divorce. Now she was nearly paralyzed by the idea that she might be making another mistake, one she would regret every minute of every day of the rest of her life.

There was not a gun in the place. There were knives hanging from the magnetized runners in the kitchen, but Jack was between her and them.

In her striving to make the right decision, to find the alternative, the bitter irony of her thoughts did not occur: an hour ago she had been asleep, firmly convinced that things were all right and soon would be even better. Now she was considering the possibility of using a butcher knife on her husband if he tried to interfere with her and her son.

At last she stood up with Danny in her arms, her legs trembling. There was no other way. She would have to assume that Jack awake was Jack sane, and that he would help her get Danny down to Sidewinder and Dr. Edmonds. And if Jack tried to do anything *but* help, God help *him*.

She went to the door and unlocked it. Shifting Danny up to her shoulder, she opened it and went out into the hall.

"Jack?" she called nervously, and got no answer.

With growing trepidation she walked down to the stairwell, but Jack was not there. And as she stood there on the landing, wondering what to do next, the singing came up from below, rich, angry, bitterly satiric:

> *"Roll me over*
> *In the clo-ho-ver,*
> *Roll me over, lay me down and do it again."*

She was frightened even more by the sound of him than she had been by his silence, but there was still no alternative. She started down the stairs.

28

"It Was Her!"

Jack had stood on the stairs, listening to the crooning, comforting sounds coming muffled through the locked door, and slowly his confusion had given way to anger. Things had never really changed. Not to Wendy. He could be off the juice for twenty years and still when he came home at night and she embraced him at the door, he would see/sense that little flare of her nostrils as she tried to divine scotch or gin fumes riding the outbound train of his exhalation. She was always going to assume the worst; if he and Danny got in a car accident with a drunken blindman who had had a stroke just before the collision, she would silently blame Danny's injuries on him and turn away.

Her face as she had snatched Danny away—it rose up before him and he suddenly wanted to wipe the anger that had been on it out with his fist.

She had no goddam right!

Yes, maybe at first. He had been a lush, he had done terrible things. Breaking Danny's arm had been a terrible thing. But if a man reforms, doesn't he deserve to have his reformation credited sooner or later? And if he doesn't get it, doesn't he deserve the game to go with the name? If a father constantly accuses his virginal daughter of screwing every boy in junior high, must she not at last grow weary (enough) of it to earn her scoldings? And if a wife secretly—and not so secretly—continues to believe that her teetotaling husband is a drunk . . .

He got up, walked slowly down to the first-floor landing, and stood there for a moment. He took his handkerchief from his back pocket, wiped his lips with it, and considered going down and pounding on the bedroom door, demanding to be let in so he could see his son. She had no right to be so goddam highhanded.

Well, sooner or later she'd have to come out, unless she planned a radical sort of diet for the two of them. A rather ugly grin touched his lips at the thought. Let her come to him. She would in time.

He went downstairs to the ground floor, stood aimlessly by the lobby desk for a moment, then turned right. He went into the dining room and stood just inside the door. The empty tables, their white linen cloths neatly cleaned and pressed beneath their clear plastic covers, glimmered up at him. All was deserted now but

(*Dinner Will Be Served at 8 P.M.*
Unmasking and Dancing at Midnight)

Jack walked among the tables, momentarily forgetting his wife and son upstairs, forgetting the dream, the smashed radio, the bruises. He trailed his fingers over the slick plastic dustcovers, trying to imagine how it must have been on that hot August night in 1945, the war won, the future stretching ahead so various and new, like a land of dreams. The bright and particolored Japanese lanterns hung the whole length of the circular drive, the golden-yellow light spilling from these high windows that were now drifted over with snow. Men and women in costume, here a glittering princess, there a high-booted cavalier, flashing jewelry and flashing wit everywhere, dancing, liquor flowing freely, first wine and then cocktails and then perhaps boilermakers, the level of conversation going up and up and up until the jolly cry rang out from the bandmaster's podium, the cry of "Unmask! Unmask!"

(*And the Red Death held sway . . .*)

He found himself standing on the other side of the dining room, just outside the stylized batwing doors of the Colorado Lounge where, on that night in 1945, all the booze would have been free.

(*Belly up to the bar, pardner, the drinks're on the house.*)

He stepped through the batwings and into the deep, folded shadows of the bar. And a strange thing occurred. He had been in here before, once to check the inventory sheet Ullman had left, and he knew the place had been stripped clean. The shelves were totally bare. But now, lit only murkily by the light which filtered through from the dining room (which was itself only dimly lit because of the snow blocking the windows), he thought he saw ranks and ranks of bottles twinkling mutedly behind the bar and syphons, and even beer dripping from the spigots of all three highly polished taps. Yes, he could even *smell* beer, that damp and fermented and yeasty odor, no different from the smell that had hung finely misted around his father's face every night when he came home from work.

Eyes widening, he fumbled for the wall switch, and the low, intimate bar-lighting came on, circles of twenty-watt bulbs emplanted on the tops of the three wagon-wheel chandeliers overhead.

The shelves were all empty. They had not even as yet gathered a good coat of dust. The beer taps were dry, as were the chrome drains beneath them. To his left and right, the velvet-upholstered booths stood like men with high backs, each one designed to give a maximum of privacy to the couple inside. Straight ahead, across the red-carpeted floor, forty barstools stood around the horseshoe-shaped bar. Each stool was upholstered in leather and embossed with cattle brands—Circle H, Bar D Bar (that was fitting), Rocking W, Lazy B.

He approached it, giving his head a little shake of bewilderment as he did so. It was like that day on the playground when . . . but there was no sense in thinking about that. Still he could have sworn he had seen those bottles, vaguely, it was true, the way you see the darkened shapes of furniture in a room where the curtains have been drawn. Mild glints on glass. The only thing that remained was that smell of beer, and Jack knew that was a smell that faded into the woodwork of every bar in the world after a certain period of time, not to be eradicated by any cleaner invented. Yet the smell here seemed sharp . . . almost fresh.

He sat down on one of the stools and propped his elbows on the bar's leather-cushioned edge. At his left hand was a bowl for peanuts—now empty, of course. The first bar he'd been in for nineteen months and the damned thing was dry—just his luck. All the same, a bitterly powerful wave of nostalgia swept over him, and the physical craving for a drink seemed to work itself up from his belly to his throat to his mouth and nose, shriveling and wrinkling the tissues as it went, making them cry out for something wet and long and cold.

He glanced at the shelves again in wild, irrational hope but the shelves were just as empty as before. He grinned in pain and frustration. His fists, clenching slowly, made minute scratchings on the bar's leather-padded edge.

"Hi, Lloyd," he said. "A little slow tonight, isn't it?"

Lloyd said it was. Lloyd asked him what it would be.

"Now I'm really glad you asked me that," Jack said, "really glad. Because I happen to have two twenties and two tens in my wallet and I was afraid they'd be sitting there until sometime next April. There isn't a Seven-Eleven around here, would you believe it? And I thought they had Seven-Elevens on the fucking *moon*."

Lloyd sympathized.

"So here's what," Jack said. "You set me up an even twenty martinis. An even twenty, just like that, kazang. One for every month I've been on the wagon and one to grow on. You can do that, can't you? You aren't too busy?"

Lloyd said he wasn't busy at all.

"Good man. You line those martians up right along the bar and I'm going to take them down, one by one. White man's burden, Lloyd my man."

Lloyd turned to do the job. Jack reached into his pocket for his money clip and came out with an Excedrin bottle instead. His money clip was on the bedroom bureau, and of course his skinny-shanks wife had locked him out of the bedroom. Nice going, Wendy. You bleeding bitch.

"I seem to be momentarily light," Jack said. "How's my credit in this joint, anyhow?"

Lloyd said his credit was fine.

"That's super. I like you, Lloyd. You were always the best of them. Best damned barkeep between Barre and Portland, Maine. Portland, *Oregon,* for that matter."

Lloyd thanked him for saying so.

Jack thumped the cap from his Excedrin bottle, shook two tablets out, and flipped them into his mouth. The familiar acid-compelling taste flooded in.

He had a sudden sensation that people were watching him, curiously and with some contempt. The booths behind him were full—there were graying, distinguished men and beautiful young girls, all of them in costume, watching this sad exercise in the dramatic arts with cold amusement.

Jack whirled on his stool.

The booths were all empty, stretching away from the lounge door to the left and right, the line on his left cornering to flank the bar's horseshoe curve down the short length of the room. Padded leather seats and backs. Gleaming dark Formica tables, an ashtray on each one, a book of matches in each ashtray, the words *Colorado Lounge* stamped on each in gold leaf above the batwing-door logo.

He turned back, swallowing the rest of the dissolving Excedrin with a grimace.

"Lloyd, you're a wonder," he said. "Set up already. Your speed is only exceeded by the soulful beauty of your Neapolitan eyes. *Salud.*"

Jack contemplated the twenty imaginary drinks, the martini glasses blushing droplets of condensation, each with a swizzle poked through a plump green olive. He could almost smell gin on the air.

"The wagon," he said. "Have you ever been acquainted with a gentleman who has hopped up on the wagon?"

Lloyd allowed as how he had met such men from time to time.

"Have you ever renewed acquaintances with such a man after he hopped back off?"

Lloyd could not, in all honesty, recall.

"You never did, then," Jack said. He curled his hand around the first drink, carried his fist to his mouth, which was open, and turned his fist up. He swallowed and then tossed the imaginary glass over his shoulder. The people were back again, fresh from their costume ball, studying him, laughing behind their hands. He could feel them. If the backbar had featured a mirror instead of those damn stupid empty shelves, he could have seen them. Let them stare. Fuck them. Let anybody stare who wanted to stare.

"No, you never did," he told Lloyd. "Few men ever return from the fabled Wagon, but those who do come with a fearful tale to tell. When you jump on, it seems like the brightest, cleanest Wagon you ever saw, with ten-foot wheels to keep the bed of it high out of the gutter where all the drunks are laying around with their brown bags and their Thunderbird and their Granddad Flash's Popskull Bourbon. You're away from all the people who throw you nasty looks and tell you to clean up your act or go put it on in another town. From the gutter, that's the finest-lookin Wagon you ever saw, Lloyd my boy. All hung with bunting and a brass band in front and three majorettes to each side, twirling their batons and flashing their panties at you. Man, you got to get on that Wagon and away from the juicers that are straining canned heat and smelling their own puke to get high again and poking along the gutter for butts with half an inch left below the filter."

He drained two more imaginary drinks and tossed the glasses back over his shoulder. He could almost hear them smashing on the floor. And goddam if he wasn't starting to feel high. It was the Excedrin.

"So you climb up," he told Lloyd, "and ain't you glad to be there. My God yes, that's affirmative. That Wagon is the biggest and best float in the whole parade, and everybody is lining the streets and clapping and cheering and waving, all for you. Except for the winos passed out in the gutter. Those guys used to be your friends, but that's all behind you now."

He carried his empty fist to his mouth and sluiced down another—four down, sixteen to go. Making excellent progress. He swayed a little on the stool. Let em stare, if that was how they got off. Take a picture, folks, it'll last longer.

"Then you start to see things, Lloydy-my-boy. Things you missed from the gutter. Like how the floor of the Wagon is nothing but straight pine boards, so fresh they're still bleeding sap, and if you took your shoes off you'd be sure to get a splinter. Like how the only furniture in the Wagon is these long benches with high backs and no cushions to sit on, and in fact they are nothing but pews with a songbook every five feet or so. Like how all the people sitting in the pews on the Wagon are these flatchested el birdos in long dresses with a little lace around the collar and their hair pulled back into buns until it's so tight you can almost hear it screaming. And every face is flat and pale and shiny, and they're all singing 'Shall we gather at the riiiiver, the beautiful, the beautiful, the *riiiiiver*,' and up front there's this reekin bitch with blond hair playing the organ and tellin em to sing louder, sing louder. And somebody slams a songbook into your hands and says, 'Sing it out, brother. If you expect to stay on this Wagon, you got to sing morning, noon, and night. Especially at night.' And that's when you realize what the Wagon really is, Lloyd. It's a church with bars on the windows, a church for women and a prison for you."

He stopped. Lloyd was gone. Worse still, he had never been there. The drinks had never been there. Only the people in the booths, the people from the costume party, and he could almost hear their muffled laughter as they held their hands to their mouths and pointed, their eyes sparkling with cruel pinpoints of light.

He whirled around again. "Leave me—"

(alone?)

All the booths were empty. The sound of laughter had died like a stir of autumn leaves. Jack stared at the empty lounge for a tick of time, his eyes wide and dark. A pulse beat noticeably in the center of his forehead. In the very center of him a cold certainty was forming and the certainty was that he was losing his mind. He felt an urge to pick up the bar stool next to him, reverse it, and go through the place like an avenging whirlwind. Instead he whirled back around to the bar and began to bellow:

> "Roll me over
> In the clo-ho-ver,
> Roll me over, lay me down and do it again."

Danny's face rose before him, not Danny's normal face, lively and alert, the eyes sparkling and open, but the catatonic, zombielike face of a stranger, the eyes dull and opaque, the mouth pursed babyishly around his thumb. What was he doing, sitting here and talking to himself like a sulky teen-ager when his son was upstairs, someplace, acting like something that belonged in a padded room, acting the way Wally Hollis said Vic Stenger had been before the men in the white coats had to come and take him away?

(*But I never put a hand on him! Goddammit, I didn't!*)

"Jack?" The voice was timid, hesitant.

He was so startled he almost fell off the stool whirling it around. Wendy was standing just inside the batwing doors, Danny cradled in her arms like some waxen horror show dummy. The three of them made a tableau that Jack felt very strongly; it was just before the curtain of Act II in some old-time temperance play, one so poorly mounted that the prop man had forgotten to stock the shelves of the Den of Iniquity.

"I never touched him," Jack said thickly. "I never have since the night I broke his arm. Not even to spank him."

"Jack, that doesn't matter now. What matters is—"

"*This matters!*" he shouted. He brought one fist crashing down on the bar, hard enough to make the empty peanut dishes jump. "*It matters, goddammit, it matters!*"

"Jack, we have to get him off the mountain. He's—"

Danny began to stir in her arms. The slack, empty expression on his face had begun to break up like a thick matte of ice over some buried surface. His lips twisted, as if at some weird taste. His eyes widened.

His hands came up as if to cover them and then dropped back.

Abruptly he stiffened in her arms. His back arched into a bow, making Wendy stagger. And he suddenly began to shriek, mad sounds that escaped his straining throat in bolt after crazy, echoing bolt. The sound seemed to fill the empty downstairs and come back at them like banshees. There might have been a hundred Dannys, all screaming at once.

"*Jack!*" she cried in terror. "*Oh God Jack what's wrong with him?*"

He came off the stool, numb from the waist down, more frightened than he had ever been in his life. What hole had his son poked through and into? What dark nest? And what had been in there to sting him?

"Danny!" he roared. "*Danny!*"

Danny saw him. He broke his mother's grip with a sudden, fierce strength that gave her no chance to hold him. She stumbled back against one of the booths and nearly fell into it.

"*Daddy!*" he screamed, running to Jack, his eyes huge and affrighted. "*Oh Daddy Daddy, it was her! Her! Her! Oh Daaaaahdeee—*"

He slammed into Jack's arms like a blunt arrow, making Jack rock on his feet. Danny clutched at him furiously, at first seeming to pummel him like a fighter, then clutching his belt and sobbing against his shirt. Jack could feel his son's face, hot and working, against his belly.

Daddy, it was her.

Jack looked slowly up into Wendy's face. His eyes were like small silver coins.

"Wendy?" Voice soft, nearly purring. "Wendy, what did you do to him?"

Wendy stared back at him in stunned disbelief, her face pallid. She shook her head.

"Oh Jack, you must know—"

Outside it had begun to snow again.

29

Kitchen Talk

Jack carried Danny into the kitchen. The boy was still sobbing wildly, refusing to look up from Jack's chest. In the kitchen he gave Danny back to Wendy, who still seemed stunned and disbelieving.

"Jack, I don't know what he's talking about. Please, you must believe that."

"I do believe it," he said, although he had to admit to himself that it gave him a certain amount of pleasure to see the shoe switched to the other foot with such dazzling, unexpected speed. But his anger at Wendy had been only a passing gut twitch. In his heart he knew Wendy would pour a can of gasoline over herself and strike a match before harming Danny.

The large tea kettle was on the back burner, poking along on low heat. Jack dropped a teabag into his own large ceramic cup and poured hot water halfway.

"Got cooking sherry, don't you?" he asked Wendy.

"What? . . . oh, sure. Two or three bottles of it."

"Which cupboard?"

She pointed, and Jack took one of the bottles down. He poured a hefty dollop into the teacup, put the sherry back, and filled the last quarter of the cup with milk. Then he added three tablespoons of sugar and stirred. He brought it to Danny, whose sobs had tapered off to snifflings and hitchings. But he was trembling all over, and his eyes were wide and starey.

"Want you to drink this, doc," Jack said. "It's going to taste frigging awful, but it'll make you feel better. Can you drink it for your daddy?"

Danny nodded that he could and took the cup. He drank a little, grimaced, and looked questioningly at Jack. Jack nodded, and Danny drank again. Wendy felt the familiar twist of jealousy somewhere in her middle, knowing the boy would not have drunk it for her.

On the heels of that came an uncomfortable, even startling thought: Had she *wanted* to think Jack was to blame? Was she that jealous? It was the way her mother would have thought, that was the really horrible thing. She could remember a Sunday when her Dad had taken her to the park and she had toppled from the second tier of the jungle gym, cutting both knees. When her father brought her home, her mother had shrieked at him: *What did you do? Why weren't you watching her? What kind of a father are you?*

(She hounded him to his grave; by the time he divorced her it was too late.)

She had never even given Jack the benefit of the doubt. Not the smallest. Wendy felt her face burn yet knew with a kind of helpless finality that if the whole thing were to be played over again, she would do and think the same way. She carried part of her mother with her always, for good or bad.

"Jack—" she began, not sure if she meant to apologize or justify. Either, she knew, would be useless.

"Not now," he said.

It took Danny fifteen minutes to drink half of the big cup's contents, and by that time he had calmed visibly. The shakes were almost gone.

Jack put his hands solemnly on his son's shoulders. "Danny, do you think you can tell us exactly what happened to you? It's very important."

Danny looked from Jack to Wendy, then back again. In the silent pause, their setting and situation made themselves known: the whoop of the wind outside, driving fresh snow down from the northwest; the creaking and groaning of the old hotel as it settled into another storm. The fact of their disconnect came to Wendy with unexpected force as it sometimes did, like a blow under the heart.

"I want . . . to tell you everything," Danny said. "I wish I had before." He picked up the cup and held it, as if comforted by the warmth.

"Why didn't you, son?" Jack brushed Danny's sweaty, tumbled hair back gently from his brow.

"Because Uncle Al got you the job. And I couldn't figure out how it was good for you here and bad for you here at the same time. It was . . ." He looked at them for help. He did not have the necessary word.

"A dilemma?" Wendy asked gently. "When neither choice seems any good?"

"Yes, that." He nodded, relieved.

Wendy said: "The day that you trimmed the hedges, Danny and I had a talk in the truck. The day the first real snow came. Remember?"

Jack nodded. The day he had trimmed the hedges was very clear in his mind.

Wendy sighed. "I guess we didn't talk enough. Did we, doc?"

Danny, the picture of woe, shook his head.

"Exactly what did you talk about?" Jack asked. "I'm not sure how much I like my wife and son—"

"—discussing how much they love you?"

"Whatever it was, I don't understand it. I feel like I came into a movie just after the intermission."

"We were discussing you," Wendy said quietly. "And maybe we didn't say it all in words, but we both knew. Me because I'm your wife and Danny because he . . . just understands things."

Jack was silent.

"Danny said it just right. The place seemed good for you. You were away from all the pressures that made you so unhappy at Stovington. You were your own boss, working with your hands so you could save your brain—all of your brain—for your evenings writing. Then . . . I don't know just when . . . the place began to seem bad for you. Spending all that time down in the cellar, sifting through those old papers, all that old history. Talking in your sleep—"

"In my sleep?" Jack asked. His face wore a cautious, startled expression. "I talk in my sleep?"

"Most of it is slurry. Once I got up to use the bathroom and you were saying. 'To hell with it, bring in the slots at least, no one will know, no one will ever know.' Another time you woke me right up, practically yelling, 'Unmask, unmask, unmask.' "

"Jesus Christ," he said, and rubbed a hand over his face. He looked ill.

"All your old drinking habits, too. Chewing Excedrin. Wiping your mouth all the time. Cranky in the morning. And you haven't been able to finish the play yet, have you?"

"No. Not yet, but it's only a matter of time. I've been thinking about something else . . . a new project—"

"This hotel. The project Al Shockley called you about. The one he wanted you to drop."

"How do you know about that?" Jack barked. "Were you listening in? You—"

"No," she said. "I couldn't have listened in if I'd wanted to, and you'd know that if you were thinking straight. Danny and I were downstairs that night. The switchboard is shut down. Our phone upstairs was the only one in the hotel that was working, because it's patched directly into the outside line. You told me so yourself."

"Then how could you know what Al told me?"

"Danny told me. Danny knew. The same way he sometimes knows when things are misplaced, or when people are thinking about divorce."

"The doctor said—"

She shook her head impatiently. "The doctor was full of shit and we both know it. We've known it all the time. Remember when Danny said he wanted to see the firetrucks? That was no hunch. *He was just a baby.* He *knows* things. And now I'm afraid . . ." She looked at the bruises on Danny's neck.

"Did you really know Uncle Al had called me, Danny?"

Danny nodded. "He was really mad, Daddy. Because you called Mr. Ullman and Mr. Ullman called him. Uncle Al didn't want you to write anything about the hotel."

"Jesus," Jack said again. "The bruises, Danny. Who tried to strangle you?"

Danny's face went dark. *"Her,"* he said. "The woman in that room. In 217. The dead lady." His lips began to tremble again, and he seized the teacup and drank.

Jack and Wendy exchanged a scared look over his bowed head.

"Do you know anything about this?" he asked her.

She shook her head. "Not about this, no."

"Danny?" He raised the boy's frightened face. "Try, son. We're right here."

"I knew it was bad here," Danny said in a low voice. "Ever since we were in Boulder. Because Tony gave me dreams about it."

"What dreams?"

"I can't remember everything. He showed me the Overlook at night, with a skull and crossbones on the front. And there was pounding. Something . . . I don't remember what . . . chasing after me. A monster. Tony showed me about redrum."

"What's that, doc?" Wendy asked.

He shook his head. "I don't know."

"Rum, like yo-ho-ho and a bottle of rum?" Jack asked.

Danny shook his head again. "I don't know. Then we got here, and Mr. Hallorann talked to me in his car. Because he has the shine, too."

"Shine?"

"It's . . ." Danny made a sweeping, all-encompassing gesture with his hands. "It's being able to understand things. To know things. Sometimes you see things. Like me knowing Uncle Al called. And Mr. Hallorann knowing you call me doc. Mr. Hallorann, he was peeling potatoes in the Army when he knew his brother got killed in a train crash. And when he called home it was true."

"Holy God," Jack whispered. "You're not making this up, are you, Dan?"

Danny shook his head violently. "No, I swear to God." Then, with a touch of pride he added: "Mr. Hallorann said I had the best shine of anyone he ever met. We could talk back and forth to each other without hardly opening our mouths."

His parents looked at each other again, frankly stunned.

"Mr. Hallorann got me alone because he was worried," Danny went on. "He said this was a bad place for people who shine. He said he'd seen things. I saw something, too. Right after I talked to him. When Mr. Ullman was taking us around."

"What was it?" Jack asked.

"In the Presidential Sweet. On the wall by the door going into the bedroom. A whole lot of blood and some other stuff. Gushy stuff. I think . . . that the gushy stuff must have been brains."

"Oh my God," Jack said.

Wendy was now very pale, her lips nearly gray.

"This place," Jack said. "Some pretty bad types owned it awhile back. Organization people from Las Vegas."

"Crooks?" Danny asked.

"Yeah, crooks." He looked at Wendy. "In 1966 a big-time hood named Vito Gienelli got killed up there, along with his two bodyguards. There was a picture in the newspaper. Danny just described the picture."

"Mr. Hallorann said he saw some other stuff," Danny told them. "Once about the playground. And once it was something bad in that room. 217. A maid saw it and lost her job because she talked about it. So Mr. Hallorann went up and he saw it too. But he didn't talk about it because he didn't want to lose his job. Except he told me never to go in there. But I did. Because I believed him when he said the things you saw here couldn't hurt you." This last was nearly whispered in a low, husky voice, and Danny touched the puffed circle of bruises on his neck.

"What about the playground?" Jack asked in a strange, casual voice.

"I don't know. The playground, he said. And the hedge animals."

Jack jumped a little, and Wendy looked at him curiously.

"Have you seen anything down there, Jack?"

"No," he said. "Nothing."

Danny was looking at him.

"Nothing," he said again, more calmly. And that was true. He had been the victim of an hallucination. And that was *all*.

"Danny, we have to hear about the woman," Wendy said gently.

So Danny told them, but his words came in cyclic bursts, sometimes almost verging on incomprehensible garble in his hurry to spit it out and be free of it. He pushed tighter and tighter against his mother's breasts as he talked.

"I went in," he said. "I stole the passkey and went in. It was like I couldn't help myself. I had to know. And she . . . the lady . . . was in the tub. She was dead. All swelled up. She was nuh-nuh . . . didn't have no clothes on." He looked miserably at his mother. "And she started to get up and she wanted me. I know she did because I could feel it. She wasn't even thinking, not the way you and Daddy think. It was black . . . it was hurt-think . . . like . . . like the wasps that night in my room! Only wanting to hurt. Like the wasps."

He swallowed and there was silence for a moment, all quiet while the image of the wasps sank into them.

"So I ran," Danny said, "I ran but the door was closed. I left it open but it was closed. I didn't think about just opening it again and running out. I was scared. So I just . . . I leaned against the door and closed my eyes and thought of how Mr. Hallorann said the things here were just like pictures in a book and if I . . . kept saying to myself . . . *you're not there, go away, you're not there* . . . she would go away. But it didn't work."

His voice began to rise hysterically.

"She grabbed me . . . turned me around . . . I could see her eyes . . . how her eyes were . . . and she started to choke me . . . I could smell her . . . *I could smell how dead she was* . . ."

"Stop now, shhh," Wendy said, alarmed. "Stop, Danny. It's all right. It—"

She was getting ready to go into her croon again. The Wendy Torrance All-purpose Croon. Pat. Pending.

"Let him finish," Jack said curtly.

"There isn't any more," Danny said. "I passed out. Either because she was choking me or just because I was scared. When I came to, I was dreaming you and Mommy were fighting over me and you wanted to do the Bad Thing again, Daddy. Then I knew it wasn't a dream at all . . . and I was awake . . . and . . . I wet my pants. I wet my pants like a baby." His head fell back against Wendy's sweater and he began to cry with horrible weakness, his hands lying limp and spent in his lap.

Jack got up. "Take care of him."

"What are you going to do?" Her face was full of dread.

"I'm going up to that room, what did you think I was going to do? Have coffee?"

"No! Don't, Jack, please *don't!*"

"Wendy, if there's someone else in the hotel, we have to know."

"Don't you dare leave us alone!" she shrieked at him. Spittle flew from her lips with the force of her cry.

Jack said: "Wendy, that's a remarkable imitation of your mom."

She burst into tears then, unable to cover her face because Danny was on her lap.

"I'm sorry," Jack said. "But I have to, you know. I'm the goddam caretaker. It's what I'm paid for."

She only cried harder and he left her that way, going out of the kitchen, rubbing his mouth with his handkerchief as the door swung shut behind him.

"Don't worry, mommy," Danny said. "He'll be all right. He doesn't shine. Nothing here can hurt him."

Through her tears she said, "No, I don't believe that."

30

217 Revisited

He took the elevator up and it was strange, because none of them had used the elevator since they moved in. He threw the brass handle over and it wheezed vibratoriously up the shaft, the brass grate rattling madly. Wendy had a true claustrophobe's horror of the elevator, he knew. She envisioned the three of them trapped in it between floors while the winter storms raged outside, she could see them growing thinner and weaker, starving to death. Or perhaps dining on each other, the way those Rugby players had. He remembered a bumper sticker he had seen in Boulder, RUGBY PLAYERS EAT THEIR OWN DEAD. He could think of others. YOU ARE WHAT YOU EAT. Or menu items. Welcome to the Overlook Dining Room, Pride of the Rockies. Eat in Splendor at the Roof of the World. Human Haunch, Broiled Over Matches *La Spécialité de la Maison*. The contemptuous smile flicked over his features again. As the number 2 rose on the shaft wall, he threw the brass handle back to the home position and the elevator car creaked to a stop. He took his Excedrin from his pocket, shook three of them into his hand, and opened the elevator door. Nothing in the Overlook frightened him. He felt that he and it were *simpático*.

He walked up the hall flipping his Excedrin into his mouth and chewing them one by one. He rounded the corner into the short corridor off the main hall. The door to Room 217 was ajar, and the passkey hung from the lock on its white paddle.

He frowned, feeling a wave of irritation and even real anger. Whatever had come of it, the boy had been trespassing. He had been told, and told bluntly, that certain areas of the hotel were off limits: the equipment shed, the basement, and all of the guest rooms. He would talk to Danny about that just as soon as the boy was over his fright. He would talk to him reasonably but sternly. There were plenty of fathers who would have done more than just talk. They would have administered a good shaking, and perhaps that was what Danny needed. If the boy had gotten a scare, wasn't that at least his just deserts?

He walked down to the door, removed the passkey, dropped it into his pocket, and stepped inside. The overhead light was on. He glanced at the bed, saw it was not rumpled, and then walked directly across to the bathroom door. A curious certainty had grown in him. Although Watson had mentioned no names or room numbers, Jack felt sure that this was the room the lawyer's wife and her stud had shared, that this was the bathroom where she had been found dead, full of barbiturates and Colorado Lounge booze.

He pushed the mirror-backed bathroom door open and stepped through. The light in here was off. He turned it on and observed the long, Pullman-car room, furnished in the distinctive early nineteen-hundreds-remodeled-in-the-twenties style that seemed common to all Overlook bathrooms, except for the ones on the third floor—those were properly Byzantine, as befitted the royalty, politicians, movie stars, and capos who had stayed there over the years.

The shower curtain, a pallid pastel pink, was drawn protectively around the long claw-footed tub.

(nevertheless they *did* move)

And for the first time he felt his new sense of sureness (almost cockiness) that had come over him when Danny ran to him shouting *It was her! It was her!* deserting him. A chilled finger pressed gently against the base of his spine, cooling him off ten degrees. It was joined by others and they suddenly rippled all the way up his back to his medulla oblongata, playing his spine like a jungle instrument.

His anger at Danny evaporated, and as he stepped forward and pushed the shower curtain back his mouth was dry and he felt only sympathy for his son and terror for himself.

The tub was dry and empty.

Relief and irritation vented in a sudden *"Pah!"* sound that escaped his compressed lips like a very small explosive. The tub had been scrubbed clean at the end of the season; except for the rust stain under the twin faucets, it sparkled. There was a faint but definable smell of cleanser, the kind that can irritate your nose with the smell of its own righteousness for weeks, even months, after it has been used.

He bent down and ran his fingertips along the bottom of the tub. Dry as a bone. Not even a hint of moisture. The boy had been either hallucinating or outright lying. He felt angry again. That was when the bathmat on the floor caught his attention. He frowned down at it. What was a bathmat doing in here? It should be down in the linen cupboard at the end of the wing with the rest of the sheets and towels and pillow slips. All the linen was supposed to be there. Not even the beds were really made up in these guest rooms; the mattresses had been zipped into clear plastic and then covered with bedspreads. He supposed Danny might have gone down and gotten it—the passkey would open the linen cupboard—but why? He brushed the tips of his fingers back and forth across it. The bathmat was bone dry.

He went back to the bathroom door and stood in it. Everything was all right. The boy had been dreaming. There was not a thing out of place. It was a little puzzling about the bathmat, granted, but the logical explanation was that some chambermaid, hurrying like mad on the last day of the season, had just forgotten to pick it up. Other than that, everything was—

His nostrils flared a little. Disinfectant, that self-righteous smell, cleaner-than-thou. And—

Soap?

Surely not. But once the smell had been identified, it was too clear to dismiss. Soap. And not one of those postcard-size bars of Ivory they provide you with in hotels and motels, either. This scent was light and perfumed, a lady's soap. It had a pink sort of smell. Camay or Lowila, the brand that Wendy had always used in Stovington.

(*It's nothing. It's your imagination.*)

(*yes like the hedges nevertheless they did move*)

(*They did not move!*)

He crossed jerkily to the door which gave on the hall, feeling the irregular thump of a headache beginning at his temples. Too much had happened today, too much by far. He wouldn't spank the boy or shake him, just talk to him, but by God, he wasn't going to add Room 217 to his problems. Not on the basis of a dry bathmat and a faint smell of Lowila soap. He—

There was a sudden rattling, metallic sound behind him. It came just as his hand closed around the doorknob, and an observer might have thought the brushed steel of the knob carried an electric charge. He jerked convulsively, eyes widening, other facial features drawing in, grimacing.

Then he had control of himself, a little, anyway, and he let go of the doorknob and turned carefully around. His joints creaked. He began to walk back to the bathroom door, step by leaden step.

The shower curtain, which he had pushed back to look into the tub, was now drawn. The metallic rattle, which had sounded to him like a stir of bones in a crypt, had been the curtain rings on the overhead bar. Jack stared at the curtain. His face felt as if it had been heavily waxed, all dead skin on the outside, live, hot rivulets of fear on the inside. The way he had felt on the playground.

There was something behind the pink plastic shower curtain. There was something in the tub.

He could see it, ill defined and obscure through the plastic, a nearly amorphous shape. It could have been anything. A trick of the light. The shadow of the shower attachment. A woman long dead and reclining in her bath, a bar of Lowila in one stiffening hand as she waited patiently for whatever lover might come.

Jack told himself to step forward boldly and rake the shower curtain back. To expose whatever might be there. Instead he turned with jerky, marionette strides, his heart whamming frightfully in his chest, and went back into the bed/sitting room.

The door to the hall was shut.

He stared at it for a long, immobile second. He could taste his terror now. It was in the back of his throat like a taste of gone-over cherries.

He walked to the door with that same jerky stride and forced his fingers to curl around the knob.

(*It won't open.*)

But it did.

He turned off the light with a fumbling gesture, stepped out into the hall, and pulled the door shut without looking back. From inside, he seemed to hear an odd wet thumping sound, far off, dim, as if something had just scrambled belatedly out of the tub, as if to greet a caller, as if it had realized the caller was leaving before the social amenities had been completed and so it was now rushing to the door, all purple and grinning, to invite the caller back inside. Perhaps forever.

Footsteps approaching the door or only the heartbeat in his ears?

He fumbled at the passkey. It seemed sludgy, unwilling to turn in the lock. He attacked the passkey. The tumblers suddenly fell and he stepped back against the corridor's far wall, a little groan of relief escaping him. He closed his eyes and all the old phrases began to parade through his mind, it seemed there must be hundreds of them,

(cracking up not playing with a full deck lostya marbles guy just went loony tunes he went up and over the high side went bananas lost his football crackers nuts half a seabag)

all meaning the same thing: *losing your mind.*

"No," he whimpered, hardly aware that he had been reduced to this, whimpering with his eyes shut like a child. "Oh no, God. Please, God, no."

But below the tumble of his chaotic thoughts, below the triphammer beat of his heart, he could hear the soft and futile sound of the doorknob being turned to and fro as something locked in tried helplessly to get out, something that wanted to meet him, something that would like to be introduced to his family as the storm shrieked around them and white daylight became black night. If he opened his eyes and saw that doorknob moving he would go mad. So he kept them shut, and after an unknowable time, there was stillness.

Jack forced himself to open his eyes, half-convinced that when he did, she would be standing before him. But the hall was empty.

He felt watched just the same.

He looked at the peephole in the center of the door and wondered what would happen if he approached it, stared into it. What would he be eyeball to eyeball with?

His feet were moving
· *(feets don't fail me now)*
before he realized it. He turned them away from the door and walked down to the main hall, his feet whispering on the blue-black jungle carpet. He stopped halfway to the stairs and looked at the fire extinguisher. He thought that the folds of canvas were arranged in a slightly different manner. And he was quite sure that the brass nozzle had been pointing toward the elevator when he came up the hall. Now it was pointing the other way.

"I didn't see that at all," Jack Torrance said quite clearly. His face was white and haggard and his mouth kept trying to grin.

But he didn't take the elevator back down. It was too much like an open mouth. Too much by half. He took the stairs.

31

The Verdict

He stepped into the kitchen and looked at them,
bouncing the passkey a few inches up off his left
hand, making the chain on the white metal tongue
jingle, then catching it again. Danny was pallid and
worn out. Wendy had been crying, he saw; her eyes
were red and darkly circled. He felt a sudden burst of
gladness at this. He wasn't suffering alone, that was
sure.

They looked at him without speaking.

"Nothing there," he said, astounded by the hearti-
ness of his voice. "Not a thing."

He bounced the passkey up and down, up and
down, smiling reassuringly at them, watching the
relief spread over their faces, and thought he had
never in his life wanted a drink so badly as he did
right now.

32

The Bedroom

Late that afternoon Jack got a cot from the first-floor storage room and put it in the corner of their bedroom. Wendy had expected that the boy would be half the night getting to sleep, but Danny was nodding before "The Waltons" was half over, and fifteen minutes after they had tucked him in he was far down in sleep, moveless, one hand tucked under his cheek. Wendy sat watching him, holding her place in a fat paperback copy of *Cashelmara* with one finger. Jack sat at his desk, looking at his play.

"Oh shit," Jack said.

Wendy looked up from her contemplation of Danny. "What?"

"Nothing."

He looked down at the play with smoldering illtemper. How could he have thought it was good? It was puerile. It had been done a thousand times. Worse, he had no idea how to finish it. Once it had seemed simple enough. Denker, in a fit of rage, seizes the poker from beside the fireplace and beats saintly

Gary to death. Then, standing spread-legged over the body, the bloody poker in one hand, he screams at the audience: "It's here somewhere and I *will* find it!" Then, as the lights dim and the curtain is slowly drawn, the audience sees Gary's body face down on the forestage as Denker strides to the upstage bookcase and feverishly begins pulling books from the shelves, looking at them, throwing them aside. He had thought it was something old enough to be new, a play whose novelty alone might be enough to see it through a successful Broadway run: a tragedy in five acts.

But, in addition to his sudden diversion of interest to the Overlook's history, something else had happened. He had developed opposing feelings about his characters. This was something quite new. Ordinarily he liked all of his characters, the good and the bad. He was glad he did. It allowed him to try to see all of their sides and understand their motivations more clearly. His favorite story, sold to a small southern Maine magazine called *Contraband* for copies, had been a piece called "The Monkey Is Here, Paul DeLong." It had been about a child molester about to commit suicide in his furnished room. The child molester's name had been Paul DeLong, Monkey to his friends. Jack had liked Monkey very much. He sympathized with Monkey's bizarre needs, knowing that Monkey was not the only one to blame for the three rape-murders in his past. There had been bad parents, the father a beater as his own father had been, the mother a limp and silent dishrag as his mother had been. A homosexual experience in grammar school. Public humiliation. Worse experiences in high school and college. He had been arrested and sent to an institution after exposing himself to a pair of little girls getting off a school bus. Worst of all, he had been dismissed from the institution, let back out onto the streets, because the man in charge had decided he was all right. This man's name had been Grimmer. Grimmer had known that Monkey DeLong was exhibiting deviant symptoms, but he had written the good, hopeful report and had let him go anyway. Jack liked and sympathized with Grimmer, too. Grimmer had to run an understaffed and underfunded institution and try to keep the whole thing together with spit, baling wire, and nickel-and-dime appropriations from a state legislature who had to go back and face the voters. Grimmer knew that Monkey could interact with other people, that he did not soil his pants or try to stab his fellow inmates with the scissors. He did not think he was Napoleon. The staff psychiatrist in charge of Monkey's case thought there was a better-than-even chance that Monkey could make it on the street, and they both knew that the longer a man is in an institution the more he comes to need that closed environment, like a junkie with his smack. And meanwhile, people were knocking down the doors. Paranoids, schizoids, cycloids, semicatatonics, men who claimed to have gone to heaven in flying saucers, women who had burned their children's sex organs off with Bic lighters, alcoholics, pyromaniacs, kleptomaniacs, manic-depressives, suicidals. Tough old world, baby. If you're not bolted together tightly, you're gonna shake, rattle, and roll before you turn thirty. Jack could sympathize with Grimmer's problem. He could sympathize with the parents of the murder victims. With the murdered children themselves, of course. And with Monkey DeLong. Let the reader lay blame. In those days he hadn't wanted to judge. The cloak of the moralist sat badly on his shoulders.

He had started *The Little School* in the same optimistic vein. But lately he had begun to choose up sides, and worse still, he had come to loathe his hero, Gary Benson. Originally conceived as a bright boy more cursed with money than blessed with it, a boy who wanted more than anything to compile a good record so he could go to a good university because he had earned admission and not because his father had pulled strings, he had become to Jack a kind of simpering Goody Two-shoes, a postulant before the altar of knowledge rather than a sincere acolyte, an outward paragon of Boy Scout virtues, inwardly cynical, filled not with real brilliance (as he had first been conceived) but only with sly animal cunning. All through the play he unfailingly addressed Denker as "sir," just as Jack had taught his own son to address those older and those in authority as "sir." He thought that Danny used the word quite sincerely, and Gary Benson as originally conceived had too, but as he had begun Act V, it had come more and more strongly to him that Gary was using the word satirically, outwardly straight-faced while the Gary Benson inside was mugging and leering at Denker. Denker, who had never had any of the things Gary had. Denker, who had had to work all his life just to become head of a single little school. Who was now faced with ruin over this handsome, innocent-seeming rich boy who had cheated on his Final Composition and had then cunningly covered his tracks. Jack had seen Denker the teacher as not much different from the strutting South American little Caesars in their banana kingdoms, standing dissidents up against the wall of the handiest squash or handball court, a super-zealot in a comparatively small puddle, a man whose every whim becomes a crusade. In the beginning he had wanted to use his play as a microcosm to say something about the abuse of power. Now he tended more and more to see Denker as a Mr. Chips figure, and the tragedy was not the intellectual racking of Gary Benson but rather the destruction of a kindly old teacher and headmaster unable to see through the cynical wiles of this monster masquerading as a boy.

He hadn't been able to finish the play.

Now he sat looking down at it, scowling, wondering if there was any way he could salvage the situation. He didn't really think there was. He had begun with one play and it had somehow turned into another, presto-chango. Well, what the hell. Either way it had been done before. Either way it was a load of shit. And why was he driving himself crazy about it tonight anyway? After the day just gone by it was no wonder he couldn't think straight.

"—get him down?"

He looked up, trying to blink the cobwebs away. "Huh?"

"I said, how are we going to get him down? We've got to get him out of here, Jack."

For a moment his wits were so scattered that he wasn't even sure what she was talking about. Then he realized and uttered a short, barking laugh.

"You say that as if it were so easy."

"I didn't mean—"

"No problem, Wendy. I'll just change clothes in that telephone booth down in the lobby and fly him to Denver on my back. Superman Jack Torrance, they called me in my salad days."

Her face registered slow hurt.

"I understand the problem, Jack. The radio is broken. The snow . . . but you have to understand Danny's problem. My God, don't you? He was nearly catatonic, Jack! What if he hadn't come out of that?"

"But he did," Jack said, a trifle shortly. He had been frightened at Danny's blank-eyed, slack-faced state too, of course he had. At first. But the more he thought about it, the more he wondered if it hadn't been a piece of play-acting put on to escape his punishment. He had, after all, been trespassing.

"All the same," she said. She came to him and sat on the end of the bed by his desk. Her face was both surprised and worried. "Jack, the bruises on his neck! Something got at him! And I want him away from it!"

"Don't shout," he said. "My head aches, Wendy. I'm as worried about this as you are, so please . . . don't . . . shout."

"All right," she said, lowering her voice. "I won't shout. But I don't understand you, Jack. Someone is in here with us. And not a very nice someone, either. We have to get down to Sidewinder, not just Danny but all of us. Quickly. And you . . . you're sitting there reading your *play!*"

" 'We have to get down, we have to get down,' you keep saying that. You must think I really am Superman."

"I think you're my husband," she said softly, and looked down at her hands.

His temper flared. He slammed the playscript down, knocking the edges of the pile out of true again and crumpling the sheets on the bottom.

"It's time you got some of the home truths into you, Wendy. You don't seem to have internalized them, as the sociologists say. They're knocking around up in your head like a bunch of loose cueballs. You need to shoot them into the pockets. You need to understand that *we are snowed in.*"

Danny had suddenly become active in his bed. Still sleeping, he had begun to twist and turn. The way he always did when we fought, Wendy thought dismally. And we're doing it again.

"Don't wake him up, Jack. Please."

He glanced over at Danny and some of the flush went out of his cheeks. "Okay. I'm sorry. I'm sorry I sounded mad, Wendy. It's not really for you. But I broke the radio. If it's anybody's fault it's mine. That was our big link to the outside. Olly-olly-in-for-free. Please come get us, Mister Ranger. We can't stay out this late."

"Don't," she said, and put a hand on his shoulder. He leaned his head against it. She brushed his hair with her other hand. "I guess you've got a right after what I accused you of. Sometimes I am like my mother. I can be a bitch. But you have to understand that some things . . . are hard to get over. You have to understand that."

"Do you mean his arm?" His lips had thinned.

"Yes," Wendy said, and then she rushed on: "But it's not just you. I worry when he goes out to play. I worry about him wanting a two-wheeler next year, even one with training wheels. I worry about his teeth and his eyesight and about this thing, what he calls his shine. I worry. Because he's little and he seems very fragile and because . . . because something in this hotel seems to want him. And it will go through us to get him if it has to. That's why we must get him out, Jack. I know that! I feel that! *We must get him out!*"

Her hand had tightened painfully on his shoulder in her agitation, but he didn't move away. One hand found the firm weight of her left breast and he began to stroke it through her shirt.

"Wendy," he said, and stopped. She waited for him to rearrange whatever he had to say. His strong hand on her breast felt good, soothing. "I could maybe snowshoe him down. He could walk part of the way himself, but I would mostly have to carry him. It would mean camping out one, two, maybe three nights. That would mean building a travois to carry supplies and bedrolls on. We have the AM/FM radio, so we could pick a day when the weather forecast called for a three-day spell of good weather. But if the forecast was wrong," he finished, his voice soft and measured, "I think we might die."

Her face had paled. It looked shiny, almost ghostly. He continued to stroke her breast, rubbing the ball of his thumb gently over the nipple.

She made a soft sound—from his words or in reaction to his gentle pressure on her breast, he couldn't tell. He raised his hand slightly and undid the top button of her shirt. Wendy shifted her legs slightly. All at once her jeans seemed too tight, slightly irritating in a pleasant sort of way.

"It would mean leaving you alone because you can't snowshoe worth beans. It would be maybe three days of not knowing. Would you want that?" His hand dropped to the second button, slipped it, and the beginning of her cleavage was exposed.

"No," she said in a voice that was slightly thick. She glanced over at Danny. He had stopped twisting and turning. His thumb had crept back into his mouth. So that was all right. But Jack was leaving something out of the picture. It was too bleak. There was something else . . . what?

"If we stay put," Jack said, unbuttoning the third and fourth buttons with that same deliberate slowness, "a ranger from the park or a game warden is going to poke in here just to find out how we're doing. At that point we simply tell him we want down. He'll see to it." He slipped her naked breasts into the wide V of the open shirt, bent, and molded his lips around the stem of a nipple. It was hard and erect. He slipped his tongue slowly back and forth across it in a way he knew she liked. Wendy moaned a little and arched her back.

(*?Something I've forgotten?*)

"Honey?" she asked. On their own her hands sought the back of his head so that when he answered his voice was muffled against her flesh.

"How would the ranger take us out?"

He raised his head slightly to answer and then settled his mouth against the other nipple.

"If the helicopter was spoken for I guess it would have to be by snowmobile."

(*!!!*)

"But we have one of those! Ullman said so!"

His mouth froze against her breast for a moment, and then he sat up. Her own face was slightly flushed, her eyes overbright. Jack's, on the other hand, was calm, as if he had been reading a rather dull book instead of engaging in foreplay with his wife.

"If there's a snowmobile there's no problem," she said excitedly. "We can all three go down together."

"Wendy, I've never driven a snowmobile in my life."

"It can't be that hard to learn. Back in Vermont you see ten-year-olds driving them in the fields . . . although what their parents can be thinking of I don't know. And you had a motorcycle when we met." He had, a Honda 350cc. He had traded it in on a Saab shortly after he and Wendy took up residence together.

"I suppose I could," he said slowly. "But I wonder how well it's been maintained. Ullman and Watson . . . they run this place from May to October. They have summertime minds. I know it won't have gas in it. There may not be plugs or a battery, either. I don't want you to get your hopes up over your head, Wendy."

She was totally excited now, leaning over him, her breasts tumbling out of her shirt. He had a sudden impulse to seize one and twist it until she shrieked. Maybe that would teach her to shut up.

"The gas is no problem," she said. "The VW and the hotel truck are both full. There's gas for the emergency generator downstairs, too. And there must be a gascan out in that shed so you could carry extra."

"Yes," he said. "There is." Actually there were three of them, two five-gallons and a two-gallon.

"I'll bet the sparkplugs and the battery are out there too. Nobody would store their snowmobile in one place and the plugs and battery someplace else, would they?"

"Doesn't seem likely, does it?" He got up and walked over to where Danny lay sleeping. A spill of hair had fallen across his forehead and Jack brushed it away gently. Danny didn't stir.

"And if you can get it running you'll take us out?" she asked from behind him. "On the first day the radio says good weather?"

For a moment he didn't answer. He stood looking down at his son, and his mixed feelings dissolved in a wave of love. He was the way she had said, vulnerable, fragile. The marks on his neck were very prominent.

"Yes," he said. "I'll get it running and we'll get out as quick as we can."

"Thank God!"

He turned around. She had taken off her shirt and lay on the bed, her belly flat, her breasts aimed perkily at the ceiling. She was playing with them lazily, flicking at the nipples. "Hurry up, gentlemen," she said softly, "time."

After, with no light burning in the room but the night light that Danny had brought with him from his room, she lay in the crook of his arm, feeling deliciously at peace. She found it hard to believe they could be sharing the Overlook with a murderous stowaway.

"Jack?"

"Hmmmm?"

"What got at him?"

He didn't answer her directly. "He does have something. Some talent the rest of us are missing. The most of us, beg pardon. And maybe the Overlook has something, too."

"Ghosts?"

"I don't know. Not in the Algernon Blackwood sense, that's for sure. More like the residues of the feelings of the people who have stayed here. Good things and bad things. In that sense, I suppose that every big hotel has got its ghosts. Especially the old ones."

"But a dead woman in the tub . . . Jack, he's not losing his mind, is he?"

He gave her a brief squeeze. "We know he goes into . . . well, trances, for want of a better word . . . from time to time. We know that when he's in them he sometimes . . . sees? . . . things he doesn't understand. If precognitive trances are possible, they're probably functions of the subconscious mind. Freud said that the subconscious never speaks to us in literal language. Only in symbols. If you dream about being in a bakery where no one speaks English, you may be worried about your ability to support your family. Or maybe just that no one understands you. I've read that the falling dream is a standard outlet for feelings of insecurity. Games, little games. Conscious on one side of the net, subconscious on the other, serving some cockamamie image back and forth. Same with mental illness, with hunches, all of that. Why should precognition be any different? Maybe Danny really did see blood all over the walls of the Presidential Suite. To a kid his age, the image of blood and the concept of death are nearly interchangeable. To kids, the image is always more accessible than the concept, anyway. William Carlos Williams knew that, he was a pediatrician. When we grow up, concepts gradually get easier and we leave the images to the poets . . . and I'm just rambling on."

"I like to hear you ramble."

"She said it, folks. She said it. You all heard it."

"The marks on his neck, Jack. Those are real."

"Yes."

There was nothing else for a long time. She had begun to think he must have gone to sleep and she was slipping into a drowse herself when he said:

"I can think of two explanations for those. And neither of them involves a fourth party in the hotel."

"What?" She came up on one elbow.

"Stigmata, maybe," he said.

"Stigmata? Isn't that when people bleed on Good Friday or something?"

"Yes. Sometimes people who believe deeply in Christ's divinity exhibit bleeding marks on their hands and feet during the Holy Week. It was more common in the Middle Ages than now. In those days such people were considered blessed by God. I don't think the Catholic Church proclaimed any of it as out-and-out miracles, which was pretty smart of them. Stigmata isn't much different from some of the things the yogis can do. It's better understood now, that's all. The people who understand the interaction between the mind and the body—study it, I mean, no one understands it—believe we have a lot more control over our involuntary functions than they used to think. You can slow your heartbeat if you think about it enough. Speed up your own metabolism. Make yourself sweat more. Or make yourself bleed."

"You think Danny *thought* those bruises onto his neck? Jack, I just can't believe that."

"I can believe it's possible, although it seems unlikely to me, too. What's more likely is that he did it to himself."

"To himself?"

"He's gone into these 'trances' and hurt himself in the past. Do you remember the time at the supper table? About two years ago, I think. We were super-pissed at each other. Nobody talking very much. Then, all at once, his eyes rolled up in his head and he went face-first into his dinner. Then onto the floor. Remember?"

"Yes," she said. "I sure do. I thought he was having a convulsion."

"Another time we were in the park," he said. "Just Danny and I. Saturday afternoon. He was sitting on a swing, coasting back and forth. He collapsed onto the ground. It was like he'd been shot. I ran over and picked him up and all of a sudden he just came around. He sort of blinked at me and said, 'I hurt my tummy. Tell Mommy to close the bedroom windows if it rains.' And that night it rained like hell."

"Yes, but—"

"And he's always coming in with cuts and scraped elbows. His shins look like a battlefield in distress. And when you ask him how he got this one or that one, he just says 'Oh, I was playing,' and that's the end of it."

"Jack, all kids get bumped and bruised up. With little boys it's almost constant from the time they learn to walk until they're twelve or thirteen."

"And I'm sure Danny gets his share," Jack responded. "He's an active kid. But I remember that day in the park and that night at the supper table. And I wonder if some of our kid's bumps and bruises come from just keeling over. That Dr.

Edmonds said Danny did it right in his office, for Christ's sake!"

"All right. But those bruises were *fingers.* I'd swear to it. He didn't get them falling down."

"He goes into a trance," Jack said. "Maybe he sees something that happened in that room. An argument. Maybe a suicide. Violent emotions. It isn't like watching a movie; he's in a highly suggestible state. He's right in the damn thing. His subconscious is maybe visualizing whatever happened in a symbolic way . . . as a dead woman who's alive again, zombie, undead, ghoul, you pick your term."

"You're giving me goose-bumps," she said thickly.

"I'm giving myself a few. I'm no psychiatrist, but it seems to fit so well. The walking dead woman as a symbol for dead emotions, dead lives, that just won't give up and go away . . . but because she's a subconscious figure, she's also *him.* In the trance state, the conscious Danny is submerged. The subconscious figure is pulling the strings. So Danny put his hands around his own neck and—"

"Stop," she said. "I get the picture. I think that's more frightening than having a stranger creeping around the halls, Jack. You can move away from a stranger. You can't move away from yourself. You're talking about schizophrenia."

"Of a very limited type," he said, but a trifle uneasily. "And of a very special nature. Because he does seem able to read thoughts, and he really does seem to have precognitive flashes from time to time. I can't think of that as mental illness no matter how hard I try. We all have schizo deposits in us anyway. I think as Danny gets older, he'll get this under control."

"If you're right, then it's imperative that we get him out. Whatever he has, this hotel is making it worse."

"I wouldn't say that," he objected. "If he'd done as he was told, he never would have gone up to that room in the first place. It never would have happened."

"My God, Jack! Are you implying that being half-strangled was a . . . a fitting punishment for being off limits?"

"No . . . no. Of course not. But—"

"No buts," she said, shaking her head violently. "The truth is, we're guessing. We don't have any idea when he might turn a corner and run into one of those . . . air pockets, one-reel horror movies, whatever they are. We have to get him *away*." She laughed a little in the darkness. "Next thing we'll be seeing things."

"Don't talk nonsense," he said, and in the darkness of the room he saw the hedge lions bunching around the path, no longer flanking it but guarding it, hungry November lions. Cold sweat sprang out on his brow.

"You didn't really see anything, did you?" she was asking. "I mean, when you went up to that room. You didn't see anything?"

The lions were gone. Now he saw a pink pastel shower curtain with a dark shape lounging behind it. The closed door. That muffled, hurried thump, and sounds after it that might have been running footsteps. The horrible, lurching beat of his own heart as he struggled with the passkey.

"Nothing," he said, and that was true. He had been strung up, not sure of what was happening. He hadn't had a chance to sift through his thoughts for a reasonable explanation concerning the bruises on his son's neck. He had been pretty damn suggestible himself. Hallucinations could sometimes be catching.

"And you haven't changed your mind? About the snowmobile, I mean?"

His hands clamped into sudden tight fists

(*Stop nagging me!*)

by his sides. "I said I would, didn't I? I will. Now go to sleep. It's been a long hard day."

"And how," she said. There was a rustle of bed-clothes as she turned toward him and kissed his shoulder. "I love you, Jack."

"I love you too," he said, but he was only mouthing the words. His hands were still clenched into fists. They felt like rocks on the ends of his arms. The pulse beat prominently in his forehead. She hadn't said a word about what was going to happen to them *after* they got down, when the party was over. Not one word. It had been Danny this and Danny that and Jack I'm so scared. Oh yes, she was scared of a lot of closet boogeymen and jumping shadows, plenty scared. But there was no lack of real ones, either. When they got down to Sidewinder they would arrive with sixty dollars and the clothes they stood up in. Not even a car. Even if Sidewinder had a pawnshop, which it didn't, they had nothing to hock but Wendy's ninety-dollar diamond engagement ring and the Sony AM/FM radio. A pawnbroker might give them twenty bucks. A *kind* pawnbroker. There would be no job, not even part-time or seasonal, except maybe shoveling out driveways for three dollars a shot. The picture of John Torrance, thirty years old, who had once published in *Esquire* and who had harbored dreams—not at all unreasonable dreams, he felt—of becoming a major American writer during the next decade, with a shovel from the Sidewinder Western Auto on his shoulder, ringing doorbells . . . that picture suddenly came to him much more clearly than the hedge lions and he clenched his fists tighter still, feeling the fingernails sink into his palms and draw blood in mystic quarter-moon shapes. John Torrance, standing in line to change his sixty dollars into food stamps, standing in line again at the Sidewinder Methodist Church to get donated commodities and dirty looks from the locals. John Torrance explaining to Al that they'd just had to leave, had to shut down the boiler, had to leave the Overlook and all it contained open to vandals or thieves on snow machines because, you see, Al, *attendez-vous,* Al, there are ghosts up there and they have it in for my boy. Goodby, Al. Thoughts of Chapter Four, Spring Comes for John Torrance. What then? Whatever then? They might be able to get to the West Coast in the VW, he supposed. A new fuel pump would do it. Fifty miles west of here and it was all downhill, you could damn near put the bug in neutral and coast to Utah. On to sunny California, land of oranges and opportunity. A man with his sterling record of alcoholism, student-beating, and ghost-chasing would undoubtedly be able to write his own ticket. Anything you like. Custodial engineer—swamping out Greyhound buses. The automotive business—washing cars in a rubber suit. The culinary arts, perhaps, washing dishes in a diner. Or possibly a more responsible position, such as pumping gas. A job like that even held the intellectual stimulation of making change and writing out credit slips. *I can give you twenty-five hours a week at the minimum wage.* That was heavy tunes in a year when Wonder bread went for sixty cents a loaf.

Blood had begun to trickle down from his palms. Like stigmata, oh yes. He squeezed tighter, savaging himself with pain. His wife was asleep beside him, why not? There were no problems. He had agreed to take her and Danny away from the big bad boogeyman and there were no problems. *So you see, Al, I thought the best thing to do would be to—*

(*kill her.*)

The thought rose up from nowhere, naked and unadorned. The urge to tumble her out of bed, naked, bewildered, just beginning to wake up; to pounce on her, seize her neck like the green limb of a young aspen and to throttle her, thumbs on windpipe, fingers pressing against the top of her spine, jerking her head up and ramming it back down against the floorboards, again and again, whamming, whacking, smashing, crashing. Jitter and jive, baby. Shake, rattle, and roll. He would make her take her medicine. Every drop. Every last bitter drop.

He was dimly aware of a muffled noise somewhere, just outside his hot and racing inner world.
He looked across the room and Danny was thrashing
again, twisting in his bed and rumpling the blankets.
The boy was moaning deep in his throat, a small,
caged sound. What nightmare? A purple woman,
long dead, shambling after him down twisting hotel
corridors? Somehow he didn't think so. Something
else chased Danny in his dreams. Something worse.

The bitter lock of his emotions was broken. He
got out of bed and went across to the boy, feeling sick
and ashamed of himself. It was Danny he had to
think of, not Wendy, not himself. Only Danny. And
no matter what shape he wrestled the facts into, he
knew in his heart that Danny must be taken out. He
straightened the boy's blankets and added the quilt
from the foot of the bed. Danny had quieted again
now. Jack touched the sleeping forehead

(what monsters capering just behind that ridge of
bone?)

and found it warm, but not overly so. And he was
sleeping peacefully again. Queer.

He got back into bed and tried to sleep. It eluded
him.

It was so unfair that things should turn out this
way—bad luck seemed to stalk them. They hadn't
been able to shake it by coming up here after all. By
the time they arrived in Sidewinder tomorrow afternoon, the golden opportunity would have evaporated—gone the way of the blue suede shoe, as an old
roommate of his had been wont to say. Consider the

difference if they didn't go down, if they could somehow stick it out. The play would get finished. One
way or the other, he would tack an ending onto it.
His own uncertainty about his characters might add
an appealing touch of ambiguity to his original ending. Perhaps it would even make him some money, it
wasn't impossible. Even lacking that, Al might well
convince the Stovington Board to rehire him. He
would be on pro of course, maybe for as long as three
years, but if he could stay sober and keep writing, he
might not have to stay at Stovington for three years.
Of course he hadn't cared much for Stovington
before, he had felt stifled, buried alive, but that had
been an immature reaction. Furthermore, how much
could a man enjoy teaching when he went through
his first three classes with a skull-busting hangover
every second or third day? It wouldn't be that way
again. He would be able to handle his responsibilities
much better. He was sure of it.

Somewhere in the midst of that thought, things
began to break up and he drifted down into sleep. His
last thought followed him down like a sounding bell:

*It seemed that he might be able to find peace here. At
last. If they would only let him.*

When he woke up he was standing in the bathroom
of 217.

(been walking in my sleep again—why?—no
radios to break up here)

The bathroom light was on, the room behind him
in darkness. The shower curtain was drawn around

the long claw-footed tub. The bathmat beside it was wrinkled and wet.

He began to feel afraid, but the very dreamlike quality of his fear told him this was not real. Yet that could not contain the fear. So many things at the Overlook seemed like dreams.

He moved across the floor to the tub, not wanting to be helpless to turn his feet back.

He flung the curtain open.

Lying in the tub, naked, lolling almost weightless in the water, was George Hatfield, a knife stuck in his chest. The water around him was stained a bright pink. George's eyes were closed. His penis floated limply, like kelp.

"George—" he heard himself say.

At the word, George's eyes snapped open. They were silver, not human eyes at all. George's hands, fish-white, found the sides of the tub and he pulled himself up to a sitting position. The knife stuck straight out from his chest, equidistantly placed between nipples. The wound was lipless.

"You set the timer ahead," silver-eyed George told him.

"No, George, I didn't. I—"

"I don't stutter."

George was standing now, still fixing him with that inhuman silver glare, but his mouth had drawn back in a dead and grimacing smile. He threw one leg over the porcelained side of the tub. One white and wrinkled foot placed itself on the bathmat.

"First you tried to run me over on my bike and then you set the timer ahead and then you tried to stab me to death but *I still don't stutter.*" George was coming for him, his hands out, the fingers slightly curled. He smelled moldy and wet, like leaves that had been rained on.

"It was for your own good," Jack said, backing up. "I set it ahead for your own good. Furthermore, I happen to know you cheated on your Final Composition."

"I don't cheat . . . and I don't stutter."

George's hands touched his neck.

Jack turned and ran, ran with the floating, weightless slowness that is so common to dreams.

"You did! You did cheat!" he screamed in fear and anger as he crossed the darkened bed/sitting room. "I'll prove it!"

George's hands were on his neck again. Jack's heart swelled with fear until he was sure it would burst. And then, at last, his hand curled around the doorknob and it turned under his hand and he yanked the door open. He plunged out, not into the second-floor hallway, but into the basement room beyond the arch. The cobwebby light was on. His campchair, stark and geometrical, stood beneath it. And all around it was a miniature mountain range of boxes and crates and banded bundles of records and invoices and God knew what. Relief surged through him.

"I'll find it!" he heard himself screaming. He seized a damp and moldering cardboard box; it split apart in his hands, spilling out a waterfall of yellow flimsies. "It's here somewhere! *I will find it!*" He plunged his hands deep into the pile of papers and came up with a dry, papery wasps' nest in one hand and a timer in the other. The timer was ticking. Attached to its back was a length of electrical cord and attached to the other end of the cord was a bundle of dynamite. *"Here!"* he screamed. *"Here, take it!"*

His relief became absolute triumph. He had done more than escape George; he had conquered. With these talismanic objects in his hands, George would never touch him again. George would flee in terror.

He began to turn so he could confront George, and that was when George's hands settled around his neck, squeezing, stopping his breath, damming up his respiration entirely after one final dragging gasp.

"I don't stutter," whispered George from behind him.

He dropped the wasps' nest and wasps boiled out of it in a furious brown and yellow wave. His lungs were on fire. His wavering sight fell on the timer and the sense of triumph returned, along with a cresting wave of righteous wrath. Instead of connecting the timer to dynamite, the cord ran to the gold knob of a stout black cane, like the one his father had carried after the accident with the milk truck.

He grasped it and the cord parted. The cane felt heavy and right in his hands. He swung it back over his shoulder. On the way up it glanced against the wire from which the light bulb depended and the light began to swing back and forth, making the room's hooded shadows rock monstrously against the floor and walls. On the way down the cane struck something much harder. George screamed. The grip on Jack's throat loosened.

He tore free of George's grip and whirled. George was on his knees, his head drooping, his hands laced together on top of it. Blood welled through his fingers.

"Please," George whispered humbly. "Give me a break, Mr. Torrance."

"Now you'll take your medicine," Jack grunted. "Now by God, won't you. Young pup. Young worthless cur. Now by God, right now. Every drop. Every single damn drop!"

As the light swayed above him and the shadows danced and flapped, he began to swing the cane, bringing it down again and again, his arm rising and falling like a machine. George's bloody protecting fingers fell away from his head and Jack brought the cane down again and again, and on his neck and shoulders and back and arms. Except that the cane was no longer precisely a cane; it seemed to be a mallet with some kind of brightly striped handle. A mallet with a hard side and soft side. The business end was clotted with blood and hair. And the flat, whacking sound of the mallet against flesh had been replaced with a hollow booming sound, echoing and reverberating. His own voice had taken on this same quality, bellowing, disembodied. And yet, paradoxically, it sounded weaker, slurred, petulant . . . as if he were drunk.

The figure on its knees slowly raised its head, as if in supplication. There was not a face, precisely, but only a mask of blood through which eyes peered. He brought the mallet back for a final whistling down-stroke and it was fully launched before he saw that the supplicating face below him was not George's but Danny's. It was the face of his son.

"Daddy"—

And then the mallet crashed home, striking Danny right between the eyes, closing them forever. And something somewhere seemed to be laughing—

(*! No !*)

He came out of it standing naked over Danny's bed, his hands empty, his body sheened with sweat. His final scream had only been in his mind. He voiced it again, this time in a whisper.

"No. No, Danny. Never."

He went back to bed on legs that had turned to rubber. Wendy was sleeping deeply. The clock on the nightstand said it was quarter to five. He lay sleepless until seven, when Danny began to stir awake. Then he put his legs over the edge of the bed and began to dress. It was time to go downstairs and check the boiler.

33

The Snowmobile

Sometime after midnight, while they all slept uneasily, the snow had stopped after dumping a fresh eight inches on the old crust. The clouds had broken, a fresh wind had swept them away, and now Jack stood in a dusty ingot of sunlight, which slanted through the dirty window set into the eastern side of the equipment shed.

The place was about as long as a freight car, and about as high. It smelled of grease and oil and gasoline and—faint, nostalgic smell—sweet grass. Four power lawnmowers were ranked like soldiers on review against the south wall, two of them the riding type that look like small tractors. To their left were posthole diggers, round-bladed shovels made for doing surgery on the putting green, a chain saw, the electric hedge-clippers, and a long thin steel pole with a red flag at the top. Caddy, fetch my ball in under ten seconds and there's a quarter in it for you. Yes, *sir*.

Against the eastern wall, where the morning sun slanted in most strongly, three Ping-Pong tables leaned one against the other like a drunken house of cards. Their nets had been removed and flopped down from the shelf above. In the corner was a stack of shuffleboard weights and a roque set—the wickets banded together with twists of wire, the brightly painted balls in an egg-carton sort of thing (strange hens you have up here, Watson . . . yes, and you should see the animals down on the front lawn, ha-ha), and the mallets, two sets of them, standing in their racks.

He walked over to them, stepping over an old eight-cell battery (which had once sat beneath the hood of the hotel truck, no doubt) and a battery charger and a pair of J. C. Penney jumper cables coiled between them. He slipped one of the short-handled mallets out of the front rack and held it up in front of his face, like a knight bound for battle saluting his king.

Fragments of his dream (it was all jumbled now, fading) recurred, something about George Hatfield and his father's cane, just enough to make him uneasy and, absurdly enough, a trifle guilty about holding a plain old garden-variety roque mallet. Not that roque was such a common garden-variety game anymore; its more modern cousin, croquet, was much more popular now . . . and a child's version of the game at that. Roque, however . . . that must have been quite a game. Jack had found a mildewed rule book down in the basement, from one of the years in the early twenties when a North American Roque Tournament had been held at the Overlook. Quite a game.

(*schizo*)

He frowned a little, then smiled. Yes, it was a schizo sort of game at that. The mallet expressed that perfectly. A soft end and a hard end. A game of finesse and aim, and a game of raw, bludgeoning power.

He swung the mallet through the air . . . *whhhoooop*. He smiled a little at the powerful, whistling sound it made. Then he replaced it in the rack and turned to his left. What he saw there made him frown again.

The snowmobile sat almost in the middle of the equipment shed, a fairly new one, and Jack didn't care for its looks at all. *Bombardier Skidoo* was written on the side of the engine cowling facing him in black letters which had been raked backward, presumably to connote speed. The protruding skis were also black. There was black piping to the right and left of the cowling, what they would call racing stripes on a sports car. But the actual paintjob was a bright, sneering yellow, and that was what he didn't like about it. Sitting there in its shaft of morning sun, yellow body and black piping, black skis and black upholstered open cockpit, it looked like a monstrous mechanized wasp. When it was running it would sound like that too. Whining and buzzing and ready to sting. But then, what else should it look like? It wasn't flying under false colors, at least. Because after it had done its job, they were going to be hurting plenty. All of them. By spring the Torrance family would be hurting so badly that what those wasps had done to Danny's hand would look like a mother's kisses.

He pulled his handkerchief from his back pocket, wiped his mouth with it, and walked over to the Ski-doo. He stood looking down at it, the frown very deep now, and stuffed his handkerchief back into his pocket. Outside a sudden gust of wind slammed against the equipment shed, making it rock and creak. He looked out the window and saw the gust carrying a sheet of sparkling snow crystals toward the drifted-in rear of the hotel, whirling them high into the hard blue sky.

The wind dropped and he went back to looking at the machine. It was a disgusting thing, really. You almost expected to see a long, limber stinger protruding from the rear of it. He had always disliked the goddam snowmobiles. They shivered the cathedral silence of winter into a million rattling fragments. They startled the wildlife. They sent out huge and pollutive clouds of blue and billowing oilsmoke behind them—cough, cough, gag, gag, let me breathe. They were perhaps the final grotesque toy of the unwinding fossil fuel age, given to ten-year-olds for Christmas.

He remembered a newspaper article he had read in Stovington, a story datelined someplace in Maine. A kid on a snowmobile, barrel-assing up a road he'd never traveled before at better than thirty miles an hour. Night. His headlight off. There had been a heavy chain strung between two posts with a NO TRESPASSING sign hung from the middle. They said that in all probability the kid never saw it. The moon might have gone behind a cloud. The chain had decapitated him. Reading the story Jack had been almost glad, and now, looking down at this machine, the feeling recurred.

(If it wasn't for Danny, I would take great pleasure in grabbing one of those mallets, opening the cowling, and just pounding until)

He let his pent-up breath escape him in a long slow sigh. Wendy was right. Come hell, high water, or the welfare line, Wendy was right. Pounding this machine to death would be the height of folly, no matter how pleasant an aspect that folly made. It would almost be tantamount to pounding his own son to death.

"Fucking Luddite," he said aloud.

He went to the back of the machine and unscrewed the gascap. He found a dipstick on one of the shelves that ran at chest-height around the walls and slipped it in. The last eighth of an inch came out wet. Not very much, but enough to see if the damn thing would run. Later he could siphon more from the Volks and the hotel truck.

He screwed the cap back on and opened the cowling. No sparkplugs, no battery. He went to the shelf again and began to poke along it, pushing aside screwdrivers and adjustable wrenches, a one-lung carburetor that had been taken out of an old lawn mower, plastic boxes of screws and nails and bolts of varying sizes. The shelf was thick and dark with old grease, and the years' accumulation of dust had stuck to it like fur. He didn't like touching it.

He found a small, oil-stained box with the abbreviation *Skid.* laconically marked on it in pencil. He shook it and something rattled inside. Plugs. He held one of them up to the light, trying to estimate the gap without hunting around for the gapping tool. Fuck it, he thought resentfully, and dropped the plug back into the box. If the gap's wrong, that's just too damn bad. Tough fucking titty.

There was a stool behind the door. He dragged it over, sat down, and installed the four sparkplugs, then fitted the small rubber caps over each. That done, he let his fingers play briefly over the magneto. They laughed when I sat down at the piano.

Back to the shelves. This time he couldn't find what he wanted, a small battery. A three- or four-cell. There were socket wrenches, a case filled with drills and drill-bits, bags of lawn fertilizer and Vigoro for the flower beds, but no snowmobile battery. It didn't bother him in the slightest. In fact, it made him feel glad. He was relieved. I did my best, Captain, but I could not get through. That's fine, son. I'm going to put you in for the Silver Star and the Purple Snowmobile. You're a credit to your regiment. Thank you, sir. I did try.

He began to whistle "Red River Valley" uptempo as he poked along the last two or three feet of shelf. The notes came out in little puffs of white smoke. He had made a complete circuit of the shed and the thing wasn't there. Maybe somebody had lifted it. Maybe Watson had. He laughed aloud. The old office bootleg trick. A few paperclips, a couple of reams of paper, nobody will miss this tablecloth or this Golden

Regal place setting . . . and what about this fine snowmobile battery? Yes, that might come in handy. Toss it in the sack. White-collar crime, Baby. Everybody has sticky fingers. Under-the-jacket discount, we used to call it when we were kids.

He walked back to the snowmobile and gave the side of it a good healthy kick as he went by. Well, that was the end of it. He would just have to tell Wendy sorry, baby, but—

There was a box sitting in the corner by the door. The stool had been right over it. Written on the top, in pencil, was the abbreviation *Skid.*

He looked at it, the smile drying up on his lips. Look, sir, it's the cavalry. Looks like your smoke signals must have worked after all.

It wasn't fair.

Goddammit, it just wasn't fair.

Something—luck, fate, providence—had been trying to save him. Some other luck, white luck. And at the last moment bad old Jack Torrance luck had stepped back in. The lousy run of cards wasn't over yet.

Resentment, a gray, sullen wave of it, pushed up his throat. His hands had clenched into fists again.

(*Not fair, goddammit, not fair!*)

Why couldn't he have looked someplace else? Anyplace! Why hadn't he had a crick in his neck or an itch in his nose or the need to blink? Just one of those little things. He never would have seen it.

Well, he hadn't. That was all. It was an hallucination, no different from what had happened yesterday outside that room on the second floor or the goddam hedge menagerie. A momentary strain, that was all. Fancy, I thought I saw a snowmobile battery in that corner. Nothing there now. Combat fatigue, I guess, sir. Sorry. Keep your pecker up, son. It happens to all of us sooner or later.

He yanked the door open almost hard enough to snap the hinges and pulled his snowshoes inside. They were clotted with snow and he slapped them down hard enough on the floor to raise a cloud of it. He put his left foot on the left shoe . . . and paused.

Danny was out there, by the milk platform. Trying to make a snowman, by the looks. Not much luck; the snow was too cold to stick together. Still, he was giving it the old college try, out there in the flashing morning, a speck of a bundled-up boy above the brilliant snow and below the brilliant sky. Wearing his hat turned around backward like Carlton Fiske.

(*What in the name of God were you thinking of?*)

The answer came back with no pause.

(*Me. I was thinking of me.*)

He suddenly remembered lying in bed the night before, lying there and suddenly he had been contemplating the murder of his wife.

In that instant, kneeling there, everything came clear to him. It was not just Danny the Overlook was working on. It was working on him, too. It wasn't Danny who was the weak link, it was him. He was the vulnerable one, the one who could be bent and twisted until something snapped.

(until i let go and sleep . . . and when i do that if i do that)

He looked up at the banks of windows and the sun threw back an almost blinding glare from their many-paned surfaces but he looked anyway. For the first time he noticed how much they seemed like eyes. They reflected away the sun and held their own darkness within. It was not Danny they were looking at. It was him.

In those few seconds he understood everything. There was a certain black-and-white picture he remembered seeing as a child, in catechism class. The nun had presented it to them on an easel and called it a miracle of God. The class had looked at it blankly, seeing nothing but a jumble of whites and blacks, senseless and patternless. Then one of the children in the third row had gasped, "It's Jesus!" and that child had gone home with a brand-new Testament and also a calendar because he had been first. The others stared even harder, Jacky Torrance among them. One by one the other kids had given a similar gasp, one little girl transported in near-ecstasy, crying out shrilly: "I *see* Him! I *see* Him!" She had also been rewarded with a Testament. At last everyone had seen the face of Jesus in the jumble of blacks and whites except Jacky. He strained harder and harder, scared now, part of him cynically thinking that everyone else was simply putting on to please Sister Beatrice, part of him secretly convinced that he wasn't seeing it because God had decided he was the worst sinner in the class. "Don't you see it, Jacky?" Sister Beatrice had asked him in her sad, sweet manner. I see your *tits,* he had thought in vicious desperation. He began to shake his head, then faked excitement and said: "Yes, I do! Wow! It *is* Jesus!" And everyone in class had laughed and applauded him, making him feel triumphant, ashamed, and scared. Later, when everyone else had tumbled their way up from the church basement and out onto the street he had lingered behind, looking at the meaningless black-and-white jumble that Sister Beatrice had left on the easel. He hated it. They had all made it up the way he had, even Sister herself. It was a big fake. "Shitfire-hellfire-shitfire," he had whispered under his breath, and as he turned to go he had seen the face of Jesus from the corner of his eye, sad and wise. He turned back, his heart in his throat. Everything had suddenly clicked into place and he had stared at the picture with fearful wonder, unable to believe he had missed it. The eyes, the zigzag of shadow across the care-worn brow, the fine nose, the compassionate lips. Looking at Jacky Torrance. What had only been a meaningless sprawl had suddenly been transformed into a stark black-and-white etching of the face of Christ-Our-Lord. Fearful wonder became terror. He had cussed in front of a picture of Jesus. He would be damned. He would be in hell with the sinners. The face of Christ had been in the picture all along. All along.

Now, kneeling in the sun and watching his son playing in the shadow of the hotel, he knew that it was all true. The hotel wanted Danny, maybe all of them but Danny for sure. The hedges had really walked. There was a dead woman in 217, a woman that was perhaps only a spirit and harmless under most circumstances, but a woman who was now an active danger. Like some malevolent clockwork toy she had been wound up and set in motion by Danny's own odd mind . . . and his own. Had it been Watson who had told him a man had dropped dead of a stroke one day on the roque court? Or had it been Ullman? It didn't matter. There had been an assassination on the third floor. How many old quarrels, suicides, strokes? How many murders? Was Grady lurking somewhere in the west wing with his ax, just waiting for Danny to start him up so he could come back out of the woodwork?

The puffed circle of bruises around Danny's neck.

The twinkling, half-seen bottles in the deserted lounge.

The radio.

The dreams.

The scrapbook he had found in the cellar.

(*Medoc, are you here? I've been sleepwalking again, my dear . . .*)

He got up suddenly, thrusting the snowshoes back out the door. He was shaking all over. He slammed the door and picked up the box with the battery in it. It slipped through his shaking fingers

(*oh christ what if i cracked it*)

and thumped over on its side. He pulled the flaps of the carton open and yanked the battery out, heedless of the acid that might be leaking through the battery's casing if it had cracked. But it hadn't. It was whole. A little sigh escaped his lips.

Cradling it, he took it over to the Skidoo and put it on its platform near the front of the engine. He found a small adjustable wrench on one of the shelves and attached the battery cables quickly and with no trouble. The battery was live; no need to use the charger on it. There had been a crackle of electricity and a small odor of ozone when he slipped the positive cable onto its terminal. The job done, he stood away, wiping his hands nervously on his faded denim jacket. There. It should work. No reason why not. No reason at all except that it was part of the Overlook and the Overlook really didn't want them out of here. Not at all. The Overlook was having one hell of a good time. There was a little boy to terrorize, a man and his woman to set one against the other, and if it played its cards right they could end up flitting through the Overlook's halls like insubstantial shades in a Shirley Jackson novel, whatever walked in Hill House walked alone, but you wouldn't be alone in the Overlook, oh no, there would be plenty of company here. But there was really no reason why the snowmobile shouldn't start. Except of course

(*Except he still didn't really want to go.*)

yes, except for that.

He stood looking at the Skidoo, his breath puffing out in frozen little plumes. He wanted it to be the way it had been. When he had come in here he'd had no doubts. Going down would be the wrong decision, he had known that then. Wendy was only scared of the boogeyman summoned up by a single hysterical little boy. Now suddenly, he could see her side. It was like his play, his damnable play. He no longer knew which side he was on, or how things should come out.

Once you saw the face of a god in those jumbled blacks and whites, it was everybody out of the pool—you could never unsee it. Others might laugh and say it's nothing, just a lot of splotches with no meaning, give me a good old Craftmaster paint-by-the-numbers any day, but *you* would always see the face of Christ-Our-Lord looking out at you. You had seen it in one gestalt leap, the conscious and unconscious melding in that one shocking moment of understanding. You would always see it. You were damned to always see it.

(*I've been sleepwalking again, my dear . . .*)

It had been all right until he had seen Danny playing in the snow. It was Danny's fault. Everything had been Danny's fault. He was the one with the shining, or whatever it was. It wasn't a shining. It was a curse. If he and Wendy had been here alone, they could have passed the winter quite nicely. No pain, no strain on the brain.

(*Don't want to leave. ?Can't?*)

The Overlook didn't want them to go and he didn't want them to go either. Not even Danny. Maybe he was a part of it, now. Perhaps the Overlook, large and rambling Samuel Johnson that it was, had picked him to be its Boswell. You say the new caretaker writes? Very good, sign him on. Time we told our side. Let's get rid of the woman and his snot-nosed kid first, however. We don't want him to be distracted. We don't—

He was standing by the snowmobile's cockpit, his head starting to ache again. What did it come down to? Go or stay. Very simple. Keep it simple. Shall we go or shall we stay?

If we go, how long will it be before you find the local hole in Sidewinder? a voice inside him asked. The dark place with the lousy color TV that unshaven and unemployed men spend the day watching game shows on? Where the piss in the men's room smells two thousand years old and there's always a sodden Camel butt unraveling in the toilet bowl? Where the beer is thirty cents a glass and you cut it with salt and the jukebox is loaded with seventy country oldies?

How long? Oh Christ, he was so afraid it wouldn't be long at all.

"I can't win," he said, very softly. That was it. It was like trying to play solitaire with one of the aces missing from the deck.

Abruptly he leaned over the Skidoo's motor compartment and yanked off the magneto. It came off with sickening ease. He looked at it for a moment, then went to the equipment shed's back door and opened it.

From here the view of the mountains was unobstructed, picture-postcard beautiful in the twinkling brightness of morning. An unbroken field of snow rose to the first pines about a mile distant. He flung the magneto as far out into the snow as he could. It went much further than it should have. There was a light puff of snow when it fell. The light breeze carried the snow granules away to fresh resting places. Disperse there, I say. There's nothing to see. It's all over. Disperse.

He felt at peace.

He stood in the doorway for a long time, breathing the good mountain air, and then he closed it firmly and went back out the other door to tell Wendy they would be staying. On the way, he stopped and had a snowball fight with Danny.

34

The Hedges

It was November 29, three days after Thanksgiving. The last week had been a good one, the Thanksgiving dinner the best they'd ever had as a family. Wendy had cooked Dick Hallorann's turkey to a turn and they had all eaten to bursting without even coming close to demolishing the jolly bird. Jack had groaned that they would be eating turkey for the rest of the winter—creamed turkey, turkey sandwiches, turkey and noodles, turkey surprise.

No, Wendy told him with a little smile. Only until Christmas. Then we have the capon.

Jack and Danny groaned together.

The bruises on Danny's neck had faded, and their fears seemed to have faded with them. On Thanksgiving afternoon Wendy had been pulling Danny around on his sled while Jack worked on the play, which was now almost done.

"Are you still afraid, doc?" she had asked not knowing how to put the question less baldly.

"Yes," he answered simply. "But now I stay in the safe places."

"Your daddy says that sooner or later the forest rangers will wonder why we're not checking in on the CB radio. They'll come to see if anything is wrong. We might go down then. You and I. And let your daddy finish the winter. He has good reasons for wanting to. In a way, doc . . . I know this is hard for you to understand . . . our backs are against the wall."

"Yes," he had answered noncommittally.

On this sparkling afternoon the two of them were upstairs, and Danny knew that they had been making love. They were dozing now. They were happy, he knew. His mother was still a little bit afraid, but his father's attitude was strange. It was a feeling that he had done something that was very hard and had done it right. But Danny could not seem to see exactly what the something was. His father was guarding that carefully, even in his own mind. Was it possible, Danny wondered, to be glad you had done something and still be so ashamed of that something that you tried not to think of it? The question was a disturbing one. He didn't think such a thing was possible . . . in a normal mind. His hardest probings at his father had only brought him a dim picture of something like an octopus, whirling up into the hard blue sky. And on both occasions that he had concentrated hard enough to get this, Daddy had suddenly been staring at him in a sharp and frightening way, as if he knew what Danny was doing.

Now he was in the lobby, getting ready to go out. He went out a lot, taking his sled or wearing his snowshoes. He liked to get out of the hotel. When he was out in the sunshine, it seemed like a weight had slipped from his shoulders.

He pulled a chair over, stood on it, and got his parka and snow pants out of the ballroom closet, and then sat down on the chair to put them on. His boots were in the boot box and he pulled them on, his tongue creeping out into the corner of his mouth in concentration as he laced them and tied the rawhide into careful granny knots. He pulled on his mittens and his ski mask and was ready.

He tramped out through the kitchen to the back door, then paused. He was tired of playing out back, and at this time of day the hotel's shadow would be cast over his play area. He didn't even like being in the Overlook's shadow. He decided he would put on his snowshoes and go down to the playground instead. Dick Hallorann had told him to stay away from the topiary, but the thought of the hedge animals did not bother him much. They were buried under snowdrifts now, nothing showing but a vague hump that was the rabbit's head and the lions' tails. Sticking out of the snow the way they were, the tails looked more absurd than frightening.

Danny opened the back door and got his snowshoes from the milk platform. Five minutes later he was strapping them to his feet on the front porch. His daddy had told him that he (Danny) had the hang of using the snowshoes—the lazy, shuffling stride, the twist of ankle that shook the powdery snow from the lacings just before the boot came back down—and all that remained was for him to build up the necessary muscles in his thighs and calves and ankles. Danny found that his ankles got tired the fastest. Snowshoeing was almost as hard on your ankles as skating, because you had to keep clearing the lacings. Every five minutes or so he had to stop with his legs spread and the snowshoes flat on the snow to rest them.

But he didn't have to rest on his way down to the playground because it was all downhill. Less than ten minutes up and over the monstrous snow-dune that had drifted in on the Overlook's front porch he was standing with his mittened hand on the playground slide. He wasn't even breathing hard.

The playground seemed much nicer in the deep snow than it ever had during the autumn. It looked like a fairyland sculpture. The swing chains had been frozen in strange positions, the seats of the big kids' swings resting flush against the snow. The jungle gym was an ice-cave guarded by dripping icicle teeth. Only the chimneys of the play-Overlook stuck up over the snow

(wish the other one was buried that way only not with us in it)

and the tops of the cement rings protruded in two places like Eskimo igloos. Danny tramped over there, squatted, and began to dig. Before long he had uncovered the dark mouth of one of them and he slipped into the cold tunnel. In his mind he was Patrick McGoohan, the Secret Agent Man (they had shown the reruns of that program twice on the Burlington TV channel and his daddy never missed them; he would skip a party to stay home and watch

"Secret Agent" or "The Avengers" and Danny had always watched with him), on the run from KGB agents in the mountains of Switzerland. There had been avalanches in the area and the notorious KGB agent Slobbo had killed his girlfriend with a poison dart, but somewhere near was the Russian antigravity machine. Perhaps at the end of this very tunnel. He drew his automatic and went along the concrete tunnel, his eyes wide and alert, his breath pluming out.

The far end of the concrete ring was solidly blocked with snow. He tried digging through it and was amazed (and a little uneasy) to see how solid it was, almost like ice from the cold and the constant weight of more snow on top of it.

His make-believe game collapsed around him and he was suddenly aware that he felt closed in and extremely nervous in this tight ring of cement. He could hear his breathing; it sounded dank and quick and hollow. He was under the snow, and hardly any light filtered down the hole he had dug to get in here. Suddenly he wanted to be out in the sunlight more than anything, suddenly he remembered his daddy and mommy were sleeping and didn't know where he was, that if the hole he dug caved in he would be trapped, and the Overlook didn't like him.

Danny got turned around with some difficulty and crawled back along the length of the concrete ring, his snowshoes clacking woodenly together behind him, his palms crackling in last fall's dead aspen leaves beneath him. He had just reached the end and the cold spill of light coming down from above when the snow *did* give in, a minor fall, but enough to powder his face and clog the opening he had wriggled down through and leave him in darkness.

For a moment his brain froze in utter panic and he could not think. Then, as if from far off, he heard his daddy telling him that he must never play at the Stovington dump, because sometimes stupid people hauled old refrigerators off to the dump without removing the doors and if you got in one and the door happened to shut on you, there was no way to get out. You would die in the darkness.

(You wouldn't want a thing like that to happen to you, would you, doc?)

(No, Daddy.)

But it *had* happened, his frenzied mind told him, it *had* happened, he was in the dark, he was closed in, and it was as cold as a refrigerator. And—

(*something is in here with me.*)

His breath stopped in a gasp. An almost drowsy terror stole through his veins. Yes. Yes. There was something in here with him, some awful thing the Overlook had saved for just such a chance as this. Maybe a huge spider that had burrowed down under the dead leaves, or a rat . . . or maybe the corpse of some little kid that had died here on the playground. Had that ever happened? Yes, he thought maybe it had. He thought of the woman in the tub. The blood and brains on the wall of the Presidential Sweet. Of some little kid, its head split open from a fall from the monkey bars or a swing, crawling after him in the dark, grinning, looking for one final playmate in its endless playground. Forever. In a moment he would hear it coming.

At the far end of the concrete ring, Danny heard the stealthy crackle of dead leaves as something came for him on its hands and knees. At any moment he would feel its cold hand close over his ankle—

That thought broke his paralysis. He was digging at the loose fall of snow that choked the end of the concrete ring, throwing it back between his legs in powdery bursts like a dog digging for a bone. Blue light filtered down from above and Danny thrust himself up at it like a diver coming out of deep water. He scraped his back on the lip of the concrete ring. One of his snowshoes twisted behind the other. Snow spilled down inside his ski mask and into the collar of his parka. He dug at the snow, clawed at it. It seemed to be trying to hold him, to suck him back down, back into the concrete ring where that unseen, leaf-crackling *thing* was, and keep him there. Forever.

Then he was out, his face was turned up to the sun, and he was crawling through the snow, crawling away from the half-buried cement ring, gasping harshly, his face almost comically white with powdered snow—a living fright-mask. He hobbled over to the jungle gym and sat down to readjust his snowshoes and get his breath. As he set them to rights and tightened the straps again, he never took his eyes from the hole at the end of the concrete ring. He waited to see if something would come out. Nothing did, and after three or four minutes, Danny's breathing began to slow down. Whatever it was, it couldn't

stand the sunlight. It was cooped up down there,
maybe only able to come out when it was dark . . . or
when both ends of its circular prison were plugged
with snow.

(*but i'm safe now i'm safe i'll just go back because now i'm*)

Something thumped softly behind him.

He turned around, toward the hotel, and looked.
But even before he looked

(*Can you see the Indians in this picture?*)

he knew what he would see, because he knew
what that soft thumping sound had been. It was the
sound of a large clump of snow falling, the way it
sounded when it slid off the roof of the hotel and fell
to the ground.

(*Can you see——?*)

Yes. He could. The snow had fallen off the hedge
dog. When he came down, it had only been a harmless lump of snow outside the playground. Now it
stood revealed, an incongruous splash of green in all
the eye-watering whiteness. It was sitting up, as if to
beg a sweet or a scrap.

But this time he wouldn't go crazy, he wouldn't
blow his cool. Because at least he wasn't trapped in
some dark old hole. He was in the sunlight. And it
was just a dog. It's pretty warm out today, he
thought hopefully. Maybe the sun just melted enough
snow off that old dog so the rest fell off in a bunch.
Maybe that's all it is.

(*Don't go near that place . . . steer right clear.*)

His snowshoe bindings were as tight as they were
ever going to be. He stood up and stared back at the

concrete ring, almost completely submerged in the snow, and what he saw at the end he had exited from froze his heart. There was a circular patch of darkness at the end of it, a fold of shadow that marked the hole he'd dug to get down inside. Now, in spite of the snow-dazzle, he thought he could see something there. Something moving. A hand. The waving hand of some desperately unhappy child, waving hand, pleading hand, drowning hand.

(*Save me O please save me If you can't save me at least come play with me . . . Forever. And Forever. And Forever.*)

"No," Danny whispered huskily. The word fell dry and bare from his mouth, which was stripped of moisture. He could feel his mind wavering now, trying to go away the way it had when the woman in the room had . . . no, better not think of that.

He grasped at the strings of reality and held them tightly. He had to get out of here. Concentrate on that. Be cool. Be like the Secret Agent Man. Would Patrick McGoohan be crying and peeing in his pants like a little baby?

Would his daddy?

That calmed him somewhat.

From behind him, that soft *flump* sound of falling snow came again. He turned around and the head of one of the hedge lions was sticking out of the snow now, snarling at him. It was closer than it should have been, almost up to the gate of the playground.

Terror tried to rise up and he quelled it. He was the Secret Agent Man, and he *would* escape.

He began to walk out of the playground, taking the same roundabout course his father had taken on the day that the snow flew. He concentrated on operating the snowshoes. Slow, flat strides. Don't lift your foot too high or you'll lose your balance. Twist your ankle and spill the snow off the crisscrossed lacings. It seemed so *slow.* He reached the corner of the playground. The snow was drifted high here and he was able to step over the fence. He got halfway over and then almost fell flat when the snowshoe on his behind foot caught on one of the fence posts. He leaned on the outside edge of gravity, pinwheeling his arms, remembering how hard it was to get up once you fell down.

From his right, that soft sound again, falling clumps of snow. He looked over and saw the other two lions, clear of snow now down to their forepaws, side by side, about sixty paces away. The green indentations that were their eyes were fixed on him. The dog had turned its head.

(*It only happens when you're not looking.*)

"Oh! Hey—"

His snowshoes had crossed and he plunged forward into the snow, arms waving uselessly. More snow got inside his hood and down his neck and into the tops of his boots. He struggled out of the snow and tried to get the snowshoes under him, heart hammering crazily now

(*Secret Agent Man remember you're the Secret Agent*)

and overbalanced backward. For a moment he lay there looking at the sky, thinking it would be simpler to just give up.

Then he thought of the thing in the concrete tunnel and knew he could not. He gained his feet and stared over at the topiary. All three lions were bunched together now, not forty feet away. The dog had ranged off to their left, as if to block Danny's retreat. They were bare of snow except for powdery ruffs around their necks and muzzles. They were all staring at him.

His breath was racing now, and the panic was like a rat behind his forehead, twisting and gnawing. He fought the panic and he fought the snowshoes.

(*Daddy's voice: No, don't fight them, doc. Walk on them like they were your own feet. Walk with them.*)

(*Yes, Daddy.*)

He began to walk again, trying to regain the easy rhythm he had practiced with his daddy. Little by little it began to come, but with the rhythm came an awareness of just how tired he was, how much his fear had exhausted him. The tendons of his thighs and calves and ankles were hot and trembly. Ahead he could see the Overlook, mockingly distant, seeming to stare at him with its many windows, as if this were some sort of contest in which it was mildly interested.

Danny looked back over his shoulder and his hurried breathing caught for a moment and then hurried on even faster. The nearest lion was now only twenty feet behind, breasting through the snow like a dog paddling in a pond. The two others were to its right and left, pacing it. They were like an army platoon on patrol, the dog, still off to their left, the scout. The closest lion had its head down. The shoulders bunched powerfully above its neck. The tail was up, as if in the instant before he had turned to look it had been swishing back and forth, back and forth. He thought it looked like a great big housecat that was having a good time playing with a mouse before killing it.

(—*falling*—)

No, if he fell he was dead. They would never let him get up. They would pounce. He pinwheeled his arms madly and lunged ahead, his center of gravity dancing just beyond his nose. He caught it and hurried on, snapping glances back over his shoulder. The air whistled in and out of his dry throat like hot glass.

The world closed down to the dazzling snow, the green hedges, and the whispery sound of his snowshoes. And something else. A soft, muffled padding sound. He tried to hurry faster and couldn't. He was walking over the buried driveway now, a small boy with his face almost buried in the shadow of his parka hood. The afternoon was still and bright.

When he looked back again, the point lion was only five feet behind. It was grinning. Its mouth was open, its haunches tensed down like a clockspring. Behind it and the others he could see the rabbit, its head now sticking out of the snow, bright green, as if it had turned its horrid blank face to watch the end of the stalk.

Now, on the Overlook's front lawn between the circular drive and the porch, he let the panic loose and began to run clumsily in the snowshoes, not daring to look back now, tilting further and further forward, his arms out ahead of him like a blind man feeling for obstacles. His hood fell back, revealing his complexion, paste white giving way to hectic red blotches on his cheeks, his eyes bulging with terror. The porch was very close now.

Behind him he heard the sudden hard crunch of snow as something leaped.

He fell on the porch steps, screaming without sound, and scrambled up them on his hands and knees, snowshoes clattering and askew behind him.

There was a slashing sound in the air and sudden pain in his leg. The ripping sound of cloth. Something else that might have—*must* have—been in his mind.

Bellowing, angry roar.

Smell of blood and evergreen.

He fell full-length on the porch, sobbing hoarsely, the rich, metallic taste of copper in his mouth. His heart was thundering in his chest. There was a small trickle of blood coming from his nose.

He had no idea how long he lay there before the lobby doors flew open and Jack ran out, wearing just his jeans and a pair of slippers. Wendy was behind him.

"Danny!" she screamed.

"Doc! Danny, for Christ's sake! What's wrong? What happened?"

Daddy was helping him up. Below the knee his snowpants were ripped open. Inside, his woollen ski sock had been ripped open and his calf had been shallowly scratched . . . . as if he had tried to push his way

through a closely grown evergreen hedge and the
branches had clawed him.

He looked over his shoulder. Far down the lawn,
past the putting green, were a number of vague,
snow-cowled humps. The hedge animals. Between
them and the playground. Between them and the
road.

His legs gave way. Jack caught him. He began to
cry.

35

The Lobby

He had told them everything except what had happened to him when the snow had blocked the end of the concrete ring. He couldn't bring himself to repeat that. And he didn't know the right words to express the creeping, lassitudinous sense of terror he had felt when he heard the dead aspen leaves begin to crackle furtively down there in the cold darkness. But he told them about the soft sound of snow falling in clumps. About the lion with its head and its bunched shoulders working its way up and out of the snow to chase him. He even told them about how the rabbit had turned its head to watch near the end.

The three of them were in the lobby. Jack had built a roaring blaze in the fireplace. Danny was bundled up in a blanket on the small sofa where once, a million years ago, three nuns had sat laughing like girls while they waited for the line at the desk to thin out. He was sipping hot noodle soup from a mug. Wendy sat beside him, stroking his hair. Jack had sat on the floor, his face seeming to grow more and more still, more and more set as Danny told his story. Twice he pulled his handkerchief out of his back pocket and rubbed his sore-looking lips with it.

"Then they chased me," he finished. Jack got up and went over to the window, his back to them. He looked at his mommy. "They chased me all the way up to the porch." He was struggling to keep his voice calm, because if he stayed calm maybe they would believe him. Mr. Stenger hadn't stayed calm. He had started to cry and hadn't been able to stop so THE MEN IN THE WHITE COATS had come to take him away because if you couldn't stop crying it meant you had LOST YOUR MAR-BLES and when would you be back? NO ONE KNOWS. His parka and snowpants and the clotted snowshoes lay on the rug just inside the big double doors.

(*I won't cry I won't let myself cry*)

And he thought he could do that, but he couldn't stop shaking. He looked into the fire and waited for Daddy to say something. High yellow flames danced on the dark stone hearth. A pine-knot exploded with a bang and sparks rushed up the flue.

"Danny, come over here." Jack turned around. His face still had that pinched, deathly look. Danny didn't like to look at it.

"Jack—"

"I just want the boy over here for a minute."

Danny slipped off the sofa and came over beside his daddy.

"Good boy. Now what do you see?"

Danny had known what he would see even before he got to the window. Below the clutter of boot tracks, sled tracks, and snowshoe tracks that marked their usual exercise area, the snowfield that covered the Overlook's lawns sloped down to the topiary and the playground beyond. It was marred by two sets of tracks, one of them in a straight line from the porch to the playground, the other a long, looping line coming back up.

"Only my tracks, Daddy. But—"

"What about the hedges, Danny?"

Danny's lips began to tremble. He was going to cry. What if he couldn't stop?

(*i won't cry I Won't Cry Won't Won't WON'T*)

"All covered with snow," he whispered. "But, Daddy—"

"What? I couldn't hear you!"

"Jack, you're cross-examining him! Can't you see he's upset, he's—"

"Shut up! Well, Danny?"

"They scratched me, Daddy. My leg—"

"You must have cut your leg on the crust of the snow."

Then Wendy was between them, her face pale and angry. "What are you trying to make him do?" she asked him. "Confess to murder? *What's wrong with you?*"

The strangeness in his eyes seemed to break then. "I'm trying to help him find the difference between something real and something that was only an hallucination, that's all." He squatted by Danny so they were on an eye-to-eye level, and then hugged him tight. "Danny, it didn't really happen. Okay? It was like one of those trances you have sometimes. That's all."

"Daddy?"

"What, Dan?"

"I didn't cut my leg on the crust. There isn't any crust. It's all powdery snow. It won't even stick together to make snowballs. Remember we tried to have a snowball fight and couldn't?"

He felt his father stiffen against him. "The porch step, then."

Danny pulled away. Suddenly he had it. It had flashed into his mind all at once, the way things sometimes did, the way it had about the woman wanting to be in that gray man's pants. He stared at his father with widening eyes.

"You know I'm telling the truth," he whispered, shocked.

"Danny—" Jack's face, tightening.

"You know because you saw—"

The sound of Jack's open palm striking Danny's face was flat, not dramatic at all. The boy's head rocked back, the palmprint reddening on his cheek like a brand.

Wendy made a moaning noise.

For a moment they were still, the three of them, and then Jack grabbed for his son and said, "Danny, I'm sorry, you okay, doc?"

"You hit him, you bastard!" Wendy cried. "You dirty bastard!"

She grabbed his other arm and for a moment Danny was pulled between them.

"*Oh please stop pulling me!*" he screamed at them, and there was such agony in his voice that they both let go

of him, and then the tears had to come and he collapsed, weeping, between the sofa and the window, his
parents staring at him helplessly, the way children
might stare at a toy broken in a furious tussle over to
whom it belonged. In the fireplace another pine-knot
exploded like a hand grenade, making them all jump.

Wendy gave him baby aspirin and Jack slipped him,
unprotesting, between the sheets of his cot. He was
asleep in no time with his thumb in his mouth.

"I don't like that," she said. "It's a regression."

Jack didn't reply.

She looked at him softly, without anger, without a
smile, either. "You want me to apologize for calling
you a bastard? All right, I apologize. I'm sorry. You
still shouldn't have hit him."

"I know," he muttered. "I know that. I don't know
what the hell came over me."

"You promised you'd never hit him again."

He looked at her furiously, and then the fury collapsed. Suddenly, with pity and horror, she saw what
Jack would look like as an old man. She had never
seen him look that way before.

(?what way?)

Defeated, she answered herself. *He looks beaten.*

He said: "I always thought I could keep my
promises."

She went to him and put her hands on his arm.
"All right, it's over. And when the ranger comes to
check us, we'll tell him we all want to go down. All
right?"

"All right," Jack said, and at that moment, at least, he meant it. The same way he had always meant it on those mornings after, looking at his pale and haggard face in the bathroom mirror. *I'm going to stop, going to cut it off flat.* But morning gave way to afternoon, and in the afternoons he felt a little better. And afternoon gave way to night. As some great twentieth-century thinker had said, night must fall.

He found himself wishing that Wendy would ask him about the hedges, would ask him what Danny meant when he said *You know because you saw—* If she did, he would tell her everything. Everything. The hedges, the woman in the room, even about the fire hose that seemed to have switched positions. But where did confession stop? Could he tell her he'd thrown the magneto away, that they could all be down in Sidewinder right now if he hadn't done that?

What she said was, "Do you want tea?"

"Yes. A cup of tea would be good."

She went to the door and paused there, rubbing her forearms through her sweater. "It's my fault as much as yours," she said. "What were we doing while he was going through that . . . dream, or whatever it was?"

"Wendy—"

"We were sleeping," she said. "Sleeping like a couple of teenage kids with their itch nicely scratched."

"Stop it," he said. "It's over."

"No," Wendy answered, and gave him a strange, restless smile. "It's not over."

She went out to make tea, leaving him to keep watch over their son.

36

The Elevator

Jack awoke from a thin and uneasy sleep where huge and ill-defined shapes chased him through endless snowfields to what he first thought was another dream: darkness, and in it, a sudden mechanical jumble of noises—clicks and clanks, hummings, rattlings, snaps and whooshes.

Then Wendy sat up beside him and he knew it was no dream.

"What's that?" Her hand, cold marble, gripped his wrist. He restrained an urge to shake it off—how in the hell was he supposed to know what it was? The illuminated clock on his nightstand said it was five minutes to twelve.

The humming sound again. Loud and steady, varying the slightest bit. Followed by a clank as the humming ceased. A rattling bang. A thump. Then the humming resumed.

It was the elevator.

Danny was sitting up. "Daddy? *Daddy?*" His voice was sleepy and scared.

"Right here, doc," Jack said. "Come on over and jump in. Your mom's awake, too."

The bedclothes rustled as Danny got on the bed between them. "It's the elevator," he whispered.

"That's right," Jack said. "Just the elevator."

"What do you mean, *just?*" Wendy demanded. There was an ice-skim of hysteria on her voice. "It's the middle of the night. *Who's running it?*"

Hummmmmmm. Click/clank. Above them now. The rattle of the gate accordioning back, the bump of the doors opening and closing. Then the hum of the motor and the cables again.

Danny began to whimper.

Jack swung his feet out of bed and onto the floor. "It's probably a short. I'll check."

"Don't you dare go out of this room!"

"Don't be stupid," he said, pulling on his robe. "It's my job."

She was out of bed herself a moment later, pulling Danny with her.

"We'll go, too."

"Wendy—"

"What's wrong?" Danny asked somberly. "What's wrong, Daddy?"

Instead of answering, he turned away, his face angry and set. He belted his robe around him at the door, opened it, and stepped out into the dark hall.

Wendy hesitated for a moment, and it was actually Danny who began to move first. She caught up quickly, and they went out together.

Jack hadn't bothered with the lights. She fumbled

for the switch that lit the four spaced overheads in the
hallway that led to the main corridor. Up ahead, Jack
was already turning the corner. This time Danny
found the switchplate and flicked all three switches
up. The hallway leading down to the stairs and the
elevator shaft came alight.

Jack was standing at the elevator station, which
was flanked by benches and cigarette urns. He was
standing motionless in front of the closed elevator
door. In his faded tartan bathrobe and brown leather
slippers with the rundown heels, his hair all in sleep
corkscrews and Alfalfa cowlicks, he looked to her like
an absurd twentieth-century Hamlet, an indecisive
figure so mesmerized by onrushing tragedy that he
was helpless to divert its course or alter it in any way.

(*jesus stop thinking so crazy*—)

Danny's hand had tightened painfully on her own.
He was looking up at her intently, his face strained
and anxious. He had been catching the drift of her
thoughts, she realized. Just how much or how little of
them he was getting was impossible to say, but she
flushed, feeling much the same as if he had caught
her in a masturbatory act.

"Come on," she said, and they went down the hall
to Jack.

The hummings and clankings and thumpings
were louder here, terrifying in a disconnected,
benumbed way. Jack was staring at the closed door
with feverish intensity. Through the diamond-shaped
window in the center of the elevator door she thought
she could make out the cables, thrumming slightly.

The elevator clanked to a stop below them, at lobby level. They heard the doors thump open. And . . .

(*party*)

Why had she thought party? The word had simply jumped into her head for no reason at all. The silence in the Overlook was complete and intense except for the weird noises coming up the elevator shaft.

(must have been quite a party)

(*???WHAT PARTY???*)

For just a moment her mind had filled with an image so real that it seemed to be a memory . . . not just any memory but one of those you treasure, one of those you keep for very special occasions and rarely mention aloud. Lights . . . hundreds, maybe thousands of them. Lights and colors, the pop of champagne corks, a forty-piece orchestra playing Glenn Miller's "In the Mood." But Glenn Miller had gone down in his bomber before she was born, how could she have a memory of Glenn Miller?

She looked down at Danny and saw his head had cocked to one side, as if he was hearing something she couldn't hear. His face was very pale.

Thump.

The door had slid shut down there. A humming whine as the elevator began to rise. She saw the engine housing on top of the car first through the diamond-shaped window, then the interior of the car, seen through the further diamond shapes made by the brass gate. Warm yellow light from the car's overhead. It was empty. The car was empty. It was empty but

(on the night of the party they must have crowded in by the dozens, crowded the car way beyond its safety limit but of course it had been new then and all of them wearing masks)

(????WHAT MASKS????)

The car stopped above them, on the third floor. She looked at Danny. His face was all eyes. His mouth was pressed into a frightened, bloodless slit. Above them, the brass gate rattled back. The elevator door thumped open, it thumped open because it was time, the time had come, it was time to say

(Goodnight . . . goodnight . . . yes, it was lovely . . . no, I really can't stay for the unmasking . . . early to bed, early to rise . . . oh, was that Sheila? . . . the monk? . . . isn't that witty, Sheila coming as a monk? . . . yes, good-night . . . good)

Thump.

Gears clashed. The motor engaged. The car began to whine back down.

"Jack," she whispered. "What is it? What's wrong with it?"

"A short circuit," he said. His face was like wood. "I told you, it was a short circuit."

"I keep hearing voices in my head!" she cried. "What is it? What's wrong? I feel like I'm going crazy!"

"What voices?" He looked at her with deadly blandness.

She turned to Danny. "Did you—?"

Danny nodded slowly. "Yes. And music. Like from a long time ago. In my head"

The elevator car stopped again. The hotel was silent, creaking, deserted. Outside, the wind whined around the eaves in the darkness.

"Maybe you are both crazy," Jack said conversationally. "I don't hear a goddamned thing except that elevator having a case of the electrical hiccups. If you two want to have duet hysterics, fine. But count me out."

The elevator was coming down again.

Jack stepped to the right, where a glass-fronted box was mounted on the wall at chest height. He smashed his bare fist against it. Glass tinkled inward. Blood dripped from two of his knuckles. He reached in and took out a key with a long, smooth barrel.

"Jack, no. Don't."

"I am going to do my job. Now leave me alone, Wendy!"

She tried to grab his arm. He pushed her backward. Her feet tangled in the hem of her robe and she fell to the carpet with an ungainly thump. Danny cried out shrilly and fell on his knees beside her. Jack turned back to the elevator and thrust the key into the socket.

The elevator cables disappeared and the bottom of the car came into view in the small window. A second later Jack turned the key hard. There was a grating, screeching sound as the elevator car came to an instant standstill. For a moment the declutched motor in the basement whined even louder, and then its circuit breaker cut in and the Overlook went unearthly still. The night wind outside seemed very loud by comparison. Jack looked stupidly at the gray metal elevator door. There were three splotches of blood below the keyhole from his lacerated knuckles.

He turned back to Wendy and Danny for a moment. She was sitting up, and Danny had his arm around her. They were both staring at him carefully, as if he was a stranger they had never seen before, possibly a dangerous one. He opened his mouth, not sure what was going to come out.

"It . . . Wendy, it's my job."

She said clearly: "Fuck your job."

He turned back to the elevator, worked his fingers into the crack that ran down the right side of the door, and got it to open a little way. Then he was able to get his whole weight on it and threw the door open.

The car had stopped halfway, its floor at Jack's chest level. Warm light still spilled out of it, contrasting with the oily darkness of the shaft below.

He looked in for what seemed a long time.

"It's empty," he said then. "A short circuit, like I said." He hooked his fingers into the slot behind the door and began to pull it closed . . . then her hand was on his shoulder, surprisingly strong, yanking him away.

"Wendy!" he shouted. But she had already caught the car's bottom edge and pulled herself up enough so she could look in. Then, with a convulsive heave of her shoulder and belly muscles, she tried to boost herself all the way up. For a moment the issue was in doubt. Her feet tottered over the blackness of the shaft and one pink slipper fell from her foot and slipped out of sight.

"*Mommy!*" Danny screamed.

Then she was up, her cheeks flushed, her forehead as pale and shining as a spirit lamp. "What about this, Jack? Is this a short circuit?" She threw something and suddenly the hall was full of drifting confetti, red and white and blue and yellow. "Is *this?*" A green party streamer, faded to a pale pastel color with age.

"And *this?*".

She tossed it out and it came to rest on the blue-black jungle carpet, a black silk cat's-eye mask, dusted with sequins at the temples.

"*Does that look like a short circuit to you, Jack?*" she screamed at him.

Jack stepped slowly away from it, shaking his head mechanically back and forth. The cat's-eye mask stared up blankly at the ceiling from the confetti-strewn hallway carpet.

37

The Ballroom

It was the first of December.

Danny was in the east-wing ballroom, standing on an over-stuffed, high-backed wing chair, looking at the clock under glass. It stood in the center of the ball-room's high, ornamental mantelpiece, flanked by two large ivory elephants. He almost expected the ele-phants would begin to move and try to gore him with their tusks as he stood there, but they were moveless. They were "safe." Since the night of the elevator he had come to divide all things at the Overlook into two categories. The elevator, the basement, the play-ground, Room 217, and the Presidential Suite (it was Suite, not Sweet; he had seen the correct spelling in an account book Daddy had been reading at supper last night and had memorized it carefully)—those places were "unsafe." Their quarters, the lobby, and the porch were "safe." Apparently the ballroom was, too.

(The elephants are, anyway.)

He was not sure about other places and so avoided them on general principle.

He looked at the clock inside the glass dome. It was under glass because all its wheels and cogs and springs were showing. A chrome or steel track ran around the outside of these works, and directly below the clockface there was a small axis bar with a pair of meshing cogs at either end. The hands of the clock stood at quarter past XI, and although he didn't know Roman numerals he could guess by the configuration of the hands at what time the clock had stopped. The clock stood on a velvet base. In front of it, slightly distorted by the curve of the dome, was a carefully carved silver key.

He supposed that the clock was one of the things he wasn't supposed to touch, like the decorative fire-tools in their brass-bound cabinet by the lobby fireplace or the tall china highboy at the back of the dining room.

A sense of injustice and a feeling of angry rebellion suddenly rose in him and

(*never mind what i'm not supposed to touch, just never mind. touched me, hasn't it? played with me, hasn't it?*)

It had. And it hadn't been particularly careful not to break him, either.

Danny put his hands out, grasped the glass dome, and lifted it aside. He let one finger play over the works for a moment, the pad of his index finger denting against the cogs, running smoothly over the wheels. He picked up the silver key. For an adult it would have been uncomfortably small, but it fitted his own fingers perfectly. He placed it in the keyhole at the center of the clockface. It went firmly home with a tiny click, more felt than heard. It wound to the right, of course; clockwise.

Danny turned the key until it would turn no more and then removed it. The clock began to tick. Cogs turned. A large balance wheel rocked back and forth in semicircles. The hands were moving. If you kept your head perfectly motionless and your eyes wide open, you could see the minute hand inching along toward its meeting some forty-five minutes from now with the hour hand. At XII.

(*And the Red Death held sway over all.*)

He frowned, and then shook the thought away. It was a thought with no meaning or reference for him.

He reached his index finger out again and pushed the minute hand up to the hour, curious about what might happen. It obviously wasn't a cuckoo clock, but that steel rail had to have some purpose.

There was a small, ratcheting series of clicks, and then the clock began to tinkle Strauss's "Blue Danube Waltz." A punched roll of cloth no more than two inches in width began to unwind. A small series of brass strikers rose and fell. From behind the clockface two figures glided into view along the steel track, ballet dancers, on the left a girl in a fluffy skirt and white stockings, on the right a boy in a black leotard and ballet slippers. Their hands were held in arches over their heads. They came together in the middle, in front of VI.

Danny espied tiny grooves in their sides, just below their armpits. The axis bar slipped into these grooves and he heard another small click. The cogs at

either end of the bar began to turn. "The Blue
Danube" tinkled. The dancers' arms came down
around each other. The boy flipped the girl up over
his head and then whirled over the bar. They were
now lying prone, the boy's head buried beneath the
girl's short ballet skirt, the girl's face pressed against
the center of the boy's leotard. They writhed in a
mechanical frenzy.

Danny's nose wrinkled. They were kissing
peepees. That made him feel sick.

A moment later and things began to run backward.
The boy whirled back over the axis bar. He flipped the
girl into an upright position. They seemed to nod
knowingly at each other as their hands arched back
over their heads. They retreated the way they had
come, disappearing just as "The Blue Danube" finished.
The clock began to strike a count of silver chimes.

(*Midnight! Stroke of midnight!*)

(*Hooray for masks!*)

Danny whirled on the chair, almost falling down.
The ballroom was empty. Beyond the double cathedral window he could see fresh snow beginning to sift
down. The huge ballroom rug (rolled up for dancing,
of course), a rich tangle of red and gold embroidery,
lay undisturbed on the floor. Spaced around it were
small, intimate tables for two, the spidery chairs that
went with each upended with legs pointing at the
ceiling.

The whole place was empty.

But it wasn't really empty. Because here in the
Overlook things just went on and on. Here in the

Overlook all times were one. There was an endless night in August of 1945, with laughter and drinks and a chosen shining few going up and coming down in the elevator, drinking champagne and popping party favors in each other's faces. It was a not-yet-light morning in June some twenty years later and the organization hitters endlessly pumped shotgun shells into the torn and bleeding bodies of three men who went through their agony endlessly. In a room on the second floor a woman lolled in her tub and waited for visitors.

In the Overlook all things had a sort of life. It was as if the whole place had been wound up with a silver key. The clock was running. The clock was running.

He was that key, Danny thought sadly. Tony had warned him and he had just let things go on.

(*I'm just five!*)

he cried to some half-felt presence in the room.

(*Doesn't it make any difference that I'm just five?*)

There was no answer.

He turned reluctantly back to the clock.

He had been putting it off, hoping that something would happen to help him avoid trying to call Tony again, that a ranger would come, or a helicopter, or the rescue team; they always came in time on his TV programs, the people were saved. On TV the rangers and the SWAT squad and the paramedics were a friendly white force counterbalancing the confused evil that he perceived in the world; when people got in trouble they were helped out of it, they were fixed up. They did not have to help themselves out of trouble.

(Please?)

There was no answer.

No answer, and if Tony came would it be the same nightmare? The booming, the hoarse and petulant voice, the blue-black rug like snakes? *Redrum?*

But what else?

(Please oh please)

No answer.

With a trembling sigh, he looked at the clockface. Cogs turned and meshed with other cogs. The balance wheel rocked hypnotically back and forth. And if you held your head perfectly still, you could see the minute hand creeping inexorably down from XII to V. If you held your head perfectly still you could see that—

The clockface was gone. In its place was a round black hole. It led down into forever. It began to swell. The clock was gone. The room behind it. Danny tottered and then fell into the darkness that had been hiding behind the clockface all along.

The small boy in the chair suddenly collapsed and lay in it at a crooked unnatural angle, his head thrown back, his eyes staring sightlessly at the high ballroom ceiling.

Down and down and down and down to—

—the hallway, crouched in the hallway, and he had made a wrong turn, trying to get back to the stairs he had made a wrong turn and now AND NOW—

—he saw he was in the short dead-end corridor that led only to the Presidential Suite and the booming sound was coming closer, the roque mallet whistling savagely through the air, the head of it embedding itself into the wall, cutting the silk paper, letting out small puffs of plaster dust.

(*Goddammit, come out here! Take your*)

But there was another figure in the hallway. Slouched nonchalantly against the wall just behind him. Like a ghost.

No, not a ghost, but all dressed in white. Dressed in whites.

(*I'll find you, you goddam little whoremastering RUNT!*)

Danny cringed back from the sound. Coming up the main third-floor hall now. Soon the owner of that voice would round the corner.

(*Come here! Come here, you little shit!*)

The figure dressed in white straightened up a little, removed a cigarette from the corner of his mouth and plucked a shred of tobacco from his full lower lip. It was Hallorann, Danny saw. Dressed in his cook's whites instead of the blue suit he had been wearing on closing day.

"If there *is* trouble," Hallorann said, "you give a call. A big loud holler like the one that knocked me back a few minutes ago. I might hear you even way down in Florida. And if I do, I'll come on the run. I'll come on the run. I'll come on the—"

(*Come now, then! Come now, come NOW! Oh, Dick I need you we all need*)

"—run. Sorry, but I got to run. Sorry, Danny ole kid ole doc, but I got to run. It's sure been fun, you son of a gun, but I got to hurry, I got to run."

(No!)

But as he watched, Dick Hallorann turned, put his cigarette back into the corner of his mouth, and stepped nonchalantly through the wall.

Leaving him alone.

And that was when the shadow figure turned the corner, huge in the hallway's gloom, only the reflected red of its eyes clear.

(There you are! Now I've got you, you fuck! Now I'll teach you!)

It lurched toward him in a horrible, shambling run, the roque mallet swinging up and up and up. Danny scrambled backward, screaming, and suddenly he was through the wall and falling, tumbling over and over, down the hole, down the rabbit hole and into a land full of sick wonders.

Tony was far below him, also falling.

(I can't come anymore, Danny . . . he won't let me near you . . . none of them will let me near you . . . get Dick . . . get Dick . . .)

"*Tony!*" he screamed.

But Tony was gone and suddenly he was in a dark room. But not entirely dark. Muted light spilling from somewhere. It was Mommy and Daddy's bedroom. He could see Daddy's desk. But the room was a dreadful shambles. He had been in this room before. Mommy's record player overturned on the floor. Her records scattered on the rug. The mattress half off the bed. Pictures ripped from the walls. His cot lying on its side like a dead dog, the Violent Violet Volkswagen crushed to purple shards of plastic.

The light was coming from the bathroom door, half-open. Just beyond it a hand dangled limply, blood dripping from the tips of the fingers. And in the medicine cabinet mirror, the word REDRUM flashing off and on.

Suddenly a huge clock in a glass bowl materialized in front of it. There were no hands or numbers on the clockface, only a date written in red: DECEMBER 2. And then, eyes widening in horror, he saw the word REDRUM reflecting dimly from the glass dome, now reflected twice. And he saw that it spelled MURDER.

Danny Torrance screamed in wretched terror. The date was gone from the clockface. The clockface itself was gone, replaced by a circular black hole that swelled and swelled like a dilating iris. It blotted out everything and he fell forward, beginning to fall, falling, he was—

—falling off the chair.

For a moment he lay on the ballroom floor, breathing hard.

> REDRUM.
> MURDER.
> REDRUM.
> MURDER.

(*The Red Death held sway over all!*)
(*Unmask! Unmask!*)

And behind each glittering, lovely mask, the as-yet unseen face of the shape that chased him down these dark hallways, its red eyes widening, blank and homicidal.

Oh, he was afraid of what face might come to light when the time for unmasking came around at last.

(*DICK!*)

he screamed with all his might. His head seemed to shiver with the force of it.

(*!!!   OH DICK OH PLEASE PLEASE PLEASE*
COME   !!!)

Above him the clock he had wound with the silver key continued to mark off the seconds and minutes and hours.

PART FIVE

Matters of Life and Death

38

Florida

Mrs. Hallorann's third son, Dick, dressed in his cook's whites, a Lucky Strike parked in the corner of his mouth, backed his reclaimed Cadillac limo out of its space behind the One-A Wholesale Vegetable Mart and drove slowly around the building. Masterton, part owner now but still walking with the patented shuffle he had adopted back before World War II, was pushing a bin of lettuces into the high, dark building.

Hallorann pushed the button that lowered the passenger side window and hollered: "Those avocadoes is too damn high, you cheapskate!"

Masterton looked back over his shoulder, grinned widely enough to expose all three gold teeth, and yelled back, "And I know exactly where you can put em, my good buddy."

"Remarks like that I keep track of, *bro.*"

Masterton gave him the finger. Hallorann returned the compliment.

"Get your cukes, did you?" Masterton asked.

"I did."

"You come back early tomorrow, I gonna give you some of the nicest new potatoes you ever seen."

"I send the boy," Hallorann said. "You comin up tonight?"

"You supplyin the juice, *bro*?"

"That's a big ten-four."

"I be there. You keep that thing off the top end goin home, you hear me? Every cop between here an St. Pete knows your name."

"You know all about it, huh?" Hallorann asked, grinning.

"I know more than you'll ever learn, my man."

"Listen to this sassy nigger. Would you listen?"

"Go on, get outta here fore I start throwin these lettuces."

"Go on an throw em. I'll take anything for free."

Masterton made as if to throw one. Hallorann ducked, rolled up the window, and drove on. He was feeling fine. For the last half hour or so he had been smelling oranges, but he didn't find that queer. For the last half hour he had been in a fruit and vegetable market.

It was 4:30 P.M., EST, the first day of December, Old Man Winter settling his frostbitten rump firmly onto most of the country, but down here the men wore open-throated short-sleeve shirts and the women were in light summer dresses and shorts. On top of the First Bank of Florida building, a digital thermometer bordered with huge grapefruits was flashing 79° over and over. Thank God for Florida, Hallorann thought, mosquitoes and all.

In the back of the limo were two dozen avocados, a crate of cucumbers, ditto oranges, ditto grapefruit. Three shopping sacks filled with Bermuda onions, the sweetest vegetable a loving God ever created, some pretty good sweet peas, which would be served with the entree and come back uneaten nine times out of ten, and a single blue Hubbard squash that was strictly for personal consumption.

Hallorann stopped in the turn lane at the Vermont Street light, and when the green arrow showed he pulled out onto state highway 219, pushing up to forty and holding it there until the town began to trickle away into an exurban sprawl of gas stations, Burger Kings, and McDonalds. It was a small order today, he could have sent Baedecker after it, but Baedecker had been chafing for his chance to buy the meat, and besides, Hallorann never missed a chance to bang it back and forth with Frank Masterton if he could help it. Masterton might show up tonight to watch some TV and drink Hallorann's Bushmill's, or he might not. Either way was all right. But seeing him mattered. Every time it mattered now, because they weren't young anymore. In the last few days it seemed he was thinking of that very fact a great deal. Not so young anymore, when you got up near sixty years old (or—tell the truth and save a lie—past it) you had to start thinking about stepping out. You could go anytime. And that had been on his mind this week, not in a heavy way but as a fact. Dying was a part of living. You had to keep tuning in to that if you expected to be a whole person. And if the fact of your own death was hard to understand, at least it wasn't impossible to accept.

Why this should have been on his mind he could not have said, but his other reason for getting this small order himself was so he could step upstairs to the small office over Frank's Bar and Grill. There was a lawyer up there now (the dentist who had been there last year had apparently gone broke), a young black fellow named McIver. Hallorann had stepped in and told this McIver that he wanted to make a will, and could McIver help him out? Well, McIver asked, how soon do you want the document? Yesterday, said Hallorann, and threw his head back and laughed. Have you got anything complicated in mind? was McIver's next question. Hallorann did not. He had his Cadillac, his bank account—some nine thousand dollars—a piddling checking account, and a closet of clothes. He wanted it all to go to his sister. And if your sister predeceases you? McIver asked. Never mind, Hallorann said. If that happens, I'll make a new will. The document had been completed and signed in less than three hours—fast work for a shyster—and now resided in Hallorann's breast pocket, folded into a stiff blue envelope with the word WILL on the outside in Old English letters.

He could not have said why he had chosen this warm sunny day when he felt so well to do something he had been putting off for years, but the impulse had come on him and he hadn't said no. He was used to following his hunches.

He was pretty well out of town now. He cranked the limo up to an illegal sixty and let it ride there in the left-hand lane, sucking up most of the Petersburg-bound traffic. He knew from experience that the limo would still ride as solid as iron at ninety, and even at a hundred and twenty it didn't seem to lighten up much. But his screamin days were long gone. The thought of putting the limo up to a hundred and twenty on a straight stretch only scared him. He was getting old.

(Jesus, those oranges smell strong. Wonder if they gone over?)

Bugs splattered against the window. He dialed the radio to a Miami soul station and got the soft, wailing voice of Al Green.

> *"What a beautiful time we had together,*
> *Now it's getting late and we must leave each*
>   *other . . ."*

He unrolled the window, pitched his cigarette butt out, then rolled it further down to clear out the smell of the oranges. He tapped his fingers against the wheel and hummed along under his breath. Hooked over the rearview mirror, his St. Christopher's medal swung gently back and forth.

And suddenly the smell of oranges intensified and he knew it was coming, something was coming at him. He saw his own eyes in the rearview, widening, surprised. And then it came all at once, came in a huge blast that drove out everything else: the music, the road ahead, his own absent awareness of himself as a unique human creature. It was as if someone had put a psychic gun to his head and shot him with a .45 caliber scream.

(!!!   *OH DICK OH PLEASE PLEASE PLEASE COME   !!!*)

The limo had just drawn even with a Pinto station wagon driven by a man in workman's clothes. The workman saw the limo drifting into his lane and laid on the horn. When the Cadillac continued to drift he snapped a look at the driver and saw a big black man bolt upright behind the wheel, his eyes looking vaguely upward. Later the workman told his wife that he knew it was just one of those niggery hairdos they were all wearing these days, but at the time it had looked just as if every hair on that coon's head was standing on end. He thought the black man was having a heart attack.

The workman braked hard, dropping back into a luckily-empty space behind him. The rear end of the Cadillac pulled ahead of him, still cutting in, and the workman stared with bemused horror as the long, rocket-shaped rear taillights cut into his lane no more than a quarter of an inch in front of his bumper.

The workman cut to the left, still laying on his horn, and roared around the drunkenly weaving limousine. He invited the driver of the limo to perform an illegal sex act on himself. To engage in oral congress with various rodents and birds. He articulated his own proposal that all persons of Negro blood return to their native continent. He expressed his sincere belief in the position the limo-driver's soul would occupy in the afterlife. He finished by saying that he believed he had met the limo-driver's mother in a New Orleans house of prostitution.

Then he was ahead and out of danger and suddenly aware that he had wet his pants.

In Hallorann's mind the thought kept repeating

(*COME DICK PLEASE COME DICK PLEASE*)

but it began to fade off the way a radio station will as you approach the limits of its broadcasting area. He became fuzzily aware that his car was tooling along the soft shoulder at better than fifty miles an hour. He guided it back onto the road, feeling the rear end fishtail for a moment before regaining the composition surface.

There was an A/W Rootbeer stand just ahead. Hallorann signaled and turned in, his heart thudding painfully in his chest, his face a sickly gray color. He pulled into a parking slot, took his handkerchief out of his pocket, and mopped his forehead with it.

(*Lord God!*)

"May I help you?"

The voice startled him again, even though it wasn't the voice of God but that of a cute little carhop, standing by his open window with an order pad.

"Yeah, baby, a rootbeer float. Two scoops of vanilla, okay?"

"Yes, sir." She walked away, hips rolling nicely beneath her red nylon uniform.

Hallorann leaned back against the leather seat and closed his eyes. There was nothing left to pick up.

The last of it had faded out between pulling in here and giving the waitress his order. All that was left was a sick, thudding headache, as if his brain had been twisted and wrung out and hung up to dry. Like the headache he'd gotten from letting that boy Danny shine at him up there at Ullman's Folly.

But this had been much louder. Then the boy had only been playing a game with him. This had been pure panic, each word screamed aloud in his head.

He looked down at his arms. Hot sunshine lay on them but they had still goose-bumped. He had told the boy to call him if he needed help, he remembered that. And now the boy was calling.

He suddenly wondered how he could have left that boy up there at all, shining the way he did. There was bound to be trouble, maybe bad trouble.

He suddenly keyed the limo, put it in reverse, and pulled back onto the highway, peeling rubber. The waitress with the rolling hips stood in the A/W stand's archway, a tray with a rootbeer float on it in her hands.

"What is it with you, a fire?" she shouted, but Hallorann was gone.

The manager was a man named Queems, and when Hallorann came in Queems was conversing with his bookie. He wanted the four-horse at Rockaway. No, no parlay, no quinella, no exacta, no goddam futura. Just the little old four, six hundred dollars on the nose. And the Jets on Sunday. What did he mean, the Jets were playing the Bills? Didn't he know who the Jets were playing? Five hundred, seven-point spread. When Queems hung up, looking put-out, Hallorann understood how a man could make fifty grand a year running this little spa and still wear suits with shiny seats. He regarded Hallorann with an eye that was still bloodshot from too many glances into last night's Bourbon bottle.

"Problems, Dick?"

"Yes, sir, Mr. Queems, I guess so. I need three days off."

There was a package of Kents in the breast pocket of Queems's sheer yellow shirt. He reached one out of the pocket without removing the pack, tweezing it out, and bit down morosely on the patented Micronite filter. He lit it with his desktop Cricket.

"So do I," he said. "But what's on your mind?"

"I need three days," Hallorann repeated. "It's my boy."

Queems's eyes dropped to Hallorann's left hand, which was ringless.

"I been divorced since 1964," Hallorann said patiently.

"Dick, you know what the weekend situation is. We're full. To the gunnels. Even the cheap seats. We're even filled up in the Florida Room on Sunday night. So take my watch, my wallet, my pension fund. Hell, you can even take my wife if you can stand the sharp edges. But please don't ask me for time off. What is he, sick?"

"Yes, sir," Hallorann said, still trying to visualize himself twisting a cheap cloth hat and rolling his eyeballs. "He shot."

"Shot!" Queems said. He put his Kent down in an ashtray which bore the emblem of Ole Miss, of which he was a business admin graduate.

"Yes, sir," Hallorann said somberly.

"Hunting accident?"

"No, sir," Hallorann said, and let his voice drop to a lower, huskier note. "Jana, she's been livin with this truck driver. A white man. He shot my boy. He's in a hospital in Denver, Colorado. Critical condition."

"How in hell did you find out? I thought you were buying vegetables."

"Yes, sir, I was." He had stopped at the Western Union office just before coming here to reserve an Avis car at Stapleton Airport. Before leaving he had swiped a Western Union flimsy. Now he took the folded and crumpled blank form from his pocket and flashed it before Queems's blood-shot eyes. He put it back in his pocket and, allowing his voice to drop another notch, said: "Jana sent it. It was waitin in my letter box when I got back just now."

"Jesus. Jesus Christ," Queems said. There was a peculiar tight expression of concern on his face, one Hallorann was familiar with. It was as close to an expression of sympathy as a white man who thought of himself as "good with the coloreds" could get when the object was a black man or his mythical black son.

"Yeah, okay, you get going," Queems said. "Baedecker can take over for three days, I guess. The potboy can help out."

Hallorann nodded, letting his face get longer still, but the thought of the potboy helping out Baedecker made him grin inside. Even on a good day Hallorann doubted if the potboy could hit the urinal on the first squirt.

"I want to rebate back this week's pay," Hallorann said. "The whole thing. I know what a bind this puttin you in, Mr. Queems, sir."

Queems's expression got tighter still; it looked as if he might have a fishbone caught in his throat. "We can talk about that later. You go on and pack. I'll talk to Baedecker. Want me to make you a plane reservation?"

"No, sir, I'll do it."

"All right." Queems stood up, leaned sincerely forward, and inhaled a raft of ascending smoke from his Kent. He coughed heartily, his thin white face turning red. Hallorann struggled hard to keep his somber expression. "I hope everything turns out, Dick. Call when you get word."

"I'll do that."

They shook hands over the desk.

Hallorann made himself get down to the ground floor and across to the hired help's compound before bursting into rich, head-shaking laughter. He was still grinning and mopping his streaming eyes with his handkerchief when the smell of oranges came, thick and gagging, and the bolt followed it, striking him in the head, sending him back against the pink stucco wall in a drunken stagger.

(!!!   PLEASE COME DICK PLEASE COME
COME QUICK   !!!)

He recovered a little at a time and at last felt capable of climbing the outside stairs to his apartment.

He kept the latchkey under the rush-plaited door-mat, and when he reached down to get it, something fell out of his inner pocket and fell to the second-floor decking with a flat thump. His mind was still so much on the voice that had shivered through his head that for a moment he could only look at the blue envelope blankly, not knowing what it was.

Then he turned it over and the word WILL stared up at him in the black spidery letters.

(*Oh my God is it like that?*)

He didn't know. But it could be. All week long the thought of his own ending had been on his mind like a . . . well, like a

(*Go on, say it*)

like a premonition.

Death? For a moment his whole life seemed to flash before him, not in a historical sense, no topography of the ups and downs that Mrs. Hallorann's third son, Dick, had lived through, but his life as it was now. Martin Luther King had told them not long before the bullet took him down to his mar-tyr's grave that he had been to the mountain. Dick could not claim that. No mountain, but he had reached a sunny plateau after years of struggle. He had good friends. He had all the references he would ever need to get a job anywhere. When he wanted fuck, why, he could find a friendly one with no questions asked and no big shitty struggle about what it all meant. He had come to terms with his blackness—happy terms. He was up past sixty and thank God, he was cruising.

Was he going to chance the end of that—the end of *him*—for three white people he didn't even know?

But that was a lie, wasn't it?

He knew the boy. They had shared each other the way good friends can't even after forty years of it. He knew the boy and the boy knew him, because they each had a kind of searchlight in their heads, something they hadn't asked for, something that had just been given.

(*Naw, you got a flashlight, he the one with the searchlight.*)

And sometimes that light, that shine, seemed like a pretty nice thing. You could pick the horses, or like the boy had said, you could tell your daddy where his trunk was when it turned up missing. But that was only dressing, the sauce on the salad, and down below there was as much bitter vetch in that salad as there was cool cucumber. You could taste pain and death and tears. And now the boy was stuck in that place, and he would go. For the boy. Because, speaking to the boy, they had only been different colors when they used their mouths. So he would go. He would do what he could, because if he didn't, the boy was going to die right inside his head.

But because he was human he could not help a bitter wish that the cup had never been passed his way.

(*She had started to get out and come after him.*)

He had been dumping a change of clothes into an overnight bag when the thought came to him, freezing him with the power of the memory as it always did when he thought of it. He tried to think of it as seldom as possible.

The maid, Delores Vickery her name was, had been hysterical. Had said some things to the other chambermaids, and worse still, to some of the guests. When the word got back to Ullman, as the silly quiff should have known it would do, he had fired her out of hand. She had come to Halloran in tears, not about being fired, but about the thing she had seen in that second-floor room. She had gone into 217 to change the towels, she said, and there had been that Mrs. Massey, lying dead in the tub. That, of course, was impossible. Mrs. Massey had been discreetly taken away the day before and was even then winging her way back to New York—in the shipping hold instead of the first class she'd been accustomed to.

Halloran hadn't liked Delores much, but he had gone up to look that evening. The maid was an olive-complected girl of twenty-three who waited table near the end of the season when things slowed down. She had a small shining, Halloran judged, really not more than a twinkle; a mousy-looking man and his escort, wearing a faded cloth coat, would come in for dinner and Delores would trade one of her tables for theirs. The mousy little man would leave a picture of Alexander Hamilton under his plate, bad enough for the girl who had made the trade, but worse, Delores would crow over it. She was lazy, a goof-off in an operation run by a man who allowed no goof-offs. She would sit in a linen closet, reading a confession magazine and smoking, but whenever Ullman went on one of his unscheduled prowls (and woe to the girl he caught resting her feet) he found her working industriously, her magazine hidden under the sheets on a high shelf, her ashtray tucked safely into her uniform pocket. Yeah, Hallorann thought, she'd been a goof-off and a sloven and the other girls had resented her, but Delores had had that little twinkle. It had always greased the skids for her. But what she had seen in 217 had scared her badly enough so she was more than glad to pick up the walking papers Ullman had issued her and go.

Why had she come to him? A shine knows a shine, Hallorann thought, grinning at the pun.

So he had gone up that night and had let himself into the room, which was to be reoccupied the next day. He had used the office passkey to get in, and if Ullman had caught him with that key, he would have joined Delores Vickery on the unemployment line.

The shower curtain around the tub had been drawn. He had pushed it back, but even before he did he'd had a premonition of what he was going to see. Mrs. Massey, swollen and purple, lay soggily in the tub, which was half-full of water. He had stood looking down at her, a pulse beating thickly in his throat. There had been other things at the Overlook: a bad dream that recurred at irregular intervals—some sort of costume party and he was catering it in the Overlook's ballroom and at the shout to unmask, everybody exposed faces that were those of rotting insects—and there had been the hedge animals.

Twice, maybe three times, he had (or thought he had) seen them move, ever so slightly. That dog would seem to change from his sitting-up posture to a slightly crouched one, and the lions seemed to move forward, as if menacing the little tykes on the playground. Last year in May Ullman had sent him up to the attic to look for the ornate set of firetools that now stood beside the lobby fireplace. While he had been up there the three lightbulbs strung overhead had gone out and he had lost his way back to the trapdoor. He had stumbled around for an unknown length of time, closer and closer to panic, barking his shins on boxes and bumping into things, with a stronger and stronger feeling that something was stalking him in the dark. Some great and frightening creature that had just oozed out of the woodwork when the lights went out. And when he had literally stumbled over the trapdoor's ringbolt he had hurried down as fast as he could, leaving the trap open, sooty and disheveled, with a feeling of disaster barely averted. Later Ullman had come down to the kitchen personally, to inform him he had left the attic trapdoor open and the lights burning up there. Did Hallorann think the guests wanted to go up there and play treasure hunt? Did he think electricity was free?

And he suspected—no, was nearly positive—that several of the guests had seen or heard things, too. In the three years he had been there, the Presidential Suite had been booked nineteen times. Six of the guests who had put up there had left the hotel early, some of them looking markedly ill. Other guests had left other rooms with the same abruptness. One night in August of 1974, near dusk, a man who had won the Bronze and Silver Stars in Korea (that man now sat on the boards of three major corporations and was said to have personally pink-slipped a famous TV news anchorman) unaccountably went into a fit of screaming hysterics on the putting green. And there had been dozens of children during Hallorann's association with the Overlook who simply refused to go into the playground. One child had had a convulsion while playing in the concrete rings, but Hallorann didn't know if that could be attributed to the Overlook's deadly siren song or not—word had gone around among the help that the child, the only daughter of a handsome movie actor, was a medically controlled epileptic who had simply forgotten her medicine that day.

And so, staring down at the corpse of Mrs. Massey, he had been frightened but not completely terrified. It was not completely unexpected. Terror came when she opened her eyes to disclose blank silver pupils and began to grin at him. Horror came when

(*she had started to get out and come after him.*)

He had fled, heart racing, and had not felt safe even with the door shut and locked behind him. In fact, he admitted to himself now as he zipped the flightbag shut, he had never felt safe anywhere in the Overlook again.

And now the boy—calling, screaming for help.

He looked at his watch. It was 5:30 P.M. He went to the apartment's door, remembered it would be heavy winter now in Colorado, especially up in the mountains, and went back to his closet. He pulled his long, sheepskin-lined overcoat out of its polyurethane dry-cleaning bag and put it over his arm. It was the only winter garment he owned. He turned off all the lights and looked around. Had he forgotten anything? Yes. One thing. He took the will out of his breast pocket and slipped it into the margin of the dressing table mirror. With luck he would be back to get it.

Sure, with luck.

He left the apartment, locked the door behind him, put the key under the rush mat, and ran down the outside steps to his converted Cadillac.

Halfway to Miami International, comfortably away from the switchboard where Queems or Queems's toadies were known to listen in, Hallorann stopped at a shopping center Laundromat and called United Air Lines. Flights to Denver?

There was one due out at 6:36 P.M. Could the gentleman make that?

Hallorann looked at his watch, which showed 6:02, and said he could. What about vacancies on the flight?

Just let me check.

A clunking sound in his ear followed by saccharine Montavani, which was supposed to make being on hold more pleasant. It didn't. Hallorann danced from one foot to the other, alternating glances between his watch and a young girl with a sleeping baby in a hammock on her back unloading a coin-op Maytag. She was afraid she was going to get home later than she planned and the roast would burn and her husband—Mark? Mike? Matt?—would be mad.

A minute passed. Two. He had just about made up his mind to drive ahead and take his chances when the canned-sounding voice of the flight reservations clerk came back on. There was an empty seat, a cancellation. It was in first class. Did that make any difference?

No. He wanted it.

Would that be cash or credit card?

Cash, baby, cash. I've got to fly.

And the name was——?

Hallorann, two *l*'s, two *n*'s. Catch you later.

He hung up and hurried toward the door. The girl's simple thought, worry for the roast, broadcast at him over and over until he thought he would go mad. Sometimes it was like that, for no reason at all you would catch a thought, completely isolated, completely pure and clear . . . and usually completely useless.

He almost made it.

He had the limo cranked up to eighty and the airport was actually in sight when one of Florida's Finest pulled him over.

Hallorann unrolled the electric window and opened his mouth at the cop, who was flipping up pages in his citation book.

"I *know*," the cop said comfortingly. "It's a funeral in Cleveland. Your father. It's a wedding in Seattle. Your sister. A fire in San Jose that wiped out your gramp's candy store. Some really fine Cambodian Red just waiting in a terminal locker in New York City. I love this piece of road just outside the airport. Even as a kid, story hour was my favorite part of school."

"Listen, officer, my son is—"

"The only part of the story I can never figure out until the end," the officer said, finding the right page in his citation book, "is the driver's-license number of the offending motorist/storyteller and his registration information. So be a nice guy. Let me peek."

Hallorann looked into the cop's calm blue eyes, debated telling his my-son-is-in-critical-condition story anyway, and decided that would make things worse. This Smokey was no Queems. He dug out his wallet.

"Wonderful," the cop said. "Would you take them out for me, please? I just have to see how it's all going to come out in the end."

Silently, Hallorann took out his driver's license and his Florida registration and gave them to the traffic cop.

"That's very good. That's so good you win a present."

"What?" Hallorann asked hopefully.

"When I finish writing down these numbers, I'm going to let you blow up a little balloon for me."

"Oh, *Jeeeesus!*" Hallorann moaned. "Officer, my flight—"

"Shhhh," the traffic cop said. "Don't be naughty."
Hallorann closed his eyes.

He got to the United desk at 6:49, hoping against
hope that the flight had been delayed. He didn't even
have to ask. The departure monitor over the incoming passengers desk told the story. Flight 901 for
Denver, due out at 6:36 EST, had left at 6:40. Nine
minutes before.

"Oh shit," Dick Hallorann said.

And suddenly the smell of oranges, heavy and
cloying, he had just time to reach the men's room
before it came, deafening, terrified:

   (!!!   *COME PLEASE COME DICK PLEASE*
              PLEASE COME   !!!)

39

On the Stairs

One of the things they had sold to swell their liquid assets a little before moving from Vermont to Colorado was Jack's collection of two hundred old rock 'n' roll and r & b albums; they had gone at the yard sale for a dollar apiece. One of these albums, Danny's personal favorite, had been an Eddie Cochran double-record set with four pages of bound-in liner notes by Lenny Kaye. Wendy had often been struck by Danny's fascination for this one particular album by a man-boy who had lived fast and died young . . . had died, in fact, when she herself had only been ten years old.

Now, at quarter past seven (mountain time), as Dick Hallorann was telling Queems about his ex-wife's white boyfriend, she came upon Danny sitting halfway up the stairs between the lobby and the first floor, tossing a red rubber ball from hand to hand and singing one of the songs from that album. His voice was low and tuneless.

"So I climb one-two flight three flight four," Danny sang, "five flight six flight seven flight

more . . . when I get to the top, I'm too tired to
rock . . ."

She came around him, sat down on one of the stair
risers, and saw that his lower lip had swelled to twice
its size and that there was dried blood on his chin.
Her heart took a frightened leap in her chest, but she
managed to speak neutrally.

"What happened, doc?" she asked, although she
was sure she knew. Jack had hit him. Well, of course.
That came next, didn't it? The wheels of progress;
sooner or later they took you back to where you
started from.

"I called Tony," Danny said. "In the ballroom. I
guess I fell off the chair. It doesn't hurt anymore. Just
feels . . . like my lip's too big."

"Is that what really happened?" she asked, looking
at him, troubled.

"Daddy didn't do it," he answered. "Not today."

She gazed at him, feeling eerie. The ball traveled
from one hand to the other. He had read her mind.
Her son had read her mind.

"What . . . what did Tony tell you, Danny?"

"It doesn't matter." His face was calm, his voice
chillingly indifferent.

"*Danny*—" She gripped his shoulder, harder than
she had intended. But he didn't wince, or even try to
shake her off.

(*Oh we are wrecking this boy. It's not just Jack, it's me
too, and maybe it's not even just us, Jack's father, my mother,
are they here too? Sure, why not? The place is lousy with
ghosts anyway, why not a couple more? Oh Lord in heaven*

he's like one of those suitcases they show on TV, run over, dropped from planes, going through factory crushers. Or a Timex watch. Takes a licking and keeps on ticking. Oh Danny I'm so sorry).

"It doesn't matter," he said again. The ball went from hand to hand. "Tony can't come anymore. They won't let him. He's licked."

"Who won't?"

"The people in the hotel," he said. He looked at her then, and his eyes weren't indifferent at all. They were deep and scared. "And the . . . the *things* in the hotel. There's all kinds of them. The hotel is *stuffed* with them."

"You can see—"

"I don't want to see," he said low, and then looked back at the rubber ball, arcing from hand to hand. "But I can hear them sometimes, late at night. They're like the wind, all sighing together. In the attic. The basement. The rooms. All over. I thought it was my fault, because of the way I am. The key. The little silver key."

"Danny, don't . . . don't upset yourself this way."

"But it's *him* too," Danny said. "It's Daddy. And it's you. It wants all of us. It's tricking Daddy, it's fooling him, trying to make him think it wants him the most. It wants me the most, but it will take all of us."

"If only that snowmobile—"

"They wouldn't let him," Danny said in that same low voice. "They made him throw part of it away into the snow. Far away. I dreamed it. And he knows that woman really is in 217." He looked at her with his dark, frightened eyes. "It doesn't matter whether you believe me or not."

She slipped an arm around him.

"I believe you, Danny, tell me the truth. Is Jack . . . is he going to try to hurt us?"

"They'll try to make him," Danny said. "I've been calling for Mr. Hallorann. He said if I ever needed him to just call. And I have been. But it's awful hard. It makes me tired. And the worst part is I don't know if he's hearing me or not. I don't think he can call back because it's too far for him. And I don't know if it's too far for me or not. Tomorrow—"

"What about tomorrow?"

He shook his head. "Nothing."

"Where is he now?" she asked. "Your daddy?"

"He's in the basement. I don't think he'll be up tonight."

She stood up suddenly. "Wait right here for me. Five minutes."

The kitchen was cold and deserted under the overhead fluorescent bars. She went to the rack where the carving knives hung from their magnetized strips. She took the longest and sharpest, wrapped it in a dish towel, and left the kitchen, turning off the lights as she went.

Danny sat on the stairs, his eyes following the course of his red rubber ball from hand to hand. He sang: "She lives on the twentieth floor uptown, the elevator is broken down. So I walk one-two flight three flight four . . ."

(—*Lou, Lou, skip to m' Lou*—)

His singing broke off. He listened.

(—*Skip to m' Lou my daarlin'*—)

The voice was in his head, so much a part of him, so frighteningly close that it might have been a part of his own thoughts. It was soft and infinitely sly. Mocking him. Seeming to say:

(*Oh yes, you'll like it here. Try it, you'll like it. Try it, you'll liiiiike it*—)

Now his ears were open and he could hear them again, the gathering, ghosts or spirits or maybe the hotel itself, a dreadful funhouse where all the sideshows ended in death, where all the specially painted boogies were really alive, where hedges walked, where a small silver key could start the obscenity. Soft and sighing, rustling like the endless winter wind that played under the eaves at night, the deadly lulling wind the summer tourists never heard. It was like the somnolent hum of summer wasps in a ground nest, sleepy, deadly, beginning to wake up. They were ten thousand feet high.

(*Why is a raven like a writing desk? The higher the fewer, of course! Have another cup of tea!*)

It was a living sound, but not voices, not breath. A man of a philosophical bent might have called it the sound of souls. Dick Hallorann's Nana, who had grown up on southern roads in the years before the turn of the century, would have called it ha'ants. A psychic investigator might have had a long name for it—psychic echo, psychokinesis, a telesmic sport. But to Danny it was only the sound of the hotel, the old monster, creaking steadily and ever more closely around them: halls that now stretched back through time as well as distance, hungry shadows, unquiet guests who did not rest easy.

In the darkened ballroom the clock under glass struck seven-thirty with a single musical note.

A hoarse voice, made brutal with drink, shouted: *"Unmask and let's fuck!"*

Wendy, halfway across the lobby, jerked to a standstill.

She looked at Danny on the stairs, still tossing the ball from hand to hand. "Did you hear something?"

Danny only looked at her and continued to toss the ball from hand to hand.

There would be little sleep for them that night, although they slept together behind a locked door.

And in the dark, his eyes open, Danny thought:

(*He wants to be one of them and live forever. That's what he wants.*)

Wendy thought:

(*If I have to, I'll take him further up. If we're going to die I'd rather do it in the mountains.*)

She had left the butcher knife, still wrapped in the towel, under the bed. She kept her hand close to it. They dozed off and on. The hotel creaked around them. Outside snow had begun to spit down from a sky like lead.

40

In the Basement

(!!! The boiler the goddam boiler !!!)

The thought came into Jack Torrance's mind full-blown, edged in bright, warning red. On its heels, the voice of Watson:

(If you forget it'll just creep an creep and like as not you an your fambly will end up on the fuckin moon . . . she's rated for two-fifty but she'd blow long before that now . . . I'd be scared to come down and stand next to her at a hundred and eighty.)

He'd been down here all night, poring over the boxes of old records, possessed by a frantic feeling that time was getting short and he would have to hurry. Still the vital clues, the connections that would make everything clear, eluded him. His fingers were yellow and grimy with crumbling old paper. And he'd become so absorbed he hadn't checked the boiler once. He'd dumped it the previous evening around six o'clock, when he first came down. It was now . . .

He looked at his watch and jumped up, kicking over a stack of old invoices.

Christ, it was quarter of five in the morning.

Behind him, the furnace kicked on. The boiler was making a groaning, whistling sound.

He ran to it. His face, which had become thinner in the last month or so, was now heavily shadowed with beardstubble and he had a hollow concentration-camp look.

The boiler pressure gauge stood at two hundred and ten pounds per square inch. He fancied he could almost see the sides of the old patched and welded boiler heaving out with the lethal strain.

(She creeps . . . I'd be scared to come down and stand next to her at a hundred and eighty . . .)

Suddenly a cold and tempting inner voice spoke to him.

(Let it go. Go get Wendy and Danny and get the fuck out of here. Let it blow sky-high.)

He could visualize the explosion. A double thunderclap that would first rip the heart from this place, then the soul. The boiler would go with an orange-violet flash that would rain hot and burning shrapnel all over the cellar. In his mind he could see the redhot trinkets of metal careening from floor to walls to ceiling like strange billiard balls, whistling jagged death through the air. Some of them, surely, would whizz right through that stone arch, light on the old papers on the other side, and they would burn merry hell. Destroy the secrets, burn the clues, it's a mystery no living hand will ever solve. Then the gas explosion, a great rumbling crackle of flame, a giant pilot light that would turn the whole center of the hotel into a broiler. Stairs and hallways and ceilings and rooms aflame like the castle in the last reel of a Frankenstein movie. The flame spreading into the wings, hurrying up the black-and-blue-twined carpets like eager guests. The silk wallpaper charring and curling. There were no sprinklers, only those outmoded hoses and no one to use them. And there wasn't a fire engine in the world that could get here before late March. Burn, baby, burn. In twelve hours there would be nothing left but the bare bones.

The needle on the gauge had moved up to two twelve. The boiler was creaking and groaning like an old woman trying to get out of bed. Hissing jets of steam had begun to play around the edges of old patches; beads of solder had begun to sizzle.

He didn't see, he didn't hear. Frozen with his hand on the valve that would dump off the pressure and damp the fire, Jack's eyes glittered from their sockets like sapphires.

(*It's my last chance.*)

The only thing not cashed in now was the life insurance policy he had taken out jointly with Wendy in the summer between his first and second years at Stovington. Forty-thousand-dollar death benefit, double indemnity if he or she died in a train crash, a plane crash, or a fire. Seven-come-eleven, die the secret death and win a hundred dollars.

(*A fire . . . eighty thousand dollars.*)

They would have time to get out. Even if they were sleeping, they would have time to get out. He believed that. And he didn't think the hedges or anything else would try to hold them back if the Overlook was going up in flames.

(*Flames.*)

The needle inside the greasy, almost opaque dial had danced up to two hundred and fifteen pounds per square inch.

Another memory occurred to him, a childhood memory. There had been a wasps' nest in the lower branches of their apple tree behind the house. One of his older brothers—he couldn't remember which one now—had been stung while swinging in the old tire Daddy had hung from one of the tree's lower branches. It had been late summer, when wasps tend to be at their ugliest.

Their father, just home from work, dressed in his whites, the smell of beer hanging around his face in a fine mist, had gathered all three boys, Brett, Mike, and little Jacky, and told them he was going to get rid of the wasps.

"Now watch," he had said, smiling and staggering a little (he hadn't been using the cane then, the collision with the milk truck was years in the future). "Maybe you'll learn something. My father showed me this."

He had raked a big pile of rain-dampened leaves under the branch where the wasps' nest rested, a deadlier fruit than the shrunken but tasty apples their tree usually produced in late September, which was then still half a month away. He lit the leaves. The day was clear and windless. The leaves smoldered but didn't really burn, and they made a smell—a fragrance—that had echoed back to him each fall when men in Saturday pants and light

Windbreakers raked leaves together and burned them. A sweet smell with a bitter undertone, rich and evocative. The smoldering leaves produced great rafts of smoke that drifted up to obscure the nest.

Their father had let the leaves smolder all that afternoon, drinking beer on the porch and dropping the empty Black Label cans into his wife's plastic floorbucket while his two older sons flanked him and little Jacky sat on the steps at his feet, playing with his Bolo Bouncer and singing monotonously over and over: "Your cheating heart . . . will make you weep . . . your cheating heart . . . is gonna tell on you."

At quarter of six, just before supper, Daddy had gone out to the apple tree with his sons grouped carefully behind him. In one hand he had a garden hoe. He knocked the leaves apart, leaving little clots spread around to smolder and die. Then he reached the hoe handle up, weaving and blinking, and after two or three tries he knocked the nest to the ground.

The boys fled for the safety of the porch, but Daddy only stood over the nest, swaying and blinking down at it. Jacky crept back to see. A few wasps were crawling sluggishly over the paper terrain of their property, but they were not trying to fly. From the inside of the nest, the black and alien place, came a never-to-be-forgotten sound: a low, somnolent buzz, like the sound of high-tension wires.

"Why don't they try to sting you, Daddy?" he had asked.

"The smoke makes em drunk, Jacky. Go get my gascan."

He ran to fetch it. Daddy doused the nest with amber gasoline.

"Now step away, Jacky, unless you want to lose your eyebrows."

He had stepped away. From somewhere in the voluminous folds of his white overblouse, Daddy had produced a wooden kitchen match. He lit it with his thumbnail and flung it onto the nest. There had been a white-orange explosion almost soundless in its ferocity. Daddy had stepped away, cackling wildly. The wasps' nest had gone up in no time.

"Fire," Daddy had said, turning to Jacky with a smile. "Fire will kill anything."

After supper the boys had come out in the day's waning light to stand solemnly around the charred and blackened nest. From the hot interior had come the sound of wasp bodies popping like corn.

The pressure gauge stood at two-twenty. A low-iron wailing sound was building up in the guts of the thing. Jets of steam stood out erect in a hundred places like porcupine quills.

(*Fire will kill anything.*)

Jack suddenly started. He had been dozing off . . . and he had almost dozed himself right into kingdom come. What in God's name had he been thinking of? Protecting the hotel was his job. He was the care-taker.

A sweat of terror sprang to his hands so quickly that at first he missed his grip on the large valve. Then he curled his fingers around its spokes. He whirled it one turn, two, three. There was a giant hiss of steam, dragon's breath. A warm tropical mist rose from beneath the boiler and veiled him. For a moment he could no longer see the dial but thought he must have waited too long; the groaning, clanking sound inside the boiler increased, followed by a series of heavy rattling sounds and the wrenching screech of metal.

When some of the steam blew away he saw that the pressure gauge had dropped back to two hundred and was still sinking. The jets of steam escaping around the soldered patches began to loss their force. The wrenching, grinding sounds began to diminish.

One-ninety . . . one-eighty . . . one seventy-five . . .

(*He was going downhill, going ninety miles an hour, when the whistle broke into a scream—*)

But he didn't think it would blow now. The press was down to one-sixty.

(*—they found him in the wreck with his hand on the throttle, he was scalded to death by the steam.*)

He stepped away from the boiler, breathing hard, trembling. He looked at his hands and saw that blisters were already rising on his palms. Hell with the blisters, he thought, and laughed shakily. He had almost died with his hand on the throttle, like Casey the engineer in "The Wreck of the Old 97." Worse still, he would have killed the Overlook. The final crashing failure. He had failed as a teacher, a writer, a husband, and a father. He had even failed as a drunk. But you couldn't do much better in the old failure category than to blow up the building you were supposed to be taking care of. And this was no ordinary building. By no means.

Christ, but he needed a drink.

The press had dropped down to eighty psi. Cautiously, wincing a little at the pain in his hands, he closed the dump valve again. But from now on the boiler would have to be watched more closely than ever. It might have been seriously weakened. He wouldn't trust it at more than one hundred psi for the rest of the winter. And if they were a little chilly, they would just have to grin and bear it.

He had broken two of the blisters. His hands throbbed like rotten teeth.

A drink. A drink would fix him up, and there wasn't a thing in the goddamn house besides cooking sherry. At this point a drink would be medicinal. That was just it, by God. An anesthetic. He had done his duty and now he could use a little anesthetic—something stronger than Excedrin. But there was nothing.

He remembered bottles glittering in the shadows.

He had saved the hotel. The hotel would want to reward him. He felt sure of it. He took his handkerchief out of his back pocket and went to the stairs. He rubbed at his mouth. Just a little drink. Just one. To ease the pain.

He had served the Overlook, and now the Overlook would serve him. He was sure of it. His feet on the stair risers were quick and eager, the hurrying steps of a man who has come home from a long and bitter war. It was 5:20 A.M., MST.

41

Daylight

Danny awoke with a muffled gasp from a terrible dream. There had been an explosion. A fire. The Overlook was burning up. He and his mommy were watching it from the front lawn.

Mommy had said: "Look, Danny, look at the hedges."

He looked at them and they were all dead. Their leaves had turned a suffocant brown. The tightly packed branches showed through like the skeletons of half-dismembered corpses. And then his daddy had burst out of the Overlook's big double doors, and he was burning like a torch. His clothes were in flames, his skin had acquired a dark and sinister tan that was growing darker by the moment, his hair was a burning bush.

That was when he woke up, his throat tight with fear, his hands clutching at the sheet and blankets. Had he screamed? He looked over at his mother. Wendy lay on her side, the blankets up to her chin, a sheaf of straw-colored hair lying against her check. She looked like a child herself. No, he hadn't screamed.

Lying in bed, looking upward, the nightmare began to drain away. He had a curious feeling that some great tragedy

(fire? explosion?)

had been averted by inches. He let his mind drift out, searching for his daddy, and found him standing somewhere below. In the lobby. Danny pushed a little harder, trying to get inside his father. It was not good. Because Daddy was thinking about the Bad Thing. He was thinking how

(*good just one or two would be i don't care sun's over the yardarm somewhere in the world remember how we used to say that al? gin and tonic bourbon with just a dash of bitters scotch and soda rum and coke tweedledum and tweedledee a drink for me and a drink for thee the martians have landed somewhere in the world princeton or houston or stokely on carmichael some fucking place after all tis the season and none of us are*)

(*GET OUT OF HIS MIND, YOU LITTLE SHIT!*)

He recoiled in terror from that mental voice, his eyes widening, his hands tightening into claws on the counterpane. It hadn't been the voice of his father but a clever mimic. A voice he knew. Hoarse, brutal, yet underpointed with a vacuous sort of humor.

Was it so near, then?

He threw the covers back and swung his feet out onto the floor. He kicked his slippers out from under the bed and put them on. He went to the door and pulled it open and hurried up to the main corridor, his slippered feet whispering on the nap of the carpet runner. He turned the corner.

There was a man on all fours halfway down the corridor, between him and the stairs.

Danny froze.

The man looked up at him. His eyes were tiny and red. He was dressed in some sort of silvery, spangled costume. A dog costume, Danny realized. Protruding from the rump of this strange creation was a long and floppy tail with a puff on the end. A zipper ran up the back of the costume to the neck. To the left of him was a dog's or wolf's head, blank eyesockets above the muzzle, the mouth open in a meaningless snarl that showed the rug's black and blue pattern between fangs that appeared to be papier-mâché.

The man's mouth and chin and cheeks were smeared with blood.

He began to growl at Danny. He was grinning, but the growl was real. It was deep in his throat, a chilling primitive sound. Then he began to bark. His teeth were also stained red. He began to crawl toward Danny, dragging his boneless tail behind him. The costume dog's head lay unheeded on the carpet, glaring vacantly over Danny's shoulder.

"Let me by," Danny said.

"I'm going to eat you, little boy," the dogman answered, and suddenly a fusillade of barks came from his grinning mouth. They were human imitations, but the savagery in them was real. The man's hair was dark, greased with sweat from his confining costume. There was a mixture of scotch and champagne on his breath.

Danny flinched back but didn't run. "Let me by."

"Not by the hair of my chinny-chin-chin," the dogman replied. His small red eyes were fixed attentively on Danny's face. He continued to grin. "I'm going to eat you up, little boy. And I think I'll start with your plump little *cock*."

He began to prance skittishly forward, making little leaps and snarling.

Danny's nerve broke. He fled back into the short hallway that led to their quarters, looking back over his shoulder. There was a series of mixed howls and barks and growls, broken by slurred mutterings and giggles.

Danny stood in the hallway, trembling.

"Get it up!" the drunken dogman cried out from around the corner. His voice was both violent and despairing. "Get it up, Harry you bitch-bastard! I don't care how many casinos and airlines and movie companies you own! I know what you like in the privacy of your own h-home! Get it up! I'll *huff* . . . and I'll *puff* . . . until Harry Derwent's *all bloowwwwn down!*" He ended with a long, chilling howl that seemed to turn into a scream of rage and pain just before it dwindled off.

Danny turned apprehensively to the closed bedroom door at the end of the hallway and walked quietly down to it. He opened it and poked his head through. His mommy was sleeping in exactly the same position. No one was hearing this but him.

He closed the door softly and went back up to the intersection of their corridor and the main hall, hoping the dogman would be gone, the way the blood on the walls of the Presidential Suite had been gone. He peeked around the corner carefully.

The man in the dog costume was still there. He had put his head back on and was now prancing on all fours by the stairwell, chasing his tail. He occasionally leaped off the rug and came down making dog grunts in his throat.

"Woof! Woof! Bowwowwow! *Grrrrrr!*"

These sounds came hollowly out of the mask's stylized snarling mouth, and among them were sounds that might have been sobs or laughter.

Danny went back to the bedroom and sat down on his cot, covering his eyes with his hands. The hotel was running things now. Maybe at first the things that had happened had only been accidents. Maybe at first the things he had seen really *were* like scary pictures that couldn't hurt him. But now the hotel was controlling those things and they *could* hurt. The Overlook hadn't wanted him to go to his father. That might spoil all the fun. So it had put the dogman in his way, just as it had put the hedge animals between them and the road.

But his daddy could come here. And sooner or later his daddy would.

He began to cry, the tears rolling silently down

his cheeks. It was too late. They were going to die, all three of them, and when the Overlook opened next late spring, they would be right here to greet the guests along with the rest of the spooks. The woman in the tub. The dogman. The horrible dark thing that had been in the cement tunnel. They would be—

(*Stop! Stop that now!*)

He knuckled the tears furiously from his eyes. He would try as hard as he could to keep that from happening. Not to himself, not to his daddy and mommy. He would try as hard as he could.

He closed his eyes and sent his mind out in a high, hard crystal bolt.

(*!!! DICK PLEASE COME QUICK WE'RE IN BAD TROUBLE DICK WE NEED*)

And suddenly, in the darkness behind his eyes the thing that chased him down the Overlook's dark halls in his dreams was *there,* right *there,* a huge creature dressed in white, its prehistoric club raised over its head:

"*I'll make you stop it! You goddam puppy! I'll make you stop it because I am your FATHER!*"

"No!" He jerked back to the reality of the bedroom, his eyes wide and staring, the screams tumbling helplessly from his mouth as his mother bolted awake, clutching the sheet to her breasts.

"*No Daddy no no no*—"

And they both heard the vicious, descending swing of the invisible club, cutting the air somewhere very close, then fading away to silence as he ran to his mother and hugged her, trembling like a rabbit in a snare.

The Overlook was not going to let him call Dick. That might spoil the fun, too.

They were alone.

Outside the snow came harder, curtaining them off from the world.

42

Mid-Air

Dick Hallorann's flight was called at 6:45 A.M., EST, and the boarding clerk held him by Gate 31, shifting his flight bag nervously from hand to hand, until the last call at 6:55. They were both looking for a man named Carlton Vecker, the only passenger on TWA's flight 196 from Miami to Denver who hadn't checked in.

"Okay," the clerk said, and issued Hallorann a blue first-class boarding pass. "You lucked out. You can board, sir."

Hallorann hurried up the enclosed boarding ramp and let the mechanically grinning stewardess tear his pass off and give him the stub.

"We're serving breakfast on the flight," the stew said. "If you'd like—"

"Just coffee, babe," he said, and went down the aisle to a seat in the smoking section. He kept expecting the no-show Vecker to pop through the door like a jack-in-the-box at the last second. The woman in the seat by the window was reading *You Can Be Your*

Own Best Friend with a sour, unbelieving expression on her face. Hallorann buckled his seat belt and then wrapped his large black hands around the seat's armrests and promised the absent Carlton Vecker that it would take him and five strong TWA flight attendants to drag him out of his seat. He kept his eye on his watch. It dragged off the minutes to the 7:00 takeoff time with maddening slowness.

At 7:05 the stewardess informed them that there would be a slight delay while the ground crew rechecked one of the latches on the cargo door.

"Shit for brains," Dick Hallorann muttered.

The sharp-faced woman turned her sour, unbelieving expression on him and then went back to her book.

He had spent the night at the airport, going from counter to counter—United, American, TWA, Continental, Braniff—haunting the ticket clerks. Sometime after midnight, drinking his eighth or ninth cup of coffee in the canteen, he had decided he was being an asshole to have taken this whole thing on his own shoulders. There were authorities. He had gone down to the nearest bank of telephones, and after talking to three different operators, he had gotten the emergency number of the Rocky Mountain National Park Authority.

The man who answered the telephone sounded utterly worn out. Hallorann had given a false name and said there was trouble at the Overlook Hotel, west of Sidewinder. Bad trouble.

He was put on hold.

The ranger (Hallorann assumed he was a ranger) came back on in about five minutes.

"They've got a CB," the ranger said.

"Sure they've got a CB," Hallorann said.

"We haven't had a Mayday call from them."

"Man, that don't *matter*. They——"

"Exactly what kind of trouble are they in, Mr. Hall?"

"Well, there's a family. The caretaker and his family. I think maybe he's gone a little nuts, you know. I think maybe he might hurt his wife and his little boy."

"May I ask how you've come by this information, sir?"

Hallorann closed his eyes. "What's your name, fellow?"

"Tom Staunton, sir."

"Well, Tom, I *know*. Now I'll be just as straight with you as I can be. There's bad trouble up there. Maybe killin bad, do you dig what I'm sayin?"

"Mr. Hall, I really have to know how you——"

"Look," Hallorann had said. "I'm telling you I *know*. A few years back there was a fellow up there name of Grady. He killed his wife and his two daughters and then pulled the string on himself. I'm telling you it's going to happen again if you guys don't haul your asses out there and stop it!"

"Mr. Hall, you're not calling from Colorado."

"No. But what difference——"

"If you're not in Colorado, you're not in CB range of the Overlook Hotel. If you're not in CB range you can't possibly have been in contact with the, uh . . ." Faint rattle of papers. "The Torrance family. While I had you on hold I tried to telephone. It's out, which is nothing unusual. There are still twenty-five miles of aboveground telephone lines between the hotel and the Sidewinder switching station. My conclusion is that you must be some sort of crank."

"Oh man, you stupid . . ." But his despair was too great to find a noun to go with the adjective. Suddenly, illumination. "Call them!" he cried.

"Sir?"

"You got the CB, they got the CB. So call them! Call them and ask them what's up!"

There was a brief silence, and the humming of long-distance wires.

"You tried that too, didn't you?" Hallorann asked. "That's why you had me on hold so long. You tried the phone and then you tried the CB and you didn't get *nothing* but you don't think nothing's wrong . . . what are you guys doing up there? Sitting on your asses and playing gin rummy?"

"No, we are not," Staunton said angrily. Hallorann was relieved at the sound of anger in the voice. For the first time he felt he was speaking to a man and not to a recording. "I'm the only man here, sir. Every other ranger in the park, *plus* game wardens, *plus* volunteers, are up in Hasty Notch, risking their lives because three stupid assholes with six months' experience decided to try the north face of King's Ram. They're stuck halfway up there and maybe they'll get down and maybe they won't. There are two choppers up there and the men who are flying them are risking their lives because it's night here and it's starting to snow. So if you're still having trouble putting it all together, I'll give you a hand with it. Number one, I don't have anybody to send to the Overlook. Number two, the Overlook isn't a priority here—what happens in the park is a priority. Number three, by daybreak neither one of those choppers will be able to fly because it's going to snow like crazy, according to the National Weather Service. Do you understand the situation?"

"Yeah," Hallorann had said softly. "I understand."

"Now my guess as to why I couldn't raise them on the CB is very simple. I don't know what time it is where you are, but out here it's nine-thirty. I think they may have turned it off and gone to bed. Now if you—"

"Good luck with your climbers, man," Hallorann said. "But I want you to know that they are not the only ones who are stuck up high because they didn't know what they were getting into."

He had hung up the phone.

At 7:20 A.M. the TWA 747 backed lumberingly out of its stall, turned, and rolled out toward the runway. Hallorann let out a long, soundless exhale. Carlton Vecker, wherever you are, eat your heart out.

Flight 196 parted company with the ground at 7:28, and at 7:31, as it gained altitude, the thought-pistol went off in Dick Hallorann's head again. His shoulders hunched uselessly against the smell of oranges and then jerked spasmodically. His forehead wrinkled, his mouth drew down in a grimace of pain.

(!!! DICK PLEASE COME QUICK WERE IN BAD TROUBLE DICK WE NEED)

And that was all. It was suddenly gone. No fading out this time. The communication had been chopped off cleanly, as if with a knife. It scared him. His hands, still clutching the seat rests, had gone almost white. His mouth was dry. Something had happened to the boy. He was sure of it. If anyone had hurt that little child—

"Do you always react so violently to takeoffs?"

He looked around. It was the woman in the horn-rimmed glasses.

"It wasn't that," Hallorann said. "I've got a steel plate in my head. From Korea. Every now and then it gives me a twinge. Vibrates, don't you know. Scrambles the signal."

"Is that so?"

"Yes, ma'am."

"It is the line soldier who ultimately pays for any foreign intervention," the sharp-faced woman said grimly.

"Is that so?"

"It is. This country must swear off its dirty little wars. The CIA has been at the root of every dirty little war America has fought in this century. The CIA and dollar diplomacy."

She opened her book and began to read. The NO SMOKING sign went off. Hallorann watched the receding land and wondered if the boy was all right. He had developed an affectionate feeling for that boy, although his folks hadn't seemed all that much.

He hoped to God they were watching out for Danny.

43

Drinks on the House

Jack stood in the dining room just outside the batwing doors leading into the Colorado Lounge, his head cocked, listening. He was smiling faintly.

Around him, he could hear the Overlook Hotel coming to life.

It was hard to say just how he knew, but he guessed it wasn't greatly different from the percep-tions Danny had from time to time . . . like father, like son. Wasn't that how it was popularly expressed?

It wasn't a perception of sight or sound, although it was very near to those things, separated from those senses by the filmiest of perceptual curtains. It was as if another Overlook now lay scant inches beyond this one, separated from the real world (if there is such a thing as a "real world," Jack thought) but gradually coming into balance with it. He was reminded of the 3-D movies he'd seen as a kid. If you looked at the screen without the special glasses, you saw a double image—the sort of thing he was feeling now. But when you put the glasses on, it made sense.

All the hotel's eras were together now, all but this current one, the Torrance Era. And this would be together with the rest very soon now. That was good. That was very good.

He could almost hear the self-important *ding!ding!* of the silver-plated bell on the registration desk, summoning bellboys to the front as men in the fashionable flannels of the 1920s checked in and men in fashionable 1940s double-breasted pinstripes checked out. There would be three nuns sitting in front of the fireplace as they waited for the check-out line to thin, and standing behind them, nattily dressed with diamond stickpins holding their blue-and-white-figured ties, Charles Grondin and Vito Gienelli discussed profit and loss, life and death. There were a dozen trucks in the loading bays out back, some laid one over the other like bad time exposures. In the east-wing ballroom, a dozen different business conventions were going on at the same time within temporal centimeters of each other. There was a costume ball going on. There were soirees, wedding receptions, birthday and anniversary parties. Men talking about Neville Chamberlain and the Archduke of Austria. Music. Laughter. Drunkenness. Hysteria. Little love, not here, but a steady undercurrent of sensuousness. And he could almost hear all of them together, drifting through the hotel and making a graceful cacophony. In the dining room where he stood, breakfast, lunch, and dinner for seventy years were all being served simultaneously just behind him. He could almost . . . no, strike the *almost*. He *could* hear them, faintly as yet, but clearly—the way one can hear thunder miles off on a hot summer's day. He could hear all of them, the beautiful strangers. He was becoming aware of them as they must have been aware of him from the very start.

All the rooms of the Overlook were occupied this morning.

A full house.

And beyond the batwings, a low murmur of conversation drifted and swirled like lazy cigarette smoke. More sophisticated, more private. Low, throaty female laughter, the kind that seems to vibrate in a fairy ring around the viscera and the genitals. The sound of a cash register, its window softly lighted in the warm halfdark, ringing up the price of a gin rickey, a Manhattan, a depression bomber, a sloe gin fizz, a zombie. The jukebox, pouring out its drinkers' melodies, each one overlapping the other in time.

He pushed the batwings open and stepped through.

"Hello, boys," Jack Torrance said softly. "I've been away but now I'm back."

"Good evening, Mr. Torrance," Lloyd said, genuinely pleased. "It's good to see you."

"It's good to be back, Lloyd," he said gravely, and hooked his leg over a stool between a man in a sharp blue suit and a bleary-eyed woman in a black dress who was peering into the depths of a singapore sling.

"What will it be, Mr. Torrance?"

"Martini," he said with great pleasure. He looked at the backbar with its rows of dimly gleaming bottles, capped with their silver siphons. Jim Beam. Wild Turkey. Gilby's. Sharrod's Private Label. Toro. Seagram's. And home again.

"One large martian, if you please," he said. "They've landed somewhere in the world, Lloyd." He took his wallet out and laid a twenty carefully on the bar.

As Lloyd made his drink, Jack looked over his shoulder. Every booth was occupied. Some of the occupants were dressed in costumes . . . a woman in gauzy harem pants and a rhinestone-sparkled brassiere, a man with a foxhead rising slyly out of his evening dress, a man in a silvery dog outfit who was tickling the nose of a woman in a sarong with the puff on the end of his long tail, to the general amusement of all.

"No charge to you, Mr. Torrance," Lloyd said, putting the drink down on Jack's twenty. "Your money is no good here. Orders from the manager."

"Manager?"

A faint unease came over him; nevertheless he picked up the martini glass and swirled it, watching the olive at the bottom bob slightly in the drink's chilly depths.

"Of course. The manager." Lloyd's smile broadened, but his eyes were socketed in shadow and his skin was horribly white, like the skin of a corpse. "Later he expects to see to your son's well-being himself. He is very interested in your son. Danny is a talented boy."

The juniper fumes of the gin were pleasantly maddening, but they also seemed to be blurring his reason.

Danny? What was all of this about Danny? And what was he doing in a bar with a drink in his hand?

He had TAKEN THE PLEDGE. He had GONE ON THE WAGON. He had SWORN OFF.

What could they want with his son? What could they want with Danny? Wendy and Danny weren't in it. He tried to see into Lloyd's shadowed eyes, but it was too dark, too dark, it was like trying to read emotion into the empty orbs of a skull.

(*It's me they must want . . . isn't it? I am the one. Not Danny, not Wendy. I'm the one who loves it here. They wanted to leave. I'm the one who took care of the snowmobile . . . went through the old records . . . dumped the press on the boiler . . . lied . . . practically sold my soul . . . what can they want with him?*)

"Where is the manager?" He tried to ask it casually but his words seemed to come out between lips already numbed by the first drink, like words from a nightmare rather than those in a sweet dream.

Lloyd only smiled.

"What do you want with my son? Danny's not in this . . . is he?" He heard the naked plea in his own voice.

Lloyd's face seemed to be running, changing, becoming something pestilent. The white skin becoming a hepatitic yellow, cracking. Red sores erupting on the skin, bleeding foul-smelling liquid. Droplets of blood sprang out on Lloyd's forehead like sweat and somewhere a silver chime was striking the quarter-hour.

(*Unmask, unmask!*)

"Drink your drink, Mr. Torrance," Lloyd said softly. "It isn't a matter that concerns you. Not at this point."

He picked his drink up again, raised it to his lips, and hesitated. He heard the hard, horrible snap as Danny's arm broke. He saw the bicycle flying brokenly up over the hood of Al's car, starring the windshield. He saw a single wheel lying in the road, twisted spokes pointing into the sky like jags of piano wire.

He became aware that all conversation had stopped.

He looked back over his shoulder. They were all looking at him expectantly, silently. The man beside the woman in the sarong had removed his foxhead and Jack saw that it was Horace Derwent, his pallid blond hair spilling across his forehead. Everyone at the bar was watching, too. The woman beside him was looking at him closely, as if trying to focus. Her dress had slipped off one shoulder and looking down he could see a loosely puckered nipple capping one sagging breast. Looking back at her face he began to think that this might be the woman from 217, the one who had tried to strangle Danny. On his other hand, the man in the sharp blue suit had removed a small pearl-handled .32 from his jacket pocket and was idly spinning it on the bar, like a man with Russian roulette on his mind.

(*I want—*)

He realized the words were not passing through his frozen vocal cords and tried again.

"I want to see the manager. I . . . I don't think he understands. My son is not a part of this. He . . ."

"Mr. Torrance," Lloyd said, his voice coming with hideous gentleness from inside his plague-raddled face, "you will meet the manager in due time. He has, in fact, decided to make you his agent in this matter. Now drink your drink."

"Drink your drink," they all echoed.

He picked it up with a badly trembling hand. It was raw gin. He looked into it, and looking was like drowning.

The woman beside him began to sing in a flat, dead voice: "Roll . . . out . . . the barrel . . . and we'll have . . . a barrel . . . of fun . . ."

Lloyd picked it up. Then the man in the blue suit. The dogman joined in, thumping one paw against the table

"Now's the time to roll the barrel—"

Derwent added his voice to the rest. A cigarette was cocked in one corner of his mouth at a jaunty angle. His right arm was around the shoulders of the woman in the sarong, and his right hand was gently and absently stroking her right breast. He was looking at the dogman with amused contempt as he sang.

"—because the gang's . . . all . . . here!"

Jack brought the drink to his mouth and downed it in three long gulps, the gin highballing down his throat like a moving van in a tunnel, exploding in his stomach, rebounding up to his brain in one leap where it seized hold of him with a final convulsing fit of the shakes.

When that passed off, he felt fine.

"Do it again, please," he said, and pushed the empty glass toward Lloyd.

"Yes, sir," Lloyd said, taking the glass. Lloyd looked perfectly normal again. The olive-skinned man had put his .32 away. The woman on his right was staring into her singapore sling again. One breast was wholly exposed now, leaning on the bar's leather buffer. A vacuous crooning noise came from her slack mouth. The loom of conversation had begun again, weaving and weaving.

His new drink appeared in front of him.

"*Muchas gracias,* Lloyd," he said, picking it up.

"Always a pleasure to serve you, Mr. Torrance." Lloyd smiled.

"You were always the best of them, Lloyd."

"Why, thank you, sir."

He drank slowly this time, letting it trickle down his throat, tossing a few peanuts down the chute for good luck.

The drink was gone in no time, and he ordered another. Mr. President, I have met the martians and am pleased to report they are friendly. While Lloyd fixed another, he began searching his pockets for a quarter to put in the jukebox. He thought of Danny again, but Danny's face was pleasantly fuzzed and nondescript now. He had hurt Danny once, but that had been before he had learned how to handle his liquor. Those days were behind him now. He would never hurt Danny again.

Not for the world.

44

Conversations
at the Party

He was dancing with a beautiful woman.

He had no idea what time it was, how long he had spent in the Colorado Lounge or how long he had been here in the ballroom. Time had ceased to matter.

He had vague memories: listening to a man who had once been a successful radio comic and then a variety star in TV's infant days telling a very long and very hilarious joke about incest between Siamese twins; seeing the woman in the harem pants and the sequined bra do a slow and sinuous striptease to some bumping-and-grinding music from the jukebox (it seemed it had been David Rose's theme music from *The Stripper*); crossing the lobby as one of three, the other two men in evening dress that predated the twenties, all of them singing about the stiff patch on Rosie O'Grady's knickers. He seemed to remember looking out the big double doors and seeing Japanese lanterns strung in graceful, curving arcs that followed the sweep of the driveway—they gleamed in soft pastel colors like dusky jewels. The big glass globe on the porch ceiling was on, and night-insects bumped and flittered against it, and a part of him, perhaps the last tiny spark of sobriety, tried to tell him that it was 6 A.M. on a morning in December. But time had been canceled.

(*The arguments against insanity fall through with a soft shurring sound / layer on layer . . .*)

Who was that? Some poet he had read as an undergraduate? Some undergraduate poet who was now selling washers in Wausau or insurance in Indianapolis? Perhaps an original thought? Didn't matter.

(*The night is dark / the stars are high / a disembodied custard pie / is floating in the sky . . .*)

He giggled helplessly.

"What's funny, honey?"

And here he was again, in the ballroom. The chandelier was lit and couples were circling all around them, some in costume and some not, to the smooth sounds of some postwar band—but which war? Can you be certain?

No, of course not. He was certain of only one thing: he was dancing with a beautiful woman.

She was tall and auburn-haired, dressed in clinging white satin, and she was dancing close to him, her breasts pressed softly and sweetly against his chest. Her white hand was entwined in his. She was wearing a small and sparkly cat's-eye mask and her hair had been brushed over to one side in a soft and gleaming fall that seemed to pool in the valley between their touching shoulders. Her dress was full-skirted but he could feel her thighs against his legs from time to time and had become more and more sure that she was smooth-and-powdered naked under her dress,

(the better to feel your erection with, my dear)

and he was sporting a regular railspike. If it offended her she concealed it well; she snuggled even closer to him.

"Nothing funny, honey," he said, and giggled again.

"I like you," she whispered, and he thought that her scent was like lilies, secret and hidden in cracks furred with green moss—places where sunshine is short and shadows long.

"I like you, too."

"We could go upstairs, if you want. I'm supposed to be with Harry, but he'll never notice. He's too busy teasing poor Roger."

The number ended. There was a spatter of applause and then the band swung into "Mood Indigo" with scarcely a pause.

Jack looked over her bare shoulder and saw Derwent standing by the refreshment table. The girl in the sarong was with him. There were bottles of champagne in ice buckets ranged along the white lawn covering the table, and Derwent held a foaming bottle in his hand. A knot of people had gathered, laughing. In front of Derwent and the girl in the sarong, Roger capered grotesquely on all fours, his tail dragging limply behind him. He was barking.

"Speak, boy, speak!" Harry Derwent cried.

"Rowf! Rowf!" Roger responded. Everyone clapped; a few of the men whistled.

"Now sit up. Sit up, doggy!"

Roger clambered up on his haunches. The muzzle of his mask was frozen in its eternal snarl. Inside the eyeholes, Roger's eyes rolled with frantic, sweaty hilarity. He held his arms out, dangling the paws.

"Rowf! Rowf!"

Derwent upended the bottle of champagne and it fell in a foamy Niagara onto the upturned mask. Roger made frantic slurping sounds, and everyone applauded again. Some of the women screamed with laughter.

"Isn't Harry a card?" his partner asked him, pressing close again. "Everyone says so. He's AC/DC, you know. Poor Roger's only DC. He spent a weekend with Harry in Cuba once . . . oh, *months* ago. Now he follows Harry everywhere, wagging his little tail behind him."

She giggled. The shy scent of lilies drifted up.

"But of course Harry never goes back for seconds . . . not on his DC side, anyway . . . and Roger is just *wild*. Harry told him if he came to the masked ball as a doggy, a *cute* little doggy, he might reconsider, and Roger is *such* a silly that he . . ."

The number ended. There was more applause. The band members were filing down for a break.

"Excuse me, sweetness," she said. "There's someone I just *must* . . . Darla! Darla, you *dear girl*, where have you *been*?"

She wove her way into the eating, drinking throng and he gazed after her stupidly, wondering how they had happened to be dancing together in the first place. He didn't remember. Incidents seemed to have occurred with no connections. First here, then there, then everywhere. His head was spinning. He smelled lilies and juniper berries. Up by the refreshment table Derwent was now holding a tiny triangular sandwich over Roger's head and urging him, to the general merriment of the onlookers, to do a somersault. The dogmask was turned upward. The silver sides of the dog costume bellowsed in and out. Roger suddenly leaped, tucking his head under, and tried to roll in mid-air. His leap was too low and too exhausted; he landed awkwardly on his back, rapping his head smartly on the tiles. A hollow groan drifted out of the dogmask.

Derwent led the applause. "Try again, doggy! Try again!"

The onlookers took up the chant—*try again, try again*—and Jack staggered off the other way, feeling vaguely ill.

He almost fell over the drinks cart that was being wheeled along by a low-browed man in a white mess jacket. His foot rapped the lower chromed shelf of the cart; the bottles and siphons on top chattered together musically.

"Sorry," Jack said thickly. He suddenly felt closed in and claustrophobic; he wanted to get out. He wanted the Overlook back the way it had been . . . free of these unwanted guests. His place was not honored, as the true opener of the way; he was only another of the ten thousand cheering extras, a doggy rolling over and sitting up on command.

"Quite all right," the man in the white mess jacket said. The polite, clipped English coming from that thug's face was surreal. "A drink?"

"Martini."

From behind him, another comber of laughter broke; Roger was howling to the tune of "Home on the Range." Someone was picking out accompaniment on the Steinway baby grand.

"Here you are."

The frosty cold glass was pressed into his hand. Jack drank gracefully, feeling the gin hit and crumble away the first inroads of sobriety.

"Is it all right, sir?"

"Fine."

"Thank you, sir." The cart began to roll again.

Jack suddenly reached out and touched the man's shoulder.

"Yes, sir?"

"Pardon me, but . . . what's your name?"

The other showed no surprise. "Grady, sir. Delbert Grady."

"But you . . . I mean that . . ."

The bartender was looking at him politely. Jack tried again, although his mouth was mushed by gin and unreality; each word felt as large as an ice cube.

"Weren't you once the caretaker here? When you . . . when . . ." But he couldn't finish. He couldn't say it.

"Why no, sir. I don't believe so."

"But your wife . . . your daughters . . ."

"My wife is helping in the kitchen, sir. The girls are asleep, of course. It's much too late for them."

"You were the caretaker. You—" *Oh say it!* "You killed them."

Grady's face remained blankly polite. "I don't have any recollection of that at all, sir." His glass was empty. Grady plucked it from Jack's unresisting fingers and set about making another drink for him. There was a small white plastic bucket on his cart that was filled with olives. For some reason they reminded Jack of tiny severed heads. Grady speared one deftly, dropped it into the glass, and handed it to him.

"But you—"

"*You're* the caretaker, sir." Grady said mildly. "You've *always* been the caretaker. I should know, sir. I've always been here. The same manager hired us both, at the same time. Is it all right, sir?"

Jack gulped at his drink. His head was swirling. "Mr. Ullman—"

"I know no one by that name, sir."

"But he—"

"The manager," Grady said. "The *hotel,* sir. Surely you realize who hired you, sir."

"No," he said thickly. "No, I—"

"I believe you must take it up further with your son, Mr. Torrance, sir. He understands everything, although he hasn't enlightened you. Rather naughty of him, if I may be so bold, sir. In fact, he's crossed you at almost every turn, hasn't he? And him not yet six."

"Yes," Jack said. "He has." There was another wave of laughter from behind them.

"He needs to be corrected, if you don't mind me saying so. He needs a good talking-to, and perhaps a bit more. My own girls, sir, didn't care for the Overlook at first. One of them actually stole a pack of my matches and tried to burn it down. I corrected them. I corrected them most harshly. And when my wife tried to stop me from doing my duty, I corrected her." He offered Jack a bland, meaningless smile. "I find it a sad but true fact that women rarely understand a father's responsibility to his children. Husbands and fathers do have certain responsibilities, don't they, sir?"

"Yes," Jack said.

"They didn't love the Overlook as I did," Grady said, beginning to make him another drink, Silver bubbles rose in the upended gin bottle. "Just as your son and wife don't love it . . . not at present, anyway. But they will come to love it. You must show them the error of their ways, Mr. Torrance. Do you agree?"

"Yes. I do."

He did see. He had been too easy with them. Husbands and fathers did have certain responsibilities. Father Knows Best. They did not understand. That in itself was no crime, but they were *willfully* not understanding. He was not ordinarily a harsh man. But he did believe in punishment. And if his son and his wife had willfully set themselves against his wishes, *against the things he knew were best for them,* then didn't he have a certain duty—?

"A thankless child is sharper than a serpent's tooth," Grady said, handing him his drink. "I do believe that the manager could bring your son into line. And your wife would shortly follow. Do you agree, sir?"

He was suddenly uncertain. "I . . . but . . . if they could just leave . . . I mean, after all, it's me the manager wants, isn't it? It must be. Because—" Because why? He should know but suddenly he didn't. Oh, his poor brain was swimming.

"Bad dog!" Derwent was saying loudly, to a counterpoint of laughter. "Bad dog to piddle on the floor."

"Of course you know," Grady said, leaning confidentially over the cart, "your son is attempting to bring an outside party into it. Your son has a very great talent, one that the manager could use to even further improve the Overlook, to further . . . enrich it, shall we say? But your son is attempting to use that very talent against us. He is willful, Mr. Torrance, sir. Willful."

"Outside party?" Jack asked stupidly.

Grady nodded.

"Who?"

"A nigger," Grady said. "A nigger cook."

"Hallorann?"

"I believe that is his name, sir, yes."

Another burst of laughter from behind them was followed by Roger saying something in a whining, protesting voice.

"Yes! Yes! Yes!" Derwent began to chant. The others around him took it up, but before Jack could hear

what they wanted Roger to do now, the band began
to play again—the tune was "Tuxedo Junction," with
a lot of mellow sax in it but not much soul.

(*Soul? Soul hasn't even been invented yet. Or has it?*)

(*A nigger . . . a nigger cook.*)

He opened his mouth to speak, not knowing what
might come out. What did was:

"I was told you hadn't finished high school. But
you don't talk like an uneducated man."

"It's true that I left organized education very early,
sir. But the manager takes care of his help. He finds
that it pays. Education always pays, don't you agree,
sir?"

"Yes," Jack said dazedly.

"For instance, you show a great interest in learning
more about the Overlook Hotel. Very wise of you, sir.
Very noble. A certain scrapbook was left in the basement for you to find—"

"By whom?" Jack asked eagerly.

"By the manager, of course. Certain other materials could be put at your disposal, if you wished
them . . ."

"I do. Very much." He tried to control the eagerness in his voice and failed miserably.

"You're a true scholar," Grady said. "Pursue the
topic to the end. Exhaust all sources." He dipped his
low-browed head, pulled out the lapel of his white
mess jacket, and buffed his knuckles at a spot of dirt
that was invisible to Jack.

"And the manager puts no strings on his largess,"
Grady went on. "Not at all. Look at me, a tenth-grade

dropout. Think how much further you yourself could go in the Overlook's organizational structure. Perhaps . . . in time . . . to the very top."

"Really?" Jack whispered.

"But that's really up to your son to decide, isn't it?" Grady asked, raising his eyebrows. The delicate gesture went oddly with the brows themselves, which were bushy and somehow savage.

"Up to Danny?" Jack frowned at Grady. "No, of course not. I wouldn't allow my son to make decisions concerning my career. Not at all. What do you take me for?"

"A dedicated man," Grady said warmly. "Perhaps I put it badly, sir. Let us say that your future here is contingent upon how you decide to deal with your son's waywardness."

"I make my own decisions," Jack whispered.

"But you must deal with him."

"I will."

"Firmly."

"I will."

"A man who cannot control his own family holds very little interest for our manager. A man who cannot guide the courses of his own wife and son can hardly be expected to guide himself, let alone assume a position of responsibility in an operation of this magnitude. He—"

"*I said I'll handle him!*" Jack shouted suddenly, enraged.

"Tuxedo Junction" had just concluded and a new tune hadn't begun. His shout fell perfectly into the gap, and conversation suddenly ceased behind him. His skin suddenly felt hot all over. He became fixedly positive that everyone was staring at him. They had finished with Roger and would now commence with him. Roll over. Sit up. Play dead. If you play the game with us, we'll play the game with you. Position of responsibility. They wanted him to sacrifice his son.

(—*Now he follows Harry everywhere, wagging his little tail behind him*—)

(*Roll over. Play dead. Chastise your son.*)

"Right this way, sir," Grady was saying. "Something that might interest you."

The conversation had begun again, lifting and dropping in its own rhythm, weaving in and out of the band music, now doing a swing version of Lennon and McCartney's "Ticket to Ride."

(*I've heard better over supermarket loudspeakers.*)

He giggled foolishly. He looked down at his left hand and saw there was another drink in it, half-full. He emptied it at a gulp.

Now he was standing in front of the mantelpiece, the heat from the crackling fire that had been laid in the hearth warming his legs.

(*a fire? . . . in August? . . . yes . . . and no . . . all times are one*)

There was a clock under a glass dome, flanked by two carved ivory elephants. Its hands stood at a minute to midnight. He gazed at it blearily. Had this been what Grady wanted him to see? He turned around to ask, but Grady had left him.

Halfway through "Ticket to Ride," the band wound up in a brassy flourish.

"The hour is at hand!" Horace Derwent proclaimed. "Midnight! Unmask! Unmask!"

He tried to turn again, to see what famous faces were hidden beneath the glitter and paint and masks, but he was frozen now, unable to look away from the clock—its hands had come together and pointed straight up.

"Unmask! Unmask!" the chant went up.

The clock began to chime delicately. Along the steel runner below the clockface, from the left and right, two figures advanced. Jack watched, fascinated, the unmasking forgotten. Clockwork whirred. Cogs turned and meshed, brass warmly glowing. The balance wheel rocked back and forth precisely.

One of the figures was a man standing on tiptoe, with what looked like a tiny club clasped in his hands. The other was a small boy wearing a dunce cap. The clockwork figures glittered, fantastically precise. Across the front of the boy's dunce cap he could read the engraved word FOOLE.

The two figures slipped onto the opposing ends of a steel axis bar. Somewhere, tinkling on and on, were the strains of a Strauss waltz. An insane commercial jingle began to run through his mind to the tune: *Buy dog food, rowf-rowf, rowf-rowf, buy dog food . . .*

The steel mallet in the clockwork daddy's hands came down on the boy's head. The clockwork son crumpled forward. The mallet rose and fell, rose and fell. The boy's upstretched, protesting hands began to falter. The boy sagged from his crouch to a prone position. And still the hammer rose and fell to the light, tinkling air of the Strauss melody, and it seemed that he could see the man's face, working and knotting and constricting, could see the clockwork daddy's mouth opening and closing as he berated the unconscious, bludgeoned figure of the son.

A spot of red flew up against the inside of the glass dome.

Another followed. Two more splattered beside it.

Now the red liquid was spraying up like an obscene rain shower, striking the glass sides of the dome and running, obscuring what was going on inside, and flecked through the scarlet were tiny gray ribbons of tissue, fragments of bone and brain. And still he could see the hammer rising and falling as the clockwork continued to turn and the cogs continued to mesh the gears and teeth of this cunningly made machine.

"Unmask! Unmask!" Derwent was shrieking behind him, and somewhere a dog was howling in human tones.

(*But clockwork can't bleed clockwork can't bleed*)

The entire dome was splashed with blood, he could see clotted bits of hair but nothing else thank God he could see nothing else, and still he thought he would be sick because he could hear the hammerblows still falling, could hear them through the glass just as he could hear the phrases of "The Blue Danube." But the sounds were no longer the mechanical *tink-tink-tink* noises of a mechanical hammer striking a mechanical head, but the soft and squashy thudding sounds of a real hammer slicing down and whacking into a spongy, muddy ruin. A ruin that once had been—

"UNMASK!"

(—*the Red Death held sway over all!*)

With a miserable, rising scream, he turned away from the clock, his hands outstretched, his feet stumbling against one another like wooden blocks as he begged them to stop, to take him, Danny, Wendy, to take the whole world if they wanted it, but only to stop and leave him a little sanity, a little light.

The ballroom was empty.

The chairs with their spindly legs were upended on tables covered with plastic dust drops. The red rug with its golden tracings was back on the dance floor, protecting the polished hardwood surface. The bandstand was deserted except for a disassembled microphone stand and a dusty guitar leaning stringless against the wall. Cold morning light, winterlight, fell languidly through the high windows.

His head was still reeling, he still felt drunk, but when he turned back to the mantelpiece, his drink was gone. There were only the ivory elephants . . . and the clock.

He stumbled back across the cold, shadowy lobby and through the dining room. His foot hooked around a table leg and he fell full-length, upsetting the table with a clatter. He struck his nose hard on the floor and it began to bleed. He got up, snuffling back blood and wiping his nose with the back of his hand. He crossed to the Colorado Lounge and shoved through the batwing doors, making them fly back and bang into the walls.

The place was empty . . . but the bar was fully stocked. God be praised! Glass and the silver edging on labels glowed warmly in the dark.

Once, he remembered, a very long time ago, he had been angry that there was no backbar mirror. Now he was glad. Looking into it he would have seen just another drunk fresh off the wagon: bloody nose, untucked shirt, hair rumpled, cheeks stubbly.

(*This is what it's like to stick your whole hand into the nest.*)

Loneliness surged over him suddenly and completely. He cried out with sudden wretchedness and honestly wished he were dead. His wife and son were upstairs with the door locked against him. The others had all left. The party was over.

He lurched forward again, reaching the bar.

"Lloyd, where the fuck are you?" he screamed.

There was no answer. In this well-padded

(*cell*)

room, his words did not even echo back to give the illusion of company.

"*Grady!*"

No answer. Only the bottles standing stiffly at attention.

(*Roll over. Play dead. Fetch. Play dead. Sit up. Play dead.*)

"Never mind, I'll do it myself, goddammit."

Halfway over the bar he lost his balance and pitched forward, hitting his head a muffled blow on the floor. He got up on his hands and knees, his eyeballs moving disjointed from side to side, fuzzy muttering sounds coming from his mouth. Then he collapsed, his face turned to one side, breathing in harsh snores.

Outside, the wind whooped louder, driving the thickening snow before it. It was 8:30 A.M.

45

Stapleton Airport, Denver

At 8:31 A.M., MST, a woman on TWA's Flight 196 burst into tears and began to bugle her own opinion, which was perhaps not unshared among some of the other passengers (or even the crew, for that matter), that the plane was going to crash.

The sharp-faced woman next to Hallorann looked up from her book and offered a brief character analysis: "Ninny," and went back to her book. She had downed two screwdrivers during the flight, but they seemed not to have thawed her at all.

"It's going to crash!" the woman was crying out shrilly. "Oh, I just know it is!"

A stewardess hurried to her seat and squatted beside her. Hallorann thought to himself that only stewardesses and very young housewives seemed able to squat with any degree of grace; it was a rare and wonderful talent. He thought about this while the stewardess talked softly and soothingly to the woman, quieting her bit by bit.

Hallorann didn't know about anyone else on 196, but he personally was almost scared enough to shit peachpits. Outside the window there was nothing to be seen but a buffeting curtain of white. The plane rocked sickeningly from side to side with gusts that seemed to come from everywhere. The engines were cranked up to provide partial compensation and as a result the floor was vibrating under their feet. There were several people moaning in Tourist behind them, one stew had gone back with a handful of fresh airsick bags, and a man three rows in front of Hallorann had whoopsed into his *National Observer* and had grinned apologetically at the stewardess who came to help him clean up. "That's all right," she comforted him, "that's how I feel about the *Reader's Digest.*"

Hallorann had flown enough to be able to surmise what had happened. They had been flying against bad headwinds most of the way, the weather over Denver had worsened suddenly and unexpectedly, and now it was just a little late to divert for someplace where the weather was better. *Feets don't fail me now.*

(*Buddy-boy, this is some fucked-up cavalry charge.*)

The stewardess seemed to have succeeded in curbing the worst of the woman's hysterics. She was snuffling and honking into a lace handkerchief, but had ceased broadcasting her opinions about the flight's possible conclusion to the cabin at large. The stew gave her a final pat on the shoulder and stood up just as the 747 gave its worst lurch yet. The stewardess stumbled backward and landed in the lap of the man

who had whoopsed into his paper, exposing a lovely
length of nyloned thigh. The man blinked and then
patted her kindly on the shoulder. She smiled back,
but Hallorann thought the strain was showing. It
had been one hell of a hard flight this morning.

There was a little ping as the NO SMOKING light
reappeared.

"This is the captain speaking," a soft, slightly
southern voice informed them. "We're ready to begin
our descent to Stapleton International Airport. It's
been a rough flight, for which I apologize. The landing may be a bit rough also, but we anticipate no real
difficulty. Please observe the FASTEN SEAT BELTS and
NO SMOKING signs, and we hope you enjoy your stay
in the Denver metro area. And we also hope——"

Another hard bump rocked the plane and then
dropped her with a sickening elevator plunge. Hallorann's stomach did a queasy hornpipe. Several
people—not all women by any means—screamed.

"——that we'll see you again on another TWA flight
real soon."

"Not bloody likely," someone behind Hallorann
said.

"So silly," the sharp-faced woman next to Hallorann remarked, putting a matchbook cover into her
book and shutting it as the plane began to descend.
"When one has seen the horrors of a dirty little
war . . . as you have . . . or sensed the degrading
immorality of CIA dollar-diplomacy intervention . . .
as I have . . . a rough landing *pales* into *insignificance*.
Am I right, Mr. Hallorann?"

"As rain, ma'am," he said, and looked bleakly out into the wildly blowing snow.

"How is your steel plate reacting to all of this, if I might inquire?"

"Oh, my head's fine," Hallorann said. "It's just my stomach that's a mite queasy."

"A shame." She reopened her book.

As they descended through the impenetrable clouds of snow, Hallorann thought of a crash that had occurred at Boston's Logan Airport a few years ago. The conditions had been similar, only fog instead of snow had reduced visibility to zero. The plane had caught its undercarriage on a retaining wall near the end of the landing strip. What had been left of the eighty-nine people aboard hadn't looked much different from a Hamburger Helper casserole.

He wouldn't mind so much if it was just himself. He was pretty much alone in the world now, and attendance at his funeral would be mostly held down to the people he had worked with and that old renegade Masterton, who would at least drink to him. But the boy . . . the boy was depending on him. He was maybe all the help that child could expect, and he didn't like the way the boy's last call had been snapped off. He kept thinking of the way those hedge animals had seemed to move . . .

A thin white hand appeared over his.

The woman with the sharp face had taken off her glasses. Without them her features seemed much softer.

"It will be all right," she said.

Hallorann made a smile and nodded.

As advertised the plane came down hard, reuniting with the earth forcefully enough to knock most of the magazines out of the rack at the front and to send plastic trays cascading out of the galley like oversized playing cards. No one screamed, but Hallorann heard several sets of teeth clicking violently together like gypsy castanets.

Then the turbine engines rose to a howl, braking the plane, and as they dropped in volume the pilot's soft southern voice, perhaps not completely steady, came over the intercom system, "Ladies and gentlemen, we have landed at Stapleton Airport. Please remain in your seats until the plane has come to a complete stop at the terminal. Thank you."

The woman beside Hallorann closed her book and uttered a long sigh. "We live to fight another day, Mr. Hallorann."

"Ma'am, we aren't done with this one, yet."

"True. Very true. Would you care to have a drink in the lounge with me?"

"I would, but I have an appointment to keep."

"Pressing?"

"Very pressing," Hallorann said gravely.

"Something that will improve the general situation in some small way, I hope."

"I hope so too," Hallorann said, and smiled. She smiled back at him, ten years dropping silently from her face as she did so.

*   *   *

Because he had only the flight bag he'd carried for luggage, Hallorann beat the crowd to the Hertz desk on the lower level. Outside the smoked glass windows he could see the snow still falling steadily. The gusting wind drove white clouds of it back and forth, and the people walking across to the parking area were struggling against it. One man lost his hat and Hallorann could commiserate with him as it whirled high, wide, and handsome. The man stared after it and Hallorann thought:

(*Aw, just forget it, man. That homburg ain't comin down until it gets to Arizona.*)

On the heels of that thought:

(*If it's this bad in Denver, what's it going to be like west of Boulder?*)

Best not to think about that, maybe.

"Can I help you, sir?" a girl in Hertz yellow asked him.

"If you got a car, you can help me," he said with a big grin.

For a heavier-than-average charge he was able to get a heavier-than-average car, a silver and black Buick Electra. He was thinking of the winding mountain roads rather than style; he would still have to stop somewhere along the way and get chains put on. He wouldn't get far without them.

"How bad is it?" he asked as she handed him the rental agreement to sign.

"They say it's the worst storm since 1969," she answered brightly. "Do you have far to drive, sir?"

"Farther than I'd like."

"If you'd like, sir, I can phone ahead to the Texaco station at the Route 270 junction. They'll put chains on for you."

"That would be a great blessing, dear."

She picked up the phone and made the call. "They'll be expecting you."

"Thank you much."

Leaving the desk, he saw the sharp-faced woman standing on one of the queues that had formed in front of the luggage carousel. She was still reading her book. Hallorann winked at her as he went by. She looked up, smiled at him, and gave him a peace sign.

(*shine*)

He turned up his overcoat collar, smiling, and shifted his flight bag to the other hand. Only a little one, but it made him feel better. He was sorry he'd told her that fish story about having a steel plate in his head. He mentally wished her well and as he went out into the howling wind and snow, he thought she wished him the same in return.

The charge for putting on the chains at the service station was a modest one, but Hallorann slipped the man at work in the garage bay an extra ten to get moved up a little way on the waiting list. It was still quarter of ten before he was actually on the road, the windshield wipers clicking and the chains clinking with tuneless monotony on the Buick's big wheels.

The turnpike was a mess. Even with the chains he could go no faster than thirty. Cars had gone off the road at crazy angles, and on several of the grades traffic was barely struggling along, summer tires spinning helplessly in the drifting powder. It was the first big storm of the winter down here in the low-lands (if you could call a mile above sealevel "low"), and it was a mother. Many of them were unprepared, common enough, but Hallorann still found himself cursing them as he inched around them, peering into his snow-clogged outside mirror to be sure nothing was

(*Dashing through the snow . . .*)

coming up in the left-hand lane to cream his black ass.

There was more bad luck waiting for him at the Route 36 entrance ramp. Route 36, the Denver-Boulder turnpike, also goes west to Estes Park, where it connects with Route 7. That road, also known as the Upland Highway, goes through Sidewinder, passes the Overlook Hotel, and finally winds down the Western Slope and into Utah.

The entrance ramp had been blocked by an over-turned semi. Bright-burning flares had been scattered around it like birthday candles on some idiot child's cake.

He came to a stop and rolled his window down. A cop with a fur Cossack hat jammed down over his ears gestured with one gloved hand toward the flow of traffic moving north on I-25.

"You can't get up here!" he bawled to Hallorann over the wind. "Go down two exits, get on 91, and connect with 36 at Broomfield!"

"I think I could get around him on the left!" Hallorann shouted back. "That's twenty miles out of my way, what you're rappin!"

"I'll rap your friggin *head!*" the cop shouted back. "This ramp's closed!"

Hallorann backed up, waited for a break in traffic, and continued on his way up Route 25. The signs informed him it was only a hundred miles to Cheyenne, Wyoming. If he didn't look out for his ramp, he'd wind up there.

He inched his speed up to thirty-five but dared no more; already snow was threatening to clog his wiper blades and the traffic patterns were decidedly crazy. Twenty-mile detour. He cursed, and the feeling that time was growing shorter for the boy welled up in him again, nearly suffocating with its urgency. And at the same time he felt a fatalistic certainty that he would not be coming back from this trip.

He turned on the radio, dialed past Christmas ads, and found a weather forecast.

"—six inches already, and another foot is expected in the Denver metro area by nightfall. Local and state police urge you not to take your car out of the garage unless it's absolutely necessary, and warn that most mountain passes have already been closed. So stay home and wax up your boards and keep tuned to—"

"Thanks, mother," Hallorann said, and turned the radio off savagely.

46

Wendy

Around noon, after Danny had gone into the bathroom to use the toilet, Wendy took the towel-
wrapped knife from under her pillow, put it in the
pocket of her bathrobe, and went over to the bathroom door.

"Danny?"

"What?"

"I'm going down to make us some lunch. 'Kay?"

"Okay. Do you want me to come down?"

"No, I'll bring it up. How about a cheese omelet
and some soup?"

"Sure."

She hesitated outside the closed door a moment
longer. "Danny, are you sure it's okay?"

"Yeah," he said. "Just be careful."

"Where's your father? Do you know?"

His voice came back, curiously flat: "No. But it's
okay."

She stifled an urge to keep asking, to keep picking
around the edges of the thing. The thing was there,

they knew what it was, picking at it was only going to frighten Danny more . . . and herself.

Jack had lost his mind. They had sat together on Danny's cot as the storm began to pick up clout and meanness around eight o'clock this morning and had listened to him downstairs, bellowing and stumbling from one place to another. Most of it had seemed to come from the ballroom. Jack singing tuneless bits of song, Jack holding up one side of an argument, Jack screaming loudly at one point, freezing both of their faces as they stared into one another's eyes. Finally they had heard him stumbling back across the lobby, and Wendy thought she had heard a loud banging noise, as if he had fallen down or pushed a door violently open. Since eight-thirty or so—three and a half hours now—there had been only silence.

She went down the short hall, turned into the main first-floor corridor, and went to the stairs. She stood on the first-floor landing looking down into the lobby. It appeared deserted, but the gray and snowy day had left much of the long room in shadow. Danny could be wrong. Jack could be behind a chair or couch . . . maybe behind the registration desk . . . waiting for her to come down . . . .

She wet her lips. "Jack?"

No answer.

Her hand found the handle of the knife and she began to go down. She had seen the end of her marriage many times, in divorce, in Jack's death at the scene of a drunken car accident (a regular vision in the dark two o'clock of Stovington mornings), and occasionally in daydreams of being discovered by another man, a soap opera Galahad who would sweep Danny and her onto the saddle of his snow-white charger and take them away. But she had never envisioned herself prowling halls and staircases like a nervous felon, with a knife clasped in one hand to use against Jack.

A wave of despair struck through her at the thought and she had to stop halfway down the stairs and hold the railing, afraid her knees would buckle.

(*Admit it. It isn't just Jack, he's just the one solid thing in all of this you can hang the other things on, the things you can't believe and yet are being forced to believe, that thing about the hedges, the party favor in the elevator, the mask*)

She tried to stop the thought but it was too late.

(*and the voices.*)

Because from time to time it had not seemed that there was a solitary crazy man below them, shouting at and holding conversations with the phantoms in his own crumbling mind. From time to time, like a radio signal fading in and out, she had heard—or thought she had—other voices, and music, and laughter. At one moment she would hear Jack holding a conversation with someone named Grady (the name was vaguely familiar to her but she made no actual connection), making statements and asking questions into silence, yet speaking loudly, as if to make himself heard over a steady background racket. And then, eerily, other sounds would be there, seeming to slip into place—a dance band, people clapping, a man with an amused yet authoritative voice who seemed to be trying to persuade somebody to make a speech. For a period of thirty seconds to a minute she would hear this, long enough to grow faint with terror, and then it would be gone again and she would only hear Jack, talking in that commanding yet slightly slurred way she remembered as his drunk-speak voice. But there was nothing in the hotel to drink except cooking sherry. Wasn't that right? Yes, but if she could imagine that the hotel was full of voices and music, couldn't Jack imagine that he was drunk?

She didn't like that thought. Not at all.

Wendy reached the lobby and looked around. The velvet rope that had cordoned off the ballroom had been taken down; the steel post it had been clipped to had been knocked over, as if someone had carelessly bumped it going by. Mellow white light fell through the open door onto the lobby rug from the ballroom's high, narrow windows. Heart thumping, she went to the open ballroom doors and looked in. It was empty and silent, the only sound that curious subaural echo that seems to linger in all large rooms, from the largest cathedral to the smallest hometown bingo parlor.

She went back to the registration desk and stood undecided for a moment, listening to the wind howl outside. It was the worst storm so far, and it was still building up force. Somewhere on the west side a shutter latch had broken and the shutter banged back and forth with a steady flat cracking sound, like a shooting gallery with only one customer.

(Jack, you really should take care of that. Before something gets in.)

What would she do if he came at her right now, she wondered. If he should pop up from behind the dark, varnished registration desk with its pile of triplicate forms and its little silver-plated bell, like some murderous jack-in-the-box, pun intended, a grinning jack-in-the-box with a cleaver in one hand and no sense at all left behind his eyes. Would she stand frozen with terror, or was there enough of the primal mother in her to fight him for her son until one of them was dead? She didn't know. The very thought made her sick—made her feel that her whole life had been a long and easy dream to lull her helplessly into this waking nightmare. She was soft. When trouble came, she slept. Her past was unremarkable. She had never been tried in fire. Now the trial was upon her, not fire but ice, and she would not be allowed to sleep through this. Her son was waiting for her upstairs.

Clutching the haft of the knife tighter, she peered over the desk.

Nothing there.

Her relieved breath escaped her in a long, hitching sigh.

She put the gate up and went through, pausing to glance into the inner officer before going in herself. She fumbled through the next door for the bank of kitchen light switches, coldly expecting a hand to close over hers at any second. Then the fluorescents were coming on with minuscule ticking and humming sounds and she could see Mr. Hallorann's kitchen—her kitchen now, for better or worse—pale green tiles, gleaming Formica, spotless porcelain, glowing chrome edgings. She had promised him she would keep his kitchen clean, and she had. She felt as if it was one of Danny's safe places. Dick Hallorann's presence seemed to enfold and comfort her. Danny had called for Mr. Hallorann, and upstairs, sitting next to Danny in fear as her husband ranted and raved below, that had seemed like the faintest of all hopes. But standing here, in Mr. Hallorann's place, it seemed almost possible. Perhaps he was on his way now, intent on getting to them regardless of the storm. Perhaps it was so.

She went across to the pantry, shot the bolt back, and stepped inside. She got a can of tomato soup and closed the pantry door again, and bolted it. The door was tight against the floor. If you kept it bolted, you didn't have to worry about rat or mouse droppings in the rice or flour or sugar.

She opened the can and dropped the slightly jellied contents into a saucepan—*plop*. She went to the refrigerator and got milk and eggs for the omelet. Then to the walk-in freezer for cheese. All of these actions, so common and so much a part of her life before the Overlook had been a part of her life, helped to calm her.

She melted butter in the frying pan, diluted the soup with milk, and then poured the beaten eggs into the pan.

A sudden feeling that someone was standing behind her, reaching for her throat.

She wheeled around, clutching the knife. No one there.

(*! Get ahold of yourself, girl !*)

She grated a bowl of cheese from the block, added it to the omelet, flipped it, and turned the gas ring down to a bare blue flame. The soup was hot. She put the pot on a large tray with silverware, two bowls, two plates, the salt and pepper shakers. When the omelet had puffed slightly, Wendy slid it off onto one of the plates and covered it.

(*Now back the way you came. Turn off the kitchen lights. Go through the inner office. Through the desk gate, collect two hundred dollars.*)

She stopped on the lobby side of the registration desk and set the tray down beside the silver bell. Unreality would stretch only so far; this was like some surreal game of hide-and-seek.

She stood in the shadowy lobby, frowning in thought.

(*Don't push the facts away this time, girl. There are certain realities, as lunatic as this situation may seem. One of them is that you may be the only responsible person left in this grotesque pile. You have a five-going-on-six son to look out for. And your husband, whatever has happened to him and no matter how dangerous he may be . . . maybe he's part of your responsibility, too. And even if he isn't, consider this: Today is December second. You could be stuck up here another four months if a ranger doesn't happen by. Even if they do start to wonder why they haven't heard from us on the CB, no one is going to come today . . . or tomorrow . . . maybe not for weeks. Are you going to spend a month sneaking down to*)

get meals with a knife in your pocket and jumping at every
shadow? Do you really think you can avoid Jack for a
month? Do you think you can keep Jack out of the upstairs
quarters if he wants to get in? He has the passkey and one
hard kick would snap the bolt.)

Leaving the tray on the desk, she walked slowly
down to the dining room and looked in. It was
deserted. There was one table with the chairs set up
around it, the table they had tried eating at until the
dining room's emptiness began to freak them out.

"Jack?" she called hesitantly.

At that moment the wind rose in a gust, driving
snow against the shutters, but it seemed to her that
there had been something. A muffled sort of groan.

"Jack?"

No returning sound this time, but her eyes fell on
something beneath the batwing doors of the Colorado Lounge, something that gleamed faintly in the
subdued light, Jack's cigarette lighter.

Plucking up her courage, she crossed to the
batwings and pushed them open. The smell of gin
was so strong that her breath snagged in her throat.
It wasn't even right to call it a smell; it was a positive
reek. But the shelves were empty. Where in God's
name had he found it? A bottle hidden at the back of
one of the cupboards? *Where?*

There was another groan, low and fuzzy, but perfectly audible this time. Wendy walked slowly to the
bar.

"Jack?"

No answer.

She looked over the bar and there he was, sprawled out on the floor in a stupor. Drunk as a lord, by the smell. He must have tried to go right over the top and lost his balance. A wonder he hadn't broken his neck. An old proverb recurred to her: God looks after drunks and little children. Amen.

Yet she was not angry with him; looking down at him she thought he looked like a horribly overtired little boy who had tried to do too much and had fallen asleep in the middle of the living room floor. He had stopped drinking and it was not Jack who had made the decision to start again; there had been no liquor for him to start with . . . so where had it come from?

Resting at every five or six feet along the horse-shoe-shaped bar there were wine bottles wrapped in straw, their mouths plugged with candles. Supposed to look bohemian, she supposed. She picked one up and shook it, half expecting to hear the slosh of gin inside it

(*new wine in old bottles*)

but there was nothing. She set it back down.

Jack was stirring. She went around the bar, found the gate, and walked back on the inside to where Jack lay, pausing only to look at the gleaming chromium taps. They were dry, but when she passed close to them she could smell beer, wet and new, like a fine mist.

As she reached Jack he rolled over, opened his eyes, and looked up at her. For a moment his gaze was utterly blank, and then it cleared.

"Wendy?" he asked. "That you?"

"Yes," she said. "Do you think you can make it upstairs? If you put your arms around me? Jack, where did you—"

His hand closed brutally around her ankle.

"Jack! What are you—"

"Gotcha!" he said, and began to grin. There was a stale odor of gin and olives about him that seemed to set off an old terror in her, a worse terror than any hotel could provide by itself. A distant part of her thought that the worst thing was that it had all come back to this, she and her drunken husband.

"Jack, I want to help."

"Oh yeah. You and Danny only want to *help*." The grip on her ankle was crushing now. Still holding onto her, Jack was getting shakily to his knees. "You wanted to help us all right out of here. But now . . . I . . . *gotcha!*"

"Jack, you're hurting my ankle—"

"I'll hurt more than your ankle, you *bitch*."

The word stunned her so completely that she made no effort to move when he let go of her ankle and stumbled from his knees to his feet, where he stood swaying in front of her.

"You never loved me," he said. "You want us to leave because you know that'll be the end of me. Did you ever think about my re . . . res . . . respons'bilities? No, I guess to fuck you didn't. All you ever think about is ways to drag me down. You're just like my mother, you milksop *bitch!*"

"Stop it," she said, crying. "You don't know what you're saying. You're drunk. I don't know how, but you're drunk."

"Oh, I know. I know now. You and him. That little pup upstairs. The two of you, planning together. Isn't that right?"

"No, no! We never planned anything! What are you—"

"You liar!" he screamed. "Oh, I know how you do it! I guess I know that! When I say, 'We're going to stay here and I'm going to do my job,' you say, 'Yes, dear,' and he says, 'Yes, Daddy,' and then you lay your plans. You planned to use the snowmobile. You planned that. But I knew. I figured it out. *Did you think I wouldn't figure it out? Did you think I was stupid?"*

She stared at him, unable to speak now. He was going to kill her, and then he was going to kill Danny. Then maybe the hotel would be satisfied and allow him to kill himself. Just like that other caretaker. Just like

(*Grady.*)

With almost swooning horror, she realized at last who it was that Jack had been conversing with in the ballroom.

"You turned my son against me. That was the worst." His face sagged into lines of selfpity. "My little boy. Now he hates me, too. You saw to that. That was your plan all along, wasn't it? You've always been jealous, haven't you? Just like your mother. You couldn't be satisfied unless you had all the cake, could you? *Could you?"*

She couldn't talk.

"Well, I'll fix you," he said, and tried to put his hands around her throat.

She took a step backward, then another, and he stumbled against her. She remembered the knife in the pocket of her robe and groped for it, but now his left arm had swept around her, pinning her arm against her side. She could smell sharp gin and the sour odor of his sweat.

"Have to be punished," he was grunting. "Chastised. Chastised . . . harshly."

His right hand found her throat.

As her breath stopped, pure panic took over. His left hand joined his right and now the knife was free to her own hand, but she forgot about it. Both of her hands came up and began to yank helplessly at his larger, stronger ones.

"*Mommy!*" Danny shrieked from somewhere. "*Daddy, stop! You're hurting Mommy!*" He screamed piercingly, a high and crystal sound that she heard from far off.

Red flashes of light leaped in front of her eyes like ballet dancers. The room grew darker. She saw her son clamber up on the bar and throw himself at Jack's shoulders. Suddenly one of the hands that had been crushing her throat was gone as Jack cuffed Danny away with a snarl. The boy fell back against the empty shelves and dropped to the floor, dazed. The hand was on her throat again. The red flashes began to turn black.

Danny was crying weakly. Her chest was burning. Jack was shouting into her face. "I'll fix you! Goddam

you, I'll show you who is boss around here! I'll show
you——"

But all sounds were fading down a long dark corridor. Her struggles began to weaken. One of her
hands fell away from his and dropped slowly until the
arm was stretched out at right angles to her body, the
hand dangling limply from the wrist like the hand of
a drowning woman.

It touched a bottle—one of the straw-wrapped
wine bottles that served as decorative candleholders.

Sightlessly, with the last of her strength, she
groped for the bottle's neck and found it, feeling the
greasy beads of wax against her hand.

(*and O God if it slips*)

She brought it up and then down, praying for aim,
knowing that if it only struck his shoulder or upper
arm she was dead.

But the bottle came down squarely on Jack Torrance's head, the glass shattering violently inside the
straw. The base of it was thick and heavy, and it made
a sound against his skull like a medicine ball dropped
on a hardwood floor. He rocked back on his heels, his
eyes rolling up in their sockets. The pressure on her
throat loosened, then gave way entirely. He put his
hands out, as if to steady himself, and then crashed
over on his back.

Wendy drew a long, sobbing breath. She almost
fell herself, clutched the edge of the bar, and managed to hold herself up. Consciousness wavered in
and out. She could hear Danny crying, but she had
no idea where he was. It sounded like crying in an

echo chamber. Dimly she saw dime-sized drops of blood falling to the dark surface of the bar—from her nose, she thought. She cleared her throat and spat on the floor. It sent a wave of agony up the column of her throat, but the agony subsided to a steady dull press of pain . . . just bearable.

Little by little, she managed to get control of herself.

She let go of the bar, turned around, and saw Jack lying full-length, the shattered bottle beside him. He looked like a felled giant. Danny was crouched below the lounge's cash register, both hands in his mouth, staring at his unconscious father.

Wendy went to him unsteadily and touched his shoulder. Danny cringed away from her.

"Danny, listen to me—"

"No, no," he muttered in a husky old man's voice. "Daddy hurt you . . . you hurt Daddy . . . Daddy hurt you . . . I want to go to sleep. Danny wants to go to sleep."

"Danny—"

"Sleep, sleep. Nighty-night."

"No!"

Pain ripping up her throat again. She winced against it. But he opened his eyes. They looked at her warily from bluish, shadowed sockets.

She made herself speak calmly, her eyes never leaving his. Her voice was low and husky, almost a whisper. It hurt to talk. "Listen to me, Danny. It wasn't your daddy trying to hurt me. And I didn't want to hurt him. The hotel has gotten into him, Danny. *The*

Overlook has gotten into your daddy. Do you understand me?"

Some kind of knowledge came slowly back into Danny's eyes.

"The Bad Stuff," he whispered. "There was none of it here before, was there?"

"No. The hotel put it here. The . . ." She broke off in a fit of coughing and spat out more blood. Her throat already felt puffed to twice its size. "The hotel made him drink it. Did you hear those people he was talking to this morning?"

"Yes . . . the hotel people . . ."

"I heard them too. And that means the hotel is getting stronger. It wants to hurt all of us. But I think . . . I hope . . . that it can only do that through your daddy. He was the only one it could catch. Are you understanding me, Danny? It's desperately important that you understand."

"The hotel caught Daddy." He looked at Jack and groaned helplessly.

"I know you love your daddy. I do too. We have to remember that the hotel is trying to hurt him as much as it is us." And she was convinced that was true. More, she thought that Danny might be the one the hotel really wanted, the reason it was going so far . . . maybe the reason it was *able* to go so far. It might even be that in some unknown fashion it was Danny's shine that was powering it, the way a battery powers the electrical equipment in a car . . . the way a battery gets a car to start. If they got out of here, the Overlook might subside to its old semi-sentient state, able to do no more than present penny-dreadful horror slides to the more psychically aware guests who entered it. Without Danny it was not much more than an amusement park haunted house, where a guest or two might hear rappings or the phantom sounds of a masquerade party, or see an occasional disturbing thing. But if it absorbed Danny . . . Danny's shine or life-force or spirit . . . whatever you wanted to call it . . . into itself—what would it be then?

The thought made her cold all over.

"I wish Daddy was all better," Danny said, and the tears began to flow again.

"Me too," she said, and hugged Danny tightly. "And honey, that's why you've got to help me put your daddy somewhere. Somewhere that the hotel can't make him hurt us and where he can't hurt himself. Then . . . if your friend Dick comes, or a park ranger, we can take him away. And I think he might be all right again. All of us might be all right. I think there's still a chance for that, if we're strong and brave, like you were when you jumped on his back. Do you understand?" She looked at him pleadingly and thought how strange it was; she had never seen him when he looked so much like Jack.

"Yes," he said, and nodded. "I think . . . if we can get away from here . . . everything will be like it was. Where could we put him?"

"The pantry. There's food in there, and a good strong bolt on the outside. It's warm. And we can eat up the things from the refrigerator and the freezer.

There will be plenty for all three of us until help comes."

"Do we do it now?"

"Yes, right now. Before he wakes up."

Danny put the bargate up while she folded Jack's hands on his chest and listened to his breathing for a moment. It was slow but regular. From the smell of him she thought he must have drunk a great deal . . . and he was out of the habit. She thought it might be liquor as much as the crack on the head with the bottle that had put him out.

She picked up his legs and began to drag him along the floor. She had been married to him for nearly seven years, he had lain on top of her countless times—in the thousands—but she had never realized how heavy he was. Her breath whistled painfully in and out of her hurt throat. Nevertheless, she felt better than she had in days. She was alive. Having just brushed so close to death, that was precious. And Jack was alive, too. By blind luck rather than plan, they had perhaps found the only way that would bring them all safely out.

Panting harshly, she paused a moment, holding Jack's feet against her hips. The surroundings reminded her of the old seafaring captain's cry in *Treasure Island* after old blind Pew had passed him the Black Spot: *We'll do em yet!*

And then she remembered, uncomfortably, that the old seadog had dropped dead mere seconds later.

"Are you all right, Mommy? Is he . . . is he too heavy?"

"I'll manage." She began to drag him again. Danny was beside Jack. One of his hands had fallen off his chest, and Danny replaced it gently, with love.

"Are you sure, Mommy?"

"Yes. It's the best thing, Danny."

"It's like putting him in jail."

"Only for awhile."

"Okay, then. Are you sure you can do it?"

"Yes."

But it was a near thing, at that. Danny had been cradling his father's head when they went over the doorsills, but his hands slipped in Jack's greasy hair as they went into the kitchen. The back of his head struck the tiles, and Jack began to moan and stir.

"You got to use smoke," Jack muttered quickly. "Now run and get me that gascan."

Wendy and Danny exchanged tight, fearful glances.

"Help me," she said in a low voice.

For a moment Danny stood as if paralyzed by his father's face, and then he moved jerkily to her side and helped her hold the left leg. They dragged him across the kitchen floor in a nightmare kind of slow motion, the only sounds the faint, insectile buzz of the fluorescent lights and their own labored breathing.

When they reached the pantry, Wendy put Jack's feet down and turned to fumble with the bolt. Danny looked down at Jack, who was lying limp and relaxed again. The shirttail had pulled out of the back of his pants as they dragged him and Danny wondered if

Daddy was too drunk to be cold. It seemed wrong to lock him in the pantry like a wild animal, but he had seen what he tried to do to Mommy. Even upstairs he had known Daddy was going to do that. He had heard them arguing in his head.

(*If only we could all be out of here. Or if it was a dream I was having, back in Stovington. If only.*)

The bolt was stuck.

Wendy pulled at it as hard as she could, but it wouldn't move. She couldn't retract the goddam bolt. It was stupid and unfair . . . she had opened it with no trouble at all when she had gone in to get the can of soup. Now it wouldn't move, and what was she going to do? They couldn't put him in the walk-in refrigerator; he would freeze or smother to death. But if they left him out and he woke up . . .

Jack stirred again on the floor.

"I'll take care of it," he muttered. "I understand."

"He's waking up, Mommy!" Danny warned.

Sobbing now, she yanked at the bolt with both hands.

"Danny?" There was something softly menacing, if still blurry, in Jack's voice. "That you, ole doc?"

"Just go to sleep, Daddy," Danny said nervously. "It's bedtime, you know."

He looked up at his mother, still struggling with the bolt, and saw what was wrong immediately. She had forgotten to rotate the bolt before trying to withdraw it. The little catch was stuck in its notch.

"Here," he said low, and brushed her trembling hands aside; his own were shaking almost as badly.

He knocked the catch loose with the heel of his hand and the bolt drew back easily.

"Quick," he said. He looked down. Jack's eyes had fluttered open again and this time Daddy was looking directly at him, his gaze strangely flat and speculative.

"You copied it," Daddy told him. "I know you did. But it's here somewhere. And I'll find it. That I promise you. I'll find it . . ." His words slurred off again.

Wendy pushed the pantry door open with her knee, hardly noticing the pungent odor of dried fruit that wafted out. She picked up Jack's feet again and dragged him in. She was gasping harshly now, at the limit of her strength. As she yanked the chain pull that turned on the light, Jack's eyes fluttered open again.

"What are you doing? Wendy? What are you doing?"

She stepped over him.

He was quick; amazingly quick. One hand lashed out and she had to sidestep and nearly fall out the door to avoid his grasp. Still, he had caught a handful of her bathrobe and there was a heavy purring noise as it ripped. He was up on his hands and knees now, his hair hanging in his eyes, like some heavy animal. A large dog . . . or a lion.

"Damn you both. I know what you want. But you're not going to get it. This hotel . . . it's mine. It's me they want. Me! Me!"

"The door, Danny!" she screamed. *"Shut the door!"*

He pushed the heavy wooden door shut with a slam, just as Jack leaped. The door latched and Jack thudded uselessly against it.

Danny's small hands groped at the bolt. Wendy was too far away to help; the issue of whether he would be locked in or free was going to be decided in two seconds. Danny missed his grip, found it again, and shot the bolt across just as the latch began to jiggle madly up and down below it. Then it stayed up and there was a series of thuds as Jack slammed his shoulder against the door. The bolt, a quarter inch of steel in diameter, showed no signs of loosening. Wendy let her breath out slowly.

"Let me out of here!" Jack raged. "Let me out! Danny, doggone it, this is your father and I want to get out! *Now do what I tell you!*"

Danny's hand moved automatically toward the bolt. Wendy caught it and pressed it between her breasts.

"You mind your daddy, Danny! You do what I say! You do it or I'll give you a hiding you'll never forget. *Open this door or I'll bash your fucking brains in!*"

Danny looked at her, pale as window glass.

They could hear his breath tearing in and out behind the half inch of solid oak.

"Wendy, you let me out! Let me out right now! You cheap nickel-plated cold-cunt bitch! You let me out! I mean it! Let me out of here and I'll let it go! If you don't, I'll mess you up! I mean it! I'll mess you up so bad your own mother would pass you on the street! *Now open this door!*"

Danny moaned. Wendy looked at him and saw he was going to faint in a moment.

"Come on, doc," she said, surprised at the calmness of her own voice. "It's not your daddy talking, remember. It's the hotel."

"Come back here and let me out right NOW!" Jack screamed. There was a scraping, breaking sound as he attacked the inside of the door with his fingernails.

"It's the hotel," Danny said. "It's the hotel. I remember." But he looked back over his shoulder and his face was crumpled and terrified.

47

Danny

It was three in the afternoon of a long, long day.

They were sitting on the big bed in their quarters.
Danny was turning the purple VW model with the
monster sticking out of the sun roof over and over in
his hands, compulsively.

They had heard Daddy's batterings at the door all
the way across the lobby, the batterings and his voice,
hoarse and petulantly angry in a weak-king sort of a
way, vomiting promises of punishment, vomiting
profanity, promising both of them that they would
live to regret betraying him after he had slaved his
guts out for them over the years.

Danny thought they would no longer be able to
hear it upstairs, but the sounds of his rage carried
perfectly up the dumb-waiter shaft. Mommy's face
was pale, and there were horrible brownish bruises on
her neck where Daddy had tried to . . .

He turned the model over and over in his hands,
Daddy's prize for having learned his reading lessons.

(. . . *where Daddy had tried to hug her too tight.*)

Mommy put some of her music on the little record player, scratchy and full of horns and flutes. She smiled at him tiredly. He tried to smile back and failed. Even with the volume turned up loud he thought he could still hear Daddy screaming at them and battering the pantry door like an animal in a zoo cage. What if Daddy had to go to the bathroom? What would he do then?

Danny began to cry.

Wendy turned the volume down on the record player at once, held him, rocked him on her lap.

"Danny, love, it will be all right. It will. If Mr. Hallorann didn't get your message, someone else will. As soon as the storm is over. No one could get up here until then anyway. Mr. Hallorann or anyone else. But when the storm is over, everything will be fine again. We'll leave here. And do you know what we'll do next spring? The three of us?"

Danny shook his head against her breasts. He didn't know. It seemed there could never be spring again.

"We'll go fishing. We'll rent a boat and go fishing, just like we did last year on Chatterton Lake. You and me and your daddy. And maybe you'll catch a bass for our supper. And maybe we won't catch anything, but we're sure to have a good time."

"I love you, Mommy," he said, and hugged her.

"Oh, Danny, I love you, too."

Outside, the wind whooped and screamed.

Around four-thirty, just as the daylight began to fall, the screams ceased.

They had both been dozing uneasily, Wendy still holding Danny in her arms, and she didn't wake. But Danny did. Somehow the silence was worse, more ominous than the screams and the blows against the strong pantry door. Was Daddy asleep again? Or dead? Or what?

(*Did he get out?*)

Fifteen minutes later the silence was broken by a hard, grating, metallic rattle. There was a heavy grinding, then a mechanical humming. Wendy came awake with a cry.

The elevator was running again.

They listened to it, wide-eyed, hugging each other. It went from floor to floor, the grate rattling back, the brass door slamming open. There was laughter, drunken shouts, occasional screams, and the sounds of breakage.

The Overlook was coming to life around them.

48

Jack

He sat on the floor of the pantry with his legs out in front of him, a box of Triscuit crackers between them, looking at the door. He was eating the crackers one by one, not tasting them, only eating them because he had to eat something. When he got out of here, he was going to need his strength. All of it.

At this precise instant, he thought he had never felt quite so miserable in his entire life. His mind and body together made up a large-writ scripture of pain. His head ached terribly, the sick throb of a hangover. The attendant symptoms were there, too: his mouth tasted like a manure rake had taken a swing through it, his ears rang, his heart had an extra-heavy, thudding beat, like a tomtom. In addition, both shoulders ached fiercely from throwing himself against the door and his throat felt raw and peeled from useless shouting. He had cut his right hand on the doorlatch.

And when he got out of here, he was going to kick some ass.

He munched the Triscuits one by one, refusing to give in to his wretched stomach, which wanted to vomit up everything. He thought of the Excedrins in his pocket and decided to wait until his stomach had quieted a bit. No sense swallowing a painkiller if you were going to throw it right back up. Have to use your brain. The celebrated Jack Torrance brain. Aren't you the fellow who once was going to live by his wits? Jack Torrance, best-selling author. Jack Torrance, acclaimed playwright and winner of the New York Critics Circle Award. John Torrance, man of letters, esteemed thinker, winner of the Pulitzer Prize at seventy for his trenchant book of memoirs, *My Life in the Twentieth Century.* All any of that shit boiled down to was living by your wits.

Living by your wits is always knowing where the wasps are.

He put another Triscuit into his mouth and crunched it up.

What it really came down to, he supposed, was their lack of trust in him. Their failure to believe that he knew what was best for them and how to get it. His wife had tried to usurp him, first by fair

(sort of)

means, then by foul. When her little hints and whining objections had been overturned by his own well-reasoned arguments, she had turned his boy against him, tried to kill him with a bottle, and then had locked him, of all places, in the goddamned fucking *pantry.*

Still, a small interior voice nagged him.

(Yes but where did the liquor come from? Isn't that really the central point? You know what happens when you drink, you know it from bitter experience. When you drink, you lose your wits.)

He hurled the box of Triscuits across the small room. They struck a shelf of canned goods and fell to the floor. He looked at the box, wiped his lips with his hand, and then looked at his watch. It was almost six-thirty. He had been in here for hours. His wife had locked him in here and he'd been here for fucking *hours*.

He could begin to sympathize with his father.

The thing he'd never asked himself, Jack realized now, was exactly what had driven his daddy to drink in the first place. And really . . . when you came right down to what his old students had been pleased to call the nitty-gritty . . . hadn't it been the woman he was married to? A milksop sponge of a woman, always dragging silently around the house with an expression of doomed martyrdom on her face? A ball and chain around Daddy's ankle? No, not ball and chain. She had never actively tried to make Daddy a prisoner, the way Wendy had done to him. For Jack's father it must have been more like the fate of McTeague the dentist at the end of Frank Norris's great novel: handcuffed to a dead man in the waste-land. Yes, that was better. Mentally and spiritually dead, his mother had been handcuffed to his father by matrimony. Still, Daddy had tried to do right as he dragged her rotting corpse through life. He had tried to bring the four children up to know right from wrong, to understand discipline, and above all, to respect their father.

Well, they had been ingrates, all of them, himself included. And now he was paying the price; his own son had turned out to be an ingrate, too. But there was hope. He would get out of here somehow. He would chastise them both, and harshly. He would set Danny an example, so that the day might come when Danny was grown, a day when Danny would know what to do better than he himself had known.

He remembered the Sunday dinner when his father had caned his mother at the table . . . how horrified he and the others had been. Now he could see how necessary that had been, how his father had only been feigning drunkenness, how his wits had been sharp and alive underneath all along, watching for the slightest sign of disrespect.

Jack crawled after the Triscuits and began to eat them again, sitting by the door she had so treacherously bolted. He wondered exactly what his father had seen, and how he had caught her out by his playacting. Had she been sneering at him behind her hand? Sticking her tongue out? Making obscene finger gestures? Or only looking at him insolently and arrogantly, convinced that he was too stupidly drunk to see? Whatever it had been, he had caught her at it, and he had chastised her sharply. And now, twenty years later, he could finally appreciate Daddy's wisdom.

Of course you could say Daddy had been foolish to marry such a woman, to have handcuffed himself to that corpse in the first place . . . and a disrespectful corpse at that. But when the young marry in haste they must repent in leisure, and perhaps Daddy's daddy had married the same type of woman, so that unconsciously Jack's daddy had also married one, as Jack himself had. Except that *his* wife, instead of being satisfied with the passive role of having wrecked one career and crippled another, had opted for the poisonously active task of trying to destroy his last and best chance: to become a member of the Overlook's staff, and possibly to rise . . . all the way to the position of manager, in time. She was trying to deny him Danny, and Danny was his ticket of admission. That was foolish, of course—why would they want the son when they could have the father?—but employers often had foolish ideas and that was the condition that had been made.

He wasn't going to be able to reason with her, he could see that now. He had tried to reason with her in the Colorado Lounge, and she had refused to listen, had hit him over the head with a bottle for his pains. But there would be another time, and soon. He would get out of here.

He suddenly held his breath and cocked his head. Somewhere a piano was playing boogie-woogie and people were laughing and clapping along. The sound was muffled through the heavy wooden door, but audible. The song was "There'll Be a Hot Time in the Old Town Tonight."

His hands curled helplessly into fists; he had to restrain himself from battering at the door with them. The party had begun again. The liquor would be flowing freely. Somewhere, dancing with someone else, would be the girl who had felt so maddeningly nude under her white silk gown.

"You'll pay for this!" he howled. "Goddam you two, you'll pay! You'll take your goddam medicine for this, I promise you! You——"

"Here, here, now," a mild voice said just outside the door. "No need to shout, old fellow. I can hear you perfectly well."

Jack lurched to his feet.

"Grady? Is that you?"

"Yes, sir. Indeed it is. You appear to have been locked in."

"Let me out, Grady. Quickly."

"I see you can hardly have taken care of the business we discussed, sir. The correction of your wife and son."

"They're the ones who locked me in. Pull the bolt, for God's sake!"

"You let them lock you in?" Grady's voice registered well-bred surprise. "Oh, dear. A woman half your size and a little boy? Hardly sets you off as being of top managerial timber, does it?"

A pulse began to beat in the clockspring of veins at Jack's right temple. "Let me out, Grady. I'll take care of them."

"Will you indeed, sir? I wonder." Well-bred surprise was replaced by well-bred regret. "I'm pained to say that I doubt it. I——and others——have really come to believe that your heart is not in this, sir. That you haven't the . . . the belly for it."

"I do!" Jack shouted. "I do, I swear it!"

"You would bring us your son?"

"Yes! Yes!"

"Your wife would object to that very strongly, Mr. Torrance. And she appears to be . . . somewhat stronger than we had imagined. Somewhat more resourceful. She certainly seems to have gotten the better of *you*."

Grady tittered.

"Perhaps, Mr. Torrance, we should have been dealing with her all along."

"I'll bring him, I swear it," Jack said. His face was against the door now. He was sweating. "She won't object. I swear she won't. She won't be able to."

"You would have to kill her, I fear," Grady said coldly.

"I'll do what I have to do. Just *let me out*."

"You'll give your word on it, sir?" Grady persisted.

"My word, my promise, my sacred vow, whatever in hell you want. If you—"

There was a flat snap as the bolt was drawn back. The door shivered open a quarter of an inch. Jack's words and breath halted. For a moment he felt that death itself was outside that door.

The feeling passed.

He whispered: "Thank you, Grady. I swear you won't regret it. I swear you won't."

There was no answer. He became aware that all sounds had stopped except for the cold swooping of the wind outside.

He pushed the pantry door open; the hinges squealed faintly.

The kitchen was empty. Grady was gone. Everything was still and frozen beneath the cold white glare of the fluorescent bars. His eyes caught on the large chopping block where the three of them had eaten their meals.

Standing on top of it was a martini glass, a fifth of gin, and a plastic dish filled with olives.

Leaning against it was one of the roque mallets from the equipment shed.

He looked at it for a long time.

Then a voice, much deeper and much more powerful than Grady's, spoke from somewhere, everywhere . . . from inside him.

(*Keep your promise, Mr. Torrance.*)

"I will," he said. He heard the fawning servility in his own voice but was unable to control it. "I will."

He walked to the chopping block and put his hand on the handle of the mallet.

He hefted it.

Swung it.

It hissed viciously through the air.

Jack Torrance began to smile.

49

Hallorann, Going up the Country

It was quarter of two in the afternoon and according to the snow-clotted signs and the Hertz Buick's odometer, he was less than three miles from Estes Park when he finally went off the road.

In the hills, the snow was falling faster and more furiously than Hallorann had ever seen (which was, perhaps, not to say a great deal, since Hallorann had seen as little snow as he could manage in his lifetime), and the wind was blowing a capricious gale—now from the west, now backing around to the north, sending clouds of powdery snow across his field of vision, making him coldly aware again and again that if he missed a turn he might well plunge two hundred feet off the road, the Electra cartwheeling ass over teapot as it went down. Making it worse was his own amateur status as a winter driver. It scared him to have the yellow center line buried under swirling, drifting snow, and it scared him when the heavy gusts of wind came unimpeded through the notches in the hills and actually made the heavy Buick slew around.

It scared him that the road information signs were mostly masked with snow and you could flip a coin as to whether the road was going to break right for left up ahead in the white drive-in movie screen he seemed to be driving through. He was scared, all right. He had driven in a cold sweat since climbing into the hills west of Boulder and Lyons, handling the accelerator and brake as if they were Ming vases. Between rock 'n' roll tunes on the radio, the disc jockey constantly adjured motorists to stay off the main highways and under no conditions to go into the mountains, because many roads were impassable and all of them were dangerous. Scores of minor accidents had been reported, and two serious ones: a party of skiers in a VW microbus and a family that had been bound for Albuquerque through the Sangre de Cristo Mountains. The combined score on both was four dead and five wounded. "So stay off those roads and get into the good music here at KTLK," the jock concluded cheerily, and then compounded Halloran's misery by playing "Seasons in the Sun." "We had joy, we had fun, we had—" Terry Jacks gibbered happily, and Halloran snapped the radio off viciously, knowing he would have it back on in five minutes. No matter how bad it was, it was better than riding alone through this white madness.

(*Admit it. Dis heah black boy has got at least one long stripe of yaller . . . and it runs raht up his ebberlubbin back!*)

It wasn't even funny. He would have backed off before he even cleared Boulder if it hadn't been for his compulsion that the boy was in terrible trouble.

Even now a small voice in the back of his skull—more the voice of reason than of cowardice, he thought—was telling him to hole up in an Estes Park motel for the night and wait for the plows to at least expose the center stripe again. That voice kept reminding him of the jet's shaky landing at Stapleton, of that sinking feeling that it was going to come in nose-first, delivering its passengers to the gates of hell rather than at Gate 39, Concourse B. But reason would not stand against the compulsion. It had to be today. The snowstorm was his own bad luck. He would have to cope with it. He was afraid that if he didn't, he might have something much worse to cope with in his dreams.

The wind gusted again, this time from the northeast, a little English on the ball if you please, and he was again cut off from the vague shapes of the hills and even from the embankments on either side of the road. He was driving through white null.

And then the high sodium lights of the snowplow loomed out of the soup, bearing down, and to his horror he saw that instead of being to one side, the Buick's nose was pointed directly between those headlamps. The plow was being none too choosy about keeping its own side of the road, and Hallorann had allowed the Buick to drift.

The grinding roar of the plow's diesel engine intruded over the bellow of the wind, and then the sound of its airhorn, hard, long, almost deafening.

Hallorann's testicles turned into two small wrinkled sacs filled with shaved ice. His guts seemed to have been transformed into a large mass of Silly Putty.

Color was materializing out of the white now, snow-clotted orange. He could see the high cab, even the gesticulating figure of the driver behind the single long wiper blade. He could see the V shape of the plow's wing blades, spewing more snow up onto the road's left-hand embankment like pallid, smoking exhaust.

WHAAAAAAAAA! the airhorn bellowed indignantly.

He squeezed the accelerator like the breast of a much-loved woman and the Buick scooted forward and toward the right. There was no embankment over here; the plows headed up instead of down had only to push the snow directly over the drop.

(*The drop, ah yes, the drop—*)

The wingblades on Hallorann's left, fully four feet higher than the Electra's roof, flirted by with no more than an inch or two to spare. Until the plow had actually cleared him, Hallorann had thought a crash inevitable. A prayer which was half an inarticulate apology to the boy flitted through his mind like a torn rag.

Then the plow was past, its revolving blue lights glinting and flashing in Hallorann's rearview mirror.

He jockeyed the Buick's steering wheel back to the left, but nothing doing. The scoot had turned into a skid, and the Buick was floating dreamily toward the lip of the drop, spuming snow from under its mudguards.

He flicked the wheel back the other way, in the skid's direction, and the car's front and rear began to swap places. Panicked now, he pumped the brake hard, and then felt a hard bump. In front of him the road was gone . . . he was looking into a bottomless chasm of swirling snow and vague greenish-gray pines far away and far below.

(*I'm going holy mother of Jesus I'm going off*)

And that was where the car stopped, canting forward at a thirty-degree angle, the left fender jammed against a guardrail, the rear wheels nearly off the ground. When Hallorann tried reverse, the wheels only spun helplessly. His heart was doing a Gene Krupa drumroll.

He got out—very carefully he got out—and went around to the Buick's back deck.

He was standing there, looking at the back wheels helplessly, when a cheerful voice behind him said: "Hello there, fella. You must be shit right out of your mind."

He turned around and saw the plow forty yards further down the road, obscured in the blowing snow except for the raftered dark brown streak of its exhaust and the revolving blue lights on top. The driver was standing just behind him, dressed in a long sheepskin coat and a slicker over it. A blue-and-white pinstriped engineer's cap was perched on his head, and Hallorann could hardly believe it was staying on in the teeth of the wind.

(*Glue. It sure-God must be glue.*)

"Hi," he said. "Can you pull me back onto the road?"

"Oh, I guess I could," the plow driver said. "What the hell you doing way up here, mister? Good way to kill your ass."

"Urgent business."

"Nothin is that urgent," the plow driver said slowly and kindly, as if speaking to a mental defective. "If you'd'a hit that post a leetle mite harder, nobody woulda got you out till All Fools' Day. Don't come from these parts, do you?"

"No. And I wouldn't be here unless my business was as urgent as I say."

"That so?" The driver shifted his stance companionably as if they were having a desultory chat on the back steps instead of standing in a blizzard halfway between hoot and holler, with Hallorann's car balanced three hundred feet above the tops of the trees below.

"Where you headed? Estes?"

"No, a place called the Overlook Hotel," Hallorann said. "It's a little way above Sidewinder——"

But the driver was shaking his head dolefully.

"I guess I know well enough where that is," he said. "Mister, you'll never get up to the old Overlook. Roads between Estes Park and Sidewinder is bloody damn hell. It's driftin in right behind us no matter how hard we push. I come through drifts a few miles back that was damn near six feet through the middle. And even if you could make Sidewinder, why, the road's closed from there all the way across to Buckland, Utah. Nope." He shook his head. "Never make it, mister. Never make it at all."

"I have to try," Hallorann said, calling on his last reserves of patience to keep his voice normal. "There's a boy up there—"

"*Boy?* Naw. The Overlook closes down at the last end of September. No percentage keepin it open longer. Too many shitstorms like this."

"He's the son of the caretaker. He's in trouble."

"How would you know that?"

His patience snapped.

"For Christ's sake are you going to stand there and flap y'jaw at me the rest of the day? *I know, I know!* Now are you going to pull me back on the road or not?"

"Kind of testy, aren't you?" the driver observed, not particularly perturbed. "Sure, get back in there. I got a chain behind the seat."

Hallorann got back behind the wheel, beginning to shake with delayed reaction now. His hands were numbed almost clear through. He had forgotten to bring gloves.

The plow backed up to the rear of the Buick, and he saw the driver get out with a long coil of chain. Hallorann opened the door and shouted: "What can I do to help?"

"Stay out of the way, is all," the driver shouted back. "This ain't gonna take a blink."

Which was true. A shudder ran through the Buick's frame as the chain pulled tight, and a second later it was back on the road, pointed more or less toward Estes Park. The plow driver walked up beside the window and knocked on the safety glass. Hallorann rolled down the window.

"Thanks," he said. "I'm sorry I shouted at you."

"I been shouted at before," the driver said with a grin. "I guess you're sorta strung up. You take these." A pair of bulky blue mittens dropped into Hallorann's lap. "You'll need em when you go off the road again, I guess. Cold out. You wear em unless you want to spend the rest of your life pickin your nose with a crochetin hook. And you send em back. My wife knitted em and I'm partial to em. Name and address is sewed right into the linin. I'm Howard Cottrell, by the way. You just send em back when you don't need em anymore. And I don't want to have to go payin no postage due, mind."

"All right," Hallorann said. "Thanks. One hell of a lot."

"You be careful, I'd take you myself, but I'm busy as a cat in a mess of guitar strings."

"That's okay. Thanks again."

He started to roll up the window, but Cottrell stopped him.

"When you get to Sidewinder—*if* you get to Sidewinder—you go to Durkin's Conoco. It's right next to the li'brey. Can't miss it. You ask for Larry Durkin. Tell him Howie Cottrell sent you and you want to rent one of his snowmobiles. You mention my name and show those mittens, you'll get the cut rate."

"Thanks again," Hallorann said.

Cottrell nodded. "It's funny. Ain't no way you could know someone's in trouble up there at the Overlook . . . the phone's out, sure as hell. But I believe you. Sometimes I get feelins."

Hallorann nodded. "Sometimes I do, too."

"Yeah, I know you do. But you take care."

"I will."

Cottrell disappeared into the blowing dimness with a final wave, his engineer cap still mounted perkily on his head. Hallorann got going again, the chains flailing at the snowcover on the road, finally digging in enough to start the Buick moving. Behind him, Howard Cottrell gave a final good-luck blast on his plow's airhorn, although it was really unnecessary; Hallorann could feel him wishing him good luck.

That's two shines in one day, he thought, and that ought to be some kind of good omen. But he distrusted omens, good or bad. And meeting two people with the shine in one day (when he usually didn't run across more than four or five in the course of a year) might not mean anything. That feeling of finality, a feeling

(*like things are all wrapped up*)

he could not completely define was still very much with him. It was—

The Buick wanted to skid sideways around a tight curve and Hallorann jockeyed it carefully, hardly daring to breathe. He turned on the radio again and it was Aretha, and Aretha was just fine. He'd share his Hertz Buick with her any day.

Another gust of wind struck the car, making it rock and slip around. Hallorann cursed it and hunched more closely over the wheel. Aretha finished her song and then the jock was on again, telling him that driving today was a good way to get killed.

Hallorann snapped the radio off.

* * *

He did make it to Sidewinder, although he was four and a half hours on the road between Estes Park and there. By the time he got to the Upland Highway it was full dark, but the snowstorm showed no sign of abating. Twice he'd had to stop in front of drifts that were as high as his car's hood and wait for the plows to come along and knock holes in them. At one of the drifts the plow had come up on his side of the road and there had been another close call. The driver had merely swung around his car, not getting out to chew the fat, but he did deliver one of the two finger gestures that all Americans above the age of ten recognize, and it was not the peace sign.

It seemed that as he drew closer to the Overlook, his need to hurry became more and more compulsive. He found himself glancing at his wristwatch almost constantly. The hands seemed to be flying along.

Ten minutes after he had turned onto the Upland, he passed two signs. The whooping wind had cleared both of their snow pack so he was able to read them. SIDEWINDER 10, the first said. The second: ROAD CLOSED 12 MILES AHEAD DURING WINTER MONTHS.

"Larry Durkin," Hallorann muttered to himself. His dark face was strained and tense in the muted green glow of the dashboard instruments. It was ten after six. "The Conoco by the library. Larry—"

And that was when it struck him full-force, the smell of oranges and the thought-force, heavy and hateful, murderous:

(*GET OUT OF HERE YOU DIRTY NIGGER THIS IS NONE OF YOUR BUSINESS YOU NIGGER TURN AROUND TURN AROUND OR WE'LL KILL YOU HANG YOU UP FROM A TREE LIMB YOU FUCKING JUNGLEBUNNY COON AND THEN BURN THE BODY THAT'S WHAT WE DO WITH NIGGERS SO TURN AROUND NOW*)

Hallorann screamed in the close confines of the car. The message did not come to him in words but in a series of rebuslike images that were slammed into his head with terrific force. He took his hands from the steering wheel to blot the pictures out.

Then the car smashed broadside into one of the embankments, rebounded, slewed halfway around, and came to a stop. The rear wheels spun uselessly.

Hallorann snapped the gearshift into park, and then covered his face with his hands. He did not precisely cry; what escaped him was an uneven huh-huh-huh sound. His chest heaved. He knew that if that blast had taken him on a stretch of road with a dropoff on one side or the other, he might well be dead now. Maybe that had been the idea. And it might hit him again, at any time. He would have to protect against it. He was surrounded by a red force of immense power that might have been memory. He was drowning in instinct.

He took his hands away from his face and opened his eyes cautiously. Nothing. If there was something trying to scare him again, it wasn't getting through. He was closed off.

Had that happened to the boy? Dear God, had that happened to the little boy?

And of all the images, the one that bothered him the most was that dull whacking sound, like a hammer splatting into thick cheese. What did that mean?

(*Jesus, not that little boy. Jesus, please.*)

He dropped the gearshift lever into low range and fed the engine gas a little at a time. The wheels spun, caught, spun, and caught again. The Buick began to move, its headlights cutting weakly through the swirling snow. He looked at his watch. Almost six-thirty now. And he was beginning to feel that was very late indeed.

50

REDRUM

Wendy Torrance stood indecisive in the middle of the bedroom, looking at her son, who had fallen fast asleep.

Half an hour ago the sounds had ceased. All of them, all at once. The elevator, the party, the sound of room doors opening and closing. Instead of easing her mind it made the tension that had been building in her even worse; it was like a malefic hush before the storm's final brutal push. But Danny had dozed off almost at once; first into a light, twitching doze, and in the last ten minutes or so a heavier sleep. Even looking directly at him she could barely see the slow rise and fall of his narrow chest.

She wondered when he had last gotten a full night's sleep, one without tormenting dreams or long periods of dark wakefulness, listening to revels that had only become audible—and visible—to her in the last couple of days, as the Overlook's grip on the three of them tightened.

(*Real psychic phenomena or group hypnosis?*)

She didn't know, and didn't think it mattered. What had been happening was just as deadly either way. She looked at Danny and thought

(*God grant he lie still*)

that if he was undisturbed, he might sleep the rest of the night through. Whatever talent he had, he was still a small boy and he needed his rest.

It was Jack she had begun to worry about.

She grimaced with sudden pain, took her hand away from her mouth, and saw she had torn off one of her fingernails. And her nails were one thing she'd always tried to keep nice. They weren't long enough to be called hooks, but still nicely shaped and

(*and what are you worrying about your fingernails for?*)

She laughed a little, but it was a shaky sound, without amusement.

First Jack had stopped howling and battering at the door. Then the party had begun again

(*or did it ever stop? did it sometimes just drift into a slightly different angle of time where they weren't meant to hear it?*)

counterpointed by the crashing, banging elevator. Then that had stopped. In that new silence, as Danny had been falling asleep, she had fancied she heard low, conspiratorial voices coming from the kitchen almost directly below them. At first she had dismissed it as the wind, which could mimic many different human vocal ranges, from a papery deathbed whisper around the doors and window frames to a full-out scream around the eaves . . . the sound of a woman fleeing a murderer in a cheap melodrama. Yet, sitting stiffly beside Danny, the idea that it was indeed voices became more and more convincing.

Jack and someone else, discussing his escape from the pantry.

Discussing the murder of his wife and son.

It would be nothing new inside these walls; murder had been done here before.

She had gone to the heating vent and had placed her ear against it, but at that exact moment the furnace had come on, and any sound was lost in the rush of warm air coming up from the basement. When the furnace had kicked off again, five minutes ago, the place was completely silent except for the wind, the gritty spatter of snow against the building, and the occasional groan of a board.

She looked down at her ripped fingernail. Small beads of blood were oozing up from beneath it.

(*Jack's gotten out.*)

(*Don't talk nonsense.*)

(*Yes, he's out. He's gotten a knife from the kitchen or maybe the meat cleaver. He's on his way up here right now, walking along the sides of the risers so the stairs won't creak.*)

(*! You're insane !*)

Her lips were trembling, and for a moment it seemed that she must have cried the words out loud. But the silence held.

She felt watched.

She whirled around and stared at the night-blackened window, and a hideous white face with circles of darkness for eyes was gibbering in at her, the face of a monstrous lunatic that had been hiding in these groaning walls all along—

It was only a pattern of frost on the outside of the glass.

She let her breath out in a long, susurrating whisper of fear, and it seemed to her that she heard, quite clearly this time, amused titters from somewhere.

(*You're jumping at shadows. It's bad enough without that. By tomorrow morning, you'll be ready for the rubber room.*)

There was only one way to allay those fears and she knew what it was.

She would have to go down and make sure Jack was still in the pantry.

Very simple. Go downstairs. Have a peek. Come back up. Oh, by the way, stop and grab the tray on the registration counter. The omelet would be a washout, but the soup could be reheated on the hotplate by Jack's typewriter.

(*Oh yes and don't get killed if he's down there with a knife.*)

She walked to the dresser, trying to shake off the mantle of fear that lay on her. Scattered across the dresser's top was a pile of change, a stack of gasoline chits for the hotel truck, the two pipes Jack brought with him everywhere but rarely smoked . . . and his key ring.

She picked it up, held it in her hand for a moment, and then put it back down. The idea of locking the bedroom door behind her had occurred, but it just didn't appeal. Danny was asleep. Vague thoughts of fire passed through her mind, and something else nibbled more strongly, but she let it go.

Wendy crossed the room, stood indecisively by the door for a moment, then took the knife from the pocket of her robe and curled her right hand around the wooden haft.

She pulled the door open.

The short corridor leading to their quarters was bare. The electric wall flambeaux all shone brightly at their regular intervals, showing off the rug's blue background and sinuous, weaving pattern.

(*See? No boogies here.*)

(*No, of course not. They want you out. They want you to do something silly and womanish, and that is exactly what you are doing.*)

She hesitated again, miserably caught, not wanting to leave Danny and the safety of the apartment and at the same time needing badly to reassure herself that Jack *was* still . . . safely packed away.

(*Of course he is.*)

(*But the voices*)

(*There were no voices. It was your imagination. It was the wind.*)

"It wasn't the wind."

The sound of her own voice made her jump. But the deadly certainty in it made her go forward. The knife swung by her side, catching angles of light and throwing them on the silk wallpaper. Her slippers whispered against the carpet's nap. Her nerves were singing like wires.

She reached the corner of the main corridor and peered around, her mind stiffened for whatever she might see there.

There was nothing to see.

After a moment's hesitation she rounded the corner and began down the main corridor. Each step toward the shadowy stairwell increased her dread and made her aware that she was leaving her sleeping son behind, alone and unprotected. The sound of her slippers against the carpet seemed louder and louder in her ears; twice she looked back over her shoulder to convince herself that someone wasn't creeping up behind her.

She reached the stairwell and put her hand on the cold newel post at the top of the railing. There were nineteen wide steps down to the lobby. She had counted them enough times to know. Nineteen carpeted stair risers, and nary a Jack crouching on any one of them. Of course not. Jack was locked in the pantry behind a hefty steel bolt and a thick wooden door.

But the lobby was dark and oh so full of shadows.

Her pulse thudded steadily and deeply in her throat.

Ahead and slightly to the left, the brass yaw of the elevator stood mockingly open, inviting her to step in and take the ride of her life.

(*No thank you*)

The inside of the car had been draped with pink and white crepe streamers. Confetti had burst from two tubular party favors. Lying in the rear left corner was an empty bottle of champagne.

She sensed movement above her and wheeled to look up the nineteen steps leading to the dark second-floor landing and saw nothing; yet there was a disturbing corner-of-the-eye sensation that things

(*things*)

had leaped back into the deeper darkness of the hallway up there just before her eyes could register them.

She looked down the stairs again.

Her right hand was sweating against the wooden handle of the knife; she switched it to her left, wiped her right palm against the pink terrycloth of her robe, and switched the knife back. Almost unaware that her mind had given her body the command to go forward, she began down the stairs, left foot then right, left foot then right, her free hand trailing lightly on the banister.

(*Where's the party? Don't let me scare you away, you bunch of moldy sheets! Not one scared woman with a knife! Let's have a little music around here! Let's have a little life!*)

Ten steps down, a dozen, a baker's dozen.

The light from the first-floor hall filtered a dull yellow down here, and she remembered that she would have to turn on the lobby lights either beside the entrance to the dining room or inside the manager's office.

Yet there was light coming from somewhere else, white and muted.

The fluorescents, of course. In the kitchen.

She paused on the thirteenth step, trying to remember if she had turned them off or left them on when she and Danny left. She simply couldn't remember.

Below her, in the lobby, highbacked chairs hulked in pools of shadow. The glass in the lobby doors was pressed white with a uniform blanket of drifted snow. Brass studs in the sofa cushions gleamed faintly like cat's eyes. There were a hundred places to hide.

Her legs stilted with fear, she continued down.

Now seventeen, now eighteen, now nineteen.

(*Lobby level, madam. Step out carefully.*)

The ballroom doors were thrown wide, only blackness spilling out. From within came a steady ticking, like a bomb. She stiffened, then remembered the clock on the mantel, the clock under glass. Jack or Danny must have wound it . . . or maybe it had wound itself up, like everything else in the Overlook.

She turned toward the reception desk, meaning to go through the gate and the manager's office and into the kitchen. Gleaming dull silver, she could see the intended lunch tray.

Then the clock began to strike, little tinkling notes.

Wendy stiffened, her tongue rising to the roof of her mouth. Then she relaxed. It was striking eight, that was all. Eight o'clock . . . *five, six, seven* . . .

She counted the strokes. It suddenly seemed wrong to move again until the clock had stilled.

. . . *eight . . . nine* . . .

(*?? Nine ??*)

. . . *ten . . . eleven* . . .

Suddenly, belatedly, it came to her. She turned back clumsily for the stairs, knowing already she was too late. But how could she have known?

Twelve.

All the lights in the ballroom went on. There was a huge, shrieking flourish of brass. Wendy screamed aloud, the sound of her cry insignificant against the blare issuing from those brazen lungs.

"Unmask!" the cry echoed. *"Unmask! Unmask!"*

Then they faded, as if down a long corridor of time, leaving her alone again.

No, not alone.

She turned and he was coming for her.

It was Jack and yet not Jack. His eyes were lit with a vacant, murderous glow; his familiar mouth now wore a quivering, joyless grin.

He had the roque mallet in one hand.

"Thought you'd lock me in? Is that what you thought you'd do?"

The mallet whistled through the air. She stepped backward, tripped over a hassock, fell to the lobby rug.

"Jack—"

"You bitch," he whispered. "I know what you are."

The mallet came down again with whistling, deadly velocity and buried itself in her soft stomach. She screamed, suddenly submerged in an ocean of pain. Dimly she saw the mallet rebound. It came to her with sudden numbing reality that he meant to beat her to death with the mallet he held in his hands.

She tried to cry out to him again, to beg him to stop for Danny's sake, but her breath had been knocked loose. She could only force out a weak whimper, hardly a sound at all.

"Now. Now, by Christ," he said, grinning. He kicked the hassock out of his way. "I guess you'll take your medicine now."

The mallet whickered down. Wendy rolled to her left, her robe tangling above her knees. Jack's hold on the mallet was jarred loose when it hit the floor. He had to stoop and pick it up, and while he did she ran for the stairs, the breath at last sobbing back into her. Her stomach was a bruise of throbbing pain.

"Bitch," he said through his grin, and began to come after her. "You stinking bitch, I guess you'll get what's coming to you. I guess you will."

She heard the mallet whistle through the air and then agony exploded on her right side as the mallet-head took her just below the line of her breasts, breaking two ribs. She fell forward on the steps and new agony ripped her as she struck on the wounded side. Yet instinct made her roll over, roll away, and the mallet whizzed past the side of her face, missing by a naked inch. It struck the deep pile of the stair carpeting with a muffled thud. That was when she saw the knife, which had been jarred out of her hand by her fall. It lay glittering on the fourth stair riser.

"Bitch," he repeated. The mallet came down. She shoved herself upward and it landed just below her kneecap. Her lower leg was suddenly on fire. Blood began to trickle down her calf. And then the mallet was coming down again. She jerked her head away from it and it smashed into the stair riser in the hollow between her neck and shoulder, scraping away the flesh from her ear.

He brought the mallet down again and this time she rolled toward him, down the stairs, inside the arc of his swing. A shriek escaped her as her broken ribs thumped and grated. She struck his shins with her body while he was offbalance and he fell backward with a yell of anger and surprise, his feet jigging to keep their purchase on the stair riser. Then he thumped to the floor, the mallet flying from his hand. He sat up, staring at her for a moment with shocked eyes.

"I'll kill you for that," he said.

He rolled over and stretched out for the handle of the mallet. Wendy forced herself to her feet. Her left leg sent bolt after bolt of pain all the way up to her hip. Her face was ashy pale but set. She leaped onto his back as his hand closed over the shaft of the roque mallet.

"*Oh dear God!*" she screamed to the Overlook's shadowy lobby, and buried the kitchen knife in his lower back up to the handle.

He stiffened beneath her and then shrieked. She thought she had never heard such an awful sound in her whole life; it was as if the very boards and windows and doors of the hotel had screamed. It seemed to go on and on while he remained board-stiff beneath her weight. They were like a parlor charade of horse and rider. Except that the back of his red-and-black-checked flannel shirt was growing darker, sodden, with spreading blood.

Then he collapsed forward on his face, bucking her off on her hurt side, making her groan.

She lay breathing harshly for a time, unable to move. She was an excruciating throb of pain from one end to the other. Every time she inhaled, something stabbed viciously at her, and her neck was wet with blood from her grazed ear.

There was only the sound of her struggle to breathe, the wind, and the ticking clock in the ballroom.

At last she forced herself to her feet and hobbled across to the stairway. When she got there she clung to the newel post, head down, waves of faintness washing over her. When it had passed a little, she began to climb, using her unhurt leg and pulling with her arms on the banister. Once she looked up, expecting to see Danny there, but the stairway was empty.

(*Thank God he slept through it thank God thank God*)

Six steps up she had to rest, her head down, her blond hair coiled on and over the banister. Air whistled painfully through her throat, as if it had grown barbs. Her right side was a swollen, hot mass.

(*Come on Wendy come on old girl get a locked door behind you and then look at the damage thirteen more to go not so bad. And when you get to the upstairs corridor you can crawl. I give my permission.*)

She drew in as much breath as her broken ribs would allow and half-pulled, half-fell up another riser. And another.

She was on the ninth, almost halfway up, when Jack's voice came from behind and below her. He said thickly: "You bitch. You killed me."

Terror as black as midnight swept through her. She looked over her shoulder and saw Jack getting slowly to his feet.

His back was bowed over, and she could see the handle of the kitchen knife sticking out of it. His eyes seemed to have contracted, almost to have lost themselves in the pale, sagging folds of the skin around them. He was grasping the roque mallet loosely in his left hand. The end of it was bloody. A scrap of her pink terrycloth robe stuck almost in the center.

"I'll give you your medicine," he whispered, and began to stagger toward the stairs.

Whimpering with fear, she began to pull herself upward again. Ten steps, a dozen, a baker's dozen. But still the first-floor hallway looked as far above her as an unattainable mountain peak. She was panting now, her side shrieking in protest. Her hair swung wildly back and forth in front of her face. Sweat stung her eyes. The ticking of the domed clock in the ballroom seemed to fill her ears, and counterpointing it, Jack's panting, agonized gasps as he began to mount the stairs.

51

Hallorann Arrives

Larry Durkin was a tall and skinny man with a morose face overtopped with a luxuriant mane of red hair. Hallorann had caught him just as he was leaving the Conoco station, the morose face buried deeply inside an army-issue parka. He was reluctant to do any more business that stormy day no matter how far Hallorann had come, and even more reluctant to rent one of his two snowmobiles out to this wild-eyed black man who insisted on going up to the old Overlook. Among people who had spent most of their lives in the little town of Sidewinder, the hotel had a smelly reputation. Murder had been done up there. A bunch of hoods had run the place for a while, and cutthroat businessmen had run it for a while, too. And things had been done up at the old Overlook that never made the papers, because money has a way of talking. But the people in Sidewinder had a pretty good idea. Most of the hotel's chambermaids came from here, and chambermaids see a lot.

But when Hallorann mentioned Howard Cottrell's name and showed Durkin the tag inside one of the blue mittens, the gas station owner thawed.

"Sent you here, did he?" Durkin asked, unlocking one of the garage bays and leading Hallorann inside. "Good to know the old rip's got some sense left. I thought he was plumb out of it." He flicked a switch and a bank of very old and very dirty fluorescents buzzed wearily into life. "Now what in the tarnal creation would you want up at that place, fella?"

Hallorann's nerve had begun to crack. The last few miles into Sidewinder had been very bad. Once a gust of wind that must have been tooling along at better than sixty miles an hour had floated the Buick all the way around in a 360° turn. And there were still miles to travel with God alone knew what at the other end of them. He was terrified for the boy. Now it was almost ten minutes to seven and he had this whole song and dance to go through again.

"Somebody is in trouble up there," he said very carefully. "The son of the caretaker."

"Who? Torrance's boy? Now what kind of trouble could he be in?"

"I don't know," Hallorann muttered. He felt sick with the time this was taking. He was speaking with a country man, and he knew that all country men feel a similar need to approach their business obliquely, to smell around its corners and sides before plunging into the middle of dealing. But there was no time, because now he was one scared nigger and if this went on much longer he just might decide to cut and run.

"Look," he said. "Please. I need to go up there and I have to have a snowmobile to get there. I'll pay your price, but for God's sake let me get on with my business!"

"All right," Durkin said, unperturbed. "If Howard sent you, that's good enough. You take this Arctic-Cat. I'll put five gallons of gas in the can. Tank's full. She'll get you up and back down, I guess."

"Thank you," Hallorann said, not quite steadily.

"I'll take twenty dollars. That includes the ethyl."

Hallorann fumbled a twenty out of his wallet and handed it over. Durkin tucked it into one of his shirt pockets with hardly a look.

"Guess maybe we better trade jackets, too," Durkin said, pulling off his parka. "That overcoat of yours ain't gonna be worth nothin tonight. You trade me back when you return the snowsled."

"Oh, hey, I couldn't—"

"Don't fuss with me," Durkin interrupted, still mildly. "I ain't sending you out to freeze. I only got to walk down two blocks and I'm at my own supper table. Give it over."

Slightly dazed, Hallorann traded his overcoat for Durkin's fur-lined parka. Overhead the fluorescents buzzed faintly, reminding him of the lights in the Overlook's kitchen.

"Torrance's boy," Durkin said, and shook his head. "Good-lookin little tyke, ain't he? He n his dad was in here a lot before the snow really flew. Drivin the hotel truck, mostly. Looked to me like the two of em was just about as tight as they could get. That's one little boy that loves his daddy. Hope he's all right."

"So do I." Hallorann zipped the parka and tied the hood.

"Lemme help you push that out," Durkin said. They rolled the snowmobile across the oil-stained concrete and toward the garage bay. "You ever drove one of these before?"

"No."

"Well, there's nothing to it. The instructions are pasted there on the dashboard, but all there really is, is stop and go. Your throttle's here, just like a motorcycle throttle. Brake on the other side. Lean with it on the turns. This baby will do seventy on hardpack, but on this powder you'll get no more than fifty and that's pushing it."

Now they were in the service station's snow-filled front lot, and Durkin had raised his voice to make himself heard over the battering of the wind. "Stay on the road!" he shouted at Hallorann's ear. "Keep your eye on the guardrail posts and the signs and you'll be all right, I guess. If you get off the road, you're going to be dead. Understand?"

Hallorann nodded.

"Wait a minute!" Durkin told him, and ran back into the garage bay.

While he was gone, Hallorann turned the key in the ignition and pumped the throttle a little. The snowmobile coughed into brash, choppy life.

Durkin came back with a red and black ski mask.

"Put this on under your hood!" he shouted.

Hallorann dragged it on. It was a tight fit, but it cut the last of the numbing wind off from his cheeks and forehead and chin.

Durkin leaned close to make himself heard.

"I guess you must know about things the same way Howie does sometimes," he said. "It don't matter, except that place has got a bad reputation around here. I'll give you a rifle if you want it."

"I don't think it would do any good," Hallorann shouted back.

"You're the boss. But if you get that boy, you bring him to Sixteen Peach Lane. The wife'll have some soup on."

"Okay. Thanks for everything."

"You watch out!" Durkin yelled. "Stay on the road!"

Hallorann nodded and twisted the throttle slowly. The snowmobile purred forward, the headlamp cutting a clean cone of light through the thickly falling snow. He saw Durkin's upraised hand in the rearview mirror, and raised his own in return. Then he nudged the handlebars to the left and was traveling up Main Street, the snowmobile coursing smoothly through the white light thrown by the streetlamps. The speedometer stood at thirty miles an hour. It was ten past seven. At the Overlook, Wendy and Danny were sleeping and Jack Torrance was discussing matters of life and death with the previous caretaker.

Five blocks up Main, the streetlamps ended. For half a mile there were small houses, all buttoned tightly up against the storm, and then only wind-howling darkness. In the black again with no light but the thin spear of the snowmobile's headlamp, terror closed in on him again, a childlike fear, dismal and disheartening. He had never felt so alone. For several minutes, as the few lights of Sidewinder dwindled away and disappeared in the rearview, the urge to turn around and go back was almost insurmountable. He reflected that for all of Durkin's concern for Jack Torrance's boy, he had not offered to take the other snowmobile and come with him.

(*That place has got a bad reputation around here.*)

Clenching his teeth, he turned the throttle higher and watched the needle on the speedometer climb past forty and settle at forty-five. He seemed to be going horribly fast and yet he was afraid it wasn't fast enough. At this speed it would take him almost an hour to get to the Overlook. But at a higher speed he might not get there at all.

He kept his eyes glued to the passing guardrails and the dime-sized reflectors mounted on top of each one. Many of them were buried under drifts. Twice he saw curve signs dangerously late and felt the snowmobile riding up the drifts that masked the dropoff before turning back onto where the road was in the summertime. The odometer counted off the miles at a maddeningly slow clip—five, ten, finally fifteen. Even behind the knitted ski mask his face was beginning to stiffen up and his legs were growing numb.

(*Guess I'd give a hundred bucks for a pair of ski pants.*)

As each mile turned over, his terror grew—as if the place had a poison atmosphere that thickened as you neared it. Had it ever been like this before? He had never really liked the Overlook, and there had been others who shared his feeling, but it had never been like this.

He could feel the voice that had almost wrecked him outside of Sidewinder still trying to get in, to get past his defenses to the soft meat inside. If it had been strong twenty-five miles back, how much stronger would it be now? He couldn't keep it out entirely. Some of it was slipping through, flooding his brain with sinister subliminal images. More and more he got the image of a badly hurt woman in a bathroom, holding her hands up uselessly to ward off a blow, and he felt more and more that the woman must be—

(Jesus, watch out!)

The embankment was looming up ahead of him like a freight train. Wool-gathering, he had missed a turn sign. He jerked the snowmobile's steering gear hard right and it swung around, tilting as it did so. From underneath came the harsh grating sound of the snowtread on rock. He thought the snowmobile was going to dump him, and it did totter on the knife-edge of balance before half-driving, half-skidding back down to the more or less level surface of the snow-buried road. Then the dropoff was ahead of him, the headlamp showing an abrupt end to the snowcover and darkness beyond that. He turned the snowmobile the other way, a pulse beating sickly in his throat.

(Keep it on the road Dicky old chum.)

He forced himself to turn the throttle up another notch. Now the speedometer needle was pegged just below fifty. The wind howled and roared. The head-lamp probed the dark.

An unknown length of time later, he came around a drift-banked curve and saw a glimmering flash of light ahead. Just a glimpse, and then it was blotted out by a rising fold of land. The glimpse was so brief he was persuading himself it had been wishful think-ing when another turn brought it in view again, slightly closer, for another few seconds. There was no question of its reality this time; he had seen it from just this angle too many times before. It was the Overlook. There were lights on the first floor and lobby levels, it looked like.

Some of his terror—the part that had to do with driving off the road or wrecking the snowmobile on an unseen curve—melted entirely away. The snow-mobile swept surely into the first half of an S curve that he now remembered confidently foot for foot, and that was when the headlamp picked out the

(*oh dear jesus god what is it*)

in the road ahead of him. Limned in stark blacks and whites, Hallorann first thought it was some hideously huge timberwolf that had been driven down from the high country by the storm. Then, as he closed on it, he recognized it and horror closed his throat.

Not a wolf but a lion. A hedge lion.

Its features were a mask of black shadow and pow-dered snow, its haunches wound tight to spring. And it did spring, snow billowing around its pistoning rear legs in a silent burst of crystal glitter.

Hallorann screamed and twisted the handlebars hard right, ducking low at the same time. Scratching, ripping pain scrawled itself across his face, his neck, his shoulders. The ski mask was torn open down the back. He was hurled from the snowmobile. He hit the snow, plowed through it, rolled over.

He could feel it coming for him. In his nostrils there was a bitter smell of green leaves and holly. A huge hedge paw batted him in the small of the back and he flew ten feet through the air, splayed out like a rag doll. He saw the snowmobile, riderless, strike the embankment and rear up, its headlamp searching the sky. It fell over with a thump and stalled.

Then the hedge lion was on him. There was a crackling, rustling sound. Something raked across the front of the parka, shredding it. It might have been stiff twigs, but Hallorann knew it was claws.

"You're not there!" Hallorann screamed at the circling, snarling hedge lion. *"You're not there at all!"* He struggled to his feet and made it halfway to the snowmobile before the lion lunged, batting him across the head with a needle-tipped paw. Hallorann saw silent, exploding lights.

"Not there," he said again, but it was a fading mutter. His knees unhinged and dropped him into the snow. He crawled for the snowmobile, the right side of his face a scarf of blood. The lion struck him again, rolling him onto his back like a turtle. It roared playfully.

Hallorann struggled to reach the snowmobile. What he needed was there. And then the lion was on him again, ripping and clawing.

52

Wendy and Jack

Wendy risked another glance over her shoulder, Jack was on the sixth riser, clinging to the banister much as she was doing herself. He was still grinning, and dark blood oozed slowly through the grin and slipped down the line of his jaw. He bared his teeth at her.

"I'm going to bash your brains in. Bash them right to fuck in." He struggled up another riser.

Panic spurred her, and the ache in her side diminished a little. She pulled herself up as fast as she could regardless of the pain, yanking convulsively at the banister. She reached the top and threw a glance behind her.

He seemed to be gaining strength rather than losing it. He was only four risers from the top, measuring the distance with the roque mallet in his left hand as he pulled himself up with his right.

"Right behind you," he panted through his bloody grin, as if reading her mind, "Right behind you now, bitch. With your medicine."

She fled stumblingly down the main corridor, hands pressed to her side.

The door to one of the rooms jerked open and a man with a green ghoulmask on popped out. *"Great party, isn't it?"* He screamed into her face, and pulled the waxed string of a party-favor. There was an echoing bang and suddenly crepe streamers were drifting all around her. The man in the ghoulmask cackled and slammed back into his room. She fell forward onto the carpet, full-length. Her right side seemed to explode with pain, and she fought off the blackness of unconsciousness desperately. Dimly she could hear the elevator running again, and beneath her splayed fingers she could see that the carpet pattern appeared to move, swaying and twining sinuously.

The mallet slammed down behind her and she threw herself forward, sobbing. Over her shoulder she saw Jack stumble forward, overbalance, and bring the mallet down just before he crashed to the carpet, expelling a bright splash of blood onto the nap.

The mallet head struck her squarely between the shoulder blades and for a moment the agony was so great that she could only writhe, hands opening and clenching. Something inside her had snapped—she had heard it clearly, and for a few moments she was aware only in a muted, muffled way, as if she were merely observing these things through a cloudy wrapping of gauze.

Then full consciousness came back, terror and pain with it.

Jack was trying to get up so he could finish the job.

Wendy tried to stand and found it was impossible. Electric bolts seemed to course up and down her back at the effort. She began to crawl along in a sidestroke motion. Jack was crawling after her, using the roque mallet as a crutch or a cane.

She reached the corner and pulled herself around it, using her hands to yank at the angle of the wall. Her terror deepened—she would not have believed that possible, but it was. It was a hundred times worse not to be able to see him or know how close he was getting. She tore out fistfuls of the carpet napping pulling herself along, and she was halfway down this short hall before she noticed the bedroom door was standing wide open.

(*Danny! O Jesus*)

She forced herself to her knees and then clawed her way to her feet, fingers slipping over the silk wallpaper. Her nails pulled little strips of it loose. She ignored the pain and half-walked, half-shambled through the doorway as Jack came around the far corner and began to lunge his way down toward the open door, leaning on the roque mallet.

She caught the edge of the dresser, held herself up against it, and grabbed the doorframe.

Jack shouted at her: "Don't you shut that door! Goddam you, don't you *dare* shut it!"

She slammed it closed and shot the bolt. Her left hand pawed wildly at the junk on the dresser, knocking loose coins onto the floor where they rolled in every direction. Her hand seized the key ring just as the mallet whistled down against the door, making it tremble in its frame. She got the key into the lock on the second stab and twisted it to the right. At the sound of the tumblers falling, Jack screamed. The mallet came down against the door in a volley of booming blows that made her flinch and step back. How could he be doing that with a knife in his back? Where was he finding the strength? She wanted to shriek *Why aren't you dead?* at the locked door.

Instead she turned around. She and Danny would have to go into the attached bathroom and lock that door, too, in case Jack actually could break through the bedroom door. The thought of escaping down the dumb-waiter shaft crossed her mind in a wild burst, and then she rejected it. Danny was small enough to fit into it, but she would be unable to control the rope pull. He might go crashing all the way to the bottom.

The bathroom it would have to be. And if Jack broke through into there—

But she wouldn't allow herself to think of it.

"Danny, honey, you'll have to wake up n—"

But the bed was empty.

When he had begun to sleep more soundly, she had thrown the blankets and one of the quilts over him. Now they were thrown back.

"I'll get you!" Jack howled. "I'll get both of you!" Every other word was punctuated with a blow from the roque hammer, yet Wendy ignored both. All of her attention was focused on that empty bed.

"Come out here! Unlock this goddam door!"

"Danny?" she whispered.

Of course . . . when Jack had attacked her. It had come through to him, as violent emotions always seemed to. Perhaps he'd even seen the whole thing in a nightmare. He was hiding.

She fell clumsily to her knees, enduring another bolt of pain from her swollen and bleeding leg, and looked under the bed. Nothing there but dustballs and Jack's bedroom slippers.

Jack screamed her name, and this time when he swung the mallet, a long splinter of wood jumped from the door and clattered off the hardwood planking. The next blow brought a sickening, splintering crack, the sound of dry kindling under a hatchet. The bloody mallet head, now splintered and gouged in its own right, bashed through the new hole in the door, was withdrawn, and came down again, sending wooden shrapnel flying across the room.

Wendy pulled herself to her feet again using the foot of the bed, and hobbled across the room to the closet. Her broken ribs stabbed at her, making her groan.

"Danny?"

She brushed the hung garments aside frantically; some of them slipped their hangers and ballooned gracelessly to the floor. He was not in the closet.

She hobbled toward the bathroom and as she reached the door she glanced back over her shoulder. The mallet crashed through again, widening the hole, and then a hand appeared, groping for the bolt. She saw with horror that she had left Jack's key ring dangling from the lock.

The hand yanked the bolt back, and as it did so it struck the bunched keys. They jingled merrily. The hand clutched them victoriously.

With a sob, she pushed her way into the bathroom and slammed the door just as the bedroom door burst open and Jack charged through, bellowing.

Wendy ran the bolt and twisted the spring lock, looking around desperately. The bathroom was empty. Danny wasn't here, either. And as she caught sight of her own blood-smeared, horrified face in the medicine cabinet mirror, she was glad. She had never believed that children should be witness to the little quarrels of their parents. And perhaps the thing that was now raving through the bedroom, overturning things and smashing them, would finally collapse before it could go after her son. Perhaps, she thought, it might be possible for her to inflict even more damage on it . . . kill it, perhaps.

Her eyes skated quickly over the bathroom's machine-produced porcelain surfaces, looking for anything that might serve as a weapon. There was a bar of soap, but even wrapped in a towel she didn't think it would be lethal enough. Everything else was bolted down. God, was there nothing she could do?

Beyond the door, the animal sounds of destruction went on and on, accompanied by thick shouts that they would "take their medicine" and "pay for what they'd done to him." He would "show them who's boss." They were "worthless puppies," the both of them.

There was a thump as her record player was overturned, a hollow crash as the secondhand TV's picture tube was smashed, the tinkle of windowglass followed by a cold draft under the bathroom door. A dull thud as the mattresses were ripped from the twin beds where they had slept together, hip to hip. Boomings as Jack struck the walls indiscriminately with the mallet.

There was nothing of the real Jack in that howling, maundering, petulant voice, though. It alternately whined in tones of selfpity and rose in lurid screams; it reminded her chillingly of the screams that sometimes rose in the geriatrics ward of the hospital where she had worked summers as a high school kid. Senile dementia. Jack wasn't out there anymore. She was hearing the lunatic, raving voice of the Overlook itself.

The mallet smashed into the bathroom door, knocking out a huge chunk of the thin paneling. Half of a crazed and working face stared in at her. The mouth and cheeks and throat were lathered in blood, the single eye she could see was tiny and piggish and glittering.

"Nowhere left to run, you cunt," it panted at her through its grin. The mallet descended again, knocking wood splinters into the tub and against the reflecting surface of the medicine cabinet—

(!! *The medicine cabinet* !!)

A desperate whining noise began to escape her as she whirled, pain temporarily forgotten, and threw the mirror door of the cabinet back. She began to paw through its contents. Behind her that hoarse voice bellowed: "Here I come now! Here I come now, you pig!" It was demolishing the door in a machine-like frenzy.

Bottles and jars fell before her madly searching fingers—cough syrup, Vaseline, Clairol Herbal Essence shampoo, hydrogen peroxide, benzocaine—they fell into the sink and shattered.

Her hand closed over the dispenser of double-edged razor blades just as she heard the hand again, fumbling for the bolt and the spring lock.

She slipped one of the razor blades out, fumbling at it, her breath coming in harsh little gasps. She had cut the ball of her thumb. She whirled around and slashed at the hand, which had turned the lock and was now fumbling for the bolt.

Jack screamed. The hand was jerked back.

Panting, holding the razor blade between her thumb and index finger, she waited for him to try again. He did, and she slashed. He screamed again, trying to grab her hand, and she slashed at him again. The razor blade turned in her hand, cutting her again, and dropped to the tile floor by the toilet.

Wendy slipped another blade out of the dispenser and waited.

Movement in the other room—

(?? *going away* ??)

And a sound coming through the bedroom window. A motor. A high, insectile buzzing sound.

A roar of anger from Jack and then—yes, yes, she was sure of it—he was leaving the caretaker's apartment, plowing through the wreckage and out into the hall.

(?? *Someone coming a ranger Dick Hallorann* ??)

"Oh God," she muttered brokenly through a mouth that seemed filled with broken sticks and old sawdust. "Oh God, oh please."

She had to leave now, had to go find her son so they could face the rest of this nightmare side by side. She reached out and fumbled at the bolt. Her arm seemed to stretch for miles. At last she got it to come free. She pushed the door open, staggered out, and was suddenly overcome by the horrible certainty that Jack had only pretended to leave, that he was lying in wait for her.

Wendy looked around. The room was empty, the living room too. Jumbled, broken stuff everywhere.

The closet? Empty.

Then the soft shades of gray began to wash over her and she fell down on the mattress Jack had ripped from the bed, semiconscious.

53

Hallorann Laid Low

Hallorann reached the overturned snowmobile just as, a mile and a half away, Wendy was pulling herself around the corner and into the short hallway leading to the caretaker's apartment.

It wasn't the snowmobile he wanted but the gascan held onto the back by a pair of elastic straps. His hands, still clad in Howard Cottrell's blue mittens, seized the top strap and pulled it free as the hedge lion roared behind him—a sound that seemed to be more in his head than outside of it. A hard, brambly slap to his left leg, making the knee sing with pain as it was driven in a way the joint had never been expected to bend. A groan escaped Hallorann's clenched teeth. It would come for the kill any time now, tired of playing with him.

He fumbled for the second strap. Sticky blood ran in his eyes.

(*Roar! Slap!*)

That one raked across his buttocks, almost tumbling him over and away from the snowmobile again. He held on—no exaggeration—for dear life.

Then he had freed the second strap. He clutched the gascan to him as the lion struck again, rolling him over on his back. He saw it again, only a shadow in the darkness and falling snow, as nightmarish as a moving gargoyle. Hallorann twisted at the can's cap as the moving shadow stalked him, kicking up snow-puffs. As it moved in again the cap spun free, releasing the pungent smell of the gasoline.

Hallorann gained his knees and as it came at him, lowslung and incredibly quick, he splashed it with the gas.

There was a hissing, spitting sound and it drew back.

"Gas!" Hallorann cried, his voice shrill and breaking. "Gonna burn you, baby! Dig on it awhile!"

The lion came at him again, still spitting angrily. Hallorann splashed it again but this time the lion didn't give. It charged ahead. Hallorann sensed rather than saw its head angling at his face and he threw himself backward, partially avoiding it. Yet the lion still hit his upper rib cage a glancing blow, and a flare of pain struck there. Gas gurgled out of the can, which he still held, and doused his right hand and arm, cold as death.

Now he lay on his back in a snow angel, to the right of the snowmobile by about ten paces. The hissing lion was a bulking presence to his left, closing in again. Hallorann thought he could see its tail twitching.

He yanked Cottrell's mitten off his right hand, tasting sodden wool and gasoline. He ripped up the hem of the parka and jammed his hand into his pants pocket. Down in there, along with his keys and his change, was a very battered old Zippo lighter. He had bought it in Germany in 1954. Once the hinge had broken and he had returned it to the Zippo factory and they had repaired it without charge, just as advertised.

A nightmare flood of thoughts flooding through his mind in a split second.

(*Dear Zippo my lighter was swallowed by a crocodile dropped from an airplane lost in the Pacific trench saved me from a Kraut bullet in the Battle of the Bulge dear Zippo if this fucker doesn't go that lion is going to rip my head off*)

The lighter was out. He clicked the hood back. The lion, rushing at him, a growl like ripping cloth, his finger flicking the striker wheel, spark, *flame,*

(*my hand*)

his gasoline-soaked hand suddenly ablaze, the flames running up the sleeve of the parka, no pain, no pain yet, the lion shying from the torch suddenly blazing in front of it, a hideous flickering hedge sculpture with eyes and a mouth, shying away, too late.

Wincing at the pain, Hallorann drove his blazing arm into its stiff and scratchy side.

In an instant the whole creature was in flames, a prancing, writhing pyre on the snow. It bellowed in rage and pain, seeming to chase its flaming tail as it zigzagged away from Hallorann.

He thrust his own arm deep into the snow, killing the flames, unable to take his eyes from the hedge lion's death agonies for a moment. Then, gasping, he

got to his feet. The arm of Durkin's parka was sooty
but unburned, and that also described his hand.
Thirty yards downhill from where he stood, the
hedge lion had turned into a fireball. Sparks flew at
the sky and were viciously snatched away by the
wind. For a moment its ribs and skull were etched in
orange flame and then it seemed to collapse, disinte-
grate, and fall into separate burning piles.

(*Never mind it. Get moving.*)

He picked up the gascan and struggled over to the
snowmobile. His consciousness seemed to be flickering in and out, offering him cuttings and snippets of
home movies but never the whole picture. In one of
these he was aware of yanking the snowmobile back
onto its tread and then sitting on it, out of breath and
incapable of moving for a few moments. In another,
he was reattaching the gascan, which was still half-
full. His head was thumping horribly from the gas-
fumes (and in reaction to his battle with the hedge
lion, he supposed), and he saw by the steaming hole
in the snow beside him that he had vomited, but he
was unable to remember when.

The snowmobile, the engine still warm, fired
immediately. He twisted the throttle unevenly and
started forward with a series of neck-snapping jerks
that made his head ache even more fiercely. At first
the snowmobile wove drunkenly from side to side,
but by half-standing to get his face above the wind-
screen and into the sharp, needling blast of the wind,
he drove some of the stupor out of himself. He
opened the throttle wider.

(*Where are the rest of the hedge animals?*)

He didn't know, but at least he wouldn't be caught unaware again.

The Overlook loomed in front of him, the lighted first-floor windows throwing long yellow rectangles onto the snow. The gate at the foot of the drive was locked and he dismounted after a wary look around, praying he hadn't lost his keys when he pulled his lighter out of his pocket . . . no, they were there. He picked through them in the bright light thrown by the snowmobile head lamp. He found the right one and unsnapped the padlock, letting it drop into the snow. At first he didn't think he was going to be able to move the gate anyway; he pawed frantically at the snow surrounding it, disregarding the throbbing agony in his head and the fear that one of the other lions might be creeping up behind him. He managed to pull it a foot and a half away from the gatepost, squeezed into the gap, and pushed. He got it to move another two feet, enough room for the snowmobile, and threaded it through.

He became aware of movement ahead of him in the dark. The hedge animals, all of them, were clustered at the base of the Overlook's steps, guarding the way in, the way out. The lions prowled. The dog stood with its front paws on the first step.

Hallorann opened the throttle wide and the snowmobile leaped forward, puffing snow up behind it. In the caretaker's apartment, Jack Torrance's head jerked around at the high, wasplike buzz of the approaching engine, and suddenly began to move laboriously toward the hallway again. The bitch wasn't important now. The bitch could wait. Now it was this dirty nigger's turn. This dirty, interfering nigger with his nose in where it didn't belong. First him and then his son. He would show them. He would show them that . . . that he . . . that he was of *managerial timber!*

Outside, the snowmobile rocketed along faster and faster. The hotel seemed to surge toward it. Snow flew in Hallorann's face. The headlamp's oncoming glare spotlighted the hedge shepherd's face, its blank and socketless eyes.

Then it shrank away, leaving an opening. Hallorann yanked at the snowmobile's steering gear with all his remaining strength, and it kicked around in a sharp semicircle, throwing up clouds of snow, threatening to tip over. The rear end struck the foot of the porch steps and rebounded. Hallorann was off in a flash and running up the steps. He stumbled, fell, picked himself up. The dog was growling—again in his head—close behind him. Something ripped at the shoulder of the parka and then he was on the porch, standing in the narrow corridor Jack had shoveled through the snow, and safe. They were too big to fit in here.

He reached the big double doors which gave on the lobby and dug for his keys again. While he was getting them he tried the knob and it turned freely. He pushed his way in.

"*Danny!*" he cried hoarsely. "*Danny, where are you?*"

Silence came back.

His eyes traveled across the lobby to the foot of the wide stairs and a harsh gasp escaped him. The rug was splashed and matted with blood. There was a scrap of pink terrycloth robe. The trail of blood led up the stairs. The banister was also splashed with it.

"Oh Jesus," he muttered, and raised his voice again. *"Danny! DANNY!"*

The hotel's silence seemed to mock him with echoes which were almost there, sly and oblique.

(*Danny? Who's Danny? Anybody here know a Danny? Danny, Danny, who's got the Danny? Anybody for a game of spin the Danny? Pin the tail on the Danny? Get out of here, black boy. No one here knows Danny from Adam.*)

Jesus, had he come through everything just to be too late? Had it been done?

He ran up the stairs two at a time and stood at the top of the first floor. The blood led down toward the caretaker's apartment. Horror crept softly into his veins and into his brain as he began to walk toward the short hall. The hedge animals had been bad, but this was worse. In his heart he was already sure of what he was going to find when he got down there.

He was in no hurry to see it.

Jack had been hiding in the elevator when Hallorann came up the stairs. Now he crept up behind the figure in the snow-coated parka, a blood- and gore-streaked phantom with a smile upon its face. The roque mallet was lifted as high as the ugly, ripping pain in his back

(*?? did the bitch stick me can't remember ??*)

would allow.

"Black boy," he whispered. "I'll teach you to go sticking your nose in other people's business."

Hallorann heard the whisper and began to turn, to duck, and the roque mallet whistled down. The hood of the parka matted the blow, but not enough. A rocket exploded in his head, leaving a contrail of stars . . . and then nothing.

He staggered against the silk wallpaper and Jack hit him again, the roque mallet slicing sideways this time, shattering Hallorann's cheekbone and most of the teeth on the left side of his jaw. He went down limply.

"Now," Jack whispered. "Now, by Christ." Where was Danny? He had business with his trespassing son.

Three minutes later the elevator door banged open on the shadowed third floor. Jack Torrance was in it alone. The car had stopped only halfway into the doorway and he had to boost himself up onto the hall floor, wriggling painfully like a crippled thing. He dragged the splintered roque mallet after him. Outside the eaves, the wind howled and roared. Jack's eyes rolled wildly in their sockets. There was blood and confetti in his hair.

His son was up here, up here somewhere. He could feel it. Left to his own devices, he might do anything: scribble on the expensive silk wallpaper with his crayons, deface the furnishings, break the windows. He was a liar and a cheat and he would have to be chastised . . . harshly.

Jack Torrance struggled to his feet.

"Danny?" he called. "Danny, come here a minute, will you? You've done something wrong and I want you to come and take your medicine like a man. Danny? *Danny!*"

54

Tony

(Danny . . .)

(Dannneee . . .)

Darkness and hallways. He was wandering through darkness and hallways that were like those which lay within the body of the hotel but were somehow different. The silk-papered walls stretched up and up, and even when he craned his neck, Danny could not see the ceiling. It was lost in dimness. All the doors were locked, and they also rose up to dimness. Below the peepholes (in these giant doors they were the size of gunsights), tiny skulls and crossbones had been bolted to each door instead of room numbers.

And somewhere, Tony was calling him.

(Dannneee . . .)

There was a pounding noise, one he knew well, and hoarse shouts, faint with distance. He could not make out word for word, but he knew the text well enough by now. He had heard it before, in dreams and awake.

He paused, a little boy not yet three years out of diapers, and tried to decide where he was, where he might be. There was fear, but it was a fear he could live with. He had been afraid every day for two months now, to a degree that ranged from dull disquiet to outright, mind-bending terror. This he could live with. But he wanted to know why Tony had come, why he was making the sound of his name in this hall that was neither a part of real things nor of the dreamland where Tony sometimes showed him things. Why, where—

"Danny."

Far down the giant hallway, almost as tiny as Danny himself, was a dark figure. Tony.

"Where am I?" he called softly to Tony.

"Sleeping," Tony said. "Sleeping in your mommy and daddy's bedroom." There was sadness in Tony's voice.

"Danny," Tony said. "Your mother is going to be badly hurt. Perhaps killed. Mr. Hallorann, too."

"No!"

He cried it out in a distant grief, a terror that seemed damped by these dreamy, dreary surroundings. Nonetheless, death images came to him: dead frog plastered to the turnpike like a grisly stamp; Daddy's broken watch lying on top of a box of junk to be thrown out; gravestones with a dead person under every one; dead jay by the telephone pole; the cold junk Mommy scraped off the plates and down the dark maw of the garbage disposal.

Yet he could not equate these simple symbols with the shifting complex reality of his mother; she satisfied his childish definition of eternity. She had been when he was not. She would continue to be when he was not again. He could accept the possibility of his own death, he had dealt with that since the encounter in Room 217.

But not hers.

Not Daddy's.

Not ever.

He began to struggle, and the darkness and the hallway began to waver. Tony's form became chimerical, indistinct.

"Don't!" Tony called. "Don't, Danny, don't do that!"

"She's not going to be dead! *She's not!*"

"Then you have to help her. Danny . . . you're in a place deep down in your own mind. The place where I am. I'm a part of you, Danny."

"You're *Tony*. You're not me. I want my mommy . . . I want my mommy . . ."

"I didn't bring you here, Danny. You brought yourself. Because you knew."

"No—"

"You've always known," Tony continued, and he began to walk closer. For the first time, Tony began to walk closer. "You're deep down in yourself in a place where nothing comes through. We're alone here for a little while, Danny. This is an Overlook where no one can ever come. No clocks work here. None of the keys fit them and they can never be wound up. The doors have never been opened and no one has ever stayed in the rooms. But you can't stay long. Because it's coming."

"It . . ." Danny whispered fearfully, and as he did so the irregular pounding noise seemed to grow closer, louder. His terror, cool and distant a moment ago, became a more immediate thing. Now the words could be made out. Hoarse, huckstering; they were uttered in a coarse imitation of his father's voice, but it wasn't Daddy. He knew that now. He knew

(You brought yourself. Because you knew.)

"Oh Tony, is it my daddy?" Danny screamed. *"Is it my daddy that's coming to get me?"*

Tony didn't answer. But Danny didn't need an answer. He knew. A long and nightmarish masquerade party went on here, and had gone on for years. Little by little a force had accrued, as secret and silent as interest in a bank account. Force, presence, shape, they were all only words and none of them mattered. It wore many masks, but it was all one. Now, somewhere, it was coming for him. It was hiding behind Daddy's face, it was imitating Daddy's voice, it was wearing Daddy's clothes.

But it was not his daddy.

It was not his daddy.

"I've got to help them!" he cried.

And now Tony stood directly in front of him, and looking at Tony was like looking into a magic mirror and seeing himself in ten years, the eyes widely spaced and very dark, the chin firm, the mouth handsomely molded. The hair was light blond like his mother's, and yet the stamp on his features was that of his father, as if Tony—as if the Daniel Anthony Torrance that would someday be—was a halfling caught between father and son, a ghost of both, a fusion.

"You have to try to help," Tony said. "But your father . . . he's with the hotel now, Danny. It's where he wants to be. It wants you too, because it's very greedy."

Tony walked past him, into the shadows.

"Wait!" Danny cried. "What can I—"

"He's close now," Tony said, still walking away. "You'll have to run . . . hide . . . keep away from him. Keep away."

"Tony, I can't!"

"But you've already started," Tony said. "You will remember what your father forgot."

He was gone.

And from somewhere near his father's voice came, coldly wheedling: "Danny? You can come out, doc. Just a little spanking, that's all. Take it like a man and it will be all over. We don't need her, doc. Just you and me, right? When we get this little . . . spanking . . . behind us, it will be just you and me."

Danny ran.

Behind him, the thing's temper broke through the shambling charade of normality.

"Come here, you little shit! Right now!"

Down a long hall, panting and gasping. Around a corner. Up a flight of stairs. And as he went, the walls that had been so high and remote began to come down; the rug which had only been a blur beneath his feet took on the familiar black and blue pattern, sinuously woven together; the doors became numbered again and behind them the parties that were all one went on and on, populated by generations of guests. The air seemed to be shimmering around him, the blows of the mallet against the walls echoing and re-echoing. He seemed to be bursting through some thin placental womb from sleep to

the rug outside the Presidential Suite on the third floor; lying near him in a bloody heap were the bodies of two men dressed in suits and narrow ties. They had been taken out by shotgun blasts and now they began to stir in front of him and get up.

He drew in breath to scream but didn't.

(*!! FALSE FACES !! NOT REAL !!*)

They faded before his gaze like old photographs and were gone.

But below him, the faint sound of the mallet against the walls went on and on, drifting up through the elevator shaft and the stairwell. The controlling force of the Overlook, in the shape of his father, blundering around on the first floor.

A door opened with a thin screeing sound behind him.

A decayed woman in a rotten silk gown pranced out, her yellowed and splitting fingers dressed with verdigris-caked rings. Heavy-bodied wasps crawled sluggishly over her face.

"Come in," she whispered to him, grinning with black lips. "Come in and we will daance the taaaango . . ."

"False face!!" he hissed. "Not real!" She drew back from him in alarm, and in the act of drawing back she faded and was gone.

"Where are you?" it screamed, but the voice was still only in his head. He could still hear the thing that was wearing Jack's face down on the first floor . . . and something else.

The high, whining sound of an approaching motor.

Danny's breath stopped in his throat with a little gasp. Was it just another face of the hotel, another illusion? Or was it Dick? He wanted—wanted desperately—to believe it *was* Dick, but he didn't dare take the chance.

He retreated down the main corridor, and then took one of the offshoots, his feet whispering on the nap of the carpet. Locked doors frowned down at him as they had done in the dreams, the visions, only now he was in the world of real things, where the game was played for keeps.

He turned to the right and came to a halt, his heart thudding heavily in his chest. Heat was blowing around his ankles. From the registers, of course. This must have been Daddy's day to heat the west wing and

(*You will remember what your father forgot.*)

What was it? He almost knew. Something that might save him and Mommy? But Tony had said he would have to do it himself. What was it?

He sank down against the wall, trying desperately to think. It was so hard . . . the hotel kept trying to get into his head . . . the image of that dark and slumped form swinging the mallet from side to side, gouging the wallpaper . . . sending out puffs of plaster dust.

"Help me," he muttered. "Tony, help me."

And suddenly he became aware that the hotel had grown deathly silent. The whining sound of the motor had stopped

(must not have been real)

and the sounds of the party had stopped and there was only the wind, howling and whooping endlessly.

The elevator whirred into sudden life.

It was coming up.

And Danny knew who—*what*—was in it.

He bolted to his feet, eyes staring wildly. Panic clutched around his heart. Why had Tony sent him to the third floor? He was trapped up here. All the doors were locked.

The attic!

There was an attic, he knew. He had come up here with daddy the day he had salted the rattraps around up there. He hadn't allowed Danny to come up with him because of the rats. He was afraid Danny might be bitten. But the trapdoor which led to the attic was set into the ceiling of the last short corridor in this wing. There was a pole leaning against the wall. Daddy had pushed the trapdoor open with the pole, there had been a ratcheting whir of counterweights as the door went up and a ladder had swung down. If he could get up there and pull the ladder after him . . .

Somewhere in the maze of corridors behind him, the elevator came to a stop. There was a metallic, rattling crash as the gate was thrown back. And then a voice—not in his head now but terribly real—called out: "Danny? Danny, come here a minute, will you? You've done something wrong and I want you to come and take your medicine like a man. Danny? *Danny!*"

Obedience was so strongly ingrained in him that he actually took two automatic steps toward the sound of that voice before stopping. His hands curled into fists at his sides.

(*Not real! False face! I know what you are! Take off your mask!*)

"*Danny!*" it roared. "*Come here, you pup! Come here and take it like a man!*" A loud, hollow boom as the mallet struck the wall. When the voice roared out his name again it had changed location. It had come closer.

In the world of real things, the hunt was beginning.

Danny ran. Feet silent on the heavy carpet, he ran past the closed doors, past the silk figured wallpaper, past the fire extinguisher bolted to the corner of the wall. He hesitated, and then plunged down the final corridor. Nothing at the end but a bolted door, and nowhere left to run.

But the pole was still there, still leaning against the wall where Daddy had left it.

Danny snatched it up. He craned his neck to stare up at the trapdoor. There was a hook on the end of the pole and you had to catch it on a ring set into the trapdoor. You had to—

There was a brand-new Yale padlock dangling from the trapdoor. The lock Jack Torrance had clipped around the hasp after laying his traps, just in case his son should take the notion into his head to go exploring up there someday.

Locked. Terror swept him.

Behind him it was coming, blundering and staggering past the Presidential Suite, the mallet whistling viciously through the air.

Danny backed up against the last closed door and waited for it.

55

That Which
Was Forgotten

Wendy came to a little at a time, the grayness draining away, pain replacing it: her back, her leg, her side . . . she didn't think she would be able to move. Even her fingers hurt, and at first she didn't know why.

(*The razor blade, that's why.*)

Her blond hair, now dank and matted, hung in her eyes. She brushed it away and her ribs stabbed inside, making her groan. Now she saw a field of blue and white mattress, spotted with blood. Her blood, or maybe Jack's. Either way it was still fresh. She hadn't been out long. And that was important because—

(*?Why?*)

Because—

It was the insectile, buzzing sound of the motor that she remembered first. For a moment she fixed stupidly on the memory, and then in a single vertiginous and nauseating swoop, her mind seemed to pan back, showing her everything at once.

Hallorann. It must have been Hallorann. Why else would Jack have left so suddenly, without finishing it . . . without finishing *her?*

Because he was no longer at leisure. He had to find Danny quickly and . . . and do it before Hallorann could put a stop to it.

Or had it happened already?

She could hear the whine of the elevator rising up the shaft.

(*No God please no the blood the blood's still fresh don't let it have happened already*)

Somehow she was able to find her feet and stagger through the bedroom and across the ruins of the living room to the shattered front door. She pushed it open and made it out into the hall.

"Danny!" she cried, wincing at the pain in her chest. "Mr. Hallorann! Is anybody there? *Anybody?*"

The elevator had been running again and now it came to a stop. She heard the metallic crash of the gate being thrown back and then thought she heard a speaking voice. It might have been her imagination. The wind was too loud to really be able to tell.

Leaning against the wall, she made her way up to the corner of the short hallway. She was about to turn the corner when the scream froze her, floating down the stairwell and the elevator shaft:

"*Danny! Come here, you pup! Come here and take it like a man!*"

Jack. On the second or third floor. Looking for Danny.

She got around the corner, stumbled, almost fell. Her breath caught in her throat. Something

(someone?)

huddled against the wall about a quarter of the way down from the stairwell. She began to hurry faster, wincing every time her weight came down on her hurt leg. It was a man, she saw, and as she drew closer, she understood the meaning of that buzzing motor.

It was Mr. Hallorann. He had come after all.

She eased to her knees beside him, offering up an incoherent prayer that he was not dead. His nose was bleeding, and a terrible gout of blood had spilled out of his mouth. The side of his face was a puffed purple bruise. But he was breathing, thank God for that. It was coming in long, harsh draws that shook his whole frame.

Looking at him more closely, Wendy's eyes widened. One arm of the parka he was wearing was blackened and singed. One side of it had been ripped open. There was blood in his hair and a shallow but ugly scratch down the back of his neck.

(*My God, what's happened to him?*)

"*Danny!*" the hoarse, petulant voice roared from above them. "*Get out here, goddammit!*"

There was no time to wonder about it now. She began to shake him, her face twisting at the flare of agony in her ribs. Her side felt hot and massive and swollen.

(*What if they're poking my lung whenever I move?*)

There was no help for that, either. If Jack found Danny, he would kill him, beat him to death with that mallet as he had tried to do to her.

So she shook Hallorann, and then began to slap the unbruised side of his face lightly.

"Wake up," she said. "Mr. Hallorann, you've got to wake up. Please . . . please . . ."

From overhead, the restless booming sounds of the mallet as Jack Torrance looked for his son.

Danny stood with his back against the door, looking at the right angle where the hallways joined. The steady, irregular booming sound of the mallet against the walls grew louder. The thing that was after him screamed and howled and cursed. Dream and reality had joined together without a seam.

It came around the corner.

In a way, what Danny felt was relief. It was not his father. The mask of face and body had been ripped and shredded and made into a bad joke. It was not his daddy, not this Saturday Night Shock Show horror with its rolling eyes and hunched and hulking shoulders and blood-drenched shirt. It was not his daddy.

"Now, by God," it breathed. It wiped its lips with a shaking hand. "Now you'll find out who is the boss around here. You'll see. It's not you they want. It's me. *Me. Me!*"

It slashed out with the scarred hammer, its double head now shapeless and splintered with countless impacts. It struck the wall, cutting a circle in the silk paper. Plaster dust puffed out. It began to grin.

"Let's see you pull any of your fancy tricks now," it muttered. "I wasn't born yesterday, you know. Didn't just fall off the hay truck, by God. I'm going to do my fatherly duty by you, boy."

Danny said: "You're not my daddy."

It stopped. For a moment it actually looked uncertain, as if not sure who or what it was. Then it began to walk again. The hammer whistled out, struck a door panel and made it boom hollowly.

"You're a liar," it said. "Who else would I be? I have the two birthmarks, I have the cupped navel, even the *pecker*, my boy. Ask your mother."

"You're a mask," Danny said. "Just a false face. The only reason the hotel needs to use you is that you aren't as dead as the others. But when it's done with you, you won't be anything at all. You don't scare me."

"I'll scare you!" it howled. The mallet whistled fiercely down, smashing into the rug between Danny's feet. Danny didn't flinch. "You lied about me! You connived with her! You plotted against me! *And you cheated! You copied that final exam!*" The eyes glared out at him from beneath the furred brows. There was an expression of lunatic cunning in them. "I'll find it, too. It's down in the basement somewhere. I'll find it. They promised me I could look all I want." It raised the mallet again.

"Yes, they promise," Danny said, "but they lie."

The mallet hesitated at the top of its swing.

Hallorann had begun to come around, but Wendy had stopped patting his cheeks. A moment ago the words. *You cheated! You copied that final exam!* had floated down through the elevator shaft, dim, barely audible over the wind. From somewhere deep in the west wing. She was nearly convinced they were on the third floor and that Jack—whatever had taken possession of Jack—had found Danny. There was nothing she or Hallorann could do now.

"Oh doc," she murmured. Tears blurred her eyes.

"Son of a bitch broke my jaw," Hallorann muttered thickly, "and my *head* . . ." He worked to sit up. His right eye was purpling rapidly and swelling shut. Still, he saw Wendy.

"Missus Torrance—"

"Shhhh," she said.

"Where is the boy, Missus Torrance?"

"On the third floor," she said. "With his father."

"They lie," Danny said again. Something had gone through his mind, flashing like a meteor, too quick, too bright to catch and hold. Only the tail of the thought remained.

(*it's down in the basement somewhere*)
(*you will remember what your father forgot*)

"You . . . you shouldn't speak that way to your father," it said hoarsely. The mallet trembled, came down. "You'll only make things worse for yourself. Your . . . your punishment. Worse." It staggered drunkenly and stared at him with maudlin selfpity that began to turn to hate. The mallet began to rise again.

"You're not my daddy," Danny told it again. "And if there's a little bit of my daddy left inside you, he knows they lie here. Everything is a lie and a cheat. Like the loaded dice my daddy got for my Christmas stocking last Christmas, like the presents they put in the store windows and my daddy says there's nothing in them, no presents, they're just empty boxes. Just for show, my daddy says. You're *it*, not my daddy. You're the hotel. And when you get what you want, you won't give my daddy anything because you're selfish. And my daddy knows that. You had to make him drink the Bad Stuff. That's the only way you could get him, you lying false face."

"Liar! Liar!" The words came in a thin shriek. The mallet wavered wildly in the air.

"Go on and hit me. But you'll never get what you want from me."

The face in front of him changed. It was hard to say how; there was no melting or merging of the features. The body trembled slightly, and then the bloody hands opened like broken claws. The mallet fell from them and thumped to the rug. That was all. But suddenly his daddy *was* there, looking at him in mortal agony, and a sorrow so great that Danny's heart flamed within his chest. The mouth drew down in a quivering bow.

"Doc," Jack Torrance said. "Run away. Quick. And remember how much I love you."

"No," Danny said.

"Oh Danny, for God's sake—"

"No," Danny said. He took one of his father's bloody hands and kissed it. "It's almost over."

Hallorann got to his feet by propping his back against the wall and pushing himself up. He and

Wendy stared at each other like nightmare survivors from a bombed hospital.

"We got to get up there," he said. "We have to help him."

Her haunted eyes stared into his from her chalk-pale face. "It's too late," Wendy said. "Now he can only help himself."

A minute passed, then two. Three. And they heard it above them, screaming, not in anger or triumph now, but in mortal terror.

"Dear God," Hallorann whispered. "What's happening?"

"I don't know," she said.

"Has it killed him?"

"I don't know."

The elevator clashed into life and began to descend with the screaming, raving thing penned up inside.

Danny stood without moving. There was no place he could run where the Overlook was not. He recognized it suddenly, fully, painlessly. For the first time in his life he had an adult thought, an adult feeling, the assence of this experience in this bad place—a sorrowful distillation:

(*Mommy and Daddy can't help me and I'm alone.*)

"Go away," he said to the bloody stranger in front of him. "Go on. Get out of here."

It bent over, exposing the knife handle in its back. Its hands closed around the mallet again, but instead of aiming at Danny, it reversed the handle, aiming the hard side of the roque mallet at its own face.

Understanding rushed through Danny.

Then the mallet began to rise and descend, destroying the last of Jack Torrance's image. The thing in the hall danced an eerie, shuffling polka, the beat counterpointed by the hideous sound of the mallet head striking again and again. Blood splattered across the wallpaper. Shards of bone leaped into the air like broken piano keys. It was impossible to say just how long it went on. But when it turned its attention back to Danny, his father was gone forever. What remained of the face became a strange, shifting composite, many faces mixed imperfectly into one. Danny saw the woman in 217; the dogman; the hungry boy-thing that had been in the concrete ring.

"Masks off, then," it whispered. "No more interruptions."

The mallet rose for the final time. A ticking sound filled Danny's ears.

"Anything else to say?" it inquired. "Are you sure you wouldn't like to run? A game of tag, perhaps? All we have is time, you know. An eternity of *time*. Or shall we end it? Might as well. After all, we're missing the party."

It grinned with broken-toothed greed.

And it came to him. What his father had forgotten.

Sudden triumph filled his face; the thing saw it and hesitated, puzzled.

"*The boiler!*" Danny screamed. "*It hasn't been dumped since this morning! It's going up! It's going to explode!*"

An expression of grotesque terror and dawning realization swept across the broken features of the thing in front of him. The mallet dropped from its fisted hands and bounced harmlessly on the black and blue rug.

"The boiler!" it cried. "Oh no! That can't be allowed! Certainly not! No! You goddamned little pup! Certainly not! Oh, oh, oh—"

"*It is!*" Danny cried back at it fiercely. He began to shuffle and shake his fists at the ruined thing before him. "Any minute now! I know it! The boiler, Daddy forgot the boiler! *And you forgot it, too!*"

"No, oh no, it mustn't, it can't, you dirty little boy, I'll make you take your medicine, I'll make you take every drop, oh no, oh no—"

It suddenly turned tail and began to shamble away. For a moment its shadow bobbed on the wall, waxing and waning. It trailed cries behind itself like wornout party streamers.

Moments later the elevator crashed into life.

Suddenly the shining was on him

(*mommy mr. hallorann dick to my friends together alive they're alive got to get out it's going to blow going to blow sky-high*)

like a fierce and glaring sunrise and he ran. One foot kicked the bloody, misshapen roque mallet aside. He didn't notice.

Crying, he ran for the stairs.

They had to get out.

56

The Explosion

Hallorann could never be sure of the progression of things after that. He remembered that the elevator had gone down and past them without stopping, and something had been inside. But he made no attempt to try to see in through the small diamond-shaped window, because what was in there did not sound human. A moment later there were running footsteps on the stairs. Wendy Torrance at first shrank back against him and then began to stumble down the main corridor to the stairs as fast as she could.

"Danny! Danny! Oh, thank God! Thank God!"

She swept him into a hug, groaning with joy as well as her pain.

(*Danny.*)

Danny looked at him from his mother's arms, and Hallorann saw how the boy had changed. His face was pale and pinched, his eyes dark and fathomless. He looked as if he had lost weight. Looking at the two of them together, Hallorann thought it was the mother who looked younger, in spite of the terrible beating she had taken.

(*Dick—we have to go—run—the place—it's going to*)

Picture of the Overlook, flames leaping out of its roof. Bricks raining down on the snow. Clang of fire-bells . . . not that any fire truck would be able to get up here much before the end of March. Most of all what came through in Danny's thought was a sense of urgent immediacy, a feeling that it was going to happen *at any time.*

"All right," Hallorann said. He began to move toward the two of them and at first it was like swimming through deep water. His sense of balance was screwed, and the eye on the right side of his face didn't want to focus. His jaw was sending giant throbbing bursts of pain up to his temple and down his neck, and his cheek felt as large as a cabbage. But the boy's urgency had gotten him going, and it got a little easier.

"All right?" Wendy asked. She looked from Hallorann to her son and back to Hallorann. "What do you mean, all right?"

"We have to go," Hallorann said.

"I'm not dressed . . . my clothes . . ."

Danny darted out of her arms then and raced down the corridor. She looked after him, and as he vanished around the corner, back at Hallorann. "What if he comes back?"

"Your husband?"

"He's not Jack," she muttered. "Jack's dead. This place killed him. *This damned place.*" She struck at the wall with her fist and cried out at the pain in her cut fingers. "It's the boiler, isn't it?"

"Yes, ma'am. Danny says it's going to explode."

"Good." The word was uttered with dead finality. "I don't know if I can get down those stairs again. My ribs . . . he broke my ribs. And something in my back. It hurts."

"You'll make it," Hallorann said. "We'll all make it." But suddenly he remembered the hedge animals, and wondered what they would do if they were guarding the way out.

Then Danny was coming back. He had Wendy's boots and coat and gloves, also his own coat and gloves.

"Danny," she said. "Your boots."

"It's too late," he said. His eyes stared at them with a desperate kind of madness. He looked at Dick and suddenly Hallorann's mind was fixed with an image of a clock under a glass dome, the clock in the ballroom that had been donated by a Swiss diplomat in 1949. The hands of the clock were standing at a minute to midnight.

"Oh my God," Hallorann said. "Oh my dear God."

He clapped an arm around Wendy and picked her up. He clapped his other arm around Danny. He ran for the stairs.

Wendy shrieked in pain as he squeezed the bad ribs, as something in her back ground together, but Hallorann did not slow. He plunged down the stairs with them in his arms. One eye wide and desperate, the other puffed shut to a slit. He looked like a one-eyed pirate abducting hostages to be ransomed later.

Suddenly the shine was on him, and he understood what Danny had meant when he said it was too late. He could feel the explosion getting ready to rumble up from the basement and tear the guts out of this horrid place.

He ran faster, bolting headlong across the lobby toward the double doors.

It hurried across the basement and into the feeble yellow glow of the furnace room's only light. It was slobbering with fear. It had been so close, so close to having the boy and the boy's remarkable power. It could not lose now. It must not happen. It would dump the boiler and then chastise the boy harshly.

"Mustn't happen!" it cried. "Oh no, mustn't happen!"

It stumbled across the floor to the boiler, which glowed a dull red halfway up its long tubular body. It was huffing and rattling and hissing off plumes of steam in a hundred directions, like a monster calliope. The pressure needle stood at the far end of the dial.

"*No, it won't be allowed!*" the manager/caretaker cried.

It laid its Jack Torrance hands on the valve, unmindful of the burning smell which arose or the searing of the flesh as the red-hot wheel sank in, as if into a mudrut.

The wheel gave, and with a triumphant scream, the thing spun it wide open. A giant roar of escaping steam bellowed out of the boiler, a dozen dragons hissing in concert. But before the steam obscured the pressure needle entirely, the needle had visibly begun to swing back.

"*I WIN!*" it cried. It capered obscenely in the hot, rising mist, waving its flaming hands over its head. "*NOT TOO LATE! I WIN! NOT TOO LATE! NOT TOO LATE! NOT—*"

Words turned into a shriek of triumph, and the shriek was swallowed in a shattering roar as the Overlook's boiler exploded.

Halloran burst out through the double doors and carried the two of them through the trench in the big snowdrift on the porch. He saw the hedge animals clearly, more clearly than before, and even as he realized his worst fears were true, that they were between the porch and the snowmobile, the hotel exploded. It seemed to him that it happened all at once, although later he knew that couldn't have been the way it happened.

There was a flat explosion, a sound that seemed to exist on one low all-pervasive note

(*WHUMMMMMMMMMM—*)

and then there was a blast of warm air at their backs that seemed to push gently at them. They were thrown from the porch on its breath, the three of them, and a confused thought

(*this is what superman must feel like*)

slipped through Halloran's mind as they flew through the air. He lost his hold on them and then he struck the snow in a soft billow. It was down his shirt and up his nose and he was dimly aware that it felt good on his hurt cheek.

Then he struggled to the top of it, for that moment not thinking about the hedge animals, or Wendy Torrance, or even the boy. He rolled over on his back so he could watch it die.

The Overlook's windows shattered. In the ballroom, the dome over the mantelpiece clock cracked, split in two pieces, and fell to the floor. The clock stopped ticking: cogs and gears and balance wheel all became motionless. There was a whispered, sighing noise, and a great billow of dust. In 217 the bathtub suddenly split in two, letting out a small flood of greenish, noxious-smelling water. In the Presidential Suite the wallpaper suddenly burst into flames. The batwing doors of the Colorado Lounge suddenly snapped their hinges and fell to the dining room floor. Beyond the basement arch, the great piles and stacks of old papers caught fire and went up with a blowtorch hiss. Boiling water rolled over the flames but did not quench them. Like burning autumn leaves below a wasps' nest, they whirled and blackened. The furnace exploded, shattering the basement's roofbeams, sending them crashing down like the bones of a dinosaur. The gasjet which had fed the furnace, unstoppered now, rose up in a bellowing pylon of flame through the riven floor of the lobby. The carpeting on the stair risers caught, racing up to the first-floor level as if to tell dreadful good news. A fusillade of explosions ripped the place. The chandelier in the dining room, a two-hundred-pound crystal bomb, fell with a splintering crash, knocking tables every which way. Flame belched out of the Overlook's five chimneys at the breaking clouds.

(*No! Mustn't! Mustn't! MUSTN'T!*)

It shrieked; it shrieked but now it was voiceless and it was only screaming panic and doom and damnation in its own ear, dissolving, losing thought and will, the webbing falling apart, searching, not finding, going out, going out to, fleeing, going out to emptiness, notness, crumbling.

The party was over.

57

Exit

The roar shook the whole facade of the hotel. Glass belched out onto the snow and twinkled there like jagged diamonds. The hedge dog, which had been approaching Danny and his mother, recoiled away from it, its green and shadow-marbled ears flattening, its tail coming down between its legs as its haunches flattened abjectly. In his head, Hallorann heard it whine fearfully, and mixed with that sound was the fearful, confused yowling of the big cats. He struggled to his feet to go to the other two and help them, and as he did so he saw something more nightmarish than all the rest: the hedge rabbit, still coated with snow, was battering itself crazily at the chainlink fence at the far end of the playground, and the steel mesh was jingling with a kind of nightmare music, like a spectral zither. Even from here he could hear the sounds of the close-set twigs and branches which made up its body cracking and crunching like breaking bones.

"Dick! Dick!" Danny cried out. He was trying to support his mother, help her over to the snowmobile.

The clothes he had carried out for the two of them were scattered between where they had fallen and where they now stood. Hallorann was suddenly aware that the woman was in her nightclothes, Danny jacketless, and it was no more than ten above zero.

(*my god she's in her bare feet*)

He struggled back through the snow, picking up her coat, her boots, Danny's coat, odd gloves. Then he ran back to them, plunging hip-deep in the snow from time to time, having to flounder his way out.

Wendy was horribly pale, the side of her neck coated with blood, blood that was now freezing.

"I can't," she muttered. She was no more than semiconscious. "No, I . . . can't. Sorry."

Danny looked up at Hallorann pleadingly.

"Gonna be okay," Hallorann said, and gripped her again. "Come on."

The three of them made it to where the snowmobile had slewed around and stalled out. Hallorann sat the woman down on the passenger seat and put her coat on. He lifted her feet up—they were very cold but not frozen yet—and rubbed them briskly with Danny's jacket before putting on her boots. Wendy's face was alabaster pale, her eyes half-lidded and dazed, but she had begun to shiver. Hallorann thought that was a good sign.

Behind them, a series of three explosions rocked the hotel. Orange flashes lit the snow.

Danny put his mouth close to Hallorann's ear and screamed something.

"What?"

"I said do you need that?"

The boy was pointing at the red gascan that leaned at an angle in the snow.

"I guess we do."

He picked it up and sloshed it. Still gas in there, he couldn't tell how much. He attached the can to the back of the snowmobile, fumbling the job several times before getting it right because his fingers were going numb. For the first time he became aware that he'd lost Howard Cottrell's mittens.

(*i get out of this i gonna have my sister knit you a dozen pair, howie*)

"Get on!" Hallorann shouted at the boy.

Danny shrank back. "We'll freeze!"

"We have to go around to the equipment shed! There's stuff in there . . . blankets . . . stuff like that. Get on behind your mother!"

Danny got on, and Hallorann twisted his head so he could shout into Wendy's face.

"Missus Torrance! Hold onto me! You understand? *Hold on!*"

She put her arms around him and rested her cheek against his back. Hallorann started the snow-mobile and turned the throttle delicately so they would start up without a jerk. The woman had the weakest sort of grip on him, and if she shifted back-ward, her weight would tumble both her and the boy off.

They began to move. He brought the snowmobile around in a circle and then they were traveling west parallel to the hotel. Hallorann cut in more to circle around behind it to the equipment shed.

They had a momentarily clear view into the Overlook's lobby. The gasflame coming up through the shattered floor was like a giant birthday candle, fierce yellow at its heart and blue around its flickering edges. In that moment it seemed only to be lighting, not destroying. They could see the registration desk with its silver bell, the credit card decals, the old-fashioned, scrolled cash register, the small figured throw rugs, the highbacked chairs, horsehair hassocks. Danny could see the small sofa by the fireplace where the three nuns had sat on the day they had come up—closing day. But this was the real closing day.

Then the drift on the porch blotted the view out. A moment later they were skirting the west side of the hotel. It was still light enough to see without the snowmobile's headlight. Both upper stories were flaming now, and pennants of flame shot out the windows. The gleaming white paint had begun to blacken and peel. The shutters which had covered the Presidential Suite's picture window—shutters Jack had carefully fastened as per instructions in mid-October—now hung in flaming brands, exposing the wide and shattered darkness behind them, like a toothless mouth yawing in a final, silent deathrattle.

Wendy had pressed her face against Hallorann's back to cut out the wind, and Danny had likewise pressed his face against his mother's back, and so it was only Hallorann who saw the final thing, and he never spoke of it. From the window of the Presidential Suite he thought he saw a huge dark shape issue, blotting out the snowfield behind it. For a moment it assumed the shape of a huge, obscene manta, and then the wind seemed to catch it, to tear it and shred it like old dark paper. It fragmented, was caught in a whirling eddy of smoke, and a moment later it was gone as if it had never been. But in those few seconds as it whirled blackly, dancing like negative motes of light, he remembered something from his childhood . . . fifty years ago, or more. He and his brother had come upon a huge nest of ground wasps just north of their farm. It had been tucked into a hollow between the earth and an old lightning-blasted tree. His brother had had a big old niggerchaser in the band of his hat, saved all the way from the Fourth of July. He had lighted it and tossed it at the nest. It had exploded with a loud bang, and an angry, rising hum—almost a low shriek—had risen from the blasted nest. They had run away as if demons had been at their heels. In a way, Hallorann supposed that demons had been. And looking back over his shoulder, as he was now, he had on that day seen a large dark cloud of hornets rising in the hot air, swirling together, breaking apart, looking for whatever enemy had done this to their home so that they—the single group intelligence—could sting it to death.

Then the thing in the sky was gone and it might only have been smoke or a great flapping swatch of wallpaper after all, and there was only the Overlook, a flaming pyre in the roaring throat of the night.

* * *

There was a key to the equipment shed's padlock on his key ring, but Hallorann saw there would be no need to use it.

The door was ajar, the padlock hanging open on its hasp.

"I can't go in there," Danny whispered.

"That's okay. You stay with your mom. There used to be a pile of old horseblankets. Probably all moth-eaten by now, but better than freezin to death. Missus Torrance, you still with us?"

"I don't know," the wan voice answered. "I think so."

"Good. I'll be just a second."

"Come back as quick as you can," Danny whispered. "Please."

Hallorann nodded. He had trained the headlamp on the door and now he floundered through the snow, casting a long shadow in front of himself. He pushed the equipment shed door open and stepped in. The horseblankets were still in the corner, by the roque set. He picked up four of them—they smelled musty and old and the moths certainly had been having a free lunch—and then he paused.

One of the roque mallets was gone.

(*Was that what he hit me with?*)

Well, it didn't matter what he'd been hit with, did it? Still, his fingers went to the side of his face and began to explore the huge lump there. Six hundred dollars' worth of dental work undone at a single blow. And after all

(*maybe he didn't hit me with one of those. Maybe one got lost. Or stolen. Or took for a souvenir. After all*) it didn't really matter. No one was going to be playing roque here next summer. Or any summer in the foreseeable future.

No, it didn't really matter, except that looking at the racked mallets with the single missing member had a kind of fascination. He found himself thinking of the hard wooden *whack!* of the mallet head striking the round wooden ball. A nice summery sound. Watching it skitter across the

(*bone. blood.*)

gravel. It conjured up images of

(*bone. blood.*)

iced tea, porch swings, ladies in white straw hats, the hum of mosquitoes, and

(*bad little boys who don't play by the rules.*)

all that stuff. Sure. Nice game. Out of style now, but . . . nice.

"Dick?" The voice was thin, frantic, and, he thought, rather unpleasant. "Are you all right, Dick? Come out now. *Please!*"

(*"Come on out now nigguh de massa callin youall."*)

His hand closed tightly around one of the mallet handles, liking its feel.

(*Spare the rod, spoil the child.*)

His eyes went blank in the flickering, fire-shot darkness. Really, it would be doing them both a favor. She was messed up . . . in pain . . . and most of it

(*all of it*)

was that damn boy's fault. Sure. He had left his own daddy in there to burn. When you thought of it, it was damn close to murder. Patricide was what they called it. Pretty goddam low.

"Mr. Hallorann?" Her voice was low, weak, querulous. He didn't much like the sound of it.

"*Dick!*" The boy was sobbing now, in terror.

Hallorann drew the mallet from the rack and turned toward the flood of white light from the snowmobile headlamp. His feet scratched unevenly over the boards of the equipment shed, like the feet of a clockwork toy that has been wound up and set in motion.

Suddenly he stopped, looked wonderingly at the mallet in his hands, and asked himself with rising horror what it was he had been thinking of doing. Murder? *Had he been thinking of murder?*

For a moment his entire mind seemed filled with an angry, weakly hectoring voice:

(*Do it! Do it, you weak-kneed no-balls nigger! Kill them! KILL THEM BOTH!*)

Then he flung the mallet behind him with a whispered, terrified cry. It clattered into the corner where the horseblankets had been, one of the two heads pointed toward him in an unspeakable invitation.

He fled.

Danny was sitting on the snowmobile seat and Wendy was holding him weakly. His face was shiny with tears, and he was shaking as if with ague. Between his clicking teeth he said: "Where were you? We were *scared!*"

"It's a good place to be scared of," Hallorann said slowly. "Even if that place burns flat to the foundation, you'll never get me within a hundred miles of here again. Here, Missus Torrance, wrap these around you. I'll help. You too, Danny. Get yourself looking like an Arab."

He swirled two of the blankets around Wendy, fashioning one of them into a hood to cover her head, and helped Danny tie his so they wouldn't fall off.

"Now hold on for dear life," he said. "We got a long way to go, but the worst is behind us now."

He circled the equipment shed and then pointed the snowmobile back along their trail. The Overlook was a torch now, flaming at the sky. Great holes had been eaten into its sides, and there was a red hell inside, waxing and waning. Snowmelt ran down the charred gutters in steaming waterfalls.

They purred down the front lawn, their way well lit. The snowdunes glowed scarlet.

"Look!" Danny shouted as Hallorann slowed for the front gate. He was pointing toward the playground.

The hedge creatures were all in their original positions, but they were denuded, blackened, seared. Their dead branches were a stark interlacing network in the fireglow, their small leaves scattered around their feet like fallen petals.

"They're dead!" Danny screamed in hysterical triumph. *"Dead! They're dead!"*

"Shhh," Wendy said. "All right, honey. It's all right."

"Hey, doc," Hallorann said. "Let's get to someplace warm. You ready?"

"Yes," Danny whispered. "I've been ready for so long—"

Hallorann edged through the gap between gate and post. A moment later they were on the road, pointed back toward Sidewinder. The sound of the snowmobile's engine dwindled until it was lost in the ceaseless roar of the wind. It rattled through the denuded branches of the hedge animals with a low, beating, desolate sound. The fire waxed and waned. Sometime after the sound of the snowmobile's engine had disappeared, the Overlook's roof caved in—first the west wing, then the east, and seconds later the central roof. A huge spiraling gout of sparks and flaming debris rushed up into the howling winter night.

A bundle of flaming shingles and a wad of hot flashing were wafted in through the open equipment shed door by the wind.

After a while the shed began to burn, too.

They were still twenty miles from Sidewinder when Hallorann stopped to pour the rest of the gas into the snowmobile's tank. He was getting very worried about Wendy Torrance, who seemed to be drifting away from them. It was still so far to go.

"*Dick!*" Danny cried. He was standing up on the seat, pointing. "*Dick, look! Look there!*"

The snow had stopped and a silver-dollar moon had peeked out through the raftering clouds. Far down the road but coming toward them, coming upward through a series of S-shaped switchbacks, was a pearly chain of lights. The wind dropped for a moment and Hallorann heard the faraway buzzing snarl of snowmobile engines.

Hallorann and Danny and Wendy reached them fifteen minutes later. They had brought extra clothes and brandy and Dr. Edmonds.

And the long darkness was over.

58

Epilogue / Summer

After he had finished checking over the salads his understudy had made and peeked in on the home-baked beans they were using as appetizers this week, Hallorann untied his apron, hung it on a hook, and slipped out the back door. He had maybe forty-five minutes before he had to crank up for dinner in earnest.

The name of this place was the Red Arrow Lodge, and it was buried in the western Maine mountains, thirty miles from the town of Rangely. It was a good gig, Hallorann thought. The trade wasn't too heavy, it tipped well, and so far there hadn't been a single meal sent back. Not bad at all, considering the season was nearly half over.

He threaded his way between the outdoor bar and the swimming pool (although why anyone would want to use the pool with the lake so handy he would never know), crossed a greensward where a party of four was playing croquet and laughing, and crested a mild ridge. Pines took over here, and the wind soughed pleasantly in them, carrying the aroma of fir and sweet resin.

On the other side, a number of cabins with views of the lake were placed discreetly among the trees. The last one was the nicest, and Hallorann had reserved it for a party of two back in April when he had gotten this gig.

The woman was sitting on the porch in a rocking chair, a book in her hands. Hallorann was struck again by the change in her. Part of it was the stiff, almost formal way she sat, in spite of her informal surroundings—that was the back brace, of course. She'd had a shattered vertebra as well as three broken ribs and some internal injuries. The back was the slowest healing, and she was still in the brace . . . hence the formal posture. But the change was more than that. She looked older, and some of the laughter had gone out of her face. Now, as she sat reading her book, Hallorann saw a grave sort of beauty there that had been missing on the day he had first met her, some nine months ago. Then she had still been mostly girl. Now she was a woman, a human being who had been dragged around to the dark side of the moon and had come back able to put the pieces back together. But those pieces, Hallorann thought, they never fit just the same way again. Never in this world.

She heard his step and looked up, closing her book. "Dick! Hi!" She started to rise, and a little grimace of pain crossed her face.

"Nope, don't get up," he said. "I don't stand on no ceremony unless it's white tie and tails."

She smiled as he came up the steps and sat down next to her on the porch.

"How is it going?"

"Pretty fair," he admitted. "You try the shrimp creole tonight. You gonna like it."

"That's a deal."

"Where's Danny?"

"Right down there." She pointed, and Hallorann saw a small figure sitting at the end of the dock. He was wearing jeans rolled up to the knee and a red-striped shirt. Further out on the calm water, a bobber floated. Every now and then Danny would reel it in, examine the sinker and hook below it, and then toss it out again.

"He's gettin brown," Hallorann said.

"Yes. Very brown." She looked at him fondly.

He took out a cigarette, tamped it, lit it. The smoke raftered away lazily in the sunny afternoon. "What about those dreams he's been havin?"

"Better," Wendy said. "Only one this week. It used to be every night, sometimes two and three times. The explosions. The hedges. And most of all . . . you know."

"Yeah. He's going to be okay, Wendy."

She looked at him. "Will he? I wonder."

Hallorann nodded. "You and him, you're coming back. Different, maybe, but okay. You ain't what you were, you two, but that isn't necessarily bad."

They were silent for a while, Wendy moving the rocking chair back and forth a little, Hallorann with his feet up on the porch rail, smoking. A little breeze came up, pushing its secret way through the pines but barely ruffling Wendy's hair. She had cut it short.

"I've decided to take Al—Mr. Shockley—up on his offer," she said.

Hallorann nodded. "It sounds like a good job. Something you could get interested in. When do you start?"

"Right after Labor Day. When Danny and I leave here, we'll be going right on to Maryland to look for a place. It was really the Chamber of Commerce brochure that convinced me, you know. It looks like a nice town to raise a kid in. And I'd like to be working again before we dig too deeply into the insurance money Jack left. There's still over forty thousand dollars. Enough to send Danny to college with enough left over to get him a start, if it's invested right."

Hallorann nodded. "Your mom?"

She looked at him and smiled wanly. "I think Maryland is far enough."

"You won't forget old friends, will you?"

"Danny wouldn't let me. Go on down and see him, he's been waiting all day."

"Well, so have I." He stood up and hitched his cook's whites at the hips. "The two of you are going to be okay," he repeated. "Can't you feel it?"

She looked up at him and this time her smile was warmer. "Yes," she said. She took his hand and kissed it. "Sometimes I think I can."

"The shrimp creole," he said, moving to the steps. "Don't forget."

"I won't."

He walked down the sloping, graveled path that led to the dock and then out along the weather-beaten boards to the end, where Danny sat with his feet in the clear water. Beyond, the lake widened out, mirroring the pines along its verge. The terrain was mountainous around here, but the mountains were old, rounded and humbled by time. Hallorann liked them just fine.

"Catchin much?" Hallorann said, sitting down next to him. He took off one shoe, then the other. With a sigh, he let his hot feet down into the cool water.

"No. But I had a nibble a little while ago."

"We'll take a boat out tomorrow morning. Got to get out in the middle if you want to catch an eatin fish, my boy. Out yonder is where the big ones lay."

"How big?"

Hallorann shrugged. "Oh . . . sharks, marlin, whales, that sort of thing."

"There aren't any whales!"

"No *blue* whales, no. Of course not. These ones here run to no more than eighty feet. Pink whales."

"How could they get here from the ocean?"

Hallorann put a hand on the boy's reddish-gold hair and rumpled it. "They swim upstream, my boy. That's how."

"Really?"

"Really."

They were silent for a time, looking out over the stillness of the lake, Hallorann just thinking. When he looked back at Danny, he saw that his eyes had filled with tears.

Putting an arm around him, he said, "What's this?"

"Nothing," Danny whispered.

"You're missin your dad, aren't you?"

Danny nodded. "You always know." One of the tears spilled from the corner of his right eye and trickled slowly down his cheek.

"We can't have any secrets," Hallorann agreed. "That's just how it is."

Looking at his pole, Danny said: "Sometimes I wish it had been me. It was my fault. All my fault."

Hallorann said, "You don't like to talk about it around your mom, do you?"

"No. She wants to forget it ever happened. So do I, but—"

"But you can't."

"No."

"Do you need to cry?"

The boy tried to answer, but the words were swallowed in a sob. He leaned his head against Hallorann's shoulder and wept, the tears now flooding down his face. Hallorann held him and said nothing. The boy would have to shed his tears again and again, he knew, and it was Danny's luck that he was still young enough to be able to do that. The tears that heal are also the tears that scald and scourge.

When he had quieted a little, Hallorann said, "You're gonna get over this. You don't think you are right now, but you will. You got the shi—"

"I wish I didn't!" Danny choked, his voice still thick with tears. "I wish I didn't have it!"

"But you do," Hallorann said quietly. "For better or worse. You didn't get no say, little boy. But the worst is over. You can use it to talk to me when things get rough. And if they get too rough, you just call me and I'll come."

"Even if I'm down in Maryland?"

"Even there."

They were quiet, watching Danny's bobber drift around thirty feet out from the end of the dock. Then Danny said, almost too low to be heard, "You'll be my friend?"

"As long as you want me."

The boy held him tight and Hallorann hugged him.

"Danny? You listen to me. I'm going to talk to you about it this once and never again this same way. There's some things no six-year-old boy in the world should have to be told, but the way things should be and the way things are hardly ever get together. The world's a hard place, Danny. It don't care. It don't hate you and me, but it don't love us, either. Terrible things happen in the world, and they're things no one can explain. Good people die in bad, painful ways and leave the folks that love them all alone. Sometimes it seems like it's only the bad people who stay healthy and prosper. The world don't love you, but your momma does and so do I. You're a good boy. You grieve for your daddy, and when you feel you have to cry over what happened

to him, you go into a closet or under your covers
and cry until it's all out of you again. That's what a
good son has to do. But see that you get on. That's
your job in this hard world, to keep your love alive
and see that you get on, no matter what. Pull your
act together and just go on."

"All right," Danny whispered. "I'll come see you
again next summer if you want . . . if you don't mind.
Next summer I'm going to be seven."

"And I'll be sixty-two. And I'm gonna hug your
brains out your ears. But let's finish one summer
before we get on to the next."

"Okay." He looked at Hallorann. "Dick?"

"Hmm?"

"You won't die for a long time, will you?"

"I'm sure not studyin on it. Are you?"

"No, *sir*. I—"

"You got a bite, sonny." He pointed. The red and
white bobber had ducked under. It came up again
glistening, and then went under again.

"*Hey!*" Danny gulped.

Wendy had come down and now joined them,
standing in back of Danny. "What is it?" she asked.
"Pickerel?"

"No, ma'am," Hallorann said, "I believe that's a
pink whale."

The tip of the fishing rod bent. Danny pulled it
back and a long fish, rainbow-colored, flashed up in a
sunny, winking parabola, and disappeared again.

Danny reeled frantically, gulping.

"Help me, Dick! I got him! I got him! Help me!"

Hallorann laughed. "You're doin fine all by yourself, little man. I don't know if it's a pink whale or a trout, but it'll do. It'll do just fine."

He put an arm around Danny's shoulders and the boy reeled the fish in, little by little. Wendy sat down on Danny's other side and the three of them sat on the end of the dock in the afternoon sun.

Not sure what to read next?

Visit Pocket Books online at
www.simonsays.com

**Reading suggestions for
you and your reading group
New release news
Author appearances
Online chats with your favorite writers
Special offers
Order books online
And much, much more!**

13456